# INSIDE OLE

## SECOND EDITION

# KRAIG BROCKSCHMIDT

PUBLISHED BY
Microsoft Press
A Division of Microsoft Corporation
One Microsoft Way
Redmond, Washington 98052-6399

Copyright © 1995 by Kraig Brockschmidt

Library of Congress Cataloging-in-Publication Data
Brockschmidt, Kraig, 1968–
    Inside OLE / Kraig Brockschmidt. -- 2nd ed.
      p.    cm.
    Includes index.
    ISBN 1-55615-843-2
    1. Object-oriented programming (Computer science)   2. Microsoft
Windows (Computer file)  I. Title.
    QA76.64.B76    1995
    005.75--dc20                              95-15969
                                                  CIP

Printed and bound in the United States of America.

1 2 3 4 5 6 7 8 9  QMQM  0 9 8 7 6 5

Distributed to the book trade in Canada by Macmillan of Canada, a division of Canada
Publishing Corporation.

A CIP catalogue record for this book is available from the British Library.

Microsoft Press books are available through booksellers and distributors worldwide. For further
information about international editions, contact your local Microsoft Corporation office. Or
contact Microsoft Press International directly at fax (206) 936-7329.

PostScript is a trademark of Adobe Systems, Incorporated. Macintosh is a registered trademark
of Apple Computer, Incorporated. Borland is a registered trademark of Borland International,
Incorporated. Sesame Street is a registered trademark of Children's Television Workshop.
CompuServe is a registered trademark of CompuServe, Incorporated. Hoover is a registered
trademark of The Hoover Company. IBM and OS/2 are registered trademarks of International
Business Machines Corporation. Slinky is a registered trademark of James Industries,
Incorporated. Microsoft, Visual Basic, Win32, and Windows are registered trademarks and
Visual C++ and Windows NT are trademarks of Microsoft Corporation. Post-it is a trademark of
Minnesota Mining and Manufacturing Company. Cookie Monster is a registered trademark of
Muppets, Incorporated. UNIX is a registered trademark of Novell, Incorporated. Unicode is a
trademark of Unicode, Incorporated. Smalltalk is a registered trademark of Xerox Corporation.

**Acquisitions Editors:** Dean Holmes and David Clark
**Manuscript Editor:** John Pierce
**Project Editor:** Kathleen Atkins
**Technical Editor:** Jim Fuchs

# CONTENTS

**CHAPTER TWO**

## Objects and Interfaces     **61**

## CHAPTER THREE

# Type Information                                                    **145**

**CHAPTER NINE**

**PART III:** DATA TRANSFER, VIEWING, AND CACHING

**CHAPTER TEN**

**CHAPTER ELEVEN**

# Viewable Objects and the Data Cache      **539**

**CHAPTER TWELVE**

# The OLE Clipboard      **565**

## CHAPTER FIFTEEN

# OLE Automation Controllers and Tools    **731**

## CHAPTER SIXTEEN

# Property Pages, Changes, and Persistence    **761**

## PART V: OLE DOCUMENTS

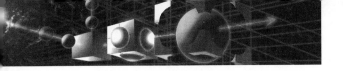

# PREFACE

Someone once said that authors write books not to be understood but so that they themselves understand. Certainly, writing the first edition of this book, *Inside OLE 2,* and now the second edition, *Inside OLE,* has been such an experience for me. It is my sincere hope, of course, that most of my understanding will also make its way into your mind and that you will find innovative ways to exploit the various OLE technologies while having loads of fun in the process.

I started working with OLE 2 in the middle of 1992. From the perspective of my job in Microsoft's Developer Relations Group, I understood the technology as merely a way to create applications that support compound documents. After all, I'd spent the previous year in the same job trying to spread the gospel about OLE version 1, which had no other purpose than the creation and management of compound documents. Because of the legacy of OLE 1, nearly everyone inside and outside Microsoft accepted OLE 2 as a refinement of OLE 1; in fact, the OLE 2 design specifications were organized around compound documents. But for some reason, the specification weighed in at more than 300 pages. There had to be something more.

For months, I plodded through prerelease information about OLE 2 in order to create some sample applications for demonstrating compound documents. With the help of various members of the OLE development team, I gave a number of classes to help others use OLE 2 to create compound document applications. In the back of my mind, however, something still told me that OLE 2 had much more than I had originally perceived. But it was hard to stop equating OLE 2 with compound documents because every available piece of documentation used the two terms synonymously.

During the first weeks of 1993, I started to see that in the process of solving the most important problems in OLE 1, the OLE 2 architects had actually created a much larger system for object-based programming. They had created an extensible technology that also solved the fundamental problems of releasing different versions of software. They had made some key innovations to the fundamental notions of objects. The problem was that the architects didn't tell anyone about these things directly — or maybe I never asked. It's taken me two editions of this book to feel that I really understand what they knew all along.

In any case, I began to see that OLE involves technologies that are quite separate from the areas specific to compound documents. In fact, I started to see exactly how one might use those other technologies without coming into contact with compound documents at all. While I'd been under the impression that OLE 2 was a set of performance improvements to OLE 1, I wasn't aware that OLE 2 was designed from the beginning to be an extensible service architecture—and a very elegant architecture at that. I was slowly beginning to discover OLE's full design, helped by my position at Microsoft, which allowed me to explore OLE in depth and even to browse the sources—letting me truly get "inside OLE."

One Sunday afternoon in mid-January 1993, while doing something totally unrelated to work, I achieved stage one of what Eric Maffei (editor of *Microsoft Systems Journal*) describes as "OLE nirvana." Everything fell into place. I saw clearly, after six months of mental fog (clouded further by the poor documentation that was available at the time), how you could exploit small pieces of OLE in incremental steps. I understood that OLE was a collection of technologies that built on one another and that the best way for me to communicate the entire vision of OLE was to write a book. I quickly fired up my notebook computer and spent the next three hours pounding out the outline. The result was the first edition of this book, published in November 1993.

The worst part about writing a book is that as soon as you get a printed copy in your hands you start finding words and phrases that you want to change. As time goes on, you begin to wish that you had written this or that section differently. With the understanding you've obtained through writing the book, you begin to have new ideas about the subject matter and about new areas you'd like to explore. In my case, I knew I needed eventually to include material about OLE Automation as well as the newest kid on the block, OLE Controls. I wanted to strengthen the earlier chapters by thoroughly discussing object-oriented principles and the important innovations to those principles that are unique to OLE. I also realized that despite my original intentions, the first edition was still mostly oriented toward compound documents. Certain topics, such as monikers, were buried in compound document chapters but deserved chapters of their own. Also, the first edition's sample code was chiefly related to 16-bit operating systems, and I needed to modify it all for 32-bit systems. A second edition was called for.

What clinched my motivation to complete this second edition was stage two of my OLE nirvana enlightenment—"groking" what OLE is really all about and how it is all organized. I understood its purpose and its future.

OLE's life purpose is—well, I won't spoil it for you. I'll let you read Chapter 1 (and Chapter 25) to find the answer, but I'll drop the hint that all of OLE has to do with empowering end users to use their computers in more productive and creative ways. It also has to do with the fact that our programming and computing paradigms are evolving in such a way that objects can truly benefit all end users. In particular, the core of OLE is what is called *component software*. Chapter 1 defines the term as I use it throughout the book. Chapter 25 describes the future of component software as I see it. Everything in between explores the technologies, the mechanisms, and the code that begin to realize it.

While writing this book of my own, I found time to read a good number of others (many of which I've quoted from at the beginning of chapters). In an intriguing case of synchronicity, one of the books I read was an extraordinary one titled *The Chalice and the Blade*, by Riane Eisler.[1] The thesis of Eisler's book is that our culture is approaching a point in history at which we will choose between a *dominator* model (a few individuals and organizations ruling and commanding the masses) and a *partnership* model (everyone working together on an equal basis). The former promises a breakdown of cultural evolution; the latter, a breakthrough. In Eisler's words, "Human evolution is now at a crossroads. Stripped to its essentials, the central human task is how to organize society to promote the survival of our species and the development of our unique potentials.... Humans [as evolutionary theorist Erwin Laszlo points out] 'have the ability to act consciously, and collectively,' exercising foresight to 'choose their own evolutionary path.' "[2]

I see a similar crossroads in the state of the software industry today. Perhaps the choices we have in the software business are merely metaphorical aspects of humanity's overall cultural evolution. (Perhaps this is stage three of OLE nirvana.) Today we have a dominator model—millions of computer users are limited by a few applications created by a few large companies. Component software, however, is a computing environment in which diverse objects created by varied groups and individuals work together, in partnership, to empower all users to solve problems themselves and to create their own software solutions. The software industry can choose either to perpetuate its excessively competitive ways or to build a market in which winning does not have to come at the expense of everything else. Our current ways seek a homogeneous end—one company's products dominating the market. Instead, we can seek an end for which diversity is the most important factor.

---

1. Harper San Francisco, 1987.
2. Eisler, p. 186.

In a component software environment, one's potential is enriched by the diversity of available components and the diversity of available tools. The greater the diversity, the greater our potential. This holds true whether we are discussing software or society.

OLE provides new programming paradigms and new techniques for dealing with object-oriented principles, and it is still struggling to be recognized for the evolutionary technology that it is. Many see OLE as tantamount to heresy, mostly because new ideas threaten change, and change can be terrifying. Many forces rise up to squelch change or to redirect it toward selfish ends. The question we face is whether change is more terrifying than the perpetuation of current conditions. As you will glean from the pages in this book, I personally believe that component software will be essential in the future and that it will eventually be recognized as one of the key innovations in computing history. OLE is the right technology to begin our journey to that undiscovered country.

## What's New in the Second Edition

All of the material that was presented in the first edition still exists in some form in the second edition. Chapters 1, 2, and 5 of this edition provide an overview of OLE, the Component Object Model, and OLE objects and interfaces. They contain information from Chapters 1 through 4 of the first edition and cover topics that didn't exist at the time the first edition was written. Chapters 7 and 8 cover structured storage, compound files, and persistent objects, material included in the single Chapter 5 of the first edition. Chapters 10 and 11 present new information about data transfer mechanisms, viewable objects, and the data cache, building on the material in Chapter 6 from the first edition. Chapter 12 (about the OLE Clipboard) and Chapter 13 (about OLE Drag and Drop) are simple revisions of the first edition's Chapters 7 and 8. Chapters 17 through 23 treat all the elements of OLE Documents and are distillations of the first edition's Chapters 9 through 16. (Some of the old Chapter 16 found its way into the new Chapter 25 as well.) Whenever possible, I've corrected errors in the first edition while making these revisions and incorporated new insights I've had since *Inside OLE 2* was first published.

The remaining chapters are entirely new. Chapters 3, 14, and 15 cover topics typically grouped as OLE Automation: type information, in particular, is given high priority as the subject of Chapter 3. Chapter 4 discusses connectable objects, or what you might know as connection points, a new set of capabilities first created for OLE Controls. Chapter 6 covers Local/Remote Transparency, colloquially called marshaling. Chapter 9 provides full coverage of naming and binding, all the stuff that involves the objects called monikers. (Parts of this were buried in Chapter 12 in the first edition.) Chapter 16 describes ways of dealing with object properties that are not part of OLE Automation, namely property pages, property sets, and property change notifications. Chapter 24 discusses OLE Controls, and Chapter 25 offers a look at the future, detailing upcoming enhancements of the current state of OLE.

My goal in writing this book was to provide an organization in which each chapter depends solely on information in previous chapters, with no dependencies on later chapters (and few forward references). I present material a little at a time in order to help you solidify your understanding before moving on. I hope the book takes you on an evolutionary path so that the work you do early in the book will be reusable in the later stages. I've always found an incremental approach more productive and rewarding than trying to understand everything at once. By concentrating on the fundamentals first, I hope you can make rapid progress through the later chapters. Once you understand what "object" means in OLE, you will see that most of OLE is nothing more than different types of objects and different interfaces that are used to communicate with the objects. Most chapters are, in fact, about a particular set of object types and the interfaces through which those objects provide their services.

It is important to realize that there isn't just one thing you can do with OLE. As a basis for component software, OLE provides many means for integrating components. Your choice of specific OLE technologies to use in order to create and implement a client or an object depends on your goals for component integration. If you have code for some sort of service provider, you need to articulate the types of clients that you want to be capable of using your service. If you are a client of a type of service, you need to consider additional services that would be useful to that client. In this book, you'll see a clear separation between the responsibilities of a provider of a service (the object implementer) and the responsibilities of a client of such a service. When you understand the role of your own products and what integration means to those products, you'll understand how you might exploit each OLE technology to its fullest extent.

So most of this book is about what you can do with OLE and how you work with it. There's also a little bit about why, but most of that is left to you — why is the creative part!

# Who Can Use This Book

In writing this book, I assumed that readers are familiar with the Windows API (primarily the Win32 API) because OLE itself, unlike Win32, is not a technology for writing a complete application (although you could build one out of OLE components). I don't describe how to use Windows API functions, nor do I describe any of the intricate details of Windows itself. The focus of this book is strictly on OLE.

I also assume that readers are at least somewhat familiar with object-oriented programming because I can spend only a paragraph or two defining terms such as *polymorphism* and *encapsulation*. (Entire books could be written about these terms.) In addition, I assume a working familiarity with C++; almost all the samples are written using basic C++ constructs. If you are a C programmer, I've included some material on the companion CD that should help you understand enough C++ to understand the samples.

This book, however, is not intended only for programmers. In fact, the chapter organization allows a designer to gain architectural knowledge of OLE without having to wade through pages of source code listings. The first half or so of each chapter (except for Chapters 1 and 2) is devoted to architectural and theoretical concepts. The latter half of each chapter contains primarily programming details, plus a detailed look at the samples and a discussion of implementation issues.

The samples are written to work on systems with Windows 95, Windows NT 3.51, and Windows 3.1x (if you're still doing 16-bit work). They compile to 16-bit systems (with a couple of exceptions) as well as 32-bit systems (both ANSI and Unicode). To that end, you'll need the following development software on your system to work with the samples in this book:

- Either Windows 95, Windows NT 3.51, or Windows 3.1 (or 3.11)

- Microsoft Visual C++ 2.0 (or later, for 32-bit platforms) or Microsoft Visual C++ 1.51 (or later, for 16-bit platforms). Both products include the Windows Software Development Kit (SDK) for their respective platforms, which is also required. The make files for the samples in this book are specific to Microsoft compilers, so some adjustment will be necessary for other environments. Elements such as compiler flags and import libraries, however, are centralized in one file. Chapter 1 includes more information about creating the appropriate build environment for the book's samples.

■ Certain samples require the OLE Control Development Kit (CDK), which is included with Visual C++ 2.0 (and later) and Visual C++ 1.51 (and later).

■ Depending on your compiler, you may need the Win32 Software Development Kit (SDK) for certain samples as well.

Let me also mention that the OLE documentation is indispensable for working with this technology. In it you'll find all the OLE API functions and interfaces fully documented, which is not possible to do in a book such as this one. Typically, I just mention an API function, sometimes providing all the arguments but never providing the complete documentation. The same is true for OLE interfaces and their member functions.

In this book, I refer to the documentation simply as the *OLE Programmer's Reference*. At the time of writing, the documentation was actually named the *OLE 2 Programmer's Reference* and was published in two volumes. (The second contains OLE Automation topics separately.) Over time, the organization of these volumes might change, new volumes might be added, or the documentation might be called something different. So when I point you to the *OLE Programmer's Reference,* I mean you should look in your development kit for the latest documentation.

One last note about writing conventions before I gush with acknowledgments. OLE interfaces are sets of member functions, and I always present them in a C++ notation. When I refer to an interface as a whole, I use a notation such as *IDataObject.* In references to a member function of an interface, I use a C++ double colon, as in *IDataObject::GetData.* Once I've introduced the interface and have established the context, I often drop the interface name and refer to the function simply as *GetData*, for example. In this case, I am not referring to a global API function named *GetData* but to a member function of the interface under discussion.

# Acknowledgments

*One hesitates between acknowledging one's obligations and implicating one's friends.*
—H. G. Wells, from the preface to *The Outline of History*

People who have read drafts of this book have asked me where I found my inspiration for writing the way I have. Influence has come from many corners, so let me list those sources as well as offer my thanks to the following groups and individuals who have helped create this tome about OLE.

My good friends Bruce Eckel and Charlie Kindel. Bruce is a wonderful source of information and a great sounding board for new ideas (enlightenment, as Bruce calls it). He is also the one person who *will* actually order decaf in Seattle, and he is probably the only person who remembers what I looked like my first time through Splash Mountain at Disneyland. My thanks to Charlie for being the primary technical reviewer for this second edition, as well as for having reviewed the first edition. Charlie and I once shared offices at Microsoft and seem to keep ending up in the same group. (We're now both program managers on the OLE team.)

The many people within Microsoft who have contributed to both editions of this book, including Phil Cooper, Nigel Thompson, Scott Skorupa, Sara Williams, Vinoo Cherian, Craig Wittenberg, Douglas Hodges, Alex Tilles, Mark Bader, Dean McCrory, David Maymudes, William Hsu, Tony Williams, Bob Atkinson, Chris Zimmerman, Mark Ryland, Nat Brown, and the entire OLE team. To all of you, thanks for all your useful real-world insights.

All the programmers in the trenches who are usually told to do too much with too little information. Without you, I'd have little incentive to write a book like this.

All the developers who devoured my draft copies as soon as I could write them and who sent words of encouragement, including Atif Aziz, Joe Najjar, Burt Harris, Brent Rector, Brian Enright, Bruce Fogelsong, Richard Watson, John A. Legelis, Brett Foster, Jurgen Heymann, Dominic Kyrie, Marc Singer, Marcellus Bucheit, Lars Nyman, Howard Chalkley, and Jim Adam, a total Python Head, who reminded me that it was *Patsy* who actually said Camelot was only a model. Thanks also to Burt Harris (again) and Thomas Holaday for setting me straight on the finer points of C++ programming.

John Pierce, Jim Fuchs, Kathleen Atkins, Shawn Peck, and the people at Microsoft Press who did all the production work for this edition and who let me get away with all the crazy things I did here. This includes Ron Lamb, Seth McEvoy, and Kathleen Atkins (take two), who did it all for the first edition. Thanks also to Dean Holmes (now retired from Microsoft Press) for helping me get this book started by saying, "Cool. Do it!"

Monty Python, Yoda, the *Harvard Lampoon,* and *MAD Magazine,* as well as authors Donald Norman, Robert Fulghum, Riane Eisler, Tom DeMarco, Timothy Lister, Douglas Adams, Piers Anthony, Richard Brodie, Roger S. Jones, Douglas Hofstadter, Marvin Harris, and Jim Stacey. Thanks for whatever it is that made me include the crazy things I wrote in this book. You've all written damn good books of your own.

Photographer Dewitt Jones, Lynette Sheppard, and the entire group from our week at HollyHock. You showed me how to enjoy and appreciate doing the crazy things I have done in this book. May you always fly with frozen eagles.

Bob Taniguchi and Viktor Grabner. Thanks to Bob for helping me get into the position at Microsoft to write this book, and to Viktor for teaching me what making my job obsolete really means and how to be a little crazy in the process.

Microsoft's Developer Relations Group. Thanks for allowing me to lock myself in my office undisturbed for months on end (or to simply work at home) while I was doing crazy things.

The guys I always seem to end up hanging out with at conferences, including Bruce "Enlightened" Eckel, Charles "I'm glad I didn't have to write an OLE book" Petzold, and Richard "Why aren't you using MFC?" Hale Shaw. They're all just plain crazy, in a good sort of way <gdr>.

And, finally, my wife and partner, Kristi, who was always there with support and encouragement, even though I'm a little crazy at times.

Kraig Brockschmidt
Redmond (and Bothell), Washington
April 1995

# PART I

# OLE AND OBJECT FUNDAMENTALS

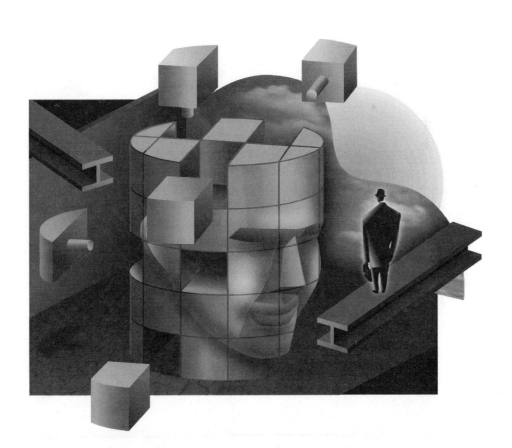

## CHAPTER ONE

# An Overview of OLE

*All evolution in thought and conduct must at first appear as heresy and misconduct.*
—George Bernard Shaw (1856–1950)

Many years from now, a Charles Darwin of computerdom might look back and wonder how the Microsoft Windows API (Application Programming Interface) evolved into an object-oriented operating system in which most of the "API" is provided through the objects. The technology known as OLE is the genesis of this transformation. It will change how you program—and eventually how you use—Windows. In the beginning, you'll probably regard it as utterly strange and difficult, no matter what your background. But don't feel too threatened. OLE doesn't ask you to throw away any knowledge you've accumulated. OLE preserves most of your knowledge and your code—extending the reach of both to help you reach new heights in software. OLE exists to facilitate and enable the integration of components, either parts of the system of applications or simply stand-alone elements, and it is the capacity for integration that creates a tremendous opportunity for innovation and growth.

Most people involved in the computer industry acknowledge the value of objects or object-oriented programming—whatever these things are. An object offers a certain set of features that define its functionality and the information it manages. Objects are powerful because a single pointer or other reference to an object provides access to all that object's functionality and content. Without objects, programs usually have to maintain multiple variables and pass them to isolated functions to achieve the same ends, adding greatly to complexity. By grouping such variables and functions in a single unit, an object, you create a layer of abstraction that simplifies many programming tasks and provides additional power. This abstraction is a key to extensibility, where new types added into a system can appear and act as existing types.

OLE's contribution to "objects" is threefold. First, OLE enables the integration of components—packages of one or more objects—that object-oriented languages such as C++ cannot, and in that way OLE strongly complements such languages. Second, OLE works independently of programming languages through a binary standard, allowing the oldest legacy code to integrate as a component alongside the newest object-oriented code. Furthermore, objects in OLE share the characteristics of all objects: they are encapsulated, they are polymorphic, and they are reusable. OLE is often denounced as heretical because of minor differences between OLE objects and other objects. OLE's language independence accounts for most of the differences. Such accusations fail to recognize the third category of OLE's tremendously powerful innovations—its concept of object "interfaces" and the idea that objects can have multiple interfaces, each of which represents support for a feature. These interfaces are, literally, different ways of communicating with an object—that is, accessing its functionality and its information. The abstraction of interfaces thus simplifies even more programming tasks, some heretofore impossible.

So while objects are very powerful because they factor functionality and information into tangible units, OLE takes it one step further and factors that functionality and information into related groups, which provides a way for the client or user of an object to ask the object—at run time—which features it supports. This arrangement makes it possible for the independent development and deployment of components over time, without requiring any recompilation of anything else in the system, without requiring a restart of the system, and without having to hassle with compatibility problems. OLE solves such problems, making evolutionary object-oriented component integration possible.

OLE is, at its core, a collection of component services accessed through objects that expose specific interfaces. You can customize some of these services with objects of your own that hook into this core, and if the services you want are not part of OLE, you can also create your own custom services using exactly the same mechanisms. In this sense, OLE is an extensible service architecture, in which a custom, or extended, service transparently becomes part of the core set of services and is immediately available to everything else in the system.

OLE is built on a foundation, the Component Object Model (COM) as it's called, that is both language independent and location independent. Language independence means that you can use any language to implement components as long as the programming tool in whatever language supports the idea of an OLE interface. With OLE, you can encapsulate an existing piece of code as an object without having to necessarily rewrite that code. Location independence means that these components and objects can be implemented and shared in separate dynamic link libraries (DLLs), or executables (EXEs) on the same machine or across machines.[1]

After defining and exploring exactly what OLE is, we'll take a look at OLE's concepts of components, objects, and interfaces. We'll then briefly examine each specific OLE feature (or technology), describing how your software might take advantage of it (that is, profit from it). By using these features today, you can begin to transform your software to take advantage more readily of the future evolution of Windows (that is, profit from it tomorrow), which is going to involve not only today's OLE but also evolutionary enhancements that Microsoft—and others—will be adding in the future. OLE might seem like heresy today. But the fact is that OLE is a powerful evolution of "objects," and someday Darwin's successor will have plenty to say about OLE—the origin of a new species of incredibly sophisticated and powerful software.

# What Is OLE?

Because this hefty tome you're holding is all about OLE, it behooves us to describe exactly what OLE is. To set the stage, we need to understand a little about the programming problems that OLE designers intend to solve.

## History: Why OLE?

Constant innovation in computing hardware and software have made a multitude of powerful and sophisticated applications available to users at their desktops and across their networks. Yet, with such sophistication have come many problems for developers, software vendors, and users. For one, such large and complex software is difficult and time-consuming to develop, maintain, and revise. Revision is a major problem for monolithic applications, even operating systems, in which features are so intertwined that they cannot be individually and independently updated or replaced. Furthermore, software is not easily integrated when written using different programming languages and when running in separate processes or on separate machines.

---

1. At the time of writing, cross-machine OLE is not yet available, although the OLE architecture is designed to anticipate such capabilities.

Even when integration facilities have been available, the programming models for working with different services across various boundaries have not been consistent. The trends of hardware downsizing and greater software complexity are driving the need for distributed component environments. This requires a generic set of facilities for finding and using services (components), regardless of who provides them or where those services run, as well as a robust method for evolving services independently over time without losing compatibility with clients of earlier versions. Any real solution to these problems must also take advantage of object-oriented concepts and be capable of working with legacy code—that is, look to the future without forgetting history.

As an example, consider the problem of creating a system service API that works with multiple providers of some service in a polymorphic fashion. In other words, you want a client of the service to be able to transparently use any particular provider of the service without any special knowledge of which specific provider—or implementation—is in use. In traditional systems, every application calls a central piece of code to access meta-operations such as selecting a service and connecting to it. Usually this code is a service, or an *object manager,* that involves function-call programming models with system-provided handles as the means for object selection. But once applications have used the object manager to connect to a service, the object manager only gets in the way like a big brick wall and forces unnecessary overhead. Yuck.

Worse yet, such traditional service models make it nearly impossible for the service provider to express new, enhanced, or unique capabilities to potential clients in a uniform fashion. A well-designed traditional service architecture, such as Microsoft's Open Database Connectivity (ODBC) API, might provide the notion of different levels of service. Applications can count on the minimum level of service and then determine at run time whether the provider supports higher levels of service in certain predefined quanta. The providers, however, are restricted to providing the levels of services defined at the outset by the API; they cannot readily provide a new capability that clients could discover at run time and access as if it were part of the original specification. To take the ODBC example, the vendor of a database provider intent on doing more than current ODBC standards permit must convince Microsoft to revise ODBC in a way that exposes that vendor's extra capabilities. In addition, the Microsoft bottleneck limits the ability for multi-vendor initiatives independent from Microsoft to exploit an existing technology for their own purposes. Thus, traditional service architectures cannot be readily extended or supplemented in a decentralized fashion—you have to go through the operating system vendor. Yuck.

Traditional service architectures also tend to be limited in their version handling. The problem with versioning is one of representing capabilities (what a piece of code can do) and identity (what a piece of code is) in an interrelated, ambiguous way. A later version of some piece of code, such as "Code version 2," indicates that it is like "Code version 1" but different in some distinct and identifiable way. The problem with traditional versioning in this manner is that it's difficult for code to indicate exactly *how* it differs from a previous version and, worse yet, for clients of that code to react appropriately to new versions—or to not react at all if they expect only the previous version. The versioning problem can be reasonably managed in a traditional system when there is only a single provider of a certain kind of service. In this case, the version number of the service is checked when the client binds to the service. The service is extended only in an upward-compatible manner (a significant restriction as software evolves over time) so that a version $n$ provider will work with consumers of versions 1 through $n-1$ as well, and references to a running instance of the service are not freely passed around by clients, all of whom might expect or require different versions. But these kinds of restrictions are unacceptable in a multivendor, distributed, modular system with polymorphic service providers. In other words, yuck.

Thus, service management, extensibility of an architecture, and versioning of services are the problems. Application complexity continues to increase as functionality becomes more and more difficult to extend. Monolithic applications are popular because it is safer and easier to collect all interdependent services and the code that uses those services into one package. Interoperability between applications suffers accordingly because monolithic applications are loath to allow outsiders to access their functionality and thus build a dependence on a certain behavior of a certain version of the code. Because end users demand interoperability, however, software developers are compelled to attempt some integration anyway, but this leads back to the problem of software complexity and completes a vicious cycle of problems that limit the progress of software development. Major yuck.

## Component Software: The Breakthrough

Object-oriented programming has long been advanced as a solution to the problems at hand. However, while object-oriented programming is powerful, it has yet to reach its full potential because, in part, no standard framework exists through which software created by different vendors can interact within the same address space—much less across address spaces—and across network and machine architecture boundaries. The major result of the object-oriented programming revolution has been the production of islands of objects that can't talk to one another across the oceanic boundaries in a meaningful way. Messages in bottles just don't cut it.

The solution is a system in which software developers create *software components*. A software component is reusable pieces of code and data in binary form that can be plugged into other software components from other vendors with relatively little effort. Software components must adhere to an external binary standard, but their internal implementation is completely unconstrained. They can be built using procedural languages as well as object-oriented languages and frameworks (although the latter usually provide many development advantages).

Software component objects are much like integrated circuit (IC) components, and component software is the integrated circuitry of tomorrow. The software industry today is very much where the hardware industry was 20 years ago. At that time, vendors learned how to shrink transistors and put them into a package so that no one had to figure out how to build a particular discrete function—a NAND gate, for example—ever again. Such functions were built into an integrated circuit, a neat package that designers could conveniently buy and design around. As the hardware functions became more complex, the ICs were further integrated to make a board of chips that provided more complex functionality and increased capability. As integrated circuits got smaller yet provided more functionality, boards of chips became just bigger chips. So hardware technology now uses chips to build even bigger chips.

The software industry is now at a point where software developers have been busy building the software equivalent of discrete transistors—software routines—for a long time.

OLE offers a solution and a future—extensible standards and mechanisms to enable software developers to package their functionality, and content, into reusable components, like an integrated circuit. Instead of worrying about how to build functions, developers can simply acquire or purchase that function without having to care about its internal implementation. Just as electronics engineers do not purchase the sources for integrated circuits and rebuild them, OLE allows you to buy a binary component and reuse it, plugging into it through its external interfaces. Not only is this component software a great benefit for developers, but it will eventually allow even end users to assemble custom applications. Users will then have the ability to solve their own problems immediately on a level they understand instead of having to wait months or years for a one-size-fits-all solution. Thus, OLE is the innovation to spark an exciting new fire in all aspects of computing.

## OLE Defined

Through its history, there have been many descriptions of OLE, ranging from the sublime to the ridiculous. At some time or another, OLE has been identified with many of its constituent technologies, such as Compound Documents, visual editing, OLE Automation, the Component Object Model, and OLE Controls. You might have seen such narrow identifications in magazines, newsletters, and books.

Each of these definitions is partially true because OLE includes all of them, but each identity misses any conception of a unified whole. A complete definition of OLE must include not only these large and visible technologies but also the minutiae that fill the gaps between them. Furthermore, the definition cannot be rigidly based on the composition of OLE at the time this book was written because Microsoft and other industry groups are continually creating new OLE technologies that are not covered in the pages of this book. Further still, OLE allows software developers to arbitrarily extend the architecture. Therefore, our definition—our framework for understanding OLE—must be flexible to accommodate new additions.

With these characteristics in mind, I define OLE as follows: *OLE is a unified environment of object-based services with the capability of both customizing those services and arbitrarily extending the architecture through custom services, with the overall purpose of enabling rich integration between components.*

Stated another way, OLE offers an *extensible service architecture,* and in addition to the architecture, OLE itself provides a number of key customizable services, one of which in turn provides for the creation of custom services of any complexity that extend the environment within the same architectural framework. All services, regardless of their complexity, point of storage, point of execution, and implementation, are globally usable by all applications, by the system, and by all other services.

Note that OLE is not a technology for writing every part of an application as the Win32 API is. Where you use the Win32 API to write code and use system resources, you use OLE to share those components with everyone else as well as to access the shared components from the rest of the world.

The collective term used to refer to all services is *component.* To be completely precise, a service is really made of one or more components, but most often a component is a service in itself. In any case, a component is itself made of one or more *objects*, where each object then provides its functionality and content through one or more *interfaces*. These interfaces, in turn, each contain one or more feature-specific member functions. It is through these member functions that one accesses everything a component can do. So while there may be simple memory-allocation services that have one component, one object, and one interface on that object (with a handful of member functions), other components might have several objects that each have several interfaces through which they expose a great number of features.

*Component software* is the practical and consumer-oriented realization of the developer-oriented principles of object-oriented programming. Component software is the vision of a computing environment in which developers and end users can incrementally add features to their applications simply by purchasing additional components, rather than by writing such components themselves or by finding more feature-laden monolithic applications.

OLE's life purpose, if you will, is to enable and facilitate component integration and component software. This makes it possible for pieces of applications to talk to one another and makes it possible to create software that involves many pieces of different applications, which is otherwise impossible to do inside a single monolithic program. As a concrete example, consider the creation of a compound document whose contents come from a variety of sources (text, graphics, charts, tables, sound, video, database queries, controls, and so forth). Providing this capability in a nonextensible monolithic application *restricts* the types of information that one can put into a document to only those types that were known to the application at build time. If a new type of content becomes available, as frequently happens, this application would have to be redeveloped, recompiled, and redeployed—a very slow and costly venture—in order to incorporate new content. In contrast, in the component software environment, the application that manages the compound document can allow the user to use content from any available component. If the component environment is designed to be extensible, as OLE is, newly installed components become available immediately to all existing components and applications. Thus, without modification of the document application, a new type of content is usable as soon as the component is installed.

OLE version 1 was created back in 1991, under the now obsolete title "Object Linking and Embedding," for the express purpose of enabling exactly this sort of compound document integration. OLE version 2 was planned originally as performance improvements and enhancements to the functionality of OLE 1, but it grew beyond the boundaries of compound documents into a much more generic service architecture. As we'll see in this chapter and throughout this book, there are many other meaningful and interesting ways to integrate components other than compound documents, such as performing a drag-and-drop operation or controlling an application programmatically. Certainly compound document technology is still part of OLE and makes a sizable topic for this book, but it no longer enjoys exclusive use of the OLE name. OLE is thus no longer an acronym for Object Linking and Embedding but is rather the name of Microsoft's component integration technology.

You may also notice that OLE is no longer given a version number. The first edition of this book was called *Inside OLE 2,* but this edition is just *Inside OLE.* The reason for this is that OLE 2 implies that there will be an OLE 3. There will not be any such product. *As an extensible service architecture, new features and technologies can be added to OLE within the existing framework without having to change the existing framework!* For example, OLE Controls, a major addition to the architecture, was released more than a year after the original release of OLE 2, but it required no changes to that original technology. Instead, OLE Controls simply builds on and enhances what existed before. This will continue to be true as Microsoft and others add technologies in the future—what exists today will retain its vitality.

## Clients and Servers

As mentioned in the previous section, a service or a component is provided through one or more objects, each object consisting of a logical grouping (or isolation) of particular features of the component. These objects make up the communication channels between the user of those objects (some piece of code) and the provider of the objects.

In this book, I use the term *client* to refer to the user of objects—the piece of code that is accessing the functionality and the content of those objects. *Client* literally means "one who uses the services of another," which is exactly what we're talking about. In some cases, I might use the term *user* or *object user* synonymously with *client*.[2] In addition, when a client also maintains the persistent states of object instances, that client is called a *container* because it contains those object instances that are entirely described by the state data. *Container* is most frequently used in the context of compound documents and custom controls.

The provider of a component and its constituent objects is known as a *server,* literally, "one who furnishes services." There is hardly a better term to describe a service provider, for in a programmatic sense a server is the

---

2. In *Inside OLE 2,* I used the term *user* much more frequently than I do in this edition. That was because the term *client* was poorly understood from the compound document definition that was used with OLE 1, and so in the transition from OLE 1 to OLE 2, *client* was ambiguous. Now that OLE 2 has established itself, it is once again safe to use *client* in the real meaning of the word.

demand-loaded code module—such as a DLL or an EXE—that makes a component and its objects available to the outside world. Without a server, the objects remain hidden from external view. The server holds them out on a silver platter and invites clients to partake of them.

The relationship between a client, a server, and the objects that make up a component or a server is illustrated in Figure 1-1. This is similar to the more general definition of any client-server relationship that might use any number of mechanisms to communicate. In the OLE relationship shown here, however, communication happens through OLE objects.

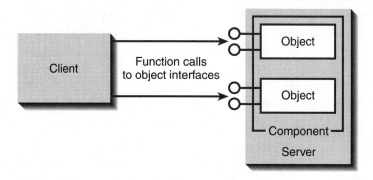

**Figure 1-1.**
*The OLE client-server relationship. A* client *uses a component or a service as provided by a* server, *and the communication between client and server happens through OLE objects.*

## Object-Based Components: COM

Our definition of OLE describes services as being "object-based." What does this mean exactly? What are "objects"—the communication medium between clients and servers—in the context of OLE? In order to answer this question, we have to look at all the various definitions of the term so we can really understand why an OLE object is what it is. The concepts that form the idea of an OLE object are collectively called the *Component Object Model,* or COM.

*Object* has to be one of the most bastardized, hackneyed, and confusing terms in the computer industry. Some argue over "real" and "fake" objects. There are academic uses of the term, end-user–oriented uses, and flat out common uses. *Objects* might refer to a methodology, specific techniques in object-oriented programming languages, or icons and other user-interface elements on a computer screen. Then, of course, you have philosophical wackos like me who will argue that the gold-plated Slinky on my desk and the model of the St. Louis Gateway Arch on my bookshelf are also objects.

## The Classical Object Definition

When you strip away all the politics, rhetoric, and other baggage and study the original concepts of object-oriented development, you find that an object is an instance of some *class* in which that object is *anything* that supports three fundamental notions:

■ *Encapsulation:* all the details about the composition, structure, and internal workings of an object are hidden from clients. The client's view is generically called the object's *interface.* The internals of the object are said to be hidden behind its interface. The interface of the computer keyboard with which I'm typing this book consists of labeled keys, in a specific layout, that I can press to generate a character in my word processor. The internal details of how a keystroke is translated into a character on the screen are encapsulated behind this interface. In the same manner, the internal implementation details of a Smalltalk string object are encapsulated behind the public member functions and variables of that Smalltalk object.

■ *Polymorphism:* the ability to view two similar objects through a common interface, thereby eliminating the need to differentiate between the two objects. For example, consider the structure of most writing instruments (pens and pencils). Even though each instrument might have a different ink or lead, a different tip, and a different color, they all share the common interface of how you hold and write with that instrument. All of these objects are polymorphic through that interface — any instrument can be used in the same way as any other instrument that also supports that interface, just as all Slinky toys, regardless of their size and material, act in many ways like any other Slinky. In computer terms, I might have an object that knows how to draw a square and another that knows how to draw a triangle. I can view both of them as having certain features of a "shape" in common, and through that "shape" interface, I can ask either object to draw itself.

■ *Inheritance:* a method to express the idea of polymorphism for which the similarities of different classes of objects are described by a common *base class.* The specifics of each object class are defined by a *derived class* — that is, a class derived from the base class. The derived class is said to *inherit* the properties and characteristics of the base class; thus, all classes derived from the same base class are polymorphic through that base class. For example, I might describe a base class called "Writing Instruments" and make derived classes of "Ballpoint Pen," "Pencil," "Fountain Pen," and so forth. If I wanted to program different "shape" objects, I could define a base class "Shape" and then derive my "Square" and "Triangle" classes from that base class. I achieve polymorphism along with the convenience of being able to centralize all the base class code in one place, within the "Shape" class implementation.

Inheritance is often a sticky point when you come to work with OLE because OLE supports the idea of inheritance only on a conceptual level for the purposes of defining interfaces. In OLE, there is no concept of an object or a class inheriting implementation from another, as there is in C++. But here is the important point: *inheritance is a means to polymorphism and reusability and is not an end in itself.* To implement polymorphic objects in C++, you use inheritance. To create reusable code in C++, you centralize common code in a base class and reuse it through derived classes. But inheritance is not the only means to these two ends! Recognizing this enables us to explore means of polymorphism and reusability that work on the level of binary components, which is OLE's realm, rather than on the level of source code modules, which is the realm of C++ and other object-oriented programming languages.

## OLE Objects and OLE Interfaces

As we will explore in this book, objects as expressed in OLE most definitely support the notions of encapsulation, polymorphism, and reusability; again, inheritance is really just a means to the latter two. OLE objects are just as powerful as any other type of object expressed in any programming language, and might be more so. While inheritance and programming languages are excellent ways to achieve polymorphism and reusability of objects or components within a large monolithic application, *OLE is about integration between binary components, and it is therefore targeted at a different set of problems.* OLE is designed to be independent of programming languages, hardware architectures, and other implementation techniques. So there really is no comparison with, and no basis for pitting OLE against, object-oriented programming languages and methodologies; in fact, such languages and methods are very helpful and complementary to OLE in solving customer problems.

The nature of an OLE object, then, is not expressed in how it is implemented internally but rather in how it is exposed externally. As a basis for illustrating the exact structures involved, let's assume we have some software object, written in whatever language (code) that has some properties (data or content) and some methods (functionality), as illustrated in Figure 1-2. Access to these properties and methods within the object and its surrounding server code is determined by the programming language in use.

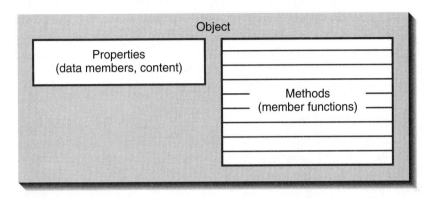

**Figure 1-2.**
*Any object can be seen as a set of properties (data members or content) and methods (member functions).*

The accessibility of the object's members in its native programming language is not of interest to OLE. What does concern OLE is how to share the object's capabilities with the outside world, which does not need to correspond at all to the object's internal structure. The external appearance of the object, that is, how clients of this object will access its functionality and content, is what OLE helps you define and implement.

In OLE, you factor an object's features into *one or more groups of semantically related functions,* where each group is called an *interface.* Again, an object can provide multiple interfaces to its client, and this capability is one of OLE's key innovations. Microsoft has already defined many interfaces representing many common features, and many of these interfaces will likely never require revision. For example, the group of functions that describes structured data exchange is easily specified and can thus be a "standard" OLE-defined interface. You are also free to define "custom" interfaces for your own needs without every having to ask Microsoft to approve the design—custom interfaces fit into the OLE architecture the way any standard interface does. We'll explore both standard and custom interfaces throughout this book.

Regardless of who defines an object's interfaces, all access to an object happens through member functions of those interfaces, meaning that OLE doesn't allow direct access to an object's internal variables. The primary reason is that OLE works on a binary component level where you would require complex protocols to control access. (In contrast, programming languages handle such control easily through source code constructs.) In addition, accessing object variables directly usually involves pointer manipulation in the client's address space, which makes it very difficult to make such access transparent across process or machine boundaries unless you stipulate language structures and compiler code generation. On the other hand, because a client gives control to the object through a function call, it is quite easy to transparently intercept that call with a "proxy" object and have it forward the call to another process or machine where the real object is running, and do so in a way independent of languages and compilers.

In the binary standard for an interface, the object provides the implementation of each member function in the interface and creates an array of pointers to those functions, called the *vtable*.[3] This vtable is shared among all instances of the object class, so to differentiate each instance, the object code allocates according to the object's internal implementation a second structure that contains its private data. The specifications for an OLE interface stipulate that the first 4 bytes in this data structure must be a 32-bit pointer to the vtable, after which comes whatever data the object wants (depending on the programming language). An *interface pointer* is a pointer to the top of this instance structure: thus a pointer to the pointer to the vtable. It is through this interface pointer that a client accesses the object's implementation of the interface—that is, calls the interface member functions but cannot access the object's private data. This interface structure is depicted in Figure 1-3.

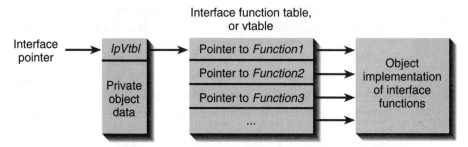

**Figure 1-3.**
*The binary standard for an OLE interface means that an object creates a vtable that contains pointers to the implementations of the interface member functions and allocates a structure in which the first 32 bits are a pointer to that vtable. The client's pointer to the interface is a pointer to the pointer to the vtable.*

---

3. For "virtual function table" because the design of an OLE interface is modeled after the structure of C++ objects that have virtual functions.

If you are familiar with the internals of C++, you'll recognize this structure as exactly that which many C++ compilers typically generate for a C++ object instance. This is entirely intentional on OLE's part, making it very convenient to write OLE objects using C++. In short, if a C++ object class is derived from an OLE interface definition, you can typecast the object's *this* pointer into an interface pointer. Chapter 2 will describe various techniques for doing so. This interface design, however, is merely convenient for C++ programmers. You can easily generate this same interface structure from straight C code, as we'll also see in Chapter 2, and even from assembly language. Since you can express it in assembly language, and because any other programming language can be reduced to an assembly equivalent, you can create an interface from any other language as long as your tools know about OLE and give you a language device through which you can implement or use an interface.

Again I'll point out that because different compilers and languages will store an object's instance data differently in the instance structure, the client cannot directly access that data through an interface pointer. In fact, the client never has any sort of pointer to the object, only to interfaces, because the notion of an object is so variable, whereas the notion of an interface is a binary standard. Besides, direct access—client code manipulating data based on a memory offset—works only when the client and the object share the same address space. In OLE, this is not always the case, so OLE's definition of an interface pointer *type* restricts the use of a pointer at compile time. The definition of the type depends, of course, on the programming language but always allows you to call functions by name through an interface pointer, such as *pInterface->MemberFunction(…)*, and provides type checking on the function's arguments. This is much more convenient than trying to call functions through an array offset with no type checking.

What is highly inconvenient is having to draw the entire binary structure whenever you want to illustrate an object. By convention, interfaces are drawn as plug-in jacks extending from the object, as illustrated in Figure 1-4. When a client wants to use the object through an interface, it must plug into that interface. The electronics analogy is that for a client to use a jack (interface), it must have a plug that fits (code that knows how to use the members of that interface).

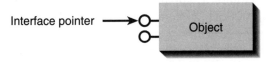

**Figure 1-4.**
*Interfaces are drawn as plug-in jacks extending from the object.*

This representation of an object and its interfaces emphasizes an important point: *an interface is not an object.* An interface is merely a channel for the object, and only one of the many channels an object might support. In a "Prolegomenon to Object Metaphysics," we might think of how the philosopher Immanuel Kant, asking how we know something is real, would differentiate objects from interfaces.[4] In such a Kantian analysis, objects are *noumena*—things-in-themselves that are in principle incapable of being known or experienced directly. Interfaces are, on the other hand, *phenomena*—manifestations of objects for sensing experience (your code). Since we can't know objects directly, we tend to refer to them and reify them as their interfaces, but strictly speaking, an object remains conceptual as far as clients of that object are concerned. The client knows only the general "type" of an object as a collection of interfaces that define that type.

As a further reinforcement of this idea, all interfaces are conventionally named with a capital *I* prefix, as in *IUnknown, IDataObject,* and so on. The symbolic name of the interface describes the feature of functionality defined in that interface. In addition, you identify an interface at run time not by its textual name but by a binary 128-bit globally unique identifier (globally unique in the real and literal sense). Contrast this to a C++ class, which is only identified at compile time by a text name that is unique only to the compilation.

You should notice that hiding the object behind its interfaces is *exactly* the fundamental notion of encapsulation. OLE also supports the idea of polymorphism between interfaces. All that is needed are two interfaces that share a common subset of functions—a base interface—in their vtables, as shown in Figure 1-5. C++ inheritance works well to define such relationships.

The interface named *Iunknown* has three functions and is the ubiquitous base interface for *every other interface* in OLE. All interfaces are polymorphic with *IUnknown,* as also illustrated in Figure 1-5. This interface represents two fundamental OLE object features. The first is the ability to control an object's lifetime by using reference counting, which happens through the member functions *AddRef* and *Release.* The second feature is navigation between multiple interfaces on an object through a function called *QueryInterface,* as we'll see shortly.

So at least at the interface level, polymorphism is clearly supported in OLE. What is left in the set of fundamental object notions that we've defined here is reusability, and it should be apparent to you that the client of any object can itself be an object. Such a client object can implement any of its

---

4. My thanks to Mark Ryland (Microsoft) for this philosophical diversion.

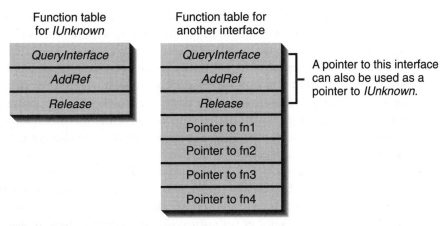

Function table
for *IUnknown*

| QueryInterface |
| AddRef |
| Release |

Function table for
another interface

| QueryInterface |
| AddRef |
| Release |
| Pointer to fn1 |
| Pointer to fn2 |
| Pointer to fn3 |
| Pointer to fn4 |

A pointer to this interface
can also be used as a
pointer to *IUnknown.*

**Figure 1-5.**
*Interfaces are polymorphic through a base interface when they both have the
same base interface functions at the top of their vtables.*

interfaces by using the implementation of another object's interfaces internally, which is reusability by *containment.* The client object contains internally
the object being reused, and external clients of the containing object are
unaware of such reuse, as it should be. Containment is by far the most common method of reusability in OLE and requires no special support in either
object. In some special circumstances, one object might want to directly
expose another object's interface pointer as its own, and this requires a special relationship known as *aggregation.* We'll explore reusability through both
means in Chapter 2, but for now we can realize that OLE objects support all
three fundamental object notions: encapsulation, polymorphism, and reusability. And as we're now ready to discuss, OLE's idea of multiple interfaces is
an important and powerful innovation.

## Multiple Interfaces and *QueryInterface*

As you read through this book, it is important to remember the difference
between an object and an interface: you can implement an object however
you want, to do whatever you want; and when you want to share its functionality and content with other components, you can provide as many interfaces as
you need, each one representing a subset of the object's features.

Now, even though OLE and C++ share the same binary structure for
accessing an object's member functions, the ability to create an object with
*multiple interfaces* is extraordinarily powerful. It represents one of OLE's

strongest architectural features and is the basis for its notion of *polymorphism between objects* in addition to polymorphism between interfaces, which we have already seen.

Because each interface is a group of semantically related functions, each interface that an object supports represents a specific feature of that object. For example, if an object supports the capability of exchanging formatted data structures, it implements the interface named *IDataObject*, whose member functions describe all the different aspects of exchanging the data, such as set data, get data, enumerate formats, and so on. It is the presence of this interface that describes the object's data exchange capacities.

Herein lies OLE's architectural advantage over single-interface models such as C++: objects can describe their features on a higher level of abstraction than individual member functions, which enables a client to ask the object whether it supports a particular feature before that client attempts to use such a feature. Contrast this to C++ techniques, which might require that a client attempt to call a function simply in order to check whether that function will work. The ability of a client to ask an object about support for a feature decouples the act of testing for functionality from the act of invoking the functionality.

The function *IUnknown::QueryInterface* (using C++ syntax) is the decoupling mechanism that a client uses to navigate through multiple interfaces. Because *QueryInterface* belongs to *IUnknown*, and because all interfaces in OLE are derived from and are polymorphic with *IUnknown*, *QueryInterface* is universally available through whatever interface pointer a client might have. The interfaces available through the same implementation of *QueryInterface* are said to be implemented *alongside* one another. If you see a reference to "interface A is implemented alongside interface B," it means that you can use *QueryInterface* to get from A to B and from B to A.

Whenever a client accesses any object, it can always obtain an initial *IUnknown* pointer for that object. But because the client can only call *IUnknown* functions through this pointer, it can't do a whole lot with the object. In order to use any other object feature—any other interface—the client must first *ask* the object whether it supports that feature by calling *QueryInterface*. In making this call, the client passes the unique identifier a globally unique identifier of the interface it would like to access. If the object supports that interface, it will return a pointer to that interface to the client; otherwise, it returns an error. If support is there, the client is given the exact interface pointer through which it can then call the member functions of that interface and access that feature. If support is not there, the object provides no such pointer, thereby disallowing all calls to unsupported features. An illustration of the *QueryInterface* process is shown in Figure 1-6.

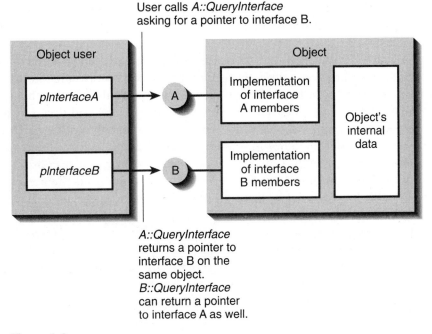

User calls *A::QueryInterface*
asking for a pointer to interface B.

*A::QueryInterface*
returns a pointer to
interface B on the
same object.
*B::QueryInterface*
can return a pointer
to interface A as well.

**Figure 1-6.**
*The* QueryInterface *function navigates through all the interfaces on
an object.*

So *QueryInterface* is a tight coupling between asking an object whether it
supports a feature and the ability to access that feature: *a client must have an
appropriate interface pointer to access a feature, and the only way to obtain the pointer
is by calling* QueryInterface—*you have to ask!*

Let this sink in for a while, and you might begin to realize the real
importance of this simple mechanism. *QueryInterface* and the idea that an
object's functionality is factored into *interfaces* rather than single *functions*
provide what is called "robust evolution of functionality over time." This is the
ability to take a component and its constituent objects, add new objects to the
component and new interfaces to its objects, and redeploy the component
into a *running* system without breaking compatibility with existing clients.
Because new features are added in the form of new uniquely identified interfaces and existing clients will never ask for interfaces that they do not understand, new interfaces do not interfere with any existing interfaces. As far as
existing clients are concerned, the objects have not changed, but new clients
that do understand those additional interfaces can take full advantage of the

new features. In this way, you have components and clients that can evolve independently over time, through many revisions, retaining full compatibility with the past without stunting future improvements.

A key point in all of this is that a change to an object or a component *requires absolutely no recompilation or changes whatsoever to existing clients.* Contrast this with a change to a C++ base class, which always requires a recompilation of any derived classes. In OLE, you never have to update an object client just because the object changes. Certainly any existing client will not use the new features of the object, but as soon as that client is independently updated to ask for those new interfaces, it can take advantage of supporting objects immediately without requiring any changes to the objects themselves.

We'll see a concrete example of this sort of independent evolution of an object and a client in Chapter 2. What is still left to mention here is the idea of polymorphism between objects. Because an interface is defined as a fixed group of member functions, an interface implemented on any object has exactly the same functions and semantics as the same interface implemented on any other object. In other words, a client can call those member functions without having to know exactly what type of object it's really talking to. This is polymorphism: any two objects are polymorphic through the interfaces they have in common. The client can always call each member function in the interface, but what the object does in response to the call can vary within the design of the interface function. For example, with the function *IViewObject2-::Draw*, a client can ask an object to draw its visual presentation to the screen or a printer. What the object will actually draw depends on the object and its state data, but the client's *intent* to draw the object is constant.

OLE takes advantage of this polymorphism in a number of its higher-level technologies, such as those dealing with compound documents and custom controls. Every OLE control, for example, supports the same set of interfaces that define a control, and so a *control container*—a client that specifically works with controls—treats all controls polymorphically through those interfaces. The container need not care about the specific types of controls: they're all just controls.

The notion of multiple interfaces for OLE objects has tremendous power and implications. To my knowledge, this extraordinary facility is not part of any other object model, programming language, or operating system technology. The idea that you can factor an object's capabilities into distinct, feature-oriented groups opens all sorts of opportunities to create innovative components and offers a promising future of interoperability and integration between components that has never before been realized.

# OLE Technologies, Features, and Services

To reiterate our definition, OLE is a unified environment of object-based services with the capability of both customizing those services and arbitrarily extending the architecture through custom services, with the overall purpose of enabling rich integration between components. Since we now understand how components express their capabilities through interfaces, we can take a look at the individual technologies within the rest of OLE.

OLE as a whole (including recent and future enhancements) is made up of a number of Win32-style API functions (those with global names that are direct calls into system DLLs) as well as a large number of interfaces. Each interface expresses a certain feature through some number of member functions. OLE currently has no fewer than 120 API functions and no fewer than 80 interfaces that average 5 to 6 member functions each. A little quick math, and you end up with almost 600 individual functions. That's a tremendous amount of functionality! But all of it falls into three categories:

- Access to OLE-implemented components (which include helper functions to make programming tasks easier)

- Customization of OLE-implemented components

- The capability of extending the environment through custom components with a wide range of possible features

In other words, OLE implements a fair amount of functionality itself and, in many cases, allows direct customization of that functionality through implementations of small isolated objects that are plugged into those components. Where OLE doesn't provide a component—most of its components are very general—OLE supports the creation of custom components, making them available to all clients through the same architecture. Many of OLE's interfaces are usually implemented on the objects in these custom components, and many of OLE's API functions assist in the operations that are involved within those interfaces.

There has been some confusion in OLE's past about who or what implements this or that interface, but this is really a meaningless question. The key question is who or what implements a particular component, and once you've answered that question, you can then ask what features that component supports and what interfaces are used to supply those features. It is true that some of OLE's components exclusively control certain types of objects and thus are the only implementers of certain interfaces. This has led some people to think that only one type of object ever implements a specific interface, but the truth is that most interfaces can be implemented by any object in any component whatsoever.

So to better understand this difference between components, the objects involved, and the interfaces on those objects, let's look at all of the various technologies within OLE, discussions of which comprise the contents of the rest of this book:

**Type Information (Chapter 3)**   A means to completely describe an object along with all of its interfaces, down to the names and types (including user-defined types) of each argument to each named function in each interface.

**Connectable Objects (Chapter 4)**   The ability to create outgoing interfaces for an object, such as notifications and event sets.

**Custom Components and COM (Chapter 5)**   The ability to create an optionally licensed component that extends the available services to clients.

**Local/Remote Transparency (Chapter 6)**   The ability to transparently integrate clients and components across process and machine boundaries as if they were all in the same process.

**Structured Storage and Compound Files (Chapter 7)**   A powerful and shareable means to deal with permanent storage that offers benefits of incremental access and transactioning.

**Persistent Objects (Chapter 8)**   The interfaces and protocols necessary to share storage between components and clients.

**Naming and Binding: Monikers (Chapter 9)**   The encapsulation of a name of an object or a process with the intelligence necessary to work with that name.

**Uniform Data Transfer (Chapter 10)**   The ability to exchange data structures between components and receive notifications about data changes.

**Viewable Objects and the Data Cache (Chapter 11)**   The ability to have an object control its visual representation on any output device and the ability of a client to cache those representations for use when the object is unavailable.

**OLE Clipboard (Chapter 12)**   Support for the familiar operations of Cut, Copy, and Paste using the mechanisms of Uniform Data Transfer.

**OLE Drag and Drop (Chapter 13)**   A mouse-oriented means of performing the same operations as the clipboard.

**OLE Automation (Chapters 14 and 15)**   The ability to expose an object's methods and properties as individual entities in a late-bound manner, also enabling cross-application macro programming.

**Property Pages, Changes, and Persistence (Chapter 16)**   A user interface for manipulating properties, a mechanism for notifying clients about property changes, and standards for the serialization of a set of properties into persistent storage.

**OLE Documents: Embedding and Linking (Chapters 17–21)**   The basic protocols for the creation and management of compound documents, by which active content objects are manipulated in windows separate from the document itself.

**OLE Documents: In-Place Activation (Chapters 22 and 23)**   An extension to embedding in which the active object is manipulated in place within the compound document. This is also called *visual editing* or *in situ editing*.

**OLE Controls (Chapter 24)**   The ability to create custom controls as OLE objects and the protocols for managing controls as in-place active objects within a document or form. OLE Controls includes events, property pages, and keyboard mnemonics.

**Futures (Chapter 25)**   A look ahead to future enhancements and additions to OLE and what they will mean to component software.

Each OLE technology is described briefly in the following sections, and the rest of the chapters in this book deal with each of these technologies in detail.

Keep in mind that absolutely all of these technologies are built on the idea of components and objects and interfaces called the Component Object Model, or COM. Each technology has specific interfaces that apply to it, and some of the higher-level protocols such as OLE Documents and OLE Controls even involve *groupings* of the interfaces from other technologies. Because of these relationships, the technologies in this list build on one another, as illustrated in Figure 1-7 on the following page.

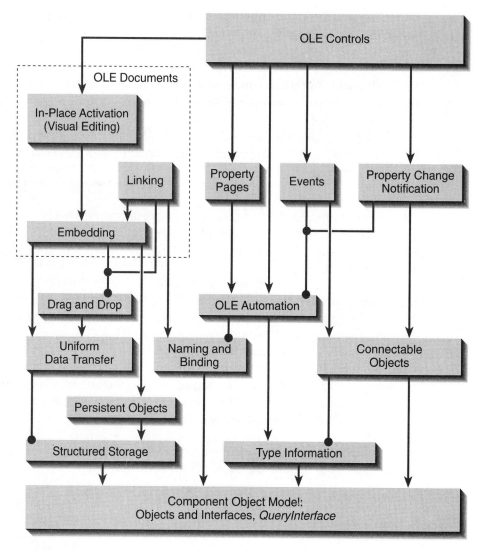

**Figure 1-7.**
*OLE technologies build on one another, with COM as the foundation.*
*An arrow indicates dependency; a circle indicates a possible use but not*
*a requirement.*

You can see that COM, as well as custom components and local/remote transparency, which are generally considered part of COM, form the underlying
basis for everything else in OLE. The lower a technology appears on this

chart, the more generic or general purpose it is and the less visible it is to an end user. The higher technologies are considered more specific; they are generally more complex, and they usually involve more user interface the higher you go. In other words, the highest technologies are the most visible to the end user, but when you set out to incorporate these technologies into a piece of software, it makes the most sense to work from the bottom up because in doing so you'll build a foundation of code that is readily usable when you work on the higher-level technologies. I most definitely encourage this sort of approach to learning OLE, as the organization of this book reflects.

## Is OLE the Only Way?

Undoubtedly you will come across situations in your development efforts in which you have a problem that perhaps some of these OLE technologies can solve. The question is then whether OLE is the *only* solution to that problem. In all likelihood, there are many possible methods that you might use to solve the problem—OLE is in no way required as the solution *unless* you are dealing with an integration problem among components from multiple vendors. In that case, you want to adhere to the standards and interfaces that make up the various OLE technologies. In other words, integration among arbitrary components that were not known to each other during development requires standards, and that is what OLE provides. If your problem involves integration among only those components that you write yourself, you can design whatever solution fits your needs. Remember, however, that everything in OLE has already been through a rigorous design and open review cycle. Using OLE in even a closed system makes sense because you do not have to struggle with the same problems that OLE solves already.

## Type Information

In the earlier material about *QueryInterface*, you might have thought of some very common questions. How can a client obtain just a list of all of an object's interfaces short of calling *QueryInterface* for every known interface under the sun? How could an object browser accomplish this without even instantiating objects in the first place? How can a client learn about the names of interface member functions as well as the names and types of the arguments to those functions? One answer to this last question is a header file that contains the function signatures for the interface in question. Header files, however, contain compile-time information. How can you obtain the same information at run time?

The answer to these questions is known as *Type Information*—literally, a collection of information about data types, interfaces, member functions (return types and arguments), object classes, and even DLL modules. Type information is really just a complex set of nested data structures: one structure describes an object and its interfaces, the interfaces have data structures describing the individual member functions, the functions have structures to describe the individual arguments, and these in turn have structures to describe their various attributes and data types. In reality, this is as much, if not more, information than you could hope to glean from any header file.

To deal with this complexity, OLE provides native services to navigate through type information as well as to create it in the first place. In other words, all creation and manipulation of type information happens through OLE-implemented objects and their interfaces, so you rarely have to deal with these complex data structures directly. These OLE components are the topic of Chapter 3.

All type information is stored in an entity called a *type library*, which can contain information for any number of objects, interfaces, data types, and modules. Creating a type library happens through an object that implements *ICreateTypeLib* and creating elements in the library happens through an object with *ICreateTypeInfo*. The implementation of these objects is provided as a standard OLE service, so you will never implement these yourself. In fact, you will generally never have occasion to even use them as a client because the OLE SDK includes a tool called MKTYPLIB.EXE (Make Type Library), which takes a text file you write in an Object Description Language (ODL), parses it, and makes all the appropriate calls to *ICreateTypeLib* and *ICreate-TypeInfo*, generating a file that contains all the binary data structures for your type library.

Accessing the information contained in a type library is accomplished through two similar OLE-provided objects. The library exposes *ITypeLib,* and the elements in it expose *ITypeInfo.* OLE offers a number of means through which you can load a type library into memory and obtain the *ITypeLib* pointer for it, as we'll see in Chapter 3. After you have an *ITypeLib* pointer, you can easily obtain the *ITypeInfo* for an object class (given a unique class identifier for the object), and through this interface you can obtain a list of the interfaces the object supports. All of this can be done without ever instantiating an object, but it does require a little information in the system registry to associate an object class with a type library.

If a client wants to retrieve the same information from an object that is already running, it can query for an interface named *IProvideClassInfo*. The presence of this interface means that the object can directly provide the client with the *ITypeInfo* that describes the object as a whole, without the bother of having to go out and find a type library.

I should point out that at the time of writing, type information is available for only a few objects outside of OLE Automation or OLE Controls (where it is required). However, type information is universal—it can describe any object and any interface, so as time passes I expect to see type information become available for most objects. Any type-related information about anything in OLE can be stored in a type library, so such a library is *the* repository for information about objects and interfaces.

## Connectable Objects

The set of interfaces that a client can access through *QueryInterface* forms an object's *incoming* interfaces when calls to those interfaces come into the object. However, this alone is not entirely sufficient to completely describe the possible features of objects: sometimes an object will want to notify external clients when events happen in the object—for example, when data changes or when a user performs an action such as clicking the mouse on the object. In order to send such notifications (or to "fire events," as it is sometimes called), the object supports *outgoing* (sometimes called *source*) interfaces, illustrated as an arrow coming out of an object, as shown in Figure 1-8.

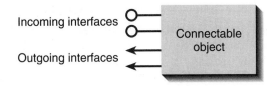

**Figure 1-8.**
*An object's outgoing interfaces are drawn as outgoing arrows alongside the jacks that represent incoming interfaces.*

Outgoing interfaces are not ones that the object implements itself. Instead, the object is a client of the interface as implemented on an external object. The most frequent use of this sort of relationship is the forming of a two-way channel of communication between two components, where each is both client and object. In order not to confuse the terminology, the object that sends the notifications is called the *source,* and the client that receives the notifications is called the *sink,* as illustrated in Figure 1-9.

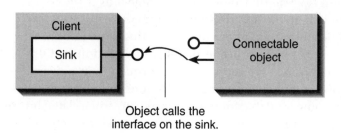

Object calls the
interface on the sink.

**Figure 1-9.**
*A client that implements an object's outgoing interface is a sink for the object's notifications and events.*

What is special in this outgoing interface relationship that differentiates it from the usual incoming interfaces is that the object generally defines the exact outgoing interface itself. This is why we still call it the *object's* interface even though the client implements it—the object defines outgoing interfaces as part of its feature set.

The exact mechanism used to establish this two-way channel of communication is the technology called Connectable Objects, which is the topic of Chapter 4. When any object wants to express the fact that it has outgoing interfaces, it implements an interface named *IConnectionPointContainer,* and in doing so it qualifies as a connectable object. When a client wants to check whether an object has outgoing interfaces, that client will call *QueryInterface,* asking for *IConnectionPointContainer.* With this interface, the client can browse through individual entities called *connection points;* each connection point represents a single outgoing interface. These connection points are small objects themselves (with their own *IUnknown* behavior), managed within the larger object, each of which implements an interface named *IConnectionPoint.* It is through this interface that the client can ask the connection point for the identifier of its outgoing interface and give the connection point the interface pointer through which the connectable object sends notifications (that is, calls interface member functions). In other words, to establish the two-way channel, the client has to be able to pass its own interface pointers to the connectable object, and connection points are the means for doing so.

Some outgoing interfaces involved in a two-way dialogue are known to both sides at compile time. These are known as standard event sets, or standard notification interfaces, which are defined in header files. In other cases, however, the client does not know the exact details of the interface until run time, which requires the object to supply type information.

The idea of events, which connectable objects provide, is a very powerful one. So many things—controls, menus, the keyboard, the mouse, modems, power failures, bothersome relatives—generate events. Anything that somehow has something to say is an event source, and connection points are how you listen. What you do when you hear that a certain event has occurred is completely open. Events are really the triggers that make things happen and that transform user actions (such as typing, moving the mouse, and speaking into a microphone) into information that a piece of software can use as a stimulus to drive a particular response. Stimulus-response makes things seem *alive*. This makes events a key to dynamic software, and connectable objects are how events are implemented in OLE.

## Custom Components and COM

The Component Object Model (COM) is a specification (hence "model") that describes, besides the notions of objects, interfaces, and *QueryInterface*, the mechanisms necessary to access a custom component given only a unique identifier.[5] This identifier, called a class identifier (or CLSID), identifies the top-level object within the component, so what COM is really providing is a mechanism to instantiate an object of a given class. This sounds a lot like the C++ *new* operator, but in OLE the client calls a COM API function *CoCreateInstance* with the CLSID to obtain an interface pointer to that object rather than calling *new* with a C++ class name, which results in an object pointer. Of course, we're talking about two different species of objects here, but the analogy still holds.

Not all objects in OLE need to support this sort of creation process, but when support is there, it is the responsibility of the object or component *server* to package the object appropriately, which is the primary topic of Chapter 5. The mechanics of this depend on whether the server is a DLL or an EXE, but a client always starts the process by calling *CoCreateInstance* with a CLSID. COM uses information stored with the CLSID in the system registry

---

5. In dealing with specific COM-related features, it is conventional to use the term *COM* in place of or interchangeably with the term *OLE* because COM identifies the core part of OLE that provides for object creation and local/remote transparency. COM API functions are all named with a *Co* prefix.

to locate the server module. It then gets that server into memory (loads the DLL or launches the EXE) and asks the server to create the object, returning an interface pointer. The act of creation involves an object known as a *class factory*, which implements the interface *IClassFactory*, whose purpose in life is to manufacture objects of a particular CLSID. This object is part of the server, not part of the component that the client is trying to access, although a client can access the class factory directly if it wants.

In any case, the client is completely isolated from how the object is structured inside a server and from all considerations about the boundaries between it and the object created. The object could be *in-proc* (in-process, from a DLL server), *local* (out-of-process, from an EXE server), or even *remote* (from a DLL or an EXE that is running on another machine).[6] In any case, COM's local/remote transparency (see the next section) means that the client doesn't have to care where the object is running — it simply accesses its features through interface pointers, and those calls are transparently routed to other processes or machines as necessary. Clients do, however, have control over what sort of boundaries are involved; for example, a client can specify only in-process or only out-process.

So far I have made no mention about what interfaces the various objects in a component might support, and this is intentional: the custom component facilities in COM make no restrictions on what interfaces an object might have (although local/remote transparency does at times). These facilities can be used anytime and anywhere a client might need to access any sort of component through a CLSID.

As part of these same mechanisms, COM also provides for what is called *emulation* of one component class by a component from a different class. This is accomplished by mapping one CLSID to another in the system registry. What this does is allow one component to be installed over another and completely replace it without requiring changes to any existing clients that might have hard-coded or persistently stored CLSIDs. When the client instantiates a component of the original CLSID, COM automatically uses the other component that is emulating the first. This is useful for providing alternative implementations of the same component and is a key factor for installing new versions of a component without breaking its existing clients.

---

6. Note that at the time of writing, OLE/COM does not yet support remote objects, also called *distributed services*, as a shipping technology because there are still some things to be worked out.

Part of the enhancements to OLE that were shipped with the set of technologies called OLE Controls is the ability to license the creation of components. This is handled through an alternative class factory interface named *IClassFactory2*, which provides a license key that is necessary to create objects later. This class factory would provide such a key only when running on a machine with a fully licensed installation. If the server is illegally copied to another unlicensed machine, the server will refuse outright to create anything.

## Local/Remote Transparency

I mentioned that OLE, or more accurately COM, allows components to be implemented in either DLL or EXE servers, which means that those components can run either in the same process as the client or in a separate process. When Microsoft enables distributed services and remote objects, components will then be able to run in another process on another machine. In all cases, COM's architecture enables a client to communicate with any object through an interface pointer in the client's address space. When the object is in-process, calls go directly to the object's implementation. When there is a process or a machine boundary between the client and the object, the call cannot be direct because the client's pointer is meaningless outside its process. How does COM route calls from the client to the object's real implementation, wherever it is running, and do so transparently to the client?

COM's Local/Remote Transparency is the technology that makes calls to a *local* or a *remote* object identical to a call to an *in-process* object as far as the client is concerned.[7] The way it works, shown in Figure 1-10 on the next page, is that the client always has a pointer to some in-process implementation of the interface in question. If the object is truly in-process, that implementation is the object's. If the object is local or remote, the implementation is part of an in-process object *proxy.* When the client makes a call to the interface, the proxy takes all the arguments to that function and packages them in some portable 32-bit data structure (which involves copying data structures, strings, and so forth) and generates some sort of remote procedure call (RPC)[8] to the other process (or machine). In that other process, a *stub,* which maintains the real interface pointers to that object, receives the call, unpacks the data structure, pushes arguments on the stack, and makes the call to the object. When

---

7. Even as COM doesn't support the remote case at the time of writing, it was intentionally designed to handle remote objects through the same architecture.

8. Under Windows 3.1 (16 bits), the mechanism is a private implementation called LRPC, for "lightweight remote procedure calls," which is strictly local to a machine. On 32-bit platforms, OLE uses the true underlying system RPC as defined by the Open Software Foundation (OSF) Distributed Computing Environment (DCE).

that call returns, the stub packages the return values and any *out-parameters* (such as structures that the function fills) and sends them back to the proxy, which unpacks that information and returns it to the client. The client never knows that any of this happens.

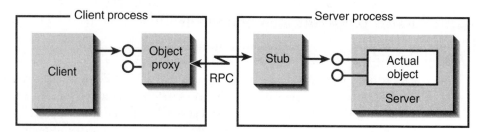

**Figure 1-10.**
*Making a cross-process call through a proxy and a stub.*

Making remote calls across process boundaries did not, of course, originate with OLE. However, OLE provides this capability on a much higher level than something like direct RPC, named pipes, Windows messages, or DDE. Furthermore, OLE makes most interface calls inherently synchronous, with the exception of certain notifications that are specifically designed to be asynchronous. This greatly simplifies programming because you don't have to sit in message loops or spin off threads to wait for things to finish—OLE waits for you and handles the messy considerations of time-outs and errors. If you need to, OLE allows you to hook into this mechanism by implementing a small object (no CLSID needed) called a *message filter* with the *IMessageFilter* interface. This is an example of a case in which you install a small object to customize an OLE-provided service.

*Marshaling* is the process of passing function arguments and return values among processes and among machines, taking any system or process differences into account. As Chapter 6 will show, you can do this through *custom marshaling* on an object-by-object basis, where the real object specifies what piece of code to use for its proxy so that it can establish a private communication channel however it wants. The other option is to use *standard marshaling* on an interface-by-interface basis, where OLE provides small interface proxies and stubs for those interfaces it defines[9] and where you can easily create

---

9. Some interfaces have function arguments, like an HDC (handle to a device context), that simply cannot be marshaled, and some interfaces do not, at the time of writing, have marshaling support, particularly those provided with OLE Controls.

the same for your own custom interfaces. Generally, this is a simple process of describing the interface in an Interface Definition Language (IDL, similar to ODL) and pumping it through the Microsoft IDL compiler (MIDL), which writes the source code for you. Then you compile this code into a DLL that fits right into OLE's standard marshaling architecture.

## Structured Storage and Compound Files

A long time ago in the computer industry, there was a one-to-one relationship between the computer and the single application that ran on it. That application had total control over all system resources, including all storage devices. It was the innovation of the operating system along with a "file system" that enabled multiple applications to share system resources. The file system was specifically responsible for allowing those applications to share the same storage device, and it did so by partitioning the disk into directories and files. Whereas the application saw a file as a flat byte array, the file system stored the information in noncontiguous sectors around the device.

A component integration environment requires something more than what a file system can offer. In such an environment, different components need to share a single disk file, just as applications once needed to share a single disk drive. OLE's Structured Storage is a specification that defines a number of storage-related interfaces to achieve exactly this, defining a "file system within a file." Instead of requiring that a single file handle with a single seek pointer manipulate a large contiguous sequence of bytes on the disk, Structured Storage describes how to treat a single file-system entity as a structured collection of two types of objects—storages and streams—that act like directories and files. Together, storages and streams provide powerful features such as transactioning and incremental access, as we'll see in more detail in Chapter 7.

A stream object, which implements the interface *IStream*, is the conceptual equivalent of a single disk file as we understand disk files today. Streams are the basic file-system component in which data lives, and each stream in itself has access rights and a single seek pointer. Streams are named by using a text string (up to 31 characters) and can contain any internal structure you want.

A storage object, using the interface *IStorage*, is the conceptual equivalent of a directory. Each storage, like a directory, can contain any number of storages (subdirectories) and any number of streams (files), as shown in

Figure 1-11. In turn, each substorage can contain any number of storages and streams until your disk is full. Storages themselves do not contain any user-defined data as do streams, but rather, storages manage the names and locations of the elements within them. Like a stream, a storage object is named with a text string and has access rights (compared with typical file-system directories, which commonly do not have access rights). Given a storage, you can ask it to enumerate, copy, move, rename, delete, or change dates and times of the elements within it, much as you can achieve through command prompts.

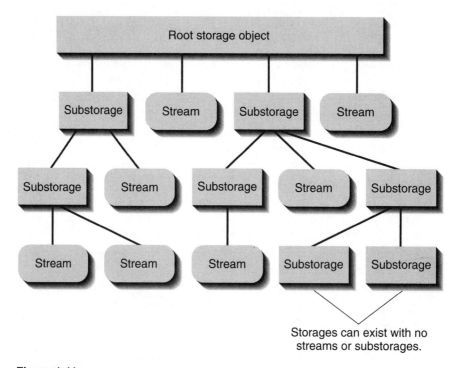

**Figure 1-11.**
*Conceptual structure of storage and stream objects.*

OLE provides as a service an implementation of structured storage that is called Compound Files.[10] You can use this technology to replace traditional file handle–based API functions such as _*lread* and _*lwrite*, as we'll see in

---

10. Formerly called "docfiles," which is considered archaic but is still in use because it rolls off the tongue so nicely. Note that "compound files" bears no relation to "compound documents" except that a compound file is an excellent medium in which to store such a document.

Chapter 7. To be perfectly accurate, Compound Files is an implementation of Structured Storage that is specifically directed to a disk file. Through a small customization called a *lockbytes* object (which implements *ILockBytes*), you can direct all the information to another location, such as memory, a database record, or even a portion of another file. In fact, Compound Files is really just a disk-based lockbytes object plugged into OLE's otherwise independent storage implementation.

Because the lockbytes object controls only the ultimate storage medium of bytes in a compound file, OLE itself controls the actual data structures and the underlying file format. As a file system makes disparate sectors on a disk appear as a contiguous byte array, OLE makes disparate blocks of data in a file appear as contiguous streams and also provides automatic garbage collection and defragmentation features. However, Microsoft recognizes that many vendors ship applications for platforms other than Windows or the Macintosh for which Microsoft has provided the Compound Files implementation itself. For that reason, Microsoft licenses the straight ANSI C++ source code for Compound Files that you can recompile for other platforms as needed.

There is one tremendous advantage to using structured storage: because the hierarchy of storage and stream elements is stored in a standard format and is accessed through a standard OLE service, anything can browse through a hierarchy in a file without having to run the code that created the file. Although the format of information in streams is still proprietary, the names and locations of those streams within the file are not. Therefore, the system shell can include browsing tools to examine the structure of the file.

This advantage is further enhanced when a standard does exist for specific types of information. The only standard that currently exists is for a stream (located off the root storage) called "\005SummaryInformation" (ASCII 5 is the first character in the name), which contains document information such as author, title, subject, keywords, comments, creation/save/print date, word count, and so on. This information is stored in a format known as a *property set* and is covered in Chapter 16 (with other property-related topics). Because the stream has a standard format, a standard location, and a standard name, anyone and anything can retrieve this information and do interesting things with it. For example, the Windows 95 Explorer allows you to search for documents and then view their summary information.

The long-term plans for structured storage include full content indexing of a file to enable shell-level searches based not only on summary information but also on content. This capability is far more powerful, yet easier to use, than requiring the end user to first find a file, then find the application that can load that file, and then use the application to open and browse files to eventually find the data. Content indexing will generally work through vendor-supplied content filter objects that crack the proprietary stream formats within a file and return indexing information to the system. The first manifestation of these types of objects (not covered in this book) are the file viewers in Windows 95, which provide a quick way to view the contents of a file without having to load the entire application that created it. It is a powerful addition, done completely through OLE, and is all part of Microsoft's *Information at Your Fingertips* philosophy.

## Persistent Objects

We've seen that structured storage is necessary to allow multiple components to share the same disk file or other mass of storage. An object indicates its ability to save its persistent state to a storage or a stream element by implementing the interface *IPersistStorage* or *IPersistStream* (or a slight enhancement, *IPersistStreamInit*). There is also an *IPersistFile* interface for components that save to separate files. An object that implements any support whatsoever for saving and loading its state is called *persistent*. In Chapter 8, we'll deal with persistent objects in detail.

The client, or, more appropriately, container, that manages persistent objects creates or obtains the *IStorage* or *IStream* pointer to pass to the objects through *IPersistStorage* or *IPersistStream[Init]*. The container tells objects when to save or load their persistent states, so the container remains in control of the overall document or file but gives each component individual control over a storage or stream within that file. This tends to make structures within a file more intelligent by placing more of the code that knows how to handle the structures in objects rather than in the container.

## Naming and Binding: Monikers

Think for a moment about a standard, mundane filename that refers to some collection of data stored somewhere on a disk. The filename essentially describes the "somewhere," and so the name identifies a file that we could call an object (in a primeval sort of way). But this is somewhat limited—filenames have no intelligence because all the knowledge about how to use and store the name exists elsewhere, in whatever application makes use of that filename. This normally hasn't been a problem because most applications can deal with files quite readily.

Now think about a name that describes the result of a query in a database, or one that describes a range of spreadsheet cells or a paragraph in a document. Then think about a name that identifies a piece of code that executes some operation on a network server. Each different name, if unintelligent, would require each application to understand the use of that name. In a component integration system, this is far too expensive. To solve the problem, OLE has Persistent, Intelligent Names, otherwise known as *monikers,* the topic of Chapter 9. Monikers are objects that encapsulate a type of name and the intelligence to work with that name behind an interface named *IMoniker.* Different moniker classes deal with different names, but they are all polymorphic through *IMoniker.* Furthermore, because *IMoniker* is itself derived from *IPersistStream,* monikers know how to store and retrieve the names they manage in a stream.

The primary intellectual operation of a moniker is called *binding,* which executes whatever operations are necessary to locate the named object and return an interface pointer to that named object. The named object, however, is not in any way related to the moniker itself—the moniker is simply doing the work of locating that object. After a client has been bound to the named object, the moniker falls out of the picture entirely. What actually happens to bind a moniker depends on the type of moniker you have, but regardless of that fact a client never needs to maintain that intelligence in itself.

OLE defines and implements five monikers itself. Four of these are "simple" monikers: File, Item, Pointer, and Anti, which are discussed fully in Chapter 9. As these simple monikers by themselves can only provide trivial names, OLE also implements a "generic composite" moniker, where the composite is a container for any number of other monikers that might themselves be simple or composite. Binding a composite basically means binding its constituent elements. The composite then enables the creation of complex names using any desired combination of other simpler names, greatly reducing the number of simple monikers necessary to create a very large number of complex names. For example, you can use a File and two Item monikers combined in a composite to name a selection of cells in a certain page of a large spreadsheet, as illustrated in Figure 1-12.

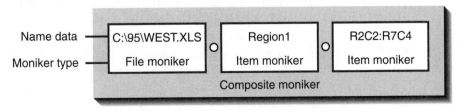

**Figure 1-12.**
*A composite moniker that contains a file moniker and two item monikers.*

Of course, if OLE's standard monikers are not suitable for your naming purposes, you can always implement your own moniker component with *IMoniker*. Because you encapsulate your functionality behind the interface, your moniker is immediately usable in any other application that knows how to work with *IMoniker*. Again, this is polymorphism on the object level, thanks to interfaces.

Working with monikers is generally called *linking*, the moniker's information being the link to some other data. OLE documents use monikers to implement linked compound document objects, which involves other user interface standards for managing links.

## Uniform Data Transfer

Structured Storage and Monikers are about integrating the storage of objects and names of objects, but clients also like to retrieve data from the objects, as well. OLE's Uniform Data Transfer mechanism is the technology for handling the exchange of "formatted data structures," that is, data with a known format. For example, the CF_TEXT format identifies a C-style string of characters. Besides data exchange, Uniform Data Transfer also handles the ability of the source of data, called the *data object*, to notify a client (or *consumer*) when data changes.

As we'll see in Chapter 10, data objects implement an interface named *IDataObject*, which includes functions to get data, set data, query and enumerate formats, and establish or terminate notifications. Notifications happen through an interface named *IAdviseSink*—a consumer interested in data changes will implement *IAdviseSink* and will pass a pointer to *IDataObject* to establish notifications.[11] It is interesting to note that *IAdviseSink* is specifically designed to be an asynchronous interface—that is, its marshaling proxy fires off an RPC call to its connected stub and immediately returns to the data object without waiting for the stub to reply. This has a few interesting consequences, as we'll also see in Chapter 10.

The "uniform" in Uniform Data Transfer arises from the fact that *IDataObject* separates exchange operations (get, set, and so on) from specific transfer protocols such as the clipboard. Thus, a data source implements one data object and uses it in any OLE transfer protocol such as the OLE Clipboard and OLE Drag and Drop (and is even usable in OLE Documents). The

---

11. Note that *IDataObject* and *IAdviseSink* were an ad hoc solution designed long before the advent of *IConnectionPointContainer* and *IConnectionPoint*, so the more generic connectable object mechanisms are not used here.

OLE protocols (unlike the existing Windows protocols) are specifically concerned with getting an *IDataObject* pointer (with the pointer representing an impending transfer) from the source to the consumer. Then the protocol disappears, and the consumer deals uniformly only with *IDataObject*. So source and consumers can implement a core set of functions based on *IDataObject* and build little protocol handlers on top of that core.

OLE makes two other significant improvements to the existing Windows mechanisms for data exchange (clipboard, DDE, and so forth): you can now describe data with more than a clipboard format, and you can exchange it using mediums other than global memory. A structure called FORMAT-ETC (literally, "format, etcetera") contains only a clipboard format, but it also has a specification about the detail (full content, thumbnail sketch, and so forth), the target device (screen, printers, and so forth), and the transfer medium. The actual reference to the data on whatever medium (for example, memory, disk file, *IStorage*, *IStream*) is passed in a STGMEDIUM structure, which is far more powerful than a simple global memory handle. Where you've traditionally been able to say only "I have a bitmap" that is always in global memory, OLE let's you say "I have, saved in a storage object, a thumbnail sketch of a bitmap rendered for a 300-dot-per-inch (dpi) black-and-white PostScript 52.3 printer." You can choose, as a source of data, the best possible medium in which to transfer data, and you can make it the preferred format, providing other mediums as backups (such as global memory, the lowest common denominator). So if you happen to generate 30-MB 24-bit bitmaps, you can keep those in disk files or storage objects, even during a data exchange. This can lead to tremendous performance gains for applications that were up to now forced to load large data sets into global memory, just to have them swapped out to the disk again (virtual memory paging)! This overhead is what OLE helps you avoid.

## Viewable Objects and the Data Cache

Closely related to data objects in Uniform Data Transfer is the capability of an object to indicate that it can draw presentations of its data directly to devices through the interface *IViewObject2*. Often a data object will use *IDataObject* to provide renderings of its presentations into bitmaps and metafiles while it implements *IViewObject2* to provide direct device renderings. When an object supports this interface to draw its own "views," it's called a *viewable object,* the topic of Chapter 11.

*IViewObject2* also contains member functions for handling notifications to a client for when an object's view, as opposed to its data, changes. For example, a bar chart has underlying data used to generate the chart, and a data change will normally also mean a view change for the chart. But changing the color of one of the bars changes the view but not the data; therefore, we have a separate notification. This notification also happens through *IAdviseSink* because *IDataObject* and *IViewObject2* are often found together, and the combination of notifications into *IAdviseSink* centralizes not only sink implementation but also the asynchronous nature of the interface. In response to the view change notification, a client displaying the object's view somewhere will normally ask the object to redraw itself.

An important point about *IViewObject2* is that it has no marshaling support: an *HDC* argument to its *Draw* function cannot be shared across process boundaries. So a "viewable" object always shares the client's process.

Closely related to an object's view is the capability of a client to *cache* one or more views (metafiles or bitmaps) in what is called a *data cache*, the implementation of which is a standard OLE service. This cache component, which always works in a client's own process, has an object that implements the interfaces *IOleCache2* and *IOleCacheControl*. Through this object, the client can control what is saved in the cache and can also connect the cache to a running local or remote object's *IDataObject* interface. Through this interface, the cache can obtain the graphics to cache and can watch for changes in those presentations in order to update the cache automatically.

## OLE Clipboard

As mentioned before, a practical use of a data object is that of exchanging data on the clipboard. OLE effectively uses the clipboard to pass an *IDataObject* pointer from the source to a consumer, setting up a proxy and stub as necessary. In this way, an application's clipboard features can benefit from all of OLE's data transfer enhancements. Chapter 12 will examine the OLE Clipboard in detail, illustrating how you can build data objects on top of any existing clipboard code you might have.

## OLE Drag and Drop

Besides the clipboard, OLE also provides another means of getting an *IDataObject* pointer from a source to a consumer: OLE Drag and Drop. Because you can exchange virtually any data through a data object, you can exchange virtually any data through this very direct and user-oriented mechanism, which is widely exploited in the Windows 95 shell.

Drag and Drop effectively streamlines whatever you might do with the clipboard. With the clipboard, the user must select the data, choose Cut or

Copy from the source menu, switch applications, mark the insertion point, and choose Paste from the consumer menu. With OLE Drag and Drop, the user selects the data, *picks* it up by holding down the mouse button, *drags* it to the insertion point in the consumer (called the *target* in this context), and then releases the mouse button to *drop* it in the target. OLE performs a Move (Cut) operation by default, which the user can modify to a Copy operation by holding down the Ctrl key or a Link operation by holding down Shift+Ctrl (assuming the source provides a moniker in the data object).

During the process, the source controls the mouse cursor and determines when a drop happens (because it knows what caused the drag), when the operation should be canceled (Esc is pressed), or when the operation should continue. The source accomplishes this through an interface named *IDropSource*. The target, on the other hand, associates an implementation of *IDropTarget* with a visible window (such as a document), with that interface being told when the mouse cursor moves in, around, or out of the window and when a drop happens. All this time, the target communicates to the source the "effect" (move, copy, link) that would happen if a drop occurred, and the source uses this information to set the mouse cursor to an appropriate image. The target usually also draws something in its own window to indicate the insertion point of the data, such as a caret or a dotted rectangle. Furthermore, the target also provides the user with the ability to scroll through the target window during the operation by holding the mouse cursor inside the window's border for a short period of time.

All of these considerations, not only for the target but also for the source, are topics for Chapter 13. There we'll see that OLE Drag and Drop is a tremendous user benefit, and if you implement a data object for the clipboard first, your drag-and-drop implementation is close to trivial.

## OLE Automation

For a long time, users have wanted the ability to write macros that would affect more than one application at a time. It is extraordinarily useful to create a script that could take data automatically from a spreadsheet, plot it in a graphics program, copy that image into a word processor document, format the document and update its fields, print 40 copies of the document merged with a mailing list, and then send a piece of e-mail to an assistant who would take the pages from the printer and mail them out. It is even more useful to run this script automatically when something like an elapsed timer custom control fires an event once a month. The whole process, with the exception of the human stuffing envelopes, can be automated in software.

The critical part of making this level of integration possible is the ability to drive components programmatically, without an end user's presence but instead with an end-user script of some sort. In more technological terms, it means having various components expose their end-user–level functionality (that is, what the user understands the components to do) through interfaces that a scripting tool can use to invoke that functionality in a user-defined sequence.

There are two sides to this picture. On the one hand, we have "programmable" components, which are called *automation objects*. These objects provide type information, through a type library associated with the object's CLSID, that describes everything the object can do: names of interfaces, their member functions and properties, and the types of properties and arguments. On the other hand, we have some component that provides a programming environment in which a developer or other user can write scripts or create applications that drive automation objects. These are called *automation controllers*. Chapters 14 and 15, respectively, deal with each.

OLE Automation is centered on the interface named *IDispatch*. Any object that implements this interface is an automation object, regardless of what other interfaces might also be available. But in and of itself, *IDispatch* doesn't do a lot—it has only a few member functions. Yet somehow a component can expose all of its methods and properties through this interface.

The answer to this puzzle is that any particular object's implementation of *IDispatch* actually implements a more complex entity known as a *dispatch interface*, or *dispinterface*, in which each method and property is given a unique identifier, called the dispID. The dispinterface is an instance of *IDispatch* that responds only to a certain set of dispIDs. The object's type information for this dispinterface, which can also be obtained through an *IDispatch* member function, provides the controller with the means to convert the names of functions and properties to dispIDs and to learn about the types of everything involved.

When a controller wants to access a property to call a function, it passes the dispID of that element to *IDispatch::Invoke*, which then either gets or sets the property, or calls the method, depending on other flags also passed to *Invoke*. Arguments to a method call are packaged and passed to *Invoke* as well. The idea of invoking a method or a property through a dispID is the crux of late binding to the dispinterface because you can easily retrieve the dispIDs and all the type information about the interface at run time. Furthermore, it is relatively easy to write an implementation of *IDispatch* that can respond to any underlying dispinterface. It is also possible to write a "dual" interface that provides the same functionality through both early-bound vtable and late-bound dispatch interfaces.

As we'll see in Chapter 14, OLE Automation includes a number of guidelines for automating an entire application, by which, instead of implementing one automation object, you're actually implementing an object hierarchy. If you have a reasonably object-oriented application already, as I have with the sample application in that chapter, adding OLE Automation support can be done in a few days, even without any additional supporting tools such as the Microsoft Foundation Classes (MFC), which would make the job even easier.

Microsoft Visual Basic (and Visual Basic for Applications) is one of the primary automation controllers available at the time of writing. Visual Basic supports specific code constructs that directly generate *IDispatch::Invoke* calls, meaning that VB can drive any other object because everything is reduced to the binary standard of interfaces. Thus VB, like any other controller for that matter, drives automation objects written in C, C++, Smalltalk, Pascal, VB, COBOL, or whatever other esoteric language might support OLE. The converse of this statement is that no matter how you implement an automation object, it's usable from any controller.

This is important because some years ago, Microsoft considered making one standard, systemwide macro language. Bad idea: it would have limited the choice of language and the choice of macro tool to one. That's a bit autocratic, wouldn't you say? OLE Automation makes it possible for anyone to write a scripting tool (controller) that works with any language whatsoever and to have complete integration with all available automation objects. This gives users the choice of language and the choice of tool. With a wide enough availability of automation controllers and objects, we'll finally be rid of the cumbersome and cryptic application-specific macro languages that we all hate to learn, and instead we'll need to learn only once how to use a tool we actually like.

## Property Pages, Changes, and Persistence

Although interfaces such as *IDispatch* and *IDataObject* can provide access to an object's data programmatically, there are occasions when the user would like to work directly with an object's properties. OLE's mechanism for doing just this — the mechanism uses a tabbed-dialog user interface, as shown in Figure 1-13 on the following page — is called Property Pages, which was introduced initially with OLE Controls. Each separate tab in the dialog box is a property page, and each page is managed by a separate object, with its own CLSID, that implements the interface, *IPropertyPage* (or *IPropertyPage2*). An object that supports property pages implements *ISpecifyPropertyPages*, which supplies a list of property page CLSIDs that it would like displayed in the dialog.

A property page isn't all that useful by itself, so whatever component wants to show the pages creates a *property frame* (which is the dialog box) and hands that frame all the CLSIDs of all the property pages to display, along with the *IUnknown* pointers to all the objects that are being affected by changes in those property pages. When the user clicks on the Apply Now button in the dialog box to apply the changes to the affected objects, the frame notifies the current property page to notify each object in turn.

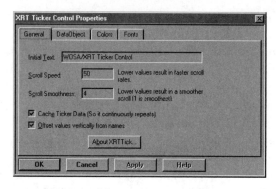

**Figure 1-13.**
*The user interface for property pages involves a tabbed dialog box in which each tab is a separate property page.*

Property pages are extremely useful for things like controls, and they will find more use for various user interface elements in future versions of Windows. As a technology, they are rather general purpose, so you'll likely find many uses for them.

Regardless of how a property changes, either programmatically or through a property page UI, some clients might be interested in knowing when certain properties (identified with a dispID) change. An object that supports notification of property changes supplies a connection point for the interface *IPropertyNotifySink*. Interested clients implement this interface and hand it to the object through the latter's connection point.

This interface handles two notifications. The first is that the property has actually changed value, in response to which the client can retrieve the new value. The second notification tells the client that the property is about to change, which allows the client to prevent the change altogether or perhaps to implement some sort of read-only behavior. Properties that support the first type of notification are called *bindable* properties, and those of the second type are *request edit* properties.

The final consideration for properties is a persistent storage method called *property sets,* by which a component can write properties into a stream in a self-describing manner. The actual structure of a property set starts with a header that describes the offsets in the stream of each property therein, and at each offset is a header describing the type of property and the offset of the actual data elsewhere in the stream. This structure is very flexible. It allows a component to write only those properties it has and allows another component or client to robustly read only the properties that are there. There are no expectations about the existence of any property—if it's in the stream, it's there completely.

Property pages, property change notification, and property sets are covered in Chapter 16.

## OLE Documents: Embedding and Linking

Whereas OLE version 1 was about nothing but the creation and management of compound documents—now called OLE Documents—this is now simply a subset of today's OLE. However, many of the other OLE technologies are used to create compound documents.

A compound document is essentially a collection site for *unstructured* data from a variety of other sources. An important part of this is that the data travels with information about what component was used to create it, along with any information necessary to return it to the exact state it was in when created. The package that works with such data is called a *compound document content object,* or simply *content object.* These objects encapsulate any sort of complex information, such as a chart, a table, a graphic, or a sound or video bite, and supply the necessary facilities for editing or otherwise manipulating that content. These objects are stored and managed inside a compound document *container* that provides the storage and display space for these objects along with the necessary user interface to expose their capabilities. The container, however, is ignorant of the data itself and simply views each piece of content as unstructured.

Unstructured data differs from formatted data (Uniform Data Transfer) and properties (OLE Automation) because the container never touches it directly, nor does it know how to modify or otherwise manipulate that data. That is the responsibility of the object, and the process of *activation*—whereby a *loaded* object is made *active*—makes any sort of editing or manipulation facilities for some content object available to the user in a separate window. Often this form of activation means that the object reappears in the original tool that was used to create it (or an emulating tool). A content object can support more than one way to activate its content as well, with each action called a *verb*. Relatively static display content, such as a graphic, usually supports a single verb called Edit. Sound and video will typically support a primary Play verb and a secondary Edit verb. The container displays the object's verb as a command in its own menus, and when the user selects a verb the container merely passes it to the object for execution.

How the content object actually gets into the container in the first place can happen in a variety of ways. The user can paste an object from the clipboard or drop one into the container using OLE Drag and Drop. The user can also create a brand-new object using the Insert Object dialog box, as we'll see in Chapter 17.

Regardless of the method used to create the object, there are two ways in which its underlying native data is stored. When the data is encapsulated within the content object itself, that object is said to be *embedded* in the container. These are also called *embedded objects*. When the data is actually stored elsewhere, the content object simply maintains a moniker to name that location, and the object is said to be *linked* to the container, a *linked object*. A linked object is for the most part identical to an embedded object, with the single exception of where its data is located—the container generally treats both types equally, using the same code.

Programmatically speaking, any such content object will support the *IOleObject* interface. Although this interface always identifies a content object, it does not supply all the functionality necessary to make compound documents work. The OLE specifications stipulate that all content objects also support *IDataObject*, *IViewObject2*, *IPersistStorage*, and those of the data cache. But don't the *IViewObject2* interface and the data cache work only in a client's process? Doesn't *IViewObject2* completely lack marshaling support? Does this mean that content objects must always be in-process?

The answer to this last, unrhetorical question is both yes and no, in a way. The complete implementation of a content object can be provided either in-process or out-of-process. However, there must *always* be at least a partial implementation of the object supplied from an in-process component, usually an *in-process handler,* and it is this partial object that implements *IViewObject2* and caching in order to draw the object in the container. Because of this hard requirement, OLE provides a *default handler* that provides these services by asking the local object's *IDataObject* for a metafile or a bitmap that it can then draw in the container. If you want more control over the visual rendering of your object, as well as of any number of other facilities, you can implement your own handler that uses much of the default handler internally through aggregation. In some cases, you might want to implement a complete in-process server, eliminating the need for a handler altogether.

In any compound document relationship, the container always talks to the in-process part of the object first, handler or otherwise. When necessary, the handler will call on a local server to complete the implementation, which is usually required only to retrieve data renderings or to execute verbs. The overall relationship is illustrated in Figure 1-14.

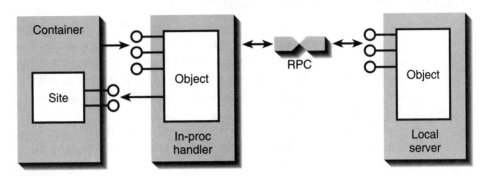

**Figure 1-14.**
*The relationship between a compound document container, an object in a handler, and an object in a local server.*

You'll notice in this illustration that the container also implements an object, called the *site,* for use in a compound document relationship. This site implements *IAdviseSink* for one, so it receives notifications of data changes, view changes, and a number of other changes in the state of the content object (when it's saved, renamed, closed, and so forth). Alongside this interface, the site provides *IOleClientSite* simply to provide some information and capabilities of the container to the content object.

All the details regarding embedding and linking, including containers, handlers, and full object implementations, take a number of chapters to cover. Chapters 17 and 18 will cover the basics of embedding for containers and objects from local servers. Chapter 19 will look into object handlers as well as the implementation of a complete in-process content object. Chapters 20 and 21 will then cover the necessary aspects of linking for containers and objects, and in Chapter 21 we'll also see how a container can support linking to objects embedded within it.

As you can imagine, OLE Documents is a fairly lengthy topic, and it is precisely the reason why OLE has the undeserved reputation of being too difficult and too complex. The fact of the matter is that OLE can be very simple on the lower levels, and once you understand those lower-level technologies there isn't too much more you need to do to extend your understanding to OLE Documents. If, however, you try to understand OLE by reading this book starting with Chapter 17, I can guarantee that you'll be confused. A technology as rich as OLE will take some time to understand, so plan your approach carefully and build your understanding from the bottom up.

## OLE Documents: In-Place Activation

In cases other than playing a sound or a video clip, activation of an object generally requires that the object display another window in which an operation such as editing takes place. For example, if you have a table from a spreadsheet embedded within a document and you want to edit that table, you would need to get the table back into the spreadsheet application to make changes. Right?

Not necessarily. OLE Documents includes a feature called in-place activation (also known as visual editing when you talk to marketing folks), which is a set of interfaces and negotiation protocols through which the container and the object merge elements of their user interface into the container's window space. In other words, in-place activation allows the object to bring its editing tools to the container instead of taking the object to the editing tools. This includes menus, toolbars, and small child windows that are all placed within the container.

The central idea of in-place activation is to create a *document*-centric work environment for the end user. The simple activation model of embedding and linking is a more *application*-centric model, in which data is taken to the application for editing. Again, in-place activation brings the editing to the document. Visually, the user never has to leave the document itself— everything is right there.

Chapters 22 and 23 cover the necessary additions to both containers and objects. The changes are almost entirely manifest in adding various interfaces that start with the *IOleInPlace* prefix. For example, a container site supports in-place activation by adding *IOleInPlaceSite*, and when activating itself, an object will query for this interface to see whether it should become active in-place or in another window. Because of this query step, objects that support in-place activation work perfectly well with containers that don't, and as soon as the container is revised to support the additional interface, the same unmodified object begins immediately to activate in place, even though it never did before. The object itself implements *IOleInPlaceObject* to indicate that it is in-place capable. Other in-place interfaces are implemented in other areas of the container and object in order to make the user interface negotiation work.

In-place activation is not limited to activating just one object at a time, or to activating objects only on user command. Objects can mark themselves to be activated in place whenever visible but without bothering the menu or toolbars. This means that each object can have an editing window in its space in the container so that it can respond immediately to mouse clicks and the like. Only one object, however, can be UI active, which means that its menus and toolbars are available and that it gets a chance to process keyboard accelerators. So while many objects might be active at once, the UI active object switches as the user moves around within the document.

With many objects active at one time within a document, you can start to imagine how useful it would be if some of those objects were things like buttons or list boxes. Why, you could create forms with such objects, and you could create an arbitrary container that could hold objects from any source and benefit from all the other integration features of OLE! This is exactly why OLE Controls technology has been invented.

## OLE Controls

In the OLE context, an OLE control is an embedded content object, with support for properties and methods through *IDispatch*, support for property pages with *ISpecifyPropertyPages*, support for type information with *IProvideClassInfo*, and support for events through *IConnectionPointContainer* and individual connection points for each event set. Controls often support property change notification as well.

A control is really a user interface device that transforms those many different types of external events, such as mouse clicks, keystrokes, and phone calls from your bothersome relatives (thank goodness for caller ID!), into meaningful programmatic events. At the occurrence of these programmatic events, some event handler, in what is called the *control container,* can execute code, such as showing another form when a button is pressed, executing a command, or telling your modem to answer the phone and immediately hang up.

For the most part, there is very little that we have not already seen that is unique to a control. In fact, a control is mostly built of other technologies, and a control container is primarily a compound document container that is also in many ways an automation controller. The few things that distinguish controls are keyboard mnemonics and what are called *ambient properties.*

Keyboard mnemonics are necessary to allow each control to display an active underlined mnemonic character so that the control can execute its default action when that keystroke is pressed, regardless of what control has the focus. Each control provides its list of mnemonics to the control container, and the control container looks through the lists of all controls whenever a mnemonic key is pressed, informing the appropriate control of the event.

Ambient properties are those that the container supplies through an *IDispatch* interface implemented on the container site. These properties define the environment or "ambience" for all controls, such as default colors and fonts. Controls generally initialize themselves with these ambient properties, although an explicit change to an object's property becomes persistent for that object and overrides the ambient value.

The facilities that manage mnemonics and ambient properties are handled through the interfaces *IOleControl* (implemented on the control) and *IOleControlSite* (implemented on the container site). Chapter 24 brings these interfaces together with all the other things we've seen to create controls and control containers.

If you look back at Figure 1-7 on page 26, you will notice that if you start from OLE Controls at the top, you can eventually work your way down through every other technology in OLE. A control is thus a superset of most other object types in OLE. For this reason, people sometimes use the word "control" to refer to objects that don't necessarily need to be implemented as full-blown controls but that use some of these other technologies. For example, you can create an object that supports an event set without it necessarily having to be a control, with property pages and in-place activation. It might make sense for something like that to be a control, depending on what sort of containers might want to use it, but you don't have to implement a control just to use the lower-level technologies. Keep that in mind when you hear talk about OLE Controls.

You can expect that the market will rapidly become full of very useful OLE controls in the near future. OLE Controls was designed to be a more powerful, flexible, and robust replacement for the VBX standard, which, as you may know, was not all that well designed. Visual Basic will work with OLE Controls in preference to VBX controls, and Microsoft is also planning for controls to take a leading role in extensible user interfaces of future versions of Windows. The technology is well worth your time today.

# Conventions

From the looks of the previous sections describing the various parts of OLE and from the sheer weight of this book, we'll see a lot of material in the chapters ahead. It will serve us well to briefly look at the conventions that apply throughout this book.

## 32 Bits vs. 16 Bits

In contrast to the first edition, *Inside OLE 2,* which was concerned only with 16-bit OLE, this second edition, *Inside OLE,* is oriented specifically toward 32-bit OLE development. Accordingly, there are some topics in this book that are available *only* on 32-bit OLE platforms such as Windows NT 3.5 and Windows 95. For the most part, however, what you'll find here is applicable to both 16-bit and 32-bit environments. The text in this book is written assuming 32-bit OLE, so where a difference exists with 16-bit OLE or where there is information relevant to 16 bits, you'll see a flag in the margin as shown next to this paragraph. This is your indication to look in the 16BITOLE.WRI file on the companion CD for more information.

One major difference between environments is that 32-bit OLE always uses Unicode strings, even on systems that don't support Unicode otherwise (such as Win95). Do keep this in mind as you work with OLE, and you'll see special-case handling in the sample code for Unicode/ANSI string conversion.

## Chapter Organization

I have attempted, probably imperfectly, to organize the chapters in this book, with the exception of some of the very early ones, in such a way that if you're reading only to gain an architectural understanding of OLE, you need read only the first third to half of each chapter. Those pages will generally describe the technology under discussion and will explain the mechanisms involved in making that technology work. These pages will not get into details about writing code. Instead, all coding details are left to the later parts of a chapter, so they remain out of your way if you want to learn only the mechanics. If you are a programmer reading this book, you might find it more helpful to read a mechanism section at the beginning of a chapter and then skip to the corresponding implementation section.

No matter how you decide to read this book, or what your purposes are in reading it, you will probably benefit by using the index and the table of contents. From the latter, you can see the structure of each chapter at a glance, which is especially useful for seeing the correlation between the mechanism and the implementation sections of each. I have strived to keep tidbits of architectural knowledge out of the code-oriented sections, but I suspect that things will creep in. If you want to be sure you don't miss anything, read through the mechanisms of all the chapters, and then return to each chapter and scan the programming sections. For readers who also have the first edition of this book, you'll notice that some chapters of this book, such as "Persistent Objects and Viewable Objects," were topics buried in the tail ends of the first edition's chapters, such as "Structured Storage" and "Uniform Data Transfer." The separation of this information into different chapters is done mostly in an attempt to make the chapter organization consistent.

Each chapter (with the exception of this one and the last chapter) also ends with a summary of the major points of the chapter that you should understand before moving on. As the various OLE technologies build on one another, so does your understanding of OLE, so it is important to be sure that you're building a mental foundation as we explore technological ones.

## Sample Code

In case you have not noticed, this book contains a companion CD as opposed to a disk, so there is a lot of sample code that we'll see discussed in the chapters ahead. The installation program on the CD will create a number of directories with the contents shown in Table 1-1. I suggest that you install these samples in a C:\INOLE directory if at all possible because the registry files assume this location. (See "Registry Files" later in this chapter.) For a description of the files in each of these directories, please refer to the CONTENTS-.TXT file in the installation directory. Most of the samples compile to both 16-bit and 32-bit OLE except for those that rely on features available only with 32-bit OLE. CONTENTS.TXT points out those samples that are 32-bit specific. As 32-bit OLE is all Unicode, all 32-bit samples compile to Unicode as well.

| Directory | Contents |
| --- | --- |
| INC | Include (H) files shared by multiple samples. You should add this directory to your INCLUDE environment variable. The most important file here is INOLE.H, which is a central include file for just about every sample that pulls in the necessary Windows and OLE headers as well as other private macros used in the samples. |

**Table 1-1.**  *(continued)*
*Directories created by the installation procedure.*

**Table 1-1.** *continued*

| Directory | Contents |
|---|---|
| LIB | Libraries (LIB files) shared by multiple samples. You should add this directory to your LIB environment variable. |
| BUILD | A repository for built DLLs and EXEs so you can add this one directory to your PATH environment variable. Because there's so much space on a CD, 32-bit builds of all the samples are included in the installation. |
| CLASSLIB | A hack-o-rama C++ class library for a basic Windows-based application that is used by the more feature-laden samples. |
| INOLE | A library of useful helper functions and UI controls. |
| INTERFAC | Template implementations for all the OLE-defined interfaces discussed in this book. |
| CHAP*xx* | Sample code for Chapter *xx*. |

When citing specific samples, this book will point to one of the directories listed in Table 1-1 followed by the subdirectory containing the sample. For example, CHAP02\QUERY is a reference to the "Query" sample of Chapter 2; INC\BOOKGUID.H points to a header file in the shared INC directory.

Many samples in this book are simple demonstrations of the ideas behind a technology or an interface. There are two sample applications— Cosmo and Patron— that you'll find in a number of chapters, both of which are based on the CLASSLIB framework.[12] These serve to illustrate how to add various OLE features to an existing application as well as a new application, and both evolve throughout the book. Cosmo, a little graphical editor shown in Figure 1-15 on the following page, starts in CHAP01\COSMO as a fully featured application that doesn't do anything with OLE. You draw a figure by simply clicking the mouse to add points, and you can change the colors and the line style used. As we progress through this book, we'll change and add features to use OLE as described in CONTENTS.TXT. In particular, this application gets a full OLE Automation treatment and also becomes a server for compound document content objects. In addition, we'll break the graphical part of Cosmo into a separate component, called Polyline, which also evolves through various chapters.

---

12. CLASSLIB exists only for these samples and should not be used in professional development efforts. See the "OLE Tools" section on page 59.

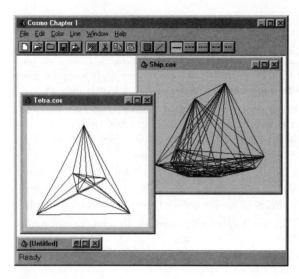

**Figure 1-15.**
*The Cosmo application with several open Polyline figures.*

Patron is a companion application that manages documents, in which each document has pages, as shown in Figure 1-16. *Webster's* defines *patron* as "one who uses the services of another establishment" or "the proprietor of an establishment (such as an inn)." As described in CONTENTS.TXT, Patron will evolve into a container for various types of objects—bitmaps, metafiles, compound document objects, and controls—that are the "tenants" that stay in the pages in the document. So this application really is running some sort of establishment and providing services to its customers. In CHAP01\PA-TRON, this application does next to nothing. All you can do is open new documents; add, remove, or navigate through pages; and format the document according to printer device information. You cannot place anything on a page, nor can you save a document. We'll add such features in later chapters, using Patron to illustrate building a new application with OLE technologies. I've left out some features initially because creating them without OLE would take a horrendous amount of code. Call it laziness if you want. I call it planning.

As Cosmo, Patron, and other samples evolve through the book, I've consistently marked the modifications made in each chapter with two comments: *//CHAPTERxxMOD* and *//End CHAPTERxxMOD*, where *xx* is the relevant chapter number. These delimiters will help you see what changes I had to make to header (H), source (CPP), and resource (RC) files in order to support the feature under discussion in that chapter. For example, if you want to

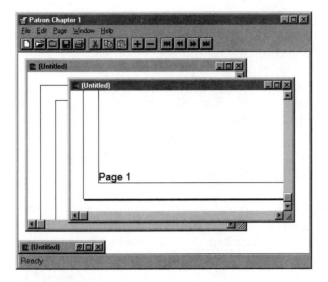

**Figure 1-16.**
*The Patron application with several open documents.*

see which variables I added to a class to support a specific feature, look in the H files, and you'll see the new ones between these comments. With these comments, you'll be able to see how a new feature fits into an overall application, especially because many OLE features make sense only in a larger application. But at the same time, you won't have to struggle to figure out which parts of the application have to do with that feature and which parts deal with other features.

I should also point out that many of the design techniques used in the sample code do not represent singular ways of accomplishing any particular goal. For example, the techniques I use to implement an object and its interfaces are not in any way part of OLE; they are simply my own techniques and do not represent Truth. "If it's Truth you're interested in," as Indiana Jones would remind us, "Dr. Tyree's philosophy class is right down the hall." What's important in OLE is that you provide the right vtable for an interface, and that's really the proverbial *it*.

## To C or Not to C (with Apologies to Shakespeare)

The sample code provided in this book is written mostly in C++, primarily because the concepts and features of OLE are best expressed in that language. Authoring a book of this sort presents a few philosophical difficulties, such as what language to use, how everything will fit on the companion disks, and how not to alienate those in your audience who do not understand C++.

C++ code is smaller and simplifies code reuse, reducing the amount of code I have to write and the amount of code you have to read. C programmers will no doubt be a little put off by this. The file APPA.WRI on the companion CD provides the necessary explanations of basic C++ concepts and notations that should help the C programmer understand the sample code. While writing the code, I tried to remember that it has to be understandable to a typical C programmer, so I've purposely kept myself from going hog-wild about everything C++ can do, such as deep multiple inheritance or long chains of virtual functions. This will no doubt put off a number of C++ programmers, but believe me, this is not as bad as forcing everyone to labor through verbose C.

For the most part, the samples are written using C++ as a better C, which is the most primitive way to use C++. This primarily means that C++ is a more convenient way to manage data structures and create OLE objects and interfaces. Some of the samples have, in fact, a C language legacy, and I have converted them to C++ mostly by switching structures into classes. I hope that those readers who are not very familiar with C++ will still be able to make sense of the samples.

## Interface Files in the INTERFAC Directory

The first step in implementing an interface is usually to create stubs for all the member functions of that interface, after which you fill in those functions with the appropriate code. Because creating function stubs is such a tedious and mundane process, the INTERFAC directory includes such stubs. For each interface that we'll explore in this book, I've provided a C++ class for an "interface implementation," in which the *CImpI<name>* class implements a single interface. For each class, there's an H file with the class declaration and a CPP file with the stub implementation. In some cases, there's a full object implementation because some objects are almost always implemented the same way. The basic idea here is that you can use these files as a starting point for implementing any interface or object you need: it is very simple to quickly search and replace the names in the file.

## Registry Files

As we will discover throughout this book, OLE makes extensive use of the system registry, and many of the samples require specific registry entries in order to operate correctly. To that end, most samples have a REG file in their respective directories that you must merge with the registry before running the sample. You do this by double-clicking on the WIN32.REG file (or WIN16.REG file) from the system shell. If you forget to do this, some samples might work only partially, and some might not work at all. This can be very confusing, so train yourself to question whether the registry is correct when something goes awry.

You might wonder why there isn't just one global registry file for everything in this book. This is because a number of the samples change between chapters and therefore require different registry entries for those changes.

OLE registry information often involves a pathname to a DLL or an EXE server for some object class, as well as pathnames of type libraries. The REG files on the CD assume that these paths are based on C:\INOLE, the default installation directory. If you install to a different directory, you'll need to edit every REG file (just text files) and change "c:\inole" to your installation directory.

## Building and Testing Environment

The installed samples include files named MAKEALL.BAT in a number of directories. Running this batch file in the installation root will build every sample in that and all subdirectories. There are a number of environment variables, such as "NODEBUG," that control various aspects of the build process. For more information, see the BUILD.TXT file in the installation directory, which also describes the environment neccessary to build the samples.

# OLE Tools

I've been asked frequently why I don't use MFC in this book, not only for the basic application framework (for which I use CLASSLIB) but also for the OLE features. In other words, why is this book (including all the samples) focused on working with OLE through the raw API and the raw interfaces? There are a number of reasons. First of all, no OLE-related tool I know, even MFC (the Microsoft Foundation Classes), has direct and explicit support for absolutely every OLE feature that we'll be covering. At the time of writing, MFC is focused on OLE Automation, OLE Documents, and OLE Controls, although as time goes by it will gain additional features. Working in MFC would not allow us to easily explore type information by itself, nor connection points, nor persistent objects, nor monikers, and so on. To study these technologies, we do have to study the raw OLE API and interfaces outside the context of any development tool. In addition, I intend this book to be of use not only to applications programmers but also to those who are interested in creating better OLE tools for the rest of us, and they need the raw information in order to make such tools.

The most important reason, however, is that even when you have a great development framework such as MFC, I strongly believe that you will benefit from at least knowing how OLE works on a mechanism level, as well as how things work on a code level (which is, again, reflected in the chapter organization as described earlier). If you use something like MFC to do OLE development, it helps to understand why you're using this or that part of OLE. This is especially important when something doesn't work, or when the framework doesn't support what you want to do—then you really need to know what's going on not only inside the framework but inside OLE as well. If this book were about MFC-OLE, you'd learn MFC but not much about OLE. You need to learn about OLE to work with it using any tool.

My favorite analogy for this argument is to compare OLE to mathematics and tools such as MFC to a calculator. A calculator makes the acts of calculating mathematical equations a helluva lot easier; it sure beats taking square roots by hand or looking up logarithms and trigonometry functions in tables. But even when you have a calculator, you really have to know why you are using those functions and what those functions do for you so that you know when it is appropriate to apply the calculator to your problem. The relationship between OLE and MFC's OLE support is the same way: know what you're trying to accomplish and what MFC can do for you so that you'll know when to apply MFC intelligently and when you might have occasion to do a little math by hand. Having knowledge of the mathematical principles will greatly increase your ability to exploit your tools.

That said, I will mention that there are an ever-growing number of tools that can help you incorporate OLE technologies into software projects. Microsoft itself offers Visual C++ with MFC, as well as Visual Basic, both of which can help write applications that use components as well as components themselves. Something like MFC, for example, makes technologies such as OLE Documents much easier because OLE Documents technology involves more than just implementing interfaces, and MFC can provide default implementations of almost all of it. Visual C++'s debugger, as another example, offers OLE debugging, by which you can step into an interface function call across a process boundary and easily debug two applications at the same time.

Microsoft is not the only provider of OLE-related tools. Borland has ObjectComponents Framework, or OCF, which simplifies many of the same technologies that MFC simplifies, with better support in some areas, less support in others. Blue Sky Software has an OLE debugging tool. I'm sure there are more, and I encourage you to scout around a little and see what might be of use. If you have an idea of what you'd like to see, let the tool vendors know. I'm sure one of them will see a great opportunity to take advantage of the growing popularity of OLE.

# CHAPTER TWO

# Objects and Interfaces

*object* n *1* **syn** *THING, article;* **rel** *doodad; gadget 2* **syn** *THING, being, entity, indi-vidual, material, matter, stuff, substance.*
— *Webster's Collegiate Thesaurus,* Merriam-Webster, 1976

Whenever you hear about objects, you probably have the same nagging question that I often do: just what is an object? For all the highly charged political and religious battles over this question, objects are simply *things.* The half-empty glass of water on my desk (my doctor says I should be drinking more) is a thing, just as the 12 CDs in the complete collection of Beethoven's piano sonatas are things, just as the button control on my computer screen is a thing.

Out of curiosity, I ventured to look up a suitable definition of *thing* in Webster's companion dictionary to my thesaurus. (These too are things.) The best of the 10 definitions given is "*3 b:* the concrete entity as distinguished from its appearances." This definition has one primary implication: my glass of water the *object* is a glass of water — the object is not its look, its feel, or any other aspect of what I might call its *interfaces,* sensory or otherwise. Yet because I perceive the world through my senses, these *interfaces* define how I interact with this object, what I can do with the object, and how I use it. In other words, the true essence of an object is unavailable to me through my senses, so I'm left with no real way to discern the true object. This is, of course, one of those dilemmas that have occupied philosophers for the last, oh, 3000 years or so.

But whether I really *know* the object's true nature is immaterial to whether I can actually make use of the object. Through the interface of my glass of water, I can certainly make use of it by picking it up, tilting it so that the water runs into my mouth, refilling it when it's empty, and so on.

The separation between what an object *is* and how that object is *used* by something external is at the core of how we understand objects in the Component Object Model (COM) (and thus OLE) sense. Again, because OLE is concerned with component integration and components are built of objects, it is our present interest to learn how these objects work, which means learning about COM, the object model. In Chapter 1, you saw what OLE calls an *interface* and learned how objects support multiple interfaces. This chapter explores these ideas further by looking at how to define and identify an interface, how to use and implement an interface in both C and C++ (proving that you can work with COM and OLE in C, although this will be the only time straight C is used in this book), and various techniques for implementing multiple interfaces, such as C++ multiple inheritance. This chapter will describe the *globally unique identifiers* (GUIDs) that are used to identify interfaces and object classes and introduce registry considerations that will be cropping up again and again in this book. We will also examine reference counting rules and considerations, standard COM task memory management, standard error types, interface properties, and some glorious details about the ever-so-important *QueryInterface* function that we met in Chapter 1. We'll see exactly how *QueryInterface* supports the notion of "robust evolution of functionality over time."

I'll refer mostly to COM instead of OLE in this chapter because COM is the primary technology involved with these topics. In addition, this chapter doesn't exactly follow the convention of placing topics unrelated to programming mechanisms in the first sections of the chapter. Some important information about memory management and special types of objects called *enumerators* appears at the beginning of some of the programming sections, and earlier sections even introduce some OLE/COM API functions that are of particular interest. The reason for this break from the convention is that the information here, as part of the Component Object Model, is central to everything else in OLE. It is all well worth your time.

Through the course of this chapter, we'll discover COM's answer to the question "What is an object?"—which will serve us well throughout this book. Then we can truly begin to see how a button control or the Beethoven CD I'm listening to (Sonata 17, Op. 31, No. 2, "Tempest") could become an object. What matters is not the nature of the thing, but how we communicate with that thing through whatever interfaces it shows us.

# The Ultimate Question of Life, the Universe, and Objects (with Apologies to Douglas Adams)

You probably already have some idea that once you have your first interface pointer for any given object, you can use *QueryInterface* to learn what else the object can do for you. But this begs a key question: Given a way to identify an object of a class, how do you obtain your first interface pointer to it?

This question is a central theme in this book: most chapters that follow generally deal with identifying different objects and components, the interfaces they support, techniques to obtain the first interface pointer, and what to do with the member functions of those interfaces. So the answer to this ultimate question (which is not "42," as it was in Douglas Adams's books) varies with each technology in OLE. In fact, there are four different answers to the question—four different ways to obtain that very important first pointer:

- Call an API function that creates an object of only one type and returns only one type of interface pointer. Many OLE and COM API functions fit into this category—for example, *CreateTypeLib*, which always creates the same type of object—a new type library—and returns the same interface pointer, *ICreateTypeLib*.

- Call a member function through an interface of an object that you already have, which returns an interface pointer to a different object. This is generally how a client navigates through multiple objects in a component. For example, opening a stream within a storage in a compound file requires that you call *IStorage::OpenStream* to obtain the *IStream* pointer you need.

- Implement on an object of your own an interface through which other objects will pass their own interface pointers. A connectable object, for example, receives pointers to sink interfaces through *IConnectionPoint::Advise*.

- Call an API function that given a class identifier creates an object and returns any type of interface pointer you request. The COM API function *CoCreateInstance*, the *new* operator for custom components, is the primary function in this category.

As you can see, both OLE and your own component and object implementations will involve most of these techniques at some time or other. In each case, there is also a difference in how you identify the object or component you're trying to use. Let's first look at object identity along with other object properties before we examine interfaces more closely.

---

### Class, Type, and Prototype

The words *class* and *type* are generally interchangeable concepts and are used that way in this book. In OLE, it is often useful to view a type as a specific instance of a *prototype* that describes the total signature of an object as the union of its supported interfaces (which must include at least *IUnknown*). Thus, a class or type is a particular implementation that supports the same interfaces as other classes of the same prototype, although each class differs in many ways. For example, the compound document content object is a prototype, but chart, table, text, sound, and video classes are specific instances (types) of that prototype. The importance of a prototype is that because objects with the same interfaces are polymorphic, a client needs to understand only how to work with a prototype to work with a wide range of different specific types. Thus, a compound document container can work with any compound document content object. Such clients are implemented according to a protocol that specifies how to work with a particular prototype, and that prototype then involves multiple interfaces.

---

## Object Identity

The "ultimate question" raised earlier had a loaded catchphrase: "Given a way to identify an object of a class…" Corresponding to the four answers to the question itself, there are four basic ways to uniquely identify a class:

- By the name of the API function that creates or retrieves an object of the class

- By an object's position within the hierarchy of a component—that is, through the name of the interface function that provides access to it

■ By some internal structure or class name provided when the object is created and then exposed to outside clients

■ By a globally unique class identifier, or CLSID

The key to all of these identifications is *uniqueness.* By design, the name of an API function is unique within the system and so is unique among all components and applications. Because interfaces are unique, so are the member functions they contain. Those functions that create new objects uniquely identify the class of object they create. Objects that are created within a client for the express purpose of communicating with another instance of an object—for example, an event sink—need be unique only within that client because there is no other way to get at the object. In such cases, a compiler will enforce a unique internal name.

The fourth method is a bit trickier: the case in which custom components are uniquely identified within an entire system and, in the future, across an entire network. The primary issue here is that distributed environments have potentially millions of components, objects, and interfaces that need unique identification. Using human-readable names for finding and binding to all of these elements (used for system APIs and internal class names) will certainly result in collision. The result of name-based identification will inevitably be the accidental connection of two or more software components that were not designed to interact with each other, and this will result in an error or a crash, even though the components and the system had no bugs and worked as designed.

The problem seems worse when you consider that many components and interfaces are developed at different times by different people in different places. How can you possibly guarantee uniqueness when there is no communication among vendors?

## Globally Unique Identifiers (GUIDs)

The problem of unique cross-network identification is not itself unique to OLE—it is, in fact, a problem that is present with basic Remote Procedure Calls (RPC). Because of this, the Open Software Foundation (OSF) created the Universally Unique Identifier, or UUID, as part of their Distributed Computing Environment (DCE), which is where the standards for the RPC used in Microsoft Windows, and thus in OLE, are defined.

A UUID, which is given the alias GUID[1] in COM and OLE, is a 128-bit (16-byte) integer that is virtually guaranteed to be unique in the world across space and time. Claiming that such an integer is unique across the universe is presumptuous. Global uniqueness is more realistic; hence the *G* in *GUID* instead of *U.* Throughout OLE, GUIDs are used to programmatically identify component classes (in which case they are called *class IDs,* or CLSIDs) and to identify interfaces (in which case they are called *interface IDs,* or IIDs).[2]

In various situations you'll need to obtain one or more GUIDs to assign to components that you implement or to new interfaces that you define. For this fundamental purpose COM provides an API function named *CoCreateGuid,* which actually calls the Win32 RPC API (acronym city!) function *UUIDCreate.* This function executes the algorithm specified by OSF DCE,[3] which uses a combination of the following information to generate the GUID:

- The current date and time

- A *clock sequence* and related persistent state to deal with retrograde motion of clocks

- A forcibly incremented counter to deal with high-frequency allocations

- The truly globally unique IEEE machine identifier, obtained from a network card (the implementation does not require a network card; if no network card is present, a machine identifier can be synthesized from highly variable machine states and stored persistently)

The chance of this carefully developed algorithm generating duplicate GUIDs in two different places at different times, even without a network card, is about the same as two random atoms in the universe colliding to form a small California avocado mated to a New York City sewer rat. In other words, don't worry about it.

---

1. Pronounced *goo-id,* similar to how you would say *gooey.* Perhaps this is why OLE can seem a little "sticky" at times. Pun definitely intended.

2. In traditional object-oriented technology, an object ID is more like an IID than a CLSID. Traditionally, objects have only a single interface, and the object ID identifies what one can access in that object, which is how interfaces are used in OLE. A CLSID in OLE identifies a component with one or more objects, each with one or more interfaces.

3. See "DEC/HP, Network Computing Architecture, Remote Procedure Call RunTime Extensions Specification, Version OSF TX1.0.11," Steven Miller, July 23, 1992. This is part of the OSF DCE documentation. Chapter 10 describes the UUID/GUID allocation algorithm.

While you might have occasion to create a GUID at run time with *CoCreateGuid,* you'll normally obtain the GUIDs you need once and assign them to the components you're developing. Your development environment will include a tool called UUIDGEN.EXE or GUIDGEN.EXE, which will give you one or more GUIDs that you can incorporate into source code. While writing this paragraph, I ran UUIDGEN, and it spit out the following:

```
3fad3020-16b7-11ce-80eb-00aa003d7352
```

This is the DCE standard for spelling out a GUID in hexadecimal text digits. (The hyphens are part of the standard as well.) To show just how unique these things can be, I ran UUIDGEN again only a few seconds later and got this result:

```
42754580-16b7-11ce-80eb-00aa003d7352
```

If you'd like to have more than one sequential GUID to make them a little more consistent, use the command-line switch *-n <number>.* For example, I ran UUIDGEN -n5, and it gave me this sequence:

```
a4f8a400-16b7-11ce-80eb-00aa003d7352
a4f8a401-16b7-11ce-80eb-00aa003d7352
a4f8a402-16b7-11ce-80eb-00aa003d7352
a4f8a403-16b7-11ce-80eb-00aa003d7352
a4f8a404-16b7-11ce-80eb-00aa003d7352
```

The sequence is counted in the first 32 bits of each value. A number of other switches for UUIDGEN can generate GUID declarations for use in C/C++ source files as well. Run UUIDGEN -? for a complete listing.

The code you'll write for OLE will use symbols to refer to whatever GUIDs you need. While the OLE header files and link libraries include every GUID that OLE defines (mostly IIDs), you'll need to define your own GUIDs somewhere in your own sources. You can do this with a C structure such as the following, which defines a symbol "MYGUID":

```
MyGUID = {  /* 891a0d90-16b7-11ce-80eb-00aa003d7352 */ 0x891a0d90
    , 0x16b7, 0x11ce, {0x80, 0xeb, 0x00, 0xaa, 0x00, 0x3d, 0x73
    , 0x52} };
```

You can also use the OLE macro DEFINE_GUID to do the same thing, as was done for this book's central repository of GUIDs used in the sample code, INC\BOOKGUID.H:

```
DEFINE_GUID(IID_ISampleOne, 0x00021141, 0, 0, 0xC0,0,0,0,0,0,0,0x46);
```

All the GUIDs used in this book's samples start with *0x000211xx* and should not be used in your own projects: you must run UUIDGEN.EXE to obtain your own GUIDs. (My GUIDs are fraught with zeros because they were allocated from a pool of GUIDs set aside for Microsoft's purposes. Unfortunately, you can't get clean GUIDs like this; you must use GUIDGEN or UUIDGEN.)

Reduced to its binary form, a GUID has the following data structure:

```
typedef struct GUID
    {
    DWORD    Data1;
    WORD     Data2;
    WORD     Data3;
    BYTE     Data4[8];
    } GUID;

typedef GUID CLSID;
typedef GUID IID;
```

Each field of the structure represents a piece of the GUID between the hyphens, giving you an easy way to address each part. For example, it can be useful in debugging to dump out the first DWORD of a GUID; if you have a sequence of GUIDs, this will be enough to indicate which one is which. For the most part, however, you'll never manipulate GUIDs directly—they are almost always manipulated either as a symbolic constant or as a variable whose absolute value is unimportant. For example, a client might enumerate all component classes registered on the system and display a list of those classes to an end user. That user selects a class from the list, which the client then maps to an absolute CLSID value. The client does not care what that value is—the client simply knows that the value uniquely identifies the user's selection.

This last example brings up an interesting question: do you really want to show the end user ugly hex strings such as *42754580-16b7-11ce-80eb-00aa003d7352*? I think not. Therefore, you can assign human-readable names to GUIDs in the system registry for the convenience of the end user—users will usually see only a few components at a time in any list, so the chances of confusion over a conflict are greatly reduced. We'll talk about the registry in a moment.

## COM API Functions for GUIDs

The basic COM and OLE system DLLs provide a number of API functions for dealing with GUIDs, CLSIDs, and IIDs, as illustrated in Table 2-1:

| Function | Purpose |
|---|---|
| *CoCreateGuid* | Allocates a new GUID |
| *IsEqualGUID* | Compares two GUIDs for equivalence |
| *IsEqualCLSID* | Typesafe version of *IsEqualGUID* for CLSIDs |
| *IsEqualIID* | Typesafe version of *IsEqualGUID* for IIDs |
| *StringFromCLSID* | Typesafe conversion of a CLSID to a text string |
| *StringFromIID* | Typesafe version of *StringFromCLSID* for IIDs |
| *StringFromGUID2* | Converts a GUID to a text string, storing the string in a caller-allocated buffer |
| *CLSIDFromString* | Converts a text string to a typesafe CLSID |
| *IIDFromString* | Typesafe version of *CLSIDFromString* for IIDs |

**Table 2-1.**
*API functions for working with GUIDs, CLSIDs, and IIDs. Strings are always in Unicode on 32-bit platforms.*

All of the string-related functions work with a GUID spelled out in hex digits as before, but they are wrapped in braces, as in *{42754580-16b7-11ce-80eb-00aa003d7352}*. This is the format of a GUID as it appears in the registry. The *StringFromCLSID* and *StringFromIID* functions allocate the returned string themselves, using what is called the *task allocator,* as we'll see in "Memory Management" later in this chapter.

In addition to the *IsEqual* functions, the OLE header files also include C++ overloaded == operators for GUIDs, CLSIDs, and IIDs, providing more convenient methods of comparison for C++ implementations. You'll see these operators used in most of this book's sample code.

One other note concerning C vs. C++: when passing any GUID as a function argument, you must pass an explicit pointer in C, whereas you can use a reference in C++. For example, in C++ you could pass something such as *IID_ISampleOne* as is, but in C you would have to pass *&IID_ISampleOne*.

### #include <initguid.h> and Precompiled Headers

Any code that ever refers to any GUID, be it a CLSID or an IID, must include a standard OLE header file, INITGUID.H, once and only once in the entire compilation of a DLL or an EXE. All clients and components should have an *#include <initguid.h>* line in one and only one source file, which comes after the other OLE headers. INITGUID.H ensures that all GUIDs (yours and OLE's) get defined as constants in your data or code segment that holds constants. If you typically use a central include file for all files in your project, wrap an *#ifdef* statement around the *#include*. The samples in this book have such a statement based on a symbol INITGUIDS that you'll see in INC\BOOKGUID.H. One file in each project defines INITGUIDS. (INITGUIDS is a symbol used in the OLE headers themselves for the same sort of purpose, but I couldn't think of another name.)

Including INITGUID.H only once is tricky when you are using precompiled headers. Create the precompiled header in a file that does not include INITGUID.H—the samples using precompilation all use the file PRECOMP.CPP, which contains only one *#include* statement. You can then use the precompiled header from this step to compile with all files *except* the one in which you *want* to include INITGUID.H. You should compile that single file without using the precompiled header to pull in the extra file.

## CLSID Registration and ProgIDs

On each host system, COM uses the system registry (also called the *registration database*) to store relevant information about components according to their CLSIDs. In the chapters ahead, we'll see the entries necessary to map a CLSID to the server that implements a component or to the type library that describes the component and its interfaces. Anytime you need to associate any information with any GUID for any reason, you'll use the registry. Such information is then available to everything else in the system without requiring the instantiation of any component. This does, of course, require some standards.

In the registry of a system in which OLE is installed, there will be a key called *CLSID* directly off the root key known as HKEY_CLASSES_ROOT. If you run the REGEDT32.EXE program with the Win32 SDK, you'll see this set of entries in a window with the caption "HKEY_CLASSES_ROOT on Local Machine." The top-level key (folder) shown in the window will be labeled

"HKEY_CLASSES_ROOT," and there will be a subkey (subfolder) labeled "CLSID." Under this subkey, you'll find all the information about component classes.

The primary entry you must make for a CLSID is a subkey under the CLSID key. Your subkey name is your CLSID spelled in hex digits within braces—such as *{42754580-16b7-11ce-80eb-00aa003d7352}*—where the value of that subkey is the human-readable name that you want to associate with the CLSID. (All characters are acceptable in the name, including spaces and punctuation.) This provides a pretty name that can be displayed by a client without scaring off the end user. The documentation convention for describing a registry entry such as this is to use a backslash for the root. Each entry below the root is indented and written as a "key = value" pair. (The "= value" can be omitted.) So the entry described here is written as follows:

```
\
    CLSID
        {42754580-16b7-11ce-80eb-00aa003d7352} = Acme Component 3.0
```

You might also want to associate your CLSID with what is called a *programmatic identifier,* or ProgID, which effectively (but less precisely) identifies the same class. A ProgID, which is not considered something that an end user should see, is a text string[4] *without spaces* that can be used in programming contexts where referring to the ugly CLSID string isn't appropriate. For example, you use ProgIDs to identify an object class in Visual Basic instead of the raw CLSID because Visual Basic doesn't have a way to define the same GUID structure and can't read C/C++ header files in order to pull in symbolic names. The ProgID is thus an alternative language-independent symbolic name.

The standard ProgID format is *<Vendor>.<Component>.<Version>*, such as *Microsoft.Chart.5* or *Lotus.AmiProDocument.4.2.* This format is reasonably unique, and if everyone follows it there will generally not be a collision. (The trademark lawyers ensure this.) There is also the *VersionIndependentProgID*, which has the same format without the version number. Both the ProgID and the VersionIndependentProgID can be registered, with a human-readable name as a value, below the root key. You should include a "CurVer = <ProgID>" entry under VersionIndependentProgID to provide a convenient mapping between ProgID and VersionIndependentProgID, and then you should include a "CLSID = <{CLSID}>" entry under ProgID to map it to the CLSID, as shown at the top of the following page.

---

4. A ProgID can contain DBCS characters, but because end users never see a ProgID, it is rather pointless to include these characters.

```
\
    Acme.Component.3 = Acme Component Version 3.0
        CLSID = {42754580-16b7-11ce-80eb-00aa003d7352}

    Acme.Component = Acme Component
        CurVer = Acme.Component.3
```

The VersionIndependentProgID is thus mapped to the ProgID, which is mapped to the CLSID. You will also want to map the CLSID itself to both ProgIDs, using additional entries such as these:

```
\
    CLSID
        {42754580-16b7-11ce-80eb-00aa003d7352} = Acme Component 3.0
        ProgID = Acme.Component.3
        VersionIndependentProgID = Acme.Component
```

OLE provides functions to look up a ProgID from a CLSID and vice versa using registry information so that you don't have to consult the registry directly:

| Function | Purpose |
| --- | --- |
| *ProgIDFromCLSID* | Returns the ProgID associated with a given CLSID |
| *CLSIDFromProgID* | Returns the CLSID associated with a given ProgID |

To create registry entries, you can either write code using the *Reg\** Win32 APIs (which is a pain) or create a REG file and simply run it to merge its entries with the registry. The file below will create all the entries that were shown above:

```
REGEDIT
HKEY_CLASSES_ROOT\Acme.Component.3 = Acme Component Version 3.0
HKEY_CLASSES_ROOT\Acme.Component.3\CLSID = {42754580-16b7-11ce-80eb-00aa003d7352}

HKEY_CLASSES_ROOT\Acme.Component = Acme Component
HKEY_CLASSES_ROOT\Acme.Component\CurVer = Acme.Component.3

HKEY_CLASSES_ROOT\CLSID\{42754580-16b7-11ce-80eb-00aa003d7352} = Acme Component 3.0
HKEY_CLASSES_ROOT\CLSID\{42754580-16b7-11ce-80eb-00aa003d7352}\ProgID = Acme.Component.3
HKEY_CLASSES_ROOT\CLSID\{42754580-16b7-11ce-80eb-00aa003d7352}\VersionIndependentProgID = Acme.Component
```

You can see that each backslash represents another level in the registration hierarchy. Also note that the spaces around the equal signs are used to separate the key name (which cannot have spaces) from the value (which can have spaces).

## What Components Need CLSIDs and Registry Information?

As you might have guessed, not all components and objects need to have a CLSID because there are other ways to uniquely identify them. In general, only those custom components that want to be created through a function such as *CoCreateInstance* require a CLSID. This includes, but is not limited to, all compound document content objects, all OLE Controls, and any OLE Automation objects providing a service (as opposed to those that just implement *IDispatch* for some other reason). These require additional entries to identify the component server, as we'll see in Chapter 5. In addition, the registry is the only way to associate an object class with type information without needing an already running instance of the object; if you want to make such information available, there are entries to map a CLSID to a type library, as described in Chapter 3. The registry is also used to associate an interface with its marshaling proxy and stub implementations, which are packaged in a component with a CLSID. Outside of these uses, a CLSID is totally unnecessary, especially for objects that are created internally within a component, such as an event sink, a client site in a compound document container, or a portion of a filename with a moniker.

# Interfaces and Interface Attributes

By now we understand that an object is an entity that can be experienced or used only through its interfaces, and those interfaces are nothing more than semantically related groups of functions. Each interface uniquely identifies an object's support for a particular feature across time and space by virtue of its IID. Although an object has its own class identity, it is really its interfaces that make that object useful. We reviewed the binary structure in Chapter 1; this is repeated in Figure 2-1 on the following page to refresh our memories. It is through this structure that a client calls interface members to access the object.

We are now ready to explore additional topics about these interfaces: identity, definition (including calling conventions and standard error types), and, most important, attributes and properties of interfaces. These define the rules of implementation that external clients will expect an object to follow.

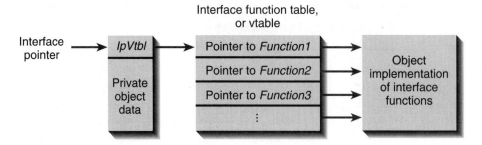

**Figure 2-1.**
*The binary interface structure.*

## Interface Identity

Like objects and component classes, every interface must have a unique identity so that clients are always clear about the functionality and features they are accessing through the interface. In contrast to the four possible ways to identify a component, an interface is *always* identified precisely with an IID. Again, an IID is equivalent to the GUID and therefore shares the same characteristic uniqueness.

Of course, it would be painful to write code that identifies an interface with a bunch of hex digits. For this reason, IIDs are usually given a compile-time symbolic constant that works in place of the exact value, which is then used at run time. These symbols are named *IID_<Interface>*, as in *IID_IConnectionPoint* or *IID_IUnknown*. However, these symbols identify the interface but not the interface pointer type. Interface pointer variables are always declared using *<Interface>* *, as in *IUnknown* * or *IStorage* *. OLE also defines aliases for these types, for example LPSTORAGE, for which you drop the *I* and the *, add *LP*, and put the rest in uppercase. Outside the context of a pointer, interface names are never used programmatically but serve only for conversation. You will never see *IUnknown* by itself in code, always *IUnknown* *. We'll refer to an object's implementation of the interface as simply *IUnknown*. Of course, all of these names, types, and symbols only matter at compile time; the actual IID value is the sole interface identifier at run time.

## Interface Definitions

There are a number of ways to define an interface. Regardless of the technique, an interface definition always reduces to either a C++ abstract base class (a class with nothing but pure virtual function signatures) or a C structure containing pointers to the interface member functions (the vtable) and a second structure containing a pointer to that vtable. The two are entirely equivalent. As examples, here are the entries for the *IUnknown* interface as taken from the Win32 SDK header file OBJBASE.H:

```
//This is a convenience for documentation.
#define interface struct

typedef /* [unique] */ IUnknown __RPC_FAR *LPUNKNOWN;
EXTERN_C const IID IID_IUnknown;

#if defined(__cplusplus) && !defined(CINTERFACE)
interface IUnknown
    {
    public:
        virtual HRESULT __stdcall QueryInterface(
            /* [in] */ REFIID riid,
            /* [out] */ void __RPC_FAR *__RPC_FAR *ppvObject) = 0;
        virtual ULONG __stdcall AddRef(void) = 0;
        virtual ULONG __stdcall Release(void) = 0;
    };

#else   /* C style interface */

typedef struct IUnknownVtbl
    {
    HRESULT ( __stdcall __RPC_FAR *QueryInterface )(
        IUnknown __RPC_FAR * This,
        /* [in] */ REFIID riid,
        /* [out] */ void __RPC_FAR *__RPC_FAR *ppvObject);

    ULONG ( __stdcall __RPC_FAR *AddRef )(
        IUnknown __RPC_FAR * This);

    ULONG ( __stdcall __RPC_FAR *Release )(
        IUnknown __RPC_FAR * This);

    } IUnknownVtbl;

interface IUnknown
    {
    CONST_VTBL struct IUnknownVtbl __RPC_FAR *lpVtbl;
    };

#endif  /* C style interface */
```

The text in this book, as well as the original OLE specifications, uses a clean C++ style syntax—without all the platform-specific embellishments and "virtual" keywords—to illustrate an interface's member functions. (Note that the IID to *QueryInterface* is passed by reference in C++ and passed as a *const* pointer in C.)

```
interface IUnknown
    {
    HRESULT QueryInterface(IID& iid, void **ppv);
    ULONG   AddRef(void);
    ULONG   Release(void);
    };
```

When you're working in C++, you can derive one interface definition from another by using C++ inheritance, illustrated in the following syntax example. This is the only place where OLE makes use of such inheritance. Different mechanisms are employed in achieving reusability, as we'll see in "Object Polymorphism and Reusability" later in this chapter.

```
interface IProvideClassInfo : IUnknown
    {
    HRESULT GetClassInfo(ITypeInfo **ppTI)
    };
```

From the puzzled look on your face, I know you have a few questions. What is all that extra junk in the Win32 definition about? What is an HRESULT?

## Interface Definition Language (IDL)

On 32-bit platforms, the preferred method for defining an interface is to write a script in the Interface Definition Language (IDL), which is based, once again, on the OSF DCE standard. In this language, you can describe interfaces, member functions, and attributes of those functions and their arguments. IDL is preferred because COM can extend it quite readily to support distributed services when the time comes.

This chapter will not discuss IDL in any detail, as that subject is covered in Chapter 6. The full specifications exist in the *Microsoft Win32 Remote Procedure Call Programmer's Guide and Reference*. For now it is enough to say that once you've written an IDL script, you run it through the Microsoft IDL compiler (MIDL.EXE, part of the Win32 SDK), which pumps out the header file mess that we saw earlier. MIDL actually does more, such as generating source code for a proxy and stub that can marshal the interface across a process boundary, but that also is a subject for Chapter 6. What is important here is that the header files are necessary for both the object's implementation of that interface and for a client's compilation of code that uses the interface. This does assume, of course, that everything is written in C or C++, which is why there are type libraries. Type libraries contain the same information as a MIDL-generated header file but are language-independent. As we'll see in the next chapter, you use the Object Description Language (ODL), which is similar to and actually a superset of IDL, to define the information that ends up in a type library.

NOTE: IDL is simply a convenience for programmers; it is not necessary to use it to define an interface or even to provide marshaling for an interface. Microsoft expects that in time there will be better tools for defining interfaces, such as point-and-click editors that generate the IDL scripts themselves.

## Calling Conventions and Parameter Types

A close look at the preceding interface definitions will show you that all the interface functions are declared using __*stdcall*, the standard for 32-bit implementations. Frequently, however, you will see use of a STDMETHOD macro that expands to include the calling convention and the standard return type, HRESULT. When implementing an interface member function, you'll frequently see the use of the macro STDMETHODIMP(*method*), which expands to HRESULT __*export* __*stdcall method*, or STDMETHODIMP_(*type, method*), which expands to *type* __*export* __*stdcall method*. You must always export all interface member functions; using the IMP macros will eliminate any chances that you'll forget to do so.

You may also have noticed the use of *[in]* and *[out]* labels before various arguments in the interface member functions. These labels identify the direction of the flow of information through these arguments, such as whether the information is exclusively input data to a function, exclusively output data from the function (such as a structure that it fills), or both. The possible variations are defined as follows, using the word *parameter* interchangeably with *argument*:

| Parameter Type | Description and Allocation Rules |
| --- | --- |
| in-parameter | Input data for a function, allocated and freed by the caller using whatever memory management is wanted. |
| out-parameter | Output data from a function, allocated by the function and freed by the caller using standard COM task memory. The called function must always fill this parameter even on failure; for example, an output pointer must be set to NULL on failure. |
| in/out-parameter | Input data for the function, modified and returned as output data on return from the function. Initially allocated by the caller, freed and reallocated by the callee if necessary, and ultimately freed by the caller as with an out-parameter. |

What is referred to as *standard COM task memory* involves the use of OLE's standard memory allocation service. This is discussed later under "Memory Management." This memory service is used for all function arguments in which a transfer of memory ownership occurs between a client and an object, which means that there must be rules on how to allocate and free this memory. Because there's no transfer of ownership with in-parameters, they do not involve the use of this memory service.

## Return Types: HRESULT and SCODE

Except in special circumstances, nearly every COM and OLE API function and nearly every interface member function returns a value of the type HRESULT. HRESULT is also called a "handle to a result" and has a structure identical to the Win32 error codes structure, as shown in Figure 2-2.

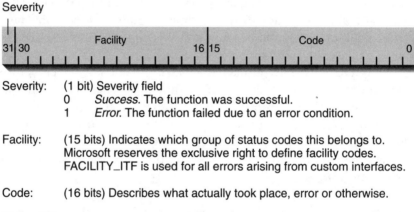

Severity

| 31 | 30 | Facility | 16 | 15 | Code | 0 |

Severity:   (1 bit) Severity field
            0    *Success.* The function was successful.
            1    *Error.* The function failed due to an error condition.

Facility:   (15 bits) Indicates which group of status codes this belongs to. Microsoft reserves the exclusive right to define facility codes. FACILITY_ITF is used for all errors arising from custom interfaces.

Code:       (16 bits) Describes what actually took place, error or otherwise.

**Figure 2-2.**
*Structure of an HRESULT and an SCODE.*

Another name for an HRESULT on 32-bit platforms is SCODE, which has exactly the same structure. Historically, these were different types on 16-bit platforms, but they have since been made identical. Because many of the samples in this book also compile to 16 bits, you'll see some 16-bit COM API functions used in the code. These compile to nothing under 32 bits.

A major benefit of this error structure is that it not only defines the error but also includes the facility or layer within the system or component that caused the error, such as whether it was an error in the RPC transport between processes or an error that occurred inside the implementation of a member function. This can help tremendously when you are trying to determine when and where the error occurred. The other big gain with HRESULT/SCODE is that the severity bit allows you to have *multiple success codes* in addition to multiple failure codes.[5] Traditionally, functions have returned only Boolean information or returned only one success code and any number of error codes. With OLE, you can write a function that returns a TRUE or FALSE value if the function works and an error code if it doesn't work.

Because there are both multiple success and multiple error codes, OLE follows a naming convention for different codes. Any name with $E\_$ in it, which may be at the beginning as in E_FAIL or RPC_E_NOTCONNECTED means that the function failed. Any name with $S\_$, as in S_TRUE, S_FALSE, or STG_S_CONVERTED, means that the function succeeded. The most common codes are listed in Table 2-2. Because there can be multiple codes in each category, there are also two macros, SUCCEEDED and FAILED, that determine whether a code falls into the appropriate category, returning a Boolean TRUE or FALSE value. (SUCCEEDED returns TRUE when FAILED returns FALSE, and vice versa.) These macros actually do nothing more than test the high bit in the code, but they are used frequently in conditional statements.

| Value | Meaning |
| --- | --- |
| S_OK | Function succeeded. Also used for functions that semantically return a Boolean TRUE result to indicate that the function succeeded. |
| S_FALSE | Used for functions that semantically return a Boolean FALSE result to indicate that the function succeeded. |
| E_NOINTERFACE | *QueryInterface* did not recognize the requested interface. |
| E_NOTIMPL | Member function contains no implementation. |
| E_FAIL | Unspecified failure. |
| E_OUTOFMEMORY | Function failed to allocate necessary memory. |

**Table 2-2.**
*Common SCODE values.*

There is one special value that has the symbol NOERROR, which is defined as 0 and is equivalent to S_OK. (Win32 also defines NO_ERROR and ERROR_SUCCESS as 0.) You'll see this used quite often as a return value for a function, but you must be careful when you use it in a conditional statement. A common mistake is to compare the return value of a function to NOERROR to see whether it worked, but if the function returns a nonzero success code,

5. Note that a function's possible *success* codes are part of that function's behavior and must be fixed when the function is first published. Error codes, however, can be added at any later time.

such as S_FALSE (which is 1), the comparison will be wrong. There are only a few cases in which you *really* want to know whether the function returns *exactly* NOERROR. Otherwise, you should always use SUCCEEDED and FAILED.

You may have occasion to display a useful message to an end user when you encounter an error represented by an HRESULT. For this purpose, OLE offers the function *FormatMessage* that returns a user-readable message for any given HRESULT, localized to the user's language as appropriate. See the *OLE Programmer's Reference* for more information on this function.

## Interface Attributes

The first and foremost concept surrounding an interface is that it is a form of contract between the client using the interface and the object implementing it. This contract means that when a client has a pointer to an interface, the client can successfully call every member function in that interface. In other words, when an object implements an interface, it must implement every member function to at least return *E_NOTIMPL*. This means that after a client has obtained a pointer to an interface from a call to *QueryInterface*, it no longer has to ask the object whether the functions in that interface are callable — they are. The functions may not actually *do* anything, but they can be called. That is the nature of the contract.

Given that, there are four other important points about interfaces:

- Interfaces are not classes. An interface is an abstract base class, so it is not instantiable. It is merely a template for the correct vtable structure for that interface, providing names and function signatures for each entry in the vtable — an interface definition carries no implementation. It must be implemented in order to be usable. Furthermore, different object classes might implement an interface differently yet be used interchangeably in binary form, as long as the behavior conforms to the interface specification (such as two objects that implement *IStack*, where one uses an array and the other a linked list).

- Interfaces are not objects. Interfaces are the means to communicate with objects, which are otherwise intangible entities. The object can be implemented in any language with any internal structure so long as it can provide pointers to interfaces according to the binary structure. Because all interfaces work through function calls, the object can expose its internal state only through such functions.

■ Interfaces are strongly typed. At compile time, the compiler will enforce unique names for interfaces that identify variable types. At run time, an interface is globally unique by virtue of its IID, thereby eliminating the possibility of collisions with human-readable names. Interface designers must consciously assign an IID to any new interface, and objects and clients must consciously incorporate this IID into their own compilations to use that interface at run time. In this way, collisions cannot happen by accident, and this leads to improved robustness.

■ Interfaces are immutable. Interfaces are never versioned; revising an interface by adding or removing functions, changing argument types, or changing semantics effectively creates a new interface because it inherently changes the contract of the existing interface. Therefore, the revision must be assigned a new IID, making it as different from the original interface as any other. This avoids conflicts with the older interface. Objects can, of course, support multiple interfaces simultaneously so that the objects have a single internal implementation of the capabilities exposed through two or more similar revisions of an interface while still fulfilling their contractual obligations to all clients. This approach of creating immutable interfaces and allowing multiple interfaces per object avoids versioning problems.

Just because a class supports one interface, there is no requirement that it support any other. Interfaces are meant to be small contracts that are independent of one another. There are no contractual units smaller than interfaces. However, specifications or protocols such as OLE Documents and OLE Controls are *higher* contractual units than interfaces; objects must implement a related set of interfaces as defined by the specification of a certain prototype. See "Class, Type, and Prototype" on page 64. It is true that all compound document objects or OLE controls will always implement the same basic set of interfaces, but those interfaces themselves do not depend on the presence of the other interfaces. It is instead the clients of those objects that depend on the presence of all the interfaces.

The encapsulation of functionality in objects accessed through interfaces makes COM/OLE an open, extensible system. It is open in the sense that anyone can provide an implementation of a defined interface and anyone can develop a client that uses such interfaces. It is extensible in the sense that new or extended interfaces can be defined without changing existing clients or components, and those clients that understand the new interfaces can exploit them on newer components while continuing to interoperate with older components through the old interfaces. Still better is the fact that no under-lying changes to COM or OLE are required to support your own custom in-terface designs, as we'll see in Chapter 6. Because of that, you can extend the system without ever having to involve Microsoft, a big change from previous service architectures in which any change in features meant a change to the system API. You don't have to wait for Microsoft any longer—you can inno-vate as fast and as often as you want and control your own destiny!

# *IUnknown*: The Root of All Evil

The *IUnknown* interface is the one interface that all objects must implement, regardless of what other interfaces are present. *IUnknown* is what defines *object-ness* in OLE. An Object's *IUnknown* pointer value is what gives that object *in-stance* its run-time identity. Implementing *IUnknown* presents little challenge because *IUnknown* is the base interface for every other interface in OLE. By virtue of implementing any interface, you'll implement *IUnknown* to boot. In some cases, as we'll see in "Object Polymorphism and Reusability" later in this chapter, you'll need to implement two different sets of *IUnknown* member functions, but most of the time you'll implement only one set.

This interface itself encapsulates two operations: the control of an object's lifetime (or life cycle, as it is sometimes called, which sounds like a piece of horrendous exercise equipment, so I prefer the first term) and the navigation of multiple interfaces:

| *IUnknown*<br>Member Function | Result |
| --- | --- |
| *ULONG AddRef(void)* | Increments the object's reference count, return-ing the new count. |
| *ULONG Release(void)* | Decrements the object's reference count, return-ing the new count. If the new count is 0, the ob-ject is allowed to free (delete, destroy) itself, and the caller must then assume that all interface pointers to the object are invalid. |
| *HRESULT QueryInterface*<br>*(REFIID riid, void **ppv)* | Asks the object whether it supports the interface identified by *riid* (an IID reference); a return value of NOERROR indicates support exists, and the necessary interface pointer is stored in the out-parameter *\*ppv*. On error, E_NOINTERFACE says the object does not support the interface. |

The following sections examine reference counting and *QueryInterface* in more detail.

## Reference Counting

In short, reference counting is the way an object controls its own lifetime. Reference counting works on the same principles as memory management. Just as a component frees memory when the memory is no longer in use, objects are destroyed when they are no longer being used. The difference is that destroying an object is not a passive operation: instead of freeing the object directly, a client must tell the object to free itself. The overall difficulty of making this work is that COM objects are dynamically allocated from within the component, yet clients must be allowed to decide when the object is no longer needed. Furthermore, objects can be simultaneously connected to multiple clients, even in different processes, and the object must wait for all clients to release their hold on the object before it can destroy itself.

Hence the reference count, which is a ULONG variable, usually called *m_cRef* inside C++ implementations. This reference count maintains the number of independent interface pointers that exist to any of the object's interfaces. If there is only a single client of an object and that client has two different interface pointers on the object, the reference count will be 2. If there are three clients, each with a single interface pointer on the object, the reference count will be 3. While the overall reference count concerns the object, that object might maintain individual interface reference counts so that it creates interfaces only when they are requested from *QueryInterface* and destroys them when their individual reference counts go to 0, even though the object itself is still around.

The concepts governing reference counting can be distilled into two fundamental rules:

■ Creation of a new interface pointer to an object must be followed by an *AddRef* call through that new pointer.

■ Destruction of an interface pointer (such as when the pointer variable goes out of scope in the client) must be preceded by a *Release* call through that pointer.

Because some objects internally use interface-specific reference counting, clients must always match *AddRef* and *Release* calls through each interface pointer.

The overall implications of these two rules are that whenever you (client or object) assign one pointer to another in some piece of code, you should call *AddRef* through the new pointer (the left operand). Before overwriting or otherwise destroying that pointer, call *Release* through it. These implications are illustrated in the client code on the following page.

```
LPSOMEINTERFACE     pISome1;      //Some1 object
LPSOMEINTERFACE     pISome2;      //Some2 object
LPSOMEINTERFACE     pCopy;

//A function that creates the pointer calls AddRef.
CreateISomeObject(&pISome1);  //Some1 ref count=1
CreateISomeObject(&pISome2);  //Some2 ref count=1

pCopy=pISome1;                //Some1 count=1
pCopy->AddRef();              //AddRef new copy, Some1=2

[Do things.]

pCopy->Release();             //Release before overwrite, Some1=1
pCopy=pISome2;                //Some2=1
pCopy->AddRef();              //Some2=2

[What kinds of things do you do?]

pCopy->Release();             //Release before overwrite, Some2=1
pCopy=NULL;

[Things that make us go.]

pISome2->Release();           //Release when done, Some2=0, Some2 freed
pISome2=NULL;
pISome1->Release();           //Release when done, Some1=0, Some1 freed
pISome1=NULL;
```

Again, an object's lifetime is controlled by all *AddRef* and *Release* calls on all of its interfaces combined. An object might use interface reference counting internally, so it is important that the *AddRef* and *Release* calls be matched through the same interface *pointer* (which can, of course, be in several client *variables* at once).

In any case, the first fundamental principle of reference counting is that any function that returns a pointer to an interface must call *AddRef* through that pointer. Functions that create an object and return the first pointer to an interface are such functions, as in the hypothetical *CreateISomeObject* function in the preceding example. Anytime you create a new copy of a pointer, you must also call *AddRef* through that new copy because you have two independent references—two independent pointer variables—to the same object. Then, according to the second principle of reference counting, all *AddRef* calls must be matched with a *Release* call. So before your pointer variables are destroyed (by an explicit overwrite or by going out of scope), you must call *Release* through each pointer. This process includes calling *Release* through any pointer copy (through which you called *AddRef*) and through the pointer you obtained from the function that created the object (and the pointer) that called *AddRef* implicitly.

## My Kingdom for Some Optimizations!

The stated rules and their effect on the code shown earlier probably seem rather harsh, and in fact, they are. However, when you have *dependent* pointer variables for the same object's interfaces and you know the relative lifetimes of those variables, you can bypass the majority of explicit *AddRef* and *Release* calls. There are two manifestations of such knowledge, nested lifetimes and overlapping lifetimes, which are illustrated in Figure 2-3.

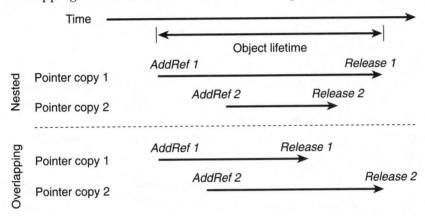

**Figure 2-3.**
*Nested and overlapping interface pointers.*

In the code fragment shown earlier, every instance of *pCopy* is nested within the lifetimes of *pISome1* and *pISome2*—that is, the copy lives and dies within the lifetime of the original. After *CreateISomeObject* is called, both objects have a reference count of 1. The lifetimes of the objects are bounded by these create calls and the final *Release* calls. Because we know these lifetimes, we can eliminate any other *AddRef* and *Release* calls through copies of those pointers:

```
LPSOMEINTERFACE     pISome1;
LPSOMEINTERFACE     pISome2;
LPSOMEINTERFACE     pCopy;

CreateISomeObject(&pISome1);    //Some1 ref count=1
CreateISomeObject(&pISome2);    //Some2 ref count=1
```

*(continued)*

```
pCopy=pISome1;              //Some1=1, pCopy nested in Some1's life

[Do things.]

pCopy=pISome2;              //Some2=1, pCopy nested in Some2's life

[Do other things.]

pICopy=NULL;                //No Release necessary

[Do anything, and then clean up.]

pISome2->Release();         //Release when done, Some2=0, Some2 freed
pISome2=NULL;
pISome1->Release();         //Release when done, Some1=0, Some1 freed
pISome1=NULL;
```

In other words, the lifetime of the first object is bounded by *CreateISome-Object(&pISome1)* and *pISome1->Release.* The lifetime of the second object is bounded by *CreateISomeObject(&pISome2)* and *pISome2->Release.* Therefore, you can make as many temporary pointers as you need as long as those variables have a scope nested within the object's lifetime. There are three instances in which you can take advantage of this optimization:

■ Local variables, whose scope is defined by a function whose scope is contained in the lifetime of an object.

■ A function that takes an interface pointer as an in-parameter has a scope defined by the caller, who is waiting for this function to return. The called function and any others it calls are nested in the original caller's scope. No *AddRef* or *Release* calls are necessary unless the called function has explicit specifications for doing so.

■ An object that is nested inside another can maintain a backpointer to the outer object without calling *AddRef* or *Release* because the nested object's lifetime is contained in the scope of the outer object.

Overlapping lifetimes are those in which the original pointer dies after the copy is born but before the copy itself dies. If the copy is alive at the original's funeral, it can inherit ownership of the reference count on behalf of the original:

```
LPSOMEINTERFACE    pISome1;
LPSOMEINTERFACE    pCopy;

CreateISomeObject(&pISome1);   //Some1 ref count=1
```

```
pCopy=pISome1;    //Some1=1, pCopy nested in Some1's life
pISome1=NULL;     //Pointer destroyed, pCopy inherits count, Some1=1

pCopy->Release(); //Release inherited ref count, Some1=0, Some1 freed
pCopy=NULL;
```

Again, the lifetime of the object is between *CreateISomeObject* and *pCopy->Release*. *Release* is still being called through the original interface *pointer;* it's just that the pointer *variable* changes.

With both of these optimizations, there are only four specific cases in which an *AddRef* must be called explicitly for a new copy of a pointer (and thus must have a *Release* call made through it when destroyed):

■ Functions that return a new interface pointer in an out-parameter or as a return value must call *AddRef* for the object through that pointer before returning. *QueryInterface* is a primary example, as are object-creation API functions and interface members.

■ Functions that accept an interface pointer as an in/out-parameter must call *Release* through the in-parameter before overwriting it and must call *AddRef* through the out-parameter. If the caller wants to maintain a copy of the pointer passed in this parameter, it must call *AddRef* through the copy before calling the function.

■ If two interface pointers to the same object have unrelated lifetimes, *AddRef* must be called through each. For example, a copy of an interface pointer given to a new thread in a multithreaded application must have an independent reference count.

■ Call *AddRef* for each local copy of a global pointer since other functions that also have copies can call *Release* while your local copy is still valid.

In all cases, some piece of code must call *Release* for every *AddRef* on a pointer. In the first of the preceding cases, the caller of an interface-creating function is responsible for the new pointer (that is, the object) and must call *Release* when finished. If the object's reference count is decreased to 0, the object can destroy itself at its leisure, although the client has to consider it gone. If you fail to call *Release,* you generally doom the object to the boredom of wasteful immortality—memory will not be freed, the object's server might not unload, and so on. Be humane to your objects; let them die with dignity: be sure to release them.

### Call-Use-Release

I want to clarify a statement you might see in the *OLE Programmer's Reference*, which describes *IUnknown::Release* as follows: "If *IUnknown::AddRef* has been called on this object's interface[s] *n* times and this is the *n+1*th call to *IUnknown::Release*, the [object] will free itself." This might be confusing because *n+1* minus *n* seems like too many calls to *Release*. This statement refers specifically to explicit *AddRef* calls from within the *client* code and implicitly assumes that *AddRef* was called within the function that initially created the interface pointer. This is a valid assumption because a creation function is required to make the call, but it is unclear in the documentation. In every case, *AddRef* and *Release* calls are perfectly paired, even when done in different places.

In addition, although the return value of *Release* is specified as returning the new reference count of an object, you really cannot use this value for anything other than debugging purposes. *Usually,* an object will be destroyed when a client's call to *Release* has returned 0. An object doesn't have to free itself when its reference count is 0, so a client cannot use the zero return value from *Release* to know whether the object has been destroyed. In cases for which this information is important, a higher-level protocol such as OLE Documents will provide the necessary information, for example an explicit notification that says, "The object has been closed."

In all of OLE, *Release* is just about the only function you'll see anywhere along the lines of destroy or delete. (There are a few close functions in OLE Documents and OLE Automation.) A very common programming pattern is for a client to call some function to get an interface pointer (which might be *QueryInterface*), then call interface member functions for whatever purpose, and then call *Release* when it's finished with that pointer. The point is that there are many interface creation functions—not only *QueryInterface*, but other interface and API functions that effectively include a *QueryInterface*. Regardless of how you get the pointer or what you do with it, you must call *Release* through it when you have finished.

This pattern isn't much different from any other resource manipulation sequences involved with Windows programming, such as *CreateWindow*, use window, *DestroyWindow*; *CreateFont*, use font, *DeleteObject*; or *OpenFile*, use file, *_lclose*. But whereas the Windows API is befuddled with many destroy/delete/close functions, the names of which hardly match their respective creation functions (for example, *OpenFile* and *_lclose*, a truly well-matched pair! <sarcasm>), OLE has only *Release*. The final *Release* can do more than simply free the object. For example, releasing the root storage of a compound file effectively closes the file; a memory allocator object that we'll see later in this chapter will free any allocations it has made; a custom component will terminate its own EXE server. Thus, *Release* makes it much easier to remember how to get rid of something.

## Circular Reference Counts

Imagine that human beings' lifetimes are determined by the number of acquaintances they have: as long as you know someone who in turn knows you, you'll both stay alive. At birth, you have an immediate acquaintance with your mother, and throughout your life you meet and befriend other people. Every new relationship is effectively a new reference count on both you and the other person. The only way the count would ever diminish would be for someone you knew to pass on, but that is impossible because you know them. Therefore, we'd all be immortal.

As appealing as this scenario might sound, there is the problem of resources: if no one ever dies, sooner or later there is not enough food, water, land, air, and so forth to maintain everyone. Then what? You simply cannot create more people—you'd need a few lightning bolts from Olympus to abruptly free a few resources.

The same is true on a computer: if objects are never destroyed and their resources are never freed, eventually there will be nothing left from which to create new objects. Hardly a workable situation. This is exactly what can happen, however, if two objects, such as a connectable object and an event sink, as we saw in Chapter 1, hold reference counts on each other! This problem is known as a *circular reference count* and requires special handling. In all cases in which such circular counts are possible, the interfaces involved are designed to include some other function besides *Release* that will force one of the two objects to call *Release* on the other.

For example, in the connectable object/event sink relationship, the client of the connectable object explicitly tells that object to terminate the notification relationship. This means that the object releases its reference to the event sink, thereby allowing the event sink to be destroyed. The client can then release the connectable object, destroying it. Other, slightly different, examples occur in OLE Documents. First, if the end user deletes an embedded or a linked object in the container, the container explicitly tells the object to close, which means that object releases any references it has to the client's site and shuts itself down. Second, if the end user directly closes the object's visible editing window, the object then releases its client references and shuts itself down.

In all cases, there is something other than *Release*, either another function call or a bolt of lightning from the Almighty End User, that causes one object in a circular relationship to terminate its relationship with another. The circle is broken, and objects can be freed.

### Artificial Reference Counts

As a final note about reference counts, let's examine the use of a technique called *artificial reference counts.* Suppose you're writing the code in method *CMyObject::Init,* and in the implementation of *Init* you invoke functions that might call your *AddRef* and then *Release.* If your reference count is 0, as happens during the creation of an object before any interfaces exist, a call to *AddRef* and *Release* would destroy the object, causing *Init* to crash. This artificial count means incrementing your reference counter directly at the beginning of the risky code and then decrementing it, usually to 0, directly afterward. Decrementing the counter directly bypasses *Release* and its potentially destructive behavior:

```
void CMyObject::Init(void)
    {
    m_cRef++;      //Increment count.

    //Risky code that might call AddRef and Release

    m_cRef--;      //Decrement count.
    return;
    }
```

The artificial reference count guarantees object stability within this function.

## *QueryInterface*

When we first met *QueryInterface,* we learned that it was the fundamental mechanism through which a client could ask an object about the features it supported, by asking for pointers to specific interfaces. The *QueryInterface* function itself is quite simple: pass an IID and an out-parameter for the pointer, and if the function returns NOERROR, you have a new interface pointer. For example, if you have an *IUnknown* pointer in a variable *pIUnknown* and you want to ask an object whether it has any type information, query for *IProvideClassInfo* as follows:

```
//pIUnknown was obtained through other means.

IProvideClassInfo    *pPCI;
HRESULT              hr;

hr=pIUnknown->QueryInterface(IID_IProvideClassInfo, (void **)&pPCI);
```

```
if (SUCCEEDED(hr))
    {
    //Use pCPI to do whatever you want.
    pCPI->Release();
    }
else
    {
    //QueryInterface failed; object doesn't support interface.
    }
```

The call to *QueryInterface* asks the object whether it supports a feature, and the feature is identified by the IID of the appropriate interface. If *Query-Interface* is successful, it will call *AddRef* through the out-parameter (*&pCPI*) before returning, so the client must call *Release* through that pointer when it is through with it.

There are a number of benefits to being able to ask this question. The first is that a client can make dynamic decisions about how to treat an object based on that object's capabilities, instead of rigidly compiling such behavior. If a query fails with one object, the client can take action different from what it would if the query succeeded. For example, a client that wants to work with any object's persistence model might first query for *IPersistStorage*. If that works, the client tells the object to save into an *IStorage*. If the query fails, the client can ask for *IPersistStream*, and if that works, have the object save into an *IStream*. Failing this second query, the client can try *IPersistFile*, and failing that, it could try to retrieve the object's native data through *IDataObject*. With this sort of code, the client would first work preferentially with storage-based persistence, then with stream-based, and then with file-based, and would then resort to other means of saving data for objects that don't support persistence at all.

A second benefit is that without successfully calling *QueryInterface* first you cannot possibly ask an object to perform any operation expressed through any interface. That is, in order to call an interface member function, you have to have a pointer to that interface. The only way to obtain such a pointer is by calling *QueryInterface* or by calling a creation function, which implicitly calls *QueryInterface*. If the object doesn't support the interface you request, it returns a NULL pointer, and you cannot make calls through a NULL pointer. Therefore, the object is always protected from malignant clients who think that they can bully objects into doing things the objects are not capable of doing. In other words, no one can insult you verbally in a language you don't understand! (I've heard people try; thankfully objects don't have emotions.) Contrast this with the traditional handle-based or structure-based sort of service APIs of the past, in which you can throw any garbage handle or any garbage structure to one of those API functions, and the function has to protect itself with all sorts of validation checks. This not only hurts performance but makes it very easy for bugs to creep into the code when you forget to validate something. In OLE, all validation on the function-call level happens in one place—*QueryInterface*—and validation is very simple to achieve, as we'll see in some code a little later.

The third benefit of *QueryInterface* lies in what we call "robust evolution of functionality over time." This deserves its own section.

## Robust Evolution of Functionality over Time

The process of asking an object about the features it supports is also called *interface negotiation,* although it is a simple negotiation. The process allows any arbitrary client to dynamically (at run time) determine the largest number of interfaces that the object implements from the set of interfaces the client knows how to use. In other words, it allows the client to determine the largest intersection between the interfaces the client knows how to call and the interfaces the object implements. The more interfaces the two share, the richer the integration the two can achieve.

As an analogy, consider each human language as an interface, which is really an accurate description. Let's say that I work at the United Nations in New York and that I speak English and German. I walk into a room with 10 international delegates with whom I need to discuss a few issues. I go up to one of the delegates and ask, "Do you speak English?" This query is met with an affirmative "Yes." Great, now we can talk. Partway through our conversation, I find that I simply cannot express one of my ideas in English, but I know I could express it in German—some languages have words without equivalents in other languages. So I ask, "Sprechen Sie Deutsch?" To this, the other person responds, "Ja." Because my partner also speaks German, I can now express my idea in that language, and the integration between us is much richer than if I were talking to someone who spoke only English. (The nice thing about *IUnknown* is that all objects speak that language, so there is always some rudimentary form of snort-and-grunt communication that you can use.)

The point is that the ability to communicate is limited by the number of languages, or interfaces, two components have in common, which is determined at run time. This is a vast improvement over building components that are hard-coded at compile time to work with some least common denominator and that are thus unable to take advantage of a richer component should it appear in the future. *QueryInterface* allows you to create a client or an object with as many features as you see fit that will work perfectly well with another component that doesn't necessarily support all of those features. For example, if I learn another language, perhaps Spanish, I don't lose any compatibility with my friend at the UN who speaks only English and German. If she goes on to learn Spanish and French, we can continue to communicate not only in English and German but now also in Spanish. If I then learn French and Russian, we add yet another language of integration, and so on.

The process whereby components add capabilities and features yet still remain compatible with one another through the changes is exactly the idea of "robust evolution of functionality over time." Not only is the idea powerful, but it is also very efficient because the negotiation happens on an interface-by-interface level, and not a function-by-function level, which would require much more overhead.

To illustrate the extent to which *QueryInterface* is a true cornerstone in COM, let's imagine that we have a client that wants to display the contents of a number of text files and that knows that for each file format (ASCII, RTF, Unicode, and so on) there is some component class associated with that format. (By "associated" I mean that we don't know what that component can do with the format, but we know that it exists.) The client's ultimate purpose is to display the contents of these files by using as much of the component as possible to do the work. We would write the client as follows:

1. Find the component class associated with a file format.

2. Instantiate an object of that class, obtaining a pointer to *IUnknown* in return.

3. Check whether the object supports loading data from a file by calling *IUnknown::QueryInterface* and requesting a pointer to *IPersistFile*. If that's successful, ask the object to load the file through *IPersistFile::Load*.

4. Check whether the object can provide a metafile or bitmap rendering of the file contents that the client could draw in its own window. Such renderings are obtained through *IDataObject*, so queries for this interface are made through either *IUnknown* or *IPersistFile* pointers. If successful, ask the object for a rendering and draw it on the screen.

If a component class exists for every file format in the client's file list, and all those objects implement all three interfaces, the client can display all the contents of all the files. But in an imperfect world, the object class for the ASCII text format might not support *IDataObject*—that is, the object can load text from a file and save the text to another file if necessary, but it can't render the text into a graphical format. When the client code, written as described above, encounters this object, the *QueryInterface* for *IDataObject* fails, and the contents are not viewable. Oh well....

The ASCII component programmers now realize that they are losing market share because they don't support graphical rendering, so they update the component to support *IDataObject*. An end user installs this new component on the machine that has the existing client there already. Nothing else changes in the entire system but the ASCII component. What happens the next time someone runs the same old client?

Because of *QueryInterface*, the client immediately begins to use *IDataObject* on the updated component. Where before the query for this interface failed, it now succeeds, and the client can now retrieve a rendering and display ASCII file contents.

This again is the raw power of *QueryInterface*: you can write a client to exploit as many interfaces and as much functionality as you want for whatever component you encounter. Ideally you would like to have components that support everything you do, but that is not generally the case. When your client encounters such less capable components, you still use as much functionality as those components actually implement. When the object is updated later to support new interfaces, the same client, without any recompilation, redeployment, or changes whatsoever, automatically takes advantage of those additional interfaces. This is true component software: components evolve independently and retain full compatibility.

This process also works in the other direction. Imagine that since the client application described above was shipped, many of the components were improved by adding support for the *IViewObject2* interface so that instead of always having to ask an object for a rendering, the client could now ask an object to draw directly in the client's window. Each component is upgraded independently of the client, but because the client never queries for *IViewObject2*, all components continue to work perfectly. By implementing this new functionality—this additional interface—the components do not lose compatibility with the existing client and require no changes at all to the client.

At a later time, however, we might notice that the client isn't taking advantage of the performance improvements that could be realized if it supported direct rendering through the improved display components. Traditionally, before COM and *QueryInterface*, we'd worry tremendously about whether we should implement the new functionality and lose compatibility with components that still don't support direct rendering or whether we should simply not implement the new functionality at all and suffer from poor performance. Either way, black-or-white decisions such as these are difficult.

However, such concerns are totally irrelevant with *QueryInterface*. We simply add step 3a to the client's earlier steps: after we have the component load the file, we query for *IViewObject2*. If that interface is supported, we call *IViewObject2::Draw* to perform the high-speed, high-quality direct rendering. If the query fails, we can still resort to the old method of using *IDataObject*. With this simple addition to the client, we work optimally with newer components while still working with old components. We didn't have to change any of the code we used for working with old objects, and so we didn't risk any loss of compatibility. Support for the new feature was accomplished entirely through the addition of code, not the modification of old code.

Of course, the client might also add support for some new interface at this time, even though no components yet support it. When they do, the client will immediately begin to be integrated with those components through the new interface. The objects can leapfrog the client once again, with even newer interfaces. This process continues, back and forth, ad infinitum.

Before COM, repeated and independent versioning of components and clients such as this was simply not possible: new features required upgrading all clients and all components together. Yuck! But now, and for all time, *QueryInterface* solves the problem and removes the barriers. Time is ripe for rapid software innovation without the growing pains.

### *QueryInterface* Rules and Properties

To wrap up our discussion of *QueryInterface*, let's look at a number of rules concerning its behavior. The first rule is that any call to *QueryInterface* asking for *IUnknown* through any interface on the object must always return the same pointer value, which is the run-time identity of the object instance. The specific reasoning for this is that given two arbitrary interface pointers, you can determine whether they belong to the same object by asking each for an *IUnknown* pointer and comparing the actual pointer values. If they match, application of this rule allows both interface pointers to refer to the same object.

The second rule is that after an object is instantiated, it must support the same interfaces throughout its lifetime: if *QueryInterface* succeeds once for a given IID, it must succeed again until that object is destroyed. This does not mean that the exact pointer *values* returned from both calls will be identical—it means only that the interface is always available. Again, this applies to a single *instantiation* of an object, not the class. Different instances of objects from the same class can support different sets of interfaces as long as the available interfaces are stable through each object's lifetime.

The third rule is that any implementation of *QueryInterface* must be reflexive, symmetric, and transitive, as described in the table on the following page (in which *IOne*, *ITwo*, and *IThree* are hypothetical).

| Property | Meaning |
|---|---|
| Reflexive | *pIOne->QueryInterface(IID_IOne)* must succeed. |
| Symmetric | If *pITwo* was obtained from *pIOne->QueryInterface(IID_ITwo)*, then *pITwo->QueryInterface(IID_IOne)* must also succeed. |
| Transitive | If *pITwo* was obtained from *pIOne->QueryInterface(IID_ITwo)* and *pIThree* was obtained from *pITwo->QueryInterface(IID_IThree)*, then *pIThree->QueryInterface(IID_IOne)* must also succeed. |

In all these cases, "must succeed" is not so strong as to imply that these calls cannot fail under the most catastrophic situations. In addition, these properties do not require that the same pointer value be always returned for a given interface, with the exception of *IUnknown*.

## Object Polymorphism and Reusability

In Chapter 1, we discussed how COM/OLE objects do not support a notion of inheritance, which we defined as a means to achieve polymorphism and reusability. Inheritance is the relationship through which you describe a class as resembling some other more generic class (the base class). When a more specific class is derived from the base class, it inherits the characteristics of that base class. The derived class can then be treated polymorphically with the base class, which is the primary purpose of inheritance. When these ideas are applied to object implementation as well as object definition, you have what is called *implementation inheritance.*

Implementation inheritance has two significant drawbacks. The first is language dependency, which is not suitable in a language-independent binary component environment such as OLE. The second problem is known as the *fragile base class problem,* which complicates the evolution of software written with implementation inheritance. This problem occurs when you have a base class B that calls one of its own virtual functions. If you create a derived class D that overrides that virtual function, the implementation of class B used for an instance of class D will now call D's override of the virtual function. This is not, however, the code that B was designed to call. Thus, class B is fragile because the implementation of D's override can easily break B, and the implementer of B has to be extremely careful and usually has to give away the source code to B so that people making derived classes know what B expects. It's also a problem when you have two unrelated pieces of code working on the same object instance and the contracts for communication between base and derived classes are very weak. This again is why base class implementers typically ship source code. Robustness depends a great deal on the discipline of human programmers.

Suffice it to say that this makes a process such as direct implementation inheritance unworkable for large component systems such as those that COM and OLE support, not just because of the fragility of base classes and the language dependence, but also because Microsoft doubts that everyone will want to ship the source code to all of their components to everyone else in the industry. Therefore, we need different component-oriented binary mechanisms to achieve both polymorphism and reusability.

## Polymorphism

Polymorphism is many things in object-oriented programming. It is the capability to treat objects from multiple classes identically because they all share one or more interfaces in common. Polymorphism means that heterogeneous objects can respond to the same interface calls from the same client, allowing that client to be written according to a prototype instead of for specific object classes. In addition, polymorphism means that you create more instances (types) of a prototype so existing clients that understand the prototype can immediately use those new classes. In OLE, objects whose classes have a common set of interfaces are polymorphic with one another, as we saw with the recent example concerning the evolution of file rendering objects.

In OLE, *QueryInterface* and the idea of multiple interfaces provide polymorphism. In C++, you would define basic characteristics in a base class and add characteristics by creating a derived class from that base class. You can derive further specific classes from the first derived class, creating a deep object hierarchy in which a derived class is polymorphic with all classes above it, all the way to the base class. In OLE, however, basic characteristics are expressed in one interface, and additional and more specific sets of characteristics are expressed through additional interfaces. Two object classes that support the same interfaces are like each other—polymorphic—across those interfaces. The classes are instances of the same prototype.

When you start designing interfaces for different sets of characteristics, you have two choices: you can actually use inheritance to derive the more specific interfaces from the more generic ones, or you can define completely separate interfaces for each set of characteristics. Which approach is better?

As an example, let's say I want to model some animals as objects, specifically rabbits and koalas. Since both are animals, I could make a base interface to represent the characteristics of a general animal (which, of course, includes *IUnknown* members).

```
interface IAnimal : IUnknown
    {
    HRESULT Eat(...);
    HRESULT Sleep(...);
    HRESULT Procreate(...);
    }
```

Here I'm saying that all animals, including humans, share the basic characteristics of eating, sleeping, and procreation. (Arguments to these functions are irrelevant to this discussion.) Now I need to create my *IRabbit* and *IKoala* interfaces. (Ideally you'd probably make *IRodent* and *IMarsupial* interfaces as well, but we'll keep things simple here.) One way to create these new interfaces would be to use C++ inheritance to derive each new interface from *IAnimal*:

```
interface IRabbit : IAnimal
    {
    HRESULT RaidGardens(...);
    HRESULT Hop(...);
    HRESULT DigWarrens(...);
    }

interface IKoala : IAnimal
    {
    HRESULT ClimbEucalyptusTrees(...);
    HRESULT PouchOpensDown(...);
    HRESULT SleepForHoursAfterEating(...);
    }
```

This technique is entirely workable, but it has a significant drawback. If for some reason a new interface, *IAnimal2*, is created (to add the function *Locomotion* or some such), it would force the creation of *IRabbit2* and *IKoala2* if we wanted to update objects to also support *IAnimal2*. In other words, the change to the base has to propagate to derived interfaces. While this is not a big deal for a two-level inheritance tree, it becomes an utter nightmare with a deep inheritance tree—a change in a base interface might force changes in hundreds of other interfaces! The additional impact of such sweeping changes is that clients and objects using these interfaces would then have to make much more sweeping changes as well.[6]

The preferred technique is to simply define each additional interface separately, deriving only from *IUnknown*:

---

6. There are only a few cases in OLE in which interface inheritance goes deeper than one level, a few of which the original OLE designers acknowledge as less than optimal choices.

```
interface IRabbit : IUnknown
    {
    HRESULT RaidGardens(...);
    HRESULT Hop(...);
    HRESULT DigWarrens(...);
    }

interface IKoala : IUnknown
    {
    HRESULT ClimbEucalyptusTrees(...);
    HRESULT PouchOpensDown(...);
    HRESULT SleepForHoursAfterEating(...);
    }
```

An object that implements *IAnimal* and *IRabbit* separately, as would be required in this technique, is functionally equivalent to one that implements a single *IRabbit* derived from *IAnimal*.[7] However, if *IAnimal2* comes out, this Rabbit object needs to amend only one of its interface implementations, leaving all others as is. This is beneficial when the object has a large number of interfaces. A client can also rest easy: to exploit *IAnimal2*, it needs only to modify its code that handles *IAnimal* to work with *IAnimal2*, and it can leave all *IRabbit* calling code unmodified.

I will point out here as well that a deep inheritance tree would be absolutely required if an object could not support multiple interfaces. It is due entirely to *QueryInterface* that we can avoid the complexity and difficulties associated with deep inheritance. A shallow interface inheritance tree is much easier to work with over time, for objects as well as for clients. Functionally it is identical to a deep inheritance tree but far more practical.

Another drawback to a deep inheritance tree is that it is less efficient to reuse some other component's implementation of base interfaces. But that requires us to look at the reusability of interface implementations.

## Reusability

According to the definition of encapsulation, a client simply does not care about the internal implementation of a component or its constituent objects. For all the client knows, the component itself might be built out of any number of other components, which in turn might themselves be built out of components. Reusability is therefore the exclusive concern of a component

---

7. Note that the derived *IRabbit* and the independent *IRabbit* are not the same interface because they have different vtable layouts and therefore must have different IIDs. *Functionally equivalent* means that the same features are available in both interfaces.

implementer. Reusability in OLE is about the implementation of objects with the desired interfaces on a binary level, where source code is not available.

The two reusability mechanisms in OLE are called *containment* and *aggregation,* and they are literally the means to reuse some other component at run time rather than inheriting implementation at compile time. (This latter method is totally valid when you are compiling your own source code but not for binary OLE components that are reusable only at run time.)[8]

Let's say we want to implement a Koala object with the *IAnimal* and *IKoala* interfaces (the separate interfaces described above). We know that our target systems will have a basic implementation of an Animal object, with only *IAnimal,* that we want to use in our implementation of Koala. The two objects are illustrated below, with an *IUnknown* interface extending out the top explicitly to show its presence. How this *IUnknown* is implemented and how the other interfaces implement their *IUnknown* members will be part of our discussion.

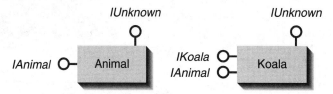

In reusability relationships, the component/object being used is called the *inner object,* whereas the component/object doing the reusing is called the *outer object.* The outer object conceptually contains the inner object and is a client of that inner object.

## Containment

Containment is by far the simplest and most frequently used method of reuse in OLE that requires no special reusability support on behalf of the object being reused. In containment, the outer object uses the inner object exactly as any other client would use the inner object. It is a simple client-object relationship, and the inner object does not know that its immediate client is an object itself.

The simplest case of this occurs when a component with multiple objects simply instantiates an object outside of itself that it incorporates into the component as a whole. When the component needs that object, it instantiates the object the same way any client would.

---

8. Everyone at Microsoft who worked on marketing OLE in the early days, myself included with the first edition of this book, placed far, far too much emphasis on aggregation, which is used much less often and is merely a convenience for certain containment cases.

A more interesting case occurs when the outer object wants to reuse the implementation of the inner object's interfaces in order to help implement its own interfaces. In our example, the Koala object implements both its *IAnimal* and its *IKoala* interface. When the Koala object is created, it internally creates an instance (however that's done) of the Animal class and queries for its *IAnimal* interface. Inside the Koala object's implementation of *IAnimal*, it makes calls to the Animal class's *IAnimal* implementation. The Koala object's implementation might do nothing more than this, or it might embellish the calls in any way it wants. The Koala object is simply using the services of the Animal class, as would any other client. This overall relationship is shown in Figure 2-4. The Koala object's client, of course, has no idea that Animal is being used internally, as Animal is entirely encapsulated within Koala.

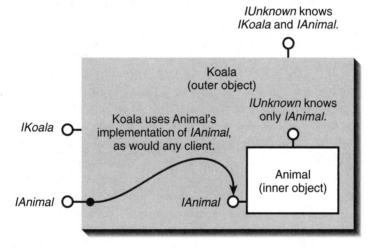

**Figure 2-4.**
*The containment relationship between the inner object and the outer object.*

## Aggregation

Containment, as mentioned earlier, is the most frequently used means of object reuse. There are circumstances, however, in which you would like to completely reuse another object's implementation of one or more interfaces without modification and without the hassle of having to code a bunch of functions that do nothing more than delegate to another interface pointer. In our example, let's say that Koala wants to completely reuse Animal's implementation of *IAnimal* without modification. In essence, Koala would like to expose Animal's interface directly, as if it came from Koala itself, as shown in Figure 2-5 on the following page.

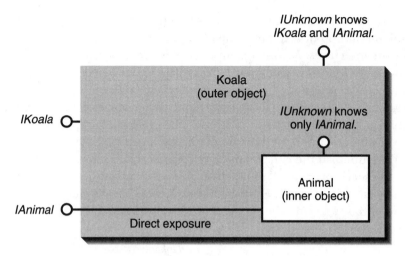

**Figure 2-5.**
*A possible relationship between the inner object and the outer object.*

To do this, Koala would create an instance of Animal during initialization, the same as it would in containment. Koala would query for Animal's *IAnimal* pointer, and when Koala itself was asked in *QueryInterface* for a pointer to *IAnimal*, it would simply return Animal's pointer. Right?

Here's the problem. Clients of the Koala object expect reflexive and transitive behavior from both *IKoala::QueryInterface* and *IAnimal::QueryInterface*. They also expect that *AddRef* and *Release* calls through both interfaces control Koala's lifetime. However, although *IKoala::QueryInterface(IID_IAnimal)* will return Animal's *IAnimal*, a subsequent *IAnimal::QueryInterface(IID_IKoala)* will fail, breaking the *QueryInterface* properties. Why? Because the implementation of this function, as well as *AddRef* and *Release*, resides in Animal when called through this *IAnimal* pointer, and the Animal class has absolutely no idea about the outer Koala object!

Somehow Animal must implement the correct behavior of Koala's *IUnknown* functions so that *QueryInterface* works and the reference count affects Koala as a whole. To accomplish this, Koala must pass a pointer to its own *IUnknown* to Animal at creation time, which is simple because Koala will exist before Animal does (top-down creation) and will readily have its own *IUnknown* pointer to pass. If an object such as Animal supports aggregation, it must provide a creation function that accepts this pointer, which is called the *outer unknown* or the *controlling unknown*. As we'll see in Chapter 5, both the custom component creation function, *CoCreateInstance*, and the *IClassFactory* interface (which we saw in Chapter 1) have arguments for this purpose. Other OLE API functions that create objects have such arguments as well.

So when Animal is created, it will be given this outer unknown pointer; if it receives a NULL pointer, it knows that aggregation is not in use. If it receives a non-NULL pointer, it must delegate all *IUnknown* calls from its own interfaces to this outer unknown. Therefore, any client's calls to the *AddRef*, *Release*, and *QueryInterface* functions of *IAnimal* are simply delegated to this Koala object's *IUnknown*, which of course provides the correct behavior of this interface for the Koala object. This relationship is shown in Figure 2-6.

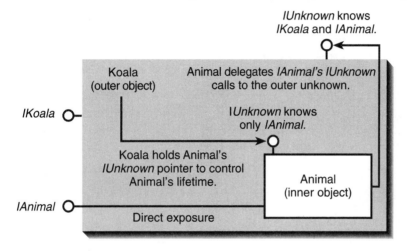

**Figure 2-6.**
*The aggregation relationship between the inner object and the outer object. The outer object provides the inner object with the outer unknown so that the inner object can delegate calls to that outer unknown. This provides the correct* IUnknown *behavior for the outer object through the inner object's own interfaces.*

There is a small complication that affects the implementation of the inner object in this relationship: somehow the outer object must still be able to individually control the inner object's lifetime. For this reason, and in light of other matters regarding this technique, there are several additional rules for the aggregation mechanism:

■ The inner object must explicitly implement a set of *IUnknown* functions that are separate from the same member functions in all the rest of its interfaces (which delegate to the outer unknown).

■ The inner object's explicit *IUnknown* must control the inner object's reference count alone as well as implement *QueryInterface* behavior for only the inner object.

■ The outer object must explicitly ask for *IUnknown* when creating the inner object. The inner object will fail to be created if this rule is not followed.

■ The inner object does not call *AddRef* when holding on to the outer unknown pointer. This is because the inner object's lifetime is entirely contained within the outer object, so it is guaranteed that the outer unknown pointer will always be valid. This rule avoids a circular reference count.

■ The outer object must protect its implementation of *Release* from reentrancy with an artificial reference count around its destruction code.

■ The outer object must call its own outer unknown's *Release* if it queries for a pointer to any of the inner object's interfaces. To free this pointer, the outer object calls its own outer unknown's *AddRef* followed by *Release* on the inner object's pointer.

■ The outer object's *QueryInterface* usually only returns *specific* pointers from the inner object's *QueryInterface*: the outer object must not blindly delegate a query for any unrecognized interface to the inner object unless that behavior is specifically the intention of the outer object.

The second to last rule in this list is specified to simplify the management of reference counts in objects aggregated across process boundaries. It exists because a *QueryInterface* on the inner object will call the outer unknown's *AddRef*, which could not be released until the outer object was destroying itself. But that destruction cannot happen, of course, because the outer *Release* will never see a zero reference count. Therefore, the rule initially fixes the outer object's reference count without affecting the lifetime of the inner object's interface (which is what's important for remote objects). The cleanup part of the rule fixes the outer object's count so that a *Release* call to the inner object will not cause reentrant destruction, which the artificial reference count also protects.

The last rule avoids problems when a client asks for a newer version of an interface that the inner object supports but the outer object supports only the old version of the interface from which the new one is derived. Without this rule, the client would talk directly to the inner object's newer interface and bypass the outer object altogether. If the outer object is aware of the new interface and wants to reuse it from the inner object, it will explicitly delegate *QueryInterface* for that case.

The point is that when implementing a particular version of an object, you want to decide ahead of time what interfaces that version will support. You should choose which interfaces your object will implement and which it will obtain from an existing object through aggregation. If the inner object is updated without your knowledge, it will suddenly change the prototype of your object in ways you did not logically expect—this can lead to problems.

In some cases, however, the outer object is intentionally trying to embellish the inner object with an interface that is otherwise unknown to the inner object. For example, a client might want to create a generic object wrapper with a custom interface that aggregates every object used from the client. This wrapper could provide a custom interface known only to that one client, thereby centralizing container-specific methods and properties within that wrapper object. This technique is used in OLE Control containers, for example, where a container creates an *extended control* that wraps the real control via aggregation. It is a highly useful technique but must be used with care.

The aggregation contract thus allows the outer object to reuse complete interfaces from an inner object, but it also requires the inner object to be written specifically to support aggregation. There is an error code for creation functions, CLASS_E_NOAGGREGATION, that an inner object returns to tell an outer object that aggregation is not supported.

A final note is that aggregation works to arbitrarily deep levels. The Animal object in use here might itself be an aggregate that obtained its *IAnimal* from some other component, and that component was an aggregate using yet another aggregate, and so on. Since object creation is top-down, Koala creates Animal, which in turn creates any object within it. If Animal is given an outer unknown pointer during creation, it must pass that pointer down to whatever object it creates, which in turn passes the pointer on down the chain. In this way, every object in every level of an arbitrarily deep aggregation will always have a pointer to the outermost unknown. No matter whose interface pointers the outer object ultimately exposes, all delegated *IUnknown* calls go directly to the outermost *IUnknown* implementation. In other words, the calls do not have to percolate up the entire aggregation chain: it's simply one quick step up to the outer unknown.

# Using an Object in C and C++

We're now at the point in this chapter where we've covered the theoretical and mechanical matters and we can take a look at some sample code. This first section will illustrate how to call interface member functions in both C and C++, illuminating the role of a client and the differences between the languages, using the context of COM's memory management facilities. As a prelude to this discussion, we'll also look into basic requirements such as COM initialization for all COM/OLE applications or components that make up a task. The next major section, "Implementing an Object in C and C++," describes an object's perspective on creating interfaces in both languages and introduces the idea of *enumerator objects*. If you are reading this book to gain an architectural understanding of OLE, you'll want to read the first parts of that section to understand these types of objects and skip the code discussion. The section "Implementing Multiple Interfaces" will examine three different ways in C++ to implement an object with multiple interfaces, giving you some options for your own work. "Implementing Reusability" will illustrate containment and aggregation in the form of sample code. "Interfaces and OLE API Functions" describes the differences among and functionality of the various OLE interfaces and API functions.

So again, this first section is primarily concerned with what it means to be a client in COM and OLE—that is, how one goes about calling interface functions, which is generally relevant to objects as well.

## COM/OLE Task Requirements

Any and all applications (EXEs) that plan to use or implement components must ensure that the COM/OLE DLLs are properly initialized in the process before attempting to use almost any function in those libraries. Only a few scattered functions can be called before initialization is complete. A component that runs from a DLL need not be concerned with any of these requirements because they apply only to modules that define a task—EXEs.

For 32-bit components, there are two initialization steps. Absolutely all tasks (such as all the sample applications in this book that compile EXEs) must do the following:

1. During startup, call *CoInitialize* or *OleInitialize*.

2. During shutdown, call *CoUninitialize* or *OleUninitialize* if and only if step 1 succeeded.

The *Co\** functions control your access to COM functions. If you use API functions or interfaces related to any type library, the clipboard, drag and drop, OLE Documents, OLE Automation, or OLE Controls, you must use the *Ole\** functions instead of their *Co\** counterparts. The *Ole\** versions perform a few more specific operations and call the *Co\** versions. For the most part, it is safest to simply call *OleInitialize* and forget it.

## Call *CoInitialize* or *OleInitialize*

On startup, an application must call *CoInitialize* or *OleInitialize* before calling any other function in their respective libraries. Most 32-bit applications should use *OleInitialize*. You need to remember whether initialization works, usually through some variable such as *m_fInitialized*:

```
if (FAILED(CoInitialize(NULL)))    //Or OleInitialize
    [Fail loading the task]

m_fInitialized=TRUE;
```

In 32-bit OLE, both initialization functions take a NULL reserved pointer and will fail with E_INVALIDARG if you pass a non-NULL value.

Any code within the same task can call *CoInitialize* or *OleInitialize* multiple times. This allows any code (usually that in a DLL) to ensure that the OLE DLLs are initialized, even if the application that loaded the DLL is OLE-ignorant and did not perform initialization. The first successful call to *[Co¦Ole]Initialize* will return NOERROR; subsequent successful calls will return S_FALSE, meaning that the call still worked but that it wasn't the first call. Because a DLL's *LibMain* is called before the application's *WinMain*, *[Co¦Ole]Initialize* will never have been called by that time. It's best to defer this code to a later DLL-specific initialization call if possible, but there's no real harm in a DLL making the first call within a task. Internally, OLE associates task information with a unique number returned from the function *CoGetCurrentProcess*, which you can use whenever you need a process-specific (as opposed to thread-specific) identifier. This identifier is considerably closer to unique than a Windows HTASK is.

Any caller to the initialization functions must remember whether initialization worked so that it knows whether to call *CoUninitialize* or *OleUninitialize* when it shuts down. In other words, every *Uninitialize* must be matched one-to-one with an *Initialize*.

## Call *CoUninitialize* or *OleUninitialize*

After an application has finished with the COM/OLE DLLs, it must call *CoUninitialize* if it previously called *CoInitialize* or *OleUninitialize* if it previously called *OleInitialize*. Neither function takes any arguments. You must uninitialize only if initialization worked, to ensure that everything is balanced inside the DLLs. The uninitialize functions check that all pending OLE calls across process boundaries have cleared, ensuring that the states of all components are cleaned up completely before a task terminates. One part of the process is a call to *CoFreeAllLibraries*, which checks that any DLL servers for components loaded into this task are properly unloaded. We'll see the effect of this unloading process in Chapter 5.

## Multithreaded COM/OLE Components

With the availability of 32-bit operating systems such as Windows NT and Windows 95, there is the question of multithreaded code that uses COM and OLE. In 32-bit OLE as shipped with Windows NT 3.5 for x86 processors, everything that you do with OLE must be done from the same thread that called *CoInitialize* or *OleInitialize*. This restriction is not absolute, however, as you can use in-process objects and their interfaces if you specifically know those interfaces are thread safe. Because Microsoft doesn't guarantee this with Windows NT 3.5 (x86) for any of its interfaces, it applies only to your own custom interfaces on this platform.

Starting with Windows 95 and Windows NT 3.51, you can use OLE from multiple threads. At the time of writing, final information about the threading model was not yet available. Check the *OLE Programmer's Reference* for a full discussion of multithreaded OLE.

## Memory Management

Earlier in this chapter, we defined rules for handling out-parameters and in/out-parameters that deal with memory allocation. We learned that OLE specifies that the caller of a function become responsible for the memory involved with those parameters. We also learned that in order to make this work, there has to be a standard allocation mechanism accessible to both object and client so that memory can pass freely between them, even across processes. This mechanism is COM's *task memory allocation* service, based on the memory management APIs of the underlying system.

The service is provided through an *allocator object* that supports the single interface *IMalloc* (which includes *IUnknown* functions, of course). All components are required to use this service whenever there is a need to exchange allocated memory between components, even across process boundaries.[9] Any code in a task accesses this service by calling the API function *CoGetMalloc* as follows:

---

9. When cross-process allocations are involved, the marshaling layer in COM takes care of copying object-task allocations into client-task allocations.

```
HRESULT    hr;
IMalloc    *pIMalloc;

hr=CoGetMalloc(MEMCTX_TASK, &pIMalloc);
//Use IMalloc functions through pIMalloc.
pIMalloc->Release();
```

*CoGetMalloc* is a function that returns a new interface pointer, so *pIMalloc* has a reference count on it when you get the pointer back; therefore, remember to call *Release* when you finish. (You must always pass MEMCTX-_TASK as the first argument.)

So what can you do with an allocator? Everything is represented through the *IMalloc* interface, which is defined as follows:

```
interface IMalloc : IUnknown
    {
    void * Alloc(ULONG cb);
    void * Realloc(void *pv, ULONG cb);
    void   Free(void *pv);
    ULONG  GetSize(void *pv);
    int    DidAlloc(void *pv);
    void   HeapMinimize(void);
    };
```

I'll leave it to your intelligence to guess what *Alloc, Realloc, Free, GetSize,* and *HeapMinimize* do, mentioning only that all allocations are referred to with a pointer, just as with the C run-time *malloc* functions. The one function to describe a little further is *DidAlloc*, which returns 1 if the memory was allocated by the allocator in question, 0 if the memory was not, and −1 if the allocator simply doesn't know.

With this service, any piece of code can, at any time, get the task allocator's *IMalloc* pointer, allocate or free memory, and call *IMalloc::Release*. You may be required to free out-parameters and in/out-parameters in this way as a client. Usually this can be something of a pain to code, having to call three functions to perform a simple operation. For this reason, OLE includes three helper functions, *CoTaskMemAlloc, CoTaskMemFree,* and *CoTaskMemRealloc,* which take the same parameters as the interface functions and internally call *CoGetMalloc,* the appropriate *IMalloc* function, and then *IMalloc::Release.*

## The Malloc1 and Malloc2 Samples

Let's now use *CoGetMalloc* and the *IMalloc* interface to illustrate the differences between C and C++ interface calls. The samples of interest here are in CHAP02\MALLOC1 and CHAP02\MALLOC2. Malloc1 is written in C and

Malloc2 in C++, serving as side-by-side examples of equivalent functionality and equivalent code structures. Both samples call *CoInitialize* and *CoUninitialize* as necessary and create a small main window with a menu from which you can access the allocator, ask it to perform various functions, release the allocator, and exit the program. Both allocate a number of consecutively larger blocks (from 100 bytes up to tens of thousands of bytes), storing the ASCII character *a* in the first block, *b* in the second, and so forth. You can use a debugging tool to look at memory and see where the allocations ended up.

Both samples call *CoGetMalloc* when you select the Allocator/CoGetMalloc menu item. They save the pointer in a variable named *m_pIMalloc*, which is part of the application structure (in C) or the C++ object. When you select the Allocator/Alloc or Realloc menu item, you'll end up in the IDM_ALLOC (or IDM_REALLOC) case of each sample's window procedure, which verifies that you've selected CoGetMalloc already and calls a *DoAllocation* function. Malloc1's C code for this is in *App_DoAllocations*, which appears as follows:

```
BOOL App_DoAllocations(PAPP pApp, BOOL fRealloc)
    {
    UINT        i;
    ULONG       iByte;
    BOOL        fResult=TRUE;
    ULONG       cb;
    LPVOID      pv;

    if (!fRealloc)
        App_FreeAllocations(pApp, FALSE);

    for (i=0; i < CALLOCS; i++)
        {
        //cb is set in the code below for later initialization.
        if (fRealloc)
            {
            pApp->m_rgcb[i]+=128;
            cb=pApp->m_rgcb[i];

            //Old memory is not freed if Realloc fails.
            pv=pApp->m_pIMalloc->lpVtbl->Realloc(pApp->m_pIMalloc
                , pApp->m_rgpv[i], cb);
            }
        else
            {
            cb=pApp->m_rgcb[i];
            pv=pApp->m_pIMalloc->lpVtbl->Alloc(pApp->m_pIMalloc, cb);
            }
```

```
            pApp->m_rgpv[i]=pv;

            [Code to fill allocations with letters]
            fResult &= (NULL!=pv);
            }

        [Other cleanup code]
        return fResult;
        }
```

Here's the equivalent code from Malloc2's (MALLOC.CPP) *CApp::Do-Allocations*:

```
BOOL CApp::DoAllocations(BOOL fRealloc)
    {
    UINT        i;
    ULONG       iByte;
    BOOL        fResult=TRUE;
    ULONG       cb;
    LPVOID      pv;

    if (!fRealloc)
        FreeAllocations(FALSE);

    for (i=0; i < CALLOCS; i++)
        {
        //cb is set in the code below for later initialization.
        if (fRealloc)
            {
            m_rgcb[i]+=128;
            cb=m_rgcb[i];

            //Old memory is not freed if Realloc fails.
            pv=m_pIMalloc->Realloc(m_rgpv[i], cb);
            }
        else
            {
            cb=m_rgcb[i];
            pv=m_pIMalloc->Alloc(cb);
            }

        m_rgpv[i]=pv;

        [Code to fill allocations with letters]
        fResult &= (NULL!=pv);
        }

    [Other cleanup code]
    return fResult;
    }
```

In each case, the array *m_ rgcb* contains a bunch of integer values to determine the size of the allocations. Each *Realloc* operation increases the size. The array *m_ rgpv* holds the allocated pointers that are freed in the samples' *FreeAllocations* functions.

To closely compare C and C++ function calls, look at the calls to *Alloc*:

```
C:      pv=pApp->m_pIMalloc->lpVtbl->Alloc(pApp->m_pIMalloc, cb);
C++:    pv=m_pIMalloc->Alloc(cb);
```

In C++, you need to call only the function through the interface pointer using a single indirection, as you would when making a member function call to any C++ object. This is because OLE interfaces are designed to have the same structure as C++ objects have in memory, and because interfaces are defined in C++ abstract base classes, the compiler hides all the complexities of making the call. In C, however, these complexities are explicit: you must state the double indirection to the function using the *lpVtbl* field of the interface structure, and you must pass the interface pointer itself as the first parameter. C++ performs this last step automatically to generate the *this* pointer inside the member function.

In even a simple client implementation, you will easily have 50 calls to interface member functions. You don't even need to multiply to see why C++ is the more convenient language in which to work with OLE, although it is no more functional. If you are using other languages, the compiler or programming environment should support some sort of language construct that represents interfaces and making calls to interfaces.

If you want to take advantage of the convenience of C++ but don't want to rewrite your existing C code, I have a suggestion. Simply rename your C files to CPP and recompile. Three weeks later, when you've added the necessary *extern "C"* statements around include files and have fixed all the type warnings that you'll get, you effectively have C++ code. Remember that C is a subset of C++. You can use this fact to your advantage to make the compiler understand that you are writing C++ code so that when you use an interface pointer you can benefit from the more concise calling structure. Investing some time up front to recompile your code as C++ is, believe me, well worth it. I've written code both ways, and it gets painful to write *lpVtbl* all over the place. If you really can't recompile your code as C++, try making sets of macros for each interface that will turn an interface call into *MACRO(<interface pointer>, <arguments>);*. It will make your source code smaller, your code more readable, and your programmers happier.

# Implementing an Object in C and C++

Now that we've seen how to call interface member functions in C and C++, we can look as well at how you implement an object with an interface in both languages. Once we have established this level of understanding, we can use the convenience of C++ in the rest of this book, assured that all of the code is possible in C as well. To set the stage for this section, we need an object to implement.

## Enumerators

A frequent programming task is to generate some sequence of items and iterate through that sequence. A number of places within COM and OLE require this sort of functionality, such as where a client wants to obtain a list of items from an object, regardless of what type of boundary exists between the two. For example, a client that is a data consumer usually wants a list of formats that a data source (that implements *IDataObject*) can render for it. When asked for such a list, the source returns an interface pointer to a separate object called an *enumerator*. Enumerators cleanly encapsulate, behind an interface, the knowledge of how to iterate through a sequence of items from the client's desire to iterate, thereby allowing the enumerator to be implemented in whatever way is most convenient—array, linked list, and so forth.[10]

Enumerators are so named because they implement a type-specific interface that always has the prefix *IEnum* followed by the name of a type. For example, OLE defines *IEnumUnknown* (to enumerate a list of objects by their *IUnknown* pointers) and *IEnumFORMATETC* (to enumerate FORMATETC structures from data objects). There is also the interface *IEnumVARIANT*, which enumerates data structures named VARIANT—a big union of different data types, as we'll see later with OLE Automation. A generic enumerator with *IEnumVARIANT* is usually called a *collection*, which is an appropriate term for any enumerator, literally a collection of things.

Regardless of the type involved, all *IEnum\** interfaces contain the same member functions, although the specific argument types vary with the enumerated type. The difference among enumerator interfaces is strictly in the types involved; the semantics are always the same. Enumerators in general can be described as a parameterized type, using a C++ template syntax (although actual templates are not used to define enumerator interfaces in header files).

---

10. Note that OLE Automation has a data type called a *Safe Array* that can be used to pass arrays along with information about the array dimensions and bounds when an enumerator is not necessary.

```
template <class ELT_T> interface IEnum : IUnknown
    {
    virtual HRESULT Next(ULONG celt, ELT_T *rgelt
        , ULONG *pceltFetched)=0;
    virtual HRESULT Skip(ULONG celt)=0;
    virtual HRESULT Reset(void)=0;
    virtual HRESULT Clone(IEnum<ELT_T> ** ppEnum)=0;
    };
```

In this template syntax, *ELT_T* stands for "ELemenT Type" and is a place-holder for whatever specific type is applicable to the enumerator, such as *IUnknown*, FORMATETC, VARIANT, and so forth. By itself, *elt* means "element."

The following table describes the member functions of an enumerator interface, omitting the omnipresent *IUnknown* members:

| Function | Description |
|---|---|
| *Next* | Returns the next *celt* elements of the list, starting at the current index. When the enumerated type is itself an interface pointer, as with *IEnumUnknown*, the *Next* function must call *AddRef* through each pointer before return, and the client must later call *Release* through each pointer. |
| *Skip* | Skips past *celt* elements in the list. |
| *Reset* | Sets the current index to 0. |
| *Clone* | Returns a new enumerator object with the same items but an independent index. The items in the clone are not guaranteed to be in the same order as the original enumerator. |

Note that enumerators are separate and independent objects, although in almost every circumstance a client obtains an enumerator by asking another object for the pointer. This is the second method that we saw earlier through which a client obtains its first interface pointer to a new object. If the object providing the enumerator doesn't have anything to enumerate, it will return S_FALSE and a NULL interface pointer from the appropriate member function.

## The EnumRect Sample

As additional proof that OLE has a language-independent binary standard, the EnumRect sample (CHAP02\ENUMRECT) implements identical enumerators for RECT structures in C and C++ but uses both of them from exactly the same C++ client code. The enumerators themselves implement an interface named *IEnumRECT*, which is defined for this sample and is not a standard OLE interface. The sample file IENUM.H contains the C and C++ definitions, using the STDMETHOD macros that expand to the appropriate calling conversion:

```
//C++ definition of an interface
#ifdef __cplusplus

typedef struct IEnumRECT IEnumRECT;
typedef IEnumRECT *PENUMRECT;

struct IEnumRECT
    {
    STDMETHOD(QueryInterface)(REFIID, PPVOID)=0;
    STDMETHOD_(ULONG,AddRef)(void)=0;
    STDMETHOD_(ULONG,Release)(void)=0;
    STDMETHOD(Next)(DWORD, LPRECT, LPDWORD)=0;
    STDMETHOD(Skip)(DWORD)=0;
    STDMETHOD(Reset)(void)=0;
    STDMETHOD(Clone)(PENUMRECT *)=0;
    };

#else    //!__cplusplus

typedef struct
    {
    struct IEnumRECTVtbl FAR *lpVtbl;
    } IEnumRECT, *PENUMRECT;

typedef struct IEnumRECTVtbl IEnumRECTVtbl;

struct IEnumRECTVtbl
    {
    STDMETHOD(QueryInterface)(PENUMRECT, REFIID, PPVOID);
    STDMETHOD_(ULONG, AddRef)(PENUMRECT);
    STDMETHOD_(ULONG, Release)(PENUMRECT);
    STDMETHOD(Next)(PENUMRECT, DWORD, LPRECT, LPDWORD);
    STDMETHOD(Skip)(PENUMRECT, DWORD);
    STDMETHOD(Reset)(PENUMRECT);
    STDMETHOD(Clone)(PENUMRECT, PENUMRECT *);
    };

#endif   //!__cplusplus
```

For convenience, we'll call the object that implements this interface a *RectEnumerator*. The part of EnumRect that is the client displays a small window with a menu that allows you to create either a C or a C++ object. There are two API-type functions that EnumRect calls to create the objects: *CreateRectEnumeratorC* and *CreateRectEnumeratorCPP*. These are typical functions

115

that create an object and return an interface pointer that must later be released, as usual. Regardless of which object you create, you can use the other menu items in EnumRect to call the various *IEnumRECT* member functions. EnumRect displays only the mundane results of the function (success or failure) in its client area, so it's most enlightening to run this sample in a debugger to step through the code and watch what happens when calls are made.

Note that IID_IEnumRECT is defined in INC\BOOKGUID.H, which is pulled in through EnumRect's inclusion of INC\INOLE.H. The ENUMRECT-.CPP file defines the INITGUIDS symbol to include this IID in the compilation.

## RectEnumerator in C: ENUMC.C

Let's look first at how we would implement a RectEnumerator object in straight C. To start, we need to define a data structure that will comprise the object, in which, according to the binary interface standard, the first 32 bits of this structure must be a pointer to the interface vtable. You can find this definition in the file ENUMRECT.H:

```
typedef struct tagRECTENUMERATOR
    {
    IEnumRECTVtbl    *lpVtbl;
    DWORD            m_cRef;        //Reference count
    DWORD            m_iCur;        //Current enum position
    RECT             m_rgrc[CRECTS]; //RECTS we enumerate
    } RECTENUMERATOR, *PRECTENUMERATOR;
```

This enumerator maintains a reference count, as expected, along with the current index of the enumeration (for implementing *Next*, *Skip*, and *Reset*) and a static array that holds the RECT structures to enumerate. This sample is somewhat contrived in that the number of structures is arbitrarily fixed at 15 (the constant *CRECTS*) and each structure contains bogus values, but it demonstrates the principles.

In addition to the object structure, we need to declare the member functions that will provide the implementation of the interface. Because we don't have the convenience of declaring member functions as we would in C++, we have to declare each one as an individually named global function:

```
PRECTENUMERATOR RECTENUM_Constructor(void);
void            RECTENUM_Destructor(PRECTENUMERATOR);

STDMETHODIMP       RECTENUM_QueryInterface(PENUMRECT, REFIID, PPVOID);
STDMETHODIMP_(ULONG) RECTENUM_AddRef(PENUMRECT);
STDMETHODIMP_(ULONG) RECTENUM_Release(PENUMRECT);
```

```
STDMETHODIMP      RECTENUM_Next(PENUMRECT, DWORD, LPRECT, LPDWORD);
STDMETHODIMP      RECTENUM_Skip(PENUMRECT, DWORD);
STDMETHODIMP      RECTENUM_Reset(PENUMRECT);
STDMETHODIMP      RECTENUM_Clone(PENUMRECT, PENUMRECT *);
```

The use of a constructor function and a destructor function is included to closely mimic the structure of the C++ version of this sample (shown below). The constructor is called from within the creation function *CreateRect-EnumeratorC*, which you'll find in ENUMC.C (along with all the other C functions):

```
BOOL CreateRECTEnumeratorC(PENUMRECT *ppEnum)
    {
    PRECTENUMERATOR      pRE;
    HRESULT              hr;

    if (NULL==ppEnum)
        return FALSE;

    //Create object.
    pRE=RECTENUM_Constructor();

    if (NULL==pRE)
        return FALSE;

    //Get interface, which calls AddRef.
    hr=pRE->lpVtbl->QueryInterface(pRE, &IID_IEnumRECT
        , (void **)ppEnum);
    return SUCCEEDED(hr);
    }
```

*RECTENUM_Constructor* has most of the interesting stuff regarding a C implementation. This function has to manually create a vtable for the object's interfaces (of which there is only one) and then allocate the object structure and store a pointer to that vtable as the first field:

```
static IEnumRECTVtbl  vtEnumRect;
static BOOL           g_fVtblInitialized=FALSE;

PRECTENUMERATOR RECTENUM_Constructor(void)
    {
    PRECTENUMERATOR      pRE;
    UINT                 i;

    if (!fVtblInitialized)
        {
        vtEnumRect.QueryInterface=RECTENUM_QueryInterface;
```

*(continued)*

```
        vtEnumRect.AddRef      =RECTENUM_AddRef;
        vtEnumRect.Release     =RECTENUM_Release;
        vtEnumRect.Next        =RECTENUM_Next;
        vtEnumRect.Skip        =RECTENUM_Skip;
        vtEnumRect.Reset       =RECTENUM_Reset;
        vtEnumRect.Clone       =RECTENUM_Clone;

        fVtblInitialized=TRUE;
        }

    pRE=(PRECTENUMERATOR)malloc(sizeof(RECTENUMERATOR));

    if (NULL==pRE)
        return NULL;

    //Initialize function table pointer.
    pRE->lpVtbl=&vtEnumRect;

    //Initialize array of rectangles.
    for (i=0; i < CRECTS; i++)
        SetRect(&pRE->m_rgrc[i], i, i*2, i*3, i*4);

    //Ref counts always start at 0.
    pRE->m_cRef=0;

    //Current pointer is first element.
    pRE->m_iCur=0;

    return pRE;
    }
```

The vtable itself needs initialization only once in this program to cover all possible instances of the object, so this structure is stored as the global variable *vtEnumRect*, with the flag *g_fVtblInitialized* indicating whether initialization has yet occurred. There is nothing sacred about filling the vtable explicitly like this; you could also declare the global variable along with the names of the functions that fill the table at compile time.

Notice that the reference count from the constructor is set initially to 0. This is because no pointer to the object's interfaces actually exists at this point. So after the constructor returns, *CreateRectEnumeratorC* will call the object's *QueryInterface* to obtain its *IEnumRECT* pointer, which in turn calls *AddRef*. This query step will call *AddRef* before returning the pointer, thereby transferring control of the object's lifetime from the creation function to the calling client:

```
STDMETHODIMP RECTENUM_QueryInterface(PENUMRECT pEnum
    , REFIID riid, PPVOID ppv)
    {
    //Always NULL the out-parameters.
    *ppv=NULL;

    if (IsEqualIID(riid, &IID_IUnknown)
        !! IsEqualIID(riid, &IID_IEnumRECT))
        *ppv=pEnum;

    if (NULL==*ppv)
        return ResultFromScode(E_NOINTERFACE);

    //AddRef any interface we'll return.
    ((LPUNKNOWN)*ppv)->lpVtbl->AddRef((LPUNKNOWN)*ppv);
    return NOERROR;
    }

STDMETHODIMP_(ULONG) RECTENUM_AddRef(PENUMRECT pEnum)
    {
    PRECTENUMERATOR        pRE=(PRECTENUMERATOR)pEnum;

    return ++pRE->m_cRef;
    }
```

You can see here that *QueryInterface* returns the same pointer for both *IUnknown* and *IEnumRECT* requests, which is perfectly normal because *IEnumRECT* is polymorphic with *IUnknown*. This shows how you don't need to implement *IUnknown* explicitly (unless you're supporting aggregation, as we'll see later). Again, the *AddRef* call made at the end of *QueryInterface* will increment the object's reference count initially to 1. The client's later *Release* call through the interface pointer will then destroy the object:

```
STDMETHODIMP_(ULONG) RECTENUM_Release(PENUMRECT pEnum)
    {
    PRECTENUMERATOR        pRE=(PRECTENUMERATOR)pEnum;

    if (0!=--pRE->m_cRef)
        return pRE->m_cRef;

    RECTENUM_Destructor(pRE);
    return 0;
    }
```

This interface member function, like all others, has to know what object is being used through this interface. In C, the first parameter to a member function is the interface pointer through which the client makes the call. Because we know internally that this pointer actually points to our RECTENUMERATOR structure, we can typecast it into our object pointer and access our data members, such as *m_cRef*. Here in *Release,* we decrement the reference count (which is trivially incremented in *AddRef*) and return the new value. If the value is 0, we call our own destructor, which simply deallocates the structure:

```
void RECTENUM_Destructor(PRECTENUMERATOR pRE)
    {
    if (NULL==pRE)
        return;

    free(pRE);
    return;
    }
```

There is no need to unravel the global vtable because we initialize it only once per task.

I will leave it to you to examine the implementation of the specific *IEnumRECT* member functions, which are pretty standard as far as enumerators are concerned. The *Clone* function, for example, simply calls our own *CreateRectEnumeratorC* again. This is a little simpler than a working enumerator because normally a cloning process can involve the duplication of the list itself. In cloning, it's important that the clone have the same state as the current enumerator. In our *Clone* implementation, this means copying the current index pointer.

## RectEnumerator in C++: ENUMCPP.CPP

Now let's look at the equivalent implementation of the C object done in C++. First the object can be defined using a C++ class that inherits the function signatures from the interface. Because the interface is an abstract base class, we have to override every member function explicitly (ENUMRECT.H):

```
class CEnumRect : public IEnumRECT
    {
    private:
        DWORD           m_cRef;         //Reference count
        DWORD           m_iCur;         //Current enum position
        RECT            m_rgrc[CRECTS]; //RECTS we enumerate

    public:
        CEnumRect(void);
        ~CEnumRect(void);
```

```
            STDMETHODIMP            QueryInterface(REFIID, PPVOID);
            STDMETHODIMP_(ULONG) AddRef(void);
            STDMETHODIMP_(ULONG) Release(void);

            //IEnumRECT members
            STDMETHODIMP Next(ULONG, LPRECT, ULONG *);
            STDMETHODIMP Skip(ULONG);
            STDMETHODIMP Reset(void);
            STDMETHODIMP Clone(PENUMRECT *);
    };
```

```
typedef CEnumRect *PCEnumRect;
```

Creating the object, which happens in *CreateRectEnumeratorCPP* (ENUM-CPP.CPP), performs the same steps as *CreateRectEnumeratorC* by using the C++ *new* operator to allocate the object, calling its constructor automatically:

```
BOOL CreateRECTEnumeratorCPP(PENUMRECT *ppEnum)
    {
    PCEnumRect  pER;
    HRESULT     hr;

    if (NULL==ppEnum)
        return FALSE;

    //Create object.
    pER=new CEnumRect();

    if (NULL==pER)
        return FALSE;

    //Get interface, which calls AddRef.
    hr=pER->QueryInterface(IID_IEnumRECT, (void **)ppEnum);
    return SUCCEEDED(hr);
    }

    ⋮

CEnumRect::CEnumRect(void)
    {
    UINT        i;

    //Initialize array of rectangles.
    for (i=0; i < CRECTS; i++)
        SetRect(&m_rgrc[i], i, i*2, i*3, i*4);
```

*(continued)*

121

```
//Ref counts always start at 0.
m_cRef=0;

//Current pointer is first element.
m_iCur=0;

return;
}
```

The big difference is that in C++ you do not have to create the vtable manually: that step is performed automatically by virtue of creating a C++ object that inherits it from an interface. What we did in C is similar to the code that the C++ compiler creates transparently. This is the second reason (apart from concise interface calling) that C++ is more convenient than C: the compiler does some of the work for you.

Let's also look at the implementation of *QueryInterface* and *Release* and show how the C++ functions automatically receive a *this* pointer instead of an extra first parameter to each member call:

```
STDMETHODIMP CEnumRect::QueryInterface(REFIID riid, PPVOID ppv)
    {
    *ppv=NULL;

    if (IID_IUnknown==riid || IID_IEnumRECT==riid)
        *ppv=this;

    if (NULL==*ppv)
        return ResultFromScode(E_NOINTERFACE);

    ((LPUNKNOWN)*ppv)->AddRef();
    return NOERROR;
    }


STDMETHODIMP_(ULONG) CEnumRect::AddRef(void)
    {
    return ++m_cRef;
    }


STDMETHODIMP_(ULONG) CEnumRect::Release(void)
    {
    if (0!=--m_cRef)
        return m_cRef;

    delete this;
    return 0;
    }
```

In C++, *QueryInterface* can use the overloaded == operator for IIDs instead of calling *IsEqualIID*. In addition, we return our *this* pointer as the interface pointer because the two are equivalent. If you singly inherit an interface into a C++ object class, you do not need explicit typecasting when assigning *this* to a *void* pointer, as we're doing here. The *CEnumRECT* pointer is an *IEnumRECT* pointer in such a case.

In the preceding code, the pointer returned for *IUnknown* is the same as the pointer returned for *IEnumRECT*, so it is tempting to think that a client that obtained an *IUnknown* pointer could typecast it into an *IEnumRECT* type. This is utterly dangerous and entirely illegal because it breaks the idea of *QueryInterface* completely. Furthermore, it cannot possibly work when a process or machine boundary separates client and object. A client's use of a pointer in this way represents intimate knowledge of the object's implementation. This goes against encapsulation and polymorphism and is a capital crime in object-oriented programming. In short, don't do it.

As we'll see later, you also must be careful with multiple inheritance. But before we look at those issues, notice that the implementation of *Release* has the odd statement *delete this*. This is C++ suicide, if you will: the object destroys itself, calling the destructor. This may look strange, but it is perfectly legal and is used frequently in OLE object implementations.

> **N O T E :**   When an object can have multiple simultaneous clients, it is best to protect *Release* from reentrancy—that is, if you're already doing *delete this*, ignore any subsequent *Release* calls (as well as most other interface members, but this is the important one), just in case. This applies to C implementations as well. The RectEnumerator objects here do not do this because an instance has only one possible client.

Viewing both the C and the C++ implementations, you can see that what is important to OLE is that the interface be a structure that contains a pointer to a vtable that contains pointers to the implementations of the member functions. How you choose to create this structure is irrelevant: C++ is more convenient, but the same thing can be accomplished almost as easily in C. If you examine the C++ code in the ENUMRECT.CPP file, you'll see that a C++ client can make calls to a C object as easily as to a C++ object—language is no barrier in OLE.

# Implementing Multiple Interfaces

In the C++ RectEnumerator sample, I used single inheritance to bring the function signatures for the *IEnumRECT* interface into the *CEnumRect* object class. This technique works quite well for single-interface, nonaggregatable objects. However, when you want to implement multiple interfaces, which includes an explicit *IUnknown* for aggregation, you need to use one of three other techniques: interface implementations, contained interface classes, and multiple inheritance, each of which are each discussed in the following sections. The C++ Query sample in CHAP02\QUERY demonstrates each of these techniques through three equivalent object implementations (*CObject1*, *CObject2*, and *CObject3*). The Query code itself acts as a client for any of these objects, and it creates a small window with a menu through which you can select which object to create, invoke the member functions of their interfaces, and release them.

Each object in this demonstration implements two interfaces, *ISampleOne* and *ISampleTwo*, which are defined as follows in INTERFAC.H, using the macros that expand to the appropriate C++ interface declarations for different target platforms:

```
DECLARE_INTERFACE_(ISampleOne, IUnknown)
    {
    //IUnknown members
    STDMETHOD(QueryInterface) (THIS_ REFIID, PPVOID) PURE;
    STDMETHOD_(ULONG,AddRef)  (THIS) PURE;
    STDMETHOD_(ULONG,Release) (THIS) PURE;

    //ISampleOne members
    STDMETHOD(GetMessage) (THIS_ LPTSTR, UINT) PURE;
    };

typedef ISampleOne *PINTERFACEONE;

DECLARE_INTERFACE_(ISampleTwo, IUnknown)
    {
    //IUnknown members
    STDMETHOD(QueryInterface) (THIS_ REFIID, PPVOID) PURE;
    STDMETHOD_(ULONG,AddRef)  (THIS) PURE;
    STDMETHOD_(ULONG,Release) (THIS) PURE;

    //ISampleTwo members
    STDMETHOD(GetString) (THIS_ LPTSTR, UINT) PURE;
    };

typedef ISampleTwo *PINTERFACETWO;
```

The IIDs for these interfaces are given in INC\BOOKGUID.H, as are all GUIDs defined for this book. Both *ISampleOne::GetMessage* and *ISampleTwo::GetString* fill a string buffer with some string that the client (QUERY.CPP) displays in its window to prove that it called the correct member function of the correct interface. It is instructive to run Query in a debugger and follow the path of execution through each object.

## Interface Implementations (*CObject1*)

This technique employs only single inheritance, where the object class itself inherits from *IUnknown* and implements those functions to control the object as a whole. Each additional interface is implemented as a separate C++ *interface implementation* class that singly inherits from the appropriate interface. Each separate class holds a backpointer to the full object class (with no *AddRef* because this is a case of nested lifetimes) and delegates all *IUnknown* calls from its interface to those of the actual object. Thus, reference counting and *QueryInterface* are centralized in the full object class, as should be the case. In general, the interface implementation classes use the backpointer to get at centralized object variables, so they are commonly declared as *friend* classes to the object class.

To implement an object with *ISampleOne* and *ISampleTwo*, we would declare classes as found in OBJECT1.H:

```
class CImpISampleOne;
typedef CImpISampleOne *PCImpISampleOne;

class CImpISampleTwo;
typedef CImpISampleTwo *PCImpISampleTwo;

//The C++ class that manages the actual object
class CObject1 : public IUnknown
    {
    friend CImpISampleOne;
    friend CImpISampleTwo;

    private:
        DWORD           m_cRef;          //Object reference count

        PCImpISampleOne m_pImpISampleOne;
        PCImpISampleTwo m_pImpISampleTwo;

    public:
        CObject1(void);
        ~CObject1(void);
```

*(continued)*

125

```
            BOOL Init(void);

            //IUnknown members
            STDMETHODIMP          QueryInterface(REFIID, PPVOID);
            STDMETHODIMP_(DWORD) AddRef(void);
            STDMETHODIMP_(DWORD) Release(void);
        };

typedef CObject1 *PCObject1;

class CImpISampleOne : public ISampleOne
    {
    private:
        DWORD       m_cRef;        //For debugging
        PCObject1   m_pObj;        //Backpointer for delegation

    public:
        CImpISampleOne(PCObject1);
        ~CImpISampleOne(void);

        //IUnknown members
        STDMETHODIMP          QueryInterface(REFIID, PPVOID);
        STDMETHODIMP_(DWORD) AddRef(void);
        STDMETHODIMP_(DWORD) Release(void);

        //ISampleOne members
        STDMETHODIMP          GetMessage(LPTSTR, UINT);
    };

class CImpISampleTwo : public ISampleTwo
    {
    private:
        DWORD       m_cRef;        //For debugging
        PCObject1   m_pObj;        //Backpointer for delegation

    public:
        CImpISampleTwo(PCObject1);
        ~CImpISampleTwo(void);

        //IUnknown members
        STDMETHODIMP          QueryInterface(REFIID, PPVOID);
        STDMETHODIMP_(DWORD) AddRef(void);
        STDMETHODIMP_(DWORD) Release(void);

        //ISampleTwo members
        STDMETHODIMP          GetString(LPTSTR, UINT);
    };
```

My personal convention is to name the interface classes with *CImp<Interface>* and the variables in the object that hold pointers to these classes with *m_pImp<Interface>*. This variable naming distinguishes interface implementations that the object manages from other interface pointers that it might store as well, which I name with *m_p<Interface>*. These are my conventions: use whatever you like because OLE itself doesn't care about such implementation details.

The Query client creates this object through the *CreateObject1* function, which looks a lot like *CreateRectEnumeratorCPP*. One addition is that after creating an instance of *CObject1* with the *new* operator, the Query client calls *CObject1::Init*, which explicitly instantiates the interface implementations:

```
CObject1::CObject1(void)
    {
    m_cRef=0;

    m_pImpISampleOne=NULL;
    m_pImpISampleTwo=NULL;

    return;
    }

    ⋮

BOOL CObject1::Init(void)
    {
    m_pImpISampleOne=new CImpISampleOne(this);

    if (NULL==m_pImpISampleOne)
        return FALSE;

    m_pImpISampleTwo=new CImpISampleTwo(this);

    if (NULL==m_pImpISampleTwo)
        return FALSE;

    return TRUE;
    }
```

The *this* pointer passed to the interface implementation constructors becomes the backpointer to the object, through which the interface implementations delegate *IUnknown* calls. Again, the interface implementations do not call *AddRef* on this pointer because their lifetimes are nested within *CObject1*'s. Thus, the object can simply call *delete* on its *m_pImp\** pointers in its destructor to clean up the allocations made inside *Init*, as shown on the following page.

```
CObject1::~CObject1(void)
    {
    DeleteInterfaceImp(m_pImpISampleTwo);
    DeleteInterfaceImp(m_pImpISampleOne);
    return;
    }
```

The destructor is called from within *Release*, which calls *delete this*, as we saw before. In the destructor, the macro DELETEINTERFACEIMP is my own creation. (You'll find it in INC\INOLE.H.) This macro calls *delete* on the given pointer and sets that pointer to NULL. I have also defined a macro, RELEASEINTERFACE, that calls *Release* on a pointer and sets it to NULL:

```
#define DeleteInterfaceImp(p)\
            {\
            if (NULL!=p)\
                {\
                delete p;\
                p=NULL;\
                }\
            }

#define ReleaseInterface(p)\
            {\
            if (NULL!=p)\
                {\
                p->Release();\
                p=NULL;\
                }\
            }
```

I have found that setting a pointer to NULL after you believe you have deleted it or released it for the last time is very useful for debugging, as it easily exposes interface calls after the interface becomes invalid. I recommend that you use this technique in your own work as well: it will save you some head banging.

Now to the real purpose of our discussion—the implementation of *QueryInterface*. *CObject1* effectively supports three interfaces: *IUnknown*, *ISampleOne*, and *ISampleTwo*. Each interface pointer comes from a different source:

```
STDMETHODIMP CObject1::QueryInterface(REFIID riid, PPVOID ppv)
    {
    *ppv=NULL;

    //IUnknown comes from CObject1.
    if (IID_IUnknown==riid)
        *ppv=this;
```

```
//Other interfaces come from interface implementations.
if (IID_ISampleOne==riid)
    *ppv=m_pImpISampleOne;

if (IID_ISampleTwo==riid)
    *ppv=m_pImpISampleTwo;

if (NULL==*ppv)
    return ResultFromScode(E_NOINTERFACE);

((LPUNKNOWN)*ppv)->AddRef();
return NOERROR;
}
```

In other words, *this* is the *IUnknown* pointer, whereas *m_pImpISampleOne* and *m_pImpISampleTwo* are the others. If the client calls any *IUnknown* function through these latter two interface pointers, the calls are delegated to *CObject1*'s implementation:

```
CImpISampleOne::CImpISampleOne(PCObject1 pObj)
    {
    m_cRef=0;
    m_pObj=pObj;
    return;
    }


STDMETHODIMP CImpISampleOne::QueryInterface(REFIID riid, PPVOID ppv)
    {
    return m_pObj->QueryInterface(riid, ppv);
    }


DWORD CImpISampleOne::AddRef(void)
    {
    ++m_cRef;
    return m_pObj->AddRef();
    }


DWORD CImpISampleOne::Release(void)
    {
    --m_cRef;
    return m_pObj->Release();
    }
```

The same thing happens in *CImpISampleTwo*. Do note that these implementations maintain their own interface reference counts simply for debugging. If you wanted to—and you are not supporting aggregation—you could have *CObject1::QueryInterface* create the interface implementations when necessary and have those implementations destroy themselves in *Release*. The technique is not allowed in aggregation, however, because there you have to ensure validity of all interface pointers until the object as a whole is destroyed, as we'll see shortly.

The primary advantage of this technique is that everything is explicit: you can trace when and where interfaces are instantiated, and you can watch everything that happens. For this reason, and because it is more readily understood by a C++ neophyte, I've used this technique in almost every multiple-interface sample in this book. Its biggest drawback is that it's rather verbose; the other techniques don't require as much source code. The extra step of *IUnknown* delegation is also a minor but usually insignificant performance degradation, and this technique generally uses more memory than others do.

## Contained Interface Classes (*CObject2*)

One reason why interface implementations are rather verbose is that you end up defining a bunch of separate classes for each object. One way to combine the classes is to use *contained* or *nested* classes for each interface, as demonstrated in the *CObject2* class in OBJECT2.H:

```
class CObject2 : public IUnknown
    {
    class CImpISampleOne : public ISampleOne
        {
        private:
            DWORD       m_cRef;         //For debugging
            CObject2    *m_pObj;        //Backpointer for delegation

        public:
            CImpISampleOne(CObject2 *pObj)
                { m_cRef=0; m_pObj=pObj; }

            ~CImpISampleOne(void)
                { }

            //IUnknown members
            STDMETHODIMP        QueryInterface(REFIID, PPVOID);
            STDMETHODIMP_(DWORD) AddRef(void);
            STDMETHODIMP_(DWORD) Release(void);

            //ISampleOne members
            STDMETHODIMP        GetMessage(LPTSTR, UINT);
        };

    class CImpISampleTwo : public ISampleTwo
```

```
        {
        private:
            DWORD       m_cRef;           //For debugging
            CObject2    *m_pObj;          //Backpointer for delegation

        public:
            CImpISampleTwo(CObject2 *pObj)
                { m_cRef=0; m_pObj=pObj; }
            ~CImpISampleTwo(void)
                { }

            //IUnknown members
            STDMETHODIMP          QueryInterface(REFIID, PPVOID);
            STDMETHODIMP_(DWORD)  AddRef(void);
            STDMETHODIMP_(DWORD)  Release(void);

            //ISampleTwo members
            STDMETHODIMP          GetString(LPTSTR, UINT);
        };

    friend CImpISampleOne;
    friend CImpISampleTwo;

    private:
        DWORD       m_cRef;           //Object reference count

        CImpISampleOne  m_ImpISampleOne;
        CImpISampleTwo  m_ImpISampleTwo;

    public:
        CObject2(void);
        ~CObject2(void);

        //IUnknown members
        STDMETHODIMP          QueryInterface(REFIID, PPVOID);
        STDMETHODIMP_(DWORD)  AddRef(void);
        STDMETHODIMP_(DWORD)  Release(void);
    };

typedef CObject2 *PCObject2;
```

The only real difference here is that instead of the object managing pointers to each interface, it directly manages the implementation objects themselves. This means that constructing an instance of *CObject2* will automatically instantiate the interface classes; destruction is automatic as well. We don't need any extra *Init* function to complete the construction of the object, but we do have to play tricks with the object constructor, as shown in the code at the top of the following page.

```
CObject2::CObject2(void)
    : m_ImpISampleOne(this), m_ImpISampleTwo(this)
    {
    m_cRef=0;
    return;
    }
```

This is the only way I found to get the object's *this* pointer into the interface classes to serve as the backpointer.

The object's *QueryInterface* implementation looks much the same as in *CObject1* except that we have to return the address of the contained objects instead of pointers:

```
STDMETHODIMP CObject2::QueryInterface(REFIID riid, PPVOID ppv)
    {
    *ppv=NULL;

    //IUnknown comes from CObject2.
    if (IID_IUnknown==riid)
        *ppv=this;

    //Other interfaces come from contained classes.
    if (IID_ISampleOne==riid)
        *ppv=&m_ImpISampleOne;

    if (IID_ISampleTwo==riid)
        *ppv=&m_ImpISampleTwo;

    if (NULL==*ppv)
        return ResultFromScode(E_NOINTERFACE);

    ((LPUNKNOWN)*ppv)->AddRef();
    return NOERROR;
    }
```

Other than that, the implementations of the contained classes are exactly the same (you'll notice that the constructor and destructor are declared in line in this sample), even the delegation of *IUnknown* calls to *CObject2*.

Contained classes are a little more concise than interface implementations, and the technique automates the creation of interface classes. This makes the creation process harder to trace, but that's not a big issue. I find the class declarations harder to read, which is why I don't use this technique in this book. You might find it beneficial in your own projects to limit the scope of an interface class to the object that uses it—especially if you have in the same source code multiple objects that implement the same interfaces but need those interface implementations to be different. This technique allows you to scope the interface class names within the object class name, whereas the interface implementations technique requires globally unique interface class names.

## Multiple Inheritance (*CObject3*)

You are probably thinking that both of the previous techniques are too verbose—they have a lot of source code and still use a bunch of classes to implement one object. Multiple inheritance in C++ is the way to cut out the extra classes and combine all the *IUnknown* implementations into one. That means no delegation and no backpointers: you have only one object. *CObject3* is the multiple-inheritance version of what we've already seen, declared in OBJECT3.H:

```
class CObject3 : public ISampleOne, public ISampleTwo
    {
    private:
        DWORD           m_cRef;             //Object reference count

    public:
        CObject3(void);
        ~CObject3(void);

        //Shared IUnknown members
        STDMETHODIMP            QueryInterface(REFIID, PPVOID);
        STDMETHODIMP_(DWORD) AddRef(void);
        STDMETHODIMP_(DWORD) Release(void);

        //ISampleOne members
        STDMETHODIMP            GetMessage(LPTSTR, UINT);

        //ISampleTwo members
        STDMETHODIMP            GetString(LPTSTR, UINT);
    };

typedef CObject3 *PCObject3;
```

This uses a lot less code to declare the object, and because there are no other classes, the total amount of memory is less. You also avoid the extra step of delegation for *IUnknown* functions.

One important factor to remember, however, is that a pointer to the object is not a direct pointer to *any* interface, even *IUnknown*. (The compiler will complain that *IUnknown* is ambiguous because it is inherited from both the other interfaces.) This means that we must use explicit typecasts in *Query-Interface* to retrieve the correct pointers for each interface, as in the following:

```
STDMETHODIMP CObject3::QueryInterface(REFIID riid, PPVOID ppv)
    {
    *ppv=NULL;

    if (IID_IUnknown==riid || IID_ISampleOne==riid)
        *ppv=(ISampleOne *)this;

    if (IID_ISampleTwo==riid)
        *ppv=(ISampleTwo *)this;

    if (NULL==*ppv)
        return ResultFromScode(E_NOINTERFACE);

    ((LPUNKNOWN)*ppv)->AddRef();
    return NOERROR;
    }
```

Because we don't have an explicit *IUnknown*, we use *ISampleOne* as our *IUnknown*. This is because *ISampleOne* has an *IUnknown* vtable itself.

It is important to realize that when multiple inheritance is involved, a typecast operation will change the pointer value. What the preceding code stores in *\*ppv* is not the same as what is stored in *this*. The reason is that C++ overloads the typecast operators to allocate the right vtable for the interface type, and thus you have to have a different pointer to that vtable as well as a different pointer to that pointer, which is what gets stored in *\*ppv*. If you are unfamiliar with how this works, please refer to the "Multiple Inheritance" section in the APPA.WRI file on the companion CD for more details.

Failure to typecast properly can result in some very strange side effects: because *ppv* is a *void \*\**, you can store any pointer you want in it without complaint from the compiler. This means that if you forget the typecast, you'll effectively give the client an interface pointer that points to the object's vtable, not the interface vtable. In multiple inheritance, this object vtable includes all object member functions, such as the constructor and destructor. I've encountered situations in which my object destructor was called from a client, which confused the heck out of me for a long time. Other people have asked me about this same problem, in which they saw a function being called twice. Any strange symptom involving a call to the wrong function indicates a possible failure to typecast in *QueryInterface*. Do be careful.

As just described, multiple inheritance has the drawback of difficult debugging, especially when vtables are not created properly. But its primary advantage is that the expression of such an object is much more concise and generally looks cleaner in code. When you involve more than a few interfaces, however, things start to get messy, and the whole technique breaks down if you have two interfaces with identically named member functions, which does occasionally occur. For most situations, multiple inheritance is a great technique for production development projects because of its concise nature. If you are planning to implement an aggregatable object, however, you will need to use one of the other techniques to make a set of *IUnknown* functions outside those inherited from all the other interfaces. In that case, you'll have the main object delegate its *IUnknown* functions to some other unknown, either the outer unknown (in aggregation) or the object's own *IUnknown* (outside of aggregation).

## Implementing Reusability

Our final topic involving sample code is reusability through both containment and aggregation. The Reuse sample (CHAP02\REUSE) demonstrates both techniques, using the Animal and Koala objects seen earlier. The KoalaC object in this sample implements its *IAnimal* interface through containment of the Animal object; KoalaA obtains *IAnimal* through aggregation. The same implementation of the Animal object is used in both cases; it was written to support either mechanism. Let's look first at how both Koala objects set up their relationships with Animal through the creation function *CreateAnimal* (found in ANIMAL.CPP). Then we'll look deeper into Animal's code to see how an object specifically supports aggregation. All of these objects use interface implementations to support multiple interfaces (even Animal, because as an aggregatable object it needs an explicit *IUnknown*).

Like the other samples we've seen, Reuse creates a small window with a menu through which you can create either Koala object and invoke the member functions of both interfaces. None of the member functions other than those in *IUnknown* actually do anything except return NOERROR, so again it is instructive to walk through this sample in a debugger. You will notice in the code that the various interface implementation classes are given a suffix to differentiate them from the various objects. This is to avoid linker errors with same-named classes.

## Containment (KOALAC.CPP)

In containment, the outer object, KoalaC, creates an instance of the inner object, Animal, during KoalaC's initialization process and requests an *IAnimal* pointer in return. (*CKoalaC::Init* is called from *CreateKoalaContainment*, which is called from Reuse's window procedure.) KoalaC will request an *IAnimal* pointer in the process:

```
BOOL CKoalaC::Init(void)
    {
    HRESULT     hr;

    m_pImpIAnimal=new CImpIAnimal_K(this);

    if (NULL==m_pImpIAnimal)
        return FALSE;

    m_pImpIKoala=new CImpIKoala_C(this);

    if (NULL==m_pImpIKoala)
        return FALSE;

    hr=CreateAnimal(NULL, IID_IAnimal, (void **)&m_pIAnimal);

    if (FAILED(hr))
        return FALSE;

    return TRUE;
    }
```

Inside KoalaC's implementation of the specific *IAnimal* member functions, KoalaC might choose to use — that is, reuse — the implementations of the same functions in the Animal object by calling them through *m_pIAnimal,* as any other client would. In this case, KoalaC is delegating all the calls after generating an output message to the debugger:

```
STDMETHODIMP CImpIAnimal_K::Eat(void)
    {
    ODS("KoalaC's IAnimal_K::Eat called");
    m_pObj->m_pIAnimal->Eat();
    return NOERROR;
    }

STDMETHODIMP CImpIAnimal_K::Sleep(void)
    {
    ODS("KoalaC's IAnimal_K::Sleep called");
    m_pObj->m_pIAnimal->Sleep();
    return NOERROR;
    }
```

```
STDMETHODIMP CImpIAnimal_K::Procreate(void)
    {
    ODS("KoalaC's IAnimal_K::Procreate called");
    m_pObj->m_pIAnimal->Procreate();
    return NOERROR;
    }
```

Animal's implementation of the interface also pumps out similar messages. (The ODS macro and others like it wrap calls to *OutputDebugString*; you can find these macros in INC\DBGOUT.H.)

When KoalaC is destroyed (from the Reuse client code calling its *Release*), the destructor calls *m_pIAnimal->Release* using the RELEASEINTERFACE macro we saw earlier. Animal's interface pointer never actually enters into KoalaC's implementation of *QueryInterface* because KoalaC has its own implementation. Everything KoalaC does with Animal's interface is exactly what any other client would do with Animal, which is the essence of containment.

## Aggregation: Outer Object (KOALAA.CPP)

You may have noticed that KoalaC passed a mysterious NULL pointer as the first argument to the *CreateAnimal* function. This argument is the means by which an outer object passes its outer unknown pointer to Animal to inform the object that it is being created as part of an aggregate. We'll see shortly what Animal does with this pointer. From KoalaA's perspective, it must pass its own *IUnknown* pointer to this function in order to create an aggregatable Animal object, and in compliance with the other aggregation rule, KoalaA must request an *IUnknown* pointer in return. Compare this with KoalaC, which asked for an *IAnimal* in return; remember that KoalaA cannot do this because Animal's *IUnknown* pointer is the only way to control Animal's lifetime properly.

Here, then, is KoalaA's code to create the aggregated Animal object in KoalaA's initialization:

```
BOOL CKoalaA::Init(void)
    {
    HRESULT     hr;

    m_pImpIKoala=new CImpIKoala_A(this);

    if (NULL==m_pImpIKoala)
        return FALSE;

    hr=CreateAnimal(this, IID_IUnknown, (void **)&m_pIUnknown);
```

*(continued)*

137

```
if (FAILED(hr))
    return FALSE;

hr=m_pIUnknown->QueryInterface(IID_IAnimal, (void **)&m_pIAnimal);

if (FAILED(hr))
    return FALSE;

m_cRef--;
return TRUE;
}
```

This initialization procedure shows not only KoalaA passing its *IUnknown* to Animal (the *this* sent to *CreateAnimal*) but also the way in which a 32-bit aggregate has to fix its reference count. In this sample, the *Query-Interface* call to retrieve *IAnimal* will bump KoalaC's reference count to 1, but it has to be 0 because we still have to provide any external pointers. Therefore, we simply decrement *m_cRef* without calling our own *Release*, which would destroy the object. If we had to call *Release* here for some reason, you would have to wrap that call in *m_cRef++* and *m_cRef--*.

We must also use *m_pIAnimal->Release* in our destructor in the following manner, as stipulated by the rules, as well as safeguard *CKoalaA::Release*:

```
CKoalaA::~CKoalaA(void)
    {
    AddRef();
    ReleaseInterface(m_pIAnimal);
    m_pIAnimal=NULL;    //Already released

    ReleaseInterface(m_pIUnknown);
    DeleteInterfaceImp(m_pImpIKoala);
    return;
    }

DWORD CKoalaA::Release(void)
    {
    if (0!=--m_cRef)
        return m_cRef;

    m_cRef++;         //Artificial count preventing reentrancy
    delete this;
    return 0;
    }
```

Because we're doing aggregation, KoalaA doesn't implement *IAnimal* itself; however, it does need to return its *IAnimal* pointer when asked for it in *QueryInterface*. This can be done in two ways: either return a cached pointer or pass the call to Animal's *IUnknown::QueryInterface* (which does not delegate). KoalaA demonstrates the latter:

```
STDMETHODIMP CKoalaA::QueryInterface(REFIID riid, PPVOID ppv)
    {
    ⋮

    //Alternatively, *ppv=m_pIAnimal; works for this case.
    if (IID_IAnimal==riid)
        return m_pIUnknown->QueryInterface(riid, ppv);

    ⋮
    }
```

Both ways implement the proper *QueryInterface* behavior for KoalaA. KoalaA's only other concern is releasing the Animal object during KoalaA's own destruction, which simply involves a call to Animal's *IUnknown::Release*. This is, again, why KoalaA must ask for Animal's *IUnknown* during creation because a *Release* call to any other interface would be routed to KoalaA's *IUnknown*, leaving no way to free Animal to the wild open spaces.

## Aggregation: Inner Object (ANIMAL.CPP)

We can now look at those parts of the Animal object that specifically concern aggregation: creation and *IUnknown* implementation. Even if you were using multiple inheritance as an implementation technique, you must still have a separate implementation of *IUnknown* functions. For Animal, we'll have its object class *CAnimal* inherit only from *IUnknown*, the implementation of which controls the object as a whole. Animal then manages an interface implementation class, *CImpIAnimal*, for the *IAnimal* interface. Notice that you could also have *CAnimal* inherit from *IAnimal* and make a *CImpIUnknown* if you wanted. This would work great if you were using multiple inheritance for multiple interfaces on *CAnimal*. Either way you have two classes: one that delegates its *IUnknown* calls and one that controls the object as a whole. In the sample, *CAnimal* implements *IUnknown*, and *CImpIAnimal_A* implements *IAnimal*. Both classes have a pointer, *m_pUnkOuter*, with which to store the outer unknown.

This arrangement allows you to play a rather elegant trick on any delegating *IUnknown* functions. In the Object1 and Object2 samples described earlier, the interface implementations held a backpointer to the main object for the purpose of both *IUnknown* delegation and access to any object members as necessary. (The samples didn't show this, but that's what backpointers are for.) When creating an aggregatable object, you can separate these two roles of the backpointer and instead pass each interface implementation a backpointer and some *IUnknown* pointer to which that interface must delegate all of its calls. The trick is this: if the object is not being used in aggregation, the object passes its own *IUnknown* to the interface implementations. In aggregation, the object instead passes the outer unknown it receives at creation time. As a result, the interface implementations are oblivious to aggregation concerns: they blindly delegate to someone else's *IUnknown*, which can be easily switched as needed.

We can now see how the Animal object uses the outer unknown passed to its creation function. If the pointer is NULL, the aggregation is not happening, and it passes its own *IUnknown* to its interface implementation and allows the caller to request any interface pointer. If the pointer is non-NULL, it passes its *IUnknown* on to the interface and checks to be sure that the caller is asking for Animal's *IUnknown* in return:

```
HRESULT CreateAnimal(IUnknown *pUnkOuter, REFIID riid, void **ppv)
    {
    CAnimal    *pObj;

    if (NULL!=pUnkOuter && riid!=IID_IUnknown)
        return ResultFromScode(CLASS_E_NOAGGREGATION);

    pObj=new CAnimal(pUnkOuter);

    if (NULL==pObj)
        return FALSE;

    if (!pObj->Init())
        return FALSE;

    return pObj->QueryInterface(riid, (PPVOID)ppv);
    }


BOOL CAnimal::Init(void)
    {
    IUnknown    *pUnkOuter=m_pUnkOuter;

    //Set up the right unknown for delegation.
    if (NULL==pUnkOuter)
        pUnkOuter=this;

    m_pImpIAnimal=new CImpIAnimal_A(this, pUnkOuter);

    if (NULL==m_pImpIAnimal)
        return FALSE;

    return TRUE;
    }
```

We can also see how *CImpIAnimal* simply stores whatever unknown it is given (no *AddRef* because the interface is always nested) so that it can delegate its *IUnknown* calls appropriately:

```
CImpIAnimal_A::CImpIAnimal_A(PCAnimal pObj, IUnknown *pUnkOuter)
    {
    m_cRef=0;
    m_pObj=pObj;
    m_pUnkOuter=pUnkOuter;   //No AddRef; we're nested.
    return;
    }
```

Supporting aggregation is not a tremendous amount of work, for both outer and inner objects, but it must be consciously supported. Remember that if the Animal object itself created additional objects, it would pass the *pUnkOuter* argument it receives on creation down to the creation functions it calls, so KoalaA's pointer is propagated through the entire aggregation.

# Interfaces and OLE API Functions

Now that we understand interfaces and the various mechanisms through which they work, we're ready to begin exploring all the other OLE services and technologies. Some of the 80 or so OLE-defined interfaces known at the time of writing are used internally within OLE, others are often used in writing components and clients, and others are less common. Most of OLE is, in fact, described, expressed, and accessed through interfaces of one kind or another, and some interfaces do no more than provide a base interface for others related to them. For most components, you'll need to implement only a few interfaces yourself, and as a client, you'll generally work with only a handful. OLE looks like a lot of technology—and it is—but you don't have to chew it all at the same time. Don't be scared of the myth that OLE is "complicated, complex, and difficult" simply because there's a lot of technology in there. Win32 as a whole is more complicated, but few people complain about that because they understand how to look at little pieces, one at a time, as each piece becomes necessary in programming. You can approach OLE the same way, and this book is structured to help you on that journey.

Part of what makes OLE so exciting is this idea of an *extensible service architecture* that allows you to arbitrarily extend what OLE does with custom components as well as with custom interfaces. You can implement a service that OLE does not for whatever reason you want. (For example, a group named the Open Market Data Council created a specification called WOSA/XRT for real-time market data exchange, using OLE technology to create a higher integration standard.) If OLE doesn't define an interface you need, you can define custom interfaces yourself. In this chapter, we've already seen six custom interfaces: *IAnimal*, *IRabbit*, *IKoala*, *ISampleOne*, *ISampleTwo*, and *IEnumRECT*. Granted, these are pretty useless interfaces for any real components, but they show you how easily you can create them, and GUIDs mean that you don't need to worry about conflicts. Remember that all these interfaces work only in-process because there is no marshaling support for them. We'll look at that topic in Chapter 6.

Besides the interfaces, OLE is also made up of more than 120 API functions. These generally fall into three categories: creation functions for components of different types such as *CoCreateInstance* and *CoGetMalloc* that access OLE-implemented components or custom components; helper functions such as *CoTaskMemAlloc* that wrap commonly used sequences of interface calls; and functions such as *CoInitialize*, *StringFromCLSID*, and *IsEqualGUID* that completely implement some useful or even vital functionality that does not create a component and is not a simple wrapper. We will see many examples of all of these functions in the chapters ahead, and as with interfaces, you'll generally use only a subset of them. Again, there's no reason to be terrified of all this technology. Each function and each interface has a specific purpose in life, and your paths need cross only when you share a common purpose.

# Summary

In OLE, a client deals with every object through one or more interface pointers. The most important question for a client is how it obtains its first pointer to any given object, which depends greatly on the way one identifies an object. In all cases, object classes are uniquely identified and will often use globally unique identifiers (GUIDs) that are also used for precisely identifying unique interfaces. These identifiers are generated with an algorithm that eliminates the chance of collision, and OLE provides various functions for both generating and manipulating these identifiers. In addition, there are rules for creating registry entries for a class identifier in which an object class can describe itself and its server.

Interfaces themselves, besides having a unique identity, are the channels of communication to an object. They are, in fact, the only way a client can know an object. Interfaces are defined as abstract base classes in C++ and as data structures in C. Interfaces can be defined in IDL. The standard return type for interface members is HRESULT, which is used in most cases but is not required. The HRESULT allows an interface member to return multiple success and error codes. Interfaces also have a number of important attributes: they are not classes or objects, but they are strongly typed groups of function signatures that an object must implement to communicate with clients. Interfaces are also immutable in that modifying an interface requires the assignment of a new unique identifier.

The most fundamental interface in OLE is *IUnknown*, which provides for reference counting and interface negotiation. Reference counting is the way a client controls an object's lifetime through the members *AddRef* and *Release*, where specific rules govern when these functions must be called and by whom. Interface negotiation is handled through the member *Query-Interface*, through which a client asks an object about its support for a feature by asking the object to return an interface pointer that represents the feature in question. Querying an object for such information solves versioning and compatibility problems, allowing for what is called "robust evolution of functionality over time."

An object's implementation is always encapsulated behind its interfaces, and when different object classes implement the same interface, those classes are polymorphic through that interface. If classes share a common set of interfaces, those classes are polymorphic through a larger prototype definition. In addition, individual interfaces that share common member functions are also polymorphic, and as all interfaces in OLE are derived from *IUnknown*, the *AddRef*, *Release*, and *QueryInterface* functions are ubiquitously available. The interface structure also supports two methods for achieving object reuse. These are called containment and aggregation. Aggregation is an optimization to containment in which one object can directly expose the interface pointer of another provided certain standard rules are followed. Overall, interfaces support the fundamental object-oriented notions of encapsulation, polymorphism, and reusability. Inheritance is a programming language–specific device for achieving the latter two, which is not practical in the domain of binary OLE components.

This chapter has explored these concepts in sample code and has also shown the need for clients and components to initialize the OLE libraries with *CoInitialize* or *OleInitialize*. It has shown how to work with OLE in both C and C++ through an exploration of OLE's standard task memory service and through the idea of enumerator objects. It has demonstrated three techniques for implementing an object with multiple interfaces and has illustrated how containment and aggregation work with reusable components.

## CHAPTER THREE

# Type Information

*SETTING THE CLOCK*
*Complete these steps to set the clock:*

1. *If the display does not show the clock, press F/C.*
2. *Press and hold down F/C.*
3. *While holding down F/C, turn TUNING counterclockwise until the display shows the correct hour.*
4. *While holding down F/C, turn TUNING clockwise until the display shows the correct minute.*
5. *When the display shows the correct time, press F/C.*

—Car stereo owner's manual

A few months ago, I finally decided to replace the broken radio/tape deck in my 1976 Datsun 610, as moving to a new house had lengthened my commute considerably. After a lot of scouting around, I found what I was looking for on one of those half-price discount tables in front of the local Radio Shack—you know, the ones with the unidentifiable bare circuit boards and the leftover firefighter's hats with the siren and the flashing red light. Anyway, I sorted through the box, and everything seemed to be there: the stereo, knobs, speaker cables, and so on. I took the radio/tape deck home and disassembled my car's dashboard (that's what you have to do with an old Datsun, which makes it damn hard for anyone to steal the stereo), and after the better part of a day I had it all in there and working. Installation was straightforward enough, and some of those electrical engineering classes I had in college seemed to pay off. The wiring "interface," if you will, was readily apparent, so I didn't bother to refer to the owner's manual.

It was only when I got around to setting the clock on this device that I discovered that I did not, in fact, have an owner's manual. I tried quite a number of button combinations, but nothing worked. Showing my lack of skill as a thorough tester, I gave up and returned to Radio Shack to get a manual. The sequence of steps required to set the clock had never occurred to me: my digital-electronics mindset told me that pressing buttons was the way to change a digital clock, rather than turning the seemingly analog (but really digital) knobs. Once I had the information, however, it seemed perfectly reasonable, and I was able to set the clock.

The point of this story is that in order to use the device properly, I needed something other than that device's own interfaces to tell me what I could do with it. The same is true of COM and OLE objects: given some arbitrary *IUnknown* pointer, there are limitations to what you can discover about an object. Just as I didn't want to spend the time articulating and attempting every possible combination of pressing buttons and turning knobs to set the time on my clock, clients generally do not want to spend the time querying an object for every possible interface just to figure out which interfaces exist. Such an operation is not exactly high performance. Furthermore, merely being told that an object has an interface doesn't tell you much about how to make calls to the interface; for example, knowing a specific function's offset in the interface vtable and what types of arguments it takes (the stack it expects) is not enough information to be able to reliably call the function. Knowing that there is an interface is about as informative as knowing that setting the clock involves one of the buttons and one of the knobs. It would have helped a little, but not completely. I really needed the owner's manual.

The rough analog of an owner's manual for an object is *type information.* An owner's manual tells me how to do something once I know that I want to do it—that is, it tells me how to carry out my intentions. In the same fashion, type information contains the necessary information about objects and their interfaces—for example, what interfaces exist on what objects (given the CLSID), what member functions exist in those interfaces, and what arguments those functions require. Type information can also describe custom types such as C-style data structures, unions, and enumerations, as well as noninterface functions that are exported from a DLL module. In fact, whatever you can store in header files (H), import libraries (LIB files for linking to DLL exported functions), and indexes to help files (HLP), you can store and retrieve through type information.

Type information, however, does not tell a client why it would want to look at an object's interfaces or call member functions, nor does it say when such things should take place. My car stereo owner's manual, in the same way, doesn't tell me why I want to set the clock or when I should do it; it only says how. With my car stereo and components alike, the *intent* of using that information exists externally, usually in the head of some human. With our current computer sophistication, only portions of that intent can be incorporated into running client code. Therefore, type information is most useful when a human can browse it and tell some client when to use which object and what member function, and what to pass those member functions. In other words, in our current technology it generally takes a human to interpret what the information means and why and when it's useful. We'll leave it to the artificial intelligence community to figure out how to get a computer to do the same.

In the meantime, plenty of useful things can happen with type information that involve interactive development tools: a developer can browse available objects, look at their interfaces and member functions, and potentially do point-and-click programming rather than text-based coding. But type information is not just for browsing: any compiler can use the information just as it would use a header file (even precompiled) or an import library, in the same way any interpreted or otherwise late-bound programming environment can.

In this chapter, we'll look at what type information is, what it can contain, and the basics of how you work with it, both in creation and in manipulation. Type information is an OLE-provided and OLE-implemented service involving a number of API functions that create and load the information as well as a number of interfaces through which you store and retrieve information. We introduced a few of these—such as *ITypeLib* and *ITypeInfo*—in Chapter 1. Here we'll explore them in more detail, although we won't actually see them used in code until later chapters, which cover topics for which type information is necessary. Hence this short chapter contains no samples.

OK, this sounds great, but you're likely not in the business of creating development tools, right? So why am I bothering to tell you about this stuff? Why is it so important that I put it here at the front of this book, in Chapter 3, without any samples? There are two reasons.

First, type information has been considered part of OLE Automation for a long time. Some have called it the essence of Automation. It was, in fact, invented out of sheer necessity for Automation's purposes. However, the technology itself has begun to assume a wider and more general role in the whole of OLE and thus has many uses entirely outside of Automation. Type information is now used heavily in a number of other important OLE technologies—for example, Connectable Objects and OLE Controls. Because type information is used so widely and can be used with any other OLE technologies (although it's not required with others as it is with Automation), what we learn here will enable us to talk about "an object's type information" in later chapters with a full understanding of what it means. I'd rather not break up our discussions about other technologies with distracting excursions into details of type information. Rather than spreading the details throughout this book, I've centralized the information here, even though some parts of it won't mean much until we look at them in context with the OLE technologies that care.

Second, because you can store so much rich type information, the technology involved will become vitally important in the next generation of development tools that are centered on the creation of applications from components rather than from source code. These tools will depend on an object's type information to show the developer what an object can do and what you might be able to connect with it. Rather than the tools having to try to read basically unstructured header files and help files, they'll use type information, which is stored in a structured, language-independent repository and is accessed through various OLE-implemented objects and their interfaces. Thus, the tools don't need to have language-specific parsers and can use other components written in any language.

When applications can be created with components instead of code, I personally believe that we'll see many more opportunities for growth in the computer industry, perhaps even a significant area of tools that enable end users to effectively "program" their own custom applications and solutions, although the users won't call it programming — they'll call it fun. But component integration tools cannot happen if components are as mysterious as the clock setting feature on my car stereo. Type information is how you publish your owner's manual.

## Does an Object Need Type Information?

Short answer: maybe, maybe not.

Long answer: whether or not an object or component requires type information depends on how it expects clients to use the information. In cases such as objects that support OLE Automation or the OLE Controls specification, the client will expect type information to be available. In fact, these are the only two *documented* and *required* uses for type information at the time of writing. However, many possibilities for additional uses outside of standard Automation or Controls scenarios have yet to be articulated. Said another way, in some cases aspects of Automation — that is, the *IDispatch* interface and the idea of late binding to methods and properties through a dispatch identifier — are useful in and of themselves without being oriented toward end-user, cross-application macro programming. In certain cases, event sets, which involve the use of the Connectable Objects technology, are useful without an OLE control lying around. It's just that today we lack development tools or other sorts of generic clients for these objects that will take advantage of such features and the mere presence of type information, regardless of whatever else the object happens to do.

As I pointed out in this book's introduction, there is an interdependent relationship between the tools available to work with objects and the general expectations of what those objects provide. An increase on one side usually leads to an increase of features on the other. No tools that really exploit type information will appear until there are sufficient objects that provide it, but objects may not provide it until there are sufficient tools to exploit it. I'm saying that you should consider the future of the components (or tools) that you put together because providing (or browsing or exploiting) type information now, which isn't very difficult to do, empowers future clients or components to achieve a higher level of integration than is available today.

It's really your choice: do you want to meet minimum requirements today or set yourself up for new possibilities in the future? Your own development cycle may ultimately determine this. You simply need to understand that although you hardly ever have to provide type information, it will become more and more useful to do so. It's worth a little time now to understand what it is and how it's used, because it will come up in other chapters of this book. And who knows? You may find a new and innovative use for this stuff and open up a new branch of the industry.

Maybe, maybe not.[1]

## The Type Library

As a single owner's manual is a book, a collection of books is called a *library*. In OLE, a collection of the type information for any number of *elements* (objects, interfaces, and so forth) is called a *type library*. OLE's type information service is really a service for creating and manipulating information that is contained in a type library. The library itself has only a little bit of its own information— it is primarily concerned with storage and retrieval of type information for the elements within it. So for the most part, the type library acts as a librarian, meaning that you, like a client or user of any library, can ask it to locate the type information for some element of interest.

A type library is nothing more than a collection of static data structures for each element within it, and those structures contain additional nested structures to describe their contents. In this sense, the library itself is not an "object," as it doesn't have any inherent functionality. OLE provides the wrapper objects—its type library service with appropriate interfaces—to let you work with these underlying structures without having to know the exact structures themselves. Because interfaces are language-independent constructs, OLE's services here are usable from any client and can be used to describe

---

1. My lunchtime reading of Robert Fulghum's book with this title has, I believe, influenced my writing here (maybe).

any object, regardless of implementation. As I mentioned before, type information is a language-independent and structured way to combine the contents of header files, help files, and import libraries.

In this section, we'll first look briefly at the types of elements that can go into a type library and the attributes that can exist for those elements. In the following section, we'll see how to create a type library. For most of us, this will involve writing a script in ODL, the Object Description Language, and running that script through a compiler called MKTYPLIB.EXE. But this is just a convenient tool: OLE actually provides a more fundamental creation service that we'll look at first. After we know how to create a library, which invariably creates a disk file containing the binary data structures, we can see how to register its location and how to load it. Once it's loaded, we can then look into the details about retrieving the information within the library.

## Type Library Elements

If you walk around a "real-life" library, you'll usually see books of many shapes and sizes that deal with a wide range of topics. That's what you'd expect for the almost limitless domain of human knowledge. Fortunately, a *type* library is somewhat simpler (reflecting the limited domain of component information). Any element in a type library falls into one of the five categories described in Table 3-1.

| Element | Purpose |
| --- | --- |
| *coclass* | Describes the interfaces and dispinterfaces implemented on a particular object (identified by a CLSID). |
| *interface* | Describes a vtable interface (identified by an IID): specifically, the names of member functions, the return types of those functions, and the names and types of the arguments to those functions. |
| *dispinterface* | Describes a dispatch interface (identified by an IID) used by OLE Automation: specifically, the names, dispIDs, and types of the methods and properties (including return types and argument names and types for methods in the interface). |
| *module* | Describes a DLL module (identified by a DLL filename), including names and ordinals for exported functions and global variables. |

**Table 3-1.** *(continued)*

*The kinds of elements in a type library.*

**Table 3-1.** *continued*

| Element | Purpose |
|---------|---------|
| *typedef* | Describes a user-defined data structure, enumeration, or union (identified by a name or an optional GUID). |

Dealing with type information is in large part finding the element you want and working with the specific information in that element. This varies, of course, from element to element.

## Type Library and Element Attributes

When we combine the data structures and elements stored in a type library and encapsulate those structures behind particular interfaces, we can refer to the library and each element in it as "objects." In doing so we raise the question of what sorts of properties these objects have.

The properties of a type library or an element are called *attributes.* The attributes that apply to the library and most of its elements are described in Table 3-2. Many of the attributes for elements are described through the bits in the *Flags* attribute.

| Attribute | Description |
|-----------|-------------|
| *Name* | The descriptive name of the type library or element without spaces or punctuation, as in *KoalaTypeLibrary*, *KoalaObject*, or *IKoala*. Every element has a name. |
| *Guid* (or *Uuid*) | A programmatic identifier for the library or element. A library GUID is different from other CLSIDs or IIDs. A *module* cannot have a GUID; it is optional for a *typedef*; it is required for all other elements. |
| *Version* | The major and minor version of the library or element. |
| *DocString* | A short piece of text describing the purpose of the library or element. |
| *HelpFileName* | The name of a help file (no path) that contains further information about all the contents of the library. There is only one help file per library, so this attribute applies only to a library and not to individual elements. |

**Table 3-2.**

*Attributes of a type library and its elements.*

*(continued)*

**Table 3-2.** *continued*

| Attribute | Description |
| --- | --- |
| *HelpContext* | The context ID inside *HelpFileName*, where specific information is found for library or element. |
| *Lcid* | A locale identifier, or *locale,* that describes the single national language used for all text strings in the type library and elements. A type library is intended to be written for a specific national language, with the exception that individual function arguments can be given a locale for the purpose of accommodating functions that might perform translations. |
| *Flags* | Bits specifying additional aspects about the library or element. Although there are many element flags, a library has only a few possibilities: no flags at all, *hidden* (not browsable through user interface), or *restricted* (controlled programmatically for security). |

You can see that the *HelpString, HelpFileName,* and *HelpContext* attributes carry help information along with a type library, but not *all* of the help information. The idea is that a user can view any element in some sort of browser and quickly get a description of its purpose from the *HelpString* attribute. If the *HelpFileName* attribute is available, the browser would also provide a Help button that, when pressed, would launch WinHelp with the *HelpContext* value to show more information about the library or element.

The *Lcid* attribute deserves some more discussion. This is usually found only on a library, but it can appear on function arguments as well. As you might expect, a type library, like an owner's manual, will contain text in a specific written language, such as English, Russian, or Arabic. This language applies to everything in the library except specific function arguments. The intention is that you support multiple languages by providing multiple localized type libraries, each of which can coexist on the same machine and can share the same GUID. Registry entries differentiate these localizations.

The *Lcid* attribute is a value of the type LCID, for *locale identifier,* which was originally created by the Unicode Consortium. Such an identifier forms the basis for all localization or globalization or internationalization or whateveryouwanttocallittodayization not only of type information but of all other language-sensitive parts of the Win32 API. As part of supporting Unicode, the Win32 API took in the LCID as part of its National Language Support (NLS) API, and OLE uses that part of the operating system to handle its own language concerns.[2]

Simply said, an LCID, or "locale," as it's called for convenience, is nothing more than a 32-bit value whose lower 16 bits contain a "language identifier," or LANGID:

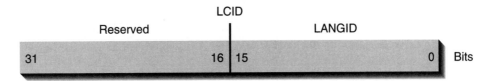

The Win32 macro MAKELCID will create one of these 32-bit values from a 16-bit LANGID through a bitwise OR with a 32-bit zero value. The LANGID itself contains a primary-language value and a sub-language value. The primary language (the lower 10 bits) identifies a generic category of languages, such as English, in which the sub-language (the upper 6 bits) identifies variations of the primary language such as American, British, Australian, Irish, New Zealand, and Canadian English:

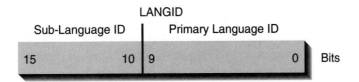

A caution: it is *very* easy to mistakenly think of the primary and sub-language fields in a LANGID as being both 8 bits because that's how we intuitively think about bits. This can get you into a lot of trouble and confusion, so take a few well-invested moments to study the 10-bit/6-bit structure of this type.

---

2. The NLS API is documented in the *Win32 Programmer's Reference*, volumes 2 and 5, particularly Appendix C of volume 2. (Note that the "String Manipulation and Unicode" chapter in volume 2 refers to Appendix C of volume 5, but this is incorrect: Appendix C is actually in volume 2.) These API functions allow you to retrieve the current user's locale identifier as well as locale-specific information.

Enough with the meditation. There are a number of macros to assist you in creating or decomposing a LANGID given values for the primary language and the sub-language:

| | |
|---|---|
| MAKELANGID(*primary, sub*) | Creates a LANGID |
| PRIMARYLANGID(*langID*) | Extracts the primary language value |
| SUBLANGID(*langID*) | Extracts the sub-language value |
| LANGIDFROMLCID(*lcid*) | Chops off the upper 16 bits of *lcid* |

The OLE and Win32 header files define constants of the form *LANG_<primarylang>* for all known primary languages as well as symbols of the form *SUBLANG_<sublang>* for all variations of the primary languages. So you can specify primary languages from Albanian to Catalan to Rhaeto-Romanic to Urdu,[3] and sub-languages from Simplified Chinese to Brazilian Portuguese to Mexican or Modern Spanish. The header files have the most up-to-date list of language IDs, more current than any documentation.

Some of the more common LANGIDs you'll see are 0x0409 for American English (English primary language 9, American sub-language 1), 0x0009 for basic English, and 0x0000 for "neutral." The neutral language is generally the one used at the programming level and not the user interface level, and so it is typically English.

For the most part, you'll localize to primary languages, taking considerations about specific regions into account much less frequently. Specifying a sub-language is usually necessary only when you need to use words like "wrench," "semitrailer," and "cookie" in American English, which translate to "spanner," "lorry," and "biscuit" in British English.

This is not meant to be an exhaustive study of language and locale identifiers, just enough of one to make you aware of them and what they contain, because they apply to type information. Locales will come into play again when we talk about OLE Automation in Chapters 14 and 15. If you're interested in learning more about locales, please refer to the OLE and Win32 programmer's references as well as *Developing International Software for Windows 95 and Windows NT,* by Nadine Kano.

---

3. OK, OK, so I picked the lesser-known languages from the list. (Urdu is actually last alphabetically.) Catalan is a Romance language used in Catalonia, Valencia, and the Balearic islands, all eastern regions of Spain (around Barcelona), as well as Andorra, the tiny country wedged between Spain and France. Rhaeto-Romanic is a Romance language of eastern Switzerland, northeastern Italy, and the adjacent parts of Austria. Urdu is an Indic language that is widely used in India and is an official literary language of Pakistan.

# The Type Library That Jack Built

You may or may not be familiar with one of the hundreds of variations of the children's poem called "The House That Jack Built," which goes something like this:

> *This is Jack.*
> *This is the house that Jack built.*
> *This is the kitchen in the house that Jack built.*
> *This is the wall in the kitchen in the house that Jack built.*
> *This is the hole in the wall in the kitchen in the house that Jack built.*
> *This is the mouse that made the hole in the wall in the kitchen in the house that Jack built.*

And so on. The fun of this particular poem for English-speaking children (and some of us adults) is that you can keep adding more and more nouns and prepositional phrases as long as you can remember the whole chain. Our concern for type libraries is similar because we need to describe a library, an interface in that library, a member function in the interface in the library, and an argument of that member function in the interface in the library.

Fortunately, OLE provides a type library creation service, or component, that you can use to describe such fine details about an object and its interfaces. Whenever you want to create type information for any purpose, you'll use this creation service in some capacity. The hard way to use the service is directly through OLE's implementation of certain interfaces. The easy way is to use an ODL script and let the MKTYPLIB compiler worry about the hard way. The following two sections describe both processes: The first will be more important to readers involved with creating OLE tools. The second will be more important to most of us, who simply want to create type information with as few hassles as possible.

## The Hard Way: *CreateTypeLib*

In Chapter 2, we learned how the provider of a component gives access to the objects and interfaces of that component through one of four mechanisms, such as a specific API function that creates one type of component and gives you back one type of interface. This is exactly the means through which OLE exposes its type library creation service.

The API function of interest here is *CreateTypeLib*, which has the arguments you see at the top of the following page.

| Argument | Description |
|---|---|
| *syskind* | A value from the SYSKIND enumeration to describe the target operating system, such as SYS_WIN16, SYS_WIN32, or SYS_MAC. |
| *szFile* | *OLECHAR* *, which provides the name of the disk file in which OLE stores the type library data structures. Type library files conventionally use TLB for the extension. |
| *ppCTLib* | *ICreateTypeLib* *, in which the function returns the interface pointer representing the new type library. |

*CreateTypeLib* doesn't really do much more than create a disk file with one top-level data structure, which happens to be empty. At this point you have, in terms of the children's poem, a vacant lot. You have a place to put the house—the type information—but there isn't anything there but rocks, weeds, and crummy fill dirt.

Building something in that vacant lot is the purpose of the *ICreateTypeLib* pointer you get back from calling *CreateTypeLib*. The member functions of this interface, described in Table 3-3, deal mostly with setting the library's attributes that we saw earlier—that is, building the basic shell of a house. As with any pointer you obtain for any object, you must call *Release* when you're finished with the type library.

| Member Function | Description |
|---|---|
| *SetName, SetGuid, SetVersion, SetLcid, SetLibFlags* | Assigns the name, GUID, version numbers, locale, and flags to a type library. |
| *SetDocString, SetHelpFileName, SetHelpContext* | Assigns help-related attributes to a type library. |
| *SaveAllChanges* | Commits all changes made to the type library (to any element within it) to the disk file. If this is not called before *Release*, the changes are lost. |
| *CreateTypeInfo* | Creates an element in the type library and returns an *ICreateTypeInfo* pointer through which that element is constructed. |

**Table 3-3.**
*Member functions of the* ICreateTypeLib *interface.*

The two functions in the interface that don't have to do with attributes—*CreateTypeInfo* and *SaveAllChanges*—are the most critical. Everything you do to the library before calling *SaveAllChanges* is the same as drawing an architectural blueprint and planning everything else that should go in a house, but the house exists only on paper. Calling *SaveAllChanges* is similar to taking those plans and giving them to a builder who will actually create something tangible. In the case of a type library, it means writing everything to disk.

*ICreateTypeLib::CreateTypeInfo* is what you use to create a *coclass, interface, dispinterface, module,* or *typedef* (*struct, union, enum*) element in the library. The type of element is identified with a value from the enumeration TYPEKIND, which can be TKIND_ALIAS (a simple *typedef* to name a new type), TKIND_COCLASS, TKIND_DISPATCH (*dispinterface*), TKIND_ENUM (*typedef enum*), TKIND_INTERFACE, TKIND_MODULE, TKIND_RECORD (*typedef struct*), and TKIND_UNION (*typedef union*). Along with the type identifier, this function also takes a name attribute (text string) for the new element.[4] *CreateTypeInfo* then returns an *ICreateTypeInfo* pointer.

The member functions of *ICreateTypeInfo* described in Table 3-4 allow you to build the rooms, the walls, and the mouse holes in your house.

| Member Function | Description |
|---|---|
| *SetGuid, SetVersion* | Assigns a GUID or version to the element. |
| *SetDocString, SetHelpContext* | Assigns help-related attributes to the element. |
| *SetTypeDescAlias* | Creates an alias for a type (a simple *typedef*). |
| *SetAlignment* | Specifies byte alignment for a data structure. |
| *DefineFuncAsDllEntry* | Defines an exported DLL function by name or by ordinal; applicable only to module elements. |
| *SetTypeFlags* | Sets additional flags for *coclass* elements, such as whether or not a *coclass* element is licensed, instantiable, or restricted from browsing. |

**Table 3-4.** *(continued)*
*Member functions of the* ICreateTypeInfo *interface.*

---

4. This is only a convenience for coclass, interface, and dispinterface elements, but necessary for typedefs and modules. The former three are programmatically identified with a GUID, which is optional for a typedef but not allowed on a module.

**Table 3-4.** *continued*

| Member Function | Description |
| --- | --- |
| *AddImplType,* *SetImplTypeFlags* | Creates information about the interfaces in a *coclass* element. *AddImplType* adds the description of the interface; *SetImplTypeFlags* assigns default, source, and restricted attributes to those interfaces. Both require information returned from *AddRefTypeInfo.* |
| *AddRefTypeInfo* | Creates an HREFTYPE that refers to a *coclass* and is necessary for calling *AddImplType* to add interfaces and dispinterfaces to a *coclass* description. This function requires an *ITypeInfo* pointer, which is obtained by calling *ICreateTypeInfo::QueryInterface.* |
| *AddFuncDesc,* *SetFuncAndParamNames,* *SetFuncDocString,* *SetFuncHelpContext* | Creates information about a member function in interface or dispinterface elements only. *AddFuncDesc* takes a pointer to a FUNCDESC structure, which contains the identifier, calling convention, return type, argument types, and permitted return codes. *SetFuncParamsAndNames* assigns names to the function and its arguments. *SetFuncDocString* and *SetFuncHelpContext* save help attributes for a function. With all of these functions you identify the member function in question by a common index. |
| *AddVarDesc, SetVarName,* *SetVarDocString,* *SetVarHelpContext* | Creates information about a global variable description to a module or a property to a dispinterface. *AddVarDesc* adds a variable through the VARDESC structure. The other functions set the variable's name and help information. |
| *SetTypeIdlDesc, SetMops* | Defines cross-process marshaling information for an interface or dispinterface. |
| *LayOut* | Assigns vtable positions for an interface element, dispatch identifiers for methods and properties in a dispinterface element, and offsets for exported global variables from a module element. This function should only be called for an element after all other information is stored and just before calling *ICreateTypeLib::SaveAllChanges.* |
| *SetSchema* | Reserved. |

The overall process of creating a type library is illustrated in Figure 3-1. The illustration shows the steps of creating the library, then creating the elements within it (you can create as many elements of each type as desired), and then saving the changes on disk through *ICreateTypeLib::SaveAllChanges*.

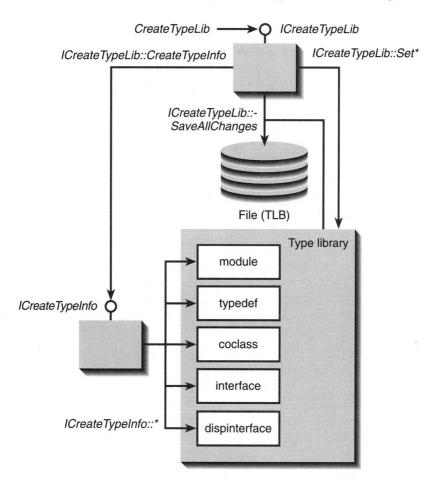

**Figure 3-1.**
*The type library creation process.*

You can see that through *ICreateTypeLib* and *ICreateTypeInfo* you can create whatever type information structures you want. These interfaces and OLE's direct type library creation service are useful mostly for development tools, but some applications or other components may find these functions useful for creating some type information on the fly. The whole process, however, is somewhat involved, and this book will not get into any other details. For more information about these functions, see the *OLE Programmer's Reference*.

> **NOTE:** You might encounter references to some data structures called INTERFACEDATA, PARAMDATA, and METHODDATA, which are an archaic way to create type information for a single dispinterface that existed before OLE's type library services were complete. Ignore these structures: they are obsolete.

## The Easy Way: MKTYPLIB and the Object Description Language

If you think about the amount of information you might want to describe for, say, one object and four interfaces, with each interface having about six member functions, you can quickly see that calling *ICreateTypeLib* and *ICreate-TypeInfo* functions directly would get tedious beyond human patience. You can also see that much of what goes into a type library is similar to what you'd put in a header file. You would figure it makes sense to have some sort of tool that would parse headerlike information and call the appropriate interfaces and member functions internally to create type information out of that header. Just such a tool exists: MKTYPLIB.EXE—literally, "Make Type Library." This small compiler is more or less a C++ preprocessor that uses a file written in ODL as input. The parser recognizes ODL keywords and syntax and in turn calls *CreateTypeLib* and the other interfaces' member functions to turn the ODL information into a real type library. MKTYPLIB can also create a C/C++ header file containing interface and GUID definitions to simplify your implementation of the interfaces and classes defined in the library. This is quite convenient, and we'll see examples of this in later chapters.

To ship type information with an object, you can either ship the type library file stand-alone, integrate it into the resources of an EXE or a DLL, or place it inside a compound file. In a later section, we'll look at deployment and use of a type library. First, however, let's look at the format of an ODL file in more detail.

The keywords you can use and the syntax of an ODL file allow you to basically describe any structures, interfaces, dispinterfaces, modules, and objects that you want, using whatever types you want. An ODL file is simply a text file that has the following general syntax structure, in which keywords are indicated with boldface:

```
[uuid(<GUID>), <helpinfo>, <attributes>]
library <name>
    {
    importlib(<path to another type library>)
```

```
typedef [<attributes>] <basename | struct | enum | union>
    {
    ⋮
    } <type>;

[attributes] module <name>
    {
    <element list>
    };

[uuid(<GUID>), <helpinfo>, <attributes>]
interface <name>
    {
    [<attributes>] <return type> [calling convention]
        <function name>(<arguments>);
    ⋮
    }

[uuid(<GUID>), <helpinfo>, <attributes>]
dispinterface <name>
    {
    Properties:
        [<attributes>] <type> <name>;
        ⋮
    Methods:
        [<attributes>] <return type> <name>(<arguments>);
        ⋮
    }

[uuid(<GUID>), <helpinfo>, <attributes>]
dispinterface <name>
    {
    interface <name>;
    }

[uuid(<GUID>), <helpinfo>, <attributes>]
coclass
    {
    [<attributes>] dispinterface  <dispinterface name>;
    ⋮
    [<attributes>] interface      <interface name>;
    }
};
```

Although the *OLE Programmer's Reference* has a complete description of ODL (it's too lengthy to repeat here), let's nonetheless take a look at this structure and point out the most important concepts.

You define the type library with the *library* keyword, assigning to it a LIBID (a GUID, the *uuid*), help information such as a descriptive string, and other attributes, all of which are specified between the square brackets preceding *library*. The *attributes* can include version information, the library LCID, and whether the entire library is hidden or restricted.

The body of a type library is contained between the braces following the *library* statement and can contain any number of each of the statements listed in Table 3-5. The most interesting statements to us so far are *coclass* and *interface*

## Head-Banging MKTYPLIB Errors

MKTYPLIB is not necessarily the friendliest tool in the world, and the error messages that it generates can be the epitome of ambiguity. Here are a few I've seen:

First, it might complain, "Error generating type library: MKTYP-LIB cannot preprocess the file." This is provoked either by a failure to find STDOLE.TLB as referenced in your *importlib* statement or by a failure to find CL.EXE, the C-compiler preprocessor, both of which have to be on your path. To avoid the preprocessing step, you can use the /nocpp switch to bypass it without consequence.

The second strange error message is MKTYPLIB complaining of "unknown types," especially about things like *boolean* and BSTR which are definitely known types. This problem is caused by mismatched OLE DLLs on your system—MKTYPLIB uses the OLE DLLs themselves, where the implementation of *CreateTypeLib* and *ICreateType[Lib | Info]* are found. If, for example, you have debug OLE DLLs in your path, you'll end up with an OLENLS.DLL that is not enabled for DBCS characters and ends up for a variety of reasons making types line *BSTR* unrecognizable.

Finally, you need to be very careful when creating a dispinterface or one marked as *oleautomation* (automation compatible). MKTYPLIB itself can accept any type you want to put in an interface, including your own *structs*, *enums*, and *unions*. However, as we've seen, these are not accepted in an automation-compatible interface which includes by design any dispinterface. Furthermore, *unsigned* is not accepted for automation-compatible interfaces, although you can use it anywhere else. The inconsistencies that arise from not understanding what automation compatible means can really drive you batty.

(and *dispinterface*). Through these statements, you describe the core of an object: its interfaces and the methods and properties of those interfaces. All of the *<type>* entries shown earlier can be a predefined standard type such as *int, long, double,* or *char* or any user-defined type created with a *typedef* statement.

| Statement | Description |
|---|---|
| *importlib* | Brings in all the information contained in another type library and makes it part of this library. The statement requires the filename of the TLB file. If a full pathname is not specified, this statement looks for the file in directories specified by the system path. All ODL files must have the statement *importlib* ("STDOLE.TLB") to pull in standard types. |
| *coclass* | Describes a component class in which *uuid* is the object's CLSID. The object can have any number of interfaces and dispinterfaces listed in its body, specifying the full set of interfaces that the object implements, both incoming and outgoing. |
| *interface* | Describes a vtable interface with the given name in which the body contains only member functions as in any other interface declaration. The *uuid* attribute is the IID. |
| *dispinterface* | Describes a dispinterface with the given name in which the body contains the list of properties and methods; properties are listed as data members in a C++ class and methods as C++ member functions. An alternative syntax can be used to distinguish a dispinterface from a vtable interface. The *uuid* attribute is the IID. |
| *typedef* | Defines a new type as an alias for an existing type or as a *struct, enum,* or *union.* The syntax is identical to the C *typedef* syntax. To be included in the final type library, a *typedef* must have at least one attribute, the most common of which is *public,* making it a public type. All *typedefs* can also have help information, a UUID, and a version number. |
| *module* | Describes exported functions and constants from a DLL just like an import library (LIB), which can be used for linking without an import library at all. |

**Table 3-5.**
*Statements that can appear in a type library.*

**The *coclass* statement**   If you'll remember back to Chapter 2, there was the question about why *IUnknown* didn't have a way to ask an object to enumerate all of its incoming interfaces short of calling *QueryInterface* for everything you knew. The answer was type information, and the *coclass* statement provides just such a listing of the interfaces an object supports. The object itself is identified with its CLSID, given in the *uuid* attribute. A client that knows this CLSID can look through the type information, with or without instantiating the object, to easily determine an object's full set of incoming and outgoing interfaces. Without type information, *QueryInterface* is the only way to learn about the incoming interfaces; *IConnectionPointContainer::EnumConnection-Points* is the only way to know an object's outgoing interfaces, and then you have to make sense of the enumerated IIDs for which you need type information anyway.

One very important attribute for *coclass* is called *licensed*. This attribute identifies the object's server as supporting an interface named *IClassFactory2*, which means the object (component) is licensed. This makes a difference with respect to how an object of the class must be instantiated, as we'll see in Chapter 5.

Each interface or dispinterface listed in a *coclass* can have only two optional attributes: *default* and *source*. If an interface or dispinterface is marked *source*, it is an outgoing interface; otherwise, it's an incoming interface. The default attribute can be used for one incoming and one outgoing interface or dispinterface. The default incoming interface is the primary interface for the object. If the interface is a dispinterface, a client can obtain its pointer with *QueryInterface(IID_IDispatch)*; all other dispinterfaces must be queried for by using their specific IIDs. The default source interface is called the primary event set for the object, but the object can have any number of event sets or other outgoing interfaces. Marking interfaces and dispinterfaces as *default* makes it convenient for a client to locate the object's most important interfaces.

**The *interface* statement**   If you want to describe a vtable interface, such as *IUnknown*, the *interface* statement lets you list all the member functions of that interface with the syntax shown earlier. Each function has optional attributes, a return type, an optional calling convention (*cdecl*, *pascal*, or *stdcall*, with or without a leading _ or __ ), the name of the member function, and its list of arguments, which can be *void* or any sequence of *[attributes]* *<type>* *<name>* entries separated by a comma. Yes, this is pretty rich stuff.

The attributes you can specify on an *interface* include its IID, help information, version information, whether it is *hidden* or *restricted,* whether the interface is what is called a *dual* interface in OLE Automation, and whether the interface uses only *oleautomation*-compatible argument types (which are restricted, as we'll see in Chapter 14). You must also always include the *odl* attribute on every *interface* to distinguish it from an IDL definition.[5] The attributes on each function in the interface include whether the function is a property get, property put, or property put-by-reference operation (*propget, propput, propputref*); whether it has variable arguments; and whether it is *hidden*. A leading underscore on a member name, as in *_NewEnum*, is equivalent to including the *hidden* attribute. In addition, the *id(xx)* attribute assigns some identifier to the member (useful for OLE Automation, especially dual interfaces). Finally, arguments themselves each have attributes such as *in, out,* and *optional,* which specify the behavior of the argument.

**The *dispinterface* statement**   You might have noticed that *dispinterface* has two forms. The first form allows you to describe methods and properties as if you were declaring a C++ class, using the keywords *Properties* or *Methods* as you would use *public* or *private*. Each property can have an *id* attribute to specify its dispatch identifier (dispID) as well as help information, whether it's *hidden,* and whether this particular property is *read-only*. Each method and argument can have the same attributes as *interface*.

The second form of the *dispinterface* statement basically picks up the functions in some interface and makes a dispinterface out of it. Whichever members in the interface had *propget, propput,* or *propputref* on them become properties in the dispinterface; other members become methods. In all cases, any *id* in the *interface* is preserved.

Having two forms for *dispinterface* was necessary before the idea of dual interfaces became available. Dual interfaces are now recommended over the definition of a dispinterface from an interface. We'll see dual interfaces in Chapter 14.

---

5. The Interface Definition Language is used to describe interfaces for marshaling purposes as we'll see in Chapter 6. ODL and IDL are very similar and have their differences, but Microsoft is currently looking at ways to merge the two. Interface descriptions in ODL without the *odl* will simply fail to compile.

The previous discussion of the most important ODL statements mentioned a fair number of attributes, but not all of them. The complete list as of the time of writing this chapter appears in Table 3-6. Entries marked with an asterisk (*) are available under Win16 with OLE 2.02 or later, and those marked with a double asterisk (**) are available only under Win16 if you have the MKTYPLIB.EXE file from the OLE Custom Controls Development Kit. Because not all of these attributes can be used with every statement or other field in an ODL file, the allowable uses of each attribute are cross-referenced in Figure 3-2 on page 168.

| Attribute | Description |
|-----------|-------------|
| *appobject* | Identifies a *coclass* as an *application object*, which is associated with a full EXE application. |
| *bindable*** | Identifies a property as supporting data binding through the *IPropertyNotifySink::OnChanged* function. |
| *control*** | Identifies a *coclass* as an OLE control. |
| *default*** | Specifies a default incoming or outgoing interface in a *coclass*. |
| *defaultbind*** | Identifies a *bindable* property that best represents the object as a whole. |
| *displaybind*** | Indicates that the binding capability of a property can be displayed in the user interface of a controller. |
| *dllname* | Identifies the name of the DLL described in a module. |
| *dual** | Marks an interface as a dual interface. |
| *entry* | Specifies an exported function or constant in a module. |
| *helpcontext* | Specifies a context ID within a help file that can be used to view information about this element. |
| *helpfile* | Specifies the filename (no path) of the help file that contains information about this element. Your installation program must save the path of the help file in the registry under TypeLib\HELPDIR; you do not want to hard code such paths into your type library. |
| *helpstring* | Contains a short description of the element, usually suitable for a status line or a similar user interface. |
| *hidden** | Indicates that the element should never be displayed in a browser in a programming environment. |
| *id* | Assigns a DISPID to a function, method, or property. |

**Table 3-6.**     *(continued)*
*Listing of ODL attributes.*

**Table 3-6.** *continued*

| Attribute | Description |
|---|---|
| *in* | Identifies an argument as an in-parameter. |
| *lcid* | Identifies the locale for a library or an argument. |
| *licensed* * * | Indicates that a *coclass* must be instantiated using *IClassFactory2*. |
| *nonextensible* * | Indicates that an interface or dispinterface includes only those methods and properties listed and cannot be extended with additional members at run time. |
| *odl* | Required for all *interface* statements to identify the description as an ODL description as opposed to IDL. |
| *oleautomation* * | Indicates that the interface or dispinterface is OLE Automation compatible. |
| *optional* | Marks an argument as optional. |
| *out* | Marks an argument as an out-parameter. |
| *propget* | Used in an interface to indicate that the named function performs a property get on a property of the same name. |
| *propput* | Used in an interface to indicate that the named function performs a property put on a property of the same name. |
| *propputref* | Same as *propput* but indicates that the put value can be passed by reference. |
| *public* | Includes a *typedef* in the type library so it can be browsed later; otherwise, treats it as a *#define*. |
| *readonly* | Marks a property as read-only. |
| *requestedit* * * | Identifies a property that will send *IPropertyNotifySink::OnRequestEdit* before changing. |
| *restricted* | Indicates that a library or members in a module or interface or dispinterface cannot be called from arbitrary clients. Usually this means that some other form of access is required to call the function. |
| *retval* * | Marks a parameter in a dual interface as the actual return value for a method when the method returns HRESULT. |
| *source* * * | Indicates that an interface or dispinterface listed in a *coclass* is outgoing. |
| *string* | Declares a string for compatibility with IDL. |
| *uuid* | Assigns a GUID to the element. |
| *vararg* | Indicates that the function takes variable arguments. |
| *version* | Specifies a version number for the element. |

| Attribute | library | importlib | typedef | module | module members | interface | dispinterface | property | method | arguments | coclass | interface in coclass | dispinterface in coclass |
|---|---|---|---|---|---|---|---|---|---|---|---|---|---|
| appobject | | | | | | | | | | | y | | |
| bindable** | | | | | | | | y | | | | | |
| control** | y | | | | | | | | | | y | | |
| default** | | | | | | | | | | | | y | y |
| defaultbind** | | | | | | | | y | | | | | |
| displaybind** | | | | | | | | y | | | | | |
| dllname | | | | y | | | | | | | | | |
| dual* | | | | | | y | | | | | | | |
| entry | | | | | y | | | | | | | | |
| helpcontext | y | y | y | y | | y | y | y | y | | y | | |
| helpfile | y | y | y | y | | y | y | y | y | | y | | |
| helpstring | y | y | y | y | | y | y | y | y | | y | | |
| hidden* | y | | | | | y | y | y | y | | y | | |
| id | | | | | | | | d | y | | | | |
| in | | | | | | | | | | y | | | |
| lcid | y | | | | | | | | | y* | | | |
| licensed* | | | | | | | | | | | y | | |
| nonextensible* | | | | | | y | y | | | | | | |
| odl | | | | | | r | | | | | | | |
| oleautomation* | | | | | | y | y | | | | | | |
| optional | | | | | | | | | | y | | | |
| out | | | | | | | | | | y | | | |
| propget | | | | | | | | | y | | | | |
| propput | | | | | | | | | y | | | | |
| propputref | | | | | | | | | y | | | | |
| public | | | y | | | | | | | | | | |
| readonly | | | | | | | | | | y | | | |
| requestedit** | | | | | | | | y | | | | | |
| restricted | y | | | | | y | y | y | | | | | |
| retval* | | | | | | | | | | y | | | |
| source** | | | | | | | | y | y | | y | y | y |
| string | | | s | | | | | y | y | y | | | |
| uuid | y | y | y | | | y | y | | | | y | | |
| vararg | | | | | y | | | | | y | | | |
| version | y | y | y | | | y | y | | | | y | | |

y   yes—can be used with this element
d   with dispinterface only
r   required
s   typedef struct only
*   only available under 16 bits with OLE 2.02 and later
**  available under 16 bits only as part of OLE Controls

**Figure 3-2.**
*Attributes and their corresponding ODL statements.*

Keep in mind that you can use C-language comments, /*...*/ and //, in an ODL file. The various samples that accompany this chapter show different ODL files that use many of these attributes in real working pieces of code.

---

### Other Type Library Generation Tools

Since MKTYPLIB is really little more than a preprocessor that ties into an OLE service, you can create other tools that generate type libraries without involving MKTYPLIB at all. You can, in fact, even bypass ODL files completely since such a file is simply input to MKTYPLIB. You can easily imagine a tool that would provide a way to specify interfaces and object classes faster and easier than writing an ODL file from scratch. You can also imagine a tool that would actually write the ODL file for you. (The ClassWizard in Microsoft Visual C++ does this.) The point is that MKTYPLIB and ODL files should not be considered the final word in creating type libraries—they're just tools.

---

## Type Library Deployment

The end result of whatever means you use to create a type library is a binary file containing nothing more than the type data structures.[6] When you ship a component that depends on this type information you must also ship this type library. You can either attach a type library to the component's server module (EXE or DLL) as a resource, store it in a stream named "\006typelib" (located in the root storage object) in a compound file, or ship the stand-alone TLB file directly.

Regardless of how you decide to ship a type library, you have to associate that type library with every component CLSID that uses it so that clients given the CLSID can retrieve your type information. This, of course, involves the registry once again. What we know about the registry so far is that any object that needs to have registry entries should have a ProgID, a Version-IndependentProgID, and a CLSID entry, as described in Chapter 2. There we mentioned that an object that didn't need a CLSID doesn't need any registry information. If you want to associate type information with an object, however, you have to assign the object a CLSID, even if it's not part of a custom

---

6. The *OLE Programmer's Reference* incorrectly states that this file is a compound file. A type library is actually a standard flat binary file.

component that could be instantiated with that CLSID—you still need it for association purposes.

In Chapter 2, we listed the following entries under the CLSID key for some hypothetical object:

```
\
    CLSID
        {42754580-16b7-11ce-80eb-00aa003d7352} = Acme Component 3.0
            ProgID = Acme.Component.3
            VersionIndependentProgID = Acme.Component
```

To associate a type library with this CLSID, you need to add the following subkey (on the same level as ProgID):

```
        TypeLib = {<LIBID>}
```

Here *{<LIBID>}* is the *uuid* attribute for the library itself. For example, if I were to assign the GUID *a4f8a400-16b7-11ce-80eb-00aa003d7352* to the library, this entry would appear as follows:

```
        TypeLib = {a4f8a400-16b7-11ce-80eb-00aa003d7352}
```

This GUID now refers to a set of entries that you must also store under the TypeLib section of the registry, which is on the same level as the CLSID section. Here is the format of the entries:

```
\
    TypeLib
        {<LIBID>} = <name of type library>
            DIR = <path of type library files; no filename!>
            HELPDIR = <path of help files; no filename!>
            <version>
                <LangID>
                    [Win16 | Win32] = <filename>
                <LangID>
                    ⋮
            <version>
                ⋮
        ⋮
```

Basically you create a key with an LIBID (all spelled out in hex with the hyphens and the braces) with the value of some readable name for the library. Under this key, you store directory information and keys for each version of the type library, demonstrating that different versions of a type library can share the same LIBID. Under each version entry, you create a subkey equal to the language ID (part of an LCID) identifying the national language of the library in question, and then you create another subkey identifying the "bitness" (16 or 32) of the library. The value of this last key is either the name of a raw TLB file, an EXE, or a DLL (in which the library is a resource), or the name of a compound file that contains the library in a stream. Let's now look at each entry in more detail.

The DIR and HELPDIR keys provide the paths on which you installed your type libraries and help files. This means that any filenames you build into code, such as those of TLB files or HLP files named in *helpfile* attributes, need not include the path because this path is known only at installation time and not at build time. The DIR key identifies the default location of any TLB, EXE, DLL, or compound file referenced farther down in the registry entries. If these files are located in another place, you should store the complete pathnames in those later entries. The HELPDIR key works much the same way, identifying where any HLP file was installed. When anyone asks the type library to return its "documentation," that is, the name of the *helpfile* attribute for any element and the *helpcontext*, OLE automatically prepends the HELP-DIR pathname to the filename in the library itself.

Each version number entry uses the form *major.minor*, as in "1.0" or "0.0" and so forth. This allows multiple versions to coexist using the same LIBID, but each registered library must have a major version number that matches the version key under which it is registered. Under each version, you create keys containing the hexadecimal representation of the LANGID of the information. The LANGID is the lower 16 bits of an LCID—that is, the primary-language ID and the sub-language ID. The language identified by this key must match the *lcid* attribute given to the library itself. The name does not include the "0x" prefix (as with ODL) and is stripped of any leading zeros. If I were writing a specifically American English type library, my language ID would be 0x0409, which is what I'd use in the *lcid* attribute. In the registry, I would use only the string "409" as the key name. If I were writing a type library in basic English (not specific to a dialect), the language ID would be 0x0009 and the registry entry simply "9" with no leading zeros. If I were writing a language-neutral library, *lcid* would be 0x0000 to match "0" in the registry.

Finally, underneath the language ID, the Win16 subkey points to a 16-bit type library location and the Win32 subkey points to the 32-bit type library location. The location path is for one of the names mentioned before, a TLB, an EXE, a DLL, or a compound file.

The biggest difficulty in creating registry entries is matching the language, and you want to use the most generic language ID you possibly can, both in the registry and in the *lcid* attribute. The OLE API functions that load the type library, which we'll see in a moment, take a language ID as an argument. These functions look first for an exact match in the registry, next for a primary language ID entry, and then for a zero ("neutral") entry, before failing completely. The more specifically you register a library, the fewer the cases in which some loading call will succeed. So again, be as generic as possible. It's a good idea to always register something under "0" so that loading will always work in some capacity.

We're now ready to look at some of the loading API functions and the interfaces that they return. Through these interfaces, both the object and any client can browse through the information in the type library.

# Loading and Using a Type Library

Type information is a resource that both objects and clients of those objects can load directly. Objects usually load type information to give it to a client through an interface such as *IProvideClassInfo*, which we'll see later. In most cases, the client is the consumer of the type information because it is trying to learn about the object—trying to make sense of its owner's manual. If the object is not running, the client can load the library itself; if the object is running, the client can ask the object to do the honors.

There are four loading-related functions in the OLE API. The first two rely on an object's registry entries and assume that the caller knows the LIBID of the type library (which the caller can load from the object's TypeLib entry under its CLSID). The first, *QueryPathOfRegTypeLib*, returns the full pathname of a type library given a version number and a language ID (both of which must match what is in the library itself), the path being the concatenation of the DIR entry and the appropriate name under Win16 or Win32 (depending on the platform). The second, *LoadRegTypeLib*, takes the same arguments and calls *QueryPathOfRegTypeLib* internally to retrieve the name of the library. It then calls one of the other two loading functions that do not depend on the registry. These are *LoadTypeLib* and *LoadTypeLibFromResource*.  *LoadTypeLib* loads the library given a filename, which is used if the library is in a stand-alone file or in a compound file. *LoadTypeLibFromResource*, on the other hand, extracts a library from a module's resources.

Both *LoadTypeLib* and *LoadTypeLibFromResource* also have one other nice side effect: they call the OLE API function *RegisterTypeLib* to patch up any problems in the registry for this library. In light of this, when a running object wants to load its own type library, as it usually does on behalf of clients, it attempts *LoadRegTypeLib* first. If that fails because of a corrupt registry, the object can load the library directly using one of the other functions as a backup.

If that backup loading succeeds, OLE will automatically correct the registry entries so that the next *LoadRegTypeLib* call succeeds.[7]

---

### *QueryPathRegTypeLib* and the BSTR Type

If you read the documentation for the *QueryPathRegTypeLib* function, you'll be told that the string it returns is a system-allocated string called a BSTR, for "Basic STRing." This string type is used particularly in OLE Automation because it is compatible with the strings used in Basic-language OLE Automation controllers, such as Microsoft Visual Basic. This data type will be described in more detail in Chapter 14; all you need to know now is that there are a number of OLE API functions of the form *Sys<action>String*, such as *SysAllocString* and *SysFreeString*, that you use to manipulate BSTRs. These functions internally use the task allocator from *CoGetMalloc* and require, like everything else, that at least *CoInitialize* (if not *OleInitialize*) has been called. The most important function to remember now is *SysFreeString*, which is used to free any BSTR that comes back from a function you might call.

---

So now the big question: what does loading give you back to represent the loaded library? You can probably guess it: an interface pointer — specifically, a pointer to an interface called *ITypeLib*. In other words, loading a type library means loading a type library object and getting your first interface pointer to it. Through this interface, you can retrieve the library's attributes or navigate to individual elements in the library and retrieve their information. Whereas the library as a whole is handled by *ITypeLib*, each element is manipulated as a separate object through *ITypeInfo*. Through *ITypeInfo*, you can retrieve anything you can create through *ICreateTypeInfo*. A consequence of having different objects is that you have to always call *Release* through any of the pointers you obtain. Calling *ITypeLib::Release* effectively closes the type library file if all *ITypeInfo* pointers have also been released.

---

7. *RegisterTypeLib* can also be useful for development environments that can both create objects and run client code against them, if only just to test the objects. The developer could create and register an object and its type library and then immediately run a client script that would use that object as any other. This would provide a nice level of integration between object development and testing, especially if the way a developer specifies the object's interfaces would allow the tool to automatically write a fair amount of the test script. Now there's a tool I'd like to see!

A simple representation of the relationship between the library, a few elements, and their interfaces is shown in Figure 3-3. You'll see that the *IType-Info* pointers for the interfaces and dispinterfaces that are specified as part of a *coclass* can be obtained either by navigating through the *ITypeInfo* interface for the *coclass* or by retrieving the *ITypeInfo* pointer for the IID directly.

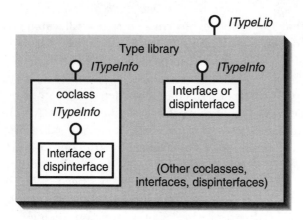

**Figure 3-3.**
*A type library has an* ITypeLib *interface through which you can navigate to* ITypeInfo *interfaces that represent the various parts of the library.*

A practical use of type information outside the scope of an instantiated object is for things called *type information browsers.* Type information browsers can look inside type libraries and present the available objects, interfaces, methods, and properties to an end user. These browsers can be the basis for powerful environments that might use drop-down list boxes and drag and drop in their programming user interfaces, greatly reducing the amount of typing that a programmer must do manually. I have not seen this sort of tool at the time of writing this text; I hope to see such innovative work in the future. However, two tools in the OLE SDK provide some sort of browsing capability. The first is TIBROWSE, for which the source code is provided as a sample. (It is also in Microsoft Visual C++.) This is a pretty simple tool, but it gives you the idea. A more complete tool, for which sources might not be provided, is OLE2VIEW. This tool allows you to peek into type libraries, among other things, through its File/View Type Library command or by locating a type library in OLE2VIEW's display of the registry. OLE2VIEW will show you just about everything that's in a library and can be very useful as a browser.

However you want to make use of all the type information available (and you're free to use it in any way you see fit—for precompiled headers, for example), you'll use the *ITypeLib* and *ITypeInfo* interfaces to navigate through the information. The following sections describe these interfaces in more detail. As a prelude, though, note that much of this information is expressed through the different data structures described in Table 3-7, many of which are used in some capacity through *ICreateTypeLib* and *ICreateTypeInfo*. Only TLIBATTR and TYPEKIND are available through *ITypeLib*; all other data structures are available only through *ITypeInfo*.

| Structure | Description |
|---|---|
| TLIBATTR | Contains a type library's LIBID (GUID), LCID, version number, flags ("restricted" being the only one), and the target operating system (Win16, Win32, Mac). |
| TYPEKIND | Enumerates the type of a particular element in the library: it could be TKIND_RECORD (*typedef struct*), TKIND_MODULE, TKIND_INTERFACE, TKIND_DISPATCH (*dispinterface*), TKIND_COCLASS, TKIND_ALIAS (*typedef*), TKIND_ENUM, or TKIND_UNION. This is *very* useful for filling in items such as tree lists with the contents of a type library.[*] |
| TYPEATTR | Contains the attributes of any TYPEKIND element: GUID (IID, CLSID, etc.), LCID, member IDs of constructor and destructor methods (*interface* and *dispinterface*), size of an instance of the type, count of methods (*dispinterface*), count of properties, variables, and data members (*interface* and *dispinterface, typedef*), count of interfaces (for *coclass*), size of the vtable (*interface* and *dispinterface*), byte alignment, and version number. Also included are TYPEDESC, TYPEFLAGS, and IDLDESC fields. (See below.) |

[*]  Using the Tree List control of Windows 95, you can easily imagine a very slick type library browser that would have top-level items with each of these names and a little + next to the name. If you clicked on the +, that item would expand to show the names of each individual element of that type, and the information you can get from *ITypeInfo* would allow further levels of expansion.

**Table 3-7.**                                                                                   *(continued)*

*Data structures and enumerations obtainable through* ITypeLib *and* ITypeInfo *member functions. The descriptions in this table are not exhaustive; see the* OLE Programmer's Reference, *for complete details.*

**Table 3-7.** *continued*

| Structure | Description |
|---|---|
| TYPEDESC | A structure that describes the type of a variable or argument or the return type of a method. Contains a VARTYPE (see Chapter 14, "VARIANT and VARIANTARG Structures") and a union that can contain either a TYPEDESC, an ARRAYDESC, or an HREFTYPE. (See below.) Nested TYPEDESCs describe nested structures. |
| ARRAYDESC | Describes an array of some type (TYPEDESC) with a specific number of dimensions and the bounds of each dimension. |
| HREFTYPE | A handle (unsigned long) that identifies a TYPEDESC. |
| TYPEFLAGS | An enumeration that contains TYPEFLAG_FAPP-OBJECT, identifying a *coclass* with the *appobject* attribute; and TYPEFLAG_FCANCREATE, which indicates whether the function *ITypeInfo::CreateInstance* will work. See "The *ITypeInfo* Interface" on page 180. |
| IDLDESC | A structure containing information used in marshaling an argument; at present, this specifies only IDLFLAGS and contains a reserved BSTR. |
| IDLFLAGS | An enumeration that identifies an argument as having the in or the out attribute, both attributes, or neither attribute. |
| ELEMDESC | A structure that describes a *typedef enum* using a TYPEDESC and an IDLDESC. |
| FUNCDESC | A structure that describes a method, including its dispID, an array and count of legal return SCODEs, the type of function (FUNCKIND), flags (FUNCFLAGS), the invocation style (INVOKEKIND), the calling convention (CALLCONV), the number of total arguments, the number of optional arguments, an array of ELEMDESC structures for each argument, the ELEMDESC of the return type, and the offset of this method in a virtual function table. |
| FUNCFLAGS | An enumeration that contains FUNCFLAG_FRESTRICTED, FUNCFLAG_FSOURCE, FUNCFLAG_FBINDABLE, FUNCFLAG_FREQUESTEDIT, FUNCFLAG_FDISPLAYBIND (*bindable* and displayed to user), and FUNCFLAG_FDEFAULTBIND (the method in an interface that best represents the object). |

*(continued)*

**Table 3-7.** *continued*

| Structure | Description |
|---|---|
| FUNCKIND | An enumeration that describes the function as either FUNC_VIRTUAL (called by an offset in a vtable), FUNC_PUREVIRTUAL, FUNC_NONVIRTUAL (called by address and takes a *this* pointer), FUNC-_STATIC (called by address and takes no *this* pointer), or FUNC_DISPATCH (member of a *dispinterface* called through *IDispatch::Invoke*). |
| CALLCONV | An enumeration that identifies the calling convention as CC_CDECL, CC_PASCAL, CC_MACPASCAL, CC_STDCALL, or CC_SYSCALL. |
| INVOKEKIND | An enumeration that identifies the types of operations available through *IDispatch::Invoke*: INVOKE_FUNC, INVOKE_PROPERTYGET, INVOKE_PROPERTYPUT, INVOKE_PROPERTYPUTREF. These map exactly to DISPATCH_* values. |
| IMPLTYPE | An enumeration containing the implementation type of *interface* or *dispinterface* in a *coclass*: IMPLTYPE-_FDEFAULT (*default*), IMPLTYPE_SOURCE (*source*), and IMPLTYPE_FRESTRICTED (*restricted*). |
| VARDESC | A structure that describes a variable, argument, constant, or data member and contains a dispID (MEMBERID), an offset or the variable within an object instance or a VARIANT with the actual value of a constant, an ELEMDESC, a value from VARFLAGS, and a type from VARKIND. |
| VARFLAGS | An enumeration that contains VARFLAG_FREADONLY, VARFLAG_FSOURCE, VARFLAG_FBINDABLE, VARFLAG_FREQUESTEDIT, VARFLAG_FDISPLAYBIND, and VARFLAG_FDEFAULTBIND. |
| VARKIND | An enumeration identifying a kind of variable or constant: VAR_PERINSTANCE (where the offset into an object in VARDESC makes sense), VAR_CONST (where the VARIANT in the VARDESC makes sense), VAR-_STATIC (a single-instance global), or VAR_DISPATCH (a property in a dispinterface). |
| MEMBERID | Same as a dispID. |

## The *ITypeLib* Interface

The member functions of the *ITypeLib* interface, as described in Table 3-8, are oriented primarily toward retrieving library attributes or retrieving information and *ITypeInfo* pointers for the elements within the library.

| Member Function | Description |
| --- | --- |
| *GetLibAttr* | Allocates, fills, and returns a pointer to the library's TLIBATTR structure. This must be freed with *ReleaseLibAttr*. |
| *ReleaseLibAttr* | Frees the TLIBATTR structure allocated in *GetLibAttr*. |
| *GetTypeInfo* | Returns the *ITypeInfo* pointer for a top-level element in the library given a zero-based index. You would use *GetTypeInfo* to iterate through all the elements in the library. |
| *GetTypeInfoCount* | Returns the number of top-level elements in the type library. |
| *GetTypeInfoType* | Returns the TYPEKIND of an element in the library given its index. This is the information you might use in creating an organized tree list of type library contents. |
| *GetTypeInfoOfGuid* | Returns the *ITypeInfo* pointer for an element in the type library given the GUID of that element. The GUID must match a *uuid* attribute for some element, be it for a *typedef, dispinterface, interface coclass*, or whatever. |
| *GetDocumentation* | Given an index, allocates and returns a BSTR with the library name (which follows the *library* keyword in the ODL file) and allocates and returns BSTR copies of the *helpstring, helpfile*, and *helpcontext* attributes of the library. The caller must free the BSTRs with *SysFreeString*. |
| *FindName* | Returns the *ITypeInfo* pointers (and member IDs) for any number of elements given the element names. |

**Table 3-8.**  *(continued)*

*Member functions of the* ITypeLib *interface.*

**Table 3-8.** *continued*

| Member Function | Description |
| --- | --- |
| *IsName* | Checks quickly whether the given names exist in the type library. *IsName* is suitable for verifying existence before calling a more expensive function such as *FindName*. |
| *GetTypeComp* | Returns an *ITypeComp* interface for the library. See "The *ITypeComp* Interface" on page 183. |

All of these functions basically give you access to the various parts of a type library that you would describe in an ODL file or create otherwise. The relationships between these member functions and a sample ODL file are shown in Figure 3-4.

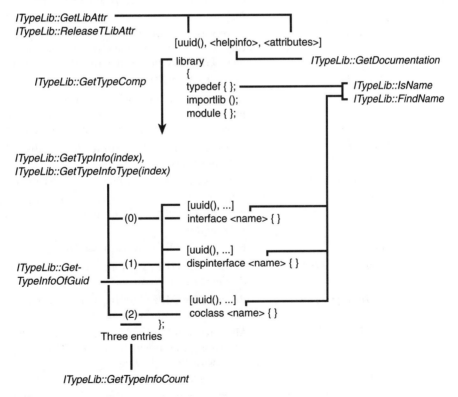

**Figure 3-4.**
*How* ITypeLib *members relate to ODL entries.*

## The *ITypeInfo* Interface

As you can probably expect from the plethora of structures you can get from *ITypeInfo*, shown in Table 3-7, there are a good number of member functions, shown in Table 3-9. As with *ITypeLib*, each of these functions relates to specific parts of an ODL file, as illustrated in Figure 3-5 on page 182.

| Member Function | Description |
| --- | --- |
| *GetContainingTypeLib* | Retrieves the *ITypeLib* pointer for the library that contains this type information as well as the index of this type information in the library. |
| *GetDocumentation* | Given an index, allocates and returns a BSTR with the item name and allocates and returns BSTR copies of the *helpstring*, *helpfile*, and *helpcontext* attributes of the item. The caller must free the BSTRs with *SysFreeString*. |
| *GetFuncDesc* | Allocates, fills, and returns the FUNCDESC structure for a method with a given index in an interface. This must be freed with *ReleaseFuncDesc*. |
| *ReleaseFuncDesc* | Frees the FUNCDESC from *GetFuncDesc*. |
| *GetNames* | Retrieves the names of properties, types, variables, methods, method arguments, and so forth in BSTR variables, which the caller frees with *SysFreeString*. |
| *GetIDsOfNames* | Maps text names of a dispinterface to dispIDs and argument IDs. |
| *GetRefTypeInfo* | Returns the *ITypeInfo* of a given HREFTYPE. |
| *GetTypeAttr* | Allocates, fills, and returns the TYPEATTR structure for this *ITypeInfo*. This must be freed with *ReleaseTypeAttr*. |
| *ReleaseTypeAttr* | Frees the TYPEATTR from *GetTypeAttr*. |
| *GetRefTypeOfImplType* | Returns the HREFTYPE for an *interface* or *dispinterface* in a *coclass*. |
| *GetImplTypeFlags* | Returns the IMPLTYPE flags of an *interface* or *dispinterface* item if it's in a *coclass*. |
| *GetVarDesc* | Allocates, fills, and returns a VARDESC structure describing the specified variable. This must be freed with *ReleaseVarDesc*. |
| *ReleaseVarDesc* | Frees the VARDESC from *GetVarDesc*. |

**Table 3-9.** *(continued)*

*The* ITypeInfo *interface.*

**Table 3-9.** *continued*

| Member Function | Description |
|---|---|
| *Invoke* | Invokes a method or accesses a property of an object that implements the interface described by this *ITypeInfo*. |
| *CreateInstance* | Attempts to create a new instance of a *coclass* using *CoCreateInstance* for the *uuid* attribute, using the process described in Chapter 5. |
| *AddressOfMember* | Retrieves the addresses of static functions or variables defined in a DLL as well as the INVOKEKIND flag. |
| *GetDllEntry* | Retrieves the DLL module name and function name (or ordinal) of an exported DLL function as well as its INVOKEKIND flag. |
| *GetMops* | Retrieves marshaling information for an argument. |
| *GetTypeComp* | Returns the *ITypeComp* interface for this *ITypeInfo*. See "The *ITypeComp* Interface" later in this chapter. |

## Alternative *ITypeLib* and *ITypeInfo* Implementations

There is nothing sacred about OLE's type information services that provide the standard implementations of type library and type information objects. You are perfectly free to implement your own objects with these interfaces that sit on top of a type library. Such custom implementations might be used to extend the available information for the purposes of a particular client. For example, if you want to extend the properties available on an object with a set of client-supplied properties and to use type information consistently throughout the controller, you can implement wrapper interfaces that filter out the specific client types before passing the calls on to OLE's standard implementations.

With *ITypeLib* and *ITypeInfo*, you can see how a client could load a type library using registry information, obtain an *ITypeLib* pointer, and then call *ITypeLib::GetTypeInfoOfGuid* to retrieve an *ITypeInfo* pointer for a *coclass*. Through *ITypeInfo::GetRefTypeOfImplType*, you then obtain the HREFTYPE for each interface or dispinterface in that class and can pass that HREFTYPE to *ITypeInfo::GetRefTypeInfo* to retrieve the *ITypeInfo* pointer for each particular interface.

From there you can call, with this new pointer, *ITypeInfo::GetTypeAttr* to retrieve the TYPEATTR structure, which contains the interface IID. This is how you retrieve the IIDs of all of an object's incoming and outgoing interfaces directly from type information. This does involve a number of iterations and is a little convoluted, I must admit, but it is the only way to retrieve this information without otherwise instantiating the object itself.

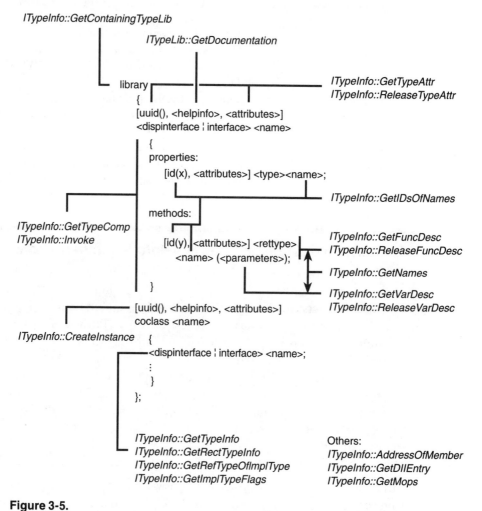

**Figure 3-5.**
*How* ITypeInfo *members relate to ODL entries. Although not drawn in this figure (to keep it readable),* AddressOfMember *and* GetDllEntry *work with* module *entries and the* appobject *coclass, and* GetMops *works with structures as well as arguments.*

## The *ITypeComp* Interface

If you've ever looked into type information before reading this chapter, you're probably still confused to death about this *ITypeComp* interface—like, what it's for in the first place and what you're supposed to do with it.[8] The name of the interface implies the type of client that might use it: "Comp" stands for "compiler." A compiler can use type information as a sort of header file or as an import library.

During the compilation process, compilers need to quickly access information about user-defined types, exported module functions, global variables and constants, and interfaces within *coclass* objects. The optimization, which works through *ITypeComp::BindType* and *ITypeComp::Bind* (the only two members besides those in *IUnknown*), allows the compiler to quickly locate this information without having to navigate through all the elements over and over, which would be tremendously slow. *Bind* is also what gets you the FUNCDESC or VARDESC structure for a variable, constant, or exported function.

Navigation through the entire library according to its structure makes perfect sense for a type information browser, for which the locations of the data in question are important. But for a compiler, location in the structure isn't of any concern—it's the data itself that's important. For example, if you wanted to locate an exported function named *arctan* in some modules that are described in a type library, you could call *ITypeLib::GetTypeComp* and then *ITypeComp::Bind*. This procedure is much easier and faster than calling *ITypeLib::FindName*, *ITypeLib::GetTypeInfo*, *ITypeInfo::GetIDsOfNames*, and *ITypeInfo::AddressOfMember*, which would accomplish the same end. If you wanted to restrict the search to a single object class, you can call *ITypeInfo::GetTypeComp* by using the *ITypeInfo* for that *coclass*. The *ITypeComp* you get in this case would ignore everything else in the library, for an even faster search.

Both *Bind* and *BindType*, as well as *ITypeLib::FindName* and *ITypeLib::IsName*, involve the use of a hash value for the name in question. The OLE API function *LHashValOfName* does the actual hashing. *LHashValOfName* is a macro that is converted to a call to *LHashValOfNameSys* inside the OLE header files, so you don't have to care what system you're working on. (The system is hard-coded into the header files for each system, which is appropriate.) In any case, before calling *Bind* or *BindType*, you hash the name you're looking for by using this function and pass it as an argument to the *ITypeComp* functions, which then race through the library looking for a match, bypassing all the tedious navigation through the various elements.

---

8. I am indebted to Burt Harris for greatly clarifying the purpose of this interface to me.

# Objects with Type Information: *IProvideClassInfo*

If a client wants to browse an object's type information without instantiating the object, the client can use the object's registry entries to load the library itself and obtain an *ITypeLib* pointer. The only complication here is that the client has to know the CLSID of the object in question, and it then has to navigate through the library to find the *ITypeInfo* pointer for the object's *coclass*. If the client already has a running instance of that class, it would make sense to simply *ask* the object for its *coclass* type information directly.

This is the purpose of the *IProvideClassInfo* interface, which an object can implement if it wants to provide this feature. The only types of objects that are currently required to implement this interface are those with custom event sets, such as OLE controls. For other objects, it's merely a convenience for interested clients, but it is an interface I strongly recommend.[9]

*IProvideClassInfo* is actually one of the simplest interfaces you'll find. Besides its *IUnknown* members, it has only one additional function, named *Get-ClassInfo*, which takes a single out-parameter in which it returns the *ITypeInfo* pointer for the object's *coclass* information:

```
interface IProvideClassInfo : IUnknown
    {
    HRESULT GetClassInfo(ITypeInfo **ppITI);
    }
```

The presence of this interface frees the client from having to load and navigate a type library itself, which is, however, what the object will generally do using code somewhat like the code on the following page to obtain the *ITypeInfo* pointer to return:

---

9. This interface was first defined as part of the OLE Controls specification itself, and at the time of writing it is not widely used outside this realm. In addition, the initial support for this interface, which was the OLE Controls Development Kit (with Microsoft Visual C++ 2.0), did not provide any marshaling support (proxy and stub) for *IProvideClassInfo*, and as a consequence, it can be implemented only on in-process objects unless you are willing to write your own proxy or stub DLL. I fully expect that this limitation will not be present by the time this book is published or shortly thereafter.

```
//Try loading from registry information.
if (FAILED(LoadRegTypeLib(LIBID_MyTypeLibrary, 1, 0
    , LANG_NEUTRAL, &pITypeLib)))
    {
    //Try loading directly, fixing registry information.
    if (FAILED(LoadTypeLib(TEXT("MYTYPES.TLB"), &pITypeLib)))
        return FALSE;
    }

//Find ITypeInfo for coclass.
pITypeLib->GetTypeInfoOfGuid(CLSID_MyObject, &m_pITI);
pITypeLib->Release();
```

In the following code, *m_pITI* would end up with the *ITypeInfo* pointer for *IProvideClassInfo::GetClassInfo*:

```
STDMETHODIMP CMyObject::GetClassInfo(ITypeInfo **ppITI)
    {
    if (NULL==ppITI)
        return ResultFromScode(E_POINTER);

    *ppITI=m_pITI;

    if (NULL!=m_pITI)
        {
        m_pITI->AddRef();
        return NOERROR;
        }

    return ResultFromScode(E_FAIL);
    }
```

In a sense, *IProvideClassInfo* represents the ability of an object to describe its interfaces and types when everything else about it is unknown. As an example, if a client received through, say, a drag-and-drop operation some arbitrary *IUnknown* pointer, it would query for *IProvideClassInfo*, and if that succeeded, it could programmatically analyze the available incoming and outgoing interfaces that the object supports. Based on this analysis, the client might determine what could be done with the object: Is it a control? A compound document content object? An OLE Automation object? Something else? What abilities does it have?

There is one deficiency in this interface that you should note: there is no way to ask the object for type information in a particular language. In other words, the interface assumes that the object will have already loaded type information appropriate to the user's international settings on the current machine. In some cases, however, this may not be adequate for the needs of all clients, so there may, in the future, be something like an *IProvideClass-Info2* that would have an additional function that takes an LCID as an argument. For the time being, however, this remains a single-locale interface.

## Summary

Many technological devices are often very hard to understand and use without a description of that device and its uses — an owner's manual. For an object or component, *type information* is the owner's manual, in which is described an object's CLSID, its interfaces, their IIDs, their member functions, and the return value and arguments of those functions. This is combined with brief help information, references to a complete help file, and even exported functions from DLLs. In short, type information is the combination of a header file, a help file, and an import library.

A *type library* is a collection of type information elements for one or more objects and one or more interfaces as well as a repository for type definitions and module export lists. The elements in a type library, including the library itself, can be given a wide range of attributes to describe their characteristics as can even the individual member functions of interfaces. A library is also assigned a locale identifier describing the national language in which the library is written.

Type libraries are created through a standard OLE service involving the interfaces *ICreateTypeLib* and *ICreateTypeInfo*. The tool MKTYPLIB.EXE works in conjunction with the Object Description Language (ODL) to automate the process of library creation, allowing the developer to define interfaces and classes in a C++ style notation. Once the library is created, clients and components access type information through another standard OLE service involving several API functions and the interfaces *ITypeLib* and *ITypeInfo*, which provide structured access to the information. The interface *ITypeComp* provides high-speed unstructured access for the purposes of compilers.

OLE defines specific registry entries to associate a type library with an object's CLSID, providing a way for clients to read up on an object before ever instantiating it. When an object already exists, the interface *IProvideClassInfo* allows the client to ask an object for its type information directly.

CHAPTER FOUR

# Connectable Objects

*It is the province of knowledge to speak, and it is the privilege of wisdom to listen.*
—Dr. Oliver Wendell Holmes

In Chapter 2, we explored the notion of incoming interfaces for an object and the *QueryInterface* function that manages these interfaces. "Incoming," in the context of a client-object relationship, implies that the object "listens" to what the client has to say. In other words, incoming interfaces and their member functions are like an object's sensory organs—its eyes, ears, nose, and nerve endings—which receive input from the outside. But there is only so much you can say in a one-sided conversation.

Objects are fairly tolerant of loquacious clients, so they usually don't mind listening. Many objects, however, have useful things to say themselves, and this requires a two-way dialogue between object and client. Such two-way communication involves *outgoing* interfaces—the different languages that an object can speak through its own mouth as opposed to those that it can understand through its incoming senses. When an object supports one or more outgoing interfaces, it is said to be *connectable*. In this chapter, we'll cover the mechanisms that make connectable objects—also, for brevity, called *sources*—work.

A source can, of course, have as many outgoing interfaces as it likes. Each interface is composed of distinct member functions, with each function representing a single *event, notification,* or *request*. Events and notifications are equivalent concepts (and interchangeable terms), as they are both used to tell the client that something interesting happened in the object—that data changed, a property changed, or the user did something such as click a button. Obviously events are very important for OLE Controls, which use the mechanisms we'll describe in this chapter. Events and notifications differ from a request in that the object expects no response from the client. A request, on the other hand, is how an object asks the client a question and expects a response. For example, an object that allows a client to override an action such as a property change will first ask the client whether it will allow that action to occur. Events and requests are quite similar to Windows messages, some of which inform a window of an event (WM_MOVE, WM_PAINT, WM_COMMAND, WM_WININICHANGE, and so forth) and others of which ask for information (WM_CTLCOLOR, WM_QUERYEND-SESSION).

In all of these cases, there must be some client that listens to what the object has to say and uses that information wisely. It is the client, therefore, that actually implements these interfaces on objects called *sinks*. From the sink's perspective, the interfaces are incoming, meaning that the sink listens through them. A connectable object plays the role of a client as far as the sink is concerned; thus, the sink is what the object's client uses to listen to that object. Confused about who is doing what? Let's look at the connectable object mechanisms to set everything straight.

# The Client-Object-Sink Relationship

The game of connectable objects has three players. First, we have the client of the connectable object, which communicates with that object as usual through the object's incoming interfaces. Second, we have the object. In order to have the object communicate with the client in the other direction, the object must somehow obtain a pointer to an outgoing interface implemented somewhere in the client. Through this pointer, the object sends events, notifications, or requests to the client.

The "somewhere" in this picture is the third player — the sink — which is an object itself but a very simple object that doesn't need anything fancy like a CLSID or type information. The client "connects" this sink to the object by passing the sink's interface pointer to the object through some other interface method. The object keeps a copy of this pointer (after calling *AddRef*) and calls the sink's member functions when necessary. The basic connection process is illustrated in Figure 4-1. Keep in mind that although the sink is conceptually a separate object (which is how its *QueryInterface* behaves in relation to the rest of the container), it is strongly tied to the rest of the client's code because that client will want to perform some action in response to the event or request. This is useful to know because sometimes you can make some other object act like a sink without making two separate objects. The separation is merely a question of the *QueryInterface* implementations.

An object doesn't necessarily have a one-to-one relationship with a sink. In fact, a single instance of an object usually supports any number of connections to sinks in any number of separate clients. This is called *multicasting*.

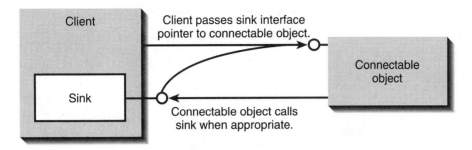

**Figure 4-1.**
*The process of connecting a client sink object to a connectable source object.*
*This allows the connectable object to make outgoing function calls to the sink.*

In addition, any sink can be connected to any number of objects. These situations, illustrated in Figure 4-2 below and Figure 4-3 on the following page, both have a myriad of uses because the notion of outgoing interfaces is quite generic.

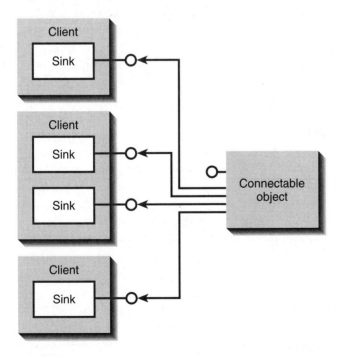

**Figure 4-2.**
*A one-to-many relationship between an object and sinks.*

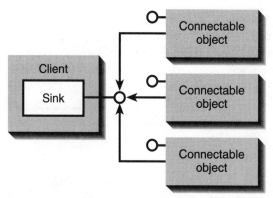

**Figure 4-3.**
*A many-to-one relationship between objects and a sink.*

Like an object, a sink can support as many outgoing interfaces as you want. That is, you can easily write a single sink that accepts a wide range of events and requests from any number of external objects, centralizing the code to handle all these calls. This sink could be connected to any number of objects, and each source could call functions in any combination of that sink's interfaces. An object, however, will never query a sink for an interface pointer unless that object is told specifically—by the container—to connect to that sink. In other words, an object considers each sink interface pointer it receives to belong to a sink that implements only that one interface and no others (except *IUnknown*, of course).

But what is the mechanism through which the client hands its sink pointers to objects? For each outgoing interface, a connectable object will manage another small object called a *connection point*, so named because these objects implement the *IConnectionPoint* interface. Through this interface, the client passes the interface pointers to its sinks. Each connection point is contained within the connectable object itself, and the connection points usually share whatever information they have from clients. In addition, a connection point's reference count is included in the object's reference count so that as long as any connection points remain, so does the containing object.

Regardless of the implementation details, the object must expose these individual connection points to clients. It does this by implementing the *IConnectionPointContainer* interface itself. Through this interface, the client asks the object about its outgoing interfaces; when it wants to connect a sink, the client asks for a connection point for one outgoing interface and then hands the sink's interface pointer to that connection point. Let's look at this mechanism in detail to see how it all works.

## The *IConnectionPointContainer* Interface

The outgoing arrows shown in the previous figures represent the fact that the object contains code to call the member functions of outgoing interfaces when necessary. In and of itself, however, this doesn't help the client know which outgoing interfaces the object supports.

*IConnectionPointContainer* allows the client to ask a connectable object a few questions about outgoing interfaces. Of course, a client must request this interface from an object by first calling *QueryInterface(IID_IConnection-PointContainer)*, which asks the object, "Are you a connectable (source) object?"— that is, "Do you have any outgoing interfaces?" If an object replies with an error, it has no outgoing interfaces at all. Otherwise, you're given a pointer through which you can ask two other questions about the outgoing interfaces, expressed through the two specific members of *IConnectionPoint-Container* (shown in this code and in Table 4-1):

```
interface IConnectionPointContainer : IUnknown
    {
    HRESULT EnumConnectionPoints(IEnumConnectionPoints **);
    HRESULT FindConnectionPoint (REFIID, IConnectionPoint **);
    };
```

| Member Function | Description |
|---|---|
| *FindConnectionPoint* | "Do you have this specific outgoing interface?" Asks the object whether it supports the outgoing interface identified with an IID, returning an *IConnectionPoint* pointer if so. |
| *EnumConnectionPoints* | "Which outgoing interfaces do you support?" Creates and returns an enumerator object that implements *IEnumConnectionPoints*, through which the client can retrieve the *IConnectionPoint* pointers for each outgoing interface. |

**Table 4-1.**
*Member functions of* IConnectionPointContainer.

To clarify the operations involved here, consider again the analogy of two humans trying to communicate with one another, as we described in Chapter 2. When I walk up to another person and perform the equivalent of

*QueryInterface* for a human language, I'm asking specifically whether that person can understand that language. I'm not asking whether the person can speak the language, only whether he or she understands it. If I query for *IConnectionPointContainer*, I'm asking, "Can you speak?" and if so, I can ask, "Do you speak *<language>*?" and "What languages do you speak?"

With a positive response to either of the latter two questions, I get back a connection point. With that connection point, I can indicate my ability to understand that language myself. Again, you'll notice a decoupling of the process of asking a question—that is, exploring an object—and the process of actually performing some action. I could, if I wanted, ask whether you speak classical Latin. If you answered yes, I might say, "That's nice, too bad I don't understand it!" (It is, of course, a waste of time to write a program that works that way.)

Getting back a connection point is similar to being handed a jack into which I can plug a set of headphones that I can use to hear what the object has to say. Unless I plug into that jack, I won't hear a thing. This socket happens to be a pointer to *IConnectionPoint*, so let's see what that interface does.

## The *IConnectionPoint* Interface

Plugging a pair of headphones into a jack is a nice analog to passing an interface pointer on a sink object to a connection point. The connection point will call *AddRef* on that pointer in order to maintain the connection as long as it needs it. Unplugging the headphones means asking the connection point to release its hold on that pointer.[1] These two operations are the purpose of two of the *IConnectionPoint* member functions, as described in Table 4-2.

```
interface IConnectionPoint : IUnknown
    {
    HRESULT GetConnectionInterface(IID *);
    HRESULT GetConnectionPointContainer(IConnectionPointContainer **);
    HRESULT Advise(IUnknown *, DWORD *);
    HRESULT Unadvise(DWORD);
    HRESULT EnumConnections(IEnumConnections **);
    }
```

---

1. Can you imagine rather temperamental headphone jacks that you must politely ask to let go of your headphones? Fortunately, objects aren't moody, and they comply with any *Release* call.

| Member Function | Description |
| --- | --- |
| *Advise* | Establishes a connection with an outgoing interface and returns a *key* (or *cookie*) to identify the connection. A connection point can support any number of connections, whatever is appropriate for the design of the connectable object. |
| *Unadvise* | Terminates a connection given a *key* or *cookie* from *Advise*. |
| *EnumConnections* | Creates and returns an enumerator with the *IEnumConnections* interface, through which the caller can iterate over every connection established through *Advise*. |
| *GetConnectionPointContainer* | Returns the *IConnectionPointContainer* pointer for the connectable object that manages this connection point. This is highly useful for clients that have an *IConnectionPoint* pointer and want to navigate up to the full object. |
| *GetConnectionInterface* | Returns the IID of the single outgoing interface that this connection point supports. This is needed when a client calls *IConnectionPointContainer::EnumConnectionPoints* and needs to know the IID of each connection point therein. |

**Table 4-2.**
*Member functions for* IConnectionPoint.

*GetConnectionPointContainer* and *GetConnectionInterface* exist because of the relationship between the connectable object and its contained connection points. Given one or the other, you can find all the information you need about which outgoing interfaces an object supports.

With both the *IConnectionPoint* and *IConnectionPointContainer* interfaces spelled out, we can see the exact sequence of steps taken by a client in order to establish a connection. For the sake of discussion, let's assume that there's an event interface named *IDuckEvents* with the members *Quack*, *Flap*, and *Paddle* and that a client would like to connect a sink with this interface to some connectable object for which it has an *IUnknown* pointer. Here are the steps the client would follow:

1. Call *IUnknown::QueryInterface(IID_ IConnectionPointContainer, &pCPC)*. If this fails, no connections are possible.

2. Call *pCPC->FindConnectionPoint(IID_ IDuckEvents, &pConnPt)*. If this fails, the object doesn't support this outgoing interface. Regardless of the success or failure of this call, the client should always call *pCPC->Release*: if the call succeeds, the connectable object will still be alive because one of its contained connection points is alive.

3. Call *pConnPt->Advise(pIDuckEvents, &dwCookie)* to establish the connection to the instance of the sink identified by the *pIDuckEvents* pointer. The connection key is returned in *dwCookie*. Now, whenever appropriate events occur in the source, or the source has reason to make a request to the client, it will call some member function in *pIDuckEvents*.

4. When the client wants to terminate the connection, it calls *pConnPt-> Unadvise(dwCookie)*, passing the same connection key that was returned from *Advise*. This is followed by *pConnPt->Release*.

The last three steps of this process are illustrated in Figure 4-4. The complete process is repeated for every connection that a client wants to make with whatever sources it's dealing with. For example, an OLE Control container will connect to the custom event sets for each control placed in a document or form.

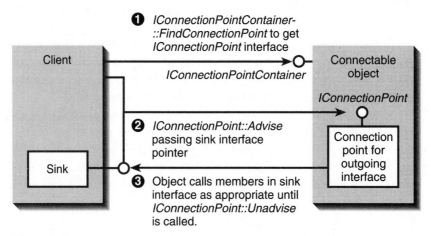

**Figure 4-4.**
*The process of connecting a sink through a connection point.*

## Why the Complexity?

You might be thinking that this connection mechanism seems unreasonably complicated for a reasonably simple operation. Wouldn't it be simpler to get rid of the connection point business altogether? Couldn't we simply put *Advise, Unadvise,* and *EnumConnections* into *IConnectionPointContainer* and add an IID argument to *Advise?* That would let us eliminate all the other junk, making everything quite a bit simpler. The primary reason for this mechanism is extensibility: the design as it stands allows the nature of the connectable object to change, perhaps with new interfaces, independently of the connection points, and allows the connection points to change without bothering the connectable object. This is intended to keep the design free of constraints in the future when this technology serves larger purposes. Such extensibility is a key part of working with OLE because evolution over time is so fundamental. A little added complication here, which isn't tremendous, saves a lot of complication years down the road. The Connectable Object technology is meant to be generic and flexible.

# Outgoing Interface Definitions and Type Information

This whole scheme of connectable objects and their relationships to clients and sinks is quite powerful, but it raises some concerns. Given an arbitrary object, a client can, by asking for *IConnectionPointContainer,* determine whether the object has any outgoing interfaces. If that client already knows about the outgoing interfaces it wants to connect—that is, it has compiled header files with the definitions of those interfaces—there is little complication: it calls *FindConnectionPoint* and goes through the steps listed earlier.

However, what if a client wants to connect to whatever outgoing interfaces there may be, regardless of whether it had compile-time knowledge about those interfaces? In this case, it has to call *EnumConnectionPoints* and then *IConnectionPoint::GetConnectionInterface* to get a list of all the outgoing interface IIDs. But what good is an IID if you don't have any information about it?

Well, an IID by itself with no other context is practically useless, which is one reason why type information is fundamentally important. Given an object and a list of its outgoing IIDs, a client can ask the source for type information by querying for *IProvideClassInfo* followed by a call to *GetClassInfo* in that interface. With the *ITypeInfo* pointer you are given back, you can use functions such as *ITypeInfo::GetRefOfImplType* and *ITypeInfo::GetRefTypeInfo* to find the *ITypeInfo* structure for the interface matching the IID you already have. Through that *ITypeInfo* structure, you can learn about all the attributes, member functions, and arguments for that interface, enough information to provide an implementation of it on a sink and connect that sink to the connectable object. This run-time process works much more easily with outgoing dispinterfaces than with outgoing vtable interfaces because dispinterfaces were designed for such late-binding considerations.[2] We'll see how to do this when we deal with OLE Control containers in Chapter 24.

Suffice it to say that if a client encounters an unknown outgoing IID in a connectable object but cannot retrieve type information for that object, it is, to put it mildly, flat out of luck. The client simply doesn't have enough information to connect to the object through that interface.

## Specific Outgoing Interfaces and Historical Trivia

As time moves on, the vast majority of connectable outgoing interfaces will be defined through type information, especially because a plethora of new OLE controls and other similar objects will be coming to market.

There are, however, a few standard interfaces defined in the OLE header files that deal with various types of object-to-client events, notifications, and requests, all of which are designed for specific purposes. These are *IAdviseSink*, *IPropertyNotifySink*, *IOleClientSite*, *IOleInPlaceSite*, *IPropertyPageSite*, and *IOleControlSite*. However, only one of them, *IPropertyNotifySink*, is handled through connection points as described in this chapter. Connections to the others are established through specific member functions of *IDataObject*, *IViewObject*, *IViewObject2*, *IOleObject*, *IOleInPlaceObject*, *IPropertyPage*, and *IOleControl*. There are two reasons for this.

---

2. A dispinterface is simpler because a sink can implement an *IDispatch* interface at compile time whose specific methods and properties are not determined until run time using type information. This involves code that executes some sequence of actions when *IDispatch::Invoke* is passed an

The first reason applies to the interface *IAdviseSink*, which contains notifications of data changes, view changes, layout changes, object closure, object renaming, and object saving. This interface was designed as part of the original OLE 2 specification way back in 1991–92. It works specifically with aspects of Uniform Data Transfer, Viewable Objects, and OLE Documents, which were defined at the same time. The interfaces *IDataObject*, *IViewObject2*, and *IOleObject* each have advise and unadvise member functions to establish and terminate connections through *IAdviseSink*. This was an ad hoc solution to the specific problems of these technologies. In 1994, the authors of the OLE Controls specification were faced with creating either another ad hoc solution only for OLE Controls or an extensible generic mechanism that would be reusable in other present and future designs. So the OLE Controls specification is the original source of all the connection point business and the *IConnection\** interfaces. Because *IAdviseSink* appeared way before OLE Controls, it remains an oddity, and it will remain so unless there's some compelling reason to change it.

The other reason applies to the *Site* interfaces, which generally contain very rich functionality for an object to use itself. In fact, *Site* interfaces represent more than just simple notifications or requests; they expose services from both containers and clients to their respective objects. These interfaces were designed specifically for the rich OLE Documents and OLE Controls integration protocols. In these protocols, bidirectional communication is *not optional*, as it is with connectable objects. Both sides need to talk to each other. Establishing a connection between an object and the site that conceptually "contains" it is a fixed part of the protocol.

As you see new interfaces—and design your own—anything using *Sink* in its name implies a simpler interface that is managed with connection points. A *Site* as part of the interface name implies a more complex relationship between an object and a container that goes beyond the scope of sinks.

---

appropriate dispID. It is far more tedious to create a run-time interface implementation that requires you to construct the vtable and create entry points for each member function that will handle a proper stack frame for that function. It is possible, but it's not nearly as trivial as implementing a run-time dispinterface.

# Using and Implementing
# a Connectable Object: CONNECT

Now that you understand the theory and mechanics of connection points, let's look at them in practice through the Connect sample, which you'll find in CHAP04\CONNECT. This is really something of a contrived example because the client, source, and sink are all contained within the same program. Connection points are most useful when you have clients and objects separated by DLL or process boundaries, but we won't see how to work with custom service components until the next chapter. Nevertheless, this sample illustrates all the principles of connection points and provides a complete reference implementation of all the interfaces (including enumerators) on appropriate objects.

For the Connect sample, we'll need some sort of interface for notifications and events. For the purpose of our sample, let's define the interface *IDuckEvents* as follows (the compiling form of which is found in the file INTERFAC.H):

```
interface IDuckEvents : IUnknown
    {
    HRESULT Quack(void);
    HRESULT Flap(void);
    HRESULT Paddle(void);
    };
```

This interface is also assigned *IID_IDuckEvents* (*00021145-0000-C000-000000000046*) in INC\BOOKGUID.H.

The main application in the Connect sample, considered the "client" portion of the program, is the C++ class *CApp*, which creates a window and processes menu commands. During initialization, *CApp* instantiates two sink objects using the C++ class *CDuckEvents*. This class inherits the member functions of *IDuckEvents* directly. Initially these sinks are not connected to any objects. The Object menu on the Connect sample window allows you to create and destroy a connectable source object (through the *CConnObject* and *CConnectionPoint* classes) as well as to connect and disconnect either sink (#1 or #2) from that source. Nothing much will happen, of course, until we can cause the source to actually fire some of its events, which is the purpose of the Trigger menu on the main window. From this menu, you can cause a *Quack*, *Flap*, or *Paddle* event and see the effect on whatever sinks are connected. If you haven't connected anything, nothing will, in fact, happen. If you have either or both sinks connected, you'll see messages in the window. If you are running on a Win32 system and have a sound board, you'll get to hear what's in the WAV files that come with this sample. Surprise![3]

> **N O T E :** To compile these samples, you'll need the OLECTL.H and OLECTLID.H header files from the Visual C++ Control Development Kit. However, you don't need any import libraries from the CDK.

## Implementing and Connecting a Sink

As mentioned earlier, the main client code in the Connect sample is contained within the *CApp* class, which is defined in CONNECT.H:

```
//Identifiers for sinks, indexes into m_rgpSink below
enum
    {
    SINK1=0,
    SINK2
    };


class CApp
    {
    friend LRESULT APIENTRY ConnectWndProc(HWND, UINT, WPARAM, LPARAM);

    protected:
        HINSTANCE       m_hInst;            //WinMain parameters
        HINSTANCE       m_hInstPrev;
        UINT            m_nCmdShow;
        HWND            m_hWnd;             //Main window handle
        PCDuckEvents    m_rgpSink[2];       //Sinks to connect

        PCConnObject    m_pObj;             //Source object

    protected:
        void            Connect(UINT);
        void            Disconnect(UINT);
        IConnectionPoint *GetConnectionPoint(void);
```

*(continued)*

---

3. I'll be honest. These sounds are only my imitations of the ducks that paddle around the lake near my house. I couldn't get one to come inside and give me voice samples.

```
public:
    CApp(HINSTANCE, HINSTANCE, UINT);
    ~CApp(void);

    BOOL        Init(void);
    void        Message(LPTSTR);
};
```

```
typedef CApp *PAPP;
```

One of the reasons I say this sample is contrived is that *CApp* maintains a pointer to the source object it creates using the C++ type instead of an interface. This lets us tell the source to trigger events when the menu commands are given. Obviously, when a real OLE client-object relationship is at work, the client would have only an interface pointer at any given time, and something outside the client would trigger events. That consideration aside, everything else is more or less what any client might have. This class has three protected member functions — *Connect, Disconnect,* and *GetConnectionPoint* — to centralize the connection process for whatever sink we might want to work with. The little enumeration of the values SINK1 and SINK2 provides names for the indexes into the array of sink objects stored in *m_ rgpSink.*

The sinks themselves are implemented using the C++ class *CDuckEvents,* also defined in CONNECT.H:

```
class CDuckEvents : public IDuckEvents
    {
    private:
        ULONG       m_cRef;     //Reference count
        PAPP        m_pApp;     //For calling Message
        UINT        m_uID;      //Sink identifier

    public:
        //Connection key, public for CApp's usage
        DWORD       m_dwCookie;

    public:
        CDuckEvents(PAPP, UINT);
        ~CDuckEvents(void);

        //IUnknown members
        STDMETHODIMP            QueryInterface(REFIID, PPVOID);
        STDMETHODIMP_(DWORD) AddRef(void);
        STDMETHODIMP_(DWORD) Release(void);
```

```
    //IDuckEvents members
    STDMETHODIMP Quack(void);
    STDMETHODIMP Flap(void);
    STDMETHODIMP Paddle(void);
};
```

This is pretty standard stuff for implementing a simple object with a single interface, which is usually all we need for sink objects. If you require a sink with multiple interfaces, feel free to use any of the three techniques for doing so described in the "Implementing Multiple Interfaces" section in Chapter 2. The implementation of this class, found in SINK.CPP, is also typical. The only interesting parts for our discussion are the *event handlers,* that is, the implementations of the specific members of *IDuckEvents,* each of which looks just like the following code for *CDuckEvents::Quack,* with nothing more than a few names changed:

```
STDMETHODIMP CDuckEvents::Quack(void)
    {
    TCHAR       szTemp[100];

    wsprintf(szTemp, TEXT("Sink #%u received Quack."), m_uID+1);
    m_pApp->Message(szTemp);

#ifdef WIN32
    PlaySound(TEXT("quack.wav"), NULL, SND_SYNC);
#endif

    return NOERROR;
    }
```

**NOTE:** The *PlaySound* function is part of the Win32 API in the import library WINMM.LIB, and it requires a sound card to operate. SND_SYNC means that *PlaySound* will not return until the sound has finished playing. This ensures that you'll be able to see and hear events in both sinks when they're both connected.

As I mentioned, the Connect sample creates two instances of *CDuckEvents* during initialization in *CApp::Init,* using the C++ *new* operator. Immediately after they're created, *CApp::Init* calls *AddRef* on both sinks to ensure that their lifetimes will be stable until Connect is closed. These references are released in *CApp::~CApp,* which will cause the sink objects to destroy themselves.

Now for the interesting parts of the client code. Object creation happens through use of the C++ *new* operator within the IDM_OBJECTCREATE case of *ConnectWndProc*, as seen in the following:

```
pObj=new CConnObject();

if (NULL!=pObj)
    {
    fRes=pObj->Init();
    pObj->AddRef();
    }
```

Again, this sample is contrived because no OLE client ever has access to a C++ object for an OLE object. All of this creation code would always be encapsulated within an object's own creation process. The call to *AddRef* here, however, allows the rest of the code to treat the object like any other OLE object, calling *Release* to free it.

With an instantiated object, you can connect either or both sinks to the source object. Selecting Connect from the menu calls *CApp::Connect,* and selecting Disconnect calls *CApp::Disconnect.* Big surprise. In either case, we need to have an *IConnectionPoint* pointer to the connection point for *IDuckEvents.* Retrieving this pointer from the object is the purpose of *CApp::GetConnectionPoint*:

```
IConnectionPoint * CApp::GetConnectionPoint(void)
    {
    HRESULT                      hr;
    IConnectionPointContainer  *pCPCont;
    IConnectionPoint           *pCP=NULL;

    hr=m_pObj->QueryInterface(IID_IConnectionPointContainer
        , (PPVOID)&pCPCont);

    if (FAILED(hr))
        return NULL;

    hr=pCPCont->FindConnectionPoint(IID_IDuckEvents, &pCP);
    pCPCont->Release();

    if (FAILED(hr))
        return NULL;

    return pCP;
    }
```

This function executes the sequence described earlier in this chapter for obtaining the connection point interface pointer for a known IID. It also demonstrates that you can call *Release* on the *IConnectionPointContainer* interface without harm to the *IConnectionPoint* pointer. This is because connection points are contained within the source object and therefore contribute to its overall reference count. (It would also be silly to destroy an object you're trying to connect to, so a client will usually have another unrelated interface pointer to the same source object that keeps it alive anyway.)

With the *IConnectionPoint* pointer for the connection point that supports *IDuckEvents, Connect* establishes the connection and *Disconnect* terminates it, as shown in the following:

```
void CApp::Connect(UINT uID)
    {
    HRESULT            hr;
    IConnectionPoint   *pCP;

    [Trivial validation code omitted]

    //Is this sink connected already?
    if (0!=m_rgpSink[uID]->m_dwCookie)
        {
        Message(TEXT("This sink is already connected."));
        return;
        }

    pCP=GetConnectionPoint();

    if (NULL!=pCP)
        {
        hr=pCP->Advise(m_rgpSink[uID]
            , &m_rgpSink[uID]->m_dwCookie);

        if (FAILED(hr))
            Message(TEXT("Connection failed."));
        else
            Message(TEXT("Connection complete."));

        pCP->Release();
        }
    else
        Message(TEXT("Failed to get IConnectionPoint."));

    return;
    }
```

*(continued)*

```
void CApp::Disconnect(UINT uID)
    {
    HRESULT                hr;
    IConnectionPoint    *pCP;

    [Trivial validation code omitted]

    //Is the sink connected at all?
    if (0==m_rgpSink[uID]->m_dwCookie)
        {
        Message(TEXT("This sink is not connected."));
        return;
        }

    pCP=GetConnectionPoint();

    if (NULL!=pCP)
        {
        hr=pCP->Unadvise(m_rgpSink[uID]->m_dwCookie);

        if (FAILED(hr))
            Message(TEXT("Disconnection failed."));
        else
            {
            Message(TEXT("Disconnection complete."));
            m_rgpSink[uID]->m_dwCookie=0;
            }

        pCP->Release();
        }
    else
        Message(TEXT("Failed to get IConnectionPoint."));

    return;
    }
```

These functions can work with either sink stored in *CApp* according to the index *uID* passed as an argument. *Connect* simply calls *IConnectionPoint-::Advise* and stores the returned connection key in the *m_dwCookie* member of *CDuckEvents*. *Disconnect* checks to be sure the connection exists and then passes that same *m_dwCookie* to *IConnectionPoint::Unadvise* to terminate the relationship.

So the stage is set. The lights are turned low. We're ready to see how the connectable object uses these connected sinks to fire events.

## Implementing a Connectable (Source) Object

The complete implementation of a source with even a single connection point is a little more complicated than the implementation of a sink because several different independent objects are on the scene. Each C++ class for the object part of the Connect sample is defined in OBJECT.H. Those dealing with the object as a whole are implemented in OBJECT.CPP, and those dealing with connection points themselves are in CONNPT.CPP. Each object class singly inherits from the interface it implements, as follows:

■ The connectable object, in this case *CConnObject*, provides *IConnectionPointContainer* and maintains a reference count and an array of *CConnectionPoint* pointers (see the third item) in *m_rgpConnPt*. It has a member function named *TriggerEvent* that is called from *ConnectWndProc* when any Trigger menu item is selected. In the Connect sample, this object manages only a single connection point, but the code is written to handle an array of such contained objects for your reference.

■ The enumerator created from *IConnectionPointContainer::EnumConnectionPoints* is implemented using *CEnumConnectionPoints*, a typical enumerator implementation that deals with the type *IConnectionPoint ∗*. This is written to manage an arbitrarily large array of pointers.

■ Each connection point (of which there is only one in this sample at any time) is an instance of the generic class named *CConnectionPoint*. This class manages an array of *IUnknown* pointers passed to it through *IConnectionPoint::Advise* and is completely generic (that is, it contains nothing specific to any outgoing interface). Its one limitation is that it fixes the number of allowed connections at compile time (to the constant CCONNMAX) instead of dynamically allocating space to store connection information. In any case, it is written to be quite usable in your own work.

■ The enumerator created from *IConnectionPoint::EnumConnections* is implemented using *CEnumConnections*, another typical enumerator based on the OLE-defined type CONNECTDATA that contains an *IUnknown* pointer and a DWORD connection key—everything needed to describe any single connection.

The following sections look at each piece of the implementation in more detail.

## The Source Object

We've seen how the client side of the Connect sample creates an instance of *CConnObject,* to which it later makes connections. It instantiates the connection points (only one of them in this case, defined by the constant CCONN-POINTS) during initialization in *CConnObject::Init*:

```
BOOL CConnObject::Init(void)
    {
    UINT    i;

    //Create our connection points.
    for (i=0; i < CCONNPOINTS; i++)
        {
        m_rgpConnPt[i]=new CConnectionPoint(this, IID_IDuckEvents);

        if (NULL==m_rgpConnPt[i])
            return FALSE;

        m_rgpConnPt[i]->AddRef();
        }

    return TRUE;
    }
```

Remember that external clients must always see these contained connection points as separate objects, which means that your source's *Query-Interface* never returns a pointer to these connection points, even if some client asks for *IConnectionPoint*. In the Connect sample, *CConnObject::Query-Interface* responds only to *IUnknown* and *IConnectionPointContainer*. If you have only a single connection point in your object, you can cheat and implement *IConnectionPoint* as an interface of the whole object itself, provided you supply the proper *QueryInterface* behavior through all the interfaces. (You can share *AddRef* and *Release* implementations as long as they all affect a single reference count.) But I find it more explicit (and easier for you to understand) to keep them as separate objects.

The implementation of *IConnectionPointContainer* is now simply a matter of returning pointers from the *m_rgpConnPt* array either singly through *Find-ConnectionPoint* or as a set through *EnumConnectionPoints*. The first approach is simplest. Using it, you query the connection point for its *IConnectionPoint*, which has the added and desirable effect of calling *AddRef* on that pointer:

```
STDMETHODIMP CConnObject::FindConnectionPoint(REFIID riid
    , IConnectionPoint **ppCP)
    {
    *ppCP=NULL;
```

```
if (IID_IDuckEvents==riid)
    {
    return m_rgpConnPt[0]->QueryInterface(IID_IConnectionPoint
        , (PPVOID)ppCP);
    }

return ResultFromScode(E_NOINTERFACE);
}
```

You can see how easily this code would expand to serve additional connection points, by adding additional conditions for other IIDs. *EnumConnectionPoints*, however, is a little more involved. We have to instantiate the enumerator by giving it copies of all the pointers:

```
STDMETHODIMP CConnObject::EnumConnectionPoints
    (LPENUMCONNECTIONPOINTS *ppEnum)
    {
    IConnectionPoint        *rgCP[CCONNPOINTS];
    UINT                    i;
    PCEnumConnectionPoints  pEnum;

    *ppEnum=NULL;

    for (i=0; i < CCONNPOINTS; i++)
        rgCP[i]=(IConnectionPoint *)m_rgpConnPt[i];

    //Create the enumerator: we have only one connection point.
    pEnum=new CEnumConnectionPoints(this, CCONNPOINTS, rgCP);

    if (NULL==pEnum)
        return ResultFromScode(E_OUTOFMEMORY);

    pEnum->AddRef();
    *ppEnum=pEnum;
    return NOERROR;
    }
```

The constructor for *CEnumConnectionPoints* takes a pointer to the object (for reference counting), a pointer to the number of connection points in the enumeration (in this case only one, but the enumerator is generic to handle any number), and a pointer to an array of *IConnectionPoint* pointers. The constructor makes a copy of this array and keeps a reference count on each connection point and is released in the destructor, as shown on the following page.

```
CEnumConnectionPoints::CEnumConnectionPoints(LPUNKNOWN pUnkRef
    , ULONG cPoints, IConnectionPoint **rgpCP)
    {
    UINT        i;

    m_cRef=0;
    m_pUnkRef=pUnkRef;

    m_iCur=0;
    m_cPoints=cPoints;
    m_rgpCP=new IConnectionPoint *[(UINT)cPoints];

    if (NULL!=m_rgpCP)
        {
        for (i=0; i < cPoints; i++)
            {
            m_rgpCP[i]=rgpCP[i];
            m_rgpCP[i]->AddRef();
            }
        }

    return;
    }

CEnumConnectionPoints::~CEnumConnectionPoints(void)
    {
    if (NULL!=m_rgpCP)
        {
        UINT        i;

        for (i=0; i < m_cPoints; i++)
            m_rgpCP[i]->Release();

        delete [] m_rgpCP;
        }

    return;
    }
```

To ensure that the object whose connection points are being enumerated sticks around as long as the enumerator itself, any *AddRef* or *Release* call to the enumerator is forwarded to the object as well. Circular references don't occur, however, because the object doesn't hold any reference to the enumerator; that responsibility belongs to the client.

One final remark about this enumerator: because it enumerates interface pointers, the reference-counting rules stipulate that any pointer returned from the *Next* member receives a reference count as well. Keep this in mind when you implement and use pointer enumerators. As far as *CEnumConnection* is concerned, the *Next* function has to call *AddRef* for any pointer it's about to return:

```
STDMETHODIMP CEnumConnectionPoints::Next(ULONG cPoints
    , IConnectionPoint **ppCP, ULONG *pulEnum)
    {
    ULONG               cReturn=0L;

    [Validation code omitted]

    while (m_iCur < m_cPoints && cPoints > 0)
        {
        *ppCP=m_rgpCP[m_iCur++];

        if (NULL!=*ppCP)
            (*ppCP)->AddRef();

        ppCP++;
        cReturn++;
        cPoints--;
        }

    [Other code omitted]
    return NOERROR;
    }
```

So besides the typical *IUnknown* members, that's all there is to *IConnectionPointContainer*. Even with the enumerator, the implementation is not terribly involved, not terribly difficult, nor terribly tricky.

## The Connection Point Object

Creating an object to implement a connection point is really no more complicated than creating a connection point container, as you can see in the implementation of *CConnectionPoint*, found in CONNPT.CPP. Let's first look at the definition of this class in OBJECT.H:

```
class CConnectionPoint : public IConnectionPoint
    {
    private:
        ULONG           m_cRef;         //Object reference count
        PCConnObject    m_pObj;         //Containing object
        IID             m_iid;          //Our relevant interface
```

*(continued)*

```
IUnknown         *m_rgpIUnknown[CCONNMAX];
DWORD            m_rgdwCookies[CCONNMAX];

UINT             m_cConn;
DWORD            m_dwCookieNext; //Counter
```

```
[Constructor, destructor, IConnectionPoint members omitted]
};
```

This implementation of a connection point, as I mentioned before, is slightly crippled because it is limited to maintaining a fixed number of connections determined at compile time through the CCONNMAX value. In the Connect sample, the number is two because that's all we'll need. A really robust and flexible connection point should maintain some kind of variable-length list for maintaining connections, if it needs to. But if your design won't require as many connections, feel free to limit their number as necessary.

*CConnectionPoint* also maintains the IID (*m_iid*) that it can connect to, the *IUnknown* interface pointers it receives through *Advise* (*m_rgpIUnknown*), the connection cookies assigned to them (*m_rgdwCookies*), the current number of connections (*m_cConn*), and the cookie to assign in the next *Advise* call (*m_dwCookieNext*). The variable *m_dwCookieNext* is basically a counter that starts at some arbitrary value (100) and is incremented in every *Advise* call. This increment is not by itself thread safe, and it must be controlled with a semaphore if you are planning to do multithreaded work. Remember also that none of these variables—and nothing in this object class or its associated enumerator—are specific to *IDuckEvents*, making this a nicely usable class in whatever connection point implementations you might run into.

Now, besides the ubiquitous *IUnknown* members, which have yet another typical implementation, we have five connection point–specific members. The first two, *GetConnectionInterface* and *GetConnectionPointContainer*, are trivial:

```
STDMETHODIMP CConnectionPoint::GetConnectionInterface(IID *pIID)
    {
    if (NULL==pIID)
        return ResultFromScode(E_POINTER);

    *pIID=m_iid;
    return NOERROR;
    }
```

```
STDMETHODIMP CConnectionPoint::GetConnectionPointContainer
    (IConnectionPointContainer **ppCPC)
    {
    return m_pObj->QueryInterface(IID_IConnectionPointContainer
        , (void **)ppCPC);
    }
```

*QueryInterface* works nicely in *GetConnectionPointContainer* because it retrieves the pointer, calls *AddRef,* and returns an HRESULT in one stroke. The *m_iid* value returned from *GetConnectionInterface* is actually stored in the *CConnectionPoint* constructor as it is passed from the source that creates this connection point. This is another means of making this implementation generic.

The *Advise* function, which receives an *IUnknown* pointer to the sink to connect, now executes the following steps:

1. Checks that there is space for another connection if space is limited. If there is no space, returns CONNECT_E_ADVISELIMIT. Otherwise, adds another space to whatever list the connection point maintains.

2. Queries the sink's *IUnknown* interface for the expected outgoing interface, which is identified in this implementation with *m_iid.* If this fails, returns CONNECT_E_CANNOTCONNECT. Otherwise, you have a pointer, at least an *IUnknown* pointer, with a reference count on it that you can store. (The implementation doesn't actually need to know the outgoing interface type; it can treat the result of the query as an *IUnknown,* which is perfectly safe.)

3. Finds an open space in whatever connection list this connection point maintains and stores the pointer from step 2. This pointer already has an *AddRef* on it, so there's no need for another.

4. Stores a new unique cookie in the out-parameter named *pdwCookie.* You should remember the value stored here along with the pointer saved in step 3 so you can correctly match the cookie to the pointer in *Unadvise* later on.

5. Increments your connection count and returns NOERROR.

We can see this process implemented in *CConnectionPoint::Advise,* as shown on the following page.

```
STDMETHODIMP CConnectionPoint::Advise(LPUNKNOWN pUnkSink
    , DWORD *pdwCookie)
    {
    UINT            i;
    IUnknown        *pSink;

    *pdwCookie=0;

    //Check whether we're already full of sink pointers.
    if (CCONNMAX==m_cConn)
        return ResultFromScode(CONNECT_E_ADVISELIMIT);

    if (FAILED(pUnkSink->QueryInterface(m_iid, (PPVOID)&pSink)))
        return ResultFromScode(CONNECT_E_CANNOTCONNECT);

    for (i=0; i < CCONNMAX; i++)
        {
        if (NULL==m_rgpIUnknown[i])
            {
            m_rgpIUnknown[i]=pSink;
            m_rgdwCookies[i]=++m_dwCookieNext;
            *pdwCookie=m_dwCookieNext;
            break;
            }
        }

    m_cConn++;
    return NOERROR;
    }
```

Here again, the code to increment the cookie counter, *m_rgdwCookies[i]-=++m_dwCookieNext*, is not thread safe. Also, this counter, which is initialized to 100, is a DWORD and doesn't have much chance of rolling over anytime soon, so it's not anything to worry about. Finally, you might think that the sink pointer value itself might be a great way to uniquely identify the sink and be tempted to return it as the cookie. Bad idea. It is possible that a connection point is given the same exact interface pointer for the sink more than once. The connection point cannot make any assumptions about this sort of thing, especially because the pointer could be for a proxy that is talking to an out-of-process object elsewhere. A pointer value is not necessarily unique, so a counter is the easiest solution, albeit not entirely perfect. I hope that we're not still using the same instance of an object by the time it's made more than 4 billion connections!

Now that we've seen how *Advise* stores a pointer and a cookie, *Unadvise*, which receives a cookie as an argument, needs to find the matching pointer, release it, clear out that entry in the connection list, and decrement the connection count:

```
STDMETHODIMP CConnectionPoint::Unadvise(DWORD dwCookie)
    {
    UINT        i;

    if (0==dwCookie)
        return ResultFromScode(E_INVALIDARG);

    for (i=0; i < CCONNMAX; i++)
        {
        if (dwCookie==m_rgdwCookies[i])
            {
            ReleaseInterface(m_rgpIUnknown[i]);
            m_rgdwCookies[i]=0;
            m_cConn--;
            return NOERROR;
            }
        }

    return ResultFromScode(CONNECT_E_NOCONNECTION);
    }
```

The *ReleaseInterface* macro is found in INC\INOLE.H. This macro calls *Release* through the given pointer and sets that pointer to NULL.

What's left to see in the *IConnectionPoint* interface is *EnumConnections*. The enumerator created through this function deals with OLE's CONNECTDATA:

```
typedef struct tagCONNECTDATA
    {
    LPUNKNOWN pUnk;
    DWORD dwCookie;
    } CONNECTDATA;
```

Everything you'd want to know about a connection! Anyway, the implementation of *EnumConnections* creates an array of such structures, and then it passes that array to the constructor for *CEnumConnections*:

```
STDMETHODIMP CConnectionPoint::EnumConnections
    (LPENUMCONNECTIONS *ppEnum)
    {
    LPCONNECTDATA       pCD;
    UINT                i, j;
    PCEnumConnections   pEnum;

    *ppEnum=NULL;

    if (0==m_cConn)
        return ResultFromScode(E_FAIL);

    pCD=new CONNECTDATA[(UINT)m_cConn];

    if (NULL==pCD)
        return ResultFromScode(E_OUTOFMEMORY);

    for (i=0, j=0; i < CCONNMAX; i++)
        {
        if (NULL!=m_rgpIUnknown[i])
            {
            pCD[j].pUnk=(LPUNKNOWN)m_rgpIUnknown[i];
            pCD[j].dwCookie=m_rgdwCookies[i];
            j++;
            }
        }

    pEnum=new CEnumConnections(this, m_cConn, pCD);
    delete [] pCD;

    if (NULL==pEnum)
        return ResultFromScode(E_OUTOFMEMORY);

    //This does an AddRef for us.
    return pEnum->QueryInterface(IID_IEnumConnections, (PPVOID)ppEnum);
    }
```

Be aware that the array passed to *CEnumConnections* is only temporary and that the connection point itself doesn't call *AddRef* on any of the pointers. This is because the enumerator will make a complete copy of this array in its own constructor, as you can see in the following code.

```
CEnumConnections::CEnumConnections(LPUNKNOWN pUnkRef, ULONG cConn
    , LPCONNECTDATA prgConnData)
    {
    UINT         i;

    m_cRef=0;
    m_pUnkRef=pUnkRef;

    m_iCur=0;
    m_cConn=cConn;

    m_rgConnData=new CONNECTDATA[(UINT)cConn];

    if (NULL!=m_rgConnData)
        {
        for (i=0; i < cConn; i++)
            {
            m_rgConnData[i]=prgConnData[i];
            m_rgConnData[i].pUnk->AddRef();
            }
        }

    return;
    }

CEnumConnections::~CEnumConnections(void)
    {
    if (NULL!=m_rgConnData)
        {
        UINT          i;

        for (i=0; i < m_cConn; i++)
            m_rgConnData[i].pUnk->Release();

        delete [] m_rgConnData;
        }

    return;
    }
```

Why go to all the trouble to make a copy? Because of the *IEnumConnections::Clone* member. Any clone of this enumerator needs its own copy in case the first enumerator is released before this clone or any later clone. Because this implementation doesn't tie all clones together with a common reference count, a copy is necessary.

Finally, like the *Next* function in *CEnumConnectionPoints* shown earlier, the *Next* function in this enumerator also needs to call *AddRef* on the pointers in each CONNECTDATA structure it enumerates:

```
STDMETHODIMP CEnumConnections::Next(ULONG cConn
    , LPCONNECTDATA pConnData, ULONG *pulEnum)
    {
    [Other code omitted]

    while (m_iCur < m_cConn && cConn > 0)
        {
        *pConnData++=m_rgConnData[m_iCur];
        m_rgConnData[m_iCur++].pUnk->AddRef();
        cReturn++;
        cConn--;
        }

    [Other code omitted]
    return NOERROR;
    }
```

This is a complete connection point implementation. How then can we use this implementation to assist in firing events?

## Triggering Events

I mentioned earlier that the Connect sample makes some compromises because the client, the object, and the sink are all part of the same program. The primary reason for these compromises is that in order for events to be demonstrated, something has to trigger them. In real sources, triggers are usually events that happen to the object directly, such as a mouse click in a window, a change in some data, or an event or a notification sent from some other source altogether. In this sample, however, the triggers are menu items that come as WM_COMMAND messages into the main *ConnectWndProc* function. To turn these messages into events, *ConnectWndProc* calls *CConnObject-::TriggerEvent*, passing an ID of the event that has been triggered. Again, an actual client-object relationship in OLE would not have this kind of a C++ mechanism; it could, however, call a trigger function that is part of some other incoming interface on the source. That's perfectly legal.

Regardless of how the trigger reaches the source, the source has to call each and every connected sink that is interested in the corresponding event. This is a perfect time for the source to call *IConnectionPoint::EnumConnections* on the appropriate connection point. It can iterate over each *IUnknown* pointer in the CONNECTDATA structures, query each pointer for the right outgoing interface, call the appropriate member function, and then call *Release* on that pointer as well as on the *IUnknown* pointer in the CONNECT-DATA structures. We can see this exact process in *CConnObject::TriggerEvent*, which can fire any of the three events in *IDuckEvents*:

```
BOOL CConnObject::TriggerEvent(UINT iEvent)
    {
    IEnumConnections    *pEnum;
    CONNECTDATA         cd;

    if (FAILED(m_rgpConnPt[0]->EnumConnections(&pEnum)))
        return FALSE;

    while (NOERROR==pEnum->Next(1, &cd, NULL))
        {
        IDuckEvents     *pDuck;

        if (SUCCEEDED(cd.pUnk->QueryInterface(IID_IDuckEvents
            , (PPVOID)&pDuck)))
            {
            switch (iEvent)
                {
                case EVENT_QUACK:
                    pDuck->Quack();
                    break;

                case EVENT_FLAP:
                    pDuck->Flap();
                    break;

                case EVENT_PADDLE:
                    pDuck->Paddle();
                    break;
                }

            pDuck->Release();
            }

        cd.pUnk->Release();
        }

    pEnum->Release();
    return TRUE;
    }
```

217

It is likely that any source will have some similar sort of event-triggering mechanism for the rest of its code to call when the right things happen. You could also make a custom interface for your own internal use with a bunch of member functions named *Fire<EventName>*. This is especially useful when your events also have arguments. A simple dispatching function such as *TriggerEvent* doesn't allow for arguments to the events, although separate functions to each event would. This is all quite unimportant, however, because the key to working with connection points is calling the right member function of any connected sink. That's what makes integration work.

## Summary

While the *IUnknown::QueryInterface* function handles access to an object's incoming interfaces, some objects need to send notifications, events, or requests back to their clients. An object of that kind is a connectable object. The interfaces that a connectable object calls are outgoing interfaces. The connectable object defines and calls interfaces itself, but its client implements these interfaces through sink objects. Through outgoing interfaces, an object carries out two-way communication with its client. One object can multicast to multiple sinks, and one sink can easily accept calls from multiple objects.

To express its outgoing interfaces, an object implements the interface *IConnectionPointContainer*, through which the client can access the object's connection points, which are small contained objects within the connectable object itself. Through *IConnectionPointContainer*, the client can enumerate the available connection points or ask for a specific one given the outgoing interface's IID. Each connection point then manages connections to one or more sinks through the interface *IConnectionPoint*. This two-level container or connection-point architecture will allow for extension of the connection-point idea through additional interfaces, if they become necessary.

This chapter has examined these interfaces, in regard to both the client and the object, through sample code.

## CHAPTER FIVE

# Custom Components and the Component Object Model

*Arthur: Camelot!*
*Galahad: Camelot…*
*Lancelot: Camelot…*
*Patsy: It's only a model….*
*Arthur: Sh!*

—From *Monty Python and the Holy Grail*

When OLE 2 was introduced, almost everyone talked about it in the context of compound documents because OLE 1 dealt with nothing but compound documents. I was one such person, and for a long time (before writing the first edition of this book) I struggled along trying to present OLE 2 as a better way to create compound documents.

But OLE 2 had all these other nagging details that remained enigmatic and confusing. In particular, there was something called COM, the Component Object Model, which apparently had something to do with the interface model that we saw in Chapter 2. COM is at the core of everything in OLE, but that nasty word "Model" just didn't fly with a lot of people. On a few occasions when I was giving an oral presentation, the mere mention of "object model" in the context of OLE interfaces brought glazed looks to many faces in the audience. Many people, especially those trained in traditional object-oriented development school of analysis, design, Booch notation, and so on, understood that an "object model" was a specific set of defined objects and their relationships in a hierarchy—in essence, a "model" or structure that represented some particular business problem. Any mention I made about the Component Object Model was interpreted in a variety of ways, and few people understood how a "model"—a specific design for a specific problem—could form the basis for an extensible service architecture in an operating system, which is what I was usually trying to talk about.

COM, if you think of it as a single word and forget to spell out the acronym, is really nothing more than a specification of how interfaces work and of the fundamental mechanisms that make the creation and use of custom components (services) possible. To use these mechanisms, a client need only know the unique identifier of a component—its class identifier, or CLSID—which it might read from the registry, extract from type information, or obtain at run time through some other means.

Given this CLSID and no other knowledge about a component (except that it supports at least the *IUnknown* interface), a client can ask some implementation of COM to retrieve for it an interface pointer to the root object of that component. From there the client can query for interfaces and check type information for more details about the component and its object. The COM implementation, called the COM Library, performs all the magic necessary to instantiate the object and establish any necessary marshaling across process or machine boundaries. So COM is quite full of some specific, and powerful, functionality. The COM Library, part of OLE32.DLL, also contains the COM API functions such as *CoInitialize* and *CoGetMalloc* and is the generic part of the specification that needs to be implemented only once per system.

The idea of a "model" was part of COM's name because the specification prescribes a certain structure on custom components servers—what exported functions a DLL should have, what an EXE server should do on startup and shutdown, and so forth. These servers implement the remaining parts of the COM specification that the COM Library does not. Between the two, they provide the complete implementation of the specification for clients.

In this chapter, we'll cover the majority of what constitutes the guts of COM as far as client and server implementations are concerned. As you might have noticed, the clients and components we've seen in sample code so far have all been contained within the same application, separated at most by a source file boundary. However, a component integration system such as OLE must facilitate communication between clients and components across arbitrary process and network boundaries. Furthermore, this communication must be transparent, so a client can always make interface member calls through a pointer in its own address space, just as for in-process objects. This is the concept of *Local/Remote Transparency*, the internal architecture of which is the topic of Chapter 6.

In this chapter, we're primarily concerned with the higher-level APIs and interfaces that are involved in establishing communication between a client and the root object of some component, regardless of the location of that component. This mechanism is centered on the instantiation of that root object based on a CLSID that is associated with a particular server module (a DLL or an EXE). A part of COM called the Service Control Manager (SCM, pronounced "scum") takes a CLSID and does all the work to find and run the server, have it create the object, set up Local/Remote Transparency, and return a meaningful and callable interface pointer to the client. After that, it gets out of the way, with the only thing standing between the client and the object being the necessary marshaling support.

This mechanism is the single most fundamental component/object creation mechanism in OLE, by which the CLSID uniquely identifies the component of interest. It is used with OLE Automation objects, OLE Document content objects, OLE Controls, and anything else that you want to act as an extended service to the existing component system. To support such a generic mechanism, a component server must follow a few standards, as we'll see, which include additional registry entries and can include licensing control and self-registration. We'll also see how to make one server emulate—that is, act in place of—another server and how you can break pieces of applications off into components. Through all of this you should gain a good understanding of what components are and how to create them. It is the implementation of components that makes OLE and COM really powerful. Without custom components, COM by itself is only a model.

# Where the Wild Things Are
# (with Apologies to Maurice Sendak)

So what exactly is a custom component? In Chapter 1, we saw how OLE is made up of a fair number of services, or components. Each component is composed of one or more objects, and each object has any number of interfaces that describe its functionality and content.

Now, OLE itself cannot possibly implement every service that clients might want. To meet the demand for additional services, a developer can create a custom component that extends the services that OLE already makes available. Through the standard mechanisms described by COM, a client written to use components of a generic prototype can create an instance of that new component and use its services without knowing anything more specific about it. For example, if you write a client that knows how to browse through an object's type information, that client can work with any component—regardless of its CLSID or anything else it does—whose objects implement *IProvideClassInfo*, through which you can obtain an *ITypeInfo* pointer. As new components are added to the system, additional entries in the system registry appear in order to identify their servers. Your client, without modification, can then immediately begin to use those new components without trouble.

So a *custom component* is any set of objects with any set of interfaces that are wrapped up inside some server module. This component is identified with a unique CLSID, and registry entries provide the association between the CLSID and the path of the server module. A client with that CLSID can then ask COM to access that component. COM does whatever it takes to make this happen and then gets out of the way (except for any necessary marshaling support). This creation process is illustrated in Figure 5-1, which shows how there really isn't much between the client and the object.

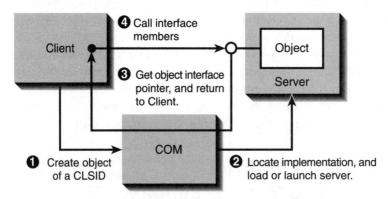

**Figure 5-1.**
*A client uses COM to access the first interface pointer for an object in some server's component.*

COM's Local/Remote Transparency allows any code acting as a client to access and use the services of components without regard to the boundaries between client and component. Some components will be located in DLLs (in-process), others in EXEs (local), and still others in such modules running on other machines (remote) by which a remote component itself might be distributed across many machines. How a server runs—in-process, local, or remote—is called its *execution context.*

A client doesn't have to care about the execution context because COM ensures that any interface calls, made in either direction, are marshaled across the applicable boundary using the appropriate magic, as illustrated in Figure 5-2. When an in-process component is in use, pointers to the interfaces of the objects within it are in the same address space as the client, so calls through such pointers are direct calls into the object code. When a greater boundary separates the client and the component, COM performs its Local/Remote Transparency magic through proxies and stubs to marshal the call to another process. The greater the distance or separation between client and component, the slower the marshaling of function calls will be, of course.

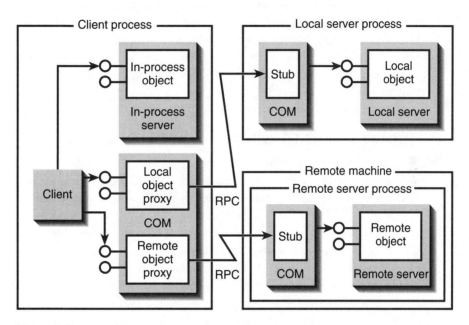

**Figure 5-2.**
*Clients can use other components across any boundary.*

Another term used to describe the role of a proxy is that of *object handler*. Structurally, a handler is no different than a proxy or an in-process server. But whereas a standard proxy usually forwards every call to a local or remote server, and whereas an in-process server completely implements the object, a handler is everything in the middle. A handler usually exposes an object with all the interfaces the client expects, but the handler itself only provides a *partial* object implementation of that object. For example, a handler might implement the performance-critical members of certain interfaces, delegating the remainder to its corresponding local server, usually through a standard proxy. A handler is also useful when an object requires an interface that can only be implemented in-process. Some interfaces involve arguments to member functions that simply cannot be shared across process boundaries (like an HDC), and some interfaces do not have marshaling support available (either by design or because such support hasn't been shipped yet). For whatever reason, a handler is necessary; it completes its implementation by establishing communication with its own local server, just as any other client would, but only when absolutely necessary. This cuts down on the total memory overhead necessary for the component at any given time.

However you choose to implement a component with whatever type of server and handler, the objects in that component can, for the most part, support any interfaces you want. The only exceptions are those interfaces that have no marshaling support, in which case you must implement those with an in-process server or handler.

# The Mechanisms of Server, Client, and COM

A *server* is a module that provides a service, or component. In other words, the server is the module—EXE or DLL—in which a component resides, and that server is responsible for exposing that component to the outside world. Now, OLE itself can be considered the "server" for many components, such as type library management, which we saw in Chapter 3, or Compound Files, which we'll see in Chapter 7. Because OLE itself is part of the operating system, it can provide uniquely named API functions, such as *CreateTypeLib*, in order to provide access to its own components. But a custom component server does not have this luxury; any exported API function for creating an instance of that component is not part of the system API, so there is no efficient way to publish such a function for clients at run time. This is a problem especially when you consider that an end user might install a component on a machine after a client is installed. For that component to be useful at all, it must become immediately available to all existing clients, as well as those clients installed later on.

The solution to this problem is to implement both client and server to a particular central standard, which is part of COM. Given a CLSID of a component, the client asks COM, through standard API functions, to create an instance of that component; COM, in turn, asks the server, through standard functions and interfaces, to create that instance and return an interface pointer that COM gives to the client (creating marshaling support as necessary). Given such a standard mechanism, a client is free from specific knowledge about servers, and servers are free from specific knowledge about clients. The simple abstraction layer of COM provides this freedom. The following sections examine the responsibilities and roles of the server, the client, and COM in implementing this standard.

One point, however, applies to both clients and servers alike when those agents are executables themselves. When any executable is run, the operating system creates a new task—a new process space—for that executable. As we saw in Chapter 2, any executable that is using OLE must call *CoInitialize* on startup and *CoUninitialize* on shutdown (or *OleInitialize* and *OleUninitialize*, as necessary). This applies not only to clients, as we've seen so far, but also to local and remote component servers, because those servers have their own processes as well. It is easy to confuse task initialization as a client-only concern, so remember that it always applies to any executable, even components.

## Server (and Handler) Responsibilities

To meet the COM standard for component instantiation, a server must provide the following, regardless of whether it's a DLL or an EXE:

- Registry entries that associate the server module with the CLSID. This can be optionally provided through self-registration and can include entries through which the server indicates that it should be used to emulate another server.

- An implementation of a class factory object that supports *IClassFactory* through which COM asks the server to create the root object in the component. This class factory can support *IClassFactory2* instead if it wants to control object creation through licensing.

- A mechanism through which COM can access the server's class factory.

- An unloading mechanism through which the server that is no longer serving any objects can be removed from memory.

Although all servers follow the generic structure shown in Figure 5-3 on the next page, the exact implementation of each of these requirements differs for DLLs and EXEs, regardless of whether those modules exist on the same machine or on a different machine from the client. The details of these requirements apply to remote servers just as they do to in-process and local servers. In addition, an object handler is structurally equivalent to a full-blown DLL server, so everything described here for DLLs also applies to handlers. The only difference between a handler and a full server is the extent of the implementation found in that component.

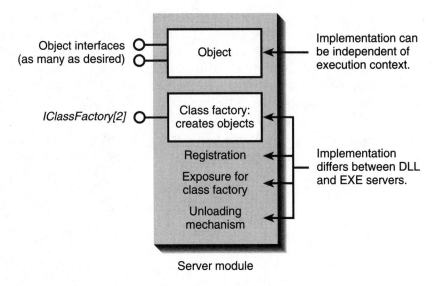

**Figure 5-3.**
*The generic structure of a server module.*

## Registry Entries

Every component class requires a unique CLSID to identify it. The registry entries under that CLSID identify the server module for that component. In Chapter 2, we saw the basic use of the CLSID in the registry, which took the following form:

```
\
    CLSID
        {42754580-16b7-11ce-80eb-00aa003d7352} = Acme Component 3.0
```

The *ProgID* and *VersionIndependentProgID* entries are omitted here because they are not particularly relevant to this discussion. In any case, COM requires that you include at least one of the following entries as an additional subkey of the hexadecimal CLSID string:

- In-process servers: *InprocServer32=<path to DLL>*

- Object handlers: *InprocHandler32=<path to DLL>*

- Local servers: *LocalServer32=<path to EXE>*

The value of each entry must be the full pathnames of the DLL or EXE in question; this way, you do not depend on those modules being in the system path. COM enforces this requirement and will fail to load a server if the full pathname is not listed. For that reason, a component's installation program usually updates these values after the exact installation location is known. In any case, any single server DLL or EXE can support as many CLSIDs as it wants because COM provides the CLSID to a class factory when asking it to instantiate an object. This means that the same DLL or EXE pathname can appear under as many CLSIDs in the registry as desired.

These keys can appear in any combination if multiple server modules for the same CLSID exist. When multiple server entries exist, COM will attempt to use them in the order *InprocServer32, InprocHandler32, LocalServer32* unless the client has specified a restriction to only in-process servers or only local servers. For a number of reasons, you might choose to supply both an in-process server and a local server. The most important of these is that a client can then choose which server it would like to use. An in-process server is faster, but if that server crashes it can potentially take down the entire client process. On the other hand, a local server, having its own process space, can crash without any ill effect on the client, thereby making the relationship more secure and robust, but slower.

A useful combination is to register a handler together with a local server. *InprocHandler32* appearing by itself implies that only a partial implementation of a component is available. In many situations, this is perfectly reasonable because partial implementation provides some basic capabilities to clients without requiring the full server. We'll see an example of this in OLE Documents later, in Chapter 19. One use for this combination is to freely distribute a handler as a sort of crippled component that encourages customers to purchase the full component.

---

### A Major Waste of Time

If you use REG files to create registry entries, be very, very careful about extra spaces preceding pathnames in that file: extra spaces make different values. In other words, an entry such as:

```
\...\...\InprocServer32 = c:\inole\chap05\dkoala1\dkoala1.dll
```

is different from:

```
\...\...\InprocServer32 =  c:\inole\chap05\dkoala1\dkoala1.dll
```

where an extra space precedes "c:\inole…" This is the sort of bug you can stare at for hours, and your brain will simply refuse to see it.

## Self-Registration

The most common way to create whatever registry entries you need is to ship a REG file with your component. However, there is always the risk that a component server might show up on a system without any such registry file and without an installation program that knows what entries to create. When a system contains potentially thousands of components, dragging around registry files and installation programs for each of them becomes highly inconvenient. For that reason, COM defines a self-registration mechanism that enables you to encapsulate registry needs into a DLL or an EXE. This provides clients, as well as future system shells, with an easy way to be sure that any given module is fully and accurately registered. In addition, COM also includes a mechanism so that a server can remove (unregister) all of its registry entries when the DLL or EXE is removed from the file system, thereby keeping the registry clean of useless trash.

Self-registration is considered optional for many components, but it is strongly encouraged for exactly the reasons stated above. When a server does support this feature, it can indicate its support in its version information resource by including an entry "OLESelfRegister" with an empty value in the "StringFileInfo" section of the version resource:

```
VS_VERSION_INFO VERSIONINFO
  [...]
  BEGIN
    BLOCK "StringFileInfo"
    BEGIN
      BLOCK "040904B0" // Lang=US English, CharSet=Unicode
      BEGIN
        [...]
        VALUE "OLESelfRegister", "\0"
      END
    END
  [...]
END
```

This entry is optional because the actual self-registration mechanisms do not depend on it. The information simply allows a caller to avoid loading a DLL or launching an EXE for no gain.

When asked to self-register, a server must create all entries for every component that it supports, including any entries for type libraries. When asked to unregister, the server must remove the entries that it created in its self-registration. For a DLL server, these requests are made through calls to the exported functions *DllRegisterServer* and *DllUnregisterServer*, which must exist in the DLL under these exact names. Both functions take no arguments and return an HRESULT to indicate the result. The two applicable error codes are SELFREG_E_CLASS (failure to register/unregister CLSID information) and SELFREG_E_TYPELIB (failure to register/unregister type library information).[1] Because exported functions cannot be used from an EXE, a local server must instead watch for two command-line arguments passed to its *WinMain* named */RegServer* and */UnregServer* (case-insensitive, they may also appear as *-RegServer* and *-UnregServer*). If either argument is detected, the server must perform the necessary registration or unregistration and immediately terminate, without ever showing a main window or executing other code.

## Server Emulation

In a number of scenarios, it is useful to have a server that supports one particular CLSID act in the place of—or emulate—the server for a different component CLSID. For example, an OLE 2 server with a new CLSID would like to replace the OLE 1 server (that is, overwrite the EXE) that uses an older CLSID, but it doesn't want to break any existing clients that use that old CLSID. Another example is a vendor that would like its component to be compatible and interchangeable with another vendor's component. This is highly useful for workgroups that exchange electronic documents that contain content objects from, for example, different graphics editors. Emulation allows an end user to create a document using one class of graphics objects so that another end user with a different but compatible graphics editor can still open the document and view and manipulate its content as if he or she had the same graphics editor as the first end user.

In both cases, obviously, the objects in question must implement the same set of interfaces to retain compatibility with existing clients. In other words, from the client's point of view, objects from either server must be polymorphic through their interfaces. The newer "emulating" server can, however, supply interfaces beyond those supported from the original server's objects. Again, *QueryInterface* keeps those interfaces isolated unless a client specifically asks for those interfaces. The end result is that new clients can use new interfaces while old clients use the original interfaces, all from within a single module. This is a vast improvement over less robust versioning schemes

---

1. SELFREG_E_CLASS and SELFREG_E_TYPELIB are defined in OLECTL.H.

in which over time you end up with an armload of different versions of the same module, like VBRUN100.DLL, VBRUN200.DLL, VBRUN300.DLL, VB-RUN400.DLL, and so on. The presence of multiple versions of a module is confusing to end users who don't know whether they can safely delete a module and free up disk space. COM's emulation facilities, along with *QueryInterface* and the idea of interfaces being the sole difference between object revisions, solves the problem by allowing a single module to handle all versions.

The biggest part of implementing this feature is ensuring that the emulating server's components are compatible with those being emulated. After that is done, however, registry entries named TreatAs and AutoTreatAs, stored under the CLSID of the server being emulated, point to the new emulating server:

```
\
    CLSID
        {42754580-16b7-11ce-80eb-00aa003d7352} = Original Component
            TreatAs = {6fa820f0-2e48-11ce-80eb-00aa003d7352}
            AutoTreatAs = {6fa820f0-2e48-11ce-80eb-00aa003d7352}
            InprocServer32 = c:\older\original.dll

        {6fa820f0-2e48-11ce-80eb-00aa003d7352} = New Emulating Component
            InprocServer32 = c:\newer\emulator.dll
```

In this example, the New Emulating Component is registered to emulate Original Component. Whenever a client asks COM to create an instance of the CLSID *{42754580-16b7-11ce-80eb-00aa003d7352}*, it detects the TreatAs key and uses the server entry under the CLSID *{6fa820f0-2e48-11ce-80eb-00aa003d7352}* instead. (A local server can emulate an in-process server and vice versa without restriction except that such a mixture is risky because clients may be restricting their use to a specific type of server. It is recommended that you match server types when implementing emulation.)

The presence of AutoTreatAs doesn't affect the functionality of *CoGetClassObject* or *CoCreateInstance*. This key is used to describe a *permanent* emulation, whereas TreatAs simply describes a *temporary* emulation. Here's how it works. When New Emulating Component is installed over Original Component (as happens when updating versions), it creates both the TreatAs and AutoTreatAs keys, the latter indicating that Original Component is simply no longer available. Now let's say another component is installed—we'll call it Third Component—that emulates Original Component but doesn't know about New Emulating Component. Third Component, however, doesn't intend to overwrite Original Component (which it would not do if Third Component is not a new version of Original Component), so it only changes the TreatAs key. Now creating an instance of the Original Component CLSID will create an instance of Third Component instead.

Imagine now that Third Component is removed from the system, or for some other reason the end user wants to end Third Component's emulation of Original Component. However, because New Emulating Component overwrote Original Component, the TreatAs value must revert to the CLSID stored with AutoTreatAs. This is the entire reason why AutoTreatAs exists: to store the permanent emulating CLSID.

We can see more of how TreatAs and AutoTreatAs work through the two COM API functions that deal with emulation. The first, *CoGetTreatAsClass*, takes a CLSID and either returns the emulating CLSID read from the TreatAs key or returns S_FALSE to indicate that no emulation exists. *CoGetClassObject* uses this function to find the correct server CLSID.

The second function, *CoTreatAsClass*, takes the old CLSID and the new CLSID. If the two CLSIDs are different, this function creates the TreatAs entry under the old CLSID with the value of the new CLSID and replaces any existing TreatAs entry. Installation programs use this function to create TreatAs, although they create AutoTreatAs manually. If, however, *CoTreatAs-Class* receives the same CLSID in both arguments, it does the following:

- If AutoTreatAs exists, it extracts the CLSID value from that key and stores it as the value for TreatAs.

- If AutoTreatAs does not exist, it deletes the TreatAs key altogether.

*CoTreatAsClass* will also delete the TreatAs entry if the new CLSID given is CLSID_NULL. This is how you turn off any temporary emulation; to turn off permanent emulation, you have to explicitly delete the AutoTreatAs key.

## The Class Factory and *IClassFactory*

Telling COM where a server lives on the file system is one thing, but to make the component useful, that server has to provide a way for COM to request the creation of a new object. This mechanism has two parts. First, the server has to implement a class factory, which is a special type of object that literally manufactures another object of a particular CLSID, as "factory" implies. Second, the server has to expose this class factory to COM, and doing this differs between a DLL and an EXE, just as with the self-registration mechanisms.

The number one concept to understand is that a class factory, while itself an object, is not the root object of the component. Every instance of a class factory is associated with a single CLSID and exists strictly to facilitate the creation of the root object of a component of that CLSID, as illustrated in Figure 5-4. This is part of the COM standard. A single implementation of a class factory, such as a C++ object class, can be written to support any number of CLSIDs, but each instance of such an implementation can create objects for only one CLSID. The reasons for this will be clearer in a moment.

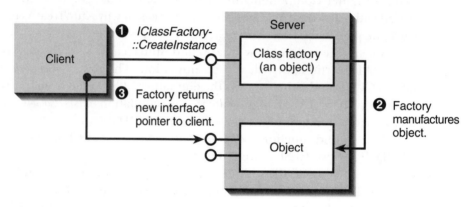

**Figure 5-4.**
*A class factory object exists to create other objects of a specific CLSID.*

A class factory object gets its name because it must implement at least *IClassFactory* (and optionally *IClassFactory2*, which we'll see later).

```
interface IClassFactory : IUnknown
    {
    HRESULT CreateInstance(IUnknown *pUnkOuter, REFIID riid
        , void **ppv);
    HRESULT LockServer(BOOL fLock);
    };
```

The *LockServer* function increments or decrements a *lock count,* which allows a client to keep a server in memory even when it is serving no objects; see "Unloading Mechanisms" later in this chapter for more details on this function. Note that you may run into the archaic belief that you need not implement this function, which is dead wrong. See the NOTE on page 242.

*CreateInstance* does what it says: it creates an *uninitialized* instance of the object associated with the class factory, returning in *\*ppv* a pointer to the interface identified with *riid.* (That is, a *QueryInterface* is built into *Create-Instance.*) The *pUnkOuter* argument is a pointer to the controlling unknown if the object is being created as part of an aggregation (as described in Chapter 2). This *pUnkOuter* is the standard means through which a new object from a custom component is given the controlling unknown pointer. If this pointer is non-NULL and the object doesn't support aggregation, *CreateInstance* should return CLASS_E_NOAGGREGATION. Otherwise the object should verify that the caller has requested *IID_IUnknown* according to the aggregation rules, returning E_NOINTERFACE if not. E_NOINTERFACE is also the return code when the requested interface is not otherwise available, and E_OUTOFMEMORY is a common error to indicate that the object could not be created.

Now you will notice that *CreateInstance* is not passed a CLSID because the association between CLSID and class factory happens elsewhere in the server. (See the section "Exposing the Class Factory" on page 237.) Other than that, the idea of a class factory and the *CreateInstance* function is like the C++ *new* operator, and in fact, C++ implementations of class factories typically use *new* internally. For example, we've already seen code in the *CreateAnimal* function of the Chapter 2 REUSE sample that does exactly what is being described here:

```
HRESULT CreateAnimal(IUnknown *pUnkOuter, REFIID riid, void **ppv)
    {
    CAnimal    *pObj;

    if (NULL!=pUnkOuter && riid!=IID_IUnknown)
        return ResultFromScode(CLASS_E_NOAGGREGATION);

    pObj=new CAnimal(pUnkOuter);

    if (NULL==pObj)
        return FALSE;

    if (!pObj->Init())
        return FALSE;

    return SUCCEEDED(pObj->QueryInterface(riid, (PPVOID)ppv));
    }
```

This code is almost exactly like most *CreateInstance* implementations you'll see and write. What is special about the class factory object is that we can expose an *IClassFactory* pointer outside the server through a standard mechanism, whereas it's much harder to directly expose some arbitrarily named function like *CreateAnimal*. In fact, *IClassFactory* is precisely how you would encapsulate a function such as *CreateAnimal* behind a binary standard so that it can be used from outside the server. In such a case, *IClassFactory-::CreateInstance* would do nothing more than call *CreateAnimal,* and it is the COM interface mechanism that allows the server to expose the pointer to this function in a standard way. This is how COM makes it simple to encapsulate legacy code in OLE objects.

*IClassFactory*, therefore, eliminates the need for any client to know the exact name of the creation function for some type of component—the client need only know the CLSID, which can be retrieved from the registry. So we can now see that the only thing standing between the server pathname in the registry and the class factory itself is a way for COM to get hold of that factory's *IClassFactory* pointer. This is the subject of "Exposing the Class Factory" beginning on page 237.

---

### Uninitialized Objects and Initialization Interfaces

The previous discussion describes *IClassFactory::CreateInstance* as creating an *uninitialized* object from the perspective of the client. This means that the client's first act should be to pass any additional information that will suitably initialize the object. Of course, some objects need no initialization, so that *CreateInstance* returns, in those cases, ready-to-use objects. Other objects, however, will support at least one interface that contains an initialization member function. *IPersistStorage::InitNew* and *IPersistStorage::Load* are interfaces of this kind; one tells an object to initialize with a new state (*InitNew*) while the other tells an object to initialize from a previously saved state (*Load*). Another example of an initialization interface is *IOleObject::SetClientSite*, through which a compound document object is given access to the functionality in the container site, which the object may need for initialization. In the course of this book, we'll see other examples of initialization interfaces.

---

## Licensing with *IClassFactory2*

A monumental problem for most software vendors is piracy—people making copies of software on multiple machines without any payment to the vendor. As more and more components become available, end users will find more opportunities to make illicit copies of those components, perhaps thinking that it's no big deal to copy just a little control or some other small component. People who would not copy a $500 word processor might not be so ethical when it comes to a $5 component, just as people today seem to have no qualms about copying a few fonts between systems. In such an environment it becomes necessary to control illegal copies.

To that end, COM supports a licensing mechanism that a server can use to control instantiations of its components. This involves differentiating between two scenarios:

- A machine (or end user) is fully licensed. Some license file or other information resides on the machine to indicate that the component was installed on the system legally and not simply copied from another source.

- A machine (or end user) is not licensed at all. In this case, a client must have a special license key to instantiate the component, which prevents clients without such a license from accessing the service.

License control means that you must have either global permission to use a component on a given machine or specific permission (the license key) to use the component on another machine.

The first scenario has been employed for some time to control application licensing and works just as well for components. The mechanism is trivial and requires no special operating system support. This is often achieved by having the installation program create some sort of license information on the machine. When the application is loaded, it checks for the presence of this information. If the information is not present, the application automatically terminates with a message politely telling the end user how to order a real copy of that application.

The second scenario is a little more complicated and comes into consideration only when applications are being developed using third-party components, such as custom controls and run-time libraries. The development machine itself is fully licensed because the developer had to purchase all those components and in doing so obtained the necessary licenses. However, any application created on that machine must be portable to other unlicensed machines along with the components, and it must take along with it the necessary permissions to use those components on the other machines. Even though the component server exists on the other machines, other clients are not allowed to use it because global license permissions do not exist. This is called *run-time licensing*.

The *license key* is the piece of information that an application must carry to other machines in order to continue using a component. When the final build of that application is generated, the development tool in use must request a license key from each component in use and save it so that the application can use it later. This key doesn't need to be anything fancy—a simple piece of text will prevent all but the most clever of end users from using illegal copies.

The heart of licensing in COM is the *IClassFactory2* interface, which is a modest enhancement of *IClassFactory*.[2] Because this interface is derived from *IClassFactory*, a server needs only to implement *IClassFactory2* to satisfy all of COM's class factory requirements:

```
interface IClassFactory2 : IClassFactory
    {
    HRESULT GetLicInfo(LPLICINFO pLicInfo);
    HRESULT RequestLicKey(DWORD dwResrved, BSTR FAR* pbstrKey);
    HRESULT CreateInstanceLic(IUnknown *pUnkOuter
        , IUnknown *pUnkReserved, REFIID riid, BSTR bstrKey
        , void **ppvObject);
    };
```

The *GetLicInfo* member function fills a LICINFO structure that describes available license information for this particular component:

```
typedef struct tagLICINFO
    {
    long cbLicInfo;
    BOOL fRuntimeKeyAvail;
    BOOL fLicVerified;
    } LICINFO;
```

The *fLicVerified* flag indicates whether the component has a global license on the machine. This is another way of saying whether *IClassFactory[2]-::CreateInstance* has any chance of succeeding on this machine. If the flag is FALSE, *CreateInstance* should return CLASS_E_NOTLICENSED; if TRUE, *CreateInstance* should work as usual.

The *fRuntimeKeyAvail* flag indicates whether the *RequestLicKey* function will succeed, for it is through this function that a client requests a license key that it can take to another machine in order to continue using the component. This key is returned in the form of a BSTR (introduced in Chapter 3 on page 173), which may, of course, contain encrypted information. This string, in any case, is exactly what a run-time licensed client would store persistently and take to another machine along with the component server.

Now, when that client is run on another machine, any call to *CreateInstance* will fail outright unless a global license also exists there. In the case of

---

2. Licensing was first provided with OLE Controls, so you'll find this interface and associated definitions in OLECTL.H.

failure, the client can instead instantiate an object through *CreateInstanceLic*, using the license key. The class factory validates this key and, if it checks out, proceeds to create the object as if a global license is present. If the key fails validation, the class factory returns CLASS_E_NOTLICENSED. Thus, only a client with a proper license key from a proper installation can hope to instantiate an object from this component on an unlicensed machine.

As a component vendor, you are free to choose as secure a mechanism as you want. Microsoft's scheme is simple: the license file is a simple text file installed with the component itself, and a license key is usually nothing more than the first line of text from that file. This stops end users from making casual copies of a component, but it is fairly weak because you need only to copy the license file as well. A more secure scheme would involve something like additional registry entries, which would make it more difficult for an end user to know how to make a copy. You can go further and incorporate unique installation identifiers and encrypted information. The more devices you employ, the fewer end users will find out how to make and use illegal copies of your software. Whatever your security measures, COM and *IClassFactory* are there to help you validate them at run time.

## Exposing the Class Factory

Now that we understand how to register a server module and what a class factory is, we can see how the server allows COM to access that class factory on behalf of calling clients. How this is accomplished is, in fact, the major difference between DLL and EXE servers, primarily because an EXE defines a task, whereas a DLL doesn't. A class factory is an object, and COM needs to obtain its *IClassFactory* or *IClassFactory2* pointer, or whatever other pointer a client wants. (Clients can request any interface for a class factory.) Let's see how this works for each module in turn.

### In-Process Server

Every DLL server must implement and export a function named *DllGet-ClassObject* with the following form:

```
STDAPI DllGetClassObject(REFCLSID rclsid, REFIID riid, void **ppv);
```

When a client asks COM to create an object and COM finds that an in-process server is available, COM will pull the DLL into memory with the COM API function *CoLoadLibrary*. COM then calls *GetProcAddress* looking for *DllGet-ClassObject*; if successful, it calls *DllGetClassObject*, passing the same CLSID and IID that the client passed to COM. This function creates a class factory for the CLSID and returns the appropriate interface pointer for the requested IID, usually *IClassFactory* or *IClassFactory2*, although the design of this function allows new interfaces to be used in the future. No straitjackets here.

*DllGetClassObject* is structurally similar to *IClassFactory::CreateInstance*, and as we'll see later in the sample code for this chapter, the two functions are almost identical: the difference is that *CreateInstance* creates the component's root object, whereas *DllGetClassObject* creates the class factory. Both query whatever object they create for the appropriate interface pointer to return, which conveniently calls *AddRef* as well.

Because *DllGetClassObject* is passed a CLSID, a single DLL server can provide different class factories for any number of different classes—that is, a single module can be the server for any number of component types. The OLE DLL is itself an example of such a server; it provides most of the internally used object classes of OLE from one DLL.

## Be Sure to Export *DllGetClassObject*

When creating an in-process server or handle, be sure to export *DllGetClassObject* as well as *DllCanUnloadNow*. (See "Unloading Mechanisms" later in this chapter.) Failure to do so will cause a myriad of really strange and utterly confusing bugs. I guarantee that you'll hate tracking these bugs down. Save yourself the trouble and write yourself a really big, hot-pink fluorescent Post-it note and stick it in the middle of your monitor so you'll remember.

### Local Server

Exposing a class factory from an EXE is somewhat different because an EXE has a *WinMain*, a message loop that defines its lifetime, and usually a main window. Whereas COM loads an in-process server and asks it for a class factory pointer, an EXE must instantiate all of its class factories on startup and register them with COM through the function *CoRegisterClassObject*—but only under the appropriate circumstances.

When COM launches an EXE, it appends the command-line argument *-Embedding*[3] (case-insensitive) to the server path stored in the registry. This flag might also appear as */Embedding*, and if you register your EXE with flags yourself, look for the flag at the end of the command line. Checking this flag

---

3. A leftover from OLE 1, in which servers did nothing more than provide an embedded compound document object.

should happen during initialization, after you've checked for *-RegServer* and *-UnregServer*. If this flag is not present, the end user has run your EXE stand-alone. If your component can't run stand-alone at all—that is, if it exists for no purpose other than to serve components—use this condition to immediately terminate the EXE. Note that if *-Embedding* is present, you should not show your main window because your component might be launched specifically to do some processing that the end user should not see. We'll see cases for which this really becomes important when we deal with OLE Documents.

When *-Embedding* is present, the server must create a separate class factory for each CLSID that it supports and pass the class factory interface pointers to *CoRegisterClassObject*. This works in the same way that we are accustomed to calling the Windows API function *RegisterClass* for each window that your application manages. With *RegisterClass*, you create a WNDCLASS structure, fill in the *lpfnWndProc* field with a pointer to your window's message procedure, and pass a pointer to that WNDCLASS to *RegisterClass*. Your window procedure is not actually called until something creates a window of that class. With *CoRegisterClassObject*, you create each class factory you support and pass an interface pointer from each to *CoRegisterClassObject* along with its associated CLSID, but those objects aren't used until some external client asks COM for an object of that CLSID.[4] If the EXE was launched because a client has already asked COM for such an object, COM is patiently waiting (for up to 5 to 10 minutes or so) for the server to register an appropriate class factory before returning to the client with a time-out error. Therefore, you should create and register class factories as soon as possible in your server, particularly before entering your message loop.

Do note that you need to register all supported class factories because, unlike *DllGetClassObject*, COM doesn't have a way to pass an EXE the desired CLSID, and in some cases a single server really has to register multiple factories at once. To see why, we need to look at the *CoRegisterClassObject* arguments:

| Argument | Description |
| --- | --- |
| *rclsid* | The CLSID associated with the class factory |
| *pUnk* | The *IUnknown* pointer to the class factory object |

*(continued)*

---

4. COM itself will actually call *AddRef* a few times when it saves your pointer internally.

*continued*

| Argument | Description |
|---|---|
| *dwContext* | A DWORD describing the execution context of this class factory—that is, the type of server that is registering the factory, which can be CLSCTX_INPROC_SERVER or CLSCTX_LOCAL_SERVER |
| *dwUsage* | A DWORD describing how many objects this class factory can create |
| *pdwReg* | A pointer to a DWORD that receives a registration "key" to use when revoking the registration |

The *dwUsage* flag explains why a server might need to register all of its factories at once: any class factory registered with *dwUsage* set to REGCLS_MULTIPLE_USE eliminates the need to launch another instance of the same EXE every time a client needs one of its components. If an EXE is launched once for one CLSID, it makes all of its other components available as well, and this increases overall performance. On the other hand, a single-use class factory registered with REGCLS_SINGLE_USE can be used only once, and COM must launch another instance of the server to get another instance of that component, which is much costlier. This is necessary when the component involves singular resources or a user interface that excludes multiple object instances.

When a local server registers a class factory with CLSCTX_LOCAL_SERVER and REGCLS_MULTIPLE_USE, that same class factory is also registered with CLSCTX_INPROC_SERVER. This makes the same class factory available to everything else in that process, preventing the need to launch another instance of the EXE. To suppress this behavior, use the REGCLS_MULTI_SEPARATE flag in *dwUsage*, which registers the class factory as strictly local.

During shutdown, a local server must reverse each call to *CoRegisterClassObject* by passing the value stored in the *pdwReg* argument to *CoRevokeClassObject*. This function tells COM to take the previously registered class factory out of service and release any reference counts to it. This will clean up the class factory object (which should delete itself when its reference count reaches zero, like most other objects) and ensure that no client can gain access to a (now) invalid class factory.

Finally, note that it is altogether allowable for an in-process server to register a class factory just as a local server does. This allows other clients to access objects of that class without having to load another DLL or launch another EXE. However, a client in another process will see the server as a local server because the server DLL is not loaded again into the other client's address space. There are some complications with this technique. The biggest one is that the DLL needs to keep the process in which it is loaded alive until all other processes have disconnected from it. This is tricky if not outright impossible at times.

## Unloading Mechanisms

Just as COM will load DLLs and launch EXEs programmatically without any user interaction, it must also have a way to unload those DLLs and terminate those EXEs. Otherwise, it would, over time fill, all available memory with servers that are no longer in use. The problem is a matter of how COM determines whether or not a server is currently servicing any objects.

The bottom line is that a server is no longer needed when there are no lock counts from *IClassFactory::LockServer* and there are no objects, excluding the class factory objects, currently being serviced. Typically, a server will maintain one or two global variables (an object count and a lock count, or one combined counter), and when both counts go to 0, the server isn't needed anymore. An EXE actually doesn't need COM to unload: it can detect the appropriate conditions and terminate itself by calling *PostQuitMessage* to exit its message loop. But DLLs have no idea of how to "quit" or unload themselves, so they must mark themselves as "unloadable" and wait for COM to ask for that condition. Let's look at each case in turn.

### In-Process Server

Being rather passive, the DLL unloading mechanism is fairly trivial. Every now and then—primarily when a client calls the function *CoFreeUnused-Libraries*—COM attempts to call an exported function named *DllCanUnload-Now* in the same manner that it calls *DllGetClassObject*. This function takes no arguments and returns an HRESULT:

```
STDAPI DllCanUnloadNow(void)
```

When COM calls this function, it is essentially asking "Can I unload you now?" *DllCanUnloadNow* returns S_FALSE if any objects or any locks exist, in which case COM doesn't do anything more. If there are no locks or objects, the function returns NOERROR (or S_OK), and COM follows by calling *CoFreeLibrary* to reverse the *CoLoadLibrary* function call that COM used to load the DLL in the first place.

NOTE: Early 16-bit versions of OLE did not implement the *CoFreeUnusedLibraries*, so *DllCanUnloadNow* was never called. This led to the belief that it was not necessary to implement this function or *IClassFactory::LockServer* because the DLL would stay in memory for the duration of the client process. This is no longer true because the COM function is fully functional and will call all DLLs in response. To support proper unloading, you must always implement *IClassFactory::LockServer* as well as *DllCanUnloadNow*.

A DLL's response to a *DllCanUnloadNow* call does not take into consideration the existence or reference counts on any class factory object. Such references are not sufficient to keep a server in memory, which is why *LockServer* exists. To be perfectly honest, an in-process server could include a count of class factories in its global object count if it wanted to, but this doesn't work with a local server, as the following section illustrates.

## Local Server

Unlike a DLL server, which waits passively for COM to ask about unloading it, the EXE server must watch actively for the following conditions and terminate itself when those conditions are met:

- The object count is currently 0 and the last lock is removed by a call to *IClassFactory::LockServer(FALSE)*.

- The lock count is 0 and the last object is destroyed with a call to its *IUnknown::Release*.

If a single combined counter is used, the server need only detect when it is decremented to 0. All of these conditions imply active detection of a decrement event, not just a zero condition. The server terminates after the final decrement, not whenever a counter happens to be 0. Otherwise, the server would start up, detect a zero count, and terminate. That sort of code is about as useful as wearing dark sunglasses for stargazing.

In addition, if an EXE server involves any kind of user interface, it must also maintain a condition called *user control*. This Boolean flag is normally FALSE but is set to TRUE if an end user does anything that "takes control" of the server. For example, a server with a Multiple Document Interface (MDI) might be servicing a document object for the purposes of another client. The end user might come along and create a new document in that server as if it had been run stand-alone. In such a case, the server should most definitely not shut itself down when the original document object is released; otherwise, the end user's new document would be prematurely destroyed without any chance to save it. Bad idea. Automatic termination should not occur unless the user control flag is FALSE. If it is TRUE, only the end user can shut down that EXE.

When an end user forcibly closes a server, other running objects may still be in service. In such a case, the server has two choices: it can either hide its main window, giving the end user the illusion of closing by not actually terminating until all objects are released (essentially setting the user control flag back to FALSE), or disconnect each of its running objects by calling the COM API function *CoDisconnectObject*. This latter solution is rather rude because it will cause any external client's interface calls to return the error RPC_E-_NOTCONNECTED—the client can still make the call because it still has a pointer to the interface proxy, but that proxy has been disconnected from its stub. In effect, *CoDisconnectObject* causes a controlled crash of the external connections to the object. Brutal as this may be, *CoDisconnectObject* gives a server control over external reference counts so it can properly free its objects on shutdown.

We can now examine why a reference count on a class factory object is not strong enough to keep an EXE server from terminating itself. Recall that you must create class factory objects during initialization and register them with *CoRegisterClassObject*. In the process of registration, there will be at least one, if not more, calls to that object's *AddRef* function. The matching calls to *Release* will not be made, however, until the server calls *CoRevokeClassObject* during shutdown. If a positive reference count could keep a class factory in memory, the EXE could not terminate until that object's reference count reached zero and it was destroyed. But the reference count will never reach zero unless we call *CoRevokeClassObject*, but we call *CoRevokeClassObject* only when we are in the shutdown process and are on the nonstop express to oblivion. We can't revoke until we're shutting down and we can't shut down until we revoke. Aaaugh! Fourth down and 100 yards to go…so we punt. Officially, a positive reference count on a class factory cannot be used to keep a server in memory. If a client wants to hold a class factory outside the scope of a function, it must rely on *LockServer* to prevent server shutdown. This is one of the few special cases of reference counting in all of OLE.

# Client Responsibilities

Now that we know and understand how COM, given a CLSID, talks to a server to create an object, we can look at how a client tells COM to do it all in the first place. There are two topics of relevance here:

- Creating and initializing objects from a CLSID with and without licensing

- Managing server lifetime to free unused servers from memory when the client is no longer using previously created objects

In addition to these two capabilities, a client can be written to also support self-registering servers. This generally means little more than supplying an end-user interface through which an end user can select one or more files and ask the client to register or unregister them. The client, in turn, attempts to load any DLL in the list to call *DllRegisterServer* or *DllUnregisterServer* (using *GetProcAddress* to get the address of the function) and attempts to launch any EXE with *-RegServer* or *-UnregServer*. The client could check the version resource to save time if it wants, but that's about all there is to self-registration.

## Creating and Initializing Objects from a CLSID

Given a CLSID, you can create objects in two ways:

- If you need only one object, call the COM API function *CoCreateInstance* with the CLSID and the IID of the interface you want on the object.

- If you need more than one object, call *CoGetClassObject* to obtain an *IClassFactory* pointer for that CLSID, and then call *IClassFactory::CreateInstance* as often as you want with the desired IID. Call *IClassFactory::Release* when you have finished.

*CoCreateInstance* is really nothing more than a convenient wrapper around *CoGetClassObject* and *IClassFactory::CreateInstance* that creates a single object. The following code shows the basic implementation of this function:

```
STDAPI CoCreateInstance(REFCLSID rclsid, LPUNKNOWN pUnkOuter
    , DWORD dwContext, REFIID iid, void **ppv)
```

```
{
HRESULT          hr;
IClassFactory *pCF;

*ppv=NULL;

hr=CoGetClassObject(rclsid, dwContext, NULL, IID_IClassFactory
    , (void **)&pCF);

if (FAILED(hr))
    return hr;

hr=pCF->CreateInstance(pUnkOuter, iid, ppv);
pCF->Release();
return hr;
}
```

What the arguments to this function mean is not hard to figure out: *rclsid* is the CLSID of interest, *pUnkOuter* points to the outer unknown if this call is being made for aggregation purposes, and *riid* and *ppv* are just like the arguments passed to *QueryInterface* that specify the type of interface pointer to obtain from the newly created object. The most interesting argument is *dwContext*, which allows the caller to restrict the types of servers used for the object: it can be CLSCTX_INPROC_SERVER, CLSCTX_INPROC_HANDLER, CLSCTX_LOCAL_SERVER, or any combination of these values. The value CLSCTX_ALL is defined as the combination of all three. So a client (or an aggregate object) can choose to use only handlers or only in-process or local servers. You can play with these flags to change the order in which COM typically looks for servers (normally, in-process, handler, local).

In looking at the code for *CoCreateInstance*, you can see where *pUnkOuter*, *riid*, and *ppv* are passed to *IClassFactory::CreateInstance*, which is the only place they are used. This leaves the function *CoGetClassObject*, whose sole purpose in life is to access a class factory for a specific CLSID, returning some interface pointer to that factory. Its complete function prototype and argument list are as follows:

```
HRESULT CoGetClassObject(REFCLSID clsid, DWORD dwContext
    , LPOLESTR pszRemote, REFIID iid, void **ppv)
```

| Argument | Description |
|---|---|
| *clsid* | A REFCLSID identifying the class factory to obtain |
| *dwContext* | A DWORD identifying the allowable execution contexts |
| *pszRemote* | An LPOLESTR to the name of the remote machine on which the remote server is to run[5] |
| *iid* | A REFIID identifying the interface to obtain on the factory object[6] |
| *ppv* | A void ** in which to store the interface pointer upon return |

Calling *CoGetClassObject* yourself is necessary in three situations:

- You want to create more than one object from the same class factory

- You need to obtain an interface other than *IClassFactory* on the class factory, such as *IClassFactory2*

- You need to call *IClassFactory::LockServer*

In all of these cases, *CoCreateInstance* is either inefficient for the task (the first case) or unable to perform the task (the second and third cases), so you must go to the class factory directly. Be sure to call *Release* when you're finished with the class factory, even if you still hold interface pointers to objects you created through it.

Note once again that *IClassFactory::CreateInstance* (and therefore *CoCreateInstance*) creates an uninitialized object, so the first act a client should perform is to query for an appropriate initialization interface and call an initialization member function. But whether this really happens depends on the type of object in question because some objects need no initialization. Usually such requirements are defined (and documented) as part of the prototype of which the object class is an instance.

One last note: if *CoCreateInstance* or *CoGetClassObject* returns REGDB_E-_CLASSNOTREG, check the registry. You might have forgotten to register a server, or those entries might have been corrupted. The registry is always a good place to start looking for problems when object creation fails.

---

5. At the time of writing, this argument was nonfunctional, as OLE's distributed services are not yet available. A NULL value must be passed in the meantime. When distributed services are available, there will be more than just *pszRemote* involved to access a remote server—for example, security and load balancing. This will most likely be handled through use of monikers that can dynamically determine which server to use and that can perform security checks. The *pszRemote* argument is really intended for later use with such monikers.

## Creating a Licensed Object

A call to *IClassFactory::CreateInstance*, or *CoCreateInstance* for that matter, might possibly fail with the error code CLASS_E_NOTLICENSED, telling the client that the component is not globally licensed on the machine. If this happens, you must resort to obtaining an *IClassFactory2* pointer from *CoGetClassObject*, followed by *IClassFactory2::CreateInstanceLic*. This assumes, of course, that the client has a license key — if not, it's completely locked out of that component.

Licensing is primarily the concern of application-building tools that can incorporate components into such an application. At design time, the development tool itself is really playing the client role of creating and manipulating objects. When this tool gets to the point of writing or compiling the final application, it must obtain the necessary license for every component it can so that the application can later run on nonlicensed machines.

This process means that the tool first calls *IClassFactory2::GetLicInfo* for each component and checks *fRuntimeKeyAvail* in each LICINFO structure returned. If this flag is TRUE, the tool can then call *IClassFactory2::RequestLicKey* to obtain a key that it saves persistently in the created application. By "saves persistently," I mean that the license key is stored in the application image so that the application, when run itself, will pass the license key in calls to *IClassFactory2::CreateInstanceLic*.

Some components will not offer a run-time license at all, in which case the generated application has to handle the absence of any of its desired components more robustly. Presumably this means warning the end user that a certain component is missing or not available, and it is beneficial to those end users to distinguish the complete nonexistence of a component from the lack of a proper license. If the component isn't there, *CoGetClassObject* will fail outright. If there is no license, *CoGetClassObject* will work but *IClassFactory::CreateInstance* will fail with CLASS_E_NOTLICENSED. If you want to check ahead of time whether *CreateInstance* will fail, call *IClassFactory2::GetLicInfo* first and check the *fLicVerified* field in LICINFO. If the field is FALSE, you know that the component is not globally licensed and *CreateInstance* will fail. In either case, you can give the end user a meaningful error message, all the better for your customer support staff.

---

6. Windows NT 3.5 allows a client to pass *IID_IClassFactory* in this argument only when a local server is going to be used. This restriction will be removed in the near future.

### Managing Servers and *CoFreeUnusedLibraries*

What you do with an object after you have obtained an interface pointer depends entirely on the object itself and is really what most of the chapters in the book are about. You must, in any case, be absolutely sure to call *Release* through that interface pointer when you have finished with the object. Otherwise, you doom the object to live in memory for all eternity—or until the universe collapses (power off or the jolly three-finger reset).

Releasing the object is not the only consideration when in-process modules (servers and handlers) are involved. Local servers, remember, will terminate themselves when they're no longer in use. DLLs, however, must wait for COM to call *DllCanUnloadNow* from within the *CoFreeUnusedLibraries* function. As a client, you are responsible for periodically calling this COM function because COM does not make the call itself. A good time to call the function is immediately after releasing what you consider to be the last interface pointer to an object. Another good choice is to call the function every minute or two during any idle-time processing your application might do.

Remember that a reference count on a class factory does not guarantee that the server will stay in memory and that you can use the class factory later. If you want to hold the class factory's pointer across function calls (especially across iterations through your message loop if you have one), you must call *IClassFactory::LockServer(TRUE)* when you save the pointer and *IClassFactory::LockServer(FALSE)* before calling its *Release*.

One additional function that a client might find useful in managing servers is *CoFreeAllLibraries*, a much more brutal version of *CoFreeUnusedLibraries* that forcibly dumps all DLLs out of memory without regard to their object counts or lock counts. This isn't a good function to call in the course of normal processing, but it exists so that a client can clean up its address space during an abnormal termination. *CoFreeAllLibraries* is called from within *CoUninitialize*, so clients generally don't need to call this function directly during shutdown.

# COM's Responsibilities

Now that we've seen both the client side and the server side of the puzzle, we can complete the picture and examine what COM does internally to make it all work. More precisely, our interest is in how COM takes a client's request for an object instance and asks the right server to create the object and return its interface pointer back to the client. Of course, because the structure of an in-process server and a local server differ, COM treats both differently, as illustrated in Figure 5-5 and Figure 5-6 on the following page. In these diagrams, the client itself is calling *CoGetClassObject* and *IClassFactory::CreateInstance*, an identical process regardless of the server used. This is an important idea of Local/Remote Transparency: the client code need not differentiate between server contexts, and the same client code works equally well for all types of server. COM automatically establishes the necessary communication elements so that the client can make interface calls across the boundaries involved.

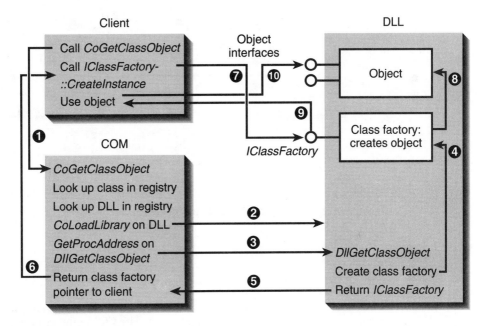

**Figure 5-5.**
*The creation process for an in-process server.*

To be precise, the COM Library itself doesn't perform *implementation location*—finding the server that provides the implementation of a particular CLSID and setting up an RPC connection as necessary. This is the role of COM's SCM. When a client asks for an object of a CLSID, the COM Library contacts the local SCM (the one on the same machine) and requests that the appropriate server be located or launched, returning a "connection" to the COM Library.

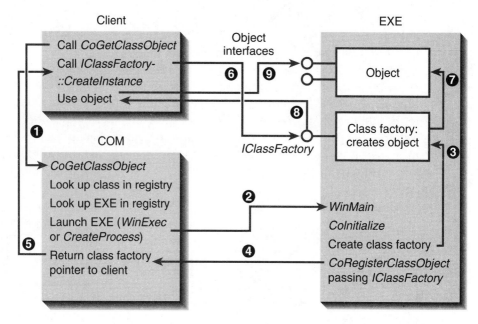

**Figure 5-6.**
*The creation process for a local server.*

The actions taken by the local SCM and the "connection" it returns depend on the type of server that is registered for the CLSID:

| Server Type | Description |
|---|---|
| In-Process | The SCM returns the pathname of the DLL containing the object server implementation. The COM Library then loads the DLL and asks it for an interface pointer to the class factory. |
| Local | The SCM starts the local executable, which registers a class factory on startup. The SCM then returns an RPC handle to the stub connected to that class factory. |
| Remote | The local SCM contacts the SCM running on the appropriate remote machine and forwards the request to the remote SCM. The remote SCM brings that server into memory (be it DLL or EXE) and sets up an RPC connection to a remote stub. |

In any of these cases, the COM Library gets back a connection. If that connection is in-process, the COM Library loads the DLL directly and obtains the necessary interface pointer from *DllGetClassObject*. Otherwise, the COM Library locates the necessary proxy or handler implementation creates an instance of that proxy object, and gives it the RPC connection. In turn, that proxy provides an interface pointer that the COM Library returns to the client. The end result is that no matter what type of server is involved, the COM Library itself needs only to load some DLL and get an in-process interface pointer from it that it can then give to a client. The whole process the SCM follows is illustrated in Figure 5-7.

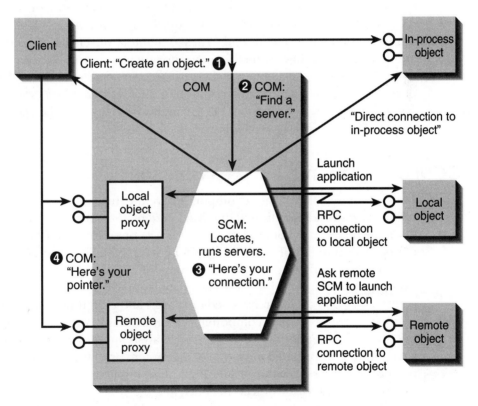

**Figure 5-7.**
*The role of the SCM.*

It is important to realize how a proxy or handler object completely encapsulates the RPC connection to the local or remote object behind its own interfaces. Local/Remote Transparency is, again, the idea that a client assumes it is always working with an in-process implementation of the object. Whether or not the object is fully or partially implemented inside some in-process module is irrelevant to the client because such a setup is entirely an object implementation issue. The one thing that is necessary to make such transparency work is that the client must transfer execution to whatever in-process element it has by making a function call. After that in-process element has control, it can perform whatever RPC it needs to complete the client's request. This is why COM does not support direct access of an object's data members—such access does not require any transfer of control because it is based on memory reads and writes to memory offsets. It is very difficult and impractical to have something monitor such memory access so that the request can be forwarded to a local or remote server. So, instead, OLE supports a number of data exchange interfaces, such as *IDataObject* (see Chapter 10) and *IDispatch* (see Chapter 14) through which data can be accessed by means of calls to interface members.

# COM Components vs. C++ Classes

In describing COM's custom component architecture and the mechanisms that make it work, I mentioned that *IClassFactory::CreateInstance*, and thus also *CoCreateInstance*, are something like C++ *new* operators for COM components. A fair number of similarities exist between C++ classes and COM components, especially when you're designing an application or other project using object-oriented principles. The analysis and design that you can use to create a C++ object hierarchy based on classes and class inheritance can also be used to create a COM component hierarchy based on CLSIDs, containment, and aggregation. Object-oriented analysis and design is a useful process to find encapsulated elements of any system, which can be turned into objects of some sort within a hierarchy. The implementation issue is how exactly to express those objects in code.

The process called *componentization* is the breaking up of a large application or system into individual COM components. It's really a matter of first identifying those elements you can isolate as separate objects and then matching each object's functionality and content to the various OLE technologies and interfaces through which you can integrate those objects.

A comparison of how "objects" work both in an object-oriented language such as C++ and in COM helps us understand why COM is designed like it is and why it's different. From experience, I know that the object-oriented paradigm in COM differs somewhat from traditional object-oriented languages, and this can seem rather intimidating.

The main reason why COM uses a different paradigm is that it's trying to solve the problem of integrating components that are developed, deployed, and revised independently so that new components can be instantly and robustly integrated into a running system. COM solves problems at the run-time binary level, through the binary standard of interfaces, and is concerned with components and objects that live and execute outside the boundaries of an application—that's what component integration is all about. Programming languages such as C++, on the other hand, are designed for solving programming problems within the scope of a single application on the source code or compile-time level. Few mechanisms are available for run-time integration of C++ objects implemented in DLLs, let alone the integration of objects in separate processes that might be written in different programming languages. Allow me to indulge in an analogy to illustrate the differences between COM and C++. Let's go traveling.

Suppose I'm a C++ application that lives in Rugby, North Dakota (the geographic center of North America), and I am bounded by the border of the continental United States, as illustrated in Figure 5-8 on the next page. I can visit freely any of 48 states, no questions asked, by driving along an interstate. Access is fast and easy, although I am subject to the laws of each state I drive through. I can also drive into Canada or Mexico to buy their goods and use their services, but I have to stop at their borders and answer a few questions; travel is a little slower but still quite easy. In programming terms, I can freely use any object class within the boundaries of my application as long as I obey the access rights of those individual objects. I can also use objects implemented in DLLs, but there is just a little more work involved in getting across the DLL boundary, even to my own DLL, such as Alaska.

**Figure 5-8.**
*Travel within North America is fairly painless.*

I might live happily for a long time while restricting my travels to a single continent. But there are six other continents and many other countries on the planet, and at some point I might want to visit them. Getting there is not easy—I have to transfer flights, go through customs, and show my passport. If I want to travel to a distant destination, such as Antananarivo, Madagascar, I would have to fly to Chicago and then to London, switch carriers to get to Nairobi, Kenya, and then catch a final flight to Antananarivo. On each segment of my journey, I would probably fly on a different airline in a different airplane (or I might be forced to travel only by boat or train) and walk through customs offices in three different countries. If I step out of line anywhere, I might find myself in trouble on the other side of the globe.

As a C++ application, I experience the same difficulty in using C++ objects implemented in other applications (countries) or code that is otherwise separated by a process boundary (oceans) or a network boundary (planets), as illustrated in Figure 5-9. The best I can hope for is to become intimately familiar with the protocols and customs of each application along my way, knowledge that can apply only to those specific applications. When I want to use the services of a different application, I must learn another new interface.

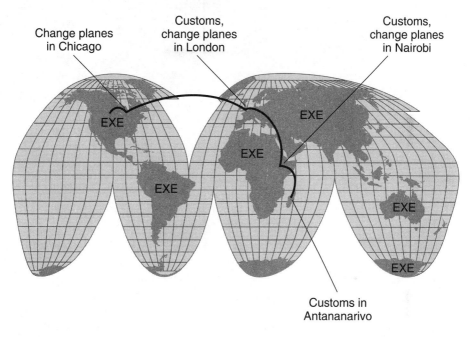

**Figure 5-9.**
*Travel abroad involves much more time, effort, and knowledge.*

COM offers you membership in the Component Club, which makes travel abroad much easier. This Club essentially standardizes the protocols for visiting any other country, so you have to learn only one set of rules. The Club offers nonstop flights to many countries (in-process components) and at worst one-stop flights to any other destination on the earth (local components) or on the moon or any of the other planets for that matter (remote components). As a member of the Component Club, travel is as easy as showing your membership card and hopping on a plane bound for whatever destination you choose. No matter where you are, there's a flight departing to any destination, as depicted in Figure 5-10 on the following page.

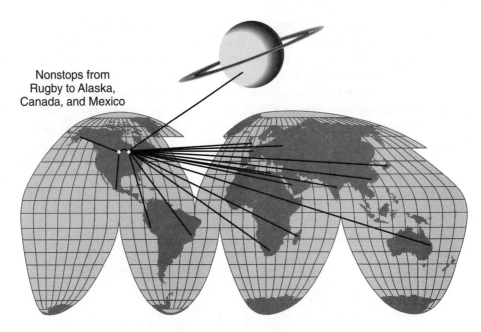

Nonstops from
Rugby to Alaska,
Canada, and Mexico

Fly through Chicago to get anywhere else in the world or off to any other planet.
Customs is identical for each destination, and the Component Club
provides interpreters no matter where you go.

**Figure 5-10.**
*The Component Club simplifies terrestrial and interplanetary travel.*

In programming terms, you join the Component Club by using the various COM (and OLE) API functions to access a specific component without concern for where its server executes. Those API functions form the protocols you learn once, and with the upcoming capability to access remote servers, you can reach servers running on any networked machine, be it figuratively or literally on another planet.

The purpose of this little exercise was to show that C++ objects are somewhat limited in scope because access to objects, being defined by the language, restricts you to objects that live in your own application and were written in that same language. COM, on the other hand, is not concerned with languages—by encapsulating object capabilities behind interfaces and providing Local/Remote Transparency for those interfaces, COM opens up a world of components to everyone.

# Implementing Basic Clients and Servers

Let's now take a look at how all of the mechanisms described earlier appear in code, which, being written in C++, illustrates how COM enables you to share language-specific implementations with the rest of the system through language-independent interfaces. We'll first look at the basic mechanisms and then at self-registration and licensing separately.

We'll use three separate samples for this discussion: a client named ObjectUser, found in CHAP05\OBJUSER, and two implementations of an object named Koala (yes, I have a certain penchant for these critters) for both DLL and EXE servers, found in CHAP05\DKOALA1 and CHAP05-\EKOALA1, respectively. Before running ObjectUser, you will need to create the registry entries for both servers using the REG files found in their respective directories. The Koala object is assigned the CLSID of *00021146-0000-0000-C000-000000000046*, which is given the name *CLSID_Koala* in INC\BOOKGUID.H.

The Koala object used in these samples is nothing more than a regular OLE object with only the *IUnknown* interface—so all that is really useful to do with this object is call *AddRef* and *Release* on it. For the record, Koala has no initialization interface, nor a need of one. In any case, Koala will illustrate the mechanisms through which each server makes this object available to ObjectUser. You can look at the Koala implementation in the KOALA.CPP and KOALA.H files in both the DKOALA1 and the EKOALA1 directories and notice that the code is identical in both. This shows how you can create an object independently of the server packaging around it.

## ObjectUser

When you start ObjectUser, you'll see (after COM is initialized) a small window with a single menu. With the menu items on this menu you can do the following:

- Select which server to use, DLL or EXE. This controls the CLSCTX flags that ObjectUser will pass to *IClassFactory::CreateInstance*. The choice is stored in the flag *CApp::m_fEXE*.

- Create a Koala object with the selected server through either *CoCreateInstance* or *CoGetClassObject* and *IClassFactory::CreateInstance*.

- Call *AddRef* and *Release* for the available Koala object, displaying its reference count as well as a "usage count" that ObjectUser maintains to track its own calls to *AddRef* and *Release*.

When you select the Create (CoGetClassObject) menu item, you end up in the IDM_OBJECTCREATECOGCO case of *ObjectUserWndProc* in OBJUSER.CPP. This selection provokes the execution of the following code (*pApp* is a pointer to the ObjectUser application structure that maintains variables such as *m_pIUnknown*, a pointer to the last Koala object created):

```
HRESULT           hr;
LPCLASSFACTORY    pIClassFactory;
DWORD             dwClsCtx;

    [Other code omitted]

case IDM_OBJECTCREATECOGCO:
    if (NULL!=pApp->m_pIUnknown)
        {
        while (pApp->m_cRefOurs--)
            ReleaseInterface(pApp->m_pIUnknown);

        CoFreeUnusedLibraries();
        }

    dwClsCtx=(pApp->m_fEXE) ? CLSCTX_LOCAL_SERVER
        : CLSCTX_INPROC_SERVER;

    hr=CoGetClassObject(CLSID_Koala, dwClsCtx, NULL
        , IID_IClassFactory, (PPVOID)&pIClassFactory);

    if (SUCCEEDED(hr))
        {
        hr=pIClassFactory->CreateInstance(NULL
            , IID_IUnknown, (PPVOID)&pApp->m_pIUnknown);

        pIClassFactory->Release();

        if (SUCCEEDED(hr))
            {
            pApp->Message(TEXT("Creation succeeded."));
            pApp->m_cRefOurs=1;
            }
        else
            pApp->Message(TEXT("Creation failed."));
        }
    else
        pApp->Message(TEXT("CoGetClassObject failed."));

    break;
```

The Create (CoCreateInstance) menu command does exactly the same thing in a more concise manner because we're creating only one instance of the object:

```
case IDM_OBJECTCREATECOCI:
    if (NULL!=pApp->m_pIUnknown)
        {
        while (pApp->m_cRefOurs--)
            ReleaseInterface(pApp->m_pIUnknown);

        CoFreeUnusedLibraries();
        }

    //Simpler creation: use CoCreateInstance.
    dwClsCtx=(pApp->m_fEXE) ? CLSCTX_LOCAL_SERVER
        : CLSCTX_INPROC_SERVER;

    hr=CoCreateInstance(CLSID_Koala, NULL, dwClsCtx
        , IID_IUnknown, (PPVOID)&pApp->m_pIUnknown);

    if (SUCCEEDED(hr))
        {
        pApp->Message(TEXT("Creation succeeded."));
        pApp->m_cRefOurs=1;
        }
    else
        pApp->Message(TEXT("Creation failed."));

    break;
```

The two sequences of code produce exactly the same result: an *IUnknown* pointer to the new Koala instance. If an instance is already available, we first call *m_pIUnknown->Release* as many times as needed to free the object (through the *ReleaseInterface* macro in INC\INOLE.H) and then call *CoFreeUnusedLibraries*. This latter call allows you to watch what happens in the DKoalal server's implementation of *DllCanUnloadNow*.

ObjectUser maintains in the variable *pApp->m_cRefOurs* a count of how many references it thinks it owns on the object. The counter is initially 0 but is set to 1 after creating an instance. ObjectUser's AddRef and Release menu items either increment or decrement this counter, after which ObjectUser displays the reference count returned from the object's function next to its own counter.

When you run ObjectUser with the DLL server option, you'll see that the object's reference count and ObjectUser's internal count are equal. But when you use the EXE server, you'll see something strange: the value returned by any call to *AddRef* might be something huge like 1336120 and remain that way no matter how many *AddRef* calls you make. In the same manner, this number is also returned from *Release* as long as the actual reference count is nonzero. Why is this? The specification for *IUnknown::Release* (described in Chapter 2) explicitly states that the client cannot attach any meaning to a nonzero return value. In addition, the client cannot really attach much meaning to a zero return value except for knowing that its own responsibility for the object is complete. In no way does the return value tell you whether the object has actually been destroyed—at most it tells you that the in-process proxy object has been destroyed and that you can no longer access the local or remote object to which you were connected. That object, however, could easily remain running if other clients are accessing it as well.

To prevent clients from reading too much into the return value from *AddRef* and *Release*, proxy objects generally return some large constant unless the proxy is destroyed, in which case *Release* returns 0. Of course, because proxy objects are not used with in-process servers such as DKoala1, a client will generally get back the actual object reference count. In any case, clients can't do very much with the information.

## DKoala1 and EKoala1

As I mentioned earlier, both the DKoala1 and the EKoala1 server contain exactly the same implementation of the Koala object. In fact, their class factory implementations are almost identical as well, and their registry entries differ only by the *InprocServer32* and *LocalServer32* entries.

As you know by now, each server has to maintain a count of its current objects so it can properly control unloading. Typically this will be a global variable. But because I don't want the Koala object tied to a global variable in some other source file, I instead have the class factory pass Koala's constructor (*CKoala::CKoala*) a pointer to an "object destroyed" function with the following prototype:

```
void ObjectDestroyed(void)
```

The Koala object stores the pointer in *m_pfnDestroy* and calls the function when destroying itself in *Release*:

```
STDMETHODIMP_(ULONG) CKoala::Release(void)
    {
    if (0L!=--m_cRef)
        return m_cRef;
```

```
if (NULL!=m_pfnDestroy)
    (*m_pfnDestroy)();

delete this;
return 0;
}
```

This little trick eliminates any compile-time relationship between the server code and the object code, making it a run-time relationship instead. Koala doesn't call *ObjectDestroyed* by name; it calls a function that matches the prototype, a pointer it receives when constructed. This trick makes such an object rather portable between different server modules, which you might find useful.

The second point about the Koala object is that it is also given a *pUnkOuter* pointer if it's created as part of an aggregation. Because Koala implements only *IUnknown*, this is pretty useless in and of itself. I included it here not only to show how the *IClassFactory* implementation should handle the aggregation scenario but also to make a clean object framework that can be easily extended with additional interfaces that might be used in aggregation. If you use this code as such a base, any additional interfaces' *IUnknown* members should delegate to the *pUnkOuter* pointer passed to Koala's constructor, which was demonstrated in Chapter 2.

## The Class Factory and the Unloading Mechanism

Both KOALA servers define for their class factory objects a C++ class *CKoalaClassFactory*, which singly inherits from *IClassFactory*. The definitions (in DKOALA1.H and EKOALA1.H) are identical, with the only member variable being a reference count. In the same manner, the *IUnknown* members in both implementations (DKOALA1.CPP and EKOALA1.CPP) are also identical: the class factory deletes itself when its reference count goes to 0, as usual. Nothing else special happens in *Release* because the class factory's existence has little to do with the server's own lifetime.

The *CKoalaClassFactory* members *CreateInstance* and *LockServer* appear as follows in DKoala1:

```
//From DKOALA1.CPP
STDMETHODIMP CKoalaClassFactory::CreateInstance(LPUNKNOWN pUnkOuter
    , REFIID riid, PPVOID ppvObj)
    {
    PCKoala            pObj;
    HRESULT            hr;
```

*(continued)*

261

```
    *ppvObj=NULL;
    hr=ResultFromScode(E_OUTOFMEMORY);

    if (NULL!=pUnkOuter && IID_IUnknown!=riid)
        return ResultFromScode(CLASS_E_NOAGGREGATION);

    pObj=new CKoala(pUnkOuter, ObjectDestroyed);

    if (NULL==pObj)
        return hr;

    if (pObj->Init())
        hr=pObj->QueryInterface(riid, ppvObj);

    if (FAILED(hr))
        delete pObj;
    else
        g_cObj++;

    return hr;
    }

STDMETHODIMP CKoalaClassFactory::LockServer(BOOL fLock)
    {
    if (fLock)
        g_cLock++;
    else
        g_cLock--;

    return NOERROR;
    }
```

Here you can see a number of features. First *CreateInstance* verifies that aggregation rules are being followed correctly if *pUnkOuter* is non-NULL. We then create an instance of the Koala object (the C++ class *CKoala*), passing to the constructor the outer unknown and a pointer to the object destroyed function named *ObjectDestroyed*. If the C++ *new* operator succeeds, we have a new C++ object but not an interface pointer, so we initialize the object and query for an interface pointer if initialization succeeds. The *QueryInterface* call conveniently calls *AddRef* as well. If all of this succeeds, we increment the global counter *g_cObj* and return. Along similar lines the *LockServer* function increments or decrements another global counter, *g_cLock*. We could have *LockServer* fiddle with *g_cObj* instead of a separate counter, but having two counters greatly simplifies debugging objects and locks separately.

Again, EKoala1's implementation is almost identical. Can you spot the differences?

```
//From EKOALA1.CPP
STDMETHODIMP CKoalaClassFactory::CreateInstance(LPUNKNOWN pUnkOuter
    , REFIID riid, PPVOID ppvObj)
    {
    PCKoala            pObj;
    HRESULT            hr;

    *ppvObj=NULL;
    hr=ResultFromScode(E_OUTOFMEMORY);

    if (NULL!=pUnkOuter && IID_IUnknown!=riid)
        return ResultFromScode(CLASS_E_NOAGGREGATION);

    pObj=new CKoala(pUnkOuter, ObjectDestroyed);

    if (NULL==pObj)
        {
        g_cObj++;
        ObjectDestroyed();
        return hr;
        }

    if (pObj->Init())
        hr=pObj->QueryInterface(riid, ppvObj);

    g_cObj++;

    if (FAILED(hr))
        {
        delete pObj;
        ObjectDestroyed();
        }

    return hr;
    }

STDMETHODIMP CKoalaClassFactory::LockServer(BOOL fLock)
    {
    if (fLock)
        g_cLock++;
    else
        {
        g_cLock--;
        g_cObj++;
        ObjectDestroyed();
        }

    return NOERROR;
    }
```

The differences exist because EKoala1 was launched for no reason other than to create an object. If creation fails, the server shuts itself down—no reason to keep hogging memory uselessly! As we'll see shortly, an EXE server has to start its own shutdown when its last object is destroyed or the last lock removed. This requirement lets us isolate shutdown initiation code inside a function such as *ObjectDestroyed*, which tests for the right conditions and posts a WM_CLOSE message to the main hidden window to generate a *PostQuit-Message* call:

```
//From EKOALA1.CPP
void ObjectDestroyed(void)
    {
    g_cObj--;

    //No more objects and no locks; shut the application down.
    if (0L==g_cObj && 0L==g_cLock && IsWindow(g_hWnd))
        PostMessage(g_hWnd, WM_CLOSE, 0, 0L);

    return;
    }
```

So anywhere else that we need to start shutdown, we can fake an object destruction by incrementing *g_cObj* and calling *ObjectDestroyed* directly as when *new* fails, when object initialization or *QueryInterface* fails, and inside *LockServer* as well. *ObjectDestroyed* worries about testing the conditions.

This is actually the full extent of how EKoala1 terminates itself when the last lock is removed and *g_cObj* is zero or when *g_cLock* is zero and the last Koala object goes away, in which case Koala incorrectly calls *ObjectDestroyed*.

DKoala1, on the other hand, doesn't unload itself but implements *DllCanUnloadNow* instead to return S_OK or S_FALSE for the same conditions under which EKoala1 terminates. Correspondingly, its *ObjectDestroyed* function does nothing more than decrement *g_cObj*:

```
//From DKOALA1.CPP
STDAPI DllCanUnloadNow(void)
    {
    SCODE   sc;

    sc=(0L==g_cObj && 0L==g_cLock) ? S_OK : S_FALSE;
    return ResultFromScode(sc);
    }

void ObjectDestroyed(void)
    {
    g_cObj--;
    return;
    }
```

## Expose the Class Factory

To expose its class factory, a DLL needs only to implement and export *DllGet-ClassObject*. This function looks quite similar to *IClassFactory::CreateInstance*:

```
//From DKOALA1.CPP
STDAPI DllGetClassObject(REFCLSID rclsid, REFIID riid, PPVOID ppv)
    {
    HRESULT             hr;
    CKoalaClassFactory *pObj;

    if (CLSID_Koala!=rclsid)
        return ResultFromScode(E_FAIL);

    pObj=new CKoalaClassFactory();

    if (NULL==pObj)
        return ResultFromScode(E_OUTOFMEMORY);

    hr=pObj->QueryInterface(riid, ppv);

    if (FAILED(hr))
        delete pObj;

    return hr;
    }
```

The only special note to make here is that *DllGetClassObject* should always validate the CLSID passed to it, as done here. You don't want to return a class factory for the wrong CLSID!

An EXE server, on the other hand, must first check for the *-Embedding* flag and register its class factories using *CoRegisterClassObject*. In EKoala1, we should do all of this in *CApp::Init*, which registers the class factory for multiple use. (Note that *-Embedding* always appears in ANSI characters, as does the entire command line.)

```
BOOL CApp::Init(void)
    {
    HRESULT    hr;

    //Fail if we're run outside of CoGetClassObject.
    if (lstrcmpiA(m_pszCmdLine, "-Embedding")
        && lstrcmpiA(m_pszCmdLine, "/Embedding"))
        return FALSE;

    if (FAILED(CoInitialize(NULL)))
        return FALSE;
```

*(continued)*

265

```
m_fInitialized=TRUE;

[Register window class and create main hidden window.]

m_pIClassFactory=new CKoalaClassFactory();

if (NULL==m_pIClassFactory)
    return FALSE;

m_pIClassFactory->AddRef();

hr=CoRegisterClassObject(CLSID_Koala, m_pIClassFactory
    , CLSCTX_LOCAL_SERVER, REGCLS_MULTIPLEUSE, &m_dwRegCO);

if (FAILED(hr))
    return FALSE;

return TRUE;
}
```

If EKoala1 served more than one CLSID, it would repeat the process of creating a class factory and calling *CoRegisterClassObject* for each CLSID. In the preceding code, the *m_dwRegCO* variable receives the registration key for our single class factory. If we had multiple class factories, we'd need to have an array of such keys, of course. Also, EKoala1 does not allow itself to run stand-alone: if *-Embedding* does not appear, EKoala1 terminates immediately. If you are writing a server that can run stand-alone, use *-Embedding* to determine whether you must register all your class factories or skip them all. A server will generally register its multiple-use class factories with or without *-Embedding*, but it only registers single-use ones when the flag is present.

Because this class factory is registered as REGCLS_MULTIPLE_USE, this same class factory is used to create objects for any number of separate clients. To demonstrate this, run two or more instances of ObjectUser, and in each choose Use EXE Object followed by Create (CoCreateInstance). Now run a tool like PView and look at the loaded modules. Because EKoala1 registers itself for multiple use, only one instance of the EXE will appear in the list. Notice that the time it takes to create the first object is longer than the time to create subsequent instances. EKoala1 is already running, so we don't have to incur the overhead of launching another instance. Now change EKoala1 to use REGCLS_SINGLE_USE, and run the same test with multiple instances of ObjectUser. This time you'll see multiple instances of EKoala1, each servicing only a single object.

The final piece of EKoala1's implementation is revoking and releasing its class factory on shutdown. This happens in the application destructor *CApp::~CApp*:

```
CApp::~CApp(void)
    {
    if (0L!=m_dwRegCO)
        CoRevokeClassObject(m_dwRegCO);

    if (NULL!=m_pIClassFactory)
        m_pIClassFactory->Release();

    if (m_fInitialized)
        CoUninitialize();

    return;
    }
```

## The "OLE Is Difficult" Myth Debunked

Take a moment to reflect on the amount of code that we've seen in the last two sections. Even if we include the implementations of the *IUnknown* members of *CKoalaClassFactory* and *CKoala*, there are really only a few dozen lines of code in DKoala1 and EKoala1 that deal with the class factory and the objects that it creates.

Such code is the core of any custom component in OLE, which includes OLE Automation objects, OLE Document objects, OLE Controls, and any other type of component you want to make with OLE and access using a CLSID. The core functionality for exposing an object in a component is very simple and occupies little code. As we have seen in the last few pages, none of this code is at all complex—it's just as simple as writing any other exported functions or creating something such as a window class. If you take the time to understand these fundamental mechanisms, most everything else you might implement with OLE will make a lot more sense and will cease to be something overly complex and foreign. More complex objects simply have more interfaces than the KOALA object has.

*(continued)*

> OLE has been called "difficult" and "hard," a myth perpetuated largely by competitive marketing efforts and by people who stand to win big if you believe the myth. Certainly the more OLE technologies you use and the more complex the problems you're trying to solve, the more complex your programming will become. But this is true of any programming.
>
> So understand that any belief you might have that OLE is just too damned hard is just that—a belief. And beliefs often do not correspond to reality.

# Self-Registration

After having looked at the details of creating and exposing a server's class factories, implementing self-registration is a snap. Three samples demonstrate this feature: SelfReg (CHAP05\SELFREG), DKoala2 (CHAP05\DKOALA2), and EKoala2 (CHAP05\EKOALA2). The two servers are simple enhancements to DKoala1 and EKoala1 to support self-registration. SelfReg is nothing more than a command-line tool (a Windows application nevertheless) with the following syntax:

```
selfreg [/e] [/u] <path to server>
```

The /e switch specifies that the path is to an EXE as opposed to a DLL, and /u instructs the server to unregister as opposed to register. The code in SELFREG.CPP parses the command line and generates the appropriate calls: when the code sees /e, it will attempt to call *WinExec* with the given path, passing /REGSERVER or /UNREGSERVER as the command line, depending on the presence of /u. If /e is not present, SelfReg calls *CoLoadLibrary* with the server specified on the path and then calls *DllRegisterServer* or *DllUnregisterServer*, depending again on /u. SelfReg displays a message box with the result of whatever sequence it executes (and calls *CoFreeLibrary* to unload the DLL).

Prior to calling *CoLoadLibrary*, SelfReg calls *CoInitialize*. It then calls *CoUninitialize* after calling *CoFreeLibrary*. SelfReg does this because in-process servers will expect that COM has been initialized by the application that owns the process. SelfReg falls into that category and so must perform the initialization.

How you actually choose to create the registry entries from within the server itself is up to you. You can use either the straight registry APIs (*RegCreateKeyEx*, *RegSetValueEx*, *RegCloseKey*, *RegDeleteKey*, and so on) as done in DKoala2 and EKoala2, or you can use another technique, such as launching

REGEDIT.EXE with an appropriate registration file. What is most important in all of this is that the *InprocServer32*, *InprocHandler32*, and *LocalServer32* entries have values equivalent to the full path of the loaded module. This is true also for any entries for your type libraries, which you should also register at this time. These paths are the only entries that depend on the directory in which the component resides, and that directory is the most important way OLE has of finding a component. This isn't hard to accomplish, mind you, as the Windows function *GetModuleFilename* gives you the full path to the loaded server, exactly what you want to store in the registry. If you perform registration using a REG file, be sure to update the keys with pathnames in them after that process is complete.

A final note to make here is that the function *RegDeleteKey* is picky: it will not delete a registry key if there are any subkeys below it. This means that just as you need to register entries one by one, you have to delete them one by one. You want to delete only the keys and subkeys that you registered from within your own server because other servers might have stored, for example, a *TreatAs* key under your CLSID. If you simply removed everything in the registry that pertained to your server, you'd obliterate this *TreatAs* key and potentially break clients that weren't using your server anyway. So delete only what you stored in the registry, and leave the rest alone.

# Licensing

Support for licensing in both a client and a server is simply a matter of supporting *IClassFactory2*, as demonstrated in the samples LicenseUser (CHAP05\LICUSER) and DKoala3 (CHAP05\DKOALA3).[7]

LicenseUser is a program similar to ObjectUser, with two top-level menus. The menu item Class Factory allows you to have the program obtain either an *IClassFactory* or an *IClassFactory2* pointer from DKoala3. If you ask for *IClassFactory2*, you can also call its *RequestLicKey* member, which stores the BSTR key in the member variable *CApp::m_bstrKey*. The menu item Clear LicKey frees this string. The Koala Object menu is enabled only when you have obtained a class factory, so you can then try to create an object with *IClassFactory::CreateInstance*. If you've used the RequestLicKey menu, you can try creation through *IClassFactory::CreateInstanceLic*. In either case, License-User tells you the result—whether the object was created or there was a "not licensed" error.

---

7. There is not a licensed version of EKoala because at the time of writing there was no marshaling support for *IClassFactory2*, restricting its use to in-process servers only.

This menu structure and these operations allow you to experiment with different licensing situations, using the server DKOALA3.DLL and its license file DKOALA3.LIC (also in CHAP05\DKOALA3). For licensing to work, the LIC file must be located in the same directory as DKOALA3.DLL. If you run into funny problems, be sure to check this requirement. In any case, here are the scenarios that you can test with these samples:

- DKoala3 is globally licensed. When loaded, it will find DKOALA3- .LIC, verify that it's the correct file, and set an internal flag. This allows any call to *IClassFactory[2]::CreateInstance* to succeed.

- DKoala3 is not globally licensed. This means that DKOALA3.LIC is not found or doesn't contain the correct contents. Any calls to *CreateInstance* will fail. To simulate this lack of a global license, you can rename DKOALA3.LIC, move it to another directory, or re- name it and make a garbage file with the name DKOALA3.LIC and see how DKoala3 detects that the contents are bad.

- DKoala3 is initially globally licensed, at which time LicenseUser obtains a license key. After this, DKoala3 is not globally licensed (*CreateInstance* fails) but an instance of the object can be created using the license key (*CreateInstanceLic* succeeds). To simulate this situation, run LicenseUser as usual, choose Obtain IClassFactory2 followed by RequestLicKey, and then choose Release to let go of the class factory while continuing to hold the license key. This will un- load DKOALA3.DLL (through *CoFreeUnusedLibraries*), after which you can move or trash DKOALA3.LIC. Now choose Obtain IClass- Factory2 again. During its initialization, DKoala3 will fail to validate a global license. Calls to *CreateInstance* will fail, but *CreateInstanceLic* will work because you still hold a license key.

Let's now see how DKoala3 validates the license and otherwise restrict access to its components. First of all, here's the contents of DKOALA3.LIC, a simple text file with Microsoft's standard license file format:

```
Koala Object #3 Copyright (c) 1993-1995 Microsoft Corp.

Warning: This product is licensed to you pursuant to the terms of the
Microsoft license agreement included with the original software, and is
protected by copyright law and international treaties. Unauthorized
reproduction or distribution may result in severe civil and criminal
penalties, and will be prosecuted to the maximum extent possible under
the law.
```

DKoala3 validates this license file during its initialization code in *Lib-Main32* in DKOALA3.CPP, in which a global variable, *g_fMachineLicensed*, indicates whether a global license is present:

```
//License key string, stored in ANSI to match contents of LIC file
char g_szLic[]="Koala Object #3 Copyright (c) 1993-1995 Microsoft Corp.";
BOOL g_fMachineLicensed=FALSE;


BOOL WINAPI LibMain32(HINSTANCE hInstance, ULONG ulReason
    , LPVOID pvReserved)
    {
    [Other code omitted]
    :

    g_fMachineLicensed=CheckForLicenseFile(hInstance
        , TEXT("DKOALA3.LIC"), (BYTE *)g_szLic, lstrlenA(g_szLic));

    :
    return TRUE;
    }

BOOL CheckForLicenseFile(HINSTANCE hInst, LPTSTR pszFile
    , LPBYTE pbLic, UINT cb)
    {
    BOOL        fFound=FALSE;
    TCHAR       szPath[_MAX_PATH];
    LPTSTR      pszTemp;
    LPBYTE      pbCompare;
    HANDLE      hFile;
    UINT        cbRead;
    ULONG       cbWasRead;

    //Get module path; then replace DLL name with LIC filename.
    GetModuleFileName(hInst, szPath, _MAX_PATH);
    pszTemp=_tcsrchr(szPath, '\\')+1;
    lstrcpy(pszTemp, pszFile);

    hFile=CreateFile(szPath, GENERIC_READ, FILE_SHARE_READ
        , NULL, OPEN_EXISTING, FILE_ATTRIBUTE_NORMAL, NULL);

    if (INVALID_HANDLE_VALUE==hFile)
        return FALSE;

    cbRead=cb*sizeof(BYTE);
    pbCompare=(LPBYTE)malloc(cbRead+4);
```

*(continued)*

```
if (NULL!=pbCompare)
    {
    ReadFile(hFile, pbCompare, cbRead, &cbWasRead, NULL);
    fFound=(0==memcmp(pbLic, pbCompare, cb));
    free(pbCompare);
    }

CloseHandle(hFile);
return fFound;
}
```

The function *CheckForLicenseFile* attempts to open the license file specified by *pszFile* in the same location as the server module identified by *hInst*. If that file is found and opened, the function loads *cb* bytes from that file and compares it with the contents at *pbLic*. If the two blocks of data match, the license is validated; otherwise, the machine is not licensed. In DKoala3, I'm comparing only the first line of the license file, which is usually suitable; however, feel free to be as secure as you want.

DKoala3's class factory *CKoalaClassFactory* (DKOALA3.CPP) now inherits from *IClassFactory2*. Because both *CreateInstance* and *CreateInstanceLic* share a lot of functionality, I broke out the core creation sequence to make a private member function, *CKoalaClassFactory::CreateAnObject*. This function is unrestrictive and will create an object whenever asked, so the other public members that are simply validating the necessary license then call *CreateAnObject*:

```
STDMETHODIMP CKoalaClassFactory::CreateInstance(LPUNKNOWN pUnkOuter
    , REFIID riid, PPVOID ppvObj)
    {
    *ppvObj=NULL;

    if (!g_fMachineLicensed)
        return ResultFromScode(CLASS_E_NOTLICENSED);

    return CreateAnObject(pUnkOuter, riid, ppvObj);
    }


STDMETHODIMP CKoalaClassFactory::CreateInstanceLic(LPUNKNOWN pUnkOuter
    , LPUNKNOWN pUnkReserved, REFIID riid, BSTR bstrKey
    , PPVOID ppvObj)
    {
    BOOL        fMatch;
    BSTR        bstrTemp;
```

```
HRESULT        hr;

*ppvObj=NULL;

//Get our own license key, which should match bstrKey exactly.
hr=RequestLicKey(0, &bstrTemp);

if (FAILED(hr))
    return hr;

fMatch=(0==memcmp(bstrTemp, bstrKey, lstrlen(bstrTemp)));
SysFreeString(bstrTemp);

if (!fMatch)
    return ResultFromScode(CLASS_E_NOTLICENSED);

return CreateAnObject(pUnkOuter, riid, ppvObj);
}
```

As you can see, *CreateInstance* will work only if the global license exists; *CreateInstanceLic* will allow creation only if it's passed a license key identical to what it returns from *RequestLicKey*. So what is the key we return? Microsoft's convention is to use the first line of the license file. In DKoala3, this is stored in *g_ szLic*, the same buffer used to validate the license file:[8]

```
STDMETHODIMP CKoalaClassFactory::RequestLicKey(DWORD dwReserved
    , BSTR *pbstrKey)
    {
OLECHAR        szTemp[256];

    //Can't give away a key on an unlicensed machine.
    if (!g_fMachineLicensed)
        return ResultFromScode(CLASS_E_NOTLICENSED);

    mbstowcs(szTemp, g_szLic, sizeof(g_szLic));
    *pbstrKey=SysAllocString(szTemp);
    return (NULL!=*pbstrKey) ? NOERROR : ResultFromScode(E_OUTOFMEMORY);
    }
```

---

8. *SysAllocString* always takes a Unicode string in Win32, so we have to convert the ANSI *g_szLic* to accommodate that condition.

Notice how this function fails if a global license is not available. If you didn't include a check like this, it would certainly make it easy for some clever person to cheat you out of an object! Of course, if you choose not to provide run-time licensing at all, *RequestLicKey* should return E_NOTIMPL.

All that's left now is to implement *GetLicInfo*, which fills a structure with appropriate information:

```
STDMETHODIMP CKoalaClassFactory::GetLicInfo(LPLICINFO pLicInfo)
    {
    if (NULL==pLicInfo)
        return ResultFromScode(E_POINTER);

    pLicInfo->cbLicInfo=sizeof(LICINFO);

    //This says whether RequestLicKey will work.
    pLicInfo->fRuntimeKeyAvail=g_fMachineLicensed;

    //This says whether standard CreateInstance will work.
    pLicInfo->fLicVerified=g_fMachineLicensed;

    return NOERROR;
    }
```

Because we implement *RequestLicKey*, and thereby support run-time licensing, we store TRUE in *fRuntimeKeyAvail* if the current machine itself is licensed, or store FALSE if otherwise. This is the same value that we store in *fLicVerified*. If we didn't support run-time licensing, *fRuntimeKeyAvail* would always be set to FALSE, with *fLicVerified* remaining variable.

## Cosmo's Polyline as a DLL Object

All of the variations of the Koala object that we've seen earlier in this chapter are pretty boring and, well, useless. I bet you'd now like a component example that does something real. To demonstrate a more useful and exciting component, I've taken the Cosmo application from Chapter 1 and turned the C++ object *CPolyline* into an OLE component. The CHAP05\POLYLINE directory contains the implementation of this component using an in-process server, POLY05.DLL. Its registry entries are stored under the CLSID *00021147-0000-0000-C000-000000000046* (*CLSID_Polyline5*). This Polyline component provides objects with an incoming interface named *IPolyline5* (which is equivalent to the C++ member functions on the original *CPolyline*) and an outgoing interface named *IPolylineAdviseSink5* (which has the same member functions as the original *CPolylineAdviseSink*). To support this outgoing interface, the objects also implement *IConnectionPointContainer* and a connection point for *IPolylineAdviseSink*, demonstrating how connection points work between a real client and a real component. Both the *IPolyline** interfaces are defined in INC\IPOLY5.H (their IIDs are defined in INC\BOOKGUID.H).

*IPolyline5* contains member functions to deal with initialization, file I/O, data exchange, positioning of its window, and setting colors and line styles. As we progress through this book, we'll replace portions of this interface with standard OLE interfaces that provide the same capabilities, eventually building Polyline into a compound document object as well as an OLE control. For example, we can replace the file I/O members with the interfaces *IPersistStorage* and *IPersistStreamInit*, as we'll do in Chapter 8, and we can replace the data exchange members with *IDataObject,* as we'll do in Chapter 10. We'll also have occasion in Chapter 10 to replace the *OnDataChange* member of *IPolylineAdviseSink5* with support for a separate outgoing interface called *IAdviseSink,* which also has an *OnDataChange* member. But throughout all these changes, the basic structure of the Polyline component, that is, its class factory, server structure, and object structure, will remain essentially the same.

*IPolyline5* and *IPolylineAdviseSink5* are examples of custom interfaces, but because we're implementing them on an in-process object we don't need any marshaling support. If we wanted to make a local server for Polyline, we'd have to create that marshaling support. The process of doing that is a topic for Chapter 6, but we'll demonstrate the mechanism on a somewhat simpler interface.

If you look at Polyline's source code, you'll notice that the *CPolyline* class still exists. The Polyline component uses this class internally to implement the object. This really demonstrates how you can take a C++ object and turn it into a shareable OLE component.

Of course, with Polyline split off into a separate component, Cosmo becomes a client of that component, which we'll now call Component Cosmo or CoCosmo. Its modified sample code is found in CHAP05\COCOSMO, in which modifications from the Chapter 1 version of Cosmo are offset by //CHAPTER5MOD and //End CHAPTER5MOD comments. This allows you to see exactly the sorts of things that a real client program would do to manage a component, including connection to an outgoing interface through connection points. Overall, Component Cosmo merely changed from being the user of a private C++ object, *CPolyline,* to being a client of the Polyline component through COM.

# Summary

The Component Object Model, or COM, is a specification that defines how interfaces work and how the root objects of components are created. The COM Library implements part of this specification to work in conjunction with custom component servers, DLLs or EXEs, that implement the rest. Through this interaction, a client can pass a CLSID to the COM Library, which locates the appropriate server implementation, brings that code into memory, and has that server create the root object of a component for the client. From that point on, the client communicates directly with the component's objects through interface pointers, with the COM Library providing transparent "marshaling," which enables the client to work with local (different process) and remote (different machine) objects as if they were in the client's own process space.

To support this architecture, a COM server must provide a class factory object (*IClassFactory*) that creates instances of objects on demand with optional support for licensing (*IClassFactory2*). A server must expose this class factory to the rest of the system and provide a means for unloading itself, the mechanisms for which depend on the type of server involved. Registry entries map the server's supported CLSID to its module location and can be used to mark one server as "emulating" another. These registry entries can be created from within the server itself if it supports self-registration. COM uses the registry to locate the implementation of a CLSID on behalf of a client in response to calls to *CoCreateInstance* or *CoGetClassObject*, the latter of which is the core means through which anything outside of a server gains access to that server's class factory.

Regardless of the type of server involved, its components can have any number of objects and those objects can have any number of interfaces. Some interfaces, however, do not have marshaling support, either because it is technically impossible or because specific marshaling support for those particular interfaces is not available in the system. This means that some interfaces can be implemented only from in-process objects, while others can be implemented in local and remote objects. The concept of an object handler provides the necessary means to supply a partial in-process object that communicates with its remaining implementation elsewhere.

This chapter includes a number of samples to demonstrate the basic mechanisms involved with COM clients and servers, as well as demonstrations of self-registration and licensing.

# CHAPTER SIX

# Local/Remote Transparency

$A$ccording to the *Handbook of Chemistry and Physics,*[1] "Transparency of a layer of material is defined as the ratio of the intensity of the transmitted light to that of the incident light. Opacity is the reciprocal of the transparency. Optical density is the common logarithm of the opacity." In other words:

$$\text{Optical density} = \log_{10}(I_i/I_t)$$

Obviously, then, a perfect transparency of 1.000 is achieved only when optical density (not necessarily physical density) is exactly 0. A total vacuum falls into this category, and high-quality lenses—for which professional photographers shell out tens of thousands of dollars—come rather close. A perfect opacity, on the other hand, has an infinite optical density. In this category, you'll find materials such as trees, concrete, electrical tape, other people's heads in movie theaters, and even the *Handbook of Chemistry and Physics.*

In the field of engineering acoustics, the notion called *transmission loss* is almost identical. Transmission loss measures sound through various types of wall construction, such as gypsum wallboard, 4-inch bricks, concrete, and piles of outdated *Handbook of Chemistry and Physics* volumes. The acoustics textbook I used in college[2] describes transmission loss with this equation:

$$\text{TL} = 10\text{dB} \log_{10}(I_i/I_t)$$

The concepts of optical density and transmission loss, even those of electrical resistance and conductivity to some extent, relate exceptionally well to the member function calls that a client of some object makes through one of that object's interface pointers. As we saw in Chapter 5, the effective optical density—the transmission loss—for a call from a client to an in-process object is 0: there is nothing standing between the call made in the

---

1. 65th ed. CRC Press, Inc., Boca Raton, Florida. 1984–85.
2. *Basic Acoustics,* by Donald E. Hall, Harper & Row Publishers, New York. 1987.

client and the code that implements that function in the object. Whatever piece of machine code in the client issues a call instruction, the next point of execution is at the beginning of the implementation of that function inside the object code itself.

With the aim of complete component integration, OLE and COM also allow clients to communicate with local and remote objects. Process and network boundaries are real and substantial, and significant work is required to change from one address space to another or to transmit information across network cables. For complete component integration to work, a function call made in a client must show up in any object as if no barrier existed at all. From the client's perspective, any function call to any object's interface is an in-process call, regardless of the boundaries between the client and the object. From the object's perspective, the object receives interface calls as if the client were in the same address space as well, and so the object enjoys perfect transmission.

The crux of Local/Remote Transparency is that somehow a server process has an interface pointer that it wants to make available to other processes. This always begins with a server's *IClassFactory* pointer—the first interface pointer of this kind that a server gives to COM. COM must then create the structures that allow clients in other processes to make function calls through this pointer. That's what ultimately matters. Of course, Local/Remote Transparency isn't at all important when a client is dealing with an in-process server. Only when a client is working with local or remote servers does sharing an interface pointer matter at all.

Fortunately, COM makes the whole process utterly trivial: the server can just hand the pointer to COM, and COM sets up everything required for the client to make calls into the object. This is why COM is so powerful: there is so much work to make Local/Remote Transparency work, but the burden is all on COM, not on the client or the server.

The whole trick to this technology is to always have the client call some in-process code when making any interface call and to always have the object receive that call from some code in its own process. This chapter is about the mechanisms and devices that COM uses to achieve this. Called *marshaling* or *remoting*, these mechanisms determine how an object in a local or remote process communicates with a *proxy* in the client process. An object can employ different marshaling mechanisms—custom marshaling, in which the object controls the interprocess communication itself, or standard marshaling, in which OLE provides a default mechanism. With standard marshaling, OLE offers some facilities to support custom interfaces for cases in which standard marshaling support is not already built into the system. To wrap it all up, we'll also see *concurrency management* (also called *message filtering*), through which clients and objects can gracefully handle time-outs and rejected calls, informing the end user of the situation.

The idea of COM's Local/Remote Transparency is to make interface calls to local and remote objects as transparent as calls to in-process objects, regardless of how the interprocess or intermachine communication occurs. Because COM itself handles all of the work involved and allows you to make specific customizations of the underlying architecture, clients, servers, components, and objects don't care how it all works—they just know that calls go through without one shred of loss in transmission. Not only are calls transparent as far as transmission is concerned, they are also effortless to both clients and objects; just as effortless, in fact, as an in-process call—that is, a simple function call through an interface pointer. You get zero opacity, perfect transmission.

> N O T E : You can accomplish quite a lot with OLE without knowing much of the information in this chapter, which is fairly detailed. If you are interested primarily in high-level concepts, feel free to skip this chapter or simply peruse it quickly, but be sure to read "The OLE UI Library and the Busy Dialog Box" on page 316, which is relevant to material in other chapters. Otherwise, come back to specific sections when you need to understand a specific topic.

# What Is Marshaling?

Marshaling is the mechanism that enables a client in one process to transparently make interface function calls to local objects in another process or to remote objects running on other machines. For convenience, this chapter refers to both local and remote objects as *remote objects* and both local and remote servers as *remote servers*.[3] Clients are not concerned with the differences. Regardless of the object's ultimate location, marshaling involves two steps. The first is to take an interface pointer in a server's own process and make the pointer available to code in the client process. This involves establishing some form of interprocess communication. The second step is to take the arguments to an interface call as passed from the client and transfer those arguments to the remote object's own implementation.

In earlier chapters, I've shown a simple diagram in which the client always makes interface calls to an in-process object of some sort. The object can be the complete object implementation, a handler, or a proxy. A handler and

---

3. Let me remind you again that remote servers and objects are not yet supported (at the time of writing). This chapter, however, is written as if such support existed.

a proxy are structurally identical and are often discussed interchangeably. A proxy, however, is completely aware of the nature of the connection it maintains to a remote object across whatever boundary is involved. A handler, on the other hand, might itself internally use a proxy to communicate with its own remote object. A handler doesn't need to be aware of the nature of the connection. From the client's perspective, however, the handler or proxy provides callable interface pointers as well as a complete in-process object. Thus, calls to remote objects are transparent because they appear in client code exactly as calls to in-process objects do.

Here is where the second step of marshaling comes into play. (We'll see the first step momentarily.) The client has pushed arguments onto the stack and made a function call through an interface pointer. If necessary, the call winds its way into the implementation of this function in a proxy. That proxy marshals the call by packing the arguments into a data structure that can be transmitted to another process or another machine. This data structure is then picked up by some piece of code in the object's own process, either a stub or the object itself, depending on the nature of the marshaling. That stub unpacks the data structure, pushes the arguments onto the stack, and then calls the actual object's implementation. On return, the stub packs the function's return value and any out-parameters into a data structure and transmits that structure back to the proxy. The proxy takes the return values, puts them in the appropriate places, and returns them to the client.

Different argument types, of course, are marshaled differently. A simple value such as a DWORD is marshaled by copying the value, but pointers to strings or structures are marshaled by copying the data pointed to. Whatever exists in the client's address space at the time of the call must be re-created in the server's address space, which is what the object will expect. This is the idea of transparency—neither client nor object can detect the boundaries between them.

The first step in marshaling determines exactly how arguments are transmitted between processes, if they need to be transmitted at all. Basic marshaling architecture, also called *custom marshaling*, is what the remote object uses to control the nature of the connection between it and whatever proxy it requires. Through custom marshaling, an object specifies the CLSID of its proxy and completely controls interprocess (or intermachine) communication for *all* its interfaces (custom or standard) as a whole. This means that the object also controls how to marshal the arguments of all those interfaces.

Various designs benefit tremendously from the object's control. Objects with an immutable state, for example, benefit because the proxy itself can simply be a complete copy of the remote object, thereby eliminating the need for any IPC at all! The next section examines the architecture that makes this possible, along with a few other cases in which custom marshaling is helpful.

Custom marshaling is the fundamental marshaling mechanism. Microsoft recognizes, of course, that it's pointless to make every object implementation supply its own marshaling mechanism, so OLE also offers *standard marshaling*. With standard marshaling, OLE provides a generic proxy and a generic stub that communicate through system-standard RPC. The proxy and the stub both understand all the standard OLE-defined interfaces (barring those that cannot be marshaled at all or those for which support doesn't otherwise exist). Each interface is represented by its own small piece of code, called an *interface marshaler*, that understands the semantics of each member of the interface and how to marshal all the arguments of those functions appropriately. The interface marshaler actually performs the packing and unpacking of argument structures. This architecture allows you to plug in your own marshalers for custom interfaces as well, making those custom interfaces appear the same as standard interfaces to the rest of the system. Thus, objects are completely relieved from marshaling burdens if standard marshaling is suitable for the design.

The generic proxy and stub objects are nothing more than containers, or managers, for interface marshalers, regardless of whether you provide the marshaler itself. Thus, a proxy is often called a *proxy manager* and a stub a *stub manager*. The marshalers themselves contain an *interface proxy*, which resides in the proxy object, and an *interface stub*, which resides in the stub object. This chapter refers to an interface proxy as a *facelet* and an interface stub as a *stublet* to eliminate any confusion about the use of *proxy* and *stub*. The latter two terms are used exclusively to refer to the proxy and stub objects as a whole, not the specific interface pieces within them.

It is vital to understand that standard marshaling is a specific instance of the generic custom marshaling architecture. With this in mind, we'll see first how custom marshaling works. But because standard marshaling is omnipresent on OLE-capable systems, we'll also spend considerable time dealing with it, especially with respect to how you create marshalers for your own custom interfaces.

# Basic Marshaling Architecture (Custom Marshaling)

The most fundamental operation in Local/Remote Transparency is to take an interface pointer to an object in one process and somehow create the structures that allow a client in another process to call member functions through that interface pointer. Marshaling, in its most literal form, is the process for making this interface pointer available. Again, OLE's standard marshaling is simply one way to achieve this. Custom marshaling is essentially the generic mechanism that lets any object specify exactly how it communicates with a proxy in another process, if such communication is even necessary.

To understand this mechanism and how standard marshaling uses it, let's begin with a server process that has an *IClassFactory* pointer that it has just passed to *CoRegisterClassObject*. We start here because the class factory is the first object that any server process will create and the class factory's interface pointer is the first pointer that requires marshaling. Inside *CoRegisterClassObject* (and within *CoGetClassObject* in the client's process), the exact sequence of operations that occurs for the first interface pointer is the same for the first interface pointer to any other object in the server—for example, the one returned from *IClassFactory::CreateInstance*.[4] In short, the basic marshaling process is used whenever a function in one interface returns the first interface pointer to a new and separate object, which must then be marshaled independently. Because custom marshaling happens on an object-by-object basis, we need the capability for an object that uses one form of marshaling to return an interface pointer to an object that might use a different form. Each object has the right to control whatever sort of marshaling it wants to use. If it wants no control, OLE's standard marshaling is used as a default.

Inside *CoRegisterClassObject*, COM has an *IClassFactory* pointer that it must somehow marshal to the other process. This happens through the following steps, which are the same for any interface pointer to any object regardless of the form of marshaling:

1. Inside *CoRegisterClassObject*, COM asks the object for the CLSID of the proxy it requires in the client's process. If the object does not provide a specific CLSID, COM will use a standard marshaling proxy.

---

4. Other examples include *IProvideClassInfo::GetClassInfo, IStorage::OpenStream* (Chapter 7), *IMoniker::BindToObject* (Chapter 9), *IDataObject::EnumFormatEtc* (Chapter 10), and many other standard and custom interfaces that you might use or design. All of these return new interface pointers to separate objects.

2. COM attempts to ask the object for a *marshaling packet,* which is a stream of bytes containing whatever information the proxy needs to create the interprocess connection to the object. If the object does not provide a packet, COM creates one appropriate for standard marshaling.

3. COM passes the proxy CLSID and the marshaling packet to the client process, where it shows up inside *CoGetClassObject.*

4. In the client's process, COM creates an instance of the proxy using the CLSID retrieved in step 1 and passes to it the marshaling packet retrieved in step 2.

5. The proxy uses whatever means necessary to connect with the object and returns an interface pointer to COM. COM then returns that pointer to the client on return from *CoGetClassObject.* This pointer is the one through which the client can now make calls that the proxy will forward to the object as necessary.

Steps 1 and 2 are wrapped inside the COM API function named *CoMarshalInterface.* Steps 4 and 5 are wrapped inside *CoUnmarshalInterface.* These two functions represent the core of marshaling.

Step 3 is entirely internal to COM. The transfer of the marshaling packet is the responsibility of the *service control manager* (SCM), which is what launched the server in the first place. In this sense, the SCM knows exactly what sort of barrier lies between the client and the server. It describes the barrier through a *marshaling context,* a combination of flags taken from the MSHCTX enumeration. This enumeration currently contains MSHCTX_NOSHAREDMEM (shared memory is not available between processes on this machine) and MSHCTX_DIFFERENTMACHINE (a network boundary exists between client and server). Obviously, these flags can restrict the form of marshaling that an object might want to employ. For example, an object that typically uses shared memory as an IPC mechanism could not do so when the context includes MSHCTX_NOSHAREDMEM. It might then use Microsoft Windows messages instead because window handles are shareable on the same machine. If MSHCTX_DIFFERENTMACHINE is also specified, the object would need to use named pipes, RPC, or some other appropriate network IPC.

Step 3 addresses the reason marshaling is happening in the first place. It depends on the design of whatever code calls *CoMarshalInterface.* The reason is described by a single flag taken from the MSHLFLAGS enumeration. MSHLFLAGS_NORMAL specifies marshaling that is being carried out to hook up a client and object immediately, as would happen in a client's call to *IClassFactory::CreateInstance* (to connect to the new object). MSHLFLAGS-_TABLESTRONG and MSHLFLAGS_TABLEWEAK, on the other hand, specify that the marshaling packet is only being stored in a global object table and that marshaling isn't happening immediately. Registering a class factory is an example of this: *CoRegisterClassObject* merely stores the object's marshaling packet and its proxy CLSID in a global table so that *CoGetClassObject* in the client's process can access it. (This might not happen at all.) This sort of registration makes the object available to other processes because the necessary marshaling information is accessible through the table. *Strong* means that COM has called *AddRef* on the object when storing its marshaling packet in the table, whereas *weak* means that COM has not made the call.[5] We'll see more about strong and weak references in the section "Strong and Weak Connections" later in this chapter.

The marshaling context and the marshaling flags are known within code such as *CoRegisterClassObject*, which has, at this point, an *IClassFactory* pointer to marshal. It passes this pointer to *CoMarshalInterface* along with the other necessary arguments, described as follows:

| Argument | Description |
| --- | --- |
| *pstm* | An *IStream* pointer to a stream (see Chapter 7) into which the object being marshaled should store its marshaling packet. This information is given to an appropriate proxy in the destination process. |
| *riid* | The IID of the interface pointer being marshaled. The interface itself must be derived from *IUnknown*. |
| *pUnk* | The interface pointer (cast to *IUnknown*) to marshal. |
| *dwDestContext* | DWORD flags from the MSHCTX enumeration. |
| *pvDestContext* | A *void* * pointing to additional information based on *dwDestContext*. (Currently this argument has no defined uses and must be set to NULL.) |
| *mshlflags* | DWORD flags from the MSHFLAGS enumeration. |

---

5. A weak reference means that the object might disappear while its marshaling packet still appears in the table, where the object is responsible for revoking the registration. *CoRegisterClassObject* always uses MSHLFLAGS_TABLESTRONG, which is why you cannot control server lifetime with a class factory, as discussed in Chapter 5. Only *CoRevokeClassObject* can remove the extra reference counts. However, other mechanisms, such as the running object table described in Chapter 9, give the object the choice between strong and weak registration.

The implementation of *CoMarshalInterface* works in conjunction with an interface named *IMarshal*. Arguments to *IMarshal*'s member functions are named similarly to those in the preceding table and also have the same usage, as shown in the following code. (*pvInterface* is the same as *pUnk*.)

```
interface IMarshal : IUnknown
    {
    HRESULT GetUnmarshalClass(REFIID iid, void *pvInterface
        , DWORD dwDestContext, void *pvDestContext, DWORD mshlflags
        , CLSID *pclsid);
    HRESULT GetMarshalSizeMax(REFIID iid, void *pvInterface
        , DWORD dwDestContext, void *pvDestContext, DWORD mshlflags
        , DWORD *pcb);
    HRESULT MarshalInterface(IStream *pstm, REFIID iid, void *pvInterface
        , DWORD dwDestContext, void *pvDestContext, DWORD mshlflags);
    HRESULT UnmarshalInterface(IStream *pstm, REFIID iid, void **ppv);
    HRESULT DisconnectObject(DWORD dwReserved);
    HRESULT ReleaseMarshalData(IStream *pstm);
    };
```

Through this interface, an object can control its own marshaling: *GetUnmarshalClass* returns the proxy CLSID to use, and *GetMarshalSizeMax* and *MarshalInterface* create the marshaling packet. If the object does not choose to implement this interface, it says, in effect, "Use standard marshaling." Here are the steps performed within *CoMarshalInterface*:

1. Query the object for *IMarshal*. If this interface is unavailable, standard marshaling will be used, in which case we query the object for *IPersist* in an attempt to call *IPersist::GetClassID*. The CLSID returned here still allows the object to specify which object handler to use in the client process, although that handler continues to use a standard marshaling proxy underneath. If *IPersist* is unavailable, COM defaults to a generic proxy CLSID (specifically, *CLSID_ StdMarshal*, whose server is the COM Library itself).

2. If *IMarshal* is available, call *IMarshal::GetUnmarshalClass* to obtain the proxy CLSID. The proxy must understand the object's marshaling packet.

3. Call *IMarshal::GetMarshalSizeMax* to retrieve the maximum size of the marshaling packet. COM can then preallocate the stream to the appropriate size. (Some streams, as described in Chapter 7, cannot automatically extend themselves.)

4. Call *IMarshal::MarshalInterface*, in which the object creates its marshaling packet by writing information into the stream (using *IStream::Write*).

At the end of this sequence, we're left with a proxy CLSID and a marshaling packet in a stream that can be either stored in a global table or passed directly to COM in a client process, depending on the marshaling flags. The former happens in the case of *CoRegisterClassObject*; the latter in most other cases. Depending on what operation is being performed, COM now picks up the marshaling packet in the client process. This might happen from within *CoGetClassObject*, which periodically checks the global class factory table for the new factory, or from within the proxy for whatever object created the new object being marshaled.[6] One way or the other, code in the client process retrieves the new proxy CLSID and the marshaling packet.

The job of this code is to turn the information into an interface pointer that can be given back to the client. After the client receives the pointer, it can transparently make function calls into the local or remote object, wherever it happens to be. This is the purpose of *CoUnmarshalInterface*. This function takes the following arguments, two of which imply a call to *QueryInterface* to return the interface pointer to give to the client:

| Argument | Description |
| --- | --- |
| *pstm* | An *IStream* pointer to the stream containing the marshaling packet |
| *riid* | The IID of the interface pointer required |
| *ppv* | A *void* ** in which to return the client-process pointer through which the client can make calls |

*CoUnmarshalInterface* then executes the following steps to create the proxy and have it establish communication with the local or remote object:

1. Call *CoCreateInstance* with the proxy CLSID, asking for *IMarshal* in return. A proxy must implement *IMarshal* in all circumstances. At this point, it doesn't matter what sort of marshaling is being used;

---

6. Specifically, a stub that has an out-parameter containing an interface pointer will return a marshaling packet to the proxy for that pointer, not a pointer itself.

the CLSID might be *CLSID_ StdMarshal* as easily as it can be a CLSID for a custom marshaling proxy.

2. Pass the marshaling packet to *IMarshal::UnmarshalInterface.* The proxy reads the information using *IStream::Read* and uses it to establish whatever connection the proxy requires to the local or remote object through the interface in question. From this function, the proxy returns in *ppv* the requested interface pointer specified in *riid.*

3. Call *IMarshal::ReleaseMarshalData* to free whatever data might be stored in the marshaling packet (for example, a piece of shared memory whose handle is in the stream or the handle to a file or a named pipe).

4. Return the pointer from *IMarshal::UnmarshalInterface* to the caller. This pointer is ultimately returned to the client.

Through the steps in *CoMarshalInterface* and *CoUnmarshalInterface,* a local or remote object is able to specify what proxy to create in the client process and to provide that proxy with the information necessary to establish a connection to the object through *all* of the object's interfaces, whatever those might be. This will often, of course, involve standard marshaling, as usually happens for a server's class factory. As we'll see in the next section, standard marshaling creates a generic proxy in the client process and a generic stub in the server process, where that stub maintains the object's actual interface pointers. Using this setup, we can follow the sequence of operations that occurs when a client calls *IClassFactory::CreateInstance* for an object that does use custom marshaling, as illustrated in Figure 6-1 on the next page. From the client's point of view, an object that uses custom marshaling (proxy) is no different from one that uses standard marshaling: both are transparent. Basic marshaling architecture gives an object control over its own marshaling for all of its interfaces, allowing it to make optimizations as it deems necessary.

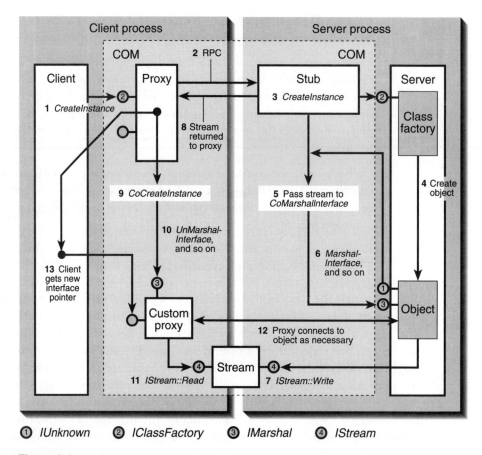

**Figure 6-1.**

*The process of establishing custom marshaling between an object and its proxy in the client's process.*

Keep in mind that this entire process can work both ways in a client-object relationship. For example, when a client passes a sink interface pointer to *IConnectionPoint::Advise,* the proxy itself is now in the position of any other remote object in that it has an interface pointer to make available to another process. The proxy calls *CoMarshalInterface* to create a client-side stub for the sink interface and passes the resulting marshaling packet to the remote process. There the *IConnectionPoint* stub will itself call *CoUnmarshalInterface* to create a proxy for the (now remote) sink object, handing an interface pointer of that new proxy to the object. The object can now call members of the remote sink in the client's process as transparently as the client calls the object's own members.

We have yet to mention *IMarshal::Disconnect*. COM uses this function to inform the custom marshaling object that some other code (in that object's server) has called *CoDisconnectObject* for it. The object must then notify its connected proxy of this disconnection so that the proxy will no longer attempt to call the object itself, returning RPC_E_NOTCONNECTED to the client instead.

---

## Four Reasons to Choose Custom Marshaling

■ If the remote object itself is a proxy to some other object, custom marshaling allows you to short-circuit this middle proxy and let the second client connect directly to the remote object. This procedure can increase performance and improve robustness—it'd be silly to have a proxy to a proxy to a proxy to a proxy, and so on.

■ Some objects keep their entire state in shared memory or in some other shareable storage medium (such as a disk). In this case, custom marshaling enables the proxy to access that shared storage directly, eliminating the need to call the remote object at all and avoiding context switches. Storage and stream objects in OLE's structured storage implementation (Chapter 7) are great examples of this.

■ After creation, some objects have an immutable state, which means no changes ever occur to their state data. Monikers (Chapter 9) are an example. With custom marshaling, such objects can make a complete copy of their internal states in both client and server processes; being immutable, the two copies are indistinguishable.

■ Some designs can cut down interprocess or network traffic by grouping several remote calls into one, thus optimizing performance. An example might be some sort of transactioning system with a commit operation, by which the proxy could cache changes until the commit is made, at which time it passes all the changes to a remote object across the network in a single call.

---

# Standard Marshaling Architecture

When an object does not want to provide its own custom marshaling, COM will automatically install standard marshaling for the object and all of its interfaces, employing specific interface marshalers as necessary. In standard marshaling, the proxy is connected to a stub that is then connected to the remote object itself. Underneath it all, both proxy and stub communicate with what is called the *RPC Channel,* an object (inside the COM Library) that encapsulates all the details about the underlying cross-process or cross-network transport, as illustrated in Figure 6-2. The RPC Channel itself makes calls into whatever RPC API exists on the system, so it only needs to control the data packets sent across the wire, so to speak, leaving the physical transport to the system.

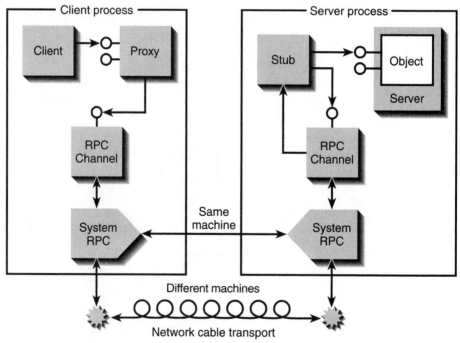

**Figure 6-2.**
*Proxies and stubs communicate with the RPC Channel, which in turn generates the necessary RPC sequences for cross-process or cross-machine communication.*

A key point here is that COM performs standard marshaling interface by interface, not object by object. In other words, COM does not create a connection between a proxy and a stub for a particular interface until the client actually has a pointer to that interface itself. In Figure 6-2, the proxy object manages *facelets,* one for each interface, that individually communicate with a corresponding *stublet* managed by the stub object, as shown in the exploded view in Figure 6-3.

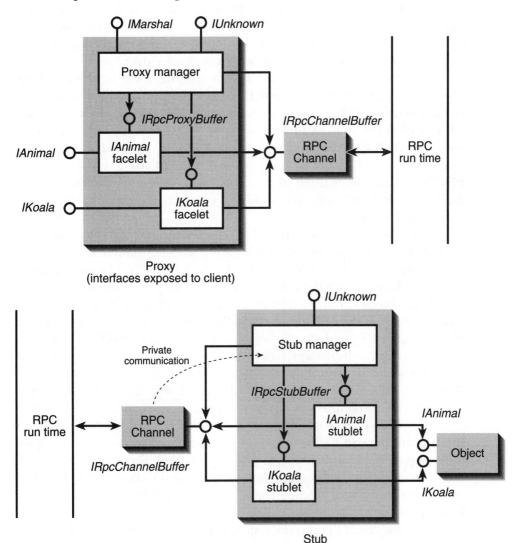

**Figure 6-3.**

*A proxy manager contains any number of facelets (one per interface); and the stub manager, any number of stublets. Client calls go directly to the appropriate facelet, which marshals the call to the stublet through the RPC Channel. The stublet maintains the pointer to the remote object's interface to make the real call.*

291

Facelets and stublets perform all the communication because they, not the proxy or stub managers, know how to marshal arguments, out-parameters, and return values correctly for their specific interfaces. In other words, the semantics of each interface member function are known somewhat to the facelet and stublet implementations. They know when an out-parameter, for example, is an interface pointer to a new and separate object, which then requires a call to *CoMarshalInterface*. An interface pointer to the same object, on the other hand, requires only a new facelet and stublet pair.

As you might expect, there are a great many details about the way proxy and stub managers are built and how they get into memory along with facelets and stublets. For interested readers, APPB.WRI on the companion CD describes the architectural objects and how they come into and out of memory. APPB.WRI discusses a short piece of client code that calls *CoGet-ClassObject*, *IClassFactory::CreateInstance*, and *IProvideClassInfo::GetTypeInfo*, an example that involves three objects, each with different interfaces. A few points, however, are worth mentioning here to help us understand other topics in this chapter.

Three members of the *IRpcChannelBuffer* interface, implemented on the RPC Channel objects shown in Figure 6-3, are important to the operation of standard marshaling. By calling the function *GetBuffer*, a facelet obtains a buffer in which it stores the function arguments to pass to its corresponding stublet. (This buffer is freed with the member function *FreeBuffer*.) When it's ready to transmit the call, the facelet calls the member function *SendReceive*. The stublet is then told to call the appropriate member function of the remote object through *IRpcStubBuffer*. When that stublet is ready to return out-parameters and return values, it calls *GetBuffer* as well and stores the data. When the stublet returns, the RPC Channel brings the data back to the facelet, which recognizes it as an out-parameter from *SendReceive*.

In most cases, the call is *synchronous*. This means that *SendReceive* will not return until the call has been completely processed in the remote object. Calls might also be *asynchronous* or *input-synchronized,* as discussed in the section "Concurrency Management" later in this chapter. When a call is blocked inside *SendReceive*, concurrency management allows the caller to control how long it is willing to wait for the call to be completed.

In some cases, the interface member that was called in this manner might create a new object and return an interface pointer to that object as an out-parameter. The stublet, knowing the semantics of that interface pointer, then has to call *CoMarshalInterface* and store the contents of the stream in the return buffer. The facelet that receives this buffer reintegrates the stream and passes it to *CoUnmarshalInterface* to obtain the correct pointer to return to the client. This mechanism is the same when the facelet has to pass an interface pointer to some object to the stublet (such as with a sink interface pointer). In this case, the facelet calls *CoMarshalInterface* and stores the stream in the buffer so that the stublet can then reintegrate the stream and call *CoUnmarshalInterface* to get the pointer to pass to the object itself. In each case, the form of marshaling is established according to the needs of the new object being marshaled.

In other cases, the interface member being called from the client returns a pointer to an interface other than the one being used, but still one that is on the same object. Here the correct proxy and stub already exist, but they now need to create a new facelet/stublet pair for the new pointer (assuming it doesn't already exist). This is one of the operations that *QueryInterface* must perform inside COM's standard *IUnknown* marshaler. Whatever code needs the new interface marshaler takes the IID and looks for a registry entry that maps to a CLSID. That CLSID then maps to a server that implements the appropriate facelet and stublet for the IID in question. The class factory in that server implements the interface *IPSFactoryBuffer*, whose members *CreateProxy* and *CreateStub* create the necessary facelet and stublet, as described in detail in APPB.WRI on the companion CD.

Interfaces that have no standard marshaling support simply do not have either the necessary registry entries or a server that provides the marshalers (which is, of course, irrelevant for objects using their own custom marshaling). The lack of marshaling support will cause any operation involving a cross-process *QueryInterface* call to fail. In other words, any facelet or stublet for any interface member that takes IID and *void* ** arguments to identify an interface pointer will fail when the appropriate registry entries for the IID in question are not found. The specific error is REGDB_E_IIDNOTREG. If the entries do exist but the server doesn't, the error is CO_E_DLLNOTFOUND. There are other possibilities, of course, and these are the errors you will see if you try to use an interface across process boundaries when marshaling support doesn't exist. The nice thing is that you can install marshalers on a running system and make marshaling suddenly work for whatever interface. The same code that failed before will now work without a hitch because the necessary marshaling support is available.

The following section describes the process of creating marshalers for custom interfaces, after which we'll look at one more topic of relevance to standard marshaling—strong and weak references.

## Custom Interfaces and Standard Marshaling

We saw earlier how the proxy and stub objects, as COM implements them internally, use registry entries to locate the necessary facelet and stublet implementations for any interface, which are assumed to be found inside an in-process server or handler. The server itself exposes a factory that implements *IPSFactory*, whereas each facelet implements *IRpcProxyBuffer* and each stublet implements *IRpcStubBuffer*.

OLE itself provides these implementations for all of its own remotable interfaces, so Local/Remote Transparency works automatically for only those interfaces. If you want to have a client and an object communicate through an interface of your own design, therefore, you must implement and register your own server for Local/Remote Transparency and plug it into the rest of COM's standard remoting facilities. There are hard ways and easy ways to accomplish this, as discussed in the following two sections. Both ways require the same registries, of the form:

```
\
    Interface
        {<IID>} = <Name of interface>
            NumMethods = <Total number of interface members>
            BaseInterface = <{IID} of base interface>
            ProxyStubClsid32 = <{CLSID} of a server for the marshaler>
```

The NumMethods entry describes the total number of members in this interface, and BaseInterface identifies the IID of the interface from which the interface is derived. If no BaseInterface is given, COM assumes the IID of *IUnknown*. Finally, ProxyStubClsid32 provides the CLSID of the server whose class factory implements *IPSFactoryBuffer*, through which COM's standard marshaling can create new facelets and stublets for this interface, as described earlier.

### The Hard Way: Manual Facelet and Stublet Implementation

As we learned in Chapter 5, implementing a DLL server is not a big deal. Implementing a server with a PSFactory is no more involved than writing a server with a class factory: you merely change the interface. Nor is it a big deal to create some skeletal facelet and stublet implementations that expose the correct interfaces and that behave properly through *QueryInterface*. All that remains is to implement the functions in *IRpcProxyBuffer* and *IRpcStubBuffer* along with the facelet's implementation of its marshaled interface. When a client calls the interface to marshal, the facelet places arguments in the RPC Channel and calls *IRpcChannelBuffer::SendReceive*. From here, COM calls the stublet's *IRpcStubBuffer::Invoke*, which extracts the arguments, calls the object, and sends all the return values back over. (This is described in APPB.WRI on the companion CD.)

How you decide to represent marshaled data for a custom interface is entirely up to you. In COM's remoting architecture, only the facelet and the stublet care about the format of the marshaled argument: therefore, you can write such code in whatever way you want. This works well for remoting within the same machine; in this case, the same server is used for facelet and stublet. When remoting occurs across a network, however, relying on the simultaneous installation of a compatible facelet/stublet server on all the different machines is no longer reasonable. Instead, facelets and stublets that support cross-network marshaling must conform to published standards for data representation. These standards are published along with Microsoft's distributed services for COM. They may or may not be available by the time you read this book.

Well, all of this doesn't sound so bad—only a few simple object implementations, right? Why do I call it the "hard way"? The truth of the matter is that for a reasonably useful and interesting interface, member functions deal with nontrivial arguments, especially when you start dealing with pointers to structures, pointers to strings, and other interface pointers that require you to create a new proxy and a new stub as well. Using the functions *CoMarshalInterface* and *CoUnmarshalInterface* along with *CoLetMarshalSizeMax*, *CoMarshalHResult*, and *CoUnmarshalHResult* is described in the *OLE Programmer's Reference.*

That said, implementing custom interface support for standard marshaling manually is entirely possible; it just takes more work.

## The Easy Way: The MIDL Compiler
Instead of you implementing all the code yourself, Microsoft provides the Microsoft Interface Definition Language, or MIDL, compiler, which can take a simple text description of an interface (including any data structures you need in that interface) and churn out C code for both facelet and stublet, along with the header file that contains the interface definition itself.[7] All you have to do afterwards is provide a DEF file and a make file, compile, link, register the server, and BOOM! Instant standard marshaling support! You even have the correct header file to include with any client or object code that you want to write using this interface.

---

7. The Win32 SDK header files for OLE-defined interfaces are defined in this manner. We saw the output in Chapter 2 for *IUnknown.*

The Microsoft Interface Definition Language itself is a set of extensions to the Open Software Foundation Distributed Computing Environment Interface Definition Language (OSF DCE IDL), the basic industry-standard RPC interface language. IDL is simply a language, and the MIDL compiler a tool, to relieve the tedium of manually creating marshaling support. The IDL documentation, the MIDL compiler, and the header files and import libraries that you need to work with MIDL are officially part of Microsoft RPC, which you'll find in the Win32 SDK. Your specific development environment (for example, Visual C++) might not include Microsoft RPC, so you might need the Win32 SDK to work with MIDL.

The IDL is similar to the Object Description Language (ODL) we saw in Chapter 3, and the two have a similar syntax. However, many keywords available in one are not available in the other to address specific problems. ODL is geared specifically to describing OLE servers and objects. IDL, on the other hand, is geared to cross-process and cross-network RPC and is capable of describing much more than is necessary to create marshaling code for some OLE interface. When describing a custom interface in IDL, you end up using only a small subset of its capabilities. For example, the following is an IDL file for the interface *IAnimal*, which we'll see later in a custom interface sample:

```
[uuid(0002114a-0000-0000-c000-000000000046),
    object
]
interface IAnimal : IUnknown
    {
    import "unknwn.idl";

    HRESULT Eat([in] LPTSTR pszFoodRecommended
        , [in, out] LPTSTR pszFoodEaten, [in] short cchEaten);
    HRESULT Sleep([in, out] short *pcMinutes);
    HRESULT Procreate([out] short *pcOffspring);
    HRESULT WhatKindOfAnimal([out] IID *pIID);
    }
```

Describing an interface is mostly a matter of setting its IID and listing the member functions, their arguments, and the attributes for those arguments. In some cases, you'll also need to describe a data type that you use in the interface. Such structures, as well as any other argument types, must be unambiguous, meaning that the size of the data must be known and pointers must have a known type. See "Marshaling Considerations for Custom Interfaces" on the facing page.

Otherwise, the most important question is whether the arguments are in-parameters, out-parameters, or in/out-parameters. These directional attributes determine what sort of marshaling code is necessary for such an argument. An in-parameter is put into the channel by the facelet and is consumed in the stublet. The opposite is true for an out-parameter. With an in/out-parameter, the facelet sends it through the channel, the stublet sends new contents back, and the facelet extracts those new contents. Of course, the MIDL compiler hides all the details from you, as long as you describe the interface accurately.

Eventually, skipping the compilation step altogether might be possible. Instead, the system could dynamically create facelets and stublets at run time directly from an IDL script. This would be especially useful in a distributed environment. COM could then pass the IDL script across the network so that you don't have to worry about installing the custom interface marshalers on every system. It would certainly be a nice feature!

## Marshaling Considerations for Custom Interfaces

The process of marshaling, especially for data structures and other pointers to data, means that a function's arguments must be re-created inside the object's address space exactly as they appear in the client's. Doing this on a single machine is relatively easy; when the process involves two different machines with potentially different operating systems and hardware architectures, implementation becomes more complicated, and it demands the unambiguous specification of your interface and associated data structures. In general, you should avoid any hardware-dependent types, such as *int*, as well as *void* * pointers, which do not specify exactly what is being pointed to.

To address this, Microsoft has listed a few rules of thumb that you should follow to best support marshaling across network boundaries:

■ Do not use *int* or *unsigned int*; use *short, unsigned short, long*, and *unsigned long*. The MIDL compiler will choke on anything containing *int*, just to keep you honest.

■ Do not use *void* *. If you need a pointer to a generic interface pointer, use *IUnknown* **. The *void* ** arguments used in *QueryInterface* are an exception because MIDL inherently understands the semantics of the function, but it doesn't understand the semantics of your own function.

■ Include as the first field of any data structure a count of bytes that describes the size of the structure itself. This makes it faster and easier to copy the structure, which will probably become necessary in the course of marshaling.

■ Be careful with pointers to structures; MIDL assumes that a pointer points to a single data item. MIDL sees a MYSTRUCT * as pointing to a single MYSTRUCT, whereas you might want to pass an array of MYSTRUCT structures; in this case, there are IDL constructs to help you include a length argument to specify the exact length of the referenced data.

■ Be careful with pointers embedded in structures; they must all be initialized or NULL. Uninitialized pointers will cause problems when a facelet attempts to copy the contents into the RPC Channel.

■ When using unions, include a description of which part of the union is being passed. This is especially important for unions that mix by-value and by-reference arguments. The facelet must know which piece to marshal. Again, IDL provides ways to describe this.

## Strong and Weak Connections

When a server passes a pointer to its class factory to a function such as *CoRegisterClassObject*, the resulting stub maintains a reference count on that class factory so that the only way to remove that reference is by calling *CoRevokeClassObject*. This sort of reference, one that will guarantee that the object stays in memory no matter what else happens, is called a *strong connection,* or *strong lock*. The adjective "strong" means that the stub maintains a pointer *and* a reference count to some object and that the stub will stay in memory as long as that reference count exists. Only a specific function call from the server itself can remove the reference.

Class factory registration, however, is not the only function in COM that creates a stub so that that stub holds a pointer. Some functions, such as *RegisterDragDrop* (which we'll see in Chapter 13), create a stub to hold the pointer but do not call *AddRef* on that pointer. Thus, a *Release* call from an external client can easily remove the last reference count on the object and destroy it along with the stub. A case in which COM holds a pointer to an object but not a reference count is called a *weak connection,* or *weak lock*. Here *weak* means that an object and a stub can disappear without any additional action on behalf of the server or whatever agent registered the object in the first place. For example, because *RegisterDragDrop* has only a weak lock on an object, that object and its stub can disappear before *RevokeDragDrop* is called.

The most critical difference between strong and weak locks is the possible disappearance of the stub while an object remains active. Whatever code created an object might itself hold reference counts to that object so that an external *Release* call doesn't actually destroy the object itself. However, such a

*Release* call will, in fact, destroy a stub that maintains only a weak lock on the object in question. When the stub is destroyed in this manner, the object, although it's still running, becomes unavailable to external clients, period. Without a stub, COM no longer has any reference to an object, and thus, any external request to open an RPC Channel to that object through a stub will fail. In other words, a weak registration function is the only chance COM has to obtain a pointer to a given object that is then held in the stub. If that stub disappears, so does that pointer as far as COM is concerned—COM simply has no way to ask the server for another pointer!

Weak locks are, in fact, useful at times, as we'll see in later chapters. The function *IRunningObjectTable::Register,* for example, actually gives you the choice of a strong lock or a weak lock. A server would choose a weak lock if it held no references to an object and wanted that object to be destroyed when all external references were removed. A server would choose a strong lock if it wanted control over object and stub lifetime; in this case, it would have to call *IRunningObjectTable::Revoke* to remove that lock.

This leaves us with two possible problems that can arise with other, less flexible, registration functions:

■ The registration function creates a strong lock, but the server needs to have it behave as a weak lock for which the last external connection causes the object to destroy itself.

■ The registration function creates only a weak lock, but the server requires it to be strong.

The solution to the first problem is an interface named *IExternalConnection.* When strong locks exist on an object, its reference count will remain positive until some other code in the server revokes the registration. In some cases, this is not the behavior you want, so you implement *IExternalConnection* on the object; this allows you to track only external connections from outside clients through the *AddConnection* (a new connection has been made) and *ReleaseConnection* (a connection has been ended) member functions. An object that wants to destroy itself does so inside *ReleaseConnection* when the last connection is torn down and the argument *fLastReleaseCloses* is TRUE, which will usually be the case. The Boolean flag exists for cases when COM is performing some operation in which an external connection is being removed before a new one is added. In these cases, COM needs a way to prevent the object from closing when it should not. If it did, the last *ReleaseConnection* would come with a FALSE flag, suppressing object destruction.

The solution to the second problem comes in two forms. You can count the number of weak locks through *IExternalConnection* and add this count to your own reference count if that suits your needs. The other solution requires a server to have some means to tell COM to add or remove a strong lock from an object. The means is a single COM API function named *CoLockObjectExternal*, which returns an HRESULT and takes the following arguments:

| Argument | Description |
| --- | --- |
| *pUnk* | Points to the object to be locked or unlocked. |
| *fLock* | Specifies whether a lock is to be added (TRUE) or removed (FALSE). Adding a lock will call *AddRef* on the object; removing a lock will call *Release*. |
| *fLastUnlockReleases* | Ignored unless *fLock* is TRUE, in which case it specifies whether the strong lock (reference) controls the object's lifetime, such that removal of the last strong lock will cause the stub to release all of its references to the object. |

If you call *CoLockObjectExternal* on an object that is already registered in the global object table through some other means, this function calls only *AddRef* and *Release*. If the object is already registered, this function will register or revoke the object from the global object table, making it suitably available or unavailable to external clients. If the object implements *IExternalConnection* as well, it can know when connections are being added and removed. Some object implementations might use this interface merely for information; others might well use a combination of self-imposed strong locks and *IExternalConnection* to control their own lifetimes.

In this context, we can better understand another COM API function that we saw in Chapter 5: *CoDisconnectObject*, which takes a single argument, the *IUnknown* pointer to the object to disconnect. We described this function as forcibly removing all external connections to an object, a useful thing to do when a user terminates a server directly. *CoDisconnectObject* has the effect of tearing down the server-side stub for the object and disconnecting the RPC Channel. Subsequent calls from the client will fail inside the RPC Channel, generating an RPC_E_NOTCONNECTED error. You can see how *CoDisconnectObject* is highly useful to ensure that external clients can no longer make any calls to an object, preventing reentrancy problems during the destruction of that object.

Along these same lines, a client might want to know whether its proxy has, in fact, an open and connected RPC Channel to the remote object. This is the purpose of another COM API function, named *CoIsHandlerConnected*. To this function the client passes its *IUnknown* pointer to what it believes is the object, which really identifies the proxy instead. This function does little more than ask the proxy whether it's connected, and the proxy then turns around and asks the RPC Channel whether it's connected.

*CoIsHandlerConnected* is useful for more than just diagnostics when a call to a remote object fails. A client might be using a true object handler (underneath which is the proxy itself) that implements much of what the client needs from the object, relying on a local server for only a few operations. If the client knows which calls would require COM (at the handler's behest) to launch the local server, it could delay making such calls until it has cached a sufficient number of them to warrant the overhead involved in launching the server. *CoIsHandlerConnected* would tell such a client whether the server is already running, allowing the client to decide when to make the optimization.

## Concurrency Management

In our discussion of standard marshaling, we tacitly assumed that a proxy's call to *IRpcChannelBuffer::SendReceive* actually works and that a remote object is ready and waiting to receive the call and process it. However, there is always the possibility that the RPC takes an intolerably long time (a network is overloaded, for example) or that the server is blocked in some modal process and cannot take the call.

For this reason, COM provides a service called *concurrency management*, or *message filtering*, through which an application (a client or a local or remote server) can filter calls or messages coming into it, allowing the application to handle or reject some calls and defer others. This applies to clients that call objects and objects that call back to a client sink through some notification or event interface.

These calls fall into three categories that help us discern why we'd want to handle certain calls in certain ways, as shown on the following page.[8]

---

8. IDL has keywords that allow you to express these call types for members of a custom interface.

- *Synchronous calls,* in which the client waits for the object to reply before continuing but can receive other messages in a controlled way while waiting. All calls are synchronous unless they fall explicitly into one of the other two categories.

- *Asynchronous notifications and events,* in which the caller proceeds without waiting for the called object to process the call. Notifications and events, as we saw in Chapter 4, are usually calls from an object back to a sink in its client. While processing an asynchronous call, COM prevents the sink from making any synchronous calls back to the calling object. For example, a sink notified of a data change in the object cannot make a synchronous call to the object to request a new data rendering. Message filtering enables the client providing the sink to know when an asynchronous call is in progress.

- *Input-synchronized calls,* in which the object must not yield in any way before the call is complete so that user interface concerns such as focus management and keyboard type-ahead will work correctly. While processing one of these calls, the object cannot call any function that has the possibility of yielding (that is, entering a message loop), which includes synchronous calls to other objects.

The vast majority of interface calls are synchronous because asynchronous ones increase programming complexity. A synchronous call means that the client process basically waits in a message loop inside *IRpcChannelBuffer::SendReceive* until the call is complete. From within this message loop, COM will notify a *message filter* when certain conditions occur, allowing the caller to time-out as well as handle any incoming calls that may occur in the meantime.

The conditions in question occur when a sequence of calls is made in the same thread of execution that eventually calls back into the original client process. Whenever a client makes a call (or an object sends a notification or fires an event), COM considers this a top-level call and assigns a logical thread ID to it, nominally the caller's HTASK. This is just some machine-unique integer and doesn't bear any relation to the multitasking system thread that is executing the caller's code. This COM thread identifies a series of calls *between* processes, which might involve multiple system threads.

Anyway, this ID travels from process to process as the recipients of this call themselves make other calls to other processes. This, of course, has the possibility of winding up in a call back to the original top-level process, which is currently waiting for the original top-level call to return. This is the exact condition that COM will detect inside this message loop; otherwise, such a situation would result in utter deadlock. Message filtering is the means by which the original caller, or any caller in between, can handle such a call and return the result through the entire chain.

The core of this mechanism is the message filter, a simple object that implements the *IMessageFilter* interface. (All of these calls return a DWORD and not an HRESULT.)

```
interface IMessageFilter : IUnknown
    {
    DWORD HandleInComingCall (DWORD dwCallType, HTASK threadIDCaller
        , DWORD dwTickCount, LPINTERFACEINFO pInterfaceInfo);
    DWORD RetryRejectedCall(HTASK threadIDCallee, DWORD dwTickCount
        , DWORD dwRejectType);
    DWORD MessagePending (HTASK threadIDCallee, DWORD dwTickCount
        , DWORD dwPendingType);
    };


/*
 * Return values for HandleInComingCall and RetryRejectedCall,
 * the latter two also being the values for dwRejectType in
 * RetryRejectedCall.
 */
typedef enum tagSERVERCALL
    {
    SERVERCALL_ISHANDLED  = 0,
    SERVERCALL_REJECTED   = 1,
    SERVERCALL_RETRYLATER = 2
    } SERVERCALL;
```

It is very important to note that *HandleInComingCall* is the object side of message filtering; *RetryRejectedCall* and *MessagePending* are client-side operations. The object-side member allows that task to handle, delay, or reject calls being made from external clients. The other operations allow the calling client to determine when the object delayed or rejected a call and also to handle other calls that might occur while waiting to try a previously rejected call. These differences apply regardless of who or what the caller and callee are.

In order to handle concurrency issues, you must implement your own simple message filter with this interface and register that filter with COM, which then calls it from within its internal message loop. By default, COM always installs its own standard message filter. Your implementation is a customization of COM's standard filtering service. This is an example of a small object, one without a CLSID and without a server or any registry entries, through which you can customize a standard OLE-provided service.

If you do implement your own message filter, you install it with COM using the function *CoRegisterMessageFilter*, which has the following arguments:

| Argument | Description |
|---|---|
| *pIMessageFilter* | The pointer to your *IMessageFilter* implementation |
| *ppIMsgFilterPrev* | A pointer to another *IMessageFilter* pointer variable that receives, as an out-parameter, the pointer to the previously installed message filter |

To unregister your message filter, call *CoRegisterMessageFilter(NULL, NULL)*. Whereas registration will call *AddRef* on the message filter, unregistration will call *Release*. Registration, however, never involves global object tables, marshaling, or anything else, even though the name of the API function is almost the same as *CoRegisterClassObject*. A message filter is a simple object that serves only to customize COM's default message filtering.

## *IMessageFilter* Member Functions

After calling *CoRegisterMessageFilter*, you can expect an occasional call to the *IMessageFilter* member functions. This section both explains how to implement each function and describes the behavior of COM's default filter.

### *IMessageFilter::HandleInComingCall*

COM calls the *HandleInComingCall* function when it detects any remote call into the process that registered the message filter. In other words, this function is a single entry point for all external calls made into this process, regardless of whether that call is from a client to an object or from an object to a client's sink.

```
DWORD HandleInComingCall(DWORD dwCallType, HTASK threadIDCaller
    , DWORD dwTickCount, LPINTERFACEINFO pInterfaceInfo);

typedef enum tagCALLTYPE   //dwCallType values
    {
    CALLTYPE_TOPLEVEL = 1,
    CALLTYPE_NESTED   = 2,
    CALLTYPE_ASYNC    = 3,
    CALLTYPE_TOPLEVEL_CALLPENDING = 4,
    CALLTYPE_ASYNC_CALLPENDING    = 5
    } CALLTYPE;
```

```
typedef struct  tagINTERFACEINFO
    {
    IUnknown *pUnk;
    IID       iid;
    WORD      wMethod;
    } INTERFACEINFO;
```

For synchronous calls (CALLTYPE_TOPLEVEL, CALLTYPE_TOP-LEVEL_CALLPENDING, and CALLTYPE_NESTED), the filter can process *HandleInComingCall* in the following ways:

■ Determine whether the called object (*pInterfaceInfo->pUnk*) can accept the call (to the *pInterfaceInfo->wMethod* member of *pInterface-Info->iid*). This gives the filter a chance to perform preparatory work required to accept the call. It is especially useful when *dwCallType* is CALLTYPE_NESTED, which indicates that the current (reentrant) call is being made in the same thread as an original top-level call from within this same process; or, when *dwCallType* is CALLTYPE-_TOPLEVEL_CALLPENDING, which indicates that this process is currently waiting inside its own outgoing call and that this new call has come in from a third party. If all goes well, the filter returns SERVERCALL_ISHANDLED to let the call proceed.

■ If the object simply cannot accept the call, the filter returns SERVERCALL_REJECTED. In this case, COM usually propagates an RPC_E_CALL_REJECTED error back to the original caller.

■ If a temporary modal state blocks processing of this call, the filter returns SERVERCALL_RETRYLATER. This shows up as a call to *RetryRejectedCall* in the caller's message filter, which, as we'll see shortly, can decide how much longer to wait before trying again, eventually causing a time-out if the call won't go through.

When the call is asynchronous (CALLTYPE_ASYNC, a new call; or CALLTYPE_ASYNC_CALLPENDING, which occurs while this process is inside another synchronous call) or input-synchronized (as determined by the filter based on INTERFACEINFO), it doesn't really matter what a filter returns—*HandleInComingCall* merely gives the filter a chance to prepare before COM forwards the call to the appropriate object.

The *dwTickCount* argument to this function indicates the time elapsed since the original call was made unless *dwCallType* is CALLTYPE_TOPLEVEL, in which case *dwTickCount* is meaningless.

**Default filter**  Returns SERVERCALL_ISHANDLED in all circumstances.

### *IMessageFilter::RetryRejectedCall*

When a client caller makes a call to a remote object (or an object makes a call back to a remote client), the recipient of that call can reject or delay the call by returning SERVERCALL_REJECTED or SERVERCALL_RETRYLATER from its implementation of *HandleInComingCall*.

When the recipient rejects a call, COM, on the caller side, first checks whether a connection to that remote process still exists, failing with RPC_E_CONNECTIONTERMINATED if one doesn't. If the connection is still valid, COM processes any pending incoming calls to the caller's process (calling *HandleInComingCall* in its own filter, of course) and tries to make the remote call again. If COM runs out of things to do on the caller side, the remote process might be in a temporary blocking state. COM then notifies the calling process by calling *RetryRejectedCall* in its filter, giving the caller the chance to wait for a while before trying again:

```
DWORD RetryRejectedCall(HTASK threadIDCallee, DWORD dwTickCount
    , DWORD dwRejectType);
```

This also gives the caller a chance to display a dialog box informing the user of the delay, allowing the end user to wait longer or cancel the call completely, avoiding deadlocks. The *dwTickCount* argument contains the time elapsed since the original call so that *RetryRejectedCall* can check the limits of its patience.

The *dwRejectType* argument contains the SERVERCALL_REJECTED or SERVERCALL_RETRYLATER value that was returned from the recipient's *HandleInComingCall*. SERVERCALL_REJECTED is usually the final word— the caller shouldn't try the call again unless it has special knowledge about the state of the remote object, which is rare.

If the caller decides to give up, either because the object rejected the call or because a time-out occurred, it should return the value –1 from this function. As a result, the original calling code will see the error RPC_E-_CALL_REJECTED.

Otherwise, the caller returns the number of milliseconds that COM should wait before trying the call again. Any value below 100, being too small for the resolution of the Windows timer (which is 55 ms), effectively means, "try again immediately," so COM doesn't bother to wait. Otherwise, COM sits in the message loop until the given time has elapsed and then tries the call again. If that call goes through, all is well; if the remote process rejects or delays the call again, COM will call *RetryRejectedCall* once again.

Eventually the caller's filter will run out of patience—usually after about 5 seconds (*dwTickCount* > 5000), the patience of a typical end user—at which time the filter can pop up a dialog box, using the task handle in *threadIDCallee*, to retrieve information about the remote task. Granted, a task handle isn't all that useful in itself, but with it you can invoke the standard UI busy dialog box shown in Figure 6-4. A standard implementation of this dialog exists in the OLE UI Library, as we'll see a little later. From this dialog, the end user can instruct *RetryRejectedCall* to return either −1 or some other value to wait once more.

**Default filter**   Fails all delays or rejections by returning −1.

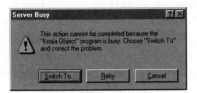

**Figure 6-4.**
*The standard busy dialog box implemented in the OLE UI Library.*

### IMessageFilter::MessagePending

While a caller is waiting for one of its own outgoing calls to be completed (the sort described by *dwPendingType*), it must still handle some additional user input, such as keystrokes and mouse clicks. If the remote application being called has taken the input focus and come to the foreground, such messages will end up in that application's message queue and in its user interface. In many cases, however, the focus does not change, so the end user continues to work in the caller application. Even if the remote application does take the focus, the end user can switch back to the caller. This introduces some complications—namely, what to do with the Windows messages that appear in the caller's queue while the caller is waiting for the remote call to finish. One way to address this is with the *MessagePending* member, as shown in the following:

```
DWORD MessagePending (HTASK threadIDCallee, DWORD dwTickCount
    , DWORD dwPendingType);

typedef enum tagPENDINGTYPE
    {
    PENDINGTYPE_TOPLEVEL = 1,
    PENDINGTYPE_NESTED   = 2
    } PENDINGTYPE;
```

*(continued)*

```
//Return values
typedef enum tagPENDINGMSG
    {
    PENDINGMSG_CANCELCALL    = 0,
    PENDINGMSG_WAITNOPROCESS  = 1,
    PENDINGMSG_WAITDEFPROCESS = 2
    } PENDINGMSG;
```

Usually the caller will want to dispatch WM_PAINT and WM_MOUSE-MOVE messages but leave others in the queue for a short length of time, about 2 or 3 seconds. This is enough time for an end user's pending keyboard actions to be processed after the call returns. However, after 2 to 3 seconds (which *MessagePending* calculates from *GetTickCount() − dwTickCount* again), end-user input is no longer considered to be of the type-ahead variety but more along the lines of this-application-seems-dead-so-perhaps-slamming-the-keyboard-and-mouse-will-fix-it. In this case, the caller should flush the message queue and show the busy dialog box once again (using *threadIDCallee* in the same manner) to give the end user a chance to do something about the problem.

Now COM is spinning in a message loop inside the caller's process while waiting for the remote call to become complete. If a Windows message appears during this time, COM will check whether the connection has failed, returning appropriate error codes such as RPC_E_CONNECTIONTERMINATED and RPC_E_SERVER_DIED (connection is still valid but the thing sure is taking forever, like more than an hour). If the connection is still valid, COM calculates the elapsed time and calls *MessagePending* without removing the message from the queue.

Within *MessagePending*, you check the message and return one of the PENDINGMSG values to tell COM what to do with it. Returning PENDING-MSG_WAITDEFPROCESS tells COM to dispatch messages related to task switching or window activation, dispatch WM_PAINT and WM_TIMER messages, discard input messages, and continue to wait for a reply. Returning PENDINGMSG_WAITNOPROCESS tells COM to simply wait some more. Returning PENDINGMSG_CANCELCALL tells COM to drop out of its loop and return RPC_E_CALL_CANCELED from the outgoing call.

**Default filter**   Returns PENDINGMSG_WAITDEFPROCESS.

## Limitations of Outgoing Calls

Besides the errors that message filtering might generate, COM places a few other restrictions on outgoing calls from any process to an object in any other process, as described in the following error list:

| | |
|---|---|
| RPC_E_CANTCALLOUT-_INASYNCCALL | An object cannot make other outgoing calls while processing an asynchronous call to itself. See the discussion that follows this table for more information. |
| RPC_E_CANTCALLOUT-_ININPUTSYNCCALL | An object cannot make other outgoing calls while processing an input-synchronous call itself. |
| RPC_E_CANTCALLOUT-_INEXTERNALCALL | It is illegal to call out while inside a message filter. |
| RPC_E_CANTCALLOUT-_AGAIN | There is no second outgoing call on a DDE channel, used when communicating with an OLE version 1 server (OLE Documents only). |

We will encounter a few of these as we progress through other subjects in this book, especially RPC_E_CANTCALLOUT_INASYNCCALL, which you will probably encounter in your own work at some time or other. The reason for this restriction is that the source of an asynchronous call is usually making a series of such calls to potentially multiple sinks. That source might also make a synchronous call after it has completed making asynchronous calls, expecting that it will not receive any incoming calls in the meantime. In such a case, the receiver (sink) of the asynchronous call is not allowed to make a synchronous call to the source. This avoids problems in which the sink calls back to the source but the source rejects the call. The sink can then go into a retry loop, during which time the source tries another asynchronous call to the same sink. These calls fail now that the sink is blocked. If the source itself goes into a retry loop, we get deadlocked. Not good. This means that you cannot make a call from within an asynchronous call—instead, you'll need to post yourself a message to make that call later.

## Implementing *IExternalConnection*

From the look of the preceding pages, you can probably guess that there's a lot we can talk about as far as implementation is concerned: concurrency management, custom interfaces, and custom marshaling. To ease us into those topics, however, let's first look at the simple implementation of the *IExternalConnection* interface, which we can use to demonstrate when COM adds and removes strong locks on objects, especially the effect of calling *CoLockObjectExternal*.

The basis for our discussion, as well as for the section about concurrency management, is the EKoala3 sample (CHAP06\EKOALA3). This is basically the EKoalal sample from Chapter 5 with the following changes (marked with //CHAPTER6MOD and //End CHAPTER6MOD comments in the sources):

■ *IExternalConnection* is implemented on and exposed from both the *CKoala* and *CKoalaClassFactory* objects, exposed through their *Query-Interface* functions, of course. Both *AddConnection* and *ReleaseConnection* display a message box with the current number of strong and weak locks.

■ The function *CApp::Init* (EKOALA3.CPP), which creates and registers the class factory with *CoRegisterClassObject*, also calls *CoLockObjectExternal(..., TRUE, TRUE)* followed by *CoLockObjectExternal(..., TRUE, FALSE)* on the class factory to show the effects of a strong lock in the class factory's *IExternalConnection*.

■ The EKoala3 server (EKOALA3.CPP) displays a main window with a menu through which you can affect incoming calls (by using the menu items Block and Delay) to demonstrate concurrency management. These menu items simply toggle the variables *m_fBlock* and *m_fDelay* in the EKoala3 application structure *CApp*.

■ The EKoala3 server creates and registers a message filter using the class *CMessageFilter* (MSGFILT.CPP). This filter will reject or delay calls inside *IMessageFilter::HandleInComingCall* depending on *CApp::m_fBlock* and *CApp::m_fDelay*.

■ Because the main window is visible, EKoala3 ignores WM_CLOSE messages to its main window unless the proper shutdown conditions are met. This prevents the end user from closing the server too soon.

■ The Koala object (KOALA.CPP), besides implementing *IExternalConnection*, also implements *IPersist* simply because standard marshaling exists for that interface, allowing us to demonstrate concurrency management.

For our discussion of *IExternalConnection*, only the first two changes are important. We cover the rest in the section "Implementing Concurrency Management and the Busy Dialog Box" later in this chapter.

To see how *IExternalConnection* works, be sure that EKoala3's registry entries are current (using its REG file—EKoala3 is not self-registering), and run the ObjectUser sample from Chapter 5. In ObjectUser, choose Use EXE

310

Server followed by either of the Create commands. This executes the following sequence in both the client and server processes, where a number of message boxes will appear from within EKoala3:

1. ObjectUser calls *CoGetClassObject*. (COM launches server.)

2. EKoala3 calls *CoRegisterClassObject*, which registers the class factory in the object table with a strong lock. COM calls the class factory's *IExternalConnection::AddConnection(EXTCONN_ STRONG)*.

3. EKoala3 displays a message for *AddConnection*, where the strong count is 1.

4. EKoala3 calls *CoLockObjectExternal(class factory, TRUE, TRUE)*, which generates another call to *AddConnection(EXTCONN_ STRONG)*.

5. EKoala3 displays a message for *AddConnection*, where the strong count is 2. EKoala3 is blocked until you close the message box; however, the message box is sitting in a message loop, so *CoGetClassObject* will return the *IClassFactory* pointer to ObjectUser.

6. ObjectUser calls *IClassFactory::CreateInstance*, which creates the object in EKoala3. COM's *IClassFactory* stublet creates a new stub for the new object using *CoMarshalInterface*.

7. The new stub registers the object in the object table, which generates a call to the Koala's *IExternalConnection::AddConnection(EXTCONN_ STRONG)*.

8. EKoala3 displays an *AddConnection* from within the Koala object, where its strong count is now 1. Close the message box to continue.

9. EKoala3 returns from its first *CoLockObjectExternal* call (step 4) and calls *CoLockObjectExternal(class factory, TRUE, FALSE)*, which generates a call to *ReleaseConnection(EXTCONN_ STRONG)*.

10. EKoala3 displays a message for *ReleaseConnection*, where the strong count is 1. Close the message box to continue.

11. ObjectUser calls *IClassFactory::Release*, which releases the external connection to the class factory, resulting in a call to the class factory's *ReleaseConnection(EXTCONN_ STRONG)*.

12. EKoala3 displays a message for *ReleaseConnection*, where the strong count is 0. Close the message box to continue.

When you now choose Release in ObjectUser to free the object, COM will call the Koala object's *ReleaseConnection*, which will display a message that its count is 0. After you close the message box, the EKoala3 server will terminate, removing its window from the screen.

This whole demonstration is somewhat contrived because neither the class factory nor the Koala object really have a reason to implement *IExternalConnection* other than to demonstrate when calls are made to its member functions. The class factory's implementation of *AddConnection* is fairly representative of *ReleaseConnection* as well as of the same functions in the Koala object (which have the same implementation but a different title on the message box):

```
STDMETHODIMP_(DWORD) CImpIExternalConnection::AddConnection
    (DWORD dwConn, DWORD dwReserved)
    {
    DWORD        dwRet;
    TCHAR        szTemp[80];

    if (EXTCONN_STRONG & dwConn)
        {
        dwRet=++m_cStrong;
        wsprintf(szTemp
            , TEXT("AddConnection cStrong=%lu"), m_cStrong);
        }

    if (EXTCONN_WEAK & dwConn)
        {
        dwRet=++m_cWeak;
        wsprintf(szTemp
            , TEXT("ReleaseConnection cWeak=%lu"), m_cWeak);
        }

    MessageBox(NULL, szTemp
        , TEXT("EKoala3: CKoalaClassFactory::IExternalConnection")
        , MB_OK);

    return dwRet;
    }
```

The implementation picks up both strong and weak locks, counting both and displaying a message for both. However, you won't see any calls with EXTCONN_WEAK when running ObjectUser and EKoala3—the code is included to illustrate the different flags in the *dwConn* argument.

Later in this book, we'll see some cases for which an in-process object really must implement *IExternalConnection* so it can lock its client in memory as well as tell the client when to shut down. There are, of course, other uses for this interface anytime you need to control an object's lifetime according to external connections, as described earlier in this chapter.

# Implementing Concurrency Management and the Busy Dialog Box

In the previous section, I mentioned some additions to the EKoala3 sample to support concurrency management—a few menu items, the implementation of the *IPersist* interface, and a message filter—all of which allow you to see what happens when a server blocks or delays incoming calls.

In talking about concurrency management, keep in mind that the *IMessageFilter::HandleInComingCall* function is used only for a process that receives external calls, while the other members, *RetryRejectedCall* and *MessagePending*, are expressly for a process that makes calls into a remote object. For this reason, EKoala3's message filter implements only *HandleInComingCall*. To demonstrate the other two functions, we'll use a modification of the ObjectUser sample—ObjectUser2—which installs its own message filter to display the busy dialog box at the appropriate times.

In this section, we'll first look at the EKoala3 modifications that allow us to simulate a blocked server or a delayed call. Then we'll take a brief look at the OLE UI library, which provides the standard implementation of the busy dialog box. We'll then see ObjectUser2 and how it employs this dialog box to tell the end user when the server is not responding to calls.

## A Server-Side Message Filter: EKoala3

A server's message filter allows it to block incoming calls if the server (as a whole) or one or more of its objects are in some state that would force them to either reject calls completely or specify that a client should try again later. For example, a server might be in the middle of a calculation using data that a client can modify through some object's interfaces—it would be best if that data didn't change during the calculation!

*IMessageFilter::HandleInComingCall* is the single entry point on the server side for all incoming calls, regardless of which object and which interface those calls are headed toward. But to see the calls as they happen, the server has to implement, instantiate, and register a message filter. EKoala3 accomplishes this through a C++ class, *CMessageFilter*, defined in EKOALA3.H (singly inheriting from *IMessageFilter*) and implemented in MSGFILT.CPP. This message filter (which needs no CLSID) has its own reference count and deletes itself on the final *Release* call, just as any other simple object does. The only interesting part of the entire object is the *HandleInComingCall* function; the other two members simply return default values because they are not used in a server that makes no outgoing calls:

```
//m_pApp set in CMessageFilter constructor

STDMETHODIMP_(DWORD) CMessageFilter::HandleInComingCall
    (DWORD dwCallType, HTASK htaskCaller, DWORD dwTickCount
    , LPINTERFACEINFO pInterfaceInfo)
    {
    if (m_pApp->m_fBlock)
        return SERVERCALL_REJECTED;

    if (m_pApp->m_fDelay)
        return SERVERCALL_RETRYLATER;

    return SERVERCALL_ISHANDLED;
    }


//These functions are not used unless you make outgoing calls.
STDMETHODIMP_(DWORD) CMessageFilter::RetryRejectedCall
    (HTASK htaskCallee, DWORD dwTickCount, DWORD dwRejectType)
    {
    return 0;
    }


STDMETHODIMP_(DWORD) CMessageFilter::MessagePending
    (HTASK htaskCallee, DWORD dwTickCount, DWORD dwPendingType)
    {
    return PENDINGMSG_WAITDEFPROCESS;
    }
```

Again, the LPINTERFACEINFO structure passed to *HandleInComingCall* identifies which interface member (the *iid* and *wMethod* fields) of which object (the *pUnk* field) is being called. EKoala3's implementation of this function, however, doesn't care which object or which interface member is being called; instead, it checks its *CApp* variables *m_fBlock* and *m_fDelay*, which EKoala3 toggles through the Block and Delay items on its Incoming Call menu.

When you tell EKoala3 to block calls, it rejects everything that comes into *HandleInComingCall* by immediately returning SERVERCALL_REJECT-ED. This generates an RPC_E_CALL_REJECTED error in the client making the call. If you tell EKoala3 to delay calls, it returns SERVERCALL_RETRY-LATER. Both these return values end up in the client message filter's

*RetryRejectedCall* function, as we'll see shortly. If neither condition is set, EKoala3 returns SERVERCALL_ISHANDLED, allowing the call to go through as usual. OLE's default message filter, remember, always returns SERVERCALL_ISHANDLED.

EKoala3 creates an instance of its message filter inside *CApp::Init* (EKOALA3.CPP) and registers the instance with *CoRegisterMessageFilter*. If for some reason it fails to instantiate the filter, EKoala3 skips the registration entirely:

```
m_pMsgFilter=new CMessageFilter(this);

if (NULL!=m_pMsgFilter)
    {
    m_pMsgFilter->AddRef();

    if (FAILED(CoRegisterMessageFilter(m_pMsgFilter, NULL)))
        ReleaseInterface(m_pMsgFilter);
    }
```

The *CMessageFilter* constructor sets the message filter's reference count to 0 initially. The explicit call to *AddRef* here gives EKoala3 control of the object's lifetime. If *CoRegisterMessageFilter* works, it will also call *AddRef* on the object. If it fails, however, the *ReleaseInterface* macro (INC\INOLE.H) will remove EKoala3's reference count and delete the object, in which case we just do without the message filter. All of this is also reversed inside *CApp::~CApp*, calling *CoRegisterMessageFilter* again to remove the filter (which calls the object's *Release*), followed by *ReleaseInterface* to destroy the object:

```
if (NULL!=m_pMsgFilter)
    {
    CoRegisterMessageFilter(NULL, NULL);
    ReleaseInterface(m_pMsgFilter);
    }
```

While the filter remains registered, you can play around with external calls, blocking and delaying them. Because EKoala3 is a multiuse server, you can run multiple instances of ObjectUser2 against it and watch calls to different objects coming in through *HandleInComingCall*. With this sample, you can make a few simple modifications to allow, reject, or delay specific calls to specific objects. By blocking one object's calls and not another's, you can watch one client make successful calls while another has to wait and, after a few seconds, display the busy dialog box. Let's now take a look at the OLE UI Library, where this dialog comes from.

## The OLE UI Library and the Busy Dialog Box

I begged and pleaded and it finally happened. When I first worked with OLE version 1, I figured that the hardest part about implementing a compound document container (the only kind of client then) was providing all of the user interface, namely a bunch of dialog boxes. When I began working with OLE 2, I tried hard to convince others that Microsoft should implement common dialog boxes. Although I initially met stiff resistance ("not enough resources"), eventually it made sense to everyone: I was going to have to implement these dialog boxes anyway, the OLE 2 team would have to provide them in their own samples, and various Microsoft product groups—including product support—were going to have to implement them for their customers. So a number of us got together to divide up the work. From that effort came the OLE UI Library, or just OLEUI, which will save you a tremendous amount of time in providing the proper OLE user interface elements in various types of applications, notably those involved with OLE Documents.

The OLE UI Library was shipped originally as a bunch of sample code containing not only the dialog boxes but a host of other helper functions that usually began with the prefix *OleStd*. Many of these functions—some renamed and others modified—have ended up in the utility library for this book's samples, found in the INOLE directory. Since that time, a reduced version of this code, containing little more than the dialogs themselves, has become part of the operating system (Microsoft Windows 95, Microsoft Windows NT 3.51, and later). It is now called OLEDLG.DLL. This book's samples attempt to link to this library. Documentation is generally found in the file OLE2UI-.HLP, but check the header file for the most accurate information.

We'll see quite a lot of OLEUI as we go through additional chapters in this book. What is of interest here is the standard busy dialog box that we saw in Figure 6-4 on page 307. To invoke this dialog box, you must fill a structure named *OLEUIBUSY* and pass it to the function *OleUIBusy*. The structure and the function are defined in OLE2UI.H as follows:

```
typedef struct tagOLEUIBUSY
    {
    //These IN fields are standard across all OLEUI dialog functions.
    DWORD           cbStruct;          //Structure size
    DWORD           dwFlags;           //IN-OUT:  flags
```

```
HWND            hWndOwner;          //Owning window
LPCTSTR         lpszCaption;        //Dialog caption bar contents
LPFNOLEUIHOOK   lpfnHook;           //Hook callback
LPARAM          lCustData;          //Custom data to pass to hook
HINSTANCE       hInstance;          //Instance for customized template
LPCTSTR         lpszTemplate;       //Customized template name
HRSRC           hResource;          //Customized template handle

//Specifics for OLEUIBUSY
HTASK           hTask;              //IN: hTask that is blocking
HWND FAR *      lphWndDialog;       //IN: dialog's HWND placed here.
} OLEUIBUSY, *POLEUIBUSY, FAR *LPOLEUIBUSY;

//API prototype
STDAPI_(UINT) OleUIBusy(LPOLEUIBUSY);
```

The first set of fields in the structure is common across all the OLEUI dialogs by design. These fields allow you to control various standard aspects of the dialog boxes, such as the caption, the layout template, and the dialog box's parent window. You can also hook the dialog box to preprocess Windows messages coming into it, with the exception of WM_INITDIALOG, for which you can perform post-processing.

Each dialog box–specific structure also includes a few extra fields as needed for that dialog box. In the case of the busy dialog box, there are only two: *hTask* is where a client stores a busy server's task handle, the exact one it receives in *IMessageFilter* members (intelligent, no?); *lphWndDialog* is a pointer to an HWND variable in which the calling client can obtain the (modal) dialog box's handle while that dialog box is visible if the client needs to cancel it for any reason.

There are four flags that you can combine and store in the *dwFlags* field of the structure. The first three, BZ_DISABLECANCELBUTTON, BZ_DIS-ABLESWITCHTOBUTTON, and BZ_DISABLERETRYBUTTON, selectively disable the dialog box's buttons, whereas the fourth, BZ_NOTRESPOND-INGDIALOG, changes the wording slightly, from a "server is busy" description to "server is not responding," and disables the Cancel button. Usually you use this flag when invoking the dialog from *IMessageFilter::MessagePending* rather than from *IMessageFilter::RetryRejectedCall*.

Let's see how we use this dialog in ObjectUser2.

## A Simple Client-Side Message Filter: ObjectUser2

A client application will want to install a message filter to determine when a server has rejected a call or is otherwise not responding or to process Windows messages that come into the application message queue while a call is in progress. As described earlier, OLE's default message filter will cancel any rejected or delayed call and discard any input message. If you want to change this behavior, you need to install a message filter.

To demonstrate the client side of message filtering, the ObjectUser2 program registers a message filter and provides a menu item to call *IPersist::GetClassID* on a Koala object obtained from EKoala3. *IPersist* is used here because it's the simplest interface for which OLE provides standard marshaling support (which means that we don't have to introduce some other complex interface into this specific sample). It is also a call that the proxy will forward to the object—we can't use *AddRef* or *Release* in this demonstration because OLE's standard proxy doesn't forward anything except the last *Release*. So *IPersist::GetClassID* fits the bill nicely.

ObjectUser2 uses a C++ class, *CMessageFilter*, which is similar to that in EKoala3 except that the version here fully implements *RetryRejectedCall*, leaves *MessagePending* the same as the default filter (returns PENDINGMSG_WAITDEFPROCESS) and returns E_NOTIMPL from *HandleInComingCall*. The application initialization code instantiates and registers the filter in *CApp::Init* and removes and releases it in *CApp::~CApp*, exactly as shown earlier with EKoala3. In other words, the registration process is identical for both clients and servers.

Inside ObjectUser2's *RetryRejectedCall*, we immediately cancel a rejected call (which returns RPC_E_CALL_REJECTED from the call itself). If the call is merely delayed, we print a message with the time elapsed since the call was made. If 5 seconds elapse, we display the busy dialog box:

```
STDMETHODIMP_(DWORD) CMessageFilter::RetryRejectedCall
    (HTASK htaskCallee, DWORD dwTickCount, DWORD dwRejectType)
    {
    UINT    uRet;
    TCHAR   szMsg[256];

    if (SERVERCALL_REJECTED==dwRejectType)
        return (DWORD)-1;

    wsprintf(szMsg, TEXT("RetryRejectedCall waiting %lu")
        , dwTickCount);
    m_pApp->Message(szMsg);

    if (dwTickCount < 5000)
        return 200;
```

```
     m_pApp->Message
        (TEXT("CMessageFilter::RetryRejectedCall showing busy dialog box"));

     uRet=DisplayBusyDialog(htaskCallee, 0L);

     switch (uRet)
         {
         case OLEUI_CANCEL:
             return (DWORD)-1;

         case OLEUI_BZ_SWITCHTOSELECTED:
             /*
              * This case won't happen without BZ_NOTRESPONDINGDIALOG,
              * but we would wait maybe 10 seconds if it did happen.
              */
             return 10000;

         case OLEUI_BZ_RETRYSELECTED:
             m_pApp->Message(TEXT("Waiting another second"));
             return 1000;

         default:
             break;
         }

     return 0;
     }

UINT CMessageFilter::DisplayBusyDialog(HTASK hTask, DWORD dwFlags)
     {
     OLEUIBUSY   bz;

     //Clear out everything we don't use.
     memset(&bz, 0, sizeof(bz));

     bz.cbStruct=sizeof(OLEUIBUSY);
     bz.dwFlags=dwFlags;
     bz.hWndOwner=m_pApp->m_hWnd;
     bz.hTask=hTask;
     bz.lphWndDialog=NULL;

     return OleUIBusy(&bz);
     }
```

The OLEUI_CANCEL and OLEUI_BZ_* flags indicate the button the user chose in the dialog box. If the user clicks on the Cancel button in the dialog box, *RetryRejectedCall* will cancel the call, generating an RPC_E-_CALL_REJECTED result. If the user clicks on Retry, we wait for another second by returning 1000 (milliseconds). If the call hasn't gone through by the time that second has elapsed, we come back into *RetryRejectedCall* and display the dialog box again as long as the user keeps clicking on Retry.

If the user chooses Switch To, the busy dialog box sets the focus to the server if possible (using the server's task handle to get at the window). If the dialog box can't find a window, it launches the Windows task manager. This tells the user to fix whatever the problem is in the server before switching back to the client. When the user does switch back, the busy dialog box automatically closes as if he or she had clicked on the Retry button, in which case our code will wait another second.

One of the little differences between the busy dialog box and the "not responding" dialog box is that choosing Switch To in the latter will, after switching to the server (or task manager), close the dialog box immediately and return OLEUI_BZ_SWITCHTOSELECTED. The client can choose to continue waiting (as the code on the preceding page would do), cancel the call, or wait for a while and then cancel the call if the server still doesn't respond (without invoking the dialog box again).

With ObjectUser2 and EKoala3, you can now fully explore how message filtering works. Run ObjectUser2 and choose Create. After going through all of EKoala3's *IExternalConnection* messages, choose the IPersist::GetClassID menu item in ObjectUser2. This call will succeed. Now choose Block in EKoala3 and try the call again. This time it fails with 0x80010001, or RPC_E-_CALL_REJECTED. Now turn off Block, turn on Delay, and try the call again. This time you'll see ObjectUser2 show the elapsed time while it's waiting through *RetryRejectedCall*. While this is going on, turn off Delay in EKoala3, and you'll see the call completed with NOERROR, showing how a client will wait for a while and, if the server responds in the right amount of time, proceed without bothering the end user.

Now turn Delay back on and make the call again, but this time let ObjectUser2's counter go past 5000; now the busy dialog box appears. If you click on Cancel, the call will fail with RPC_E_CALL_REJECTED. If you click on Retry, you'll see a message in ObjectUser2, after which the busy dialog box appears again. You can keep choosing Retry as long as you want, to no avail. Now choose Switch To, which will place you in EKoala3. Turn Delay off and switch back to ObjectUser2, where you'll see the busy dialog box disappear. After waiting another second, you'll see the call succeed. You can see the same thing happen if, after you click on Retry, you quickly switch to EKoala3 and turn off Delay. (Or turn Block on and watch the call fail immediately.)

In all, these two samples let you take a look at the variations of rejected and delayed calls. If you watch ObjectUser2's *IMessageFilter::MessagePending* function as well, you'll see that it gets called during any waiting period if you press a key or do anything with the mouse in ObjectUser2's window, even moving the mouse over it. The preceding code doesn't generate any kind of message in such a case because it would overwrite those messages shown in *RetryRejectedCall*. But you can prove that calls are being made by inserting the following line into the code:

```
m_pApp->Message(TEXT("MessagePending called."));
```

ObjectUser2 is itself a pretty lame application. It doesn't really care about input messages from the mouse and keyboard, so default processing from *MessagePending* is fine. But what if you want to preserve messages?

## Handling *IMessageFilter::MessagePending*

One of the pieces of sample code found in the original OLEUI sources is a sort of standard message filter implementation—not the default one, but a more typical sort that shows the sort of thing you can do within *Message-Pending* to process additional input. (This code is cleaned up a little from the actual sources, with some bits omitted to simplify our discussion.)

```
/*
 * Macro checks for WM_LBUTTONDOWN, WM_LBUTTONDBLCLK,
 * WM_NCLBUTTONDOWN, WM_NCLBUTTONDBLCLK, WM_KEYDOWN, and WM_SYSKEYDOWN
 * through PeekMessage calls with PM_NOREMOVE | PM_NOYIELD.
 */
#define IS_SIGNIFICANT_MSG(lpmsg)  [Expansion omitted]

STDMETHODIMP_(DWORD) OleStdMsgFilter_MessagePending(LPMESSAGEFILTER lpThis
    , HTASK htaskCallee, DWORD dwTickCount, DWORD dwPendingType)
    {
    LPOLESTDMESSAGEFILTER    this=(LPOLESTDMESSAGEFILTER)lpThis;
    DWORD                    dwReturn=PENDINGMSG_WAITDEFPROCESS;
    MSG                      msg;
    BOOL                     fIsSignificantMsg=IS_SIGNIFICANT_MSG(&msg);
    UINT                     uRet;

    if (dwTickCount > 5000 && fIsSignificantMsg
        && !this->m_bUnblocking)
        {
        this->m_bUnblocking=TRUE;

        //Eat messages in our queue that we do NOT want dispatched.
```

*(continued)*

```
while (PeekMessage(&msg, NULL, WM_CLOSE, WM_CLOSE
  , PM_REMOVE | PM_NOYIELD))
    ;

[Invoke the dialog box with BZ_NOTRESPONDING.]
uRet=OleUIBusy(&bz);

this->m_bUnblocking = TRUE;
return PENDINGMSG_WAITNOPROCESS;
}

if (this->m_bUnblocking)
    return PENDINGMSG_WAITDEFPROCESS;

if (this->m_lpfnMessagePendingCallback)
    {
    MSG msg;

    if (PeekMessage(&msg, NULL, 0, 0, PM_NOREMOVE | PM_NOYIELD))
        {
        if (this->m_lpfnMessagePendingCallback(&msg))
            dwReturn=PENDINGMSG_WAITNOPROCESS;
        else
            dwReturn=PENDINGMSG_WAITDEFPROCESS;
        }
    }

return dwReturn;
}
```

This implementation displays the "not responding" version of the busy dialog box if a significant message (mouse click or keystroke) has occurred and we've waited more than 5 seconds (which you may want to make as little as 2 seconds) for a call to complete. Note that the *m_fUnblocking* flag protects against reentrant calls. Anyway, only significant messages are considered good enough to warrant the dialog box because something like a mouse move shouldn't really be considered input. Before the dialog box appears, this implementation removes any messages that might be in the queue and that it doesn't want dispatched from the message loop within the Windows *DialogBox* function (called from *OleUIBusy*). In this case, the implementation removes WM_CLOSE to prevent the client from disappearing when it's inside this busy state. Not a bad idea!

What happens *before* the waiting period is over is most interesting. As described earlier in this chapter, you should try to process or cache an end user's pending work (keystrokes and mouse clicks) while waiting for a call to be completed. The preceding code calls an application-supplied hook (a *callback*) to process the next message in the queue. The hook returns, indicating (by a TRUE or a FALSE) whether the message was processed. If it was processed, the return value from *MessagePending* tells COM to discard the message; otherwise, COM performs its default action with it.

For your own implementation, you can take this basic code and replace the callback material with whatever message processing you want.

# Implementing a Custom Interface with MIDL

The most beautiful thing about the MIDL compiler is that you can create standard marshalers for a custom interface without writing any code at all! The overall process is really very simple:

1.  Describe your interface in an IDL file, specifying the IID as an attribute of the interface.

2.  Write a DEF file for the proxy/stub DLL that exports *DllGetClassObject*, *DllCanUnloadNow*, and a function named *GetProxyDllInfo*.

3.  Write a make file that pumps the IDL file through MIDL and compiles the resulting files.

4.  Write a REG file containing the registry information for the compiled DLL.

For examples of using MIDL, I've included four (yes, four) relevant samples in this chapter. First is yet another variation of the EKoala server, this time EKoala4 (CHAP06\EKOALA4). This is another modification of Chapter 5's EKoala1. The only changes are two custom interfaces added to the Koala object. These interfaces are *IAnimal* (*0002114a-0000-0000-c000-000000000046*) and *IKoala* (*0002114b-0000-0000-c000-000000000046*). We'll see the member functions of these interfaces shortly. To work with EKoala4, I've included ObjectUser3 (CHAP06\OBJUSER3), which knows how to call the functions in *IAnimal* and *IKoala*. This is basically a modification of Chapter 5's ObjectUser.

The code in both of these samples is pretty similar to everything we've seen before. EKoala4 serves up the Koala object, and the Koala object provides its interfaces and implements their member functions. (Unlike EKoala3, the EKoala4 server doesn't show a main window because it has no menu items itself.) ObjectUser3 queries for those interfaces, calls their member functions, and displays the results. In fact, none of the code in either sample knows that *IAnimal* and *IKoala* are custom interfaces—it treats them as if they were OLE-defined interfaces, taking their marshaling support for granted.

How we create the marshalers for *IAnimal* and *IKoala* is of interest to us here. In the CHAP06\IANIMAL directory, you'll find only a few files: a make file, a DEF file, a REG file, and IANIMAL.IDL, the interface definition. You'll find similar files in CHAP06\IKOALA. The make files in these directories will produce IANIMAL.DLL and IKOALA.DLL, which are set with the REG files as InprocServer32 for *CLSID_PSIAnimal* and *CLSID_PSIKoala*, respectively (the same values as *IID_IAnimal* and *IID_IKoala*, for reasons we'll see later).

Let's look briefly at each step we have to take to create these necessary sources.

## Get the Right RPC SDK Files

The MIDL compiler, RPC header files, and RPC import libraries that are necessary to build interface marshalers might not be a part of your development environment. They are really part of Microsoft's RPC development kit. They can be found in the Win32 SDK but are not included with compilers such as Visual C++. Specifically, you need the following files from the Win32 SDK in order to work with MIDL:

| | |
|---|---|
| MIDL.EXE | The MIDL compiler |
| RPCPROXY.H | The header file for interface marshalers |
| UNKWN.IDL | Contains the IDL description for *IUnknown* that you include in your own IDL files; pulls in WTYPES.IDL |
| WTYPES.IDL | Contains IDL descriptions of Windows types, structures, and so on |
| RPCRT4.LIB | A mixed static-link and import library that provides the rest of the interface proxy/stub implementation you'll need |

In addition, the Win32 SDK contains full documentation for MIDL and the IDL language. This book doesn't document them beyond what is in the following section.

## Write the IDL File

An IDL file for an OLE interface uses only a small portion of IDL, which is designed for much broader RPC applications. IDL simply happens to serve us well for our own little interfaces. When you set out to describe an interface, you must include at least the IID to assign to the interface, the *interface* keyword and the name of the interface, the statement *import "unknwn.idl"*, and the list of your member functions. Any single IDL file can contain as many interface

definitions as you'd like, but in the case of *IAnimal* and *IKoala* only one interface is in each file:

```
//CHAP06\IANIMAL\IANIMAL.IDL
[uuid(0002114a-0000-0000-c000-000000000046),
    object
]
interface IAnimal : IUnknown
    {
    import "unknwn.idl";

    HRESULT Eat([in] LPTSTR pszFoodRecommended
        , [in, out] LPTSTR pszFoodEaten, [in] short cchEaten);
    HRESULT Sleep([in, out] short *pcMinutes);
    HRESULT Procreate([out] short *pcOffspring);
    HRESULT WhatKindOfAnimal([out] IID *pIID);
    }


//CHAP06\IKOALA\IKOALA.IDL
[uuid(0002114b-0000-0000-c000-000000000046),
    object
]
interface IKoala : IUnknown
    {
    import "unknwn.idl";

    HRESULT ClimbEucalyptusTree([in] short iTree);
    void    PouchOpensDown(void);
    HRESULT SleepAfterEating([in] short cMinutes);
    }
```

You can see that much of IDL is similar to ODL, such as the format for
attributes. Some of the attributes, however, don't appear in ODL. The *object*
attribute, for example, is an IDL attribute to identify the script as MIDL-
specific. Check the MIDL reference for others.

One useful member function attribute is *[async]*, which lets you describe
the call as asynchronous as opposed to the default synchronous. Most important of all, however, are the *[in]*, *[out]*, and *[in, out]* attributes on the
function arguments. These determine the type of marshaling code that
MIDL will write for that member function. If you make a mistake here, the
MIDL-generated code might not properly copy arguments, especially the
contents of strings, across the process boundary.

On the whole, a number of attributes and other statements are available
in ODL. For a full list, check the documentation.

## Write a DEF File

Because you're going to be compiling and linking MIDL-generated code, you'll have to provide a module definitions file for the linker, which MIDL does not generate itself. Specifically, you need to name the resulting module and export the functions *DllGetClassObject*, *DllCanUnloadNow*, and *GetProxy-DllInfo*, as shown here for IANIMAL.DLL:

```
LIBRARY         IANIMAL
DESCRIPTION     'IAnimal Interface Proxy/Stub DLL Chapter 6'

CODE            PRELOAD DISCARDABLE
DATA            PRELOAD SINGLE

EXPORTS
                DllGetClassObject       @2
                DllCanUnloadNow         @3
                GetProxyDllInfo         @4
```

You don't actually have to implement these exported functions because RPCRT4.LIB provides them—you need only to export them. But failure to do so will lead to some quite ugly problems that you'd be happier avoiding altogether.

## Write a Make File for MIDL-Generated Files

Once you have an IDL file and a DEF file, you're ready to compile the DLL. However, you need to know the names of the MIDL-generated source files before you can write a make file to build them all. So you need the appropriate MIDL command in the make file as well. For both IANIMAL.DLL and IKOALA.DLL, I've used the following command line for MIDL:

```
midl /ms_ext /app_config /c_ext <name>.idl
```

where */ms_ext* and */c_ext* enable Microsoft extensions to IDL (necessary with OLE interfaces) and */app_config* allows certain attributes to appear in the IDL file instead of having to be present in another *attribute configuration file,* or ACF. This is something that you might want to try if you have a lot of interfaces to define.

With this simple command line, MIDL generates the following files by default, assuming that *<name>* identifies the name of the IDL file, as in the command line above:

| | |
|---|---|
| <name>_p.c | Source code for the interface proxy and interface stubs |
| <name>_i.c | Interface information, such as the structure containing the IID |

<name>.h            The header file that defines the interface for both C and
                    C++ compilers

dlldata.c           An auxiliary file that contains added information about
                    the DLL

If you run MIDL on IANIMAL.IDL, you'll end up with IANIMAL_P.C, IANIMAL_I.C, IANIMAL.H, and DLLDATA.C (assuming your operating system supports long filenames). With IKOALA.IDL, you'll have IKOALA_P.C, IKOALA_I.C, IKOALA.H, and DLLDATA.C. MIDL does have a number of command-line options to suppress generation of the proxy or stub side of the code, to suppress generation of header and auxiliary files, and to rename each of these output files. Run MIDL /? or check the MIDL documentation for more information about these options.

Now that you know which files MIDL will generate, you can write a make file to compile these files as you would any other standard C code. You'll probably want to place the MIDL command underneath a dependency on the IDL file, as follows:

```
ianimal.h ianimal_p.c ianimal_i.c dlldata.c: ianimal.idl
    midl /ms_ext /app_config /c_ext ianimal.idl
```

Both the IANIMAL and IKOALA samples also include the file LIB-MAIN.CPP with a custom DLL entry point. This is just to work with this book's make file system and isn't included for any other reason.

If you take a look at the MIDL-generated code, you'll see a lot of calls to *Ndr* (Network Data Representation) functions in the _p suffix file that the MIDL-generated proxy and stub use to stuff information into the RPC Channel. In addition, the _i suffix file will contain the interface's ID, defined with a structure instead of a macro such as DEFINE_GUID:

```
typedef struct _IID
{
    unsigned long  x;
    unsigned short s1;
    unsigned short s2;
    unsigned char  c[8];
} IID;

const IID IID_IAnimal =
{{0x0002114a,0x0000,0x0000,{0xc0,0x00,0x00,0x00,0x00,0x00,0x00,0x46}}};
```

As far as the DLL itself is concerned, there is no reason to store this IID anywhere else. However, clients and servers that are going to implement this interface will need a definition of the IID elsewhere, and for this reason you'll find *IID_IAnimal* and *IID_IKoala* listed in INC\BOOKGUID.H. Both EKoala4 and ObjectUser3 include these interfaces. In that same directory, you'll also find copies of MIDL-generated IANIMAL.H and IKOALA.H, which the client and server samples need as well, but they don't care who wrote the header file; nor do they care that these are custom interfaces. From a compiler's point of view, a custom interface header contains the same material as the OLE headers themselves, all interfaces being equal.

## Write a Registration File

Earlier in this chapter, we saw the entries necessary to map an IID to a CLSID that implements the marshalers for that IID, which essentially amounts to the following:

```
\
    Interface
        {0002114a-0000-0000-c000-000000000046} = IAnimal
            NumMethods = 7
            ProxyStubClsid32 = {0002114a-0000-0000-c000-000000000046}

\
    CLSID
        {0002114a-0000-0000-c000-000000000046} = IAnimal Proxy/Stub Factory
            InprocServer32 = c:\inole\chap06\ianimal\ianimal.dll
```

The strange part about these entries (essentially the contents of CHAP06\IANIMAL\WIN32.REG) is that the CLSID is the same as the IID of the interface. When using the MIDL compiler, you pull in all the CLSID-dependent code, such as *DllGetClassObject* from RPCRT4.LIB, which means that you can't really set the CLSID to anything you want. Specifically, the standard *DllGetClassObject* implementation recognizes the IID of any interface contained in the DLL as a suitable CLSID. This allows you to place marshalers for any number of interfaces inside the same DLL.

This little game with the IID and CLSID is an issue only when MIDL is in the picture—it has nothing to do with standard marshaling itself.[9] If you implement marshalers manually, you also implement *DllGetClassObject* and can use any CLSID you want, whether or not it matches an IID.

---

9. The IID and CLSID do not conflict because they are used in totally different circumstances. An IID is used only in calls to *QueryInterface* and such, and a CLSID is used only in calls to *CoGetClassObject* and *CoCreateInstance*. The two simply don't overlap in usage.

# Implementing Custom Marshaling

Our final sample for this chapter illustrates custom marshaling, in which an object can tell COM to bypass all its standard marshaling support and use the object's implementation of the *IMarshal* interface. The EKoala5 server (CHAP06\EKOALA5) contains the same Koala object as EKoala4, with the same *IAnimal* and *IKoala* interfaces, but it also has an implementation of *IMarshal* to specify custom marshaling. *IMarshal::GetUnmarshalClass* returns *CLSID_KoalaProxy* (*0002114c-0000-0000-c000-000000000046*), which is then implemented in KOALAPRX.DLL (CHAP06\KOALAPRX). This DLL also provides an implementation of the same Koala object with the same public interfaces to show the client, except that most functions are implemented by making custom-marshaled calls to the object in EKoala5.

The sample client to use with EKoala5 and its proxy is ObjectUser3, the same one that we used to demonstrate custom interface marshalers in the previous section. In other words, a change in the marshaling technique for any given object class does not affect clients at all. ObjectUser3 was oblivious to the existence of marshalers for a custom interface in the previous section; here it's oblivious to the presence of custom marshaling.

Earlier in this chapter, we discussed the many ways to perform custom marshaling: shared memory, private RPC connections, and so on. KOAL-APRX and EKoala5 in this sample communicate through Windows messages, specifically through WM_COMMAND messages that the proxy sends or posts to a window connected to the object within the server process. This works well on any single machine and also works between 16-bit and 32-bit processes because window handles (HWNDs) are global within a system. While this technique will work in the absence of shared memory, it will not work across a network.

The proxy implemented here doesn't blindly forward every call into *IAnimal* and *IKoala*, however. The proxy can handle a lot of implementation itself because it has intimate knowledge about the local object. For example, the proxy can fully implement *IAnimal::WhatKindOfAnimal* because COM will load that proxy only when the local Koala object specifies it through *IMarshal*. The proxy, therefore, knows the object is a Koala object and that it can hard code the IID returned from *WhatKindOfAnimal*. In addition, the proxy knows that the local object doesn't do anything with *IKoala::ClimbEucalyptusTree* or with *IKoala::PouchOpensDown*. Thus, the proxy doesn't bother to send these on to the local object because performing a useless context switch would simply be a waste of time.

This knowledge shared between the proxy and the local object is precisely what makes custom marshaling so useful—you can make any optimizations you want to cut down on cross-process or cross-machine calls and thus improve overall performance. In this specific example, the proxy passes only *IAnimal::Eat*, *IAnimal::Sleep*, *IAnimal::Procreate*, and *IKoala::SleepAfterEating* calls to the local object along with the final call to *Release* (but no other *AddRef* or *Release* calls because the proxy knows that the object is alive as long as there's a reference count of 1). The proxy makes these calls by sending or posting a WM_COMMAND message to the object's window with one of the following command IDs:

```
#define MSG_RELEASE            1000
#define MSG_EAT                1001
#define MSG_SLEEP              1002
#define MSG_PROCREATE          1003
#define MSG_SLEEPAFTEREATING   1004
```

Let's see how EKoala5 prepares to receive these messages and how the proxy obtains the window handle to which it sends the messages.

## The Custom Marshaling Object: EKoala5

The EKoala4 sample that worked with custom interfaces and standard marshaling actually implemented all of the entry points for each interface member function. In EKoala5, with custom marshaling, these entry points are no longer necessary: calls from the client process come into a window procedure because that's the communication channel between the processes. The Koala object (KOALA.CPP) in this sample implements only one interface: *IMarshal* (which includes *IUnknown*). In addition, it creates a window for itself inside its *CKoala::Init* function (called from EKoala5's *IClassFactory::CreateInstance*). The Koala object eventually passes the handle to this window to the proxy in a marshaling packet:

```
BOOL CKoala::Init(HINSTANCE hInst, HWND hWndParent)
    {
    m_hWnd=CreateWindow(TEXT("KoalaObject"), TEXT("KoalaObject")
        , WS_CHILD, 35, 35, 35, 25, hWndParent, NULL
        , hInst, this);

    if (NULL==m_hWnd)
        return FALSE;

    return TRUE;
    }
```

By the time *IClassFactory::CreateInstance* returns an interface pointer to this Koala object, the object will have created a window for itself. (EKoala5's initialization code, *CApp::Init*, registers the KoalaObject window class.)

Now COM's *IClassFactory* stublet knows that it has to create a new stub for this object unless that object supports custom marshaling. The stublet calls *CoMarshalInterface* to do the honors, which in turn queries for *IMarshal* and, finding it, calls *IMarshal::GetMarshalSizeMax*. To make a connection with its proxy, the Koala object knows that it needs to send the proxy only its window handle, which thus forms the entire contents of the marshaling packet for which the Koala object defines this structure:

```
typedef struct
    {
    HWND        hWnd;        //Message window
    } KOALAMARSHAL, *PKOALAMARSHAL;
```

The implementation of *GetMarshalSizeMax* merely returns the size of this structure:

```
STDMETHODIMP CKoala::GetMarshalSizeMax(REFIID riid, LPVOID pv
    , DWORD dwDestCtx, LPVOID pvDestCtx, DWORD dwFlags
    , LPDWORD pdwSize)
    {
    if (dwDestCtx & MSHCTX_DIFFERENTMACHINE)
        return ResultFromScode(E_FAIL);

    *pdwSize=sizeof(KOALAMARSHAL);
    return NOERROR;
    }
```

Notice how we check the marshaling context in use here for MSHCTX-_DIFFERENTMACHINE. Because we know that we use a window handle for communication, a machine boundary disallows our custom marshaling, so we fail this call. This tells *CoMarshalInterface* to fail, so *CreateInstance* will also fail: marshaling simply isn't available in such a case.

Assuming that we're on the same machine, *GetMarshalSizeMax* then returns the size of the KOALAMARSHAL structure. *CoMarshalInterface* creates the marshaling packet stream and calls our *IMarshal::GetUnmarshalClass*, where we return the proxy CLSID:

```
STDMETHODIMP CKoala::GetUnmarshalClass(REFIID riid
    , LPVOID pv, DWORD dwCtx, LPVOID pvCtx, DWORD dwFlags
    , LPCLSID pClsID)
```

*(continued)*

```
{
/*
 * If context is on different machine, we cannot use
 * our custom marshaling based on SendMessage.
 */
if (dwCtx & MSHCTX_DIFFERENTMACHINE)
    return ResultFromScode(E_FAIL);

//Same proxy for all interfaces
*pClsID=CLSID_KoalaProxy;
return NOERROR;
}
```

Then *CoMarshalInterface* calls our *IMarshal::MarshalInterface* function, in which we create our marshaling packet structure and write it into the stream:

```
STDMETHODIMP CKoala::MarshalInterface(LPSTREAM pstm
    , REFIID riid, LPVOID pv, DWORD dwDestCtx, LPVOID pvDestCtx
    , DWORD dwFlags)
    {
    KOALAMARSHAL          km;

    if (dwDestCtx & MSHCTX_DIFFERENTMACHINE)
        return ResultFromScode(E_FAIL);

    //Proxy needs to know only where to send messages.
    km.hWnd=m_hWnd;

    //This is for the client that will call Release when needed.
    AddRef();

    //Write marshaling packet to stream.
    return pstm->Write((void *)&km, sizeof(KOALAMARSHAL), NULL);
    }
```

Nothing fancy is going on here except the extra *AddRef* call, which is really quite necessary because there is no stub that actually holds a reference to the Koala object itself. Usually a stub will maintain a reference count for an object, but with custom marshaling there is no stub. Therefore, the Koala object holds a reference count on itself, which its proxy actually controls. In other words, the object and the proxy have an unwritten agreement that the proxy will not send a *Release* call until the client has released the proxy for the final time. We'll see shortly where Koala makes the *Release* call that reverses this *AddRef*.

Once we return from *MarshalInterface*, COM has all the information it needs to create the proxy in the client process, and all we do now is wait for WM_COMMAND messages, which are handled in *CKoala::HandleCall*, to show up in the object's window procedure:

```
DWORD CKoala::HandleCall(UINT iMsg, LPARAM lParam)
    {
    DWORD       dw;
    short       iRet=0;

    switch (iMsg)
        {
        case MSG_RELEASE:              //Last IUnknown::Release
            Release();
            break;

        case MSG_EAT:
            m_fJustAte=TRUE;
            break;

        case MSG_SLEEP:                //IAnimal::Sleep
            //Client's in-parameter in LOWORD(lParam)
            iRet=LOWORD(lParam)+m_cSleepAfterEat;
            m_fJustAte=FALSE;          //Probably want to eat again.
            break;

        case MSG_PROCREATE:            //IAnimal::Procreate
            dw=GetTickCount()/100;

            iRet=((dw/10)*10==dw) ? 1 : 0;
            break;

        case MSG_SLEEPAFTEREATING: //IKoala::SleepAfterEating
            m_cSleepAfterEat=LOWORD(lParam);
            break;

        default:
            break;
        }

    return iRet;
    }
```

The *HandleCall* function actually contains the entire implementation of the object's member functions that are not otherwise handled in the proxy. Most of the code you see in each message case is what the Koala object in EKoala4 had in its individual interface member functions. From this, you can thus see how custom marshaling allows you to put this code wherever is most convenient for your implementation.

Notice that the MSG_RELEASE case contains the *Release* call to match the *AddRef* call we made in *IMarshal::MarshalInterface*. This is how the proxy effectively calls *Release*, illustrating why we had to call *AddRef* on ourselves in the first place.

The final point to make about this custom marshaling Koala is that it doesn't do anything in the other *IMarshal* member functions. Specifically, *Disconnect* is never called because EKoala5 never calls *CoDisconnectObject*, and COM never calls *UnmarshalInterface* or *ReleaseMarshalData* because they have meaning only for the client-side proxy. To see the corresponding implementation of these functions, we examine the sources for KOALAPRX.DLL.

## The Custom Marshaling Proxy: KoalaPrx

With custom marshaling, the local object can get away with not implementing any of the interfaces it supposedly provides. However, this is absolutely required for the proxy because it must expose the correct interfaces to the client. The KOALAPRX DLL that manages such a proxy contains much of the same code that we previously had in EKoala4, which means that its Koala object implementation does explicitly implement *IAnimal* and *IKoala* to provide the client with the proper entry points. What differs is how the proxy actually implements these functions.

COM loads the proxy DLL and asks it to create an instance of the CLSID returned from the local object's *IMarshal::GetUnmarshalClass*, just as anything else creates an instance of an in-process object. In calling our DLL's *IClassFactory::CreateInstance*, however, COM asks for an *IMarshal* interface, considered to be the initialization interface for a proxy. That pointer in hand, COM calls *IMarshal::UnmarshalInterface*, which the proxy implements in IMARSHAL.CPP:

```
STDMETHODIMP CImpIMarshal::UnmarshalInterface(LPSTREAM pstm
    , REFIID riid, LPVOID *ppv)
    {
    KOALAMARSHAL    km;

    pstm->Read((void *)&km, sizeof(KOALAMARSHAL), NULL);
    m_pObj->m_hWndLocal=km.hWnd;

    //Get the pointer to return to the client.
    return QueryInterface(riid, ppv);
    }
```

This function has two responsibilities. First, it extracts the necessary connection information from the marshaling packet stored in the stream (the *pstm* argument). This contains only the local object's window handle, to which we can post messages. We extract that handle and save it. The second responsibility is that we have to return, in *ppv*, the pointer that COM eventually returns to the client, the type of which is specified in *rid*. All we need to do is call our own *QueryInterface* to get the correct pointer and call our own *AddRef* as required.

After you return from *UnmarshalInterface*, COM calls *IMarshal::ReleaseMarshalData*, giving you the chance to clean up any resources that the local object might have saved in the stream. No such resources are in this example, so this function just returns NOERROR. In addition, this proxy object also returns E_NOTIMPL from all the other *IMarshal* member functions, which are called only in the server process. We don't need to worry about them in the proxy.

Let's now look at how this proxy implements the interfaces as seen by the client:

```
DWORD CKoala::CallLocal(UINT iMsg, LPARAM lParam, BOOL fAsync)
    {
    DWORD    dwRet=0;

    if (fAsync)
        PostMessage(m_hWndLocal, WM_COMMAND, (WPARAM)iMsg, lParam);
    else
        {
        dwRet=SendMessage(m_hWndLocal, WM_COMMAND, (WPARAM)iMsg
            , lParam);
        }

    return dwRet;
    }



STDMETHODIMP_(ULONG) CKoala::Release(void)
    {
    if (0L!=--m_cRef)
        return m_cRef;

    CallLocal(MSG_RELEASE, 0, TRUE);

    if (NULL!=m_pfnDestroy)
        (*m_pfnDestroy)();

    delete this;
    return 0;
    }
```

*(continued)*

335

```
STDMETHODIMP CImpIAnimal::Eat(LPTSTR pszFoodRecommended
    , LPTSTR pszFoodEaten, short cchEaten)
    {
    _tcsncpy(pszFoodEaten, TEXT("Eucalyptus Leaves"), cchEaten);
    m_pObj->CallLocal(MSG_EAT, 0L, FALSE);
    return NOERROR;
    }

STDMETHODIMP CImpIAnimal::Sleep(short *pcMinutes)
    {
    DWORD        dwRet;

    //Pass the client's value.
    dwRet=m_pObj->CallLocal(MSG_SLEEP, (LPARAM)*pcMinutes, FALSE);

    if (FAILED((HRESULT)dwRet))
        return (HRESULT)dwRet;

    //Store the return value in the client's variable.
    *pcMinutes=LOWORD(dwRet);
    return NOERROR;
    }

STDMETHODIMP CImpIAnimal::Procreate(short *pcOffspring)
    {
    DWORD        dwRet;

    dwRet=m_pObj->CallLocal(MSG_PROCREATE, 0, FALSE);

    if (FAILED((HRESULT)dwRet))
        return (HRESULT)dwRet;

    *pcOffspring=(short)LOWORD(dwRet);
    return ResultFromScode(0==dwRet ? S_FALSE : S_OK);
    }

STDMETHODIMP CImpIAnimal::WhatKindOfAnimal(IID *pIID)
    {
    //No need to ask the local object for something we know.
    *pIID=IID_IKoala;
    return NOERROR;
    }

STDMETHODIMP CImpIKoala::ClimbEucalyptusTree(short iTree)
    {
    //We know that the server doesn't need this.
    return NOERROR;
    }
```

```
STDMETHODIMP CImpIKoala::PouchOpensDown(void)
    {
    //We know that the server doesn't need this.
    return NOERROR;
    }

STDMETHODIMP CImpIKoala::SleepAfterEating(short cMinutes)
    {
    DWORD   dwRet;

    dwRet=m_pObj->CallLocal(MSG_SLEEPAFTEREATING
        , (LPARAM)cMinutes, TRUE);

    if (FAILED((HRESULT)dwRet))
        return (HRESULT)dwRet;

    return NOERROR;
    }
```

You can see in this code how the proxy completely implements some member functions while depending on the local object for others, using the *CallLocal* function to generate the message to the object's window.

*IAnimal::Eat* is an interesting function because the implementation is split between the proxy and the local object. The proxy knows what Koalas eat, so it fills the client's out-parameter, *pszFoodEaten*, with the appropriate text. It doesn't bother trying to marshal text back to and from the server. However, because this proxy knows that the local object modifies one of its state variables, it still generates a call to that object. As we saw earlier, the object does nothing more with the call than set its $m\_fJustAte$ variable to TRUE. (See EKoala5's *HandleCall* code in the previous section.)

All of the other members that generate calls to the local object rely on that object for the full implementation. Two of these, *Release* and *IKoala::SleepAfterEating*, are implemented as asynchronous calls, for which we use *PostMessage* instead of the synchronous *SendMessage*. *SleepAfterEating* is asynchronous simply for demonstration, whereas *Release* is asynchronous by design: we have no need to wait for the server to disappear within our own self-destruction code, so we post the message and forget it. This might not work with other designs, however, particularly ones in which a more complex interaction occurs between the proxy and the local object, especially if any synchronization of resources is going on. In that case, you might want to wait for the server to complete its shutdown before finishing the proxy's own cleanup.

# Summary

The most important concept in COM's Local/Remote Transparency is that somehow a server process has an interface pointer that it wants to make available to other processes. The mechanism called *marshaling* is the means to make this pointer available and to pass arguments from the client's process to the server's process through whatever interprocess communication is established. In all cases, a client calls interface member functions that are located inside a *proxy* object. The proxy then forwards those calls to a local or remote object as necessary.

An object can use custom marshaling by implementing the *IMarshal* interface. Through this interface, the object specifies exactly which proxy should be created in the client process (using a CLSID) and provides a *marshaling packet* for that proxy. The packet contains whatever information is necessary to connect to the remote object—a window handle, a named pipe handle, and so on. The entire sequence of operations involved is neatly encapsulated inside the COM API functions *CoMarshalInterface* and *CoUnmarshalInterface*. If an object doesn't want to control its own marshaling, it can simply not implement *IMarshal*. In this case, COM establishes a connection using standard marshaling, which involves a client-side generic proxy that communicates with a server-side generic stub, which in turn communicates with the local or remote objects.

The generic proxy and stub objects are nothing more than containers, or managers, of marshalers: individual interface proxy and interface stub objects are called *facelets* and *stublets* in this book. To support standard marshaling of a custom interface, the interface provider must also provide an implementation of the marshalers for that interface, a process that is nearly automated using the Microsoft-supplied MIDL compiler.

Within the context of standard marshaling, both client and object can perform what is called *message filtering*, or *concurrency management*. Message filtering gives an object a single entry point through which it can process, reject, or delay all calls coming to it from other processes. Message filtering gives clients the capability to process pending messages while a synchronous call is being completed as well as the capability to time-out and fail the call when it takes too long. This latter facility involves the standard OLE busy dialog box, provided in the OLE UI Library.

Concurrency management, the busy dialog box, standard marshaling of custom interfaces, and custom marshaling, are all topics demonstrated in this chapter's samples.

# PART II

# STORAGE
# AND NAMING
# TECHNOLOGIES

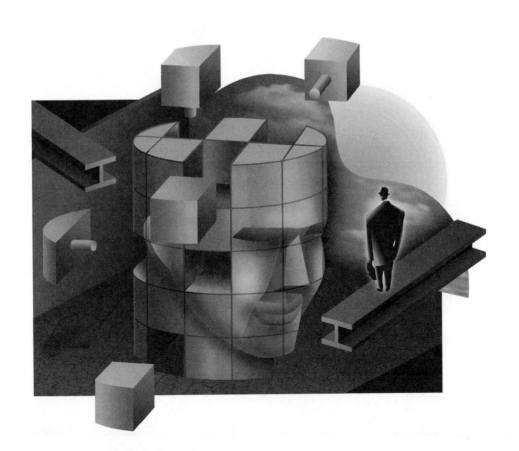

**CHAPTER    SEVEN**

# Structured Storage
# and Compound Files

Through their history, computer storage technologies have evolved to allow more and more separate agents—applications and components, for example—to simultaneously share a common storage device such as a disk drive or a database. Where once an application owned the entire computer and all its resources, operating systems have for some time now allowed multiple applications to share those resources using the concept of files. In the next stage of computing, as end users understand component software, a need will develop for many components to share a single file. The first section of this chapter justifies this need more clearly.

Assuming that the need to share the contents of a file among components truly exists, OLE defines an *architecture* called *Structured Storage,* which enables this kind of sharing. OLE also implements this architecture in a service called *Compound Files.*[1] All of this effectively creates a "file system within a file," in which two types of named elements, *storages* and *streams,* encapsulate the functionality that you find today in directories and files on existing file systems. A storage acts like a directory in that it manages other storages and streams but holds no data itself; a stream acts like a file in that it can hold information but not other storage elements.

The Structured Storage and Compound Files implementations support many features that can simplify the way an application—especially one created from arbitrary components—deals with its underlying storage. For example, storage elements can be direct (changes are permanent when written) or transactioned (changes are not permanent until explicitly committed to storage). Incremental access, including saving and loading, is also the

---

1. Microsoft licenses the ANSI C++ source code for Compound Files as a reference implementation for those who want to use the technology on other platforms, such as UNIX and OS/2. Microsoft provides the implementation for Windows and Macintosh as part of OLE.

default mode of operation: if all you want to read is the information from one stream at a particular point in the storage (directory) tree, you need only to navigate the hierarchy and open that stream—no need to search through the whole file yourself. To provide these features, OLE requires control over the absolute positioning (seek offsets) of information within the bounds of a file, just as a file system takes over the absolute positioning (sectors) of file contents on a storage device.

What? Microsoft is asking me to change my file format? Have those people had too much espresso or something? This is a response I heard often when Microsoft first presented Structured Storage. Surely we can all heartily agree that file systems are a good and powerful innovation, right? Thus, in this chapter, I intend to convince you that doing the same thing to files as we know them—creating a "file system within a file"—is a good and powerful innovation itself. OLE doesn't intend to dictate what information you store in a file or the elements within that file; it merely intends to standardize the means of accessing units of information, whatever the internal format of that information happens to be. In other words, OLE takes control of managing any hierarchy of storage and stream elements, in the same way that a file system manages any hierarchy of directories and files. In exchange, you're given the freedom to build any sort of hierarchy you want and to store any information you want with however many streams you want.

The general and most fundamental implication of such standardization is that information stored in a compound file can be browsed by code other than the application that originally created the file. Most file formats today are proprietary—only the application that wrote the file (or one with intimate knowledge of that application) can examine its contents. On the other hand, because OLE, a central service, maintains the hierarchy of elements in a compound file, any arbitrary agent can browse the storage and stream elements within that file. That is, anyone else can examine the hierarchy; however, they cannot crack the proprietary information contained inside individual streams. (Not yet at least, but further technology is under development to make such information browsable as well.) If a stream, however, has a standard name and contains information in a standard format, anyone can find that stream in a file and extract its information regardless of the presence of the code that originally wrote that information.

As we'll see in Chapter 16, there is a standard for a stream named SummaryInformation that contains a document's title, subject, author, keywords, and so forth. This standard allows an end user to issue a query to a search tool, for example "find all documents that I wrote after 14 September 1994 with the word *vegetarian* in the title or keywords," and the shell goes off and searches for all files, regardless of origin, whose summary information matches the criteria. For the end user, this eliminates a host of application-specific features used to search through files, which usually apply exclusively to that application's files. The standards that Structured Storage brings to the scene allow consolidation of such features in the system shell, a boon for the end user and the developer alike—end users need not learn so many different user interfaces, and developers need not write them in the first place (unless they want to improve on the system shell, a legitimate market).

Just as the invention of file systems paid off big for the computer industry, you can expect that OLE's Compound Files, if put into practice, will pay off big once again. As we'll see in this chapter, simple use of the technology is quite similar to what you understand about files today. In the same manner as a file system makes disparate sectors on a disk appear as a contiguous byte array through the infamous file handle, OLE makes disparate fragments within a file appear as a contiguous byte array through a stream element. Indeed, there is almost a one-to-one correlation between how you work with a file handle and how you work with a stream.

After we examine the benefits and features of Structured Storage and Compound Files, we'll take a look at storage and stream elements more closely. These elements are objects with specific interfaces, namely *IStorage* and *IStream*. We'll spend some time learning how you access these objects and obtain your first interface pointer to them, showing examples in code as we apply the technology to the Patron and Cosmo samples.

This discussion will set the stage for the many uses of Structured Storage in other parts of OLE, such as Persistent Objects (Chapter 8), Monikers (Chapter 9), Uniform Data Transfer (Chapter 10, as well as Clipboard and Drag and Drop in Chapters 12 and 13), Property Sets (Chapter 16), OLE Documents (Chapters 17 through 23), and OLE Controls (Chapters 24 and 25). Obviously, Structured Storage plays a very supportive role in much of OLE, and just as storage has played a key role in the evolution of computers and software in general, this part of OLE is central to the evolution of component software.

# Motivation I: Sharing Files Between Components

The first computers, whether mechanical like an abacus or electronic like ENIAC, really didn't have the idea of "storage" of any kind: they were nothing more than mechanical or electronic calculators. The idea of a computer brought with it the idea of some sort of physical storage device—punch cards, paper tape, and magnetic media such as disks, drums, and reel tapes— on which the computer could write information and recall it at a later time. The idea of an application at this time was the code that ran on the computer: one computer, one application. The singular application was the heart of the computer, and it controlled all aspects of reading and writing information to the storage device, as illustrated in Figure 7-1.

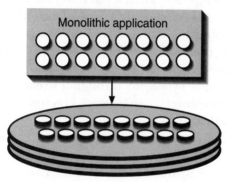

Monolithic application

Storage device (no "file" concept)

**Figure 7-1.**
*When computers ran only one application, the application had complete control over the storage device. On a hard disk, the application controlled the absolute sectors in which it stored information.*

In that era, computer programming gurus were skilled at optimizing throughput by taking into account the rotation speed of a disk or a drum. When the program needed the next set of data from the device, those sectors would be directly under the read head. Such were the days of *real* programming. None of this wimpy user interface glitz. (Just kidding.)

But these skills became obsolete with the advent of the operating system, which took control of system resources in order to allow multiple applications to run together on the same computer. Those applications now had to share system resources—such as the storage device—to ensure that they didn't overwrite one another's data. For these reasons, applications had to ask the operating system—or more accurately the file system—for a file handle. The file handle represented space on the storage device set aside for the exclusive use of the application that opened the file and owned the file handle. When the application wrote information to that file, the file system found free sectors on the disk in which to store the information and kept a table describing which sectors contained the contents of the file and in what order. The idea of a file is unknown to the storage device itself, which understands only sectors. The file system is a piece of code that manages the allocation of those sectors, requiring applications to work through a conceptual file that maps information to certain sectors on the storage device, as shown in Figure 7-2. In this way, the file system prevented conflicts between applications.

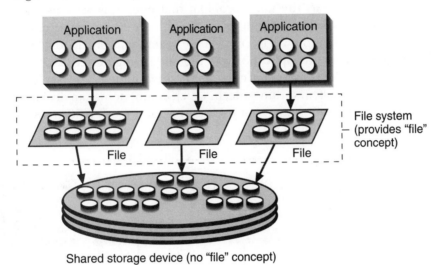

**Figure 7-2.**
*The file system introduced the concept of files to prevent conflicts between applications that shared a common storage device.*

The idea of a file system was a boon to application developers. They no longer needed to understand the intricate details of disk controllers and sectors. Instead, they could ask for a file—which appeared as a flat, contiguous array of bytes—in which they could create any structures they wanted. Applications relinquished control of the device in order to gain this convenient way to share it.

For a long time, operating system APIs and language-based run-time libraries have provided applications with many satisfactory ways of working with singular file entities. Using these technologies, applications have made some incredible innovations in the ways they deal with a single stream of information, providing features such as incremental fast saves and garbage collection within a file.

But OLE as a technology changes the scene drastically. In a component software environment, an application is no longer a monolith that controls every aspect of its storage. Instead, an application might be built from many different components, written by different developers at different points in time. But those components still require a way to store their own persistent information. At the same time, all that information has to end up in a single file, as the end user understands it, because users perceive applications as unified entities rather than as an aggregation of disparate components.

Thus, component integration requires the ability for multiple components to share storage contained within a single file on the underlying file system. This is *exactly* the same problem that operating systems had to solve when they enabled multiple applications to share system resources. The operating system solution was to create a file system that provided a level of indirection between an application and the underlying device. That abstraction was the file. The solution for component integration is another level of indirection: a file system within a file, in which components can deal with entities called *storages* and *streams* that each correspond to specific areas within the file, as shown in Figure 7-3.

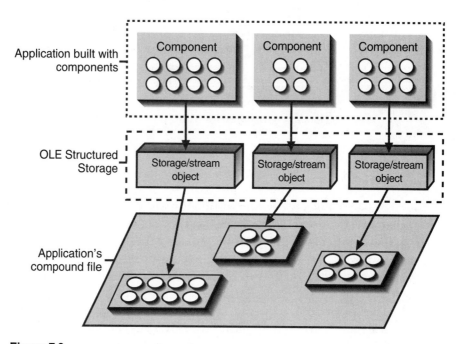

**Figure 7-3.**
*A file system within a file enables multiple components to share the resources of a single file.*

OLE's Structured Storage is the model that defines this second layer of abstraction, which involves not only streams that act like files but also storages that act like directories on a file system. Just as a file system removes from applications the burden of managing disk sectors, Structured Storage removes from components the burden of sharing a file and is a very powerful way to manage files even for an application that is not built of components. Where components are involved, Structured Storage is a necessity; where they are not, this technology is a gift. In either case, OLE has provided the next step in the evolution of storage.

# Motivation II: More Powerful Files

A man and his 16-year-old daughter were traveling through Seattle on their way back from a long hiking trip in Alaska's Denali National Park. During the entire trip, the man had to live with the horrible, plastic taste of cheap instant coffee. Still, he put up with it because he enjoyed the extra caffeine boost that allowed him to keep up with his daughter. While in Seattle, the man remembered the lore about the Emerald City's espresso habits. With espresso carts on every street, he didn't have any trouble finding one quickly. As he ordered a latte, he knew darn well that the tasty caffeine bomb would give him the jitters, but he really wanted one nonetheless. He would have enjoyed it too, had his daughter not asked a simple but probing question, one that would change pleasure to guilt and for which he had no answer. She asked with a menacing stare, "What exactly does that *do* for you?"

If after reading the previous section you feel that your particular development efforts won't involve component-based applications, you may still want to ask the same question: "What does OLE's Compound Files technology *do* for me?" In a manner of speaking, compound files give you the energy boost of caffeine without the jitters. While you are not required to indulge, there are certainly benefits to starting the habit, so to speak. Let's explore this in the context of how we might add file I/O capabilities to the Patron sample, which prior to this point has none.

## Patron Files with the Jitters

Patron is designed to manage a document composed of pages, with each page eventually managing any number of tenants—bitmaps, metafiles, compound document content objects, and controls. If we were to implement Patron using traditional file I/O, we would create a file with the three primary structures listed on the following page and illustrated in Figure 7-4.

■ File (document) header: contains the document's page count, the printer configuration (a DEVMODE structure), and an offset to the first page.

■ Page: contains the tenant count, the offset of the next page, and a variable-length list of offsets to the tenants. All page structures are stored sequentially in the file before any tenant structures.

■ Tenant: contains the type of tenant, the length of tenant-specific data, and the tenant's data itself.

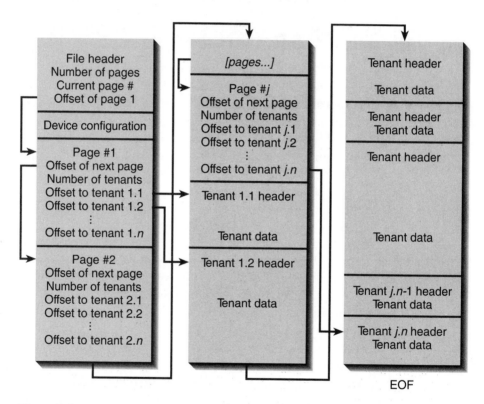

**Figure 7-4.**
*A possible Patron file with traditional file I/O.*

Certainly this sort of layout is manageable, albeit tedious. To write such a file, we would first write the file header, then all the page headers, and then all the tenants. Writing the file header is simple because we know its size and can easily calculate the offset of the first page to store in this header. Before writing the page headers, however, we need to build the entire list in memory to determine the total size of the page list and store the appropriate tenant offsets in each page structure. When we have this list, we write it all out to disk at once and then write each tenant in turn. Besides a little tedium in calculating the offsets, this code would be simple enough and performance would be good—all the pages are at the front of the file, and large seeks occur only when a particular tenant is accessed.

Let's say now that an end user deletes a page and then saves the file again. We have two alternatives. We can rewrite the entire file (typically the easiest option), or we can mark the structure for the deleted page as "unused" and mark its tenant structures as "unused" as well. The second option would not reduce the file size but would allow a fast save. This is a highly demanded feature in today's applications, so we opt for the second choice.

Now the end user adds a page in the middle of the document and adds a few tenants to that page. The end user saves again, giving us the following three choices for where to put this page:

- In "unused" space from a previous deletion

- At the end of the file

- In line with existing page structures, which would require rewriting the entire file

The first two options would allow an incremental fast save again, but they negate the idea that all the page structures would be stored sequentially in the file introducing the complexities of a fragmented file. The third option has the potential to be horrendously slow, especially if some tenants (a true color bitmap, for instance) have large amounts of data.

At this point, we perform the engineering exercise called "compromise" and weigh the possible options: we can have fast saves with file fragmentation, or we can have files efficient to read but slower than molasses to save. In a performance-driven market, we choose fast saves to get good timing reviews in trade magazines. Get a few developers to put in some overtime, and you'll have a wonderfully elaborate garbage collection scheme for managing free space in your files as best you can, just as you would handle free space in any memory manager. You would allow fast saves for performance and give the user the option of a full save, which would rewrite the file completely, effectively defragmenting the whole thing. Cool. We just turned a problem into a couple of features by writing a great deal of file management code. Yes! Gives us the satisfaction of a Double Tall Macho Grande Latte.

On an actual system, all of our garbage collection and defragmentation work buys us very little unless the end user defragments the hard disk. A defragmentation scheme managed by an application works on what the application sees as the contents of the file, faithfully reproduced by the file system. But that same file system probably has the actual file contents spread all over the physical disk itself. All the work we did to make the file look good has little to do with real performance on a fragmented disk: a 128-byte seek in the file might equate to a 128-MB seek on disk, and a 10-MB seek in the file might actually seek only 10 KB on disk.

After we've put in all the work—and compromised a number of other features we really wanted in the application—we find that our cool file management code does little more than keep the file size to a minimum. It bought us little in the way of real performance. In other words, we missed the design goal completely and the jitters set in, making us truly pay for that latte.

## The Decaffeinated Alternative

If we had the luxury of designing Patron for a closed system (one in which no one ever copies files off the system), we would save an enormous amount of trouble by writing all our data structures into various files in a directory tree:

- The "document" would be a base directory, named as any other document would be, and all the information in that directory would be considered part of the document. In this directory are files that contain the "file header" information: the count of pages, the name (subdirectory of the first page), and printer configuration.

- Each page is itself a subdirectory named PAGE*nnnn.nnn* (under the "document" directory), which would allow up to 10 million pages per document. No problem. Each page directory contains files with the page information, such as the names of tenants. (This eliminates the need to manage the offsets to them.)

- Each tenant is itself a subdirectory named TEN*nnnnn.nnn* (100 million per page), which allows the tenant to create any files it wants and to store any information within that directory. This would even make it easy for other applications to manage the tenants because those other applications could easily write information into this directory.

Overall, this promising scheme would look like the layout shown in Figure 7-5. To add a page or a tenant, we create another subdirectory off the appropriate directory and write its specific files. Deleting a page or a tenant is as simple as deleting a directory. In both cases, we let the file system worry about free space, garbage collection, and defragmentation. We inherently let the end users control overall performance by their choice of underlying file system and defragmentation tools. More power to them!

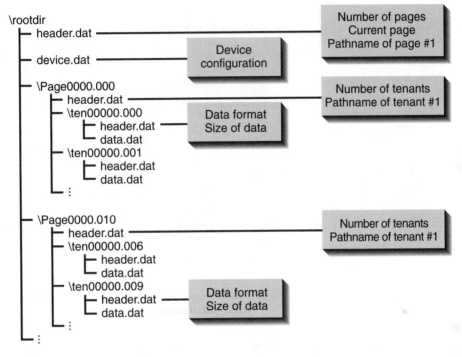

**Figure 7-5.**

*A possible Patron storage scheme using directories.*

And, even better, incremental access, for saving *and* loading information, is always the primary mode of operation. Changing the contents of one tenant means rewriting a part of a single file without bothering anything else in the entire "document." Reading in the contents of a tenant, or retrieving the count of pages in the document, requires us to access only a few relevant files in the right place in the hierarchy, all of which can be done very fast. Overall, this incremental capability means that we probably never have to rewrite the entire file, even to change its name. (We can just rename the base directory.)

But there is a snag: someone kindly points out that this design assumes a closed system, a far cry from anything our customers are using. Reality check! End users will despise having the information for a single "document," as they understand it, be spread around a bunch of directories, meaning that they have to do complicated backup procedures to simply copy a document to a network location or send it to a colleague in a piece of e-mail. We're reminded that an application implemented this way will sell about as well as Double Tall Macho Grande *Decaffeinated* Latte in downtown Seattle. That is, not at all. So now what?

## Energy Boosts Without the Jitters: Compound Files

Up to now, we've had two rather unappealing choices: drink caffeinated coffee and risk the jitters, or drink decaf and miss out on that energy hit that got you drinking coffee in the first place. What we really want is some energy-boosting java with no side effects—we want the efficiency and benefits of using a directory-oriented document structure, but we want it all within the confines of a single file that is critical on an open system. In other words, we want a powerful file system implemented within a file. In fact, we want OLE Structured Storage. More specifically, we decide that compound files are the way to go: we can build the same directory and file hierarchy using storage and stream elements, as shown in Figure 7-6. We gain all the benefits of incremental access, automatic garbage collection, and free space management— as well as a number of other features—without doing much work at all. We preserve the single file notion that the end user has come to expect, yet we don't have to spend time on complex development efforts, giving us the opportunity to improve the product in other ways or to get it to market sooner. Wow! A great buzz with no jitters!

---

## Must You Use Structured Storage and Compound Files?

If you are implementing objects that require a persistent state, you will generally need to use storage and stream elements for storing object data, as described in Chapter 8. The client or container application that deals with persistent objects will then need to provide objects with the appropriate storage or stream elements. As we'll see, these elements need not come from a compound file and can be built on top of an application's private file format. But there are many advantages to using Compound Files directly, especially because future versions of Windows will use this sort of model as the native file system. Applications that store their data in compound files will integrate better with the rest of the system.

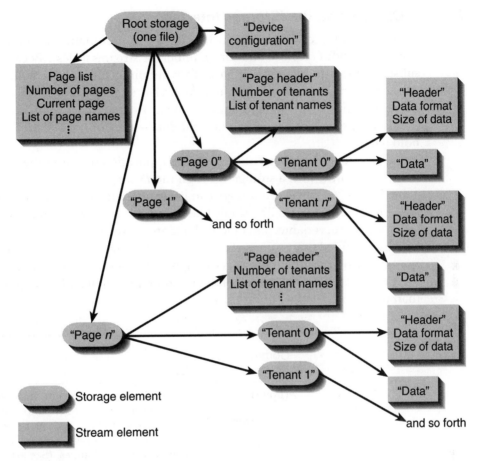

**Figure 7-6.**
*Patron's storage scheme, using structured storage.*

# Structured Storage Objects and Interfaces

In the last two sections, we saw many of the reasons for OLE's Structured Storage as well as the general idea of a file system within a file, a hierarchy composed of storage objects (*IStorage*) and stream objects (*IStream*). Let's now explore these two interfaces to see the full extent of their capabilities.

## Storage Objects and the *IStorage* Interface

Again, a storage object is like a directory: it can contain any number of storages (subdirectories) and any number of streams (files). Because any substorage is a storage in itself, just as any subdirectory is always a directory, substorages might themselves contain more storages and more streams—ad nauseam—until you deplete your available storage space. But in and of themselves, storage objects do not hold data—they only hold streams that hold data.

The client of a storage object, be it an application or some other component itself, works with a storage through the *IStorage* members described in Table 7-1. As you can see, a storage can perform many of the operations that you'll find in command-line shells like COMMAND.COM, such as enumerate, copy, move, rename, and delete elements, as well as change the creation and last modified time stamps of those elements. Combined with the fact that storages also have their own access rights (read-only, read/write, and so forth), a storage is more powerful than a command shell and more powerful than traditional file I/O libraries.

| *IStorage* Member | Command-Line Equivalent | Description |
|---|---|---|
| *Release* (last reference count only) | (none) | Closes the storage element. If the storage is a root object attached to a file, *Release* closes the file and can optionally delete it. If the storage is transacted, *Release* discards changes. (See also *Revert*.) |
| *CreateStream* | Copy | Creates and opens a stream within the storage, returning an *IStream* pointer. |
| *OpenStream* | Copy, Type | Opens an existing stream within the storage, returning an *IStream* pointer. |
| *CreateStorage* | Mkdir, Chdir | Creates and opens a new substorage within the storage, returning an *IStorage* pointer. |
| *OpenStorage* | Chdir | Opens an existing substorage within the storage, returning an *IStorage* pointer. |
| *CopyTo* | Copy | Copies the entire contents from the storage into another storage, removing excess unused space in the process. |

**Table 7-1.**
*The* IStorage *interface.*

*(continued)*

**Table 7-1.** *continued*

| *IStorage* Member | Command-Line Equivalent | Description |
|---|---|---|
| *Commit* | (none) | Ensures that all changes made to a storage are reflected to the parent storage (or to the device itself in the case of a root storage); also flushes buffers. |
| *Revert* | (none) | Discards any changes made to a transacted storage since the last *Commit*. |
| *EnumElements* | Dir | Returns a STATSTG enumerator object (implementing *IEnumSTATSTG*), which enumerates information relating to the substorages and streams within the storage. |
| *MoveElementTo* | Copy (+Del) | Copies or moves a substorage or a stream from the storage into another storage. |
| *DestroyElement* | Del, Deltree | Removes a specified substorage or stream from within the storage. If a substorage is destroyed, all elements contained within it are also destroyed. |
| *RenameElement* | Rename | Changes the name of a stream or a substorage. |
| *SetElementTimes* | (none) | Sets the modification, last access, and creation date and time of a substorage or stream, subject to file-system support. |
| *SetClass* | (none) | Assigns a CLSID to the storage, which can be retrieved by using *Stat*. The CLSID identifies code associated with the contents of the storage. |
| *SetStateBits* | Attrib | Marks the storage with various flags. |
| *Stat* | (varies) | Retrieves a STATSTG structure describing storage statistics and attributes. |

It is important to realize that all storage objects that implement *IStorage* are the same as far as the interface is concerned, regardless of whether they are a substorage deep in a hierarchy or a root storage attached to the underlying file system or storage medium itself. So, for example, the *MoveElementTo* member can move or copy a stream between storages in different points in the same storage hierarchy or between storages in different hierarchies. *CopyTo* can copy all the elements under a root storage to a substorage in some other hierarchy. In other words, all storages are peers without regard to their position within a hierarchy.

As we can see from Table 7-1, *IStorage::CreateStorage* and *IStorage::Open-Storage* return an *IStorage* pointer, and these functions are the only means to obtain such a pointer to a substorage anywhere in a hierarchy. This is another example of the third way to obtain an interface pointer for a new object, which we described in Chapter 2. But how does one obtain the pointer to the root storage object? That depends on the implementation of Structured Storage, and as we'll see a little later in this chapter, OLE's Compound Files provide a few API functions through which you obtain that first *IStorage* pointer. But let's first see how a stream works.

## Stream Objects and the *IStream* Interface

As we've seen already, in Structured Storage a stream is the equivalent of a file in which you can store any bits you want. Like a file, a stream maintains its own seek pointer. But instead of reading and writing through a file handle, you work with an *IStream* interface pointer, as described in Table 7-2. Through this pointer, a client always views the stream as a contiguous byte array; the actual data, however, might be spread around within the storage medium.

The *SetSize* function is included in *IStream* as an optimization allowing a client to preallocate space in the stream. Usually a stream will allocate more space if a *Write* operation extends past the current end of the stream. However, this allocation might fail, so *SetSize* allows the client to preallocate space and handle errors outside the process of writing data. Note, however, that *SetSize*, like the *CopyTo* function, is often slow. (*CopyTo*, for example, has to deal with potentially overlapping streams.) In contrast, the most common operations—performed by *Read*, *Write*, and *Seek*—are usually optimized as much as possible to provide the best performance most of the time.

As shown in Table 7-2, many stream functions equate to existing file functions. The practical upshot of this is that most code written to use files through *_lread* and *_lwrite* are easily rewritten to work with *IStream::Read* and *IStream::Write*. Streams also have the same access rights as files do (read-only, read/write, share-exclusive, and so forth), as well as their own seek pointer. One advantage of a stream over a file, however, is that you can open as many streams as you want without hogging a lot of file handles: only the root storage of a structured storage file requires a file handle—everything else is simply a memory structure. Because of this efficiency, you might find many new ways in which multiple streams can improve an application's storage architecture that were simply too expensive with file handles.

| *IStream* Member | File Equivalent* | Description |
|---|---|---|
| *Release* (last reference count only) | _ *lclose* | Closes the stream, discarding changes if the stream is transacted (equivalent of *Revert*). |
| *Read* | _ *lread* | Reads into memory a given number of bytes from the current seek offset. |
| *Write* | _ *lwrite* | Writes a number of bytes from memory to the stream, starting at the current seek offset. |
| *Seek* | _ *llseek* | Moves the seek offset to a new position from the beginning of the stream, from the end of the stream, or from the current position. |
| *SetSize* | _ *chsize* | Preallocates space for the stream but does not preclude writing outside that stream. (See the discussion that follows.) |
| *CopyTo* | *memcpy* | Copies the number of bytes from the current seek offset in the stream either to the current seek offset in another stream or to the one in a clone of the same stream. |
| *Commit* | (none) | Publishes all changes to the parent storage and flushes all internal buffers. |
| *Revert* | (none) | Discards any changes made to a transacted stream since the last *Commit*. |
| *LockRegion* | _ *locking* | Restricts access to a byte range in the stream instead of the stream as a whole. |
| *UnlockRegion* | _ *locking* | Frees restrictions set with *LockRegion*. |
| *Stat* | _ *stat* | Retrieves a STATSTG structure describing stream statistics and attributes. |
| *Clone* | _ *dup* | Creates a new stream object that works with the same actual bytes but manages an independent seek offset. This allows you to access different parts of the same stream with multiple clones rather than work with a single seek offset. |

\* Both Windows API and C run-time functions are shown here.

**Table 7-2.**
*The* IStream *interface.*

You will notice that *IStream*, unlike *IStorage*, has no functions to deal with any other structure within the stream: *Read* and *Write* simply expose a byte array. To obtain a pointer to a stream within a storage hierarchy, you call either *IStorage::CreateStream* or *IStorage::OpenStream*; the stream always ends a branch in the hierarchy.

## Streams on Memory

As we saw in the discussion of custom marshaling in Chapter 6, OLE provides a stand-alone stream object that works on a piece of global memory. The function *CreateStreamOnHGlobal* will construct such a stream on any memory block you give it, returning an *IStream* pointer that you can use in the same way as an *IStream* pointer in some other storage hierarchy. Memory streams can be extremely useful for tasks such as making a memory snapshot of a stream within a storage hierarchy. In other cases, it is convenient to work with memory through an *IStream* pointer instead of through a *BYTE* * pointer — a stream is a higher-level abstraction than an array of bytes.

*CreateStreamOnHGlobal* takes a Boolean argument indicating whether the stream is to take control of the underlying memory such that the last *IStream::Release* call will free the memory in addition to freeing the stream itself. This means that the client of a memory stream needs only to hold an *IStream* pointer instead of the pointer and the HGLOBAL underneath it. In other words, the following code has no memory leaks because *GlobalFree* is contained inside *IStream::Release*:

```
IStream    *pIStream;
HGLOBAL    hMem;

hMem=GlobalAlloc(...);
CreateIStreamOnHGlobal(hMem, &pIStream, TRUE);
[Use stream as long as necessary.]
pIStream->Release();    //Memory freed.
```

The function *GetHGlobalFromStream* exists in case you need to retrieve the memory handle from the stream at some later time. Even if the client retains control of the memory, it still doesn't have to hold the handle itself: the stream holds the handle regardless of ownership.

## Streams on Existing Files

Because streams and files are so close in nature, it seems natural that you should be able to create a stream object that accesses a file through *IStream* instead of through a file handle. OLE doesn't currently provide a simple API function for this exact purpose, although for small files you can easily load the file into memory and create a stream on that memory.

Structured Storage does, however, define a special access mode that allows a client to open an existing file as if it were a root storage, and the contents of the existing file are exposed through a stream named CONTENTS (big surprise). So while you can't simply open a stream on top of a file, you can open a root storage and then open a stream.

## The *Stat* Member Function and STATSTG

As we've seen in the last two sections, both *IStorage* and *IStream* have a member function named *Stat*, along with *IStorage::EnumElements*, which returns an *IEnumSTATSTG* pointer. All of these functions deal with the STATSTG structure, which contains information such as the name of the element, creation and modification times, the type of object (storage or stream), the access mode under which the object is opened, and whether the object supports region locking:

```
typedef struct FARSTRUCT tagSTATSTG
    {
    char FAR        *pwcsName;            //Name of element
    DWORD           type;                 //Type of element
    ULARGE_INTEGER  cbSize;               //Size of element
    FILETIME        mtime;                //Last mod date/time
    FILETIME        ctime;                //Creation date/time
    FILETIME        atime;                //Last access date/time
    DWORD           grfMode;              //Mode element opened in
    DWORD           grfLocksSupported;    //Support region locking?
    CLSID           clsid;                //CLSID of element
    DWORD           grfStateBits;         //Current state
    DWORD           reserved;
    } STATSTG;

//For type field
typedef enum tagSTGTY
    {
    STGTY_STORAGE   = 1,    //Storage object
    STGTY_STREAM    = 2,    //Stream object
    STGTY_LOCKBYTES = 3,    //Byte array object (Compound Files)
    } STGTY;

//For grfLocksSupported
typedef enum tagLOCKTYPE
    {
    LOCK_WRITE     = 1,
    LOCK_EXCLUSIVE = 2,
    LOCK_ONLYONCE  = 4
    } LOCKTYPE;
```

The *mtime, ctime, atime,* and *clsid* fields are meaningful only for storage elements, whereas *grfLocksSupported* is meaningful only for streams. Furthermore, *grfMode* is not meaningful in the context of *IEnumSTATSTG*, only in *Stat* calls.

The *mtime* field (modification time) will contain a different time stamp depending on whether the mode of the storage is direct or transacted. (See the next section.) The value of *mtime* for a transacted storage will be the time of the last commit. For a direct storage, *mtime* will contain the time of the last call to *IStorage::Commit* or the last call to *IStorage::Release* because *Commit* has no impact on a direct-mode storage other than flushing buffers.

You might have noticed the STGTY_LOCKBYTES flag that crept in here: this specifically identifies a LockBytes object that is peculiar to Compound Files, OLE's storage implementation. It is not strictly part of the general Structured Storage specification.

One more important point to remember about a STATSTG structure is that *pwcsName* points to a buffer allocated with the task allocator from *CoGetMalloc*. The client that calls *Stat* or *IStorage::EnumElements* becomes responsible for this memory, so you must free it with *CoTaskMemFree*.

In looking through the *IStorage* and *IStream* members, we've seen a number of references to access modes such as transacted and direct. It's time now to look at all of these modes along with the other features of this technology.

# Structured Storage Features

The design of Structured Storage provides for a number of significant features not expressly described in the *IStorage* and *IStream* interfaces:

- ▣ Access modes. Elements can be opened in a variety of ways, including the usual read/write permissions and sharing exclusions. In addition, elements can be opened as transacted or direct and can be manipulated in a few other ways as well.

- ▣ Shareable elements. Storages and streams are shareable across process boundaries.

■ Element naming. Storages and streams can have names up to 31 characters long.

■ Incremental access. Modifications to any element do not require a complete rewrite of a file, and elements can be read as little as necessary.

Again, this technology is not a rigid requirement for doing any other work with OLE, but these features, which are described in more detail in the following sections, can greatly simplify how an application or a component manages its storage. Incremental access, for example, comes almost for free, and a "revert to saved" feature is easily provided with transactioning.

## Access Modes

Storage and stream objects support access modes like those found with traditional handle-based files. These modes, used with any function that creates or opens a storage or a stream, are defined with flags beginning with STGM_*, as shown in Table 7-3. Many of these access modes match exactly the OF_* flags used with the Windows API function *OpenFile* and, in fact, share the same integer values. As with *OpenFile*, you can combine any of these flags with a bitwise OR operation, producing the same effects that *OpenFile* has on a traditional file. Beyond that, moreover, OLE offers additional flags with special functions that are not available elsewhere, as described in Table 7-4 on the following page.

| Structured Storage Flag | Definition Using *OpenFile* Flags |
| --- | --- |
| STGM_READ (default) | OF_READ |
| STGM_WRITE | OF_WRITE |
| STGM_READWRITE | OF_READWRITE |
| STGM_SHARE_DENYNONE | OF_SHARE_DENY_NONE |
| STGM_SHARE_DENYREAD | OF_SHARE_DENY_READ |
| STGM_SHARE_DENYWRITE | OF_SHARE_DENY_WRITE |
| STGM_SHARE_EXCLUSIVE | OF_SHARE_EXCLUSIVE |
| STGM_CREATE | OF_CREATE |

**Table 7-3.**
*Basic available access modes and their Windows API* OpenFile *equivalents.*

| Structured Storage Flag | Description |
|---|---|
| STGM_DIRECT (default) | Opens the element for direct access. |
| STGM_TRANSACTED | Opens the element so that changes are buffered and not saved until the element is committed. |
| STGM_FAILIFTHERE (default) | Fails to create an element of a given name if one having that name already exists. |
| STGM_CONVERT (storages only) | Allows an application to convert any traditional file to a storage that contains a single stream named "CONTENTS"; this stream contains exactly the same data as the original file. If the file is opened with STGM_DIRECT, the old file is immediately and permanently converted on disk, and therefore STGM_CONVERT always requires STGM_WRITE. To prevent permanent conversion, use STGM_TRANSACTED. |
| STGM_DELETEONRELEASE | Deletes the file underneath a root storage when the object is destroyed through *Release*. This flag is highly useful for temporary files. |
| STGM_PRIORITY | Allows an application to open a direct, read-only storage or stream for a short time to quickly read some data. This flag tells the storage implementation to internally avoid extra buffering and processing, making the operation much faster. For more information, see the *OLE Programmer's Reference*. |

**Table 7-4.**
*Additional Structured Storage flags.*

When using these flags, remember that a stream is always restricted by the access mode of its parent storage. If the storage is read-only, streams within that storage are also read-only. Transactioning, however, is not a limitation— you can have direct streams inside a transacted storage. From the stream's point of view, changes are permanent, but from the view of the whole storage, that stream is transactioned in the scope of its parent storage.

Be aware that Structured Storage offers a finer granularity of file sharing than traditional files can provide. Multiple applications (run by multiple end users) can easily open different elements within the same storage hierarchy using exclusive access. They can even open the same element as long as STGM_SHARE_EXCLUSIVE is not specified.[2] In such a case, transactioning allows each application to know whether another application has already changed the contents of that element since it was opened.

## Transactioning

The most interesting and powerful access mode is STGM_TRANSACTED, which means that any changes made to that storage are not published to its own parent until the client calls *Commit*. (An element opened with STGM-_DIRECT publishes changes immediately.) If that parent is a storage element itself, these changes are scoped by that parent's own access mode. If that parent is a disk file, changes are then written to disk. Changes include the creation, deletion, or modification of any of the elements in the storage, regardless of whether they are substorages, streams, or streams within the substorage of a substorage of a substorage.

In other words, transactioning is a relationship between the transactioned element and its parent element or file. When multiple levels of transactioning exist, changes at the lowest level are not permanent until they percolate upward to the root and the root is committed. In other words, a *Commit* only publishes changes to the next layer up. This is very important in File Save (and File Save As) operations because a client must be sure to commit every transacted element from the bottom up. If it doesn't, changes will be lost when the root storage is committed.

To illustrate this concept, let's say we have three element objects—A, B, and C—all opened with STGM_TRANSACTED:

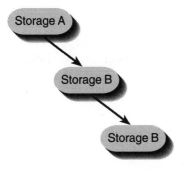

If we modify information in C and call its *Commit*, only B becomes aware of those changes. B is now considered dirty in the eyes of A, so we must commit B in order to save its changes within the scope of A:

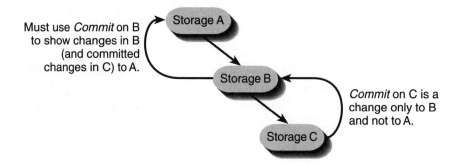

Must use *Commit* on B
to show changes in B
(and committed
changes in C) to A.

*Commit* on C is a
change only to B
and not to A.

On the other hand, if B is opened in direct mode, it immediately publishes the changes in C up to A. If A is a direct mode root storage, those changes go directly to the underlying storage medium.

The whole trick with multilevel transactioning is to walk through the hierarchy and commit everything that has been changed, starting from the bottom and working your way up. The Patron sample we'll see later distributes a Save command from the document to each page, and each page distributes the command to each tenant. When each tenant has committed its storage, each page can commit its storage, and the document can perform the final commit.

An interesting feature of transactioning is that you can open an element as read-only transacted and manipulate it as if it were read/write. The only operation that will not succeed is *Commit*.

### Commit Flags

The *Commit* member functions in *IStorage* and *IStream* support a number of different semantics depending on a combination of the following flags passed as the only argument to *Commit*:

| Flag | Description |
|------|-------------|
| STGC_DEFAULT | No special semantics; simply commit changes. |
| STGC_ONLYIFCURRENT | When an element is shared between two threads (or processes), this flag prevents one thread from overwriting changes made by another thread or process that has already committed changes. *Commit* will return STG_E_NOTCURRENT when another commit has already happened. In this case, the calling thread has to reconcile its changes with the new contents of the element before calling *Commit* without the STGC_ONLYIF-CURRENT flag. This flag allows a finer granularity of sharing to occur between end users on a network than was previously available through traditional files — multiple applications can open the same element as read/write as long as they don't specify exclusive access. |
| STGC_OVERWRITE | Allows new data to overwrite old data, resulting in smaller space requirements. This should be used only in a low-memory situation or when the storage medium is already full. It is risky because the status of the element is in limbo during the commit, so a failure to complete the operation (such as a power failure) would result in data corruption — the element would contain a mixture of old and new information. |
| STGC_DANGEROUSLY-COMMITMERELY-TODISKCACHE | OLE designers never said they couldn't be verbose. This flag specifies that the commit should not attempt to flush buffers after changes are written (which would ensure that the data ends up on the storage medium before *Commit* returns). Using this flag will make *Commit* faster but riskier because for a short time the data will exist only in whatever cache is being used on the underlying medium. Using this flag is not any riskier than using traditional file I/O today because such file I/O is always at the whim of the file-system caching. |

### Discarding Changes: *Revert*

Closely related to the *Commit* function and equally important in the scheme of transactioning is *Revert*. This function discards any changes that have been made to a transacted element since the last *Commit* (or open); it is a mere no-op when direct mode is in operation. It is very important to remember that calling a transacted element's *Release* without calling *Commit* first implicitly calls *Revert*.

A *Revert* call on a storage object will effectively revert down the hierarchy all changes to everything within it, so a *Revert* call to a root storage would effectively reset everything to the last committed state. When that root storage is connected to a file, this makes for an easy implementation of a Revert To Last Save command and makes it simple to close a file without saving changes—just call *Release*.

When you revert a storage, all open substorages and streams underneath that storage in the hierarchy must be closed (you must call *Release*) and reopened; otherwise, subsequent calls to those objects will fail outright with an STG_E_REVERTED code.

### Transacted Streams as Memory Structures

Transacted mode enables a new technique in application design. Because changes made to transacted storages and streams will be recorded in memory or in temporary files, making changes to a transacted element might be only slightly slower than writing directly to memory. Applications usually need to read structures out of a disk file into memory, modify them in memory, and then write them back to the disk file during a save. Transactioning allows these structures to remain in the file as a stream with little effect on overall performance. In using streams for such structures, you also gain a number of benefits:

- Writing past the end of the stream automatically expands the stream instead of causing a crash.

- Saving the data requires only a call to *Commit* instead of copying the data from memory into the stream before the commit.

- An Undo operation is a simple call to *Revert*. An undo stack could be implemented by making temporary copies of the stream being modified in a temporary storage with all the individual changes recorded in separate streams. Before changing the current stream, simply call *IStream::CopyTo* to copy the data into a stream on the undo stack.

When a memory structure contains pointers, keeping the pointers in a stream makes committing the stream senseless. However, even for small structures that you will store persistently in a file, this technique can save you from keeping the same data in a memory structure. When you need it, load it from a stream. When you change it, write it to the stream. When you save, commit everything. Because you want the data in permanent storage anyway, why not leave it there?

Configuration structures, such as LOGFONT, and any structure that is likely to grow over time are great candidates for this technique. An application seldom reads and writes configuration data, but such data is always written to storage. Keeping things in the streams they occupy in the permanent file can greatly simplify or eliminate the tedious memory management code that we all hate to write ourselves.

## Element Naming

Each storage and stream is identified by a name, which can be up to 31 characters long. The sole exception is a root storage associated with a disk file, which can have a name as long as the file system allows and must obey any file-system restrictions on the name. Otherwise, all other element names can contain any characters above value 32 except ., \, /, :, and !.

Prefix characters below 32 have a special meaning at the beginning of the name of any element. All of these values mark an element as being owned and managed by some agent other than the owner of the particular storage element in question:

- ■ \000, \001, and \002 specify an OLE-managed element. OLE has special uses for each of these values, as we'll see in later chapters.

- ■ \003 marks an element as owned by the code that manages the parent storage of that element. This is useful when a client is handing out *IStorage* pointers to other components so that those components can store their data inside the client's storage hierarchy. A client can save extra information for each instance of a component within such a storage by using the \003 prefix.

- ■ \004 is for the exclusive use of the Structured Storage implementation (and not by any other part of OLE). Such elements are useful if the implementation, for example, supports interfaces (besides *IStorage*) that require persistent data.

- ■ \005 through \01F are reserved for OLE and the operating system.

Whatever code owns the storage in which elements appear with these prefixed names must generally leave that information alone. One exception to this is the permanent conversion of OLE 1 embedded compound document objects to be compatible with the current OLE, as described in the OLE1.WRI file on the sample CD.

The actual names of elements in a storage hierarchy are generally not intended to be shown directly to an end user and therefore don't need to be localized. When such an arrangement becomes necessary in a future release of Windows, there will be a standard place to store a localized name.

## Incremental Access

As we described earlier in this chapter, an incremental or a fast save is a greatly demanded feature, which applies just as well to incremental loads. I mentioned before that access to elements within Structured Storage is inherently incremental in the same way that access to individual directories and files in a typical file system is incremental. In a file system, saving information in a file requires only a change to that file, leaving everything else in the file system untouched. In the same manner, changing the name of a directory or shuffling files around within it affects only that directory and its contents. Because Structured Storage is a file system within a file, the same ideas apply. Changes to an individual stream don't affect any other element in the entire storage hierarchy. Changing the name of a storage element or fudging with its contents leaves the rest of the hierarchy untouched.

The real impact of incremental access is the time it takes to perform a read or write operation to the final disk file. Without incremental access, loading a file means loading all of it into memory; saving a file means writing all of it back to disk. These operations can take an enormous amount of time. With incremental access, however, the time it takes to do all of this is not only spread over a longer period but also minimized a great deal—it takes zero time to read and write information that you aren't going to use and don't need to modify in any way. The idea of "incremental" really means "as needed."

If the changes you're making to a document, for example, mean changing a few characters in a block of text on a particular page, you need only to change the contents of the stream that holds that block of text. All other data on that page—and all other pages in the document—remain unaffected. As a result, saving these changes is very quick: rewrite one stream and you've finished. This chapter's Patron sample uses this idea—only the page being viewed is opened.

The real trick to doing all this in a storage hierarchy is navigating the hierarchy to get to the stream that contains the information you want. This means a sequence of *IStorage::OpenStorage* (or *CreateStorage*) calls to navigate to the stream and an *IStorage::OpenStream* (or *CreateStream*) call to open the stream that you need to read or write. Of course, this does take time, and Structured Storage doesn't provide any sort of shortcut. Once you get there, however, you can read and write that stream in isolation without disturbing any other parts of the hierarchy, even if you write new information past the end of that stream. Structured Storage simply finds new space for the new information, requiring no modification to the rest of the file. If you delete information or even whole elements, the storage implementation simply marks that space as free and uses that space to write new information later. In other words, it performs garbage collection as necessary.

Of course, things can become fragmented in this manner, and to combat this you can create a storage and copy the existing file contents into it with *IStorage::CopyTo*. OLE will eliminate all unused space in the process. This is faster than rewriting the entire file, but it doesn't necessarily defragment stream contents within the file. If you repeat the *CopyTo* operation or manually rewrite the entire file, you'll defragment the contents as well. We'll see an example of how this works in "Compound File Defragmentation" at the end of this chapter.

## Shareable Elements

The final important characteristic of Structured Storage, a characteristic that benefits other OLE technologies, is that storage and stream objects are shareable across process boundaries. This means that multiple processes can write to the same elements on a storage medium at the same time. This enables components to share information without having to load the information into memory or make copies across process boundaries. This improves performance dramatically for technologies such as the Clipboard, Drag and Drop, and OLE Documents.[3] This kind of sharing means that the benefits of incremental access are realized across components.

OLE achieves storage and stream sharing through custom marshaling of storage and stream objects, as we saw in Chapter 6. A storage is the perfect example of a component whose entire state is kept on a shareable medium such as a hard disk. Therefore, a proxy and the actual object can work simultaneously with the elements in the storage without any need for interprocess calls or context switches. Custom marshaling is obviously the best possible way to implement this sort of sharing.

---

3. Structured Storage was originally invented to solve performance problems with OLE 1 compound documents. It grew into a technology in its own right, with implications much deeper than simply compound documents.

# OLE's Implementation: Compound Files

What we've seen to this point, with the exception of custom marshaling for storage and stream objects, is the specification for Structured Storage. In other words, we've seen the architectural model of storage and stream objects, their interfaces, and how transactioning works. But a model is of little more than academic interest until it's actually implemented as something usable. The implementation of storage and stream objects is what OLE calls Compound Files, which involves a few additions to the architecture as well as a few features, such as transactioned streams and region locking, that are left unsupported.

The sections that follow describe the additions, mainly a LockBytes object that implements an interface named (what else) *ILockBytes*, the API functions through which a client creates a compound file and obtains the *IStorage* pointer to the root object within that file, and an interface named *IRootStorage*. Following discussion of the additions is a hit list of differences between the model and the implementation of Compound Files, and a few other notes of interest about this OLE-provided service.

## The LockBytes Object and *ILockBytes*

The Structured Storage model doesn't make any stipulation about the storage device that is hidden behind the root storage object. OLE's compound files use an object named LockBytes to abstract any storage device into a generic byte array. This object implements *ILockBytes*, which supports operations such as "read so many bytes from this part of the array" and "write these bytes at this address." A LockBytes object doesn't know what information is being placed in the array; it simply makes any potentially noncontiguous storage medium appear as a long flat byte array, exactly the same way a file system presents a file and just the way a stream looks to its client. In short, a LockBytes object acts like a sort of device driver, isolating the rest of the compound files implementation from any specific knowledge about the device, as illustrated in Figure 7-7.

With compound files, OLE provides a default LockBytes implementation that works with a handle-based file from the local file system. The API functions that we'll discuss install this LockBytes object as part of their functionality, but you can implement your own object with *ILockBytes* and create a compound file on top of it. Or you can use a standard OLE-provided implementation that works on global memory. In both of these cases, an alternative LockBytes is a customization of OLE's service that gives you control over where the bits finally end up.

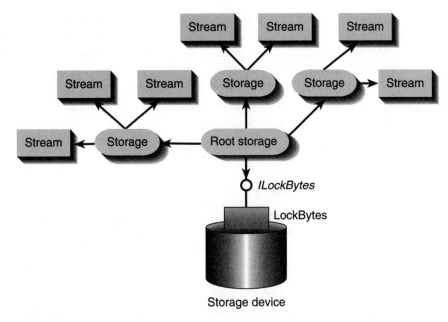

**Figure 7-7.**
*A LockBytes object sits on a device, a root storage builds on the LockBytes*
*object, and streams and storages live below that root storage.*

The global-memory LockBytes implementation is provided through the API function *CreateILockBytesOnHGlobal,* to which you can pass a section of global memory or let the function allocate the memory itself. You can tell the LockBytes object to free the memory automatically when the object itself is destroyed. The function *GetHGlobalFromILockBytes* then returns the global-memory handle underneath the object. This allows you to manage the LockBytes object as you would a memory stream obtained through *Create-StreamOnHGlobal*—you need only to maintain a pointer, retrieving the memory from the object if you need it. In the future, you can expect to see functions to create a LockBytes object on top of a traditional file, just like the APIs that would allow you to open a stream on top of a file.

Although an implementation of *ILockBytes* lets you control where the bits are stored, it does not give you the ability to determine what is contained in those bits. As we can see in Table 7-5 on the following page, the *ILockBytes* member functions *ReadAt* and *WriteAt* must blindly read or write blocks of data without any interpretation of what those blocks contain. These read and write mechanisms are similar to those in a stream, but a LockBytes object maintains no seek offset—it is always told where to read and where to write in every call. So although a LockBytes object controls the physical location of bits, which need not be contiguous (they might span multiple physical files, multiple global-memory allocations, multiple database fields, and so forth), OLE retains control of the compound file data structures. The LockBytes object isolates OLE from the physical aspects of the storage device, presenting that device as a contiguous byte array.

| ILockBytes Member | Description |
| --- | --- |
| ReadAt | Reads a number of bytes from a given location in the byte array. If there are not enough bytes on the device to satisfy the request, ReadAt returns as many bytes as can be read. |
| WriteAt | Writes a number of bytes to a given location in the byte array, expanding the allocations on the device to accommodate the request. |
| Flush | Ensures that any internal buffers are written to the device. |
| SetSize | Preallocates a specific amount of space on the device. |
| LockRegion | Locks a range of bytes on the device for write access or exclusive access. |
| UnlockRegion | Reverses a LockRegion call. |
| Stat | Fills a STATSTG structure with information about the object, which in turn reflects information about the device. |

**Table 7-5.**
*The* ILockBytes *interface.*

## Compound File API Functions

Now for the moment we've all been waiting for. You've likely been reading this chapter wondering just how a client obtains an *IStorage* pointer to the root object of a hierarchy. The answer is simple: OLE provides four API functions that create a compound file on whatever LockBytes object you want. Two of the functions create a new file, and two open an existing file:

| API Function | Description |
|---|---|
| *StgCreateDocfile** | Opens a new compound file, given a filename and access mode flags, using the default file-based LockBytes. A compound file can be opened as transacted or direct. This function will generate a temporary file if a NULL filename is specified. If the file already exists, this function can either fail or overwrite the existing file, depending on the flags you pass. |
| *StgCreateDocfileOnILockBytes* | Opens a new compound file on a given LockBytes object; otherwise, acts the same as *StgCreateDocfile*. |
| *StgOpenStorage* | Opens an existing compound file given a filename or creates a new file in the same way as *StgCreateDocfile*. |
| *StgOpenStorageOnILockBytes* | Opens an existing compound file whose bits exist in a given LockBytes object; otherwise, acts the same as *StgOpenStorage*. The STGM_CREATE flag is not allowed with this function. You must use *StgCreateDocfileOnILockBytes* to create a new storage, after which this function can open that storage. |

\* The name *Docfile* is an archaic term for a compound file and has been preserved in these function names for compatibility with the initial beta releases of OLE 2.

The *OnLockBytes* functions give you the ability to create a compound file anywhere you want instead of on the file system. For example, you might want to send the data across a network to a database without ever having to bother the storage object about the details. No matter what your LockBytes does, the *IStorage* pointer you get back from any of these four functions is equivalent to any other: the available functionality is identical.

Both *StgOpenStorage* and *StgOpenStorageOnILockBytes* take some extra arguments to deal with transaction optimizations, allowing a client to exclude specific elements in the storage hierarchy from being transacted even though the compound file itself is transacted. By excluding such elements, you reduce the overall amount of memory necessary to record changes to your data. For more information, refer to the *OLE Programmer's Reference*. This chapter does not go into more detail about this topic.

Besides the four create/open functions, OLE provides three other useful functions:

| API Function | Description |
| --- | --- |
| *StgIsStorageFile* | Tests whether a given file is a compound file |
| *StgIsStorageLockBytes* | Tests whether the data in a given LockBytes object contains a compound file |
| *StgSetTimes* | Provides the *SetElementTimes* equivalent for a root storage without having to open the storage |

An important note is that a compound file stores the filename as provided by the calling client without converting it to uppercase or lowercase. However, all filename comparisons made under Windows are case insensitive. In addition, OLE will typically use three file handles in opening a transacted compound file—one for the file, one for a temporary file in which changes are recorded, and one preallocated handle for low-memory save situations. Let's see why this third handle is important.

## Low-Memory Save As and *IRootStorage*

A typical Save operation with a compound file is usually a matter of committing changes and writing memory information into the necessary streams. OLE's implementation of compound files is quite robust under low-memory conditions in that *Commit* uses no extra memory. Microsoft went to great lengths to make *Commit* this robust because the only thing an end user really cares about when memory is full is saving data.

Although there's no trouble with a Save operation, a low-memory Save As presents a different problem. When using a transacted compound file, the user's data is split between the original storage contents and a bunch of uncommitted changes being held in a temporary file. To save this information in another storage, the application must call *IStorage::CopyTo*, which copies the current state of the original storage to the new one, including uncommitted changes. However, *CopyTo* could not be written to use no extra memory, so there is the possibility that *CopyTo* will fail, leaving you with a bunch of uncommitted changes to the file you originally opened.

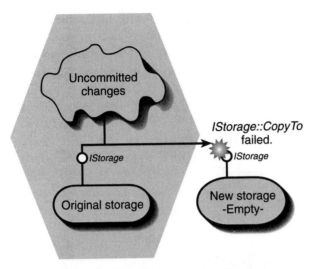

Current state of data is split between unchanged parts
in the original storage and changed parts in memory.

In such a situation, you want to be able to take all uncommitted changes that live in memory and all unchanged parts of the storage that still live on disk and write them all to a new storage without taking up any more memory. In other words, you want to make a copy of the original disk file to the new file and then commit the changes into that new file.

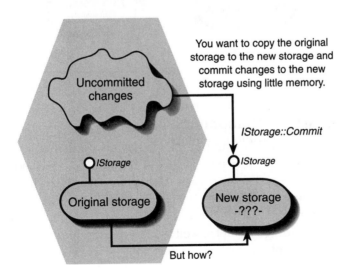

You can do this by using the *IRootStorage* interface, which OLE provides alongside *IStorage* on a root storage object (the one connected to the file underneath). You can obtain a pointer to this interface by calling *IStorage::QueryInterface*, with *IID_IRootStorage* on a storage object from *StgOpenStorage* or *StgCreateDocfile*. *IRootStorage* has one member function, *SwitchToFile(pszNewFile)*, in which *pszNewFile* is the name of the new file to associate with the storage object. This function effectively makes a disk copy of the original file and associates your *IStorage* object internally with that new file. This uses no extra memory and requires no new file handles—hence the reason for the third handle allocated for a transacted compound file. So after *SwitchToFile* returns, you can call *IStorage::Commit* to save changes to that new file, again using no extra memory, and perform a successful Save As even under zero memory conditions.

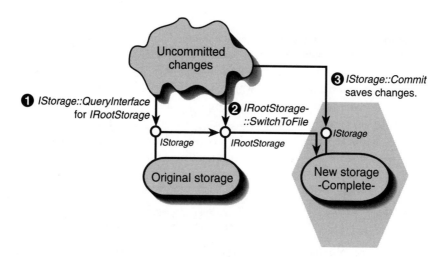

## Limitations and Features of Compound Files

As mentioned earlier, OLE's Compound Files is an implementation that doesn't support absolutely every part of the Structured Storage model—it's one of those things you call *engineering*—certain features were left out because of time constraints and the fact that few developers would be interested in those features anyway. Here then are the aspects of Compound Files that differ from the ideal storage model as well as a few notes regarding the implementation of this technology:

■ Storage objects completely implement all the functions in *IStorage* except *SetStateBits*, which doesn't do anything because no legal state bits are defined at this time. Do not be tempted to use this function with custom flags.

■ Infrequently used operations such as *IStorage::EnumElements* (as well as *MoveElementTo*, *RenameElement*, and *DestroyElement*) are not optimized for performance—they can be very slow. Microsoft recommends that you *not* use *EnumElements* to manage a list of substorages and streams but rather that you store an extra stream that contains a cache of that list. You'll realize much faster performance in that way, with only a little extra coding.

■ Stream objects in compound files do not support region locking, nor do they support being opened in transacted mode themselves. Thus, the *IStream* members *LockRegion*, *UnlockRegion*, and *Revert* are no-ops, while *Commit* does nothing more than flush internal buffers. When you make a change to a stream, you will not be able to revert to the previous contents unless you've made a separate copy.

■ The Structured Storage specifications allow streams to contain up to $2^{64}$ bytes—that is, the seek offset is a 64-bit value. OLE's implementation is limited to $2^{32}$ bytes, using a 32-bit seek offset instead. Microsoft didn't see a 4-gigabyte limit as a problem.

■ Stream allocation happens on a granularity of 512 bytes, so a stream with 10 bytes of data will occupy 512 bytes in the file, and a stream of 513 bytes will occupy 1024 bytes in the file.

■ Seeking backward in a stream is somewhat slower than a forward seek because OLE's implementation uses a singly linked list to manage noncontiguous blocks of space in the file that makes up the stream.

■ All element names are stored as Unicode characters regardless of platform.

Besides performance issues, the only real limitations in compound files are the absence of region locking and transactioning for streams. Keep these in mind when you design an application that uses this technology. The 512-byte granularity for streams is also an important design consideration: it becomes very inefficient to store many small data structures in individual streams because you'll end up with a lot of unused space in a file. If at all possible, design your use of compound files so that you use as much space in each 512-byte block of a stream as you can, which you can do simply by combining a few structures in the same stream. You can then use *IStream::Clone* to keep *IStream* pointers positioned at the beginning of each structure within the same stream. This way you don't have to make a large number of *Seek* calls to go from one structure to another.

# Associating Code with Storage

Being the experienced Windows user that you are, you know that Windows allows you to associate an application with a file so that when you double-click the filename in the system shell, you automatically launch the associated application and it opens the file. OLE, in fact, takes file association a little further, allowing you to assign to a file the CLSID of some code that can work with that file. In addition, OLE provides essentially the same association capabilities for storage and stream elements within a hierarchy (including the root storage). This again associates some CLSID with those elements to identify the code that can read and write the data.

When some client (or the system shell) wants to run code that knows how to work with the information in that element, it can take the CLSID and call *CoCreateInstance*. The interfaces this caller might request are the topic of Chapter 8. They will be from among *IPersistFile*, *IPersistStorage*, *IPersistStream*, and *IPersistStreamInit*. Through these interfaces, the client can make the object aware of the filename, storage element, or stream element in which the data resides.

To this end, OLE provides a few API functions to assign and retrieve the CLSID associated with some type of storage:

| API Function | Description |
| --- | --- |
| *WriteClassStg* | Serializes a CLSID into an OLE-controlled stream within a given storage, associating that CLSID with the storage. This API calls *IStorage::SetClass*, which creates a stream named "\001CompObj", in which it writes the CLSID. Calling *WriteClassStg* for a root storage associates the entire compound file with that CLSID. |
| *ReadClassStg* | Reads the CLSID from the stream created through *WriteClassStg*. This API calls *IStorage::Stat* and returns the *clsid* field of the STATSTG structure. |

| API Function | Description |
|---|---|
| *WriteClassStm* | Serializes a CLSID into a stream starting at the current seek offset. By convention, a CLSID must appear before any application or component-specific data within a stream.* |
| *ReadClassStm* | Reads a CLSID from the current seek offset in a stream, expecting the format written by *WriteClassStm*. Again, by convention the CLSID appears before any custom information does. |
| *GetClassFile* | Returns a CLSID associated with a particular filename. (See the discussion that follows.) |

* As we'll see in Chapter 8, a client can have multiple components write their persistent data into the same stream, writing a CLSID before each object's private data. The first CLSID in the entire stream should identify the client that understands the remaining stream contents.

In addition, OLE offers two other API functions for writing and reading format information into a storage object. This information consists of a clipboard format value (a CF_* value or a registered one) and a "user type," which is a user-readable string describing the data type as the end user understands it—for example, "Rich Text". Such information is quite useful for servers that want to emulate others because it describes the internal format of information in streams. We'll see where these functions become important in the samples of later chapters.

| | |
|---|---|
| *WriteFmtUserTypeStg* | Serializes a clipboard format and a user-readable name describing the format of the contents of the storage. If the clipboard format is a registered one, this function stores the registered string instead of the value. |
| *ReadFmtUserTypeStg* | Reads the clipboard format and the string previously written by *WriteFmtUserTypeStg*. If the clipboard format is a string, it registers the format and returns the value. |

The matter of associating a CLSID with a storage or stream object is entirely handled through *[Read ¦ Write]Class[Stg ¦ Stm]*. Associating a CLSID with a file presents a few additional concerns. First of all, if the file is a compound file, *[Read ¦ Write]ClassStg* apply perfectly well to the root storage in that file, as they do to any other storage element. But what if the file is not a compound file? OLE still allows you to create an association in two other ways, using additional registry entries.

The first method is to create a registry entry for the file's extension of the form:

```
\
    .<ext> = <ProgID>

    <ProgID> = <Name of class>
        CLSID = {<CLSID in hex>}

    CLSID
        {<CLSID in hex>}
            [Inproc ¦ Local]Server32 = <path to server module>
```

The first entry in this list is a file extension with a period. (The string ".doc" is an example.) The value of this key is the ProgID under which OLE can locate the CLSID associated with this file type. The .*<ext>* entry is the same one that Windows itself uses to associate extensions with applications. What differs with OLE is the entries under the *<ProgID>* entry. Whereas Windows stores varied information under a shell subkey, OLE needs only the CLSID entry.

The second method of association is a little more involved. OLE defines a root registry key named *FileType,* under which appear entries in the following form:

```
\
    FileType
        {<CLSID in hex>}
            <type id> = <offset>,<cb>,<mask>,<value>
            <type id> = <offset>,<cb>,<mask>,<value>
            <type id> = <offset>,<cb>,<mask>,<value>
            ⋮
```

Each *<type id>* key, which is some integer unique for the CLSID, describes a byte pattern *<value>* that will match *<cb>* bytes in an associated file found at *<offset>* (from the beginning of that file) when a bitwise AND operation has been performed on those file bytes with *<mask>* (which may be omitted to indicate that no mask is necessary). Here are the patterns for Microsoft Word 6.0 as an example:

```
\
    FileType
        {00020900-0000-0000-C000-000000000046}
            0 = 0,2,FFFF,DBA5
            1 = 0,2,FFFF,9BA5
```

The *GetClassFile* function will use these byte patterns in their registered order if the given file is not a compound file with a CLSID in it already. If *GetClassFile* cannot match these byte patterns, it will attempt to associate the file by extension; otherwise, it fails with MK_E_INVALIDEXTENSION.

# Compound Files in Practice

Now that we've thoroughly pounded into the deep earth all the interfaces and API functions related to compound files, we can look at how to actually apply it all to implementing file functions in an application. For this chapter, I have modified the Chapter 1 version of Cosmo to write its data into a compound file, demonstrating the simplest use of compound files: open, read or write, and then close. This version of Cosmo also retains compatibility with old versions of its files by using the conversion feature of compound files, which allows it to treat old files as storages. I have also added compound file support to Patron. Patron has a much more complicated storage scheme because we implement parts of the storage model shown earlier in Figure 7-6 on page 353.

## Simple Storage: Cosmo

Cosmo (CHAP07\COSMO) requires only a few changes to use compound files instead of traditional files as the Chapter 1 version does (or as does Chapter 5's Component Cosmo). The changes are simple. Instead of opening a regular file with which to read or write data, we open a root storage. Instead of using file I/O functions such as _*lread* and _*lwrite*, we obtain a stream pointer and use *IStream* member functions. These changes affect the functions *CCosmoDoc::Load* and *CCosmoDoc::Save* in DOCUMENT.CPP as well as new functions we add to the Polyline object, *CPolyline::ReadFromStorage* and *CPolyline::WriteToStorage* (POLYLINE.CPP). These latter functions are similar to the existing *CPolyline* members of *ReadFromFile* and *WriteToFile*.

To write a simple file with a single stream, Cosmo makes the following calls, in which steps 1, 2, and 6 occur in *CCosmoDoc::Save*, and steps 3, 4, and 5 occur in *CPolyline::WriteToStorage*:

1. *StgCreateDocfile*, using STGM_DIRECT ¦ STGM_CREATE, creates a new compound file, overwriting any file that already exists. This returns an *IStorage* pointer for this new file. Because we use STGM-_DIRECT, there is no need to call *IStorage::Commit* later.

2. *WriteClassStg* and *WriteFmtUserTypeStg* set various flags on the storage and save standard class information.

3. *IStorage::CreateStream*, using the name "CONTENTS", returns an *IStream* pointer.

4. *IStream::Write* saves the data, passing a pointer to the data and the size of the data to go into the stream.

5. *IStream::Release* closes the stream, matching *IStorage::CreateStream.*

6. *IStorage::Release* closes the storage, matching *StgCreateDocfile.*

We can see these steps in the following code. You'll see that Cosmo handles multiple versions of its data (it has a legacy of an OLE 1 version as well as its file-based version of Chapter 1), but the specific code to handle the different cases has been omitted here for brevity:

```
UINT CCosmoDoc::Save(UINT uType, LPTSTR pszFile)
    {
    LONG        lVer, lRet;
    UINT        uTemp;
    BOOL        fRename=TRUE;
    HRESULT     hr;
    LPSTORAGE   pIStorage;

    if (NULL==pszFile)
        {
        fRename=FALSE;
        pszFile=m_szFile;
        }

[Determine version of data to write in lVer.]
[Ask whether user wants to change versions if necessary.]


    /*
     * Use old WriteToFile code for version 1 data; otherwise,
     * use Structured Storage through WriteToStorage.
     */
    if (lVer==MAKELONG(0, 1))
        lRet=m_pPL->WriteToFile(pszFile, lVer);
    else
        {
        hr=StgCreateDocfile(pszFile, STGM_DIRECT | STGM_READWRITE
            | STGM_CREATE | STGM_SHARE_EXCLUSIVE, 0, &pIStorage);

        if (FAILED(hr))
            return DOCERR_COULDNOTOPEN;

        //Mark this as one of our class.
        WriteClassStg(pIStorage, CLSID_CosmoFigure);

        //Write user-readable class information.
        WriteFmtUserTypeStg(pIStorage, m_cf
            , PSZ(IDS_CLIPBOARDFORMAT));
```

```
        lRet=m_pPL->WriteToStorage(pIStorage, lVer);
        pIStorage->Release();
        }

    if (POLYLINE_E_NONE!=lRet)
        return DOCERR_WRITEFAILURE;


    FDirtySet(FALSE);
    m_lVer=lVer;

    if (fRename)
        Rename(pszFile);

    return DOCERR_NONE;
    }

LONG CPolyline::WriteToStorage(LPSTORAGE pIStorage, LONG lVer)
    {
    ULONG           cb;
    ULONG           cbExpect=0;
    WORD            wVerMaj=HIWORD(lVer);
    WORD            wVerMin=LOWORD(lVer);
    POLYLINEDATA    pl;
    LPSTREAM        pIStream;
    HRESULT         hr;

    if (NULL==pIStorage)
        return POLYLINE_E_READFAILURE;

    //Get copy of our data in version we're going to save.
    DataGet(&pl, lVer);

    [Set cbExpect to size of appropriate version.]

    hr=pIStorage->CreateStream(SZSTREAM, STGM_DIRECT ! STGM_CREATE
        ! STGM_WRITE ! STGM_SHARE_EXCLUSIVE, 0, 0, &pIStream);

    if (FAILED(hr))
        return POLYLINE_E_WRITEFAILURE;

    hr=pIStream->Write(&pl, cbExpect, &cb);
    pIStream->Release();

    if (FAILED(hr) !! cbExpect!=cb)
        return POLYLINE_E_WRITEFAILURE;

    return POLYLINE_E_NONE;
    }
```

In a similar fashion, Cosmo makes the following calls to open and read the data saved previously during a File Open operation. Steps 1, 2, and 7 occur in *CCosmoDoc::Load*; and steps 4, 5, and 6 occur in *CPolyline::Read-FromStorage*:

1. *StgIsStorageFile* determines whether the filename refers to a compound file by looking for a specific OLE-generated signature at the beginning of the disk file.

2. If the file is a compound file, *StgOpenStorage* opens the storage for reading and returns an *IStorage* pointer. Otherwise, *StgCreateDocfile*, using STGM_TRANSACTED | STGM_CONVERT, opens a non-compound file as a storage object and returns an *IStorage* pointer.

3. At the application's option, *ReadClassStg* loads the CLSID previously saved from *WriteClassStg*, and *IsEqualCLSID* compares the expected class to the one in the file. If the two don't match, you didn't write this file, and you can read the data any way you want. Cosmo does not perform this step.

4. *IStorage::OpenStream* is passed the name "CONTENTS" and returns an *IStream* pointer to the data.

5. *IStream::Read* loads the data from the file into the memory structures.

6. *IStream::Release* closes the stream, matching *IStorage::OpenStream*.

7. *IStorage::Release* closes the storage, matching the *StgOpenStorage* or *StgCreateDocfile* call.

These steps are apparent in the following code:

```
UINT CCosmoDoc::Load(BOOL fChangeFile, LPTSTR pszFile)
    {
    HRESULT        hr;
    LPSTORAGE      pIStorage;

    if (NULL==pszFile)
        {
        //For new untitled document, just rename ourselves.
        Rename(NULL);
        m_lVer=VERSIONCURRENT;
        return DOCERR_NONE;
        }
```

```
pIStorage=NULL;

if (NOERROR!=StgIsStorageFile(pszFile))
    {
    hr=StgCreateDocfile(pszFile,STGM_TRANSACTED | STGM_READWRITE
        | STGM_CONVERT | STGM_SHARE_EXCLUSIVE, 0, &pIStorage);

    if (FAILED(hr))
        {
        //If denied write access, try to load the old way.
        if (STG_E_ACCESSDENIED==GetScode(hr))
            m_lVer=m_pPL->ReadFromFile(pszFile);
        else
            return DOCERR_COULDNOTOPEN;
        }
    }
else
    {
    hr=StgOpenStorage(pszFile, NULL, STGM_DIRECT | STGM_READ
        | STGM_SHARE_EXCLUSIVE, NULL, 0, &pIStorage);

    if (FAILED(hr))
        return DOCERR_COULDNOTOPEN;
    }

if (NULL!=pIStorage)
    {
    m_lVer=m_pPL->ReadFromStorage(pIStorage);
    pIStorage->Release();
    }

if (POLYLINE_E_READFAILURE==m_lVer)
    return DOCERR_READFAILURE;

if (POLYLINE_E_UNSUPPORTEDVERSION==m_lVer)
    return DOCERR_UNSUPPORTEDVERSION;

if (fChangeFile)
    Rename(pszFile);

//Importing a file makes things dirty.
FDirtySet(!fChangeFile);

return DOCERR_NONE;
}
```

*(continued)*

```
LONG CPolyline::ReadFromStorage(LPSTORAGE pIStorage)
    {
    POLYLINEDATA    pl;
    ULONG           cb=(ULONG)-1;
    ULONG           cbExpect=0;
    LPSTREAM        pIStream;
    HRESULT         hr;
    LARGE_INTEGER   li;

    if (NULL==pIStorage)
        return POLYLINE_E_READFAILURE;

    //Open CONTENTS stream.
    hr=pIStorage->OpenStream(SZSTREAM, 0, STGM_DIRECT | STGM_READ
        | STGM_SHARE_EXCLUSIVE, 0, &pIStream);

    if (FAILED(hr))
        return POLYLINE_E_READFAILURE;

    //Read version numbers and seek back to file beginning.
    hr=pIStream->Read(&pl, 2*sizeof(WORD), &cb);

    LISet32(li, 0);
    pIStream->Seek(li, STREAM_SEEK_SET, NULL);

    if (FAILED(hr) || 2*sizeof(WORD)!=cb)
        {
        pIStream->Release();
        return POLYLINE_E_READFAILURE;
        }

    [Code to set cbExpect according to version omitted.]

    if (0==cbExpect)
        {
        pIStream->Release();
        return POLYLINE_E_UNSUPPORTEDVERSION;
        }

    hr=pIStream->Read(&pl, cbExpect, &cb);
    pIStream->Release();

    if (cbExpect!=cb)
        return POLYLINE_E_READFAILURE;

    DataSet(&pl, TRUE, TRUE);
    return MAKELONG(pl.wVerMin, pl.wVerMaj);
    }
```

The most interesting aspects of this code are the correspondence between stream operations and traditional file operations and the use of STGM_CONVERT to deal with an old file format. We'll cover these topics in the next two sections. Although Cosmo writes a CLSID to the storage, it does not check it during File Open using *ReadClassStg*. I do this so Cosmo and Component Cosmo (CoCosmo, modified for storage objects a little later) retain file compatibility. Because the two applications write different CLSIDs into their storages, we skip the *ReadClassStg* step. Using *ReadClassStg* is an extra check that you can perform to validate a file before loading potentially large amounts of data.

## Streams vs. Files

Earlier in this chapter, I mentioned that a strong parallel exists between traditional file I/O functions (in both the Windows API and the C run-time library) and the member functions of the *IStream* interface. In the implementation of Cosmo's *CPolyline* class, we can see these similarities by comparing its *ReadFromFile* member used in the Chapter 1 version of Cosmo to the *ReadFromStorage* member used here. The two functions, *ReadFromFile* and *ReadFromStorage*, are shown side by side here to illustrate the similarities between the two implementations:

```
LONG CPolyline::ReadFromFile          LONG CPolyline::ReadFromStorage
    (LPSTR pszFile)                       (LPSTORAGE pIStorage)
    {                                     {
    OFSTRUCT       of;                    HRESULT        hr;
    HFILE          hFile;                 LPSTREAM       pIStream;
    POLYLINEDATA   pl;                    POLYLINEDATA   pl;
    UINT           cb=-1;                 ULONG          cb=-1;
    UINT           cbExpect=0;            ULONG          cbExpect=0;
    LARGE_INTEGER  li;

    if (NULL==pszFile)                    if (NULL==pIStorage)
        return POLYLINE_E_READFAILURE;        return POLYLINE_E_READFAILURE;

    hFile=OpenFile(pszFile, &of          hr=pIStorage->OpenStream("CONTENTS", 0
        , OF_READ);                          , STGM_DIRECT | STGM_READ
                                             | STGM_SHARE_EXCLUSIVE, 0
                                             , &pIStream);

    if (HFILE_ERROR==hFile)               if (FAILED(hr))
        return POLYLINE_E_READFAILURE;        return POLYLINE_E_READFAILURE;

    cb=_lread(hFile, (LPSTR)&pl          hr=pIStream->Read((LPVOID)&pl
        , 2*sizeof(WORD));                    , 2*sizeof(WORD), &cb);
```

*(continued)*

```
_llseek(hFile, 0L, 0);            LISet32(li, 0);
                                  pIStream->Seek(li, STREAM_SEEK_SET, NULL);

if (2*sizeof(WORD)!=cb)           if (FAILED(hr) || 2*sizeof(WORD)!=cb)
    {                                 {
    _lclose(hFile);                   pIStream->Release();
    return POLYLINE_E_READFAILURE;    return POLYLINE_E_READFAILURE;
    }                                 }

[Code here to calculate cbExpect  [Code here to calculate cbExpect
 based on version number]          based on version number]

cb=_lread(hFile, (LPSTR)&pl       hr=pIStream->Read((LPVOID)&pl
    , cbExpect);                      , cbExpect, &cb);
_lclose(hFile);                   pIStream->Release();

if (cbExpect!=cb)                 if (cbExpect!=cb)
    return POLYLINE_E_READFAILURE;     return POLYLINE_E_READFAILURE;

DataSet(&pl, TRUE, TRUE);         DataSet(&pl, TRUE, TRUE);
return MAKELONG(pl.wVerMin        return MAKELONG(pl.wVerMin
    , pl.wVerMaj);                    , pl.wVerMaj);
}                                 }
```

We can see how a call to *OpenFile* maps to a call to *IStorage::OpenStream*; we treat the storage object as we'd treat the file system. Then all of the old file I/O functions called with the file handle map to *IStream* calls; in this case, the standard return type of HRESULT means that we have to pass pointers to out-parameters of *IStream* functions that are generally the straight return values of traditional file I/O calls (such as the *cb* returned from _ *lread*).

One glaring difference between traditional files and streams is seeking. Because the Structured Storage definition of *IStream* allows a stream to contain up to $2^{64}$ addressable bytes of data, we can't just use a DWORD to indicate the new seek offset. For this reason, OLE defines the type LARGE_INTEGER, a 64-bit value of two LONGs, together with the macro LISet32, which fills such a structure with a 32-bit value:

```
LARGE_INTEGER   li;

LISet32(li, 0);
pIStream->Seek(li, STREAM_SEEK_SET, NULL);
```

There is also a ULARGE_INTEGER, composed of two (unsigned) DWORDs, with the associated macro ULISet32. The third parameter to *IStream::Seek* could be a ULARGE_INTEGER, which would receive the prior seek offset before the call. In the code shown above, the NULL means that we're not interested in this information.

## Pulling Rabbits from a Hat with STGM_CONVERT

Cosmo is capable of reading and writing two different versions of its files; in Chapter 1, both formats were typical MS-DOS files. For this chapter and later ones, Cosmo uses a compound file for its version 2 files, but it remains compatible with old files (both the version 1 files and the version 2 files generated by the Chapter 1 version of Cosmo) and is able to read and write the old formats. Cosmo preserves its old file-writing code for this reason, but reading files of either format can be centralized using the STGM_CONVERT flag. We could, of course, test a file with *StgIsStorageFile* first and call the appropriate code to handle whichever version of the file is present. Doubtless many applications have this code already. But let's see what we can do with OLE's automatic conversion.

When Cosmo sees a noncompound file while loading, it calls *StgCreate-Docfile*, passing STGM_CONVERT instead of STGM_CREATE, and this causes OLE to open the file as a compound file with a single stream named "CONTENTS" (in uppercase). If this operation succeeds, the HRESULT returned from *StgCreateDocfile* will contain STG_S_CONVERTED, which is a success code (_S_) but different from NOERROR. Therefore, using the FAILED macro is a valid test for errors.

```
LPSTORAGE    pIStorage;
HRESULT      hr;

hr=StgCreateDocfile(pszFile, STGM_TRANSACTED ¦ STGM_READWRITE
    ¦ STGM_CONVERT ¦ STGM_SHARE_EXCLUSIVE, 0, &pIStorage);

if (FAILED(hr))
    {
    if (STG_E_ACCESSDENIED==GetScode(hr))
        [Try loading file using traditional file I/O.]
    }
```

When using *StgCreateDocfile* for conversion, we purposely pass STGM_TRANSACTED ¦ STGM_READWRITE but never bother to commit anything. The semantics of STGM_CONVERT in *StgCreateDocfile* mean "convert the file now." If we use STGM_DIRECT in this case, the old file will be immediately overwritten with a compound file. By specifying STGM_TRANS-ACTED, we create the conversion in a separate temporary storage, leaving the original disk image unaffected. Calling *IStorage::Commit* would then change the actual file on the disk.

Because conversion is a potential Write operation, we must specify at least STGM_WRITE along with STGM_CONVERT. If the file is marked as read-only, however, *StgCreateDocfile* will fail with STG_E_ACCESSDENIED.

In this situation, you can default to loading the file with old code that restricts you to read-only access. For this reason, Cosmo preserves its original *CPolyline- ::ReadFromFile* function as a backup.

It is no coincidence that I chose to use the stream name "CONTENTS" for Cosmo's native compound files. My choice means that the code in *CPoly- line::ReadFromStorage* doesn't have to care whether the storage is a native compound file or a converted traditional file. It is, however, perfectly fine to use whatever stream names you want, especially if you need to distinguish between versions of data elsewhere in your code. The choice of "CON- TENTS" in Cosmo is completely arbitrary, made only to match what OLE creates with STGM_CONVERT.

> **NOTE:** STGM_CONVERT can be used only with *StgCreateDocfile* and *StgCreateDocfileOnILockBytes*. It is not supported with *StgOpen- Storage* or *StgOpenStorageOnILockBytes*.

## Complex Compound Files: Patron

English grammar defines a number of sentence structures. A simple sentence expresses one idea, such as "The rabbit sat in its form."[4] Compound sen- tences express more than one independent idea, such as "The rabbit sat in its form, and the photographer set up her camera." These sentences have a vague notion of concurrency but no hard evidence of it. A complex sentence, however, defines such a relationship, as in "The rabbit sat in its form while the photographer set up her camera." A complex compound sentence is more on the order of "Although the rabbit felt trepidation about most humans, it calmly sat in its form, and the photographer continued to set up her camera."

The idea of a single flat traditional file is an analog of the simple sen- tence structure. A compound file, one with a single storage and a single stream, is much like a compound sentence: two elements that are related by being in the same place at the same time. When we add more streams in the root storage, we make things more complex—the meaning of the data in one stream might be partially or completely defined by the context of the data in another stream. As we use even more complex structures, we add substorages alongside these streams and new streams under those substorages. We can build any complexity we want, and thus we can call such structures complex compound files.

For this chapter's version of Patron (CHAP07\PATRON), we'll imple- ment the storage structure shown in Figure 7-8, which is the same as that

---

4. A form is a rabbit's resting place.

shown in Figure 7-6 on page 353, but without the page header streams or tenant storages because we haven't yet added the capability of creating tenants. Each Patron file is a root storage, underneath which live two streams. The first contains the printer configuration; the second contains the list of pages within the document, including the number of pages, the current page (the one to view when opening the file), and any number of page identifiers. Each page is assigned a unique DWORD according to the order of creation, and the page list stream contains the next ID to use. The ordering of pages in the document is determined by the sequence of IDs in the page list, not by the ID values themselves, because the fourth page created might have been inserted at the beginning of the document. Each page is given its own substorage under the root; the substorage name is Page <*ID*>, where <*ID*> is the ASCII representation of the identifier. For this chapter, these substorages will not contain anything else — they do, however, provide the structure in which we can create tenants later on.

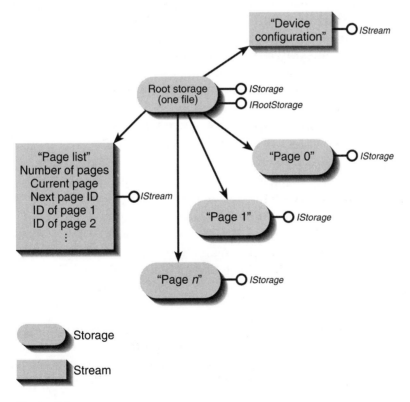

**Figure 7-8.**
*Exact layout of Patron's compound files as described in this chapter, prior to adding tenant support.*

Adding file I/O capabilities using compound files requires considerable modifications and additions to Patron: filling out its *CPatronDoc* members *Load* and *Save* (DOCUMENT.CPP), adding structural support in the *CPages* class (PAGES.CPP), and adding functionality to the *CPage* class (PAGE.CPP). All the code is available on the companion CD and need not be shown here. For the most part, Patron follows the same sorts of call sequences for saving and loading files that were described for Cosmo earlier in this chapter, except that not everything happens at the same time and in the same place. Patron's file handling is summarized as follows:

- *CPatronDoc::Load* either opens an existing file (*StgOpenStorage*) or creates a temporary file (using *StgCreateDocfile* with a NULL filename). It passes the resulting *IStorage* pointer to *CPages::Storage-Set*, which uses the pointer when creating or opening the page substorages.

- *CPages::StorageSet* reads the Page List stream in the storage given to it and creates all the necessary pages described by that stream. (This is more efficient than calling *IStorage::EnumElements* to find all the page names directly. The information in the stream is sufficient to re-create those names more quickly.) If this is a new file, *StorageSet* creates the "Page List" stream, setting the next ID counter to 0. This function then creates or reads the device configuration stream, switches to the current page, and returns. When a repaint occurs, the user will see the current page.

- *CPatronDoc::Save*, when performing a simple Save operation, tells each page to update its storages by calling *CPages::StorageUpdate*, followed by a call to *IStorage::Commit(STGC_DEFAULT)*. If performing a Save As operation, *CPatronDoc::Save* creates a new compound file, updates all the page storages, calls *CopyTo* to store all the information in the new file, and then calls *Commit* to make it all permanent. If *CopyTo* fails due to lack of memory, Patron queries for *IRootStorage* and calls *IRootStorage::SwitchToFile* followed by *IStorage::Commit*. In either case, the new file is saved properly.

- *CPages::StorageUpdate* calls *CPage::Update* for the current page, closes that page, and rewrites the "Page List" stream. This function needs only to update the current page: when the user switches to another page, Patron ends up in *CPages::CurPageSet*, calling *CPage::Close*, which tells the page to commit its changes. That page's substorage then contains the current copy of its information, so we can release that substorage and open the new page to view. In other words, changing pages commits the previous one and opens the new one, so when we save the entire file we need only commit the changes to the current page. In this manner, Patron performs the necessary commits on each level of its storage, which we'll expand in a later chapter when adding tenants.

■ The functions *CPatronDoc::Print* and *CPatronDoc::PrinterSetup*, along with *CPages::DevModeSet*, *CPages::DevModeGet*, *CPages::ConfigureForDevice*, and *CPages::Print* — all of which you can find in PRINT.CPP — manage the printer information inside the "device configuration" stream. This is an example of keeping an infrequently used data structure in a stream at all times instead of loading it into memory. The only drawbacks are that Patron ties a document to a specific printer device and that the DEVMODE structure it stores in this stream is not portable between platforms. Both design decisions would be silly in a shipping software product, but I use DEVMODE here as a matter of convenience for this sample, whose fundamental purpose is not sales but demonstration of concepts.[5]

■ Deleting a page calls *CPages::DeletePage*, which calls *CPage::Destroy*. This in turn calls *IStorage::DestroyElement* to delete its own substorage. (Remember that the *CPage* class is a run-time C++ object in memory, which is here destroying its own substorage in the compound file. This is not a case of the object destroying itself, only its storage.)

I encourage you to follow through the code and see where each piece of Patron's architecture (I don't call it ideal by any means) works with its piece of the storage hierarchy. The *CPatronDoc* and *CPages* classes both work with the root storage, whereas instances of *CPage* work with their own substorage. Let's look at two of the more interesting parts of this implementation.

---

5. Patron does not gracefully handle the case in which a document created for one printer, with a specific DEVMODE, is taken to another machine without that printer installed. What will happen is that Patron will call *CreateIC* with that information and will fail to find the driver specified in DEVMODE. As a result, the user gets blasted with one of those ugly "Cannot find MSHPPCL5-.DRV" messages. If you encounter this, remember it's just a sample.

## The Root Storage and Temporary Files

Patron always keeps the root storage open. If a new file is created (from a File New command), Patron uses a temporary compound file created by passing a NULL to *StgCreateDocfile* along with STGM_DELETEONRELEASE, which should be the default for temporary files:

```
hr=StgCreateDocfile(NULL, STGM_TRANSACTED | STGM_READWRITE
    | STGM_SHARE_EXCLUSIVE | STGM_CREATE | STGM_DELETEONRELEASE
    , 0, &m_pIStorage);
```

If a file is loaded from disk (opened with the File Open command), Patron opens it with *StgOpenStorage* and keeps that storage open. One of these two functions is called from *CPatronDoc::Load*, depending on whether the end user chose File New or File Open.

Keeping a transacted storage open in this manner is a little expensive in terms of file handles. It allows us, however, to open any number of sub-storages and streams at any other time and in any other place in the code. If you are able to tolerate the cost of the file handles, this can be very conve-nient for application design, especially if you are running on a system for which file handles are not a scarce system resource.

The temporary file created in *StgCreateDocfile* will appear on the file sys-tem in your environment's TEMP directory with a pseudorandom name (such as ~DF4C8.TMP). If you specify STGM_DELETEONRELEASE, OLE will clean the files out of the directory, but if the application crashes (as it will under development, no doubt) or if the user turns off the machine without closing files, the TEMP directory can become cluttered with garbage files. I suggest that you check for these files periodically during your development work and warn your end users in the application's documentation.

## Managing Substorages

As mentioned earlier, Patron manages a substorage for each page in the over-all document. This, of course, requires somewhat more complex code when pages are created or destroyed. Whenever Patron creates a new page in the document, it calls *IStorage::CreateStorage* using the name Page<*ID*>, where <*ID*> is the page identifier in ASCII. When Patron opens an existing page, it calls *IStorage::OpenStorage* with the appropriate name as well. Both operations occur in *CPage::Open*. The member *CPage::GetStorageName* simply generates the text name to use in both calls:

```
BOOL CPage::Open(LPSTORAGE pIStorage)
    {
    BOOL        fNULL=FALSE;
    HRESULT     hr=NOERROR;
    DWORD       dwMode=STGM_TRANSACTED | STGM_READWRITE
                   | STGM_SHARE_EXCLUSIVE;
    OLECHAR     szTemp[32];

    if (NULL==m_pIStorage)
        {
        fNULL=TRUE;

        if (NULL==pIStorage)
            return FALSE;

        GetStorageName(szTemp);

        hr=pIStorage->OpenStorage(szTemp, NULL, dwMode, NULL, 0
            , &m_pIStorage);

        if (FAILED(hr))
            {
            hr=pIStorage->CreateStorage(szTemp, dwMode, 0, 0
                , &m_pIStorage);
            }
        }

    ⋮
    }


UINT CPage::GetStorageName(LPOLESTR pszName)
    {
    return wsprintf(pszName, TEXT("Page %lu"), m_dwID);
    }
```

The *CPages* class assigns the page ID through the *CPage* constructor, which saves the value in *m_dwID*. The *CPages* class, once again, keeps a persistent DWORD counter for page IDs in the Page List stream. IDs are not recycled when a page is destroyed, but the DWORD counter would overflow only if you sat down and created (for example) one page every second until the year 2129. I desperately hope this software is obsolete by then!

Speaking of destroying a page, this operation requires a call to *IStorage-::DestroyElement* to counter the *IStorage::CreateStorage* in the preceding code. The function *CPage::Destroy* takes care of this in Patron:

```
//pIStorage is document's root storage.
void CPage::Destroy(LPSTORAGE pIStorage)
    {
    if (NULL!=pIStorage)
        {
        OLECHAR   szTemp[32];

        Close(FALSE);
        GetStorageName(szTemp)
        pIStorage->DestroyElement(szTemp);
        }

    return;
    }


void CPage::Close(BOOL fCommit)
    {
    if (NULL==m_pIStorage)
        return;

    if (fCommit)
        Update();

    if (0L==m_pIStorage->Release())
        m_pIStorage=NULL;

    return;
    }

BOOL CPage::Update(void)
    {
    if (NULL!=m_pIStorage)
        m_pIStorage->Commit(STGC_DEFAULT);

    return TRUE;
    }
```

# Compound File Defragmentation

Compound files provide incremental saves inherently, so the physical size of a compound file on disk will typically be larger than necessary. This is because the size of the file is determined by the amount of space between the first and last sectors used by that file. This is like calculating free space on your hard disk by using the location of the first and last files stored on it instead of by the number of actual unused sectors: with this method, you could have two 1-KB files on a 1-GB disk, but because they are located at opposite ends of the drive, the disk is considered full.

Although this does not actually happen on hard disks, it can happen within the confines of a storage hierarchy. There might be plenty of unused space inside the storage medium itself, but the size of that medium, as reported by the operating system for something like a file, is defined by the first and last sectors used, regardless of the amount of internal free space. This means that the possibility of internal fragmentation and larger than necessary files (or other mediums) always exists, as shown in Figure 7-9.

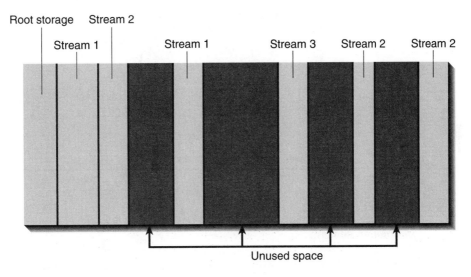

**Figure 7-9.**
*A fragmented storage that takes up more room than necessary.*

The *IStorage::CopyTo* function will remove all the dead space in the process of copying the contents of one storage to another and will order the contents of streams sequentially, as shown in Figure 7-10.

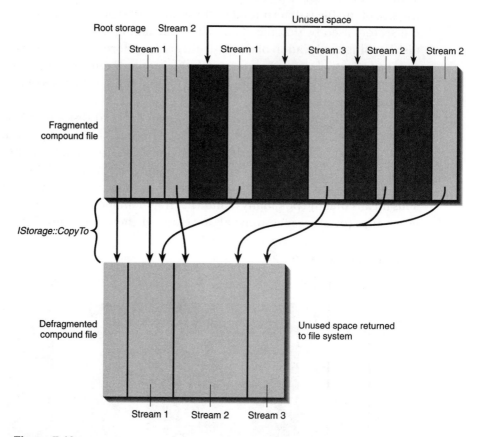

**Figure 7-10.**
IStorage::CopyTo *removes dead space and orders stream contents within the destination storage.*

The Fragmenter sample (CHAP07\FRAGMENT) illustrates this process. Compile and run this program. You won't see any main window—instead you'll see a message appear after a little while that says "FRAGMENT.BIN created." This means that Fragmenter has finished creating a compound file with 26 streams, each of which contains 5120 characters. The first stream, called Stream A, contains A characters, Stream B contains B characters, and so on. These streams are not written sequentially; rather, they are written 256 characters at a time through 20 iterations of the alphabet. When the first message appears, you can look at the contents of the file to see that there are essentially 10 sections of 512 characters each because streams are allocated to a 512-byte granularity. At this point, the file itself will be 219,136 bytes.

Now close the message box, and after a short time Fragmenter will display the message "Space has been freed in FRAGMENT.BIN." After you closed the first message, Fragmenter deleted the streams C, E, G, H, J, M, N, T, and X, freeing a significant portion of the space in the file before closing it again. Now look at the binary contents of the file once more. You'll see that all the original information is there. What gives? OLE only *marked* the space occupied by those streams as unused, but it doesn't need to bother overwriting their contents. (If you want deleted information to be secure, overwrite the stream before deleting it.) All the original information still exists, the file is the same size, and all that have changed are a few bytes marking blocks of data as used or unused.

Now close this second message box. After another pause, you'll see the message "Defragmentation complete on FRAGMENT.BIN." Here is where Fragmenter created a new file, then called the *IStorage::CopyTo* function to copy the storage contents to that new file, and then deleted the old file and renamed this new file to FRAGMENT.BIN. If you look at the file again, you'll now see that not only are all the unused blocks (all the deleted character streams) gone, but also all the characters—all 5120 of each type—are sequential in the file. The file itself is now only 91,136 bytes.

This process illustrates how to defragment any compound file. You can use this technique to compress files from your own application or perhaps build an end-user tool that will do the same.

## Summary

OLE Structured Storage is a specification of a "file system within a file" in which storage elements (objects with the *IStorage* interface) act like directories and stream elements (objects with the *IStream* interface) act like files. There are strong parallels between the capabilities of each element and the same type of element in a file system. The motivation behind this technology is the need for multiple components constituting an application to share an underlying disk file in the same way that multiple applications running on the same computer need to share the underlying storage device. Besides meeting this fundamental need, Structured Storage also provides a powerful way for an application to deal with its own files, in which it can benefit from incremental access, a hierarchy of named elements (of which some named elements are reserved), and built-in transactioning. By giving up absolute control over the disk file format, an application greatly benefits from the "file system within a file," especially because you don't need to run applications anymore in order to browse the elements of data within a file. This difference produces a number of significant and useful side effects, such as a "Summary Information" property set (described in Chapter 16) that could be used to run shell-level document search queries.

OLE's implementation of this storage architecture is called Compound Files, the ANSI C++ implementation of which can be licensed from Microsoft for porting to other platforms (to retain application file format compatibility). This implementation supports the Structured Storage features of shareable and named elements, incremental access, and a host of access modes, including transactioning facilities. This implementation is built on the concept of a LockBytes object (using the *ILockBytes* interface) that acts as a device driver for an underlying storage device, shielding the rest of the implementation from the actual device. This makes it easy to redirect bytes to and from mediums other than disks, such as a database record or global memory. Clients access the services provided by OLE's Compound Files through a few OLE API functions, such as *StgCreateDocfile* and *StgOpenStorage*, which return *IStorage* pointers to the root storage objects in the hierarchy. From here, the client can navigate through the rest of the hierarchy, and the root storage object itself also supports *IRootStorage* for the purposes of low-memory saves.

OLE also provides the ability to associate a CLSID with data in a storage or stream element so that you can use the CLSID to locate an object that can load and work with that data. In addition, registry entries can be used to map a noncompound file to a CLSID based either on the file extension or on byte patterns within the file.

This chapter examines these principles in the context of the Cosmo and Patron samples. Cosmo is converted from using traditional files to using compound files, thus offering a comparison between the two models. Patron is given file capabilities using Compound Files from the beginning and implements a reasonably complex storage mechanism. In addition, a small sample named Fragmenter demonstrates OLE's built-in defragmentation facility to keep compound files to their smallest necessary size.

**C H A P T E R   E I G H T**

# Persistent Objects

*For the soul there is never birth nor death. It is not slain when the body is slain.*
—Lord Krishna, Bhagavad Gita, 2:25

*Do not be afraid of those who kill the body but cannot kill the soul.*
—Jesus, The NIV Bible, Matthew 10:28a

*If I am killed, it destroys merely the clay garment, the body. But if I kill, it injures the reality, the soul!*
—Peace Pilgrim, being questioned by the FBI[1]

The concept of an eternal soul is part of the doctrines of many world religions and reflected in the writings of many mystics. The body is temporary, the soul is enduring—or what we might call persistent. Whatever another person might do to your body, they cannot touch the soul.

Without wandering off too much into theological speculation, we can think of many objects as having a body and a soul. The body is the volatile instantiation of the object's data structures and function tables in memory. These are volatile—that is, temporary—because they are destroyed when the computer is turned off or when a process simply terminates. Granted, for many objects this is no problem—their entire state is re-created as needed from instantiation to instantiation. These are objects without a soul.

Other objects, however, need to preserve some of their state information from instantiation to instantiation, much like a soul in the Vedic and Hindu traditions of reincarnation transmigrates from being to being, life after life, carrying with it the saintly or sinful acts of all past lives. In OLE, we call the information carried across object lifetimes the *persistent state* of that

---

1. From *Peace Pilgrim, Her Life and Works in Her Own Words*, Ocean Tree Books, Santa Fe, NM. Peace Pilgrim was a woman (known by no other name) who walked across countries and continents (primarily the United States) from 1953 to 1981 carrying the message "This is the way of peace—overcome evil with good, and falsehood with truth, and hatred with love. When enough of us find inner peace, our institutions will become more peaceful and there will be no more occasion for war."

object. This muddles our understanding of an object—is it simply a set of memory structures, is it this persistent state, or is it both? To be precise, what we call a persistent object is some object that can somehow save its persistent state so that a later instantiation of the same class can reload that state and re-create the original object exactly. The memory structures that hold the information will change in the process, but the state remains the same. The body changes, but the soul is steady.

When an object exists as nothing more than its persistent state (that is, it occupies no memory and no pointers exist to its interfaces), we still call it an object for convenience, but we call it *passive*. When we create an instance of that object's class and ask it to initialize itself with the persistent state, that object is *loaded*, or *running*. The loading process brings the object's persistent state into memory, loads code that knows how to work with it, and makes interface pointers available to clients so they can access the running object.

In Chapter 7, we described OLE's implementation of the Structured Storage model and how to work with storage and stream elements. In the early part of that chapter, we saw how the idea of a "file system within a file" is necessary to allow multiple components to write their persistent information into the same underlying disk file. But a few important questions remain. How does a component or an object in a component become aware of the *IStorage* or *IStream* pointer that it should use in order to read and write its information? How does a client tell an object to make a transition between passive and active states?

The answers to these questions are what we call *persistence models,* described through the interfaces *IPersistStorage, IPersistStream,* and *IPersistStream-Init,* as well as the interface *IPersistFile* (which works along lines similar to the other interfaces but outside the scope of storage and stream elements). Whenever an object provides any of the *IPersist\** interfaces through its *QueryInterface* function, that object tells the world that it can read and write its persistent state to a storage, stream, or file according to the contract implied by the interface. In other words, the object says that it has some things it would like to take with it into its next life, and the client is responsible for telling the object to write or read its persistent state at the appropriate times. (The client declares which persistence model is used.) The process of running a persistent object from its passive state is simply one of creating an instance of the object with *CoCreateInstance* and having that object initialize itself from the contents of some storage medium, through member functions of the *IPersist\** interfaces.

After we take a look at the *IPersist\** interfaces themselves, their member functions, and their rules of use and implementation, we'll see all but *IPersist-File* implemented in the Polyline component that we first saw in Chapter 5.

Component Cosmo is also updated from the Chapter 5 version to work with this new Polyline, through both storage-based and stream-based persistence models. The sample code in this chapter forms a good framework for other implementations of these interfaces that we'll see in later chapters. As for *IPersistFile*, we'll see an implementation of it in Chapter 9, as file monikers are particularly interested in that interface.

An object's persistent state, of course, really isn't as eternal as various religions' descriptions of the soul. As Buddhists might tell you, the soul, being changeable, cannot be permanent because there is no immortal survival for a changing thing. Certainly the persistent state of an object may change, and it may disappear altogether. A client (or end user) that ultimately controls the storage may, at any time, obliterate that persistent state. But until that time, an object wants to keep its soul alive through many transitions between its passive and running states. The various *IPersist\** interfaces are the means to such endurance.

## Persistent Object Interfaces

When a client wants to ask an object whether it can read or write its persistent data to some type of medium—either a storage, a stream, or a file—that client queries for one of four interfaces that begin with *IPersist* and, in fact, derive from the *IPersist* interface we saw first in Chapter 6. All of these interfaces can be marshaled between processes:[2]

| | |
|---|---|
| *IPersistStorage* | The object can read and write its information in a storage hierarchy in which the object is allowed to create additional substorages and streams to any depth it requires. The object can also open elements and hold their pointers outside the scope of calls to this interface. |
| *IPersistStream* | The object can read and write its information in a single stream and must do so within the scope of calls to this interface. |
| *IPersistStreamInit* | Same as *IPersistStream*, but this interface means the object would like to be informed when it is newly created and has no persistent state as yet. The member function for this purpose does not exist in *IPersistStream*. |
| *IPersistFile* | The object can read and write its information into a completely separate file (traditional or compound) outside the scope of Structured Storage. |

2. At the time of writing, *IPersistStreamInit* did not have marshaling support. Check your current system.

All of these interfaces are considered *initialization* interfaces as described in Chapter 5. Each has specific member functions that perform the initialization; each one has a *Load* member for this purpose, and *IPersistStorage* and *IPersistStreamInit* have an additional *InitNew* member to distinguish new initializations from an initialization based on existing data. This existing data does not need to have come from a previous instantiation of the object—a client is perfectly free to create the data itself in a storage hierarchy, a stream, or a file prior to calling any initialization function. As long as the client knows about the object's persistent state structures, the client can fabricate data and initialize objects from the object all it wants.[3]

Each interface is derived from *IPersist*, so they all share the *GetClassID* member function. This call identifies the CLSID of the code that knows how to work with the persistent data. This is particularly useful for OLE, which uses the CLSID to determine what proxy or handler to load in another process that can also work with the data, as we saw in Chapter 6.

*GetClassID* is not the only member function that these interfaces have in common. All the interfaces also share two common operations: *Load* and *Save*. We'll see these functions as we look at *IPersistStream[Init]*, then *IPersistFile*, and finally *IPersistStorage*, which has a more complex behavior than the others, introducing a specific set of rules that both object and client must follow.

## *IPersistStream* and *IPersistStreamInit*

The simplest persistence model for an object is for it to read and write its information from a single stream. A moniker is an example of such an object (as we'll see in Chapter 9), as are a variety of OLE controls. The *IPersistStream* interface describes the semantics of simple load and save operations, and *IPersistStreamInit* improves on this idea slightly by adding the extra *InitNew* initialization function:

```
interface IPersistStream : IPersist
    {
    //IUnknown members and GetClassID from IPersist
    HRESULT IsDirty(void);
    HRESULT Load(IStream *pStm);
    HRESULT Save(IStream *pStm, BOOL fClearDirty);
    HRESULT GetSizeMax(ULARGE_INTEGER *pcbSize);
    };
```

---

3. An instance of this technique is the function *OleCreateFromFile*, which we'll use in Chapters 17 and 20 to create embedded and linked compound document objects based on the contents of an existing file. It doesn't mean that such objects had to exist before: we're using the file contents for initialization purposes.

```
interface IPersistStreamInit : IPersist
    {
    [All other functions identical to IPersistStream]
    HRESULT InitNew(void);
    };
```

These functions behave as follows:[4]

| Member Function | Description |
|---|---|
| *IsDirty* | Indicates whether the object considers itself dirty. If the object is dirty, the client should call *Save* before releasing the object. |
| *Load* | Instructs the object to load its persistent data from the current seek offset of the given stream. Clients are allowed to serialize the data from multiple objects into a single stream. The object must read its data and return, and it cannot hold the *IStream* pointer outside this function. |
| *Save* | Instructs the object to save its persistent data at the current seek offset of the given stream. The object must save its data and return without holding the *IStream* pointer. The *fClearDirty* argument tells the object whether it should consider itself clean after this call—a client may be making a copy of the object as opposed to saving its data permanently, and this flag distinguishes the cases. |
| *GetSizeMax* | Asks the object to return the maximum amount of information it would possibly write through a call to *Save*. This allows a calling client to preset the size of a stream (*IStream::SetSize*), especially if it is saving the data of multiple objects in the same stream or is otherwise planning to provide an *IStream* that cannot enlarge itself automatically. For this reason, the implementation of *GetSizeMax* should return the maximum upper boundary of the object's storage requirements. |
| *InitNew* (*IPersistStreamInit*) | Initializes the object after creation, giving one object an opportunity to set its initial state. |

---

4. While *IPersistStreamInit* is not derived directly from *IPersistStream*, it has exactly the same member function signatures as the members of *IPersistStream*. Therefore, *IPersistStreamInit* is polymorphic with *IPersistStream*. A pointer to *IPersistStreamInit* can be used as a pointer to *IPersistStream*.

*IPersistStream* and *IPersistStreamInit* can both act as initialization interfaces. The *Load* function of either interface and the *InitNew* function of *IPersistStreamInit* are the specific initialization functions. *IPersistStreamInit* was specially created to provide a stream-based object with a way to know that it has been newly created and has no persistent data as yet, a requirement for certain OLE controls.

It is important to understand the locality of *Load* and *Save* calls. First, the object cannot hold a copy of the *IStream* pointer outside the scope of these functions, and second, the object is allowed to work only with the stream between the current seek offset on entry to the function and that offset plus whatever the object returns from *GetSizeMax*. In short, these rules mean that the calling client has ultimate control over which object's data is stored in what parts of the stream. As mentioned in Chapter 7, a stream in a compound file is allocated on a 512-byte granularity, so clients generally try to utilize all those bytes if they can. The locality of *Load* and *Save* enables clients to do this even with multiple stream-based objects, each of which may need only a few dozen bytes of the overall stream. These rules also work well with functions such as *ReadClassStm* and *WriteClassStm*, so a client can associate CLSIDs for each object's data, anywhere in the stream. In addition, the client can write its own CLSID at the beginning of the stream, identifying itself as the code that understands the layout of information in the rest of the stream.

OLE provides two API functions that wrap these various sequences. *OleSaveToStream* calls *WriteClassStm* followed by *IPersistStream::Save* on a given object. *OleLoadFromStream* will call *ReadClassStm* on a given stream, instantiate an object of that class with *CoCreateInstance*, then have that new object initialize itself through *IPersistStream::Load*. A client can use both these API functions to save and load sequential objects in a single stream.

## *IPersistFile*

Another simple persistence model for an object is for it to read and write its information from a separate file, be it a traditional file or a compound file. Components that support linking through a file moniker (as many do when supporting linked objects with OLE Documents) will implement this interface. Through it a client can ask a component to load or save a file that might contain other instances of object data of interest to that client. As we'll see in practice in Chapter 9, when we deal with file moniker binding, the *IPersistFile* interface describes load and save semantics for a separate file, illustrated in the following:

```
interface IPersistFile : IPersist
    {
    //IUnknown members and GetClassID from IPersist
    HRESULT IsDirty(void);
    HRESULT Load(LPCOLESTR pszFile, DWORD dwMode);
    HRESULT Save(LPCOLESTR pszFile, BOOL fRemember);
    HRESULT SaveCompleted(LPCOLESTR pszFile);
    HRESULT GetCurFile(LPCOLESTR *ppszFile);
    };
```

These functions behave as follows:

| Member Function | Description |
|---|---|
| *IsDirty* | Indicates whether the object considers itself dirty. If the object is dirty, the client should call *Save* before releasing the object, as with *IPersistStream[Init]*. |
| *Load* | Instructs the object to load its persistent data from the file with the given filename, using the given access flags. The object is allowed to keep this file open, and if the file is a compound file, the object can open and hold pointers to any storage and stream elements for incremental access. |
| *Save* | Instructs the object to save its persistent data in the file of the given name. If *pszFile* is NULL, this works like a File Save operation: the object saves data into the file opened in *Load*. Otherwise, the call is equivalent to Save As or Save Copy As, where the *fRemember* flag distinguishes the behavior: TRUE saves the file under a new name, which becomes the current file for the object; FALSE saves a copy but doesn't change the current file. For any operation other than the Save Copy As case, *Save* must clear the object's dirty flag (as returned from *IsDirty*) and release any open pointers or handles to the file. See also *SaveCompleted*. |
| *SaveCompleted* | Informs the object that the calling client has completed its overall save procedure and that the object can reopen files and storage or stream elements. The relationship of *Save* and *SaveCompleted* allows a client to manipulate the file itself between the two calls without having to worry about sharing violations that might arise because the object has kept the file open. If the *pszFile* argument is NULL, the object reopens its known file; if it is non-NULL, the object opens the named file as the current file. |

*(continued)*

*continued*

| Member Function | Description |
|---|---|
| *GetCurFile* | Returns a copy of the object's current absolute pathname, allocated with the task memory allocator (*CoTaskMemAlloc*). The caller becomes responsible for the memory. |

As mentioned earlier, *IPersistFile* can act as an initialization interface, with *Load* being the only member available for this purpose.

The relationship between *Save* and *SaveCompleted* deserves a little more clarification. After a persistent object is initialized through *IPersistFile::Load*, it is allowed to scribble into that file—that is, read and write incrementally as it sees fit. If the object wants to scribble, it can keep a file open and hold as many handles or pointers as it needs. When the object is told to save (in the current file or a new current file), it must write its current state and turn off this scribbling mode until *SaveCompleted* is called. Turning off scribbling means releasing any open handles or pointers that the object can reopen only during *SaveCompleted*. In this way, a client can avoid sharing violations or other access problems with that file, especially if the client needs to move that file or rename it. The *pszFile* argument to *SaveCompleted* is the way the client identifies the file that the object can reopen; a NULL means "current file," and a non-NULL name can identify the same file that has been moved to another location or a different file altogether.

Keep in mind that if the client calls *Save(pszFile, FALSE)*, it is simply making a new copy of the data in another file and will always call *SaveCompleted-(NULL)* afterward. In this case, the object need not close the original file.

## *IPersistStorage*: A Heavy Dose of Protocol

The persistence model of *IPersistFile* introduces a few of the complications that arise when an object is allowed incremental access to its persistent data—that is, allowed to scribble in its storage. The persistence model of *IPersistStorage* is even more complicated because it allows an object to read and write its information to a storage hierarchy that begins with an arbitrary storage element (*IStorage*) as well as to handle low-memory save situations. As with *IPersistFile*, a client of an object that implements *IPersistStorage* has to be able to tell that object when to release its pointers to open storage and stream elements so that the client can manipulate the storage, change an underlying file location, and so on.

So the *IPersistStorage* interface describes not only load and save semantics but also includes initialization semantics such as *IPersistStreamInit* and the operations necessary to determine when the object can scribble to its storage:

```
interface IPersistStorage : IPersist
    {
    HRESULT IsDirty(void);
    HRESULT InitNew(IStorage *pstg);
    HRESULT Load(IStorage *pstg);
    HRESULT Save(IStorage *pstg, BOOL fSameAsLoad);
    HRESULT SaveCompleted(IStorage *pstg);
    HRESULT HandsOffStorage(void);
    };
```

These functions behave as follows:

| Member Function | Description |
| --- | --- |
| *IsDirty* | Same semantics as in *IPersistStream[Init]* and *IPersistFile*. |
| *InitNew* | Instructs the object to fully initialize a new storage identified by *pstg*. The object should create and open every storage and stream element into which it would like to scribble, as well as any element that it will require in a low-memory save situation. It should also preallocate stream space (*IStream::SetSize*) that it will need in a save operation in case the storage medium is full. It may also hold a reference on *pstg* itself. |
| *Load* | Instructs the object to load its persistent data from the storage element identified by *pstg*. The object should hold open any element it may want (for scribbling) or require (for low-memory saves) as described for *InitNew*. *Load* is always called in lieu of *InitNew* to initialize the object. |
| *Save* | Instructs the object to save its persistent data in either its current storage or a different storage, depending on the *fSameAsLoad* flag (*pstg* will always be non-NULL). If *fSameAsLoad* is TRUE, the object can write changes incrementally; otherwise, the object must completely rewrite all of its data. In either case, the object continues to hold its present pointers to open elements, although it cannot scribble until *SaveCompleted* is called. The object clears its dirty flag on *Save*. |

*(continued)*

409

*continued*

| Member Function | Description |
|---|---|
| | *Save* is not allowed to fail as the result of an out-of-memory condition, which means that the object must open and hold pointers to any element it might need in order to complete a save during *InitNew* and *Load*. Creating and opening elements requires memory that might not be available. |
| | The object should never call *IStorage::Commit* on the *pstg* passed to this function nor write a CLSID with *WriteClassStg*; the client owns those operations. |
| *SaveCompleted* | Informs the object that the calling client has completed its overall save procedure. If *pstg* is NULL, the object can once again scribble to its open elements. If *pstg* is non-NULL, the object must release its pointers and reopen its elements underneath *pstg*. |
| *HandsOffStorage* | Instructs the object to release all of its pointers to any and all elements, including the pointer passed to *InitNew* or *Load*. This call can follow *Save* and precede *SaveCompleted* to allow the client to manipulate the storage without possibility of access violations (see the following discussion). |

As with *IPersistStreamInit*, both the *Load* and *InitNew* functions can initialize the object as well as its storage. *InitNew* is called only if the object as yet has no persistent storage; otherwise, *Load* is always called. The two will never be used on the same instance of an object. *InitNew* should, however, preallocate stream space with *IStream::SetSize*. It's silly to go to all the trouble to save pointers for a low-memory save just to run out of disk space at the same time![5]

The relationship between *Save*, *SaveCompleted*, and *HandsOffStorage* is a little more complex than with *IPersistFile*. These functions provide an object with incremental access to its storage (including access needed for low-memory saves) but allow the client to temporarily suspend that right in order to rename the storage element, save a file and reopen it, move a file, and so on. The nature of *IPersistStorage* allows an object to hold an *IStorage* pointer for its own use, which it may access incrementally throughout its lifetime. When that client wants to perform a complete save, or when that client wants

---

5. Do not depend on the stream having a 512-byte allocation granularity as with compound files because it is not necessarily true that the stream is part of a compound file. It could be implemented on global memory or a database field with a different granularity.

to save everything into a new file, it has to have some way of telling the persistent object to release whatever pointers it holds to open storage and stream elements.

To illustrate the process, let's assume that we have a client in control of a root storage, which in turn contains a substorage. The client instantiates some object to which it hands the *IStorage* pointer to that substorage, allowing the object to create whatever hierarchy it wants within that substorage. At this point the object is uninitialized. If the storage is brand-new, the client initializes the object (and its storage) through *IPersistFile::InitNew*; if the storage is opened within an existing file, initialization occurs with *IPersistStorage::Load*:

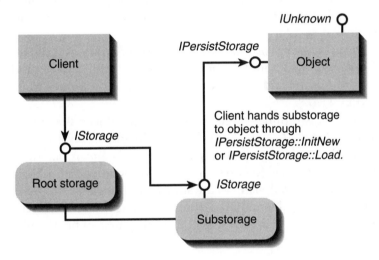

In either case, the client hands an *IStorage* pointer to the object, which is now in the scribble state, in which it can open and hold any pointers to any elements in the storage (it must call *AddRef* on the *pstg* passed to *Load* or *InitNew* to hold that pointer):

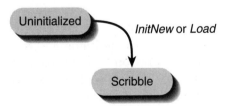

At some later time, the client tells the object to save its data through *IPersistStorage::Save*, to perform either a full save or an incremental save. In both cases, the object is passed the *IStorage* in which to save, using *fSameAsLoad* to distinguish the operations to perform. Again, *IPersistStorage::Save* is contractually obligated to save its data without failing as a result of out-of-memory conditions. This last statement has some heavy implications. It means that to fulfill this requirement, the object must not attempt to create new streams or substorages from within *Save* because creating them requires memory. Again, this means that in its implementation of both *Load* and *InitNew*, the object must not only hold onto the *IStorage* pointer, but it must also create and hold open any element it might need in a subsequent incremental save. This ensures that a user's data can be saved with zero available memory, which is all that matters in such conditions. Of course, if you are not interested in robustness of this kind, feel free to ignore the rules...and then train your product support teams in the fine art of soothing horribly irate customers! Best to follow the rules.

Again, after *InitNew* or *Load* is called, the object is in its scribble state, in which it reads and writes in the storage as necessary. In scribble mode, additional calls to *InitNew* and *Load* are illegal (client error) and should return E_UNEXPECTED.

Now one of two things might happen to the object: the client can call either *Save* or *HandsOffStorage*. As mentioned already, *Save* instructs the object to perform either an incremental or a full save. After *Save* is called, the object enters into a zombielike (or no-scribble) state. A zombified object cannot perform any incremental writes to the storage, although it can still read from the storage without problem. When the client wants to allow scribbling again, it calls *SaveCompleted*, freeing the object from the curse of being undead:

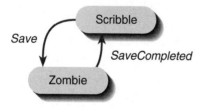

In some situations, a client requires the object to release any of its open storage or stream pointers, for example when the client is going to rename the underlying file or when it is reverting to a previously saved state. This is the purpose of *HandsOffStorage*, which tells the object to get its grubby little mitts off any elements within the storage. If this call occurs before *Save*, the object must shrug its shoulders, heave a heavy sigh, and blindly call *Release* on all its pointers. However, the client later makes the same bits available through *SaveCompleted*, which the object was looking at when *HandsOffStorage* was called. In other words, the object doesn't lose any data and doesn't have to reinitialize its internal state—it can just reopen its needed elements.

When the client calls *HandsOffStorage*, the object enters the *hands-off* state. In this state, it cannot read from *or* write to a storage—it has no pointers! When the client has finished partying on the storage, it must then call *SaveCompleted*, passing the *IStorage* pointer from which the object can reopen its elements. *SaveCompleted* means a return to the scribble state.

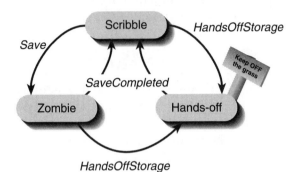

Obviously, the client must always pass an *IStorage* pointer to *SaveCompleted* when the object is in the hands-off state. The storage must always contain the object's expected hierarchy because the object will attempt to reopen its elements. Granted, the storage may or may not be the same as the one passed to *InitNew*, *Load*, or even *Save*. But the same data will be in whichever storage the object receives. Keep in mind as well that a sequence of calls to *HandsOffStorage* and *SaveCompleted* should clear the object's dirty flag.

We'll see all of this protocol reduced to code a little later in this chapter.

## Persistent Storage and Emulation

Chapter 5 described how one server could mark itself to emulate another CLSID using the *TreatAs* and *AutoTreatAs* registry keys. In that discussion, emulation was related only to a component's objects and interfaces—that is, its run-time functionality. But what if those objects implement *IPersistStorage*, *IPersistStream[Init]*, or *IPersistFile*? In that case, not only must the emulating object match the original's functionality, it must also emulate the original's storage. In other words, the emulating object must be able to read and write the same data formats as the original. This means that the object has knowledge about the original object's persistence model and data structures in order for it to read and write those structures.

When an emulating object overwrites the original object's storage, the object (the CLSID and the persistent data) is said to be permanently *converted* to the newer CLSID. This means that if emulation were removed, the original object could no longer work with the data in the storage. This process is currently limited to compound document objects and OLE controls that support *IPersistStorage*. The user interface elements and API functions that deal with conversion are found in OLE Documents. We'll see them in Chapters 17–19. The client and object must cooperate to make conversion work, and the only standards defined for that cooperation are part of OLE Documents.

# Objects with Multiple Persistence Models

Any object can, as it sees fit, implement multiple persistence models by implementing a combination of the four *IPersist\** interfaces. However, each of these interfaces is considered mutually exclusive in that a client will use only one of them, depending on the client's prioritization of each model.

Generally speaking, *IPersistStorage* is the most powerful of the four interfaces, so a client might ask for it first when attempting to save or reload an object. However, storage-based persistence is expensive, so a client might request *IPersistStreamInit* or *IPersistStream*, and then *IPersistStorage*. Or it can give *IPersistFile* preference over the others.

Regardless of the client's prioritization, it must use only one of the interfaces with any given instance of an object, although it is allowed to use a different interface with different instances. The object must enforce this rule by remembering which interface was used to initialize it. If *IPersistStorage::InitNew* or *IPersistStorage::Load* has been called, the object must fail any calls to *IPersistStream[Init]* and *IPersistFile*. If *IPersistStream[Init]::Load* or *IPersistStreamInit::InitNew* has been called, the object fails calls to *IPersistStorage* and *IPersistFile*, and so on.

Remember that an object implementing all of these interfaces can use them to implement each other regardless of what the client does. For example, an implementation of *IPersistFile* can open a compound file and pass the *IStorage* pointer to its own *IPersistStorage* implementation, which may in turn do little more than open streams and pass them to *IPersistStream*. In this way, objects can support as many persistence models as they like without having a lot of redundant code.

Furthermore, an object's implementations of *IPersistStorage* and *IPersistStream[Init]* are completely independent of how the client obtains *IStorage* and *IStream* pointers. The client might be passing pieces of a storage hierarchy created on an *ILockBytes*, or it might pass an *IStream* implemented on a piece of global memory or some other medium. The object cannot assume that the storage and stream elements refer to a portion of a compound file in which a stream is at least 512 bytes. A stream implemented on a database field may be only 10 bytes by default, so writing 500 bytes of information to it can potentially fail if there is no more memory or no more space in the storage medium. This is why *IPersistStorage::InitNew* should call *IStream::SetSize* after opening the stream. This is not necessary with *IPersistStream[Init]*, however, because the client is responsible for preallocating any streams based on what objects return from *IPersistStream::GetSizeMax*.

# Of Clients and Persistent Objects: CoCosmo

Our earlier discussion of *IPersistStorage* outlined some of a client's responsibilities when dealing with an object using this persistence model. To demonstrate this, we'll use the Component Cosmo sample for this chapter (CHAP08\COCOSMO) as the client and a modification of Polyline (CHAP-08\POLYLINE) as the object.

CoCosmo now uses compound files as its native file format, just as the Cosmo sample from Chapter 7 does. In order to save or load Polyline's data, CoCosmo queries Polyline for *IPersistStorage*. Failing that, it will query for *IPersistStreamInit* and then *IPersistStream*. Whichever interface it finds, CoCosmo follows the appropriate protocol, as the fragments of code shown in this section (taken from DOCUMENT.CPP) will illustrate.

To facilitate the handling of multiple persistence models, I've defined the following flags and data structure in the INC\INOLE.H file to hold one of the *IPersist\** pointers in a union:

```
typedef enum
    {
    PERSIST_UNKNOWN=0,
    PERSIST_STORAGE,
    PERSIST_STREAM,
    PERSIST_STREAMINIT,
    PERSIST_FILE
    } PERSIST_MODEL;

typedef struct
    {
    PERSIST_MODEL    psModel;
    union
```

*(continued)*

415

```
        {
        IPersistStorage    *pIPersistStorage;
        IPersistStream     *pIPersistStream;
        IPersistStreamInit *pIPersistStreamInit;
        IPersistFile       *pIPersistFile;
        } pIP;
    } PERSISTPOINTER;
```

This work is merely an implementation convenience for CoCosmo and later samples. CoCosmo includes a PERSISTPOINTER in its *CCosmoDoc* class named *m_pp*. This holds whatever pointer it obtained from the Polyline object along with the specific type of pointer it happens to be. The *m_pp* variable is set inside *CCosmoDoc::Init* through a series of *QueryInterface* calls:

```
BOOL CCosmoDoc::Init(...)
    {
    ⋮

    hr=CoCreateInstance(CLSID_Polyline8, NULL, CLSCTX_INPROC_SERVER
        , IID_IPolyline8, (PPVOID)&m_pPL);

    if (FAILED(hr))
        [Show error and return.]

    [Other initialization omitted]

    hr=m_pPL->QueryInterface(IID_IPersistStorage
        , (PPVOID)&m_pp.pIP.pIPersistStorage);

    if (SUCCEEDED(hr))
        m_pp.psModel=PERSIST_STORAGE;
    else
        {
        hr=m_pPL->QueryInterface(IID_IPersistStreamInit
            , (PPVOID)&m_pp.pIP.pIPersistStreamInit);

        if (SUCCEEDED(hr))
            m_pp.psModel=PERSIST_STREAMINIT;
        else
            {
            hr=m_pPL->QueryInterface(IID_IPersistStream
                , (PPVOID)&m_pp.pIP.pIPersistStream);

            if (SUCCEEDED(hr))
                m_pp.psModel=PERSIST_STREAM;
```

```
        else
            return FALSE;
        }
    }

    return TRUE;
    }
```

Whatever pointer we obtain here is released in *CCosmoDoc::~CCosmoDoc* along with the member *m_pIStorage*, which refers to the document's open compound file.

When loading an existing file or creating a new file in *CCosmoDoc::Load*, CoCosmo follows its responsibilities and passes an *IStorage* pointer to Polyline's *IPersistStorage::Load* or *IPersistStorage::InitNew*, or it passes an *IStream* pointer to *IPersistStream::Load* or calls *IPersistStreamInit::InitNew*. When CoCosmo has to call *IPersistStream::Load*, the code it uses to open the stream is exactly what would appear in an object's *IPersistStorage::Load* function, as we'll see later in our discussion of Polyline.

In all cases, CoCosmo holds onto the open *IStorage* pointer itself, regardless of what Polyline does with it. CoCosmo is the owner of that storage, but Polyline needs it in order to create any of its own streams or substorages. As the following code shows, CoCosmo saves the pointer after calling *StgCreateDocfile* (for a new file) or *StgOpenStorage* (for an existing file):

```
//From CCosmoDoc::Load

//For new files
hr=StgCreateDocfile(NULL, STGM_DIRECT | STGM_READWRITE
    | STGM_CREATE | STGM_DELETEONRELEASE
    | STGM_SHARE_EXCLUSIVE, 0, &pIStorage);

if (FAILED(hr))
    return DOCERR_COULDNOTOPEN;

if (PERSIST_STORAGE==m_pp.psModel)
    m_pp.pIP.pIPersistStorage->InitNew(pIStorage);
else
    {
    if (PERSIST_STREAMINIT==m_pp.psModel)
        m_pp.pIP.pIPersistStreamInit->InitNew();
    }

m_pIStorage=pIStorage;

⋮
```

*(continued)*

```
//For existing files
hr=StgOpenStorage(pszFile, NULL, STGM_DIRECT | STGM_READWRITE
    | STGM_SHARE_EXCLUSIVE, NULL, 0, &pIStorage);

if (FAILED(hr))
    return DOCERR_COULDNOTOPEN;

if (PERSIST_STORAGE==m_pp.psModel)
    hr=m_pp.pIP.pIPersistStorage->Load(pIStorage);
else
    {
    LPSTREAM    pIStream;

    hr=pIStorage->OpenStream(SZSTREAM, 0, STGM_DIRECT
        | STGM_READWRITE | STGM_SHARE_EXCLUSIVE, 0, &pIStream);

    if (SUCCEEDED(hr))
        {
        //This also works for PERSIST_STREAMINIT
        hr=m_pp.pIP.pIPersistStream->Load(pIStream);
        pIStream->Release();
        }

m_pIStorage=pIStorage;
```

Within *CCosmoDoc::Save*, CoCosmo calls *IPersistStorage::Save* or *IPersist-Stream[Init]::Save*, passing the appropriate pointer. Again, the extra step of opening a stream in which to save through *IPersistStream* is what the object would do inside *IPersistStorage* itself. The difference between the interfaces is mostly where that stream creation occurs. Anyway, in the case of *IPersist-Storage*, CoCosmo passes either the existing *IStorage* pointer obtained when loading the document (for File Save) or a new *IStorage* pointer from *StgCreate-Docfile* when writing a new file (File Save As). It sets *fSameAsLoad* to TRUE in the former case, FALSE in the latter. After calling *IPersistStorage::Save*, we have to complete the protocol by calling *IPersistStorage::SaveCompleted* with a NULL if *fSameAsLoad* was TRUE; otherwise, we have to pass the *IStorage* of the new file we saved so that Polyline can reinitialize its pointers:

```
//From CCosmoDoc::Save
LPSTORAGE           pIStorage;
BOOL                fSameAsLoad;

//If Save or Save As under the same name, do Save.
if (NULL==pszFile || 0==lstrcmpi(pszFile, m_szFile))
    {
    fRename=FALSE;
```

```
    pszFile=m_szFile;
    fSameAsLoad=TRUE;
    }
else
    {
    hr=StgCreateDocfile(pszFile, STGM_DIRECT | STGM_READWRITE
        | STGM_CREATE | STGM_SHARE_EXCLUSIVE, 0, &pIStorage);

    if (FAILED(hr))
        return DOCERR_COULDNOTOPEN;

    fSameAsLoad=FALSE;
    m_pIStorage->Release();
    m_pIStorage=pIStorage;
    }

if (PERSIST_STORAGE==m_pp.psModel)
    {
    hr=m_pp.pIP.pIPersistStorage->Save(m_pIStorage, fSameAsLoad);

    if (SUCCEEDED(hr))
        {
        hr=m_pp.pIP.pIPersistStorage->SaveCompleted(fSameAsLoad
            ? NULL : m_pIStorage);
        }
    }
else
    {
    LPSTREAM    pIStream;

    hr=m_pIStorage->CreateStream(SZSTREAM, STGM_DIRECT
        | STGM_CREATE | STGM_WRITE | STGM_SHARE_EXCLUSIVE
        , 0, 0, &pIStream);

    if (SUCCEEDED(hr))
        {
        //This also works for PERSIST_STREAMINIT.
        hr=m_pp.pIP.pIPersistStream->Save(pIStream, TRUE);
        pIStream->Release();
        }
    }
```

Through this little bit of code, CoCosmo can handle an object with any persistence model except *IPersistFile*. To demonstrate this ability, we'll look at two implementations of Polyline: one with *IPersistStorage* and the other with *IPersistStreamInit*. But first, as a close to this section, note that CoCosmo never has occasion to place Polyline in the hands-off state, so it never calls *IPersistStorage::HandsOffStorage*. In addition, when saving a stream-based object, CoCosmo could fail to create the stream because of an out-of-memory condition. To be more robust, it would create and cache the stream when it found a stream-based object, just as a storage-based object would cache a pointer inside its *InitNew* or *Load*.

# Of Persistent Objects: Polyline

In Chapter 5's version of Polyline, the *IPolyline5* interface had two member functions, *ReadFromFile* and *WriteToFile*. Because CoCosmo now uses compound files, these *IPolyline5* members are no longer useful. (This sample doesn't retain backward compatibility with the traditional file–based version of Chapter 5.) In their place, Polyline uses implementations of both the *IPersistStorage* and *IPersistStreamInit* interfaces.[6] This code is found in CHAP-08\POLYLINE. To support and manage the additional interfaces, Polyline requires a few minor modifications to its *QueryInterface* and its initialization and cleanup code. The primary changes are the interface implementations themselves, in IPERSTOR.CPP and IPERSTMI.CPP. Note also that Polyline now uses *IPolyline8* and *IPolylineAdviseSink8* (instead of the Chapter 5 versions), which are defined in INC\IPOLY8.H.

Now, according to CoCosmo's initialization code, which we saw in the last section, CoCosmo will ask Polyline for *IPersistStorage* first and then use that interface exclusively if it's found. Because Polyline implements that interface and *IPersistStreamInit* (thus *IPersistStream* also), CoCosmo will never touch the stream-based implementation if you run the code as is. To test the stream interaction, either modify CoCosmo to not ask for *IPersistStorage* or modify Polyline to not respond to *IID_IPersistStorage* in its *QueryInterface*. Either change will cause CoCosmo to use *IPersistStreamInit*. You can make another modification to turn off this interface and have CoCosmo use *IPersistStream*. To avoid recompilation, run CoCosmo in a debugger and skip over the *QueryInterface* calls in *CCosmoDoc::Init* for the interfaces you want to omit.

The *IPersistStream* implementation is simple, as you can see in Listing 8-1. The *GetClassID* member returns a CLSID, *IsDirty* returns the right

---

6. *IPersistFile* was not used for two reasons. First, CoCosmo manages the document and has an *IStorage* pointer for it (or an *IStream*), and we want Polyline's data to be part of that document, not in a separa te file. Second, Polyline is a good code base for a compound document content object (as we'll make it in Chapter 18) as well as an OLE control (Chapter 24). Implementing these interfaces now saves us work later.

HRESULT depending on Polyline's dirty flag, *GetSizeMax* returns the size of Polyline's data structure, and *InitNew* doesn't do anything at all. (Polyline has no other state to initialize.) The bulk of the work happens in *Load* and *Save*, which do little more than call *IStream::Read* and *IStream::Write*.

```
IPERSTMI.CPP
/*
 * IPERSTMI.CPP
 * Polyline Component Chapter 8
 *
 * Copyright (c)1993-1995 Microsoft Corporation, All Rights Reserved
 */

#include "polyline.h"

[Constructor, Destructor, IUnknown members omitted]

STDMETHODIMP CImpIPersistStreamInit::GetClassID(LPCLSID pClsID)
    {
    *pClsID=m_pObj->m_clsID;
    return NOERROR;
    }



STDMETHODIMP CImpIPersistStreamInit::IsDirty(void)
    {
    return ResultFromScode(m_pObj->m_fDirty ? S_OK : S_FALSE);
    }



STDMETHODIMP CImpIPersistStreamInit::Load(LPSTREAM pIStream)
    {
    POLYLINEDATA    pl;
    ULONG           cb;
    HRESULT         hr;

    if (NULL==pIStream)
        return ResultFromScode(E_POINTER);

    //Read all data into the POLYLINEDATA structure.
    hr=pIStream->Read(&pl, CBPOLYLINEDATA, &cb);
```

**Listing 8-1.**                                                          *(continued)*
*The* IPersistStreamInit *interface implementation for the Polyline object.*

**Listing 8-1.** *continued*

```
    if (FAILED(hr) !! CBPOLYLINEDATA!=cb)
        {
        pIStream->Release();
        return hr;
        }

    m_pObj->m_pImpIPolyline->DataSet(&pl, TRUE, TRUE);
    return NOERROR;
    }

STDMETHODIMP CImpIPersistStreamInit::Save(LPSTREAM pIStream
    , BOOL fClearDirty)
    {
    POLYLINEDATA    pl;
    ULONG           cb;
    HRESULT         hr;

    if (NULL==pIStream)
        return ResultFromScode(E_POINTER);

    m_pObj->m_pImpIPolyline->DataGet(&pl);

    hr=pIStream->Write(&pl, CBPOLYLINEDATA, &cb);
    pIStream->Release();

    if (FAILED(hr) !! CBPOLYLINEDATA!=cb)
        return ResultFromScode(STG_E_WRITEFAULT);

    m_pObj->m_fDirty=fClearDirty;
    return NOERROR;
    }

STDMETHODIMP CImpIPersistStreamInit::GetSizeMax(ULARGE_INTEGER
    *pcbSize)
    {
    if (NULL==pcbSize)
        return ResultFromScode(E_POINTER);

    ULISet32(*pcbSize, CBPOLYLINEDATA);
    return NOERROR;
    }

STDMETHODIMP CImpIPersistStreamInit::InitNew(void)
    {
    return NOERROR;
    }
```

You can see why *IPersistStream[Init]* is the simplest persistence model. The implementation of *IPersistStorage*, which is shown in Listing 8-2, is more complicated. This code is a basic framework for any *IPersistStorage* implementation, in which values starting with "PSSTATE" identify the various object states such as scribble and zombie. The values are defined as follows in an enumerator in the common header file INC\INOLE.H because many other samples in the rest of this book will include similar implementations of *IPersistStorage*:

```
typedef enum
    {
    PSSTATE_UNINIT,      //Uninitialized
    PSSTATE_SCRIBBLE,    //Scribble
    PSSTATE_ZOMBIE,      //No-scribble
    PSSTATE_HANDSOFF     //Hands-off
    } PSSTATE;
```

Overall, the *IPersistStorage* implementation in Polyline demonstrates the correct changes in the object's storage state when it shifts among all the states. The only differences between this code and code for a more complex storage scheme are in the number of open elements managed by the object and in the complexity of the data stored in those elements. Thus, this implementation works as a solid framework for your own development needs.

**IPERSTOR.CPP**

```
/*
 * IPERSTOR.CPP
 * Polyline Component Chapter 8
 *
 * Copyright (c)1993-1995 Microsoft Corporation, All Rights Reserved
 */

#include "polyline.h"

CImpIPersistStorage::CImpIPersistStorage(PCPolyline pObj
    , LPUNKNOWN pUnkOuter)
    {
    [Other initialization omitted]
    m_psState=PSSTATE_UNINIT;
    return;
    }
```

**Listing 8-2.** *(continued)*

*The* IPersistStorage *interface implementation for the Polyline object.*

**Listing 8-2.** *continued*

```
    [Destructor and IUnknown members omitted]

STDMETHODIMP CImpIPersistStorage::GetClassID(LPCLSID pClsID)
    {
    if (PSSTATE_UNINIT==m_psState)
        return ResultFromScode(E_UNEXPECTED);

    *pClsID=m_pObj->m_clsID;
    return NOERROR;
    }


STDMETHODIMP CImpIPersistStorage::IsDirty(void)
    {
    if (PSSTATE_UNINIT==m_psState)
        return ResultFromScode(E_UNEXPECTED);

    return ResultFromScode(m_pObj->m_fDirty ? S_OK : S_FALSE);
    }


STDMETHODIMP CImpIPersistStorage::InitNew(LPSTORAGE pIStorage)
    {
    HRESULT           hr;
    ULARGE_INTEGER  uli;

    if (PSSTATE_UNINIT!=m_psState)
        return ResultFromScode(E_UNEXPECTED);

    if (NULL==pIStorage)
        return ResultFromScode(E_POINTER);

    hr=pIStorage->CreateStream(SZSTREAM, STGM_DIRECT
        | STGM_CREATE | STGM_READWRITE | STGM_SHARE_EXCLUSIVE
        , 0, 0, &m_pObj->m_pIStream);

    if (FAILED(hr))
        return hr;

    //Preallocate stream space.
    ULISet32(uli, CBPOLYLINEDATA);
    m_pObj->m_pIStream->SetSize(uli);
```

*(continued)*

**Listing 8-2.** *continued*

```
    //We expect that client has called WriteClassStg.
    WriteFmtUserTypeStg(pIStorage, m_pObj->m_cf
        , (*m_pObj->m_pST)[IDS_USERTYPE]);

    m_pObj->m_pIStorage=pIStorage;
    pIStorage->AddRef();

    m_psState=PSSTATE_SCRIBBLE;
    return NOERROR;
    }


STDMETHODIMP CImpIPersistStorage::Load(LPSTORAGE pIStorage)
    {
    POLYLINEDATA    pl;
    ULONG           cb;
    LPSTREAM        pIStream;
    HRESULT         hr;

    if (PSSTATE_UNINIT!=m_psState)
        return ResultFromScode(E_UNEXPECTED);

    if (NULL==pIStorage)
        return ResultFromScode(E_POINTER);

    //We don't check CLSID to remain compatible with other chapters.

    hr=pIStorage->OpenStream(SZSTREAM, 0, STGM_DIRECT
        | STGM_READWRITE | STGM_SHARE_EXCLUSIVE, 0, &pIStream);

    if (FAILED(hr))
        return ResultFromScode(STG_E_READFAULT);

    //Read all data into the POLYLINEDATA structure.
    hr=pIStream->Read(&pl, CBPOLYLINEDATA, &cb);

    if (FAILED(hr) || CBPOLYLINEDATA!=cb)
        {
        pIStream->Release();
        return hr;
        }
```

*(continued)*

**Listing 8-2.** *continued*

```
    m_pObj->m_pIStream=pIStream;
    m_pObj->m_pIStorage=pIStorage;
    pIStorage->AddRef();

    m_pObj->m_pImpIPolyline->DataSet(&pl, TRUE, TRUE);
    m_psState=PSSTATE_SCRIBBLE;
    return NOERROR;
    }


STDMETHODIMP CImpIPersistStorage::Save(LPSTORAGE pIStorage
    , BOOL fSameAsLoad)
    {
    POLYLINEDATA    pl;
    ULONG           cb;
    LPSTREAM        pIStream;
    HRESULT         hr;

    //Have to come here from scribble state.
    if (PSSTATE_SCRIBBLE!=m_psState)
        return ResultFromScode(E_UNEXPECTED);

    //Must have an IStorage if we're not in SameAsLoad.
    if (NULL==pIStorage && !fSameAsLoad)
        return ResultFromScode(E_POINTER);

    if (fSameAsLoad)
        {
        LARGE_INTEGER   li;

        pIStream=m_pObj->m_pIStream;
        LISet32(li, 0);
        pIStream->Seek(li, STREAM_SEEK_SET, NULL);

        //This matches the Release below.
        pIStream->AddRef();
        }
    else
        {
        hr=pIStorage->CreateStream(SZSTREAM, STGM_DIRECT
            ¦ STGM_CREATE ¦ STGM_WRITE ¦ STGM_SHARE_EXCLUSIVE
            , 0, 0, &pIStream);

        if (FAILED(hr))
            return hr;
```

*(continued)*

**Listing 8-2.** *continued*

```
        //Do this only with new storages.
        WriteFmtUserTypeStg(pIStorage, m_pObj->m_cf
            , (*m_pObj->m_pST)[IDS_USERTYPE]);
        }

    //DataGet does not make allocations; it's just a memory copy.
    m_pObj->m_pImpIPolyline->DataGet(&pl);

    hr=pIStream->Write(&pl, CBPOLYLINEDATA, &cb);
    pIStream->Release();

    if (FAILED(hr) || CBPOLYLINEDATA!=cb)
        return ResultFromScode(STG_E_WRITEFAULT);

    m_psState=PSSTATE_ZOMBIE;
    return NOERROR;
    }


STDMETHODIMP CImpIPersistStorage::SaveCompleted(LPSTORAGE
    pIStorage)
    {
    HRESULT     hr;
    LPSTREAM    pIStream;

    //Must be called in no-scribble or hands-off state.
    if (!(PSSTATE_ZOMBIE==m_psState
        || PSSTATE_HANDSOFF==m_psState))
        return ResultFromScode(E_UNEXPECTED);

    //If we're in hands-off state, we'd better get storage.
    if (NULL==pIStorage && PSSTATE_HANDSOFF==m_psState)
        return ResultFromScode(E_UNEXPECTED);

    if (NULL!=pIStorage)
        {
        hr=pIStorage->OpenStream(SZSTREAM, 0, STGM_DIRECT
            | STGM_READWRITE | STGM_SHARE_EXCLUSIVE, 0
            , &pIStream);

        if (FAILED(hr))
            return hr;
```

*(continued)*

**Listing 8-2.** *continued*

```
            if (NULL!=m_pObj->m_pIStream)
                m_pObj->m_pIStream->Release();

            m_pObj->m_pIStream=pIStream;

            if (NULL!=m_pObj->m_pIStorage)
                m_pObj->m_pIStorage->Release();

            m_pObj->m_pIStorage=pIStorage;
            m_pObj->m_pIStorage->AddRef();
            }

        m_psState=PSSTATE_SCRIBBLE;
        return NOERROR;
        }


STDMETHODIMP CImpIPersistStorage::HandsOffStorage(void)
    {
    /*
     * Must be in scribble or no-scribble state. A repeated call
     * to HandsOffStorage is an unexpected error (bug in client).
     */
    if (PSSTATE_UNINIT==m_psState || PSSTATE_HANDSOFF==m_psState)
        return ResultFromScode(E_UNEXPECTED);

    //Release held pointers.
    if (NULL!=m_pObj->m_pIStream)
        ReleaseInterface(m_pObj->m_pIStream);

    if (NULL!=m_pObj->m_pIStorage)
        ReleaseInterface(m_pObj->m_pIStorage);

    m_psState=PSSTATE_HANDSOFF;
    return NOERROR;
    }
```

You can see that most of the implementation is fairly simple. *GetClassID* and *IsDirty* are trivial, and *InitNew*, *SaveCompleted*, and *HandsOffStorage* need only to manage *IStorage* and *IStream* pointers for use in *Save*. These three functions demonstrate how you should maintain these pointers so that you do not need to create any new objects in *Save* under a low-memory scenario. *InitNew* and *Load* also demonstrate preallocation of the object's needed stream space to avoid problems with a full storage medium later on.

Polyline's *IPersistStorage::Load* function simply opens the "CONTENTS" *stream* (the symbol SZSTREAM is defined as this string), reads the data, makes the data current, and holds on to the *IStream* pointer for *Save*. Because *IStorage::OpenStream* returns an *IStream* pointer with a reference count, we do not need an extra call to *AddRef* when we store that pointer in *m_pIStream*.

The implementation of *IPersistStorage::Save* is the interesting part. If *fSameAsLoad* is TRUE, we're writing into the storage we received during *InitNew* or *Load*, so we already have the *IStream* pointer in which to write our current data. If you look carefully at the implementation of *Save* in Listing 8-2, you will notice that it allocates no memory (and creates no new objects), fulfilling the requirement that *Save* will not fail because of an out-of-memory condition. When *fSameAsLoad* is FALSE, however, we have to write data into the *IStorage* passed to *Save*, so we have to create new streams. Again, the object is allowed to fail in this case if no memory is left. If the new storage object that we're writing into is to become the current one, we'll see it again in *SaveCompleted*.

Inside *SaveCompleted*, you can see that what we do depends on whether *pIStorage* is NULL or not. If it is NULL, we can just switch back to the scribble state, using all the same pointers we currently hold. Otherwise, we have to release those pointers and replace them with ones we open in the new storage, making this new storage current. Also, the implementation of *HandsOff-Storage* does what it must, of course, by releasing the *IStorage* and *IStream* pointers to our open elements.

Finally, the storage created through these implementations of Co-Cosmo and Polyline is identical to those generated by Chapter 7's Cosmo, with the exception of the exact CLSID and format tags. A file from either sample can be opened in the other.

## Summary

A *persistent object* is one that supports a model through which a client can ask the object to save and load the object's state data to some storage medium. Each model is described by an interface whose name begins with *IPersist*, for example, *IPersistStorage* (the medium is a storage element plus any streams or storages within the element), *IPersistStream[Init]* (the medium is a single stream), and *IPersistFile* (the medium is a separate file altogether). Specifically, *IPersistStorage* and *IPersistStream[Init]* provide the basic means through which multiple components can share a compound file.

Of these models. stream-based persistence is the simplest to use, followed by file-based persistence. Storage-based persistence offers an object the ability to keep storage and stream elements open for incremental access while other components might have different elements in the same compound file open as well. The way *IPersistStorage* and *IPersistStreamInit* work is demonstrated through the Polyline component and its interactions with Component Cosmo. Your understanding of this will be useful in many other areas of OLE, including the use of monikers, OLE Documents, and OLE Controls.

**C H A P T E R   N I N E**

# Naming and Binding: Monikers

*"Why do they call it a Ferris wheel?"*

*This question was put to me by my twelve-year-old as we swayed high above the cotton candy stands at a recent summer carnival. I gave it two seconds' thought. "It was invented by a guy named Ferris."*

*"Amazing, Dad. What was his first name? Did he work in a carnival? When did he—"*

*"Eat your cotton candy," I advised. "When we get home you can look it up."*

*"You always say that," he grumbled. I had been pitching him this Stengelism lately—Casey [Stengel] was fond of capping his baseball stories with the tag line "You could look it up"—and he had begun to resent it. What he didn't know was that, in this particular case, I had no choice. For all I knew, Ferris was an acronym or somebody's pet piranha.*

—Tad Tuleja, Marvelous Monikers[1]

Not long ago I was listening to a radio interview with a scientist who was asked about the most important elements in human evolution. One of the elements the scientist listed was symbolic thinking—the ability to create symbols that represent things much more complex. Symbols allow us to encapsulate a tremendous amount of meaning and intelligence in a single entity. A person raised around county fairs, for example, understands a Ferris wheel not only as a specific object but also as a term that represents a host of feelings and images associated with amusement parks, childhood, cotton candy, farm animals, and the dime toss. Symbols sometimes also become rallying points for political action, even though very few of the people involved really understand the meaning of the symbol. Witness the Information Superhighway or, for that matter, OLE. (This book is supposed to clear up misconceptions about the latter.)

Symbols are thus very powerful abstractions that encapsulate potentially very large amounts of meaning. Because languages are built with tens of thousands of symbols, they form the basis for our ability to communicate

---

1. Harmony Books, 1990.

(and miscommunicate) as richly as we do. Without symbols, you could not be reading this book, right? If you think about it, a symbol in a human language is a great example of an *object* in terms of object-oriented programming. It encapsulates both information (meaning) and functionality (intelligence or knowledge of a process). Words are obviously reusable, and they are polymorphic: grammatically similar symbols can be interchanged with one another to radically alter the meaning of a phrase or sentence without changing the grammatical structure at all.

An object that can act like a symbol is a powerful abstraction to introduce into a computing environment—so powerful, in fact, that fully exploring the philosophical nature of such symbols is beyond the scope of this book. What we can explore, however, is the nature and utility of a *naming* architecture built on such interchangeable and polymorphic symbols, an architecture in which we can assign some rich symbolic unit to name an object, a set of objects, or a process involving objects.

These symbolic names for things are of practical use only when you can resolve the name into the actual thing it names. The process of resolution— which is the same as the process implied in the name itself—is called *binding*. If the name refers to an object, binding results in an interface pointer to that object. If the name refers to a process, binding carries out that process, and the result is also some interface pointer to some object. In this latter case, however, the object isn't as important as the process used to create or access it.

So the ability to create and manage names for things and the ability to resolve those names into interface pointers on the objects they refer to is what OLE's naming and binding architecture is all about. This is sometimes referred to as *linking*, as it is in OLE Documents. A linked compound document object is really a type of proxy that manages the name of some real object. It is important to understand the term *link* in a generic capacity: any client that holds any sort of symbolic reference to or name of something else is said to have a link to that something else. A link is just another synonym for a name.

In the same way that Local/Remote Transparency has a number of distinct architectural objects, OLE's naming and binding architecture also has a number of such objects. From the perspective of a client that uses a name to access an object, only the name itself is important. The name, which is an object, encapsulates all the necessary binding knowledge behind an interface and has to be able to store arbitrary information (perhaps persistently) and run arbitrary code when asked to bind to its named object. When such a name is finished binding, it falls out of the picture entirely, just as such portions of COM as the Service Control Manager fall out of the picture after locating a new object created in response to a client's request.

OLE calls such a name a *moniker,*[2] which is any OLE or COM object that implements at least the interface *IMoniker.* Because *IMoniker* itself is derived from *IPersistStream,* a moniker also knows how to read and write its persistent state to a stream object. This persistent state is the information that the moniker needs in order to intelligently bind to the object or process that it names — monikers are also called *persistent, intelligent names* for this reason. In addition, monikers can provide a *display name* that is suitable to show in a user interface, such as in a list of links shown in a list box. Monikers also support parsing a display name into internal moniker state data, enabling an application to create a moniker from some text a user types into a dialog box.

Although the exact state data and binding process differ between different types of monikers, the way a client tells a moniker to bind is always the same: it uses *IMoniker::BindToObject,* a function that does whatever is necessary to access the object named by the moniker and return some interface pointer to the client. This member function, along with the closely related *IMoniker::BindToStorage* (which accesses the object's storage), represents the core of OLE's naming and binding architecture. All the other members of *IMoniker,* as well as the other architectural objects and their interfaces, are really the details of making the entire binding process work.

In examining naming and binding architecture in this chapter, we'll see the various objects and interfaces involved, such as the *bind context* object and its *IBindCtx* interface, the *running object table* (*IRunningObjectTable*), and *composite monikers.* In addition, we'll look at four specific types of monikers that OLE provides as well as how to create your own custom moniker when the need arises. In all of this, we'll see how monikers are just about as powerful as cultural symbols themselves. And just as symbols play an important role in human evolution, you can expect that in time monikers will be important in the evolution of computing.

The Ferris wheel, by the way, was created by a civil engineer named George Washington Gale Ferris for the 1893 World's Colombian Exposition in Chicago. It was created as a show of American ingenuity to rival the Eiffel Tower, which was built for the same exposition in Paris four years earlier by another engineer, Alexandre Gustave Eiffel. The original $385,000 wheel was several hundred feet in diameter and carried over 2000 passengers at a time in 36 cars. After the craze settled down, it was sold in 1898 as scrap iron for a mere $2,000.

---

2. Something of a symbol itself, which people in the United Kingdom understand but most Americans do not. Moniker generally means *nickname.*

# Why Monikers? The Need for an Architecture

Think for a moment about a standard, mundane filename. That filename refers to a collection of data that happens to be stored somewhere on disk. We can call the file's contents an object—the contents are information, and there's probably some code lying around that knows how to provide some functionality for that information. An object such as this would allow clients to manipulate its contents through interface pointers.

Now, the filename itself is not the object but is merely a reference to where the object exists in a passive state. The intelligence about how to use that name is concerned with bringing the object—the file—from its passive state to its running state. But a filename by itself is unintelligent; all the knowledge about how to run the object and how to manage that filename persistently must be coded into the client that intends to use the file object. Usually this isn't much of a problem because applications have been working with file objects for a long time.

In a component software environment, however, there are many more types of objects than those whose data exists in a file. There are objects that passively reside in databases, in e-mail messages, and in specific locations inside other files as well. Other objects represent some running process and don't have a passive state at all. Nevertheless, clients need to maintain symbolic links—that is, clients need persistent names that they can bind in order to run objects and retrieve interface pointers for them. Clients also need names to describe specific parts of a file (or parts of parts of files), database queries, remote computations, administrative operations, and so on. Literally any data set and any process or function in a computing environment can be given a name, and a naming and binding architecture allows clients to exploit those resources in efficient and powerful ways.

This is why unintelligent names are such a problem and are, in fact, antithetical to component software. The addition of a new type of name into the environment requires revisions to all the clients that want to make use of that new type of name. In other words, each client has to contain specific code in order to work with any particular type of name for particular resources. If they don't know how to use the name, the resource is unavailable to them. This is completely impractical in a component software system, in which we have the ability to change, modify, update, and redeploy software components independently of any other component and in which *QueryInterface* allows us to add new interfaces and new features without losing compatibility with existing clients.

## So, Monikers

In light of this problem, it makes sense that new names are themselves components that play by the same rules as all other components. Instead of these names being mere repositories for persistent data (the name data), they must also encapsulate the intelligence to work with that name behind a standard interface. Thus, all clients only need to include code to work with the standard name interface, not with each particular type of name. The solution is a persistent, intelligent name—a moniker.

A moniker encapsulates all of its capabilities behind the *IMoniker* interface, which includes both binding methods and persistence methods (from *IPersistStream*). Clients only need to know how to use the *IMoniker* member functions, and because all objects that implement the same interface are polymorphic, all monikers are polymorphic as well. Clients that know how to use one moniker know how to use all monikers.

Let this sink in for just a moment. Yes, I mean lift your eyes from this page and stare at the wall while you think about what this encapsulation means. You're still reading, aren't you? I'll stop writing for a minute.

Again, the problem with unintelligent names is that adding a new type of unintelligent name into a system means that only those clients updated to understand that new name can take advantage of it. With monikers, however, clients that know how to work with existing monikers can immediately and transparently work with any new moniker—with any new intelligent name—that is added to the system. A new name requires absolutely no changes whatsoever to existing clients. In short, OLE's naming and binding is extensible in all directions, requiring no changes to clients nor of the programming model.

## An Example

Imagine that we have a client that wants to maintain a list of links to objects and that the code and data for those objects are located outside the client's own code and storage so that the client maintains only a link or a name in its own storage while the real data exists elsewhere. When an end user gives a command such as View Description, this client would like to:

- Obtain an interface pointer to the object identified by a selected name—that is, bind the moniker.

- Retrieve a piece of user-readable text from the object that describes the object and its purpose.

- Display that text to the user in a little pop-up window. Each object implements a hypothetical interface, *IDescription*, with a single member function, *GetText*, for this purpose.

Let's say the client has in its list a *file* moniker that manages a simple filename such as C:\DATA\BOOKS\CHALICE.DOC. When the user selects View Description, the client calls *IMoniker::BindToObject*. The moniker, understanding that it has a filename, calls *GetClassFile* (as we saw in Chapter 7) to find the CLSID of the code related to this file type. The moniker then calls *CoCreateInstance*[3] with that CLSID, requesting *IPersistFile*, and then passes its filename to *IPersistFile::Load*, bringing the file into memory. After this, the moniker calls *IPersistFile::QueryInterface(IID_ IDescription)*, returning that *IDescription* pointer as an out-parameter from *IMoniker::BindToObject*. The client then calls *IDescription::GetText*, which returns a string such as "Notes from January 1995 reading of *The Chalice and the Blade,* by Riane Eisler," which is the sort of thing I might have typed into a Summary Information comments field.

In all of what went on, the client made only two calls in order to retrieve the descriptive text: *IMoniker::BindToObject* to get the named object's *IDescription* pointer and *IDescription::GetText* to get the text. Nowhere did the client know that the moniker actually referred to a file-based object that contained a document. Nowhere does the client actually do any work itself to resolve the name into an interface pointer. All of that is done inside the moniker itself— that's where the intelligence lies. (Keep in mind that the file object probably has more interfaces than the ones this client happens to use. The same moniker could be used by some other client that wanted to do something different with the same object!)

Now let's say the user selects View Description for another name in the client's list. This time it's a hypothetical network connection moniker that contains the name *http://www.gardens.com/bunnykins.carrotpatch!eatweeds*, where the ! delimiter separates the name of the World Wide Web page from the password needed to access that page. The client, of course, doesn't know this. It simply executes the same code as before, calling *IMoniker::BindToObject* to get *IDescription* and then calling *IDescription::GetText*. This moniker, however, does something completely different from the file moniker we saw before, calling *CoCreateInstance* with a hypothetical *CLSID_WWWBrowser*, asking for a hypothetical *IWWWPage* interface pointer in return. The object here represents the connection itself so that when released it will disconnect from that page. On return from *CoCreateInstance*, the moniker passes the share name and password to something like *IWWWPage::SetConnection*, which might store that information but not actually make the connection (until something like *IWWWPage::Connect* is called).

---

3. *Moniker::BindToObject* calls *CoCreateInstance* with CLSCTX_ALL, meaning that all server types are allowable for moniker binding.

The moniker then queries the connection object for *IDescription* and returns to the client. When that client calls *IDescription::GetText*, the connection object calls functions in the Win32 WinSockets API to connect to the World Wide Web page. The object then grabs the first 512 characters found on the Web page and returns that text to the client as the descriptive text. This might contain something like "Bunnykin's private garden of goodies—raptors not welcome."

It is important to see that in these examples the client, using exactly the same code, retrieved the descriptive text for radically different objects without any specific knowledge of those objects. All that knowledge is hidden in the moniker, encapsulated behind the *IMoniker* interface. The monikers themselves are not the objects of interest but merely symbols that wrap all the meaning and knowledge of those objects in interchangeable units. As such, monikers are extraordinarily powerful, capable of doing far more than you might think when you first work with them.

## Naming and Binding Architecture

In a nutshell, OLE's naming technology can be described as a client having an *IMoniker* pointer to some moniker where calling *IMoniker::BindToObject* does whatever is necessary to access the named object and returns one of that object's interface pointers to the client, as illustrated in Figure 9-1.

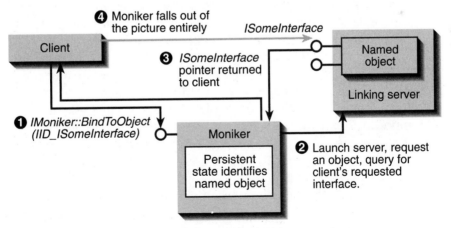

**Figure 9-1.**
*A client asks a moniker to bind to the object named by the moniker.*

From the client's perspective, this process is as simple as calling an interface member function for a local or remote object is. To make the process even simpler, OLE offers a wrapper function named *BindMoniker* with the following signature:

```
HRESULT BindMoniker(IMoniker *pmk, DWORD grfOpt, REFIID riid, void **ppv);
```

where *pmk* is the moniker (name) to bind, *grfOpt* is reserved and must be 0, and *riid* and *ppv* specify the interface pointer that the client wants for the object named by this moniker. Thus the entire idea of naming and binding is wrapped up inside this single API function, which represents the extent to which a simple client has to concern itself with monikers.

Well, if it were that simple we wouldn't need a whole chapter on the subject, would we? As you probably expect, there is actually much more to this picture than meets the eye because a binding operation can take a significant amount of time to execute and can involve any number of intermediate objects and their servers—binding can load any number of DLLs, launch any number of EXEs, load any number of files or objects, and so on.

Therefore, we must first know how a client obtains a moniker in the first place, which happens through any of the four techniques that we saw in Chapter 2: call a specific API function, call a generic API function, call an interface member function in some other object, or receive the pointer through your own object's interface. Which technique applies depends on the type of moniker or the origin of that moniker. In some cases, a client can create a new moniker itself. In other cases, some other source or server of links will create the name and make it available to the client through a data transfer mechanism such as the clipboard or drag and drop.

The most important type of name is called a *composite moniker,* which is little more than a collection of other monikers (including other composites). A composite moniker allows creation (or *composition*) of arbitrarily complex names, and its *IPersistStream* implementation simply asks each contained moniker to save or load in turn. An example of a very complex name is one for a specific paragraph in a specific section of a specific document in a specific database on a specific network server in a specific network domain on a specific network system.

Creating the name is only half of naming and binding: we also need to see what it means to bind a moniker. Our discussion will be specifically oriented to binding a composite because any other moniker is really just a degenerate form of a composite. Binding a composite means binding all of its contained monikers in a particular sequence to avoid as much extra work as possible. Once we have examined this binding, we'll have a good overall picture of what naming and binding are all about.

OLE also goes beyond the basic architecture and provides a few mechanisms to optimize the binding process. The first optimization is to track objects that are already in a running state through what is called the running object table. If an object is already running, binding to it is nothing more than extracting its pointer from the table and querying for the desired interface pointer, and this saves a tremendous amount of time.

In addition, maintaining some sort of state through the entire composite binding process is advantageous, and for that reason OLE provides an object called the *bind context*. This object holds flags controlling the binding and acts as a repository of the intermediate objects that have already been bound in the entire process. The intermediate objects and servers can also save properties or parameters inside the bind context that remain active as long as the binding is in progress.

But before we get into the details, let me introduce an analogy that will help us understand how monikers work—a treasure map. When you read the words "treasure map," what comes to mind? Probably some old piece of crusty parchment with a series of instructions or directions scrawled on it, telling you how to navigate through a hazardous terrain to get to the big X, where the treasure lies. The data stored in a moniker is like a treasure map, but the moniker also contains the intelligence to follow the map and return with the treasure. The client of such a treasure map needs only to ask the map, "Go get the treasure and bring it back." A moniker will do this without any reservation, returning an interface pointer to the object, which is indeed a treasure to a client.

As a specific example of this analogy, let's imagine that we spent a day in my kitchen baking some cookies and that we then placed them in a cookie jar. We set the jar on the third shelf of the pantry in my house (not sure how I'd talk you into letting me keep them) in the city of Bothell, in the state of Washington, in the United States of America (which is on the continent of North America, on the planet Earth, and so on). As cookie junkies, we want to make treasure maps that tell us exactly where these cookies are, so no matter where we go, we know how to get back to them.

## The Origin of Monikers

How do you write a treasure map? In other words, how does one *create* a new moniker? This can happen either in the server of the object being named or directly inside a client. In the former case, the server creates the moniker and makes it available to the client through a data transfer mechanism such as the clipboard. The client then performs a Paste Link to obtain that moniker for its own use—that is, to get an *IMoniker* pointer. In this way, a client obtains a moniker without knowing anything at all about the treasure map itself. In some cases, however, the client knows the location of the treasure and can simply create a moniker itself. In this sense, the client is using a moniker as a convenient encapsulation, perhaps so the rest of the client's code can use monikers for all names instead of having code to use monikers in some cases and specific code for other cases. Dealing with all names as monikers can greatly simplify design and improve performance and efficiency.

Both clients and servers use the same means to create a moniker. The means depend on the moniker class in question, which is either a standard OLE-provided moniker class or a custom moniker class. Both categories include *simple* monikers and *composite* monikers; the simple monikers are generally useful only inside a composite.

Regardless of the means of creation, all moniker types must have a run-time identity. So, every moniker class must be assigned its own CLSID, standard and custom monikers alike. At run time, this CLSID is retrieved through *IMoniker::GetClassID* (which comes from *IPersist*). In addition, *IMoniker::IsSystemMoniker* returns a flag from the MKSYS enumeration, identifying whether the moniker is a standard or a custom type:

```
enum tagMKSYS
    {
    MKSYS_NONE              = 0,
    MKSYS_GENERICCOMPOSITE  = 1,
    MKSYS_FILEMONIKER       = 2,
    MKSYS_ANTIMONIKER       = 3,
    MKSYS_ITEMMONIKER       = 4,
    MKSYS_POINTERMONIKER    = 5
    } MKSYS;
```

All custom monikers must return MKSYS_NONE from this function, whereas OLE's standard implementations are allowed to return the other values. (Microsoft reserves the right to add new values in the future—don't depend on this list to be permanent.) With that in mind, let's see a few details of these standard monikers.

## Standard Simple Moniker Classes

What? More classes? I thought I finished all my classes in college! Ah, but they never told you about monikers. Actually, OLE implements four simple moniker classes: file moniker, item moniker, pointer moniker, and anti-moniker.[4]

---

4. Two other types, *DDECompositeMoniker* and *PackagerMoniker*, are used internally in OLE for the same reasons mentioned previously regarding centralization of naming intelligence. I mention them because you will see their CLSIDs in the registry.

Of these, the file and pointer monikers are useful outside a composite, and only file and item monikers have a persistent state. Anti-monikers and pointer monikers have no persistent states, and the anti-moniker is not even bindable. We'll see what the anti-moniker does later in this chapter.

OLE exports a different creation function for each simple moniker, as described in Table 9-1. Each function returns the new moniker in an out-parameter *ppmk* (of type *IMoniker* **); other arguments provide the monikers with their state data, which for the file and item monikers becomes the information they can read and write persistently. Each moniker also has its own CLSID of the form *0000030x-0000-0000-C000-000000000046*, where *x* is 3 for file monikers, 4 for item, 5 for anti, and 6 for pointer.

| Function | Description |
|---|---|
| *CreateFileMoniker(pszPath, ppmk)* | Creates a file moniker, given any portion of a pathname in *pszFile*. The portion can be as short as a drive letter or as long as a complete path. The file moniker converts *pszPath* to a standard UNC path. Anything the operating system understands as a path is suitable for a file moniker. |
| *CreateItemMoniker(pszDelim, pszItem, ppmk)* | Creates an item moniker for which *pszItem* identifies the item's name and *pszDelim* identifies a delimiter string (usually a single character such as !), which does not occur elsewhere in *pszItem*. This delimiter is used to prefix the item's display name, allowing it to be combined with other items in the same string and parsed out of that string again. |
| *CreatePointerMoniker(pIUnknown, ppmk)* | Creates a pointer moniker to encapsulate the pointer passed in *pIUnknown*. This makes any object look like a moniker. |
| *CreateAntiMoniker(ppmk)* | Creates an anti-moniker, which needs no extra information. |

**Table 9-1.**
*OLE API functions that create simple monikers.*

Because a file moniker manages a pathname, it is useful by itself. Binding a single file moniker finds a CLSID associated with the file, instantiates an object of that class, and has it load the file through *IPersistFile::Load*. A pointer moniker is also useful by itself but only as an encapsulation of the object it names. Binding a pointer moniker simply calls the object's *QueryInterface*, allowing you to write code that can treat all passive or running objects exclusively through *IMoniker*.

Item monikers, on the other hand, must be part of a composite. By design, an item moniker depends on whatever moniker precedes it in a composite (the moniker to its left) in order to define the item's context—that is, to uniquely identify what the item is part of. For example, say our treasure map indicates, "Cookie jar is on the third shelf in the pantry in the kitchen of the house at 723 East Satori Street." If we made this sequence from individual item monikers, the "third shelf" makes no sense outside of "pantry," which must be found in a kitchen, which is not unique unless you define the house. Even then, the address isn't unique. As an item moniker, that address also requires a city, state, and country, such as a file moniker containing USA-\Washington\Bothell.[5] A composite with all these elements would uniquely identify which cookie jar we're talking about.

Binding an item moniker depends on some implementation of *IOleItem-Container*, specifically its members *GetObject* and *GetObjectStorage*, to interpret the name in the item and return the object it refers to. When asked to bind, an item moniker asks the moniker to its left to bind and return an *IOleItem-Container* pointer through which the item can then resolve its data into a pointer to return to the client.

## Custom Moniker Classes

The standard file and item monikers are sufficient for the vast majority of naming situations. An implementation of *IOleItemContainer::GetObject* can encapsulate any sort of process or intelligence it wants for any item. For example, you could write a server to process a composite file and item moniker that actually names a database query. The file names the database, and the item names the query.

---

5. I do actually live in this city, but this is not my address. (I'm not crazy enough to publish it.) But don't worry, I'll watch the cookies.

In rare situations, however, you may want to use a more efficient moniker to encapsulate more intelligence within the moniker instead of within an *IOleItemContainer* implementation. This is the case where you might use a custom moniker, which is nothing more than an in-process object that implements *IMoniker* (and possibly *IROTData*; see "The *IROTData* Interface and Custom Monikers" on page 464). In other words, a custom moniker has nothing special over the standard run-of-the-mill custom component that we saw in Chapter 5. You implement the object, stuff it in an in-process server, and register that server. Anything that wants an instance of your moniker requires only the CLSID (or ProgID) to pass to *CoCreateInstance.*

When you are tempted to create a custom moniker, ask yourself whether you really, *really* have to resort to that. You may find that some composite moniker is good enough. The few cases where you really do need a custom moniker are those in which the persistent state of the moniker is binary (file and item monikers work with text strings) or when you require special behavior when creating a composite moniker with a custom moniker.

As you know, a client's call to *CoCreateInstance* creates an uninitialized object, so how is that client to get initialization arguments to the custom moniker? You can do this in a number of ways. First, you could ship your own API function to create the custom moniker and forgo the component business altogether. A second option is to create a custom interface and implement it on the class factory with a "create instance with this data" function. You can also add another initialization interface on the moniker itself, for example *IDataObject*, *IDispatch*, or a custom interface. The other option is to take advantage of the fact that *IPersistStream* is the base interface for *IMoniker* and that *IPersistStream::Load* is an initialization function. If the client knows the correct stream format for your custom moniker, it can create a stream, store arguments in it (which will be exactly the same as your moniker's persistent state), and then call your *IMoniker::Load.* This solution (and those dealing with other standard interfaces) requires you to publish only a data structure as opposed to a custom interface (all of which can be done in type information, of course). Which method you choose depends on your potential customers. At the time of writing, Microsoft has not set any sort of standard because there are so many other satisfactory means.

## Custom Monikers and Custom Marshaling

Once created, the persistent state of a moniker usually remains constant, or the moniker has no persistent state at all. In either case, you can call the state immutable, making a moniker a prime candidate for custom marshaling, through which both the client and the server of the named object use identical copies of the moniker in their own processes. Simply said, a moniker can write its own persistent data into its marshaling packet (a stream) in *IMarshal::MarshalInterface*. The proxy is just another copy of the same moniker that initializes itself with the same data. No interprocess communication is necessary because both monikers are equivalent.

### Composite Monikers

Once again, a composite moniker is a collection of any other monikers, including other composites, that knows how to manage the relationships between its constituent monikers. A composite is the mechanism through which you create an arbitrary name of any size and complexity. A composite moniker allows each simple moniker within it to concentrate on one sort of naming and binding mechanism, completely eliminating redundant implementation in different moniker types. For example, creating a separate "part-of-a-file" moniker isn't necessary because you can create a composite with the existing file and item monikers to achieve the same goal. In mathematical terms, composites form the set of all possible permutations and combinations of the set of simple monikers.

OLE provides a standard implementation called the *generic composite* moniker, which is created through the OLE API function *CreateGeneric-Composite*:

```
HRESULT CreateGenericComposite(IMoniker *pmkFirst, IMoniker *pmkRest
    , IMoniker **ppmkComposite);
```

This function basically glues together *pmkFirst* and *pmkRest*, returning the composite in *ppmkComposite*. (*CreateGenericComposite* does not call *Release* in *pmkFirst* or *pmkRest*. The caller is still responsible for them.)

A composite moniker stores its constituent monikers left to right, as shown in Figure 9-2. Just as a treasure map is made up of many individual instructions, a composite is a collection of individual monikers that each represent an instruction. Some of those instructions can be simple; others may be more complex. In any case, the composition is considered associative in

that composing moniker A with B and composing that result with C—
(A•B)•C—produces the same moniker as composing B with C and composing the result with A—that is, A•(B•C).

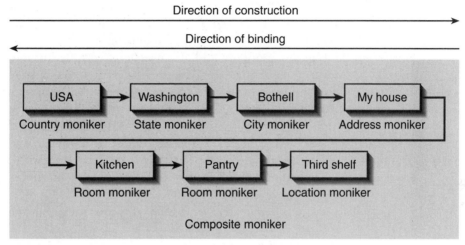

**Figure 9-2.**

*A composite moniker stores other monikers inside it in a left to right sequence.*

The persistent state of a composite moniker is nothing more than a
stream containing the persistent states of every constituent moniker. The generic composite implements its *IPersistStream::Save* by calling *OleSaveToStream*
for each moniker within it; *IPersistStream::Load* simply calls *OleLoadFromStream*
on each moniker, which instantiates and initializes all those monikers without the composite having to do any other work.

OLE's generic composite knows nothing about the specific monikers
inside it. You may, however, find occasion to create a composite moniker of
your own that understands more about its constituents and their relationship, making optimizations based on the types of monikers therein. This is
the reason why each moniker class must have a unique CLSID obtainable at
run time through *IMoniker::GetClassID*—there is no other robust way for a
nongeneric composite to know its own contents.

A number of member functions in the *IMoniker* interface are relevant to
composites. *ComposeWith* tells any moniker to create a composite using itself
and another moniker to attach to its right. Some monikers, such as the file
moniker, do not use the generic composite to implement their *ComposeWith*
member. It would be silly to attach two filenames together. Because the file
moniker implementation of *ComposeWith* understands what filenames are

445

and how they act, it will merge the two filenames into a single file moniker, a degenerate nongeneric composite. The composites in this case are called *nongeneric.*

The *Enum* member of *IMoniker* returns an enumerator through which the caller can iterate through the individual monikers in the composite, using the *IEnumMoniker* interface. (The enumerated elements are *IMoniker* pointers.) *Inverse* asks any given moniker for another moniker so that a composite containing the moniker and its inverse effectively annihilates the moniker. For example, the inverse of the path\DATA\OLE is\..\..— the composite of the two yields nothing. The concept of an inverse is the purpose of the anti-moniker, which really acts as a handy generic inverse for simple monikers—such as item and pointer monikers—that have no special internal structure (which a file moniker does). Composing an anti-moniker with a simple moniker annihilates them both. When composed with another composite, the anti-moniker effectively removes the last moniker in that composite.

Finally there is *IMoniker::Reduce*, which asks the moniker to create an equivalent moniker with a more efficient form. This can effectively mean *decompress* or *compress* depending on the type of composite. For example, you might have some sort of moniker that is nothing more than an alias for two others. Reducing this alias is the same as resolving it into the real value—that is, into the other monikers that make a precise name.

## Composite Notation

The discussions that follow describe a composite according to the types of monikers contained within it. We've seen a few examples of this notation already. The first convention for naming a composite is *<Type>!<Type>!-<Type>!…*, where *<Type>* might be File, Item, Anti, Pointer, Comp[osite], or whatever custom name you want, with an exclamation point—pronounced "bang"—serving as the delimiter between types ("!" is typically used in generating display names from a composite).

So a File!Item moniker—pronounced "file-bang-item"—is a composite with one file and one item moniker. File!Item!Item has one file and two item monikers, whereas File!Item!Item!Pointer!Anti is effectively the same as File!Item!Item, but it describes exactly what is contained in the composite. It is also useful to number multiple items of the same type to distinguish those items, as in File!Item1!Item2. Finally, because a composite can contain other composites, Comp!Item is also a suitable notation.

A second notation uses a character such as • to denote "composed with," as in File•Item. This notation is used most often in the context of creating a composite, and the use of the ! delimiter refers to the structure of a composite after it's been created.

## Binding a Composite Moniker

The individual binding operations of most simple monikers make sense only in the context of a composite. The binding processes for those simple monikers that can stand alone are also quite simple, as we've already seen with the file and pointer monikers. You might expect that because a composite usually contains more than one element within it, binding is just a matter of following the map, right? You only have to follow each step in order to get to the right place…or do you? There are, in fact, many reasons why following the entire sequence isn't necessary.

Composite monikers actually bind in a right to left order (instead of left to right), which has the practical effect of doing only as much binding as necessary. When following a map, you do not always start at the beginning—if your present location is already partway down the map. A composite moniker achieves this by reading the map in reverse order until it comes to a deterministic point. From that point, it can bind forward again.

A composite actually delegates most of its binding to the monikers within it by using the following algorithm, executed in its *IMoniker::BindToObject* (and *IMoniker::BindToStorage*):

1. (*BindToObject* only) Check whether the object named by this composite is currently registered in the running object table. If so, the object's *IUnknown* pointer is available from there, so the composite retrieves it and calls *QueryInterface* to obtain the pointer to return to the client. See "Binding Optimizations I: The Running Object Table" later in this chapter for more details about the running object table.

2. Separate the composite into two pieces: a *rightmost,* or *last,* moniker (*pmkRight*) and a composite containing the *left,* or *all but last,* moniker (*pmkLeft*). The composite as a whole can be viewed as AllButLast!Last or Left!Right for this purpose.

3. Call *pmkRight->BindToObject*, passing *pmkLeft* as an argument. Whatever this rightmost moniker returns from *BindToObject* is what the composite returns from its own *BindToObject*.

The result of separating a composite into Left!Right is depicted in Figure 9-3 on the next page. In general, the Right moniker requires some services of the Left moniker in order to bind itself, which is why the composite passes Left as an argument to Right's *BindToObject*. Thus, Right usually calls *pmkLeft->BindToObject* again, and if Left is itself a composite, we'll go right back through this algorithm again.

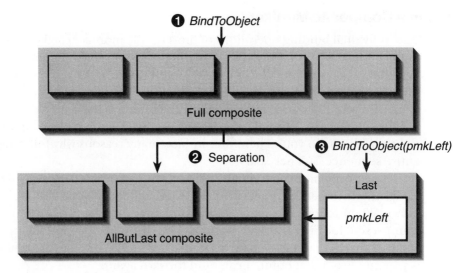

**Figure 9-3.**
*Binding a composite moniker splits the moniker into left and right pieces and then calls* BindToObject *on the right moniker passing the left moniker. (The services of the left moniker may be required by the right.)*

This algorithm effectively walks backward through the composite, asking each piece to bind in turn. Three conditions will stop this right to left progression:

- The moniker to the left refers to a running object, in which case calling *BindToObject* on that left piece returns immediately. This does not apply to *BindToStorage*.

- Binding reaches the first moniker in the original composite, which cannot depend on anything to its left because there is nothing to the left. Only a file, pointer, or suitable custom moniker can bind in the absence of a moniker to the left.

- Partway through the original composite, binding reaches a moniker that does not depend on the moniker to the left at all. For example, binding a File!Item!File!Item composite would need to progress only as far as the rightmost file moniker. A File!Item!Pointer would end at the pointer moniker.

## A Composite Binding Example

To illustrate this process, let's walk through the binding of a File!Item1!Item2 composite, in which the names Item1 and Item2 help us to distinguish which moniker is which. Let's say we have a client with a pointer to this moniker in the variable *pmkComp*. That client wants to obtain an *IProvideClassInfo* pointer for the object named by this moniker, so it calls *pmkComp->BindToObject(...,* *IID_ IDescription, (void \*\*)&pIDesc)* to get the pointer. No problem.

Now we enter what we'll call the *outer* composite's *BindToObject*. According to the algorithm, *BindToObject* checks the running object table first. Let's say the object is not running (or else it would take all the fun away). The composite divides itself into left and right pieces, where the left piece is a File!Item1 composite and the right piece is simply Item2. The outer composite then calls Item2's *BindToObject*, passing File!Item1 as *pmkLeft*.

As described before, an item moniker must have a context in which to make sense of its persistent name. It depends on the *pmkLeft* it receives to provide that context in the form of an *IOleItemContainer* interface. So Item2 now calls *pmkLeft->BindToObject(..., IID_ IOleItemContainer, (void \*\*)&pCont2)*, which puts us into the File!Item1 composite. Once again, this second composite checks whether the object is running, and failing that, it splits itself into File and Item1 monikers. It then calls Item1's *BindToObject*, passing File as *pmkLeft*. Item1, being an item moniker, also needs a context in which to make sense of its persistent name, so it calls *pmkLeft->BindToObject(..., IID_ IOleItemContainer, (void \*\*)&pCont1)*, where *pmkLeft* is the File moniker.

At this point, we are four levels deep into various *BindToObject* calls. The outer composite called Item2, which then called Item1, which has now called the File moniker. Fortunately, this File moniker doesn't depend on anything to its left, so it takes its filename, calls *GetClassFile, CoCreateInstance*, and *IPersistFile::Load(pszFile)*. After loading is complete, the File moniker calls *IPersistFile::QueryInterface(riid1, ppv1)*, where *riid1* and *ppv1* are the same arguments that the File moniker received in its *BindToObject* call. These arguments will be *IID_ IOleItemContainer* and *pCont1* as passed from Item1.

The object that implements *IPersistFile* must also support *IOleItemContainer* to support binding this File!Item1!Item2 moniker. This should not be a surprise to that object because its server (the source) is probably what gave away the composite moniker in the first place. Either that, or the client synthesized the moniker knowing that the object supported such binding. This is the big rule about implementing any link-source server: if you give away the moniker, you have to provide the support for binding it.

Anyway, the File moniker succeeds in obtaining the *IOleItemContainer* pointer, which it now returns to Item1. This item moniker calls *IOleItem-Container::GetObject(pszItem1, riid2, ppv2)*, where *riid2* and *ppv2* are the arguments that Item1's *BindToObject* received from Item2. The *GetObject* member now must find the object named by *pszItem1*, which is the name stored in Item1. In something like a File!Item!Item moniker this name might be for a specific sheet in a workbook or for a specific page in a document—that is, an item in the overall file that is itself a container for still other items. This *GetObject* member will find the correct object for *pszItem1* and return whatever interface pointer it was asked for. In this example, we have one implementation of *IOleItemContainer* returning a pointer to the same interface but on a different object. In other words, Item2 requires an *IOleItemContainer* pointer from Item1, which also required the same pointer from File. But the containers named by File and Item1 are completely separate. It is only because we have two item monikers in a row that *IOleItemContainer* comes up twice.

So the file object's *IOleItemContainer* resolves *pszItem1* into another *IOleItemContainer* interface on the Item1 object, and this pointer is returned to Item2. This item then calls *IOleItemContainer::GetObject(pszItem2, riidOrg, ppvOrg)*, where *pszItem2* is Item2's persistent name and *riidOrg* and *ppvOrg* are the arguments originally passed from the client, in this case *IID_IDescription* and *&pIDesc*. The implementation of *GetObject* (which is part of the object named by Item1) finds the object identified with *pszItem2* and returns the correct interface pointer to it. This interface pointer is implemented on the object named by Item2, in the context of File!Item1, which is exactly the object named by the File!Item1!Item2 composite. Item2 then returns this pointer from its own *BindToObject*, which the outer composite returns all the way back to the client.

This process is illustrated in Figure 9-4, assuming that a single server implements the File, Item1, and Item2 objects within the same process, which is usually the case when such a source hands out a File!Item!Item moniker.

Through the binding process, you can see how a composite delays as much work as possible, especially when we add the optimizations discussed in the next section. If, for example, the server in this example had already opened the file described by the File moniker and registered it in the running object table, the File moniker would not have had to call *CoCreate-Instance* at all. It would only need to extract the file object's *IUnknown* from the running object table and call its *QueryInterface*. Furthermore, if the server had had the file open and had been already viewing whatever object is described by Item1 (page, sheet, and so on), the File!Item1 moniker would have been registered as running; thus, binding File!Item1 would have gone no further than to extract a pointer and a query for *IOleItemContainer*.

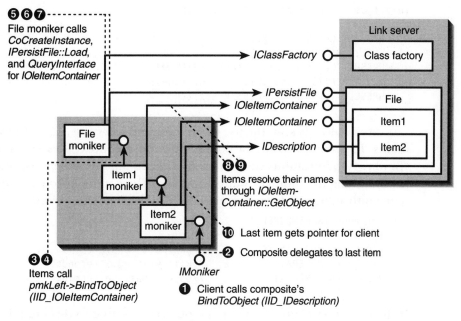

**Figure 9-4.**
*Binding a File!Item1!Item2 moniker.*

## The *IOleItemContainer, IOleContainer,* and *IParseDisplayName* Interfaces

Before we look at the running object table and the bind context, let's first look at *IOleItemContainer,* which plays such a prominent role in binding an item moniker. This interface derives from an interface named *IOleContainer,* which is itself derived from one named *IParseDisplayName*:

```
interface IParseDisplayName : IUnknown
    {
    HRESULT ParseDisplayName(IBindContext *pbc, LPOLESTR pszDisplayName
        , ULONG *pchEaten, IMoniker **ppmkOut);
    };


interface IOleContainer : IParseDisplayName
    {
    HRESULT EnumObjects(DWORD grfFlags, LPENUMUNKNOWN *ppEnum);
    HRESULT LockContainer(BOOL fLock);
    };
```

*(continued)*

451

```
interface IOleItemContainer : IOleContainer
    {
    HRESULT GetObject(LPOLESTR pszItem, DWORD dwSpeedNeeded
        , IBindCtx *pbc, REFIID riid, void **ppv);
    HRESULT GetObjectStorage(LPOLESTR pszItem, IBindCtx *pbc
        , REFIID riid, void **ppvStorage);
    HRESULT IsRunning(LPOLESTR pszItem);
    };
```

We've already seen the use of *GetObject* and its *pszItem*, *riid*, and *ppv* arguments. Its *pbc* argument is a pointer to a bind context, described later in "Binding Optimizations II: The Bind Context," and *dwSpeedNeeded* indicates just how long the moniker wants to wait for the container to parse the item name into an object, taken from the BINDSPEED enumeration:

```
typedef enum tagBINDSPEED
    {
    BINDSPEED_INDEFINITE  = 1,   //Can wait forever.
    BINDSPEED_MODERATE    = 2,   //Will wait ~2.5 seconds.
    BINDSPEED_IMMEDIATE   = 3    //Object must be running.
    } BINDSPEED;
```

If the container cannot retrieve the object according to this limit, it should return MK_E_EXCEEDEDDEADLINE.

The other two members of *IOleItemContainer* are quite straightforward. *GetObjectStorage* is to *IMoniker::BindToStorage* as *GetObject* is to *IMoniker::Bind-ToObject*. *IsRunning* asks the container whether the object identified with the item name is already up and running so that requesting a pointer to it is immediate.

*IOleContainer* has only two members specific to itself. The first, *Enum-Objects*, is asked to create an enumerator with *IEnumUnknown*, which iterates over a specific set of object types in the container according to the combination of OLECONTF flags passed in *grfFlags*:

```
typedef enum tagOLECONTF
    {
    OLECONTF_EMBEDDINGS    = 1,    //OLE Document embeddings only
    OLECONTF_LINKS         = 2,    //OLE Document linkings only
    OLECONTF_OTHERS        = 4,    //Anything outside OLE Documents
    OLECONTF_ONLYUSER      = 8,    //Objects visible to end user
    OLECONTF_ONLYIFRUNNING = 16    //Running objects
    } OLECONTF;
```

(OLECONTF_OTHERS is basically the set of all objects that are not otherwise included with OLECONTF_EMBEDDINGS and OLECONTF_LINKS.)

The other function in *IOleContainer* is *LockContainer*, which gives any object inside this container a way to tell the container to stay in memory (when *fLock* is TRUE) or to release itself if necessary (when *fLock* is FALSE). A container will typically call *CoLockObjectExternal* to create or remove a strong lock on itself in response to this call.

Finally we come to *IParseDisplayName* and its single member *ParseDisplay-Name*. This function is asked to turn a display name string into a moniker. More precisely, the container is asked to parse as much of the display name as it can, from left to right, returning an appropriate moniker for what it parsed. The out-parameter *pchEaten* specifies how many characters were parsed out of the display name; if more remain, the caller will need to parse the rest of that name. We'll see later how this comes into play when we look at display names in the context of the *IMoniker* interface in "*IMoniker*: Display Name Group."

## Binding Optimizations I: The Running Object Table

Binding a moniker does not mean that the moniker must always run some object to get the object from the passive state into the running state. There are two scenarios in which we can avoid excess work (and time):

- The object might be running when a client asks to bind to it. The moniker only needs to connect to that running object and query for the interface as requested by the client.

- The client might want to connect to an object named by a moniker when that object enters the running state.

The running object table handles the first scenario. When the source of linked objects runs those objects (for example, when a server opens a file in response to some other action), that source registers those objects in the table as running. Composite monikers and file monikers routinely use this table to avoid redundant actions.

What is called the *alert object table* would handle the second scenario, notifying interested clients when objects appeared in the running object table. However, this service is not implemented at this time, although it is described in the original OLE design specification.

OLE provides the running object table through a single object that implements—surprise, surprise—an interface named *IRunningObjectTable*. Through this interface, servers register the monikers for their running objects, and clients (and monikers) check whether an object is running. What this table really does (which is not exactly a binding optimization) is distinguish between passive objects and running objects. The table holds only those objects that are running, and anything not in the table is considered passive.

Both clients and link-source servers access the table by calling *Get-RunningObjectTable*, which returns an *IRunningObjectTable* pointer. Be sure to call *Release* through this pointer when you are finished with it. This interface has the following member functions:

```
interface IRunningObjectTable : IUnknown
    {
    HRESULT Register(DWORD grfFlags, IUnknown *pUnkObject
        , IMoniker *pmkObject, DWORD *pdwRegister);
    HRESULT Revoke(DWORD dwRegister);
    HRESULT IsRunning(IMoniker *pmkObject);
    HRESULT GetObject(IMoniker *pmkObject, IUnknown **ppUnkObject);
    HRESULT NoteChangeTime(DWORD dwRegister, FILETIME *pft);
    HRESULT GetTimeOfLastChange(IMoniker *pmkObject, FILETIME *pft);
    HRESULT EnumRunning(IEnumMoniker **ppEnum);
    };
```

The *Register* function places an object's *IUnknown* pointer into the running object table along with a moniker to identify it. If you register the same moniker twice, the table will still keep the pointer in the table but will return MK_S_MONIKERALREADYREGISTERED to indicate that you've made a redundant call. If *Register* returns this code or NOERROR, it gives back a registration key that can then be passed either to *Revoke* to remove the object from the table or to *NoteChangeTime*.

The *grfFlags* argument passed to *Register* indicates the type of lock—strong or weak—that the running object table should make on *pUnkObject*. If this flag is 0, the lock is weak and the table will not call *AddRef* on the object. If this flag is ROTFLAGS_REGISTRATIONKEEPSALIVE, the table will call *AddRef*, as befits a strong lock. Remember from Chapter 6 that which sort of lock you need depends greatly on how this object will be used and how you will remove it from the table.

*NoteChangeTime* is the function a server can use to store a time stamp with the object in the table. Clients that are interested can call *GetTimeOfLast-Change* to retrieve that time stamp. In both cases, the time stamp is a 64-bit OLE structure named FILETIME:

```
typedef struct _FILETIME
    {
    DWORD dwLowDateTime;
    DWORD dwHighDateTime;
    }  FILETIME;
```

To assist the server in filling one of these structures, OLE provides the API function *CoFileTimeNow*, which takes a *FILETIME* \* argument identifying the structure to fill. Because many applications, both servers and clients, still deal with 16-bit MS-DOS time stamps, OLE provides two functions to convert between them: *CoDosDateTimeToFileTime* and *CoFileTimeToDosDateTime*. See the *OLE Programmer's Reference* for details about these functions.

Besides time changes, clients are usually interested in whether an object is currently running, and if so they may want to connect to it. The *IsRunning* and *GetObject* members of this interface serve these two needs, and both functions take a moniker to identify the object. In addition, clients might want to look at all running objects, in which case they can call *EnumRunning* to obtain an enumerator with *IEnumMoniker*. If you use this enumerator, be sure to call *Release* through every *IMoniker* pointer returned from *IEnumMoniker::Next*.

Obviously, the running object table is of great use to composite and file monikers in their binding processes and may also be of use to a custom moniker implementation. Monikers, however, inside their *BindToObject* and *Bind-ToStorage* functions, are not allowed to call *GetRunningObjectTable*. Instead, they access the table through the bind context that flows throughout the entire binding process.

## Server Requirements for Running Objects and Wildcard Monikers

The running object table is the sole place where objects are differentiated between passive and running states on a systemwide basis, so servers that bring possibly linked objects into memory are strongly recommended to register those objects as running. This is required only for objects in servers that supply link monikers and support binding to them; it is not necessary to register objects that are never named with any moniker.

This recommendation can seem complicated for something like a Microsoft Excel workbook that supports linking to individual cell ranges within it. Does the server need to register separate monikers for every possible combination of cell ranges in that spreadsheet?

*(continued)*

455

*continued*

> Obviously there isn't enough memory to do this for a 16,384-by-16,384-by-256-cell workbook! Does this mean the server should try to remember what has possibly been linked? Not at all. OLE supports what is called a *wildcard* item moniker that you can compose with a file moniker to name "this file and everything in it." A wildcard item moniker has the text "\" (a single backslash). When the server opens a file, it can register a single File!Item moniker with a wildcard item. This ties into the item moniker's implementation of *IMoniker::IsRunning*, which checks whether Left•"\" (the moniker to its left with a \ item) is running. If it is, there is a wildcard match. The use of "\" in an item is peculiar to the standard item monikers. Custom monikers that support wildcards must define their own convention.

## Binding Optimizations II: The Bind Context

More than half the member functions of *IMoniker* take an argument of type *IBindCtx \**, which points to the bind context object for the current binding operation. The bind context carries information that applies to the entire binding underway, as opposed to the binding action of a single moniker. In other words, the bind context carries information global to the entire outer composite being bound and thus all other monikers within it, regardless of the complexity of the composite.

OLE provides bind context objects as a standard service. To create a bind context, call the API function *CreateBindCtx* as follows (the first argument is reserved and must be 0):

```
IBindCtx *pbc;
HRESULT   hr;

hr=CreateBindCtx(0, &pbc);
⋮
pbc->Release();
```

This creates a default initialized bind context that can be passed to various *IMoniker* functions. A bind context is, in fact, the first argument to *IMoniker::BindToObject*; creation of the context is one of the steps that the API function *BindMoniker* performs:

```
HRESULT BindMoniker(IMoniker *pmk, DWORD grfOpt, REFIID riid, void **ppv)
    {
    IBindCtx *pbc;
    HRESULT   hr;
```

```
hr=CreateBindCtx(0, &pbc);

if (SUCCEEDED(hr))
    {
    hr=pmk->BindToObject(pbc, NULL, riid, ppv)
    pbc->Release();
    }

return hr;
}
```

So one bind context travels through a binding procedure regardless of the monikers involved, as shown in Figure 9-5.

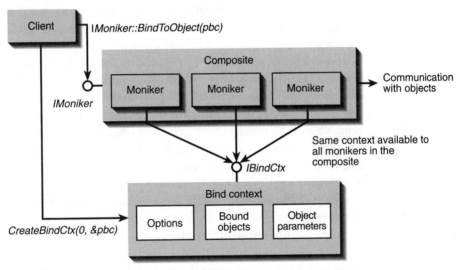

**Figure 9-5.**
*The role of the bind context when binding a composite moniker. It acts as a centralized repository for information available to all monikers used in the process.*

*CreateBindCtx* is the extent to which clients usually have to deal with these objects. Monikers, on the other hand, deal with them frequently during binding, always through the *IBindCtx* interface:

```
interface IBindCtx : IUnknown
    {
    HRESULT RegisterObjectBound IUnknown *pUnk);
    HRESULT RevokeObjectBound(IUnknown *pUnk);
    HRESULT ReleaseBoundObjects(void);
```

*(continued)*

```
HRESULT SetBindOptions(BIND_OPTS *pbindopts);
HRESULT GetBindOptions(BIND_OPTS *pbindopts);

HRESULT GetRunningObjectTable(IRunningObjectTable **ppROT);

HRESULT RegisterObjectParam(LPOLESTR pszKey, IUnknown *pUnk);
HRESULT GetObjectParam(LPOLESTR pszKey, IUnknown **ppUnk);
HRESULT EnumObjectParam(IEnumString **ppEnum);
HRESULT RevokeObjectParam(LPOLESTR pszKey);
};
```

As you can see, four groupings of functions represent the basic capabilities of a bind context:

- *RegisterObjectBound*, *RevokeObjectBound*, and *ReleaseBoundObjects* manage a list of intermediate objects that have been bound during the entire binding process. When a moniker binds to an object, it calls *RegisterObjectBound*; it can remove the object from the bind context at will with *RevokeObjectBound*. The simple act of registration creates an extra reference count on the object (a strong lock), which ensures that the object stays running throughout the bind operation. This really means that once a moniker binds its *pmkLeft*, for example, and registers it as bound, any further uses of *pmkLeft* that might also require binding will execute quickly because the object is still running. Only when the object is revoked and released can it destroy itself. *ReleaseBoundObjects* revokes all registered objects, which the bind context calls within its own destructor. Some monikers and sophisticated clients might use this sweeping release function without releasing the bind context itself, to free any object pointers without destroying the rest of the information in the bind context.

- *SetBindOptions* and *GetBindOptions* store and retrieve a BIND_OPTS structure in the bind context that controls various binding aspects. (See the discussion that follows.)

- *GetRunningObjectTable* returns an *IRunningObjectTable* pointer appropriate to the bind context. The design point is that a moniker should access all state information through the bind context instead of depending on a global state such as the running object table. OLE's bind context actually calls *GetRunningObjectTable* itself simply to encapsulate this global dependency.

■ *RegisterObjectParam, RevokeObjectParam, GetObjectParam,* and *Enum-ObjectParam* manage a table of miscellaneous object pointers, in which each pointer is associated with a specific key (a string). *RegisterObjectParam* revokes any object that is already registered under the same key and calls *AddRef* on the object. *RevokeObject-Param* removes the object from the table and calls its *Release. Get-ObjectParam* retrieves the pointer for any key (it also calls *AddRef* on that object before returning), and *EnumObjectParam* creates an enumerator with *IEnumString,* which enumerates the existing registered key names. (These strings are managed inside the enumerator—do not free the strings obtained through *IEnumString::Next!*) Releasing the bind context will clear the table and call *Release* on each object therein.

These last four *\*ObjectParam* functions enable the monikers involved in the binding to store custom information that remains valid throughout the operation. A moniker can place a pointer to any object whatsoever in this table as long as it supports *IUnknown.* Only the moniker that stores the object knows what the object means, and these objects are always in the same process as the moniker. This means you can use as many custom interfaces as you want to store whatever information you want with the object. You can even get away with storing a C++ object pointer here as long as that object's vtable starts with *IUnknown.* In short, this is a very nice little object repository.[6]

The bind options described in a BIND_OPTS structure remain fixed throughout binding. This structure contains a set of flags, sharing flags, and a timer count that establishes the client's deadline for binding to complete:

```
typedef struct tagBIND_OPTS
    {
    DWORD       cbStruct;
    DWORD       grfFlags;
    DWORD       grfMode;
    DWORD       dwTickCountDeadline;
    } BIND_OPTS;
```

The *cbStruct* field describes the size of this structure. The default bind context sets *grfFlags* to 0, but the client can store other options from the enumeration BINDFLAGS, as you see in the code at the top of the following page.

---

6. It is worthwhile to point out that if you have a need for some generic list management service, you could use the *\*ObjectParam* members in a bind context, just as you might use a Windows list box control for the same purpose.

```
typedef enum tagBINDFLAGS
    {
    BIND_MAYBOTHERUSER    = 1,
    BIND_JUSTTESTEXISTENCE = 2
    } BINDFLAGS;
```

The BIND_MAYBOTHERUSER option tells monikers that they can in-corporate user interface in their binding process; for example, they can display a dialog box that a user must type a password in, or they can ask the user to make a network connection manually. If this option is not present, monikers must either use a binding algorithm that requires no user interac-tion or return MK_E_MUSTBOTHERUSER to fail the binding.

The BIND_JUSTTESTEXISTENCE flag allows the client requesting the binding to indicate that it wants to know only whether binding is possible but not to actually carry out the operation. Usually this ends up being as expensive as performing the actual binding, especially because monikers themselves may completely ignore this flag if they choose to. This flag enables a sophisticated client to create a populated bind context ahead of time and hold that bind context until it really does want to bind at some time shortly thereafter. Because the bind context would still have all the registered bound objects inside it, the actual binding operation would be much faster than the test.

The flags allowed for *grfMode* are taken from the STGM enumeration that we saw in Chapter 7—that is, storage-mode flags. These flags communi-cate to the object being bound, as well as to any intermediate objects, the types of access mode to use for any storages that need to be opened in the process. This is especially useful for *IMoniker::BindToStorage* and is critical if there is an issue with concurrent access. By default, a new bind context will set this option to STGM_READWRITE | STGM_SHARE_EXCLUSIVE.

Finally, the *dwTickCountDeadline* field gives the client a way to say how long it is willing to wait for binding to be complete—clients who need bind-ing to occur rapidly can ensure that they won't get locked up inside a moniker for too long. The value 0 in *dwTickCountDeadline*, which is the default value, means "no deadline." A client that wants to set a deadline must call the Win-dows API *GetTickCount* and add to it the number of milliseconds it is willing to wait, taking wraparound of the DWORD tick count into consideration. That value then goes into this field.

Monikers that might perform a potentially time-consuming operation should check the deadline frequently; monikers such as a pointer moniker—which just call *QueryInterface*—need not pay attention to this. Those that do pay attention do not have to be completely accurate in the timing (it being difficult to predict how long some operation might take) as long as they stay in the ballpark of the deadline. It is allowable to exceed it a little, say by a few hundred milliseconds at most. When the deadline is passed, the moniker should fail with MK _ E _ EXCEEDEDDEADLINE.

If a moniker exceeds the deadline because one or more intermediate objects that it would like to use in binding are not running, it can save the monikers of these objects with *IBindCtx::RegisterObjectParam*. This tells the client that if these objects had been running, the binding might have happened faster. The client can then force the objects into the running state with the *OleRun* API function and try again. The monikers themselves are stored with the key names *ExceededDeadline, ExceededDeadline1, ExceededDeadline2,* and so on.

## Up Close with the *IMoniker* Interface

In our discussion of OLE's naming and binding architecture, we've seen some of the member functions of *IMoniker* and the parts of the architecture that use those members. We're now in a position to look at the entirety of this rather large interface, which, again, is derived from *IPersistStream:*[7]

```
interface IMoniker : IPersistStream
    {
    HRESULT BindToObject(IBindContext *pbc, IMoniker *pmkToLeft
        , REFIID riid, VOID **ppvResult);
    HRESULT BindToStorage(IBindContext *pbc, IMoniker pmkToLeft
        , REFIID riid, void **ppvObj);
    HRESULT Reduce (IBindContext *pbc, DWORD dwReduceHowFar
        , IMoniker **ppmkToLeft, IMoniker **ppmkReduced);
    HRESULT ComposeWith(IMoniker **pmkRight, BOOL fOnlyIfNotGeneric
        , IMoniker **ppmkComposite);
    HRESULT Enum(BOOL fForward, IEnumMoniker **ppEnum);
    HRESULT IsEqual(IMoniker *pmkOtherMoniker);
    HRESULT Hash(DWORD *pdwHash);
    HRESULT IsRunning(IBindContext *pbc, IMoniker *pmkToLeft
        , IMoniker *pmkNewlyRunning);
    HRESULT GetTimeOfLastChange(IBindContext *pbc, IMoniker *pmkToLeft
        , FILETIME *pFileTime);
```

*(continued)*

---

7. The OLE architects admit that a moniker might benefit from a more flexible choice of persistence model, so they have at times regretted using *IPersistStream* as a base interface for *IMoniker,* chaining monikers to stream persistence. At the time they were designed, interfaces and monikers were so scary that trying to explain a multiple-interface component as complicated as a moniker was simply not acceptable. At that time, it was easier to understand objects with single interfaces, so that's what a moniker came out to be. Of course, in hindsight and with a better understanding of interfaces, this is not an optimal design.

```
HRESULT Inverse(IMoniker **ppmk);
HRESULT CommonPrefixWith(IMoniker *pmkOther, IMoniker **ppmkPrefix);
HRESULT RelativePathTo(IMoniker *pmkOther, IMoniker **ppmkRelPath);
HRESULT GetDisplayName(IBindContext *pbc, IMoniker *pmkToLeft
    , LPOLESTR *ppszDisplayName);
HRESULT ParseDisplayName(IBindContext *pbc, IMoniker *pmkToLeft
    , LPOLESTR pszDisplayName, ULONG *pchEaten, IMoniker **ppmkOut);
HRESULT IsSystemMoniker(DWORD pdwMksys);
};
```

Holy cow! *IMoniker* alone has 15 specific members and as many as 23 members if you count all the base interfaces. This makes *IMoniker* one of the largest interfaces in all of OLE. Fortunately, we can group the specific *IMoniker* members so that looking at them in detail isn't such a drag.

| Group | Related Members |
|-------|-----------------|
| Binding | *BindToObject, BindToStorage* |
| Composite | *Reduce, ComposeWith, Inverse, Enum, CommonPrefixWith, RelativePathTo, IsSystemMoniker* |
| Table | *IsEqual, Hash, IsRunning, GetTimeOfLastChange* |
| Display Name | *GetDisplayName, ParseDisplayName* |

We've already explored the members of the Binding group except to note that not all named objects have storage, so the function *BindToStorage* can easily fail with MK_E_NOSTORAGE. That said, the following sections look in more detail at the functions in the Table, Composite, and Display Name groups. Do note that understanding *IMoniker* is generally necessary only if you are developing custom monikers and sophisticated clients. If this is not what you plan to be doing, feel free to skip the rest of this detailed section.

## *IMoniker*: Table Group

Two monikers that compare as equal through *IsEqual* must also return the same value from *Hash*—both of these functions should be developed with the other in mind. The reason is that *Hash* makes a convenient value to use as an index for a moniker table (like the running object table) and *IsEqual* is commonly used to match a moniker to a moniker entry in such a table.

Hashing is not a difficult proposition. For example, the file moniker merely runs through the characters in the pathname and munges the characters with some XOR operations (this is code based on Unicode):

```
HRESULT CFileMoniker::Hash(LPDWORD pdwHash)
    {
    DWORD   dwTemp = m_cAnti;
    WCHAR   *pch;
    WCHAR   ch;

    [Set pch to path string, converting to Unicode if needed.]

    while (*pch)
        {
        dwTemp *= 3;
        ch = *pch++;
        dwTemp ^= ch;
        }

    *pdwHash = dwTemp;
    return NOERROR;
    }
```

OLE's item monikers do exactly the same thing with their strings. For your own monikers, any suitable hash algorithm is fine.

Another important note about the hash value is that it must be consistent across processes—that is, the hash value can be marshaled. Be sure to take this into account when you're writing *Hash* because you cannot use the value of a pointer as part of the algorithm.

For *IsRunning*, its *pmkNewlyRunning* argument is the moniker of the last object registered as running in the running object table. If this argument is NULL, the moniker can use the running object table to implement this function directly (using *IBindCtx::GetRunningObjectTable*, of course). If *pmkNewlyRunning* is non-NULL, the return value from *IsRunning* is NOERROR only if *pmkNewlyRunning* is the same moniker as *this*. You can make this assumption because of the nature of composite binding and because servers will register newly running objects as they are bound in the process. This means that a moniker doesn't need to perform an exhaustive search to see that the object is running. At most, the moniker needs to look in the running object table. The documentation for *IsRunning* in the *OLE Programmer's Reference* has a number of sample implementations of this function that also account for "wildcard," as described earlier.

*IMoniker::GetTimeOfLastChange* can generally use *IRunningObjectTable::GetTimeOfLastChange* to implement itself. This function should not attempt to run an object to obtain information but should rely instead on any cached information the moniker might already have. The reason to keep change times in the first place is to help clients decide whether to bother binding to the object. For example, if the object has not changed for a long time, binding to it to get an update is not necessary. You can optimize the implementation of this member if the *pmkToLeft* passed to this function is non-NULL because then the moniker can assume that it cannot have changed any later than the moniker to its left, so it can pass this function call to *pmkLeft->Get-TimeOfLastChange*. If *pmkLeft* is NULL, the moniker can try the running object table and then pursue other means such as checking file time stamps.

---

### The *IROTData* Interface and Custom Monikers

The running object table in OLE under Windows NT 3.5 exhibited poor performance when calling *IMoniker::IsEqual*. To solve the performance question, monikers that are going to be registered in the running object table must implement a second interface, named *IROTData*. This interface has a single member—*GetComparisonData*—through which the table asks the moniker for data it can use to compare with another moniker in lieu of calling *IsEqual*. All of OLE's standard monikers will follow this rule, as should custom monikers. Monikers that do not implement this interface will not be allowed to register as running. This rule will affect custom monikers on Windows 95, Windows NT 3.51, and later platforms. Check your documentation for the details.

---

### *IMoniker*: Composite Group

A number of *IMoniker* members apply specifically to composites. This means that simple monikers can leave many of these functions unimplemented. We have seen the operation of *Enum* and *IsSystemMoniker*; all we need to add to our discussion of *Enum* is that *fForward* specifies the direction of enumeration, left to right (when *fForward* is TRUE) or right to left (when *fForward* is FALSE), depending on the needs of the caller.

The core member in the Composite group is *ComposeWith*. Even simple monikers (including the anti-moniker) implement it. The function is given a "suffix"—that is, a moniker to its right (*pmkRight*)—and is asked to create a composite containing itself and that suffix. *ComposeWith* basically gives a moniker the chance to control the type of composite used, generic or nongeneric. The moniker being asked to compose can call *pmkRight->GetClassID* (or use some other means, such as querying for a particular custom interface) to determine whether that type would be understood by a nongeneric composite. If not, the *fOnlyIfNotGeneric* flag controls what should happen. If this flag is TRUE, *ComposeWith* should return a NULL in *\*ppmkComposite* and the result MK_E_NEEDGENERIC. This basically says that the moniker and *pmkRight* support only generic composition. If *fOnlyIfNotGeneric* is FALSE, the same two monikers could be combined generically with *CreateGeneric-Composite*.

It is interesting that if *pmkRight* happens to be an anti-moniker or something that completely negates the moniker being called, *ComposeWith* returns a NULL in *\*ppmkComposite* and the NOERROR result, regardless of the value of *fOnlyIfNotGeneric*.

The functionality of the *IMoniker::Inverse* function is closely related to this idea of negation. An inverse of a moniker (which can be written as ~moniker or moniker$^{-1}$) is defined as a moniker such that a NULL composition results when that inverse is passed to the moniker's *ComposeWith* (moniker•inverse). Some monikers, such as the anti-moniker, have no inverse at all, and most inverse monikers have no inverses themselves. The reason is that an inverse of one specific moniker is usually the inverse of a certain superset of monikers with the same structure as the original one. For example, a file moniker with the path DATA\OLE\SLIDES has an inverse of ..\..\... Composing the two results in nothing at all. Well, ..\..\.. is also the inverse of \TEXT\2ND_ED\FIGURES as well as FOO\BAR\BAZ, literally anything in the form <x>\<y>\<z>.

The inverse of a composite moniker is basically a composite that contains the inverses of each contained moniker in reverse order. That is, the inverse of File!Item1!Item2 would be Item2$^{-1}$!Item1$^{-1}$!File$^{-1}$, which may be nothing more than Anti!Anti!File$^{-1}$. The anti-moniker is again the generic inverse of any simple moniker that has no internal structure.

### *CommonPrefixWith* and *RelativePathTo*

The member functions *CommonPrefixWith* and *RelativePathTo* are related to inverses but exist primarily for dealing with composites that contain a file moniker. When a client maintains a link to some object in another file, it is useful for that client to retain two monikers for that link: one absolute, the other relative. This is exactly how a linked compound document object stores its link information, as we'll see in Chapter 20. *CommonPrefixWith* and *Relative-PathTo* provide the means to create a relative moniker.

*CommonPrefixWith* asks a moniker to determine how much it has in common with the moniker passed to it in *pmkOther*, returning the result (which can be a composite) in *\*ppmkPrefix*. For example, a composite containing C:\DATA\OLE\SPEC.DOC!Page2!Table1 and a file moniker with C:\DATA-\NOTES\1995.DOC would have the common prefix C:\DATA in a single file moniker. C:\DATA\OLE\SPEC.DOC!Page2!Table1 and C:\DATA\OLE-\SPEC.DOC!Page2!Table7 would have the common prefix C:\DATA\OLE-\SPEC.DOC!Page2 in a File!Item composite. A few return codes for this function indicate special relationships—for example, MK_S_NOPREFIX (no common prefix exists), MK_S_HIM (*pmkOther* is already the prefix of *this* moniker), and MK_S_US (*this* and *pmkOther* are equal).

The *RelativePathTo* function works along similar lines: the moniker is asked to return a relative moniker so that moniker•relative results in the moniker passed in *pmkOther*. So if we ask C:\DATA\OLE\SPEC.DOC!Page2-!Table1 to return the relative that would result in C:\DATA\OLE\SPEC.DOC, it could return an Anti!Anti composite. Or if asked for the relative to produce C:\DATA, it would return Anti!Anti!File, in which the file moniker contains "..". If *RelativePathTo* returns a meaningful relative, it should return the NOERROR result; if *pmkOther* is the only relative form of the moniker called, it returns MK_S_HIM to say so.

In both of these functions, *pmkOther* is often the moniker for the container document (or file, spreadsheet, and so on) that manages the link. If I have a container document C:\DATA\OLE\SPEC.DOC in which is linked C:\DATA\PICTURES\PUFFINS.BMP, we can create a relative moniker that contains ..\PICTURES\PUFFINS.BMP. To do this, we call the absolute path moniker's *CommonPrefixWith* with the container's moniker to get C:\DATA and then call *RelativePathTo* on the container moniker passing the common prefix to get "..". We then strip the common prefix from the linked object's moniker and compose the remainder with the relative path moniker. The result is a moniker describing the linked object in relation to the document.

If all of this sounds like a lot of work for a moniker to implement, you're right. For that reason, OLE provides default implementations through the API functions *MonikerCommonPrefixWith* and *MonikerRelativePathTo*. A moniker should first check whether it has intimate knowledge of *pmkOther*—that is, whether the moniker knows that it can handle *pmkOther* in a special way. If not, the moniker should use these two API functions for its implementation in order to handle generic composites correctly. *MonikerRelativePathTo* can also be called from a client as a simple wrapper for *IMoniker::RelativePathTo*. This is not true of *MonikerCommonPrefixWith*; clients should call *IMoniker-::CommonPrefixWith* directly.

## Reduce

The final member of the composite group, *Reduce*, asks a moniker to rewrite itself into an equivalent but more efficient form, which has several uses:

■ It enables the construction of new moniker classes that act as user-defined macros or aliases. When these are reduced, the moniker evaluates the macro or alias returning a moniker to the real object. This evaluation would normally happen if the macro or alias moniker were asked to bind, so the reduction allows the caller to separate the work of evaluation from the actual binding and improve overall binding speed.

■ It enables the construction of a kind of moniker that tracks data as it moves about so that the reduction results in the current location. This is really a special case of an alias or a macro moniker.

■ It enables a file moniker created on one operating system to translate itself into a moniker suitable for a different operating system—for example, translating from an addressing scheme based on filenames to one based on identifiers.

A somewhat contrived example of reduction is shown in Figure 9-6. It may not look like a reduction, but it illustrates the evaluation of various sorts of alias monikers into their appropriate values in the host environment. The particular classes of monikers shown here are illustrative only—OLE does not implement such monikers. In any case, you can see that many monikers in this example reduce to something totally different, whereas others do not.

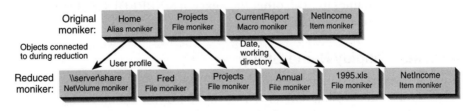

**Figure 9-6.**
*An example of moniker reduction.*

467

In this example, the top moniker is essentially decompressed into its exact form. Other monikers might reduce to something that is actually smaller, performing garbage collection. For example, a composite that contains three file monikers (some relative, some absolute) can reduce a mess like \\BUNNY-KINS\CDRIVE\DATA\OLE2\OLD\..\..\OLE\..\..\TEXT\2ND_ED\CH09.DOC to \\BUNNYKINS\CDRIVE\DATA\OLE\CH09.DOC.

Many monikers, especially simple ones, reduce to themselves, in which case *Reduce* returns MK_S_REDUCED_TO_SELF. Otherwise, *dwReduce-HowFar*, taken from the MKRREDUCE enumeration, indicates to what extent the reduction should proceed:

```
typedef enum tagMKREDUCE
    {
    MKRREDUCE_ONE        = 3<<16,
    MKRREDUCE_TOUSER     = 2<<16,
    MKRREDUCE_THROUGHUSER = 1<<16,
    MKRREDUCE_ALL        = 0
    } MKRREDUCE;
```

MKRREDUCE_ONE instructs the moniker to reduce "one step," which usually means the caller has intimate knowledge of what that step will accomplish. MKRREDUCE_TOUSER asks the moniker to reduce to something whose display name would be meaningful to an end user — that is, a display name that uses filenames, bookmarks, cell ranges, database queries, and other recognizable item names that appear in the link source's user interface. Internal names (like aliases) should not be part of such a display. Closely related is MKRREDUCE_THROUGHUSER, which tells the moniker to reduce to the point at which any further reduction would render an unrecognizable display name from the user's point of view. This is often the same thing that MKRREDUCE_TOUSER does. Finally, MKRREDUCE_ALL tells the moniker to reduce as far as possible so that any later requests to reduce return MK_S_REDUCED_TO_SELF. Monikers that have no user-readable display names treat all other flags except MKRREDUCE_ONE exactly as they would treat MKRREDUCE_ALL.

## *IMoniker*: Display Name Group

The final two member functions of *IMoniker*, *GetDisplayName* and *ParseDisplay-Name*, deal with a textual representation of the moniker that can be used in a user interface. *GetDisplayName* asks a moniker for this display name, but this might actually be as costly an operation as binding the object altogether, which it might require anyway. For this reason, *GetDisplayName* takes *as arguments* a bind context and the moniker to its left in a composite. The resulting display name is returned in *∗ppszDisplayName*, which the moniker allocates with *CoTaskMemAlloc*; thus, the caller is responsible for freeing that memory with *CoTaskMemFree*.

For example, a file moniker that contains the path \\BUNNYKINS-\CDRIVE\DATA\OLE\CH09.DOC will generally use that string for the display name unless it can resolve the \\*machine\volume* part into a local drive letter, which results in C:\DATA\OLE\CH09.DOC, for example. An isolated item moniker (*pmkLeft* is NULL) will do nothing more than return its item string, and pointer monikers and anti-monikers have no display name, so they fail this function altogether.

A composite moniker creates a display name out of the strings of each constituent moniker. A File!Item!Item moniker will create a display name like C:\DATA\OLE\CH09.DOC!Section5!Graphic6. Keep in mind that when the composite asks an item moniker for its display name, it will pass a non-NULL *pmkLeft* to that moniker. In such a case, the item moniker will prefix its item string with the delimiter character originally passed to *CreateItemMoniker*. This character thus separates the item from whatever comes before it in the display name.

This separation not only is useful for providing a user with a visual separation but also provides for parsing a display string into a moniker — that is, for performing the opposite of *GetDisplayName*. The function *IMoniker::ParseDisplayName* does this — the moniker called names the object that knows how to parse the display name. In other words, the moniker called is not parsing its own display name but some display name that is relevant to the object named by the moniker. The *pszDisplayName* argument is thus the string to parse, *∗ppmkOut* is the resulting moniker, and *pchEaten* is filled with the number of characters parsed from *pszDisplayName* in the process of creating *∗ppmkOut*.

Some monikers might understand enough about their named objects to actually perform some of this parsing themselves. Most monikers, however, including file, item, and pointer monikers, depend on the objects they themselves name to perform the parsing. More specifically, these monikers bind to their named objects (calling their own *BindToObject*) and request the *IParseDisplayName* interface. The monikers then call *IParseDisplayName::ParseDisplayName* to do the honors, which returns the new moniker and the value to store in *pchEaten*, which the moniker called originally and then returns to the client.

Because this parsing will generally bind to the named object anyway, the operation can be just as expensive as binding is already. Usually parsing is needed only when the user has provided some name to an application and has told the application to create a link from it. We'll see examples when we talk about OLE Document containers in Part V of this book.

Parsing a display name almost always happens on a composite, which asks each of its constituent monikers to parse in turn. This is the whole reason why *IMoniker::ParseDisplayName* takes arguments such as *pchEaten*: the composite must track each moniker as it gets parsed from the name. In addition, simple monikers will call *IBindCtx::RegisterObjectBound* in the process to optimize possible later uses of the same object for parsing.

A client that wants to parse a user-provided string into a moniker doesn't actually have a composite moniker to call in the first place! This is the reason for the OLE API function *MkParseDisplayName* (the *Mk* stands for "moniker"), which has the following signature:

```
HRESULT MkParseDisplayName(IBindCtx *pbc, LPCWSTR pszName
    , ULONG *pchEaten, IMoniker **ppmk)
```

Here the caller must create a new bind context before calling, passing that pointer in *pbc* along with the display string in *pszName*. On return, *pchEaten* will specify how far the parsing was successful, and *ppmk* will have a moniker for whatever was successfully parsed. You can use *pchEaten* to show the user how much of a string was parsed (with a highlight) and where the first parsing error occurred, allowing the user to correct the name if necessary.

*MkParseDisplayName* has the challenge to figure out exactly what type of moniker to start with, after which it can call *IMoniker::ParseDisplayName* as often as needed. Because of this, the display name passed to *MkParseDisplayName* must contain one of two initial patterns: a UNC pathname or the character @. If a UNC path is found, this function creates a file moniker and calls its *ParseDisplayName* to get the ball rolling down the rest of the string. (The file parses the next moniker in the string, which is asked to parse the rest, and so on.) If the string begins with @, *MkParseDisplayName* assumes the next string of characters is a ProgID, up to the next character that is not legal for a ProgID (such as \ or ! or anything other than 0–9, a–z, A–Z, and a period). With this ProgID, *MkParseDisplayName* looks up the CLSID registered for it and calls *CoCreateInstance(clsid, NULL, CLSCTX_ALL, IID_IParseDisplayName, &pIPDN)*. The resulting object is given the entire display name to parse, so it must understand what sort of moniker to create initially. *MkParseDisplayName* then asks this initial moniker to parse its display name, and this continues until the whole string is parsed or an error occurs.

# Creating and Using Standard Monikers: LinkUser

Now that we understand what monikers are and how they are used to name objects and link to those objects, we can look at monikers in action through three samples—LinkSource, LinkUser, and IDescription.

- LinkSource (CHAP09\LINKSRC) has two modes of operation. When it is run stand-alone, you will see a window and a menu from which you can create a file named GOOP.LKS (for lack of a better name) that is bindable through a file moniker. The rest of Link-Source exists to support binding File, File!Item, and File!Item!Item monikers that identify the file or pieces within that file. (The pieces are substorages from the root, or substorages of substorages.)

- LinkUser (CHAP09\LINKUSER) manages three monikers: a file moniker to the LinkSource file (GOOP.LKS), a File!Item moniker naming the Object 2 piece of that file, and a File!Item!Item moniker naming Sub-Object 3 in Object 2 of that file. LinkUser shows the display name of each moniker in a list box; double-clicking on that item (or using the Link/Show Description menu item) attempts to bind the moniker by asking for *IDescription*, through which LinkUser then asks for a piece of descriptive text from the object. You can also ask LinkUser to take that display name and attempt to parse it into a moniker (the Link/Parse Display Name And Bind menu item) and then bind that moniker.

- IDescription (CHAP09\IDESCIP) is a custom interface that allows us to ask an object for a piece of descriptive text through its *GetText* member function. This simple interface has the same semantics as that described earlier in this chapter.

In this section, we'll use LinkUser to look at the client side of monikers. The next section will examine LinkSource in more detail. Because IDescription is simply an IDL file for the custom interface, it contains nothing that we didn't already see in Chapter 6. However, be sure to compile and register both LinkSource and IDescription before running LinkUser, or else nothing will work. If you forget, you'll have a good opportunity to see what will happen in the absence of the link-source server or the interface marshaler.

These three samples work together to illustrate the entire binding process as well as to show parsing. From LinkUser's point of view (the client's, that is), these processes are very simple: binding is encapsulated entirely within *BindMoniker* and *IMoniker::BindToObject*, and parsing is executed entirely within *MkParseDisplayName*. Most of LinkUser, in fact, is code that calls these functions and does something with whatever comes back from them. But the first major issue is how LinkUser comes into the monikers in the first place. After we know that, we can examine its code to bind those monikers and then the code to parse display names.

## Creating or Obtaining Monikers and Display Names

The first interesting question for LinkUser is how it will come by the monikers it holds in its lists. We could have LinkSource copy a moniker for one of its objects to the clipboard where the data is essentially a piece of global memory containing a moniker's persistent stream. In other words, LinkSource might call *CreateStreamOnHGlobal*, save a moniker into it with *OleSaveToStream*, and then put that memory on the clipboard; LinkUser could then paste the global memory, call *CreateStreamOnHGlobal* itself, and then call *OleLoadFromStream* to re-create the moniker. LinkSource could also copy a display name to the clipboard, which LinkUser could paste as text and then parse into a moniker (which would be very expensive for just a paste!). Either solution would work perfectly fine, in fact, but as we'll see in the next few chapters, OLE has a specific stream-based moniker format that allows us to copy links via the clipboard as well as through OLE Drag and Drop.

So for now, LinkUser creates the monikers itself because it has intimate knowledge of LinkSource. As we discussed earlier in this chapter, however, you can create an identical moniker with the same sequence of function calls. So while we could have LinkSource create monikers and pass them to LinkUser, simplicity argues to have LinkUser do it. This is, of course, not feasible when you have a client that wants to use links to a variety of sources of which it does not have intimate knowledge—that's the whole idea behind linked objects in OLE Documents.

LinkUser creates its monikers from hard-coded strings inside *CApp::CreateMonikers* (LINKUSER.CPP), in which the strings assume knowledge of LinkSource (such as the proper delimiter and the filename—do change the filename if you installed these samples in a directory other than C:\INOLE):

```
BOOL CApp::CreateMonikers(void)
    {
    TCHAR      szFile[]=TEXT("c:\\inole\\chap09\\linksrc\\goop.lks");
    TCHAR      szItem1[]=TEXT("Object 2");
```

```
TCHAR        szItem2[]=TEXT("Sub-Object 3");
TCHAR        szDelim[]=TEXT("!");
IMoniker     *pmkItem;
HRESULT      hr;

//Create simple file moniker.
if (FAILED(CreateFileMoniker(szFile, &m_rgpmk[0])))
    return FALSE;

//Create File!Item moniker--item first, then composite.
if (FAILED(CreateItemMoniker(szDelim, szItem1, &pmkItem)))
    return FALSE;

//The output here will be File!Item moniker.
hr=m_rgpmk[0]->ComposeWith(pmkItem, FALSE, &m_rgpmk[1]);
pmkItem->Release();

if (FAILED(hr))
    return FALSE;

/*
 * Now create File!Item!Item by appending another item
 * to the File!Item just created.
 */
if (FAILED(CreateItemMoniker(szDelim, szItem2, &pmkItem)))
    return FALSE;

hr=m_rgpmk[1]->ComposeWith(pmkItem, FALSE, &m_rgpmk[2]);
pmkItem->Release();

if (FAILED(hr))
    return FALSE;

return TRUE;
}
```

You can see that the basic idea is to create the simplest moniker first and then compose more specific monikers to append to the first in order to create more complex names. Stripped to the bare minimum, the sequence is essentially as follows:

```
CreateFileMoniker(..., &pmkFile);
CreateItemMoniker(..., &pmkItem1);
pmkFile->ComposeWith(pmkItem1, ..., &pmkComp1);
CreateItemMoniker(..., &pmkItem2);
pmkComp1->ComposeWith(pmkItem2, ..., &pmkComp2);
```

Note that to create a composite we're always calling one moniker's *ComposeWith* member instead of directly creating a generic composite. Because we're using nothing but OLE's standard file and item monikers, we actually know that each of them will create a generic composite internally, so we might do the same ourselves. However, this is not a valid assumption for other moniker types or for composing a file moniker to another file moniker, which results in a single file moniker. For this reason, clients that are not familiar with the types of monikers they are fabricating should always use *ComposeWith*. A source that understands those monikers can use *CreateGeneric-Composite* directly if you want it to, but that is hardly more efficient than calling *ComposeWith*. I recommend the latter.

With these three monikers in hand (inside the array *CApp::m_rgpmk*), LinkUser places their display names in a list box that fills its client area, as shown in Figure 9-7. This all happens in *CApp::ListInitialize*, which makes a call to *IMoniker::GetDisplayName*:

```
BOOL CApp::ListInitialize(void)
    {
    UINT        i;

    for (i=0; i < CMONIKERS; i++)
        {
        LPOLESTR    pszName;
        HRESULT     hr;
        IBindCtx    *pbc;

        if (FAILED(CreateBindCtx(0, &pbc)))
            return FALSE;

        hr=m_rgpmk[i]->GetDisplayName(pbc, NULL, &pszName);
        pbc->Release();

        if (FAILED(hr))
            return FALSE;

        SendMessage(m_hWndList, LB_ADDSTRING, 0, (LPARAM)pszName);
        CoTaskMemFree((void *)pszName);
        }

    return TRUE;
    }
```

You'll see that because *GetDisplayName* needs a bind context, we create a default one here, and the output string must be freed with *CoTaskMemFree*.

LinkUser will hold these three monikers until termination, at which point cleanup is a simple call to *IMoniker::Release.*

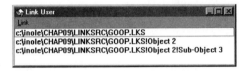

**Figure 9-7.**
*LinkUser's list of moniker display names.*

## Binding a Moniker

From the client's perspective, binding couldn't be much easier: call the API function *BindMoniker* or call *IMoniker::BindToObject* if you want more control over the bind context. LinkUser centralizes this process in *CApp::BindAndShow* (LINKUSER.CPP), which binds the moniker to obtain an *IDescription* interface for the object and then asks that object to render its text description with *IDescription::GetText*:

```
void CApp::BindAndShow(IMoniker *pmk, IBindCtx *pbc)
    {
    HRESULT         hr;
    IDescription    *pIDescription;

    if (NULL==pbc)
        {
        hr=BindMoniker(pmk, 0, IID_IDescription
            , (void **)&pIDescription);
        }
    else
        {
        hr=pmk->BindToObject(pbc, NULL, IID_IDescription
            , (void **)&pIDescription);
        }

    if (SUCCEEDED(hr))
        {
        const long   cch=512;
        TCHAR        szText[cch];

        hr=pIDescription->GetText(szText, cch);
        pIDescription->Release();
```

*(continued)*

475

```
    [Show appropriate message on success or failure.]
    }
else
    [Show appropriate error message.]

return;
}
```

That's it—a client needs to do nothing more than ask the moniker to perform its magic. As we'll see shortly, LinkSource does considerable work through the process, but this encapsulation is exactly what makes monikers such a powerful technology. The moniker is a treasure map, and all a client needs to do is ask the moniker for the treasure.

## Parsing a Display Name

The other action a client can take is to parse a display name into a moniker, either to simply test whether the moniker is valid or to actually go all the way and bind the moniker. LinkUser does the latter in *CApp::ParseAndBind* in response to the Link/Parse Display Name And Bind menu item:

```
void CApp::ParseAndBind(void)
    {
    HRESULT         hr;
    IBindCtx        *pbc;
    IMoniker        *pmk;
    int             i;
    TCHAR           szName[512];
    ULONG           chEaten=0;

    i=(int)SendMessage(m_hWndList, LB_GETCURSEL, 0, 0L);

    if (LB_ERR==i)
        return;

    SendMessage(m_hWndList, LB_GETTEXT, i, (LPARAM)(LPTSTR)szName);

    if (FAILED(CreateBindCtx(0, &pbc)))
        [Error message and return]

    hr=MkParseDisplayName(pbc, szName, &chEaten, &pmk);

    if (SUCCEEDED(hr))
        {
        MessageBox(m_hWnd, TEXT("Name parsed. Press OK to bind.")
            , TEXT("Link User"), MB_OK);
```

```
        BindAndShow(pmk, pbc);
        pmk->Release();
        }
    else
        {
        //Tell user how far parsing got.
        wsprintf(szName, TEXT("Parsing failed after %lu characters.")
            , chEaten);

        MessageBox(m_hWnd, szName, TEXT("Link User"), MB_OK);
        }

    pbc->Release();
    return;
    }
```

Just as with binding, *MkParseDisplayName* encapsulates all the magic for us. Because this API function takes a bind context and because the parsing process will contain registered bound objects after parsing is complete, we can use this same bind context to bind the moniker and show its description, thereby making the extra binding step more efficient. In other words, the server that did the parsing will still be running until we release the bind context, so subsequent binding with that same context is more efficient.

The *pchEaten* argument that comes back from *MkParseDisplayName* is important because it would allow a client to display where the parsing encountered an error. We'll see specific use of this value in Chapter 20, when we look at the Links dialog box standard for linked objects in OLE Documents.

# Implementing a Linking Server: LinkSource

A server's implementation of binding and name parsing is stipulated by the types of monikers it supports. In actual applications, this means that the server must be able to bind or parse any moniker it creates and hands to other clients through the clipboard or some other transfer mechanism; it may, of course, fail to parse any moniker that it didn't originally provide or one that has more elements than the server can support.

LinkSource, in particular, supports binding of File, File!Item, and File!Item!Item monikers, in which the File item is related to a file object, the first item is related to objects contained in first-level substorages of that file, and the second item is related to objects contained in substorages below those of the first level, as illustrated in Figure 9-8 on the next page. The file object has to support binding to a file moniker as well as the resolution of a first-level item moniker, so it must implement *IPersistFile* and *IOleItem-Container*. The "Container Item" object (named with such a File!Item moniker) needs to support only the resolution of the second-level item moniker, so it needs only *IOleItemContainer*. The second-level object itself, called here the "Simple Item," needs no special interfaces for binding because that's all handled by its container. All three of these objects also implement *IDescription* to allow LinkUser to retrieve some interesting information from the objects for its own demonstrative purposes.

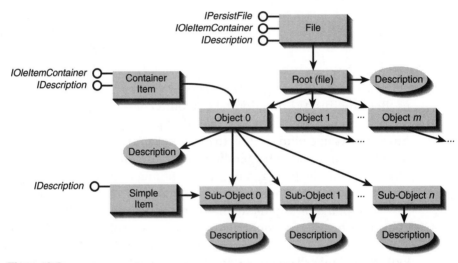

**Figure 9-8.**
*LinkSource's object implementations as they relate to pieces of its storage.*

The implementation of LinkSource's three objects is found in the classes *CFileObject* (FILEOBJ.CPP), *CContainerItem* (CONTITEM.CPP), and *CSimpleItem* (SIMPITEM.CPP). Although these are separate objects as far as reference counting is concerned, LinkSource actually centralizes some of their code inside common interface implementations. The *CImpIOleItem-Container* class (IOLECONT.CPP) implements *IOleItemContainer* for both *CFileObject* and *CContainerItem*—a Boolean flag in the interface class differentiates the two. As we'll see, much of the implementation of any *IOleItem-Container* interface for any object is somewhat independent of the actual object. This is even more true with the *IDescription* interface. As shown in Figure 9-8, the descriptive text for every object is stored in a stream named "Description" under the object's dedicated storage. The *CImpIDescription* class

(IDESCRIP.CPP) doesn't care what *IStorage* it should look at; it simply implements *GetText* by attempting to read the description stream. Each object that exposes this interface instantiates a *CImpIDescription* and hands it its particular *IStorage* pointer; thus, we need only one piece of code for each object, showing one case in which the interface implementation technique is highly useful and actually more efficient and robust than a deep multiple-inheritance technique.

You will also notice that *CContainerItem* and *CSimpleItem* are so much alike (the former implements one additional interface) that you may wonder why I haven't used *CSimpleItem* as a base class for *CContainerItem*. My reason is that the similarity is an artifact of the relationship of these objects to the hierarchy in LinkSource's compound file. Real-world scenarios will likely not be this simple, so I'd rather illustrate a framework with distinct object classes. In later chapters, we'll be adding link-source capabilities to the Patron sample in which its Document, Page, and Tenant objects act in the same ways that LinkSource's three objects act here. But the Page and Tenant objects are so dissimilar that they share no implementation at all.

The following sections look at this implementation in more detail, specifically those parts related to binding and name parsing. First, however, we need to create a file so that LinkUser can name it with a file moniker.

## Creating the Source File

LinkUser will create a file moniker with the hard-coded pathname C:\INOLE\CHAP09\LINKSRC\GOOP.LKS, so someone had better create that file. If you run LinkSource by itself, it will display a window with a File /Create GOOP.LKS menu item that does exactly this. If you are interested in the exact code, look at *CApp::CreateSampleFile*, *CApp::CreateStore*, and *CApp::WriteDescription* in LINKSRC.CPP. Besides being a demonstration of the use of Structured Storage, this procedure also creates a compound file with five first-level substorages named "Object *m*," under each of which are five more substorages named "Sub-Object *n*." Overall, the file will contain 26 distinct storage elements (including the root), and each will contain a description stream with some relevant text. You can easily modify the code to create more storage elements on either level if you want.

Obviously, this file is a contrived example that gives us some persistent data to which we can bind through monikers. A real-world application, of course, would use many different files, but typically those files will all have the same internal structure. The names might be more variable, and data might not be structured perfectly in isolated storage elements and streams, but you get the idea. The benefit of using a storage hierarchy in the manner that LinkSource does is that the item names in a long composite moniker are nothing more than the substorage names in the file. The Patron implementation we'll see later works in the same way. Of course, this is not efficient for all types of applications, for example a spreadsheet, which uses item names to identify sections of data within a particular stream.

The final note about the file is that LinkSource marks it with its own CLSID, specifically *CLSID_ LinkedFile*, by calling *IStorage::SetClass*. This allows the file moniker to easily retrieve this CLSID and launch LinkSource to get at its file object. Let's see how that works.

## Implementing Binding Support

LinkSource as a server supports binding to File, File!Item, and File!Item!Item monikers. What is common in all of these names is that they each begin with a File moniker, so all binding in LinkSource starts with binding a file moniker. Any item binding happens relative to the object named by such a file moniker, so LinkSource needs to serve only a single CLSID. In other words, a LinkSource file is a component with three objects: File, Container Item, and Simple Item. The one CLSID, *CLSID_ LinkedFile* identifies the file object, which is the root of the Linked File component.

Thus, LinkSource will create and register a class factory (using *CFileObjectFactory* in LINKSRC.CPP) and will include all the registry entries needed to list LINKSRC.EXE under *CLSID_ LinkedFile*. There is nothing more to all of this class factory and registration business that we have not already learned from Chapter 5. The important point is that there is only one registered CLSID. Note also that LinkSource registers the class factory regardless of *-Embedding* on the command line; this enables you to run LinkSource in a debugger and trace through it easily when LinkUser attempts to bind a moniker or parse a display name, without having to otherwise struggle to get the server launched into a debugger.

### Binding Support for the File Moniker

As we know, a file moniker's *BindToObject* will call *GetClassFile* to associate its filename with a CLSID, then call *CoCreateInstance(..., IID_ IPersistFile)* with that CLSID, then call *IPersistFile::Load*, and finally call *IPersistFile::Query-Interface* to get the interface to return to the client. When LinkUser attempts to obtain the description for a stand-alone file moniker, this last *QueryInterface* will ask for *IDescription*.

To support this binding, LinkSource must first associate its file with its CLSID, which is the reason why it calls *IStorage::SetClass* as described earlier. The object instantiated through this CLSID, *CFileObject*, supports *IPersistFile* (*CImpIPersistFile* in FILEOBJ.CPP). The implementation is quite simple: *GetClassID* returns *CLSID_LinkedFile*, *IsDirty* returns S_FALSE (LinkSource makes no changes), *Save* and *SaveCompleted* return NOERROR (no reason to save), and *GetCurFile* makes a copy of the filename.

The implementation of *IPersistFile::Load* is where most of the action takes place:

```
STDMETHODIMP CImpIPersistFile::Load(LPCOLESTR pszFile, DWORD grfMode)
    {
    const int    cch=512;
    HRESULT      hr;

    if (NULL!=m_pObj->m_pmk)
        return ResultFromScode(E_UNEXPECTED);

    hr=StgOpenStorage(pszFile, NULL
        , STGM_DIRECT | STGM_READ | STGM_SHARE_DENY_WRITE, NULL, 0
        , &m_pObj->m_pIStorage);

    if (FAILED(hr))
        return hr;

    m_pObj->m_pImpIDescription->SetStorage(m_pObj->m_pIStorage);
    lstrcpyn(m_pObj->m_szFile, pszFile, cch);

    if (SUCCEEDED(CreateFileMoniker(pszFile, &m_pObj->m_pmk)))
        {
        IRunningObjectTable    *pROT;

        if (SUCCEEDED(GetRunningObjectTable(0, &pROT)))
            {
            //Register as weak so clients can free us.
            pROT->Register(0, m_pObj, m_pObj->m_pmk
                , &m_pObj->m_dwRegROT);
            pROT->Release();
            }
        }

    return NOERROR;
    }
```

If *Load* successfully opens the file, it then hands that *IStorage* to its *IDescription* interface (which does not call *AddRef* because it's a contained class), saves the filename, and registers the file as running in the running object table. This last step is very important for servers to complete, especially those that potentially service links from any number of clients. For example, if you ran two instances of LinkUser against the same instance of LinkSource, the second attempt to bind any moniker would be faster because the file object is already running and is registered. Wherever the server creates the registered moniker, it generally holds onto that moniker for potential later uses. In LinkSource, we use the moniker to know whether or not *Load* has already been called so we can prevent reentrancy.

If we successfully return from *Load*, the file moniker will query the file object for whatever interface it wants, which in this scenario is *IDescription*. Thus, we've followed the map and found the treasure with only a little bit of code and a simple implementation of *IPersistFile*.

## Binding Support for the File!Item Moniker

When LinkUser binds a File!Item composite and asks for *IDescription*, the composite will specifically call the item's *BindToObject* and ask for that same interface. Item monikers know that they require the services of the moniker to their left, in this case the file moniker. So the item calls *pmkLeft->BindToObject(..., IID_IOleItemContainer, ...)*. This *BindToObject* call appears to LinkSource's file object exactly as if LinkUser were binding a file moniker by itself except that the final *QueryInterface* will now ask for *IOleItemContainer*. Thus, the file object in LinkSource must also implement this interface, which is again a shared implementation in *CImpIOleItemContainer* (IOLECONT.CPP). In this case, the interface will know that it's part of the file object through its internal flag *m_fFileObj*.

LinkSource implements all the member functions in this interface except for *EnumObjects*, which for binding purposes can return E_NOTIMPL. We need to implement *ParseDisplayName* and *LockContainer* specifically for parsing support, as we'll see a little later on. The other members, *GetObject*, *GetObjectStorage*, and *IsRunning*, are important to the binding process. In particular, *GetObject* has to create or access the correct object as specified by an item name:

```
STDMETHODIMP CImpIOleItemContainer::GetObject(LPOLESTR pszItem
    , DWORD dwSpeed, LPBINDCTX pbc, REFIID riid, PPVOID ppv)
    {
    HRESULT        hr;
    IStorage       *pIStorage;
```

```
    PCContainerItem    pCI;
    PCSimpleItem       pSI;
    BOOL               fSuccess;
    IUnknown           *pUnk;

    *ppv=NULL;

    hr=GetRunning(pszItem, pbc, riid, ppv, FALSE);

    if (BINDSPEED_IMMEDIATE==dwSpeed && NOERROR!=hr)
        return ResultFromScode(MK_E_EXCEEDEDDEADLINE);

    //If object was running, we're done!
    if (NOERROR==hr)
        return NOERROR;

    //Otherwise, we need to get storage.
    hr=GetObjectStorage(pszItem, pbc, IID_IStorage
        , (void **)&pIStorage);

    if (FAILED(hr))
        return hr;

    fSuccess=FALSE;

    if (m_fFileObj)
        {
        pCI=new CContainerItem(m_pObjFile, m_pObjFile->m_pfnDestroy);

        pUnk=pCI;

        if (NULL!=pCI)
            {
            pUnk->AddRef();
            fSuccess=pCI->Init(m_pObjFile->m_pmk, pbc, pszItem
                , pIStorage);
            }
        }
    else
        {
        pSI=new CSimpleItem(m_pObjCont, m_pObjCont->m_pfnDestroy);

        pUnk=pSI;
```

*(continued)*

```
        if (NULL!=pSI)
            {
            pUnk->AddRef();
            fSuccess=pSI->Init(m_pObjCont->m_pmk, pbc, pszItem
                , pIStorage);
            }
        }

    if (!fSuccess)
        {
        if (NULL!=pUnk)
            pUnk->Release();

        return ResultFromScode(E_OUTOFMEMORY);
        }

    g_cObj++;

    //If QueryInterface fails, this Release destroys object.
    hr=pUnk->QueryInterface(riid, ppv);
    pUnk->Release();

    if (FAILED(hr))
        return hr;

    return NOERROR;
    }
```

On entry to *GetObject*, you should always check whether the object is already running and return its pointer if so. The internal member *CImpIOle-ItemContainer::GetRunning* performs this step, which conveniently provides us with the implementation for *IsRunning* as well. *GetRunning* does nothing more than create an appropriate moniker and call *IRunningObjectTable-::IsRunning* or *IRunningObjectTable::GetObject*, depending on a Boolean flag. The call we're making to *GetRunning* here within *GetObject* attempts the latter.

Now comes an important step: if the object is running, we can return successfully even if the bind context specified BINDSPEED_IMMEDIATE. If the object is not running, we have to return MK_E_EXCEEDEDDEAD-LINE—we should not attempt to load or run the object under such a time limitation.

If we can use more time, we check the existence of the particular object named in *pszItem* by calling our own *GetObjectStorage*. Our ability to do this stems from the fact that LinkSource's items are all contained within storage elements already—a server that handles objects whose data resides in other structures will, of course, take different steps here and potentially have to

Naming and Binding: Monikers

parse much more out of *pszItem*. The way you handle this string is entirely up to the nature of your server and the complexity of that string. With the binding speed being the only constraint, you can execute any code you want inside *GetObject* and *GetObjectStorage*.

Anyway, if *GetObjectStorage* is successful, we know the object exists, and we get back its *IStorage* pointer. We then hand the pointer to a new instantiation of *CContainerItem* or *CSimpleItem*, the choice of which is controlled by the interface's *m_fFileObj* flag. When the flag is FALSE, the interface is part of a *CContainerItem* object and is being used to bind a second item moniker. In our present example, this code will create a *CContainerItem*. (You can see how similar it is to *CSimpleItem* as well, because creation and initialization of both are nearly identical.)

The function *CContainerItem::Init* performs steps similar to the file object's *IPersistFile::Load*: it sets up the *IDescription* interface and registers the object as running. The code here looks just like the code shown earlier for *Load* with a slight change in variables. Nothing fancy.

That leaves us to glance quickly at *IOleItemContainer::GetObjectStorage*, which in our case can supply only an *IStorage* for the object:

```
STDMETHODIMP CImpIOleItemContainer::GetObjectStorage(LPOLESTR pszItem
    , LPBINDCTX pbc, REFIID riid, PPVOID ppv)
    {
    IStorage        *pIStorageObj;
    IStorage        *pIStorageNew;
    HRESULT          hr;

    if (IID_IStorage!=riid)
        return ResultFromScode(MK_E_NOSTORAGE);

    pIStorageObj=m_fFileObj ? m_pObjFile->m_pIStorage
        : m_pObjCont->m_pIStorage;

    hr=pIStorageObj->OpenStorage(pszItem
        , NULL, STGM_TRANSACTED | STGM_READ | STGM_SHARE_EXCLUSIVE
        , NULL, 0, &pIStorageNew);

    if (FAILED(hr))
        {
        IUnknown    *pUnk;

        if (STG_E_ACCESSDENIED!=GetScode(hr))
            return hr;
```

*(continued)*

```
    if (FAILED(pbc->GetObjectParam(SZOPENSTORAGE, &pUnk)))
        return ResultFromScode(STG_E_ACCESSDENIED);

    hr=pUnk->QueryInterface(IID_IStorage
        , (void **)&pIStorageNew);
    pUnk->Release();
    *ppv=pIStorageNew;
    return hr;
    }

*ppv=pIStorageNew;
pbc->RegisterObjectParam(SZOPENSTORAGE, pIStorageNew);
return NOERROR;
}
```

Here you can see an example of a use of *IBindCtx::RegisterObjectParam* and *IBindCtx::GetObjectParam*. When LinkScr is run in order to parse a name and bind the resulting moniker, LinkUser maintains the same bind context throughout the whole process. The problem we run into is that the first *CSimpleItem* object created for parsing is still alive in the bind context and is still holding the storage open using STGM_SHARE_EXCLUSIVE. So the *CSimpleItem* created during binding will not be able to open this storage itself. To solve this problem, we register the open storage as an object parameter during the parsing step so that we can access it again during the binding step. (Sharing is not a problem because this is all in the same server.)

With that, we have all the support necessary for File!Item moniker binding. If LinkUser were binding such a moniker, *IOleItemContainer::GetObject* would be followed by a *QueryInterface* to the new *CContainerItem* asking for *IDescription*.

### Binding Support for the File!Item!Item Moniker

When LinkUser now binds a File!Item!Item composite asking for *IDescription*, the composite once again asks the rightmost item to bind and return that interface. Once again, this item calls *pmkLeft->BindToObject(..., IID_IOleItem-Container, ...)*, which in this case asks the first-level item moniker to bind as described in the previous section. However, the final *QueryInterface* to the *CContainerItem* object will ask for *IOleItemContainer*. Now *CContainerItem* uses exactly the same *IOleItemContainer* implementation that we've already seen except that it creates an instance of *CSimpleItem* as the object being named. *CSimpleItem* also sets up its *IDescription* implementation and registers itself as running.

Because *CSimpleItem* implements only *IDescription*, any attempt to bind a File!Item!Item!Item moniker through LinkSource will fail. If we added *IOle-ItemContainer* to this object, we would support that additional layer of items.

In short, as long as each intermediate item supports *IOleItemContainer*, you can support arbitrarily long composite monikers, with many treasures along the way.

## Implementing Parsing Support

For the most part, asking a server to parse moniker strings works very similarly to the binding process except that we do, of course, parse the display name from left to right. *MkParseDisplayName* will check for a filename or a string starting with @ in order to determine the CLSID of the first object in the name. So let's say LinkUser wants to parse "C:\INOLE\CHAP09\LINK-SRC\GOOP.LKS!Object 2!Sub-Object 3". *MkParseDisplayName* will parse out the filename and create a file moniker out of it; this file moniker is the base to which *MkParseDisplayName* will attempt to add more individual monikers. Somehow it has to take the remaining string, "!Object 2!Sub-Object 3", and find someone to parse it. Well, because it knows that the file object named with the file moniker also understands the items within it, *MkParseDisplayName* asks that file object to do the parsing. It finds the CLSID for the filename already parsed and calls *CoCreateInstance* and asks for *IParseDisplayName*.

In the case of LinkSource, this will once again go all the way through the class factory to instantiate a *CFileObject*. When LinkSource is queried or when *IParseDisplayName* is called, we return our *IOleItemContainer* because the latter is derived from the former. When *MkParseDisplayName* gets this interface back from *CoCreateInstance*, it will pass the remaining string to parse to *IParseDisplayName::ParseDisplayName*:

```
STDMETHODIMP CImpIOleItemContainer::ParseDisplayName(LPBC pbc
    , LPOLESTR pszName, ULONG *pchEaten, LPMONIKER *ppmk)
    {
    OLECHAR    ch;
    ULONG      chEaten=0;
    TCHAR      szName[256];
    TCHAR      szComp[15];
    LPTSTR     psz;
    UINT       cch;

    *ppmk=NULL;
    *pchEaten=0;
    psz=szName;

    ch=*pszName++;
    chEaten++;
```

*(continued)*

```
if ((OLECHAR)'!'!=ch)
    return ResultFromScode(MK_E_SYNTAX);

ch=*pszName++;

while ((OLECHAR)0!=ch && (OLECHAR)'!' !=ch)
    {
    *psz++=(TCHAR)ch;
    chEaten++;
    ch=*pszName++;
    }

*psz=(TCHAR)0;

lstrcpy(szComp, m_fFileObj ? TEXT("Object ")
    : TEXT("Sub-Object "));

//Does szName start with szComp?
cch=lstrlen(szComp);

if (0!=_tcsncicmp(szName, szComp, cch))
    {
    *pchEaten=1;    //Parsed ! at least.
    return ResultFromScode(MK_E_SYNTAX);
    }

//Check for number in szName.
if ((TCHAR)'0' != szName[cch])
    {
    if (0==_ttoi(szName+cch))
        {
        *pchEaten=cch;  //Got past name.
        return ResultFromScode(MK_E_SYNTAX);
        }
    }

*pchEaten=chEaten;
return CreateItemMoniker(TEXT("!"), szName, ppmk);
}
```

LinkSource knows that it separates item monikers with a ! delimiter, so this code needs only to scan for strings between those delimiters. The *pszName* argument should be initially pointing to a !, so if that is absent we return MK_E_SYNTAX. Otherwise, we copy the remaining characters into a buffer up to the next ! or to the end of the string. We then confirm that this string has the format "Object *m*" or "Sub-Object *n*," depending on the *m_fFileObj* flag in this interface, return MK_E_SYNTAX in case of error, and ensure that an appropriate value is stored in *∗pchEaten* to indicate where the error occurred. We do not, however, verify that an object exists—parsing is meant to check syntax, leaving binding to check existence.

After we finish parsing and validation, we need to return an appropriate moniker. In this example, that is always an item moniker, but there are no restrictions as to the moniker type. (*IParseDisplayName* does not depend on *IOleItemContainer*; it's the other way around.)

The final part of this implementation is the *IOleContainer::LockContainer* function, which *MkParseDisplayName* will call to stabilize the object doing the parsing—that is, to ensure that the object doesn't disappear as long as the bind context remains alive. You can implement *LockContainer* with a simple *AddRef* and *Release*, depending on the *fLock* argument:

```
STDMETHODIMP CImpIOleItemContainer::LockContainer(BOOL fLock)
    {
    if (fLock)
        AddRef();
    else
        Release();

    return NOERROR;
    }
```

You might also consider using *CoLockObjectExternal* in this function if your implementation calls for managing the object on the basis of external connections rather than through a reference count. Because no other strong locks are involved with LinkSource, we can use just a reference count.

## Summary

OLE's Naming and Binding technology is centered around a type of object called the moniker, which acts as a symbol or a name for some other object. The purpose of this technology is to enable applications to use a wide variety of names in a polymorphic, and thus extensible, manner, keeping specific code for specific types of names out of those applications.

A moniker maintains persistent data that describes the name itself and provides the intelligence (code) that knows how to bind that name. These operations are encapsulated behind the interface *IMoniker*, whose *BindTo-Object* member resolves the moniker's name as an interface pointer to the named object, returning that pointer to whoever asked the moniker to bind itself. *IMoniker* itself is derived from *IPersistStream*, meaning that monikers know how to read and write their persistent data (their names) into a stream. Thus monikers are also called *persistent, intelligent names*.

Monikers can be created in many ways, either by the source of the object being named or by a client who wants to fabricate a name for some known object. OLE supplies five standard monikers: file, item, pointer, anti, and generic composite. The composite moniker is nothing more than a container for other monikers, but with it you can create arbitrarily complex names using the other simple monikers. Simple monikers themselves name only things like an entire file. It is also worthwhile at times to implement a custom moniker, which is simply an object that implements *IMoniker* structured inside a server and given a CLSID. Implementing *IMoniker*, a rather large interface, is nontrivial, but in this chapter we explore the purpose of its member functions.

Binding a composite moniker is the process of binding its constituent pieces in a right to left manner, thereby eliminating any extra overhead. Two optimizations, the running object table and the bind context, are available to improve binding performance. The server that supports linking to its objects through monikers must implement the necessary structures and interfaces to support the binding process of a composite as well as a single file moniker. This chapter demonstrates how this works to the level of complexity of a File!Item!Item moniker, which is a composite containing a file and two levels of items, whereby the composite as a whole names a specific piece of a compound file.

Finally, monikers can generate a display name from their persistent data (to show the user) as well as parse such a display name back into an appropriate moniker. These capabilities are also demonstrated in this chapter's samples.

# PART III

# DATA TRANSFER, VIEWING, AND CACHING

CHAPTER TEN

# Uniform Data Transfer and Notifications

*Have you ever flown up in an airplane and thought about all the little houses down there? If you look at them really close, they're just little piles of people's stuff.*

—Comedian George Carlin

In this book, we've used the general definition of an object as an entity that manages data as well as functionality to manipulate that data in some way. Programming languages such as C++ allow an object's client to call its member functions and to possibly access its data directly. On the other hand, objects in COM and OLE are always manipulated through interface pointers, and those interfaces have nothing in them except functions. Still, OLE and COM objects, like objects in any programming language, have data—the object's stuff—that may be useful to the client. The question is, will that object let you look at its stuff?

In OLE, the answer concerns how you (playing the role of the client) want to look at that stuff. Do you want to see formatted data structures, graphical representations of that data, or individual fields or properties? Perhaps you really don't care about the actual data at all and would rather see it as an unstructured blob that you can store without knowing its internal format. Much of the rest of this book concerns the various ways to get at an object's stuff, as well as some of its functionality, through a variety of interfaces. In this chapter, we are concerned particularly with formatted data structures that contain any number of individual fields. Chapter 11 looks at the graphical side of things, and Chapters 12 and 13 explore two user interface mechanisms for data exchange, the clipboard and OLE Drag and Drop. Part IV (Chapters 13 through 15) looks into OLE Automation and the idea of individual properties, and Part V (Chapters 17 through 23) details OLE Documents, through which a client generally sees an object's data as unstructured blobs.

A *data object,* or the *source* of data, is any object that implements the interface named *IDataObject.* Through this interface, OLE handles all exchanges of formatted data structures between that data source and its client, which we call the *consumer* in this context. All sources of structured data, as far as consumers are concerned, are polymorphic through this interface, regardless of how the consumer comes to obtain an *IDataObject* pointer. There are several ways to obtain such a pointer: the consumer can query for one, it can receive it from a drag-and-drop operation, or it can ask for one from OLE's clipboard APIs.

Some objects might implement *IDataObject* as their primary interface, representing their overall purpose for existence. For example, a stand-alone, in-process data object can be a great way to expose the information collected from data acquisition hardware that's attached to your computer (via serial port, parallel port, custom board, and so on). Usually this hardware comes with some complex custom API in a DLL or offers its data only through cumbersome DDE (Dynamic Data Exchange) protocols. With a data object, the vendor could ship a component DLL so that any interested client would need only to call *CoCreateInstance* with the right CLSID (easily retrieved from the registry using a ProgID that can be entered into a consumer at run time) and ask for *IDataObject* in return. Through that interface, the consumer could enumerate the available data and retrieve whatever structures it wants. The result? Fewer API functions for everyone to design, implement, deploy, and learn. Being a component, such a DLL could be replaced and updated at will, without endangering existing clients. This is Plug and Play not only for the hardware, but also for the software!

You can see that a data object can either be very specialized or be a generic expression of the contents of some other data store, such as the clipboard, or the contents of some other, much richer, object, such as an OLE control. (*IDataObject* is one of a control's requisite interfaces.) Whenever formatted data structures need to be exchanged, *IDataObject* is there.

In this chapter, we'll define data objects and explain how they behave — that is, we'll define the semantics of *IDataObject.* All of the functionality embodied in the Windows clipboard and DDE APIs (even OLE 1, a data transfer API of sorts) is brought together in *IDataObject.* Regardless of the way a consumer obtains such a pointer, it can always treat it polymorphically, which is exactly why I coined the term (or moniker, we might say) *Uniform Data Transfer.* This term means that the way a consumer uses an *IDataObject* pointer is entirely removed from the way it obtains that pointer. The method of obtaining the pointer is called the *transfer protocol.* Mechanisms such as the OLE

Clipboard and OLE Drag and Drop are *protocols* because they are concerned only with communicating information about the data object along with the *IDataObject* pointer—they are not concerned with the actual data. The source and the consumer use a protocol to agree on the data format and exchange rules; data transfer is the actual exchange of real, tangible bits.

Up to this time, the Windows API has intertwined the act of transfer with each protocol (clipboard, DDE, and so on). Uniform Data Transfer ends this shotgun marriage and simplifies and homogenizes the way in which both sources and consumers deal with data exchange. In addition, some features (such as dynamic data change notifications) have previously been supported only for one protocol. The other part of *Uniform* means that these features are enabled for all protocols because they exist as part of *IDataObject*.

Another problem with the existing Windows API in this area is that data formats are limited to a single WORD clipboard format (a CF_* value) that describes only the layout of the bits in the data structure. This data structure must also reside in global memory—no standards exist for data exchange using any other storage medium. To counter this problem, OLE introduces two new data structures, FORMATETC and STGMEDIUM, that enable far more descriptive formats and a choice of storage mediums, in which the WORD format and the HGLOBAL medium form a small subset. These structures are the first topic in this chapter. This topic is followed by a look at the *IDataObject* interface and its member functions. Three of these member functions, along with an interface named *IAdviseSink* (the original sink, predating connection points), allow the consumer to receive notifications when the data changes in the source. Through *IAdviseSink*, the consumer can either have new data sent with each notification or simply be notified that data changed so that it can request an update later.

These notifications have some parallels with the old (and rather worn-out) DDE protocol. This chapter will also take a look at these parallels, how the OLE model differs from DDE, and how to reconcile those differences. We'll look at a real-world situation in which a DDE-oriented design was replaced with a more efficient design based on OLE. Along with the exploration of the other methods of later chapters, we'll see that OLE offers a complete architecture for data exchange between source and consumer, all of which is centered on, or employs in some fashion, the single *IDataObject* interface. So no matter how high you are flying, no matter how complex the code, Uniform Data Transfer and the *IDataObject* interface let you see every object down below as just a little pile of stuff.

# New and Improved Ultra-Structures!

The following is a paid commercial announcement.

*Hello, friends. Ole' Bob Data here. Are you cranky because the only way to describe data is by using a lousy little clipboard format? Are you irritable because the only way to exchange data is by using a crummy global-memory handle? Are you tired of waiting around while you try to copy a 30-MB, 24-bit, device-independent bitmap, listening to your disk chug like Grandma's old Hoover? Well, friends, I can end your misery forever. What I have here can end hard disk swapping that sounds like a Studebaker lug nut in a meat grinder! It's New and Improved Ultra-Structures, free with every purchase of OLE and free with every instance of a data object! No longer do you just say, "Bitmap"! No longer do you just say, "Metafile"! Be free! Be fresh! Send me your paycheck! Tell your data object not only that you want a bitmap but that you want it to be just a thumbnail sketch! Tell your data object not only that you want that metafile but that you want it created for a PostScript device! Tell your data object that you want every known translation of the Bible, Koran, Torah, I Ching, Bhagavad-Gita, and the collected thoughts of Mao Tse-tung, and not just as a lousy temperamental piece of global memory but in a compound file!!! The choice is yours! How much would you be willing to pay? Five API functions? Twenty API functions? A hundred new API functions? No! These are yours free with your qualified use of a data object! Available at a data object supplier near you.*

Taxlicensinganddestinationchargesapplicablebutvoidwhereprohibitedanddoesnotincludedealerprep-markuportheoverheadofpayingforridiculousadvertisementslikethisorthetendollarsaminuteweautomat-icallychargetoeverycreditcardinyournamejustforlisteningtous.

Now back to our scheduled programming.

Every version of Windows since version 1 back in 1985 has performed all data exchange (the clipboard and DDE) using a simple clipboard format and a global-memory handle. To copy data to the clipboard, you call *SetClipboard-Data*, passing a clipboard format and a global-memory handle. To paste, you call *GetClipboardData* with a clipboard format and get back a global-memory handle. DDE is restricted in the same fashion: WM_DDE_DATA messages carry with them only a global-memory handle containing the data and an item that describes what might be in that memory.

OLE 1 employed this same scheme for its data transfer needs and suffered accordingly. As happens with the clipboard and DDE, many copies of the same data generally sat in memory at any given moment. Small data were tolerable, but large 24-bit DIBs rapidly drained the system of free memory. Often a source would load a large block of data into memory from disk, and it promptly ended up back on the disk as virtual memory. The consumer would then load this data back from the disk through virtual memory, eventually writing it somewhere else on the disk. I think all of us have experienced a good 15 minutes' worth of serious grinding noises coming from a hard drive in these cases. OLE 1 merely exacerbated the problem because it did this for both a graphical presentation and a content object's native data, which was often just as large.

The OLE architects realized that this was an area for major improvement when they began designing OLE 2. In fact, Structured Storage grew out of the need to have an efficient shareable storage medium that different components could access incrementally. The architects were also set on adding OLE Drag and Drop and didn't want another protocol to suffer the same performance problems as the others.

Thus, it became necessary to extend the allowable mediums for data exchange beyond global memory and to expand the format definition beyond the clipboard format. At the same time, the designers needed to preserve compatibility with existing mechanisms, making the clipboard format and memory handle a subset of the new order of things. Enter two new structures, FORMATETC and STGMEDIUM.

## The FORMATETC Structure

FORMATETC (pronounced "format et cetera") is a generalization—and an improvement—of the clipboard format and contains a rich description of data. The name comes from the idea that it contains a clipboard format and some more stuff—the et cetera:

```
typedef WORD CLIPFORMAT;

typedef struct tagFORMATETC
    {
    CLIPFORMAT      cfFormat;
    DVTARGETDEVICE *ptd;
    DWORD           dwAspect;
    LONG            lindex;
    DWORD           tymed;
    } FORMATETC;

enum tagDVASPECT
    {
    DVASPECT_CONTENT    = 1,
    DVASPECT_THUMBNAIL  = 2,
    DVASPECT_ICON       = 4,
    DVASPECT_DOCPRINT   = 8
    } DVASPECT;
```

Its fields carry information as follows:

- *cfFormat*: The clipboard format identifying the data structure. This can be a standard format such as CF_TEXT or a format that both source and consumer register with the Windows API *RegisterClipboardFormat*. The use of "clipboard" here is archaic—the identified structures themselves have nothing to do with the clipboard. The name stuck because the clipboard was the first data exchange protocol in Windows and the first to use a simple integer identification of structures.

- *ptd*: Information about the device, such as a screen or a printer, for which the data was rendered. The DVTARGETDEVICE structure looks and acts similar to the Windows DEVNAMES structure. It contains a header for a variable-length block of data, and each offset in the structure points to a specific piece of information in the block, where all strings are stored in Unicode under 32-bit OLE:

```
typedef struct FARSTRUCT tagDVTARGETDEVICE
    {
    DWORD    tdSize;
    WORD     tdDriverNameOffset;
    WORD     tdDeviceNameOffset;
    WORD     tdPortNameOffset;
    WORD     tdExtDevmodeOffset;
    BYTE     tdData[1];    //Contains the names and DEVMODE
    } DVTARGETDEVICE;
```

  *tdSize* always holds the size of the entire structure, including all additional bytes that occur after the DVTARGETDEVICE header. This simplifies copying the structure when necessary. Each *td...Offset* field is an offset from the start of the entire structure, not from the start of *tdData*. Because offsets start at the top of the structure, a 0 means "not present," or a NULL value for that name.

- *dwAspect*: The detail contained in the rendering, particularly useful for graphical formats. Values are taken from the DVASPECT enumeration: DVASPECT_CONTENT specifies "full content," as would normally be shown in some kind of document; DVASPECT_THUMBNAIL means "thumbnail sketch," as would be used in a print preview or document preview window; DVASPECT_ICON describes an icon view appropriate for small presentations as an attachment to an e-mail message; and DVASPECT_DOCPRINT identifies the rendering as a full "printer document" that includes all page numbers, headers,

and footers, just as if the data were printed as a document from its
native application.

- *lindex*: Identifier for the piece of the data when the data must be
  split across page boundaries. An *lindex* of −1 identifies the entire
  data and is the most common value. Otherwise, *lindex* has meaning
  only in DVASPECT_CONTENT, in which it identifies a piece of data
  for extended layout negotiation, and in DVASPECT_DOCPRINT, in
  which it identifies the page number.[1]

- *tymed*: The medium in which the data lives with values taken from
  the TYMED enumeration. See "The STGMEDIUM Structure" later
  in this chapter.

Obviously, filling out a structure like this every time you want to describe
a data format will become tedious; you need five lines of code simply to fill
the structure. To address this, I have defined two macros in INC\INOLE.H
that facilitate filling a FORMATETC: *SETFormatEtc*, which allows you to set
every field in a FORMATETC structure explicitly, and *SETDefFormatEtc*, which
allows you to set *cfFormat* and *tymed* while filling the other fields with defaults
(a common operation):

```
#define SETFormatEtc(fe, cf, asp, td, med, li)    \
    {\
    (fe).cfFormat=cf;\
    (fe).dwAspect=asp;\
    (fe).ptd=td;\
    (fe).tymed=med;\
    (fe).lindex=li;\
    };

#define SETDefFormatEtc(fe, cf, med)    \
    {\
    (fe).cfFormat=cf;\
    (fe).dwAspect=DVASPECT_CONTENT;\
    (fe).ptd=NULL;\
    (fe).tymed=med;\
    (fe).lindex=-1;\
    };
```

I encourage you to use these macros when dealing with FORMATETC
because they are far more convenient than writing each line of code separately.

---

1. Page layout capabilities might not be supported in the version of OLE you are working with.
In the original OLE 2 and all shipping versions up to the time of writing in early 1995, *lindex* must
always be −1. Newer interfaces will be using this field in the near future according to its original
purpose described here. See your current *OLE Programmer's Reference* for more information.

## Handling DVTARGETDEVICE

As described above, the *ptd* field of a FORMATETC structure is a pointer to a DVTARGETDEVICE structure. A NULL *ptd* always means "screen device," which is, of course, the easiest to handle. Printer devices, on the other hand, are more complex. Applications and components that deal with device-specific data will end up performing a few basic operations with such a structure: creating a structure, copying or comparing two structures, and creating a device context or an information context from a structure.

To that end, the sample code for this chapter provides a number of standard implementations of these functions, which you can find in CHAP10-\TARGDEV\TARGDEV.CPP.[2] In this file are the functions *TargetDeviceToDC*, *TargetDeviceFromPrintDlg*, *TargetDeviceCopy*, and *TargetDeviceCompare*. *TargetDeviceToDC* calls *CreateDC* or *CreateIC* with the information in a DVTARGET-DEVICE structure. *TargetDeviceFromPrintDlg* creates a DVTARGETDEVICE structure (using the task memory allocator through *CoTaskMemAlloc*) from the PRINTDLG structure filled by the Windows *PrintDlg* API function. Applications generally use *PrintDlg* to obtain printer information in the first place, so it's convenient to be able to send that data to *TargetDeviceFromPrintDlg* and get back the OLE structure you need.

The other two functions are actually quite simple and manipulate the structure on little more than a binary level. In any case, I hope you find this code useful in your own work.

## Copying and Comparing FORMATETC Structures

Whenever you want to copy or compare FORMATETC structures, keep the following in mind. When copying one structure to another, be sure to copy the entire DVTARGETDEVICE structure as well, using code such as that found in the sample *TargetDeviceCopy* function. Other than that, copying is a straightforward duplication of each field.

Comparing two FORMATETC structures presents a slightly different problem. First of all, the *cfFormat* and *lindex* fields must match exactly for equivalence. In addition, both structures must have the same target device structure, which is where the sample *TargetDeviceCompare* function comes in handy. Both *dwAspect* and *tymed* require special handling, however. You can compare these either for exact equivalence or on a subset basis. For example, if one FORMATETC has DVASPECT_CONTENT | DVASPECT_THUMB-NAIL, another with only DVASPECT_CONTENT could be considered equivalent but not an exact match. The same applies to TYMED_* flags. Why

---

2. These functions are portable between ANSI (16-bit) and Unicode (32-bit) to handle both versions of DVTARGETDEVICE.

you'd choose either form of comparison depends on why you're making the comparison in the first place. If you want to determine whether one FORMAT-ETC is a subset of a supported set of formats, use a subset comparison. If you need an exact match for a specific rendering, you want an exact comparison.

## The STGMEDIUM Structure

FORMATETC is merely half of the picture, of course, because it describes only the data format but says nothing about where the data actually is. This reference is provided by the STGMEDIUM (storage medium) structure, a generalization of the global-memory handle, which holds a mixture of different data references:

```
typedef struct tagSTGMEDIUM
    {
    DWORD tymed;
    union
        {
        HBITMAP         hBitmap;
        HMETAFILEPICT   hMetaFilePict;
        HENHMETAFILE    hEnhMetaFile;
        HGLOBAL         hGlobal;
        LPOLESTR        lpszFileName;
        IStream         *pstm;
        IStorage        *pstg;
        } u;
    IUnknown *pUnkForRelease;
    } STGMEDIUM;

enum tagTYMED
    {
    TYMED_HGLOBAL   = 1,
    TYMED_FILE      = 2,
    TYMED_ISTREAM   = 4,
    TYMED_ISTORAGE  = 8,
    TYMED_GDI       = 16,
    TYMED_MFPICT    = 32,
    TYMED_ENHMF     = 64,
    TYMED_NULL      = 0
    }   TYMED;
```

The STGMEDIUM fields store the following information:

■ *tymed*: An identifier for the type of medium used, taken from the TYMED enumeration: TYMED_HGLOBAL for global memory, TYMED_FILE for a traditional disk file, TYMED_ISTREAM for any stream object, TYMED_ISTORAGE for a storage object (it doesn't matter whether the storage medium is a compound file), TYMED-_GDI for a Windows GDI object, TYMED_MFPICT for a META-FILEPICT structure in global memory, TYMED_ENHMF for an enhanced metafile in global memory, or TYMED_NULL for no medium (that is, no data).

- *hBitmap, hMetafilePict, hEnhMetaFile, hGlobal, lpszFileName, pStg, pStm*: A union that refers to the actual data. The meaningful element in the union is determined by *tymed*.

- *pUnkForRelease*: If non-NULL, identifies the pointer through which to call *Release* and free the data. This allows control over the ownership of the data, whereby a source can hand out the same data multiple times and track the number of consumer references to that data. See the following discussion of *ReleaseStgMedium*.

Consumers of data (that is, of a storage medium) are usually responsible for freeing the data after they have finished with it. The richness of STGMEDIUM would typically make this process quite complex — you should have the image of a big ugly *switch(stm.tymed)* statement floating in your head. Don't bother — OLE itself provides a single cleanup function named *ReleaseStgMedium*, which does all the right things according to the contents of the structure:

| tymed | Freeing Mechanism in *ReleaseStgMedium* |
| --- | --- |
| Any | *pUnkForRelease->Release()* if *pUnkForRelease* is non-NULL |
| TYMED_HGLOBAL | *GlobalFree(hGlobal)* |
| TYMED_FILE | *DeleteFile(lpszFileName)* followed by *CoTaskMem-Free(lpszFileName)*; the filename is assumed to be allocated with the task allocator |
| TYMED_ISTORAGE | *pStg->Release()* |
| TYMED_ISTREAM | *pStm->Release()* |
| TYMED_GDI | *DeleteObject(hBitmap)* |
| TYMED_MFPICT | *LPMETAFILEPICT pMFP;*<br>*pMFP=GlobalLock(hMetaFilePict);*<br>*DeleteMetaFile(pMFP->hMF);*<br>*GlobalUnlock(hMetaFilePict);*<br>*GlobalFree(hMetaFilePict)* |
| TYMED_ENHMF | *DeleteEnhMetaFile(hEnhMetaFile)* |

The *ReleaseStgMedium* API is exactly the reason why the *tymed* fields of both STGMEDIUM and FORMATETC differentiate between handles for global memory, GDI objects, and metafile pictures. Only with such precise identification can *ReleaseStgMedium* know how to perform cleanup correctly.

---

### The Practical Impact of FORMATETC and STGMEDIUM

The FORMATETC and STGMEDIUM structures open up a wide range of possibilities in data transfer and solve a number of the key problems with previous protocols and data transfer techniques. The most fundamental benefit of these richer descriptions is that data no longer has to live in global memory. If the data is better suited to a disk file, use TYMED_FILE; if a storage or stream element is preferable, use TYMED_ISTORAGE or TYMED_ISTREAM. For example, persistent moniker data—which is easily written to and read from a stream (using *OleSaveToStream* and *OleLoadFromStream*)—is ideally exchanged in TYMED_ISTREAM. In fact, we'll see a standard clipboard format for this named "LinkSource" (CFSTR_LINKSOURCE). In addition, you can easily exchange marshaling data for any interface pointer, where the source would write the stream with *CoMarshalInterface*, and the consumer would call *CoUnmarshalInterface*.

Very large data sets that do not fit in memory can be kept on disk even during a data transfer operation, either in a traditional file or in an element of a compound file. Data that exists in a database need not be extracted until called for because the act of transferring an *IDataObject* pointer doesn't transfer any data, only the means to get at the data. If the data itself is stored in a disk file or in a storage or stream element, the consumer has the advantage of incremental access. Overall, these two structures vastly improve data transfer; any particular data can remain on its most optimal medium until the consumer chooses to copy it elsewhere.

---

# Data Objects and the *IDataObject* Interface

Any component that is a source of formatted data structures is a data object if it implements *IDataObject*. Any and all code that in one way or another has data to share can do so with a data object. The great benefit of doing this is that once you have a data object implementation around, you can use that data object in any transfer protocol, be it clipboard, drag and drop, compound documents,

OLE Automation, and so on, and any new format you might support is instantly provided through all the protocols. A source can centralize the code that renders data into this data object implementation; a consumer can centralize the code necessary to check available formats in a data object and also centralize the code used to paste that data. Centralization reduces both the overall amount of code you must implement and the number of different API functions for dealing with each protocol.

Centralization is possible because the *IDataObject* interface combines the functionality of the existing data transfer protocols, thereby providing more functionality in an OLE data transfer than is available for any other existing protocol. The definition of the *IDataObject* interface is as follows:

```
interface IDataObject : IUnknown
    {
    HRESULT GetData(LPFORMATETC pFEIn, LPSTGMEDIUM pSTM);
    HRESULT GetDataHere(LPFORMATETC pFE, LPSTGMEDIUM pSTM);
    HRESULT QueryGetData(LPFORMATETC pFE);
    HRESULT GetCanonicalFormatEtc(LPFORMATETC pFEIn
        , LPFORMATETC pFEOut);
    HRESULT SetData(LPFORMATETC pFE, LPSTGMEDIUM pSTM, BOOL fRelease);
    HRESULT EnumFormatEtc(DWORD dwDirection, LPENUMFORMATETC *ppEnum);
    HRESULT DAdvise(LPFORMATETC pFE, DWORD grfAdv, LPADVISESINK pAdvSink
        , LPDWORD pdwConnection);
    HRESULT DUnadvise(DWORD dwConnection);
    HRESULT EnumDAdvise(LPENUMSTATDATA *ppEnum);
    };
```

Many of the member functions have equivalents in specific Windows API functions; keep in mind, however, that data objects are used to describe data transferred by means of *any* protocol, and thus they provide the ability to treat data in a uniform fashion regardless of how you obtained the *IDataObject* pointer. The following list describes each *IDataObject* member in more detail and lists the similar (but not always exact) functionality that exists in the clipboard, DDE, and outdated OLE 1 transfer protocols:

■ *GetData* renders the data described by a FORMATETC and returns it in the out-parameter STGMEDIUM, which then becomes the caller's responsibility.

| Protocol | Similar API Function or Message |
|----------|--------------------------------|
| Clipboard | *GetClipboardData* |
| DDE | WM_DDE_REQUEST, WM_DDE_DATA |
| OLE 1 | *OleGetData* |

■ *SetData* provides data to the source described by a FORMATETC and referenced by the in-parameter STGMEDIUM. The data object is responsible for releasing the data if the *fRelease* flag is TRUE. When you call *SetData*, the *tymed* fields in both FORMATETC and STGMEDIUM structures must match.

| Protocol | Similar API Function or Message |
| --- | --- |
| Clipboard | *SetClipboardData* |
| DDE | WM_DDE_POKE |
| OLE 1 | *OleSetData* |

■ *GetDataHere* allows the caller to provide a preallocated medium in which to render the data. For example, if the caller provides an *IStream* object and asks for CF_BITMAP, the source should serialize its bitmap into that stream instead of allocating a new stream on its own as it would through *GetData*. This capability is not found in any existing protocol.

■ *QueryGetData* answers whether the data object can render data described by the given FORMATETC. The caller can be as specific as desired. *QueryGetData* returns NOERROR for "yes" or S_FALSE for "no," so *don't* use the SUCCEEDED or FAILED macro to test return values; compare directly with NOERROR.

| Protocol | Similar API Function or Message |
| --- | --- |
| Clipboard | *IsClipboardFormatAvailable* |
| DDE | None (perhaps handled through WM_DDE_CONNECT, WM_DDE_ADVISE) |
| OLE 1 | None |

■ *GetCanonicalFormatEtc* provides a different but logically equivalent FORMATETC structure, allowing the caller to determine whether a rendering it has already obtained is identical to what would be obtained by calling *GetData* with a different FORMATETC. There is no equivalent to this function in any existing protocol.

■ *EnumFormatEtc* instantiates and returns a FORMATETC enumerator object through which the caller can determine all available formats that the object can provide. There must be a unique element in the enumeration for each *cfFormat*, *dwAspect*, and *ptd* variation, although you can combine TYMED_* values in *tymed*. The enumerator object implements the single *IEnumFORMATETC* interface, and the caller is responsible for calling *IEnumFORMATETC::Release* when it has finished so the object can free itself. The caller can ask for an enumerator for either "direction," *GetData* or *SetData*. See the section "FORMATETC Enumerators and Format Ordering" beginning on page 508 for more details on this enumerator.

| Protocol | Similar API Function or Message |
| --- | --- |
| Clipboard | *EnumClipboardFormats* (get direction only) |
| DDE | None |
| OLE 1 | None |

■ *DAdvise*[3] sets up an advisory connection between the data object and a caller, providing an advise sink in which the caller indicates the data of interest in a FORMATETC. The data object calls *IAdviseSink::OnDataChange* when a change occurs, possibly sending the data along with the notification.

| Protocol | Similar API Function or Message |
| --- | --- |
| Clipboard | None |
| DDE | WM_DDE_ADVISE |
| OLE 1 | None |

■ *DUnadvise* terminates an advisory connection previously established with *DAdvise*.

| Protocol | Similar API Function or Message |
| --- | --- |
| Clipboard | None |
| DDE | WM_DDE_UNADVISE |
| OLE 1 | None |

---

3. The *D* in the function names identifies these functions as belonging to *IDataObject*. Prior to the release of OLE 2, both *IDataObject* and *IOleObject* had the member functions *Advise*, *Unadvise*, and *EnumAdvise*, which played havoc with OLE Document content objects that used multiple inheritance. To ensure that the names will not conflict, *IDataObject*'s members are *DAdvise*, *DUnadvise*, and *EnumDAdvise*, whereas those in *IOleObject* remain *Advise*, *Unadvise*, and *EnumAdvise*.

■ *EnumDAdvise* returns an enumerator with the *IEnumSTATDATA* interface. There is no equivalent to this function in any existing protocol. A STATDATA structure holds information pertaining to each advisory connection to the data object:

```
typedef struct   tagSTATDATA
    {
    FORMATETC    formatetc;
    DWORD        advf;
    IAdviseSink *pAdvSink;
    DWORD        dwConnection;
    }   STATDATA;
```

You can see from the preceding list that no existing protocol supports the full range of functionality that *IDataObject* provides for all protocols. This is not to say that any arbitrary data object that a client might obtain actually implements the full functionality of every member function. Some data objects—such as a static bitmap on the clipboard—will refuse any advisory connections. Others might not support any *SetData* calls. But you are always allowed to try to learn the data object's capabilities through error return values. With existing protocols, you are not even allowed to play a little.

Related to *IDataObject* is an OLE API function that you might find useful in your work: *OleDuplicateData*. This function will copy any global-memory—based format, including metafiles, bitmaps, and palettes. Its signature is as follows:

```
HANDLE OleDuplicateData(HANDLE hSrc, CLIPFORMAT cf, UINT uiFlags);
```

where *hSrc* is the handle of the source data, *cf* identifies the format of the data, and *uiFlags* specifies the flags to pass to *GlobalAlloc* if such memory needs allocation. If *uiFlags* is 0, the function assumes GMEM_MOVEABLE.

*OleDuplicateData* will perform a bytewise duplication of the data except in the case of CF_METAFILEPICT, CF_ENHMETAFILE, CF_PALETTE, and CF_BITMAP, for which special handling is required. Accordingly, *hSrc* must be a global-memory handle for any bytewise duplication, whereas it is the appropriate handle type when used with these other four formats.

## What Does It Mean, "Canonical"?

The word "canonical" means "the simplest form of something," which is the basic idea behind *GetCanonicalFormatEtc*. This function allows a consumer to obtain a FORMATETC structure that describes exactly the same rendering of a difficult FORMATETC. In general, the canonical FORMATETC should contain the most general information possible for a specific rendering. For example, a data source that always provides the same metafile for any device, for either DVASPECT_CONTENT or DVASPECT_THUMBNAIL aspects, would return from this function a structure with *cfFormat* set to CF_META-FILEPICT, *dwAspect* set to content and thumbnail, *ptd* set to NULL (device independent), and *lindex* set to −1 (*tymed* is irrelevant). All other FORMAT-ETC descriptions with a specific target device are more specific instances of this basic, canonical FORMATETC.

The simplest implementation of *GetCanonicalFormatEtc* copies the input structure to the output structure, sets the output *ptd* field to NULL, and returns DATA_S_SAMEFORMATETC. This says that the data object doesn't care about target devices for the specific FORMATETC. If, on the other hand, the source does care, it returns NOERROR, filling the output FORMATETC as generally as it can.

The entire reason for *GetCanonicalFormatEtc* is to give a consumer a way to compare whether two calls to *GetData* with two different FORMATETC structures will produce exactly the same rendering. If so, the consumer can bypass the second *GetData* call and use the data obtained from the first. This cuts down on memory wasted for duplicate renderings and improves overall performance.

## FORMATETC Enumerators and Format Ordering

*IDataObject::EnumFormatEtc* is responsible for creating and returning an enumerator object for FORMATETC structures, in which the object implements *IEnumFORMATETC*. The data consumer can ask *EnumFormatEtc* for an enumerator that knows the formats obtainable from *IDataObject::GetData*— the get direction— or the formats that can be sent to *IDataObject::SetData*— the set direction. Directions are taken from the DATADIR enumeration:

```
typedef enum tagDATADIR
    {
    DATADIR_GET = 1,
    DATADIR_SET = 2
    } DATADIR;
```

As with all enumerators we've seen, *IEnumFORMATETC* implements the same member functions as all other enumerators: *Next, Skip, Reset,* and *Clone.* They merely deal with FORMATETC structures instead of some other type.

What is most important about a FORMATETC enumerator is its logical equivalence to the Windows API function *EnumClipboardFormats,* meaning that the order of formats enumerated through *IEnumFORMATETC* should proceed from the highest-detail, highest-fidelity formats to the lowest. A consumer will enumerate the available formats, looking for an acceptable one;

the first such format is assumed to be the best the consumer can obtain from the source. The enumerated formats usually start with the most precise private data structures and proceed through other standard interchange formats (such as those for compound documents), picture or graphic formats such as CF_METAFILEPICT and CF_BITMAP, and simple link information such as a moniker. Link information is always considered to be the lowest-priority format so that the user has to explicitly ask for a link in order to have the consumer use such a format.

*IEnumFORMATETC* is one of the few enumerators that you may actually need to implement yourself in a data source unless you have a fixed list of formats. In that case, you can let OLE implement the enumerator for you provided you have registry entries describing the formats available in both get and set directions. Because the registry holds somewhat fixed information, the available formats are also relatively fixed. If you can live with this restriction, which many data sources can, you can use OLE's services provided through the API function *OleRegEnumFormatEtc*, which has the following signature:

```
HRESULT OleRegEnumFormatEtc(CLSID clsid, DWORD dwDirection
    , LPENUMFORMATETC *ppEnum);
```

Here *clsid* identifies where to find the appropriate registry entries, *dwDirection* identifies the direction of the enumeration, and *ppEnum* is where the enumerator's *IEnumFORMATETC* pointer is returned. With this function and appropriate registry entries, a data object's implementation of *IDataObject::EnumFormatEtc* is reduced to the following:

```
HRESULT CImpIDataObject::EnumFormatEtc(DWORD dwDirection
    , LPENUMFORMATETC *ppEnum);
    {
    //m_clsID is the object's CLSID.
    return OleRegEnumFormatEtc(m_clsID, dwDirection, ppEnum);
    }
```

This API function will look for registry entries in the following format:

```
\
CLSID
    {<CLSID>} = <Name>
        DataFormats
            GetSet
                0 = <format,aspect,medium,direction>
                1 = <format,aspect,medium,direction>
                2 = <format,aspect,medium,direction>
                <n> = <format,aspect,medium,direction>
```

You can list as many formats as you want, provided each is given a unique integer key name under *GetSet*. Note that *DataFormats* and *GetSet* are literal keywords in registry entries of this type.

Each format entry is made of a clipboard format value or string, followed by any combination of DVASPECT values (−1 means "all"), then by any combination of TYMED values (be specific; no wildcards allowed), and finally by any one of the DATADIR values. Take, for example, the following entry:

```
1 = 3,-1,32,1
```

This entry describes CF_METAFILEPICT (3) for all aspects (−1) on the TYMED_MFPICT medium (32) available in the get direction (*DATADIR-_GET*, which equals 1). Another example is the following entry:

```
2 = 2,1,16,1
```

This entry describes CF_BITMAP (2) for only DVASPECT_CONTENT (1) in TYMED_GDI (16) for the get direction. Remember that the format can also be a string (spaces allowed) to identify a registered clipboard format. You can see this in the following entry:

```
0 = Polyline Figure,3,5,3
```

Here a registered format "Polyline Figure" for DVASPECT_CONTENT ¦ DVASPECT_THUMBNAIL (3) in TYMED_HGLOBAL¦TYMED_ISTREAM (5) is available in both get and set directions (DATADIR_GET ¦ DATA DIR_SET, which equals 3).

The integer key given to each format determines their order. The format described by key 0 is the preferred format, followed by key 1, then key 2, and so on. In the three examples shown here, we have the format order of "Polyline Figure," CF_METAFILEPICT, and CF_BITMAP. This is the information that a consumer would obtain through the *IEnumFORMATETC* interface that it would obtain through *IDataObject::EnumFormatEtc*.

It's not always the case that a data source can fix its available formats in stone. For example, a data object representing information on the clipboard has to work with a variable data set, so each enumerator it creates might have a different list of formats. Even so, given an array of FORMATETC structures, you can use a reasonably standard implementation—such as that found in the *CEnumFormatEtc* class in INTERFAC\IENUMFE.CPP—which is also used in some of this chapter's samples. This particular implementation takes an array of FORMATETC structures in its constructor, which it copies as the list to enumerate.

```
CEnumFormatEtc::CEnumFormatEtc(ULONG cFE, LPFORMATETC prgFE)
    {
    UINT        i;

    m_cRef=0;

    m_iCur=0;
    m_cfe=cFE;
    m_prgfe=new FORMATETC[(UINT)cFE];

    if (NULL!=m_prgfe)
        {
        for (i=0; i < cFE; i++)
            m_prgfe[i]=prgFE[i];
        }

    return;
    }

CEnumFormatEtc::~CEnumFormatEtc(void)
    {
    if (NULL!=m_prgfe)
        delete [] m_prgfe;

    return;
    }
```

As an independent object, *CEnumFormatEtc* enjoys the luxury of managing its own private reference count because it doesn't depend on the data object to stick around to provide the list of current formats. If you implement an enumerator that has such a dependency, it's best to have the enumerator hold a single reference count to the data object until the enumerator itself is destroyed. This is merely an implementation technique and has no impact whatsoever on the consumer, which will consider the data object destroyed when it releases its final pointer to that object.

Between *OleRegEnumFormatEtc* and this standard implementation, you shouldn't have to spend much time writing your own enumerator except in very special circumstances. Just remember to get the formats ordered the way you want consumers to see them.

## Data Change Notifications with *IAdviseSink*

A consumer of data from a particular source frequently wants to know when the data changes in that source so that the consumer can request a new rendering. For example, a client application that displays real-time market data would want to know when certain stock issues change their value or volume. In this sort of relationship, the source must notify the consumer when data changes occur, which means the consumer must provide some sort of sink implementation to absorb these notifications.

We've already explored the general concept of a sink object in Chapter 4; for the purposes of change notification, a data object needs an *IAdviseSink* pointer to the sink:

```
interface IAdviseSink : IUnknown
    {
    void OnDataChange(FORMATETC *pFE, STGMEDIUM *pSTM);
    void OnViewChange(DWORD dwAspect, LONG lindex);
    void OnRename(LPMONIKER pmk);
    void OnSave(void);
    void OnClose(void);
    };
```

Only the *OnDataChange* member function of *IAdviseSink* has relevance to data objects. *OnViewChange* has relevance to viewable objects, which we'll see in Chapter 11, and the other members have relevance to OLE Documents. (See Chapters 17 and 18.) There is also an *IAdviseSink2* interface with one more member function—*OnLinkSourceChange*—that is used in OLE Document linking scenarios, but that does not concern us here.

A client interested in data change notifications implements a small object with *IAdviseSink* and nothing more. Like other sinks, this object needs no CLSID and no component structure around it—the object serves no other purpose than to accept notification calls. But two major differences exist between the sink for data change notifications and the sinks we saw in Chapter 4. First, *IAdviseSink* is a completely asynchronous interface—that is, OLE's standard marshalers are built to send these notifications asynchronously. Second, data objects do not use connection points to establish a connection with a sink. To make a long story short, *IDataObject* and a few other interfaces were designed before *IConnectionPointContainer* and *IConnection-Point*, so *IDataObject* has its own private member functions through which it handles notification: *DAdvise*, *DUnadvise*, and *EnumDAdvise*. *DAdvise* receives the client's sink and establishes a connection, *DUnadvise* terminates a connection, and *EnumDAdvise* enumerates current connections, as described earlier. *DAdvise* is somewhat richer than *IConnectionPoint::Advise*, as we can see by its arguments:

```
HRESULT DAdvise(LPFORMATETC pFE, DWORD grfAdv, LPADVISESINK pAdvSink
    , LPDWORD pdwConnection);
```

Here *pAdvSink* specifies the client's sink object, and *pdwConnection* receives the connection key for later use with *DUnadvise*. The *pFE* argument describes the specific format and aspect for which the client would like to receive notifications, meaning that a consumer can ask for notifications concerning a single format in the data source as opposed to all formats. In addition, the consumer can ask for notifications on a specific aspect of a specific format because these can, in fact, be different renderings. In short, the notification is established for whatever format and aspect you specify in *pFE*. This is important, of course, because consumers typically use only one of many formats and aspects that the source is able to provide and thus want a change notification only for specific ones. A consumer can establish notifications for multiple formats using the same sink by calling *DAdvise* multiple times. If the consumer wants a wildcard notification, it can fill the fields of the FORMATETC structure by using *cfFormat=0*, *ptd=NULL*, *dwAspect=−1*, *lindex=−1*, and *tymed=−1*. The sink will then receive a notification for any change in any format, where the *pFE* structure sent to *OnDataChange* will identify the exact format that changed.

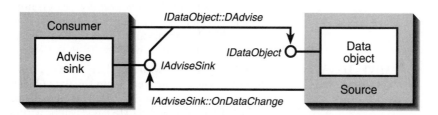

The *grfAdv* argument specifies how the notifications should occur. The values for *grfAdv* are listed in the ADVF enumeration (shown below) and can be combined as needed. The effects of the flags relevant to *IDataObject-::DAdvise* are described in Table 10-1 on the following page.[4]

```
typedef enum tagADVF
    {
    ADVF_NODATA             = 1,
    ADVF_PRIMEFIRST         = 2,
    ADVF_ONLYONCE           = 4,
    ADVF_DATAONSTOP         = 64,
    ADVFCACHE_NOHANDLER     = 8,
    ADVFCACHE_FORCEBUILTIN  = 16,
    ADVFCACHE_ONSAVE        = 32
    } ADVF;
```

---

4. These are also the same flags that can appear in the *advf* field of the STATDATA structure that comes through *EnumDAdvise* and *IEnumSTATDATA*. The ADVFCACHE_* flags are related to caching, as we'll see in Chapter 11.

| Flag | Description |
|---|---|
| ADVF_NODATA | Prevents the data object from sending data along with the *OnDataChange* notification, the default mode of operation. When ADVF_NODATA is specified, the *tymed* field of the STGMEDIUM passed to *OnDataChange* will usually contain TYMED_NULL. Some data objects might still send data anyway and *tymed* will contain another value, in which case *OnDataChange* is still responsible for freeing the STGMEDIUM contents. Be sure to check. |
| ADVF_PRIMEFIRST | Causes an initial *OnDataChange* call even when the data has not changed from its present state. If you combine ADVF_PRIMEFIRST with ADVF_ONLYONCE, you create a single asynchronous *IDataObject::GetData* call. |
| ADVF_ONLYONCE | Automatically terminates the advisory connection after the first call to *OnDataChange*. It is not necessary to call *DUnadvise* when you use this flag. You can still, however, call *DUnadvise* if you have not yet received a notification. |
| ADVF_DATAONSTOP | When provided with ADVF_NODATA, causes the last *OnDataChange* sent from the data object (before that object was destroyed) to actually provide the data—that is, *pSTM->tymed* will be a value other than TYMED_NULL. This flag is meaningless without ADVF_NODATA. |

**Table 10-1.**
*The advise flags usable with* IDataObject::DAdvise.

A consumer must design carefully around the use of ADVF_NODATA when the source exists in another process: that consumer cannot call *IDataObject::GetData* for a new rendering from within *IAdviseSink::OnDataChange*. Recall from Chapter 6 that COM does not allow external calls to be made from within an asynchronous call, and that rule applies here. Any attempt to make such a call will result in RPC_E_CANTCALLOUT_INASYNCCALL. This means the consumer must post itself a message and return from *OnDataChange* and then call *IDataObject::GetData* later in response to that message. This allows the consumer, however, to cache multiple data change notifications together until it really needs a new rendering of the data for a repaint, which can significantly improve overall performance. The source doesn't need to render the data for each notification.

The next point regarding *IAdviseSink* is that like a connection point, a data object must support multicasting of data change notifications when multiple consumers can connect to that same source. OLE, however, provides a convenient service in the form of a standard *data advise holder* object that implements the interface *IDataAdviseHolder*:

```
interface IDataAdviseHolder : IUnknown
    {
    HRESULT Advise(LPDATAOBJECT pDataObject, FORMATETC *pFE
        , DWORD advf, LPADVISESINK pAdvise, DWORD *pdwConnection);
    HRESULT Unadvise(DWORD dwConnection);
    HRESULT EnumAdvise(LPENUMSTATDATA *ppEnum);
    HRESULT SendOnDataChange(LPDATAOBJECT pDataObject
        ,DWORD dwReserved, DWORD advf);
    };
```

The OLE API function *CreateDataAdviseHolder* instantiates and returns a data advise holder object with this interface, exposing this particular OLE service. With this object, a source can delegate the *IDataObject* functions of *DAdvise, DUnadvise,* and *EnumDAdvise* directly to the *Advise, Unadvise,* and *EnumAdvise* members of *IDataAdviseHolder.* OLE's implementation will hold on to all of the *IAdviseSink* pointers itself, freeing the data object from the burden. When the data object wants to send a notification, it passes its own *IDataObject* pointer along with some ADVF_* flags to *SendOnDataChange.* The data advise holder then checks the flags for every one of the advise sinks it holds and calls *IAdviseSink::OnDataChange* for each matching one. If the flags do not include ADVF_NODATA, *SendOnDataChange* calls *IDataObject::GetData* first to obtain a rendering and sends that rendering to the sink.

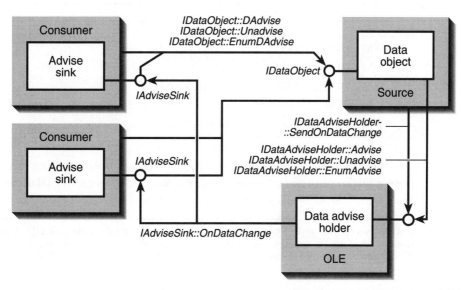

The data advise holder thus makes the implementation of a data object's notification members trivial, as we will see later in this chapter when we look at some sample code. Note that this standard data advise holder is not exactly the fastest possible implementation of this service. If performance is really important to you, you can implement your own holder or eliminate it altogether. The latter choice is optimal if you know that the data object will have only a fixed number of connections to it, making a generic mechanism unnecessary.

The final point in this discussion about *IAdviseSink* is that a data object should generally call only *IAdviseSink::OnDataChange* through the pointers it received in *IDataObject::DAdvise*. According to the basic rule of interfaces, the data object could actually call any of the other members. However, this is not part of the defined relationship between *IDataObject* and *IAdviseSink*, and you can use the other notifications only when you have a consumer that expects them. So calling other data members is not a good practice when a consumer expects that only *OnDataChange* notifications will come from a data object.

# *IDataObject*, DDE, and the Real-Time Market Data Council

In the previous section, we saw that much of the *IDataObject* interface encompasses the capabilities of Dynamic Data Exchange. As a result, OLE is poised to displace DDE as a standard for dynamic interapplication data transfer.[5] The table below summarizes the parallels between DDE and *IDataObject*:

| DDE Message | *IDataObject* Member Function |
|---|---|
| WM_DDE_POKE | *IDataObject::SetData* |
| WM_DDE_REQUEST | *IDataObject::GetData* |
| WM_DDE_ADVISE | *IDataObject::DAdvise* |
| WM_DDE_UNADVISE | *IDataObject::DUnadvise* |
| WM_DDE_DATA | *IAdviseSink::OnDataChange* |

On the surface, one could seemingly write a simple mapping layer to expose a DDE conversation through *IDataObject* or to generate DDE messages

---

5. DDE Execute (the WM_DDE_EXECUTE message) is entirely displaced with OLE Automation. However, the OLE Documents technology has a low-level DDE layer for the express purpose of communicating with OLE 1 clients and servers, as OLE 1 was entirely based on DDE.

from events in a data object that could be picked up by some consumer's sink. But there are three differences between DDE and OLE *IDataObject* members. The first is that everything in DDE is inherently asynchronous, and DDE applications have come to depend on this fact. *IDataObject* members themselves are synchronous, while only the act of notification through *IAdviseSink::OnDataChange* is asynchronous.[6]

The second difference is in how to obtain an *IDataObject* pointer for a specific data set. Under DDE, a consumer initiates a conversation using only a general specification for the source, a *service* and a *topic* such as the service *Excel* and the topic *NASDAQ.XLS*. With OLE, you generally have a file moniker to perform the same process.

Once connected, a DDE consumer can send a WM_DDE_REQUEST message to the source to ask for a rendering of a specific subset or *item* of the data represented by the topic, such as *R4C5:R8C20*. In other words, the act of requesting data includes the ability to specify the item of interest. However, the arguments to *IDataObject::GetData* do not have a concept of item. If you bound a NASDAQ.XLS file moniker asking for *IDataObject* and then called *IDataObject::GetData*, the source would need to render the entire spreadsheet. The FORMATETC structure passed to *GetData* simply does not have an item field. (The *lindex* member is specifically for graphical renderings that involve multiple disparate parts and cannot be used to specify an item.)

Of course, you could bind a File!Item moniker that specifies the exact data you want, but the data object you get back would know only about that specific cell range in the spreadsheet. If you wanted data from another part of the spreadsheet, you'd have to bind another moniker, thus creating another data object. Obviously, this is expensive with respect to memory for a large number of cell ranges, making the data object solution much more costly than the equivalent DDE connection, because there isn't a way through the *IDataObject* interface to tell the data object to switch the item it will render in a *GetData* call.

This really boils down to the third difference in the concept of an item in DDE and OLE. In DDE an item is inherently specified during the act of a data request, but in OLE it's inherently part of creating the data object initially. You can see that there isn't a simple way to map DDE to OLE and vice versa.

Does this mean that it is impossible to create a DDE-type solution using OLE? Not at all—it simply means that the data source has to implement some interface other than *IDataObject* so that the consumer can have that data object

---

6. Calling *DAdvise* with ADVF_ONLYONCE ¦ ADVF_PRIMEFIRST is essentially an asynchronous *IDataObject::GetData* call, but that's a special case and works only for the get direction.

switch to another item at run time. This was precisely the problem faced by the Open Market Data Council, a group of representatives from over 75 software corporations involved with electronic stock market services. They needed an efficient way of using OLE to exchange very sparse subsets of all available quotes in real time. A consumer of such data needed a way to ask for a single quote or for a specific batch of quotes from a single source that knew all market quotes; that consumer also needed to create a notification connection so that it knew when any number of specific values for some set of issues changed. Obviously, it was not agreeable to have the source render the entire market state for each request, which is what it would have to do through *IDataObject* alone.

The Council's solution, called the WOSA Extensions for Real-Time Market Data Transfer (WOSA/XRT), uses *IDataObject* and *IAdviseSink* for all of the data exchange and notification. However, the data source also implements an OLE Automation dispinterface (an implementation of *IDispatch*, described in more detail in Chapter 14) through which the consumer can specify the current item to watch. Through this dispinterface, the consumer has a way to tell the source to switch items, as shown in Figure 10-1. Not only does this provide all the functionality of the DDE solution, it is also more efficient: once the consumer specifies the item, that item remains in effect until it is changed again. The consumer doesn't need to specify the item in every call, and the source doesn't have to send the item along with every change notification, as happens with DDE. Through OLE Automation dispatch interfaces, the council was able to take advantage of all the capabilities of OLE, greatly improving the overall efficiency of the real-time market data systems.

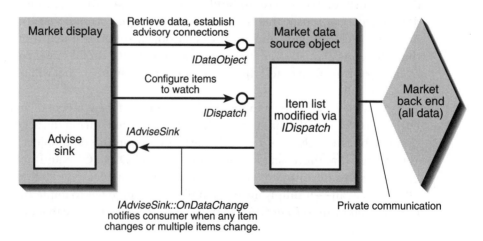

**Figure 10-1.**
*The WOSA/XRT solution for dynamically specifying items in a data object.*

It is no crisis then that OLE can't completely supplant DDE. OLE will prove over time to be a more efficient, powerful, and robust means of doing whatever DDE could do but through an object-oriented programming model. For all intents and purposes, consider DDE to be obsolete—the only applications that should be using it are those that need backward compatibility with legacy code. New designs should strive for solutions based on OLE.

# Implementing a Data Object: DDataObj and EDataObj

This section explores the concepts of Uniform Data Transfer through code samples, looking at data objects (single objects in a component server) based on both a DLL and an EXE. (These samples are found in CHAP10\DDATA-OBJ and CHAP10\EDATAOBJ.) The next section, "Implementing a Consumer: DataUser," looks at a sample (CHAP10\DATAUSER) that works in conjunction with the data objects here.

Both DDataObj and EDataObj servers share a common object implementation in the C++ class *CDataObject*, which has only the *IDataObject* interface. Its implementation is found in the files DATAOBJ.CPP (the object's core), IDATAOBJ.CPP (the *IDataObject* interface), and RENDER.CPP (specific code for rendering individual formats). This data object, which is independent of the DLL or EXE server structure (like the Koala objects of Chapter 5), uses the *CEnumFormatEtc* implementation mentioned earlier in this chapter for its handling of *IDataObject::EnumFormatEtc* and also uses OLE's data advise holder service.

The data object itself supports full-content renderings (DVASPECT-_CONTENT) for the formats of CF_TEXT, CF_BITMAP, and CF_META-FILEPICT. The text is a certain number of characters, the bitmap is an image (see CHAP10\RES for the BMP files), and each metafile is a series of rectangles filled with various shades of blue. Both DDataObj and EDataObj actually support three CLSIDs corresponding to three sizes of data:

| CLSID | Text (Characters) | Bitmap ($x * y$) | Metafile (*FillRect* Records) |
|---|---|---|---|
| CLSID_DataSmall | 64 | $16 * 16$ | 16 |
| CLSID_DataMedium | 1024 | $64 * 64$ | 128 |
| CLSID_DataLarge | 16,384 | $256 * 256$ | 1024 |

All three classes are handled with the same class factory, named *CData-ObjectClassFactory*, which tells each data object it creates about which data set to render for the consumer. The servers described here are good examples of supporting multiple CLSIDs—DDataObj creates a different class factory instance for each CLSID, whereas EDataObj creates all three of them on startup, registering them separately.

The *CDataObject* implementation (DATAOBJ.CPP) has a number of features worth mentioning. First, only the get direction is supported. *SetData* always returns E_NOTIMPL, as does *GetDataHere*, because *CDataObject* doesn't support any variable-length formats:

```
STDMETHODIMP CImpIDataObject::GetData(LPFORMATETC pFE
    , LPSTGMEDIUM pSTM)
    {
    UINT            cf=pFE->cfFormat;

    //Check aspects we support.
    if (!(DVASPECT_CONTENT & pFE->dwAspect))
        return ResultFromScode(DATA_E_FORMATETC);

    switch (cf)
        {
        case CF_METAFILEPICT:
            if (!(TYMED_MFPICT & pFE->tymed))
                break;

            return m_pObj->RenderMetafilePict(pSTM);

        case CF_BITMAP:
            if (!(TYMED_GDI & pFE->tymed))
                break;

            return m_pObj->RenderBitmap(pSTM);

        case CF_TEXT:
            if (!(TYMED_HGLOBAL & pFE->tymed))
                break;

            return m_pObj->RenderText(pSTM);

        default:
            break;
        }

    return ResultFromScode(DATA_E_FORMATETC);
    }
```

```
STDMETHODIMP CImpIDataObject::GetDataHere(LPFORMATETC pFE
    , LPSTGMEDIUM pSTM)
    {
    return ResultFromScode(E_NOTIMPL);
    }


STDMETHODIMP CImpIDataObject::SetData(LPFORMATETC pFE
    , LPSTGMEDIUM pSTM, BOOL fRelease)
    {
    return ResultFromScode(DATA_E_FORMATETC);
    }
```

The *CDataObject* member functions *RenderText*, *RenderBitmap*, and *RenderMetafilePict* are found in RENDER.CPP. The first function allocates global memory and writes a stream of characters into it, the second loads a bitmap from the server's resources, and the third creates a metafile device context into which it makes a number of *FillRect* calls. Again, the number of characters in the text, the dimensions of the bitmap, and the number of *FillRect* calls made into the metafile depend on the size of the data object as determined by the CLSID that was used to create it in the first place (a DOSIZE_* value as defined in DATAOBJ.H). The large metafile, for example, looks much like the shaded blue background you see in Microsoft's standard setup program; each rectangle is only a few pixels high, and each rectangle's color differs only slightly from the previous one. The small metafile, on the other hand, has only four rectangles of very different shades.

It is very important for *GetData* to fill the entire STGMEDIUM structure. It's easy to forget to fill the *tymed* field and to set the *pUnkForRelease* field to NULL when necessary. If you forget to set *tymed*, OLE will not marshal the data rendering between processes correctly—it has to know the exact nature of that data to copy it correctly. If you place an invalid pointer in *pUnkForRelease*, OLE can cause a fault inside *ReleaseStgMedium*, especially with an in-process data object.

By definition, *GetDataHere* tries to render data into a caller-allocated storage medium but does not attempt to reallocate space itself. Generally the only storage mediums you need to support in this function are TYMED_ISTORAGE, TYMED_ISTREAM, and TYMED_FILE. If you don't support these mediums, you don't need to support this function; if you do, return STG_E_MEDIUMFULL if writing to such storage fails.

The implementation of *QueryGetData* in the samples responds only to CF_TEXT, CF_BITMAP, and CF_METAFILEPICT, as you might expect, and *GetCanonicalFormatEtc* always returns DATA_S_SAMEFORMATETC, indicating that all renderings are identical for each format:

```
STDMETHODIMP CImpIDataObject::QueryGetData(LPFORMATETC pFE)
    {
    UINT            cf=pFE->cfFormat;
    BOOL            fRet=FALSE;

    //Check aspects we support.
    if (!(DVASPECT_CONTENT & pFE->dwAspect))
        return ResultFromScode(DATA_E_FORMATETC);

    switch (cf)
        {
        case CF_METAFILEPICT:
            fRet=(BOOL)(pFE->tymed & TYMED_MFPICT);
            break;

        case CF_BITMAP:
            fRet=(BOOL)(pFE->tymed & TYMED_GDI);
            break;

        case CF_TEXT:
            fRet=(BOOL)(pFE->tymed & TYMED_HGLOBAL);
            break;

        default:
            fRet=FALSE;
            break;
        }

    return fRet ? NOERROR : ResultFromScode(S_FALSE);
    }

STDMETHODIMP CImpIDataObject::GetCanonicalFormatEtc
    (LPFORMATETC pFEIn, LPFORMATETC pFEOut)
    {
    if (NULL==pFEOut)
        return ResultFromScode(E_INVALIDARG);

    pFEOut->ptd=NULL;
    return ResultFromScode(DATA_S_SAMEFORMATETC);
    }
```

For the purposes of *EnumFormatEtc*, *CDataObject* keeps its supported formats ordered in the array *m_rgfeGet*, which is initialized in the object's constructor. This array is passed to the *CEnumFormatEtc* constructor from within *EnumFormatEtc*. (We could, of course, achieve the same end with registry entries.)

```
CDataObject::CDataObject(LPUNKNOWN pUnkOuter
    , PFNDESTROYED pfnDestroy, UINT iSize)
    {
    UINT        i;

    [Other initialization omitted]
    m_cfeGet=CFORMATETCGET;

    SETDefFormatEtc(m_rgfeGet[0], CF_METAFILEPICT, TYMED_MFPICT);
    SETDefFormatEtc(m_rgfeGet[1], CF_BITMAP, TYMED_GDI);
    SETDefFormatEtc(m_rgfeGet[2], CF_TEXT, TYMED_HGLOBAL);

    [Other code omitted]
    }


STDMETHODIMP CImpIDataObject::EnumFormatEtc(DWORD dwDir
    , LPENUMFORMATETC *ppEnum)
    {
    switch (dwDir)
        {
        case DATADIR_GET:
            *ppEnum=new CEnumFormatEtc(m_pObj->m_cfeGet
                , m_pObj->m_rgfeGet);
            break;

        case DATADIR_SET:
            *ppEnum=NULL;
            break;

        default:
            *ppEnum=NULL;
            break;
        }

    if (NULL==*ppEnum)
        return ResultFromScode(E_FAIL);
    else
        (*ppEnum)->AddRef();

    return NOERROR;
    }
```

You can see how this implementation supports only the get direction through *EnumFormatEtc*, failing requests for the set direction. In addition, it uses the *CEnumFormatEtc* class found in IENUMFE.CPP for the enumerator implementation.

The object then uses *CreateDataAdviseHolder* and the *IDataAdviseHolder* interface to implement the members of *IDataObject* related to notification, creating the advise holder once inside *DAdvise* and releasing it in the object's destructor:

```
STDMETHODIMP CImpIDataObject::DAdvise(LPFORMATETC pFE, DWORD dwFlags
    , LPADVISESINK pIAdviseSink, LPDWORD pdwConn)
    {
    HRESULT            hr;

    if (NULL==m_pObj->m_pIDataAdviseHolder)
        {
        hr=CreateDataAdviseHolder(&m_pObj->m_pIDataAdviseHolder);

        if (FAILED(hr))
            return ResultFromScode(E_OUTOFMEMORY);
        }

    hr=m_pObj->m_pIDataAdviseHolder->Advise((LPDATAOBJECT)this, pFE
        , dwFlags, pIAdviseSink, pdwConn);

    return hr;
    }


STDMETHODIMP CImpIDataObject::DUnadvise(DWORD dwConn)
    {
    HRESULT            hr;

    if (NULL==m_pObj->m_pIDataAdviseHolder)
        return ResultFromScode(E_FAIL);

    hr=m_pObj->m_pIDataAdviseHolder->Unadvise(dwConn);

    return hr;
    }


STDMETHODIMP CImpIDataObject::EnumDAdvise(LPENUMSTATDATA *ppEnum)
    {
    HRESULT            hr;

    if (NULL==m_pObj->m_pIDataAdviseHolder)
        return ResultFromScode(E_FAIL);

    hr=m_pObj->m_pIDataAdviseHolder->EnumAdvise(ppEnum);
    return hr;
    }
```

```
CDataObject::~CDataObject(void)
    {
    [Other cleanup omitted]

    ReleaseInterface(m_pIDataAdviseHolder);

    [Other code omitted]
    }
```

Finally, each data object creates a small visible window, as shown in Figure 10-2, for the purposes of demonstrating data change notifications and comparable exchange rates for in-process and local data objects. Each window has only a caption bar (specifying the server as a DLL or an EXE) and an Iterations menu, but no system menu. (The window is destroyed only when the object is destroyed.) From the Iterations menu, you can tell the data object to fire off a small number to a large number of *IAdviseSink::OnDataChange* calls to any connected consumer. The data object counts the time it takes to make all of the calls and reports that time along with an average time per call in a message box when the iterations are complete.

**Figure 10-2.**
*A window created by an instance of* CDataObject *for the small data set.*

All the notifications are sent through *IDataAdviseHolder::SendOnDataChange* inside *AdviseWndProc* in DATAOBJ.CPP:

```
LRESULT APIENTRY AdvisorWndProc(HWND hWnd, UINT iMsg
    , WPARAM wParam, LPARAM lParam)
    {
    PCDataObject    pDO;
    DWORD           i;
    DWORD           iAdvise;
    DWORD           dwTime;
    DWORD           dwAvg;
    TCHAR           szTime[128];
    TCHAR           szTitle[80];
    HCURSOR         hCur, hCurT;

    pDO=(PCDataObject)GetWindowLong(hWnd, 0);
```

*(continued)*

```
switch (iMsg)
    {
    case WM_NCCREATE:
        pDO=(PCDataObject)(((LPCREATESTRUCT)lParam)
            ->lpCreateParams);
        SetWindowLong(hWnd, 0, (LONG)pDO);
        return (DefWindowProc(hWnd, iMsg, wParam, lParam));

    case WM_CLOSE:
        //Forbid task manager to close us.
        return 0L;

    case WM_COMMAND:
        if (NULL==pDO->m_pIDataAdviseHolder)
            break;

        //Send IAdviseSink::OnDataChange many times.
        i=(DWORD)(LOWORD(wParam)-IDM_ADVISEITERATIONSMIN+1);
        iAdvise=(i*i)*16;

        hCur=LoadCursor(NULL, MAKEINTRESOURCE(IDC_WAIT));
        hCurT=SetCursor(hCur);
        ShowCursor(TRUE);

        dwTime=GetTickCount();

        i=0;
        while (TRUE)
            {
            [A PeekMeesage loop in the 16-bit EXE server only]
            pDO->m_pIDataAdviseHolder->SendOnDataChange
                (pDO->m_pImpIDataObject, 0, ADVF_NODATA);

            if (++i >= iAdvise)
                break;
            }

        dwTime=GetTickCount()-dwTime;
        dwAvg=dwTime/iAdvise;

        SetCursor(hCurT);
        ShowCursor(FALSE);

        wsprintf(szTime
            , TEXT("Total\t=%lu ms\n\rAverage\t=%lu ms")
            , dwTime, dwAvg);

        GetWindowText(hWnd, szTitle, sizeof(szTitle));
```

```
            MessageBox(hWnd, szTime, szTitle, MB_OK);
            break;

        default:
            return (DefWindowProc(hWnd, iMsg, wParam, lParam));
        }

    return 0L;
    }
```

These iterations give you the chance to test the relative performance of data change notifications between DLL and EXE servers. As you'd expect, the DLL rates are much faster because nothing exists between the object and the consumer with the in-process case. In this sample, *CDataObject* accepts only ADVF_NODATA advises, so we can determine the flat-out notification time independently and not have to include the time it actually takes to render the data, which would skew the results.

## Implementing a Consumer: DataUser

A consumer is any piece of code that obtains and uses an *IDataObject* pointer. As we'll see in Chapters 12 and 13, the OLE Clipboard and OLE Drag and Drop technologies are two methods of obtaining this pointer. In this chapter, however, we can demonstrate a number of consumer features through a client for the DDataObj and EDataObj samples. This client is DataUser, found in CHAP10\DATAUSER, where all the code is in DATAUSER.CPP. When you run this sample, you'll see the window shown in Figure 10-3. Here the Data Object menu allows you to select the type of object to use (server and data size) as well as to send either *GetData* or *QueryGetData* calls to that object's *IDataObject* interface.

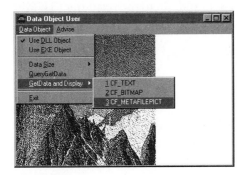

**Figure 10-3.**
*The DataUser program showing the Data Object menu.*

DataUser initially creates three in-process data objects from DDataObj by using *CoCreateInstance*: one for the small data set (*CLSID_DataSmall*), one for the medium data set (*CLSID_DataMedium*), and one for the large data set (*CLSID_DataLarge*). The Use EXE Object menu item will destroy these three objects and create new ones from the local server, EDataObj, instead. The Use DLL Object menu item will destroy the objects once again and switch back to DDataObj.

One of these three objects is always marked as the current object (stored in *CApp::m_pIDataObject*) so that any *IDataObject* call you select through the Data Object menu will be sent to that object. The small data object is the default. You can change the current object—the data size under consideration—through the Data Size menu item, which has the subitems Small, Medium, and Large. Any change in the server being used will reset the current object to the small one.

## Calling *QueryGetData* and *GetData*

When you select *QueryGetData*, DataUser generates five calls to *IDataObject::QueryGetData*, passing FORMATETC structures containing CF_TEXT, CF_BITMAP, CF_DIB, CF_METAFILEPICT, and CF_WAVE. DataUser displays the result (and whether that was the expected result) in its window. Each call to *QueryGetData* itself is isolated in the function *CApp::TryQueryGetData*.

Those calls to *QueryGetData* specifying the CF_DIB and CF_WAVE formats should fail, while the others succeed. Remember that *QueryGetData* will return either S_OK or S_FALSE success codes depending on the format's availability. An error code means that the query operation itself failed and the answer is indeterminate.

When you select one of the GetData And Display menu items, DataUser will retrieve a rendering of the specified format from the current object and display it in the client area. DataUser holds on to the resulting STGMEDIUM in *CApp::m_stm* until it calls *GetData* again or until you close the program entirely.

```
//In the WM_COMMAND message case of DataUserWndProc

case IDM_OBJECTGETDATATEXT:
case IDM_OBJECTGETDATABITMAP:
case IDM_OBJECTGETDATAMETAFILEPICT:
    if (NULL==pApp->m_pIDataObject)
        break;
```

```
//Clean up whatever we currently have.
pApp->m_cf=0;
ReleaseStgMedium(&pApp->m_stm);

if (IDM_OBJECTGETDATATEXT==wID)
    SETDefFormatEtc(fe, CF_TEXT, TYMED_HGLOBAL);

if (IDM_OBJECTGETDATABITMAP==wID)
    SETDefFormatEtc(fe, CF_BITMAP, TYMED_GDI);

if (IDM_OBJECTGETDATAMETAFILEPICT==wID)
    {
    SETDefFormatEtc(fe, CF_METAFILEPICT
        , TYMED_MFPICT);
    }

hr=pApp->m_pIDataObject->GetData(&fe
    , &(pApp->m_stm));

if (SUCCEEDED(hr))
    pApp->m_cf=fe.cfFormat;

InvalidateRect(hWnd, NULL, TRUE);
UpdateWindow(hWnd);
break;
```

Repaints performed by DataUser happen in the function *CApp::Paint*, which calls *DrawText* for CF_TEXT data, *BitBlt* for CF_BITMAP data, and *PlayMetaFile* for CF_METAFILEPICT data. Because DataUser holds the data until it calls *GetData* again, you can resize the window as necessary and the data will still be visible.

## Establishing an Advisory Connection

You may have noticed by now that DataUser has an Advise menu on which appear the items shown in Figure 10-4 on the following page. Through this menu, you can tell DataUser to call *IDataObject::DAdvise* on the current object with any of the three data formats. The GetData On Change and Paint On Change items are enabled only for in-process objects and allow you to control what happens inside DataUser's implementation of *IAdviseSink*, which is found in the file IADVSINK.CPP.

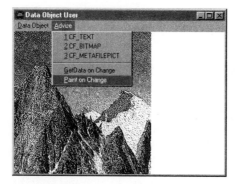

**Figure 10-4.**
*The DataUser program showing the Advise menu along with the large bitmap.*

DataUser implements the advise sink through the class *CAdviseSink*, creating one such object on startup and using that same instance throughout DataUser's lifetime. DataUser holds the sink's *IAdviseSink* pointer in the variable *m_pIAdviseSink*, releasing it on shutdown. The implementation of *CAdviseSink* holds a backpointer to the main application class *CApp* to tell the application when to repaint or change its data, but otherwise, it is an independent object with its own *QueryInterface* behavior and a *Release* function that destroys it when no more references are extant.

When you tell DataUser to create an advisory connection, it passes its *m_pIAdviseSink* pointer to *IDataObject::DAdvise* along with the FORMATETC matching the menu item you select and the ADVF_NODATA flag (allowing us to time the raw notification rates exclusive of the time it takes to render data). The connection key is stored in *m_dwConn* inside *CApp*. DataUser makes all of these formats mutually exclusive, so selecting one will tear down any existing advisory connection for another:

```
//In the WM_COMMAND message case of DataUserWndProc

case IDM_ADVISETEXT:
case IDM_ADVISEBITMAP:
case IDM_ADVISEMETAFILEPICT:
    if (NULL==pApp->m_pIDataObject)
        break;

    //Terminate old connection
    if (0!=pApp->m_dwConn)
        {
        pApp->m_pIDataObject->DUnadvise(pApp
            ->m_dwConn);
        }
```

```
CheckMenuItem(hMenu, pApp->m_cfAdvise
    +IDM_ADVISEMIN, MF_UNCHECKED);
CheckMenuItem(hMenu, wID, MF_CHECKED);

//New format is wID-IDM_ADVISEMIN.
pApp->m_cfAdvise=(UINT)(wID-IDM_ADVISEMIN);
fe.cfFormat=pApp->m_cfAdvise;
pApp->m_pIDataObject->DAdvise(&fe, ADVF_NODATA
    , pApp->m_pIAdviseSink, &pApp->m_dwConn);

break;
```

Keep in mind that an advise connection is always associated with not only a specific data format but also the *dwAspect* contained in the FORMAT-ETC structure passed to *DAdvise*. If the data object does not support that aspect, it can refuse the connection; otherwise, it uses that aspect to determine when it needs to send a notification.

## Inside the Advise Sink

The GetData On Change and Paint On Change menu items allow you to control how *IAdviseSink::OnDataChange* behaves. Two flags in *CApp*, *m_fGetData* and *m_fRepaint*, hold the current state of your menu selections. DataUser disables both of these menu items and sets these flags to FALSE unless it's using the in-process server DDataObj as the source of the data objects. Reasons for this will become clear shortly.

As you might expect, only the implementation of *OnDataChange* is important in the advise sink (besides the *IUnknown* members) because the other notifications are not relevant to data objects themselves. The bulk of code in the sink is contained in this single function:

```
STDMETHODIMP_(void) CAdviseSink::OnDataChange(LPFORMATETC pFE
    , LPSTGMEDIUM pSTM)
    {
    BOOL        fUsable=TRUE;
    UINT        cf;

    STGMEDIUM   stm;

    if (!m_pApp->m_fGetData && !m_pApp->m_fEXE)
        return;

    //See whether we're interested in format and aspect that changed.
    cf=pFE->cfFormat;
```

*(continued)*

```
if ((CF_TEXT!=cf && CF_BITMAP!=cf && CF_METAFILEPICT!=cf)
    !! !(DVASPECT_CONTENT & pFE->dwAspect))
    return;

//Check medium if we got data.
switch (cf)
    {
    case CF_TEXT:
        fUsable=(BOOL)(TYMED_HGLOBAL & pFE->tymed);
        break;

    case CF_BITMAP:
        fUsable=(BOOL)(TYMED_GDI & pFE->tymed);
        break;

    case CF_METAFILEPICT:
        fUsable=(BOOL)(TYMED_MFPICT & pFE->tymed);
        break;

    default:
        break;
    }

if (!fUsable)
    return;

if (NULL==m_pApp->m_pIDataObject)
    return;

if (m_pApp->m_fEXE)
    {
    ReleaseStgMedium(&(m_pApp->m_stm));
    m_pApp->m_cf=cf;
    m_pApp->m_stm.tymed=TYMED_NULL;

    InvalidateRect(m_pApp->m_hWnd, NULL, TRUE);
    return;
    }

if (FAILED(m_pApp->m_pIDataObject->GetData(pFE, &stm)))
    return;

//Get rid of old data and update.
ReleaseStgMedium(&(m_pApp->m_stm));

m_pApp->m_cf=cf;
m_pApp->m_stm=stm;
```

```
InvalidateRect(m_pApp->m_hWnd, NULL, TRUE);

if (m_pApp->m_fRepaint)
    UpdateWindow(m_pApp->m_hWnd);

return;
}
```

On entry, this function immediately checks whether the *m_fGetData* flag is FALSE (and whether we're specifically using DDataObj so that *CApp::m_fEXE* is FALSE), and if so, it returns immediately, doing nothing else. If you remove the additional check on *m_fEXE* in the first line, you can run basic performance tests between DDataObj and EDataObj as far as raw notification rates are concerned. To run such a test, start DataUser, select Advise for any format (it doesn't matter which format), switch to the Small DLL Advisor #1 window, and select 572 from the Iterations menu. This causes that object to send 572 *OnDataChange* calls, but because you probably have a fast machine (486/66), you'll end up with a short elapsed time—perhaps 90 ms—with an average time per call of less than 1 ms (0.16 ms), or 6350 calls per second. Now select DataUser's Use EXE Object menu item, select Advise for any format, switch to the Small EXE Advisor #1 window, and select 572 from the Iterations menu again. After a considerably longer time lapse, you'll get a message box reporting the total time, on the relative order of 1532 ms, for an average of 2.7 ms per call, or 370 calls per second. You can see that working with an in-process data object is somewhat faster than working with a local one, simply because there is no marshaling overhead involved. This overhead, in fact, is where most of the extra time is spent: even with the extra *m_fEXE* condition intact (and the calls to *ReleaseStgMedium* and *InvalidateRect*), the total time for a local object to send 572 notifications was 1603 ms on my machine, hardly different from before. Still, 370 notifications per second is a fast rate, good enough for most notification purposes.

Anyway, if *OnDataChange* proceeds past this first check, it then ensures that the data object sent a notification for the format, aspect, and storage medium you're interested in watching. If there are any differences, it ignores the call altogether. Otherwise, what it does next depends on the server in question. If you're using EDataObj, *OnDataChange* frees whatever data it currently holds (by calling *ReleaseStgMedium*) and saves the format that changed inside *CApp::m_stm.cf* but marks that storage medium as TYMED_NULL. After this, it invalidates but does not update the main window. *OnDataChange* is telling the main application that it should repaint itself but that it has to call *IDataObject::GetData* when repainting occurs because the data is not yet available.

TYMED_NULL indicates the absence of data, and the call to *InvalidateRect* basically posts a WM_PAINT to the main window. Therefore, when painting next occurs, DataUser will no longer be inside *IAdviseSink::OnDataChange*. It detects that it doesn't have a rendering, so it must ask the data object for one before painting, which all occurs in *CApp::Paint*:

```
void CApp::Paint(void)
    {
    [Other code omitted]

    if (m_fEXE)
        {
        if (TYMED_NULL==m_stm.tymed && 0!=m_cf)
            {
            SETDefFormatEtc(fe, m_cf, TYMED_HGLOBAL
                | TYMED_MFPICT | TYMED_GDI);

            if (NULL!=m_pIDataObject)
                m_pIDataObject->GetData(&fe, &m_stm);
            }
        }

    [Other code omitted]
    }
```

You can see how this works when you run iterations from one of the EXE object windows. When the notifications have all been sent, DataUser draws the data in whatever format you selected. With a large number of iterations, you might also see a repaint occur during the iterations themselves because DataUser gets a chance to process some of its own messages, one of which could be WM_PAINT.

If DataUser is talking to an in-process data object, it can turn around and request a new rendering right away by calling *IDataObject::GetData*. Because there is no marshaling with an in-process object, there is no chance of such a call being rejected. If it gets the new data and then releases the old rendering that's held in *CApp:m_stm*, it replaces that rendering with the new one and invalidates the window to post a WM_PAINT message. Furthermore, if you've selected the Paint On Change menu item, DataUser calls *UpdateWindow* to force an immediate repaint. This gives you an opportunity to evaluate performance differences between a delayed repaint scheme and a synchronous one. Of course, repainting every time makes the whole process take longer because the data object will be waiting for all of this to occur before the call to *OnDataChange* returns.

It is a worthwhile exercise to modify these samples in order to send the data along with each notification and then to compare the relative performance in each case. For all cases except when DataUser asks the in-process object for a rendering inside *OnDataChange,* you will see a noticeable performance drop. In the cases outlined earlier, very few actual calls were sent into *IDataObject::GetData.* Sending the data with every notification means rendering the data each time and also freeing the data each time. This can get very expensive where large bitmaps or metafiles are concerned. The techniques demonstrated in DataUser and the two data objects represent more efficient implementations.

# *IDataObject* as a Standard for Object Data Transfer

As I mentioned, *IDataObject* is the standardized interface for data exchange. It makes sense for any object capable of performing any type of data transfer to do as much as it can through *IDataObject* instead of through custom interfaces. We can see this in practice with the Polyline component object we've used in earlier chapters. In Chapter 8, we eliminated the private members of the *IPolyline5* interface that had to do with file input and output and replaced those members with the *IPersistStorage* and *IPersistStreamInit* interfaces. Now we can do the same thing in CHAP10\POLYLINE, replacing the data exchange members of *IPolyline8,* shown in the following, with *IDataObject*:

```
//From Chapter 8's Polyline
interface IPolyline8 : public IUnknown
    {
    [Other members]

    STDMETHOD(DataSet)        (THIS_ LPPOLYLINEDATA, BOOL, BOOL) PURE;
    STDMETHOD(DataGet)        (THIS_ LPPOLYLINEDATA) PURE;
    STDMETHOD(DataSetMem)     (THIS_ HGLOBAL, BOOL, BOOL, BOOL) PURE;
    STDMETHOD(DataGetMem)     (THIS_ HGLOBAL FAR *) PURE;
    STDMETHOD(RenderBitmap) (THIS_ HBITMAP FAR *) PURE;
    STDMETHOD(RenderMetafile) (THIS_ HMETAFILE FAR *) PURE;
    STDMETHOD(RenderMetafilePict) (THIS_ HGLOBAL FAR *) PURE;

    [Other members]
    }
```

In other words, we can eliminate from *IPolyline8* all the separate functions for exchange of its native data in both get and set directions because FORMATETC allows us to specify different formats and different mediums through *IDataObject* calls directly. The new interface, *IPolyline10*, for this chapter's version of Polyline no longer has these specific member functions.

In addition, Polyline has been working with its own private notification interface, *IPolylineAdviseSink8*, with members such as *OnDataChange*, *OnPoint-Change*, and so on. With the addition of *IDataObject* to the Polyline object, we can remove the *OnDataChange* member from the updated *IPolylineAdvise-Sink10* interface and instead use *IAdviseSink* for this notification. Any client can now use Polyline for data exchange and notification without having to be aware of the custom *IPolyline10* and *IPolylineAdviseSink10* interfaces.

Along with these changes to Polyline are the necessary changes to Component Cosmo (CHAP10\COCOSMO), as follows:

- Polyline has one additional file, IDATAOBJ.CPP, which implements the *IDataObject* interface for the *CPolyline* class.

- Polyline maintains a data advise holder object internally for implementing the advise members of *IDataObject*. Where Polyline used to call *IPolylineAdviseSink8::OnDataChange*, it now calls *IDataAdvise-Holder::SendOnDataChange*.

- *IPolyline8::DataSet* and *IPolyline8::DataGet* are now private member functions of the C++ *CPolyline* class because they are used internally by the Polyline object in the rest of its implementation.

- Polyline now registers a private clipboard format ("Polyline Figure") to identify its native data.

- Polyline implements *IDataObject::EnumFormatEtc* using *OleRegEnum-FormatEtc* and registry entries for its native Polyline Figure format, CF_METAFILEPICT, and for CF_BITMAP.

- CoCosmo adds the file IADVSINK.CPP, in which it receives *OnData-Change* notifications from Polyline. CoCosmo implements the *IAdviseSink* interface as part of its *CCosmoDoc* object, which now uses multiple inheritance from both its normal base class *CDocument* and *IAdviseSink*. Take a look at *CCosmoDoc::QueryInterface* to see why you must be careful to correctly typecast the pointers you assign to the *void* ** out-parameter. Failure to do this can cause all sorts of strange problems, such as premature calls to the document destructor, as we described in Chapter 2.

- CoCosmo implements a set of *IUnknown* members on its *CCosmoDoc* class to support the interface implementation of *IAdviseSink*.

■ All of CoCosmo's clipboard handling in *CCosmoDoc::RenderFormat* and *CCosmoDoc::Paste* now work through Polyline's *IDataObject*, which CoCosmo queries for when needed.

None of the code to implement these features is much different from the code we've seen so far, so there's no need to show any of it here. However, with the addition of *IDataObject* along with *IPersistStorage*, the Polyline object is now very close to an embedded content object. What it lacks are the interfaces *IViewObject2*, which we'll see in the next chapter, and *IOleObject*, which we'll see in Chapter 19. Even when we make those changes, Component Cosmo can still use Polyline as before, totally ignoring any additional interfaces. This shows the flexibility of the multiple interface paradigm made possible by *QueryInterface*. In later chapters, we'll see how Polyline can support two different types of client (CoCosmo with inside knowledge and a container with no knowledge outside OLE Documents) merely by implementing a number of interfaces for both.

# Summary

Because objects in OLE are accessed exclusively through interface pointers, a client needs ways to access an object's data. One such way is through the interface *IDataObject*, which exposes an object's structured information. Any object that implements this interface is called a *data object*.

Data exchange through *IDataObject* works with two structures named FORMATETC and STGMEDIUM. The FORMATETC structure improves on the idea of a clipboard format by adding an *aspect* (content, icon, thumbnail, and so on), a device description, and a transfer medium indicator. The STGMEDIUM structure improves on a global-memory handle, allowing data exchange to occur in a variety of mediums such as memory, storage elements, stream elements, and disk files. Through these structures, a data object and a data consumer can exchange rich data in a very efficient manner.

The *IDataObject* interface itself incorporates the best of all existing transfer protocols in Windows, such as the clipboard and DDE. Through its member functions, a client of a data object can get or set data, query and enumerate formats, get data in a preallocated medium, check format equivalency, and manage a notification loop with the data object. That all of this functionality is centrally located in one interface makes data transfer through the interface a uniform operation regardless of how a pointer to that interface is communicated between a data source and its consumer. This is where the name "Uniform Data Transfer" comes from.

Enumerating formats involves an enumerator for the FORMATETC structure that implements *IEnumFORMATETC*. OLE provides a standard implementation of such an enumerator that uses an object's registry entries to find the list of formats. A notification loop with a data object involves an interface named *IAdviseSink*, specifically its member *OnDataChange*. Through this asynchronous call, a client can know when data changes occur in any number of sources. OLE also provides a service for data objects that manages multiple sinks and sends notifications to them.

OLE's Uniform Data Transfer is a new, very flexible standard that will find broad application in many areas. It can also supplant Dynamic Data Exchange (DDE), although the two exchange mechanisms are slightly different. This chapter examines a situation in which an industry group for real-time market data replaced a DDE-based solution with an OLE-based solution, showing the flexibility of this OLE technology.

In this chapter, we also examine the considerations and issues surrounding the implementation of data objects in both in-process and local servers. We also take a look at a data consumer (a client) that also works with data change notifications.

## CHAPTER ELEVEN

# Viewable Objects and the Data Cache

In real estate, you can distinguish between properties with a view and properties without one (or, say, with a view of the hind end of a grocery store). You can say the same thing about vacation destinations. There's a big difference between places with grand views of natural wonders and those with a view of the backside of a grocery store.

Now, we've all received those postcards from so-called friends—postcards that show the most fabulous views in the world along with the note, "Wish you were here." Yeah, right. While a picture is worth a thousand words, a picture still doesn't come close to being there. Small, two-dimensional photographs have nowhere near the latitude for color and contrast that can be seen with the human eye. They're just not the same.

In Chapter 10, I mentioned that most objects have information of some kind. That information is commonly called the object's *properties*. Through the *IDataObject* interface, you can ask an object for those properties directly, or you can ask for a graphical rendering of that data. As far as seeing the "real thing" goes, these graphical renderings are akin to asking friends for photographs of the view from their own property. Having a data object send you a new rendering with a data change notification is somewhat like a friend sending you a postcard.

These renderings are, of course, very useful—a consumer of data will often incorporate such pictures into its own user interface—but they do have some limitations, just as a photograph is limited in comparison to the human eye. First of all, you can work with only limited graphical formats, such as CF_METAFILEPICT, CF_BITMAP, CF_DIB, and CF_TIFF. While you can create any image you want in a bitmap or TIFF format, these formats are typically large and bulky and consume a lot of memory and disk space. Metafiles are more efficient with respect to storage, but they also have their limitations because certain graphical operations cannot be written into a metafile format. In all of these cases, it is also difficult to fully exploit the target device.

While a data object can create graphics appropriate to the device (that is, for the colors and resolution available), it cannot use the services of that device directly. For example, a data object that knows about PostScript and is asked to render itself for a PostScript device cannot simply send PostScript commands directly to the device.

To accomplish direct rendering to a device—and to optimize the quality of the output—the object itself must have access to the device context, the Windows *hDC* for whatever screen or printer the consumer (or client) wants to show the object's image. To that end, OLE defines the interfaces named *IViewObject* and *IViewObject2*, through which an object tells its clients that it can render directly to a device. The primary member of these interfaces, named *Draw*, takes an *hDC* as an argument, giving what we called the *viewable object* direct access to the device. So instead of a client asking a data object for a graphical rendering, that client can ask the object to draw itself here. Instead of asking the object for a photograph, the client asks to see the real thing with its own eyes, without limitations in detail, quality, and so on.

*IViewObject* and *IViewObject2* are the primary topics of this chapter. Besides the *Draw* function, these interfaces express the ability to freeze and unfreeze an object's view (so as to stabilize it during printing), expose the colors used in the rendering, set the size of the rendering, and allow a client to request notifications from the viewable object through *IAdviseSink::OnViewChange*. This kind of notification allows a client to redraw the object only when the view has changed (as opposed to a data change, which might not affect the view) and keeps the client's image up to date with the object.

All of this is not to say that graphical renderings in the metafile or bitmap formats are entirely useless. One look around will tell you that photographs and other static images are highly valuable and have many uses. In fact, having a client cache one or more object images in a document or other such file is often very useful because then the object need not be present to view its data. This is an important consideration. A client doesn't want its own presentation to be altogether dependent on the presence of objects. If that client is run on a machine without those objects, it can't do anything more than show a bunch of ugly gray boxes saying, "There was once an interesting picture here; please use your imagination." Can you hear your customer support phones ringing off the hook?

A second case in which a cache is important occurs when obtaining a new rendering for an object would otherwise be very expensive, with or without *IViewObject2* in the picture. Let's say that a client asks a data object for a metafile rendering that contains something like 50,000 distinct graphical elements—a large rendering indeed. Let's also say that the object in question executes from a local server that takes at least 20 seconds to run. Without a cache, the client would have to continually run this huge local server and have it repeatedly render this large graphic whenever that client wanted to display or even repaint the image.

To address these concerns, OLE provides the implementation of a service called the *data cache,* whose object implements the interfaces named *IOleCache2* (with the base interface *IOleCache*) and *IOleCacheControl.* The data cache also implements three other interfaces: *IDataObject,* which lets the client send data to the cache and retrieve the same later; *IPersistStorage,* so that the client can have the cache save its data and load it again; and *IViewObject2,* which lets the client ask the cache to draw a stored graphic to the screen or printer. If you have any experience with compound documents, you'll recognize that the needs described here are also common needs for compound documents themselves. In fact, OLE's data cache and the *IOleCache\** interfaces were originally created for OLE Documents. But the cache is still a useful service in and of itself, just as a viewable object is useful by itself. A viewable data object gives us the experience of seeing natural wonders with our own eyes, and caching allows us to archive photographs that help us to remember those experiences—even if they are only those of the hind end of a grocery store.

# Viewable Objects: *IViewObject* and *IViewObject2*

Simply put, an object's support of either *IViewObject* or *IViewObject2* makes that object viewable. In other words, when a client queries for these interfaces it is asking whether the object can draw itself directly to a device. These interfaces are often found alongside *IDataObject,* giving a client the capability of obtaining renderings directly or from a storage medium. *IViewObject2* is the same as *IViewObject* with one extra member:

```
interface IViewObject : IUnknown
    {
    HRESULT Draw(DWORD dwAspect, LONG lindex, void *pvAspect
        , DVTARGETDEVICE *ptd, HDC hicTargetDev, HDC hDC
        , LPCRECTL prcBounds, LPCRECTL prcWBounds
        , BOOL (CALLBACK *pfnContinue)(DWORD), DWORD dwContinue);

    HRESULT GetColorSet(DWORD dwAspect, LONG lindex, void *pvAspect
        , DVTARGETDEVICE *ptd, HDC hicTargetDev
        , LPLOGPALETTE *ppColorSet);
    HRESULT Freeze(DWORD dwDrawAspect, LONG lindex, void *pvAspect
        , DWORD *pdwFreeze);
```

*(continued)*

```
    HRESULT Unfreeze(DWORD dwFreeze);
    HRESULT SetAdvise(DWORD dwAspects, DWORD dwAdvf
        , IAdviseSink *pAdvSink);
    HRESULT GetAdvise(DWORD *pAspects, DWORD *pdwAdvf
        , IAdviseSink *ppAdvSink);
    };

interface IViewObject2 : IViewObject
    {
    HRESULT GetExtent(DWORD dwAspect, LONG lindex, DVTARGETDEVICE *ptd
        , LPSIZEL pszl);
    };
```

The *IViewObject2* interface was created because asking an object for its size — *GetExtent* — is a common request. The original *IViewObject* did not have this capability, and the only other interface that does is *IOleObject*, a large interface found on compound document objects. It is pointless to make an object implement *IOleObject* simply to tell a client how large it is, so *IViewObject2* is a necessity. Objects should always implement *IViewObject2* where the object's *QueryInterface* will also return the base interface *IViewObject*. Any viewable object implemented by OLE itself (such as the data cache) implements *IViewObject2*, and it is silly for an object to implement *IViewObject* alone unless for some odd reason its extents make no sense for it. *IViewObject* is not wholly obsolete, however, because clients that do not need the extents might ask only for this lesser interface. But by virtue of supporting *IViewObject2*, objects support *IViewObject*. For all of these reasons, the rest of this chapter (and book) is concerned with *IViewObject2*.

You probably noticed that a number of the member functions of *IViewObject2* take arguments that are found inside the FORMATETC structure that we saw in Chapter 10: an aspect (*dwAspect*; all DVASPECT_* values are legal), a piece index (*lindex*), and a target device (*ptd*).[1] These arguments identify the exact data concerned with the member. This means you can ask *Draw*, for example, to render a thumbnail sketch or an icon for whatever device is appropriate. *IViewObject2* doesn't require a FORMATETC because we're not at all concerned with data formats or storage mediums. The format is always "the object's view," and the medium, important only in *Draw*, is always the *hDC* device.

---

1. The *pvAspect* argument provides extended information for the object according to *dwAspect*. At the time of writing, no definitions for such information exist, so this value is always NULL. It does allow future extension, however.

The *hDC* brings up a significant restriction for both of these interfaces. An *hDC* is not shareable between processes under any Windows operating system, so *IViewObject* and *IViewObject2* can be implemented only on in-process objects! In other words, no marshaling support exists for these interfaces because an *hDC* cannot be marshaled. Only those objects provided from in-process servers and in-process handlers can implement these interfaces. *IViewObject2* is, in fact, one of the major reasons why you might need to implement an in-process handler that communicates with a local server: the handler implements *IViewObject2*, delegating all other interfaces to its local server.

Two types, found in *Draw* and *GetExtent*, respectively, deserve mention here because we have not yet encountered them, but we will in later chapters. LPCRECTL, used for *prcBounds* and *prcWBounds* in *Draw*, is a pointer to a constant RECTL structure:

```
typedef struct _RECTL
    {
    LONG left;
    LONG top;
    LONG right;
    LONG bottom;
    } RECTL;
```

This is a 32-bit version of the standard Windows RECT type, and under 32-bit systems a RECTL is actually identical to a RECT. However, you cannot simply assign a RECTL value to a RECT because the compiler recognizes them as different structures. For this reason, you'll find two macros in INC\INOLE.H to convert one value to the other, as well as a macro to set a RECTL structure, similar to the Windows *SetRect* function:

```
RECTLFROMRECT(rcl, rc)
RECTFROMRECTL(rc, rcl)

#define SETRECTL(rcl, l, t, r, b) \
    {\
    (rcl).left=l;\
    (rcl).top=t;\
    (rcl).right=r;\
    (rcl).bottom=b;\
    }
```

The SETRECTL macro takes a RECTL structure itself, not a pointer, as the first argument.

The *pszl* argument to *GetExtent* is a pointer to the SIZEL structure, which has no existing Windows analog but is simply a structure containing general horizontal and vertical dimensions:

```
typedef struct  tagSIZEL
    {
    LONG cx;
    LONG cy;
    } SIZEL;
```

The file INC\INOLE.H also includes the macro SETSIZEL (which takes a structure, not a pointer), but because nothing else like it exists, conversion macros aren't necessary:

```
#define SETSIZEL(szl, h, v) \
    {\
    (szl).cx=h;\
    (szl).cy=v;\
    }
```

Now that we have some background, let's look at the various *IViewObject2* members.

## *IViewObject2::Draw*

Because the *Draw* member function encompasses such rich functionality, it probably has the longest argument list in all of OLE. It allows a client to tell an object exactly what to draw (*dwAspect, lindex, pvAspect*), where to draw it (*hDC, prcBounds, prcWBounds*), and how to draw it (*ptd, hicTargetDev*). In addition, a client can supply a callback function to break out of long repaints (*pfnContinue* and *dwContinue*). We'll first look at the basic form of *Draw* and then at the specific areas of handling a device, drawing into a metafile, and breaking out of long repaints.

The simplest way to call *Draw* is expressed in the following code:

```
pIViewObject2->Draw(DVASPECT_CONTENT, -1, NULL, NULL, 0, hDC, &rcBounds
    , NULL, NULL, 0);
```

This statement says, "Draw the full rendering of the object (*DVASPECT-_CONTENT, −1*) in this rectangle (*rcBounds*) on this device context (*hDC*)." The object draws its full-content rendering (whatever it is) directly to *hDC*, scaled to fit into *rcBounds*. The rectangle must be expressed in the current mapping mode of *hDC*, which can be a screen, a printer, a metafile, or a memory device context. An object that typically generates bitmaps can implement this function with a simple *StretchBlt* call; if it normally uses a metafile, it can call *PlayMetafile* after setting the extents properly for the rectangle. The object is also required (as common sense would dictate) to leave *hDC* in the same state as it was received. If the object needs to change mapping modes or another state of *hDC*, it must call the Windows API *SaveDC* on entry to *Draw* and match it with *RestoreDC* on exit.

Again, the RECTL pointed to by *prcBounds* specifies the scaling rectangle in units appropriate to *hDC*. This is not a clipping rectangle: the object is required to draw its full presentation into this rectangle. Where the scaling percentage is the ratio of the *prcBounds* dimensions to the object's extents:

$$xScale = \frac{prcBounds\text{ -}>right - prcBounds\text{ -}>left}{xExtent} * 100\%$$

$$yScale = \frac{prcBounds\text{ -}>bottom - prcBounds\text{ -}>top}{yExtent} * 100\%$$

If the client actually wants a clipped rendering, it must create a clipping rectangle, select it into *hDC* before calling *Draw*, and specify *prcBounds* so that the intersection of the clipping rectangle and *prcBounds* results in the correct viewing window, as shown in Figure 11-1. In short, clipping is always the client's concern, never the viewable object's.

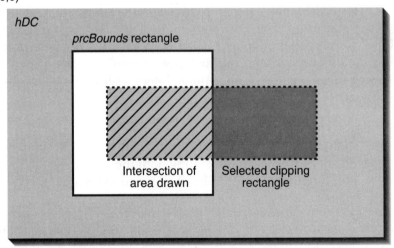

**Figure 11-1.**
*Clipping through* IViewObject2::Draw *is achieved through a combination of a* prcBounds *and a clipping rectangle selected into* hDC.

Because a client often wants no more than to specify the aspect, the device context, and the bounding rectangle for any drawing operation, OLE provides the API function *OleDraw*, whose implementation is as follows:

```
STDAPI OleDraw(LPUNKNOWN pIUnknown, DWORD dwAspect, HDC hDC
    , LPCRECTL prcBounds);
    {
    HRESULT        hr;
    LPVIEWOBJECT pIViewObject;

    if (NULL!=pIUnknown)
        {
        hr=pIUnknown->QueryInterface(IID_IViewObject
            , (VOID **)&pIViewObject);

        if (SUCCEEDED(hr))
            {
            pIViewObject2->Draw(dwAspect, -1, NULL, NULL, 0
                , hDC, prcBounds, NULL, NULL, 0);

            pIViewObject2->Release();
            }
        }

    return;
    }
```

This API function is a convenient wrapper because a client does not need to query for *IViewObject* or hold onto some *IViewObject* pointer for later drawing. But *OleDraw* doesn't help in cases in which you want more control over the exact rendering. In those cases—rendering for a specific device, drawing into a metafile, and stopping long repaints—you can always query for *IViewObject[2]* and call *Draw*.

## Rendering for a Specific Device

Many applications, especially high-end graphics and desktop publishing packages, are concerned about getting both the highest quality and the fastest possible output on a printer. Two arguments to *Draw* allow applications to tell a viewable object about the intended device:

- *ptd (DVTARGETDEVICE \*)*: Identical to the *ptd* field in a FORMATETC, which describes the exact device for which the object is to render its image. A NULL means the display.

■ *hicTargetDev (hDC)*: An information context for a target device other than the screen. By using this context, the object can extract device metrics, test the device's capabilities, and retrieve any other relevant parameters. Objects ignore this argument if *ptd* is NULL; if *hicTarget-Dev* is non-NULL, it specifies the information context for a printer; if NULL, it means the client is drawing to the screen what would appear on the printer.

There are two primary cases in which a client might pass non-NULL values in these arguments. The first and most obvious occurs when *hDC* is a printer device context and you want the objects to render as accurately as possible for that printer. In this case, you can describe the printer device in *ptd* and pass either an information context you have on hand in *hicTargetDev* or pass your *hDC* as this argument. (A device context is an information context.) When *ptd* is non-NULL, a client must pass something in *hicTargetDev* to tell the object that the device context in *hDC* is for a printer. As an example of when you might use these arguments, consider printing to a PostScript printer for an object that understands PostScript directly. The object, knowing that *hDC* is a real printer device context, could send PostScript commands directly to the printer (through the Windows *Escape* function) instead of calling Windows GDI functions. The result is better performance and highly optimized output.

The second use of these arguments is for situations such as print preview, in which the client wants the object to draw to the screen what that object would draw to the printer. In this case, *ptd* points to a valid DVTARGETDEVICE, but *hicTargetDev* is NULL. This means that the object should call GDI functions on *hDC* to draw itself but should use colors and resolution appropriate for the device described by *ptd*. For example, an object that normally shows a magenta shading on the screen would print a dither pattern on a black-and-white printer. In this situation, the object creates its own information context according to *ptd* in order to know the color capability of that device and in order to modify its output to *hDC* accordingly.

## Drawing into a Metafile

A metafile device context is a rather special beast when it comes to drawing the object at a specific location within that metafile. The object in this case needs to know both the window extents and the window origin of the *hDC* to draw itself in the correct location within the scope of the entire metafile. To do this, the *prcWBounds* argument to *Draw* contains the window extent and the window origin for the metafile, not a real rectangle. This argument will be non-NULL only if *hDC* is a metafile device context.

The origin is the point (*prcWBounds->left*, *prcWBounds->top*). The horizontal extent is *prcWBounds->right*, and the vertical extent is *prcWBounds->bottom*. To account for these values, a viewable object must offset its GDI calls into the metafile by the origin coordinates and must scale the points it passes to those GDI calls according to the ratio of the window extents to the object's own extents. Do not call the Windows API *SetWindowsOrgEx* or *SetWindowExtEx* for this purpose.

The *prcWBounds* argument really matters when an object plays another metafile as part of its own rendering. Usually each record in such a metafile will assume a certain origin and extent, so to account for those assumptions the object must enumerate the metafile and massage each record individually to modify the origin and scaling appropriately.

## Stopping Long Repaints

The *pfnContinue* and *dwContinue* arguments to *IViewObject2::Draw* give a client the ability to terminate long repaints for complicated drawings:

- ■ *pfnContinue (BOOL (CALLBACK *)(DWORD))*: A pointer to a callback function that the viewable object will call periodically during a lengthy drawing process. The callback function returns TRUE to continue drawing or FALSE to abort the operation (usually if the user hits Esc). If the drawing operation is canceled, *Draw* returns DRAW_E_ABORT.

- ■ *dwContinue (DWORD)*: An extra 32-bit value to pass as the argument to *pfnContinue*. Typically, this value is a pointer to some client-defined structure needed inside the callback function.

A typical client implements the continue function to test the Esc key status:

```
BOOL CALLBACK ContinuePaint(DWORD dwContinue)
    {
    return !(GetAsyncKeyState(VK_ESCAPE) < 0);
    }
```

How often this function is actually called depends on the object and how it draws itself. As a general guideline, an object should call the function once for every 16 operations, an operation being a GDI call or the playing of a metafile record. Obviously this will not work to break out of a single, time-consuming call to *StretchBlt*, but if the object draws more than one large bitmap, it should call the function after each *BitBlt* or *StretchBlt*. A really kind object might even try to draw a large bitmap in separate bands. In any case, call the continuation function if possible, and if the object draws quickly, you can ignore it altogether.

## *IViewObject2::GetColorSet* and *GetExtent*

*IViewObject2::GetColorSet* allows a client to obtain an object's logical palette used during *Draw*, which the client can try to match as closely as possible when the object's image is considered background. For example, a client that displays multiple images in separate windows would consider the object shown in the foreground window to own the palette; all other objects would have to render using that same palette. If the object uses a particular palette, it should fill the LOGPALETTE structure pointed to by *ppColorSet* with the colors it would use if *Draw* were called with the rest of the arguments passed to *GetColorSet*. Objects that are not palette sensitive return S_FALSE. In general, the palette here is identical to what the object might pass to the Windows API functions *SetPaletteEntries* and *CreatePalette*.

*IViewObject2::GetExtent*, the function not found in *IViewObject* itself, fills the SIZEL structure with the object's natural size. The extents are always expressed in HIMETRIC units—not the MM_HIMETRIC mapping mode, but the same units used in that mode. In other words, both the horizontal and vertical extents returned from this function are positive values scaled according to 100 logical units per millimeter; on the screen, positive $x$ is left, and positive $y$ is down. (It is negative with the MM_HIMETRIC mapping mode.) Be careful that you use the correct units but not the mapping mode.

## *IViewObject2::Freeze* and *Unfreeze*

*Freeze* and *Unfreeze* (the latter of which I've always thought should be *Thaw*) let the client control whether the object is allowed to change what it would render on subsequent calls to *Draw*. *Freeze* works on one aspect at a time— freezing DVASPECT_CONTENT does not freeze a call to *Draw* for DV-ASPECT_ICON. Calling *Freeze* returns a DWORD key, which you later pass to *Unfreeze* to bring the object back from the Ice Age.

Freezing a viewable object is comparable to creating a bitmap copy of the current view of the object and always using that bitmap to show the object. Underneath, the actual data might have changed, but the image does not. Because we're always using the snapshot bitmap to show the object, calls to *Draw* don't show any changes. The utility of frozen views is that they stabilize an object's rendering during printer banding so that multiple calls to *Draw* work with the same underlying view. Without freezing that view, it could change between *Draw* calls, and that would totally louse up any attempt at printer banding.

## *IViewObject2::SetAdvise* and *GetAdvise*

The final two members of *IViewObject2*— *SetAdvise* and *GetAdvise*—work with *IAdviseSink::OnViewChange* independently of *IAdviseSink::OnDataChange*, which we saw in Chapter 10. *SetAdvise* establishes or ends a notification loop, and *GetAdvise* retrieves the last *IAdviseSink* pointer seen in *SetAdvise*.

*IAdviseSink::OnViewChange* informs a client that an object's view changed, not necessarily some underlying data. This is why a client calls *IDataObject- ::DAdvise* for data change notifications and *IViewObject2::SetAdvise* for view changes. As an example, consider a data object attached to a spreadsheet whose view is also that spreadsheet. A change in one of the cells would fire *OnDataChange* but would fire *OnViewChange* for DVASPECT_CONTENT only if that cell is visible in the rendering. A change to the spreadsheet does not, however, change a DVASPECT_ICON rendering, which is unrelated to the actual data underneath. A change to the actual spreadsheet filename, on the other hand, might change the icon aspect (if the filename is the icon's label) but not the content aspect, which shows only the spreadsheet cells. In addition, a change to the rotation of a chart might fire *OnViewChange*, although the actual data is the same. When data and view changes occur together, which notification is fired first is variable between objects. Clients should not depend on any particular order.

Clients call *IViewObject2::SetAdvise* with *dwAspect* set to whatever aspects it is displaying in an active fashion. A view object that doesn't support notifications at all returns NOTIFY_E_ADVISENOTSUPPORTED. Otherwise, the *dwAdvf* flags (the same ADVF_* flags as for *IDataObject::DAdvise*) describe the nature of the notifications desired; 0 means "normal notification," ADVF- _PRIMEFIRST generates an *OnViewChange* call immediately, and ADVF- _ONLYONCE will have the object release the advise sink after the first *OnViewChange* call. No other ADVF_* flags are relevant. Furthermore, *pAdvSink* points to the client's *IAdviseSink* implementation. A client will generally invalidate some region of its window inside *IAdviseSink::OnViewChange* and then call *IViewObject2::Draw* later during a repaint. A client calls *SetAdvise* with a NULL in *pAdvSink* to terminate the advisory connection.

Another point about *SetAdvise* is that each viewable object maintains only a single *IAdviseSink* pointer. A viewable object does not support multicasting. Any call to *SetAdvise* will release the formerly installed sink and install the new one. This will not cause a conflict for multiple clients because

*IViewObject2* can be implemented only on an in-process object and there will generally be only one client for any one instantiation of such an object. There is no conflict with multiple remote clients. The possibility exists, of course, that multiple components in a process will try to access the same instance of a viewable object, but that has not been shown to be a problem. Because components are usually isolated from one another, each would use its own instance of the viewable object. Only components with intimate knowledge of each other could be in conflict, in which case it is entirely their responsibility to determine how to handle notifications.

### Synchronizing with a Local Server

As mentioned earlier, a viewable object must be in-process, and as part of an in-process handler it works in conjunction with a local server. To keep the two synchronized, the handler object needs to know when the local object changes data. The handler object can then generate an *IAdviseSink::OnViewChange* call to the client if necessary. To do this, the handler object must implement a sink of its own and connect it to the local object through *IDataObject::DAdvise*. When this handler sink receives *IAdviseSink::OnDataChange*, it can check whether the change affects any current view for which the client wants a notification. If so, the handler object turns around and calls the client's *IAdviseSink-::OnViewChange*, which it can do directly from within the handler object's own *OnDataChange* because the handler is in the client process already. The handler's sink is a separate object from the viewable object in that same handler, so they must have separate implementations of *QueryInterface*.

## The OLE Data Cache

Clients often find it useful, especially in the context of OLE Documents, to cache an object's image or presentation for use later when that object is no longer available. To assist in this matter, OLE provides a *data cache* service, which consists of one object that implements *IDataObject*, *IPersistStorage*, *IViewObject2*, *IOleCache2* (derived from *IOleCache*), and *IOleCacheControl*. The data cache is accessed through the OLE API function *CreateDataCache*:

```
HRESULT CreateDataCache(IUnknown *pUnkOuter, REFCLSID rclsid
    , REFIID riid, void **ppv)
```

Here *pUnkOuter* allows another object to aggregate on the cache, *rclsid* represents the CLSID used to generate icon labels (this is usually CLSID-_NULL), and *riid* and *ppv* are the same as for *QueryInterface*. The reason the data cache supports aggregation so directly is that in-process objects commonly expose one or more of the cache's own interfaces directly (for example, *IPersistStorage* or *IDataObject*) when the object doesn't want to modify the behavior of the cache itself.

## The Cache's *IDataObject*, *IPersistStorage*, and *IViewObject2*

The presence of *IDataObject* describes the cache as a source of data. *GetData*, *GetDataHere*, and *QueryGetData* are implemented as you would expect and deal with the contents of the cache. *SetData* delegates to *IOleCache2::SetData*, as we'll see shortly, and format enumeration and advisory connections are not supported at all. On the other hand, *IPersistStorage* is fully implemented so that *Save* will write any data in the cache to separate streams (regardless of that data's native storage medium) and *Load* will read information from those streams back into the cache. Those streams are named "\002OlePres<*xxx*>", where <*xxx*> varies from 000 to 999. *IViewObject2* is also fully implemented, which means a client can ask the cache to draw any presentation within it. In addition, the cache will notify the client through *IDataObject::SetData* or *IOleCache2::Cache* any time a view is changed. Overall, the behavior of the cache's *IDataObject*, *IPersistStorage*, and *IViewObject* interfaces is summarized in Tables 11-1, 11-2, and 11-3.

| IDataObject Member Function | Behavior |
| --- | --- |
| *DAdvise* | Returns OLE_E_ADVISENOTSUPPORTED. |
| *DUnadvise* | Returns OLE_E_NOCONNECTION. |
| *EnumDAdvise* | Returns OLE_E_ADVISENOTSUPPORTED. |
| *EnumFormatEtc* | Returns E_NOTIMPL. |
| *GetCanonicalFormatEtc* | Returns E_NOTIMPL. |
| *GetData* | Attempts to find the data in the cache, which must use the mediums TYMED_HGLOBAL, TYMED-_MFPICT, TYMED_GDI, TYMED_ISTORAGE, |

**Table 11-1.**
*Behavior of the data cache's* IDataObject *interface.*

*(continued)*

**Table 11-1.** *continued*

| IDataObject Member Function | Behavior |
|---|---|
| | and TYMED_ISTREAM. DV_E_TYMED is returned for any other medium. OLE_E_BLANK is returned for data that is not found in the cache. |
| *GetDataHere* | Same as for *GetData* but supports only TYMED_HGLOBAL, TYMED_ISTORAGE, and TYMED_ISTREAM. |
| *QueryGetData* | Returns NOERROR if the format is present in the cache; otherwise, returns S_FALSE. |
| *SetData* | Delegates to *IOleCache2::SetData*. |

| IPersistStorage Member Function | Behavior |
|---|---|
| *GetClassID* | Returns E_NOTIMPL. |
| *IsDirty* | Returns S_OK if the cache contents have been changed; otherwise, returns S_FALSE. |
| *InitNew* | Returns NOERROR but saves the *IStorage* pointer, calling *AddRef* on it. |
| *Load* | Loads information about cached data from streams in *IStorage* and saves the *IStorage* pointer. No data is actually loaded until required through *IDataObject::GetData* or *IViewObject2::Draw*. |
| *Save* | Saves any presentations that have changed since the call to *Load*, as well as an information block describing what is cached. Data is stored in streams named "\002OlePres<*xxx*>", where <*xxx*> varies from 000 to 999. |
| *SaveCompleted* | Releases and replaces any held pointers as necessary and returns NOERROR. |
| *HandsOffStorage* | Releases any held pointers and returns NOERROR. |

**Table 11-2.**
*Behavior of the data cache's* IPersistStorage *interface.*

| IViewObject2 Member Function | Behavior |
|---|---|
| *Draw* | Attempts to draw using a presentation from the cache; otherwise, returns OLE_E_BLANK. |
| *GetColorSet* | Tries to determine the color set from the metafile or bitmap in the cache. Returns OLE_E_BLANK if there is no presentation; otherwise, returns NOERROR or S_FALSE, depending on the success of the function. |
| *Freeze* | Adds the aspect to an internal list that affects the behavior of *Draw* and returns NOERROR if successful or OLE_E_BLANK if not. Returns VIEW_S_ALREADY_FROZEN if this is a repeat request. |
| *Unfreeze* | Removes an entry from the internal list of frozen aspects and frees any duplicate presentation. Returns OLE_E_NOCONNECTION if the aspect was not frozen; otherwise, returns NOERROR. |
| *SetAdvise* | Saves the *IAdviseSink* pointer and returns NOERROR. |
| *GetAdvise* | Returns the last *IAdviseSink* from *SetAdvise* and returns NOERROR. |
| *GetExtent* | Returns the size of a known presentation (extents from a METAFILEPICT or the size of a bitmap) and returns NOERROR; otherwise, returns OLE_E_BLANK. |

**Table 11-3.**
*Behavior of the data cache's* IViewObject2 *interface.*

## The *IOleCache2* Interface

The *IOleCache2* interface is the interface a client uses to control what actually gets cached. The *IOleCache* interface expresses the basic functionality, with *IOleCache2* adding the capability of the client to update any cached data that is maintained. The following shows the definitions of the interfaces; the member functions of both interfaces are described in Table 11-4.

```
interface IOleCache : IUnknown
    {
    HRESULT Cache(FORMATETC *pFE, DWORD dwAdvf, DWORD *pdwConnection);
    HRESULT Uncache(DWORD dwConnection);
    HRESULT EnumCache(IEnumSTATDATA **ppEnum);
    HRESULT InitCache(IDataObject *pIDataObject);
```

```
        HRESULT SetData(FORMATETC *pFE, STGMEDIUM *pSTM, BOOL fRelease);
        };

interface IOleCache2 : IOleCache
    {
    HRESULT UpdateCache(IDataObject *pIDataObject, DWORD dwgrfUpdf
        , void **pvReserved);
    HRESULT DiscardCache(DWORD dwDiscardOptions);
    }
```

| IOleCache and IOleCache2 Member Function | Behavior |
|---|---|
| *Cache* | Adds the given format to the list of those cached. If *FORMATETC::cfFormat* is 0, all formats are cached. If CF_BITMAP is cached, the cache will also save CF_DIB and vice versa. The ADVF_* flags specify how the cache relates to a remote object. (See "The *IOleCacheControl* Interface" later in this chapter.) *Cache* returns a connection key for use with *Uncache*. |
| *Uncache* | Removes a format from the list to cache by using the key returned from *Cache* and releases any data of this format from the cache. Also terminates any connection to a local or remote object for the format. |
| *EnumCache* | Enumerates the present cached formats (not the data) through *IEnumSTATDATA*, as described for *IDataObject::EnumDAdvise* in Chapter 10. The *pAdvSink* field of the enumerated structures holds *IAdviseSink* pointers to sinks implemented in the cache that are connected to a local or remote object. |
| *InitCache* | Fills the cache with all the data available from a data object. This is easily implemented by enumerating the formats in the data object, calling *IDataObject::GetData* for each and then saving each one by calling *IOleCache2::SetData*. |
| *SetData* | Saves a specific piece of data in the cache. The *fRelease* flag acts like the same argument to *IDataObject::SetData*. |

**Table 11-4.**

*(continued)*

*Behavior of the data cache's* IOleCache2 *interface.*

**Table 11-4.** *continued*

| IOleCache and IOleCache2 Member Function | Behavior |
|---|---|
| *UpdateCache* (*IOleCache2* only) | Updates the data in the cache in bulk from the data available in a data object according to *dwgrfUpdf*. These flags are fully described in the *OLE Programmer's Reference*. |
| *DiscardCache* (*IOleCache2* only) | Flushes any data from memory but does not delete it from the cache. Only information about available formats remains in memory. The *dwDiscardOptions* flag allows the caller to save any data that has been changed or to simply discard it. |

Basically, the data cache keeps data on disk as long as possible, bringing it into memory only when necessary. The *IOleCache2::Cache* and *IOleCache2-::Uncache* members control the information list that determines what is available. Other than that, *InitCache*, *SetData*, *UpdateCache*, and *DiscardCache* do nothing more than control what will actually be saved, and *EnumCache* describes what is there.

Using the data cache, you can save any number of pieces of data that you want as long as each has a different FORMATETC (except for *tymed*). This means you can save CF_METAFILEPICT data for any number of aspects and for any number of target devices per aspect. You can also save an object's presentations for any number of printers, allowing the client to fully control the presentations and output quality that will be available when the object is not available itself. This is a tremendous benefit for OLE Documents because a client can save a cache for each embedded or linked object so that the cached presentations travel with the document wherever it goes. Even when the object's code is unavailable or when the source of linked data is unavailable, the client will still be able to view and print appropriate images.

## The *IOleCacheControl* Interface

Describing *IOleCache2*, I made several references to a local or remote object, by which I mean an object running in a local or remote server. The remaining interface on the data cache, *IOleCacheControl*, has two members through which the client of the cache makes the cache aware of this object:

```
interface IOleCacheControl : IUnknown
    {
    HRESULT OnRun(IDataObject *pIDataObject);
```

```
HRESULT OnStop(void);
};
```

The *OnRun* function tells the cache that the object identified with *pIDataObject* is now running, and *OnStop* tells the cache that the same object has stopped running. (The data cache manages only one remote object at a time.) When the data cache becomes aware of this remote object, it establishes advisory connections for any cached format using the ADVF_* flags previously passed to *IOleCache2::Cache* for those formats, as shown in Figure 11-2. The sink objects here are simple objects with *IAdviseSink*; their pointers are enumerated through *IOleCache2::EnumCache*.

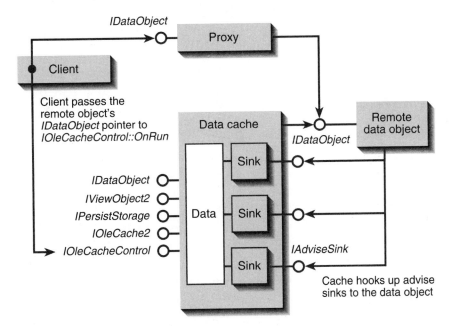

**Figure 11-2.**
*Through* IOleCacheControl, *the data cache becomes connected with an object running in a local or remote server.*

When these connections are active, the cache updates its cached formats whenever the remote object sends an *IAdviseSink::OnDataChange*. The various flags that you can pass to *IOleCache2::UpdateCache* determine which formats are updated according to the type of advisory connection they use with the remote object. For example, UPDFCACHE_ALLBUTNODATACACHE updates all the data formats that were cached with flags other than ADVF-_NODATA.

We can now understand the other values of the ADVF enumeration that we glossed over in Chapter 10. ADVFCACHE_NOHANDLER itself is reserved for future use, so you will have occasion to use it presently. ADVFCACHE-_FORCEBUILTIN restricts cached presentation data to that which OLE itself can handle, namely metafiles and bitmaps (both CF_BITMAP and CF_DIB). ADVFCACHE_ONSAVE causes the cache to update data only when the remote object is itself saved—that is, when and if the data source object calls *IAdviseSink::OnSave*. Obviously, the client using this flag should have some knowledge about the nature of the data source.

# Freeloading from the Data Cache

The data cache is a rich service that can do quite a lot for whatever happens to be using it. With the cache, you get a service that knows how to draw, save, and load a variety of presentation formats as well as how to connect itself to a remote object and automatically update its data when that object's data changes. The data cache obviously has a number of potential uses.

The primary use is that of implementing an object in an in-process handler, especially in OLE Documents. I mentioned earlier how a handler object must synchronize data changes with its local server to keep its implementation of *IViewObject2::Draw* up to date. If that handler object doesn't have reason to implement *Draw* itself, it can rely entirely on the cache for its implementation. The cache can then manage its own internal state by connecting to a remote object, asking for presentations through *IDataObject-::GetData*, and watching for changes in those presentations through *IAdviseSink::OnDataChange*. The handler object doesn't even need its own advise sink! Because the data cache has such great utility in this manner, a handler object can aggregate on the cache for any interfaces it finds useful to expose. The handler object customizes only those interfaces that it really wants to control.

The second use of the data cache is as a cache for static graphics. In this case, it is never connected to a remote object. Instead, you can store and retrieve metafiles and bitmaps and take advantage of the cache's drawing and persistence capabilities. In Chapter 12, when we look at the OLE Clipboard, we'll add *tenants* to the Patron sample (last seen in Chapter 7) that can contain static metafiles or bitmaps. (This lends itself well to enabling tenants to contain compound document content objects, which we'll see in Chapter 17.) Many applications, especially word processors and business graphics applications, do something similar because their users like to integrate graphics into documents and slide shows. When I thought about adding these features to Patron, I felt a tad queasy: I would first have to write code to draw metafiles and bitmaps (not too bad) and then more code to save that data in a disk file and load it back into memory again. I don't know about you, but serializing graphics to a file and then figuring out how to load them again involve a degree of tedium that I avoid like the plague.

This is exactly what the data cache is good at doing already. The trick is to figure out how to freeload from OLE in the right way. This isn't all that hard because OLE supports two CLSIDs, named *CLSID_ Picture_ Metafile (00000315-0000-0000-C000-000000000046)* and *CLSID_ Picture_Dib (00000316-0000-0000-C000-000000000046)*, that are specific instances of the data cache that manage a single presentation format. OLE supports these CLSIDs for the purposes of static compound document objects, which are presentations without a known source.

To test how much I could take advantage of OLE's inherent services, I came up with the sample named Freeloader (CHAP11\FREELOAD), shown in Figure 11-3. This handy application can copy or paste any metafile or bitmap from the clipboard and load or save it to a compound file with the FRE extension. Freeloader is built on the sample code CLASSLIB, as are Patron and Cosmo, in which each document can contain one graphic. Freeloader demonstrates the use of the data cache and the client side of *IViewObject2*. We'll see an implementation of *IViewObject2* in Chapter 19, where we implement a handler for use in conjunction with an OLE Documents server.

**Figure 11-3.**
*The Freeloader program, with three open presentations.*

In Freeloader, all the relevant code for working with the cache and its interfaces is found in DOCUMENT.CPP. In particular, this file includes the functions dealing with the clipboard: *Clip*, *RenderFormat*, and *Paste* members in the class *CFreeloaderDoc*. The *Load* and *Save* members call the cache's *IPersistStorage* members according to the contract described for this interface in Chapter 7, so there's little need to look at the code. More to the point, a Freeloader document saves itself by creating a compound file and asking the cache to save its data in that storage through *IPersistStorage::Save*. Loading is a matter of opening that file, creating a cache, and telling it to load through *IPersistStorage::Load*.

The *CFreeloaderDoc::FMessageHook* function shows how to call *IViewObject2::Draw* with a continuation function (for which *OleDraw* doesn't suffice):

```
BOOL CFreeloaderDoc::FMessageHook(HWND hWnd, UINT iMsg
    , WPARAM wParam, LPARAM lParam, LRESULT *pLRes)
    {
    PAINTSTRUCT     ps;
    HDC             hDC;
    RECT            rc;
    RECTL           rcl;
    LPVIEWOBJECT2   pIViewObject2;
    HRESULT         hr;

    if (WM_PAINT!=iMsg)
        return FALSE;

    hDC=BeginPaint(hWnd, &ps);
    GetClientRect(hWnd, &rc);

    if (NULL!=m_pIUnknown)
        {
        hr=m_pIUnknown->QueryInterface(IID_IViewObject2
            , (PPVOID)&pIViewObject2);

        if (SUCCEEDED(hr))
            {
            //Put "Hit Esc to stop" in status line.
            m_pFR->StatusLine()->MessageSet(PSZ(IDS_HITESCTOSTOP));

            RECTLFROMRECT(rcl, rc);
            pIViewObject2->Draw(DVASPECT_CONTENT, -1, NULL, NULL
                , 0, hDC, &rcl, NULL, ContinuePaint, 0);
            pIViewObject2->Release();

            m_pFR->StatusLine()->MessageDisplay(ID_MESSAGEREADY);
            }
        }
```

```
    EndPaint(hWnd, &ps);
    return FALSE;
    }

BOOL CALLBACK ContinuePaint(DWORD dwContinue)
    {
    return !(GetAsyncKeyState(VK_ESCAPE) < 0);
    }
```

In all truth, the *Clip* and *RenderFormat* functions do very little. *Clip* opens the clipboard, asks *RenderFormat* for a presentation, and sticks that presentation on the clipboard. *RenderFormat* does its thing by calling the cache's *IDataObject::GetData*:

```
HGLOBAL CFreeloaderDoc::RenderFormat(UINT cf)
    {
    LPDATAOBJECT        pIDataObject;
    FORMATETC           fe;
    STGMEDIUM           stm;

    if (NULL==m_pIUnknown)
        return NULL;

    [Set up fe and stm appropriately for format.]

    m_pIUnknown->QueryInterface(IID_IDataObject
        , (PPVOID)&pIDataObject);
    pIDataObject->GetData(&fe, &stm);
    pIDataObject->Release();

    return stm.hGlobal;
    }
```

But how on earth did we originally obtain the pointer to the object? The answer lies in *CFreeloaderDoc::Paste*:

```
BOOL CFreeloaderDoc::Paste(HWND hWndFrame)
    {
    UINT                cf=0;
    BOOL                fRet=FALSE;
    HRESULT             hr;
    DWORD               dwConn;
    LPUNKNOWN           pIUnknown;
    LPOLECACHE          pIOleCache;
    LPPERSISTSTORAGE    pIPersistStorage;
    FORMATETC           fe;
    STGMEDIUM           stm;
    CLSID               clsID;
```

*(continued)*

```
if (!OpenClipboard(hWndFrame))
    return FALSE;

/*
 * Try to get data in order of metafile, dib, bitmap.  We set
 * stm.tymed up front so that if we actually get something a
 * call to ReleaseStgMedium will clean it up for us.
 */

stm.pUnkForRelease=NULL;
stm.tymed=TYMED_MFPICT;
stm.hGlobal=GetClipboardData(CF_METAFILEPICT);

if (NULL!=stm.hGlobal)
    cf=CF_METAFILEPICT;

if (0==cf)
    {
    stm.tymed=TYMED_HGLOBAL;
    stm.hGlobal=GetClipboardData(CF_DIB);

    if (NULL!=stm.hGlobal)
        cf=CF_DIB;
    }

if (0==cf)
    {
    stm.tymed=TYMED_GDI;
    stm.hGlobal=GetClipboardData(CF_BITMAP);

    if (NULL!=stm.hGlobal)
        cf=CF_BITMAP;
    }

CloseClipboard();

//Didn't get anything?  Then we're finished.
if (0==cf)
    return FALSE;

//This now describes data we have.
SETDefFormatEtc(fe, cf, stm.tymed);

hr=CreateDataCache(NULL, CLSID_NULL, IID_IUnknown
    , (PPVOID)&pIUnknown);
```

```
if (FAILED(hr))
    {
    ReleaseStgMedium(&stm);
    return FALSE;
    }

pIUnknown->QueryInterface(IID_IPersistStorage
    , (PPVOID)&pIPersistStorage);
pIPersistStorage->InitNew(m_pIStorage);
pIPersistStorage->Release();

pIUnknown->QueryInterface(IID_IOleCache, (PPVOID)&pIOleCache);
pIOleCache->Cache(&fe, 0, &dwConn);

hr=pIOleCache->SetData(&fe, &stm, TRUE);
pIOleCache->Release();

if (FAILED(hr))
    {
    ReleaseStgMedium(&stm);
    pIUnknown->Release();
    return FALSE;
    }

//Now that that's all done, replace our current with the new.
ReleaseObject();
m_pIUnknown=pIUnknown;
m_dwConn=dwConn;

FDirtySet(TRUE);

InvalidateRect(m_hWnd, NULL, TRUE);
UpdateWindow(m_hWnd);
return TRUE;
}
```

The first half of *Paste* looks like a reasonably normal piece of Windows code that gets a graphics image from the clipboard. The slightly odd thing about it is that I'm storing the data handle directly into a STGMEDIUM (because it's there). I also initialize a FORMATETC with the description of the data I actually pasted. I call *CreateDataCache* to create a cache object and tell it to initialize itself through *IPersistStorage::InitNew*. I then tell the cache object to cache the format I found on the clipboard through *IOleCache::Cache*, stuff that data into it with *IOleCache::SetData*, and then clean everything up.

Freeloader also uses *IViewObject2::GetExtent* to size the window to match the graphic when reopening a file. This occurs in *CFreeloaderDoc::SizeTo-Graphic*, (also called from Freeloader's Edit/Size To Graphic menu item).

That's really all there is to it, and it seems much simpler than having to write so much more code. (Code I don't need to write to make Patron functional in Chapter 12.) All compliments of OLE.

## Summary

A viewable object is any object that implements *IViewObject2* alongside any other interfaces. (*IViewObject2* is a refinement of *IViewObject*, an earlier OLE interface.) Through *IViewObject2*, a client can have an object draw graphical presentations directly to a screen or printer device, using the member function named *Draw*. *Draw* gives a viewable object direct access to a device, defines how the object should scale its output, and provides for drawing into metafiles and breaking out of long repaints. Because *Draw* takes an *hDC* argument, however, *IViewObject2* can be implemented only from an in-process object. A Windows *hDC* cannot be shared across process boundaries.

Nevertheless, *IViewObject2* is a powerful interface. Other member functions allow the client to control changes to graphic presentations (for printer banding) and also to receive asynchronous notifications when a view changes. These notifications occur through *IAdviseSink::OnViewChange* and are distinct from data change notifications sent through *IAdviseSink::OnData-Change*. The latter function is useful for synchronizing an in-process implementation of a viewable object with a data source in a local server.

Related to an object's ability to draw its own presentations is its ability to cache those presentations in a piece of storage. A client can use such cached information to later display or print object presentations without requiring the object code to be present. OLE itself provides a data cache service. The cache is an object that implements not only *IViewObject2* but also *IPersist-Storage*, *IDataObject*, *IOleCache2*, and *IOleCacheControl*. Through these interfaces, the cache can save and load presentations, render the presentations as data formats, control what is stored in the cache, and connect to a running object in a local server from which the cache can automatically obtain updated presentations.

This chapter demonstrates the use of the cache as well as the client side of *IViewObject2* by showing how an application can display, print, save, and reload metafiles and bitmaps without doing much work at all. The chapter's example sets the stage for enhancements to the Patron application in later chapters.

CHAPTER TWELVE

# The OLE Clipboard

*What do you do with a data object?*
*What do you do with a data object?*
*What do you do with a data object?*
*Put it on the clipboard!*

—Version 2 of an old sea chantey

As we saw in Chapter 10, data objects encompass the functionality of all the existing data transfer protocols. Using raw data objects by themselves to exchange information between applications is rich enough to describe anything you could do with existing Windows APIs, and more. In this chapter, we'll focus on how you can use data objects to implement clipboard operations.

Conceptually the operations are simple: to place data on the clipboard, you pass an *IDataObject* pointer to OLE, which enumerates that object's available formats and calls *IDataObject::GetData* when a consumer requests data. To retrieve information from the clipboard, you ask OLE for a data object that represents whatever is currently on the clipboard and then call *IDataObject-::GetData*.

Simple? On the surface, yes, but having to create an entire data object and FORMATETC enumerator to do something as simple as copy a small piece of text to the clipboard seems like overkill. Accordingly, the first part of this chapter describes how much of a data object you need for clipboard transfers and discusses implementation of a *data transfer* component that provides a generic data object for such transfers. We'll then see how Cosmo and Patron incorporate this component to implement their clipboard support. Through Cosmo, we'll see how clipboard code based on the Windows API is converted to use the OLE Clipboard. Through Patron, we'll see the addition of new clipboard code that enables this application to paste both bitmaps and metafiles using the concepts from the Freeloader sample in Chapter 11. In addition, we'll discuss the Paste Special dialog box from the OLE UI Library and see how Component Cosmo implements clipboard support using a snapshot copy of the Polyline component (because Polyline already implements *IDataObject*). In essence, this involves the same techniques as working with the data transfer object but on a more application-specific basis.

Using the OLE Clipboard protocol is not a requirement for your application unless you want it to take advantage of Uniform Data Transfer through the FORMATETC and STGMEDIUM structures. In other words, unless you need to exchange data with formats and mediums other than those you can use with the Windows API, you do not need to use OLE. But as we'll see in later chapters, the transfer of compound document objects and OLE Controls requires specific storage mediums that make use of the OLE Clipboard. Because the protocol itself is rather simple and you gain so much flexibility in making the change, I encourage you to follow the guidelines in this chapter.

With that bit of preaching out of the way, let's look at the mechanisms for the OLE Clipboard and then dive into code examples. This chapter is light on theory and heavy on coding because all we're concerned with here is the creative use of a data object.

## The OLE Clipboard Protocol

A transfer protocol in the OLE sense is a mechanism for communicating an *IDataObject* pointer from a source to a consumer. The OLE Clipboard is one such protocol, supported through four OLE API functions:

| OLE API Function | Description |
| --- | --- |
| *OleSetClipboard* | Places a data object on the clipboard; that data object wraps all the data to copy or cut. OLE calls *AddRef* on this object and asks it to enumerate its formats. OLE makes these formats available to potential consumers. |
| *OleGetClipboard* | Retrieves a data object that represents the data available on the clipboard, calling *AddRef* on the *IDataObject* pointer returned. The consumer must call *Release* when it is done with the object. |
| *OleFlushClipboard* | Clears the clipboard, calling *Release* on the data object passed to *OleSetClipboard*. |
| *OleIsCurrentClipboard* | Answers whether a given data object is the one currently on the clipboard. |

The overall mechanism of a clipboard data transfer in OLE is shown in Figure 12-1. The source creates a data object (including its FORMATETC enumerator) and calls *OleSetClipboard*. OLE calls the Windows function *OpenClipboard*, followed by *IDataObject::AddRef* and *IDataObject::EnumFormat-Etc*. For each enumerated format that uses TYMED_HGLOBAL, OLE calls the Windows function *SetClipboardData(formatetc.cfFormat, NULL)* to make the format available using delayed rendering. OLE finishes by calling the Windows function *CloseClipboard*. When any consumer, aware of OLE or not, calls the Windows function *GetClipboardData* for any of these formats, Windows, according to delayed rendering, sends a WM_RENDERFORMAT message.

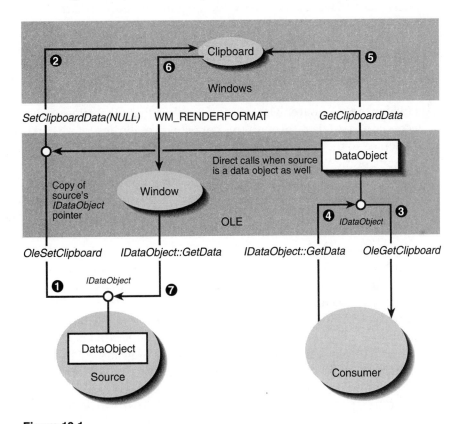

**Figure 12-1.**
*The OLE Clipboard involves* OleGetClipboard, OleSetClipboard, *and a data object.*

567

But to which window is the message sent? It is sent to one inside OLE itself, the handle to which OLE passes in its call to *OpenClipboard*. This window is always hidden and is created inside *OleInitialize*. If you plan to use the OLE Clipboard, you must use *OleInitialize* instead of *CoInitialize*. Failure to do this will cause clipboard operations to fail.

When this window receives WM_RENDERFORMAT, OLE generates calls to *IDataObject::QueryGetData* (to validate the format) and to *IDataObject-::GetData*. In other words, OLE provides delayed clipboard rendering by means of data objects. Delayed rendering, however, means that the source must make a snapshot of the data it places on the clipboard so that the data object placed there is not tied to changing information. (I'll treat this subject in more detail momentarily.)

The consumer that pastes data from the clipboard doesn't have to care about complications like this: it just calls *OleGetClipboard* to obtain an *IDataObject* pointer for the clipboard. This pointer is not the one the source might have provided; instead, it is an OLE-provided data object made especially for the clipboard. The reason for this is that OLE allows consumers to access clipboard data through this data object regardless of whether the data was copied to the clipboard using OLE. OLE's data object reflects the conceptual state of the Windows clipboard, not the state of any source's data object.

With the data object, the consumer can call the *IDataObject* members *EnumFormatEtc*, *QueryGetData*, and *GetData*, as it would call the *EnumClipboard-Formats*, *IsClipboardFormatAvailable*, and *GetClipboardData* functions in Windows. Through the *IDataObject* interface, a consumer can access not only the TYMED_HGLOBAL-based data on the Windows clipboard but also any other data based on other mediums that the data source provides itself. When the consumer asks for data through *IDataObject::GetData*, OLE will either access data from the Windows clipboard itself or simply forward the call to the source's *IDataObject* interface. So the consumer has access to all the possible data on the clipboard, regardless of whether that data came from an OLE data object or from a non-OLE Windows application. The effort needed to obtain clipboard data through OLE is minimal.

I should mention that OLE's clipboard data object does not implement *IDataObject::SetData* or any of the advise-related members. Also, its *GetData-Here* will work only with limited formats. The data object itself exposes only *IDataObject* and *IUnknown*, so don't expect anything fancy.

# But All I Want to Do Is Copy Some Simple Data!

I imagine that at this point you are screaming or cursing that OLE makes the clipboard far too complex. To copy even the simplest piece of data—maybe a short, but passionate, string such as "Why is Microsoft doing this to me?"—requires an implementation of a data object, a FORMATETC enumerator that supports cloning, and the complexity of taking a snapshot of the data involved so as to support delayed rendering. Ouch! Whatever happened to *OpenClipboard*, *SetClipboardData*, and *CloseClipboard*?

Well, in reality, the Windows API has never been quite that simple because somewhere along the way you have to allocate global memory and copy your data into it. Before calling *SetClipboardData* with a string, for example, you usually call some function to make a copy of it:

```
HGLOBAL CopyStringToHGlobal(LPTSTR psz)
    {
    HGLOBAL    hMem;
    LPTSTR     pszDst;

    hMem=GlobalAlloc(GHND, (DWORD)(lstrlen(psz)+1));

    if (NULL!=hMem)
        {
        pszDst=GlobalLock(hMem);
        lstrcpy(pszDst, psz);
        GlobalUnlock(hMem);
        }

    return hMem;
    }
```

With this function, the code to copy the text to the clipboard would appear as follows:

```
HGLOBAL    hMem;

hMem=CopyStringToHGlobal(TEXT("Why is Microsoft doing this to me?"));

if (NULL!=hMem)
    {
    if (OpenClipboard(hWndMain))
        {
        SetClipboardData(CF_TEXT, hMem);
        CloseClipboard();
        }
```

*(continued)*

569

```
else
    GlobalFree(hMem);  //We must clean up.
}
```

Under OLE, however, we would like to write simple code that takes advantage of data objects:

```
IDataObject      *pIDataObject;
HRESULT          hr;
FORMATETC        fe;
STGMEDIUM        stm;

stm.tymed=TYMED_HGLOBAL;
stm.hGlobal=
    CopyStringToHGlobal(TEXT("Why is Microsoft doing this to me?"));

if (NULL!=stm.hGlobal)
    {
    hr=FunctionToCreateADataObject(&pIDataObject)

    if (SUCCEEDED(hr))
        {
        SETDefFormatEtc(fe, CF_TEXT, TYMED_HGLOBAL);
        pIDataObject->SetData(&fe, &stm);
        OleSetClipboard(pIDataObject);
        pIDataObject->Release();
        }
    else
        GlobalFree(stm.hGlobal);
    }
```

This code shows how we would *like* to translate existing Windows API code into OLE-based code. *SetClipboardData(cf, hMem)* becomes *IDataObject::SetData(&fe, &stm)*, followed by *OleSetClipboard*. *CloseClipboard* turns into *IDataObject::Release*. But what about *FunctionToCreateADataObject*? Where does this come from? Certainly something like this would be quite convenient, but alas, my friends, OLE does not supply such an implementation. You could cheat and use *CreateDataCache* for this purpose, except for the small problem that the data cache does not implement *IDataObject::EnumFormatEtc*. Bummer.

What we need is a function to create a data object that we can stuff through *IDataObject::SetData*, and then we need to throw that data object on the clipboard. The data object would maintain all the data until the object was released, and then it would free all that data automatically. So I wrote such a component, named DataTran, found in CHAP12\DATATRAN.

## A Data Transfer Component

An object that would simplify clipboard transfers is essentially a data cache with *IDataObject* slapped on it, one that you could grab with a quick call to *CoCreateInstance*. DataTran is a server for such an object; its *CLSID_Data-TransferObject* is defined in INC\BOOKGUID.H. Be sure to create registry entries for DataTran using the REG file in the sample's directory before you attempt to run Cosmo or Patron from this or any subsequent chapter. Both Cosmo and Patron call *CoCreateInstance* with this CLSID in place of *Function-ToCreateADataObject* in the code listed earlier.

DataTran is simply an archetypal in-process component server for a single object, implemented in a C++ class named *CDataObject* in DATAOBJ.H, DATAOBJ.CPP, and IDATAOBJ.CPP. The FORMATETC enumerator is in IENUMFE.CPP.

During initialization, the data object creates a hidden list box control. In the list, it stores whatever renderings you care to stuff in it using a custom data structure named RENDERING (DATAOBJ.H). This structure manages a FORMATETC, a STGMEDIUM, and an *IUnknown* pointer to the data's real owner:

```
typedef struct tagRENDERING
    {
    FORMATETC       fe;             //Format
    STGMEDIUM       stm;            //Actual data
    LPUNKNOWN       pUnkOrg;        //Real owner
    } RENDERING, *PRENDERING;
```

DataTran allocates and stores a RENDERING structure in each call to its *IDataObject::SetData* (IDATAOBJ.CPP); the structure holds a copy of the FOR-MATETC and STGMEDIUM structures passed to *SetData*, with one exception. DataTran replaces the *STGMEDIUM::pUnkForRelease* field with its own *IUnknown* so that DataTran can share that rendering with multiple consumers. It uses its own reference count to keep the data valid. However, we must still preserve the original *pUnkForRelease*, which ends up in the *RENDERING-::pUnkOrg* field. DataTran restores this pointer before calling *ReleaseStg-Medium* to free the data. Through all of this, DataTran's *SetData* member acts a lot like the Windows *SetClipboardData*, with the added feature that calling *SetData* with NULL pointers cleans out the entire data object:

```
STDMETHODIMP CImpIDataObject::SetData(LPFORMATETC pFE
    , LPSTGMEDIUM pSTM, BOOL fRelease)
    {
    PRENDERING      prn;
```

*(continued)*

```
//We have to remain responsible for data.
if (!fRelease)
    return ResultFromScode(E_FAIL);

if (NULL==pFE || NULL==pSTM)
    {
    m_pObj->Purge();
    return NOERROR;
    }

prn=new RENDERING;

if (NULL==prn)
    return ResultFromScode(E_OUTOFMEMORY);

prn->fe=*pFE;
prn->stm=*pSTM;
prn->pUnkOrg=pSTM->pUnkForRelease;
prn->stm.pUnkForRelease=this;

SendMessage(m_pObj->m_hList, LB_ADDSTRING, 0, (LONG)prn);
return NOERROR;
}
```

With a list of RENDERING structures, the implementations of *QueryGet-Data* and *EnumFormatEtc* need only to look in the list for their formats. *EnumFormatEtc* creates an enumerator object that copies the FORMATETC structures from each RENDERING in the list into its own array for enumeration.

That leaves *GetData* and *Release*. *GetData* walks through the list looking for a match on the requested FORMATETC. (*GetDataHere* is the same as *GetData* except that it is restricted to *IStorage* mediums.) If the format exists, *GetData* copies the STGMEDIUM structure for that format into the caller's structure and then calls *AddRef* on itself:

```
STDMETHODIMP CImpIDataObject::GetData(LPFORMATETC pFE
    , LPSTGMEDIUM pSTM)
    {
    UINT        i, cItems;
    PRENDERING  pRen;
    DWORD       cb;
    HWND        hList;

    if (NULL==m_pObj->m_hList || NULL==pFE || NULL==pSTM)
        return ResultFromScode(DATA_E_FORMATETC);

    hList=m_pObj->m_hList;
    cItems=(UINT)SendMessage(hList, LB_GETCOUNT, 0, 0L);
```

```
for (i=0; i < cItems; i++)
    {
    cb=SendMessage(hList, LB_GETTEXT, i, (LPARAM)&pRen);

    if (LB_ERR!=cb)
        {
        if (pFE->cfFormat==pRen->fe.cfFormat
            && (pFE->tymed & pRen->fe.tymed)
            && pFE->dwAspect==pRen->fe.dwAspect)
            {
            *pSTM=pRen->stm;
            AddRef();
            return NOERROR;
            }
        }
    }

return ResultFromScode(DATA_E_FORMATETC);
}
```

The *AddRef* call accounts for the *Release* call that will come from inside the consumer's later call to *ReleaseStgMedium*.[1] The consumer doesn't know that we're not giving it an independent copy, but because of the *pUnkForRelease* field in FORMATETC, we can control the data with a simple reference count. Only when we reset or free the entire data object will we actually free the data. This happens in *CDataObject::Purge*:

```
void CDataObject::Purge(void)
    {
    UINT        i, cItems;
    PRENDERING  pRen;
    DWORD       cb;

    if (NULL==m_hList)
        return;

    cItems=(UINT)SendMessage(m_hList, LB_GETCOUNT, 0, 0L);

    for (i=0; i < cItems; i++)
        {
        cb=SendMessage(m_hList, LB_GETTEXT, i, (LPARAM)&pRen);
```

*(continued)*

---

1. Because *ReleaseStgMedium* will call DataTran's *Release* to free the data, we do not need to make an extra *AddRef* call to *IStorage* or *IStream* pointers in the medium. The consumer will not call these objects' *Release* members. Only our call to *ReleaseStgMedium* in *CDataObject::Purge* can do it.

```
       if (LB_ERR!=cb)
          {
          pRen->stm.pUnkForRelease=pRen->pUnkOrg;
          ReleaseStgMedium(&pRen->stm);
          delete pRen;
          }
       }

   SendMessage(m_hList, LB_RESETCONTENT, 0, 0L);
   return;
   }
```

In this way, DataTran shows a good use for *pUnkForRelease*: to control the ownership of the data, taking over from the real source until the time when the data must really be freed.

DataTran handles probably the most common case in which you need a data object to work with the OLE Clipboard. But in the case of Component Cosmo, having a data object isn't necessary.

## If You Already Have a Data Object...Component Cosmo

If a source is about to copy an object that is already a data object, it's not necessary to use an entirely different class as does DataTran. For example, the Polyline object used by CoCosmo implements *IDataObject*, so CoCosmo can make another Polyline and copy data directly into it. Any data object works as well as any other. The copying is necessary to create a snapshot of the current, visible Polyline so changes to it will not cause problems with delayed rendering. End users will expect that the data they paste is exactly the same data they copied. If CoCosmo places the visible Polyline on the clipboard, the data is *live,* so any change made to the Polyline object will show up when the data is pasted later. What the end user copied and what that user pasted is not the same. Not good.

Instead, CoCosmo instantiates an extra hidden Polyline with the same dimensions as the visible one and copies the visible object's data into it. A perfect snapshot. CoCosmo then tosses the hidden Polyline onto the clipboard, as shown in the following code (taken from CHAP12\COCOSMO-\DOCUMENT.CPP, which continues to use the Polyline implementation from Chapter 10):

```
BOOL CCosmoDoc::Clip(HWND hWndFrame, BOOL fCut)
    {
    PPOLYLINE               pPL;
    LPDATAOBJECT            pDataSrc, pIDataObject;
    FORMATETC               fe;
    STGMEDIUM               stm;
```

```
BOOL                    fRet=TRUE;
HRESULT                 hr;
RECT                    rc;

hr=CoCreateInstance(CLSID_Polyline10, NULL, CLSCTX_INPROC_SERVER
    , IID_IPolyline10, (PPVOID)&pPL);

if (FAILED(hr))
    return FALSE;

m_pPL->RectGet(&rc);

if (FAILED(pPL->Init(m_hWnd, &rc, WS_CHILD, ID_POLYLINE)))
    {
    pPL->Release();
    return FALSE;
    }

m_pPL->QueryInterface(IID_IDataObject, (PPVOID)&pDataSrc);

SETDefFormatEtc(fe, m_cf, TYMED_HGLOBAL);
fRet=SUCCEEDED(pDataSrc->GetData(&fe, &stm));
pDataSrc->Release();

if (!fRet)
    {
    pPL->Release();
    return FALSE;
    }

pPL->QueryInterface(IID_IDataObject, (PPVOID)&pIDataObject);
pPL->Release();

pIDataObject->SetData(&fe, &stm, TRUE);

fRet=SUCCEEDED(OleSetClipboard(pIDataObject));

if (NULL!=m_pIDataClip)
    m_pIDataClip->Release();

m_pIDataClip=pIDataObject;

//Delete our current data if "cut" succeeded.
if (fRet && fCut)
    {
    m_pPL->New();
    FDirtySet(TRUE);
    }

return fRet;
}
```

The preceding code handles both Cut and Copy operations with identical vigor, but Cut removes the affected data from the document. Keep in mind, however, that you still need to create a snapshot of the data regardless of whether you are cutting it or copying it.

### If You Already Have Extensive Clipboard Handling Code

Some applications (one of which might be yours) have a great deal of highly optimized clipboard code already in place. This is especially true if you already have a scheme to handle delayed rendering and snapshot copies of your data. If that's the case, you can implement a data object on top of your existing code, one that implements *IDataObject* using code such as that which handles the WM_RENDERFORMAT message.

This technique allows you to preserve all your existing code, perhaps restructuring it only to make it more generally accessible to a data object.

## Simple Data Source and Consumer: Cosmo

With DataTran, we have the necessary means to simplify clipboard operations, so we can demonstrate how to convert existing clipboard code to OLE Clipboard code by using the Cosmo sample (CHAP12\COSMO). This involves a few steps for startup/shutdown, for the Copy/Cut and Paste operations, and for enabling the Edit/Paste menu item.

### Startup/Shutdown

Applications using the OLE Clipboard must tell OLE to create a clipboard window on startup and to free any OLE-owned renderings on shutdown. The following steps are handled in Cosmo's *CCosmoFrame::Init* and *CCosmoFrame-::~CCosmoFrame* functions in COSMO.CPP, respectively:

1. At startup, call *OleInitialize* instead of *CoInitialize* so that OLE creates its clipboard window.

2. During shutdown, first call *OleFlushClipboard* to free the data object on the clipboard (which happens only if that data object belongs to the application), then destroy the data object, and then call *OleUninitialize* to destroy OLE's clipboard window.

At the time of initialization (*CCosmoFrame::Init*), Cosmo also obtains Data-Tran's class factory and calls *IClassFactory::LockServer*, which is reversed in the frame destructor. This is so later instantiations of DataTran will happen very quickly, improving the performance of clipboard (and later drag-and-drop) operations. This procedure exemplifies an intelligent use of *IClassFactory-::LockServer*.

## Copy/Cut

A Copy or a Cut operation entails gaining access to the clipboard, copying the data renderings, and releasing the clipboard. (Cut deletes the data from the source afterward.) The OLE version of this process is a bit different because there are no analogs to opening or closing the clipboard. Instead, there's just *OleSetClipboard*:

1. Create a data object (such as DataTran), and store the appropriate data in it. This is similar to calling *OpenClipboard* followed by *SetClipboardData* as many times as needed. Calling *EmptyClipboard* is unnecessary here: OLE does it within *OleSetClipboard*.

2. Pass the data object to *OleSetClipboard*. This calls the object's *AddRef* followed by *IDataObject::EnumFormatEtc* to place each format on the Windows clipboard.

3. The source is now finished with its own data object and can release it if desired. The object remains alive until OLE calls its *Release*. This step is much like calling *CloseClipboard*.

4. For a Cut operation only, remove the affected data from the source.

Cosmo performs these steps in *CCosmoDoc::Clip* (DOCUMENT.CPP). At least half of the code and the *structure* of the function are unaffected by the changes. These deal primarily with creating a data object, stuffing it with data, and placing it on the clipboard. *CCosmoDoc::RenderFormat* creates the renderings to give to DataTran:

```
BOOL CCosmoDoc::Clip(HWND hWndFrame, BOOL fCut)
    {
    BOOL            fRet=TRUE;
    HGLOBAL         hMem;
    UINT            i;
    static UINT     rgcf[3]={0, CF_METAFILEPICT, CF_BITMAP};
    const UINT      cFormats=3;
    static DWORD    rgtm[3]={TYMED_HGLOBAL, TYMED_MFPICT, TYMED_GDI};
    LPDATAOBJECT    pIDataObject;
    HRESULT         hr;
    STGMEDIUM       stm;
    FORMATETC       fe;
```

*(continued)*

577

```
hr=CoCreateInstance(CLSID_DataTransferObject
    , NULL, CLSCTX_INPROC_SERVER
    , IID_IDataObject, (PPVOID)&pIDataObject);

if (FAILED(hr))
    return NULL;

rgcf[0]=m_cf;

for (i=0; i < cFormats; i++)
    {
    //Copy private data first.
    hMem=RenderFormat(rgcf[i]);

    if (NULL!=hMem)
        {
        stm.hGlobal=hMem;
        stm.tymed=rgtm[i];
        stm.pUnkForRelease=NULL;

        SETDefFormatEtc(fe, rgcf[i], rgtm[i]);
        pIDataObject->SetData(&fe, &stm, TRUE);
        }
    }

fRet=SUCCEEDED(OleSetClipboard(pIDataObject));
pIDataObject->Release();

if (fRet && fCut)
    {
    m_pPL->New();
    FDirtySet(TRUE);
    }

return fRet;
}
```

The order in which we store formats in a DataTran object is the same order in which it will enumerate those formats. This means we stuff formats with the highest integrity first.

## Enabling Edit/Paste

Any programmer who has ever implemented Paste functionality in an application has gone through the rite of processing WM_INITMENUPOPUP and deciding whether to enable the Paste menu item depending on the formats available on the clipboard. This user interface does not change with OLE; what does change is the way you can implement it using data objects.

I want to stress the phrase "can implement" because OLE does not force you to use data objects for enabling paste or for performing a paste. OLE is simply a convenient way of doing it. The big advantage is that once you write a piece of code to enable pasting or to paste from a data object, that same code can be used in OLE Drag and Drop, which we'll cover in Chapter 13. By adding support for additional formats to your code, you expand the capabilities of both protocols to enable the pasting of things such as compound document objects and controls.

As you can see in the following code, the OLE method is only a matter of asking the data object to go through this sequence:

1. Call *OleGetClipboard* to retrieve an *IDataObject* pointer for the clipboard.

2. Call *IDataObject::QueryGetData* for each format you would pass to the Windows function *IsClipboardFormatAvailable*. If successful, enable the Edit/Paste menu item. If no formats are available, disable the item.

3. Call *IDataObject::Release* when finished.

```
BOOL CCosmoDoc::FQueryPaste(void)
    {
    LPDATAOBJECT    pIDataObject;
    BOOL            fRet;

    if (FAILED(OleGetClipboard(&pIDataObject)))
        return FALSE;

    fRet=FQueryPasteFromData(pIDataObject);
    pIDataObject->Release();
    return fRet;
    }


BOOL CCosmoDoc::FQueryPasteFromData(LPDATAOBJECT pIDataObject)
    {
    FORMATETC       fe;

    SETDefFormatEtc(fe, m_cf, TYMED_HGLOBAL);
    return (NOERROR==pIDataObject->QueryGetData(&fe));
    }
```

Cosmo's *CCosmoDoc::FQueryPaste* function, which used to call *IsClipboardFormatAvailable*, now retrieves the clipboard's *IDataObject* and sends it to *CCosmoDoc::FQueryPasteFromData*, which determines whether it can be pasted with *IDataObject::QueryGetData* before releasing the pointer. I strongly encourage you to implement a function like *FQueryPasteFromData*. With such a function in place, you can pass any data object to it, whether you get the pointer from *OleGetClipboard*, from a drag-and-drop operation, or from some *QueryInterface*. A function like this gives you a single place to add new formats that you might support with additional OLE work.

## Paste

Paste is essentially the same operation as checking pastability except that instead of calling *IDataObject::QueryGetData* we call *IDataObject::GetData* with the following steps:

1. Obtain a data object pointer by calling *OleGetClipboard*, which calls *AddRef* through the pointer before returning.

2. Call *IDataObject::GetData* to retrieve whatever data you want. As a consumer, you now own the data, so call *ReleaseStgMedium* when you finish with it. Also, you must not hold on to this data—copy it as necessary. This is no different from what is required with data obtained from the clipboard using *GetClipboardData*.

3. Call *IDataObject::Release* to match the *AddRef* called in *OleGetClipboard*.

Cosmo implements these steps in *CCosmoDoc::Paste*:

```
BOOL CCosmoDoc::Paste(HWND hWndFrame)
    {
    LPDATAOBJECT    pIDataObject;
    BOOL            fRet;

    if (FAILED(OleGetClipboard(&pIDataObject)))
        return FALSE;

    fRet=PasteFromData(pIDataObject);
    pIDataObject->Release();
    return fRet;
    }
```

```
BOOL CCosmoDoc::PasteFromData(LPDATAOBJECT pIDataObject)
    {
    FORMATETC       fe;
    STGMEDIUM       stm;
    BOOL            fRet;

    SETDefFormatEtc(fe, m_cf, TYMED_HGLOBAL);
    fRet=SUCCEEDED(pIDataObject->GetData(&fe, &stm));

    if (fRet && NULL!=stm.hGlobal)
        {
        m_pPL->DataSetMem(stm.hGlobal, FALSE, FALSE, TRUE);
        ReleaseStgMedium(&stm);
        FDirtySet(TRUE);
        }

    return fRet;
    }
```

As we did for Cosmo's *FQueryPaste*, *Paste* obtains the data object pointer from *OleGetClipboard* and passes it to *PasteFromData*. A function such as *PasteFromData* is reusable (like *FQueryPasteFromData*), and I encourage you to make such a function because it will become useful in later work.

## Paste Special and a Functional Patron

With an understanding of the OLE Clipboard, we can bring it together with the techniques for using the data cache we saw in Chapter 11 and make Patron (CHAP12\PATRON) do something useful. The changes are extensive, so we'll focus on the important elements of the code. Besides adding a number of functions to the *CPatronDoc*, *CPages*, and *CPage* classes, I've added two important source files, TENANT.CPP and PAGEMOUS.CPP. This work primarily supports the pasting of metafiles and bitmaps into a page as tenants, which the data cache will draw and serialize for us. The result is that Patron finally displays something visible, as shown in Figure 12-2 on the following page. All that's left is for us to provide storage for each tenant, to ensure that each tenant is saved to a file we can reload later, and to provide the ability to copy or cut a tenant back to the clipboard.

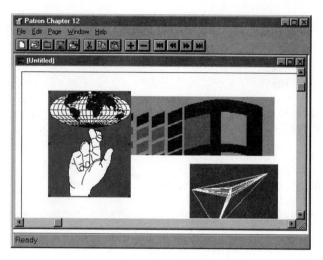

**Figure 12-2.**
*Patron with a number of tenants on a page.*

Patron also contains a few user interface components; mouse hit-testing that selects a tenant, a menu item to delete a tenant, and code to provide functional resizing handles on the selected object, as shown in Figure 12-3. (I won't go into much detail about these non-OLE features in Patron. One part of the existing code that will become important for OLE Drag and Drop is a technique for mouse *debouncing* that we'll see in Chapter 13.)

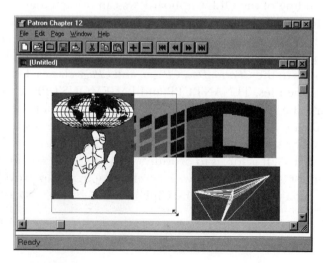

**Figure 12-3.**
*Resizing a tenant in Patron.*

The other feature of Patron that concerns us here is the Paste Special dialog box. This dialog box allows the end user to selectively paste either a bitmap or a metafile. By default, Patron prefers to paste a metafile rather than a bitmap, but with Paste Special the end user can choose a format. The Paste Special dialog box, as it appears in Figure 12-4, is provided as part of the OLE UI Library and readily expands to support OLE Documents, including the Display As Icon check box (disabled for now). If you skipped Chapter 6, read the section called "The OLE UI Library and the Busy Dialog Box" starting on page 316. That section explains the nature of the OLE UI Library, and you may want to glance through that information again for review in any case.

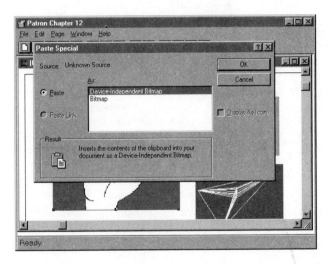

**Figure 12-4.**
*The Paste Special dialog box in Patron.*

## The Paste Special Dialog Box

To invoke the Paste Special dialog box, you first fill an OLEUI-PASTESPECIAL structure (shown in the code on the following page) and call the function *OleUIPasteSpecial*. On return, the dialog box will indicate the index of the format the end user chose from the list. Patron uses this format to determine whether to create a data cache for *CLSID_Picture_Dib* or *CLSID_Picture_Metafile*. The real trick, however, is filling the OLEUIPASTE-SPECIAL structure.

```
typedef struct tagOLEUIPASTESPECIAL
    {
    [Standard header common to all OLE UI dialogs]

    //Specifics for OLEUIPASTESPECIAL
    //IN fields
    LPDATAOBJECT     lpSrcDataObj;        //Source IDataObject* (on
                                          //clipboard) for data to paste

    LPOLEUIPASTEENTRY arrPasteEntries;    //Array of OLEUIPASTEENTRYs
                                          //of acceptable formats
    int              cPasteEntries;       //Number of OLEUIPASTEENTRYs

    [These are not important for this chapter.]
    UINT        FAR *arrLinkTypes;
    int              cLinkTypes;

    //OUT fields
    int              nSelectedIndex;      //User-selected arrPasteEntries
    BOOL             fLink;               //Paste or Paste Link selected?
    HGLOBAL          hMetaPict;           //Icon and icon title
    } OLEUIPASTESPECIAL, *POLEUIPASTESPECIAL, FAR *LPOLEUIPASTESPECIAL;
```

The Paste Special dialog box needs to present the end user with a list box containing text descriptions of all the available formats. This lets the application control which formats are allowed at all. First the dialog box needs to know the data object that exists on the clipboard. You store that object in the *lpSrcDataObj* field of OLEUIPASTESPECIAL, as shown in the code in *CPatronDoc::PasteSpecial* (DOCUMENT.CPP):

```
OLEUIPASTESPECIAL   ps;

_memset(&ps, 0, sizeof(ps));

if (FAILED(OleGetClipboard(&ps.lpSrcDataObj)))
    return FALSE;
```

You must also fill the *cbStruct* field with the size of the structure (used to verify versions) and identify the window that owns it:

```
ps.cbStruct=sizeof(ps);
ps.hWndOwner=hWndFrame;
```

In the *dwFlags* field, you can specify any of these flags: PSF_SHOW-HELP, PSF_SELECTPASTE, PSF_SELECTPASTELINK, and PSF_CHECK-DISPLAYASICON. We'll use the latter two in the chapters about OLE

Documents. To use the dialog box for simple pasting, specify the PSF_SELECT-PASTE flag (including PSF_SHOWHELP if you want):

```
ps.dwFlags=PSF_SELECTPASTE;
```

Now you need only to describe the allowable formats and provide text descriptions for those formats by filling the *cPasteEntries* and *arrPaste-Entries* fields:

```
OLEUIPASTEENTRY      rgPaste[4];

ps.arrPasteEntries=rgPaste;
ps.cPasteEntries=4;
```

The *arrPasteEntries* field is a pointer to an array of OLEUIPASTE-ENTRY structures. Each structure describes the format and holds the description string:

```
typedef struct tagOLEUIPASTEENTRY
    {
    FORMATETC   fmtetc;
    LPCSTR      lpstrFormatName;
    LPCSTR      lpstrResultText;
    DWORD       dwFlags;
    DWORD       dwScratchSpace;
    } OLEUIPASTEENTRY, *POLEUIPASTEENTRY, FAR *LPOLEUIPASTEENTRY;
```

The following table lists the meanings of these fields:

| Field | Description |
| --- | --- |
| *fmtetc* | The FORMATETC for this entry. |
| *lpstrFormatName* | A text description of the FORMATETC. For example, a string for a CF_DIB-based format (regardless of the aspect, storage medium, or other FORMATETC values) is "Device-Independent Bitmap". |
| *lpszResultText* | A string that describes the data resulting from a Paste Special operation. Typically this is "a" or "an" prepended to the format description, as in "a Device-Independent Bitmap". |
| *dwFlags* | Flags indicating what operations are allowed on this particular format. The only one of relevance for now is OLEUIPASTE_PASTEONLY, indicating that Paste is allowed. Other options enable the Paste Link and Display As Icon options. |
| *dwScratchSpace* | Reserved for internal dialog use. |

Patron can paste any of four formats. The preferred format is a structure named PATRONOBJECT (see PAGES.H). This describes a tenant in a way that a Copy or Paste operation between Patron documents places the object in the same location as it had in the source document if possible. PATRONOBJECT is followed in preference by CF_METAFILEPICT, CF__DIB, and CF_BITMAP. Therefore, Patron fills an array of four OLEUI-PASTEENTRY structures (*rgPaste*), as is shown in the following for its private format:

```
SETDefFormatEtc(rgPaste[0].fmtetc, m_cf, TYMED_HGLOBAL);
rgPaste[0].lpstrFormatName="Patron Object";
rgPaste[0].lpstrResultText="a Patron Object";
rgPaste[0].dwFlags=OLEUIPASTE_PASTEONLY;

[Similar code for other formats]
```

After Patron has filled these structures, it can call *OleUIPasteSpecial*:

```
uTemp=OleUIPasteSpecial(&ps);

if (OLEUI_OK==uTemp)
    {
    fRet=PasteFromData(ps.lpSrcDataObj
        , &rgPaste[ps.nSelectedIndex].fmtetc
        , TENANTTYPE_STATIC, NULL, 0L);
    }

ps.lpSrcDataObj->Release();
return fRet;
```

If *OleUIPasteSpecial* returns OLEUI_OK, the end user has pressed the OK button, and we execute a Paste with the selected format, in which the *nSelectedIndex* field of OLEUIPASTESPECIAL matches the index of OLEUI-PASTEENTRY. Patron calls its "paste from data" function before releasing the data object it obtained from *OleGetClipboard*.

## Tenant Creation, Paste

The difference between Paste Special and the typical Paste operation is that Paste does not allow selection of the specific format. For Paste, Patron conducts a series of checks to find the best format on the clipboard by calling *IDataObject::QueryGetData*; when it finds a suitable format, it uses the same "paste from data" function that Paste Special uses. Checking for formats occurs in *CPatronDoc::FQueryPasteFromData*, which returns the FORMATETC of the best format to paste. Actual pasting occurs in *CPatronDoc::Paste*:

```
BOOL CPatronDoc::FQueryPasteFromData(LPDATAOBJECT pIDataObject
    , LPFORMATETC pFE, LPTENANTTYPE ptType)
    {
    FORMATETC       fe;
    HRESULT         hr;

    if (NULL!=(LPVOID)ptType)
        *ptType=TENANTTYPE_STATIC;

    //Any of our specific data here?
    SETDefFormatEtc(fe, m_cf, TYMED_HGLOBAL);
    hr=pIDataObject->QueryGetData(&fe);

    if (NOERROR!=hr)
        {
        //Try metafile, DIB, and then bitmap, setting fe each time.
        SETDefFormatEtc(fe, CF_METAFILEPICT, TYMED_MFPICT);
        hr=pIDataObject->QueryGetData(&fe);

        if (NOERROR!=hr)
            {
            SETDefFormatEtc(fe, CF_DIB, TYMED_HGLOBAL);
            hr=pIDataObject->QueryGetData(&fe);

            if (NOERROR!=hr)
                {
                SETDefFormatEtc(fe, CF_BITMAP, TYMED_GDI);
                hr=pIDataObject->QueryGetData(&fe);
                }
            }
        }

    if (NOERROR==hr && NULL!=pFE)
        *pFE=fe;

    return (NOERROR==hr);
    }


BOOL CPatronDoc::Paste(HWND hWndFrame)
    {
    LPDATAOBJECT    pIDataObject;
    BOOL            fRet=FALSE;
    FORMATETC       fe;
    TENANTTYPE      tType;
```

*(continued)*

```
    if (NULL==m_pPG)
        return FALSE;

    if (FAILED(OleGetClipboard(&pIDataObject)))
        return FALSE;

    //Go get type and format we *can* paste; then paste it.
    if (FQueryPasteFromData(pIDataObject, &fe, &tType))
        fRet=PasteFromData(pIDataObject, &fe, tType, NULL, 0L);

    pIDataObject->Release();
    return fRet;
    }


BOOL CPatronDoc::PasteFromData(LPDATAOBJECT pIDataObject
    , LPFORMATETC pFE, TENANTTYPE tType, LPPATRONOBJECT ppo
    , DWORD dwData)
    {
    BOOL            fRet;
    HRESULT         hr;
    PATRONOBJECT    po;
    STGMEDIUM       stm;

    if (NULL==pFE)
        return FALSE;

    //If we're not given any placement data, see if we can retrieve it.
    if (pFE->cfFormat==m_cf && NULL==ppo)
        {
        hr=pIDataObject->GetData(pFE, &stm);

        if (SUCCEEDED(hr))
            {
            ppo=(LPPATRONOBJECT)GlobalLock(stm.hGlobal);

            po=*ppo;
            ppo=&po;
            GlobalUnlock(stm.hGlobal);
            ReleaseStgMedium(&stm);
            }
        }

    fRet=m_pPG->TenantCreate(tType, (LPVOID)pIDataObject, pFE
        , ppo, dwData);

    if (fRet)
        {
        //Disable Printer Setup once we've created a tenant.
```

```
    if (m_fPrintSetup)
        m_fPrintSetup=FALSE;

    FDirtySet(TRUE);
    }

return fRet;
}
```

*PasteFromData* first checks to see whether it was given explicit placement data for whatever it pastes. This way we can allow an end user to simply move a tenant on a page instead of copying it and pasting it. Placement data consists of a point for the upper left corner of the tenant on the page and the tenant extents. I separated the corner point and the extents so that they can be manipulated independently—changing the size of a tenant doesn't necessarily change the upper left corner; moving a tenant doesn't necessarily change the extents.[2]

In any case, during pastes from the clipboard the *ppo* parameter to *PasteFromData* will always be NULL. This means that if the clipboard holds our private Patron Object data, *PasteFromData* pastes the best available graphic format at the point specified by any present positioning information. In this chapter, Patron always passes a NULL in *ppo* to this function—a preparation for Chapter 13's work. In all honesty, I implemented this differently on my first pass through this chapter's code, and after finding it deficient for drag and drop, I came back and modified it. This is a worthy consideration for your own designs.

Now let's look at what actually creates a tenant, which is an object of the C++ class *CTenant* and has member functions such as *Open, Load, Update, Destroy, Select, Activate, Draw,* and *SizeSet,* to name a few. This tenant class will expand into a compound document site in Chapter 17 and a control site in Chapter 25. In this chapter, a tenant already does much of what it needs in OLE Documents: it holds some object's *IUnknown* pointer, asks that object to draw through *IViewObject2,* and uses the OLE functions *OleSave* and *OleLoad* to save and load the object and its presentations to and from a piece of storage. (We'll see these APIs in Chapter 17.)

Each tenant's storage is a uniquely named storage element created in the storage element for the tenant's page. This happens in *CTenant::Open*, if you care to look, which opens the storage of a given name if it exists or, failing

---

2. The code that disables Printer Setup after creating a tenant is simply to accommodate my own laziness—I didn't want to introduce the complication of reformatting a page to a new paper size after tenants have been placed on that page. This hack has nothing to do with OLE.

that, creates a new storage of that name. The names are "Tenant *n*" (*n* is the value of a persistent counter kept in each page). The page saves this counter with a list of tenants, just as the *CPages* implementation saves lists of pages to its own storage element, as we saw in Chapter 7.

When Patron creates a tenant (a process that usually begins at the document level and works through *CPages* and then to *CPage*), it instantiates the tenant with *new CTenant* (see *CPages::TenantAdd*) and then asks that tenant to initialize itself (*CTenant::Create*) to obtain the *IUnknown* pointer for whatever object is stored in the tenant. *Create* is the only piece of code that knows how to take something like an *IDataObject* pointer and create an object with whatever is there. Exactly what it should try is determined by the TENANTTYPE (see TENANT.H) argument. For this chapter, the type is always TENANT-TYPE_STATIC, so *Create* generally uses the same technique as Chapter 11's Freeloader to create a static picture. In later chapters, we'll add more types, such as compound document objects and controls.

## Saving and Loading Tenants

In Chapter 7, we added basic compound file functionality to Patron. This enabled a document to maintain a list of pages, and each page committed its storage before the end user switched away from it. When we saved the entire document, we wrote a "Page List" stream off the root storage that contained the number of pages in the document, the currently viewed page, the next ID to use for a page, and the list of pages—that is, the list of page IDs from which Patron can re-create the name of the page's storage.

For this chapter, we extend the same idea to each page. A page can maintain a list of tenants and write a stream containing the number of tenants, the next tenant ID, and a list of tenant IDs that exist in the page. We base the name of the tenant's storage on the tenant ID, just as we do for the pages. Managing the storages, however, is a little different. When the page is open, all the tenants on that page are also considered loaded in the sense that Patron has a pointer to the object in that tenant. When you switch away from the page, each tenant's storage is committed before the page's storage is committed. Still, nothing is written to the disk because we have yet to commit the root storage. But as far as each page is concerned, we don't have to try to keep pointers to any tenant that has been modified; instead, we save those objects to storage when closing the page and reload them from memory when the page is reopened.

In the Freeloader sample in Chapter 11, we explicitly used the object's *IPersistStorage* interface to affect the saving and loading of the objects and their presentations. Patron instead uses *OleSave* and *OleLoad*—OLE API function wrappers—which reproduce exactly, and I mean exactly (I looked), the sequence of operations that we performed in Freeloader. *OleSave* saves all the presentations in the cache and stores the object's class ID to its storage. *OleLoad* reinitializes the cache from the saved presentations and creates a pointer to the object. When we reload a tenant and its object, we do not need to use *Create*. That latter function is exclusively for first-time creation of the object residing in the tenant.

Patron's whole storage scheme really shows off the power of transacted storage. By simple virtue of having the root storage transacted, we can write the rest of the application to think that its data is always on disk. In other words, when we create a new object in a tenant, we immediately save that object to its storage. (See the *OleSave* call in *CTenant::CreateStatic*.) When any tenant is asked to update itself in its storage, it writes a small stream containing its FORMATETC and position information and then calls *OleSave* to write all the messy data, followed by a *Commit*. In all, the storage management on the tenant level is minimal, and the page needs only to ensure that each tenant is given the chance to update itself before the page closes.

The most beautiful part of this storage mechanism is that we now have in place everything we need to handle storage for a compound document content object. When we enable this feature in Patron in Chapter 17, you'll see that we need no modifications to our storage model.

## Copy and Cut

The final feature that I want to discuss here is Copy and Cut operations for the currently selected tenant. I will not discuss exactly how I implemented the sizing functionality because that's just a lot of straight Windows programming that's pretty clear from the source code itself. I admit that the sizing code took about three times as long to write and debug as any part of this application that is using OLE, but I don't want to sedate you with the details.

Patron uses the technique developed in Cosmo at the beginning of this chapter. The data for the object is stuffed into one of our data transfer component objects, and it is that object that we put on the clipboard. The Copy and Cut operations start in *CPatronDoc::Clip*, which simply calls *CPages::TenantClip*, which then calls the current page's *CPage::TenantClip*. Inside this last function, the page calls its internal *TransferObjectCreate* function. *TransferObjectCreate* places two data formats in the data transfer object. The first is a PATRONOBJECT structure that describes where the object lives on the page. If we paste into a Patron document later, we can use this data to try to put the tenant in the same place that it was in the source. We'll use this as well in Patron's drag-and-drop implementation in the next chapter. In addition to this placement data, we include the graphical presentation we're using for the object in the tenant. A rendering of this graphic is readily available through the object's *IDataObject::GetData*. Mostly harmless, I would say, and when *TransferObjectCreate* is finished, *CPage::TenantClip* calls *OleSetClipboard* and possibly destroys the selected tenant if we're doing a Cut operation.

Note that I created the separate *TransferObjectCreate* function because we'll want to use it again when we need a data object as a drag-and-drop source. This is why there's the *pptl* parameter to *TransferObjectCreate*, which describes the offset from the top left of the tenant's rectangle, where it was picked up in the drag and drop.

## Summary

OLE makes it possible to work with all clipboard data through the *IDataObject* interface. The API function *OleGetClipboard* retrieves a data object that encapsulates the data on the clipboard, regardless of whether that data was placed there by an OLE-aware application or a non-OLE Windows application. An OLE-aware source application copies data to the clipboard by packaging that data inside a data object and passing that object's *IDataObject* pointer to the API function *OleSetClipboard*. This makes all global-memory—based data in that object available to all applications (OLE and non-OLE alike) and makes any other data based on other mediums available to OLE-aware consumers. Through the OLE Clipboard, then, applications can achieve higher-performance data exchange without losing compatibility with any other non-OLE applications.

In this chapter, we examine the methods for working with the OLE Clipboard protocol and see how simple OLE code can easily replace other code to manipulate the clipboard through the existing Windows API. Both the Cosmo and Patron samples show all this, and Patron also demonstrates the use of the OLE UI Library's Paste Special dialog box, in which the user can specifically select a data format to paste. This work in Patron enables it to store meaningful information in its documents.

## CHAPTER THIRTEEN

# OLE Drag and Drop

When I first began looking for OLE enlightenment, I watched a number of videotapes from early OLE seminars and demonstrations (early as in 1991). At one point, bored out of my skull, I decided to fast-forward through some of them. I noticed during that fit of impatience how often the presenter would select data in some application, pull down the Edit menu to choose Cut or Copy, switch to another application, and then pull down the Edit menu and choose Paste. This is to be expected: the clipboard is a great way to transfer data between a source and a consumer. It is a protocol that works.

I realized at that time, as did other designers, that a drag-and-drop technique would streamline many of these Cut/Copy and Paste operations. In drag and drop, the end user selects some data in the source, *picks* it up by clicking and holding down a mouse button in a specific region of that data, *drags* that data from the source's window to the consumer's window, and *drops* it into the consumer by releasing the mouse button. Keys such as Ctrl and Shift determine whether the operation moves, copies, or links the data, as you can accomplish through the clipboard. Move, copy, link, and even no-drop are each called an *effect* of the drag-and-drop operation.

This *pick-drag-drop* sequence, with its keyboard modifiers, has the same result as using the clipboard. The big difference is that drag and drop is direct and immediate—the entire data transfer operation happens in one swift stroke of the mouse, making drag and drop more efficient and easier to understand. The clipboard is most useful for storing data for an undetermined amount of time and pasting it repeatedly or not at all. With drag and drop, the source and the consumer perform a single transfer without touching the clipboard at all—that is, the clipboard contents remain intact.

OLE Drag and Drop, like the OLE Clipboard, is a transfer protocol that involves moving an *IDataObject* pointer from a source to a consumer. As part of the protocol, the source implements a simple object (no CLSID, no persistence, and so on) called the *drop source*, which implements the interface *IDropSource*. The consumer, which in the drag-and-drop context is called a *target*, implements a *drop target* object with the *IDropTarget* interface. Through these two objects, the source and the target communicate various events that occur from the pick to the drop.

This chapter first explains how OLE Drag and Drop works through source and target objects to communicate with a data object. As a demonstration, we'll add simple drag-and-drop support to Cosmo to show how easy it is to support this feature. In fact, OLE Drag and Drop can be so simple for certain applications that you can implement and test the feature in a day—and gain quite a lot of power and flexibility for your customers. A more complex implementation that involves additional user interface elements, mouse debouncing, and scrolling during a drag-and-drop operation will take longer, and we'll see why as we add drag and drop to Patron. These features are useful not only in exchanging data with other applications (such as a metafile from Cosmo) but also for simply moving tenants around on the same page—all with the same code. This is the power of OLE Drag and Drop: with one implementation, you can move data within an application, between documents or windows in that application, and between different applications.

Let me again stress that by implementing OLE Clipboard support and the "[query] paste from data" functions, as we saw in Chapter 11, you build a code base that makes for a fast implementation of drag and drop. The time you take to work with data objects and the clipboard will reduce a drag-and-drop implementation to perhaps only a few hours or a few days, depending on the level of complexity you want. (C'mon, Kraig, you think we *want* complexity?) If you do this, customers watching your video demonstrations on fast-forward won't know what hit them.

## Sources and Targets: The OLE Drag and Drop Protocol

To illustrate how OLE Drag and Drop works, let's begin with an end user who wants to transfer selected data from a source to a consumer. The source and the consumer might be different applications, different windows (documents, say) in the same application, or the same window inside a single application. As shown in Figure 13-1, OLE sits between the two, so there really isn't any distinction. As with the clipboard, the source must wrap its selected data into a data object.

The problem for drag and drop is how to get the *IDataObject* pointer from the source to the consumer or target. To prepare for this, the source first requires an implementation of the *IDropSource* interface, as shown in Figure 13-2, in which the object in question needs only to support this one interface. *IDropSource* has two specific member functions, as shown in the table on the facing page.

**Figure 13-1.**
*Prior to a drag-and-drop operation, the source has a data object for the selected
data. The source and the consumer can be different applications, different
documents in the same application, or the same document.*

| Function | Description |
|---|---|
| *QueryContinueDrag* | Determines what conditions continue or cancel an operation. Also determines what causes a drop because only the source knows what started the operation. |
| *GiveFeedback* | Sets the mouse cursor appropriate for an *effect* flag that indicates what would happen if the data were dropped in the target under the mouse cursor. The source can also control other user interface elements within this function. |

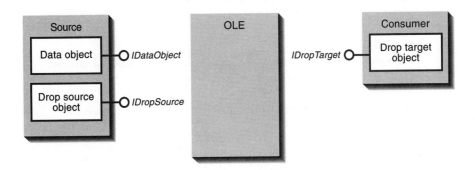

**Figure 13-2.**
*Objects necessary in both the source and the target to facilitate a drag-
and-drop operation.*

The target, in order to accept data from a drag-and-drop operation, must provide an object implementing *IDropTarget*, also shown in Figure 13-2. This object must then be attached to some window so that OLE can retrieve the *IDropTarget* pointer from the HWND it finds under the mouse cursor during a drag-and-drop operation. This association is accomplished through the OLE API function *RegisterDragDrop*, as shown in Figure 13-3. *RegisterDragDrop* takes an HWND and an *IDropTarget* pointer, calls *IDropTarget::AddRef*, and attaches that pointer as a window property to the HWND (using the Windows API *SetWindowProp*). At this point, the window is an open target. When the consumer no longer wants to be a target, it calls *RevokeDragDrop*, which removes the window property and releases the pointer.

NOTE: *IDropTarget* members are given the current mouse position in screen coordinates (in a POINTL structure). The target usually needs to call *ScreenToClient* before hit-testing the mouse position against other client-area coordinates.

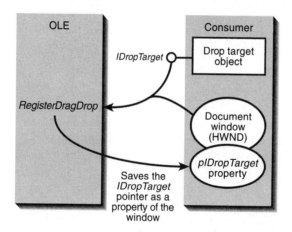

**Figure 13-3.**
*A consumer registers itself as a drop target by passing a window handle and an* IDropTarget *pointer to* RegisterDragDrop.

*IDropTarget* itself has four specific member functions:

| Function | Description |
|----------|-------------|
| *DragEnter* | Indicates that the mouse has entered the window associated with this drop target. The target initializes its drag-and-drop state and provides visible feedback to the user. |
| *DragOver* | Indicates that the mouse has moved within the window, the keyboard state has changed, or an internal OLE timer has expired. This function provides the target with a *pulse* through which it controls user feedback and indicates the effect of a drop if it occurred at this very moment. The source is given this effect flag through *IDropSource::GiveFeedback*, in which it controls the mouse cursor. |
| *DragLeave* | Indicates that the mouse has moved out of the window. The target cleans up its state from *DragEnter* and *DragOver* and removes any visual feedback. |
| *Drop* | Indicates that the source's *IDropSource::QueryContinueDrag* said "drop." The target performs a paste and cleans up as in *DragLeave.* |

The stage is now set for the operation to commence. The source must provide some means for starting a drag-and-drop operation, which is typically a WM_LBUTTONDOWN (or other mouse button message) on a particular region of the selected data, such as the outer edge of a rectangle. When this event occurs, the source passes its *IDropSource* and *IDataObject* pointers to the OLE function *DoDragDrop*, as shown in Figure 13-4.

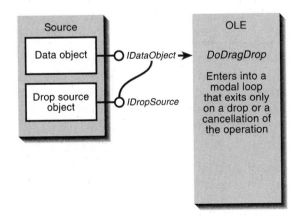

**Figure 13-4.**
*A source starts a drag-and-drop operation by passing its* IDataObject *and* IDropSource *to* DoDragDrop.

Internally, *DoDragDrop* enters a loop that monitors changes in the state of the mouse and the keyboard, executing the following sequence, as illustrated in Figure 13-5:

1. Call *WindowFromPoint* (Win32) with the current mouse coordinates, and then attempt to retrieve the *IDropTarget* associated with the window if it exists. If not, *DoDragDrop* passes DROPEFFECT_NONE to the source's *IDropSource::GiveFeedback*, which displays a no-drop mouse cursor. If OLE doesn't find a drop target for a child window, it will attempt to find one for the parent window of the child, up to the top-level window of any such ancestry.

2. Call *IDropTarget::DragEnter*, passing the source's *IDataObject* (marshaled if necessary). The target determines whether there is usable data in the data object and returns an appropriate effect flag (DROPEFFECT_*) after initializing the data object's internal state.

3. *DoDragDrop* passes the effect flag to *IDropSource::GiveFeedback*. This changes the mouse cursor to indicate the effect and provides whatever feedback is appropriate in the source (such as indicating that a drop would delete the source data).

4. When the mouse moves within the target window, or when the Ctrl or Shift key is pressed, or when an internal pulse timer elapses, *DoDragDrop* calls *IDropTarget::DragOver*. *IDropTarget::DragOver* displays user feedback, scrolls the target window if necessary, and returns an effect flag (which OLE passes to the source). If the mouse moves out of the window, *DoDragDrop* calls *IDropTarget::DragLeave* for that target, possibly calling *DragEnter* for a new target (back to step 1).

5. If the Esc key is pressed or there is a change in a mouse button state, *DoDragDrop* calls *IDropSource::QueryContinueDrag*, which tells OLE to continue the operation, cancel it (if the Esc key is pressed), or perform a drop (if the correct mouse conditions are met to reverse the pick). A cancellation will result in a call to the current target's *IDropTarget::DragLeave*, whereas a drop calls *IDropTarget::Drop*.

6. The loop repeats until a drop or a cancellation occurs.

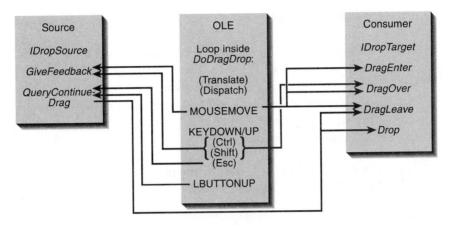

**Figure 13-5.**
*The execution sequence of* DoDragDrop.

Why does the source always maintain control of the mouse cursor? The reasoning is that when a drag-and-drop operation begins, the user is staring at the mouse cursor. From that point on, the cursor should consistently reflect any move, copy, or link effects regardless of the target under the mouse cursor. In other words, the three effects should have the same mouse cursor no matter what target specified that effect. The cursor should not change in different ways for different targets as a result of the same effect because the same cursor might then be used twice to indicate different effects. The only single agent in an entire operation is the source, so it retains control over this user interface element.

## Two Issues

One issue related to drag and drop is that the user needs to see the target to drag data to it. At the time of writing, however, OLE does not itself define a way to bring covered windows to the foreground during a drag-and-drop operation—end users have to arrange windows manually.

An issue for which OLE does provide a solution arises when a target window is visible but the location in that target where the end user would like to drop the data is not visible. If *DoDragDrop* is eating the keyboard messages and has the mouse capture, how can the user cause the target window to scroll? (Obviously the target cannot simply assume that if the mouse is off the edge of a particular window, the window should scroll in that direction.) The target, not having the mouse capture, would never see the mouse messages that do this. Even if the target could get the messages, it would mean that every running target would be wildly scrolling in the direction of the mouse!

Although this would conform to the second law of thermodynamics, entropy is not user friendly.[1]

OLE's solution defines a small *inset region* inside each document window, usually on the order of 11 pixels, as shown in Figure 13-6. If the end user holds the mouse in this region for an appropriate period of time (about 50 ms), the target then scrolls the contents of the window in the direction of the mouse at a rate of one scroll every 50 ms. Scrolling ends when the mouse moves out of the inset region.

**Figure 13-6.**
*The inset region within a target window.*

The initial delay before scrolling allows the user to pass the mouse over the inset region without causing any scrolling—in other words, moving the mouse around the screen doesn't cause all potential targets to jump around. Usability testing has shown 50 ms to be about the right delay, 11 pixels to be the right size for the inset region, and 50 ms to be the right scroll rate. These values are defined as the WIN.INI settings DragScrollDelay, DragScrollInset, and DragScrollInterval under the [windows] section. OLE defines the default values with the symbols DD_DEFSCROLLDELAY, DD_DEFSCROLLINSET, and DD_DEFSCROLLINTERVAL.

---

1. OK, OK, so you didn't take thermodynamics in college. The law states that the amount of entropy, $S$ (disorder, chaos), in the universe is increasing—that is, $\Delta S > 0$.

## Source and Target Responsibilities

From the previous discussion, we can identify specific responsibilities for the source and the target in a drag-and-drop relationship. The source has the following responsibilities:

1. Provide a data object with the selected data.

2. Provide an object with *IDropSource*, which need not be instantiated until immediately before calling *DoDragDrop* and can be deleted after the operation is finished.

3. Call *DoDragDrop* to start the operation, debouncing the mouse if necessary, and control its duration through *IDropSource::QueryContinueDrag*.

4. Control the mouse cursor and end-user feedback through *IDropSource::GiveFeedback*.

The target's responsibilities consist of the following:

1. Implement an object with *IDropTarget*.

2. Associate the object with a target window with *RegisterDragDrop*, usually when creating the window or making it visible. Disassociate the object when the window is destroyed or hidden with *RevokeDragDrop*. The object also requires a strong lock, which is not created in *RegisterDragDrop*, so the target must also call *CoLockObjectExternal* before registering or revoking the object.

3. Check for usable data in *IDropTarget::DragEnter* and *IDropTarget::DragOver* and determine the effect (which may be "no drop allowed").

4. Provide optional end-user feedback in the target within *DragEnter* and *DragOver*. The implementation of this can be done after the other steps have been completed.

5. Scroll the target window as appropriate, using the inset region, scroll delay, and scroll rate. This step is also optional and can be postponed until other parts of the implementation are complete.

6. Perform a Paste operation in *IDropTarget::Drop*.

These two lists define all that sources and targets must do to support OLE Drag and Drop. In many cases, you will need to implement only a subset of these responsibilities.

# Simple Drag and Drop, Step by Step: Cosmo

To demonstrate a basic drag-and-drop implementation, we'll add the feature to the Cosmo sample (CHAP13\COSMO). These changes apply to Component Cosmo as well (CHAP13\COCOSMO), but because both share the same code, we'll see only Cosmo's code in this section. Cosmo's idea of a document is a single Polyline figure that never has scroll bars, so there is no reason to worry about scrolling as a target. In addition, there is already an 8-pixel border around the figure that serves as a perfect pick region. This is the only area of Cosmo's document window class that is visible, so we can say that any mouse button down event in that window causes a pick. Because of this, there is no reason to support mouse debouncing. We'll leave these topics to "Advanced Drag and Drop: Patron" later in this chapter.

Even with these simplifications, we'll make a Cosmo document both the source and the target for Cosmo's private Polyline format. (Instances of Cosmo and CoCosmo will also work together.) Most applications will usually be a source and a target for a private format because those applications can usually copy, cut, and paste private formats using the clipboard within a document window, between document windows, or between applications. OLE Drag and Drop is just as flexible, and in Cosmo's implementation, we'll set up the feature in four source steps and three target steps. We'll do the source side first because it's simpler and because the data object includes graphical formats (metafile and bitmap) that can be dropped into a variety of existing targets that you probably have on your machine (such as an OLE-aware word processor).

The source steps are as follows:

1. Design the user interface for the operation, including the mouse cursors for each effect and any feedback in the source. (OLE provides default cursors.)

2. Determine the pick event (for example, left mouse button down) and the drop event (left mouse button up).

3. Implement the object with *IDropSource*, which is usually trivial.

4. Call *DoDragDrop* when the pick event occurs, and handle both copy and move effects after a drop occurs.

Implementation steps for the target are the following:

1. Design and implement the end-user feedback code to indicate the result of the drop. Do this first so that step 2 can use it.

2. Implement the object with *IDropTarget*. Functions such as *DragEnter* and *DragLeave* use the end-user feedback code created in step 1.

3. Call *RegisterDragDrop* and *RevokeDragDrop*, along with *CoLockObjectExternal*, to manage availability and stability of the target's *IDropSource* object.

The following sections look at each of the steps in detail. The *CDropSource* class, which singly inherits members from *IDropSource* in COSMO.H and is implemented in DROPSRC.CPP, implements the source side. The *CDropTarget* class, defined in COSMO.H and implemented in DROPTGT-.CPP, provides the target side. Both objects have trivial constructors, destructors, and *IUnknown* members. The objects maintain their own reference counts and delete themselves in *Release* as usual. (There is no need to do anything more.)

A few changes to DOCUMENT.CPP fill out Cosmo's drag-and-drop responsibilities. One special note about the document class (*CCosmoDoc*): it now has a BOOL member named *m_fDragSource* that is set to TRUE when the user picks up data in that document. Because the same document might be a target, this flag allows Cosmo to detect a drag and drop within the same document. Cosmo doesn't need to do anything when a drop happens on the same source document, so we can avoid unnecessary code and processing with this simple flag.

## Design and Implement Drop Source User Feedback

The first step in implementing a source for drag and drop is to determine what kind of user feedback to provide during the operation. The minimal requirement is to set the mouse cursor appropriately. You might also want to indicate that a move operation will delete the data in the source, but there are no user interface standards for that. In Cosmo, we'll worry only about the mouse cursor. If the standard OLE cursors for each possible effect are sufficient for your needs, your implementation of *IDropSource::GiveFeedback* will be trivial. (See the screen shot on the following page.)

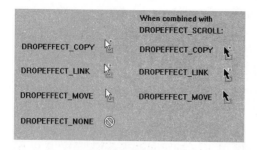

The DROPEFFECT_SCROLL flag can be included with the move, copy, and link effect flags to indicate that the target is currently scrolling. This flag is just a modifier of the basic effect and has no other impact on the data transfer itself.

If your implementation requires other cursors, you are free to use whatever you feel is appropriate. You could draw a big skull and crossbones for DROPEFFECT_NONE, a moving van for DROPEFFECT_MOVE, or a camera for DROPEFFECT_COPY. The people who will see these cursors are your customers—do what is best for them.

## Determine the Pick Event

The pick event is the mouse action that starts a drag-and-drop operation with a call to *DoDragDrop*. You need to know what starts the operation in order to know what ends it, and you must know this to implement *IDropSource::QueryContinueDrag*.

Most often the pick event will be a WM_LBUTTONDOWN message about some meaningful point. As mentioned earlier, this can be anywhere in Cosmo's document window; only 8 pixels of it are visible around the outside of the Polyline figure. This is convenient because it eliminates any hit-testing. Therefore, Cosmo's pick event is any WM_LBUTTONDOWN message in the document window. We'll see how Cosmo detects this message and calls *DoDragDrop* later. But we have to implement and instantiate the object with *IDropSource* in order to call *DoDragDrop*.

> NOTE: A source can use any mouse button for a pick event and can even combine the mouse action with the Alt key because you can detect changes in the state of any button and the Alt key within *QueryContinueDrag* in order to detect a drop event.

## Implement a Drop Source Object with *IDropSource*

As mentioned earlier, Cosmo's drop source object is *CDropSource* in DROP-SRC.CPP. Because Cosmo's needs are trivial, so is the implementation of the important *IDropSource* members:

```
STDMETHODIMP CDropSource::QueryContinueDrag(BOOL fEsc
    , DWORD grfKeyState)
    {
    if (fEsc)
        return ResultFromScode(DRAGDROP_S_CANCEL);

    if (!(grfKeyState & MK_LBUTTON))
        return ResultFromScode(DRAGDROP_S_DROP);

    return NOERROR;
    }


STDMETHODIMP CDropSource::GiveFeedback(DWORD dwEffect)
    {
    return ResultFromScode(DRAGDROP_S_USEDEFAULTCURSORS);
    }
```

The arguments to *QueryContinueDrag* describe the current keyboard and mouse states. The *fEsc* flag will be TRUE if the Esc key is pressed, meaning that we cancel the operation by returning DRAGDROP_S_CANCEL. This tells *DoDragDrop* to clean up and end the operation without the exchange of any data having occurred. The *grfKeyState* argument contains the states of the Ctrl, Alt, and Shift keys as well as the states of the left, middle, and right mouse buttons. All of these have corresponding MK_* values from WINDOWS.H (MK_LBUTTON, MK_RBUTTON, MK_MBUTTON, MK_SHIFT, and MK_CONTROL) except for MK_ALT, which is defined by OLE itself. The flags that appear in *grfKeyState* indicate the keys and buttons that are currently pressed.

Cosmo's implementation above checks whether the left mouse button is no longer pressed, and if it is, Cosmo returns DRAGDROP_S_DROP to cause a call to *IDropTarget::Drop* in order for *DoDragDrop* to return successfully. You can use any mouse button to cause a drop, modified with the Alt key if desired. However, you cannot use Ctrl and Shift because they modify the operation as a whole and might change during the operation without causing a drop. They are included in *grfKeyState* for the source's information. In any case, if the source does not detect appropriate drop conditions, it returns NOERROR from *QueryContinueDrag* to continue the operation.

If you think *QueryContinueDrag* is trivial (as it will be for most applications!), *GiveFeedback* is even simpler. If you want to use the standard mouse cursors, return DRAGDROP_S_USEDEFAULTCURSORS as shown earlier, which tells *DoDragDrop* to call the Windows function *SetCursor* with the appropriate mouse cursor. Otherwise, you can load your own cursor and call *SetCursor* yourself. If you need to know where the mouse is, call the Windows function or *GetCursorPos*.

> NOTE: *GiveFeedback* is called many times during the course of an operation, so you should keep the code optimized and preload any needed cursors elsewhere to avoid the overhead here.

## Call *DoDragDrop*

We're now ready to call *DoDragDrop* on the pick event, which happens in the WM_LBUTTONDOWN case of *CCosmoDoc::FMessageHook*:

```
if (WM_LBUTTONDOWN==iMsg)
    {
    LPDROPSOURCE    pIDropSource;
    LPDATAOBJECT    pIDataObject;
    HRESULT         hr;
    SCODE           sc;
    DWORD           dwEffect;

    pIDropSource=new CDropSource(this);

    if (NULL==pIDropSource)
        return FALSE;

    pIDropSource->AddRef();
    m_fDragSource=TRUE;

    //Go get data and start the ball rolling.
    pIDataObject=TransferObjectCreate(FALSE);

    if (NULL!=pIDataObject)
        {
        hr=DoDragDrop(pIDataObject, pIDropSource
            , DROPEFFECT_COPY | DROPEFFECT_MOVE, &dwEffect);
        pIDataObject->Release();
        sc=GetScode(hr);
        }
```

```
else
    sc=E_FAIL;

pIDropSource->Release();
m_fDragSource=FALSE;

if (DRAGDROP_S_DROP==sc && DROPEFFECT_MOVE==dwEffect)
    {
    m_pPL->New();
    FDirtySet(TRUE);
    }

return TRUE;
}
```

We first instantiate the drop source object, failing to do anything more if instantiation fails. We then set the document's *m_fDragSource* to avoid unnecessary processing and then create the data object to use in the transfer. The *CCosmoDoc::TransferObjectCreate* function is the one we added for the OLE Clipboard in Chapter 12. This shows the benefit of writing such a function: it makes the initiation of a drag-and-drop operation simple because we just pass the *IDataObject* and *IDropSource* pointers as the first two arguments to *DoDragDrop*. The third argument to this function is a value that represents the source's allowable effects, which can be any combination of DROPEFFECT-_MOVE, DROPEFFECT_COPY, and DROPEFFECT_LINK. If you don't want to allow a move, you need not include that flag. In Cosmo, we don't support linking (we don't provide CFSTR_LINKSOURCE), so we don't include the link effect.

The fourth argument to *DoDragDrop* is an out-parameter that will receive the final effect of the operation after *DoDragDrop* returns. After the operation is finished, Cosmo cleans up the data object and the drop source object and checks what happened. If the final effect was a copy, we have finished. If it was DROPEFFECT_MOVE, we have to delete the source data, which in this case means clearing the Polyline data. Remember that a move operation modifies the source document, so you should set your dirty flag.

This code in *CCosmoDoc::FMessageHook*, along with the drop source object, is the complete source implementation—very simple! Because Cosmo is a source of metafiles and bitmaps as well as its Polyline data, this code allows you to drag and drop a Polyline figure as a static picture into a suitable drop target. Now let's see how we can make Cosmo itself a target.

## Design and Implement Drop Target User Feedback

The first step for a target is to decide how it will indicate what might happen in a drop operation. There are many ways to do this. A word processor, for example, might show a shaded caret at the point where text would be dropped.

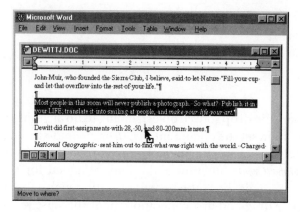

An application such as Patron, which pastes graphics, might show a rectangle of the exact size and at the location the dropped data would occupy.

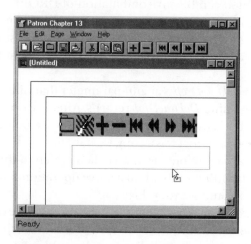

For Cosmo, pasting any Polyline data replaces the data in the window with the new data, so we can highlight the Polyline window itself with inverted edges.

This feedback is generated in the new function *CCosmoDoc::DropSelect-TargetWindow*, which inverts a 3-pixel frame around the window. This function is a toggle: we'll turn the highlight on in *IDropTarget::DragEnter* and turn it off in *IDropTarget::DragLeave* and *IDropTarget::Drop*:

```
void CCosmoDoc::DropSelectTargetWindow(void)
    {
    HDC       hDC;
    RECT      rc;
    UINT      dd=3;
    HWND      hWnd;

    hWnd=m_pPL->Window();
    hDC=GetWindowDC(hWnd);
    GetClientRect(hWnd, &rc);

    //Top
    PatBlt(hDC, rc.left, rc.top, rc.right-rc.left, dd, DSTINVERT);

    //Bottom
    PatBlt(hDC, rc.left, rc.bottom-dd, rc.right-rc.left, dd
        , DSTINVERT);

    //Left, excluding regions already affected by top and bottom
    PatBlt(hDC, rc.left, rc.top+dd, dd, rc.bottom-rc.top-(2*dd)
        , DSTINVERT);
```

*(continued)*

```
//Right, excluding regions already affected by top and bottom
PatBlt(hDC, rc.right-dd, rc.top+dd, dd, rc.bottom-rc.top-(2*dd)
    , DSTINVERT);

ReleaseDC(hWnd, hDC);
return;
}
```

The *DropSelectTargetWindow* function (like all such feedback functions) has two responsibilities. First, it needs to determine where to place the feedback. For Cosmo, we can use the rectangle of the Polyline window, but for applications such as word processors, you might need to calculate the line and character nearest the mouse cursor. For a spreadsheet, you would have to determine the closest range of cells.

Second, the function must draw the visuals at that location. Cosmo does this with *PatBlt* and DSTINVERT. Normally you'll use some sort of XOR operation so that you can show an image and remove it quickly and easily, but it's always your choice.

## Implement a Drop Target Object with *IDropTarget*

The next step for a target implementation is to implement the drop target object. In Cosmo, this is *CDropTarget*, found in COSMO.H and DROPTGT-.CPP. This object maintains a backpointer to the *CCosmoDoc* object because this object will be associated with the document window. In addition, *CDrop-Target* maintains an *IDataObject* pointer, specifically the one it receives in *IDropTarget::DragEnter*. This lets Cosmo examine the data object during calls to *DragOver*, which do not include a data object as an argument. Thus, we need to remember the data object in *DragEnter*.

### *IDropTarget::DragEnter*

This function is called whenever the mouse moves into a registered target window. It receives the following arguments:

| Argument | Description |
|---|---|
| *pIDataSource* | (*IDataObject \**): A pointer to the source's data object (marshaled as necessary). |
| *grfKeyState* | (DWORD): MK_* flags describing the current state of the Ctrl, Alt, and Shift keys as well as each mouse button (as with *IDropSource::QueryContinueDrag*). |

| Argument | Description |
|----------|-------------|
| *pt* | (POINTL): The current location of the mouse, in screen coordinates. |
| *pdwEffect* | (DWORD *): A pointer to a DWORD containing the allowable effects as specified by the source. On output, the target stores the effect a drop would have with the mouse at the current position in *pt*. |

With these arguments, you implement *DragEnter* as follows:

1. Call *pIDataSource->EnumFormatEtc* and *pIDataSource->QueryGetData* to determine whether the source has usable data, generally the same data that the target would be able to paste from the clipboard. If no usable data is found, store DROPEFFECT_NONE in *\*pdwEffect* and return NOERROR.

2. Determine whether *pt* is a suitable drop point. If not, store DROPEFFECT_NONE in *\*pdwEffect* and return NOERROR.

3. If *pt* is a suitable drop point, determine what effect will occur and store that flag in *\*pdwEffect*.

4. If you want to access *pIDataSource* in *DragOver*, save the pointer and call its *AddRef*.

5. Provide user feedback and return NOERROR.

You'll notice that *DragEnter* generally returns NOERROR, even for unusable data. OLE will always call *DragEnter* when the mouse moves into your window and will continue to call *DragOver* and eventually *DragLeave*, even if you continually return DROPEFFECT_NONE in *\*pdwEffect*. Saying "no drop" doesn't prevent additional *DragOver* calls. Here is Cosmo's *DragEnter*:

```
STDMETHODIMP CDropTarget::DragEnter(LPDATAOBJECT pIDataSource
    , DWORD grfKeyState, POINTL pt, LPDWORD pdwEffect)
    {
    HWND        hWnd;

    m_pIDataObject=NULL;

    if (!m_pDoc->FQueryPasteFromData(pIDataSource))
```

*(continued)*

```
        {
        *pdwEffect=DROPEFFECT_NONE;
        return NOERROR;
        }

    *pdwEffect=DROPEFFECT_MOVE;

    if (grfKeyState & MK_CONTROL)
        *pdwEffect=DROPEFFECT_COPY;

    m_pIDataObject=pIDataSource;
    m_pIDataObject->AddRef();

    hWnd=m_pDoc->Window();
    BringWindowToTop(hWnd);
    UpdateWindow(hWnd);
    m_pDoc->DropSelectTargetWindow();

    return NOERROR;
    }
```

In Chapter 12, we gave Cosmo a suitable "query paste from data" function: *CCosmoDoc::FQueryPasteFromData*. Again, a function such as this is very useful and centralizes clipboard, drag-and-drop, and compound document data transfers. We can see that step 1 in the preceding code calls this function and returns DROPEFFECT_NONE if it fails. If there is usable data, Cosmo continues at step 3 by storing DROPEFFECT_MOVE or DROPEFFECT-_COPY, depending on the state of the Ctrl key. If Cosmo supported linking (which it does not), it would check the state of the Shift and Ctrl keys and store DROPEFFECT_LINK if the Shift key were pressed.

But why did we skip step 2? Well, Cosmo accepts a drop anywhere in its document window—including the Polyline window—so it's not picky about the drop point. Also note that *DoDragDrop* calls the Windows API function *WindowFromPoint* to find the drop target. If the window is a child window but is not registered for drag and drop, OLE checks its parent window to see whether the parent is a target. If not, it will continue up the chain, checking each parent window.

That leaves us with step 4, in which we simply store the *pIDataSource* pointer in the drop target object (calling its *AddRef* like a good citizen), and then step 5, in which we give some visual feedback about what might happen if a drop occurred. We designed *CCosmoDoc::DropSelectTargetWindow* for this purpose in Cosmo, so we call that function here.

Before this, however, the calls to *BringWindowToTop* and *UpdateWindow* ensure that the target window is fully visible. Using *BringWindowToTop* has a nice effect: when you drag across document windows, Cosmo will bring the current target window to the foreground. This means that the end user can effectively switch document windows during this operation using only the mouse. Of course, if the intended target window is not visible, none of this helps—the user has to rearrange windows before the operation.

### IDropTarget::DragOver

*DoDragDrop* calls this function frequently: whenever the mouse moves, a key or button changes state, or a pulse timer elapses. Again, the "pulsing" is necessary to support scrolling in a target document, as we'll see later in Patron.

*DragOver* should be optimized to avoid costly operations, keeping the user interface crisp instead of sluggish. In general, you should perform hittesting on the mouse location, determine a new effect flag, and update your user feedback similar to the way you did in *DragEnter*. OLE passes only three arguments to this function—*grfKeyState*, *pt*, and *pdwEffect*—with the same types and meanings as for *DragEnter*. (Again, *pt* is in screen coordinates.) If you need to access the source's data object, perhaps to check a format, you must save that pointer in *DragEnter*. If you only need to check a format again, you can just as well check it with *DragEnter* and save a flag, avoiding another call to *IDataObject::QueryGetData*. If you need a rendering of the data for any reason, ask for it in *DragEnter*; doing so in *DragOver* will perform a lot of unnecessary work.

In any case, there are three steps to perform in *DragOver*:

1. Check whether *pt* is an allowable drop point given the effect defined by *grfKeyState* and the availability of data from the source. If no drop is allowed, return DROPEFFECT_NONE and NOERROR.

2. If a drop is allowed, determine the effect as in *DragEnter* and store it in *pdwEffect*. If you allow scrolling, check those conditions and add DROPEFFECT_SCROLL to the effects.

3. Update your user feedback (if any) appropriate for the effect and return NOERROR.

Cosmo's implementation is quite simple:

```
STDMETHODIMP CDropTarget::DragOver(DWORD grfKeyState, POINTL pt
    , LPDWORD pdwEffect)
    {
    if (NULL==m_pIDataObject)
        {
        *pdwEffect=DROPEFFECT_NONE;
        return NOERROR;
        }

    //We can always drop; return effect flags based on keys.
    *pdwEffect=DROPEFFECT_MOVE;

    if (grfKeyState & MK_CONTROL)
        *pdwEffect=DROPEFFECT_COPY;

    return NOERROR;
    }
```

If Cosmo returned DROPEFFECT_NONE in *DragEnter*, the *IDataObject* pointer we might have saved is NULL. If that pointer is NULL, we know that no usable formats were in the data object, so we immediately return from *DragOver* with DROPEFFECT_NONE again. This is a fast means to check whether there is usable data. Otherwise, Cosmo simply updates the effect flags and returns. And because we don't care where the mouse is inside the document window, we leave the inverted border created in *DragEnter* where it stands, doing nothing else in *DragOver*.

### IDropTarget::DragLeave

All good things come to an end; so too with drag and drop, in which a call to *DragLeave* tells a target the disappointing news that no drop will occur in it this time. The target must then clean up whatever state it has from *DragEnter* and *DragOver*. *DragLeave* itself takes no arguments, so you need to do only three things:

1. Remove any UI feedback in the target window.

2. Release any *IDataObject* held from *DragEnter*.

3. Return NOERROR.

Cosmo performs step 1 by calling *CCosmoDoc::DropSelectTargetWindow* again. This reverses the inversion done in *DragEnter*, leaving no visual feedback in the document. Cosmo then calls *Release* on the data object pointer and returns. The implementation of this is straightforward:

```
STDMETHODIMP CDropTarget::DragLeave(void)
    {
    if (NULL!=m_pIDataObject)
        {
        m_pDoc->DropSelectTargetWindow();
        ReleaseInterface(m_pIDataObject));
        }

    return NOERROR;
    }
```

### IDropTarget::Drop

This must be the target's lucky day! It's been chosen to accept a drop when *IDropTarget::Drop* is called, and for the most part, all it needs to do is perform a paste and then clean up its state, as occurs in *DragLeave*. *Drop* is called with the same arguments as *DragEnter*. (Once again, *pt* is in screen coordinates.) The value of *pIDataSource* is the same as in *DragEnter*, but the values of the other parameters will likely change (unless the mouse did not move). Following are the steps that the target should perform in *Drop*:

1. Remove any end-user feedback in the target window and release any held pointer, as described for *DragLeave*. (You can simply call *DragLeave* if appropriate.)

2. Validate that a drop can occur at the location of the mouse (*pt*) and whether the source has the right data. If not, store DROPEFFECT_NONE in *pdwEffect* but then return E_FAIL from the function.

3. Perform a Paste operation from the data object, returning DROPEFFECT_NONE and E_FAIL on error. Otherwise, store the effect flag according to *grfKeyState* and return NOERROR.

Cosmo's code is once again simple, exploiting the existing *CCosmoDoc::PasteFromData* to perform most of step 3:

```
STDMETHODIMP CDropTarget::Drop(LPDATAOBJECT pIDataSource
    , DWORD grfKeyState, POINTL pt, LPDWORD pdwEffect)
    {
    BOOL        fRet=TRUE;

    *pdwEffect=DROPEFFECT_NONE;

    if (NULL==m_pIDataObject)
        return ResultFromScode(E_FAIL);
```

*(continued)*

```
DragLeave();

//No point in drag and drop to oneself (for Cosmo, at least)
if (m_pDoc->m_fDragSource)
    return ResultFromScode(E_FAIL);

fRet=m_pDoc->PasteFromData(pIDataSource);

if (!fRet)
    return ResultFromScode(E_FAIL);

*pdwEffect=DROPEFFECT_MOVE;

if (grfKeyState & MK_CONTROL)
    *pdwEffect=DROPEFFECT_COPY;

return NOERROR;
}
```

Cosmo's implementation of *Drop* also has one other oddity—checking the document's *m_fDragSource* flag. If Cosmo detects that the end user dropped the data into the same window that it came from, there's nothing to do. We can simply return a failure code. For an application such as Patron, dragging data in the same document is useful for moving the data within a page—but Cosmo has no need for such a feature.

## Register and Revoke the Drop Target Object

The last step for making Cosmo a full target is to register the drop target object to associate it with the document window. Cosmo both creates and registers the object in *CCosmoDoc::Init*:

```
m_pDropTarget=new CDropTarget(this);

if (NULL!=m_pDropTarget)
    {
    m_pDropTarget->AddRef();
    CoLockObjectExternal(m_pDropTarget, TRUE, FALSE);
    RegisterDragDrop(m_hWnd, m_pDropTarget);
    }
```

The *hWnd* passed to *RegisterDragDrop* identifies the target window for the drop target object. If creation of the object fails or if registration fails, Cosmo does without drag and drop.

But what in tarnation is *CoLockObjectExternal* here for? *RegisterDragDrop* is another example of a weak registration function—OLE will create a stub

616

that holds the *IDropTarget* pointer but does not call *AddRef* through it. Without *CoLockObjectExternal*, when *DoDragDrop* accesses the target pointer from the source's process, everything works fine until *DoDragDrop* releases the pointer. This destroys the proxy in the source process and also destroys the stub in the target's process. The next time you drag into the same target window, no stub is available, so *DoDragDrop* quits—it doesn't simply ignore the window; it fails with an error. As we learned in Chapter 6, *CoLockObjectExternal* will force a strong lock and keep a stub in memory, so Cosmo needs to call this function here. It is unfortunate that *RegisterDragDrop* doesn't do this itself.

Of course, the process must be reversed when the document isn't a target any longer. This means removing the strong lock, revoking the registration, and releasing the target object, which happens in the processing for the WM_DESTROY case in *CCosmoDoc::FMessageHook*:

```
if (NULL!=m_pDropTarget)
    {
    RevokeDragDrop(m_hWnd);
    CoLockObjectExternal(m_pDropTarget, FALSE, TRUE);
    ReleaseInterface(m_pDropTarget);
    }
```

Cosmo removes the strong lock on WM_DESTROY and not in the document destructor because by the time the destructor is called, the window is long gone and *RevokeDragDrop* cannot remove its property from that window.

# Intermission

*Ole MacDonald's document was
E-I-E-I-E-OLE
In it was a data source and
E-I-E-I-E-OLE
(With) drag and drop here
And drag and drop there
And drag and drops going everywhere...
Ole MacDonald's document was
E-I-E-I-E-OLE!*

*Sung to "Ode to Joy" theme, Beethoven's Ninth Symphony, fourth movement.
Lyrics inspired by Robert Fulghum.*

# Advanced Drag and Drop: Patron

If you've been playing with the Patron sample from Chapter 11, you've probably noticed the annoying absence of a way to simply move a tenant on a page in one step. You can resize a tenant from one corner and then resize it from the opposite corner, but that's a pretty lame way to carry out what should be a single action. With OLE Drag and Drop, we can add the capability to do this in one step. Not only that, with the same code, we can also copy tenants to other documents either in the same instance of Patron, in a different instance, or to a different application altogether (particularly one that understands a graphics format). To do this, we need to make Patron both a source and a target, where dragging and dropping within the same document doesn't need to copy anything but can only reposition the tenant.

Patron (CHAP13\PATRON) implements the same steps as described for Cosmo, using similar source and target objects found in DROPSRC.CPP and DROPTGT.CPP. In fact, Patron's *CDropSource* is identical to Cosmo's. *CDropTarget* is structurally the same, but we have to do more work to support scrolling and additional user feedback in the target window. Other modifications to Patron include the file DRAGDROP.CPP, which contains some helper functions in the *CPages* class for performing hit-testing, scrolling, and end-user feedback. These are the functions *CPages::UTestDroppablePoint*, *CPages::DrawDropTargetRect*, and *CPages::AdjustPosition*. Finally, *CPage::OnLeftDown* (PAGEMOUS.CPP) is where we begin a drag and drop, so we perform hit-testing as well as mouse debouncing here.

## Tenant Pick Regions and Drop Sourcing

In Patron, I've defined the outer rectangular boundary of any tenant as the pick region, excluding those areas already occupied by sizing handles. The width and height of the region are the same as the dimensions of sizing handles.

In Chapter 12, we added the *CPage::OnNCHitTest* (PAGEMOUS.CPP) function to Patron to determine when the mouse was over a sizing handle. We used the return value from this function in *CPage::SetCursor* to show an appropriate mouse cursor for each sizing handle. For drag and drop, we modify *OnNCHitTest* to also check for the pick region (after the sizing) and modify *CPage::SetCursor* to show a four-pointed move cursor:

When *OnNCHitTest* determines that the mouse is within a pick region, it stores the code HTCAPTION in *CPage::m_uHTCode*, which *CPage::SetCursor* uses to set the move cursor. When *CPage::OnLeftDown* detects the HTCAPTION code, it calls *CPage::DragDrop* to create the data object (*CPage::TransferObjectCreate*) and the drop source object and then calls *DoDragDrop*. When the latter function returns, Patron checks whether a move effect occurred and handles the selected data appropriately.

## Da Bears, Da Bulls, Da Bounce

Often end users accidentally press a mouse button so that it stays down for only a short period of time. This is called a mouse bounce. It is preferable for an application to avoid executing actions on accidental mouse clicks by debouncing the mouse.[2] In Patron, we want to avoid the extra work to set up a drag-and-drop operation unless the end user really does want to do one. To do this, we need to debounce the mouse in the following way:

1. When the mouse button is pressed in the pick region, start a delay timer with a period defined by the DragDelay value in the [windows] section of WIN.INI. OLE's default DD_DEFDRAGDELAY value is 200 ms.

2. If the mouse moves a small distance away from its button down point before the timer expires, start the drag-and-drop operation. (Enough mouse movement means that the end user wants to drag the data.) The "small distance" is the number of pixels defined by the DragMinDist value in the [windows] section of WIN.INI. OLE's default DD_DEFDRAGMINDIST value is 2.

3. When the timer elapses, start the drag-and-drop operation.

---

2. Some applications perform different actions on selected data depending on whether the end user quickly clicked the mouse button or clicked it and held it down for a little while. Microsoft Word 6, for example, will start a drag and drop if you click and hold the mouse button in a block of selected text for 200 ms or so. If you click quickly, it will remove the selection and place the text caret at the click point.

The version of Patron in Chapter 12 contains code to do this for the sizing handles as well. Here's how it works. The *CPage* constructor (PAGE.CPP) reads the delay and distance values and stores them in the page object. It also initializes size pending and drag pending flags:

```
m_fDragPending=FALSE;
m_fSizePending=FALSE;

m_cxyDist=GetProfileInt(TEXT("windows"), TEXT("DragMinDist")
    , DD_DEFDRAGMINDIST);
m_cDelay=GetProfileInt(TEXT("windows"), TEXT("DragDelay")
    , DD_DEFDRAGDELAY);
```

When the left mouse button is pressed in a sizing handle or the pick region, *CPage::OnLeftDown* sets the type of operation pending, saves the exact location of the click, and starts a timer, as shown in the code for the drag operation. (The FALSE return value indicates that the mouse event doesn't modify the tenant.)

```
if (HTCAPTION==m_uHTCode)
    {
    m_fDragPending=TRUE;
    m_ptDown.x=x;
    m_ptDown.y=y;
    m_uKeysDown=uKeys;
    m_fTimer=TRUE;
    SetTimer(m_hWnd, IDTIMER_DEBOUNCE, m_cDelay, NULL);
    return FALSE;
    }
```

When the timer expires, Patron's pages window (managed in *CPages*) picks up a WM_TIMER message and calls *CPage::OnTimer* (PAGEMOUS-.CPP), which kills the timer and starts the type of operation that was pending:

```
void CPage::OnTimer(UINT uID)
    {
    if (m_fSizePending || m_fDragPending)
        {
        BOOL        fSize=m_fSizePending;
        BOOL        fDrag=m_fDragPending;

        m_fSizePending=FALSE;
        m_fDragPending=FALSE;

        KillTimer(m_hWnd, IDTIMER_DEBOUNCE);
        m_fTimer=FALSE;

        if (fDrag)
```

```
        {
        POINT        pt;

        GetCursorPos(&pt);
        m_pPG->m_fDirty |= DragDrop(m_uKeysDown
            , m_ptDown.x, m_ptDown.y);
        return;
        }

    if (fSize)
        StartSizeTracking();
    }

return;
}
```

If the mouse moves during this delay period, *CPage::OnMouseMove* is
called. If there is a pending size or drag and the mouse has moved more than
the minimum distance, the appropriate operation is started:

```
void CPage::OnMouseMove(UINT uKeys, int x, int y)
    {
    ⋮

    if (m_fSizePending || m_fDragPending)
        {
        int     dx, dy;

        dx=(x>m_ptDown.x) ? (x-m_ptDown.x) : (m_ptDown.x-x);
        dy=(y>m_ptDown.y) ? (y-m_ptDown.y) : (m_ptDown.y-y);

        if (dx>m_cxyDist || dy>m_cxyDist)
            {
            [Code like that in OnTimer to start a drag or a size]
            }
        [Other code omitted]
        }

    [Other code omitted]
    }
```

The final thing to remember is to kill the timer if the mouse button is
released before the timer elapses. This is done in *CPage::OnLeftUp*, which also
resets both pending operation flags to FALSE.

## Moving a Tenant on a Page

After a drag-and-drop operation is finished, Patron checks to see whether the source and the target were the same window, using the *m_fDragSource* flag as we did in Cosmo to avoid extra work. This flag is stored in the *CPages* class. Patron also has a flag in *CPages* named *m_fMoveInPage*, initially set to FALSE. Now look at *IDropTarget::Drop* in DROPTGT.CPP—if *m_fDragSource* is TRUE and the last effect was DROPEFFECT_MOVE, we can set *m_fMoveInPage* to TRUE. In all other cases, *m_fMoveInPage* remains FALSE. Setting *m_fMoveInPage* to TRUE tells *CPage::DragDrop* to do nothing more than move a tenant after *DoDragDrop* returns. This invalidates the tenant's old position (for repaint) and ensures that the new tenant position is clipped to the page boundaries. The following sequence of code performs all the operations necessary for this special case:

```
//In CPage::DragDrop
m_pPG->m_fDragSource=TRUE;
m_pPG->m_fMoveInPage=FALSE;
hr=DoDragDrop(...);

//In CDropTarget::Drop
if (m_pDoc->m_pPG->m_fDragSource && !(grfKeyState & MK_CONTROL))
    {
    *pdwEffect=DROPEFFECT_MOVE;
    m_pDoc->m_pPG->m_fMoveInPage=TRUE;
    m_pDoc->m_pPG->m_ptDrop=po.ptl;
    return NOERROR;
    }

//In CPage::DragDrop
if (m_pPG->m_fMoveInPage)
    {
    m_pTenantCur->Invalidate();

    [Code to clip the rectangle to page boundaries]

    m_pTenantCur->RectSet(&rcl, TRUE);
    m_pTenantCur->Repaint();
    return TRUE;
    }
```

If *m_fMoveInPage* is not set after *DoDragDrop*, Patron knows that the end user is either copying a tenant on the same page or accepting a drop from something external. In either case, *CDropTarget::Drop* pastes a new tenant by calling *CPatronDoc::PasteFromData*—that manifestly useful function. *PasteFrom-*

*Data* doesn't know or care about the source of the data; it simply makes a new copy. Therefore, no special cases are needed to copy a tenant within the same page:

```
//In CDropTarget::Drop
m_pDoc->m_pPG->m_fMoveInPage=FALSE;
fRet=m_pDoc->FQueryPasteFromData(pIDataSource, &fe, &tType);

if (fRet)
    {
    po.fe=(m_pDoc->m_cf==fe.cfFormat) ? m_fe : fe;
    fRet=m_pDoc->PasteFromData(pIDataSource, &fe, tType, &po, 0);
    }

if (!fRet)
    return ResultFromScode(E_FAIL);

*pdwEffect=DROPEFFECT_MOVE;

if (grfKeyState & MK_CONTROL)
    *pdwEffect=DROPEFFECT_COPY;

return NOERROR;
```

Finally, *CPage::DragDrop* must delete the originally picked tenant if a move occurred to an external target. It accomplishes this by calling *CPage-::TenantDestroy*:

```
if (DROPEFFECT_MOVE==dwEffect)
    {
    TenantDestroy();
    return TRUE;
    }
```

## More Advanced Drop Target Hit-Testing

In Cosmo, every point in a document window is a valid drop point. However, in a Patron document (the *CPages* window, to be exact), a page has unusable margins and is also surrounded by a border. We don't want to allow drops to happen in these areas, so *CPages::UTestDroppablePoint* (DRAGDROP.CPP) handles this more complex hit-testing. It returns a code from the UDROP_* values Patron defines in PAGES.H. The two most important values are UDROP_NONE (can't drop here) and UDROP_CLIENT (drop is allowed). Other values are for scrolling. (See "Scrolling the Page" later in this chapter.) Basically, *UTestDroppablePoint* returns UDROP_CLIENT if the mouse is within

623

the intersection of the document's client area and the client-relative rectangle of the usable page regions. Otherwise, it returns UDROP_NONE.

```
UINT CPages::UTestDroppablePoint(LPPOINTL pptl)
    {
    POINT       pt;
    RECT        rc, rcT, rcC;
    UINT        uRet;

    POINTFROMPOINTL(pt, *pptl);
    ScreenToClient(m_hWnd, &pt);

    CalcBoundingRect(&rc, FALSE);

    GetClientRect(m_hWnd, &rcC);
    IntersectRect(&rcT, &rc, &rcC);

    //Check for at least a client area hit.
    if (!PtInRect(&rcT, pt))
        return UDROP_NONE;

    uRet=UDROP_CLIENT;

    [Code here for scrolling considerations]

    return uRet;
    }
```

*UTestDroppablePoint* is first called from *IDropTarget::DragEnter* to set the initial effect. It's then called on entry into *IDropTarget::DragOver* to set the effect as well as to determine whether further checks for feedback and scrolling are necessary. (See the next sections.) Finally, it's called again from *IDropTarget::Drop* to ensure that our application doesn't attempt to perform a Paste operation on an invalid drop point. (Note that a POINTL structure, like the RECTL and SIZEL structures described in Chapter 12, is made of 32-bit fields.) Other Windows API functions use the POINT type (which varies with the operating system), so the POINTFROMPOINTL macro (INC\INOLE.H) converts a POINTL to a POINT. The same header file also has POINTLFROMPOINT to go the other way.

## A Feedback Rectangle

The version of Patron in Chapter 12 defined a private clipboard format named *Patron Object,* which contained necessary information about the original position of an object within a page:

```
typedef struct tagPATRONOBJECT
    {
    POINTL      ptl;        //Location of object
    POINTL      ptlPick;    //Pick point from drag-and-drop operation
    SIZEL       szl;        //Extents of object (absolute)
    FORMATETC   fe;         //Actual object format
    } PATRONOBJECT, *PPATRONOBJECT;
```

This structure contains not only the location of the original tenant but also its size (extents). We can use this information to draw the same-size rectangle in the target window to show the space that the data would occupy if a drop happened. In addition, the field *ptlPick* is used to store the exact location of the mouse in relation to the upper left corner of the tenant, specifically for a drag and drop. This way we can draw a feedback rectangle in relation to the mouse in the same way as shown below. In Chapter 11, Patron always stored (0,0) in this field. Now *CPage::DragDrop* calculates these offsets and stores them in the PATRONOBJECT structure included with the data object. This is all so that the feedback rectangle will first appear exactly over the object that is picked up.

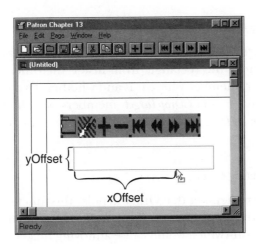

The offset is picked up in *CDropTarget::DragEnter* and used to place the rectangle properly. If the PATRONOBJECT structure is unavailable, we punt and show a default rectangle size, although the representation obviously will not be true to the size of the graphic. This approach lets us avoid having the source render data simply to determine the size. In later chapters, we'll add some code to also check for a structure named OBJECTDESCRIPTOR, which is defined in OLE2UI.H for the CFSTR_OBJECTDESCRIPTOR format. This structure has information similar to PATRONOBJECT but lacks a field with the offset point of the cursor from the upper left corner of the object itself. As a result, Patron will continue to look for its own structure later on, using OBJECTDESCRIPTOR as a backup.

*CDropTarget::DragEnter* then copies the pick point offset (into *m_ptPick*) and the extents of the object (into *m_szl*) for later use in *DragOver*. *DragEnter* now also draws the first feedback rectangle through *CPages::DrawDropTargetRect* (DRAGDROP.CPP), which then calls the Windows function *DrawFocusRect* to draw a dotted rectangle with an XOR operation. The upper left corner of this rectangle is simply the mouse coordinates minus the offset of the pick point:

```
//In CDropTarget::DragEnter
pt.x-=m_ptPick.x;
pt.y-=m_ptPick.y;

m_ptLast=pt;
m_fFeedback=TRUE;
m_pDoc->m_pPG->DrawDropTargetRect(&pt, &m_szl);
```

*DrawDropTargetRect* is a toggle function because *DrawFocusRect* is a toggle function. Therefore, to remove the rectangle from inside the other *CDropTarget* functions, we have to remember where it is and whether it's currently visible. That's the purpose of the *CDropTarget* members *m_ptLast* and *m_fFeedback*. Early in *DragOver*, *DragLeave*, and *Drop*, we remove the old rectangle if it's showing:

```
if (m_fFeedback)
    ppg->DrawDropTargetRect(&m_ptLast, &m_szl);
```

In *DragOver*, we have to remember that OLE will pulse this function even if the mouse doesn't move. In such a case, we don't want to remove the feedback rectangle only to redraw it (which would cause annoying flicker). So we leave it be if the point passed to *DragOver* differs from *m_ptLast*:

```
if ((pt.x-m_ptPick.x==m_ptLast.x) && (pt.y-m_ptPick.y==m_ptLast.y))
    return NOERROR;
```

626

## Scrolling the Page

I saved this topic for last because it involves a few tricks. To be honest, it took me about six working days to figure out Patron's scrolling code. I hope this experience can save you some time because, on the surface, scrolling seems simple enough. If the mouse is held in the inset region (inside the edge of the *window,* not the droppable region) for the right amount of time, the target starts combining DROPEFFECT_SCROLL with any other effect flag. (This tells the user that scrolling will begin shortly.) When the mouse has stayed in the inset region for the set time, the target starts scrolling its window in the appropriate direction, using the *DragOver* pulse to continue scrolling if the mouse doesn't move. Inside *DragOver,* you scroll only if the scroll repeat rate time has elapsed since the last time you scrolled.

Patron first reads the DragScrollInset value from WIN.INI in the *CPages* constructor:

```
m_uScrollInset=GetProfileInt(TEXT("windows"), TEXT("DragScrollInset")
    , DD_DEFSCROLLINSET);
```

*CPages::UTestDroppablePoint* uses *m_uScrollInset* to check whether the mouse coordinates are within the inset region of the pages window:

```
//In CPages::UTestDroppablePoint
UINT    uRet;
RECT    rcC;

GetClientRect(m_hWnd, &rcC);

[Code to store UDROP_NONE or UDROP_CLIENT in uRet]

//Scroll checks happen on client area.
if (PtInRect(&rcC, pt))
    {
    //Check horizontal inset.
    if (pt.x <= rcC.left+(int)m_uScrollInset)
        uRet |= UDROP_INSETLEFT;
    else if (pt.x >= rcC.right-(int)m_uScrollInset)
        uRet |= UDROP_INSETRIGHT;

    //Check vertical inset.
    if (pt.y <= rcC.top+(int)m_uScrollInset)
        uRet |= UDROP_INSETTOP;
    else if (pt.y >= rcC.bottom-(int)m_uScrollInset)
        uRet |= UDROP_INSETBOTTOM;
    }
```

UDROP_INSETLEFT and UDROP_INSETRIGHT are inclusive with both UDROP_INSETTOP and UDROP_INSETBOTTOM, but LEFT is mutually exclusive with RIGHT and TOP is mutually exclusive with BOTTOM. This means that Patron can scroll horizontally and vertically at the same time if the mouse is within both the horizontal and vertical inset regions. Patron will not, however, attempt to scroll up and down or left and right at the same time. That would be an interesting sight!

As mentioned earlier, *UTestDroppablePoint* is called each time in *CDropTarget::DragEnter*, *CDropTarget::DragOver*, and *CDropTarget::Drop*. The important call is the one in *DragOver*, in which the variable *uRet* contains the current UDROP_* combination and *m_uLastTest* (in *CPages*) contains the code from the last cycle through *DragOver* (or from *DragEnter*). So in any pass through *DragOver*, we know whether the cursor was outside the inset region and moved in, whether it was in the inset region and moved out, or whether we haven't changed from the last pass in or out of the region.

But *CDropTarget* has to be sensitive to the initial scroll delay so as to allow the user to move the mouse over the edge of the window without causing a scroll. This value is first loaded in *CPages::CPages*:

```
m_uScrollDelay=GetProfileInt(TEXT("windows"), TEXT("DragScrollDelay")
    , DD_DEFSCROLLDELAY);
```

The default value for DD_DEFSCROLLDELAY is defined as 50 ms. Unfortunately, this is shorter than the 55-ms resolution of the Windows timer. It's a little hard to test a delay this short—create a *DragScrollDelay=300* in the [windows] section of WIN.INI for testing purposes; this lets you move through things more slowly and test your timer counting.

Now we have to count the time from the moment the mouse entered the inset region in each iteration through *DragOver*. The best way to do this is with *GetTickCount*. A Windows timer does work because a timer requires you to be in your message loop calling *GetMessage* and *DispatchMessage*. But *DoDragDrop* does this only for mouse and keyboard messages. I tried using timers for implementing scrolling, but because my message loop never had a chance to run and dispatch WM_TIMER (or have *DispatchMessage* call a timer callback function), I never saw the timer expire.

Instead, *DragOver* saves in *m_dwTimeLast* the value from *GetTickCount* when the mouse first moved into the inset region. On every later call to *DragOver*, *GetTickCount* is called again and *m_dwTimeLast* is subtracted from it. If this difference is greater than the scroll rate, Patron scrolls a little and stores the current time in *m_dwTimeLast*. Through more calls to *DragOver*, Patron counts beyond the scroll rate again, scrolls a little more, resets as the base counter, and continues. If the mouse moves out of the region, Patron, of course, stops scrolling. To indicate this condition, *DragOver* sets *m_dwTimeLast* to 0 (meaning "no scroll under any circumstances").

All of this is wrapped up in some repetitive-looking code in *DragOver*, in which *uLast* is the value in *m_uLastTest* and *ppg* is the current *CPages* pointer:

```
if ((UDROP_INSETHORZ & uLast) && !(UDROP_INSETHORZ & uRet))
    ppg->m_uHScrollCode=0xFFFF;

if (!(UDROP_INSETHORZ & uLast) && (UDROP_INSETHORZ & uRet))
    {
    ppg->m_dwTimeLast=GetTickCount();
    ppg->m_uHScrollCode=(0!=(UDROP_INSETLEFT & uRet))
        ? SB_LINELEFT : SB_LINERIGHT; //Same as UP and DOWN codes
    }

if ((UDROP_INSETVERT & uLast) && !(UDROP_INSETVERT & uRet))
    ppg->m_uVScrollCode=0xFFFF;

if (!(UDROP_INSETVERT & uLast) && (UDROP_INSETVERT & uRet))
    {
    ppg->m_dwTimeLast=GetTickCount();
    ppg->m_uVScrollCode=(0!=(UDROP_INSETTOP & uRet))
        ? SB_LINEUP : SB_LINEDOWN;
    }

if (0xFFFF==ppg->m_uHScrollCode && 0xFFFF==ppg->m_uVScrollCode)
    ppg->m_dwTimeLast=0L;

//Set the scroll effect on any inset hit.
if ((UDROP_INSETHORZ | UDROP_INSETVERT) & uRet)
    *pdwEffect |= DROPEFFECT_SCROLL;
```

This block of code checks for a change in the mouse's position relative to the inset region—in to out or out to in. It then sets up the *CPages* variables *m_uHScrollCode* and *m_uVScrollCode* with the codes to send with WM_HSCROLL and WM_VSCROLL messages, in which 0xFFFF is a flag that means "no scrolling."

*DragOver* then checks for expiration of the scroll rate timer. If the timer has elapsed, *DragOver* sends the appropriate scroll messages as follows:

```
if (ppg->m_dwTimeLast!=0
    && (GetTickCount()-ppg->m_dwTimeLast) > (DWORD)ppg->m_uScrollDelay)
    {
    if (0xFFFF!=ppg->m_uHScrollCode)
```

*(continued)*

```
      {
      m_fPendingRepaint=TRUE;
      SendMessage(ppg->m_hWnd, WM_HSCROLL, ppg->m_uHScrollCode, 0L);
      }

  if (0xFFFF!=ppg->m_uVScrollCode)
      {
      m_fPendingRepaint=TRUE;
      SendMessage(ppg->m_hWnd, WM_VSCROLL, ppg->m_uVScrollCode, 0L);
      }
  }
```

This will send both WM_HSCROLL and WM_VSCROLL messages in the same pass through *DragOver* if necessary. This brings us to repainting. In Patron, drag-and-drop scrolling should be fast and should not require a repaint on every scroll. With many tenants on a page, especially tenants with bitmaps, each scroll would be painfully slow. To prevent the repaints, the *m_fPendingRepaint* flag is set to FALSE unless a scroll has occurred, in which case, it's set to TRUE. This flag is used in *DragOver*, *DragLeave*, and *Drop* to repaint the page when scrolling has stopped. The last two cases are obvious: moving out of the window or dropping stops scrolling. In *DragOver*, however, we have to determine whether the last *SendMessage* did, in fact, change the scroll position of the page. Therefore, before executing the preceding code, we save the current scroll positions in local variables:

```
xPos=ppg->m_xPos;
yPos=ppg->m_yPos;
```

After we have possibly sent WM_*SCROLL messages, we check the previous scroll positions against the new ones. If they are the same and a repaint is pending, we repaint:

```
if (xPos==ppg->m_xPos && yPos==ppg->m_yPos && m_fPendingRepaint)
    {
    UpdateWindow(ppg->m_hWnd);
    m_fPendingRepaint=FALSE;
    }
```

*DragLeave* and *Drop* always call *UpdateWindow* if the *m_fPendingRepaint* flag is TRUE.

One last consideration caused me much consternation. When I first implemented this scrolling business on a 16-bit platform, I tested it mostly by moving tenants around on the same page or among different documents. Everything worked great. Then I tried to drag something in from another application, such as Cosmo. Things fell apart because, with remote calls going on, my message loop had a chance to run. This didn't happen before because there's no yielding when both the source and the target are the same application!

The result was that Patron would occasionally receive WM_PAINT messages because scrolling, of course, invalidates regions of my client area. Normally this would not have been a problem except for my little end-user feedback rectangle. This is what happened: my *CDropTarget::DragOver* was called, I removed the previous feedback rectangle, I scrolled the page, and then I drew the new feedback rectangle over a possibly invalid region of the window. When WM_PAINT came along, it repainted that invalid region, erasing parts of my feedback rectangle. Then I came back into *DragOver* and attempted to erase the old feedback rectangle again. Because part of it was already gone and because my rectangle drawing is based on an XOR, I ended up with rectangle fragments on the screen. U-G-L-Y. I tried a number of things—ignoring the WM_PAINT messages, for example (which didn't work at all, as I should have known)—and finally arrived at a solution after a few more days of going nowhere. I maintain a flag in *CPages::m_fDragRectShown* that is modified only in *DrawDropTargetRect*: the flag is TRUE if the rectangle is visible, FALSE otherwise. If this flag is set when *PagesWndProc* in PAGEWIN.CPP is processing WM_PAINT, I call *DrawDropTargetRect* to erase the current rectangle, do the painting as usual, and then call *DrawDropTargetRect* again to reinstate the feedback. Finally everything came out clean. Yes, we all struggle at times with some aspects of programming for Windows!

## Summary

The OLE Drag and Drop protocol is a streamlined technique for transfering data through direct mouse action rather than through the clipboard. The protocol itself is nothing more than a way to bring an *IDataObject* pointer from a source to a consumer, or target. Any distance can separate the source and the consumer: they can be the same document, different documents in the same application, or two different documents or sets of data in two completely different applications. The same code handles all cases, and because you can exchange any data through *IDataObject*, you can exchange any data through OLE Drag and Drop.

To facilitate the exchange of an *IDataObject* pointer, the source implements a second object called the drop source, which implements the *IDropSource* interface. The target, on the other side of the picture, implements an object called the drop target using the interface *IDropTarget*. The target must attach this object to a window with the OLE API function *RegisterDragDrop*.

When the source wants to start a drag-and-drop operation, it passes its *IDataObject* and *IDropSource* pointers to the OLE API *DoDragDrop*. This function then enters a modal loop that watches the mouse and the keyboard. Any mouse movement into a target window will call *IDropTarget::DragEnter*; movement within a target window calls *IDropTarget::DragOver*, and movement out of such a window calls *IDropTarget::DragLeave*. In the *DragEnter* and *DragOver* cases, the target checks the available data, displays any desired user feedback to indicate what will happen if a drop occurs, and returns an effect flag to OLE. The effect describes what should happen when a drop occurs: a move, a copy, or a link. The default effect is move, whereas holding down the Ctrl key during an operation changes the meaning to copy, and holding down Shift+Ctrl changes it to link.

This effect shows up in *IDropSource::GiveFeedback*, which changes the mouse cursor accordingly. Now, when the Esc key is pressed or there is a change in the state of any mouse button, *DoDragDrop* calls *IDropSource::QueryContinueDrag*, which decides whether to continue the operation, cancel the operation (which calls *IDropTarget::DragLeave*), or cause a drop. The latter calls the target's *IDropTarget::Drop*, at which point the target performs a Paste operation using what's available in the data object originally passed to *DoDragDrop*.

This chapter explores how to implement drag-and-drop features through the simple example of Cosmo and the more complex example of Patron. Specifically, Patron allows the user to scroll a target document by holding the mouse just inside the window border for a short period of time. Patron also demonstrates how to "debounce" the mouse when it is accidentally clicked in a region that would normally cause a drag and drop to commence.

# PART IV

# OLE AUTOMATION AND PROPERTIES

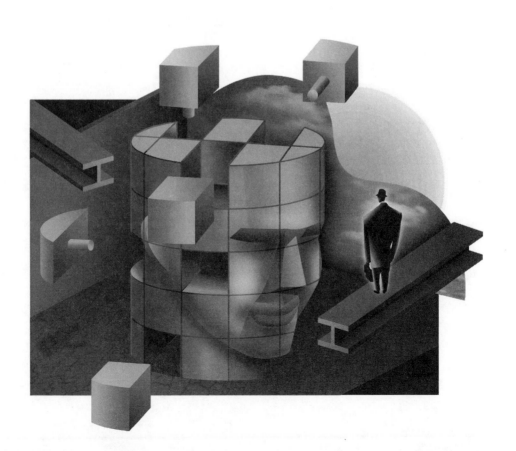

**CHAPTER FOURTEEN**

# OLE Automation and Automation Objects

*At the height of the Industrial Revolution, two workers watched with awe as a huge backhoe rapidly scooped up tremendous amounts of earth.*

*"If it wasn't for that blasted machine," said one worker, "there could be five hundred of us working here with shovels!"*

*"That is true," replied the other, "and if it wasn't for our shovels, there could be a million of us working here with spoons."*

The ever changing landscape of technology has repeatedly introduced new means of automating the labor-intensive tasks of the previous generation. This has, of course, given rise to the seemingly perpetual conflict between business owners, who see automation as a means to higher profitability, and labor forces, who see automation as a means of making a large number of workers obsolete. One of the greatest concerns is that the automation of a manufacturing process, for example, transfers the hard-earned skills of a group of workers to a machine. With the machine, the same process can be carried out without those skilled workers. In general, the automation of a task allows the same task to be performed by fewer people with fewer skills.

Leaving the subject of labor issues to sociology texts, we can at least acknowledge that because an automated task requires fewer skills to perform, a much larger number of people can effectively perform that task. Once automated, a task that was the privilege of a few becomes a possibility for all. Call it freedom and democracy.

As an example, consider 35mm photography. When 35mm single-lens reflex (SLR) cameras first appeared decades ago, only a small number of expert photographers actually knew how to manipulate the controls necessary to produce a good photograph. As time passed, tasks such as measuring available light or synchronizing a flash to the click of a shutter became automated and integrated features of the camera. These simplifications opened 35mm photography to a much larger number of people. In the past 20 years, other camera operations have become automated: film wound with a motor drive, exposure determined with integrated shutter and aperture control, focus accomplished with auto-focus lenses. In the 1990s, computers with large memories have become small enough to fit inside a camera. At the time of writing, those computers have integrated the expert advice of hundreds of professional photographers and the experience of a hundred thousand lighting situations to the point that high-quality 35mm photography has become nearly idiot proof. Good thing, too, because there seem to be a lot of us idiots out there, a good number of whom are using computers as well.

The history of the computer is also riddled with new automated technologies. Operating systems have automated the task of managing a computer's resources. Programming tools have automated the task of turning high-level languages into machine code, and more recent tools have even automated the task of writing programs in high-level languages.

Personal computers have been a tool in many homes and offices for some years now, and end users are becoming more mature and more comfortable with what computers can do for them. A few short years ago, many users found that they frequently repeated the same sequence of operations within a particular application, and they wanted a way to automate those sequences. This spawned the idea of *macro programming*, by which the user could list the steps in a sequence and essentially make the sequence a single operation in itself, called the *macro*. That single operation could then be attached to a keystroke or other command-giving device. Within corporations, instead of each end user creating his or her own macros or custom solutions, corporate developers usually do the job. The result is consistency in the execution of tasks (fewer errors) and more overall productivity—workers can concentrate on the business task, not the operation of a computer application.

More recently, end users and corporate developers have been finding that many of the macros they want to create involve multiple applications. For example, once a month someone might want to take raw numbers from a database, perform calculations on them in a spreadsheet, color a regional sales map with the results, place that map in a word processor document, and send a report via e-mail to the company's nationwide sales manager. By automating this task, one person could give the appropriate command on the last day of each month to generate the report, instead of having a dozen people spend a frantic week doing the same thing manually. Furthermore, if you could somehow rig an alarm clock control to automatically give the command on the right day of each month, even the person assigned to give the command could be freed from that chore.

OLE Automation, or just Automation with a capital *A,* is Microsoft's technology for solving the problem of cross-application macro programming, but it goes much deeper than that. In the past, Microsoft explored the idea of building a standard macro-programming language and programming tool into Windows itself. In a country built on free-market economics, this was a wretched idea: it would have limited the choice of macro-programming languages to one and the choice of tools to one. Instead, Microsoft chose a more open path and created OLE Automation, in which components with shared functionality or content become *automation objects,* and clients that can integrate those objects become *automation controllers.* Because Automation is a protocol, any automation controller can use every automation object, and any automation object can be integrated with every automation controller. Thus consumers—end users and corporate developers alike—can be given a full range of choices. Microsoft, of course, has produced its own set of automation objects (components contained in Microsoft Office applications and others) and its own set of controllers (centered around the Basic language in Microsoft Visual Basic, Visual Basic for Applications, and Access Basic).

This lengthy chapter will look at the mechanisms that make Automation work and then examine the design and implementation of automation objects. In the implementation section, we'll see a number of different ways to implement a simple object, and then we'll look at automating an entire application with a hierarchy of objects, using the version of Cosmo from Chapter 12. This latter section also includes a few design notes, and I want to stress that even if you do not intend to automate an application today, you may still want to read this information to get a sense of how you can structure your application to make it readily adaptable for OLE Automation later.

The architectural part of this chapter is quite long, so you may find it best to skim these sections and then follow through one of the samples under "Five Variations on the Theme of Implementing a Simple Automation Object" before coming back to reread more of the earlier material. I warn you against any attempt to pick up Automation in one sitting.

In this chapter and in Chapter 15, we will see that Automation has only a few interfaces and a few OLE API functions. So why is this chapter one of the longest in this book? The reason is that through the single *IDispatch* interface, a client can access a tremendous amount of functionality and content. Accordingly, *IDispatch* is a very rich interface, and it will take a while to look at all the details. In doing so, we'll see that the implications of OLE Automation for application design and the possibilities that it creates can be tremendous. Like automation in other industries, the automation of working with software can significantly change the nature of how people perform tasks. OLE Automation is really the software equivalent of beating spoons into shovels and shovels into backhoes. Then we can figure out what to do with the backhoes.

---

### A Note About Automation Testing Tools

In order to test an automation object, you generally need an automation controller. For most of the samples in this chapter, the AutoCli sample in Chapter 15 serves well. Otherwise, you can use Microsoft Visual Basic (version 3 or later) using the projects in the CHAP14-\BEEPTEST and CHAP14\COSMOTST directories. In addition, the 16-bit OLE SDK included a tool named DispTest, a stripped-down version of Visual Basic 3. Note, however, that both DispTest and VB3 are 16 bit only, so you cannot use them to test a 32-bit object—automation is subject to the limitations of Local/Remote Transparency between such models. If you're working on a 32-bit platform, a later 32-bit version of Visual Basic will run with 32-bit builds of this chapter's samples.

---

## The Mechanics of OLE Automation

OLE Automation involves a controller, usually an application with a programming environment of some kind (either language or graphics based; it doesn't matter), and one or more automation objects. Because these objects can be driven from an external programming environment, they are also called *programmable* objects. When an entire application is structured in a way that a controller can drive it through Automation, the application is also programmable. This terminology simply means that the mechanics of Automation are involved.[1]

---

1. If you have an early version of the *OLE Programmer's Reference* for Windows 3.1 or Windows NT 3.5, you'll find apparent contradictions between this text and that reference. Believe this text; the original version of the reference was written when OLE and Automation were not well understood. Later versions of the reference, such as that for Windows 95, are much more solid.

A controller is a client of one or more automation objects, for which the most important interface is *IDispatch*. Any object that implements this interface is said to support Automation, regardless of whether that object is packaged in a server and has a CLSID. Many automation objects are structured this way, but it is not required. Our focus here is specifically on objects with *IDispatch*, which is simply another mechanism through which an object shares its functionality and content but by using a *late-bound* mechanism. You can also use an early-bound mechanism or use type information when compiling. The capability of cross-application macro programming is an intentionally higher-level result of this mechanism.

We've seen how objects have functionality (both incoming and outgoing interfaces) and content. So far, however, we've seen only how to access an object's content as formatted data structures by using *IDataObject*. With *IDispatch*, we now have a formalized notion of *individual properties*—small pieces of information that work like single data members of an object. Instead of our having to ask an object for a structure of a particular format through *IDataObject::GetData*, we can ask for a property by name—for example, we can specify BackColor or Caption. Properties are an equivalent expression of get and put functions for data members, and they can be read-only, write-only, or read/write.

By now you know that you can easily write a custom interface that can expose an object's methods (incoming and outgoing functions) and properties in any way you like. Later in this chapter, we'll see cases in which this knowledge is useful. However, custom interfaces work best in an early-bound or compile-time manner, although they can be used in a late-bound manner with more work. The better late-bound mechanism uses the *dispatch interface*, or *dispinterface* (pronounced dis-pin-ter-face) for short.

## The Dispinterface

To illustrate how a dispinterface works and how it differs from a vtable interface, let's consider a simple object named Beeper. The object has one property, named *Sound*, and one method, named *Beep*. We can implement this object in C++ as follows, sharing this implementation with the rest of the world through OLE:

```
class CBeeper
    {
    public:
        long        m_lSound;     //"Sound" property

    public:
        long        Beep(void);   //"Beep" method
    };
```

To share *CBeeper* through a custom interface, we'd define something such as *IBeeper*, shown in the following code, and a pointer to this interface would provide access to six member functions, as shown in Figure 14-1.

```
interface IBeeper : IUnknown
    {
    long get_Sound(void);
    void put_Sound(long lSound);
    long Beep(void);
    };
```

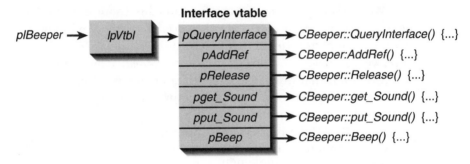

**Figure 14-1.**
*Vtable binding of the* IBeeper *custom interface to* CBeeper *functionality.*

The limitation of vtable interfaces such as *IBeeper* is that any client of this object must bind to the interface members on the basis of their locations in the vtable. A line of client source code such as *pIBeeper->Beep()* would be compiled into a call instruction to a specific offset from the value in *pIBeeper*. While this works great for compiled code, it's not as useful from an interpreted language. For the latter, we want to share the object through a late-bound dispinterface (with its own IID) whose properties are expressed directly (shown here in ODL syntax, as described in Chapter 3):

```
dispinterface DIBeeper
    {
    properties:
        [id(0)] long Sound;

    methods:
        [id(1)] long Beep(void);
    };
```

The *Sound* property is assigned a dispID of zero, and the *Beep* method is assigned a dispID of one. A controller (client) can use these dispIDs at run time to *dispatch* method calls and property manipulations to the real implementation of the object, as illustrated in Figure 14-2. Instead of accessing object services by calling a member function directly, a controller passes a dispID to some magic member of a dispinterface along with whatever parameters are needed for the property or method. That magic member then maps the dispID to the correct piece of implementation.

**Figure 14-2.**
*Binding a dispinterface means mapping the dispID to the implementation.*

The object must implement this generic mapping function as part of the early-bound *IDispatch* interface. Late binding comes from the fact that the actual method or property invoked is determined by arguments passed to the mapping function in this interface.

## The *IDispatch* Interface

The magic mapping function that invokes a method or a property according to a dispID is *IDispatch::Invoke*. When a controller has a pointer to a dispinterface, it really has a pointer to an implementation of *IDispatch* that responds to a set of dispIDs specific to that implementation. If a controller has two *IDispatch* pointers for two different objects, for example, dispID 0 may mean something completely different to each object. So while a controller will have compiled code to call *IDispatch::Invoke*, the actual method or property invoked is not determined until run time. This is the nature of late binding.

*IDispatch::Invoke* is the workhorse of OLE Automation, and besides a dispID it takes a number of other arguments to pass on to the object's implementation, as shown in Figure 14-3 on the following page. The other member functions of *IDispatch* exist to assist the controller in determining the dispIDs and types for methods and properties through type information.

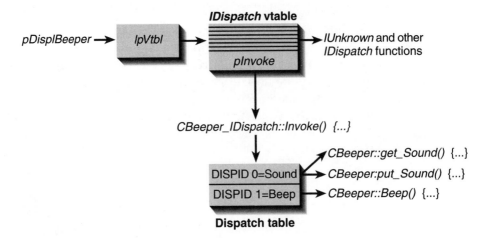

**Figure 14-3.**
*The accessing of methods and properties in a dispinterface is routed through* IDispatch::Invoke. *This calls the object's internal functions as necessary based on the dispID passed from the controller.*

Because a controller is usually a programming environment, it is generally a script or program running in that controller that determines which dispID gets passed to which object's *IDispatch*. The controller, however, needs only *one* piece of code that knows how to call *IDispatch* members polymorphically, letting its interpreter or processing engine provide the appropriate arguments for *IDispatch* members on the basis of the running script. This processing will generally involve all four of the specific *IDispatch* members:

```
interface IDispatch : IUnknown
    {
    HRESULT GetTypeInfoCount(unsigned int *pctinfo);
    HRESULT GetTypeInfo(unsigned int itinfo, LCID lcid
        ITypeInfo **pptinfo);
    HRESULT GetIDsOfNames(REFIID riid, OLECHAR **rgszNames
        , unsigned int cNames, LCID lcid, DISPID *rgdispid);
    HRESULT Invoke(DISPID dispID, REFIID riid, LCID lcid
        , unsigned short wFlags, DISPPARAMS *pDispParams
        , VARIANT *pVarResult, EXCEPINFO *pExcepInfo
        , unsigned int *puArgErr);
    };
```

| Member Function | Description |
| --- | --- |
| *Invoke* | Given a dispID and any other necessary parameters, calls a method or accesses a property in this dispinterface |
| *GetIDsOfNames* | Converts text names of properties and methods (including arguments) to their corresponding dispIDs |
| *GetTypeInfoCount* | Determines whether there is type information available for this dispinterface, returning 0 (unavailable) or 1 (available) |
| *GetTypeInfo* | Retrieves the type information for this dispinterface if *GetTypeInfoCount* returned successfully |

You can implement the *IDispatch* interface in various ways (as we'll see later in this chapter), including the use of OLE API functions such as *DispInvoke*, *DispGetIDsOfNames*, and *CreateStdDispatch*. Regardless of the implementation technique, *Invoke* always requires the same arguments, which include the following:

- *dispID*, a DISPID, to identify the method or the property to invoke.

- *wFlags*, an unsigned short identifying the *Invoke* call as a property get (DISPATCH_PROPERTYGET), a property put (DISPATCH_PROPERTYPUT), a property put by-reference (DISPATCH_PROPERTYPUTREF), or a method invocation (DISPATCH_METHOD).

- *pDispParams*, a pointer to a DISPPARAMS structure, which contains the new property value in a property put, array indices for a property get, or method arguments in VARIANTARG structures (same as a VARIANT). Each argument is an element in an array of VARIANTARGs contained inside DISPPARAMS. Arguments to a method can be optional as well as named.

- *lcid*, a locale identifier (*LCID*) identifying the national language in use at the time of the call so sensitive methods and properties can behave appropriately to the locale.

- *pVarResult*, a pointer to a VARIANT structure, a union of many different types along with a value identifying the actual type in which is stored the value of a property get or the return value of a method. This return value is separate from the return value of *Invoke* and is only meaningful if *Invoke* succeeds.

■ *pExcepInfo*, a pointer to a structure named EXCEPINFO through which the object can raise custom errors above and beyond the failure codes that *Invoke* can return.

■ *puArgErr*, in which *Invoke* stores the index of the first mismatched argument in *pDispParams* if a type mismatch occurs.

Given the dispID of a dispinterface member and the necessary information about property types and method arguments, a controller can access everything in the dispinterface. But how does a controller obtain the dispID and the arguments in the first place?

Using our Beeper object as an example, consider a little fragment of code in a Basic-oriented automation controller (DispTest or Visual Basic). This code sets Beeper's *Sound* property and instructs the object to play that sound by calling the *Beep* method. (Obviously, this is not the only way to access an automation object through a controller language; Basic is just an example.)

```
Beeper.Sound = 32    '32=MB_ICONHAND, a system sound
Beeper.Beep
```

The controller has to turn both of these pieces of code into *IDispatch::Invoke* calls with the right dispID and other parameters. To convert the names "Sound" and "Beep" to their dispIDs, the controller can pass those names to *IDispatch::GetIDsOfNames*. Passing "Sound," for example, to our Beeper's implementation of this function would return a dispID of 0. Passing "Beep" would return a dispID of 1.

You must also give the right type of data to the Beeper object to assign to the *Sound* property. The value 32 (defined for C/C++ programmers, at least, as MB_ICONHAND in WINDOWS.H) is an integer. The Basic interpreter must perform type checking to ensure that the type of the argument is compatible with the *Sound* property. This is accomplished either at run time (pass the arguments to *Invoke* and see whether the object rejects it) or through the object's type information as obtained through *IDispatch::GetTypeInfo* (if *IDispatch::GetTypeInfoCount* returns a 1). A well-behaved controller wants to use type information when it is available. If it is not, *IDispatch::Invoke* will perform type coercion and type checking itself, returning type mismatch errors as necessary.

## Standard dispIDs

The same dispID passed to different objects may result in a completely different method or property invocation. In general, specific dispinterfaces themselves are not polymorphic, although Microsoft has standardized a few dispIDs with defined semantics, as described in Table 14-1. We'll see a number of these throughout the rest of this chapter. Each of these standard dispIDs has a zero or negative value, and Microsoft reserves all negative dispID values (those with the high bit set) for future use.

| dispID (Value)* | Value and Description |
|---|---|
| DISPID_VALUE (0) | The default member for the dispinterface — that is, the property or method invoked if the object name is specified by itself without a property or a method in a controller script. |
| DISPID_UNKNOWN (−1) | Value returned by *IDispatch::GetIDsOfNames* to indicate that a member or parameter name was not found. |
| DISPID_PROPERTYPUT (−3) | Indicates the parameter that receives the value of an assignment in a property put. |
| DISPID_NEWENUM (−4) | The _*NewEnum* method of a collection. (See "Collections" later in this chapter.) |
| DISPID_EVALUATE (−5) | A method named *Evaluate* that a controller implicitly invokes when it encounters arguments in square brackets. For example, the following two lines are equivalent:<br>`x.[A1:C1].value = 10`<br>`x.Evaluate("A1:C1").value = 10` |
| DISPID_CONSTRUCTOR (−6) | The method that acts as the object's constructor. Reserves for future use. |
| DISPID_DESTRUCTOR (−7) | The method that acts as the object's destructor. Reserves for future use. |

\* The dispID −2 ran off and became a gypsy. You might see it at a rest stop along some European motorway someday. Actually, −2 is called ID_DEFAULTINST and is used specifically in *ITypeComp::Bind* to identify an implicitly created or default variable. The value was assigned from the dispID pool at a time when member IDs of arguments and interface members were not clearly distinct from dispIDs of methods and properties in a dispinterface.

**Table 14-1.**

*Standard dispID values and their meanings.*

## The BSTR and the Safe Array

Two special data types are specified as part of OLE Automation, although like much else, they are usable outside an *IDispatch* implementation. These types are the BSTR and the Safe Array.

A BSTR is a Basic STRing in which the string is stored as a DWORD count of characters followed by the characters themselves, as illustrated below. In OLE Automation, these strings are NULL-terminated, so a pointer to the beginning of the character array is the same as a C string pointer; in C or C++, a BSTR type always points to the characters, but the character count always precedes it in memory.

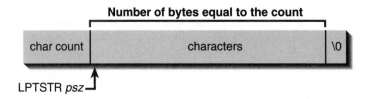

OLE provides a special set of API functions to allocate, manage, and free BSTR types: *SysAllocString, SysAllocStringLen, SysFreeString, SysReAllocString, SysReAllocStringLen,* and *SysStringLen.* You can easily guess what each function does. (The *OLE Programmer's Reference* holds the complete documentation for these functions.)

An important reason why Automation employs BSTR types for strings is that Automation was designed and implemented for the most part in the group at Microsoft that also produces Visual Basic, and Basic stores strings in a BSTR format. In addition, a BSTR is faster to copy across a process boundary because the length of the string is already known. As we'll see later in this chapter, it is quite simple to deal with BSTR variables. In fact, it can often be more convenient than working with C strings.

A Safe Array is an array of other types. The reason they are *safe* is that the array itself is a data structure that contains boundary information for the array as well as the actual reference to the data. Here's how the SAFEARRAY type is defined in the Automation header files:

```
typedef struct tagSAFEARRAY
    {
    USHORT    cDims;      //Count of array dimensions
    USHORT    fFeatures;  //Flags describing array
    USHORT    cbElements; //Size of each element
    USHORT    cLocks;     //Number of locks on array
```

```
HANDLE      handle;     //HGLOBAL to actual array
void *      pvData;     //Pointer to data valid when cLocks > 0
SAFEARRAYBOUND     rgsabound[]; //One bound for each dimension
} SAFEARRAY;

typedef struct tagSAFEARRAYBOUND
    {
    ULONG     cElements; //Number of elements in dimension
    long      lBound;    //Lower bound of dimension
    } SAFEARRAYBOUND
```

The various flags, symbols prefixed with FADF_, identify the array elements as BSTRs, *IDispatch* or *IUnknown* pointers, or VARIANT structures (see the following section). There are two flags that also indicate whether the array is allocated on the stack or allocated statically, which means that the array does not need to be freed explicitly when the SAFEARRAY structure is freed.

As with BSTRs, OLE provides a number of API functions, 19 in all, for creating, accessing, and releasing safe arrays: *SafeArrayAccessData, SafeArray-AllocData, SafeArrayAllocDescriptor, SafeArrayCopy, SafeArrayCreate, SafeArrayDestroy, SafeArrayDestroyData, SafeArrayDestroyDescriptor, SafeArrayGetDim, SafeArrayGet-Element, SafeArrayGetElemsize, SafeArrayGetLBound, SafeArrayGetUBound, Safe-ArrayLock, SafeArrayPtrOfIndex, SafeArrayPutElement, SafeArrayRedim, SafeArray-UnaccessData,* and *SafeArrayUnlock.* Again, see the *OLE Programmer's Reference* for more information about all of these functions.

## The VARIANT and VARIANTARG Structures

The VARIANT is a structure that can contain any kind of data. With *IDispatch::Invoke,* a VARIANT carries the return value from a property get or a method call; a VARIANTARG carries the arguments to a property put or a method call. Both structures have exactly the same format, shown in the following, and you'll often see the two types used interchangeably:

```
typedef struct tagVARIANT VARIANT;
typedef struct tagVARIANT VARIANTARG;

typedef struct tagVARIANT
    {
    VARTYPE          vt;         //Identifies the type
    unsigned short   wReserved1;
    unsigned short   wReserved2;
    unsigned short   wReserved3;
```

*(continued)*

```
union
    {
    //by-value fields
    short           iVal;
    long            lVal;
    float           fltVal;
    double          dblVal;
    VARIANT_BOOL    bool;
    SCODE           scode;
    CY              cyVal;      //Currency
    DATE            date;
    BSTR            bstrVal;
    IUnknown FAR *  punkVal;
    IDispatch FAR*  pdispVal;
    SAFEARRAY FAR*  parray;

    //by-reference fields
    short FAR*           piVal;
    long FAR*            plVal;
    float FAR*           pfltVal;
    double FAR*          pdblVal;
    VARIANT_BOOL FAR*    pbool;
    SCODE FAR*           pscode;
    CY   FAR*            pcyVal;
    DATE FAR*            pdate;
    BSTR FAR*            pbstrVal;
    IUnknown FAR* FAR*   ppunkVal;
    IDispatch FAR* FAR*  ppdispVal;
    VARIANT FAR*         pvarVal;
    void FAR*            byref;
    };
};
```

You can see that while this structure is actually quite small—16 bytes—it can hold just about any type of value or pointer within it. We've already seen the BSTR and SAFEARRAY types, which leaves the CY (currency) and DATE structures as the only newcomers. These two are very simple:

```
typedef struct tagCY
    {
    unsigned long Lo;
    long          Hi;
    } CY;


typedef double DATE;
```

On systems that use big-endian microprocessors—like the Macintosh—the ordering of the CY structure's fields is reversed. In any case, the currency type is an 8-byte fixed-point number, and the DATE type is a *double* that contains the number of days since December 30, 1899, in the whole part and the time in the fractional part. The time is expressed as a fraction of a day.[2]

The VARTYPE field, an *unsigned short,* at the beginning of the structure identifies the actual type that is held in the structure itself—that is, which one of the many fields of the *union* has meaning. The value in *vt* is drawn from the enumeration VARENUM, which defines not only the possible VARIANT types but also the types that are used in type information and persistent property sets, which we'll see in a Chapter 16. (See Table 16-1 on page 784.) The following is the comment for VARENUM, taken from the OLE header files, that describes the enumeration (the actual values of the symbols are unimportant):

```
/*
 * VARENUM usage key,
 *
 * * [V] - may appear in a VARIANT
 * * [T] - may appear in a TYPEDESC
 * * [P] - may appear in an OLE property set
 * * [S] - may appear in a Safe Array
 *
 *
 *   VT_EMPTY          [V]    [P]      nothing
 *   VT_NULL           [V]             SQL-style Null
 *   VT_I2             [V][T][P][S]    2-byte signed int
 *   VT_I4             [V][T][P][S]    4-byte signed int
 *   VT_R4             [V][T][P][S]    4-byte real
 *   VT_R8             [V][T][P][S]    8-byte real
 *   VT_CY             [V][T][P][S]    currency
 *   VT_DATE           [V][T][P][S]    date
 *   VT_BSTR           [V][T][P][S]    binary string
 *   VT_DISPATCH       [V][T]   [S]    IDispatch FAR*
 *   VT_ERROR          [V][T]   [S]    SCODE
 *   VT_BOOL           [V][T][P][S]    True=-1, False=0
 *   VT_VARIANT        [V][T][P][S]    VARIANT FAR*
 *   VT_UNKNOWN        [V][T]   [S]    IUnknown FAR*
 *   VT_I1                [T]          signed char
 *   VT_UI1            [V][T]   [S]    unsigned char
 *   VT_UI2               [T]          unsigned short
 *   VT_UI4               [T]          unsigned short
```

*(continued)*

---

2. There are two functions for converting an OLE Automation DATE type to the same information stored in an MS-DOS–compatible format (that is, the format used in the file system): *DosDateTimeToVariantDateTime* and *VariantTimeToDosDateTime.*

```
    *  VT_I8                [T][P]    signed 64-bit int
    *  VT_UI8               [T]       unsigned 64-bit int
    *  VT_INT               [T]       signed machine int
    *  VT_UINT              [T]       unsigned machine int
    *  VT_VOID              [T]       C-style void
    *  VT_HRESULT           [T]
    *  VT_PTR               [T]       pointer type
    *  VT_SAFEARRAY         [T]       (use VT_ARRAY in VARIANT)
    *  VT_CARRAY            [T]       C-style array
    *  VT_USERDEFINED       [T]       user-defined type
    *  VT_LPSTR             [T][P]    null-terminated string
    *  VT_LPWSTR            [T][P]    wide null-terminated string
    *  VT_FILETIME             [P]    FILETIME
    *  VT_BLOB                 [P]    Length-prefixed bytes
    *  VT_STREAM               [P]    Name of the stream follows
    *  VT_STORAGE              [P]    Name of the storage follows
    *  VT_STREAMED_OBJECT      [P]    Stream contains an object
    *  VT_STORED_OBJECT        [P]    Storage contains an object
    *  VT_BLOB_OBJECT          [P]    Blob contains an object
    *  VT_CF                   [P]    Clipboard format
    *  VT_CLSID                [P]    A Class ID
    *  VT_VECTOR               [P]    simple counted array
    *  VT_ARRAY          [V]          SAFEARRAY*
    *  VT_BYREF          [V]
    */
```

You'll notice that the types you can specify in a VARIANT are mostly the generic types. The others are useful in describing type information or in describing persistent binary data such as a BLOB. The VT_BYREF flag is what differentiates a VARIANTARG from a VARIANT: only a VARIANTARG is allowed to use this flag in order to pass parameters by reference. In that case, all of the by-reference fields in the VARIANTARG structure have no meaning in the VARIANT itself. For all intents and purposes, however, the two structures are otherwise the same.

OLE provides a few functions to initialize and otherwise manage both structures. These generally simplify your work with these structures and reduce the need for you to access fields of the structures directly.

In addition, OLE provides a host of functions to deal with the conversion between types, the topic of the next section. There are also a great number of macros that eliminate the need to refer to individual fields in a VARIANT or a VARIANTARG. V_I2(*var*) performs the equivalent of *var->iVal*, and V_BSTRREF(*var*) is the same as *var->pbstrVal*. The macro V_VT extracts the *vt* field, V_ISBYREF checks whether *vt* has the VT_BYREF flag, and

V_ISARRAY and V_ISVECTOR do the same check for VT_ARRAY and VT_VECTOR. Using these macros isn't necessary; there is no magic here. They are provided simply to make your source code more readable if you prefer this sort of syntax.

| Function | Description |
|---|---|
| *VariantClear* | Clears the VARIANT[ARG] by releasing any resources within it and setting the type to VT_EMPTY. If the structure contains a BSTR or SAFEARRAY, that element is freed with *SysFreeString*, *SafeArrayDestroyData*, or *SafeArrayDestroy*; if the element is an *IUnknown* or an *IDispatch* pointer, this calls *IUnknown::Release*. It does not recurse deeper if the type is VT_VARIANT. |
| *VariantCopy* | Copies the contents from one VARIANT[ARG] to another. The destination structure is cleared with *VariantClear*; BSTRs and SAFEARRAYs are copied in their entirety, and *AddRef* is called through any *IUnknown* or *IDispatch* pointers. |
| *VariantCopyInd* | Indirect version of *VariantCopy* that copies a by-reference VARIANTARG to a by-value VARIANT. The contents of the destination VARIANT are cleared with *VariantClear*. |
| *VariantInit* | Initializes the fields of a VARIANT[ARG], for example a field declared as a stack variable. It sets *vt* to VT_EMPTY and the *wReserved\** fields to 0, but it does not change the union value. |

## Type Coercion of VARIANTs and VARIANTARGs

Inside an implementation of *IDispatch::Invoke*, an object will generally find it necessary to *coerce* into the necessary type the variables passed to a method or put in a property. The reason is that a controller, because of its language structure (especially for weakly typed languages such as Basic), may pass arguments or properties in a type other than that specified in an object's type information. Certainly a sophisticated controller can provide some type checking before calling *Invoke* at run time, but this is not required. Ultimately it is the object's responsibility to ensure that the information it receives is converted to the type that it needs.

Now *Invoke* will receive in its DISPPARAMS argument an array of VARIANTARG structures. These structures hold every argument to a method or the value to put in a property. Where *Invoke* might expect a BSTR it gets a *long*, or a BOOL where it needs a *double*, or even an *IDispatch* pointer where it really wants CY or DATE. Type coercion is the process of converting one type to a compatible type. This might include conversion of strings to numbers and vice versa, and it may even involve getting or setting a property through another object's *IDispatch*.

To assist with this process, OLE comes with two basic functions, *Variant-ChangeType* and *VariantChangeTypeEx*. (The *Ex* brand is sensitive to localization concerns such as date and currency formats.) You can throw a VARIANT to one of these functions and see whether OLE can convince it to become a different type (inside another VARIANT). Of course, OLE is not so heavy-handed that it will try to force a square peg through a round hole, so some types simply cannot be converted to others. How, for example, does one convert an array of *IUnknown* pointers to a currency value? If I were dealing with my bank account, I'd be happy for it to max out the currency value, but I don't think my bank would appreciate that. In the interests of honesty, OLE doesn't convert incompatible types; it returns the programmer's nemesis, a type mismatch error. Rats.

In any case, OLE can coerce many types into many others. Each conversion actually has its own function with a name like *Var<type>From<type>*, as in *VarR4FromI2*, which is used internally inside *VariantChangeType[Ex]* through one massive double switch statement. There are conversion functions for every combination of *short, long, float, double,* BOOL, CY, DATE, BSTR, and *IDispatch ***, as is accurately documented in the *OLE Programmer's Reference*. These conversions are not necessarily trivial either; converting a BOOL to a BSTR, for example, gives you the string "True" or "False" as appropriate; converting dates and currency values with BSTRs does all the formatting and parsing according to the user's international settings.

What is most interesting is that you can often convert between these types and an *IDispatch* pointer. What the *IDispatch* pointer really represents is another object whose DISPID_VALUE property is the value to convert. The conversion functions that work with *IDispatch* pointers—named *Var<type>FromDisp*—call that interface's *Invoke* with a property get on DISPID_VALUE and then attempt to coerce any simple value to another type. "Simple" means that if *Invoke* returns another *IDispatch* pointer, for example, and we're trying to coerce into a *long*, the final converted value will be the numeric value of that pointer, losing any sense of it being a pointer to anything. If we were converting to a *short*, we'd end up with only the lower 16 bits of that pointer. In other words, this final conversion does not recurse into *VariantChangeType*—it just extracts the value to return out of the VARIANT that comes back from *Invoke*. This simple conversion will always work, but it may result in a useless value.

As a further assistance to implementation of *IDispatch::Invoke*, OLE offers the function *DispGetParam*, which retrieves a value from a VARIANTARG buried within *Invoke*'s DISPPARAMS argument. To use this function, you pass the DISPPARAMS pointer, the position of the argument, and the type you want to retrieve. *DispGetParam* will extract the appropriate argument and try to coerce it into the type you want by using *VariantChangeType*. If this function fails, it gives you back the error information to return to the controller that originally called *Invoke*.

I'm sure you'd like to know of a way to avoid messing with VARIANTs and performing all this tedious muck with type coercion, with or without *DispGetParam*. You might figure that because all the argument and property types you support through an implementation of *IDispatch::Invoke* are described in an object's type information, OLE can handle all this coercion automatically. In fact, you are absolutely correct. OLE provides automatic type coercion and checking directly through the *ITypeInfo* interface, specifically the function *ITypeInfo::Invoke*. We'll see how to use this feature later in this chapter, when we look at the various techniques for implementing *IDispatch*.

## Using Variant Coercion Outside Automation and OLE

Shhhh! Wanna hear a secret? You can use all the VARIANT functions as nothing more than a rich type conversion API. Nowhere in the Win32 API will you find functions to parse a date or time or currency string into an actual numeric value using the current international settings or to convert a value to a string. Nowhere else will you find functions to conveniently convert an integer to a "True" or "False" string. All the VARIANT manipulation functions are essentially a stand-alone library of useful functions that require only a prior call to *CoInitialize* as the BSTR and SAFEARRAY types use COM's memory allocation service.

## DISPPARAMS: Optional and Named Arguments

Now that we know about the VARIANT[ARG] and about coercing one type of VARIANT[ARG] into another, we can understand the DISPPARAMS structure that is passed as *pDispParams* to *IDispatch::Invoke*. This structure contains all the arguments for a method call or a property put and has the following structure:

```
typedef struct tagDISPPARAMS
    {
    VARIANTARG FAR*  rgvarg;              //Array of arguments
    DISPID FAR*      rgdispidNamedArgs;   //dispIDs of named arguments
    unsigned int     cArgs;               //Number of total arguments
    unsigned int     cNamedArgs;          //Number of named arguments
    } DISPPARAMS;
```

In the simplest cases, the *rgvarg* array has the VARIANTARG structures that make up the arguments to the method or property. For a property put, there is only one argument; for a method invocation, there may be zero or more arguments. Every VARIANTARG element in *rgvarg* is considered read-only unless it has VT_BYREF set in its *vt* field. In that case, the argument can be used as an out-parameter when necessary. Simple enough.

But of course, there are some tricks involved with DISPPARAMS that introduce more complications. First of all, any strings or other pointers to possibly allocated resources that are passed as arguments in this structure are always the *caller's* responsibility. In other words, *Invoke* should never free arguments itself. If *Invoke* wants to hold a copy of a by-reference value, for example a BSTR or an *IUnknown* or *IDispatch* pointer, it must copy the data or call *AddRef* through the pointer, respectively.

The order of the arguments inside the *rgvarg* array is from last to first—that is, a right to left stacking order. Say, for example, that you invoke a method with three arguments as follows:

```
Object.Method(arg1, arg2, arg3)
```

You would then have the value 3 in *pDispParams->cArgs*, with *arg1* at *rgvarg[2]*, *arg2* at *rgvarg[1]*, and *arg3* at *rgvarg[0]*.

Next, a method can support optional arguments. Such arguments are specifically marked in a dispinterface's type information as optional, but they must always be sent to *Invoke* inside the DISPPARAMS structure. To check whether an optional argument was sent or not, an implementation of *Invoke* checks whether the VARIANTARG has type VT_ERROR and the contents of DISP_E_PARAMNOTFOUND in the *scode* field. If so, the controller didn't provide the argument; otherwise, the argument is there and the object has to coerce it to the proper type. A method always gets its full complement of arguments, but some of them may not be available. Also, some older controllers might set the type of a nonexistent optional argument to VT_EMPTY instead of VT_ERROR.

If any argument cannot be coerced into a usable type, *Invoke* must return DISP_E_TYPEMISMATCH. Of course, it is highly useful for a controller, and ultimately the programmer or user of that controller, to know which argument was mismatched. To provide that information, the automation object must store the *rgvarg* index or the bad argument in the location pointed to by the *Invoke* parameter *puArgErr*.

Both the required and optional arguments mentioned so far are called *positional* arguments—they always appear in the same position in the *rgvarg* array. *IDispatch::Invoke*, more appropriately an automation object, can also support *named* arguments that appear first in the *rgvarg* array. In other words, they occupy the low positions in the array where the positional arguments come at the end. The *pDispParams->cNamedArgs* field tells you whether you have any named arguments. If this value is 0, everything is positional.

What are named arguments? They are arguments that can be placed anywhere in a method's argument list and are identified by a name that has meaning to the method itself. For example, consider a method named *Find-RockBand* for a music database. The method has one positional argument containing the number of members in the band and three named arguments, named *LeadGuitar*, *BassGuitar*, and *Percussion*, which are strings possessing the last names of the band members. (To complete this type of query function, we might add optional parameters such as *Vocals* and *RhythmGuitar*, which would be noted with the count argument being higher than 3, but we don't need to complicate matters here.) This method, which might return a *long* identifier to the database record, would be declared in the object's type information as follows:

```
LONG FindRockBand(int cMembers, BSTR LeadGuitar, BSTR BassGuitar
    , BSTR Percussion)
```

MKTYPLIB will assign each argument its own *member identifier* in the order declared, starting with 0. So *cMembers* would be ID 0, *LeadGuitar* ID 1, *BassGuitar* ID 2, and *Percussion* ID 3. Do not confuse these member ID values with the dispID values of methods and properties: the identifiers simply mark the argument.

With named arguments, you can invoke *FindRockBand* in a controller such as Visual Basic as follows:

```
id=Database.FindRockBand(3, LeadGuitar="Lifeson", BassGuitar="Lee"
    , Percussion="Peart")
```

Because named arguments are used, you can employ any other permutation as an exact equivalent, as in the following:

```
id=Database.FindRockBand(3, Percussion="Peart", LeadGuitar="Lifeson"
    , BassGuitar="Lee")
```

or

```
id=Database.FindRockBand(3, BassGuitar="Lee", Percussion="Peart"
    , LeadGuitar="Lifeson")
```

Inside *Invoke*, the DISPPARAMS structure for any of these calls will have *cArgs*=4 (the total count) and *cNamedArgs*=3. The first (and in this case the only) positional argument in *rgvarg* would be *rgvarg[3]*— that is, at the end of the array. The three named arguments will occupy *rgvarg[3−cNamedArgs+0]*, *rgvarg[3−cNamedArgs+1]*, and *rgvarg[3−cNamedArgs+2]*. I'm using 3 here to denote the last element in the array, subtracting *cNamedArgs* to get the beginning of the named arguments, and then adding 0, 1, and 2 to get to the first, second, and third named arguments.

Keep in mind, that you cannot depend at all on the ordering of the named arguments inside *rgvarg*. Generally the controller will just throw them in DISPPARAMS in the order they appear in the controller code, but to an automation object the order is not an order at all, only a random sequence. How you actually determine which element in *rgvarg* contains which named argument is the purpose of the final field of DISPPARAMS, *rgdispidNamedArgs*. This is an array of member identifiers, those dispIDs assigned to arguments based on their order in the method declaration. This is how an implementation of *Invoke* identifies the arguments because only the IDs, not the names themselves, are passed in DISPPARAMS. The *rgdispidNamedArgs[0]* field will always contain the ID of the argument in *rgvarg[0]*, *rgdispidNamedArgs[1]* will contain the ID of the argument in *rgvarg[1]*, and so on. So if the controller executes the following code:

```
id=Database.FindRockBand(3, LeadGuitar="Lifeson", BassGuitar="Lee"
    , Percussion="Peart")
```

the *rgvarg* and *rgdispidNamesArgs* arrays will appear as follows (lower memory to the left):

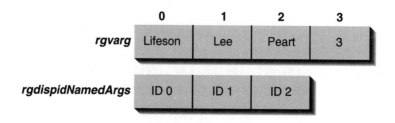

If the controller executes the following:

```
id=Database.FindRockBand(3, Percussion="Peart", LeadGuitar="Lifeson"
    , BassGuitar="Lee")
```

the *rgvarg* and *rgdispidNamesArgs* arrays will instead appear as this:

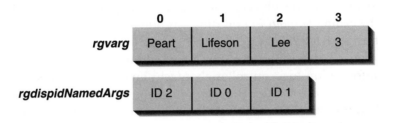

It is up to the automation object supporting named arguments to match elements in *rgvarg* with the proper argument value. The object itself can reject any attempt to pass named arguments by failing *Invoke* with DISP_E-_NONAMEDARGS if *cNamedArgs* is nonzero.

There is one special case with named arguments. Any property put operation is considered to involve a named argument when the argument is the property itself. Inside *Invoke*, you'll see *cArgs=1*, *cNamedArgs=1*, and *rgdispidNamedArgs[0]* with DISPID_PROPERTYPUT, and *rgvarg[0]* with the VARIANT containing the new property value. A controller is responsible for generating this specific DISPPARAMS structure, and an automation object considers it an error to see a property put with anything different, returning DISP_E_PARAMNOTOPTIONAL to tell the controller so. This is required because some controllers, as a result of their language structure, cannot differentiate between a property get or put and a method call. This means the *wFlags* parameter to *Invoke* will indicate both operations. The object must use this special named argument case to determine what is actually going on.

## Method and Property Return Values and Out-Parameters

Whereas the DISPPARAMS argument to *Invoke* handles all the arguments to a method or the new value for a property put, the VARIANT named *pVarResult* handles the return value of a method or the return value of a property get. This *pVarResult* exists because *Invoke* returns an HRESULT so it can describe errors; only if *Invoke* returns NOERROR does the result in *pVarResult* have meaning.

If the result is an allocated type such as a BSTR or an interface pointer, the object is responsible for allocating the resource or calling *AddRef*, whereas the controller must free the resource or call *Release*. You can see from this that combined with the rule that the object never frees arguments passed in

DISPPARAMS, an automation object never frees any resources it shares with its controller, with the exception of in/out-parameters involved in a method invocation. As I mentioned earlier, arguments in DISPPARAMS are read-only unless they are passed by reference, and then they are read/write only if the method knows that they are, in fact, in/out-parameters themselves. With such in/out-parameters, the object must be sure to free whatever arguments were passed by calling *VariantClear* on those arguments, before overwriting them and returning from *Invoke*.

Because *Invoke* can return only a limited number of SCODEs, how can it give information to a controller about why an operation failed above and beyond a simple error code? How can you get *Invoke* to say, "This property set failed because the allowable range for this value is 1 through 5," instead of returning DISP_E_OVERFLOW or some terribly undetailed information such as E_FAIL? The answer is that the object can raise an OLE Automation exception.

## Exceptions

In OLE Automation, an exception is really a form of rich and detailed error reporting. It's not the same thing as structured exception handling in C++, Win32, and so on. Although the controller can do what it wants with automation exceptions—having chains of exception handlers, for example—raising an exception from an automation object simply involves filling the fields of the EXCEPINFO structure passed to *Invoke* in the *pExcepInfo* argument and having *Invoke* return DISP_E_EXCEPTION. Controllers that don't handle exceptions will pass a NULL in *pExcepInfo*.

The EXCEPINFO itself is defined as follows:

```
typedef struct tagEXCEPINFO
    {
    unsigned short wCode;       //Object exception code, excludes scode
    unsigned short wReserved;
    BSTR           bstrSource;       //ProgID of object
    BSTR           bstrDescription; //Text description of error
    BSTR           bstrHelpFile;    //Full path to a help file
    unsigned long  dwHelpContext;   //Help context ID to display
    void FAR*      pvReserved;

    //An object function for delayed filling of structure
    HRESULT (STDAPICALLTYPE *pfnDeferredFillIn)
        (struct tagEXCEPINFO FAR*);

    SCODE          scode;    //scode for error, excludes wCode
    } EXCEPINFO, FAR* LPEXCEPINFO;
```

When an object raises an exception, it stores an error code inside either *wCode* or *scode* but not in both. A 0 in *wCode* means that the *scode* has the error. After storing the code, the object can choose either to fill in the rest of the fields as necessary except for *pfnDeferredFillIn* or to set everything to NULL and store a function pointer in *pfnDeferredFillIn*. If the controller sees an exception with a pointer in this field, it calls (*pfnDeferredFillIn*) (*&excepInfo*) when it wants the information. This allows the object to defer all of the potential costs of loading strings for the source and description fields until the controller actually wants it. The structure passed to this deferred filling function will have the *wCode* or *scode* originally stored within *Invoke* so that the filling function knows which exception was raised.[3]

The other four fields in the structure—however the controller obtains them—are used to display information about the exception to the user of that controller. The *bstrSource* string should contain the object's Version-IndependentProgID. If the field is non-NULL, the controller can then extract the value of this VersionIndependentProgID (a readable name) from the registry and display a message box with a message in the form "Error *<code>* in *<readable name>* : *<bstrDescription>*" provided *bstrDescription* is also valid. For example, the Beeper object we used before had a *Sound* property that is played through *MessageBeep* when the object's *Beep* method is invoked. Because this sound has to be meaningful to *MessageBeep*, it can have only the value MB_OK (0), MB_ICONHAND (16), MB_ICONQUESTION (32), MB__ICONEXCLAMATION (48), or MB_ICONASTERISK (64). If a controller attempts to give this object a value outside this range, the object raises an exception because there is no SCODE sufficiently rich to describe the actual error. The object will store its error code in *wCode* or *scode*, its Version-IndependentProgID of "Beeper.Object" in *bstrSource*, and the error description in *bstrDescription*. The controller will then display this information as shown in Figure 15-2 on page 755.

This message box will have an OK button by default, but if the object provides a non-NULL *bstrHelpFile*, the message box will also have a Help button. Pressing the Help button tells the controller to launch WinHelp, specifying the help file and context ID in the EXCEPINFO structure:

```
WinHelp(NULL, pExcepInfo->bstrHelpFile, HELP_CONTEXT
    , pExcepInfo->dwHelpContext);
```

---

3. DispTest and Visual Basic 3.0 do not support deferred exception filling, but later versions of Visual Basic and other controllers do. If you want to make a flexible object that fills the exception structure now for potential Visual Basic 3 customers, it is very useful to still write a deferred filling function and call it from within your *Invoke* to fill a structure. When customers shift to a newer controller, you can, if you want to support deferred filling, replace that call from inside *Invoke* and simply store the function pointer in *pExcepInfo->pfnDeferredFillIn*.

The result is that the user can get even more detailed information on the exception, as shown in Figure 14-4.

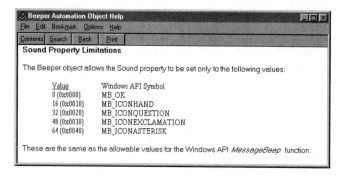

**Figure 14-4.**
*Exception information displayed in a help file.*

It is the controller's responsibility to call *SysFreeString* for all the BSTR fields of the EXCEPINFO structure.

As we explore various means of implementing *IDispatch* later in this chapter, we'll employ another error-reporting mechanism involving error objects. These are created with the API function *CreateErrorInfo* and the interface *ICreateErrorInfo*, set with the function *SetErrorInfo*, and accessed using *GetErrorInfo* and *IErrorInfo*. An object identifies its support for error objects by implementing *ISupportErrorInfo*. These functions and interfaces are basically a thread-safe mechanism for returning the same exception information to a controller that also ties into parts of OLE Automation itself.

## Supporting Locales

In Chapter 3, we saw how a locale identifier serves as the basis for performing case mapping, string comparison, sorting, and conversion of date, time, and currency formats to and from strings. In addition, a locale identifier can form the basis for localized method, property, and event names for an automation object. For example, a user in Germany who would like to use our Beeper object would not necessarily understand what the *Sound* property really was or what action the *Beep* method would perform. In German, the object is better described as a *Pieper* (pronounced "peeper") with the property *Ton* (as in *tone*) and the method *Piep*. Instead of writing an automation script in English, a German user could write it in German:

```
Pieper.Ton = 32
Pieper.Piep
```

The *lcid* argument passed to the *IDispatch* members *GetTypeInfo, GetIDs-OfNames*, and *Invoke* makes it possible for an *IDispatch* implementation to know which language is in use. It can use that information to return localized type information, convert localized member names to dispIDs, and invoke those members with the understanding that certain parameters, especially strings and time, date, or currency values, will be expressed in the language or format appropriate for that locale. In addition, it makes sense that any exception raised inside *Invoke* will provide information that is also sensitive to *lcid*—a user would not appreciate seeing an otherwise informative error message and help file show up in the wrong language!

You can support different locales from within an *IDispatch* implementation in a number of ways. We'll see some later in this chapter. The most flexible method of implementation is to have an automation object accept and support any locale from within a single version of the code. Then the object can be installed on any machine in the world and be immediately useful to any user.

This is, of course, the ideal case for an automation object, but it takes the most work. You can also choose an alternative approach that would not take as much time to implement and localize but that would still be flexible. The next-best technique, which is easily extensible to an arbitrary number of languages, is to support two languages—one localized, one neutral. (I'll illustrate this technique later with code.) An object like this allows a user to write a script in his or her own language while allowing the object to work with scripts written in the neutral language. This comes into play most often for automation objects that are useful to corporate or other developers. From what I've heard, programmers want to program in English, and this is understandable because all the system APIs are in English and all the lower-level programming tools and languages express their capabilities in English. As far as I know, the neutral language of choice is basic English (without a specific sublanguage).

Two-language support becomes very important with automation objects that can be accessed by multiple controllers at once. This means that the same instance of the object, one that is tied to a running application, for example, can be driven by two different controllers in two languages at the same time. One call to *Invoke* might use German, the next English, the next German, and so on. This would happen in the case in which the object was being driven both from an end-user script written in his or her local language and from a corporate developer's script written in English (the neutral language).

In my mind, the two-language approach is the best option because it's relatively easy to implement as well as to localize, and it addresses almost all of the important localization scenarios. Even so, there are two other techniques for handling locales; they are somewhat less flexible, but they might be the right choice in certain circumstances. In the first, an object can choose to support only a single locale, whatever the default is for the user or the machine, and return an error (DISP_E_UNKNOWNLCID) if a controller attempts to use it through any other language. This is fairly easy to implement, but it means that a script written for one language cannot be used on a machine that is operating with a different language, which, of course, shows why supporting a neutral language is advantageous. But if the automation object you're implementing is designed much more for an end user and not for corporate developers, this may be a reasonable choice.

On the other hand, you can implement an automation object that is not targeted to end users at all but targeted only to other developers (or perhaps advanced users). In that case, you can write an object that supports only one language, usually English, but also accepts any locale. This means you ignore any and all localization concerns, which is perfectly acceptable for objects that don't deal with time, date, or currency formats or with text that is displayed in a user interface or that would otherwise need translation. An automation object that performs 3-D graphics rendering, for example, is a good candidate for such an implementation. The more an implementation is potentially useful to an end user, the more important it becomes to support localization.

## Collections

For the most part, the methods and properties you expose through an *IDispatch* interface are entirely your design. The *OLE Programmer's Reference* describes some guidelines for objects such as those representing an application or a document, which we'll see later in this chapter in Table 14-4, under "Automation Object Hierarchy Design." While that section primarily covers design guidelines, there is one other standard for what are called *collections* or *collection objects*—objects that allow a controller to work with a set of similar things as a single group instead of as independent entities.

The simplest example of a collection is the group of open documents in an application. Although each document might have a *document object* to represent it alone, it would be grouped within a *documents collection*. If you are familiar with the Multiple Document Interface (MDI) for managing document windows, think of the MDI client window as the collection that holds all the MDI document windows. Collections, however, are not exclusively about documents: a document itself may have a *pages collection* that groups all the individual pages of a document. In the Patron sample, for example, the *CPages* class is essentially a collection of *CPage* objects. (These are C++ objects, mind you, but the concept still holds.) Each *CPage* is also a collection of *CTenant* objects.

A collection object itself is an automation object, with its own *IDispatch* interface and its own methods and properties. Usually it will have *Add* and *Remove* methods, as you would expect for managing any group of things. For example, a documents collection generally includes methods such as Add (File New) and Open (File Open) to create or open a document. Collections have a few stringent requirements, however, that allow controllers to iterate over the elements in the collection. The first is a standard property named *Count*, which returns a *long* describing the number of elements in the collection. The second is a standard method named *Item*. This takes an index[4] as an argument and returns any type desired, whatever is appropriate for the element of that index in the collection. So, for example, if you have a collection of integers, you can perform a summation on that collection in Visual Basic with code such as the following:

```
sum = 0
for I = 1 to NumberSet.Count
    sum = sum + NumberSet.Item(I)
next I
```

Here *NumberSet* is the collection itself. If you have a collection of documents in which each document is an automation object with a *Visible* property, you can hide all the document windows in that collection with the same construct:

```
for I = 1 to DocumentCollection.Count
    set doc = DocumentCollection.Item(I)
    doc.Visible = False
next I
```

---

4. The index can be zero-based or one-based, depending on what sort of controllers you might target. A C/C++ controller prefers zero-based indexes; a Basic controller prefers one-based indexes. The choice is, unfortunately, left up to the object implementer. No standard exists at the time of writing.

The problem with a construct such as this is that the collection itself may not necessarily support an index to the *Item* method, in which case the loop would fail. In addition, it is not necessarily true that all collections have items stored with sequential index values or that an item of a particular index will always have that same index. The unpredictability of an item's position is what distinguishes a collection from a simple array.

Visual Basic for Applications (VBA) and later versions of Visual Basic and other controllers support a collection without indexes through the *for...each* loop, which makes iteration of this sort more concise:[5]

```
for each doc in DocumentCollection
    doc.Visible = False
next doc
```

The *for...each* construct doesn't require any intermediate variables. It also doesn't require that the controller know the number of elements in the collection or depend on the collection's support for an item index.

To support iteration over the collection in this manner, a collection object must support a third standard method (or property) named *_NewEnum* (DISPID_NEWENUM). The leading underscore, according to OLE Automation, means that the method or property is hidden and should not be shown in any user interface that a controller might present. *_NewEnum* takes no arguments (which is why it can be a property or a method) and returns an *IUnknown* pointer. But a pointer to what object? This return pointer does not give access to the collection object, but instead it points to an enumerator object with the interface *IEnumVARIANT*.[6] As we know from other enumerator interfaces we've seen in earlier chapters, this interface is concerned with enumerating an array—or group—of VARIANT structures that can contain just about any kind of data, from an integer to a character string to even other objects referenced through their *IUnknown* or *IDispatch* pointers—exactly what we want to support an iteration construct. We'll see more details about this in the next section.

---

5. DispTest and Visual Basic 3.0 do not support the *for...each* construct. To do the same operation from these controllers, you must use the more traditional approach to iteration as described earlier. This limitation is strictly a feature deficiency of these specific controllers and should in no way deter you from implementing a proper collection object and a proper enumerator.

6. Older versions of the *OLE Programmer's Reference* are confusing about who implements what interface. The collection object itself implements *IDispatch* (which includes *IUnknown*) as well as any other interfaces it wants. However, *_NewEnum* returns the *IUnknown* pointer for a separate

Any *for...each* language construct will call *_NewEnum* internally to obtain the *IEnumVARIANT* pointer and then call *IEnumVARIANT::Next* to access the next element in the collection. It applies whatever code is in the body of the *for...each* statement to that element—for example, using a number in an expression or invoking another object's properties and methods—and continues looping until *IEnumVARIANT::Next* returns an error. When the loop is complete, Visual Basic calls *IEnumVARIANT::Release*.

The final standard for collections is naming: the name of a collection object should be the plural of the objects it collects. For example, a collection of Word objects should be called the Words collection; a collection of Vertex objects should be the Vertices collection; a collection of Mouse objects should be the Mice collection. So what if you have Moose objects? Append "Collection," as in MooseCollection.

## Active Automation Objects

When writing an automation script, a developer or a user might want to connect to an instance of some object type that is already running. One might, for example, want to try to connect to the automation object attached to a running application so one can ask it to create a new document in which one can execute another task. One might also want to connect to a document that is already open and extract information from it instead of trying to reload that document, which would most likely fail.

To facilitate connections to a running object, which is optional for an automation object, OLE utilizes the running object table, as we saw in Chapter 9, to maintain an *active* object for each CLSID that is running. The choice of the word *active* is an unfortunate one because object activation has a much different meaning in the context of OLE Documents. In the context of Automation, the active object would be better called the *running* object for a given CLSID. But we're stuck with the *active* name, which is part of the three

---

enumerator object. As we've seen before, an enumerator is a separate object that is generally tied to the collection itself, but because the collection can provide any number of separate enumerator objects, and because enumerators can make copies of themselves through *IEnum<Type>::Clone*, the enumerator cannot be the same as the collection. The older documentation even mentions how the collection doesn't implement *IClassFactory*. We all know better at this point in this book because we understand the role of the class factory and its separation from the class of objects it instantiates.

API functions dealing with active object instances. These functions are nothing but simple wrapper functions around the *GetRunningObjectTable* API and the *IRunningObjectTable* interface:

| Function | Description |
| --- | --- |
| *RegisterActiveObject* | Registers an object (given its *IUnknown* pointer and CLSID) as active by creating a moniker from the CLSID (converted to a string) and registering it in the running object table with *IRunningObjectTable::Register*. This returns a DWORD registration key that is returned from *RegisterActiveObject*. |
| *RevokeActiveObject* | Given the DWORD key from the registration, unregisters an object. This function employs *IRunningObjectTable::Revoke*. |
| *GetActiveObject* | Retrieves the *IUnknown* pointer for the most recently registered active object or a given CLSID through *IRunningObjectTable::GetObject*. |

It is an automation object that calls *RegisterActiveObject* and *RevokeActive-Object* and usually an automation controller that calls *GetActiveObject*, as you might expect. But as OLE API functions, any program can call these functions at any time for whatever reason.

How does this facilitate connections to running objects? When an application starts, it generally registers its application-level automation object with *RegisterActiveObject*. At this point a controller, executing some script, can call *GetActiveObject* with that application object's CLSID and get an *IUnknown* pointer to it. The controller can then query for *IDispatch* and drive that application programmatically. When the application shuts down, it calls *RevokeActiveObject*, which removes it from the running object table and makes it unavailable to controllers. An application can do exactly the same thing for a document that it opens: when creating the document, register its automation object as active (meaning the document class has its own CLSID), and revoke that object when closing the document. In this way, a controller can call *GetActiveObject* to connect to the open document.

It is very likely, of course, that the application might create and register additional documents; it is also possible that the user would launch another instance of the application. In these cases, the most recently registered object will be the active one as stipulated by the behavior of the running object table itself. So if an application created three documents and registers each one on creation, the last document created will be the active document object. If that document is closed, the second document created will become active because it is the next most recently registered. If the first document is closed, the active object does not change because the second document is still the most recently registered. If, however, the application were to create another new document, it would become the new active object. The same principle applies to instances of applications or to any other type of object that is being registered and revoked in this manner.

Simple enough? Well, as you might expect, there is one catch when using the running object table. If I have a document object with a reference count, I will usually use that reference count to destroy the document when the reference count goes to 0. However, *RegisterActiveObject* itself usually creates a strong lock by calling *AddRef* on the object you register, and that reference count is released only in *RevokeActiveObject*. You would call *RevokeActiveObject* only if the document were being destroyed, but you can't destroy the document because it has a reference count on it. The same problem applies to the application object and the application itself. Sound familiar? We discussed similar problems in Chapter 6. The solution is to use a strong or weak lock as necessary.

When calling *RegisterActiveObject*, you can specify either ACTIVEOBJECT_STRONG or ACTIVEOBJECT_WEAK to control the type of lock kept in the running object table. This works similarly to the first argument to *IRunningObjectTable::Register*. If you register a strong lock, the table calls *AddRef* on your object and that reference can be removed only with a call to *IRunningObjectTable::Revoke*. This isn't a problem when you don't need to destroy the object (and accordingly destroy a document or shut down an application). In these cases, the user is explicitly closing a window associated with the object, and the reference count is quite meaningless. If, however, you want to allow a zero reference count to destroy the object, you have to register a weak lock or you have to implement the *IExternalConnection* interface on the object, as we discussed in Chapter 6.

## Registry Entries for Automation Objects

As for any object with a CLSID, an automation object requires a few basic registry entries to tell OLE where its server is located. It is also necessary to tell automation controllers where to find your type information given your CLSID. Knowing this, controllers don't have to instantiate an object of your class just to see what the object can do.

Three basic sets of entries for each automation object fall under the CLSID key, the TypeLib key, and your ProgID key or keys. These entries are necessary for each separate object CLSID, which is true for any other object server.

Under your CLSID entry, you should register the following:

```
\CLSID
    {<CLSID>} = <name of object>
        [Inproc | Local]Server[32] = <path to DLL or EXE> [/Automation]
        InprocHandler[32] = <handler path or OLE2.DLL/OLE32.DLL>
        ProgID = ...
        VersionIndependentProgID = ...
        TypeLib = {<LIBID> spelled out as a CLSID}
        Programmable
```

We've already seen the entries for type information in Chapter 3. Here NotInsertable keeps the object out of Insert Object dialog boxes in OLE Documents containers. If an object can be inserted as well as embedded, this will be Insertable. I suggest, as an extension to OLE Automation, the *Programmable* key to indicate that the object supports OLE Automation, in the same way that Insertable marks a compound document object and Control marks an OLE Control, as we'll see later. You won't find Programmable in any other documentation. I suggest it as a means of identifying object classes that can be driven through Automation. Without such a key, you cannot differentiate these objects from a regular COM component that doesn't support *IDispatch*. Programmable is useful for controllers that would like to display a list of only automation-capable objects, but it is not a standard part of OLE.

The only other part of these registry entries related specifically to Automation is the optional */Automation* command-line flag. If you are registering an application object for automation using LocalServer[32], you will want to include this flag to tell your EXE that it is being launched in order to create the application object. You don't put this flag on any other LocalServer[32] entries for other objects, even with the same EXE name, because you'll use it to determine whether you must create and register a single-use class factory for the application object's CLSID. Because the object will usually be created as part of application startup, you don't want to register a class factory for that CLSID unless OLE is going to specifically use it right away (and thus exhaust its single use). Otherwise, some client might come along and try to instantiate your application object at some later time. If your class factory has not been used, it would be called at that time, but it could not create a new application.

Also note that your ProgID entry provides for a convenient mapping from a textual object name like "Beeper.Object" to a CLSID. This might or might not be useful to certain controllers. Visual Basic and its various derivatives allow the user to write a piece of Basic code to create an object as follows:

```
Dim X as Object
Set X = CreateObject("Beeper.Object")
```

When executing this code, Visual Basic goes to the registry and looks for a ProgID named "Beeper.Object" and then finds "CurVer". It then looks under that versioned ProgID to find the CLSID, and with that CLSID it can call *CoCreateInstance(...IID_IDispatch)* to instantiate the automation object and obtain its *IDispatch* pointer.

When OLE first establishes remote connections through a dispinterface, it automatically creates entries for *IDispatch* under the Interface key. If you have a dual interface and want to provide your own standard marshaling support, you can create your own entries under Interface as well using the IID of *IDispatch* as the BaseInterface entry.

# Design Considerations

Now that we've seen what OLE Automation and the *IDispatch* interface are all about, we can look at a number of practical design considerations involving this technology. After we discuss performance, we'll describe Automation-compatible interfaces, which restrict the types of data structures you can pass through a dispinterface. This leads to various indirect means of exchanging data structures. We'll then look at the choices you have between dispinterfaces and custom interfaces and take a brief look at what *IDispatch* means for outgoing interfaces and event sets.

## *IDispatch* Performance and Restrictions

With all the argument handling, type coercion, localization support, and exceptions that are involved with a function such as *IDispatch::Invoke*, you've probably recognized at least once that accessing the functionality and content—that is, the methods and properties—of an object through a dispinterface is not exactly fast. Hence, the topic of performance.

If you compare Figure 14-3 with Figure 14-1, you'll notice that when a client accesses the functionality in, say, *CBeeper::Beep* through a dispinterface, both client and object are executing a lot more code than if the client were accessing it through a custom interface such as *IBeeper*. The client has more overhead because instead of calling the function directly, it has to push a fair number of parameters on the stack before calling *IDispatch::Invoke*. If the function itself took additional parameters (*Beep* takes none itself), the client would also have to create the appropriate DISPPARAMS and VARIANTARG structures first, then push pointers to those parameters on the stack, and then call *Invoke*. In contrast, making a direct call to a vtable interface function allows the client to push values on the stack instead of first stuffing them into other structures. In general, the client will always execute more instructions to set up the call, resulting in lower performance. While this may or may not be significant with respect to the execution time of the called function, it is the trade-off of late binding.

The object itself also incurs additional overhead because it receives its parameters through DISPPARAMS and VARIANTARG structures. It must not only unpack those parameters from the structures but also perform type checking on each parameter. When function calls are early-bound, the compiler does type checking. In late binding, the object has to enforce types at run time. So not only is there an extra function call to get from *IDispatch-::Invoke* to, in this case, *CBeeper::Beep*, there is more overhead to manage the parameters and the return value.

In general, you will find that accessing a dispinterface that is implemented on an in-process object is anywhere from 5 percent to more than 90 percent slower—depending on the object—than accessing a custom vtable interface that implements the same features. When the object exists in a local server and marshaling is involved, a custom interface is still faster but not as much because the marshaling overhead comes into the picture. Still, is there any way to improve performance, especially for in-process objects?

## The Dual Interface

The way to improve performance for a dispinterface is somehow to cut down the per-call overhead for each property and method while still preserving the ability to perform late binding. In truth, however, you can't do much to speed up calls to *IDispatch::Invoke*: you still have to create the necessary structures for *Invoke* on the client side, and you still have to perform type checking on the object side.

What is called dual interface isn't as much an improvement on late binding to a dispinterface as it is a technique to combine a dispinterface, which has the *IDispatch* vtable, with the vtable for the equivalent custom interface, where the two share a common implementation of *IUnknown* members. A controller aware of dual interfaces can then choose to access the methods and properties either through *IDispatch::Invoke* or through direct calls to vtable entries, as illustrated in Figure 14-5. With a dual interface, a controller can choose to perform early binding or late binding to improve performance as it deems necessary, especially with in-process objects.

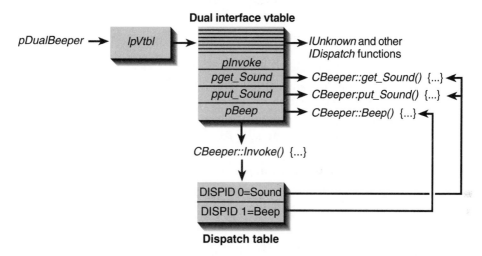

**Figure 14-5.**
*Dual interfaces combine the* IDispatch *vtable with a custom interface, allowing access to methods and properties through either route.*

One benefit of implementing a set of functions as a dual interface for local objects is that OLE provides automatic marshaling of all the functions in the custom vtable portion of the interface. This can occur because OLE will have access to the type information for this interface, as it does for any other dispinterface. Tests show, however, that performance is about the same through the vtable portion of a dual interface as it is for the *IDispatch* portion—the reason is that generic marshaling code, which has to examine type details to determine how to actually marshal each parameter, takes a considerable amount of time. In fact, when making cross-process *IDispatch::Invoke* calls, most of the time is spent in the marshaling code, and OLE employs this same code for all parts of a dual interface. Therefore the performance is about equivalent.

Remember, a straightforward custom interface is still faster than a dispinterface across process boundaries. If performance in such cases is of prime importance to you, a dual interface is not necessarily the best option. The argument and return value types that you can use within a cross-process dispinterface and a dual interface also affect your decision here. These types are limited to what are called *automation-compatible* types, which means you cannot pass arbitrary data structures by reference through these interfaces because OLE's generic marshaling service can handle only a basic set of types. OLE doesn't handle pointers to structures that may contain pointers to other structures, ad infinitum. If you want to pass data structures in this fashion, you should use either custom marshaling or standard marshaling with a custom interface.

## Automation-Compatible Interfaces and Types

When a client packages parameters in VARIANT[ARG] structures to pass to methods and properties through *IDispatch::Invoke*, some proxy and stub must marshal those parameters as well as the return value. Because OLE itself implements the proxy and stub for the *IDispatch* interface, OLE provides the generic marshaling code to handle any VARIANT structure. However, you can store only a limited number of data types in a VARIANT, and this limits the types you can employ through a dispinterface or a dual interface. These types are *int, short, long, boolean, char, wchar_t, float, double, IUnknown \*, IDispatch \**, CY (currency), DATE, BSTR, VARIANT (containing a compatible type), NULL, SCODE, and a Safe Array of any of these types. You can also have a custom *typedef enum <type>* that is the same as an *int*, but the size is also system dependent.

When you limit methods and properties to these types, you have an automation-compatible interface. As we saw in Chapter 3, you can use the *oleautomation* attribute in an ODL to enforce the restrictions listed here.

## Passing Data Structures

Certainly you can pass a lot of useful information when you follow the restrictions for an automation-compatible interface. However, you might want to pass some sort of data structure between processes through a dispinterface or a dual interface without having to provide your own custom interface.

You can accomplish the exchange of structured data through two methods. The first and most common method is to implement another object with *IDispatch* that wraps the data structure and turns each field into a property. For example, suppose I had a structure as follows:

```
typedef struct
    {
    int        Lengthcm;    //Length in centimeters
    int        Radiuscm;    //Top radius in centimeters
    int        Weightg;     //Weight in grams
    COLORREF   Shade;       //Exact color shade
    } PARSNIP;
```

I could then create a dispinterface with each field described as a property:

```
dispinterface DIParsnip
    {
    properties:
        [id(0)]  int     Lengthcm;
        [id(1)]  int     Radiuscm;
        [id(2)]  int     Weightg;
        [id(3)]  long    Shade;
    };
```

Wherever I want to have a PARSNIP * argument[7] to a method in my interface (or as a return value), I can use an *IDispatch* * instead. Whenever I need to access a field in the data structure, I can call *IDispatch::Invoke* with the dispID of the property associated with that field.

One obvious drawback to passing data structures in this manner—especially across process boundaries—is that it is *slow*. It potentially requires a cross-process call for each field in a data structure. For small structures, this generally isn't a problem, but for larger structures or when performance really matters, the faster alternative is to have your original automation object return structures as *IUnknown* pointers so that each pointer refers to an object that also implements *IDataObject* (which can be the automation object itself). Through *IDataObject*, you can provide data structures in their entirety with one call. You might also find it useful to implement a separate data structure object that has both an *IDataObject* implementation for fast access to data and an *IDispatch* implementation for flexible late-bound access to each field. To be really flexible, you could make your *IDispatch* implementation part of a dual interface for in-process objects or also provide a custom interface for local objects.

## Dispinterface, Custom Interface, or Dual Interface?

Now that you understand what dispinterfaces and dual interfaces are in relation to a custom interface, we can look at when you would choose one or the other. In most cases, you will want to implement a dual interface simply because it allows both COM clients (usually written in C, C++, or other compiled languages) and automation controllers (usually interpreted languages that run in a tool such as Visual Basic) to access your functions and data equally. When you have an in-process dual interface, you benefit from both high speed through the custom interface and high flexibility through the

---

7. Based on a part of the winter vegetable stew that I made for dinner last night. Yes, I actually find time to cook, even when writing a book.

late-binding *IDispatch*. When you have an out-of-process object, you benefit from automatic marshaling and can improve performance with a custom proxy/stub implementation. (Although a custom proxy/stub has the risk of *RegisterTypeLib*—and *LoadTypeLib*—overwriting its registry entries, thereby eliminating the performance gain.)

A dual interface, however, has the restrictions imposed by automation compatibility: no data structures (other than implementing another property object), no unsigned arguments, having to use BSTRs, and so on. One alternative is to implement both an *IDispatch* interface and a custom interface without combining them and have the custom interface take advantage of the full range of possible argument types. This allows COM clients to communicate in the best way possible while still allowing automation controllers to access the same stuff but in a less efficient manner.

Picking one interface or the other depends mostly on your target client and the bandwidth you want—as well as on how much time you want to spend in implementation. If you are making a high-speed, in-process object, a custom interface is easiest, but *IDispatch* is somewhat easier when you have to go out-of-process because then you don't have to make a proxy and stub. If each function in the interface executes rapidly, you want to cut down the per-call overhead as much as possible (especially for the in-process case), so you should use a custom interface. If you're implementing a large object hierarchy, however, with perhaps dozens of objects, the additional implementation cost of a custom interface is considerable.

When you take potential clients into consideration, you also have to think about the ease of calling your interfaces, which is again where dual interfaces are nice. Nevertheless, a vtable interface is more easily called from a C/C++ client; a dispinterface is easier from an interpreted automation controller, but it takes a lot longer to process the call.

From a design perspective, the flexibility of an interface is also an important consideration. When you define a custom vtable interface, you carve it in stone. A revision to that interface (which makes a new interface) requires recompilation of clients that want to take advantage of the changes. On the other hand, a dispinterface can almost revise itself at run time by adding new methods and properties as necessary. The cost of modifying the interface is much less. From a client's point of view, you can always count on *IDispatch* being there over time, but old custom interfaces can disappear in a newly updated object. In addition, an object that has methods and properties is more easily expressed through a dispinterface. But a related group of functions, such as those in *IDataObject*, are best expressed through a vtable interface, especially when that group is not expected to change in the future. This is best when you want an interface contract to enforce a rigid standard of some kind, the sort where flexibility is a dirty word. Then there is the design point about late binding vs. early binding, which is, of course, blurred by dual interfaces but is an important consideration nevertheless.

So a plethora of questions must be considered for how you choose which interfaces you want. I can't attempt to answer all the questions that might arise and hope that this short section has given you a good number of strengths and weaknesses of each type of interface. If you're planning on an implementation of a large object hierarchy, you can expect to spend some time with these issues before you come to your final design.

## Outgoing Interfaces and *IDispatch*

Everything we've seen so far regarding *IDispatch* and Automation, along with type information, applies to an object's incoming interface as well as its outgoing interfaces or event sets. As we saw in Chapter 3, interfaces and disp-interfaces listed for a *coclass* in an ODL file can have the *source* attribute, marking that interface as outgoing. An object with one or more outgoing interfaces supports connection points that a client can use to hook up sinks to catch events and notifications.

When an event set is a vtable interface, the object fires the event by calling *Interface::<Event>* through whatever pointers it has been given from its clients. When an event set is a dispinterface, however, the object has to call *IDispatch::Invoke* because each event sink will implement that event set through *IDispatch*. In this case, the object becomes a client of *IDispatch* and must pass the right arguments and parameters, such as DISPPARAMS and LCID. However, because the object itself defined the dispinterface, it already knows exactly which dispIDs correspond to which events as well as the proper argument types. The object, therefore, doesn't have to mess with its own type information and the event sink doesn't have to implement any function in *IDispatch* except *Invoke* and the *IUnknown* members. The relationship is a lot simpler, at least for the object. If a client or a controller wants to be able to handle arbitrary events from arbitrary objects, it has to browse the object's type information in order to find the names and dispIDs of each event as well as the types necessary to correctly understand and coerce the arguments that may accompany those events.

Handling arbitrary events in this manner as a client is a topic for Chapter 24, where we'll look at containers for OLE controls that will want to attach specific code to individual control events. Making calls to dispinterfaces, be it from an automation controller or an object firing events, is the topic of Chapter 15.

# Five Variations on the Theme of Implementing a Simple Automation Object

A few short steps from where I'm writing this chapter sits a piano. I often take breaks and play for a while to let my brain incubate and organize the next stage of writing. It happens that my current practice includes Beethoven's Fifteen Variations with Fugue on a Theme from the Eroïca Symphony, op. 35, and Brahms's Variations and Fugue on a Theme by Handel for Pianoforte, op. 24. Fabulous pieces, but perhaps they have influenced me a bit too much as I've worked on Automation. The samples in this chapter seem to follow a similar pattern: a number of variations (only five of them!) on a theme of a simple automation object, followed by a longer and more complex fugue in the form of an automated version of our dear friend Cosmo. What's scary is that the musical analogy holds better than you might think.

To illustrate a simple automation object, let's fully define the Beeper object used as an example earlier in this chapter. This object, implemented in a DLL, has one property and one method in its incoming interface. Furthermore, we'll support both English and German interfaces in all but the last variation. Our theme is specified as follows:

**Property:** *Sound* (German: *Ton*), a *long* that can be set to 0, 16, 32, 48, or 64, corresponding to the allowable values that can be sent to the *MessageBeep* function.

**Method:** *Beep* (German: *Piep*), takes no arguments (*void*) and returns a *long*, the sound that was played.

 We'll examine five different ways to implement the *IDispatch* interface through which *Sound* and *Beep* can be invoked, progressing as follows. (The name in the parentheses is the directory of the associated sample.)

**Variation I** (BEEPER1) A completely raw and manual implementation of *IDispatch* that supports simultaneous access to the dispinterface in either English or German, with full help in either language. This variation raises an exception if the controller tries to change the *Sound* property to an incorrect value, but it does not have any type information.

**Variation II**   (BEEPER2) A more convenient implementation of *IDispatch* that takes advantage of type information to perform type coercion and name-to-dispID mapping. This variation supports English and German simultaneously and raises exceptions. The exception handling mechanism, however, works only for a single-threaded model.

**Variation III**   (BEEPER3) Solves the single-thread exception problem of Variation II through the error object mechanisms that OLE provides.

**Variation IV**   (BEEPER4) Implements our dispinterface through a dual interface, illustrating the special techniques involved.

**Variation V**   (BEEPER5) A reprise of Variation III that takes advantage of an OLE-provided Standard Dispatch object to free us from having our own *IDispatch* entry points at all. However, this allows us to support only one language.

Beeper2 and Beeper3 will usually be the most common of these implementation techniques because they are the most flexible and are easy to implement (depending on what sort of threading you use). Beeper4 will be the next most common, suitable for when you need more performance. Beeper5 is easier to implement than the others but is restricted to a single language. Lastly, although Beeper1 won't be too useful for most automation objects, it is useful when you need to implement only a simple *IDispatch* interface — to use with an event sink, for example — because you have no need for type information or even for implementing *IDispatch::GetIDsOfNames.* These five techniques will show us the full set of options when it comes to *IDispatch.* Choose the method that makes sense for you.

To let you play these variations, the BEEPTEST\DISPTEST directory in this chapter contains a DispTest/Visual Basic 3 program for thoroughly pummeling each Beeper. BEEPTEST\NEWVB has the same program saved in the format of the next version of Visual Basic. If you want to watch what happens with one of these objects in a controller's source code, you can use the AutoCli sample from Chapter 15, which is written specifically for using a Beeper object.

Before looking at each variation, note that the DLL server code surrounding the object is the same in all of them (with one minor exception for multithreading concerns). The files DBEEPER.CPP and DBEEPER.H contain the standard DLL entry point and exported functions as well as the class factory implementation. The Beeper's CLSID in all cases is {00021125-0000-0000-C000-000000000046}, defined as CLSID_Beeper in INC\BOOKGUID.H. In each sample, the most important files are BEEPER.CPP, BEEPER.H, and the ODL files that are present. BEEPER.CPP contains the implementation of the object in the class *CBeeper*; BEEPER.H contains the definitions; and the ODL files provide type information. *CBeeper* is usually defined as follows in BEEPER.H:

```
class CBeeper : public IUnknown  //Possibly a different base interface
    {
    //Possible friend declarations

    protected:
        ULONG           m_cRef;             //Object reference count
        LPUNKNOWN       m_pUnkOuter;        //Controlling unknown
        PFNDESTROYED    m_pfnDestroy;       //To call on closure


        long            m_lSound;           //Type of sound

        //Some kind of IDispatch implementation pointer and other
        //variables are needed to manage implementation.

    public:
        CBeeper(LPUNKNOWN, PFNDESTROYED);
        ~CBeeper(void);

        BOOL Init(void);

        //Nondelegating object IUnknown
        STDMETHODIMP            QueryInterface(REFIID, PPVOID);
        STDMETHODIMP_(ULONG) AddRef(void);
        STDMETHODIMP_(ULONG) Release(void);

        //Possibly other member functions
    };


typedef CBeeper *PCBeeper;
```

The comments in the code above mark where we'll generally modify for the variations of the object. In all cases, however, the *CBeeper* class has a set of *IUnknown* functions, a reference count, an *m_lSound* value, and the other members shown here.

## Variation I: A Raw Multilingual *IDispatch*

The first technique for implementing *IDispatch* is to implement the entire interface yourself. You process all the arguments to *Invoke* for each method and property, manually implement *GetIDsOfNames*, and implement degenerate *GetTypeInfoCount* and *GetTypeInfo* functions. This *IDispatch* technique involves no type information and requires that the controller call *GetIDsOfNames* to convert names to dispIDs. Of course, this requires the controller to assume that the name exists until the controller tries to invoke the name. If *GetIDsOfNames* fails, the invocation fails. In addition, the controller cannot perform any type or argument checking prior to making a call to *Invoke* and has to pass whatever it has from the script that it's executing. So the controller depends on *Invoke* to return errors if there is a problem. This is, in fact, exactly how Visual Basic 3 and DispTest work: they don't make direct use of an object's type information, and they depend on the object's *IDispatch* to provide dispIDs as well as type checking.

The Beeper1 sample (CHAP14\BEEPER1) implements *IDispatch* in this way and contains no type information. The interface is implemented in a separate class, *CImpIDispatch*, which is defined in BEEPER.H and implemented in BEEPER.CPP. This class maintains a backpointer to the *CBeeper* object and delegates all *IUnknown* calls to *CBeeper's IUnknown* members. *CBeeper* itself instantiates *CImpIDispatch* in the *Init* function, storing the pointer in a field *m_pImpIDispatch*; this pointer is deleted in *CBeeper's* destructor.

### *QueryInterface* Behavior

Take a look at *CBeeper::QueryInterface*:

```
STDMETHODIMP CBeeper::QueryInterface(REFIID riid, PPVOID ppv)
    {
    *ppv=NULL;

    if (IID_IUnknown==riid)
        *ppv=this;

    if (IID_IDispatch==riid || DIID_DIBeeper==riid)
        *ppv=m_pImpIDispatch;

    if (NULL!=*ppv)
        {
        ((LPUNKNOWN)*ppv)->AddRef();
        return NOERROR;
        }

    return ResultFromScode(E_NOINTERFACE);
    }
```

For the most part, this is a typical *QueryInterface* implementation except that it recognizes two IIDs as our *IDispatch* implementation: *IID_IDispatch* and *DIID_DIBeeper*. The latter IID is the one that the Beeper object assigns to its dispinterface, hence the extra *D*s in the name. You can find this IID defined in INC\BOOKGUID.H as *{00021127-0000-0000-C000-000000000046}*. Because an object can implement multiple dispinterfaces, each interface must be available through *QueryInterface* given the specific DIID of that dispinterface. Only one, however, is considered the default dispinterface, and only that one is available through a query for *IID_IDispatch*. Because this Beeper object has only one dispinterface, both IIDs can be used to query for that dispinterface. If Beeper implemented a second interface—something such as *DIID_DITweeter*—we would add only the following line of code to *QueryInterface*:

```
if (DIID_DITweeter==riid)
    *ppv=m_pImpIDispTweeter;
```

Here *m_pImpIDispTweeter* would be a separate *IDispatch* implementation from *m_pImpIDispatch*.

### *IDispatch::GetTypeInfo* and *IDispatch::GetTypeInfoCount*

When an automation object doesn't support type information, implementing *GetTypeInfo* and *GetTypeInfoCount* is a snap:

```
STDMETHODIMP CImpIDispatch::GetTypeInfoCount(UINT *pctInfo)
    {
    *pctInfo=0;
    return NOERROR;
    }


STDMETHODIMP CImpIDispatch::GetTypeInfo(UINT itinfo, LCID lcid
    , ITypeInfo **pptInfo)
    {
    *pptInfo=NULL;
    return ResultFromScode(E_NOTIMPL);
    }
```

Because there's no type information, *GetTypeInfoCount* honestly returns a 0 in the *pctInfo* out-parameters. Because the count is 0, a controller cannot expect *GetTypeInfo* to succeed, and, in fact, our implementation fails here (although according to the out-parameter rules, we have to set the return pointer to NULL anyway).

### IDispatch::GetIDsOfNames

As we learned earlier, *GetIDsOfNames* is used to convert the names of properties and methods, as well as arguments to those methods, to the dispIDs that refer to those elements. *GetIDsOfNames* has the following signature:

```
STDMETHOD IDispatch::GetIDsOfNames(REFIID riid, OLECHAR **rgszNames
    , UINT cNames, LCID lcid, DISPID *rgDispID)
```

Here *riid* must always be *IID_NULL*, *rgszNames* is an array of pointers to the strings to convert to dispIDs, *cNames* indicates the size of the *rgszNames* array, *lcid* is the language to use in translation, and *rgDispID* is an array of dispIDs (of size *cNames* as well) in which this function returns the converted dispIDs.

When *cNames* is 1, this function needs only to convert a method or a property name to a dispID. When *cNames* is greater than 1, the additional names are for arguments to a method. All the Beeper objects in this chapter bother only with the first name because the *Beep* method doesn't have any arguments. In any case, if any name in *rgszNames* cannot be converted, we store DISPID_UNKNOWN in the same position in *rgDispID* and return DISP-_E_UNKNOWNNAME from this function. This way the controller knows which names were unrecognized.

Beeper1's implementation of *GetIDsOfNames* supports both English and German names. More precisely, Beeper1 supports primary German, primary English, and a neutral language, which is the same as English. If any other locale is given in *lcid*, we return DISP_E_UNKNOWNLCID, as required. Otherwise, we iterate through the known method and property names in the appropriate language and look for a match (case insensitive). If one is found, the dispID is stuffed into *rgDispID[0]*, and we return with NOERROR. Otherwise, we return with DISP_E_UNKNOWNNAME. Here's the actual code:

```
STDMETHODIMP CImpIDispatch::GetIDsOfNames(REFIID riid
    , OLECHAR **rgszNames, UINT cNames, LCID lcid, DISPID *rgDispID)
    {
    HRESULT     hr;
    int         i;
    int         idsMin;
    LPTSTR      psz;

    if (IID_NULL!=riid)
        return ResultFromScode(DISP_E_UNKNOWNINTERFACE);
```

*(continued)*

```
//Set up idsMin to the right stringtable in our resources.
switch (PRIMARYLANGID(lcid))
    {
    case LANG_NEUTRAL:
    case LANG_ENGLISH:
        idsMin=IDS_0_NAMESMIN;
        break;

    case LANG_GERMAN:
        idsMin=IDS_7_NAMESMIN;
        break;

    default:
        return ResultFromScode(DISP_E_UNKNOWNLCID);
    }

/*
 * The index in this loop happens to correspond to the DISPIDs
 * for each element and also matches the stringtable entry
 * ordering, where i+idsMin is the string to compare. If we
 * find a match, i is the DISPID to return.
 */
rgDispID[0]=DISPID_UNKNOWN;
hr=ResultFromScode(DISP_E_UNKNOWNNAME);

psz=m_pObj->m_pszScratch;

for (i=0; i < CNAMES; i++)
    {
    LoadString(g_hInst, idsMin+i, psz, 256);
    if (0==lstrcmpi(psz, rgszNames[0]))
        {
        //Found a match; return the DISPID.
        rgDispID[0]=i;
        hr=NOERROR;
        break;
        }
    }

return hr;
}
```

The buffer *m_pszScratch* is a 256-character array preallocated in *CBeeper-::Init*. This improves the performance of *GetIDsOfNames* and reduces the number of error conditions that might occur. The strings for each language are contained in separate stringtables in the DLL's resources, DBEEPER.RC:

```
STRINGTABLE
    BEGIN
        ⋮
        IDS_0_SOUND,                    "Sound"
        IDS_0_BEEP,                     "Beep"
    END

STRINGTABLE
    BEGIN
        ⋮
        IDS_7_SOUND,                    "Ton"
        IDS_7_BEEP,                     "Piep"
    END
```

There are a few other strings in each stringtable for exceptions, as we'll see shortly. The symbols used for the strings also indicate the language so that we can keep them straight.

Now, after the controller translates names into dispIDs (0 for *Sound* and 1 for *Beep*, the same as in other languages), there are no more locale-specific concerns anywhere in this object, as we'll see by looking at *Invoke*.

### IDispatch::Invoke

*Invoke* is the real workhorse of Automation. Because we already know the purpose of all the arguments to this function, let's start with Beeper1's implementation code:

```
STDMETHODIMP CImpIDispatch::Invoke(DISPID dispID, REFIID riid
    , LCID lcid, unsigned short wFlags, DISPPARAMS *pDispParams
    , VARIANT *pVarResult, EXCEPINFO *pExcepInfo, UINT *puArgErr)
    {
    HRESULT        hr;

    //riid is supposed to be IID_NULL always.
    if (IID_NULL!=riid)
        return ResultFromScode(DISP_E_UNKNOWNINTERFACE);

    switch (dispID)
        {
        case PROPERTY_SOUND:
            if (DISPATCH_PROPERTYGET & wFlags
                !! DISPATCH_METHOD & wFlags)
                {
                if (NULL==pVarResult)
                    return ResultFromScode(E_INVALIDARG);
```

*(continued)*

683

```
            VariantInit(pVarResult);
            V_VT(pVarResult)=VT_I4;
            V_I4(pVarResult)=m_pObj->m_lSound;
            return NOERROR;
            }
        else
            {
            //DISPATCH_PROPERTYPUT
            long        lSound;
            int         c;
            VARIANT     vt;

            if (1!=pDispParams->cArgs)
                return ResultFromScode(DISP_E_BADPARAMCOUNT);

            c=pDispParams->cNamedArgs;
            if (1!=c || (1==c && DISPID_PROPERTYPUT
                !=pDispParams->rgdispidNamedArgs[0]))
                return ResultFromScode(DISP_E_PARAMNOTOPTIONAL);

            VariantInit(&vt);
            hr=VariantChangeType(&vt, &pDispParams->rgvarg[0]
                , 0, VT_I4);

            if (FAILED(hr))
                {
                if (NULL!=puArgErr)
                    *puArgErr=0;

                return hr;
                }

            lSound=vt.lVal;

            if (MB_OK!=lSound && MB_ICONEXCLAMATION!=lSound
                && MB_ICONQUESTION!=lSound && MB_ICONHAND!=lSound
                && MB_ICONASTERISK!=lSound)
                {
                if (NULL==pExcepInfo)
                    return ResultFromScode(E_INVALIDARG);

                pExcepInfo->wCode=EXCEPTION_INVALIDSOUND;
                pExcepInfo->scode=
                    (SCODE)MAKELONG(EXCEPTION_INVALIDSOUND
                    , PRIMARYLANGID(lcid));
```

```
                    FillException(pExcepInfo);
                    return ResultFromScode(DISP_E_EXCEPTION);
                    }

                //Everything checks out: save new value.
                m_pObj->m_lSound=lSound;
                }

            break;

        case METHOD_BEEP:
            if (!(DISPATCH_METHOD & wFlags))
                return ResultFromScode(DISP_E_MEMBERNOTFOUND);

            if (0!=pDispParams->cArgs)
                return ResultFromScode(DISP_E_BADPARAMCOUNT);

            MessageBeep((UINT)m_pObj->m_lSound);

            //The result of this method is the sound we played.
            if (NULL!=pVarResult)
                {
                VariantInit(pVarResult);
                V_VT(pVarResult)=VT_I4;
                V_I4(pVarResult)=m_pObj->m_lSound;
                }

            break;

        default:
            ResultFromScode(DISP_E_MEMBERNOTFOUND);
        }

    return NOERROR;
    }
```

One argument we didn't see earlier is *riid*. This must always be IID-_NULL, or else you must return DISP_E_UNKNOWNINTERFACE. In other words, *riid* doesn't do anything for us. When OLE Automation was first being developed, the specifications indicated that the dispinterface ID was passed in this argument to support multiple dispinterfaces. But because you can query for secondary dispinterfaces using a DIID directly, this is not used. It wasn't removed from the specifications because Automation was already in beta at the time of the decision. It was left in and specified as a reserved value that must be IID_NULL.

The next few steps in our implementation are pretty intuitive: check which dispID is being invoked, check and coerce the types, and then attempt to get or put the property or execute the method, raising exceptions if necessary. You should not coerce types in *pDispParams->rgvarg* in place—use a local variable as shown here.

PROPERTY_SOUND, which is defined as dispID 0 (in BEEPER.H), can be invoked with the DISPATCH_PROPERTYGET, DISPATCH_METHOD, or DISPATCH_PROPERTYPUT flag. Because some controllers cannot differentiate a property get from a method call, we have to treat these as equivalent. In either case, we set the return VARIANT in *pVarResult* to contain the current value of *m_lSound*, and we're done. Easy!

To invoke METHOD_BEEP (defined as dispID 1 in BEEPER.H), we need first to ensure that the caller is actually trying to use this dispID as a method. Otherwise, we return DISP_E_MEMBERNOTFOUND. (This is, incidentally, the same error we return for an unrecognized dispID, as is the default case.) We also want to tell the controller that we don't take any parameters. If *pDispParams->cArgs* is nonzero, we fail with DISP_E_BADPARAM-COUNT; otherwise, we pass our *m_lSound* to *MessageBeep* to execute the method, store the sound played in *pVarResult* (just as a property get), and return successful.

With a property put operation, first protect any read-only properties you have, returning DISP_E_MEMBERNOTFOUND. I know this error isn't terribly informative, so it's likely that you'll see a DISP_E_ACCESSDENIED error added to OLE in the near future. You might also raise an exception as described on the following pages.

*Sound* is a writable property, so we first verify that we received one and only one argument in *pDispParams*, that the argument is named, and that the dispID of that argument is DISPID_PROPERTYPUT. If these conditions are not met, we return DISP_E_PARAMNOTOPTIONAL.

Next we attempt to coerce the argument we did get into a *long* because we require the use of *VariantChangeType*. The nice thing about using *VariantChangeType* is that if coercion doesn't work, this function returns the error code that we can return immediately to the controller to describe the error. In the case of an error, we have to specify which argument is in error in *\*puArgErr* before returning. This example has only one argument, so the problem is always with the 0th position argument.

If we get this far, we have the right type of data, but we need to be sure that it is a value we can accept. This sample extracts the argument's value from the VARIANT through a direct dereferencing of *pDispParams->rgvarg[0].lVal*. This works fine for simple arguments. For more complex arguments to method calls, it is advisable to use the helper *DispGetParam* to address each argument by position in the method's argument list and combine the type coercion step. In other words, *DispGetParam* hides the grunge; a call to it would look like the following:

```
VARIANT    vtNew;

hr=DispGetParam(pDispParams, 0, VT_I4, &vtNew, puArgErr));

if (FAILED(hr))
    return hr;

lSound=V_I4(vtnew);    //Same as lSound=vtNew.lVal
```

In any case, we get the new value of the property and compare it against the possible MB_* values that allow for this property. If this checks out, we save the new value in *m_ lSound* and return successful. If the validation fails, we have two choices: either fail *Invoke* trivially (with some useful error such as DISP_E_OVERFLOW or E_INVALIDARG) or raise an exception.

Raising an exception means filling the EXCEPINFO structure that the controller gave us and returning DISP_E_EXCEPTION. If the controller passes a NULL in *pExcepInfo*, you *cannot* raise exceptions and can only fail trivially. Fortunately, even DispTest asks for exception information, as do all versions of Visual Basic. You can choose to fill the exception structure at that time or fill in either the *wCode* or *scode* field and the *pfnDeferredFillIn* field for delayed filling. DispTest and Visual Basic 3 do not support deferred filling, but later versions do. You'll need a better controller than DispTest to try this feature. The code used in this sample to perform such a test is as follows:

```
INITEXCEPINFO(*pExcepInfo);
pExcepInfo->scode=(SCODE)MAKELONG(EXCEPTION_INVALIDSOUND
    , PRIMARYLANGID(lcid));
pExcepInfo->pfnDeferredFillIn=FillException;
```

INITEXCEPINFO is a macro in INC\INOLE.H that clears an EXCEP-INFO structure in one nice tidy line of code.

In both this code fragment and the previous listing of *Invoke*, I'm playing with fire by storing a 16-bit exception code and a 16-bit language ID in the *scode* field because there is no easy way to pass a locale to a deferred filling function. This is risky because I'm using *scode* in an unapproved way—it would be better if I had *Invoke* return different filling functions, depending on the language, or if I defined a set of error codes for each language so that the filling function knew what language to use. In any case, you can take a look at my shortcut lazy man's *FillException* function beginning on the following page.

```c
HRESULT STDAPICALLTYPE FillException(EXCEPINFO *pExcepInfo)
    {
    SCODE       scode;
    LANGID      langID;
    USHORT      wCode;
    HRESULT     hr;
    LPTSTR      psz;
    LPOLESTR    pszHelp;
    UINT        idsSource
    UINT        idsException;

    if (NULL==pExcepInfo)
        return ResultFromScode(E_INVALIDARG);

    /*
     * Parts of our implementation that raise exceptions; put the
     * WORD exception code in the loword of scode and the LANGID
     * in the hiword.
     */
    scode=pExcepInfo->scode;
    langID=HIWORD(scode);
    wCode=LOWORD(scode);

    //Allocate BSTRs for source and description strings.
    psz=(LPTSTR)malloc(1024*sizeof(TCHAR));

    if (NULL==psz)
        return ResultFromScode(E_OUTOFMEMORY);

    hr=NOERROR;

    switch (wCode)
        {
        case EXCEPTION_INVALIDSOUND:
            //Fill in unused information; macro in inole.h.
            INITEXCEPINFO(*pExcepInfo);
            pExcepInfo->wCode=wCode;
            pExcepInfo->dwHelpContext=HID_SOUND_PROPERTY_LIMITATIONS;

            //Set defaults.
            pszHelp=OLETEXT("c:\\inole\\chap14\\beephelp\\beep0000.hlp");
            idsSource=IDS_0_EXCEPTIONSOURCE;
            idsException=IDS_0_EXCEPTIONINVALIDSOUND;

            //Get the localized source and exception strings.
            switch (langID)
```

```
                   {
               case LANG_GERMAN:
                   idsSource=IDS_7_EXCEPTIONSOURCE;
                   idsException=IDS_7_EXCEPTIONINVALIDSOUND;
               pszHelp=OLETEXT("c:\\inole\\chap14\\beephelp\\beep0007.hlp");
                   break;

               case LANG_ENGLISH:
               case LANG_NEUTRAL:
               default:
                   break;
               }

           break;

       default:
           hr=ResultFromScode(E_FAIL);
       }

   if (SUCCEEDED(hr))
       {
       pExcepInfo->bstrHelpFile=SysAllocString(pszHelp);

       LoadString(g_hInst, idsSource, psz, 1024);
       pExcepInfo->bstrSource=SysAllocString(psz);
       LoadString(g_hInst, idsException, psz, 1024);
       pExcepInfo->bstrDescription=SysAllocString(psz);
       }

   free(psz);
   return hr;
   }
```

We store all the information necessary to describe the exception, including a help file, in the EXCEPINFO structure. The source and description strings for each language we support are in the stringtables in DBEEPER.RC:

```
//English
IDS_0_EXCEPTIONSOURCE: "Beeper.Object"
IDS_0_EXCEPTIONINVALIDSOUND: "The 'Sound' property can be set only\
to MB_OK (0), MB_ICONHAND (16), MB_ICONQUESTION (32)\
, MB_ICONEXCLAMATION (48), or MB_ICONASTERISK (64)."

//German
IDS_7_EXCEPTIONSOURCE: "Pieper.Objekt"
IDS_7_EXCEPTIONINVALIDSOUND: "Das 'Ton' Property kann nur die Werte\
MB_OK (0), MB_ICONHAND(16), MB_ICONQUESTION (32)\
, MB_ICONEXCLAMATION (48), oder MB_ICONASTERISK (64) erhalten."
```

Keep in mind that DispTest and Visual Basic 3 (but not later versions) ignore the help file and context ID that you provide through the exception. Controllers that pay attention to these fields will display a Help button in the same message box that displays the exception source and the description string that you also return from here. If the user clicks Help, the controller launches WinHelp with the help file and the context ID to display the correct help topic. If you run Beeper1 with the AutoCli sample from Chapter 15, you can see this working. The BEEPHELP directory in this chapter has the sources for the small help files (English and German) used with this example.

As a final note, an object should generally store only "<filename>.hlp" in *bstrHelpFile*, depending on the HELPDIR registry entry under the object's TypeLib entry to give controllers the installation path of the help files. Because Beeper1 doesn't have type information, there's no registry entry for the directory. Thus, we store the full path, and Chapter 15's AutoCli checks for a path before prepending the HELPDIR value.

## Variation II: Exploit Your Type Information

There has just got to be an easier way to implement *IDispatch::GetIDsOfNames* and *Invoke*, right? The amount of code shown in Variation I for just one property and one method is obnoxious enough—now imagine a complex object with 30 methods and 50 properties! If you don't like 300-page switch statements, it's time to create a type library. In Beeper2 (CHAP14\BEEPER2), the files BEEP0000.ODL and BEEP0007.ODL describe the object's dispinterface in English and German, through use of an interface description. Here's the core of BEEP0000.ODL. (BEEP0007.ODL uses German strings.)

```
[attributes]
library BeeperTypeLibrary
    {
    :

    [attributes]
    interface IBeeper : IUnknown
        {
        //Properties
        [propget, helpstring("The current sound")]
            long Sound(void);

        [propput]
            void Sound([in] long lSound);

        //Methods
        [helpstring("Play the current sound")]
            long Beep(void);
        }
```

```
[attributes]
dispinterface DIBeeper
    {
    interface    IBeeper;
    }

⋮
}
```

In the ODL files, we define the object class, *CLSID_ Beeper*, as implementing the dispinterface *DIBeeper* and the interface *IBeeper*. *DIBeeper* is defined as a dispinterface that obtains its methods and properties from *IBeeper*. *IBeeper* is defined as having a *Sound* (*Ton*) property and a *Beep* (*Piep*) method. The same property name is listed twice: once with *propget* and once with *propput*.

To see why we're doing this, let's look at what happens when we run the MKTYPLIB tool (described in Chapter 3) on one of these ODL files.

## MKTYPLIB and Generated Headers

The most common command line for MKTYPLIB, which is used in the samples for this chapter, is as follows:

```
mktyplib /h <header>.H /l <errors>.LOG /o <library>.TLB <file>.ODL
```

You'll find the batch file MAKELIB in the BUILD directory of the sample code. MAKELIB lets you generate a header, a log, and a type library from a given ODL file; the files created will have the same name as the ODL file.

When you build Beeper2, its make file calls MKTYPLIB for BEEP0000-.ODL with a special command-line switch, */h ibeeper.h,* which instructs MK-TYPLIB to create that header file.[8] The IBEEPER.H output from compiling BEEP0000.ODL is shown in Listing 14-1 beginning on the following page. (This is a built file, so you won't find it on the companion CD until you've actually built Beeper2.) Because the ODL files define an *interface* and a *dispinterface*, the header ends up with two interface definitions. In addition, MKTYPLIB automatically turns whatever *uuid* attributes you defined into DECLARE_GUID statements so that you don't have to define them elsewhere.[9]

---

8. MKTYPLIB is very aggressive when you tell it to create a header with the */h* switch: it will overwrite any existing file of that name without warning.

9. The central INC\BOOKGUID.H file used for all the samples in this book redundantly defines these same GUIDs for use from samples such as Beeper1 and AutoCli (in Chapter 15) that don't use a MKTYPLIB-generated header. To prevent compiling errors, the GUIDs in BOOKGUID.H are conditionally excluded from compiling if the symbol GUIDS_FROM_TYPELIB is defined. This symbol is specific to these samples — it's not anything you'll find documented, and you'll see it defined, for example, in Beeper2's BEEPER.H before Beeper2 includes INOLE.H, which in turn includes BOOKGUID.H.

```
IBEEPER.H
/* This header file machine-generated by mktyplib.exe */
/* Interface to type library: BeeperTypeLibrary */

#ifndef _BeeperTypeLibrary_H_
#define _BeeperTypeLibrary_H_

DEFINE_GUID(LIBID_BeeperTypeLibrary,0x0002115E,0x0000,0x0000,0xC0
    ,0x00,0x00,0x00,0x00,0x00,0x00,0x46);

DEFINE_GUID(IID_IBeeper,0x0002115C,0x0000,0x0000,0xC0,0x00,0x00
    ,0x00,0x00,0x00,0x00,0x46);

/* Definition of interface: IBeeper */
DECLARE_INTERFACE_(IBeeper, IUnknown)
{
#ifndef NO_BASEINTERFACE_FUNCS

    /* IUnknown methods */
    STDMETHOD(QueryInterface)(THIS_ REFIID riid,
        LPVOID FAR* ppvObj) PURE;
    STDMETHOD_(ULONG, AddRef)(THIS) PURE;
    STDMETHOD_(ULONG, Release)(THIS) PURE;
#endif

    /* IBeeper methods */
    STDMETHOD_(long, get_Sound)(THIS) PURE;
    STDMETHOD_(void, put_Sound)(THIS_ long lSound) PURE;
    STDMETHOD_(long, Beep)(THIS) PURE;
};

DEFINE_GUID(DIID_DIBeeper,0x0002115D,0x0000,0x0000,0xC0,0x00
    ,0x00,0x00,0x00,0x00,0x00,0x46);

/* Definition of dispatch interface: DIBeeper */
DECLARE_INTERFACE_(DIBeeper, IDispatch)
{
#ifndef NO_BASEINTERFACE_FUNCS

    /* IUnknown methods */
    STDMETHOD(QueryInterface)(THIS_ REFIID riid
        , LPVOID FAR* ppvObj) PURE;
```

**Listing 14-1.**    *(continued)*

*MKTYPLIB-generated header file from BEEP0000.ODL.*

**Listing 14-1.** *continued*

```
    STDMETHOD_(ULONG, AddRef)(THIS) PURE;
    STDMETHOD_(ULONG, Release)(THIS) PURE;

    /* IDispatch methods */
    STDMETHOD(GetTypeInfoCount)(THIS_ UINT FAR* pctinfo) PURE;

    STDMETHOD(GetTypeInfo)(
      THIS_
      UINT itinfo,
      LCID lcid,
      ITypeInfo FAR* FAR* pptinfo) PURE;

    STDMETHOD(GetIDsOfNames)(
      THIS_
      REFIID riid,
      OLECHAR FAR* FAR* rgszNames,
      UINT cNames,
      LCID lcid,
      DISPID FAR* rgdispid) PURE;

    STDMETHOD(Invoke)(
      THIS_
      DISPID dispidMember,
      REFIID riid,
      LCID lcid,
      WORD wFlags,
      DISPPARAMS FAR* pdispparams,
      VARIANT FAR* pvarResult,
      EXCEPINFO FAR* pexcepinfo,
      UINT FAR* puArgErr) PURE;
#endif

/* Capable of dispatching all methods of interface IBeeper */
};

DEFINE_GUID(CLSID_Beeper,0x0002115B,0x0000,0x0000,0xC0,0x00,0x00
    ,0x00,0x00,0x00,0x00,0x46);

class Beeper;

#endif
```

What we now have in the IBEEPER.H file is the definition of a disp-interface that is nothing more than *IDispatch* and the definition of a custom interface, *IBeeper*, which inherits from *IUnknown*. The functions in *IBeeper*, however, are a bit odd: where did those *get_* and *put_* prefixes come from? In the ODL file, the definition of *IBeeper* listed the *Sound* function twice: one had the *propget* attribute, and the other, *propput*. MKTYPLIB uses these attributes to prepend *get_* or *put_* to the function name to avoid name conflicts. Method names, of course, need no munging.

But now that we have this custom interface, what are we supposed to do with it? The answer requires that we first look at how we actually get our type information into memory and then look at some of the powerful benefits of OLE's *ITypeInfo* implementation.

## Load Your Type Information

We now have type information, so we can implement *IDispatch::GetTypeInfoCount* and *IDispatch::GetTypeInfo*, as shown in Beeper2's BEEPER.CPP file:

```
STDMETHODIMP CImpIDispatch::GetTypeInfoCount(UINT *pctInfo)
    {
    //We implement GetTypeInfo, so return 1.
    *pctInfo=1;
    return NOERROR;
    }


STDMETHODIMP CImpIDispatch::GetTypeInfo(UINT itInfo, LCID lcid
    , ITypeInfo **ppITypeInfo)
    {
    HRESULT      hr;
    ITypeLib    *pITypeLib;
    ITypeInfo  **ppITI=NULL;

    if (0!=itInfo)
        return ResultFromScode(TYPE_E_ELEMENTNOTFOUND);

    if (NULL==ppITypeInfo)
        return ResultFromScode(E_POINTER);

    *ppITypeInfo=NULL;

    switch (PRIMARYLANGID(lcid))
        {
        case LANG_NEUTRAL:
        case LANG_ENGLISH:
            ppITI=&m_pITINeutral;
            break;
```

```
        case LANG_GERMAN:
            ppITI=&m_pITIGerman;
            break;

        default:
            return ResultFromScode(DISP_E_UNKNOWNLCID);
        }

//Load a type lib if we don't have information already.
if (NULL==*ppITI)
    {
    hr=LoadRegTypeLib(LIBID_BeeperTypeLibrary, 1, 0
        , PRIMARYLANGID(lcid), &pITypeLib);

    if (FAILED(hr))
        {
        switch (PRIMARYLANGID(lcid))
            {
            case LANG_NEUTRAL:
            case LANG_ENGLISH:
                hr=LoadTypeLib(OLETEXT("BEEP0000.TLB"), &pITypeLib);
                break;

            case LANG_GERMAN:
                hr=LoadTypeLib(OLETEXT("BEEP0007.TLB"), &pITypeLib);
                break;
            }
        }

    if (FAILED(hr))
        return hr;

    hr=pITypeLib->GetTypeInfoOfGuid(DIID_DIBeeper, ppITI);
    pITypeLib->Release();

    if (FAILED(hr))
        return hr;
    }

(*ppITI)->AddRef();
*ppITypeInfo=*ppITI;
return NOERROR;
}
```

This code is perhaps more convoluted than it really needs to be. It is written so that after we've loaded our type information once, we never have to load it again for this instance of the object. The *CImpIDispatch* class in Beeper2 (BEEPER.H) maintains two *ITypeInfo* pointers in *m_pITINeutral* and *m_pITIGerman*. The *switch* statement in *GetTypeInfo* is used to set *ppITI* to the appropriate *CImpIDispatch* variable (depending on the language), and if that variable is NULL, we have to load the type library.

The easiest way to load a type library is to call *LoadRegTypeLib*, which looks for the LIBID you specify under the TypeLib key in the registry and tries to find an LIBID that matches the version number (in our case, 1.0) and the LANGID you specify (9 for English or 7 for German). It also attempts to load the type library listed for either Win16 or Win32 (as appropriate for the environment). If the file listed is a TLB file, *LoadRegTypeLib* loads it directly. If an EXE[10] or a DLL is listed, it extracts the file from that module's resources. Failing that, it attempts to open the file as a compound file and extract the type library from the "\006typelib" stream. In addition, *LoadRegTypeLib* first looks for an exact match to the LANGID you pass. If that fails, it looks for a match with only the primary LANGID (which we're starting with immediately in this code). If that fails, it looks for LANGID_NEUTRAL (0) as a last resort.

If *LoadRegTypeLib* does fail, we try to load our TLB files directly with *LoadTypeLib* as a backup. This function tries to locate the given type library file in the registered DIR key that you place under your type library registration alongside HELPDIR. (See Chapter 3 for a review.)

If *LoadTypeLib* loads a type library successfully, it automatically creates the proper registry entries for the type library. This is the other reason that using *LoadTypeLib* as a backup to *LoadRegTypeLib* is good practice. If we ever get to *LoadTypeLib*, the next call to *LoadRegTypeLib* will work.

After we load the type library, we have an *ITypeLib* pointer. That's not, however, what we need to return from *IDispatch::GetTypeInfo*; we need instead an *ITypeInfo* pointer that describes our dispinterface. To get this, we must call *ITypeLib::GetTypeInfoOfGUID* passing *DIID_DIBeeper*, the IID of our dispinterface. This returns the *ITypeInfo*, which we save in our own *m_pITI** variable (and, therefore, we call *AddRef*) and return to the controller. Even though we call *ITypeLib::Release*, the type library is still loaded because we have an *ITypeInfo* pointer to the same structure; therefore, we don't need to worry about reloading it later.

---

10. Prior to OLE 2.02 (September 1994), *LoadRegTypeLib* doesn't work properly with an EXE.

## Your Friend: *ITypeInfo*

After you retrieve an *ITypeInfo* pointer for your dispinterface's type information, the implementation of *IDispatch::GetIDsOfNames* becomes considerably easier. Take a look at Beeper2's *GetIDsOfNames*:

```
STDMETHODIMP CImpIDispatch::GetIDsOfNames(REFIID riid
    , OLECHAR **rgszNames, UINT cNames, LCID lcid, DISPID *rgDispID)
    {
    HRESULT     hr;
    ITypeInfo   *pTI;

    if (IID_NULL!=riid)
        return ResultFromScode(DISP_E_UNKNOWNINTERFACE);

    hr=GetTypeInfo(0, lcid, &pTI);

    if (SUCCEEDED(hr))
        {
        hr=DispGetIDsOfNames(pTI, rgszNames, cNames, rgDispID);
        pTI->Release();
        }

    return hr;
    }
```

What happened to matching strings to dispIDs? All that information is contained within our type information, and because we have an *ITypeInfo* pointer to that information (which *GetIDsOfNames* obtains from *GetTypeInfo* in the same *IDispatch*), we can actually ask *ITypeInfo* to do all the work for us. The OLE API function *DispGetIDsOfNames* takes an *ITypeInfo* pointer and the rest of the *GetIDsOfNames* parameters and performs all the necessary mapping. *DispGetIDsOfNames* is, however, nothing more than a trivial wrapper around *ITypeInfo::GetIDsOfNames*:

```
STDAPI DispGetIDsOfNames(ITypeInfo FAR* ptinfo
    , OLECHAR FAR* FAR* rgszNames, unsigned int cNames
    , DISPID FAR* rgdispid)
    {
    return ptinfo->GetIDsOfNames(rgszNames, cNames, rgdispid);
    }
```

You could simply call the *ITypeInfo* function directly and skip the overhead if you wanted. Internally, *ITypeInfo* uses its own member functions to extract the names and attributes of the properties, methods, and arguments in the dispinterface, matching names to *id* values. It's very similar to what we did in Beeper1's manual implementation.

## *ITypeInfo* and Your Custom Interface

If *ITypeInfo::GetIDsOfNames* can do so much for name mapping, can it do as much for our implementation of *Invoke*? Absolutely. In fact, in the implementation of *Invoke* in Beeper1, almost all of the type coercion and argument extraction is generic enough that a central piece of code could perform those steps based on the type information. What a generic function such as *GetIDsOfNames* cannot do, of course, is interpret what to do with the properties and methods. Somehow we have to break out the specific dispinterface code from *Invoke* and structure it so that a central piece of type manipulation code can call it when necessary.

This is the reason why the header file generated by MKTYPLIB defined a custom interface—in our case, *IBeeper*. This interface describes *exactly* those operations that are specific to the dispinterface. Beeper2's definition of *CBeeper* in BEEPER.H actually inherits from the *IBeeper* interface in IBEEP-ER.H, and *CBeeper*'s *QueryInterface* also responds to *IID_IBeeper* as well as *DIID_DIBeeper*. The implementation of the *get_Sound*, *put_Sound*, and *Beep* functions is found in BEEPER.CPP:

```
STDMETHODIMP_(long) CBeeper::get_Sound(void)
    {
    return m_lSound;
    }


STDMETHODIMP_(void) CBeeper::put_Sound(long lSound)
    {
    if (MB_OK!=lSound && MB_ICONEXCLAMATION!=lSound
        && MB_ICONQUESTION!=lSound && MB_ICONHAND!=lSound
        && MB_ICONASTERISK!=lSound)
        {
        m_pImpIDispatch->Exception(EXCEPTION_INVALIDSOUND);
        return;
        }

    m_lSound=lSound;
    return;
    }

STDMETHODIMP_(long) CBeeper::Beep(void)
    {
    MessageBeep((UINT)m_lSound);
    return m_lSound;
    }
```

This is fabulous news! These three simple functions are the only object-specific parts of the listing of *IDispatch::Invoke* that we saw with Beeper1. The rest of it can be handled in a central piece of code. That central piece is *IType-Info::Invoke*, which is trivially wrapped by the OLE API *DispInvoke*, the same as *DispGetIDsOfNames*. The question to answer is, how do we tie our custom *IBeeper* implementation to whatever *ITypeInfo::Invoke* does for us? To do that, let's look at Beeper2's *Invoke*:

```
STDMETHODIMP CImpIDispatch::Invoke(DISPID dispID, REFIID riid
    , LCID lcid, unsigned short wFlags, DISPPARAMS *pDispParams
    , VARIANT *pVarResult, EXCEPINFO *pExcepInfo, UINT *puArgErr)
    {
HRESULT      hr;
ITypeInfo   *pTI;

    if (IID_NULL!=riid)
        return ResultFromScode(DISP_E_UNKNOWNINTERFACE);

    hr=GetTypeInfo(0, lcid, &pTI);

    if (FAILED(hr))
        return hr;

    m_wException=EXCEPTION_NONE;

    //This is exactly what DispInvoke does, so skip the overhead.
    hr=pTI->Invoke((IBeeper *)m_pObj, dispID, wFlags
        , pDispParams, pVarResult, pExcepInfo, puArgErr);

    if (EXCEPTION_NONE!=m_wException)
        {
        pExcepInfo->scode
            =(SCODE)MAKELONG(m_wException, PRIMARYLANGID(lcid));
        FillException(pExcepInfo);
        hr=ResultFromScode(DISP_E_EXCEPTION);
        }

    pTI->Release();
    return hr;
    }
```

As we did for *GetIDsOfNames*, we use our own *GetTypeInfo* to retrieve the *ITypeInfo* pointer we want. When we call *ITypeInfo::Invoke*, the first argument is a pointer to the custom interface from which the dispinterface was defined. In our case, the *m_pObj* variable in *CImpIDispatch* is a backpointer to *CBeeper*. Casting it to *(IBeeper *)* gives us the correct *IBeeper* vtable pointer. After *ITypeInfo::Invoke* performs type coercion and argument extraction, it passes the necessary values to the *CBeeper* members that implement the *Sound* property and the *Beep* method.

Personally, I like the services that *ITypeInfo* provides: they allow you to implement your functionality as a clean custom interface and eliminate the need for all the grungy work of implementing *Invoke* yourself. Not every implementation of *IDispatch*, however, will necessarily use *ITypeInfo*. For example, an event sink that has to respond to an arbitrary event set cannot install a bunch of arbitrary custom interface functions in a vtable at run time simply to get *ITypeInfo* to invoke those functions. It's much easier to implement the event handling code inside *Invoke* manually. There are times and places for both Beeper1 and Beeper2 techniques, which is why I've shown each of them in this chapter.

## Exceptions and *ITypeInfo::Invoke*

You might have noticed that *CBeeper::put_Sound* performs the same argument validation in Beeper2 that it did in Beeper1. In Beeper1, we raised an exception when the wrong value was sent to the *Sound* property, which was easy because the exception occurred inside *Invoke*. But *CBeeper::put_Sound* doesn't have a direct way to return an exception code—the return value of the function is a *void*, as is required for a property put function. How, then, can it raise an exception?

In Beeper2, I've added a function named *Exception* to its *CImpIDispatch* class and a member variable named *m_wException* for the purpose of supporting some kind of exception model that can be used from within the custom interface implementation. Before calling *ITypeInfo::Invoke*, *CImpIDispatch::Invoke* clears exceptions by setting *m_wException* to EXCEPTION_NONE (0). If a function called from within *ITypeInfo::Invoke* wants to raise an exception, it calls *CImpIDispatch::Exception* with the exception code, and *Exception* just stuffs the exception code into *m_wException*. When *ITypeInfo::Invoke* returns, *CImpIDispatch::Invoke* checks for a nonzero *m_wException*. If *CImpIDispatch::Invoke* finds one, it calls our old friend *FillException* (the same function we have in Beeper1, except now we rely on HELPDIR) to fill the EXCEPINFO structure. *Invoke* then returns DISP_E_EXCEPTION. This type of mechanism is necessary because *ITypeInfo::Invoke* has no knowledge of the semantics of our dispinterface, only the syntax.

This solution works well only in a single-threaded operating system, however, or, more appropriately, with a single-threaded controller. This is perfectly acceptable for a Microsoft Windows 3.1 target, but it is not acceptable for a Microsoft Windows NT or Microsoft Windows 95 target, which offers preemptive multitasking. To support multiple threads, we have to maintain some sort of exception code inside *CImpIDispatch* on a per-thread basis. Fortunately, OLE has just the solution—*error objects*.

## Variation III: Exceptions Through Error Objects

A mechanism such as the one used in Beeper2 isn't suitable in a multiple-thread environment. To address this problem, the 32-bit versions of OLE support error objects, standard multithreaded devices for raising exceptions. These devices are also known to the 32-bit versions of *ITypeInfo::Invoke*, so you don't need your own postprocessing after that *Invoke* returns. We'll use the Beeper3 sample (CHAP14\BEEPER3) to demonstrate how to use error objects.

Each error object is basically an EXCEPINFO structure and an IID (of the dispinterface or interface raising the exception) wrapped in the interfaces *ICreateErrorInfo* and *IErrorInfo*. The member functions in *ICreateErrorInfo*—for example, *SetHelpFile*—store a value in the underlying EXCEPINFO structure. The functions in *IErrorInfo*—for example, *GetHelpFile*—retrieve those values, as illustrated in Figure 14-6.

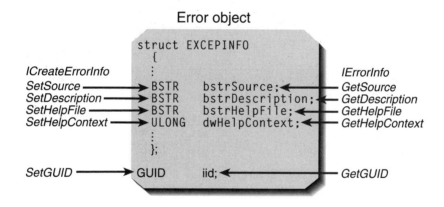

**Figure 14-6.**
*An error object wraps an EXCEPINFO structure and an IID.*

To raise an exception using error objects, you perform the following steps:

1. Before calling *ITypeInfo::Invoke*, call the OLE API function *SetErrorInfo(0L, NULL)* to clear the error object for the current thread. OLE manages a list of error objects on a per-thread basis through this function.

2. When an exception occurs from within a custom interface function called from *ITypeInfo::Invoke*, call *CreateErrorInfo(&pICreateErrorInfo)* to obtain the *ICreateErrorInfo* pointer for a new error object.

3. Call *ICreateErrorInfo* functions to set your exception information in the object.

4. Call *pICreateErrorInfo->QueryInterface(IID_IErrorInfo &pIErrorInfo)* to obtain an *IErrorInfo* pointer that you pass to *SetErrorInfo(0L, pIErrorInfo)*. (This function takes an *IErrorInfo* pointer, not an *ICreateErrorInfo* pointer.) This assigns the error object to the current thread, which releases any previous object.

5. Release both your *IErrorInfo* and your *ICreateErrorInfo* pointer. *SetErrorInfo* will call *AddRef* as required to hold on to the pointer.

6. Return from your custom interface function. *ITypeInfo::Invoke* will then call *GetErrorInfo* to retrieve the *IErrorInfo* pointer for the current thread. If you do not raise an exception, this returns S_FALSE, and *Invoke* proceeds normally. Otherwise, *Invoke* extracts the information in the error object into the EXCEPINFO structure that you were given in your own *IDispatch::Invoke* and returns DISP_E_EXCEPTION.

In Beeper3's *IDispatch* implementation (found in BEEPER3\BEEPER.CPP), we can follow this procedure. First comes the Beeper's *IDispatch::Invoke*:

```
STDMETHODIMP CImpIDispatch::Invoke(DISPID dispID, REFIID riid
    , LCID lcid, unsigned short wFlags, DISPPARAMS *pDispParams
    , VARIANT *pVarResult, EXCEPINFO *pExcepInfo, UINT *puArgErr)
    {
    HRESULT      hr;
    ITypeInfo    *pTI;

    [Code to check for errors and obtain pTI omitted]

    //Clear exceptions.
    SetErrorInfo(0L, NULL);

    hr=pTI->Invoke((IBeeper *)m_pObj, dispID, wFlags
        , pDispParams, pVarResult, pExcepInfo, puArgErr);

    pTI->Release();
    return hr;
    }
```

The implementation of *CBeeper::put_Sound* is the same in Beeper3 as in Beeper2, but the implementation of *CImpIDispatch* is much different because it implements the remaining steps in the preceding list:

```
void CImpIDispatch::Exception(WORD wException)
    {
    HRESULT             hr;
    ICreateErrorInfo    *pICreateErr;
    BOOL                fSuccess;
    LPTSTR              psz;
    LPOLESTR            pszHelp;
    UINT                idsSource;
    UINT                idsException;
    DWORD               dwHelpID;

    [Other code omitted]

    //Not much we can do if this fails.
    if (FAILED(CreateErrorInfo(&pICreateErr)))
        return;

    psz=(LPTSTR)malloc(1024*sizeof(TCHAR));

    if (NULL==psz)
        {
        pICreateErr->Release();
        return;
        }

    fSuccess=FALSE;

    switch (wException)
        {
        case EXCEPTION_INVALIDSOUND:
            pICreateErr->SetGUID(DIID_DIBeeper);
            dwHelpID=HID_SOUND_PROPERTY_LIMITATIONS;

            pszHelp=OLETEXT("beep0000.hlp");
            idsSource=IDS_0_EXCEPTIONSOURCE;
            idsException=IDS_0_EXCEPTIONINVALIDSOUND;

            switch (langID)
                {
                case LANG_GERMAN:
                    idsSource=IDS_7_EXCEPTIONSOURCE;
                    idsException=IDS_7_EXCEPTIONINVALIDSOUND;
                    pszHelp=OLETEXT("beep0007.hlp");
                    break;
```

*(continued)*

703

```
                        case LANG_ENGLISH:
                        case LANG_NEUTRAL:
                        default:
                            break;
                        }

                    fSuccess=TRUE;
                    break;

                default:
                    break;
                }


        if (fSuccess)
            {
            IErrorInfo *pIErr;

            pICreateErr->SetHelpFile(pszHelp);
            pICreateErr->SetHelpContext(dwHelpID);

            LoadString(g_hInst, idsSource, psz, 1024);
            pICreateErr->SetSource(psz);

            LoadString(g_hInst, idsDescri, psz, 1024);
            pICreateErr->SetDescription(psz);

            hr=pICreateErr->QueryInterface(IID_IErrorInfo
                , (PPVOID)&pIErr);

            if (SUCCEEDED(hr))
                {
                SetErrorInfo(0L, pIErr);
                pIErr->Release();
                }
            }

        free(psz);

        pICreateErr->Release();
        return;
        }
```

This is all quite similar to the exception filling functions we've already seen. The only difference is in how we set the EXCEPINFO fields.

## Localized Error Objects

If you have a sharp eye, you might have caught an ambiguity in the implementation of the *Exception* function. Where does that little *langID* value come from? It's not listed anywhere, yet I use it to determine the language in which to report the error information.

The source of *langID* is the *lcid* parameter in *CImpIDispatch::Invoke*—that's the only function that receives it during an invocation. Somehow we have to get that value from *Invoke* to *Exception*. We could use a member variable in *CImpIDispatch*, but that would make our whole implementation unsuitable for multiple threads—which is exactly what we are trying to avoid by doing this fancy error object stuff in the first place!

Because error objects are used primarily on Win32 platforms, we can take advantage of what is known as *thread-local storage* (TLS). TLS allows us to attach a pointer to a thread so that the system maintains one pointer per thread, just as OLE maintains one error object per thread. In order to use TLS, we have to obtain a TLS index with the Win32 API function *TlsAlloc*. This occurs, along with the reverse step, *TlsFree*, in the Beeper DLL's entry point found in DBEEPER.CPP:

```
DWORD        g_dwTLS;         //For thread-local storage

BOOL WINAPI LibMain32(HINSTANCE hInstance, ULONG ulReason
    , LPVOID pvReserved)
    {
    g_hInst=hInstance;

    if (DLL_PROCESS_DETACH==ulReason)
        {
        TlsFree(g_dwTLS);
        return TRUE;
        }
    else
        {
        if (DLL_PROCESS_ATTACH!=ulReason)
            return TRUE;

        g_dwTLS=TlsAlloc();
        }

    return TRUE;
    }
```

The TLS index is stored in the global variable *g_dwTLS*, which is declared as an extern in Beeper3's BEEPER.CPP file. This gives us the means to assign a pointer to the thread by calling *TlsSetValue* and to retrieve that pointer elsewhere by calling *TlsGetValue*. Both functions take the index as the first parameter. So to communicate the LANGID from *Invoke* to *Exception*, *Invoke* declares a LANGID on the stack (which is already thread-local), saves the language from *lcid* in it, and assigns its pointer to the thread:

```
STDMETHODIMP CImpIDispatch::Invoke(...)
    {
    ⋮
    LANGID        langID=PRIMARYLANGID(lcid);

    TlsSetValue(g_dwTLS, &langID);
    ⋮
    }
```

Inside *Exception*, we can then retrieve the same value that is currently on *Invoke*'s stack, which is where we get the right *langID* value:

```
void CImpIDispatch::Exception(WORD wException)
    {
    ⋮
    LANGID              langID=LANG_NEUTRAL;
    LANGID              *pLangID;

    pLangID=(LANGID *)TlsGetValue(g_dwTLS);

    if (NULL!=pLangID)
        langID=*pLangID;

    ⋮
    }
```

No magic—just straightforward multithreaded Win32 programming!

### The *ISupportErrorInfo* Interface

One final piece of the error object framework that I have not mentioned yet is the *ISupportErrorInfo* interface, which lets an object say, "Hey, I support error objects!" You implement this interface on the same object as *IDispatch* and your custom interface.[11] It has a single function (besides *IUnknown*) named

---

11. Older documentation is *very* misleading on this point. It mentions that this interface is put on the same object as *IErrorInfo*, but you don't implement that interface on your automation object! It should say that the interface goes alongside *IDispatch*.

*InterfaceSupportsErrorInfo.* This function gives the consumer of a thread's error object—for example, *ITypeInfo::Invoke* or a controller itself—a way to check whether the interface that's being called uses error objects to report exceptions. In other words, you can use this function to determine whether *GetErrorInfo* will return something meaningful or just plain trash—such as an exception raised long ago by something else in the same thread. *ITypeInfo::Invoke* should call *QueryInterface* for *IID_ISupportErrorInfo* through your custom interface pointer (the first argument to *ITypeInfo::Invoke*, remember?) and then call *InterfaceSupportsErrorInfo* with the dispinterface IID. If either step fails, *Invoke* should not call *GetErrorInfo*.[12]

In any case, Beeper3 implements this interface on its *CBeeper* object using the class *CImpISupportErrorInfo*—which is about as degenerate as you can get. The real core of this interface—its singular interesting member function—is very simple to implement:

```
STDMETHODIMP CImpISupportErrorInfo::InterfaceSupportsErrorInfo
    (REFIID riid)
    {
    if (DIID_DIBeeper==riid)
        return NOERROR;

    return ResultFromScode(S_FALSE);
    }
```

## Variation IV: A Dual Interface

Both Beeper2 and Beeper3 have a dispinterface and a custom interface that provide exactly the same methods and properties. It makes sense to combine them into a dual interface, which we'll do in the Beeper4 sample (CHAP14-\BEEPER4).

For the most part, we make a dual interface by pulling the *IDispatch* member functions that are part of *CImpIDispatch* in the previous Beepers and making them part of *CBeeper* along with all the *IBeeper* functions. (This includes pulling *Exception* straight from Beeper3 with all the TLS handling intact.) Most of the code in Beeper4's BEEPER.H file looks the same, but it's been reorganized a little and is slightly different in a few ways as well.

---

12. At the time of writing, *ITypeInfo::Invoke* never asks for this interface, let alone calls it: *Invoke* simply calls *GetErrorObject*, which could potentially report bogus exceptions if you don't call *SetErrorObject(0L, NULL)* and if something else in your thread calls *SetErrorObject* at some point with other garbage.

The first trick with a dual interface is to define the beast in your ODL file. This step is a little more concise than defining an interface and a disp-interface separately, as shown in the following:

```
[Attributes]
library BeeperTypeLibrary
    {
    ⋮

    [..., dual]
    interface IBeeper : IDispatch
        {
        //Properties
        [propget, helpstring("The current sound")]
            HRESULT Sound([out, retval] long *plSound);

        [propput]
            HRESULT Sound([in] long lSound);

        //Methods
        [helpstring("Play the current sound")]
            HRESULT Beep([out, retval] long *plSoundPlayed);
        }

    ⋮
    }
```

The interesting feature of a dual interface is that it is a custom interface and a dispinterface at the same time because the dual interface is polymorphic with *IDispatch*. You'll also notice that our *coclass* refers only to *IBeeper* now because *DIBeeper* no longer exists.

In making *IBeeper* a dual interface, however, the most significant change is that all of the member functions are now required to return an HRESULT for OLE's automatic marshaling support to work properly. This means that for methods and property get functions to return a value, they have to declare an extra argument with the attributes *out* and *retval*, which becomes, in effect, the actual return value. The *retval* attribute can apply to only one argument, of course, because it implies a return value from a property or a method.

The function signatures in your ODL file will also end up in a header generated by MKTYPLIB, so the implementations of your custom interface functions will change as well. These are minor changes, however, as you can see in Beeper4's version of *get_ Sound*, *put_ Sound*, and *Beep*:

```
STDMETHODIMP CBeeper::get_Sound(long *plSound)
    {
    if (NULL==plSound)
        return ResultFromScode(E_POINTER);

    *plSound=m_lSound;
    return NOERROR;
    }

STDMETHODIMP CBeeper::put_Sound(long lSound)
    {
    if (MB_OK!=lSound && MB_ICONEXCLAMATION!=lSound
        && MB_ICONQUESTION!=lSound && MB_ICONHAND!=lSound
        && MB_ICONASTERISK!=lSound)
        {
        Exception(EXCEPTION_INVALIDSOUND);
        return ResultFromScode(DISP_E_EXCEPTION);
        }

    m_lSound=lSound;
    return NOERROR;
    }

STDMETHODIMP CBeeper::Beep(long *plSoundPlayed)
    {
    if (NULL==plSound)
        return ResultFromScode(E_POINTER);

    *plSound=m_lSound;
    MessageBeep((UINT)m_lSound);
    return NOERROR;
    }
```

The only other point to make about dual interfaces is that you might want to improve the performance of the marshaling of the custom portion of the dual interface. To do this, you can create your own proxy/stub object server DLL, as described in Chapter 6, and register that DLL under your dual interface's IID in the Interface section of the registry. You must list *IDispatch*, IID *{00020400-0000-0000-C000-000000000046}*, as your BaseInterface so that OLE will use its own marshaling for the *IDispatch* portion and instantiate your proxy/stub objects for the remaining member functions. And just as a reminder, all dual interfaces must be completely automation compatible. Even if you provide your own proxy/stub objects, the dispinterface portion must always be compatible.

## Variation V: The Standard Dispatch

All of our variations on the Beeper object so far have supported both English and German. If you don't need to support more than one language in an automation object, you can simplify your implementation even more by completely eliminating your own *IDispatch* entry points, as demonstrated in the Beeper5 sample, which is English-only (CHAP14\BEEPER5).

This is made possible through a standard implementation of *IDispatch* that OLE provides through the function *CreateStdDispatch*. This function creates an object on which your own object must aggregate, as you learned in Chapter 2. In other words, the standard dispatch object provides only an *IDispatch* interface, and in order for it to provide the correct behavior through its *IUnknown* functions, it has to know about your object—the outer object.

The standard dispatch object supports only one locale because you have to pass a language-specific *ITypeInfo* pointer to *CreateStdDispatch*, so this is the only language that the object will recognize. If you need to support multiple languages from within a single instance of an object, it is best to stick with implementing *IDispatch* using *ITypeInfo*'s help. This doesn't mean that you can make only a binary that supports a single language with *CreateStdDispatch*; it's just that each instance will be fixed for a particular language, and at creation time you do not yet know which language the controller will ask for later. But if you want to support only a neutral language or the user's local language, *CreateStdDispatch* is a great convenience.

Some documentation says that the standard dispatch object doesn't support custom exceptions, the kind of exceptions we've been raising in the last few variations. With the advent of the error object feature, this is no longer true. Internally, the standard dispatch looks about the same as the *IDispatch* in Beeper3 except that it doesn't handle multiple locales in *GetTypeInfo*. But it still uses *ITypeInfo::Invoke*, which in turn looks for an error object, so you can support exceptions now when using the standard dispatch object.

I got on a cleaning binge when I removed the *CImpIDispatch* class from Beeper5, so I also got rid of all the exception handling code to keep Beeper5 as simple as possible. What is left to show is how we create the standard dispatch object and how we have to modify *CBeeper::QueryInterface*. The rest of the implementation is the same as for Beepers 2 and 3, using an implementation of *IBeeper* (although *put_ Sound* no longer raises exceptions).

To call *CreateStdDispatch*, as we do in *CBeeper::Init*, we must first have a pointer to the correct *ITypeInfo*, which we obtain using code similar to what we used in our *IDispatch::GetTypeInfo*:

```
BOOL CBeeper::Init(void)
    {
    LPUNKNOWN         pIUnknown=this;
    ITypeLib          *pITypeLib;
    HRESULT           hr;

    if (NULL!=m_pUnkOuter)
        pIUnknown=m_pUnkOuter;

    if (FAILED(LoadRegTypeLib(LIBID_BeeperTypeLibrary, 1, 0
        , LANG_NEUTRAL, &pITypeLib)))
        {
        if (FAILED(LoadTypeLib(OLETEXT("BEEP0000.TLB"), &pITypeLib)))
            return FALSE;
        }

    hr=pITypeLib->GetTypeInfoOfGuid(IID_IBeeper, &m_pITINeutral);
    pITypeLib->Release();

    if (FAILED(hr))
        return FALSE;

    hr=CreateStdDispatch(pIUnknown, (IBeeper *)this, m_pITINeutral
        , &m_pIUnkStdDisp);

    if (FAILED(hr))
        return FALSE;

    return TRUE;
    }
```

You'll see that *CreateStdDispatch* also takes a pointer to our controlling unknown—our custom interface (which in turn is given to *ITypeInfo-::Invoke*)—and always returns an *IUnknown* pointer. This last point is true because our Beeper object aggregates the *IDispatch* interface from the standard dispatch object. According to the aggregation rules, a newly created object in an aggregate must return an *IUnknown* pointer initially.

This *IUnknown* pointer is then used in the implementation of *Query-Interface* as follows:

```
STDMETHODIMP CBeeper::QueryInterface(REFIID riid, PPVOID ppv)
    {
    *ppv=NULL;

    if (IID_IUnknown==riid)
        *ppv=this;
```

*(continued)*

```
    if (IID_IDispatch==riid || IID_IBeeper==riid)
        return m_pIUnkStdDisp->QueryInterface(IID_IDispatch, ppv);

    if (NULL!=*ppv)
        {
        ((LPUNKNOWN)*ppv)->AddRef();
        return NOERROR;
        }

    return ResultFromScode(E_NOINTERFACE);
    }
```

You might be slightly surprised to know that *CreateStdDispatch* also works with a dual interface implementation. The standard dispatch object still implements *IDispatch* for you, although in having a dual interface you'll still have your own set of *IDispatch* entry points. Those entry points, however, need do nothing more than delegate the call to the standard dispatch's *IDispatch*, which you query for from the *IUnknown* returned from *CreateStdDispatch*. After you obtain this pointer, you should release that original *IUnknown* to keep your outer object's reference count correct.

# Fugue: Automating an Application

Now that we've thoroughly pureed *IDispatch* to a smooth consistency with only a simple dispinterface, let's see how to apply what we know to something more complicated and create automation interfaces for an entire application. As an example, we'll automate the version of Cosmo from Chapter 12 (so we don't need to worry about drag and drop). I won't carry these additions forward into later chapters, however, to keep those samples cleaner and to avoid having to continually add new properties and methods to the dispinterfaces as we add new features to Cosmo.

Like most other major features of an application, adding support for OLE Automation involves both design and implementation work. Because this book primarily covers mechanisms and implementation details, it won't provide a detailed account of design. The material presented here is to give you a head start in your own work.

## Design of an Object Hierarchy

When you add complete OLE Automation support to an application, you're doing more than making a single object with a few properties and methods, as we've been doing with the Beeper variations. Instead, you're trying to fully describe the functionality, features, and capabilities of your application through programmatic interfaces.

Your user interface is a good place to start your design because it already describes the capabilities of your application as well as how users access those capabilities. Much of what you try to accomplish in automating an application is to allow people to write macro scripts in an automation controller that can drive your application. It makes good sense to design your automation objects and interfaces to provide the same conceptual model as your user interface. So, for example, if you have an object that represents the application as a whole, you should be able to tell that application programmatically to change the position of a window, the window's visibility, or the contents of the status line or caption bar. You can see already that through a programmatic interface, you can provide a way to affect elements of the application for which there might not be a user interface. Windows doesn't offer an element by which a user can change a caption bar directly, but it's easy to provide the capability through a programmatic interface.

Analyzing your application and breaking it into objects of different sorts results in some kind of *object hierarchy,* or what some might call an *object model.* There are plenty of academic methodologies for object-oriented analysis that easily apply to formulating your object hierarchy. No matter how you find the objects you want to expose, each object will represent some functionality and some content or information. Naturally the functionality maps well to methods and the content to properties. Some of the methods and properties might be restricted or hidden (such as methods named with a leading underscore—for example, _NewEnum); others might be intended primarily for the eyes of a developer or an end user. With the richness of ODL, you can describe detailed and complex object hierarchies.

Your object hierarchy will also invariably involve collections. For example, an MDI application should have a documents collection that manages the group of singular document objects. This is simply a way of programmatically exposing the functionality of the MDI client window and the MDI child window. So just as you ask the MDI client window to create an MDI child, so too will you ask a documents collection to perform a task with a document object. The relationship between a document, a documents collection, and the application object in which all of these are contained generally forms the basic automation model for applications. The *OLE Programmer's Reference* has a chapter on standards and guidelines for document-centric applications.

You should understand that *document* is used here as a generic term to describe whatever your application uses as a file or an individual entity of data (a spreadsheet, a presentation, a drawing, and so on). When naming objects, you do not have to use *Document* at all—Cosmo, for example, uses *Figure* for the document-level object and *Figures* for the collection of figure objects. Use names that are appropriate and that will be most meaningful to the target users of your objects. That is what is most important in all of this.

The next sections describe OLE's guidelines for document-centric applications. These are intended primarily for user interfaces. If you have a single-document interface or an application that is generally not user interactive, many of these guidelines will not be that useful or important to you, and your design will be basically an object hierarchy with a lot of truly custom dispinterfaces. But if the functionality or content you want to expose matches a standard method or property in these guidelines, you are encouraged to conform to them. Don't forget, however, that they are just guidelines and are not enforced in any way.

One topic you might find missing in most of the guidelines is security; only one standard method for opening a file takes a password argument. This means that the design of security is up to you. You can enforce a password on many function calls or have a security checkpoint function that has to be called before any other method or property succeeds. You can enable security in many ways, but the guidelines themselves don't deal with these issues.

Before looking at the details, let's cover some concerns with the naming of objects, properties, methods (and events), arguments, constants, and enumerations. Keep in mind that all of these names (including arguments when the controller supports named arguments) will generally be visible to developers and end users alike. Because of that, keep names as whole, readable, and grammatically correct as possible. For example, use *application* instead of *app*, *document* instead of *doc*, *window* instead of *wnd*. If you must abbreviate, you can use shorter names sparingly to keep the length of the name at a reasonable size, using whole syllables as much as possible. You should also use mixed case names without underscores, such as *ActiveDocument* rather than *activeDocument*, *Active_Document*, *Activedocument*, or, horror of horrors, AC-TIVEDOCUMENT. In addition, match the names in your automation interfaces to the names a user will be familiar with in your visible user interface. This can only enhance a user's understanding. Finally, remember that these names are important only in your type information—internally you can use whatever names you want.

## A Basic Automation Hierarchy

Many current applications operate through the MDI interface that Windows provides, so the basic standards for an automation object hierarchy were written assuming that model: one application object, one or more documents collection objects, and any number of document objects, as illustrated in Figure 14-7. Obviously, if you have a single-document interface, you can merge the capabilities of the documents collection into the application object because there is no need to manage a group of one document. In cases in which you also have different collections of different document types within the same application, you can have multiple collections. OLE Automation defines a few standard properties and methods for each type of object shown in Figure 14-7.

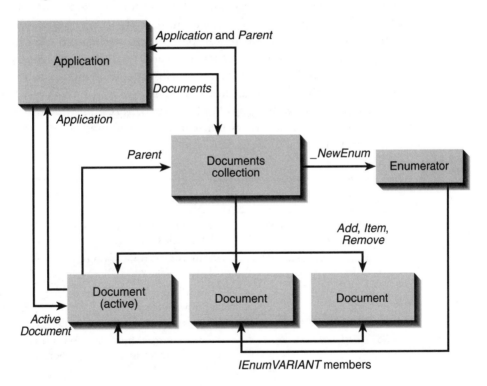

**Figure 14-7.**
*The basic MDI object hierarchy, including the application and document levels.*

All objects in an application hierarchy of this sort support two basic read-only properties: *Application* and *Parent*, both of which are *IDispatch* pointers. *Application* is the way to navigate from any object in the hierarchy back to the top, to the application object. *Parent* is the way to navigate from one object up to the next level. Obviously, for an object such as a documents collection, *Parent* and *Application* are the same thing. The only object for which these properties make little sense is the application object. You might want to provide them for consistency, in which case the application object just returns itself.

**The application object**    This object represents what you can do with the application's frame window and also provides the means to navigate down the object hierarchy shown in Figure 14-7. It is also the object through which a controller can access any sort of global state variables in the entire hierarchy. In an ODL file, this object should be given the *appobject* attribute to mark it with this special role. The recommended properties for an application object are shown in Table 14-2; the recommended methods are shown in Table 14-3. You'll notice that most of the properties have to do with either window position or the name, caption, or default path of the application. The methods are few; the most important ones are *Help* and *Quit.* Probably the foremost element of the whole set is the *Documents* property (which can be named more appropriately for your application, as in *Figures*), which allows the controller to navigate to other objects where the interesting functionality lies. The *ActiveDocument* property (which can also be named differently) is the next most important.

| Property | Description |
|---|---|
| [read-only] *IDispatch* * *ActiveDocument* | The *IDispatch* of the active document object, or VT_EMPTY if none. |
| [read-only] *IDispatch* * *Application* | Returns the application object. |
| *BSTR Caption* | Sets or returns the title of the application window. Setting the caption to VT_EMPTY returns control to the application. |
| *BSTR DefaultFilePath* | Sets or returns the default path specification used by the application for opening files. |

**Table 14-2.**                                                                              *(continued)*

*Guidelines for application object properties. Properties not marked* [read-only] *can be modified from a controller. Note that* Name *is the default property with DISPID_VALUE.*

**Table 14-2.** *continued*

| Property | Description |
|---|---|
| [read-only] *IDispatch * Documents* | Returns the documents collection object. |
| [read-only] *BSTR FullName* | Returns the full path of the application EXE, as in C:\INOLE\CHAP14\COSMO14.EXE. |
| [read-only] *BSTR Path* | Returns the path of the application's EXE, as in C:\INOLE\CHAP14. |
| [read-only] *BSTR Name* | (Default property: DISPID_VALUE.) Returns the name of the application — for example, "Cosmo Chapter 14". |
| *boolean Interactive* | Sets or returns whether the application accepts actions from the user regardless of visibility. |
| *boolean Visible* | Sets or returns whether the application is visible to the user. |
| *BSTR StatusBar* | Sets or returns the text displayed in the application's status bar. |
| *long Left* | Distance between the left edge of the screen and the left edge of the application window. Setting this property moves the window (as does setting *Width*, *Top*, and *Height*). |
| *long Width* | Width of the application window, including all borders. |
| *long Top* | Distance between the top of the screen and the top edge of the application window. |
| *long Height* | Height of the application window, including borders, menu, caption, and so on. |

| Method | Description |
|---|---|
| *void Help([optional] BSTR HelpFile, [optional] long HelpContext, [optional] BSTR HelpString)* | Displays help information for the application. If *HelpFile* and *HelpContext* are given, the application launches WinHelp. The help string is another way of specifying the context, in addition to *HelpContext*. |

**Table 14-3.** *(continued)*
*Guidelines for application object methods.*

**Table 14-3.** *continued*

| Method | Description |
|---|---|
| *void Quit(void)* | Terminates the application, closing all documents. If the user has taken control of the application while it is being driven programmatically, this method must be ignored. Otherwise, you face the possibility that the user has independently created a new document through your user interface, in which case the user must now close the document and the application manually. |
| *void Repeat(void)* | Repeats the previous action in the user interface. This method can be part of a document object instead if you want. |
| *void Undo(void)* | Reverses the previous action in the user interface. This method can be part of a document object instead if you want. |

**The documents collection object**   Earlier in this chapter, we saw some basic requirements for a generic collection object. These are summarized in Table 14-4. In addition to the *Parent* and *Application* properties, OLE defines a few standards for collections of documents, as described in Table 14-5 on page 720. The default member, DISPID_VALUE, is the *Item* method in all cases so that a piece of controller code such as *Collection(index)* can be used in place of *Collection.Item(index)*.

| Method/Property | Description |
|---|---|
| [read-only] *long Count* | The number of items in the collection. |
| Property: [read-only] *IUnknown * _ NewEnum* Method: *IUnknown * _ NewEnum(void)* | Returns the *IEnumVARIANT* enumerator for the collection. (Older OLE documentation incorrectly states the return value here as *IDispatch *, which enumerators do not implement. The correct return type is *IUnknown *.) |

**Table 14-4.**                                                                    *(continued)*
*Guidelines for generic collection objects.*

**Table 14-4.** *continued*

| Method/Property | Description |
|---|---|
| *<type> Add(void)*<br>or *void Add(<type>)* | Adds a new item to the collection. If the item cannot exist outside the collection, the collection itself should create the item and return its value (first syntax). For example, adding a new object will return that object's *IDispatch* pointer. If the item can exist separately, the collection simply maintains it in the group (calling *AddRef* for *IUnknown* or *IDispatch* items) but does not create it or destroy it. In this case, the item's value is an argument to *Add*, and the method itself has either no return value or a *boolean* to indicate success or failure. |
| *IDispatch * Item([optional] long Index, [optional] BSTR Name)* | Returns the item identified by its ordered position (*Index*) or its name (*Name*). Both arguments are optional. *Item* can also take a VARIANT to support both types with one argument. If no argument is given, returns the documents collection pointer itself. |
| *void Remove(<index>)* | Removes an item from the collection; *<index>* is the same argument list as for *Item*. For items that cannot exist outside the collection, this also destroys the item. If the item is another object, that object should support some sort of *Close* or *Destroy* method in lieu of the collection supporting *Remove*.<br><br>*Remove* takes out of the list any item that exists outside the collection, calling *Release* for *IUnknown* or *IDispatch* pointer items. |

You'll notice that a collection's methods vary slightly if the items in the collection can or cannot exist outside the collection. In some cases, the collection creates the items within it, thus acting as the only way to create the items. This means that the items can exist only as part of the collection and not outside it. If the items in the collection are objects themselves, the collection should not support *Remove* but should depend instead on a *Close* or a *Destroy* method in the subordinate object. A document object in a documents collection is such an example. For nonobject items, which by virtue of not being objects have no methods, the collection should support *Remove*. Older

| Method/Property | Description |
|---|---|
| *IDispatch * Add(void)* | Creates a new hidden document and adds it to the collection, returning that document's *IDispatch*. |
| *(Remove)* | Should not be part of a collection; instead, the document object should support a *Close* method. |
| *void Close([optional] boolean AskSave)* | Closes all documents in the collection, optionally prompting the user to save changed documents. |
| *IDispatch * Open(BSTR File, [optional] BSTR Password)* | Opens an existing document and adds it to the collection, returning the document object's *IDispatch* pointer (or VT_EMPTY on error). |
| *IDispatch * Item([optional] long Index, [optional] BSTR Name)* | Same as a generic collection's *Item* except that *Name* identifies the document filename rather than a generic name. |

**Table 14-5.**
*Additional guidelines for documents collection objects.*

OLE documentation is unclear on this point because it assumes that a collection contains other objects, when in fact a collection can contain anything you can enumerate with a VARIANT.

**The document object**  In the context of the OLE guidelines shown in Tables 14-6 and 14-7, the document object is the richest object of them all, which you would expect because a document is where most of the action takes place within an application. Again, *document* is used generically to describe a child window with meaningful stuff—it doesn't have to contain text or whatever else you might associate with a document.

A note about method names: if you try working with an automated application using DispTest or Visual Basic 3, these controllers might complain about the use of the *Print* and *Close* methods on a document object and the *Close* method on a documents collection. In these controllers, you need to wrap the member name in square brackets—for example, *[Close]* and *[Print]*—to make things work properly.

| Property | Description |
|---|---|
| [read-only] *BSTR FullName* | The full pathname of the document. |
| [read-only] *BSTR Name* | The filename of the document, not including the path. |
| [read-only] *BSTR Path* | Same as *FullName* without *Name*. |
| [read-only] *boolean ReadOnly* | TRUE if the file is read-only; otherwise, FALSE. |
| [read-only] *boolean Saved* | TRUE if the document has not been changed since creation or loading; FALSE if the document is dirty. |
| *boolean Interactive* | Sets or returns whether the application accepts actions from the user regardless of visibility. |
| *boolean Visible* | Sets or returns whether the application is visible to the user. |
| *long Left* | Distance between the left edge of the parent window's client area and the left edge of the document window. Setting this property moves the window (as does setting *Width*, *Top*, and *Height*). |
| *long Width* | Horizontal width of the document window, including all borders. |
| *long Top* | Distance between the top of the parent window's client area and the top edge of the document window. |
| *long Height* | Vertical height of the document window, including borders, caption, and so on. |
| *BSTR Author*<br>*BSTR Comments*<br>*BSTR Keywords*<br>*BSTR Subject*<br>*BSTR Title* | The fields in document summary information. |

**Table 14-6.**

*Guidelines for document object properties.*

| Method | Description |
|---|---|
| *void Activate(void)* | Activates the first window associated with the document. |
| *void Close([optional] boolean SaveChanges, [optional] BSTR File)* | Closes all windows associated with the document and removes the document from the documents collection. *SaveChanges* indicates whether to save changes; *File* indicates the file in which to save those changes. *File* appears only if *SaveChanges* is TRUE. |
| *void NewWindow(void)* | Creates a new window for the document. |
| *void Print([optional] short FromPage, [optional] short ToPage, [optional] short Copies)* | Prints the document from the range of *FromPage* and *ToPage*. *Copies* specifies the number of copies to print. Can also be called *PrintOut*. |
| *void PrintPreview(void)* | Previews the pages and page breaks of the document. Equivalent to choosing Print Preview from the File menu. |
| *void RevertToSaved(void)* | Discards changes to the document and reloads it. |
| *void Save(void)* | Saves changes to the document under the *FullName* property. |
| *void SaveAs(BSTR SaveFile)* | Saves the document's contents to the file specified by *SaveFile*, which might or might not include a path. |

**Table 14-7.**
*Guidelines for document object methods.*

## Cosmo's Automation Hierarchy

The Cosmo example for this chapter (in the COSMO directory) is a sample implementation of the basic hierarchy described in the previous section. The ODL file describing these objects is found in COSMO\COSMO000.ODL.

Cosmo's application object supports the *Application, Caption, FullName, Name, Left, Top, Width, Height, Visible,* and *StatusBar* properties and the *Quit* method, as described in the guidelines. But Cosmo calls these properties *ActiveFigure* and *Figure* instead of *ActiveDocument* and *Documents*; this is more appropriate to the type of information in each document window.

Cosmo's figures collection is the same as the documents collection described earlier, with the *Application, Parent,* and *Count* properties and the *Add, Open, Item,* and *_NewEnum* methods.

Each figure in the collection supports most of the standard document methods and properties, with the exception of *Interactive, Author, Comments, Keywords, Subject, Title, NewWindow, Print,* and *PrintPreview,* mostly because Cosmo doesn't have summary information or printing capabilities. In addition, each figure supports a number of custom properties and methods, shown in Table 14-8, that express the specific functionality for which we're implementing OLE Automation in Cosmo in the first place. You can see from the contents of Table 14-8 that everything you can achieve through Cosmo's user interface is available through this automation interface.

| Property/Method | Description |
| --- | --- |
| [read-only] *short NumberOfPoints* | The number of points in the figure. |
| *long BackColor* | The background color of the figure. |
| *long LineColor* | The line color of the figure. |
| *short LineStyle* | The style of line drawn in the figure (a Windows GDI pen style, PS_*, value). |
| *boolean AddPoint(short x, short y)* | Adds a point to the figure, where $(x,y)$ is expressed on a (32,767, 32,767) grid. Equivalent to a mouse click in the figure window. |
| *void RemovePoint(void)* | Removes the last point added to the figure, equivalent to Cosmo's *Undo* command. |

**Table 14-8.**
*Cosmo's custom properties and methods on a figure object.*

## Deeper Automation Object Hierarchies

Most applications will probably have a deeper object hierarchy than the basic object hierarchy described in the previous sections. An example is illustrated in Figure 14-8 on the following page, in which each document itself has a collection of things (call them objects) and each object can have various rich properties that it makes sense to manipulate as separate objects as well. Rich properties are complex to the extent that they have many subproperties and even their own methods. (Usually they include only properties.) A font property of a title text object on a presentation slide is a good example—in fact, the OLE guidelines spell out some standards for font objects of this kind. A graphical object may have a complex palette object with subproperties.

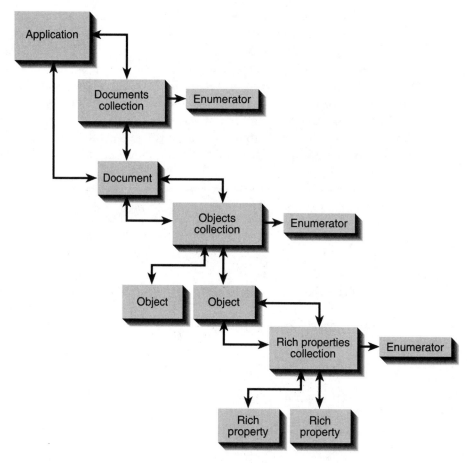

**Figure 14-8.**
*A deeper automation object hierarchy.*

For complex applications such as Microsoft Word and Microsoft Excel, you can easily end up with several dozen or more different objects in the entire hierarchy. Word and Excel, for example, include automation interfaces to their custom macro (WordBasic and Visual Basic for Applications) and dialog box features, meaning that these applications provide quite a complex object hierarchy that includes individual controls that you might have in a custom dialog box. If you do not have such facilities, it is unnecessary to provide interfaces to control elements of predefined dialog boxes—you don't need to allow a user to write a script that would essentially describe placing this or that information in this or that dialog box control unless you wanted to make a really nice CBT system. But for the most part, your automation objects and interfaces should describe the user's intent of driving your application, not the details of each minute operation. This is why a documents collection object has an *Open* method instead of the application having a menu object with an *Open* method that shows the dialog box and gives you an *IDispatch* pointer through which you could get at each individual control and enter the pathname of the file and click OK. The latter would be a ludicrous number of steps just to open a file; the former expresses the user's real intent.

As you might expect, there is a lot of extra code involved in making such a rich set of objects, and the more your application's internal structure reflects that hierarchy, the easier it will be for you to add automation support. Cosmo, for example, had a frame-client-document structure that made it *very* easy and, in fact, noninvasive to add automation support. I implemented this support in two days. Yes, two days, and most of it worked the first time. (Most of what the OLE Automation interfaces did was call member functions of objects that already existed in the application and were already tested.) This is what I mean by noninvasive: I changed almost nothing in Cosmo's existing code—my automation work simply called the code the way an external client would, exactly what I was trying to achieve. The Automation layer is simply providing a standard programmatic way to access Cosmo's functionality.

In your own automation work, the time you spend making a good application architecture will make Automation a lot easier and a lot cleaner and your entire application faster. If you've been waiting for a reason to rework your application's architecture, now is the time. If you're creating a new application from scratch and plan to add support for Automation, be sure that accessibility through Automation is considered in your design from the very early phases of development.

One final note of caution: do not use Microsoft Excel 5 as a model of how to implement arguments to methods and properties. Excel 5, developed at the same time as OLE, uses VARIANTs for absolutely all arguments to properties and methods. A VARIANT is necessary only when you want to support an optional argument or an argument that can take a variety of types. Otherwise, use as specific a type as you see fit. Using VARIANTs everywhere will only add unnecessary code in every property or method implementation.

## Notes on Implementation of Cosmo

As mentioned earlier, the Cosmo sample in this chapter implements a three-level automation object hierarchy: application–figures (collection)–figure. Rather than labor over the code here, take a look at the list beginning on the following page, which details the major points of interest in the implementation. You can look through the source code for all the details.

■ Cosmo's type information is provided only in English in COSMO-000.ODL, although the structure of the code would allow a multilingual version quite easily.

■ The automation objects are implemented by C++ classes named *CAutoApp* (AUTOAPP.CPP), *CAutoFigures* (AUTOFIGS.CPP), and *CAutoFig* (AUTOFIG.CPP). These classes all inherit from the common abstract base class *CAutoBase* (AUTOBASE.CPP), which provides the *IDispatch* and *IExternalConnection* implementations but forces the derived class to implement *IUnknown* members. *IDispatch* is implemented through the technique shown in Beeper2 using *ITypeInfo::Invoke* and other functions; Cosmo does not raise exceptions.

■ Each automation object is attached to one of Cosmo's existing framework classes: *CAutoApp* to *CCosmoFrame*, *CAutoFigures* to *CCosmoClient*, and *CAutoFigure* to *CCosmoDocument*. *CAutoBase* maintains a backpointer from the automation object to the framework object so that the automation implementation can call the various framework member functions to implement the correct automation behavior.

■ Cosmo is registered as the server for two CLSIDs: CLSID_CosmoApplication and CLSID_CosmoFigure. The registry entries for the application object include the */Automation* switch. This switch tells *CCosmoFrame::Init* (COSMO.CPP) whether to register a class factory for CLSID_CosmoApplication on startup: only if the switch is present does a single-use registration happen because that's the only instance in which anyone should ever have access to the class factory. If */Automation* is not present but */Embedding* is, Cosmo was launched to serve an instance of CLSID_CosmoFigure. In this case, Cosmo's main window is hidden until told otherwise (through *CAutoApp::put_Visible* if the caller navigates up through *CAutoFigure::get_Application*). Otherwise, Cosmo is being launched as a standalone. In any launch scenario, Cosmo always registers a multiple-use class factory for CLSID_CosmoFigure.

■ Regardless of how Cosmo is launched, it always instantiates *CAutoApp* on startup and registers it as active (that is, running) with *RegisterActiveObject*. Cosmo removes this registration during shutdown with *RevokeActiveObject*. To control reference-counting problems with active-object registration, Cosmo registers using a strong reference and exposes *IExternalConnection* through *CAutoApp*. (See AUTOBASE.CPP.) This interface simply calls *CAutoApp::Release* when the last external connection goes away. This reverses the *AddRef* from *RegisterActiveObject* and starts shutdown. *CAutoApp* is not destroyed until the *CCosmoFrame* destructor is called, so *RevokeActiveObject* will have no problem calling *Release* itself.

■ A document always instantiates *CAutoFigure* on creation and deletes it on closure. This automation object is also registered with a strong lock with *RegisterActiveObject* and uses the same *IExternalConnection* device to close the document when necessary (just as *CAutoApp* uses it). If Cosmo was launched to create a figure object, the communication from *CAutoFigure::Release* to the *ObjectDestroyed* function in COSMO.CPP initiates full shutdown of the application when the last OLE-controlled document is closed.

■ Both *CAutoApp* and *CAutoFigure* have an additional private member function named *MoveSize*. This function handles all the variations with the *Left, Top, Width,* and *Height* properties.

■ *CAutoFigures* uses a list box of current documents maintained in *CCosmoClient* (through its base class *CClient* in CLASSLIB) to maintain the documents in the collection. The class *CEnumFigures* (AUTOFIGS.CPP) handles enumerations using the copy of this list that it makes when the enumerator is instantiated from *CAutoFigures::_NewEnum*.

■ *CAutoFigures::Item* gives a good example of handling multiple optional arguments because it accepts either no arguments, a *long* index, or a BSTR name of the document to return. *CAutoFigure::Close* is another example of optional arguments.

■ *CAutoFigures::AddPoint*, which adds another point to the figure and repaints it, is implemented by converting the (32,767, 32,767) scaled point to the size of the figure window itself. It then sends the figure (class *CPolyline*, in POLYLINE.CPP and POLYWIN.CPP) a WM_LBUTTONDOWN message with the scaled coordinates in *lParam*. This simulates a user's mouse click exactly, in response to which the figure adds the point to its data and repaints.

■ The only code changes to Cosmo's framework classes that were necessary to support Automation concerned object creation, management, and shutdown. No changes were necessary to implement the member functions of any automation interface. Again, this is utterly noninvasive, made possible by the fact that Cosmo's framework was already structured in a parallel fashion with the automation object hierarchy it exposes.

■ For a non-debug Win32 compilation, the executable increased from 68,608 bytes to 84,432 bytes, an increase of 23 percent. This is roughly the amount of code added to support Automation, but the larger an application and the more complex its functionality, the smaller this percentage will be. In Cosmo, the non-OLE functionality is so simple that another set of objects to access that functionality is a significant addition. If Cosmo were much more complex in terms of internal computation, for example, the percentage would be quite a bit smaller. This measure of Cosmo is possibly the worst-case scenario for code expansion.

If you want to give Cosmo a whirl, you can use test programs in the COSMO-TST directory.

## Optional: Implement *IPersistFile* and Register as Running

You might want to add the *IPersistFile* interface to your document object, associate your file type (through extension or a CLSID in a compound file) with your document object's CLSID, and register a file moniker for any loaded document in the running object table. This allows controllers to access an object that represents the contents of the file instead of a new document, whether or not the document is already loaded. For example, Visual Basic supports an object-creation function that can take a filename as an argument:

```
Dim doc as Object
set doc = CreateObject("sample.doc")
```

The *CreateObject* function takes the filename in the argument, creates a file moniker with it, and then calls that moniker's *BindToObject(IID_ IDispatch)* to get the *IDispatch* pointer for an object that has that document loaded. To support this construct, you have to support the binding action of a file moniker, as we've seen in Chapter 9. This means implementing *IPersistFile* right next to your document's *IDispatch*. Without this sort of support, you would require controllers to first create an instance of your application object, then get the documents collection, and then ask that collection to open the same file:

```
Dim app as Object
Dim doc as Object
set app = CreateObject("Name.Application")
set doc = app.Documents.Open("sample.doc")
```

Granted, this isn't much more code, but it is more confusing to the controller's user because it is much more indirect. Users like to specify their intentions as directly as possible, and getting at a document through the application → collection → document sequence is not as direct as asking for the document in the first place.

When you do load a document, you should create a file moniker for the name with *CreateFileMoniker* and register that moniker along with your document object's *IUnknown* in the running object table. This allows a controller to support some syntax that would allow run-time connection to a running instance. Visual Basic supports this through the *GetObject* function, which creates a moniker based on the arguments given to the function and checks whether that moniker is in the running object table. If so, it connects immediately. If not, it binds that moniker, which will launch your application and work with your *IPersistFile* interface to get the document loaded.

Of course, you might want to support binding to more than just the document as a whole, which involves composite monikers and implementations of other interfaces such as *IOleItemContainer* to support binding to item monikers in the composite. This is great when you have a deep hierarchy. If you have addressable objects within a document, it makes sense to allow a controller to access these objects directly, without having to navigate the hierarchy.

# Summary

OLE Automation is a technology through which a component or an entire application can expose the functionality (methods) and content (individual properties) of any automation objects within it in a late-bound, programmatic manner. Late binding means that method and property names are resolved into dispatch identifiers (dispIDs) at run time and then passed to a function that will invoke the appropriate code for any given dispID. This allows interpreted macro-programming languages and other tools running a script of some sort to access and manipulate objects without having compile-time knowledge of vtable layouts. Such tools, called *automation controllers,* can create objects from any components or applications as necessary, thus enabling end users or developers to write cross-application macros, a longtime user demand.

The core of automation is the dispatch interface, or dispinterface for short, which is a specific implementation of the interface named *IDispatch,* which responds only to certain dispIDs. Through *IDispatch,* a controller can retrieve the object's type information for the dispinterface, map names to dispIDs, and invoke methods and properties. The latter happens through *IDispatch::Invoke.* This function has a fixed compile-time signature by which it can accept any number of arguments for the invocation of a method call, including named and optional arguments. In return, *Invoke* can provide any type of return value as well as rich error information. This chapter explores the nuances of the various arguments of *IDispatch::Invoke* and describes how it works internally.

Arguments and return values handled through *Invoke* use the types VARIANTARG and VARIANT. Both types, which are structurally identical, contain a type identifier (VARTYPE) and a value appropriate to that type, whether it is a pointer, an integer, a string pointer, a date or currency value, and so on. The value is stored in one field of a large union of types within the VARIANT. Two of these types are used frequently in OLE Automation—the BSTR (Basic string) and the Safe Array (an array that carries its bounds with it). OLE provides services to coerce a VARIANT of one type into another, compatible, type if the conversion is at all possible.

An important class of automation object is called a *collection,* which is a grouping of other objects. Collections implement specific methods and properties to navigate their contained elements, including the interface *IEnumVARIANT,* which enumerates those elements.

Making a method call or accessing a property through *IDispatch::Invoke* is a process with a good deal of overhead, which results in much slower performance than the same functionality expressed through a vtable interface. For this reason, OLE Automation defines what is called a *dual interface,* which is a custom vtable interface that derives from *IDispatch.* A dual interface allows a client that can perform vtable binding to call functions in the interface efficiently without losing compatibility with automation controllers that can call only *IDispatch* members. A dual interface comes with the added benefit that OLE Automation provides its own marshaling for both *IDispatch* and custom portions of the interface as long as the interface uses only a limited number of automation-compatible types.

This chapter also examines five different techniques for implementing an automation object: a straight manual implementation of *IDispatch*; an implementation using the service of *ITypeInfo*; one using error objects for rich error reporting; one with a dual interface; and one that employs OLE's standard dispatch object, eliminating the need to have any of your own explicit *IDispatch* entry points.

This is all topped off with a discussion of fully automated applications, including a review of a few design principles, standards, and guidelines for methods and properties. These are applied in a demonstration of how to automate Chapter 12's version of the Cosmo sample.

**C H A P T E R   F I F T E E N**

# OLE Automation
# Controllers and Tools

$V$arious airlines, at least in the United States, pipe the communications between the pilot and the air traffic controller, allowing passengers to listen to their exchanges. Before I listened to one of these exchanges, I never thought of how pilots decide when to reduce speed or altitude on their approach to an airport. When I did listen the first time, I was mildly surprised—mostly from my ignorance of how a pilot and an air traffic controller work together. Every change in the status of the airplane was directed by the air traffic controller, who was keeping track of all the airplanes around that airport and coordinating their approach for landing. The controller in charge is the only person who understands where all the airplanes are, the only person who is aware of the relationship between the planes and of how to keep them from crashing into one another. The pilots of each airplane might be aware of one or two other planes—when visual contact is established—but they are otherwise too busy flying their own machine to think about the big picture.

I was struck most by how the controller would call an order to the pilot of my airplane, the pilot would acknowledge the order, and then I would feel the plane move...all the way to landing. The controller doesn't really know how the pilot moves the airplane; the pilot doesn't know how the controller knows what orders to give. Each of them trusts the other to understand his or her role in landing an airplane safely at a busy airport.

The relationship between an air traffic controller and an airplane pilot is the same as the relationship between an OLE Automation controller—or any client—and an object. The controller understands the big picture and how the objects (the pilots) are integrated into that whole. With that understanding, the controller can send the right commands at the right time to each object involved and keep everything running perfectly. No object is aware of the big picture—each is perhaps aware of only a few other objects—but each otherwise concentrates on making the internals of the encapsulated object (and there's no doubt that an airplane is encapsulated) work smoothly and without error. The controller and the object communicate through a standard interface. With airplanes, it's the specific terminology defined by the Federal Aviation Administration; with OLE, it's the interfaces and dispinterfaces we know and love so well.

This chapter will first look in more detail at the relationship between an automation controller and an object and at how this relationship can affect design decisions for both. We'll then look at the implementation of the AutoCli sample, which illustrates the way a controller calls *IDispatch* functions and handles exceptions. This sample is written specifically to work with the Beeper objects from Chapter 14; it doesn't have a generic language structure in which you can write automation scripts. (A more complex sample, one in which you could write automation scripts, is outside the scope of this book as well as its author.) That won't stop us from looking at the features of a much richer and generic controller, however, and at the ways those features might be implemented using automation objects.

Although half of this chapter is focused on the design and features of tools and other sophisticated controllers, much of what we'll see is relevant to a fair number of objects themselves, especially OLE controls that fire events by calling someone else's *IDispatch* implementation. That is, an object might implement both incoming and outgoing dispinterfaces, so it must know not only how to receive *IDispatch* calls but also how to call them. Even if you don't need outgoing interfaces, you will create the best and most powerful objects when you understand how a controller asks an object to perform various operations. Both sides need to understand the role of the other, just as air traffic controllers and airplane pilots need to understand each other.

# The Controller-Object Relationship

To design both automation objects and controllers well, you need to understand the optimal relationship between them. Knowing that, you can reduce redundant programming as much as possible, which is, after all, the point of any object-oriented relationship.

In general, the design process entails finding the answers to *who, what, why, when, where,* and *how.* Of course, *who* is the question we're trying to answer in looking at the object-controller relationship. The answer to *how* and *where* is the object's domain, *what* it does is expressed in its interfaces, and *when* and *why* those capabilities are used are the controller's domain. Therefore, the common medium between object and controller is what the object can actually do because that will generally determine where it happens and when and why. So as with any design project, you have to start with what you want to accomplish and then decide the best ways of making it happen.

As an example, let's suppose that what we want to accomplish is the capability to draw and view from any angle a square that is transcribed within the equatorial plane of a sphere of a certain radius. It follows that we want to be able to specify rotation and declination of the sphere, which simulates our moving around it, and we want to specify the radius of the sphere, which simulates moving closer to or farther away from it.

The most difficult part of this problem is the transformation of a few three-dimensional points on a sphere into two-dimensional points on a screen. This sounds like a great place to encapsulate that functionality in an object of some kind. We could easily create one function to do this and export the function from a DLL. The function would take a radius, declination, and rotation and pump out four POINT structures. Hardly a reason to create an object—but this design would require the client of the object to manage all the variables. Besides that inconvenience, only programs that knew about our DLL would be able to use this function.

The next best solution would be to make the transformation functionality part of an object in a DLL or an EXE (because we can do EXE-based objects in OLE) and create an interface for it. Depending on our target clients, we might make a custom interface, a dispinterface, or a dual interface. For the purposes of this discussion, let's assume we want a dispinterface. With a dispinterface, we can express functionality and information—that is, methods and properties. A square object, as we might call it, can thus manage all the information necessary to draw itself. This is great because it relieves a client of having to maintain a bunch of related variables separately—by making them part of an object, we enable the client to treat those variables as a related group. So we can give a square object the properties *Radius*, *Declination*, and *Rotation*, each of which could be of type *double* for a high degree of accuracy. The object could also have other properties through which the client could retrieve each point on the basis of the object's current state, or the object could have a method that would return the entire point set at once. Because all the points form a cohesive unit, allowing them to be read in bulk rather than individually is a better design. This eliminates the possibility of the client getting one point, changing a parameter, and then getting another point that is now completely unrelated to the first.

So we've taken care of the problem of computation. We have a design that allows us to specify parameters and to retrieve the calculated points, and the points and parameters together form one object that manages all that information as a single entity. We now have to decide how to turn those points into a visual rendering on the screen. We have two choices as to where on the screen this will happen: in a location of the client's choice (inside its own window) or in the location of the object's choice (inside another window that the object creates). We also have to decide who will actually generate the GDI calls to draw the necessary lines. Here are the possible choices:

- Client draws the lines in its own space.

- Client draws the lines in the object's space.

- Object draws the lines in the object's space.

- Object draws the lines in the client's space.

It should be obvious that the second option is brain-dead because it breaks any notion of object orientation: the object would have certain expectations about the client using it. Bad bad bad. If the object allows the client to retrieve the set of calculated points in bulk, the first option is entirely the client's choice and doesn't affect the design of the relationship we're working on.

That leaves the third and fourth options, and deciding between the two is another major choice. Before we explore these, however, pause a moment to think of when drawing should actually take place in either situation. This should ultimately be the choice of the client—the controller—meaning that the object should provide a method named *Draw* that gives the client a way to tell the object when drawing should happen. This is a better design, I think, than overloading the semantics of the object's *Radius*, *Declination*, and *Rotation* properties to mean "change variable and repaint" instead of simply "change variable." Doing so allows us to change all three variables before drawing actually happens. There are, of course, other ways to accomplish this, for example overloading the properties and providing another Boolean property named *RepaintOnChange*. Either way works.

With a *Draw* method, however, we can specify where the drawing should take place, which allows control over options three and four. Such a method can take an optional *hWnd* argument (which can be shared across process boundaries); its absence means "draw into your own window with whatever scaling you choose," and its presence means "draw into the client area of the specified window." A second optional Boolean argument can control whether the drawing is scaled. (Otherwise, the *Radius* property wouldn't do anything if scaling were always on.) In addition, we'd probably want to specify how the drawing is centered in the window in which it's being drawn—which might require additional method arguments for a center point and an additional *CenterPoint* property.

Besides providing for the first option—the client draws the lines in its own space—it is best that the object can perform the drawing step as well because then it can perform optimizations if it wants, or provide extra features such as shading one side differently from the other so you'll see when the square flips over. Additional properties can let the client manipulate the colors used for the shading, or for drawing the background or the lines.

Are we done now? Possibly. We have an object that does what we set out to do: draw different views of a square inscribed in a sphere. But, of course, creeping featurism, featuritis, or whatever you want to call it, inevitably infects us, and we start to think of additional features. For example, we could make this object support animation; we could tell it to change its rotation and declination at a certain rate every so often and then tell it to start and stop the animation. We'd also want dynamic control over the radius so we could make this rotating and pulsating square appear somewhere on the screen.

We must stop here and ask whether this object is deviating from its original purpose. Adding animation support might sound cool, but adding features creates a bigger, bulkier, and slower object. This doesn't sound like what we want. As far as this simple object is concerned, animation is a feature that spans a single computation or a single rendering, and because of that, the object requires some knowledge of the big picture, some knowledge of why and when—but these are the realm of a controller. Therefore, we should stop the design of this object right here and now and keep it small. Let the controller determine how often and how much to change the parameters; let the object simply manage the current state and draw itself on request. This is the best separation of responsibilities.

You see, what we naturally and very easily slipped into was changing the original specification of the problem we wanted to solve. This is creeping featurism at its finest: stealthy guerrilla warfare. When we thought of adding animation, we had to either change the specification, which means going back to the very beginning of the design process, or state a new problem, write a new specification, and start the process over. In object-oriented design, the latter is the much better choice because we already have a component that knows how to draw the square we want. Our new specification can state the problem as one of creating an animation object that drives a calculation and rendering object that already exists. Trying to modify the original specification would hopelessly intermingle the act of controlling the animation and the acts of drawing and calculating. The problem statement is much easier when we rely on an object we've already built—that is, reusability—than when we decide to go back and redesign everything.

So the end design involves a simple calculation and rendering object (which itself could be broken into two pieces, mind you) that can be driven from any controller. We also have a value-added animation object that is itself a controller for the calculation and rendering object but that can also be driven by another controller. End users can choose which object to use depending on what they want to accomplish: if they want static views, the smaller object is best. If they want animation, the larger object is best. In each case, the user gets to choose the right object for the job, depending on the interfaces through which those objects expose their features. The larger the object, the more likely that it will have a higher-level set of interfaces that will be more appropriate for less skilled end users.

As a demonstration of the ideas discussed in this section, you can play around with the SphereSquare sample object (CHAP15\SQUARE), which implements the features described here, and use the DispTest/Visual Basic controller script (CHAP15\VBSQUARE) to drive that object. We won't look at SphereSquare in this chapter in any more detail—I merely include it for your own exploration.

The point of this exercise is to show that the design of objects and controllers is not haphazard and that objects that expose functionality and content —through OLE Automation, for example—can themselves be controllers of other objects. How you design a controller depends greatly on who you believe will use that tool and what sort of components will be most applicable for those users to integrate with that tool. So let's look at the sorts of features that controllers generally implement, and then we can look at the technical details that make it all work.

## Features of Automation Controllers

Writing a simple controller is mostly a matter of calling the *IDispatch* members correctly. We'll cover this in "Calling *IDispatch*: A Simple Automation Client" later in this chapter. However, a controller that actually allows an end user to write, run, and debug a script needs to be more sophisticated. Features that sophisticated controllers generally have include the following:

- Syntax structures that express property gets and puts, method calls (required, optional, and named arguments), and object creation and destruction in whatever programming language your controller supports

- User interface for browsing and creating automation objects

- Type information browsing—the ability to look at the capabilities of an object before and after creation

■ Compiling of a script into an executable, optimized for execution speed

The following two sections discuss the first two of these features; the last two features are primarily centered on type information we discussed in Chapter 3. Now is a good time to review that material. The type library (*ITypeLib*) and type information (*ITypeInfo*) objects that OLE can provide for any type library resource provide the browsing capabilities, and the act of compiling a script involves *ITypeComp*.

The information in these sections is intended to give you ideas—not to be a design primer or anything that precise. These are simply the things you'll want to think about that have direct correlation to the technical parts of OLE Automation.

## Language Integration: Syntax Structures

If you are planning to create a general purpose automation controller that allows a user to write a script to drive objects, you'll need code structures or other such commands to identify the following operations:

■ Object creation: A way to identify an object class and create an instance of it. Ideally, the class identification is tied as closely as possible to the CLSID. Storing the name in the registry as the value of the CLSID is a good technique for doing this. Sometimes, however, these names are unwieldy, so another choice—albeit a less precise one—is to identify a class using the ProgID or Version-IndependentProgID. Another way to find a class is by specifying a filename that is associated with the class. In this case, the object creation sequence is really meant to get at the document object that has loaded the contents of that file.

As an example, Visual Basic has an instrinsic function, *GetObject*, that takes either a ProgID—as in "Cosmo.Figure"—or a filename such as "C:\INOLE\CHAP14\COSMO\TEST\SAMP1.COS" and creates the object. In both cases, the information given is mapped to a CLSID and is passed to *CoCreateInstance*; in the latter case, the controller should create a file moniker with the name and bind to it, asking for *IDispatch* (which will launch the server, load the file, and so on, as we saw in Chapter 9). It is nice that users don't need to see CLSIDs. If you provide a user interface through which the user can specify the object to create (see the next section), the user doesn't have to type in any code.

■ Object destruction: A way for the user to say, "This object is no longer needed," which internally calls the object's *Release* function followed by *CoFreeUnusedLibraries* if wanted. In Visual Basic, the expression *Set doc = nothing* accomplishes this for the object referenced by the *doc* variable, as does letting a local variable go out of scope.

■ Connect to an active object: Some function or command that ties into the *GetActiveObject* API function that we saw in Chapter 14. *GetActiveObject* itself works only on a CLSID, but that doesn't mean you are limited to working with running objects based only on classes. Because the active object capability in OLE uses the running object table, you can support connecting to objects of any kind as long as you can create a moniker for that object and check for that moniker in the running object table. In Visual Basic, for example, the *GetObject* command can take either a pathname to a file or a classname (the ProgID), the same as its *CreateObject* function. If you specify a ProgID, Visual Basic uses the *GetActiveObject* function. If you specify a filename, Visual Basic creates a file moniker from that name and binds that file moniker. If the document is already loaded somewhere, the binding process will find it in the running object table and connect to it immediately. Otherwise, binding launches the application that can load the document, just as an object creation process would do.

You do not have to stop with the idea of binding to a running document—if you want to support additional syntax, you can allow the user to create a composite moniker by specifying additional information, such as a filename and one or more item names. When you bind the moniker successfully, you'll get an interface pointer to a portion of the document. This works very well in deeper object hierarchies, as described in "Design of an Object Hierarchy" in Chapter 14.

■ Set a property: This should happen whenever an *Object::Property* reference is on the *left* side of an expression, as in *Cosmo.LineStyle = 3*. How your language expresses the *Object::Property* relationship is up to you. Visual Basic uses the dot operator, as we've seen, but there's nothing sacred about it. You could use *::* or *->* or *( )* or *[ ]* or *{ }* or whatever else you want, as long as it's consistent and fits the programming language of the controller. A controller can also support any number of array indices with a property set.

■ Get a property: This should happen whenever an *Object::Property* reference is on the *right* side of an expression, as in *curStyle = Cosmo- .LineStyle*. As with a property put, you have a choice over how the

738

user expresses the *Object::Property* relationship, and you will probably want to include some sort of array index operator as well.

■ Call a method with arguments (possibly optional and named): Method calls are always on the *right* side of an expression, which makes them similar to property get operations. This is why some languages, Basic being one of them, cannot differentiate between property get operations and method calls. In Visual Basic, for example, *Object.Property* has the same syntax as *Object.Method* when the method has no arguments and has a return value. In any case, a method is always on the right side of an expression even when used alone: *Object.Method* is the same as *temp=Object.Method* without requiring the *temp* variable.

Your language must allow the user to express optional arguments as well as named arguments. A language such as Basic is good with optional arguments: if they're in the script, send those values to the object; if not, send empty arguments. Other languages may be more precise about the specification of such options. As far as named arguments are concerned, you must allow the user to specify the name and assign some value to it, as in *Name=value, Name:=value, Name:Value*, or whatever syntax best suits your language.

■ Event sinks: Assign script code to the events that an object might fire, using the object's type information to find outgoing interfaces and displaying the functions in those interfaces. The user can then specify actions to perform when those events occur through additional script or code.

■ *QueryInterface*: Include a way for a user to write a script that exploits the idea of multiple interfaces on an object. As we saw in Chapter 14, an object can have multiple dispinterfaces as easily as it can have multiple vtable interfaces. Providing the capability for a script to create a *QueryInterface* call to an object is as important here for robust evolution of functionality as it is anywhere else in OLE. In short, the script should be able to test the existence of functionality before attempting to execute that functionality.

With some sort of syntactical convention for each of these eight operations, you'll allow a user to fully exploit an object's interfaces, incoming and outgoing, through *IDispatch* and even through custom interfaces. There is also the possibility of creating controllers that have a graphically based programming environment, but even these have some way of expressing these operations and object-to-object relationships.

## User Interface for Object Browsing and Creation

As described in the previous section, controllers with programming languages should support some sort of syntax through which a user can give a "create this object" command. Although this works, it is not by any means the only way to create an object.

As we'll see in the chapters about OLE Documents and OLE Controls, there are basic dialog box standards through which container applications (controllers of a different nature) present the user with a list of available compound document objects or controls. When the user selects a control, for example, he or she can then draw a rectangle on the container's form that the control will occupy. The container then creates the initial control in that rectangle, holding on to whatever pointers are necessary. (Visual Basic 3 works with VBX controls; later versions of Visual Basic work with OLE controls.) The user then assigns to that control object a container-managed name, which is used to refer to the control in the container's source code. Whenever the container executes a script that contains references to the object's name, it knows which interface pointers to use. This eliminates the need for a user to write the tedious code to create and position objects. However, this doesn't mean a user might not want to create an object at some other time for temporary use—you can support this sort of automatic object creation in addition to a language syntax for the same thing.

In the same way that OLE Documents and OLE Controls object selection dialog boxes use the Insertable and Control registry keys, automation controllers can try to use something like the Programmable key to search for objects that implement *IDispatch*. (As I mentioned in Chapter 14, this key is not actually documented in OLE, but I recommend it for automation objects so controllers can identify specific objects that support automation using only registry information.)[1] Browsing the registry in this way allows the user to see what's there without having to find a ProgID in some other way. The same sort of dialog box might also allow the user to browse for names of document files and use those names in object creation as well. Even if you don't use a dialog box in this manner to automatically create objects, a dialog box is still useful for determining the argument for a command such as Visual Basic's *CreateObject*. (Visual Basic 3 doesn't actually do this, but it would be nice if you didn't have to hunt for ProgIDs.)

---

1. A further note about a *Programmable* key: controllers that decide to use this key and ship after other known servers have shipped can add the *Programmable* key to the registry entries for known servers without harm. This is because the servers and anything else that doesn't know about the key will ignore it entirely. This is one way a controller can create a new user interface and bring existing servers into that interface.

# Calling *IDispatch*: A Simple Automation Client

After reading Chapter 14, you should already understand much of what a controller will do when it calls an object's automation interfaces. Here we can take a look at this topic from the controller's point of view. First we'll examine the initialization steps involved in creating the object, loading an LCID, retrieving its type information, and finding the object's help directory. Then we'll look at calling the *IDispatch* member functions *GetIDsOfNames* and *Invoke*. We won't deal with type information because that is outside the scope of this sample. Calling *IDispatch* functions means that we're dealing with a dispinterface but not the custom part of a dual interface. To call the latter, either we'd hard code the vtable offsets by including the IBEEPER.H file from the Beeper4 sample in Chapter 14, or we'd have to manually build the correct stack frame based on type information. We'll look at a process such as this later, but it is not demonstrated by a sample program in this book. Finally we'll look at how a controller handles exceptions that come back from *IDispatch::Invoke*.

The AutoCli sample discussed here (CHAP15\AUTOCLI) will work with the dispinterface of any of the Beeper object variations in Chapter 14. The only parts that AutoCli does not exercise are the custom portion of the dual interface of Beeper4 and the *IProvideClassInfo* implementation of Beeper5. In any case, be sure to create the proper registry entries for each Beeper object using the REG files included with each of those samples before attempting to run AutoCli with them.

For whatever Beeper variation is used, AutoCli displays the same menu commands as shown in Figure 15-1. These commands allow you to get the value of the *Sound* property, set that property to its legal values, set *Sound* to a bogus value to generate an exception, and call the object's *Beep* method. AutoCli also displays the return value of a property get or a call to *Beep* in its client area as well as any error codes that come back, such as DISP_E_EXCEPTION.

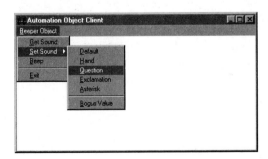

**Figure 15-1.**
*AutoCli and its menu structure.*

## MFC's *COleDispatchDriver*

One thing you will notice in this section is that it takes considerable C or C++ code to make any call or to access a property through *IDispatch::Invoke*. Tools such as Visual Basic hide much of the complexity by providing a simpler language structure that translates into *IDispatch* calls. For controllers written in C++, the Microsoft Foundation Classes provide a class called *COleDispatchDriver* that makes *IDispatch* calls just as easy. Instead of having to fill all the structures to call *IDispatch::Invoke* yourself, you can pass arguments to members of this class on the stack. In other words, *COleDispatchDriver* can make calling members of a dispinterface as simple as calling members of a custom interface, where MFC does the dirty work of filling all the structures required by *Invoke*.

## Initialization

At some point in executing a script, a controller will have to create the automation object that it wants to drive. This usually happens through *CoCreateInstance*, but it might occur through other means, such as binding a file moniker. For whatever reason, the controller will want to obtain information about the object and its environment for use when invoking methods and properties.

AutoCli instantiates the currently installed Beeper object during startup (after calling *CoInitialize*, of course). This example is somewhat contrived—AutoCli runs one script, which creates the object on startup, invokes methods and properties based on menu selections, and then destroys the object on shutdown. Controllers that are programming tools will generally create, manipulate, and destroy objects while running a script. Other controllers might perform the same action in response to various user commands. No matter how the controller is designed, it must create the object at some point, as AutoCli does in *CApp::Init* (AUTOCLI.CPP):

```
hr=CoCreateInstance(CLSID_Beeper, NULL, CLSCTX_INPROC_SERVER
    , IID_IDispatch, (PPVOID)&m_pIDispatch);
```

If this call fails, AutoCli displays a message and terminates. Obviously, this isn't the most friendly way for an application to behave, but because AutoCli cannot continue without a Beeper, it is appropriate here. A more general purpose controller would encounter this sort of error only when trying to execute a script, in which case it would inform the user of the error and perhaps give possible solutions to the problem.

After successfully creating the object, AutoCli loads the object's HELP-DIR value from its TypeLib registry entries. (This is the directory in which the object installed any help files that might be named in an exception.) The *HelpDirFromCLSID* function accomplishes this; it is written to be a stand-alone piece of code that you can cut and paste.

```
void HelpDirFromCLSID(CLSID clsID, LPTSTR pszPath)
    {
    TCHAR      szCLSID[80];
    TCHAR      szKey[512];
    UINT       cch;
    long       lRet;

    if (NULL==pszPath)
        return;

    *pszPath=0;

    cch=sizeof(szCLSID)/sizeof(TCHAR);
    StringFromGUID2(clsID, szCLSID, cch);
    wsprintf(szKey, TEXT("CLSID\\%s\\TypeLib"), szCLSID);

    //Get LIBID from under CLSID.
    if (ERROR_SUCCESS==RegQueryValue(HKEY_CLASSES_ROOT, szKey
        , szCLSID, &lRet))
        {
        //Get HELPDIR from under TypeLib.
        wsprintf(szKey, TEXT("TypeLib\\%s\\HELPDIR"), szCLSID);
        RegQueryValue(HKEY_CLASSES_ROOT, szKey, pszPath, &lRet);
        }

    return;
    }
```

In your own code, you'll probably want the object's type information, at least for its dispinterface. Although AutoCli doesn't demonstrate this, a quick call to *IDispatch* will get you the *ITypeInfo* you want:

```
ITypeInfo *pITypeInfoDispInt;
UINT       cTypeInfo;

if (SUCCEEDED(pIDispatch->GetTypeInfoCount(&cTypeInfo)))
    pIDispatch->GetTypeInfo(0, lcid, &pITypeInfoDispInt);
```

If you want to get the object's type information for the purpose of looking at both its incoming and outgoing interfaces, you can try using the *IProvideClassInfo* interface:

```
IProvideClassInfo    *pIPCI;
ITypeInfo            *pITypeInfoObject;

if (SUCCEEDED(pIDispatch->QueryInterface(IID_IProvideClassInfo
    , (void**)&pIPCI)))
    {
    pIPCI->GetClassInfo(&pITypeInfoObject);
    pIPCI->Release();
    }
```

Another alternative is to use *ITypeInfo::GetContainingTypeLib* and *ITypeInfo::GetTypeInfoOfGUID*, which would look like the following, assuming you have *pITypeInfoDispInt* from the code above:

```
ITypeLib     *pITypeLib;
ITypeInfo    *pITypeInfoObject;

if (SUCCEEDED(pITypeInfoDispInt->GetContainingTypeLib(&pITypeLib, 0)))
    {
    pITypeLib->GetTypeInfoOfGUID(CLSID_Beeper, &pITypeInfoObject);
    pITypeLib->Release();
    }
```

There is one more little snag: in the previous call to *IDispatch::GetTypeInfo* is that little *lcid* parameter. We need a locale to pass to most of the *IDispatch* functions, especially *GetIDsOfNames*. With AutoCli, we always use basic English with LANGID_ENGLISH and SUBLANGID_NEUTRAL. The LCID for this is stored in the variable *m_lcid* in the application's constructor, *CApp::CApp*, and is passed later to *IDispatch* members.

AutoCli uses English because the method and property names that it employs elsewhere are hard-coded for English. Obviously, this isn't the best solution for a general purpose controller.

A better solution is to load the current user language with *GetUserDefaultLCID*. This is best for creating new scripts for the controllers; the user probably wants to work in his or her national language whenever possible. You might also want to allow some way for the user—who may be a developer—to specify the use of a neutral language, especially if that person is writing a script that is expected to be executed in different countries using different languages.

In either case, when a controller saves a script, it should also save the LCID under which a script was written because it is likely that the names of methods and properties saved in that script are also expressed in that language. This would allow the controller running under a different language to check whether type information for the original language is available when the script is loaded—a much better solution than telling the user that a name cannot be resolved at run time because it's in the wrong language (which isn't necessarily known at run time).

Now that we have the information necessary for driving an object, we can invoke the object's methods and properties. When we're finished with the object, we simply call *IDispatch::Release*, and the object takes care of deleting itself and shutting down its application or unloading its DLL as necessary. And when our program shuts down, it calls *CoUninitialize* as usual.

## Call the Dispinterface

While executing an automation script, a controller will get or put properties and call object methods. Which operation is performed depends on how an expression such as *Object.Property* or *Object.Method* is used in the controller's scripting language. A specific controller that drives a specific object (such as AutoCli) may not have a language script, in which case the controller's structure and code determine which operation is used. We'll look at each case in turn, but first we have to know which dispID to send to *Invoke* in order to perform the operation.

### Mapping a Name to a dispID

Mapping the text names (which are used in scripting languages) of methods and properties to a dispID is the first step in late binding to the object's features. There are two ways to accomplish this. The first, demonstrated in AutoCli and also used in DispTest and Visual Basic 3, is to call *IDispatch::GetIDsOfNames* before calling *Invoke*. AutoCli has the function *CApp::NameToID* that performs the lookup:

```
    ⋮
//Elsewhere
hr=pApp->NameToID(OLETEXT("Sound"), &dispID);
    ⋮

HRESULT CApp::NameToID(OLECHAR *pszName, DISPID *pDispID)
    {
    HRESULT    hr;
    TCHAR      szMsg[80];

    hr=m_pIDispatch->GetIDsOfNames(IID_NULL, &pszName, 1
```

*(continued)*

745

```
        , m_lcid, pDispID);

    if (FAILED(hr))
        {
        wsprintf(szMsg
            , TEXT("GetIDsOfNames on '%s' failed with 0x%1X")
            , pszName, hr);
        Message(szMsg);
        }

    return hr;
    }
```

This is about the least efficient way, however, to accomplish the name-to-dispID mapping, especially when an out-of-process object is being used. In that case, it is wasteful to call across the process boundary twice for every property or method invocation.

One optimization would be to load the object's type information yourself (with *LoadRegTypeLib* or *LoadTypeLib*) and use *ITypeInfo::GetIDsOfNames* (which is usually called from within *IDispatch::GetIDsOfNames* anyway, but in the other process).[2] Because the type information would be loaded in your controller's process, you would avoid all the extra cross-process calls, and you could do all this before creating the object. There is no gain in calling *IDispatch::GetTypeInfo* at run time and performing the dispID lookups through the returned *ITypeInfo*—this *ITypeInfo* is itself tied to an out-of-process object, and as a result, you aren't saving anything.

Of course, an object might not have type information (Beeper1 in Chapter 14, for example) for you to load, in which case you have no choice but to call *IDispatch::GetIDsOfNames* after the object has been created, as is done in AutoCli.

With or without type information, there is still one more optimization—instead of mapping the name to a dispID before each call, map all the names in the controller script before execution begins, and keep the dispIDs in a cached table. You will then not only avoid two function calls (potentially across a process boundary) for each invocation, but you will eliminate all redundant calls to *GetIDsOfNames*. Later versions of Visual Basic use this sort of technique to improve run-time performance.

Whichever operation is being performed—property get, property set, or method call—your program ends up with a dispID for the method or

---

2. This technique will not work for *ITypeInfo::Invoke* because you'd need the object's custom interface in order to call the function. The interface might not be exposed and probably would not marshal anyway. So it's not an option.

property being invoked. Let's see how each different operation appears in a call to *IDispatch::Invoke*. In AutoCli, the actual call to *Invoke* happens through *CApp::Invoke*, which centralizes the *IDispatch* call as well as exception handling:

```
HRESULT CApp::Invoke(DISPID dispID, WORD wFlags, DISPPARAMS *pdp
    , VARIANT *pva, EXCEPINFO *pExInfo, UINT *puErr)
    {
    HRESULT    hr;
    ⋮

    if (NULL==m_pIDispatch)
        return ResultFromScode(E_POINTER);

    hr=m_pIDispatch->Invoke(dispID, IID_NULL, m_lcid, wFlags
        , pdp, pva, pExInfo, puErr);

    ⋮
    }
```

This function is called from specific cases within the WM_COMMAND handling code (for the menu items) in *AutoClientWndProc*. This procedure declares as stack variables the various structures that we'll need to make the *Invoke* call:

```
DISPID         dispID, dispIDParam;
DISPPARAMS     dp;
VARIANTARG     va;
EXCEPINFO      exInfo;
UINT           uErr;
HRESULT        hr;
```

Let's look at each *Invoke* case separately.

## A Property Get

Retrieving a property is about the easiest thing for an automation controller to accomplish because it involves no arguments to pass to *Invoke* and is concerned only with the return value of the property:

```
hr=pApp->NameToID(OLETEXT("Sound"), &dispID);

if (FAILED(hr))
    break;

SETNOPARAMS(dp);
hr=pApp->Invoke(dispID, DISPATCH_PROPERTYGET
    , &dp, &va, &exInfo, NULL);
```

In this code, AutoCli is finding the dispID of the *Sound* property (which is why this doesn't work in a language other than English or the neutral language) and passing that dispID to *Invoke* with the flag DISPATCH_PROPERTYGET to identify the operation. The return value comes back in the *va* parameter, in which *va.lVal* will have the sound. (AutoCli makes a string out of this sound and displays that string in its client area.) You'll notice that we must still pass a DISPPARAMS structure to *Invoke* here, but because there are no arguments, the structure is empty. The macro SETNOPARAMS, which you will find in the sample code file INC\INOLE.H, stores the appropriate NULLs and zeros in the structure using a more general macro, which is named SETDISPPARAMS:

```
#define SETDISPPARAMS(dp, numArgs, pvArgs, numNamed, pNamed) \
    {\
    (dp).cArgs=numArgs;\
    (dp).rgvarg=pvArgs;\
    (dp).cNamedArgs=numNamed;\
    (dp).rgdispidNamedArgs=pNamed;\
    }

#define SETNOPARAMS(dp) SETDISPPARAMS(dp, 0, NULL, 0, NULL)
```

These macros are simply a convenient way to save tedious typing. Note that if a property involves indices into an array, the controller can pass those indices in DISPPARAMS as arguments to the property get.

## A Property Put

Setting a property to a new value is a little more complex than retrieving its current value. As we learned in Chapter 14, a controller must pass the new value for the property in a VARIANTARG structure in DISPPARAMS, and that one argument must be named with DISPID_PROPERTYPUT. Functions such as *ITypeInfo::Invoke* will enforce this, returning DISP_E_PARAMNOTFOUND, which is a difficult error to track down. (Additional arguments are allowed if the controller is passing array indices.)

In the following code, AutoCli again finds the dispID for *Sound*, packs up the new sound value—which is either the menu command value itself in *wID* or the value 0—in the *va* variable, puts that VARIANTARG into DISPPARAMS as a VT_I4, sets the rest of the DISPPARAMS structure, and then calls *Invoke*:

```
hr=pApp->NameToID(OLETEXT("Sound"), &dispID);

if (FAILED(hr))
    break;
```

```
VariantInit(&va);
va.vt=VT_I4;
va.lVal=(IDM_SETSOUNDDEFAULT==wID)
    ? 0L : (long)(wID);

dispIDParam=DISPID_PROPERTYPUT;
SETDISPPARAMS(dp, 1, &va, 1, &dispIDParam);

hr=pApp->Invoke(dispID, DISPATCH_PROPERTYPUT
    , &dp, NULL, &exInfo, NULL);
```

You'll notice again that the controller has to set both the *cArgs* and *cNamedArgs* fields in DISPPARAMS to 1 in a property put operation. Also, because a property put has no return value, there is no reason to pass a VARI-ANT to *Invoke* for that purpose, which is why the fourth parameter to *Invoke* here is NULL.

## A Method Call with No Arguments

When AutoCli invokes the *Beep* method, it executes almost exactly the same sequence of steps that were used in the property put case:

```
hr=pApp->NameToID(OLETEXT("Beep"), &dispID);

if (FAILED(hr))
    break;

SETNOPARAMS(dp);
hr=pApp->Invoke(dispID, DISPATCH_METHOD, &dp
    , &va, &exInfo, &uErr);
```

In fact, if we used the dispID for *Sound* here instead of the one for *Beep* and changed the DISPATCH_METHOD flag to DISPATCH_PROPERTY-GET, we'd have the equivalent of a property get. You can see from this why controllers that can't discern a property get from a method invocation have no trouble—they simply get the dispID and pass both DISPATCH-_METHOD and DISPATCH_PROPERTYGET to *Invoke*. Even the return value is the same.

## A Method Call with Arguments

The method call demonstrated in AutoCli is a degenerate one in which the situation is not complicated by those petty annoyances called arguments. Let's look at a hypothetical example of a method call for which arguments are involved. Let's assume we're working with Chapter 14's Cosmo as the automation server and that we want to invoke the *Figure::AddPoint* method, which takes two arguments. The hypothetical automation script the controller is running might have a line such as the following — in this case, we must parse the line and generate the right method call:

```
Figure.AddPoint 15000,43200
```

In parsing this code, we know first that *Figure* refers to a specific *IDispatch* pointer. We then find the name *AddPoint*, and given the dispinterface's type information, we know *AddPoint* is a method. In parsing the remainder of this line, we find two arguments — 15000 and 43200 — that we can assume are of type *short*. For the most part, the actual type is unimportant as long as the object can convert it to the correct type. In this example, we could send *short*, *long*, *float*, *double*, or BSTR types, and the object would probably be able to convert it. This is, of course, the lazy man's controller — the best thing you can actually do is to check the types that are present in the type information and try to match the type of your arguments to what the controller is expecting. That greatly increases the chances that the object will be able to use what you send.

So we have two *short* values that we now need to send to *Invoke*. We allocate two VARIANTARG structures and stuff them into DISPPARAMS:

```
//Assume dispID has "AddPoint" method ID.
//Assume xArg and yArg are the values we have from parsing.

DISPPARAMS     dp;
VARIANTARG     *pva;

pva=/(VARIANTARG*)malloc(sizeof(VARIANTARG)*2);

if (NULL==pva)
    [memory error]

VariantInit(pva[0]);
pva[0].vt=VT_I2;
pva[0].iVal=xArg;
VariantInit(pva[1]);
pva[1].vt=VT_I2;
pva[1].iVal=yArg;

//cArgs=2, cNamesArgs=0
SETDISPPARAMS(dp, 2, pva, 0, NULL);
hr=pFigure->Invoke(dispID, DISPATCH_METHOD, &dp
    , &vaRet, &exInfo, &uErr);

free(pva);
⋮
```

This code demonstrates the steps necessary to call the *AddPoint* method. Most likely a controller that does any kind of language parsing will have a generic function to create the correct argument list from any method signature and would not have specific code written as this is. In any case, this example — although limited — does illustrate passing more than one argument.

You may have a situation in which you need to pass the address of a variable for use as an out-parameter or for any other by-reference passing convention. If you do, the VARIANTARG you create will simply include the VT_BYREF flag and the right pointer value in the correct field of the VARIANTARG union. For example, if we passed *xArg* by reference in the preceding example, we'd set the argument this way:

```
VariantInit(pva[0]);
pva[0].vt=VT_I2 ! VT_BYREF;
pva[0].piVal=&xArg;
```

## A Method Call with Optional Arguments

Calling a method that takes optional arguments requires that you actually send one VARIANTARG to the function for each optional argument. For those arguments that are not present, the VARTYPE must be set to VT_ERROR and the *scode* field must be set to DISP_E_PARAMNOT-FOUND. For example, consider the standard document *Close* method that takes two optional parameters, *SaveChanges* and *SaveFile*. The code that appears in the controller can take one of any three forms, here using Cosmo's Figure object as an example:

```
Figure.Close
Figure.Close (False)
Figure.Close (True, "saveit.cos")
```

Let's assume that we encounter the first form of the call. We know from the object's type information that *Close* takes two optional arguments that we need to supply, but we know from parsing the running script that we have nothing to send it. We need to allocate two VARIANTARG structures anyway and fill them as follows:

```
pva=malloc(sizeof(VARIANTARG)*2);
⋮
VariantInit(pva[0]);
pva[0].vt=VT_ERROR;
pva[0].scode=DISP_E_PARAMNOTFOUND;
VariantInit(pva[1]);
pva[1].vt=VT_ERROR;
pva[1].scode=DISP_E_PARAMNOTFOUND;
```

The object will see these empty arguments and simply perform the default action for *Close*.

If we encounter the second form of the call, we know from parsing the line that we have one argument that we store in, say, *fSave*. We still have to allocate both VARIANTARGs, filling the first with actual data:

```
VariantInit(pva[0]);
pva[0].vt=VT_BOOL;
pva[0].bool=fSave;        //fSave is a variable from parsing.
VariantInit(pva[1]);
pva[1].vt=VT_ERROR;
pva[1].scode=DISP_E_PARAMNOTFOUND;
```

The object will see that it should not save changes in this case and will ignore the second argument because it is irrelevant.

In the third form of the call, our parsing gives us a Boolean (*fSave*) and a string (*pszFile*). To pass the string we have to create a BSTR, which we free ourselves after *Invoke* returns:

```
VariantInit(pva[0]);
pva[0].vt=VT_BOOL;
pva[0].bool=fSave;        //fSave is a variable from parsing.
VariantInit(pva[1]);
pva[1].vt=VT_BSTR;
pva[1].bstrVal=SysAllocString(pszFile);

[Set up DISPPARAMS and call Invoke.]
SysFreeString(pva[1].bstrVal);
⋮
```

## A Method Call with Named Arguments

Dealing with methods that require named arguments is probably the hardest case in all the possible types of method calls because it involves more work with *IDispatch::GetIDsOfNames*. An example of this kind of method was given in Chapter 14, the *FindRockBand* method in the dispinterface of a database-type object:

```
[id(7)] long FindRockBand(int cMembers, BSTR LeadGuitar, BSTR BassGuitar
    , BSTR Percussion)
```

When this line of ODL script was compiled into the object's type information, the arguments were given member IDs of 0, 1, 2, and 3, based on the order listed in the function signature. Now let's imagine a line of code in the automation controller's script in which these named arguments are not necessarily given in the same order:

```
id=Database.FindRockBand(3, BassGuitar="Lee", LeadGuitar="Lifeson"
  , Percussion="Peart")
```

When we call *GetIDsOfNames* to find the dispID for *FindRockBand*, we have to pass the names *BassGuitar*, *LeadGuitar*, and *Percussion* to get their member IDs as well. This makes the call to *GetIDsOfNames* more complicated because you must create an array of string pointers to each name (method and arguments) as well as allocate an array of DISPIDs, one for each method and argument. Then you can retrieve the dispIDs:

```
//Assume we know we have 4 names (1 method, 3 arguments).
LPTSTR  *ppsz;
DISPID  *rgDispID;

ppsz=(DISPID *)malloc(sizeof(LPOLESTR)*cNames);
ppsz[0]=pszMethod;        //Points to "FindRockBand" from parsing
ppsz[1]=pszArg1;          //Points to "BassGuitar," the first parsed
ppsz[2]=pszArg2;          //Points to "LeadGuitar," the second parsed
ppsz[3]=pszArg3;          //Points to "Percussion," the third parsed

pDispID=malloc(sizeof(DISPID)*cNames);
pDatabase->GetIDsOfNames(IID_NULL, ppsz, cNames, lcid, pDispID);
```

On return, the *pDispID* array will contain the numbers 7 (dispID of *FindRockBand*), 2 (member ID of *BassGuitar*), 1 (member ID of *LeadGuitar*), and 3 (member ID of *Percussion*).

When we call *Invoke*, we have to allocate four VARIANTARG structures (three names plus the argument *cMembers*, which will have the value 3) and stuff them into the DISPPARAMS structure. Each string, of course, will have to be allocated as a BSTR. Assuming we've created the argument structures, we will fill DISPPARAMS as follows:

```
dp.cArgs=4;
dp.rgvarg=pva;
dp.cNamedArgs=3;
dp.rgdispidNamedArgs=&(pDispID[1]);  //Skip method name!
```

The object will see that it has been sent named arguments and will use *rgdispIDNamedArgs* to determine which argument is which in the *rgvarg* array. For a controller, this means that you must absolutely match the order of the *rgdispIDNamedArgs* array with the order of VARIANTARG structures in *rgvarg*. Failure to do this will cause, well, mayhem. The order in which the arguments appear in the object's type information and the order in which they appear in the actual running script are both completely irrelevant: all that matters is that you precisely identify which argument is in what element of *rgvarg*.

## Handle Exceptions

Now that you understand the different scenarios for making calls to *IDispatch::Invoke*, we can look at what happens after *Invoke* returns. If a call returns NOERROR, everything worked, and you can use the contents of the VARIANT that contains the value of a property get or the return value of a method call. In addition, you can use whatever values might be contained in out-parameters.

*Invoke*, of course, can return many different errors, for example, DISP_E_TYPEMISMATCH. For any error other than DISP_E_EXCEPTION, you should have the controller display meaningful error messages and give the user guidance as to how to fix the problem.

If a call returns DISP_E_EXCEPTION, the object itself has chosen to provide you with the necessary information about the problem in the EXCEPINFO structure you passed it. (Of course, if you didn't pass this structure, you cannot obtain exception information.) A controller that receives this information and wants to display it to the user should perform the following steps; each field mentioned is part of EXCEPINFO:

1. Check whether the *pfnDeferredFillIn* is non-NULL. If so, call that function passing your EXCEPINFO structure again.[3]

2. Format a message string containing the source of the error (the value of the ProgID in *bstrSource*), the error code (either *wCode* or *scode*), and the description of the exception (*bstrDescription*). A typical format is "Error <code> in <source name>: <description>". The *scode* field is valid only when *wCode* is 0, and it is best to format *wCode* in decimal but *scode* in hexademical. As you probably know by now, SCODEs are far easier to read in hex.

3. Display the message in a message box with at least the MB_OK and MB_ICONEXCLAMATION styles, as shown in Figure 15-2. If the *bstrHelpFile* field is non-NULL, however, also include a Help button. Under Windows 3.1 and Windows NT 3.5, doing this requires that you make your own dialog box template. Blech! Under Windows 95 and later versions of Windows NT, you can use a new style, MB_HELP, which gets *MessageBox* to include the Help button.

---

3. If the controller supports error objects, it can query the automation object for *ISupportErrorInfo* and call *ISupportErrorInfo::InterfaceSupportsErrorInfo* to check for available error information in an error object. If any is, the controller can then call *GetErrorInfo* and various *IErrorInfo* members to retrieve that exception information. Note that AutoCli does not demonstrate this process.

4. If the user clicks the Help button, you must launch *WinHelp* with the full pathname for *bstrHelpFile* along with the context ID *dwHelpContext*. This is where the HELPDIR we read from the registry earlier in this chapter comes into play. If we are able to read a help directory, we can assume that the object does not put a full path in the *bstrHelpFile* field. Therefore, we must prepend HELPDIR to *bstrHelpFile* to form the path to send to *WinHelp*. If we were not able to read a directory name earlier, we can only assume that the object has put the full path in *bstrHelpFile* and should send it unmodified to *WinHelp*.

5. Free *bstrSource*, *bstrDescription*, and *bstrHelpFile* with calls to *SysFreeString*.

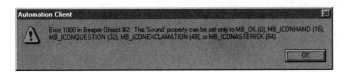

**Figure 15-2.**
*A typical controller display of an exception.*

In AutoCli, most of the code in the helper function *CApp::Invoke* is for the single purpose of handling exceptions. You can see in the following code that AutoCli implements each of the steps mentioned previously:

```
HRESULT CApp::Invoke(DISPID dispID, WORD wFlags, DISPPARAMS *pdp
    , VARIANT *pva, EXCEPINFO *pExInfo, UINT *puErr)
    {
    HRESULT     hr;
    LPTSTR      pszMsg=NULL;
    LPTSTR      pszFmt=NULL;
    UINT        uRet;
    UINT        uStyle;
    TCHAR       szSource[80];

    if (NULL==m_pIDispatch)
        return ResultFromScode(E_POINTER);

    hr=m_pIDispatch->Invoke(dispID, IID_NULL, m_lcid, wFlags
        , pdp, pva, pExInfo, puErr);
```

*(continued)*

```
if (DISP_E_EXCEPTION!=GetScode(hr))
    return hr;

//If we're given a deferred filling function, fill now.
if (NULL!=pExInfo->pfnDeferredFillIn)
    (*pExInfo->pfnDeferredFillIn)(pExInfo);

//Go get the real source name from ProgID.
lstrcpy(szSource, TEXT("Unknown"));

if (NULL!=pExInfo->bstrSource)
    {
    LONG    lRet;

    //If this doesn't work, we'll have "Unknown" anyway.
    RegQueryValue(HKEY_CLASSES_ROOT, pExInfo->bstrSource
        , szSource, &lRet);

    SysFreeString(pExInfo->bstrSource);
    }

if (NULL!=pExInfo->bstrDescription)
    {
    pszFmt=(LPTSTR)malloc(CCHSTRINGMAX*sizeof(TCHAR));
    pszMsg=(LPTSTR)malloc((CCHSTRINGMAX+lstrlen(szSource)
        +lstrlen(pExInfo->bstrDescription))*sizeof(TCHAR));

    if (0==pExInfo->wCode)
        {
        //Formatting for SCODE errors
        LoadString(m_hInst, IDS_MESSAGEEXCEPTIONSCODE, pszFmt
            , CCHSTRINGMAX);
        wsprintf(pszMsg, pszFmt, (long)pExInfo->scode
            , (LPTSTR)szSource
            , (LPTSTR)pExInfo->bstrDescription);
        }
    else
        {
        //Formatting for wCode errors
        LoadString(m_hInst, IDS_MESSAGEEXCEPTION, pszFmt
            , CCHSTRINGMAX);
        wsprintf(pszMsg, pszFmt, (UINT)pExInfo->wCode
            , (LPTSTR)szSource
            , (LPTSTR)pExInfo->bstrDescription);
        }

    free(pszFmt);
```

```
        }
    else
        {
        pszMsg=(LPTSTR)malloc(CCHSTRINGMAX*sizeof(TCHAR));
        LoadString(m_hInst, IDS_MESSAGEUNKNOWNEXCEPTION, pszMsg
            , CCHSTRINGMAX);
        }

    uStyle=MB_OK | MB_ICONEXCLAMATION;

#ifdef MB_HELP
    uStyle |=(NULL!=pExInfo->bstrHelpFile) ? MB_HELP : 0;
#else
    uStyle |=(NULL!=pExInfo->bstrHelpFile) ? MB_OKCANCEL : 0;
#endif

    //CApp::Message(string, style) displays message box.
    uRet=Message(pszMsg, uStyle);

    if (NULL!=pszMsg)
        free(pszMsg);

#ifdef MB_HELP
    if (IDHELP==uRet)
#else
    if (IDCANCEL==uRet)
#endif
        {
        TCHAR       szHelp[512];

        if ((TCHAR)0!=m_szHelpDir[0])
            {
            wsprintf(szHelp, TEXT("%s\\%s"), m_szHelpDir
                , pExInfo->bstrHelpFile);
            }
        else
            lstrcpy(szHelp, pExInfo->bstrHelpFile);

        WinHelp(NULL, szHelp, HELP_CONTEXT, pExInfo->dwHelpContext);
        }

    SysFreeString(pExInfo->bstrDescription);
    SysFreeString(pExInfo->bstrHelpFile);

    return ResultFromScode(DISP_E_EXCEPTION);
    }
```

This code conditionally compiles use of the MB_HELP style for versions of Windows that support the flag (Windows 95 and Windows NT 3.51). If you compile for earlier versions of Windows, cheat and use a Cancel button instead of a Help button because you do not want to complicate this sample with a custom dialog box that would have to dynamically resize itself based on the message length, something *MessageBox* does automatically.[4]

The two strings used to format the messages are defined in an AUTO-CLI.RC stringtable as "Error %u in %s: %s" (for *wCode* errors) and "Error %lX in %s: %s" (for *scode* errors). If there isn't a *bstrDescription* string, AutoCli uses a generic error message—"An unspecified error occurred in the automation object." This is generic because we have only one object: a more complete controller would probably have another name for the object (instead of "automation object") that it could put in such a message.

> NOTE: If you run AutoCli with Beeper 2, 3, 4, or 5 and then try to run AutoCli with Beeper1, viewing the help file will not work. The reason is that AutoCli uses the presence of HELPDIR in the registry to determine whether it should prepend a path to *bstrHelpFile* before calling *WinHelp*. If you register the entries for any of the later Beeper samples, you will create the necessary TypeLib entries, including HELPDIR. If you then register Beeper1 again, those entries will still exist, causing AutoCli to attempt to prepend a path to the full help file path already specified in *bstrHelpFile*. Swapping registry versions for objects will not happen like this in real practice. If you run into this, you'll have to hack out the TypeLib entries for Beeper by hand.

## Custom and Dual Interfaces

All of the previous discussion has to do with calling methods and accessing properties through *IDispatch*. If you have a controller that understands enough about type information to generate arbitrary calls to *IDispatch*, then it will probably also be sophisticated enough to generate calls to vtable-based

---

4. If you've ever hit a general protection fault under Windows NT, you'll see a similar use of the Cancel button, which starts WinDebug to look at the location of the fault. The message in the dialog box says that Cancel starts the debugger, but I've always found that a little confusing. A Debug button would be better. But *MessageBox* is designed to work under very low memory conditions, whereas a custom dialog box is not. Therefore, it is in the best interest of the system to display the message even under the worst possible conditions, and because Windows NT 3.5 doesn't have the MB_HELP style, MB_CANCEL is the next best thing. If you really want to, you can probably get away with using Cancel in the same way, but you should put some sort of message in the message box indicating that clicking Cancel will bring up the appropriate help. It's best, however, to make a real Help button if you can.

functions in either custom or dual interfaces. This is a bit trickier, of course, because calling these functions requires you to build a stack frame and process return values from registers—operations that are usually machine dependent.

I can't say that I've actually tried to make a generic vtable calling routine, but I suspect that it could be done with an assembly language function that took the interface pointer to call, the offset in the vtable of the function to call, the calling convention to use, and an array of VARIANTARG structures. This function would push each VARIANTARG onto the stack in the order appropriate for the calling convention, make the actual call, clean up the stack as necessary (for the *cdecl* calls, for example), and put the return value in the correct registers. This would be the only machine-dependent piece of code in the whole application.

I also suspect that you could get away with a similar scheme involving the use of a variable argument C function with some in-line assembly. The act of calling this function would possibly generate most of the stack frame automatically, whereas the function itself would tweak the stack, make the call, do some cleanup, and return.

In either of these cases, it's possible to call vtable functions in custom and dual interfaces without having machine-dependent assembly invade your source code.

## Summary

An OLE Automation controller is simply a client of automation objects—that is, a client that uses an object's services by calling the member functions of *IDispatch*, particularly *IDispatch::Invoke*. A general purpose controller, which might be a development tool such as Microsoft Visual Basic, will have some sort of integrated programming language. Different syntax structures of this programming language each correspond to a method call, a property get, or a property put operation, where method calls might include optional and named arguments as well. The general syntax structures work in conjunction with an object's type information, which the controller can use to ensure that methods and properties exist and that the types involved are compatible with those types specified in type information.

A general controller such as this also needs syntax structures for object creation and object destruction. Creation of objects can include user interfaces for browsing available objects as well as their type information. A controller can, of course, load an object's type information without having to instantiate the object itself.

A controller, or any client of *IDispatch,* does not necessarily have to involve a complex programming environment. Any code that calls *IDispatch* members in any capacity is a simple controller. For example, OLE controls typically use dispinterfaces for their event sets, so in order to fire events, such controls have to know how to call *IDispatch::Invoke.* This chapter examines how to call *Invoke* from a client's perspective for the various operations: property put, property get, and method calls with fixed, optional, and named arguments. All these constructs are demonstrated using a sample named AutoCli, which works with any of the Beeper objects from Chapter 14. AutoCli also demonstrates a controller's handling of exceptions, displaying the necessary information to the user and invoking the object's help file if necessary.

This chapter also spends a few pages examining the relationship between an automation object and a controller, which raises a number of important questions to do with design. How much should an object do? How much work can a controller do? Is a feature best implemented as an object service or as part of a controller? Pondering such questions can lead to valuable insights and more robust designs, creating an optimal partnership of controllers and objects.

**CHAPTER SIXTEEN**

# Property Pages, Changes, and Persistence

*The best ideas are common property.*
—Lucius Annaeus Seneca, c. 4 B.C.–A.D. 65

*My guiding star always is, Get hold of portable property.*
—John Huffam in *Great Expectations,* by Charles Dickens

Throughout many of the preceding chapters, we've explored ways through which a client and an object share their functionality and their information. In Chapters 2, 4, 5, and 6, we saw how clients and objects communicate. In Chapter 3, we saw how an object describes itself. In Chapters 7 and 8, we explored information storage, and in Chapter 9, we dealt with the naming of such information as well as the process of binding back to it again. In Chapters 10 through 13, we examined the means of exchanging structured data formats as well as the rendering and caching of graphic views of data. And in Chapters 14 and 15, we saw how an object can expose its functionality through late-bound methods and its information through individual properties using a dispID to identify a property in the context of an object.

Again, the common theme is that objects have functionality and content to share—objects share them in many ways. This chapter, the last before we explore the larger and more complex protocols of OLE Documents and OLE Controls, examines a number of additional considerations for an object's properties.

First we'll examine the user interface called *property sheets,* used for manipulating properties directly. Although property sheets have been seen in a number of applications for some time, no general mechanisms for creating them had been developed until recently. Windows 95 introduces this user interface on a system level, and OLE has its own set of interfaces and standards—namely property page components—that let you create property sheets in a more self-contained way. OLE-based property pages were introduced with OLE Controls as a standard means of manipulating a control's properties. The user interface, however, extends down to any object with properties, no matter how mundane that object. The key is that OLE's mechanism lets the object specify exactly which property pages to display, and those property pages can then communicate with the object in whatever way they want.

Next we'll discuss the use of an outgoing interface named *IPropertyNotify-Sink* through which a client can receive property change requests and property change notifications. This interface is especially useful when a mechanism such as property pages or an object's own user interface (such as for an OLE control) can change properties without the client itself having initiated the change. Because *IPropertyNotifySink* was designed at the same time as connection points (Chapter 4), a client uses that generic mechanism to connect its sink to the object and can then check for specific attributes in an object's type information in order to know which properties support the notifications in this interface.

Finally we'll look at a standard for the persistent storage of properties in what are called *property sets*. These are basically a sparse, flexible, and extensible stream format in which you can serialize almost any information you want. We will also see the specific property set named Summary Information, which, when attached to a compound file's root storage object, allows system shells such as that in Windows 95 to display such properties without otherwise opening the file or running the application that created it.

So as in earlier chapters we've seen how to exchange formatted data structures, how to notify a client of changes in such data, and how to access properties programmatically, here we'll see the standards for notifying a client of changes in individual properties, the standards for showing and accessing properties through a user interface, and the standards for accessing properties that exist in persistent storage.[1] Thus we complete the picture, sharing an object's properties through code, user interface, and storage, and essentially making properties not only common but also portable.

# Property Sheets, Property Pages

Most likely, you've already seen the user interface known as the *tabbed dialog box* or *property sheet*, a dialog box containing one or more individual *property pages*, in which each page itself works as a single dialog box. The collection of

---

1. At the time of writing, marshaling support does not exist for any of the interfaces introduced in this chapter.

pages in a single place allows the end user to work with different properties of one kind or another without having to skip around between different, singular dialog boxes. In a property sheet, each page is displayed as an individual tab; clicking on a tab brings the various controls on that page to the foreground.

You'll see property sheets employed quite often in the Windows 95 user interface, not only in applications but also in the system shell and in development tools. For example, let's say I'm using a programming tool to create a push-button control on a form. When I ask to view the properties of that button, I get a Button Control Properties property sheet, as shown in Figure 16-1. The General page is currently displayed. I can use this page to set the button's caption. If I click the Fonts tab, I see a different page, shown in Figure 16-2 on the following page. And if I click on the Colors tab, that page comes to the foreground, as shown in Figure 16-3 on the following page. So within the context of the button control object, I can manipulate its different groups of related properties within a single dialog box. Keep in mind that in all these figures, the OK, Cancel, Apply Now, and Help buttons—as well as the labeled tabs—are owned by the frame dialog. All other controls belong to the pages themselves.

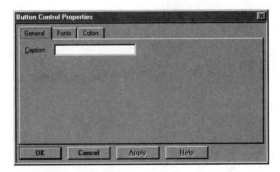

**Figure 16-1.**
*A General property page in a Button Control Properties property sheet.*

Usability testing has shown that end users work well with the grouping of related sets of properties in the same top-level dialog box. One dialog box with multiple pages reinforces the fact that all the properties apply to the same underlying object, and in many ways, factoring properties in a user interface is much like factoring an object's functionality into multiple programmatic interfaces, as we've seen throughout this book.

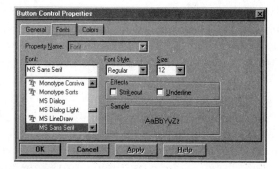

**Figure 16-2.**
*A Fonts property page in a Button Control Properties property sheet.*

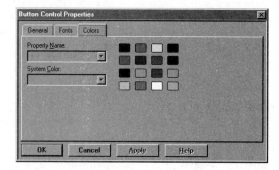

**Figure 16-3.**
*A Colors property page in a Button Control Properties property sheet.*

Windows 95 introduced the capability to create property sheets as part of the system API, allowing applications to create this user interface for their own properties. In general, each property sheet represents some conceptual object as the user sees it. For example, the Windows 95 Control Panel is a conceptual system-settings object that has groups of properties for the display, device drivers, peripherals, the network, and so on. Within the property sheet for these system settings, each group of related settings has its own page.

In a component integration environment such as OLE, we want OLE components to be able to specify which property pages they want displayed for themselves and to be able to supply the implementation of those pages. This allows a client to display the appropriate property sheet for an object being maintained in that client—or even for multiple objects simultaneously. The Windows 95 API for creating property sheets is not wholly sufficient for OLE's purposes because that API is oriented toward a single application displaying its own properties. In OLE, we need a client to display the properties of any group of objects and have changes in the property pages applied directly to those objects without the client's intervention.

The group of technologies introduced with OLE Controls includes a number of new interfaces and an API function that creates and manages component-specific property sheets. We call this set of interfaces and functions the *OLE Property Pages* technology. This technology is oriented toward a client that has *IUnknown* pointers for one or more objects and that wants to display the appropriate property sheet for any subset of those objects. (*Client* here also applies to an object that wants to display its own property pages in response to a programmatic request such as a method call to its primary dispinterface.) In any case, the property sheet manages to communicate property changes in the user interface to the objects being affected. The mechanism that makes this possible between arbitrary objects involves four parts:

1. Each object specifies which property pages should appear in its own property sheet through the interface *ISpecifyPropertyPages*, where each property page is identified by its own CLSID. This interface is necessary only to support the display of a property sheet within an object's external client — objects that want exclusive control over the display of properties should not implement this interface.

2. Whoever wants to display the property sheet (the client or the object) calls the OLE API function *OleCreatePropertyFrame* (or *OleCreatePropertyFrameIndirect*), passing an array of property page CLSIDs along with an array of *IUnknown* pointers (one for each affected object). This function creates the modal dialog frame and manages the individual property page objects themselves until the user closes the dialog box.

3. Each property page is an in-process object that implements *IPropertyPage*. Through this interface, the frame tells each page when to show or hide itself as the user selects different tabs. In addition, the frame passes the client's array of *IUnknown* pointers to each page so that those pages can send changes directly to the affected objects.

4. Each tab in the frame dialog is a *page site* that appears to each property page as the interface *IPropertyPageSite*. The pages use *IPropertyPageSite* to retrieve information about the property sheet as a whole.

The relationship between these parts is illustrated in Figure 16-4. Be aware that property changes are communicated directly from the property pages to the affected objects; they require no interaction on behalf of whoever invokes the dialog box. Because each object specifies exactly which property pages to display, those pages expect to communicate changes through specific interfaces or dispinterfaces. In some cases, having a standard property page for common properties (such as Fonts and Colors) makes sense. A standard page expects objects to support standard dispIDs for related properties through their *IDispatch* interfaces.

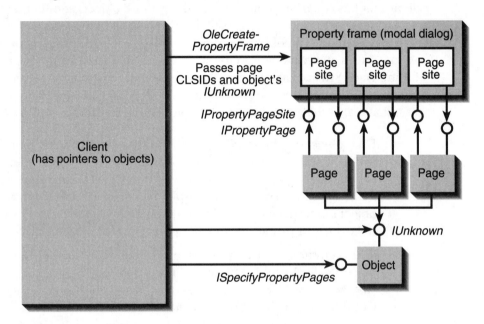

**Figure 16-4.**
*The architecture of OLE Property Pages.*

The following four sections take a closer look at each part of OLE Property Pages. In addition, we'll look at a few other interfaces, namely *IPerProperty-Browsing* and *IPropertyPage2*, that provide for more specific user interface access to an object's properties.

## Specifying Property Pages Through *ISpecifyPropertyPages*

An object expresses its ability to interact with one or more property pages by implementing the interface *ISpecifyPropertyPages*. A client can use the presence of this interface to determine whether an object supports property pages at all, enabling something like a Properties menu item or toolbar button if it does. The interface itself is quite simple, having only one specific member function:

```
interface ISpecifyPropertyPages : IUnknown
    {
    HRESULT GetPages(CAUUID *pPages);
    };
```

The type CAUUID is a "counted array of UUIDs":

```
typedef struct tagCAUUID
    {
    ULONG cElems;
    GUID *pElems;
    } CAUUID;
```

Simply stated, the client calls *ISpecifyPropertyPages::GetPages* to retrieve a counted array of the CLSIDs that together describe the property pages that the object wants displayed for itself. Whereas the client allocates the CAUUID structure before calling *GetPages*, the object allocates and fills the actual GUID array using *CoTaskMemAlloc*. The object stores a pointer to this array in the *pElems* field of the structure and fills the *cElems* field with the size of the array. When the function returns, the client is responsible for the GUID array and must be sure to free it later with *CoTaskMemFree*.

If the client is displaying properties for a single object, it can take the GUID array and proceed to create a property frame (described in the following section). This is always the case when an object is displaying its own property sheet. If a client is trying to display a sheet for multiple objects, however, it must first call *ISpecifyPropertyPages::GetPages* for each object and then build a separate array containing only those property page CLSIDs that are common to all the objects. This is because each object expects only its own specified pages to send changes. Obviously, you cannot have an object's page that understands dispID 102 to mean "edit control style bits" pass a new value to another object for which dispID 102 means "enabled nuclear power plant safety devices." In short, the client must display only those property pages that all objects in the selection understand, which does require standard page implementations (such as for fonts and colors). The user will expect that all changes he or she makes to a multiple selection will apply to the entire selection in a predictable way. Building a common set of page CLSIDs is how a client meets these expectations.

## Creating a Property Frame

When a client or an object is ready to display a property sheet, it calls the function *OleCreatePropertyFrame*, which takes a large number of arguments:

```
STDAPI OleCreatePropertyFrame(HWND hWndOwner, UINT x, UINT y
    , LPCOLESTR lpszCaption, ULONG cObjects, IUnknown **lplpUnk
    , ULONG cPages, CLSID *lpPages, LCID lcid
    , DWORD dwReserved, LPVOID pvReserved);
```

Alternatively, the caller can put these arguments and an extra dispID into an OCPFIPARAMS structure and call *OleCreatePropertyFrameIndirect*:

```
typedef struct tagOCPFIPARAMS
    {
    ULONG       cbStructSize;
    HWND        hWndOwner;
    int         x;
    int         y;
    LPCOLESTR   lpszCaption;
    ULONG       cObjects;
    IUnknown    **lplpUnk;
    ULONG       cPages;
    CLSID       *lpPages;
    LCID        lcid;
    DISPID      dispidInitialProperty;
    } OCPFIPARAMS;

STDAPI OleCreatePropertyFrameIndirect(LPOCPFIPARAMS pParams);
```

The common arguments and fields work as follows:

| Argument/Field | Description |
|---|---|
| *hWndOwner* | The parent window of the modal dialog. |
| *x, y* | The position of the dialog in relation to *hWndOwner*. |
| *lpszCaption* | The caption to show in the dialog. |
| *cObjects, lplpUnk* | The array of objects affected by this property sheet; *lplpUnk* points to the array, and *cObjects* specifies the size of the array. |
| *cPages, lpPages* | The array of CLSIDs specifying which pages to display; *lpPages* points to the array of CLSIDs, and *cPages* specifies the size of the array. |

| Argument/Field | Description |
| --- | --- |
| *lcid* | The locale specifying the national language that should be shown. |
| *dispIDInitialProperty* | The property that gets the initial focus in per-property browsing. (See "Per-Property Browsing" later in this chapter.) Clients can pass such a dispID only through *OleCreatePropertyFrameIndirect,* as *dwReserved* must be 0 in *OleCreatePropertyFrame.* Specifying DISPID_UNKNOWN in this field results in behavior identical to that of *OleCreateProperty-Frame,* so the first control on the first page receives the initial focus. |

Both the *OleCreatePropertyFrame* and *OleCreatePropertyFrameIndirect* functions create a modal dialog and attempt to instantiate and initialize each property page using the CLSIDs in *lpPages.* From that point, the dialog communicates with the pages, telling them when to show or hide themselves and when to apply changes to the affected objects. Because a modal dialog is involved, neither API function returns until the user closes the dialog box. The HRESULT return value may contain any error code, including those prefixed with CTL_E_ to specify problems with the arguments or structure fields.

## The Property Page: *IPropertyPage*

In OLE, a property page is an in-process object that implements *IPropertyPage.* Through this interface, the property frame provides the necessary information and commands to each page in the sheet:

```
interface IPropertyPage : IUnknown
    {
    HRESULT SetPageSite(IPropertyPageSite *pPageSite);
    HRESULT Activate(HWND hWndParent, LPCRECT prc, BOOL fModal);
    HRESULT Deactivate(VOID);
    HRESULT GetPageInfo(PROPPAGEINFO *pPageInfo);
    HRESULT SetObjects(ULONG cObjects, IUnknown **ppUnk);
    HRESULT Show(UINT nCmdShow);
    HRESULT Move(LPCRECT prc);
    HRESULT IsPageDirty(VOID);
    HRESULT Apply(VOID);
    HRESULT Help(LPCOLESTR pszHelpDir);
    HRESULT TranslateAccelerator(LPMSG pMsg);
    };
```

*(continued)*

```
typedef struct tagPROPPAGEINFO
    {
    size_t  cb ;
    LPOLESTR pszTitle;
    SIZE     size;
    LPOLESTR pszDocString;
    LPOLESTR pszHelpFile;
    DWORD    dwHelpContext;
    } PROPPAGEINFO;
```

These member functions behave as follows:

| Member Function | Description |
| --- | --- |
| *SetPageSite* | The initialization function for a property page through which the page receives an *IPropertyPageSite* pointer. This page should make a copy of the pointer and call *AddRef* through it. A NULL can be passed to this function to instruct the page to release whatever pointer it has. |
| *Activate* | Instructs the page to create its display window as a child of *hWndParent* and to position it according to *prc*. The *fModal* flag indicates that the modality of the dialog frame is always TRUE. This function will be called whenever the user clicks the page's tab in the dialog box. |
| *Deactivate* | Instructs the page to destroy the window created in *Activate*. |
| *GetPageInfo* | Asks the page to fill a PROPPAGEINFO structure, with the text to show in its tab (such as "Fonts" or "Colors") in *pszTitle*, the pixel dimensions of the page in *size*, a help string in *pszDocString*,* and the name and context ID for a help file in *pszHelpFile* and *dwHelpContext*. The property page allocates all strings with *CoTaskMemAlloc*, and they become the frame's responsibility. If a help filename is given, the frame will enable its Help button. |
| *SetObjects* | Provides the page with the objects being affected by changes. This function will be called after *SetPageSite* but always before *Activate* so that the page can retrieve initial values as necessary. The page must make copies of all passed pointers, calling *AddRef* on each. |

* This is currently not used by the standard property frame, but it could be used in a status line or in a tool tip to describe the page itself.

| Member Function | Description |
|---|---|
| *Show* | Asks the page to show or hide its window according to *nCmdShow*. |
| *Move* | Asks the page to relocate and resize itself to a position other than what was specified through *Activate*. |
| *IsPageDirty* | Asks the page whether it has changed its state, returning S_OK or S_FALSE. This is used to determine whether to enable the Apply Now button in the dialog, as described in the next section. |
| *Apply* | Instructs the page to send its changes to all the objects passed through *SetObjects*. The page queries for whatever interface (vtable or dispatch, custom or standard) it requires and informs the objects of new values. |
| *Help* | Instructs the page that the Help button was clicked; *pszHelpDir* is the default Help directory. If the object wants to invoke its own help information, it should return a success code. If *Help* returns an error code (E_NOTIMPL), the frame will launch WinHelp using the help information returned through *GetPageInfo*. |
| *TranslateAccelerator* | Informs the page of keyboard events, allowing it to implement its own keyboard interface. |

The size returned through *GetPageInfo* specifies the pixel dimensions of the page in question. When multiple pages are involved, the frame will create a page area large enough for the largest page (as shown earlier in Figures 16-1, 16-2, and 16-3). Those dimensions are then used in calculating the rectangle passed to both *Activate* and *Move*.

The frame will call the *Apply* member of each page either when the user clicks the Apply Now button or when the user clicks OK to close the dialog box. How a property page chooses to implement *Apply* depends entirely on what it knows about the objects that might specify the page. General purpose pages used by different object classes—such as the Fonts and Colors pages shown earlier—must specify in their documentation exactly how they intend to send changes to an object. This is done most often through standard dispIDs for various properties. Other pages that are private to an object class can use whatever mechanism is most convenient—for example, a custom interface. Whatever the means, successfully applying changes should clear the page's dirty flag so that *IsPageDirty* will return S_FALSE. If errors occur, the state should remain dirty.

The window created in *Activate* should be a child window of the frame. This child window has no border and no caption, but otherwise, it contains all the controls to display for that page. The most convenient implementation method is to define a dialog template for the page layout specifying the WS_CHILD style bit but without the WS_CAPTION and WS_THICKFRAME bits. You can then implement *Activate* by creating a modeless dialog box from this template through the Windows function *CreateDialog*. We'll see an example later in this chapter.

## The Property Page Site: *IPropertyPageSite*

As the property frame itself manages some state global to all property pages, the *IPropertyPageSite* pointer passed to *IPropertyPage::SetPageSite* provides each page with access to this information:

```
interface IPropertyPageSite : IUnknown
    {
    HRESULT OnStatusChange(DWORD flags);
    HRESULT GetLocaleID(LCID *pLocaleID);
    HRESULT GetPageContainer(IUnknown **ppUnk);
    HRESULT TranslateAccelerator(LPMSG pMsg);
    };
```

The first global state in the frame is the locale identifier that the client originally passed to *OleCreatePropertyFrame*. A property page retrieves this identifier through *IPropertyPageSite::GetLocaleID* and uses it to determine the language of the text returned through *IPropertyPage::GetPageInfo* and the localization of the controls in the page itself.

The other important global state is whether or not the Apply Now button is enabled. Initially the button is disabled. To enable it, the page first calls *IPropertyPageSite::OnStatusChange*, in response to which the frame calls *IPropertyPage::IsPageDirty*. If the latter function returns S_OK, the frame enables the button, allowing calls to *IPropertyPage::Apply*. Through this interaction, the user knows when there is a change to make permanent. It is the responsibility of a page to call *OnStatusChange* when changes occur and to implement its own *IsPageDirty* member properly. *OnStatusChange* itself takes either the flag PROPPAGESTATUS_DIRTY to indicate that a change has occurred or the flag PROPPAGESTATUS_VALIDATE to indicate that now is a good time to perform data validation.

Of the other two functions, *GetPageContainer* currently has no defined functionality. It could be used to retrieve an interface for the property sheet frame as a whole, but as yet the frame has no defined interface, so this function will always fail. *TranslateAccelerator*, on the other hand, works in conjunction with the function of the same name in *IPropertyPage*. The protocol here is that the frame first notifies the current page of a keystroke by calling *IProperty-PageFrame::TranslateAccelerator*. If the page does not want to override a key that the frame usually processes, it should call the page site's *TranslateAccelerator* for that key and then process it normally. In short, the site gives the page the ability to preprocess keys before eating them.

## Per-Property Browsing: *IPerPropertyBrowsing* and *IPropertyPage2*

The functionality described in the previous sections provides the capability to work with properties on an object-by-object basis. Sometimes, however, a client might want to display the same user interface for a specific property, which means that it must have a way to tell the property frame to go to a particular page in the property sheet and to tell the page to highlight a specific property.

This is the purpose of the *dispIDInitialProperty* field in the OCPFIPARAMS structure used with *OleCreatePropertyFrameIndirect*. When the frame is created in this manner, it will query the objects specified in the structure's *lplpUnk* field for the interface *IPerPropertyBrowsing*:

```
interface IPerPropertyBrowsing : IUnknown
    {
    HRESULT GetDisplayString(DISPID dispid, BSTR *pbstr);
    HRESULT MapPropertyToPage(DISPID dispid, LPCLSID pClsID);
    HRESULT GetPredefinedStrings(DISPID dispid
        , CALPOLESTR *pcaStringsOut, CADWORD *pcaCookiesOut);
    HRESULT GetPredefinedValue(DISPID dispid, DWORD dwCookie
        , VARIANT *pVarOut);
    };

typedef struct tagCALPOLESTR
    {
    ULONG    cElems;
    LPOLESTR *pElems;
    } CALPOLESTR;

typedef struct tagCADWORD
    {
    ULONG  cElems;
    DWORD *pElems;
    } CADWORD;
```

In particular, the frame will call *IPerPropertyBrowsing::MapPropertyToPage*. The object will then decide whether it supports the property in question. If the property is not available, the object returns CTL_E_NOPAGEAVAIL-ABLE. Otherwise, the object stores the proper page CLSID in *pClsID* and returns S_FALSE. (S_OK has a special meaning, as we'll see in a moment.) Also, when multiple objects are being affected, asking one object in the set is as good as asking all of them: because only property pages common to all the objects are being used, all the objects will specify the same page for the same property. This means the frame needs to ask only the first object.

When the frame successfully retrieves the property page CLSID for the desired property, it queries that page for *IPropertyPage2* instead of *IPropertyPage*:

```
interface IPropertyPage2 : IPropertyPage
    {
    HRESULT EditProperty(DISPID dispid);
    };
```

If this interface is not available, the frame will still activate this page first, and the focus will be on the first control in that page. If the interface is available, the frame passes the property's dispID to *EditProperty* to tell the page to set the focus to the control containing that property. If the page returns an error, the first control on the page will get the focus.

The other member functions of *IPerPropertyBrowsing* support a client's ability to display an object's properties in some sort of user interface other than a property page. The S_OK return code from *IPerPropertyBrowsing::MapPropertyToPage* indicates not only that a specific page is available for this property (so that the client can invoke a frame with only this page showing) but that the property can also be manipulated outside the property page altogether, for example in a property sheet of the client's own design that lists client-specific and object-specific properties together.

The function *IPerPropertyBrowsing::GetDisplayString* provides the property label to show in such a list, and the function *GetPredefinedStrings* allows the client to retrieve what should appear in a drop-down list box for this property. The counted arrays involved here are again filled by the object using *CoTaskMemAlloc* and become the client's responsibility. The array of DWORDs from *GetPredefinedStrings* specifies the values attached to each string when the property itself is an integer type. Finally, *GetPredefinedValue* supplies the client with a default value for the property in question.

You can see that per-property browsing, combined with the general Property Pages technology, allows for a very complete and detailed user interface surrounding the direct end-user manipulation of an object's properties. A client (or the object) can choose to show all properties in all pages at once, a single property page by itself, or simply a single property outside property pages altogether.

# Property Change Notification

In our discussion about property pages, the client has usually been left out of the picture entirely: interaction between a property page and the affected objects is direct. However, a client will often want to know when changes occur to properties so it can update the properties' internal state. For example, imagine a case in which a client is using an object, say an OLE control, as a sort of Font/Color control panel. The client could create this control with its CLSID and display its property pages easily enough when necessary. The client would then want to know when the user applies changes in the property frame so that the client could alter its own color scheme and change its current font. To do this, we need a means through which an object can inform a client of changes to both individual properties and multiple properties.[2] In all cases, the properties involved are called *bindable* because the client can bind its own specific behavior to change notifications.

In addition, having an object send a request to a client asking whether a property is allowed to change is also widely useful. It gives the client an opportunity not only to save the old state of a property but also to enforce a read-only state. In other words, the object sends a request for permission to change a property and uses the client's response to control what happens afterward. The properties for which an object supports this protocol are called *request edit* properties.

To support bindable and request edit properties, OLE provides specific flags that appear in type information as well as the interface *IPropertyNotify-Sink*, which contains an *on changed* notification and a *can edit* request. A dispID identifies the property in question, as shown in the following:

```
interface IPropertyNotifySink : IUnknown
    {
    HRESULT OnChanged(DISPID dispid);
    HRESULT OnRequestEdit(DISPID dispid);
    };
```

---

2. Imagine how much simpler it would be for applications to deal with changes in the Windows Control Panel if Control Panel told only interested applications only about the changes to those properties that have changed, instead of broadcasting WM_WININICHANGE to every application, whether it cares or not. In response to this, applications have to recheck any property of interest, a tedious and time-consuming process.

When a client wants to connect to an object so that the client can receive these notifications and requests, it must go through the connection point mechanism described in Chapter 4. If the object does not support *IConnection-PointContainer*, or if the object does not support *IPropertyNotifySink* as an outgoing interface, the client cannot receive these calls from the object at all.

When support is present, a change in a bindable property will generate a call to the sink's *OnChanged* member with the dispID of the property. If *dispID* happens to be DISPID_UNKNOWN, the object is saying that more than one bindable property changed. The client must then retrieve the properties it cares about from the object and check for changes itself. The only defined return code for *OnChanged* is NOERROR.

When changes are about to occur to a request edit property, the object must pass the dispID of that property to *OnRequestEdit*. The object can also ask whether it is allowed to change anything at all by calling *OnRequestEdit* with DISPID_UNKNOWN. The client can do whatever it wants inside this call—save existing states, for example—before it returns. If the client returns NOERROR, it tells the object that changes are allowed. Otherwise, S_FALSE or an error code tells the object that it is not allowed to change anything. An object should not mark a property as "request edit" unless it can fulfill this contract—that is, the object must not change properties when the client denies permission. Of course, if a request edit property is also bindable, the object must call *OnRequestEdit* before any call to *OnChanged*.

Keep in mind that when the client receives the call to *OnRequestEdit*, the property has not yet changed. This means that the client cannot ask the object for the new value and that *OnRequestEdit* cannot be used to perform data validation, which requires the new value. At the time of writing, validation is considered to be a feature that an object supports through its own custom events or requests.

Marking a property as "bindable" and "request edit" is accomplished through an object's type information. In Chapter 3, we saw four related attributes for properties: *bindable, requestedit, defaultbind,* and *displaybind*. The *defaultbind* attribute indicates the one bindable property that best represents the bindable state of the object overall. This is useful for clients whose user model is based on object binding rather than on property binding. The *displaybind* attribute, on the other hand, can be used to mark any number of otherwise bindable properties as suitable for showing to an end user. This gives the object a means of differentiating between programmatic properties and end-user–oriented ones.

A sophisticated client, automation controller, or OLE control container that exploits type information can use the presence of the *bindable* and *request-*

*edit* attributes to allow a programmer or user to determine what should happen when changes or requests occur. This can be as simple as having Update On Change and Read-Only menu items or as complex as letting the user attach code to execute whenever these events occur for whatever properties are important.

# Persistence Through Property Sets

At the beginning of this chapter, I described a property set as a "sparse, flexible, and extensible stream format in which you can serialize almost any information you want." By *stream format,* I mean a format for a series of bytes stored in a stream object and accessed through the *IStream* interface, although the same property set format can be used anywhere that byte streams are in use. In fact, the format also accommodates property sets spanning multiple streams that are all contained within a single storage object. We will see how this can be done shortly. First, however, what do I mean by sparse, flexible, and extensible?

■ Flexible. You can store any type of data whatsoever inside this format, be it a single character, a floating-point value, a VARIANT, a BLOB, and so forth. Every piece of information is tagged in the format with a VT_* value from the VARTYPE enumeration that we saw in Chapter 14 on page 649.

■ Sparse. The format is specified so that any code that attempts to read information from a property set can attempt to read only what is there. In other words, reading code will not attempt to extract nonexistent information. Instead of an object writing a large data structure containing its properties that might have invalid fields, it can write only those properties with meaningful values, essentially storing a sparse structure without taking up unnecessary space. Code that reads this property set reads only those values that were written.

■ Extensible. The property set format can accommodate new data types simply by adding new VARTYPE flags. New data structure types composed of existing types can be stored as a sequence of those existing types while still retaining structural identity. If a new type is added to an existing property set, code that knows how to read the old version of the property set will robustly skip the new unknown type.

In one sentence, a general property set is a serial collection of property values in which each property is tagged with a type (a VT_* value) and a 32-bit *property identifier,* or PID. This information is stored in the order PID, type, value so that any code reading the property set can first check the identifier to see whether the property is of interest, and if so, it can read the type. That type then describes the format and length of the value that follows in the stream. This sort of structure means that the semantics of the type are easily determined, although the meaning of the value is left to the program to decide. The property set writer can also include a dictionary that maps binary PIDs to human-readable strings for display in the user interface.

Individual properties are grouped into a *format,* or *section.* Each section, tagged with a *format identifier,* or FMTID, represents a particular set of properties, although any code reading this format will again attempt to read only those properties that exist.

Obviously, because a property set is intended to be used as a data exchange format, you'd think some standards must exist as far as property identifiers and format identifiers are concerned, yes? Well, yes and no. Take a quick look through the standard OLE header files on your machine for any value that starts with PID_. (Include a space before the P so that you don't pick up DISPID_ values.) You didn't find any, did you? Now look for anything containing FMTID. Didn't find any for that either. So do any standards exist? What use is this format specification if there are no standard property or format identifiers?

The fact of the matter is that the plural *property sets* describes a general format in which you can store any information. A singular *property set* describes a named collection of specific information. The specifications for that single property set are responsible for defining which identifiers are used for which formats and properties, giving each property a name that is meaningful in the context of that single property set. The format identifiers themselves are GUIDs, and the designer of the specific property set is responsible for assigning a GUID as the FMTID. For example, I mentioned the Summary Information property set at the beginning of this chapter. This set is assigned the FMTID *F29F85E0-4FF9-1068-AB91-08002B27B3D9* and is defined to contain strings for a document title, a subject, an author, keywords, and comments; integers for page count, word count, and character count; time stamps for creation, modification, and print times; and so on. In the Summary Information set, the symbol PID_TITLE, for example, is assigned the value 2 and has the type VT_LPSTR. In another property set, the PID 2 might be for something completely different, but because the second set has its own FMTID, no one will attempt to interpret that property as if it belonged to a different format. So while the specific contents of any two sets differ, the means of storing individual values in a PID/type/value triplet is the same. In other words, a VT_LPSTR will always have the same layout in the stream regardless of the specific property set.

## The General Property Set Layout

At the highest level, a property set is composed of three major pieces, illustrated in Figure 16-5. These pieces are a property set header, a list of FMTID/Offset pairs identifying sections (each offset points to the location of a separate section from the beginning of the stream), and the serialized sections themselves. When a property set has only a single format, as Summary Information does, there is only one FMTID/Offset pair and only one section.

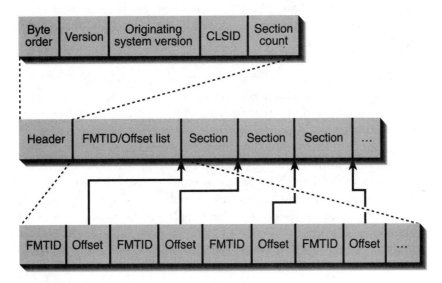

**Figure 16-5.**
*The top-level property set layout.*

A property set structure is thus defined generically as follows. (This is not an actual structure but simply a model of the property set layout.)

```
struct
    {
    PROPHEADER        ph;
    FORMATIDOFFSET    rgFIDO[cSections];
    PROPERTYSECTION   rgSections[cSections];
    };
```

You can see that a property set is a header followed by an array of FMTID/Offset pairs followed by an array of sections. Both arrays have the same number of elements. The PROPHEADER structure itself is defined as follows:[3]

```
typedef struct
    {
    WORD    wByteOrder ;  // Always 0xFFFE
    WORD    wFormat ;     // Always 0
    DWORD   dwOSVer ;     // System version
    CLSID   clsID ;       // Source CLSID
    DWORD   cSections ;   // Number of sections (must be at least 1)
    } PROPHEADER;
```

The *wByteOrder* field indicates whether the property set is written in big endian or little endian. The OLE specifications state that all property sets must be written in little-endian (Intel) ordering. This means that the value 0xFFFE appears in the stream as 0xFE and 0xFF—in that exact order—regardless of the originating operating system stored in *dwOSVer*. Currently this can be 0 for 16-bit Windows, 1 for the Macintosh, or 2 for 32-bit Windows. (Other system codes will be added as necessary.)

As indicated in the structure, the *wFormat* version number is always 0 for the specification of property sets defined here. If someone creates a new general property set layout that is different from the one described here, *wFormat* will contain another value. Code that reads a property set must always check this value to read the rest of the stream robustly. Either the CLSID field identifies the code that knows how to read and display the information in this property set, or it contains the FMTID of the property set itself if only one format is contained within it. For example, because Summary Information is defined to be generic across many applications, its FMTID will always appear here.

Finally, the *cSections* field defines how many FMTID/Offset pairs exist following this header, and this defines the number of overall sections. Each pair is a structure of the following sort:

---

3. This structure and those that follow are (unless noted otherwise) taken from the source code for the OLE Control Development Kit (CDK) shipped with Visual C++ 2.0. You won't find this structure and the others in any standard OLE header file, only in places that implement a property set. The CDK happens to be one of those places; it also includes some convenient classes for working with property sets.

```
typedef struct
    {
    GUID        formatID;
    DWORD       dwOffset;
    } FORMATIDOFFSET;
```

Again, the offset in each pair is a seek offset from the beginning of the entire property set stream to the beginning of a section. We can see why a piece of code attempting to read a property set can safely ignore sections it doesn't understand—for example, new extensions to an existing property set. If the reader doesn't recognize the FMTID in a given pair, it can simply read the next pair to see whether that one makes sense. Whenever this code finds a format it does understand, it can seek to the offset of that section and read its contents.

## The Section Layout

At any given section offset, you'll find a header and PID/Offset pairs. Each offset points to a property in the bytes that follow. Furthermore, each property is a type/value pair in which the real data is stored. This structure is similar to the property set structure itself, as shown in Figure 16-6.

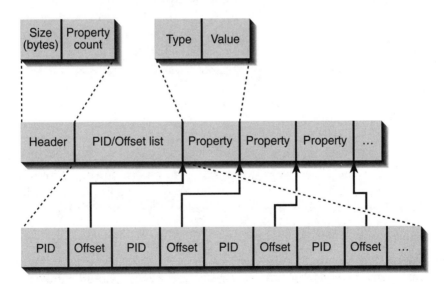

**Figure 16-6.**
*The section layout nested within a property set.*

781

You can look at a section through a generic structure, as we did for the entire property set:

```
struct
    {
    SECTIONHEADER       sh;
    PROPERTYIDOFFSET    rgPIDO[cProperties];
    PROPERTY            rgProperties[cProperties];
    };
```

The SECTIONHEADER structure has only two fields. One describes the size of the section as a whole, and the second describes the number of properties within it. Together they describe the size of the PID/Offset list that follows it in the stream:

```
typedef struct
    {
    DWORD       cbSection ;
    DWORD       cProperties ;
    } SECTIONHEADER;
```

Having the size of the section first allows anyone either to skip over this section entirely or to copy it wholesale from the stream without having to know anything more about the contents of the section. When someone is interested in the internals of the section, he or she can look at the properties it contains by using the list of PROPERTYIDOFFSET structures:

```
typedef struct
    {
    DWORD       propertyID;
    DWORD       dwOffset;
    } PROPERTYIDOFFSET;
```

Just as code that is reading a property set can skip unrecognized FMTIDs in the property set structure, code can skip unrecognized PIDs contained in this list in the section structure. Once again, if the reading code doesn't recognize the PID, it simply reads the next one. The code attempts to extract information for a property only when it understands the PID in the context of the FMTID. It then seeks to the offset written after the PID and at the offset finds information that it can use. Note that all properties must begin on a 32-bit boundary within the stream; extra zeros pad the leftover bytes.

## The Property Type/Value Layout

When you get to the bottom of a property set, you're faced with a variable length structure that contains the data type of the property and the bytes that make up its value:

```
struct
    {
    DWORD       dwType;       //From VARTYPE
    BYTE        rgbValue[cbValue];
    };
```

The type is always described with some VT_* value from the VARTYPE enumeration that we saw in Chapter 14. This type is followed by the number of bytes appropriate for the type. If *dwType* is VT_I2, the next 2 bytes contain the value. If the type is VT_BSTR, the bytes contain a character count followed by the characters. Other types, such as VT_BLOB and VT_STORAGE-_OBJECT, also have a specific format of the bytes that follow. Any type combined with VT_VECTOR specifies that an array of that type follows, in which the first DWORD specifies the number of elements and the bytes that follow contain the elements themselves. (Each element is aligned to a DWORD boundary, which matters only for VT_I2 and VT_BOOL because all other types are naturally DWORD aligned.) The list of available types and their data formats, taken from the *OLE Programmer's Reference,* is given in Table 16-1 beginning on the following page.

For various reasons, there is no provision for adding new VT_* values to define new types — that is, new data structures. Say you want to store a structure such as PARSNIP, as shown in the following:

```
typedef struct
    {
    short       Lengthcm;     //Length in centimeters
    short       Radiuscm;     //Top radius in centimeters
    short       Weightg;      //Weight in grams
    COLORREF    Shade;        //Exact color shade
    } PARSNIP;
```

To do this, you would need to write each field as a separate VARIANT structure and define the entire structure as VT_VARIANT ¦ VT_VECTOR. In the stream, you would have the following:

```
DWORD = VT_VARIANT ¦ VT_VECTOR11
DWORD = 4 (Count of elements)
DWORD = VT_I2  (Element 1)
WORD  = Lengthcm value
DWORD = VT_I2  (Element 2)
WORD  = Radiuscm value
DWORD = VT_I2  (Element 3)
WORD  = Weightg value
DWORD = VT_I4  (Element 4)
DWORD = Shade value (32-bit COLORREF)
WORD  = 0 (padding to DWORD align)
```

Two special properties always have the same PID regardless of the property set. PID 0 is defined as a dictionary that maps other PID values to user-readable strings, as described in the next section. PID 1 is a code page indicator (VT_I2) identifying the character set in which strings are stored, depending on the originating operating system.[4] Programs that don't understand the code page should not attempt to read any string-oriented data in the section. Modifying a code page property means that you must also modify all other string properties in the section according to the new code page. If no code page is present, the program must assume the system default code page.

| Type | Value | Description |
|------|-------|-------------|
| VT_EMPTY | 0 | None. A property set with a type indicator of VT_EMPTY has no data associated with it. The size of the value is 0. |
| VT_NULL | 1 | None. This is like a pointer to NULL. |
| VT_I2 | 2 | 2-byte signed integer value zero-padded to a 32-bit boundary. |
| VT_I4 | 3 | 4-byte signed integer value. |
| VT_R4 | 4 | 4-byte 32-bit IEEE floating-point value. |
| VT_R8 | 5 | 8-byte 64-bit IEEE floating-point value. |
| VT_CY | 6 | 8-byte two's complement integer (scaled by 10,000) as commonly used for currency amounts. |
| VT_DATE | 7 | 64-bit time format, a floating-point number representing seconds since January 1, 1900. This is stored in the same representation as VT_R8. |
| VT_BSTR | 8 | Counted, zero-terminated binary string; represented as a DWORD byte count (including the terminating null character) followed by the bytes of data. |
| VT_BOOL | 11 | 2 bytes representing a Boolean (WORD) value containing 0 (FALSE) or −1 (TRUE), zero-padded to a 32-bit boundary. |

**Table 16-1.** *(continued)*

*OLE property types that can appear in property sets.*

---

4. See the Win32 *GetACP* function for legal values for Windows-originated properties. For the Macintosh, see *Inside Macintosh Volume VI §14-111,* Addison-Wesley, 1991.

**Table 16-1.** *continued*

| Type | Value | Description |
|------|-------|-------------|
| VT_VARIANT (only with VT_VECTOR) | 12 | DWORD type indicator followed by the corresponding value. |
| VT_I8 | 20 | 8-byte signed integer. |
| VT_LPSTR | 30 | Same as VT_BSTR; used for most strings. |
| VT_LPWSTR | 31 | A counted and zero-terminated Unicode string; a DWORD character count (in which the count includes the terminating null character) followed by the same number of Unicode (16-bit) characters. The count is not a byte count but a WORD count. |
| VT_FILETIME | 64 | 64-bit FILETIME structure as defined in Win32. |
| VT_BLOB | 65 | DWORD count of bytes, followed by the same number of bytes of data. The byte count does not include the 4 bytes for the length of the count itself; an empty BLOB would have a count of 0, followed by 0 bytes. This is similar to VT_BSTR, but it does not guarantee a null byte at the end of the data. |
| VT_STREAM | 66 | A VT_LPSTR (DWORD count of bytes followed by a zero-terminated string of the same number of bytes); it names a stream containing the actual property value. The stream is a sibling of the stream holding this type indicator; this stream must be named "CONTENTS". |
| VT_STORAGE | 67 | A VT_LPSTR (DWORD count of bytes followed by a zero-terminated string of the same number of bytes); it names a substorage that contains the real property value. The substorage is a sibling of the stream containing this type. The stream itself must be named "CONTENTS". |

*(continued)*

**Table 16-1.** *continued*

| Type | Value | Description |
|---|---|---|
| VT_STREAMED-_OBJECT | 68 | Same as VT_STREAM (same requirements) but indicates that the named stream contains a serialized object, which is a CLSID followed by initialization data for the class. The object can be instantiated with *OleLoadFromStream*. |
| VT_STORED-_OBJECT | 69 | Same as VT_STORAGE (same requirements) but indicates that the named substorage contains an object that can be loaded through *OleLoad* or *ReadClassStg* and *IPersistStorage::Load*. |
| VT_BLOB_OBJECT | 70 | An array of bytes containing a serialized object in the same representation as would appear in a VT_STREAMED-_OBJECT (VT_LPSTR). The only significant difference between this type and VT_STREAMED_OBJECT is that VT_BLOB_OBJECT does not have the system-level storage overhead that VT_STREAMED_OBJECT has. VT-_BLOB_OBJECT is more suitable for scenarios involving numerous small objects. |
| VT_CF | 71 | An array of bytes containing a clipboard format identifier followed by the data in that format. In other words, following the VT_CF identifier is the data in the format of a VT_BLOB. This is a DWORD count of bytes followed by the indicated number of bytes of data. A LONG followed by an appropriate clipboard identifier and a property whose value is plain text should use VT_LPSTR, not VT_CF, to represent the text. Also, an application should choose a single clipboard format for a property's value when using VT_CF. |
| VT_CLSID | 72 | A CLSID, which is a DWORD, two WORDs, and 8 bytes. |

*(continued)*

**Table 16-1.** *continued*

| Type | Value | Description |
|------|-------|-------------|
| VT_VECTOR | 0x1000 | If the type indicator is one of the previous values in addition to this bit being set, the value is a DWORD count of elements followed by the indicated number of repetitions of the value. When VT_VECTOR is combined with VT_VARIANT (VT_VARIANT must be combined with VT_VECTOR), the value contains a DWORD element count, a DWORD type indicator, the first value, a DWORD type indicator, the second value, and so on. Examples: VT_LPSTR ¦ VT_VECTOR has a DWORD element count, a DWORD byte count, the first string data, a DWORD byte count, the second string data, and so on. VT_I2 ¦ VT_VECTOR has a DWORD element count followed by a sequence of 2-byte integers, with no padding between them. |

## Dictionaries

As mentioned earlier, the property with PID 0 is always an optional dictionary that is generically defined as the following structure:

```
struct
    {
    DWORD    cEntries;
    ENTRY    rgEntry[cEntries];
    };
```

Each entry is a structure containing the PID along with what is essentially a BSTR:

```
struct
    {
    DWORD    propertyID;
    DWORD    cbName;          //Includes the null terminator
    char     szName[cbName];
    };
```

The count of entries in a dictionary is the one exception to the usual property structure of a type/value pair. The count of entries in the dictionary sits in the place of the type indicator. In addition, if a dictionary exists, it must contain at least one entry describing PID 0 with the name of the property set itself. Other than that, a dictionary can contain any entries it wants, and it doesn't need to include entries for every last property in the rest of the set. Some PIDs are implicitly understood by any other code that knows how to read the set in the first place.

## Naming and Storing Property Sets

The purpose of having a property set is to facilitate data exchange between components and applications. I shouldn't need to say too much to convince you that a property set isn't necessarily the most efficient way to store your own internal data. You need to use a property set primarily when you want to share persistent information.

A property set is always considered an attachment to a compound file. It is contained either as a single stream in that file or as a substorage in that file if the property set spans multiple streams in that substorage. The reason is simple: any other code can navigate through your compound file and locate property sets. In Chapter 7, we saw that OLE reserves any storage or stream element name from ASCII 5 through ASCII 31 for its own use. Naming a property set is one use for a reserved prefix. Specifically, the ASCII 5 prefix (usually written as \005) identifies a common property set in a storage or stream. *Common* means that the property set is known to many applications and to the system. The Summary Information stream is an example of this.

When property sets are stored in a substorage, the primary stream of the set should be named "CONTENTS" and the CLSID of the storage should be identical to the CLSID written into the property set. Only when the property set takes up an entire substorage are properties of type VT_STREAM, VT_STORAGE, VT_STREAMED_OBJECT, VT_STORED_OBJECT, and VT_BLOB_OBJECT legal. Specific substorages or streams containing those other properties are siblings of the "CONTENTS" stream itself.

## The Summary Information Property Set

At the time of writing, Microsoft has defined only a single standard property set, Summary Information. This property set is defined as a stream named "\005SummaryInformation" (saving it as a storage is not allowed), and its FMTID is *F29F85E0-4FF9-1068-AB91-08002B27B3D9*. As we described earlier, a specific property set defines the meaning of each property within it and assigns the PIDs. Those for Summary Information are listed in Table 16-2.

| Property Name | Property ID | PID | Type |
|---|---|---|---|
| Title | PID_TITLE | 2 | VT_LPSTR |
| Subject | PID_SUBJECT | 3 | VT_LPSTR |
| Author | PID_AUTHOR | 4 | VT_LPSTR |
| Keywords | PID_KEYWORDS | 5 | VT_LPSTR |
| Comments | PID_COMMENTS | 6 | VT_LPSTR |
| Template | PID_TEMPLATE | 7 | VT_LPSTR |
| Last Saved By | PID_LASTAUTHOR | 8 | VT_LPSTR |
| Revision Number | PID_REVNUMBER | 9 | VT_LPSTR |
| Total Editing Time | PID_EDITTIME | 10 | VT_FILETIME |
| Last Printed | PID_LASTPRINTED | 11 | VT_FILETIME |
| Create Time/Date | PID_CREATE_DTM | 12 | VT_FILETIME |
| Last Saved Time/Date | PID_LASTSAVE_DTM | 13 | VT_FILETIME |
| Number of Pages | PID_PAGECOUNT | 14 | VT_I4 |
| Number of Words | PID_WORDCOUNT | 15 | VT_I4 |
| Number of Characters | PID_CHARCOUNT | 16 | VT_I4 |
| Thumbnail | PID_THUMBNAIL | 17 | VT_CF |
| Name of Creating Application | PID_APPNAME | 18 | VT_LPSTR |
| Security | PID_SECURITY | 19 | VT_I4 |

**Table 16-2.**

*The Summary Information property set.*

PID_CREATE_DTM is considered a read-only value once it is present in a property set. In other words, the creation date of whatever file this property set is attached to is determined only once. No one has the need to change the value later. Also, PID_THUMBNAIL should contain a metafile or bitmap (device-dependent or device-independent); a metafile is recommended. A final note is that PID_SECURITY is a set of suggested access-control flags, shown in the following table. The code that reads the property set and the document should honor these flags:

| Security Level | Value |
| --- | --- |
| None | 0 |
| Password protected | 1 |
| Read-only recommended | 2 |
| Read-only enforced | 4 |
| Locked for annotations | 8 |

The way an application obtains much of the information that it writes into this property set is up to that application. Various applications in Microsoft Office have a Summary Info command on the File menu; choosing this command displays a dialog box in which the user can enter most of the string-related information. Information such as word count and a thumbnail sketch can be obtained without the user's direct input.

Regardless of how an application obtains the information, Microsoft is strongly encouraging developers of applications that write information into compound files to include the Summary Information property set as a stream underneath the file's root storage. And for good reasons. Historically, the properties contained in Summary Information have always been wrapped inside an application's proprietary file format. If a user wanted to view or otherwise use that information, he or she had to run the application that created it. Besides simply looking at the information, users often search for files on the basis of a set of criteria, such as "search for all documents written by Terry White after 6/17/94 that contain the phrases 'west region' or 'central region' in either the title, subject, or keywords." When summary information data is locked in a proprietary file format, users have to search through each application's file type individually, a tedious process at best.

To facilitate systemwide document searches, Microsoft has used OLE's Property Sets and Compound Files to specify a standard structure for this information (the property set) and a standard place to store it (the compound file). Any application can retrieve these properties and use them for display or searching purposes. The Windows 95 Explorer, for example, allows you to view the summary information attached to any compound file without running the application that created that file. Future versions of Windows will use this information to perform file searches. In such a system, the shell allows the user to specify criteria that are then matched against summary information to generate a list of matching files. All of this happens quickly because there is no need to load more than a small block of data from any file.

## Property Set Wrap-Up

You can imagine that a structure as detailed as a property set is not all that easy to write into a single stream, not to mention managing one that spans multiple streams. Figuring out how to serialize or deserialize every last data type and how to handle all cases robustly is not trivial. You learned how to work with stream and storage elements in Chapter 7, so this book will not describe other sample code that attempts to read and write property sets such as Summary Information. There are two reasons for this.

First, Microsoft Visual C++ and the Microsoft Developer's Library service have sufficient samples and facilities to simplify your dealings with property sets. For example, the OLE Control Development Kit (CDK) includes a few classes as part of the Microsoft Foundation Classes (MFC), namely *CPropertySet*, *CPropertySection*, and *CProperty*. These classes wrap the functionality in the major pieces of any property set, sheltering you from the complexities of messing with seek offsets and byte ordering. The CDK is the source of the data structures we've seen in this section. Using these classes, you should not have to touch the structures yourself.

These same products also contain sample code for a Summary Information dialog box along with code to read and write this specific stream (as opposed to the general classes that work with any property set). If you have an application that already maintains the type of information you would store in the Summary Information property set, integrating a user interface and storage code around that information won't be too much work. You may already have code to do something similar. The only two samples in this book that write files, Patron and Cosmo, do not maintain any of the information described in the property set, nor do they have the capacity for half of it. Because there are sufficient external samples, we will not add the Summary Information feature to these samples themselves.

The second reason we'll eschew specific property set samples is that one of the future enhancements to OLE will be an OLE-provided service to encapsulate property sets behind specific interfaces related to property storage. You can easily think of how one might wrap a property set into an *IProperty-Set* interface along with *IPropertySection* and *IPropertyStorage*. When this service is available, you'll have as little need to worry about the guts of a property set as you do now with type information—let OLE take care of all the picky details.

As you might have noticed, OLE currently contains no services that deal with property sets, either to generate them or to make use of them in any way. The format described here is as far as it goes. An OLE service for manipulating property sets will be a welcome addition to all the other technologies we have.

That said, we can look at some implementation details concerning the other parts of this chapter, namely property change notifications and property pages.

## Using and Implementing *IPropertyNotifySink*

An interface as simple as *IPropertyNotifySink* is not that complicated to work with in code. In fact, the bulk of the code within this interface exists for the purpose of working with *IConnectionPointContainer* and *IConnectionPoint*, as we saw in Chapter 4. The samples AutoCli2 (CHAP16\AUTOCLI2) and Beeper6 (CHAP16\BEEPER6) provide a quick demonstration of this interface. (Be sure to register Beeper6 before running AutoCli2.) Beeper6 is a modification of Beeper2 from Chapter 14. The first change is to include a few of the necessary flags in type information, as we can see in BEEP0000.ODL, where the interface *IBeeper* is defined:

```
⋮
interface IBeeper : IUnknown
    {
    [propget, helpstring("The current sound")
        , bindable, defaultbind, displaybind, requestedit
    ]
        long Sound(void);

    [propput
        , bindable, defaultbind, displaybind, requestedit
    ]
        void Sound([in] long lSound);

    [helpstring("Play the current sound")]
        long Beep(void);
    }
```

When you define an interface in which specific member functions represent properties, you must mark both *propget* and *propput* members with the same attributes. MKTYPLIB will complain that you've defined a duplicate property name otherwise.

Supporting a bindable or request edit property from within the object itself is first a matter of implementing the necessary connection point support. Beeper6 uses the same sort of code that we've seen in other samples (such as CHAP05\POLYLINE). When Beeper6 does have an *IPropertyNotify-Sink* pointer in hand, it calls *OnRequestEdit* and *OnChanged* as appropriate from within its *IBeeper::put_Sound* method (BEEPER.CPP):

```
STDMETHODIMP_(void) CBeeper::put_Sound(long lSound)
    {
    if (MB_OK!=lSound && MB_ICONEXCLAMATION!=lSound
        && MB_ICONQUESTION!=lSound && MB_ICONHAND!=lSound
        && MB_ICONASTERISK!=lSound)
        {
        m_pImpIDispatch->Exception(EXCEPTION_INVALIDSOUND);
        return;
        }

    if (NULL!=m_pIPropNotifySink)
        {
        //If we didn't get permission, stop now.
        if (NOERROR!=m_pIPropNotifySink->OnRequestEdit(PROPERTY_SOUND))
            return;
        }

    m_lSound=lSound;

    if (NULL!=m_pIPropNotifySink)
        m_pIPropNotifySink->OnChanged(PROPERTY_SOUND);

    return;
    }
```

Because the *Sound* property is marked *requestedit*, we must first call *On-RequestEdit* for permission to change. Because the request returns S_OK or S_FALSE, we have to compare the return value against NOERROR directly. If the request is denied, we stop processing at this point and do not change the property at all. Otherwise, we make the change and follow it up with a call to *OnChanged*.

For Beeper6, this is all there is to it. This sample, of course, is simple—more complex components that support *IPropertyNotifySink* will have many more places where they must make requests and send change notifications. The process of sending the request before changing a property and then sending a notification after changing it, however, is always the same. Remember also that the object can send the request and notification with DISPID-_UNKNOWN to specify multiple objects.

On the client side, AutoCli2 provides a sink object with the necessary interface. Its two specific member functions are implemented in AUTOCLI2-.CPP as follows, using the class *CPropertyNotifySink*:

```
STDMETHODIMP CPropertyNotifySink::OnChanged(DISPID dispID)
    {
    TCHAR       szTemp[200];

    wsprintf(szTemp
        , TEXT("OnChanged notification received for DISPID=%lu")
        , dispID);

    m_pApp->Message(szTemp);
    return NOERROR;
    }

STDMETHODIMP CPropertyNotifySink::OnRequestEdit(DISPID dispID)
    {
    TCHAR       szTemp[200];

    wsprintf(szTemp
        , TEXT("OnRequestEdit received for DISPID=%lu"), dispID);
    m_pApp->Message(szTemp);

    return ResultFromScode(m_pApp->m_fReadOnly ? S_FALSE : S_OK);
    }
```

AutoCli2 displays a message in its client area within *OnChanged* to show that it received the notification. When you change the Beeper object's *Sound* property from AutoCli2's menu, you'll see change notifications come through. The return value for *OnRequestEdit* is controlled through another menu item, named Enforce Read-Only, which toggles the value of the *m_fRead-Only* flag in the code above. If you activate this option, *OnRequestEdit* will deny changes, so setting a new sound value in the Beeper object will not actually change anything, and no *OnChanged* notifications will occur.

# Displaying Property Pages

Playing with AutoCli2, you will notice a Properties menu item. When you select this item, AutoCli2 asks the Beeper object within it for a list of property page CLSIDs and then calls *OleCreatePropertyFrame* to display those property pages. As we saw earlier in this chapter, property pages involve the client, one or more objects, and the property page objects themselves. AutoCli2 and Beeper6 supply the first two pieces of the picture, and the sample BeepProp (CHAP16\BEEPPROP) contains the property page implementation, which we'll cover in the next section. (Before attempting to ask AutoCli2 to display the property pages, be sure to compile and register BeepProp.)

When we select the Properties menu item in AutoCli2, we end up in the function *CApp::ShowProperties* in AUTOCLI2.CPP:

```
void CApp::ShowProperties(void)
    {
    ISpecifyPropertyPages   *pISPP;
    CAUUID                  caGUID;
    HRESULT                 hr;

    if (FAILED(m_pIDispatch->QueryInterface
        (IID_ISpecifyPropertyPages, (void **)&pISPP)))
        {
        Message(TEXT("Object has no property pages."));
        return;
        }

    hr=pISPP->GetPages(&caGUID);
    pISPP->Release();

    if (FAILED(hr))
        {
        Message(TEXT("Failed to retrieve property page GUIDs."));
        return;
        }

    hr=OleCreatePropertyFrame(m_hWnd, 10, 10, OLETEXT("Beeper")
        , 1, (IUnknown **)&m_pIDispatch, caGUID.cElems
        , caGUID.pElems, m_lcid, 0L, NULL);

    if (FAILED(hr))
        Message(TEXT("OleCreatePropertyFrame failed."));

    //Free GUIDs.
    CoTaskMemFree((void *)caGUID.pElems);
    return;
    }
```

Here we execute the steps described earlier: query for *ISpecifyProperty-Pages*, call *ISpecifyPropertyPages::GetPages*, pass those page CLSIDs and the object pointers to *OleCreatePropertyFrame*, and on return from that function free the CLSID array allocated in *GetPages*. That's it. Barring failure at one point or another, you'll see the Beeper object's private property page. (See Figure 16-7 on page 799.)

In AutoCli2, you'll notice that the Properties menu item is always enabled and that we first check for the presence of *ISpecifyPropertyPages* in this series of operations. A slightly more sophisticated client would query for this interface within WM_INITMENUPOPUP processing to enable or disable the menu item accordingly. If the client also allowed the user to select multiple objects, it would query each selected object and enable the menu item only when everything in the selection supports property pages. A sophisticated client could also retrieve the property page CLSIDs from each object at the same time and verify that at least one property page exists in common before enabling the menu item. As stated earlier, a client should display only the set of property pages common to every object in a selection so as not to display pages that could send unexpected information to unsuspecting objects.

There are, of course, many algorithms through which the client determines the common subset of property pages for multiple objects. If you need to determine this in your own work, realize that you don't need to compare an *entire* CLSID to initially determine equality. You can make a significant optimization by comparing only the first DWORD of any two CLSIDs (the *Data1* field in the GUID structure). Even sequentially allocated GUIDs differ in that first DWORD, although they are identical everywhere else. If those DWORDs are different, the CLSIDs must be different. You will usually eliminate most of the unmatched CLSIDs in this manner. Only when a match exists in the first DWORD should you worry about comparing the entire structure for perfect equality.

As for Beeper6's implementation of *ISpecifyPropertyPages*, it needs only to allocate an array of GUIDs, store the CLSIDs of the pages it wants, and return as shown in the following code, from BEEPER.CPP:

```
STDMETHODIMP CImpISpecifyPP::GetPages(CAUUID *pPages)
    {
    GUID    *pGUID;

    pPages->cElems=0;
    pPages->pElems=NULL;

    pGUID=(GUID *)CoTaskMemAlloc(CPROPPAGES*sizeof(GUID));
```

```
if (NULL==pGUID)
    return ResultFromScode(E_OUTOFMEMORY);

//Fill array now that we allocated it.
pGUID[0]=CLSID_BeeperPropertyPage;

//Fill structure and return.
pPages->cElems=CPROPPAGES;
pPages->pElems=pGUID;
return NOERROR;
}
```

No great challenges here. *CLSID_BeeperPropertyPage* is defined in INC-\BOOKGUID.H. BeepProp is the server for that CLSID, as we'll see shortly.

If you are creating a client that supports per-property browsing, you will skip all this business with arrays of CLSIDs. Instead, you'll query the object in question for *IPerPropertyBrowsing* and pass the dispID of the single property to its *MapPropertyToPage*. You'll stuff the single CLSID that you get back into an OCPFIPARAMS structure along with the dispID and then throw the entire structure at *OleCreatePropertyFrameIndirect*.

As you can see, the responsibilities of both a client and an object displaying property pages are minimal, even when per-property browsing is involved. The bulk of the work happens between the property frame and the property page itself.

## The Standard Font, Color, and Picture Property Pages

The run-time library for OLE Controls (shipped with the OLE Control Development Kit) provides three standard property pages: one for font selection, one for color selection, and one for manipulating picture types. The Font and Color pages were shown in Figures 16-2 and 16-3. The predefined CLSIDs for these pages are *CLSID_CFontPropPage*, *CLSID_CColorPropPage*, and *CLSID_CPicturePropPage*, which are defined in the CDK header file OLECTLID.H. These property pages are designed to be generic implementations for any objects that might have such properties. As standard pages, they send changes to the affected objects through *IDispatch::Invoke*, using standard (negative) dispIDs to identify the various properties involved. This means that you can use these pages for your own objects as long as you support these standard dispIDs. For more information on the specific values involved, see the documentation provided with the CDK.

# Implementing a Property Page

When Beeper6 is asked for its list of property page CLSIDs, it specifies only *CLSID_BeeperPropertyPage*, whose server is BEEPPROP.DLL. BeepProp is a normal in-process server for an object that implements *IPropertyPage* and supports both English and German in its user interface. Its registry entries are extremely simple; we require only an entry for *InprocServer32* under the appropriate CLSID subkey. Because a property page is always specified by its CLSID, there is no need to assign a ProgID or VersionIndependentProgID or to create registry entries for them. A property page also has no need for type information (at least at this point in time).

The source code for BeepProp is contained in BEEPPROP.CPP, including the class factory, required in-process server exports, and the property page object. In addition, BEEPPROP.RC contains the dialog templates for the property page itself, in both English and German, as well as the title strings that appear in the frame's tab for this page:

```
//From BEEPPROP.RC

STRINGTABLE
    BEGIN
     IDS_0_PAGETITLE,        "General"
     IDS_7_PAGETITLE,        "Allgemein"
    END

IDD_BEEPERPROPS_0 DIALOG DISCARDABLE  0, 0, 172, 88
STYLE WS_CHILD
FONT 8, "MS Sans Serif"
BEGIN
    CONTROL        "&Default",IDC_BEEPDEFAULT,"Button",
                   BS_AUTORADIOBUTTON | WS_GROUP,13,8,84,12
    CONTROL        "&Hand",IDC_BEEPHAND,"Button",BS_AUTORADIOBUTTON,
                   13,23,84,12
    CONTROL        "&Question",IDC_BEEPQUESTION,"Button",
                   BS_AUTORADIOBUTTON,13,38,84,12
    CONTROL        "&Exclamation",IDC_BEEPEXCLAMATION,"Button",
                   BS_AUTORADIOBUTTON,13,53,84,12
    CONTROL        "&Asterisk",IDC_BEEPASTERISK,"Button",
                   BS_AUTORADIOBUTTON,13,68,84,12
    DEFPUSHBUTTON  "&Test",IDOK,118,8,50,14
END
```

```
IDD_BEEPERPROPS_7 DIALOG DISCARDABLE  0, 0, 172, 88
STYLE WS_CHILD
FONT 8, "MS Sans Serif"
BEGIN
    CONTROL         "&Standard",IDC_BEEPDEFAULT,"Button",
                    BS_AUTORADIOBUTTON ¦ WS_GROUP,13,8,84,12
    CONTROL         "&Hand",IDC_BEEPHAND,"Button",BS_AUTORADIOBUTTON,
                    13,23,84,12
    CONTROL         "&Frage",IDC_BEEPQUESTION,"Button",
                    BS_AUTORADIOBUTTON,13,38,84,12
    CONTROL         "&Ausruf",IDC_BEEPEXCLAMATION,"Button",
                    BS_AUTORADIOBUTTON,13,53,84,12
    CONTROL         "Ste&rn",IDC_BEEPASTERISK,"Button",
                    BS_AUTORADIOBUTTON,13,68,84,12
    DEFPUSHBUTTON   "&Test",IDOK,118,8,50,14
END
```

Notice the inclusion of WS_CHILD and the conspicuous lack of WS-_CAPTION and WS_THICKFRAME styles on both dialog templates—creating a dialog box from either of the templates will create a window displaying the listed controls, but the dialog window itself will have no other embellishments. We can then create a dialog from a template as a child window of the frame dialog itself. This results in the proper user interface, as shown in Figure 16-7.

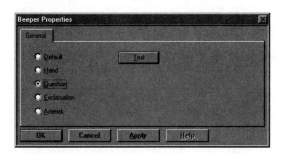

**Figure 16-7.**
*The Beeper property page inside a property frame. The page itself is a modeless dialog created inside the frame dialog.*

Deciding which template to load (and which page title string to use) occurs at run time within BeepProp's implementation of *IPropertyPage::SetPageSite*, the page's initialization function. Here it saves the LCID returned from *IProperty-PageSite::GetLocaleID* and initializes its variable *m_uIDTemplate* accordingly. It then calculates the size of the page on the basis of the dialog template and uses it later within *IPropertyPage::GetPageInfo*:

```
STDMETHODIMP CBeeperPropPage::SetPageSite
    (LPPROPERTYPAGESITE pPageSite)
    {
if (NULL==pPageSite)
    ReleaseInterface(m_pIPropertyPageSite)
else
    {
    HWND        hDlg;
    RECT        rc;
    LCID        lcid;

    m_pIPropertyPageSite=pPageSite;
    m_pIPropertyPageSite->AddRef();

    if (SUCCEEDED(m_pIPropertyPageSite->GetLocaleID(&lcid)))
        m_lcid=lcid;

    switch (PRIMARYLANGID(m_lcid))
        {
        case LANG_GERMAN:
            m_uIDTemplate=IDD_BEEPERPROPS_7;
            break;

        case LANG_NEUTRAL:
        case LANG_ENGLISH:
        default:
            m_uIDTemplate=IDD_BEEPERPROPS_0;
            break;
        }

    hDlg=CreateDialogParam(m_hInst
        , MAKEINTRESOURCE(m_uIDTemplate), GetDesktopWindow()
        , (DLGPROC)BeepPropPageProc, 0L);

    //If creation fails, use default values set in constructor.
    if (NULL!=hDlg)
        {
        GetWindowRect(hDlg, &rc);
        m_cx=rc.right-rc.left;
        m_cy=rc.bottom-rc.top;

        DestroyWindow(hDlg);
        }
    }
```

```
      return NOERROR;
      }

STDMETHODIMP CBeeperPropPage::GetPageInfo(LPPROPPAGEINFO pPageInfo)
      {
      IMalloc      *pIMalloc;

      if (FAILED(CoGetMalloc(MEMCTX_TASK, &pIMalloc)))
          return ResultFromScode(E_FAIL);

      pPageInfo->pszTitle=(LPOLESTR)pIMalloc->Alloc(CCHSTRINGMAX);

      if (NULL!=pPageInfo->pszTitle)
          {
          UINT          ids=IDS_0_PAGETITLE;

          if (PRIMARYLANGID(m_lcid)==LANG_GERMAN)
              ids=IDS_7_PAGETITLE;

          LoadString(m_hInst, ids, pPageInfo->pszTitle, CCHSTRINGMAX);
          }

      pIMalloc->Release();

      pPageInfo->size.cx      = m_cx;
      pPageInfo->size.cy      = m_cy;
      pPageInfo->pszDocString = NULL;
      pPageInfo->pszHelpFile  = NULL;
      pPageInfo->dwHelpContext= 0;
      return NOERROR;
      }
```

Notice how *SetPageSite* creates the page dialog, retrieves its dimensions, and destroys the dialog immediately. This is done only to initialize *m_cx* and *m_cy* for use in *GetPageInfo*, which will be called before this page is activated, if ever. Creating the dialog and calling the Windows function *GetWindowRect* is much easier than loading the dialog template directly and trying to calculate the extents on the basis of the dialog units in the template. This would involve creating a font, mucking with font sizes and extents, and converting all the values. Windows does this automatically when you create a dialog from the same template, so here I'm simply taking advantage of that convenience. I destroy the dialog immediately because I don't want to hog extra resources by keeping this page in memory when it might not be displayed at all. We want the *IPropertyPage::Activate* and *Deactivate* functions to control our use of these resources, in which we create the appropriate dialog or destroy it:

```
STDMETHODIMP CBeeperPropPage::Activate(HWND hWndParent
    , LPCRECT prc, BOOL fModal)
    {
    if (NULL!=m_hDlg)
        return ResultFromScode(E_UNEXPECTED);

    m_hDlg=CreateDialogParam(m_hInst, MAKEINTRESOURCE(m_uIDTemplate)
        , hWndParent, BeepPropPageProc, (LPARAM)this);

    if (NULL==m_hDlg)
        return ResultFromScode(E_OUTOFMEMORY);

    //Move page into position and show it.
    SetWindowPos(m_hDlg, NULL, prc->left, prc->top
        , prc->right-prc->left, prc->bottom-prc->top, 0);

    return NOERROR;
    }


STDMETHODIMP CBeeperPropPage::Deactivate(void)
    {
    if (NULL==m_hDlg)
        return ResultFromScode(E_UNEXPECTED);

    DestroyWindow(m_hDlg);
    m_hDlg=NULL;
    return NOERROR;
    }
```

Nothing fancy going on, simply straight Windows programming, which applies equally for the *Show* and *Move* members of *IPropertyPage* as well:

```
STDMETHODIMP CBeeperPropPage::Show(UINT nCmdShow)
    {
    if (NULL==m_hDlg)
        ResultFromScode(E_UNEXPECTED);

    ShowWindow(m_hDlg, nCmdShow);

    //Take the focus.
    if (SW_SHOWNORMAL==nCmdShow || SW_SHOW==nCmdShow)
        SetFocus(m_hDlg);

    return NOERROR;
    }
```

```
STDMETHODIMP CBeeperPropPage::Move(LPCRECT prc)
    {
    SetWindowPos(m_hDlg, NULL, prc->left, prc->top
        , prc->right-prc->left, prc->bottom-prc->top, 0);

    return NOERROR;
    }
```

Before *Activate* is called, however, the frame will pass the array of *IUn-known* pointers for the affected objects to our *IPropertyPage::SetObjects*. Here we must free any object selection we might already have and then copy the pointers we need, being sure to call *AddRef* through them. BeepProp specifically queries for *IBeeper*, through which it knows it can access the necessary features of the Beeper object:

```
STDMETHODIMP CBeeperPropPage::SetObjects(ULONG cObjects
    , IUnknown **ppUnk)
    {
    BOOL        fRet=TRUE;

    FreeAllObjects();

    if (0!=cObjects)
        {
        UINT        i;
        HRESULT     hr;

        m_ppIBeeper=new IBeeper * [(UINT)cObjects];

        for (i=0; i < cObjects; i++)
            {
            hr=ppUnk[i]->QueryInterface(IID_IBeeper
                , (void **)&m_ppIBeeper[i]);

            if (FAILED(hr))
                fRet=FALSE;
            }
        }

    //If we didn't get one of our objects, fail this call.
    if (!fRet)
        return ResultFromScode(E_FAIL);

    m_cObjects=cObjects;
    return NOERROR;
    }
```

The internal function *CBeeperPropPage::FreeAllObjects* calls *Release* on every pointer in *m_ppIBeeper* and deletes the *m_ppIBeeper* array itself.

After we know the objects for which this property page is being displayed, we can use those objects to set up the initial state of the control on the page. This happens in the WM_INITDIALOG case of *BeepPropPageProc*, which is the dialog procedure for the property page. (The local variable *pObj* inside this dialog procedure is the *CBeeperPropPage* pointer, managed with the Windows API functions *SetProp* and *GetProp*.) We retrieve the current sound from the underlying Beeper object and check the appropriate radio button:

```
case WM_INITDIALOG:
    ⋮
    if (1==pObj->m_cObjects)
        {
        UINT        iButton;

        iButton=(UINT)pObj->m_ppIBeeper[0]->get_Sound();

        if (0==iButton)
            iButton=IDC_BEEPDEFAULT;

        CheckRadioButton(hDlg, IDC_BEEPDEFAULT
            , IDC_BEEPASTERISK, iButton);

        pObj->m_uIDLastSound=iButton;
        }
    ⋮
```

This code initializes the dialog state only if there is a single object— otherwise, it leaves the state uninitialized. A more sophisticated property page would try to reconcile the states of all underlying objects in a way that if they all have the same state, some of the dialog controls could be initialized.

The variable *m_uIDLastSound* in *CBeeperPropPage* is used to keep track of changes that occur in the radio button selection in this property page. In the WM_COMMAND message processing of *BeepPropPageProc*, we execute the following code whenever a radio button is selected:

```
if (pObj->m_uIDLastSound==wID)
    break;

//Save most recently selected sound.
pObj->m_uIDLastSound=LOWORD(wParam);
pObj->m_fDirty=TRUE;

if (NULL!=pObj->m_pIPropertyPageSite)
```

```
{
pObj->m_pIPropertyPageSite
    ->OnStatusChange(PROPPAGESTATUS_DIRTY);
}
```

In short, if the newly selected sound is different from the last selection, we consider the page to be dirty by setting *m_fDirty*. At the same time, we have to notify the page site of the change by calling *IPropertyPageSite::OnStatus-Change* with PROPPAGESTATUS_DIRTY. Now our dirty flag will affect the return value from *IPropertyPage::IsPageDirty* in this way:

```
STDMETHODIMP CBeeperPropPage::IsPageDirty(void)
    {
    return ResultFromScode(m_fDirty ? S_OK : S_FALSE);
    }
```

This function is called when the user closes the dialog box with the OK button. If our page is dirty, the frame will call *IPropertyPage::Apply* before deactivating this page and destroying the object. Of course, we might receive an *Apply* call before this time because our call to *IPropertyPageSite::OnStatus-Change* will tell the frame to enable its Apply Now button. The frame will call *Apply* when the user presses this button. In response, we send the current sound value (*m_uIDLastSound*) to the affected objects:

```
STDMETHODIMP CBeeperPropPage::Apply(void)
    {
    UINT        i;
    UINT        lSound, lSoundNew;
    BOOL        fChanged;

    if (0==m_cObjects)
        return NOERROR;

    lSound=(IDC_BEEPDEFAULT==m_uIDLastSound) ? 0L : m_uIDLastSound;
    fChanged=TRUE;

    for (i=0; i < m_cObjects; i++)
        {
        m_ppIBeeper[i]->put_Sound(lSound);
        lSoundNew=m_ppIBeeper[i]->get_Sound();

        fChanged &= (lSound==lSoundNew);
        }

    m_fDirty=!fChanged;
    return NOERROR;
    }
```

Because this property page knows that the Beeper object implements the interface *IBeeper* (defined in ..\BEEPER6\IBEEPER.H, an output file from MKTYPLIB), we can call its *put_Sound* member to apply the changes. However, because *put_Sound* doesn't return an error code, we must call *get_Sound* afterward to check whether the sound actually did change. For example, if you choose Enforce Read-Only in AutoCli2 before choosing Properties, changes made in the property page will not affect the Beeper object at all. Our implementation of *Apply* here will not clear its dirty flag unless changes are applied successfully. What is the result? After calling *Apply*, the frame will immediately call *IsPageDirty* to see whether the changes made the page clean. If so, it disables the Apply Now button until another call to *IPropertyPageSite-::OnStatusChange*. If we do not clear the dirty flag within *Apply*, the Apply Now button will remain enabled, as it should be to indicate a dirty state.

Remember, the way a property page applies its changes to the affected objects is decided between the page and the object. In this sample, BeepProp knows about Beeper6's custom interface, so it uses that interface directly, which has the nice side effect of being independent of localization concerns. We could accomplish the same thing by calling *IDispatch::GetIDsOfNames* for the *Sound* property (or *Ton* in German) followed by a call to *IDispatch::Invoke*. It doesn't matter when a custom property page is involved. A standard property page — one that is intended to be used for different object classes — must specify exactly how it intends to apply changes to the objects. The standard font, color, and picture pages in the OLE Control Development Kit will always send standard dispID values to the object's *IDispatch::Invoke* and assume that the object knows what to do with the new values.

Only three things are left in this implementation. First, the Test button in our property page is really only a convenience for the user. To implement it, we call *MessageBeep* with *m_uIDLastSound* because we know exactly what the Beeper object does with a sound. This is appropriate because the object may, in fact, not be allowed to change its properties at all if the client is disallowing changes through *IPropertyNotifySink::OnRequestEdit*. But even if changes were allowed, we'd have to save the existing sound value, set the new one, have the object play the sound, and then restore the original — a big waste of time. We already assume knowledge about the object, so we might as well use it.

The final two items are the *Help* and *TranslateAccelerator* members of *IPropertyNotifySink*. We don't implement any help, so this function returns E_NOTIMPL, but it will never be called because our *GetPageInfo* didn't provide any help information. BeepProp also returns E_NOTIMPL from *Trans-*

*lateAccelerator,* which means that this page lacks a keyboard interface. You'll notice that the Tab key does nothing and that mnemonics do not work (except for the buttons that the frame owns). Supporting these requires that *TranslateAccelerator* watch for Alt key combinations as well as for Tab and Shift+Tab, setting the focus to the appropriate control for the various keystrokes. This is necessary because the frame's message loop sees all keyboard messages first and can't do anything more than send the keystrokes to the active page. The page dialog will not handle this automatically; you have to implement the keyboard interface directly. The OLE Control Development Kit has facilities for creating property pages with little effort, and MFC provides the implementation of a keyboard interface based on your dialog template.

# Summary

Much of OLE is concerned with different ways to exchange data between an object and a client. As part of the set of available methods, OLE offers three property-oriented technologies.

The first is the user interface standard called *property sheets.* Property sheets allow an end user to directly manipulate an object's properties, complementing the comparable programmatic ability that is exposed through an object's custom interfaces and dispinterfaces. A property sheet is a dialog—invoked through an OLE API function—that contains one or more property pages. Each page displays a collection of properties. In OLE, each page is a separate component with its own CLSID. Each component has one object that implements the interface *IPropertyPage.* Through this interface, the property page is given pointers to the objects being manipulated and is also told when to send changes to those objects. Because an object has to know what changes to expect from property pages, it implements the interface *ISpecifyPropertyPages* to provide the CLSIDs of the pages it supports. Property pages of this sort are demonstrated using an enhancement of the Beeper object from Chapter 14 and the AutoCli sample from Chapter 15.

Objects can also support per-property browsing by implementing *IPerPropertyBrowsing.* Through this interface, a client can ask an object for a specific property to highlight when that object's property sheet appears. Property pages that also support this feature implement *IPropertyPage2* so the object can be told to set the focus to a particular field for the appropriate property. In addition, a client can use *IPerPropertyBrowsing* to retrieve lists of information from an object that are appropriate to display in user interface elements such as drop-down list boxes.

The second property-oriented technology is an interface named *IProperty-NotifySink.* Through *IPropertyNotifySink,* a client can receive change requests and change notifications from an object for any number of properties. To receive requests and notifications, a client implements a sink object with *IPropertyNotifySink* and connects it to an object through the connection point interfaces described in Chapter 4. For any object property marked "request-edit" in the object's type information, the object will call *IPropertyNotifySink-::OnRequestEdit,* giving the client a chance to allow or deny a change to the property. For any property marked "bindable" (regardless of whether it is marked "requestedit"), the object will call *IPropertyNotifySink::OnChanged* when that property changes. A client can do whatever it wants with this notification.

The third property technology is a standard for persistent stream (or storage) layout called *property sets,* a sparse, flexible, and extensible stream format. A specific property set is a specification of a certain collection of properties that might appear in a stream. Each property set is assigned a format identifier (FMTID), which is a GUID that sets it off from all others. Within a property set, individual sections are stored, and each section contains a list of properties. Each property is marked with a type from the VARTYPE enumeration, followed by a variable length stream of bytes that determines the value of that property. Literally any type of property can be stored in this manner, and the sparse layout concept means that any code reading a property set can easily and robustly skip over those properties or sections that it does not recognize.

One property set of general interest to operating systems such as Windows 95 is named Summary Information (contained in a stream with the name "\005SummaryInformation"). This stream contains a document's title, subject, author, keywords, comments, creation time, last saved time, last printed time, and so forth—in other words, general document properties. The Windows 95 shell can display these properties on request, and future systems will use them to match a user's specified search criteria. Because a property set is easily extracted from a stream in a compound file, the application that created that file does not need to be launched simply to display or otherwise read the contents in that stream. This gives the user full and fast access to document properties.

# PART V

# OLE DOCUMENTS

**C H A P T E R   S E V E N T E E N**

# OLE Documents and Embedding Containers

*There are things, and there are places to put things.*
—Tony Williams, Microsoft OLE Architect

In our kitchen, my wife and I have about 150 resealable plastic storage units in all shapes and sizes, from tiny ones that hold barely a quarter cup to ones that should hold enough salad to feed a cast of thousands. (OK, so I'm exaggerating slightly.) Some are square, some are round, some have such unusual shapes that they can't be stacked in our freezer. Some are clear, some are bold seventies colors (such as avocado), and some are recycled yogurt containers that say, "Sell by June 1, 1962." (OK, so I'm exaggerating again.) Some we obtained as gifts from Mom, some we bought ourselves, and at least one I found at a campground in the Cascade Mountains. (No, I'm *not* exaggerating.)

Besides the ubiquitous plastic, there are boxes, bins, pots, jugs, jars, cans, bags, baskets, bottles, and small paper packets containing powders with ingredient lists long enough to choke a toastmaster. What lives inside these various storage units is just as diverse. Some contain dry goods such as assortments of beans, lentils, split peas, stone-ground whole wheat flour, rye flour, brown rice, couscous, millet, Wheat Chex, and spinach grown according to the California Organic Foods Act of 1990. Others, in the refrigerator, hold at least five different kinds of soups, last week's radishes, tomorrow's lunch, and usually some sort of edible yet unidentifiable leftover.

The problem with kitchen storage is that the stuff you want to put in a given container might not necessarily fit the container. Carrots, for example, do not lend themselves to storage in an egg carton. What we would really like is that any container have at least a basic set of attributes that allow it to contain any kind of stuff, regardless of how otherwise bizarre that container might be. In addition, we would really like to have foods that all share a basic set of attributes that would allow them to fit into any of these standardized containers, regardless of how otherwise fantastic the food might be.

I doubt this will ever happen with food storage, but the same problem exists in computing when we are trying to integrate arbitrary or unstructured data from different sources into one centralized place, which we call a *compound document.* By *unstructured* data I mean information whose internal format is not known to the application that manages the compound document—the data is simply seen as a blob of bytes. Now, it has always been relatively easy to have two specific applications exchange specific structured data when both applications understand the exact data formats in question. Such intimate knowledge allows the applications to fit together as well as eggs fit in an egg carton. But just as an egg carton really doesn't work well to store anything but eggs, such a specialized interface between applications is not all that useful to other applications.

How, then, can we create applications that can deal in a generic way with unstructured data from any other application? How can we create a container application—the one that manages a compound document—that uses information from any source without intimate knowledge of the source or the information itself? And how can we create a source of such data that needs no intimate knowledge about potential containers? The obvious solution is some sort of central standard that both sides recognize. In other words, a container application needs to view all sources as conforming to some generic prototype so that the container can treat all sources polymorphically. In the same manner, all sources need to see all containers as conforming to a prototype of their own. In this way, any container can use any source; any source can work with any container. Information is then freely shareable among them all.

OLE Documents is the specification that defines these two prototypes: one for *compound document containers,* or simply *containers,* and the other for *compound document servers,* also called *sources* or *servers.* OLE Documents is the means of integrating unstructured data from any arbitrary source in any arbitrary compound document (the persistent file) being managed by the container. The unit of exchange is called the *compound document content object,* or simply *content object.* (In the context of this and most of the chapters that follow, *object* is used to mean the same thing.) Each content object has its own identity—a CLSID—to uniquely mark its type as well as to identify the server code that knows how to manipulate that data at the container's request. Content objects encapsulate their internal data formats and manipulation code behind a set of interfaces that define the prototype. These interfaces provide for persistence, structured data exchange, viewing, caching, and what we call *activation* of the user interface in which the user can manipulate that data.

OLE Documents is the last of the various means that OLE provides to share and integrate information. In Chapter 10, we saw how to exchange structured data through *IDataObject.* Chapter 11 explored how to view and cache graphical data, and Chapters 12 and 13 examined the exchange of structured data through the OLE Clipboard and OLE Drag and Drop. With

OLE Automation, discussed in Chapters 14 and 15, we saw how data is shared through individual properties, and in Chapter 16, we saw how to share properties through persistent property sets as well as through the user interface of property pages. OLE Documents completes the picture, exchanging information through unstructured blobs. In fact, OLE Documents uses many of these other technologies to fulfill the necessary parts of its own protocol.

Nevertheless, OLE Documents is a rich technology, and we'll take the next seven chapters to explore it all. Overall, the number of new interfaces is relatively small. We'll see, for example, *IOleObject, IOleClientSite,* and *IRunnableObject.* Most of what this and the following chapters discuss are the protocols for how applications interact through these and other interfaces we've seen to make OLE Documents work. In addition, the user interface involved in object activation will be a significant topic in these chapters.

In this chapter, we'll look specifically at the architecture for OLE Documents as a whole, including additional object states we have not yet encountered. We'll then examine *embedded content objects,* a mechanism in which an object's unstructured data is stored inside the compound file directly, using storage-based persistence. Embedding is the most basic form of OLE Documents, and it forms the basis for everything else in this technology. Once we look at what embedded objects are and how they behave, we'll see the details of container-side implementation as we enhance the Patron sample to work with OLE Documents.

In Chapter 18, we'll look at the implementation details of a local server as we enhance the Cosmo sample to serve up Polyline Figures as embeddable objects. In Chapter 19, we'll complete our discussion of the basic embedded object by looking at object handlers and in-process servers for embedded objects, creating a rendering handler for Cosmo and also enhancing the Polyline sample to serve embedded objects as well. We'll see that both in-process handlers and servers have some special issues when dealing with the data cache and other container-side considerations.

Chapters 20 and 21 will build on what we know about embedded objects and explore *linked content objects,* in which the object's unstructured data is not stored directly in the compound document itself. Rather, that data is stored somewhere else, and the compound document includes a moniker that names that other place. Servers that support linking must supply these monikers and must also support the necessary mechanisms to bind those monikers, just as we saw in Chapter 9. So while we understand how monikers themselves work, Chapters 20 and 21 will show us how we move them from source to container to set up a link relationship.

Chapters 22 and 23 wrap up OLE Documents through a detailed discussion of *in-place activation,* which is a more document-centric user interface model than the one used for basic activation of an embedded object that we'll see in this chapter. In-place activation actually forms the basis for OLE Controls, so these chapters will lead naturally into Chapter 24, which covers the remaining details of OLE Controls.

Through these chapters, you'll see that OLE Documents truly enables any container to work with the data from any source—the server that provides that data—and that any server can provide data to any container, regardless of the nature of the compound document in that container. This means that we can, by analogy, fit lasagna noodles in a vinegar bottle, carrots in an egg carton, and ancho chile peppers in an ice-cube tray, without any trouble whatsoever. We can't do that in the kitchen, but, hey, this is just software...anything is possible.

## Why MFC Is So Popular for OLE Documents

I imagine that you've already concluded that OLE Documents, let alone much of the other material we've seen and you have yet to see in this book, is complex. A set of protocols as powerful as OLE Documents, to be flexible enough to handle all the demands that are made of it, will be complex. The protocols themselves involve only a handful of functional interfaces, many of which we've already seen. If implementing an object with a few interfaces were all there was to it, everything in OLE would be easy. To make OLE Documents work, however, containers and servers need to not only implement and use various interfaces but also perform specific actions in a number of places around the rest of their code. For example, containers have to do certain things when they create, open, close, save, or rename a file. Servers have to do specific things when showing or hiding their window, working with files, and so on. What makes OLE Documents complex are all these little requirements strewn around an application, and that's mostly what the implementation sections in this and following chapters deal with. The Microsoft Foundation Classes (MFC) makes OLE Documents much easier by controlling the application framework itself, so it already has these pieces of code built in. Then you need only to implement the necessary customizations through virtual function overrides of the various C++ classes involved, thereby reducing the complexity tremendously. MFC is fabulously fit for working with OLE Documents and is well worth your time and investigation. This book will help you understand what MFC is doing by exploring the complete OLE Documents protocol in the raw.

# Why Compound Documents?

To understand how OLE Documents as a whole works, we need to understand why compound documents exist and what sorts of requirements they have. It should be fairly obvious that much of the information generated today uses formats from a variety of sources. In this book, for example, the text was written using a word processor and the graphics were created with a drawing tool. An e-mail message might include graphics as well as other sorts of attachments, such as sound recordings or video clips. A presentation might include not only word processor text but also charts and tables from a spreadsheet, graphics, sounds, video, and all sorts of other interesting content. These collections of stuff—document, e-mail message, or presentation—are all things we call compound documents because they contain pieces of arbitrary information. We use the term *document* in a generic way to refer to any such collection (as opposed to a word processor document specifically).

Compound documents are not in any way new. Five-thousand-year-old pictures and hieroglyphics on the walls of Egyptian tombs are examples of a compound document, as are the illuminated manuscripts of the Middle Ages. Even in the twentieth century, compound documents have been created in much the same way as pyramid carvings and manuscripts—that is, manually. Before the computer age, one typically created a compound document by carefully typing or printing the text on a page, leaving spaces for various other forms of data, primarily graphics, photographs, or other clippings. A layout artist then literally cut those other elements to the right size and pasted them into the document with glue. These actions gave us the clipboard metaphor and its ubiquitous Copy, Cut, and Paste commands.

Using the computer's clipboard by itself—without OLE Documents— you can create very good compound documents, benefiting from automatic layout and easy positioning of elements within the document. To insert pieces of content in the document, you can run the application to create the content you want, create the data, select it, and then copy it to the clipboard and paste it into the document. The result is that in the document you have a rectangle that displays some meaningful data—text, graphics, and so on. Each rectangle is an *object* as far as the user is concerned. You insert content as many times as necessary to assemble all the data you want in that document. This is simple enough, but consider a few complications, some of which are especially difficult for novice users:

1.  The user has to know what applications are available to create content in the first place. The user must manually locate those applications and run them.

2. Pasting data from the clipboard can result in a loss of information. Pasting a metafile drawing as a bitmap, for example, loses the individuality of lines, curves, and other graphical operations. Output quality can suffer accordingly.

3. The data pasted into the document does not retain any information about the program used to create it in the first place. To edit that data, the user must locate the correct application, run it, and then attempt to copy data from the document back into the editing application.

4. Copying data back is not always possible, and if information was lost in the paste, it might not be possible to edit the data as it was originally created.

5. To get around this last problem, the user must remember to save individual files containing the original source data. To edit the data, the user must remember not only the editing application but also the source file. Searching for files is a tedious process.

All in all, these complications make the process of creating and managing compound documents fragile and time-consuming. This was why Microsoft created OLE in the first place. OLE 1, which was then called Object Linking and Embedding, was specifically designed to solve the problems described earlier. OLE 2 was originally intended to improve the performance of various OLE 1 bottlenecks and to add the capability for in-place activation. In the process, Microsoft created the component architecture that we've been exploring in this book, which we now simply call OLE. OLE Documents is specifically the subset of OLE technologies that deals with creating and managing compound documents.

Here's how OLE Documents solves the problems outlined in the previous list, tremendously easing the burden on end users:

1. Through a standard Insert Object dialog box, shown in Figure 17-1 on page 818, users can choose from a list the type of content they want to insert into the document as an embedded or a linked content object. The list is full of the names of registered content objects—those marked with a key named Insertable—each of which maps to a CLSID. This CLSID is then used to launch a server that knows how to edit and manipulate that content type. This means

that the user never has to search for applications manually. As the user edits the data, changes are reflected in the container. When the user closes the editor, the data is automatically saved in the compound document; no copy and paste is necessary.

2. If the user has an editing application already running, copying and pasting data from it (if it supports OLE Documents) results in an embedded or a linked content object in the container. (The Paste Special dialog box can be used to choose alternative formats.) The object maintains its CLSID and all of its native data (or a moniker that names the location of that data) so that information is not lost. The container shows the result of this paste as a graphical representation of the object's data. The representation is cached along with the object's native data in the compound document itself. If the object provides an in-process handler (or server), it can control output quality directly.

3. When a user wants to edit or manipulate the data, the user tells the container to execute one of the object's *verbs,* specific actions such as Edit and Play. The container tells the object to activate itself using the verb, and in response, the object runs the editing code again, initializing the user interface with the native data stored previously (not the graphical representation). The user is automatically brought back to the original editing facilities with the original data. The user doesn't need to manually launch an application or attempt to manually copy data back to it.

4. Because the object knows where it came from (its CLSID) and maintains its original data, editing is always possible if the object's server is available on the machine. Even when the server is not available, other servers might be capable of emulating that CLSID so that they can work with the data. In the absence of all editing facilities, the cached graphical representations ensure that the user can always view and print the data in the document.

5. Embedded objects always maintain their own native data directly in the compound document itself. Linked objects maintain their own moniker to their original source file. In neither case is the user required to remember where source files are located, if they are necessary at all.

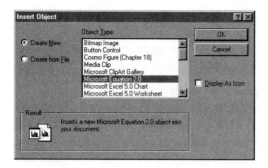

**Figure 17-1.**
*The standard Insert Object dialog box as provided by the OLE UI Library.*

To make this work, both the container and the object (and its server) must support their respective pieces of the OLE Documents protocol, much of which involves other OLE technologies. The basic process of launching a server given a CLSID and then setting up communication with it was covered in Chapters 5 and 6. As we saw in Chapter 7, the ability to share a file between a container and components is handled through a compound file, in which each embedded or linked object supports storage-based persistence through *IPersistStorage* (as we saw in Chapter 8). In particular, linked objects maintain a reference to their source information using a moniker, and the binding procedures we explored in Chapter 9 apply perfectly to the needs of OLE Documents. A content object supports *IDataObject*, *IViewObject2*, *IOleCache2*, and, optionally, *IOleCacheControl* (Chapters 10 and 11) to render data formats, draw presentations directly in the container, and cache presentations. Given additional clipboard formats, the OLE Clipboard and OLE Drag and Drop can be used to copy an embedded or a linked object from a source to a container's document, where the object's data is exchanged using an *IStorage* medium instead of global memory for more efficiency. To all of these interfaces, we add *IOleObject* and *IRunnableObject*, which fill out the capabilities of all content objects.

An object with these interfaces, as illustrated in Figure 17-2, is exactly what a container sees in its own process as a basic embedded content object. (Additional interfaces appear for linked objects and for objects that support in-place activation.) We are now ready to see how these interfaces make OLE Documents work.

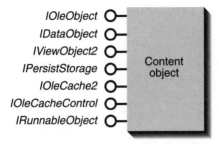

IOleObject
IDataObject
IViewObject2
IPersistStorage
IOleCache2
IOleCacheControl
IRunnableObject

Content
object

**Figure 17-2.**
*How a basic embedded content object appears to a container.*

# Object States and Activation

OLE Documents introduces a few object states above and beyond the simple passive, loaded, and running states that we've seen in earlier chapters. The following table explains how OLE defines and differentiates these states:

| State | Description |
|---|---|
| Passive | The object exists only as a persistent representation in some storage medium (disk, memory, and so on). |
| Loaded | Some in-process code is loaded for the object in the client's process and can access the persistent data as necessary. This state indicates that at least an in-process handler is loaded for the object. Loading an object does not mean launching a local or remote server. |
| Running | The object's server is fully loaded and running and has complete access to its persistent data. The object is registered in the running object table. The object has created its user interface, but that UI is not visible to the end user. |
| Active | The object's user interface is visible to the end user. |

We've seen many objects in earlier chapters that blur the distinction between these states: some objects make no distinction between loaded and running; others make no distinction between running and active. In OLE

Documents, however, all of these states are distinct for both embedded and linked objects. (Objects that are also in-place capable have additional states, as we'll see in Chapters 22 and 23.) Also, specific actions on behalf of the client control how the object moves from state to state. OLE Documents is primarily concerned with the control of active objects, as activation is one of its primary features.

The sequence of *CoCreateInstance* followed by *IPersistStream::Load* or *IPersistStorage::Load* moves a passive object into at least the loaded state, depending on the object. These sequences are encapsulated in API functions such as *OleLoadFromStream* and *OleLoad*, both of which return a new interface pointer to the newly loaded object. Calling this object's *Release* member will take the object back to the passive state. (A client usually does this after saving the object with *OleSaveToStream* or *OleSave*.)

In OLE Documents, the loaded state means that only some in-process code is loaded for the object. If the object has an in-process server, that server DLL is in memory. If an in-process server is not available, OLE will try to load an in-process handler, be it a custom handler or the OLE default handler. In OLE Documents, the default handler is always loaded in the absence of a custom handler. Outside OLE Documents, of course, the most that is loaded is a simple object proxy. In any case, a client always has an interface pointer to a loaded object and can call members in that interface as desired.

The client, or container, can now precisely move the object into the running state through an interface named *IRunnableObject*, which includes member functions named *Run*, *IsRunning*, *LockRunning*, and *SetContainedObject*. Calls to these members are wrapped for convenience in the OLE API functions *OleRun*, *OleIsRunning*, *OleLockRunning*, and *OleSetContainedObject*. When *Run* is called on an in-process server that supports OLE Documents (as we'll see in Chapter 19), the object initializes any user interface it needs when active and registers itself in the running object table. It does not, however, show itself. When called on a handler or the generic proxy, *Run* causes that handler to launch the local server (through *CoCreateInstance*). Servers that support OLE Documents will use the presence of *-Embedding* on the command line as a signal that the object in question has now entered the running state but should not be visible. This is why servers, such as those we saw with OLE Automation, are not generally supposed to make themselves visible on startup when *-Embedding* is present.

Some other means are necessary to make the object visible. In OLE Automation, this is usually controlled through an object's *Visible* property—setting *Visible* to TRUE makes the object visible, and setting it to FALSE hides the object. In cases outside OLE Documents, having the user close the object's UI directly or having the client release the object programmatically is the only way to get an object out of the running state and all the way back to passive.

OLE Documents, however, gives an added layer of control, represented through two member functions of the interface *IOleObject*. As we'll see later in this chapter, this interface represents objects that understand OLE Documents. Two of its member functions interest us here. The first is *IOleObject::DoVerb*, which takes an integer verb identifier. A *verb* is a specific action the object can execute that has meaning to the end user. Typical verbs are Edit, Open, Show, Hide, and Play. A container uses an object's registry information to determine which verbs to display to the end user on an object-specific pop-up menu. When the user selects one of these items, the container calls *IOleObject::DoVerb*, which will run an object first if the object is not already in that state.

The Show verb moves the object from the invisible running state into the visible active state. This verb has a value named OLEIVERB_SHOW and can be implicit in some of the object's other custom verbs at the object's choosing. In any case, Show makes the object visible so that the end user can now manipulate the object directly. Once the object is visible, the Hide verb, OLEIVERB_HIDE, tells the object to move back to the invisible running state and stay there. By using these verbs, passed to the object through *IOleObject::DoVerb*, a container can precisely control an object's transitions between hidden and visible.

The other function of interest is *IOleObject::Close*, which takes an active or a running object back to the loaded state—but not as far back as passive. After *IOleObject::Close*, the container will still have valid interface pointers to the object because that object is still loaded. The container can then call *OleRun* or *IOleObject::DoVerb* again to get the object running or active.

With this basic understanding of the various states of content objects, we're now ready to see the compound document architecture as a whole.

# The Basic OLE Documents Architecture

Whenever any object is in the loaded, running, or active state, a client or a container has at least one interface pointer for that object. To have this pointer, some in-process piece of code must be loaded for that object. The code can be the object server itself, a handler, or simply a proxy. In OLE Documents, the object exposes at least those interfaces shown in Figure 17-2 on page 819: *IOleObject*, *IDataObject*, *IPersistStorage*, *IViewObject2*, *IRunnableObject*, *IOleCache2*, and, optionally, *IOleCacheControl*. This is not to say that any embedded object implementation must manually implement all of these interfaces directly. There are, in fact, three basic ways to create the proper in-process objects:

- If the object is implemented entirely in a local server and has no custom handler or other in-process piece registered, OLE will use an instance of the *default handler* as the in-process object. The default handler will internally create a data cache to store presentations, thereby relying on a local server to supply an object with *IDataObject* through which the handler can retrieve presentations. The default handler also relies on a local server for the implementation of *IOleObject::DoVerb*.

- If the object wants to provide an in-process handler to work with its local server, that handler will typically aggregate on the default handler for most of these interfaces through the OLE API function *OleCreateDefaultHandler*. This is discussed in Chapter 19. We'll see how such a handler typically relies on a local server just as the default handler does.

- If the object is implemented completely in an in-process server, it can aggregate on an instance of the OLE data cache through *CreateDataCache*, as was demonstrated in Chapter 11. The object exposes at least *IOleCache2* directly from the cache. The object also delegates various member functions of *IDataObject*, *IViewObject2*, and *IPersistStorage* to the cache for handling graphical formats or display aspects that the object doesn't otherwise render itself (such as an iconic presentation). Because the object is implemented completely in-process, there is no dependency on a local server. This is also discussed in Chapter 19.

Regardless of the technique in use, the container always sees the same interfaces. Many of these interfaces are strictly in-process or container-side interfaces—namely, *IViewObject2*, *IOleCache2*, *IOleCacheControl*, and *IRunnableObject*. Accordingly, a content object implemented in a local server does not bother with these interfaces; the object implements only *IOleObject*, *IDataObject*, and *IPersistStorage*. *IDataObject* exists mostly so that the container-side cache can retrieve presentations. This process is illustrated in Figure 17-3.

The presence of *IPersistStorage* means that each embedded (or linked) object, regardless of what sort of server implements it, requires its own storage element in the container's underlying file. It also means that the object will maintain incremental access to this storage unless told otherwise through various *IPersistStorage* members. Obviously, the easy way to provide individual storage elements is for the container to use a compound file, as discussed in Chapter 7, but this is not strictly required. Using *ILockBytes* and the functions *StgCreateDocfileOnILockBytes* and *StgOpenStorageOnILockBytes*, a container can wrap individual pieces of its own storage medium inside *IStorage* pointers. The content object doesn't know the difference. Thus, a container can have objects read and write to a piece of some private file, to a database record, to a piece of global memory, and so on. When implementing a container, one of your first steps should be to define exactly how you will provide a separate *IStorage* pointer to each content object.

A major benefit of using a compound file as the compound document is that objects in both in-process handlers and local servers can simultaneously maintain incremental access to the object's storage while the container itself maintains access to the rest of the file. This relationship also is shown in Figure 17-3.

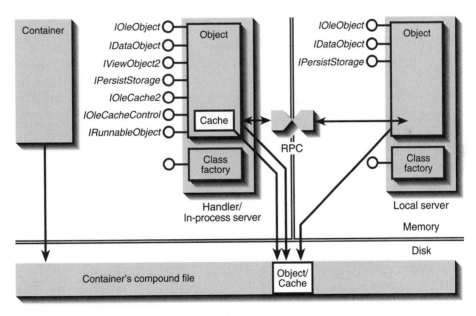

**Figure 17-3.**
*The container, the cache, and the objects inside in-process handlers and local servers can all access the object's storage simultaneously as needs arise.*

The container itself can store custom streams inside the object's storage as long as those streams are named with an ASCII 3 prefix. As described in

Chapter 7, this naming convention marks the stream as "container owned" so that the content object as well as OLE will never touch or mangle the stream in any way. OLE itself uses other specifically named streams to store its own information in the object's storage, as shown in the following table:

| Stream Name | Contents |
|---|---|
| \001CompObj | The CLSID of the object written with *WriteClassStg*. *ReadClassStg* opens this stream to retrieve the CLSID. |
| \001Ole | Contains information about the object, such as whether it's linked or embedded. |
| \002OlePres000 | The primary cached presentation for this object. If there are no cached presentations, this stream will not be present. |
| \002OlePres*nnn* | Additional cached presentations. |

## The Container Site

However a container decides to provide storage elements, it will also need some sort of data structure or internal C++ object to manage that storage and all the other information about the content object itself. This structure or object is called a *client site,* or *container site.* For every content object in a compound document, the container creates a site to manage that content object. The site itself also exposes container-side functionality to the content object in question through two interfaces of its own: *IOleClientSite* and *IAdviseSink,* as illustrated in Figure 17-4.

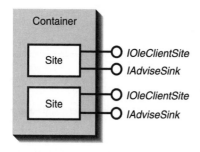

**Figure 17-4.**
*The structure of a container site. The container creates one site for each content object in the compound document.*

The member functions of both of these interfaces are either notifications or requests. *IAdviseSink* is full of notifications, as we saw in Chapters 10 and 11. *IOleClientSite* has a few notifications, a few requests, and a few members that simply provide information about the container:

```
interface IOleClientSite : IUnknown
    {
    HRESULT SaveObject(void);
    HRESULT GetMoniker(DWORD dwAssign, DWORD dwWhichMoniker
        , IMoniker **ppmk);
    HRESULT GetContainer(IOleContainer **ppContainer);
    HRESULT ShowObject(void);
    HRESULT OnShowWindow(BOOL fShow);
    HRESULT RequestNewObjectLayout(void);
    };
```

*SaveObject* is a request that allows the object to ask the container to fully save all the object's information. Why can't the object save itself? Well, the object's storage includes not only the object's native data but also the entire cache, various other OLE-managed streams, and any private streams that the container might want to save. Much of this information, especially when the object is running in another process, is not available to the object at all. This request tells the container not only to save the object's native data through *IPersistStorage::Save* but also to update the cache and save container streams.

*GetMoniker* and *GetContainer* are specific requests for information about the container itself. *GetMoniker* asks the container for either the name of the compound document or the name of the object in the container. (We'll see more of this when we discuss linking.) *GetContainer* provides the object with an *IOleContainer* interface through which one can enumerate other objects in the container and lock the container in memory if necessary. This too applies mostly in linking, so we'll come back to it in later chapters.

*ShowObject* is a request that tells the container to make the object's presentation area visible in the compound document. For example, if the object image is currently scrolled out of view, *ShowObject* must scroll it back into view. A content object will call *ShowObject* in the course of activation before the object's own user interface becomes visible. When that UI does become visible, the object will send the notification *OnShowWindow(TRUE)*. At this time, the container draws a hatch pattern across the image of the object in the compound document to indicate that the content is active, as shown in Figure 17-5 on the following page. (When in-place activation is used, the object does not appear in a separate window for editing, so a thin hatch border appears around the object in the document itself, as discussed in Chapter 22.)

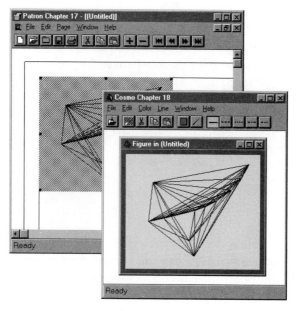

**Figure 17-5.**
*Activating a content object will bring the object's image into view in the
container and will draw a hatch pattern across it to indicate its active status.*

When the user closes or otherwise hides the object's user interface, the object
calls *OnShowWindow(FALSE)*, at which time the container removes the hatching.

The final member of *IOleClientSite* is *RequestNewObjectLayout*, which OLE
Documents does not currently use. It is, however, used with OLE Controls, so
we'll examine this member in Chapter 24.

As for *IAdviseSink*, we've already seen the use of its *OnDataChange* and
*OnViewChange* members. A container will receive these notifications for a
content object if it wants. *OnDataChange* is actually not all that interesting to a
container because a container generally doesn't deal with the object's native
data directly. This member is useful only when a container has more intimate
knowledge about the object type and can understand the object's private formats. *OnViewChange* is of more interest. This function tells the container to
redraw the object in the compound document. Doing so results in a call to
the object's *IViewObject2::Draw*, causing the image of the object to be updated
in the document. The primary use of this notification in OLE Documents is
to synchronize the image of the object in the document with its image in
whatever editing user interface the object displays when active. If we added
another point to Cosmo's polyline data in Figure 17-5, Cosmo would send
*OnViewChange* to Patron, which would then redraw the object to reflect the

change. In this way, the user always sees the same data in both the document (with the hatching) and the object's own user interface.

The other members of *IAdviseSink* also notify the container of important events in the object's user interface. *OnSave* tells the container that the object has been completely saved and is always sent after the object calls *IOle-ClientSite::SaveObject*. *OnClose* tells the container that the user has closed the object's user interface, at which time the container can clean up whatever state it manages for an active object as opposed to a loaded object. Finally, *OnRename* tells the container that a linked object was saved to a different location, as we'll see in Chapter 20.

## The *IOleObject* Interface

As a container site implements *IOleClientSite* and *IAdviseSink*, these pointers must somehow find their way into the content object itself. We already know that the object will obtain an *IAdviseSink* through both *IDataObject::DAdvise* and *IViewObject2::SetAdvise*, but these connections only indicate that the container is interested in *OnDataChange* and *OnViewChange* notifications. Various members of the *IOleObject* interface, the presence of which marks an object as a content object, allow the container to pass its site pointers to the object:

```
interface IOleObject : IUnknown
    {
    HRESULT SetClientSite(IOleClientSite *pClientSite);
    HRESULT GetClientSite(IOleClientSite **ppClientSite);

    HRESULT SetHostNames(LPCOLESTR pszContainerApp
        , LPCOLESTR pszContainerObj);

    HRESULT Close(DWORD dwSaveOption);

    HRESULT SetMoniker(DWORD dwWhichMoniker, IMoniker *pmk);
    HRESULT GetMoniker(DWORD dwAssign, DWORD dwWhichMoniker
        , IMoniker **ppmk);

    HRESULT InitFromData(IDataObject *pDataObject, BOOL fCreation
        , DWORD dwReserved);

    HRESULT GetClipboardData(DWORD dwReserved
        , IDataObject **ppDataObject);

    HRESULT DoVerb(LONG iVerb, LPMSG lpmsg
        , IOleClientSite *pActiveSite, LONG lindex
        , HWND hwndParent, LPCRECT prc);
```

*(continued)*

827

```
HRESULT EnumVerbs(IEnumOLEVERB **ppEnumOleVerb);
HRESULT Update(void);
HRESULT IsUpToDate(void);
HRESULT GetUserClassID(CLSID *pClsid);
HRESULT GetUserType(DWORD dwFormOfType, LPOLESTR *pszUserType);

HRESULT SetExtent(DWORD dwDrawAspect, SIZEL *psizel);
HRESULT GetExtent(DWORD dwDrawAspect, SIZEL *psizel);

HRESULT Advise(IAdviseSink *pAdvSink, DWORD *pdwConnection);
HRESULT Unadvise(DWORD dwConnection);
HRESULT EnumAdvise(IEnumSTATDATA **ppenumAdvise);

HRESULT GetMiscStatus(DWORD dwAspect, DWORD *pdwStatus);
HRESULT SetColorScheme(LOGPALETTE *pLogpal);
};
```

This interface rivals *IMoniker* for the distinction of having the most member functions around! It obviously has a lot of functionality, all of which has its purpose in the architecture of OLE Documents, as described in Table 17-1.

| Member | Purpose |
|---|---|
| *SetClientSite, GetClientSite* | Provides the object with the container's *IOleClientSite* pointer or retrieves that pointer from the object. |
| *SetHostNames* | Provides the object with display names of its container and the compound document, which it displays in its caption bars and as menu items. (A caption bar is visible in Figure 17-5 on page 826.) |
| *Close* | Instructs the object to close, optionally saving changes or discarding them. |
| *SetMoniker, GetMoniker* | Provides the object with the moniker that names its location in the compound document or retrieves that moniker from the object. Used only for linking. |
| *InitFromData* | Instructs the object to perform a Paste operation from a given *IDataObject*. This allows the container to paste into an embedded object if it wants to. |

**Table 17-1.**

*(continued)*

*The* IOleObject *interface.*

**Table 17-1.** *continued*

| Member | Purpose |
|---|---|
| *GetClipboardData* | Retrieves an *IDataObject* pointer from the object that encapsulates what the object would place on the clipboard if the user copied it directly. |
| *DoVerb* | Instructs the object to execute a verb. |
| *EnumVerbs* | Returns an enumerator for the OLEIVERB type. The container uses this to build a pop-up menu of available verbs. |
| *Update* | Ensures that the object is up-to-date. Embedded objects by themselves are always up-to-date unless they themselves contain other embeddings, in which case, this call is recursive to those other embeddings. Linked objects might be out-of-date if the source has changed since the last update. |
| *IsUpToDate* | Asks whether the object is up-to-date. |
| *GetUserClassID* | Returns the CLSID of the object that the user believes he or she is working with. This might change when emulation is being used. |
| *GetUserType* | Returns a user-readable string identifying the object type. |
| *SetExtent, GetExtent* | Instructs the object to change its size (reflected in its editing user interface) or retrieves the size of the object. |
| *Advise, Unadvise, EnumAdvise* | Manages a connection between the object and the site's *IAdviseSink*, specifically for the *OnClose*, *OnSave*, and *OnRename* members. |
| *GetMiscStatus* | Asks the object for its miscellaneous status flags from the enumeration OLEMISC, which describe small behavioral aspects. |
| *SetColorScheme* | Provides the object with the container's preferred color set. The object should use this set if it can. The color set is not a rendering palette but rather a set of preferred foreground, background, and fill colors. |

Much of what we'll be doing in the rest of this chapter and in those that follow will be exploring how this interface is used and where some of the information comes from. One source of such information is the registry, which holds a great deal of content object data.

## Registry Entries for Content Objects

From previous chapters, we know about registry entries such as those that appear under an object's ProgID, VersionIndependentProgID, and CLSID. Additional entries hold information relevant to OLE Documents. (This example is taken from the version of Cosmo we'll implement in Chapter 18.)[1]

```
\
    Cosmo.Figure.2 = Cosmo Figure (Chap 18)
        CLSID = {002114E-000-0000-C000-000000000046}
        Insertable
\
    CLSID
        {002114E-000-0000-C000-000000000046} = Cosmo Figure (Chap 18)
            LocalServer32 = c:\inole\chap18\cosmo\cosmo18.exe
            InprocHandler32 = OLE32.DLL
            ProgID = Cosmo.Figure.2
            VersionIndependentProgID = Cosmo.Figure
            Insertable
            DataFormats
                GetSet
                    0 = Polyline Figure,1,1,3
                    1 = Embed Source,1,8,1
                    2 = 3,1,32,1
                    3 = 2,1,16,1
            DefaultIcon = c:\inole\chap18\cosmo\cosmo18.exe,0
            verb
                0 = &Edit,0,2
                -1 = Show,0,0
                -2 = Open,0,0
                -3 = Hide,0,1
            AuxUserType
                2 = Cosmo
                3 = Cosmo from Chapter 18
            MiscStatus = 16
                1 = 17
            Conversion
                Readable
                    Main = Cosmo1.0,Polyline Figure
                Readwritable
                    Main = Cosmo1.0,Polyline Figure
```

---

1. An entry named *protocol* can also appear here for compatibility with OLE 1 containers. This key has a subkey named *StdFileEditing*, which itself has two subkeys. The first is an entry named *server*, whose value is a path to the OLE 2 local server. (Only local servers are allowed.) The other is named *verb* and contains any number of subkeys 0, 1, 2, and so on, each with a value of a verb string to show in the OLE 1 container. You can look in the REG files of Chapter 18's Cosmo sample for details about these entries.

We've seen many of these entries already, including *DataFormats*, which we first encountered in Chapter 10 along with the *OleRegEnumFormatEtc* function that worked with such entries. Also, these entries mark OLE32.DLL as the object handler for this particular object type. OLE32.DLL is the default handler itself. If you do not include an *InprocHandler32* entry, OLE uses the default handler anyway.

The new entries for OLE Documents are described in the following table:

| Key | Subkeys and Values |
|---|---|
| *Insertable* | Marks the object as one that supports OLE Documents, meaning that it should appear in a container's Insert Object dialog box. |
| *DefaultIcon* | A path to a module and the index of an icon in that module to use by default when the user checks Display As Icon in the container's Insert Object and Paste Special dialog boxes. If no entry is given or if the path is invalid, the dialog boxes will show a default icon (a sheet of paper with a corner folded down, your standard document icon). |
| *verb* | This key has no value, but each subkey is of the form *<verb identifier>* = *<text>,<menu flags>,<verb flags>*. This list of keys identifies the object's supported verbs; those with zero or positive identifiers can appear in a container's pop-up menu. As a whole, this list defines the supported verbs that can be passed to *IOleObject::DoVerb*. In the value for each identifier is first a text string suitable for user interface. This can include an ampersand if the verb is allowed to appear in a menu. The *<menu flags>* provide MF_* values from WINDOWS.H that should be used for this item in a menu. Usually, this value is MF_STRING ¦ MF_ENABLE ¦ MF_UNCHECKED, which translates to 0. The *<verb flags>* are values taken from the enumeration OLEVERBATTRIB and can include OLEVERBATTRIB_NEVERDIRTIES (value 1, which indicates that the verb does not modify the object in any way) and OLEVERBATTRIB_ONCONTAINERMENU (value 2, which indicates that the verb should appear on a pop-up menu). |
| *AuxUserType* | This key has no value itself but instead has subkeys of the format *<form number>* = *<string>*; *<form number>* is either 2 or 3 (never 1, for reasons known only to the gods)* and *<string>* is some user-readable name of the object. Form number 2 should always be a short name (under 10 characters) that describes the type of the object, as in "Cosmo". Form number 3 is a longer application name, such as "Cosmo from Chapter 18", used specifically with the Paste Special dialog box. |

---

*  Actually, 1 is defined as the name stored as the value of the object's CLSID, so it need not be stored here.

*(continued)*

continued

| Key | Subkeys and Values |
| --- | --- |
| *MiscStatus* | The value of this key is the default set of flags for the object. Each subkey is of the form *<aspect>* = *<status>*, where *<aspect>* is a DVASPECT value and *<status>* is an integer flag. |
| *Conversion* | Under this key, the object describes the other data formats that it can either convert to its own (listed under *Readable*) or emulate (listed under *Readwritable*). The subkey *Main* has a value of the form *<format,format,format,format,...>*. Each format is either a clipboard format string, as in "Polyline Figure", or an OLE 1 server ProgID, as in "Cosmo1.0".† These entries are used to populate a container's Convert dialog box, as will be explained later. |

† Specific considerations for OLE 1 conversion can be found in the file OLE1.WRI on the sample CD.

The OLE API functions *OleRegEnumVerbs*, *OleRegGetUserType*, and *OleRegGetMiscStatus* will read some of these entries for you effortlessly. *OleRegEnumVerbs* returns an enumerator for the OLEIVERB type (*IEnumOLEIVERB*), *OleRegGetUserType* returns a string, and *OleRegGetMiscStatus* returns a DWORD with the MiscStatus bits. The MiscStatus values come from the C++ enumeration OLEMISC and are the same flags that an object will return from *IOleObject::GetMiscStatus*:

```
enum tagOLEMISC
    {
    OLEMISC_RECOMPOSEONRESIZE    = 1,    //Run object to resize.
    OLEMISC_ONLYICONIC           = 2,    //Object only appears iconic.
    OLEMISC_INSERTNOTREPLACE     = 4,    //Paste instead of delete.
    OLEMISC_STATIC               = 8,    //Static object
    OLEMISC_CANTLINKINSIDE       = 16,   //No linking to embedding
    OLEMISC_CANLINKBYOLE1        = 32,   //Too complex for OLE 1
    OLEMISC_ISLINKOBJECT         = 64,   //Object is linked.
    OLEMISC_INSIDEOUT            = 128,  //In-place activation
    OLEMISC_ACTIVATEWHENVISIBLE  = 256,  //In-place activation
    OLEMISC_RENDERINGISDEVICEINDEPENDENT = 512
    } OLEMISC;
```

Many of these flags are self-explanatory, and we'll see them in context as we go along. OLEMISC_RECOMPOSEONRESIZE specifically tells a container to run the object whenever its space is changed in the compound document, allowing the object to control its output quality when scaling is used. OLEMISC_INSERTNOTREPLACE tells a container that performing a Paste operation with this object selected should not replace the object but rather paste *into* it through *IOleObject::InitFromData*. OLEMISC_CANTLINKBYOLE1 says that an object uses link source information that is too complicated for OLE 1 containers to handle—OLE 1 can work with a File or a File!Item moniker, but nothing more.

Besides the flags shown here, OLE Controls adds a large number of other OLEMISC flags for its various uses, as we'll see in Chapter 24. For the most part, a simple embedding container or an embedded object will deal with only a few of these.

## Mommy, Daddy, Where Do New Content Objects Come From?

Um, well, ah, you see, there's, ah, a stork. Yeah. The Object Stork.

Sure, an explanation like this might work for a two-year-old, but I don't think it works for programmers—there must be a better explanation. How does a container create a new content object or obtain a copy of one? It is not simply a matter of calling *CoCreateInstance* with a CLSID because with persistent storage, a cache, and related matters, there are additional initialization concerns. For this reason, OLE provides a number of API functions for creating or loading content objects.

The most fundamental of these functions is *OleCreate*, which is the equivalent of *CoCreateInstance* for embedded objects. This function will create the object (using *CoCreateInstance* internally), initialize it through *IPersistStorage::InitNew*, send the object the container's *IOleClientSite* pointer if it's wanted, and initialize the cache. *OleCreate* takes an object from a nonexistent state into a loaded state, from which the container can run and activate it as necessary. Closely related to this is *OleCreateFromFile*, which uses the information in a file to initialize the new embedded object (which itself must implement *IPersistFile* as well to support this ability).[2] If a server for the file type is not available, *OleCreateFromFile* creates what is called a *Package* object, which maintains a copy of the file as its native data. Activating a package object causes it to write that file to a temporary location and try to run it as if the user double-clicked that file in the system shell.

A container can also paste an embedded object from the clipboard or by using drag and drop. In both cases, the container will have an *IDataObject* pointer that encapsulates the embedded object's data formats. OLE defines several formats for this purpose. CFSTR_EMBEDDEDOBJECT and CFSTR_EMBEDSOURCE, whose formats are registered using the strings "Embedded Object" and "Embed Source", are both copies of the object's persistent storage inside a separate storage element (that is, TYMED_STORAGE).

---

2. The version of Cosmo in Chapter 18 does not implement this support and will not work with *OleCreateFromFile*. The version of Cosmo in Chapter 21 does include the necessary support.

The presence of either format in a data object means that an embedded object is available. The function *OleQueryCreateFromData* checks for this availability, and *OleCreateFromData* creates an embedded object from that data. Afterward, the object is no different from what is created through *OleCreate*. Another data format, CFSTR_OBJECTDESCRIPTOR (the string "Object Descriptor") usually travels along with the embedded object to provide more information about the data—for example, its extents and its pick point if the data is used in drag and drop.

Linked objects have several functions analogous to the ones for embedded objects: *OleCreateLink*, *OleCreateLinkToFile*, *OleCreateLinkFromData*, and *OleQueryCreateLinkFromData*. The latter two deal with data of the format CFSTR_LINKSOURCE ("Link Source") and CFSTR_LINKSRCDESCRIPTOR ("Link Source Descriptor").

When any linked or embedded object exists in its passive state, the *OleLoad* function brings it to the loaded state and returns an interface pointer, performing all of the necessary initialization steps done in *OleCreate* and others. *OleLoad* will always work, even if no object-specific code exists. In that case, OLE creates an instance of the default handler. Because the handler works with the data cache, the container can always view and print the object using the cached presentations. Activating the object, however, will not work.

### Containers/Servers and Embedding in Yourself

Many high-end business applications such as word processors and spreadsheets are the sorts of applications that can act both as compound document containers and as servers for material such as text, tables, charts, and so forth. This brings up an interesting possibility: the application can register itself as Insertable so that its own name will appear in its own Insert Object dialog box. This creates the possibility of inserting an object into its own application, called a *container/server*. Each half of the application, however, should still be able to work with the other half as if the object or the container came from a separate application. It doesn't make any sense to run another instance of the application under any circumstances, so using the default handler in such a situation is risky and wasteful. For this reason, OLE provides a hobbled handler called the *embedding helper,* created through the API function *OleCreateEmbeddingHelper,* which provides an efficient mediator to facilitate a container/server's own communication with itself through the standard protocol of OLE Documents. For further information, see the *OLE Programmer's Reference.*

# The Structure and the User Interface of an Embedding Container

We've now seen the basic architecture, interfaces, and API functions involved in OLE Documents and have alluded to a number of user interface elements. Once again, a container has to provide a site object for each content object in the compound document, and each site object implements *IOleClientSite* and *IAdviseSink*. This is the easy part of a container. Much of the rest of the implementation involves elements of the user interface:

1. Shading the site when an object is active; unshading it when it reverts to the running or loaded state.

2. Invoking and handling the Insert Object dialog box. (One view of this is shown in Figure 17-1 on page 818.)

3. Asking the object to draw and print its view when necessary, watching for view changes.

4. Creating an object verb menu in both the container's main menu and a pop-up context menu, which is displayed when the user clicks the right mouse button on the content object. When the user selects a verb, the container activates the object with that verb. The container also activates the object with the *primary verb* (OLEIVERB_PRIMARY) when the user double-clicks the object's rectangle.

5. Pasting content objects, including content object formats in the Paste Special dialog box, from the clipboard and from drag-and-drop operations.

6. Copying the necessary content object formats back into a data object for use with the clipboard or with drag and drop. This lets the user copy objects from within the container.

7. Handling conversion and emulation of objects through the Convert dialog box. This includes changes between content and iconic presentations.

8. Optionally installing a message filter to invoke the Busy dialog box when a local server is occupied, as discussed in Chapter 6.

This list includes only those elements of the user interface relevant to embedded objects or to all content objects. In later chapters, we'll see additional requirements for linked objects as well as in-place activation. I won't include screen shots of all the various dialog boxes because they are fully documented in the *OLE Programmer's Reference* as well as in other Microsoft Windows documentation.

With these things in mind, you should think through the structure of an application before attempting to turn it into a container. Doing so will help you understand where these user interface elements, as well as other container requirements, affect that application. To understand the role of the container, let me indulge in what I call "The Allegory of the Cookie Jar."[3]

A content object is like a batch of cookies. Different cookies have their own form and taste, just as different objects have different classes and behavior. Cookies are great by themselves right out of the oven, but eventually we need to store the rest of the batch somewhere or the cookies will quickly get stale or be devoured by a pack of ravenous hounds (other members of the household). Where we decide to store these cookies depends on how we later want to get at them. Embedded Cookies are always stored inside a cookie jar; Linked Cookies are stored elsewhere, and what you put in the cookie jar is a treasure map (that is, a moniker) that describes where elsewhere is.

A container site is like a cookie jar because it holds (in both its variables and the storage it manages) whatever information makes up the content object. On the outside of this cookie jar is generally some sort of representation of the cookies inside. For our purposes, let's imagine a high-tech cookie jar with a video camera on the inside that transmits a picture of the current cookies to a small screen on the outside. This lets us see at any time exactly what's in the jar. This is equivalent to an always up-to-date graphical presentation for an object, and the video camera represents the availability of code that we can run to obtain new presentations for the object. However, such code is not always available—users take compound documents to other machines on which, perhaps, only the default handler is available. In this case, we have a broken video camera, so as a backup, the cache saves a photograph of the cookies taken at some time in the past (which *might* be out-of-date). Thus, we always have some reminder—perhaps a lower-quality one—of what is stored in the cookie jar.

What is now important for a container application to decide is where this cookie jar lives: the site must have a home in the rest of the application. Just as a cookie jar needs a shelf or a countertop, a site needs a page, a sheet, a document, or whatever. This is vitally important to decide before embarking on the task of implementing a container because the location will likely determine how the site provides storage to its object.

---

3. With apologies to Plato and his allegory of the cave.

For example, the Patron sample that we'll make a container in the next section has internal objects called *tenants*. Each tenant lives on a page, each page lives in a document, and the document works with a compound file. The document owns the root storage for the compound file and gives each page a substorage. Each page then creates a deeper substorage for each tenant. In this way, Patron already has a substorage assigned to each tenant, and this is exactly the type of thing we can give to a content object. In fact, back in Chapter 12, we added this sort of support to enable tenants to contain static metafiles and bitmaps, using OLE's data cache as the object. In this chapter, we're ready to store active content objects in these tenants, so the tenants will become our container sites.

# Embedding Containers Step by Step: Patron

The remainder of this chapter will follow modifications I made to Patron (CHAP17\PATRON) to make it a container for embedded objects. Patron includes most of those items listed in the previous section, but it does not implement message filtering or the Busy dialog box. Such support is easily added using the code illustrated in Chapter 6.

Support for embedding requires changes at many levels, much of it having to do with the user interface. If we return to our cookie jar metaphor for a moment, the cookies need to define the user interface only to account for how they look, feel, and taste—very cookie-oriented sorts of stuff. The cookie jar has to define how it opens and how it looks from the outside. In the same manner, the shelf on which the cookie jar rests has its own interface of color and dimension, just as the kitchen and the house have to define their own characteristics. So, in much the same way that most of the user interface in a house is shown in rooms, shelves, and storage devices, most of the user interface in OLE Documents falls on the container.

Nevertheless, we can reduce implementation to the following sequence of steps; all of the steps except step 1 are elaborated in the following sections. These steps are organized so that you can at least compile after coding the step. In most cases, you will also have something you can run and test. I strongly recommend that you test as much as you can in the early steps because the later ones build on these foundations; testing simplifies the overall task of writing a container.[4]

---

4. There are a few additional concerns for dealing with OLE 1 servers, as documented in the file OLE1.WRI on the companion CD.

1. Initialize OLE on startup and uninitialize on shutdown using *OleInitialize* and *OleUninitialize.*

2. Implement *IOleClientSite* and *IAdviseSink* on your site object and add variables to manage the content object that will be stored in each site.

3. Implement site shading to be used from *IOleClientSite::OnShow-Window,* and draw the object to a screen or printer.

4. Invoke the Insert Object dialog box, and create and initialize objects on return.

5. Activate the object on a double click, and add an object verb menu. Also implement a right mouse button pop-up menu.

6. Add the ability to paste an object from the clipboard (through the Paste Special command if desired), or accept one through drag and drop.

7. Provide new data formats to copy an embedded object back to the clipboard or to source it in a drag-and-drop operation.

8. Delete objects from the document, and call *CoFreeUnusedLibraries.*

9. Save and load documents containing embedded objects.

10. Invoke the Convert dialog box, and handle the Convert To case, the Activate As case, and the Display As Icon changes. Handling iconic presentations includes working with the cache.

## Implement Site Interfaces and Add Site Variables

We first add to whatever we decide is a suitable site the necessary variables to manage an embedded object and implement the *IOleClientSite* and *IAdvise-Sink* interfaces. In Patron, I already have the *CTenant* class, which I've converted here to an object with a reference count and so on, but because this object is only a site, it needs no CLSID, no class factory support, and no registry entries: it's only a simple object with some interfaces. One effect of this change is that I had a few places around my code that called the C++ *delete* operator directly on a tenant. Now that the tenant object has a reference count and an *IUnknown* implementation, these *delete* calls are replaced with *Release.*

I added a few variables to the *CTenant* class to maintain the reference count ($m\_cRef$), the interface implementations ($m\_pImpIOleClientSite$ and $m\_pImpIAdviseSink$), and various interfaces we hold on the embedded object ($m\_pIOleObject$ and $m\_pIViewObject2$). The other new variable is $m\_tType$ of type TENANTTYPE, an enumeration that identifies the type of embedded content object in this site:

```
typedef enum
    {
    TENANTTYPE_NULL=0,
    TENANTTYPE_STATIC,
    TENANTTYPE_EMBEDDEDOBJECT,
    TENANTTYPE_EMBEDDEDFILE,
    TENANTTYPE_EMBEDDEDOBJECTFROMDATA
    } TENANTTYPE, *PTENANTTYPE;
```

In later chapters, we'll add more flags to this set to identify linked objects as well. In any case, Patron initializes these variables to 0 or NULL in *CTenant::CTenant*. In *CTenant::Open*, Patron creates the site's interfaces, deleting them in its destructor. The object's pointers themselves are initialized when we create an object (as we'll see later) and released in *CTenant::Close*.

I also added a number of new member functions to *CTenant*: *StorageGet*, *ShowAsOpen*, *ShowYourself*, *AddVerbMenu*, *TypeGet*, *CopyEmbeddedObject*, *NotifyOfRename*, *ObjectClassFormatAndIcon*, *SwitchOrUpdateDisplayAspect*, and *EnableRepaint*. Several of them are used from within the implementations of the site interfaces that are found in *CImpIOleClientSite* (ICLISITE.CPP) and *CImpIAdviseSink* (IADVSINK.CPP).

Patron makes use of only two members of *IAdviseSink*: *OnViewChange* and *OnClose*. When a site receives *OnViewChange* for the aspect that you display (content, icon, and so on), you only need to repaint the site (thus, redraw the object) and set your document's dirty flag, in whatever way you do that:

```
STDMETHODIMP_(void) CImpIAdviseSink::OnViewChange(DWORD dwAspect
    , LONG lindex)
    {
    //Repaint only if this is the right aspect.
    if (dwAspect==m_pTen->m_fe.dwAspect)
        {
        m_pTen->m_pPG->m_fDirty=TRUE;
        m_pTen->Repaint();
        }

    return;
    }
```

As pointed out in Chapter 11, *OnViewChange* tells the site that the object's presentation as opposed to its data has changed. Because a container shows an object's presentation in the site, we want to watch view changes, not data changes, in order to keep the image in the site current. In Patron,

*CTenant::Repaint* invalidates the site's area in the container's client area and forces a redraw. This calls the embedded object's *IViewObject2::Draw*, as we'll see later. Then, when an object is running and sending us these notifications, we'll immediately redraw the object's image as changes happen to it. In that way, the site image keeps up-to-date with the object's own user interface.[5]

In *IAdviseSink::OnClose*, I've included a single call to *CTenant::ShowYourself(FALSE)* to deal with some potentially misbehaving OLE 1 servers as described on OLE1.WRI on the companion CD:

```
STDMETHODIMP_(void) CImpIAdviseSink::OnClose(void)
    {
    m_pTen->ShowAsOpen(FALSE);
    return;
    }
```

The other *IAdviseSink* members, *OnDataChange, OnSave,* and *OnRename,* are not important to a container, but they are important to an object handler and the data cache being used in the container's process. Such notifications are used to update the handler's internal state, but we don't need to take an interest in them ourselves.

The behavior of *IAdviseSink::OnClose* is similar to that of *IOleClientSite::OnShowWindow*, which is one of the members we need to implement in that interface. In Patron, we also implement *SaveObject* and *ShowObject*, leaving *GetMoniker, GetContainer*, and *RequestNewObjectLayout* unimplemented for now (returning E_NOTIMPL). We will return to these functions in later chapters as we make further enhancements to Patron.

As described earlier in this chapter, *OnShowWindow* tells the container to draw a hatch pattern across the site after repainting the object. The function *CTenant::ShowAsOpen* toggles this state and repaints the object with a hatch pattern across it, as described in the next section. So *IOleClientSite::OnShowWindow* simply delegates to this function in the tenant, as does *IAdviseSink::OnClose*, discussed earlier:

```
STDMETHODIMP CImpIOleClientSite::OnShowWindow(BOOL fShow)
    {
    m_pTen->ShowAsOpen(fShow);
    return NOERROR;
    }
```

The implementation of *IOleClientSite::SaveObject* also delegates to a function in *CTenant*, that function being *Update*:

---

5. An OLE 1 server does not send notifications for every modification, so in this case, you won't see updates as frequently.

```
STDMETHODIMP CImpIOleClientSite::SaveObject(void)
    {
    m_pTen->Update();
    return NOERROR;
    }
```

*CTenant::Update* ensures that the object in this site is fully saved by querying for *IPersistStorage* and calling *OleSave*, then *IPersistStorage::SaveCompleted,*
and then *IPersistStorage::Release.* Patron has been doing this since Chapter 12,
and the code requires no modification:

```
BOOL CTenant::Update(void)
    {
    LPPERSISTSTORAGE     pIPS;

    if (NULL!=m_pIStorage)
        {
        m_pObj->QueryInterface(IID_IPersistStorage, (PPVOID)&pIPS);

        //This fails for static objects, so improvise if that happens.
        if (FAILED(OleSave(pIPS, m_pIStorage, TRUE)))
            {
            //This is essentially what OleSave does.
            WriteClassStg(m_pIStorage, m_clsID);
            pIPS->Save(m_pIStorage, TRUE);
            }

        pIPS->SaveCompleted(NULL);
        pIPS->Release();

        m_pIStorage->Commit(STGC_DEFAULT);
        }

    return FALSE;
    }
```

*OleSave* can fail, but because all it does is call *WriteClassStg* and
*IPersistStorage::Save,* we can duplicate its behavior here as needed.

Finally, *ShowObject* tells the container to bring the object (that is, the
site) into view if at all possible, scrolling only if necessary. An object calls this
function before it calls *OnShowWindow* when it's activated in a separate window. Bringing the site into view ensures that the user can see the changes reflected in the site as they happen in the object's window. Of course, because
*ShowObject* concerns only the user interface, it's not truly necessary for the
actual embedding operation. If it's too much trouble or not applicable to
your container, feel free to ignore it altogether. Patron doesn't see scrolling as

a problem, so it implements this feature through *CTenant::ShowYourself,* to which *ShowObject* delegates:

```
STDMETHODIMP CImpIOleClientSite::ShowObject(void)
    {
    m_pTen->ShowYourself();
    return NOERROR;
    }


void CTenant::ShowYourself(void)
    {
    RECTL       rcl;
    RECT        rc;
    POINT       pt1, pt2;

    //Scrolling deals in device units; get our rectangle in those.
    RectGet(&rcl, TRUE);

    //Get window rectangle offset for current scroll position.
    GetClientRect(m_hWnd, &rc);
    OffsetRect(&rc, m_pPG->m_xPos, m_pPG->m_yPos);

    //Check whether object is already visible. (Macro in bookguid.h.)
    SETPOINT(pt1, (int)rcl.left, (int)rcl.top);
    SETPOINT(pt2, (int)rcl.right, (int)rcl.bottom);

    if (PtInRect(&rc, pt1) && PtInRect(&rc, pt2))
        return;

    //Check whether upper left is within upper left quadrant.
    if (((int)rcl.left > rc.left
        && (int)rcl.left < ((rc.right+rc.left)/2))
        && ((int)rcl.top > rc.top
        && (int)rcl.top < ((rc.bottom+rc.top)/2)))
        return;

    //These are macros in INC\BOOK1632.H.
    SendScrollPosition(m_hWnd, WM_HSCROLL, rcl.left-8);
    SendScrollPosition(m_hWnd, WM_VSCROLL, rcl.top-8);
    return;
    }
```

A good rule of thumb here is to avoid scrolling if at all possible, so *ShowYourself* first checks to see whether the site's rectangle (which is the same as the object's rectangle in the container) is already visible—that is, whether both upper left and lower right corners are already visible in the page window. If so, nothing needs to happen and we can exit the routine. If this first check fails, either the site is not visible at all or the site is too big to be entirely shown in the window. If the upper left corner of the site is in the upper left quadrant of the window, it must be true that the site is not completely visible but that enough of it is visible that we would still want to avoid scrolling. If this second check fails, *ShowYourself* capitulates and scrolls the window so that the upper left corner of the site is visible just below the upper left corner of the window. The *SendScrollPosition* macros (defined in INC\BOOK1632.H) send WM_*SCROLL messages with SB_THUMBPOSITION messages, which are processed in *PagesWndProc* of PAGEWIN.CPP.

At this point, you'll have completed the site interfaces for a container—which is the simple part—with the exception of shading the site when necessary. That is our next task.

## Implement Site Shading and Draw the Object

The user interface guidelines for OLE indicate that the container should draw a hatch pattern across its site when the object in that site is active—that is, when it is open in another window. This shading appears as shown in Figure 17-6. We add this shading when *IOleClientSite::OnShowWindow(TRUE)* is called and remove it when the same function is called with FALSE:

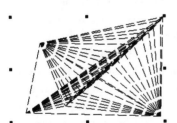 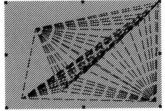

**Figure 17-6.**
*The typical appearance of a site with a loaded object and shaded with an open object. The sizing handles are optional.*

Again, Patron accomplishes this shading in *CTenant::ShowAsOpen*, for which the *fOpen* argument specifies to shade or not to shade:

```
void CTenant::ShowAsOpen(BOOL fOpen)
    {
    BOOL        fWasOpen;
    DWORD       dwState;
    RECT        rc;
    HDC         hDC;
```

*(continued)*

```
fWasOpen=(BOOL)(TENANTSTATE_OPEN & m_dwState);

dwState=m_dwState & ~TENANTSTATE_OPEN;
m_dwState=dwState ¦ ((fOpen) ? TENANTSTATE_OPEN : 0);

//If this was not open, just hatch; otherwise, repaint.
if (!fWasOpen && fOpen)
    {
    RECTFROMRECTL(rc, m_rcl);
    RectConvertMappings(&rc, NULL, TRUE);
    OffsetRect(&rc, -(int)m_pPG->m_xPos, -(int)m_pPG->m_yPos);

    hDC=GetDC(m_hWnd);
    UIDrawShading(&rc, hDC, UI_SHADE_FULLRECT, 0);
    ReleaseDC(m_hWnd, hDC);
    }

if (fWasOpen && !fOpen)
    Repaint();

return;
}
```

Besides doing the shading, the tenant also remembers the open state with TENANTSTATE_OPEN. This flag is used in its drawing function (*CTenant::Draw*) so that the shading is preserved across repaints.

The hatching itself is accomplished using a helper function, *UIDraw-Shading*, that you'll find in the INOLE.DLL library. (Sources are in INOLE-\UIEFFECT.CPP.) This function basically creates a hatch brush and paints over a given rectangle with the GDI call *PatBlt* using an ROP code of *0x00A000C9*, which performs the logical AND operation between the black pattern and whatever is on *hDC*. We get a black hatch pattern across whatever is underneath. Because this hatching is destructive, going from an open state into a loaded state requires that we repaint the entire object to remove the hatching. Fortunately for Patron, *CTenant::Repaint* does exactly that.

Drawing and printing an object in a site always happen inside *CTenant-::Draw*. This does little more than call *IViewObject2::Draw*, but it also includes grab handles and the hatch pattern as necessary. An important point to remember is that site shading applies only to on-screen presentations! Do not draw such shading if you are sending information to the printer. That would certainly look strange.

## Invoke the Insert Object Dialog Box and Create an Object

We're now at the point at which we can create an object to put in the site. To do so, we need to retrieve a CLSID to pass to the *OleCreate* function. This is the purpose of the standard Insert Object dialog box provided in the OLE UI Library. As shown in Figure 17-1 on page 818, this dialog box has two modes. The first is Create New, in which the user selects the name of an object type to create. In return, the container receives the appropriate CLSID for that type. The other mode of this dialog box, shown in Figure 17-7, lets the user enter or browse for a filename. In response to this option, the container[6] calls *Ole-CreateFromFile* to create either an initialized object or a package. (In Chapter 20, we'll enable a Link check box in this part of the dialog box and call *OleCreateLinkToFile* when that box is checked.)

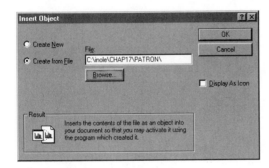

**Figure 17-7.**
*The Insert Object dialog box, with Create From File selected.*

The OLE UI Library once again provides us with the dialog implementation, which is available through the *OleUIInsertObject* API function. The dialog scans the registry for anything marked "Insertable" and populates its Create New list box with those entries.

Dealing with this dialog means that we first need a menu command for it. Patron adds an Insert Object item on its Edit menu for this purpose. If you have a top-level Insert menu already, make an Object item instead. Now, when the user selects this command, Patron invokes the dialog from within *CPatronDoc::InsertObject*. On return, it checks to see which option was selected and passes the necessary information down to *CPages::TenantCreate*, which

---

6. Note again that a server must implement basic file moniker binding support for *OleCreateFromFile* to create something other than a package. Cosmo, for example, doesn't have this capability until Chapter 21.

delegates to *CPage::TenantCreate*, which creates a new tenant and calls its *CTenant::Create* function. Inside *CTenant::Create*, we then call *OleCreate* or *OleCreateFromFile* and initialize the object. This initialization also handles iconic aspects when the Display As Icon box is checked in the dialog.

Calling *OleUIInsertObject* is a matter of filling an OLEUIINSERTOBJECT structure. Most of the work comes in handling what we get back, as you can see in *CPatronDoc::InsertObject*:[7]

```
BOOL CPatronDoc::InsertObject(HWND hWndFrame)
    {
    OLEUIINSERTOBJECT    io;
    DWORD                dwData=0;
    TCHAR                szFile[CCHPATHMAX];
    UINT                 uTemp;
    BOOL                 fRet=FALSE;

    if (NULL==m_pPG)
        return FALSE;

    memset(&io, 0, sizeof(io));

    io.cbStruct=sizeof(io);
    io.hWndOwner=hWndFrame;

    szFile[0]=0;
    io.lpszFile=szFile;
    io.cchFile=CCHPATHMAX;

    io.dwFlags=IOF_SELECTCREATENEW | IOF_DISABLELINK;

    uTemp=OleUIInsertObject(&io);

    if (OLEUI_OK==uTemp)
        {
        TENANTTYPE           tType;
        LPVOID               pv;
        FORMATETC            fe;

        SETDefFormatEtc(fe, 0, TYMED_NULL);
```

---

7. When I create an object, I disable Patron's Printer Setup command. This has nothing to do with OLE and is here only because I'm lazy and didn't want to write code to reposition every object on a page after changing the paper size. In Patron, you can change the printer setup until you put something on a page, and then you're locked into that configuration.

```
if (io.dwFlags & IOF_SELECTCREATENEW)
    {
    tType=TENANTTYPE_EMBEDDEDOBJECT;
    pv=&io.clsid;
    }
else
    {
    tType=TENANTTYPE_EMBEDDEDFILE;
    pv=szFile;
    }

if ((io.dwFlags & IOF_CHECKDISPLAYASICON)
    && NULL!=io.hMetaPict)
    {
    fe.dwAspect=DVASPECT_ICON;
    dwData=(DWORD)(UINT)io.hMetaPict;
    }

fRet=m_pPG->TenantCreate(tType, pv, &fe, NULL, dwData);

//Free this regardless of what we do with it.
INOLE_MetafilePictIconFree(io.hMetaPict);

if (fRet)
    {
    //Disable Printer Setup once we've created a tenant.
    m_fPrintSetup=FALSE;
    FDirtySet(TRUE);
    }
}

return fRet;
}
```

The *lpszFile* and *cchFile* fields in the OLEUIINSERTOBJECT structure describe a buffer in which the dialog will return the filename if Create From File was selected. The IOF_CREATENEW flag forces initial selection of Create New, and IOF_DISABLELINK disables the linking abilities of this dialog (for now). On return, the *dwFlags* field tells us which option was selected. If it was Create New, we pass the CLSID of the user's selection from the list to *CPages::TenantCreate*. If Create From File was selected, we pass the filename instead. The TENANTCREATE_* flag differentiates the two cases. In addition, we initialize a FORMATETC structure to indicate whether the user wants an iconic display, in which case the structure field *hMetaPict* contains a metafile with the iconic representation in it. This data must always be freed when you have finished using it, which the helper function *INOLE_ Metafile-PictIconFree* (INOLE\HELPERS.CPP) does for us.

Down in *CPage::TenantCreate*, we create a new tenant, have that tenant create the object, position that tenant on the page, repaint it, and select it. In addition, we activate that new object immediately if it was created in response to the Create New option in the dialog. This means that we ask the tenant to call the object's *IOleObject::DoVerb(OLEIVERB_ PRIMARY)* function and immediately update the object's storage. We do this because a new blank object is worthless and the first thing a user will do is activate the object to put some data in it. This step does exactly that. We'll see how the tenant performs this step later. We're interested here in what *CTenant::Create* does to create the new embedded object.

```
UINT CTenant::Create(TENANTTYPE tType, LPVOID pvType
    , LPFORMATETC pFE, PPOINTL pptl, LPSIZEL pszl
    , LPSTORAGE pIStorage, PPATRONOBJECT ppo, DWORD dwData)
    {
    HRESULT             hr;
    LPUNKNOWN           pObj;
    UINT                uRet=CREATE_GRAPHICONLY;

    [Validate arguments and determine placement using ppo.]

    hr=ResultFromScode(E_FAIL);

    //Now create object based specifically on type.
    switch (tType)
        {
        case TENANTTYPE_NULL:
            break;

        case TENANTTYPE_STATIC:
            hr=CreateStatic((LPDATAOBJECT)pvType, pFE, &pObj);
            break;

        case TENANTTYPE_EMBEDDEDOBJECT:
            hr=OleCreate(*((LPCLSID)pvType), IID_IUnknown
                , OLERENDER_DRAW, NULL, NULL, m_pIStorage
                , (PPVOID)&pObj);
            break;

        case TENANTTYPE_EMBEDDEDFILE:
            hr=OleCreateFromFile(CLSID_NULL, (LPTSTR)pvType
                , IID_IUnknown, OLERENDER_DRAW, NULL, NULL
                , m_pIStorage, (PPVOID)&pObj);
```

```
            break;

        case TENANTTYPE_EMBEDDEDOBJECTFROMDATA:
            hr=OleCreateFromData((LPDATAOBJECT)pvType, IID_IUnknown
                , OLERENDER_DRAW, NULL, NULL, m_pIStorage
                , (PPVOID)&pObj);
            break;

        default:
            break;
        }

//If creation didn't work, get rid of the element Open created.
if (FAILED(hr))
    {
    Destroy(pIStorage);
    return CREATE_FAILED;
    }

//We don't get size if PatronObject data was seen already.
if (!ObjectInitialize(pObj, pFE, dwData))
    {
    Destroy(pIStorage);
    return CREATE_FAILED;
    }

if (0==pszl->cx && 0==pszl->cy)
    {
    SIZEL   szl;

    //Try to get real size of object; default to 2" x 2".
    SETSIZEL((*pszl), 2*LOMETRIC_PER_INCH, 2*LOMETRIC_PER_INCH);
    hr=ResultFromScode(E_FAIL);

    //Try IViewObject2 first and then IOleObject as a backup.
    if (NULL!=m_pIViewObject2)
        {
        hr=m_pIViewObject2->GetExtent(m_fe.dwAspect, -1, NULL
            , &szl);
        }
    else
        {
        if (NULL!=m_pIOleObject)
            hr=m_pIOleObject->GetExtent(m_fe.dwAspect, &szl);
        }
```

*(continued)*

```
    if (SUCCEEDED(hr))
        {
        //Convert HIMETRIC to our LOMETRIC mapping.
        SETSIZEL((*pszl), szl.cx/10, szl.cy/10);
        }
    }

return uRet;
}
```

A tenant can create an embedded object in three ways: *OleCreate*, *OleCreateFromFile*, and *OleCreateFromData*. The first, *OleCreate*, creates a new embedded object from a CLSID. We pass to it the CLSID from the Insert Object dialog box, the interface we want (*IUnknown*), a render option (OLERENDER_DRAW), a pointer to a FORMATETC structure (NULL because we're using OLERENDER_DRAW), a pointer to an *IOleClientSite* interface (NULL because we'll give it to the object later), the storage element for this object (*m_pIStorage*), and the address in which to store the interface pointer that we want in return.

The second way to create an object, *OleCreateFromFile*, creates a new embedded object or a Package object using the file contents. You always pass CLSID_NULL along with the filename from the Insert Object dialog; the other arguments are the same.

The third way to create an object is from existing data in a data object through *OleCreateFromData*. We'll use this function when pasting a new object from the clipboard or accepting one through drag and drop. In this case, the data identifies the object to create, but otherwise the arguments are the same.

In all three cases, we get back the first interface pointer to a new and loaded object. We must now initialize the object. This event occurs in *CTenant::ObjectInitialize*, which happens to be the same initialization we need to do when loading an object again later:

```
BOOL CTenant::ObjectInitialize(LPUNKNOWN pObj, LPFORMATETC pFE
    , DWORD dwData)
    {
    HRESULT         hr;
    LPPERSIST       pIPersist=NULL;
    DWORD           dw;
    PCDocument      pDoc;
    TCHAR           szFile[CCHPATHMAX];

    if (NULL==pObj || NULL==pFE)
        return FALSE;
```

```
    m_pObj=pObj;
    m_fe=*pFE;
    m_fe.ptd=NULL;
    m_dwState=TENANTSTATE_DEFAULT;

    m_tType=TENANTTYPE_EMBEDDEDOBJECT;

[Code to handle static objects omitted]

    m_pIViewObject2=NULL;
    hr=pObj->QueryInterface(IID_IViewObject2
        , (PPVOID)&m_pIViewObject2);

    if (FAILED(hr))
        return FALSE;

    m_pIViewObject2->SetAdvise(m_fe.dwAspect, 0, m_pImpIAdviseSink);

    //We need an IOleObject most of the time, so get one here.
    m_pIOleObject=NULL;
    hr=pObj->QueryInterface(IID_IOleObject
        , (PPVOID)&m_pIOleObject);

    if (FAILED(hr))
        return TRUE;

    m_pIOleObject->GetMiscStatus(m_fe.dwAspect, &m_grfMisc);

    if (OLEMISC_ONLYICONIC & m_grfMisc)
        m_fe.dwAspect=DVASPECT_ICON;

    m_pIOleObject->SetClientSite(m_pImpIOleClientSite);
    m_pIOleObject->Advise(m_pImpIAdviseSink, &dw);

    OleSetContainedObject(m_pIOleObject, TRUE);

    pDoc=(PCDocument)SendMessage(GetParent(m_hWnd), DOCM_PDOCUMENT
        , 0, 0L);

    if (NULL!=pDoc)
        pDoc->FilenameGet(szFile, CCHPATHMAX);
    else
        szFile[0]=0;

    NotifyOfRename(szFile, NULL);
```

*(continued)*

```
if (DVASPECT_ICON & m_fe.dwAspect)
    {
    DWORD           dw=DVASPECT_CONTENT;
    IAdviseSink    *pSink;

    pSink=(NULL==dwData) ? NULL : m_pImpIAdviseSink;

    INOLE_SwitchDisplayAspect(m_pIOleObject, &dw
        , DVASPECT_ICON, (HGLOBAL)(UINT)dwData, FALSE
        , (NULL!=dwData), pSink, NULL);
    }

return TRUE;
}
```

Initialization consists of the following steps:

1. Remember the type of the object (static, embedded, linked, and so on).

2. Establish a view change notification by calling *IViewObject::SetAdvise*, passing your *IAdviseSink* pointer and the aspect of interest. By doing this, you'll receive notifications for view changes in whatever you have displayed.

3. Pass your *IOleClientSite* pointer to the object by calling *IOleObject-::SetClientSite*. You can also pass the pointer as an argument to *OleCreate\** functions, but you also need to call *SetClientSite* when loading an object with *OleLoad*, and *OleLoad* does not take such an argument. So to keep it all central (as well as explicit), the call is made here.

4. Pass your *IAdviseSink* pointer to *IOleObject::Advise* to receive other notifications. This is necessary for proper operation of the handler.

5. Call *OleSetContainedObject* to mark the object as stored in a container. This is generally to facilitate linking to embeddings that we'll support in Chapter 21, but calling it now does no harm. This function is really just a wrapper for *IRunnableObject::SetContainedObject*.

6. Provide the object with strings for its user interface by sending your application and document names to *IOleObject::SetHostNames*. Patron does this through *CTenant::NotifyOfRename*, which passes "Patron" as the application name and the filename of the document or "Untitled" as the document name (no path).

7. Handle iconic displays, which we'll look at later in this chapter.

In addition to these steps, Patron holds on to the object's *IOleObject* and *IViewObject2* pointers simply because we'll use them often and would like to avoid excess *QueryInterface* calls.

At this point, Patron has created and initialized an object. When we get back into *CPage::TenantCreate*, Patron will activate the object, which runs the server and displays the new object in its user interface. As changes occur to that object, they'll be reflected in the container when someone next calls *IViewObject2::Draw*, as happens in *CTenant::Draw*. Keep in mind that *CTenant::Draw* remembers whether the object is open, so it draws the site shading when necessary.

---

### Resizing *Objects: IOleObject::SetExtent* and *IOleObject::GetExtent*

While managing objects, your container might resize the site in which the object lives, as Patron does. In this situation, you should call *IOleObject::SetExtent* to let it know the exact size of its display. If the object is marked with OLEMISC_RECOMPOSEONRESIZE, you must also call *OleRun* before calling *IOleObject::SetExtent*. You then call *IOleObject::Update* and *IOleObject::Close* to bring the object back to the running state if it wasn't originally running. This sequence, which you can see in *CTenant::SizeSet*, allows even objects in local servers to redraw themselves for new scaling as best they can. In-process objects receive this call directly, so they are automatically optimized. In some cases, a container might not want to control an object's size, letting it be whatever size it wants. In this case, *IOleObject::GetExtent* asks the object how large it would like to be. Patron calls *GetExtent* after creating a new object to set the initial size of the site, but thereafter it will always tell the object the new extents when the site is resized by calling *SetExtent*.

---

## Activate Objects and Add the Object Verb Menu

In the introduction to this chapter, we described how the activation of an object is a primary feature of OLE Documents. Activation is what separates an embedded or a linked object from a static one. To activate an object means to

tell it to execute a verb through *IOleObject::DoVerb*. This might show a user interface in which the user can edit the object, or it might play a sound or a video
clip. This function does whatever is appropriate for the object itself. In Patron,
all activation goes through *CTenant::Activate*:[8]

```
BOOL CTenant::Activate(LONG iVerb)
    {
    RECT        rc, rcH;
    CHourglass *pHour;
    SIZEL       szl;

    [Just beep for static objects.]

    RECTFROMRECTL(rc, m_rcl);
    RectConvertMappings(&rc, NULL, TRUE);
    XformRectInPixelsToHimetric(NULL, &rc, &rcH);

    pHour=new CHourglass;

    [If a prior SetExtent failed,
     run the server and execute the verb now.]

    m_pIOleObject->DoVerb(iVerb, NULL, m_pImpIOleClientSite, 0
        , m_hWnd, &rcH);

    delete pHour;

    //If object changes, IAdviseSink::OnViewChange will see it.
    return FALSE;
    }
```

Here we show an hourglass in case *DoVerb* takes a while, and then we pass
the verb value to *DoVerb* along with our client site, a window handle, and a
rectangle.[9] These latter two arguments provide a way for certain objects to
*play in place* completely within the confines of the call to *DoVerb*. This is not in-
place activation, but simply a way for something such as a video clip to play
itself in the container's window—clipped to the rectangle—before returning

---

8. In the sample code, you'll see a call to *OleRun* and *IOleObject::SetExtent* if an *m_fSetExtent* flag is
TRUE. This flag will be set if resizing a tenant earlier did not pass the call all the way through to
the running object. This happens only for objects marked OLEMISC_RECOMPOSEONRESIZE.
The call to *SetExtent* here simply ensures that the extents are set right before we activate the object.

9. The NULL is a pointer to a MSG structure used with in-place activation.

from *DoVerb*. After the object returns, it is not allowed to leave anything in the container and is not allowed to hold on to the window handle. For a container, we want to pass these arguments to all objects whether or not they use them.

Somehow the container has to know when to activate an object. In some cases, the container can deliberately show or hide an object's user interface with OLEIVERB_SHOW and OLEIVERB_HIDE, or it can specifically request that the object open itself in a window for editing through OLEIVERB_OPEN. (There are also verbs for in-place activation, as we'll see in Chapter 22.) An object's custom verbs, however, are sent to *DoVerb* only in response to user action, which includes the creation of a new object, as we saw earlier.

There are two other suitable actions besides creation. The first occurs when the user double-clicks on an object in the container, which tells the container to execute the object's primary, or default, verb. This is accomplished by calling *IOleObject::DoVerb(OLEIVERB_PRIMARY)*, in which OLEIVERB-_PRIMARY has the value 0. The meaning of this verb changes from object to object, but it is generally what the user expects. Sound and video objects will play, text or graphical objects will edit, and so on. Whatever the behavior is, Patron handles this case in *CPage::OnLeftDoubleClick* (in PAGEMOUS.CPP):

```
BOOL CPage::OnLeftDoubleClick(UINT uKeys, UINT x, UINT y)
    {
    if (HTNOWHERE!=m_uHTCode)
        return m_pTenantCur->Activate(OLEIVERB_PRIMARY);

    return FALSE;
    }
```

The second user action that invokes a verb is its selection from a menu that the container populates with the verbs found for the object in the registry. The pop-up menu must appear in two places: on the container's Edit menu and on an object context menu, displayed when the user clicks the right mouse button over the site. In either case, the menu displays the available verbs along with an item called Convert, which is used to invoke the Convert dialog box, as discussed later in this chapter. An example of this menu for a Sound object with two verbs is shown in Figure 17-8 on the following page.

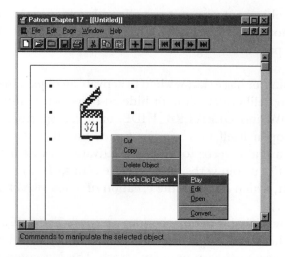

**Figure 17-8.**
*The object verb menu shown in response to a right mouse button click.*

Fortunately a container doesn't have to do much work to create this pop-up menu because of the handy OLE UI Library function named *OleUI-AddVerbMenu*:

```
STDAPI_(BOOL) OleUIAddVerbMenu(LPOLEOBJECT lpOleObj
    , LPCTSTR lpszShortType, HMENU hMenu, UINT uPos
    , UINT uIDVerbMin, UINT uIDVerbMax, BOOL bAddConvert
    , UINT idConvert, HMENU FAR *lphMenu);
```

You pass to this function the object's *IOleObject* pointer, a string describing its type (if NULL, *OleUIAddVerbMenu* will use the *AuxUserType* form 2 entry in the registry), the menu on which the pop-up menu is to appear, the position on the menu to create the pop-up, the minimum and maximum WM_COMMAND identifiers to assign to the verbs, a flag indicating whether to add the Convert item, the ID to assign to the Convert item, and a pointer to a variable that receives the pop-up menu handle on return. Patron calls this function within *CTenant::AddVerbMenu* whenever it needs to build a menu in this manner:

```
void CTenant::AddVerbMenu(HMENU hMenu, UINT iPos)
    {
    HMENU        hMenuTemp;
    LPOLEOBJECT  pObj=m_pIOleObject;

    //If we're static, say we have no object.
    if (TENANTTYPE_STATIC==m_tType)
```

```
        pObj=NULL;

OleUIAddVerbMenu(pObj, NULL, hMenu, iPos, IDM_VERBMIN
    , IDM_VERBMAX, TRUE, IDM_EDITCONVERT, &hMenuTemp);

return;
}
```

When the user selects a verb from this menu, the container's main window sees a WM_COMMAND message (*CPatron::OnCommand* in PATRON-.CPP) with a command ID equal to IDM_VERBMIN+*<verb index>*, so we would call *DoVerb* using *commandID−IDM_VERBMIN*. When the user selects the Convert item, we'll see a WM_COMMAND with IDM_EDITCONVERT.

Patron creates this pop-up menu whenever it sees WM_INITPOPUP in the main window's message procedure. We eventually end up in *CPage::F-QueryObjectSelected* (in PAGE.CPP), which calls *CTenant::AddVerbMenu* if there is a tenant selected. If there are no tenants at all, we still call *OleUIAdd-VerbMenu* but pass a lot of NULLs, which causes the function to create a single disabled menu item named Object.

Patron also creates this menu item inside *CPage::OnRightDown* (in PAGEMOUS.CPP). When a right click happens, Patron selects the tenant under the mouse, builds a context menu, adds to it the object's verbs with *CTenant::AddVerbMenu*, and then displays that menu with the Windows API *TrackPopupMenu*. Any command selected from this menu will also appear in the container's main window procedure, as do all other menu commands. The commands themselves are routed through *CPatronDoc::ActivateObject*, *CPages::ActivateObject*, *CPage::ActivateObject*, and finally *CTenant::Activate*. (I didn't say Patron had the most elegant design!)

> **NOTE:** If your application has a status line, you might want to have it display status information for these verbs as the user selects them from the menu. Patron does this by watching for WM-_MENUSELECT messages in *CPatronFrame::FMessageHook* with the appropriate identifiers. The recommended strings are documented in the Windows user interface guidelines.

## Create Objects from the Clipboard and Drag-and-Drop Transfers

As you know, creating an object using the Insert Object dialog box is only one of the ways to get an object into a container. It is also possible to paste an object by using data from the clipboard or to accept an embedded object dropped on the container. In either case, we receive a data object's

*IDataObject* pointer and pass it to *OleCreateFromData*, as occurs in *CTenant-::Create*. To work with embedded object data, we need to register the OLE-specific clipboard formats with the Windows API *RegisterClipboardFormat*, which we do in the *CPatronDoc* constructor (DOCUMENT.CPP) and other places around Patron.

The three formats that concern us here are described in this table:

| Symbol | String | Format |
|---|---|---|
| CFSTR_EMBED-DEDOBJECT | "Embedded Object" | An *IStorage* containing the object's native data |
| CFSTR_EMBED-SOURCE | "Embed Source" | Same as CFSTR_EMBEDDED-OBJECT |
| CFSTR_OBJECT-DESCRIPTOR | "Object Descriptor" | An OBJECTDESCRIPTOR structure in global memory that contains the object's size, aspect (iconic, content, and so on), class, and other information in which a potential consumer might be interested* |

* OBJECTDESCRIPTOR is meant to solve problems similar to those we solved with the PATRON-OBJECT structure in Patron in Chapter 13, in which we wanted a graphic on the clipboard to be accompanied by data that indicates the size and placement of the object. In addition, we wanted to store the pick point of an object in drag and drop relative to its upper corner to show the feedback rectangle in the right place. PATRONOBJECT contains all this data, whereas OBJECT-DESCRIPTOR contains only extents (because placement data is generally meaningless between different applications). Patron still looks for its own format first using OBJECTDESCRIPTOR as a backup.

Now, given any data object pointer, you can determine whether an embedded object is available by calling *OleQueryCreateFromData*, passing the *IDataObject* pointer. This function basically checks for CFSTR_EMBEDDED-OBJECT and CFSTR_EMBEDSOURCE, returning S_OK if either is available or if OLE 1 embedded object data is available. Patron calls this function in *CPatronDoc::FQueryPasteFromData*, which we use not only to enable the Edit Paste menu item but also to determine whether we can accept an embedded object from a drag-and-drop operation. If we can paste such data, *FQuery-PasteFromData* returns the exact information that we need in *CTenant::Create* to create an object from the data. When we create the object, we do not activate it initially as we do for new, uninitialized objects. This is because the object already has meaningful data in it, so the user might be fully satisfied with its contents.

You'll make very few changes to the rest of your clipboard and drag-and-drop code if you centralize format checks and object creation as I've done in Patron. With drag and drop, the only change I made was to use CFSTR-_OBJECTDESCRIPTOR as a backup format with placement data; otherwise, the rest of the code stayed the same. This really shows the flexibility of drag and drop and how capable it is of working with any data formats that come along.

If you are using the Paste Special dialog box, you will need to add a new entry to the list of acceptable formats so that the dialog box shows an embedded object if one is available. This new entry should have the format CFSTR-_EMBEDDEDOBJECT and the flag OLEUIPASTE_PASTE, which we include in *CPatronDoc::PasteSpecial:*

```
SETDefFormatEtc(rgPaste[1].fmtetc, m_cfEmbeddedObject
    , TYMED_ISTORAGE);
rgPaste[1].lpstrFormatName="%s Object";
rgPaste[1].lpstrResultText="%s Object";
rgPaste[1].dwFlags=OLEUIPASTE_PASTE | OLEUIPASTE_ENABLEICON;
```

Be careful to use OLEUIPASTE_PASTE for this entry and not OLEUIPASTE_PASTEONLY. If you use the latter (as we did for other static formats), you will not see this entry in the dialog box at all. This can increase your job stress by a few orders of magnitude. Believe me. I took six hours to figure this out. Also, no matter where you put this entry in your array of pasteable formats, the Paste Special dialog box will always list embedded objects first. This is the user interface standard.

## *IOleObject::InitFromData*

When a user chooses to paste with data already selected in a document, the usual behavior is to replace that selection with the new data. If the selection is an embedded object marked with OLEMISC-_INSERTNOTREPLACE, the container should call *IOleObject::InitFromData* to perform the paste instead of replacing the selected object. This allows the object to incorporate that data into itself. Patron does not support this feature.

An alternative use of this function, differentiated by a flag named *fCreation*, is to use a data object to initialize a newly created embedding. After calling *OleCreate*, you can send initial data to the object with *InitFromData*. This data might be a selection of data in the container itself or some other data from the clipboard or from a drag-and-drop operation.

## Copy and Source Embedded Objects

It's sure nice to have cookies in a cookie jar, but that's not the only place you might want to store them. You might want to move some of them from one container to another. Similarly, if end users can paste an embedded object into a container, they will probably expect to be able to copy or cut those same objects from that container and put them into another container. (It would be nice to *copy* cookies, huh?) To do this, a container must provide the CFSTR_EMBEDDEDOBJECT and CFSTR_OBJECTDESCRIPTOR formats whenever it is a source of data transfer itself, either for the clipboard or for drag and drop.

It might seem as if you could simply use *QueryInterface* on the embedded object for its *IDataObject* and use the result for a data transfer, but this is not a good idea. Instead of copying the object, you are passing a pointer to the real object, which could result in unpredictable things happening to it beyond the control of the container. So you truly need to duplicate the whole object.

This affects Patron in *CPage::TransferObjectCreate*, which is called whenever we need a data object for some transfer operation. The only modification here is to now call *CTenant::CopyEmbeddedObject* (after we've copied higher-priority formats), which creates both of the new formats and stuffs them into our transfer object. To create CFSTR_EMBEDDEDOBJECT, we create a temporary compound file (with STGM_DELETEONRELEASE) and save the object into it. If the object is dirty, we call *OleSave* and then *IPersistStorage::SaveCompleted(NULL)*, which makes a copy but doesn't change the underlying storage that the object itself is accessing. (See Chapter 8.) If the object is clean, we can call *IStorage::CopyTo*. If that succeeds, we then create CFSTR_OBJECTDESCRIPTOR data using a helper function, *INOLE_ObjectDescriptorFromOleObject* (in INOLE\HELPERS.CPP).

The details of doing all this are plain to see from the source code, so I won't belabor the point here. With this data, other containers (or our own) can paste or drop a copy of the object that is currently in our container.

## Close and Delete Objects

We would quickly fill our hard disks with large compound documents if we could never remove objects from them. So now we must add some way to delete an object from a document. This is similar to, but not exactly the same as, closing an object when the document is being closed and the object still exists—that is, the object moves from the loaded state to the passive state. Deleting an object means taking it from the running or the loaded state to outright nonexistence.

Closing an embedded object requires two actions: ensuring that the object's storage is updated and calling *IOleObject::Close*. The latter tells the object's local server to completely shut down and purge itself from memory if no other containers are using it. As far as our container is concerned, however, this object is now in the passive state, so we must call *OleLoad* to bring it back to the loaded state.

*IOleObject::Close* takes one argument—the Save option—which instructs the object how to proceed. OLECLOSE_SAVEIFDIRTY tells the object to call *IOleClientSite::SaveObject* if it's dirty before closing. OLECLOSE_NOSAVE simply closes the object regardless of its dirty state. OLECLOSE_PROMPTSAVE closes the object if it is not dirty; otherwise, it displays a Yes/No/Cancel message box asking the user whether he or she wants to save the object. In this case, *Close* will return OLE_E_PROMPTSAVECANCELLED to indicate that the user did not want to close the object after all.

Destroying an object (as Patron does when selecting Delete Object from the Edit menu), still involves *IOleObject::Close* but always with OLECLOSE_NOSAVE. This is in addition to destroying the storage element for this object, which your site manages. Finally, after destroying an object, you should call *CoFreeUnusedLibraries* as a matter of habit.

## Save and Load the Document with Embedded Objects

At some point, it would be nice to save all the objects we've been creating and editing so that we can reload them at a later time. We've by and large covered all the steps for saving an object in a document: providing an *IStorage*, calling *OleSave* when asked through *IOleClientSite::SaveObject* or when closing the object, and doing the same through *CTenant::Update*.

On a larger scale, Patron's document saving starts in *CPatronDoc::Save*, which first asks *CPages* to update, which in turn asks the currently open *CPage* to update, which in turn asks each tenant to update by using the preceding code. After all that, the document commits itself, and because it is the owner of the root storage, that commitment writes the file to disk. Little of this storage code has changed from previous versions of Patron.

Patron, by the way, is designed—and I won't argue that this is the best design—to keep only the current page open. This means that when you switch pages, all open or running objects on the old page are closed to the passive state and all objects on the new page are opened to the loaded state.

Loading a document in Patron starts with opening a root storage for the document and initializing the pages. Then Patron opens the current page by using *CPage::Open*. This, in turn, re-creates all the tenants on the page, but instead of calling *CTenant::Create*, Patron calls *CTenant::Load*, indicating the object's storage, what is in this storage, and the rectangle occupied by the tenant on the page:

```
BOOL CTenant::Load(LPSTORAGE pIStorage, PTENANTINFO pti)
    {
    HRESULT          hr;
    LPUNKNOWN        pObj;
    DWORD            dwState=TENANTSTATE_DEFAULT;

    if (NULL==pIStorage || NULL==pti)
        return FALSE;

    /*
     * If we already initialized once, clean up, releasing
     * everything before we attempt to reload. This happens
     * when using the Convert dialog.
     */
    if (m_fInitialized)
        {
        //Preserve all states except open.
        dwState=(m_dwState & ~TENANTSTATE_OPEN);
        m_cRef++;   //Prevent accidental closure.

        //This should release all holds on our IStorage as well.
        if (NULL!=m_pIViewObject2)
            {
            m_pIViewObject2->SetAdvise(m_fe.dwAspect, 0, NULL);
            ReleaseInterface(m_pIViewObject2);
            }

        ReleaseInterface(m_pIOleObject);
        ReleaseInterface(m_pObj);

        m_pIStorage=NULL;   //We'll have already released this.
        m_cRef--;           //Match safety increment above.
        }

    m_fInitialized=TRUE;

    //Open storage for this tenant.
    if (!Open(pIStorage))
        return FALSE;

    hr=OleLoad(m_pIStorage, IID_IUnknown, NULL, (PPVOID)&pObj);

    if (FAILED(hr))
```

```
    {
    Destroy(pIStorage);
    return FALSE;
    }

m_fSetExtent=pti->fSetExtent;
ObjectInitialize(pObj, &pti->fe, NULL);

//Restore original state before reloading.
m_dwState=dwState;

RectSet(&pti->rcl, FALSE, FALSE);
return TRUE;
}
```

Most of this is unchanged from previous versions. *OleLoad* brings passive objects into the loaded state and returns an interface pointer. Now, however, to support embedded objects, we call *ObjectInitialize* to perform the same initialization sequence as was required after *OleCreate* and to position the object on the page before repainting. In addition, we check to ensure that we are not simply reloading this object from an already initialized state, which might occur when we deal with conversion and emulation. We'll see why this is important shortly.

Patron's file handling still has one small modification that you can find in *CPatronDoc::Rename*. This is called whenever the user does a File Save As or otherwise changes the name of a document. After doing the usual document renaming work, Patron calls *CPage::NotifyTenantsOfRename*, which cycles through all the tenants in the current page, calling *CTenant::NotifyOfRename* with the new filename. The tenant now uses this information to call *IOleObject::SetHostNames* once again, updating the information it passed through object initialization:

```
void CTenant::NotifyOfRename(LPTSTR pszFile, LPVOID pvReserved)
    {
    TCHAR        szObj[40];
    TCHAR        szApp[40];

    if (NULL==m_pIOleObject)
        return;

    if (TEXT('\0')==*pszFile)
        {
        LoadString(m_pPG->m_hInst, IDS_UNTITLED, szObj
            , sizeof(szObj));
        }
```

*(continued)*

863

```
else
    GetFileTitle(pszFile, szObj, sizeof(szObj));

LoadString(m_pPG->m_hInst, IDS_CAPTION, szApp, sizeof(szApp));
m_pIOleObject->SetHostNames(szApp, szObj);
return;
}
```

If you leave out this small part, your current document name will not be reflected in open server windows, which is not very user friendly.

## Handle Iconic Presentations (Cache Control)

I admit that when I first looked at the handling of iconic aspects, I was so intimidated that I wanted to defer it to a later chapter. After whacking myself in the head a few times with the 40-ounce Louisville Slugger I keep in my office, I got myself to write about it in this chapter. It really didn't turn out to be all that hard.

The trick to iconic aspects is a special case of the more general issue of controlling the object's cached presentations through *IOleCache*. When we come back from either the Insert Object dialog or the Paste Special dialog with the Display As Icon box checked, we need to draw the object as DVASPECT_ICON instead of DVASPECT_CONTENT. The trouble is that most servers do not supply an iconic representation themselves, so in order to make this work, a container has to put one in the cache directly. What goes in the cache is a metafile with the iconic representation that both the Insert Object and Paste Special dialogs will create for us. This metafile contains both an icon and a label. Again, the helper function *INOLE_ Metafile-PictIconFree* will clean up one of these metafiles for us.

Inside *CTenant::Create* and *CTenant::ObjectInitialize*, we detect whether the chosen display aspect is DVASPECT_ICON. If so, we need to put the icon in the cache. We saw the code for this earlier:

```
if (DVASPECT_ICON & m_fe.dwAspect)
    {
    DWORD           dw=DVASPECT_CONTENT;
    IAdviseSink     *pSink;

    pSink=(NULL==dwData) ? NULL : m_pImpIAdviseSink;

    INOLE_SwitchDisplayAspect(m_pIOleObject, &dw
        , DVASPECT_ICON, (HGLOBAL)(UINT)dwData, FALSE
        , (NULL!=dwData), pSink, NULL);
    }
```

The helper function *INOLE_ SwitchDisplayAspect* (in INOLE\HELPERS-.CPP) removes any DVASPECT_CONTENT information from the cache, stores the icon as the cache for DVASPECT_ICON, and sets up a new advisory connection for that view aspect. All this is simply standard cache manipulation.

With this cache set, we need to be sure to pass DVASPECT_ICON to *IViewObject2::Draw*, which happens in *CTenant::Draw.* When copying the object to a data object, we have to set this aspect as well so that other containers will know what to paste. We also need to remember the aspect when we save the objects so we can initialize it properly when loading it again.

These considerations for differentiating content and icon aspects apply equally well for managing other aspects, including other device-specific renderings for the same aspect. In all cases, after you tell the cache what to do, *OleSave* and *OleLoad* do the appropriate thing. It's mostly a matter of your structures indicating the correct aspect.

The missing piece of this icon story is how you either change the icon at a later time or switch back to viewing DVASPECT_CONTENT for the object. The answer lies in the Convert dialog box, which is the final topic to examine for a basic container.

## The Convert Dialog Box: Conversion and Emulation

Earlier in this chapter, we saw how a server can mark itself as capable of converting data from another server or capable of emulating another server. In OLE Documents, conversion and emulation involve more than simply mapping the CLSIDs because persistent storage is involved. An emulating server must not only be functionally equivalent to those servers it wants to emulate, but it must also be able to both read and write foreign storage formats. A server that can read foreign data and then write it in its own format can convert objects from other servers to its own type, changing the persistent object's CLSID. The way a server handles this is covered in Chapter 18. In that chapter's sample, Cosmo is capable of converting and emulating data from its OLE 1 version server as well as from the Polyline component that we'll work with in Chapter 19.

To facilitate conversion and emulation, a container is responsible for providing the user interface necessary to show the user what conversion and emulation support exists for a given object type. This allows a user to create a compound document with one type of object from one particular server and give it to another user who does not have that server installed. When the second user attempts to activate the object, no server will be available. In that case, the container can display the Convert dialog box, shown in Figure 17-9 on the following page, through which the user can either permanently convert the object to a different type or indicate which server to use to emulate that object type not only now but for all such encounters in the future.

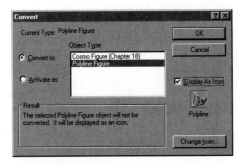

**Figure 17-9.**
*The Convert dialog box invoked for a Polyline object (Chapter 19) showing that Cosmo (Chapter 18) can convert it.*

For a container, conversion means that we have to unload the object, mark it with a new CLSID, reload it using the new server, and have that server munge the storage into the new object type. This is the Convert To case. Emulation requires making the necessary *TreatAs* entries in the registry and also that we unload the object completely and then reload it to load any handlers needed by the new type. This is the Activate As case. In addition, the Convert dialog box can be used to simply switch between DVASPECT_ICON and DVASPECT_CONTENT views of an object.

In all of these cases, we must first invoke the Convert dialog with *OleUIConvert*. This happens in response to two events: either the user selects the Convert menu item from the object's verb menu or some other attempt to activate the object failed and we now want to give the user the chance to convert or emulate. In Patron, either case winds up in the function *CPage::ConvertObject*, in which the *fNoServer* argument, when TRUE, specifies that we're coming here because of a failed activation. In all honesty, Patron doesn't use this flag at all, but it demonstrates what you would do in that case:

```
BOOL CPage::ConvertObject(HWND hWndFrame, BOOL fNoServer)
    {
    HRESULT        hr;
    OLEUICONVERT   ct;
    TENANTTYPE     tType;
    FORMATETC      fe;
    TENANTINFO     ti;
    UINT           uRet;
    HCURSOR        hCur;
```

```
BOOL            fActivate=fNoServer;
RECTL           rcl;

[Validation; exit immediately for static objects.]

//Get object information we might want.
m_pTenantCur->GetInfo(&ti);

//Fill the structure.
memset(&ct, 0, sizeof(ct));
ct.cbStruct=sizeof(OLEUICONVERT);
ct.hWndOwner=hWndFrame;
ct.fIsLinkedObject=FALSE;
ct.dvAspect=ti.fe.dwAspect;

m_pTenantCur->ObjectClassFormatAndIcon(&ct.clsid, &ct.wFormat
    , &ct.lpszUserType, &ct.hMetaPict, &ct.lpszDefLabel);

uRet=OleUIConvert(&ct);

[Code to handle the three cases goes here.]

CoTaskMemFree((void*)ct.lpszUserType);
INOLE_MetafilePictIconFree(ct.hMetaPict);
return TRUE;
}
```

The function *CTenant::ObjectClassFormatAndIcon* retrieves information about the object needed in the dialog: the CLSID, the format of the data (a clipboard format, whatever would appear in the registry under a server's Conversion entries), a string with the object's user type, the current iconic presentation (if any), and a default label for the icon. The tenant uses the helper function *INOLE_GetUserTypeOfClass* and the OLE API function *OleGetIconOfClass* to retrieve this information. You can see the details in the source code.

Now the Convert dialog box, inside *OleUIConvert*, will display any other servers that have registered conversion formats matching the values in the *wFormat* field of OLEUICONVERT. This may, in fact, be an empty list, and if you want to prevent the user from possibly seeing an empty list, you can call the function *OleUICanConvertOrActivateAs*, using the result to disable the Convert menu in the first place. I don't use this function in Patron because we change iconic aspects through the Convert dialog box.

Anyway, in the dialog the user can either change the icon, select a new format to convert to, or choose to emulate the existing object with a new server. These three cases are differentiated by the *dwFlags* field in the OLEUICONVERT structure on return. We'll see what we do in response to each, but first remember that in all of these cases, the flag *m_fRepaintEnabled* in *CTenant* is used to suppress repaints through this whole process because we might be unloading, reloading, and running servers. Turning off repaints is a great way to cut down on flicker.

## Switch Display Aspects

The first thing we do when we get back from the Convert dialog box in *CPage-::ConvertObject* is execute the following code:

```
if ((DVASPECT_ICON==ct.dvAspect && ct.fObjectsIconChanged)
    !! ct.dvAspect!=ti.fe.dwAspect)
    {
    HGLOBAL     hMem=NULL;

    //Only pass non-NULL handle for icon aspects.
    if (DVASPECT_ICON==ct.dvAspect)
        hMem=ct.hMetaPict;

    m_pPG->m_fDirty=m_pTenantCur->SwitchOrUpdateAspect(hMem
        , FALSE);
    }
```

This code handles two cases: either we switched display aspects or we simply changed the icon, leaving the aspect the same. (The latter is indicated with the Convert dialog box's *fObjectsIconChanged* flag.) *CTenant::SwitchOr-UpdateAspect* handles both cases. In the former, it switches the contents of the cache, getting an update from the object if necessary. In the second case, it merely stuffs the new icon in the cache using the helper function *INOLE-_SetIconInCache*. All of this is again basic cache manipulation.

When we do change the aspect, the tenant reinitializes its size using *IViewObject2::GetExtent* or *IOleObject::GetExtent*. When we switch to an icon, we want the tenant to show up with a reasonable size for the icon. Switching back to a content aspect should revert to a larger object size.

## Handle the Convert To Case

If the end user selects Convert To in the dialog box and then chooses OK, *OleUIConvert* will return with CF_SELECTCONVERTTO in the *dwFlags* field. A container must then execute four steps:

1. Unload the object, taking it back to the passive state.

2. Modify the class and format saved in the object's persistent storage by calling *WriteClassStg*, *WriteFmtUserTypeStg*, and *SetConvertStg*.

3. Reload the object with *OleLoad* and force an update. (This means set the document's dirty flag and force a repaint.)

4. If the Convert dialog box was invoked as a result of a failed activation, activate the object now.

These steps can be seen in the following code, taken from Patron's *CPage-::ConvertObject*:

```
BOOL            fActivate=fNoServer;
RECTL           rcl;
  ⋮
if ((CF_SELECTCONVERTTO & ct.dwFlags)
    && ct.clsid!=ct.clsidNew)
    {
    LPSTORAGE   pIStorage;

    m_pTenantCur->StorageGet(&pIStorage);
    m_pTenantCur->Close(TRUE);

    hr=INOLE_DoConvert(pIStorage, ct.clsidNew);
    pIStorage->Commit(STGC_DEFAULT);
    pIStorage->Release();

    if (SUCCEEDED(hr))
        {
        LPUNKNOWN   pObj;
        LPOLEOBJECT pIOleObject;

        //Reload and update.
        m_pTenantCur->Load(m_pIStorage, &ti);

        m_pTenantCur->ObjectGet(&pObj);
        pObj->QueryInterface(IID_IOleObject
            , (PPVOID)&pIOleObject);
        pIOleObject->Update();
        pIOleObject->Release();
        pObj->Release();
        }

    m_pPG->m_fDirty=TRUE;
    }

m_pTenantCur->Repaint();

if (fActivate)
    m_pTenantCur->Activate(OLEIVERB_SHOW);
```

It's necessary to close and reload the object because the new class we're converting to might have a specific object handler, and we have to be sure that handler is now loaded for this object. The process of taking the object to the passive state and then reloading it does the trick.

The helper function *INOLE_DoConvert* handles the calls to *WriteClassStg*, *WriteFmtUserTypeStg*, and *SetConvertStg* for us. The latter function, which we haven't seen before, specifically marks the *IStorage* for this object as being converted to a new CLSID, which a server will use to detect that conversion is happening when it loads the object data in its *IPersistStorage::Load*. We'll see this in Chapter 18.

After we have marked the object's storage appropriately, we can reload the object (*CTenant::Load*) and update it with *IOleObject::Update*, which will send *IAdviseSink::OnViewChange* notifications as necessary. The final step is that if we invoked the Convert dialog because an activation failed (REG_E_CLASSNOTREG or CO_E_APPNOTFOUND from *IOleObject::DoVerb*), we should not activate the newly converted object because that's what the user wanted to do originally.

## Handle the Activate As Case

The Convert dialog box might also return the CF_SELECTACTIVATEAS in *dwFlags*, in which case, we need to perform the following four steps:

1. Add the *TreatAs* entry in the registry by calling call *CoTreatAsClass*.

2. Unload all objects of the old CLSID that you have loaded. You can do this before step 1 if necessary.

3. Reload all the unloaded objects as necessary.

4. Set your document's dirty flag to TRUE, activate the current object, and repaint.

These steps also are shown in the code from Patron's *CPage::ConvertObject*:

```
BOOL            fActivate=fNoServer;

if (CF_SELECTACTIVATEAS & ct.dwFlags)
    {
    hr=CoTreatAsClass(ct.clsid, ct.clsidNew);
```

```
    if (SUCCEEDED(hr))
        {
        LPTENANT    pTenant;
        UINT        i;

        for (i=0; i < m_cTenants; i++)
            {
            if (TenantGet(i, &pTenant, FALSE))
                {
                pTenant->GetInfo(&ti);
                pTenant->Close(FALSE);
                pTenant->Load(m_pIStorage, &ti);
                }
            }

        fActivate=TRUE;
        }
    }
    ⋮
m_pTenantCur->Repaint();

if (fActivate)
    m_pTenantCur->Activate(OLEIVERB_SHOW);
```

*CoTreatAsClass*, as we saw in Chapter 5, establishes a permanent emulation from the old CLSID to the new CLSID. After that, we unload and reload every tenant in the current page (all that are loaded) to ensure that they are now using the right class. We unload all the tenants because we cannot be certain that one object isn't using an object of the old class that is now being emulated. So we unload everything. In addition, we always activate the object on which the Convert dialog box was originally invoked. The user saw Activate As in the dialog and expects that activation will now take place. It's a good idea to meet that expectation.

# Summary

OLE Documents is a standard protocol for the creation, exchange, and management of blocks of unstructured data, which are called compound document content objects, or simply content objects for short. A container that conforms to OLE Documents can incorporate any content object into a compound document, regardless of the data contained in that object or the source of that object. A server that supplies such objects also conforms to OLE Documents so that those objects can be stored in any other container's compound document. As a whole, OLE Documents is designed to eliminate a number of end-user difficulties in the creation and management of compound documents, such as locating the necessary server for a particular type of content and moving data between source and container with a high degree of fidelity. Through the standard Insert Object dialog box, a user can directly choose the type of content to create—OLE Documents will locate the correct server to run, and it will connect the container and server. After an object is created, the user can choose to "activate" the object by selecting an object "verb" or "action." This choice automatically runs the correct server for performing the action.

Content objects can exist in a compound document two ways: they can be embedded or linked. An embedded content object is one whose native data and cached graphical presentations of that data are stored entirely in the compound document itself. Where the document goes, the object's data goes also. A linked object is one whose native data resides in another location outside the document, although it still carries cached presentations in the compound document. A linked object manages a moniker to refer to the outside location of its native data, but it's possible that such a link can be broken.

In either case, the basic set of interfaces for an embedded object include *IDataObject*, *IViewObject2*, *IPersistStorage*, *IOleCache2* (optionally *IOleCacheControl*), *IRunnableObject*, and the mainstay of OLE Documents, *IOleObject*. These interfaces are the means by which a container sees an embedded object. (Linked objects add the interface *IOleLink*.) Depending on how an object is implemented, it might or might not need to support all these interfaces. For each object, a container has to provide certain services through a site object itself, where this site implements the interfaces *IAdviseSink* and *IOleClientSite*. Most of the member functions in these interfaces deal with notifications of various events that occur during the lifetime of an object.

OLE Documents adds a number of additional states to those already known. Besides being passive or loaded, an object can also be running, which means its server is fully loaded and is being used for all necessary services; or it can be active, which means the object's user interface is available so that the user can directly edit or manipulate the object. When the object is being serviced by an in-process server, the difference between and loaded and running states is minimal. The difference is more important for objects from local servers; in this case, the local server is not in memory unless the object is in the running state. When such a local object is merely loaded, there is always

872

an in-process handler in memory for it, which might be either a custom handler or an instance of the default handler, the latter of which provides generic services for all objects in the absence of a specific custom handler.

This chapter details the architecture of OLE Documents, the role of the interfaces with all the different objects involved, and the information in the registry that pertains specifically to this protocol. The latter half of this chapter focuses on the step-by-step implementation of an embedding container, which is mostly concerned with various pieces of user interface such as the Insert Object and Convert dialogs, shading a site when its object has been activated, dealing with the clipboard and drag and drop, and handling different display aspects for objects. These features are added to the Patron sample, which now becomes capable of managing embedded objects in a compound document. This chapter is thus the first step in the full treatment of OLE Documents, which continues through Chapter 23 and builds a foundation for OLE Controls in Chapter 24.

# OLE Documents and Local Embedding Servers

*COO-KIES!*

—Cookie Monster

In Chapter 17, I compared embedded objects and a batch of cookies in a cookie jar and described how, figuratively, to create the cookie jar. That leaves us with the question of how to bake cookies. At least some of us, I'm sure, have at one time or another gotten out all the ingredients—flour, sugar, eggs, butter, shortening, baking soda, salt, and vanilla (maybe also an obscene number of chocolate chips)—to mix up and bake a batch of cookies. (OK, I'll admit that once or twice I didn't bother to bake them.) Later we remove them from the oven, let them cool, and put them in the cookie jar.

Baking cookies is a good analogy for what's involved in creating a server for embedded compound document content objects. As bakers, we first create the cookies by mixing the dough, and then we manage the cookies by baking, cooling, and storing them. As bakers, we are cookie *servers*. In the case of embedded objects, a server must create objects and then manage those objects. Object creation, as we saw in Chapter 5, is the responsibility of a class factory. Object management is the responsibility of all the object's interfaces, including *IOleObject*, *IDataObject*, and *IPersistStorage*.

This chapter deals exclusively with local servers that provide embedded content objects. Those objects need to implement only the three interfaces mentioned above. As an example, we'll follow a step-by-step approach for adding OLE Documents support to the Cosmo application. We'll turn its internal Polyline object into a shareable content object that can be embedded while still keeping that object inside the executable itself. In Chapter 19, we'll cover additional issues surrounding in-process servers and object handlers, which are a bit more complicated than a local server. Even then, Cosmo and the samples in Chapter 19 will not explore every facet of OLE Documents. There are so many recipes for objects that we'd go crazy trying to look at them all at once. We need to start with the OLE equivalent of your basic chocolate chip cookie. That will be enough to satisfy a container as well as a furry, blue, ball-eyed maniac from Sesame Street.

# The Structure of a Local Content Object (and Server)

In Chapter 17, we learned that an object in a local server must implement *IOleObject*, *IDataObject*, and *IPersistStorage* to support its half of the OLE Documents protocol, as illustrated in Figure 18-1. Each of these interfaces has a specific purpose in the overall architecture. *IPersistStorage* provides for the object's storage of its native data, allowing that object incremental access. Because the container will pass nothing more than an *IStorage* pointer through this interface, the object does not load data until absolutely necessary. Keep in mind that a local object deals only with its own native data in storage because all other information that might be present is owned either by the container or by OLE itself. In all cases, those streams have special names and are relevant to the container process only.

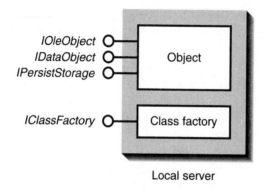

Local server

**Figure 18-1.**
*The structure of a content object in a local server.*

*IDataObject*, as we know from Chapter 17 as well as from the discussion of caching in Chapter 11, is the interface the container-side data cache uses to retrieve from the object presentation formats such as bitmaps and metafiles. Through this interface, the local object must supply these formats in addition to its own native formats and the standard OLE formats CFSTR_EMBED-SOURCE and CFSTR_EMBEDDEDOBJECT. (Also linked object formats, as we'll see in Chapter 21.) Containers can also retrieve other specific data formats through *IDataObject* if they know more about the object class itself.

The third interface is *IOleObject*, which, as we saw in Chapter 17, makes an object a content object. For the most part, many of the members in this interface need little or no implementation for basic embedding support, and some of them are utterly trivial to implement. The most important of all members is, of course, *IOleObject::DoVerb*.

Like all other servers, a server that works with OLE Documents must provide a class factory and registry entries that map its CLSID to the server code. In Chapter 17, we saw the additional registry entries that are necessary for OLE Documents. Also, the inclusion of an active state for the object means that the user interface might be visible, in which case server shutdown must be controlled not only with an object count and a factory lock count but also with a *user control* flag, especially if the server is able to support both multiple objects and independent documents at the same time. The last section of this chapter discusses some considerations regarding MDI (Multiple Document Interface) servers.

Besides implementing the necessary interfaces on the object, a local server must also modify its own user interface in a few small ways when it's working with an embedded object. In particular, because the object is not a file, the server must remove file-related user interface elements from its menus and toolbars and change its caption bar to reflect the name of the compound document itself (which the container passes to *IOleObject::SetHostNames*). In addition, the object is required to send a number of notifications for events that occur during its active lifetime, particularly notifications contained in *IOleClientSite* and *IAdviseSink*, as you would expect.

Other than that, the server should also be able to create embedded objects for clipboard and drag-and-drop operations, supplying the embedded object formats along with CFSTR_OBJECTDESCRIPTOR. The server can also choose to install a message filter to block or delay calls if it needs to do so.(Chapter 6 discusses the details of message filtering for a server.)

In designing a content object server, you'll need to think about what it is that your class factory will create. What is the embedded object inside your server? Is it simply a C++ wrapper class that communicates with other parts of the application, or is it some existing object class that you'll augment with the necessary interfaces? Either case is perfectly fine. What matters is that you provide the appropriate interfaces when they're asked for. In Cosmo, I've added a new C++ class named *CFigure*, which manages all the stuff related to OLE Documents, leaving almost all of the existing *CPolyline* class untouched. This demonstrates how you can encapsulate any sort of legacy code in an object and have it appear as a content object to the outside world.

Now, before we dive into Cosmo's implementation, let's consider three other issues that deserve a little thought.

## Linking Support and Miniservers vs. Full Servers

Support for embedded objects is only half of the linking and embedding capability of OLE Documents. Some servers, however, have no need to support linking, nor do they need to run stand-alone, regardless of whether they are in-process or local servers. These servers are called *miniservers* and generally run only within the context of embedding. In other words, the usual way to run the server is to create an instance of an object through a container's Insert Object dialog box (and later by activating the object again).

Miniservers work well for small visual data, such as font effects or a simple drawing. Because they support embedding only, miniservers should not require a great deal of storage—each object from a miniserver takes up space in the container's document. Simple drawings, for example, can be stored in a metafile of a few hundred bytes. However, because a miniserver cannot usually run stand-alone, it typically has no user interface with which to create, load, and save individual files, so it seldom has the ability to link to such persistent sources. For this reason, miniservers are generally considered embedding-only servers.

Obviously this is not a great choice when the object data itself is large, for example a 24-bit bitmap that occupies megabytes of storage. It is very costly to embed an object with data this large. For that reason, servers of potentially large data should be *full servers,* which can always run stand-alone and support both embedding and linking. Usually this means that the server is a local server because only EXEs can run by themselves. (Although providing an EXE shell to load an in-process server stand-alone is not difficult.) In any case, because a full server can run stand-alone and independently create files, there is a suitable persistent source that the server can name with a moniker as a link source. Thus, the end user has the choice of whether to link or to embed when storage space is a factor.

Most existing applications that you might consider making a server probably read and write their own files already and should become full servers as a result. If, however, you are designing a new type of lightweight content, a miniserver, especially one implemented as an in-process server, is a great choice for speed and efficiency.

## Version Numbers, Conversion, and Emulation

If you ever plan to release a new version of your application, which more or less all of us do, you will want to use version numbers with all instances of data that might be stored persistently, such as a content object's native data streams. A later version of your server might be asked to load and edit an old version of a content object through conversion and emulation if your object is registered for such use.

In designing a server, you should think about what other data formats your server might support besides its own. This includes not only old versions of your application but also your competitors' similar applications.[1] You'll need to decide which formats you want to read but write back in your own format. These are the types you can convert. Then you'll need to find the formats that you can both read and write, the types you can emulate. Your object's implementation of *IPersistStorage* is responsible for handling the differences among whatever storage formats you support. If you're dealing with competitive sources, you'll have to obtain information about their data formats. The nice thing is that those competitors will want your formats as well, and it is a benefit to all users that your servers are cross-compatible.

## Installation

Installing an OLE Documents server involves a large number of registry entries, as you might well expect, but you also need to be prepared to handle a previous version of your server or the existence of a server you know how to emulate. In these cases, you'll also need to create the necessary conversion and emulation entries in the registry, not only under your own CLSID but also under those of the other servers. For example, if you install a new version of your own server, you will need to write TreatAs and AutoTreatAs keys under the CLSID of the old server (as described in Chapter 5), depending on whether you overwrote the old server itself. If you install a server that can emulate another server, you can ask whether the user wants to set up an automatic emulation relationship, in which case you can store the necessary registry entries for that other server as well. The user interface guidelines in the *OLE Programmer's Reference* include additional information about the messages to display to the user in this circumstance.

In addition to the TreatAs and AutoTreatAs keys, a server can also include a registry key named AutoConvertTo that tells functions such as *OleLoad* to automatically use a different CLSID when loading an object. This key should be accompanied by one named NotInsertable under both the ProgID and the CLSID of the original server. NotInsertable overrides any Insertable keys found there, which means the old object class does not appear in a container's Insert Object dialog box. This is exactly what you want when

---

1. See the file OLE1.WRI on the companion CD for conversion information about OLE 1 versions of compound document servers.

installing a new version of a server. Over time, it would be silly for the container's Insert Object dialog box to show "Object 1.0," "Object 2.0," "Object 3.0," and so on. NotInsertable allows the latest version to ensure that only it will appear in the list of objects in that dialog.

# Step-by-Step Embedding with Local Servers: Cosmo

The remainder of this chapter will follow modifications I've made to Cosmo (CHAP18\COSMO) so that it can now serve embedded objects of CLSID-_CosmoFigure. Unlike a container, a server has very little user interface to contend with: instead, most of the work is functional and deals with rendering and exchanging data. In other words, the server has to define how a cookie looks, how it tastes, what kind of ingredients it needs, and how to mix together all those ingredients. It does not, however, have to worry about the cookie jars, counters, kitchens, and houses in which the cookie jars would sit. Its only concerns are the cookies.

Implementing a basic embeddable object and its server involves the following steps:

1. Initialize and uninitialize OLE on startup and shutdown with *OleInitialize* and *OleUninitialize*, as usual.

2. Create the necessary registry entries for the object and its server, as discussed in Chapter 17.

3. Implement a class factory for your embedded object class with all the usual shutdown conditions (described in Chapter 5) along with an extra user control flag if necessary.

4. Implement the object class that will be the embedded object itself.

5. Implement *IPersistStorage* on the object, adding necessary conversion and emulation support. Much of this code can use existing functions that read and write your data to *IStorage* objects if such code already exists.

6. Implement *IDataObject* on the object. If you have already written code to handle the clipboard by means of a data object, this implementation will be straightforward and will require only the addition of other OLE formats.

7. Implement *IOleObject* on the object, including verb handling. Most of the members in this large interface are easy to implement.

8. Modify your server's user interface when editing an embedded object to eliminate or disable various menu commands. You should also change the window's caption bar to reflect the embedding state. This also affects your implementation of File Save As and File Close commands.

9. Send notifications of data change, closure, saving, and renaming at various times in the object's life.

10. (Full servers) Augment your server's clipboard code to create embedded objects.

11. (MDI full servers) Provide alternative user interface for MDI applications, which adds another shutdown condition.

We've seen plenty of examples of steps 1, 2, and 3 in previous chapters, so we won't go into detail here about class factories, the registry, and what to do with *-Embedding* on the command line—for example, not showing the main window until something such as *IOleObject::DoVerb(OLEIVERB_ SHOW)* is called. In this chapter, Cosmo registers its class factory only if *-Embedding* appears, and it uses REGCLS_SINGLEUSE to avoid some of the complications of an MDI server, as described in step 11. However, because Cosmo is generally an MDI application, it does allow the user to create new documents while Cosmo is otherwise visible to serve an embedded object. In this case, Cosmo sets its user control flag, *g_fUser*, to TRUE to prevent automatic shutdown when the embedded object is itself closed.

Cosmo's registry entries include a single verb visible to the end user, that being Edit. This is Cosmo's primary verb. In addition, Cosmo marks itself with OLEMISC_CANTLINKINSIDE because we don't deal with monikers yet. (We'll change this in Chapter 21.) The MiscStatus bits for DVASPECT-_CONTENT also include OLEMISC_RECOMPOSEONRESIZE so we can see exactly how that works with a container such as Patron. It is interesting to note that the server itself doesn't have to do anything to support this option—the burden is entirely on the container. Whenever Patron resizes a Cosmo object, you'll see a delay in which Cosmo is launched and asked to render the object before being asked to close. Cosmo never becomes visible to the user through this sequence.

Cosmo also registers itself as capable of both converting and emulating the Polyline objects from Chapter 19's Polyline sample (the "Polyline Figure" format) and those from Cosmo's old OLE 1 version (ProgID of "Cosmo1.0"). You can find the source for this version of Cosmo in CHAP18\COSMO1.0. A discussion of what's involved is included in OLE1.WRI on the companion CD.

## Implement the Basic Object Class

If you're following through this chapter to add server support to an application, you should start here after you've dealt with the initialization, registry, and class factory issues in steps 1, 2, and 3. Now, having a class factory by itself and no objects to create is useful, for example, only for testing what happens when *IClassFactory::CreateInstance* fails. You can use this to ensure that your server unloads itself from memory on such an error.

The next step is to begin implementing your embedded object. I say "begin implementing" because implementing the object in pieces is a little less painful than attempting to implement the entire thing at once. So let's start by implementing an object with only the *IUnknown* interface.

Cosmo's embedded object is a class named *CFigure*, which is a wrapper for the rest of Cosmo's internals. In other words, *CFigure* is noninvasive, requiring few changes to most of the other parts of Cosmo. *CFigure* is defined in COSMOLE.H to implement *IOleObject*, *IDataObject*, and *IPersistStorage* using interface implementation classes as usual. It includes an *IStorage* pointer and an *IStream* pointer for the purposes of implementing *IPersistStorage*, an *IDataAdviseHolder* variable and FORMATETC arrays for dealing with *IDataObject*, and *IOleAdviseHolder* and *IOleClientSite* pointers for dealing with *IOleObject* and the container.

The base implementation of *CFigure* is found in FIGURE.CPP, including its constructor, destructor, *IUnknown* members, and a few other utility functions. One interesting facet of this implementation is that its *Release* function does not delete the object itself. When the reference count is 0, it does call the *ObjectDestroyed* function in COSMO.CPP to start shutdown, but the object itself is deleted in the destructor of *CCosmoDoc*. This occurs because Cosmo's class factory actually creates a document that in turn creates an instance of *CFigure*, but the object holds no reference count. Instead, an external reference count is kept. When the figure is released to a zero reference count, it starts server shutdown. This destroys the document and deletes the figure in turn. In this way, the document maintains precise control over the lifetime of *CFigure* because it needs some of the figure's variables during destruction.

It doesn't necessarily take a zero reference count to start shutdown. If the user closes the document through Cosmo's user interface, the container will still have references to it. In this case, the document is destroyed first. In its destructor, it does the following:

```
//In CCosmoDoc::~CCosmoDoc
if (NULL!=m_pFigure)
    {
    m_pFigure->AddRef();
```

```
CoDisconnectObject((LPUNKNOWN)m_pFigure, 0L);
m_pFigure->Release();  //Starts shutdown if necessary
delete m_pFigure;
}
```

The *AddRef* call on the figure will initially safeguard the object. We then call *CoDisconnectObject* to remove all external connections. As a result, the figure will have a reference count of 1. When we call *Release*, the figure will start server shutdown through *ObjectDestroyed*. The document then deletes the figure and completes its destruction. As shutdown of the server is already under way, the server itself will eventually terminate completely.

This little game that I play inside Cosmo with the *CFigure* pointer — as opposed to its external reference count — allows me to keep the figure valid until the document is entirely done with it, regardless of whether the user closes the Cosmo document directly or deletes the figure object in the container. In the latter case, server shutdown begins with a zero reference count on the figure object itself. We don't want to delete the figure at this time because the document still expects it to be of value. This is nothing but an internal design choice for Cosmo and has no external bearing on Cosmo's integration with containers.

## Implement *IPersistStorage*

It's best to first implement *IPersistStorage* on an embedded object because the first thing *OleCreate* or *OleLoad* will do is call member functions in this initialization interface. For the most part, the code is similar to the code we implemented for Polyline back in Chapter 8. Inside *InitNew* and *Load*, this implementation of *IPersistStorage* creates or opens streams as necessary, holding on to those pointers for low-memory saves, releasing those pointers as needed in *HandsOffStorage*, and so forth.

*IPersistStorage::IsDirty* is implemented by calling *CFigure::FIsDirty*, which in turn asks the document holding the figure if the document is dirty. The document, however, always returns FALSE when it is open in order to edit an embedded object. Why is this? Remember that an embedded object continually notifies its container about changes, so the object in the server's user interface and the object image in the container always match. From the user's point of view, the object is never actually dirty, although we still need to ask the container to save it before we close, as we'll see.

The core implementation of *IPersistStorage::Load* and *IPersistStorage::Save* delegates its functionality to *CPolyline::ReadFromStream* and *CPolyline::WriteToStream*. These functions contain code that I broke out of the implementations of *CPolyline::ReadFromStorage* and *CPolyline::WriteToStorage* that we added in

Chapter 7. The core functionality of Cosmo's *CPolyline* class, then, stays exactly the same. All we've done here is reorganize that code to make it more accessible from an interface implementation.

We also handle conversion and emulation considerations inside *Load* and *Save*.[2] First we handle emulation of the Polyline class because both Cosmo and the Polyline component from Chapter 19 share the same stream name and stream format. Thus, we need not make any special consideration. The conversion case is more interesting. If you read through the container side of these features in Chapter 17, you'll know that the container calls the function *SetConvertStg* before reloading a newly converted object. When we enter *Load*, we call *GetConvertStg* to see if this is, in fact, a conversion case. We also read whatever CLSID is in the storage so we can return it from *IPersistStorage::GetClassID* when we're doing emulation:

```
STDMETHODIMP CImpIPersistStorage::GetClassID(LPCLSID pClsID)
    {
    if (PSSTATE_UNINIT==m_psState)
        return ResultFromScode(E_UNEXPECTED);


    *pClsID=m_pObj->m_clsID;
    return NOERROR;
    }



STDMETHODIMP CImpIPersistStorage::Load(LPSTORAGE pIStorage)
    {
    [Validation code omitted]

    //The next statement tells us whether we're
    //coming from another class storage.
    m_fConvert=(NOERROR==GetConvertStg(pIStorage));

    ReadClassStg(pIStorage, &m_pObj->m_clsID);
    ⋮
    }
```

From here we simply load the data as necessary from whatever streams are present in the storage. When we now go to save, we have to ensure that the storage format is converted to our own. The *m_fConvert* flag we saved in *Load* tells us to do this. We first write our own streams as necessary, delete the original object's streams (which amounts to nothing when we're converting a Polyline object because the streams are identical), update the format and user type in the storage, and turn off the convert bit:

---

2. This includes OLE 1 version handling. Again, see OLE1.WRI on the companion CD.

```
STDMETHODIMP CImpIPersistStorage::Save(LPSTORAGE pIStorage
    , BOOL fSameAsLoad)
    {
    ⋮
    if (m_fConvert)
        {
        UINT    cf;

        cf=RegisterClipboardFormat((*m_pObj->m_pST)[IDS_FORMAT]);
        WriteFmtUserTypeStg(pIStorage, cf
            , (*m_pObj->m_pST)[IDS_USERTYPE]);

        SetConvertStg(pIStorage, FALSE);
        m_fConvert=FALSE;
        }
    ⋮
    }
```

After this process, the object's persistent storage will be fully a Cosmo figure no matter what it was originally. The code we've demonstrated in Cosmo is perhaps artificially simple because Cosmo and Polyline share the same storage formats. This might be true of different versions of your own server. It should be obvious, however, that handling different formats from other competitive servers, through both conversion and emulation, will involve the handling of more streams with different data, in both *Load* and *Save*. Nevertheless, the same pattern of operations holds. In conversion, load the storage that is there and write your own formats when saving. In emulation, you need to both load and save the same format.

To finish up *IPersistStorage*, the implementations of *SaveCompleted* and *HandsOffStorage* are pretty standard except for one thing. Just before we return from *SaveCompleted*, we make a call to any connected container's *IAdviseSink::OnSave*. (This happens through *CFigure::SendAdvise*, which we'll look at later.) This tells containers that a save has been completed, which some older containers (in particular Microsoft Excel 5) use to know that saving succeeded. The call is benign for containers that don't care otherwise, but it is a wise call to include for maximum compatibility.

## Implement *IDataObject*

We saw in Chapter 17 how the data cache maintains a presentation cache in the container's storage. Somehow, however, that cache must obtain presentations to store in itself. For that reason, a content object in a local server must implement *IDataObject*, through which the cache can retrieve rendering in at least the CF_METAFILEPICT format (TYMED_MFPICT) and preferably in

CF_DIB (or CF_BITMAP) as well. Technically speaking, implementing *IData-Object::GetData* for one of these formats is the absolute bare minimum support an object must have for OLE Documents.

An object will, however, also want to support its native data format through both *GetData* and *SetData*. A container that knows more about your object might ask for your object's data or might give your object some data to integrate into it. If you don't foresee a reason why someone would want to use *GetData* or *SetData* for your private format, you have no reason to support such functionality in *IDataObject*. One case in which you must support *GetData* on your native format occurs when you have your own object handler. The object handler can then synchronize its data with that of the local object. (We'll cover this in Chapter 19.)

It is best to also include support for CFSTR_EMBEDSOURCE through both *GetData* and *GetDataHere*. In the former, you create a new storage object and save the object's data to it, using your own *IPersistStorage::Save* if you want. In the latter case, the container has provided a storage object already, so you can save the object directly to it. Either way, you should write your object's exact persistent representation to the storage. A container can use this data to create a new copy of the object, and the storage is passed that new instance through *IPersistStorage::Load*. You really do want to be sure it's the same data.

Here's how Cosmo's figure handles all supported formats through *GetData* and *GetDataHere*:

```
STDMETHODIMP CImpIDataObject::GetData(LPFORMATETC pFE
    , LPSTGMEDIUM pSTM)
    {
    UINT        cf=pFE->cfFormat;
    BOOL        fRet=FALSE;

    //Another part of us already knows whether the format is good.
    if (NOERROR!=QueryGetData(pFE))
        return ResultFromScode(DATA_E_FORMATETC);

    if (CF_METAFILEPICT==cf || CF_BITMAP==cf || m_pObj->m_cf==cf)
        {
        if (CF_METAFILEPICT==cf)
            {
            pSTM->tymed=TYMED_MFPICT;
            }
        else
            pSTM->tymed=TYMED_HGLOBAL;
```

```
            pSTM->pUnkForRelease=NULL;
            pSTM->hGlobal=m_pObj->m_pDoc->RenderFormat(cf);
            fRet=(NULL!=pSTM->hGlobal);
            }
    else
            fRet=m_pObj->m_pDoc->RenderMedium(cf, pSTM);

    return fRet ? NOERROR : ResultFromScode(DATA_E_FORMATETC);
    }


STDMETHODIMP CImpIDataObject::GetDataHere(LPFORMATETC pFE
, LPSTGMEDIUM pSTM)
    {
    UINT    cf;
    LONG    lRet;

    cf=RegisterClipboardFormat(CFSTR_EMBEDSOURCE);

    //Aspect is unimportant to us here, as are lindex and ptd.
    if (cf==pFE->cfFormat && (TYMED_ISTORAGE & pFE->tymed))
        {
        //We have an IStorage we can write to.
        pSTM->tymed=TYMED_ISTORAGE;
        pSTM->pUnkForRelease=NULL;
        lRet=m_pObj->m_pPL->WriteToStorage(pSTM->pstg
            , VERSIONCURRENT);

        if (lRet >= 0)
            return NOERROR;

        return ResultFromScode(STG_E_WRITEFAULT);
        }

    return ResultFromScode(DATA_E_FORMATETC);
    }
```

*GetDataHere* is implemented entirely by calling *CPolyline::WriteToStorage* —that's all there is to it. In *GetData*, we use the function *CPatronDoc::Render-Format* to generate the necessary rendering. The document turns around and uses code in *CPolyline* to fulfill the request because the Polyline object already knows how to copy its data into global memory and how to draw itself into metafiles and bitmaps. We can see this in the code on the following page.

```
HGLOBAL CCosmoDoc::RenderFormat(UINT cf)
    {
    HGLOBAL    hMem;

    if (cf==m_cf)
        {
        m_pPL->DataGetMem(VERSIONCURRENT, &hMem);
        return hMem;
        }

    switch (cf)
        {
        case CF_METAFILEPICT:
            return m_pPL->RenderMetafilePict();

        case CF_BITMAP:
            return (HGLOBAL)m_pPL->RenderBitmap();
        }

    return NULL;
    }
```

This is another example of how an embedded object implementation can be built on top of existing code. The implementation of *SetData* is much the same because it passes the data on to *CPolyline::DataSetMem*.

The other member functions have trivial implementations. *GetCanonical-FormatEtc* is the standard "all formats are the same" implementation that we saw in Chapter 10. *EnumFormatEtc* is implemented as follows:

```
STDMETHODIMP CImpIDataObject::EnumFormatEtc(DWORD dwDir
    , LPENUMFORMATETC *ppEnum)
    {
    return ResultFromScode(OLE_S_USEREG);
    }
```

Because this interface is implemented on a local content object, it is always some part of OLE that is calling us, never the container directly. By returning OLE_S_USEREG, we tell OLE to implement this function for us using our own registry entries. In other words, OLE calls *OleRegEnumFormatEtc* on our behalf. Things are so easy around here!

Finally, we implement the three amigos—*DAdvise, DUnadvise,* and *Enum-DAdvise*—using an OLE-provided data advise holder. The advise holder is created in *DAdvise* with *CreateDataAdviseHolder*. All of these members simply delegate to the advise holder, as we've seen before.

## Implement *IOleObject*

In some ways, *IOleObject* looks like the interface from hell, a dumping ground for every function that didn't seem to have any better home. Intimidating? You bet! Is it a problem? Not really. For the most part, the member functions in this interface have either trivial or optional implementations. Only about 15 of the 21 member functions, excluding those in *IUnknown*, require some implementation for embedded objects. Twelve of those 15 either are trivial to implement or use defaults from the registry. The remaining 6 (of the 21) functions either are optional or are not used for embedded objects themselves. (They will become more important later on.) The following table lists the implementation requirements for *IOleObject* members:

| Group | Members |
|---|---|
| Require real programming | *SetHostNames, Close, DoVerb* |
| Trivial implementations | *SetClientSite, GetClientSite, Update, IsUpToDate, GetExtent, Advise, Unadvise, EnumAdvise, GetUserClassID* |
| Implemented using registry | *EnumVerbs, GetUserType, GetMiscStatus* |
| Optional | *SetExtent, InitFromData, GetClipboardData, SetColorScheme* |
| Used for linking | *SetMoniker, GetMoniker* |

Members in the real programming group will be the focus of our discussion here. Those with trivial implementations will generally require only a few lines of code, and standard code at that. Those using the registry can simply return OLE_S_USEREG, as we did with *IDataObject::EnumFormatEtc*. OLE implements these using *OleRegEnumVerbs*, *OleRegGetUserType*, and *OleRegGetMiscStatus*, respectively. For the others, you can simply return E_NOTIMPL if you don't need them. Otherwise, functions such as *InitFromData* and *SetColorScheme* can easily require nontrivial code.

Cosmo implements *IOleObject* through the class *CImpIOleObject*, found in IOLEOBJ.CPP. So that you can see the varying complexity of these members, I've included the entire file in Listing 18-1 beginning on the following page. The next three sections cover the trivial, required, and optional members in more detail.

**IOLEOBJ.CPP**

```
/*
 * IOLEOBJ.CPP
 * Copyright (c)1993-1995 Microsoft Corporation, All Rights Reserved
 */

#include "cosmo.h"

[Constructor, destructor, IUnknown members omitted]

STDMETHODIMP CImpIOleObject::SetClientSite
    (LPOLECLIENTSITE pIOleClientSite)
    {
    if (NULL!=m_pObj->m_pIOleClientSite)
        m_pObj->m_pIOleClientSite->Release();

    m_pObj->m_pIOleClientSite=pIOleClientSite;
    m_pObj->m_pIOleClientSite->AddRef();
    return NOERROR;
    }


STDMETHODIMP CImpIOleObject::GetClientSite(LPOLECLIENTSITE
    *ppSite)
    {
    //Be sure to call AddRef on new pointer you are giving away.
    *ppSite=m_pObj->m_pIOleClientSite;
    m_pObj->m_pIOleClientSite->AddRef();

    return NOERROR;
    }


STDMETHODIMP CImpIOleObject::SetHostNames(LPCOLESTR pszApp
    , LPCOLESTR pszObj)
    {
    m_pObj->m_fEmbedded=TRUE;
    m_pObj->m_pFR->UpdateEmbeddingUI(TRUE, m_pObj->m_pDoc
        , pszApp, pszObj);
    return NOERROR;
    }
```

**Listing 18-1.**                                          *(continued)*

*Cosmo's implementation of* IOleObject.

**Listing 18-1.** *continued*

```
STDMETHODIMP CImpIOleObject::Close(DWORD dwSaveOption)
    {
    HWND    hWnd;
    BOOL    fSave=FALSE;

    hWnd=m_pObj->m_pDoc->Window();

    //If object is dirty and we're asked to save, save it and close.
    if (OLECLOSE_SAVEIFDIRTY==dwSaveOption && m_pObj->FIsDirty())
        fSave=TRUE;

    /*
     * If asked to prompt, do so only if dirty; if we get a
     * YES, save as usual and close. On NO, just close. On
     * CANCEL, return OLE_E_PROMPTSAVECANCELLED.
     */
    if (OLECLOSE_PROMPTSAVE==dwSaveOption && m_pObj->FIsDirty())
        {
        UINT    uRet;

        uRet=MessageBox(hWnd, (*m_pObj->m_pST)[IDS_CLOSECAPTION]
            , (*m_pObj->m_pST)[IDS_CLOSEPROMPT], MB_YESNOCANCEL);

        if (IDCANCEL==uRet)
            return ResultFromScode(OLE_E_PROMPTSAVECANCELLED);

        if (IDYES==uRet)
            fSave=TRUE;
        }

    if (fSave)
        {
        m_pObj->SendAdvise(OBJECTCODE_SAVEOBJECT);
        m_pObj->SendAdvise(OBJECTCODE_SAVED);
        }

    //We get here directly on OLECLOSE_NOSAVE.
    PostMessage(hWnd, WM_CLOSE, 0, 0L);
    return NOERROR;
    }
```

*(continued)*

**Listing 18-1.** *continued*

```
STDMETHODIMP CImpIOleObject::SetMoniker(DWORD dwWhich
    , LPMONIKER pmk)
    {
    return ResultFromScode(E_NOTIMPL);
    }


STDMETHODIMP CImpIOleObject::GetMoniker(DWORD dwAssign
    , DWORD dwWhich, LPMONIKER *ppmk)
    {
    return ResultFromScode(E_NOTIMPL);
    }


STDMETHODIMP CImpIOleObject::InitFromData(LPDATAOBJECT pIDataObject
    , BOOL fCreation, DWORD dwReserved)
    {
    BOOL    fRet;

    fRet=m_pObj->m_pDoc->PasteFromData(pIDataObject);
    return fRet ? NOERROR : ResultFromScode(E_FAIL);
    }


STDMETHODIMP CImpIOleObject::GetClipboardData(DWORD dwReserved
    , LPDATAOBJECT *ppIDataObj)
    {
    *ppIDataObj=m_pObj->m_pDoc->TransferObjectCreate(FALSE);
    return (NULL!=*ppIDataObj) ? NOERROR : ResultFromScode(E_FAIL);
    }


STDMETHODIMP CImpIOleObject::DoVerb(LONG iVerb, LPMSG pMSG
    , LPOLECLIENTSITE pActiveSite, LONG lIndex, HWND hWndParent
    , LPCRECT pRectPos)
    {
    HWND       hWnd, hWndT;

    //Find the uppermost window.
    hWndT=GetParent(m_pObj->m_pDoc->Window());

    while (NULL!=hWndT)
        {
        hWnd=hWndT;
        hWndT=GetParent(hWndT);
        }
```

*(continued)*

**Listing 18-1.** *continued*

```
    switch (iVerb)
        {
        case OLEIVERB_HIDE:
            ShowWindow(hWnd, SW_HIDE);
            m_pObj->SendAdvise(OBJECTCODE_HIDEWINDOW);
            break;

        case OLEIVERB_PRIMARY:
        case OLEIVERB_OPEN:
        case OLEIVERB_SHOW:
            ShowWindow(hWnd, SW_SHOW);
            SetForegroundWindow(hWnd);
            SetFocus(hWnd);

            m_pObj->SendAdvise(OBJECTCODE_SHOWOBJECT);
            m_pObj->SendAdvise(OBJECTCODE_SHOWWINDOW);
            break;

        default:
            return ResultFromScode(OLEOBJ_S_INVALIDVERB);
        }

    return NOERROR;
    }


STDMETHODIMP CImpIOleObject::EnumVerbs(LPENUMOLEVERB *ppEnum)
    {
    return ResultFromScode(OLE_S_USEREG);
    }


STDMETHODIMP CImpIOleObject::Update(void)
    {
    //We're always updated since we don't contain.
    return NOERROR;
    }


STDMETHODIMP CImpIOleObject::IsUpToDate(void)
    {
    //We're always updated since we don't contain.
    return NOERROR;
    }


STDMETHODIMP CImpIOleObject::GetUserClassID(LPCLSID pClsID)
    {
    *pClsID=m_pObj->m_clsID;
    return NOERROR;
    }
```

*(continued)*

**Listing 18-1.** *continued*

```
STDMETHODIMP CImpIOleObject::GetUserType(DWORD dwForm
, LPOLESTR *ppszType)
    {
    return ResultFromScode(OLE_S_USEREG);
    }


STDMETHODIMP CImpIOleObject::SetExtent(DWORD dwAspect, LPSIZEL pszl)
    {
    RECT     rc;
    SIZEL    szl;

    if (!(DVASPECT_CONTENT & dwAspect))
        return ResultFromScode(E_FAIL);

    XformSizeInHimetricToPixels(NULL, pszl, &szl);

    //This resizes the window to match the container's size.
    SetRect(&rc, 0, 0, (int)szl.cx, (int)szl.cy);
    m_pObj->m_pPL->SizeSet(&rc, TRUE);

    return NOERROR;
    }

STDMETHODIMP CImpIOleObject::GetExtent(DWORD dwAspect, LPSIZEL pszl)
    {
    RECT     rc;
    SIZEL    szl;

    if (!(DVASPECT_CONTENT & dwAspect))
        return ResultFromScode(E_FAIL);

    m_pObj->m_pPL->RectGet(&rc);
    szl.cx=rc.right-rc.left;
    szl.cy=rc.bottom-rc.top;

    XformSizeInPixelsToHimetric(NULL, &szl, pszl);
    return NOERROR;
    }
```

*(continued)*

**Listing 18-1.** *continued*

```
STDMETHODIMP CImpIOleObject::Advise(LPADVISESINK pIAdviseSink
    , LPDWORD pdwConn)
    {
    if (NULL==m_pObj->m_pIOleAdviseHolder)
        {
        HRESULT   hr;

        hr=CreateOleAdviseHolder(&m_pObj->m_pIOleAdviseHolder);

        if (FAILED(hr))
            return hr;
        }

    return m_pObj->m_pIOleAdviseHolder->Advise(pIAdviseSink
        , pdwConn);
    }


STDMETHODIMP CImpIOleObject::Unadvise(DWORD dwConn)
    {
    if (NULL!=m_pObj->m_pIOleAdviseHolder)
        return m_pObj->m_pIOleAdviseHolder->Unadvise(dwConn);

    return ResultFromScode(E_FAIL);
    }


STDMETHODIMP CImpIOleObject::EnumAdvise(LPENUMSTATDATA *ppEnum)
    {
    if (NULL!=m_pObj->m_pIOleAdviseHolder)
        return m_pObj->m_pIOleAdviseHolder->EnumAdvise(ppEnum);

    return ResultFromScode(E_FAIL);
    }



STDMETHODIMP CImpIOleObject::GetMiscStatus(DWORD dwAspect
    , LPDWORD pdwStatus)
    {
    return ResultFromScode(OLE_S_USEREG);
    }


STDMETHODIMP CImpIOleObject::SetColorScheme(LPLOGPALETTE pLP)
    {
    return ResultFromScode(E_NOTIMPL);
    }
```

### Trivial Functions

Let's look at the simple implementations first because we'll need some of the information from these functions to implement the more complex ones. The functions in this set are *SetClientSite, GetClientSite, Update, IsUpToDate, GetExtent, GetUserClassID,* and the triumvirate *Advise, Unadvise,* and *EnumAdvise.*

*SetClientSite* is the only way through which the embedded object gets an *IOleClientSite* pointer to the container's site object. You must hold on to this pointer for the lifetime of your object, saving it in a variable and calling *AddRef* on it, of course. In the rare case that your object receives multiple calls to *SetClientSite,* release whatever pointer you are currently holding before overwriting it with the new one.

*GetClientSite* is the direct sibling of *SetClientSite.* It simply needs to copy the last *IOleClientSite* pointer seen in *SetClientSite* to the out-parameter \*\**ppSite. GetClientSite* is a function that returns a new copy of a pointer, so be sure to call *AddRef* on the *IOleClientSite* pointer again.

*Update* and *IsUpToDate* are a pair of functions that a container can use to be sure that the presentation in its cache matches the current state of the object. *IsUpToDate* asks, "Are you current?" whereas *Update* tells your application, "Make yourself current." I mentioned before that embedded objects are always up-to-date unless they actually contain other objects themselves (especially links). This is because singular embedded objects always call *IAdviseSink::OnViewChange* when a change occurs, so the cache and the container are visibly updated. If the object is a container itself, however, it has to recursively call *Update* or *IsUpToDate* on its contained objects to implement these members.

*GetExtent* asks the object, "How big is this aspect?" by asking the object to fill a SIZEL structure with the horizontal and vertical dimensions of the object in HIMETRIC units that are sensitive to the requested aspect. These extents are in absolute units—that is, the vertical value is not negative, as it would be if you were dealing in the MM_HIMETRIC mapping mode. Because no *hDC* is anywhere in sight, there is no conception of a mapping mode in this function. Cosmo implements a mapping mode by retrieving the rectangle of the current Polyline window (in pixels) and using the helper function *XformSizeInPixelsToHimetric* (which is in INOLE.DLL, file INOLE-\XFORM.CPP) to convert the values before returning.

*GetUserClassID* has to return the emulated CLSID—just as *IPersistStorage-::GetClassID* does—if the present object is being used in this capacity. In Cosmo, *IPersistStorage::Load* stores the emulated CLSID in *CFigure::m_clsID,* so that's what we return here. In emulation scenarios, the CLSID that users think they are working with is not the CLSID of your object itself. This means *GetUserClassID* gives the container (and OLE) a way of knowing what the object actually is.

You can implement the three advise functions using an advise holder created with *CreateOleAdviseHolder*. This advise holder implements the interface *IOleAdviseHolder*, through which we can multicast the *OnSave*, *OnRename*, and *OnClose* calls to *IAdviseSink* interfaces. We create the advise holder in *Advise* and release it in the *CFigure* destructor. *Advise*, *Unadvise*, and *EnumAdvise* then delegate to this holder. When we need to send notifications, we call members such as *IOleAdviseHolder::SendOnSave* and others, as we'll see later.

## Required Functions

In this set, we find *DoVerb*, *Close*, and *SetHostNames*, the three most important members (in that order) of *IOleObject*. *DoVerb* asks an object to execute one of its verbs. If *DoVerb* didn't exist, activation wouldn't exist, so it is really the crux of OLE Documents. The whole process of in-place activation begins with this function, as we'll see in Chapters 22 and 23.

As discussed in Chapter 17, the *DoVerb* function takes an object from the loaded or running state to the active state, or from the active state to the running state. This function receives a number of arguments, the first of which, *iVerb*, is the number of the verb to execute. This will be either OLEIVERB-_PRIMARY (value 0), one of the object's custom verbs as selected from the verb menu created for this object in the container (a positive value), or one of the following standard verbs:[3]

| | |
|---|---|
| OLEIVERB_ SHOW (–1) | "Make the object visible." The object calls *ShowWindow(hWnd, SW_ SHOW)*, in which *hWnd* is the topmost window that is necessary to show to make this object visible. After *ShowWindow*, the object calls *SetFocus(hWnd)* followed by calls to *IOleClientSite::ShowObject* and *IOleClientSite::OnShowWindow(TRUE)*. *IOleClientSite* is the client site returned from *SetClientSite*. |
| OLEIVERB_OPEN (–2) | "Open the object for editing." Outside of in-place activation, this has the same semantics as OLEIVERB_SHOW. |

*(continued)*

---

3. We'll see other standard verbs in the context of in-place activation.

OLEIVERB_HIDE (−3)   "Hide the object." The object calls *Show-Window(hWnd, SW_HIDE)*, in which *hWnd* is the topmost window that is suitable for hiding the object's user interface, such as the main application window (for a single-object server) or a document window (when multiple objects or documents are open). The object also calls *IOleClientSite::OnShowWindow(FALSE)*. *IOleClientSite* is the client site returned from *SetClientSite*.

All embedded objects should support at least these three verbs along with OLEIVERB_PRIMARY. Any other unsupported verb should cause *DoVerb* to return OLE_E_INVALIDVERB. The exact meaning of any positive verb, as well as OLEIVERB_PRIMARY, is something known only to the object and the end user. Cosmo's single (and primary) verb is Edit. Invoking Edit shows Cosmo's window, as with OLEIVERB_SHOW and OLEIVERB_OPEN. Another type of object, for example a sound object that has a Play verb, would only play the sound and not actually show any windows, nor would it call anything in *IOleClientSite*.

The other arguments to *DoVerb* provide the object with information that it can use to modify its behavior. The argument *lpMsg* tells the object what message (for example, WM_LBUTTONDBLCLK) actually caused the *DoVerb* call from the container. This information is important mostly for a type of in-place object called *inside-out*, which is covered in Chapters 22 and 23. The *IOleClientSite* pointer *pActiveSite* is used in other special cases that are not yet important in our discussion. The argument *lindex* is always 0 and is reserved for future use. Finally, *hWndParent* and *pRectPos* are useful to objects such as video clips, which temporarily play in the context of the container without having to implement full in-place activation. An object is allowed to temporarily create a window inside *hWndParent* in which to play or to call *GetDC-(hWndParent)*. It is also allowed to draw directly onto the container's window. The *pRectPos* parameter provides you with the position of your object (that is, the container's site) in *hWndParent*. Although you can create a window that is larger than this rectangle, you should never draw outside the rectangle on the container's *hDC*. Also, it is important to know that anything you do with these two parameters must be done entirely within *DoVerb*. If you need any other type of in-place capabilities, you need to implement in-place activation.

The next most important member of *IOleObject* is *Close*, which moves an object from the running or active state to the loaded state. *Close* is also called either when the container closes the compound document that contains the object or when the user deletes the object from that document altogether. In any case, the object generally closes its user interface, calls *IOleClientSite::On-ShowWindow(FALSE)*, and starts server shutdown as necessary.

I said that the object "generally" does these things because the *dwSave-Option* argument can modify this behavior:

| Value | Description |
|---|---|
| OLECLOSE_SAVEIFDIRTY | If the object is dirty, it should save itself before closing. |
| OLECLOSE_NOSAVE | Close the object without saving. |
| OLECLOSE_PROMPTSAVE | Display a message box with a message something like, "This object has been changed. Do you want to update *<container document>* before closing?"* and Yes, No, and Cancel buttons. If the user chooses Yes, save the object and close. If the user chooses No, simply close. On Cancel, return OLE_E_PROMPTSAVECAN-CELLED without doing anything else. The *<container document>* string is obtained through *IOleObject::SetHostNames*, as we'll see shortly. |

* I could find no standard for this message, so I'm making an educated guess based on an old OLE 1 standard.

The process of saving, when necessary, has two steps:

1. If the object has been modified, call *IOleClientSite::SaveObject* using the most recent pointer seen in *SetClientSite*. In Cosmo, this is accomplished by calling *CFigure::SendAdvise* with OBJECTCODE-_SAVEDOBJECT.

2. Call *IAdviseSink::OnSave* through your advise holder's *IOleAdvise-Holder::SendOnSave*. Again, Cosmo handles this through *CFigure-::SendAdvise* with OBJECTCODE_SAVED.

The final required function in *IOleObject* with a sizable implementation is *SetHostNames*. This function informs the object that it's being embedded in a container and is a signal to the server to show the appropriate user interface for embedding. At this point in our discussion, it's not necessary to fully implement this function, so we'll come back to it later in this chapter in "Modify the Server's User Interface."

## Optional Functions

The four functions in this group—*SetExtent*, *InitFromData*, *GetClipboardData*, and *SetColorScheme*—are not required for standard operation of compound documents, so you can implement them as suits your fancy.

*SetExtent* adds a nice touch to the interaction between a container and a server, so I do recommend that you implement it. A container will call this function when it resizes an object in one of its documents if your object is running or if you have marked it with OLEMISC_RECOMPOSEONRESIZE. Handling *SetExtent* ensures that your object always looks good in the container—no matter what the scale—because you can render the object as appropriate for that scale. When the object is active in its own user interface, this call can also be used to reduce or enlarge the object in its editing window as the user resizes it in the container. Cosmo, for example, scales the Polyline window (and the document window in which it lives) in such a way that it's as close to the size of the container's site as possible (and within reason). *SetExtent* works best for graphical objects; it does not work as well for text or table objects for which scale is much less important than the textual or numeric data. *SetExtent* is also sensitive to the display aspect that is passed in the *dwAspect* parameter.

*InitFromData* allows a container to either paste into your object directly or provide initial data during creation. This function is passed an *IDataObject* pointer, which you can use to retrieve the data, and the flag *fCreation*, which indicates the scenario in which this function is being called. If *fCreation* is FALSE, you should integrate the data in the data object with your current data, as if Edit Paste had been performed in the server itself. If *fCreation* is TRUE, the container is attempting to create a new instance of your object on the basis of a selection in the container that is described by the data object. Cosmo happens to treat both cases identically by passing the data object to *CCosmoDoc::PasteFromData*. Again, I highly recommend that you make a function that pastes data from any arbitrary data object, such as those you can get from the clipboard, from drag and drop, or from a function such as *InitFromData*.

*GetClipboardData*, on the other hand, asks the object for an *IDataObject* pointer that is identical to the one the server would place on the clipboard if the user performed an Edit Copy operation. This allows a caller to get a snapshot of the object—as opposed to the *IDataObject* interface on the object itself—that always reflects the most recent data. If you implement this function, you have to return an *IDataObject* pointer for an object whose data will not change. Cosmo has the handy function *CCosmoDoc::TransferObjectCreate*, which does the job for us.

Finally, *SetColorScheme* provides the object with the container's recommended palette. The object might choose to ignore this without any dire consequences, but if you can, try to use the colors provided. Now, the colors provided in the LOGPALETTE structure are not actually colors in a GDI palette. The first palette entry in the structure actually specifies the foreground color recommended by the container. The second palette entry specifies the background color. The first half of the remaining palette entries are fill colors, and the second half are colors for the lines and text. Container applications typically specify an even number of palette entries. When there is an uneven number of entries, the server should round up to the fill colors. In other words, if there are five entries, the first three should be interpreted as fill colors and the last two as line and text colors.

## But It Still Doesn't Work

After implementing and compiling this mammoth interface, you have most of the server side complete. Now, when you use Insert Object from a container, it will launch your application, obtain your class factory, create an object, and fire off calls such as *IPersistStorage::InitNew*, *IOleObject::SetClientSite*, *IOleObject::GetExtent*, *IOleObject::SetHostNames*, and *IOleObject::DoVerb*. Your window will appear ready for editing. If you have implemented *IOleObject::Close* along with a call to *IOleClientSite::SaveObject*, you see a call to *IPersistStorage::Save* when you close your application. When you activate the object from the container (with a quick double click), you see a call to *IPersistStorage::Load*, followed by the same calls to *IOleObject* as before. Your application should at this point be visible again, with the previously saved data ready for editing.

The container, however, has no presentation, or whatever presentation there is is not being updated as it should be when you make changes to the object. In addition, when you close your application, you probably get a prompt that says, "Document has changed; do you want to save?" If you answer "Yes," you get a File Save dialog box. Well, that's not part of the OLE user interface for embedded object servers. In fact, there's nothing else to tell you that you are working with an embedded object (as opposed to an untitled file). To solve both these problems, we have to modify the server to show a user interface that is appropriate for an embedded object and to complete the notifications we send to the container.

## Modify the Server's User Interface

I admit that I seriously loathe writing user interface code because it's the one place that you cannot be the least bit wrong without someone noticing. In addition, user interface specifications seldom identify who is responsible for doing what, and sometimes the specs don't articulate all possible cases. I guess that's why they're called *guidelines*. The situation in which you execute *IOle-Object::DoVerb* and show a server window is one such case that is not exactly well defined. User interface guidelines for OLE Documents typically devote all their discussion to in-place activation. Such is life for us in the trenches, shooting in the dark at an unknown and unseen target.

So what I'm describing here is not official. It is pieced together from what I've seen other applications do. (That's how we get standards in the first place, isn't it?)

All the following changes to the user interface should take place when *IOleObject::SetHostNames* is called. That function tells you that your application is an embedded object, as well as the names of the container application and the container document for which you need to make these changes. *SetHostNames* is always called before *DoVerb*, so these changes should be in effect before you show an editing window:

1. Remove the New, Open, Close, and Save commands from your File menu. (Remove any toolbar buttons that invoke the same commands as well.)

2. Change the name of the Save As command on the File menu to Save Copy As. You can usually keep the same command identifier for this modified item. You might also want to remove any toolbar button for this function, but that's up to you. Save Copy As essentially creates an export function that does not remember the filename after the copy is written. In addition, if you have an import function, as Cosmo does, you can leave that on the menu and the toolbar. If you have a status line, you might also want to change the message displayed for this item (which Cosmo does not do).

3. Change the Exit command on the File menu to Exit And Return To *<container document>*; the string *<container document>* is pointed to by the *pszObj* argument of *SetHostNames*. Again, you might want to change any toolbar and status line UI to accommodate this. (I know it seems silly that the argument containing the document name is called *pszObj*, but, hey, it's only software—call it anything you like.)

4. Change your caption bar to read "*<object type>* in *<container document>*"; *<object type>* is the user-readable name of your object, such as "Cosmo Figure", and *<container document>* is the *pszObj* argument from *SetHostNames*. If your application is an SDI application or if it is MDI but the document is maximized, this string appears in the main application window's title bar prefixed with "*<application name>* -". If your application is an MDI application without a maximized document window, the frame caption remains the same, and this string appears in the document's title bar. (MDI automatically handles the maximized document case by concatenating the frame window's caption with the - character and the document's caption.)

Cosmo makes these changes from within *IOleObject::SetHostNames* by calling *CCosmoFrame::UpdateEmbeddingUI* because the frame controls the menus and the toolbar. *UpdateEmbeddingUI* is actually capable of switching between an embedding state and a nonembedding state in case I ever decide to allow Cosmo to service multiple objects as well as other nonobject documents, as described in "(Optional) MDI Servers, User Interface, and Shutdown" near the end of this chapter.

```
void CCosmoFrame::UpdateEmbeddingUI(BOOL fEmbedding
    , PCDocument pDoc, LPCTSTR pszApp, LPCTSTR pszObj)
    {
    HMENU       hMenu;
    TCHAR       szTemp[256];

    //First let's play with File menu.
    hMenu=m_phMenu[0];

    //Remove or add File New, Open, and Save items.
    if (fEmbedding)
        {
        DeleteMenu(m_phMenu[0], IDM_FILENEW,   MF_BYCOMMAND);
        DeleteMenu(m_phMenu[0], IDM_FILEOPEN,  MF_BYCOMMAND);
        DeleteMenu(m_phMenu[0], IDM_FILECLOSE, MF_BYCOMMAND);
        DeleteMenu(m_phMenu[0], IDM_FILESAVE,  MF_BYCOMMAND);

        //Save As->Save Copy As
        ModifyMenu(m_phMenu[0], IDM_FILESAVEAS, MF_BYCOMMAND
            , IDM_FILESAVEAS, PSZ(IDS_SAVECOPYAS));
        }
```

*(continued)*

903

```
else
    {
    InsertMenu(m_phMenu[0], 0, MF_BYPOSITION, IDM_FILENEW
        , PSZ(IDS_NEW));
    InsertMenu(m_phMenu[0], 1, MF_BYPOSITION, IDM_FILEOPEN
        , PSZ(IDS_OPEN));
    InsertMenu(m_phMenu[0], 2, MF_BYPOSITION, IDM_FILESAVE
        , PSZ(IDS_SAVE));
    InsertMenu(m_phMenu[0], 3, MF_BYPOSITION, IDM_FILECLOSE
        , PSZ(IDS_SAVE));

    //Save Copy As->Save As
    ModifyMenu(m_phMenu[0], IDM_FILESAVEAS, MF_BYCOMMAND
        , IDM_FILESAVEAS, PSZ(IDS_SAVEAS));
    }

//Change Exit to Exit & Return to xx or vice versa for SDI.
if (fEmbedding)
    wsprintf(szTemp, PSZ(IDS_EXITANDRETURN), (LPSTR)pszObj);
else
    lstrcpy(szTemp, PSZ(IDS_EXIT));

ModifyMenu(m_phMenu[0], IDM_FILEEXIT, MF_STRING, IDM_FILEEXIT
    , szTemp);
DrawMenuBar(m_hWnd);

//Now let's play with toolbar.
m_pTB->Show(IDM_FILENEW,   !fEmbedding);
m_pTB->Show(IDM_FILEOPEN,  !fEmbedding);
m_pTB->Show(IDM_FILECLOSE, !fEmbedding);
m_pTB->Show(IDM_FILESAVE,  !fEmbedding);

//Enable what's left appropriately.
UpdateToolbar();

//Now let's play with title bar.

//IDS_EMBEDDINGCAPTION is MDI/SDI sensitive in COSMO.RC.
wsprintf(szTemp, PSZ(IDS_EMBEDDINGCAPTION), pszObj);

/*
 * Remember that in MDI situations, Windows takes care of
 * frame window caption bar when document is maximized.
 */
```

```
#ifdef MDI
    SetWindowText(pDoc->Window(), szTemp);
#else
    SetWindowText(m_hWnd, szTemp);
#endif

 return;
 }
```

When Cosmo is in the embedding state, it appears as shown in Figure 18-2. You'll see that the Import command is still on the File menu and the toolbar.

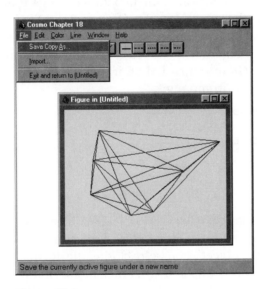

**Figure 18-2.**
*Cosmo, sporting its embedded object user interface.*

Because we modified the appearance of certain menu items, we also need to modify the behavior of those commands. First, to change Save As to Save Copy As, you can either implement a new function or modify your existing save function. In either case, Save Copy As performs the same operation as Save As except that you don't use the filename as the active document or anything to that effect. In other words, you write the file and forget the filename, without changing any other part of your user interface to reflect the filename. It's simply a way for the user to make a disk copy of the object.

In Cosmo, we modify *CCosmoDoc::Save* so that performing a Save Copy As does not make the document clean, as a typical Save As would. We also do this so that we don't store the filename in the document's structure or change the caption bar. *Save* determines that we're in an embedding state by calling *CFigure::FIsEmbedded* (which returns the value of *CFigure*'s *m_fEmbedded* flag, set to TRUE in *IOleObject::SetHostNames*). You can see these changes in COSMO\DOCUMENT.CPP.

We also change Exit to Exit And Return To *<container document>*. There's no big change to the actual process of closing a document and closing the application. But when running normally, Cosmo always checks to see whether the document is dirty when it closes the document before exiting the application. If it is dirty, Cosmo asks the user to save the document to a file.

Because saving the object to a file makes no sense in the case of embedding (we removed File Save altogether), we need to prevent this prompt. So we modify *CCosmoDoc::FDirtyGet* to return FALSE if we're in the embedded state, which effectively prevents prompting:

```
BOOL CCosmoDoc::FDirtyGet(void)
    {
    if (m_pFigure->FIsEmbedded())
        return FALSE;

    return m_fDirty;
    }
```

Now you are probably asking, "What if the object really is dirty? How do we ensure that the container saves the object before we destroy it?" We need to tell the container to save the object when we're closing the document holding the object by calling *IOleClientSite::SaveObject*, which is done in the *CCosmoDoc* destructor:

```
CCosmoDoc::~CCosmoDoc(void)
    {
    m_pFigure->SendAdvise(OBJECTCODE_SAVEOBJECT);

    ⋮
    }
```

And because I know you're getting sick of seeing this *CFigure::SendAdvise* function without knowing what it does, it's about time we looked at it and its notifications in general.

## Send Notifications

In the context of OLE Documents, an object can send a number of notifications and requests to both the container's *IAdviseSink* and *IOleClientSite* interfaces. The only true asynchronous notifications are calls to *IAdviseSink*, whereas others are synchronous calls to *IOleClientSite::SaveObject*. Nevertheless, lumping these together as notifications in an embedded object implementation is quite convenient. It enables us to make one function for our object that will send the proper notification to the appropriate interface whenever asked. That function is *CFigure::SendAdvise*, which accepts any of these codes defined in COSMOLE.H:

```
//Codes for CFigure::SendAdvise
//......Code...................Method called in CFigureSendAdvise...
#define OBJECTCODE_SAVED        0 //IOleAdviseHolder::SendOnSave
#define OBJECTCODE_CLOSED       1 //IOleAdviseHolder::SendOnClose
#define OBJECTCODE_RENAMED      2 //IOleAdviseHolder::SendOnRename
#define OBJECTCODE_SAVEOBJECT   3 //IOleClientSite::SaveObject
#define OBJECTCODE_DATACHANGED  4 //IDataAdviseHolder::SendOnDataChange
#define OBJECTCODE_SHOWWINDOW   5 //IOleClientSite::OnShowWindow(TRUE)
#define OBJECTCODE_HIDEWINDOW   6 //IOleClientSite::OnShowWindow(FALSE)
#define OBJECTCODE_SHOWOBJECT   7 //IOleClientSite::ShowObject
```

Each code is implemented using an appropriate site interface or advise holder:

```
//FIGURE.CPP
void CFigure::SendAdvise(UINT uCode)
    {
    switch (uCode)
        {
        case OBJECTCODE_SAVED:
            if (NULL!=m_pIOleAdviseHolder)
                m_pIOleAdviseHolder->SendOnSave();

            break;

        case OBJECTCODE_CLOSED:
            if (NULL!=m_pIOleAdviseHolder)
                m_pIOleAdviseHolder->SendOnClose();

            break;

        case OBJECTCODE_RENAMED:
            //Call IOleAdviseHolder::SendOnRename (later)
            break;
```

*(continued)*

907

```
case OBJECTCODE_SAVEOBJECT:
    if (FIsDirty() && NULL!=m_pIOleClientSite)
        m_pIOleClientSite->SaveObject();

    break;

case OBJECTCODE_DATACHANGED:
    //No flags are necessary here.
    if (NULL!=m_pIDataAdviseHolder)
        {
        m_pIDataAdviseHolder->SendOnDataChange(m_pIDataObject
            , 0, 0);
        }

     break;

case OBJECTCODE_SHOWWINDOW:
    if (NULL!=m_pIOleClientSite)
        m_pIOleClientSite->OnShowWindow(TRUE);

    break;

case OBJECTCODE_HIDEWINDOW:
    if (NULL!=m_pIOleClientSite)
        m_pIOleClientSite->OnShowWindow(FALSE);

    break;

case OBJECTCODE_SHOWOBJECT:
    if (NULL!=m_pIOleClientSite)
        m_pIOleClientSite->ShowObject();

    break;
    }

return;
}
```

This function eliminates the need to check for NULL pointers anywhere else and distills all notifications down to one function and one argument. Then we don't have to remember which interface—*IAdviseSink, IOleClientSite, IOleAdviseHolder,* or *IDataAdviseHolder*—we used to send which notification to the container.

We've seen a number of places in this chapter to which we send various notifications. These are listed in Table 18-1. The only events we haven't covered so far are those for closing a document and for data changes.

| Event | Notifications (in the Order Shown) |
|---|---|
| Closing a document (*CCosmoDoc::~CCosmoDoc*) | *IOleClientSite::SaveObject* *IOleClientSite::OnShowWindow(FALSE)* *IOleAdviseHolder::SendOnClose* (all of this before *CoDisconnectObject*) |
| Data changes (*CCosmoDoc::FDirtySet*) | *IDataAdviseHolder::SendOnDataChange* |
| *IOleObject::Close* (if saving) | *IOleClientSite::SaveObject* *IOleAdviseHolder::SendOnSave* |
| *IOleObject::DoVerb(HIDE)* | *IOleClientSite::OnShowWindow(FALSE)* |
| *IOleObject::DoVerb(SHOW)* (includes any verb that shows) | *IOleClientSite::ShowObject* *IOleClientSite::OnShowWindow(TRUE)* |

**Table 18-1.**
*When to send notifications from an embedded object.*

You'll notice that we don't use or implement OBJECTCODE_RE-NAMED anywhere because it's used only for linking and requires a moniker, which we won't add until Chapter 21. In addition, you'll notice that the server never calls *IAdviseSink::OnViewChange* because a local server never implements *IViewObject2*. Instead, the data cache watches *IAdviseSink::OnDataChange* and generates *OnViewChange* notifications itself.

I should point out that you might need to optimize the code when you actually send *OnDataChange* to advise sinks. The preceding table describes this situation as any time data changes in your application. To reflect that in a container, OLE must call your *IDataObject::GetData* to request a new presentation. If your presentation is complex—perhaps a metafile with 5000 records—this operation will not be fast. In such cases, you might want to defer sending the notification for a specific time after the most recent change—maybe 1 or 2 seconds. This would allow end users to make rapid changes without having to continually wait for you to generate a new presentation. Only when they stop making changes will you actually send an *OnData-Change*. You can also consider making updates part of your idle time processing. If you do defer the *OnDataChange* notification in any way, send one immediately upon shutdown to ensure that OLE can get a final presentation from you.

And now, as the stork would say, "Congratulations! You're a mother!" Well, at least a mother of an embedded object server that is fully functional with a container application. At this point, you should be able to run Insert Object from a container to launch your server, make changes in the object, and see those changes reflected in a shaded object site. If changes are not being reflected in the container, either it's displaying a different aspect than the one you are changing, or, when your *IDataObject::GetData* is asked for CF_METAFILEPICT or CF_BITMAP, you're returning the wrong STG-MEDIUM. In developing Cosmo, I tore my hair out trying to understand why the container was not reflecting changes. I discovered that the *tymed* I was storing in *GetData*'s STGMEDIUM was TYMED_HGLOBAL instead of TYMED-_MFPICT for the CF_METAFILEPICT format. Subtle, but ever so important.

If the container site is not shading itself, you might not be calling *IOleClientSite::OnShowWindow* at the appropriate times, or the container itself might be at fault. To determine whether you are doing it correctly, try your server with a dependable container, such as Chapter 17's version of Patron.

When you close your server, you should see no prompts asking to save unless you get OLECLOSE_PROMPTSAVE in *IOleObject::Close*. In this case and in the case in which you delete the running object from a container, your server should be completely purged from memory. If not, your shutdown conditions are not being met, and you are not closing your main window and exiting *WinMain*. If you are shutting down completely, you should see your object's presentation in the container's document. Double-clicking on that object should again launch your server, but this time you are asked to reload that saved object and edit that data instead.

## (Full Servers) Add OLE 2 Clipboard Formats

If you have read through Chapter 17, you already know that a container can create an object if it is pasted from the clipboard or through a drag-and-drop operation using the *OleCreateFromData* function. (If you didn't know this, now you do.) For this to happen, something has to put the embedded object data on the clipboard in the first place. This is the responsibility of a server application, regardless of whether it's running to service an embedded object or running stand-alone.

Embedded object data is made of two formats: CFSTR_EMBED-SOURCE and CFSTR_OBJECTDESCRIPTOR.[4] From Cosmo, we need to provide these formats in the data object we place on the clipboard whenever we perform a Copy or a Cut. A miniserver might not have any clipboard user interface, which is why such a feature is generally only for full servers.

In Cosmo, this means modifying *CCosmoDoc::TransferObjectCreate*, which is used in calling *OleSetClipboard*, in a drag-and-drop operation and, as we saw in this chapter, in *IOleObject::GetClipboardData*. Creating the two formats we're adding here is accomplished in *CCosmoDoc::RenderMedium*, which uses helper functions in the INOLE.DLL library (for example, *INOLE_CreateStorageOnHGlobal* and *INOLE_AllocObjectDescriptor*) to create the necessary formats. These formats should be placed in the data object after your private data but before any presentations.

## (Optional) MDI Servers, User Interface, and Shutdown

If you want to support multiple objects in one instance of your application through an MDI interface, you have to consider a few additional issues and follow different procedures from those we've covered in this chapter. These are especially important for applications that can run only a single instance.

1. Only full servers can use MDI because miniservers are always single-object servers.

2. Register your class factory with REGCLS_MULTIPLEUSE, and remove any code in *IClassFactory::CreateInstance* that prevents creation of multiple objects.

3. When modifying your user interface on *IOleObject::SetHostNames*, save the container's application and document string with your document's variables (for step 4). Do not remove File New and File Open, but remove File Close and File Save and modify the File Save As and File Exit items as described earlier. File New and File Open simply create new file-based documents as they always have, which does not interfere with the document holding the embedded object.

---

4. When you pass *OleSetClipboard* a data object that contains CF_EMBEDSOURCE, OLE will create the OLE 1 formats "Native" and "OwnerLink" and place those on the clipboard as well. This allows OLE 1 containers to also paste in your object, a fact of which you remain blissfully ignorant.

4. If you have multiple documents open, you need to switch your user interface between the embedded and nonembedded states as you change document windows. This means that switching to an embedded object document installs the embedded object UI, while switching to a normal document reinstates your normal UI. Because you will be switching the UI, you should hold on to the strings from *IOleObject::SetHostNames* because this function will not be called again.

5. Do not shut down when the last embedded object document is closed if the user has at any time in the life of this application used File New or File Open. Invoking either function passes control of the application to the user. Generally, this means you should set your user control flag to TRUE on any File New or File Open operation. When you test for shutdown in a function such as *ObjectDestroyed*, don't close if this flag is TRUE. You should also be sure that you close only when the last object is closed—that is, your object count is truly 0.

6. Hiding an object through *IOleObject::DoVerb(OLEIVERB_ HIDE)* should hide only its document window unless that's the only object. If it is, you should also hide the frame window. If another object is created before the existing one is shown again, you must show the frame window and the new document but not the existing document. In addition, whenever the visible document is closed and there is still a hidden document, hide the frame window again so that the whole server is in the state expected by the container that sent OLEIVERB_ HIDE.

You will find that I did not implement these MDI features in Cosmo, even though Cosmo can compile into an MDI application. My reason is that Microsoft is slowly moving away from encouraging the MDI interface, although support for MDI applications will remain in Windows for a long time to come. Microsoft is doing this because the document-centric user interface possible with in-place activation can eliminate all document management from applications, making it the sole responsibility of the system shell. At that point, individual applications don't need MDI. We'll see why in Chapter 25.

# Summary

A local server for embedded content objects is primarily responsible for defining what an object looks like, how it behaves, and what sort of native data is required to generate and regenerate that content object whenever necessary. The structure of a content object in a local server is considerably simpler than the structure of an in-process handler. Specifically, such an object needs to implement only *IPersistStorage*, *IDataObject*, and *IOleObject*.

*IPersistStorage* gives the object the ability to incrementally access its native data in persistent storage, that is, inside the container's compound document itself. The object does not need to load any data until absolutely necessary, and it can also write incremental changes. When an object wants to save itself, it actually asks the container to do so first by calling *IOleClient-Site::SaveObject*, which gives the container a chance to save the cache and any other information the container maintains for that object. In turn, the container will tell the object to save its own data by calling *IPersistStorage::Save*. It is also through *IPersistStorage* that a server supports conversion as well as emulation—the server's implementation of this interface must be able to read and possibly write foreign formats in order to support the conversion and emulation features.

*IDataObject* is how the cache on the container side of the picture retrieves graphical presentations from the object for whatever display aspect is used in the container. Correspondingly, a content object in a local server must supply at least CF_METAFILEPICT, CF_BITMAP, or CF_DIB through *IDataObject-::GetData*. Any other formats are optional but usually include CFSTR-_EMBEDSOURCE or CFSTR_EMBEDDEDOBJECT.

*IOleObject* is the workhorse of OLE Documents, but of its 21 member functions, only 3 really require nontrivial implementations. The most notable is *IOleObject::DoVerb*, which instructs an object to activate. Activation is, of course, one of the key elements of OLE Documents as a technology. The other most important member function is *IOleObject::Close*, which tells an object to move from the active or running state to the loaded state. Other member functions can be left unimplemented, delegated to helper functions in OLE, or implemented by returning a value that tells OLE to provide a default implementation. So overall, even this large interface doesn't present a major problem to the implementation of a local server for OLE Documents.

Besides the differences between local and in-process servers, there is also a difference between miniservers and full servers. The former are typically written for the express purpose of servicing an embedded object; that is, the user cannot run a miniserver as a stand-alone server but only to create a new object or to manipulate an existing one. As a consequence, miniservers typically do not support linking. Full servers, on the other hand, can run as stand-alone servers, outside OLE Documents altogether, and can easily support linking.

This chapter takes a brief look at the structure of local servers and the considerations that influence uses of miniservers and full servers. The implementation of a local server for embedded content objects is detailed in step-by-step fashion, using the Cosmo sample for demonstration. The treatment of in-process servers for OLE Documents is left to Chapter 19.

## CHAPTER NINETEEN

# In-Process Object Handlers and Servers

*Style and structure are the essence of a book; great ideas are hogwash.*
— Vladimir Nabokov (1899–1977), Russian-American novelist

Follow this silver watch with your eyes. Back and forth it moves. Moving… moving…. You are feeling sleepy. You are feeling hungry. When I count to three, you will forget about any lengthy chapter introduction and awake starving for information about these handler things. One. Two. Two and a half…

## The Structure of In-Process Modules

As we know from earlier chapters, all in-process modules, whether handlers or servers with objects or proxies, are structured identically. As far as OLE Documents are concerned, an in-process content object, be it supplied from the default handler, a custom handler, or a complete in-process server, exposes the interfaces *IOleObject, IDataObject, IViewObject2, IPersistStorage, IOleCache2* (optionally *IOleCacheControl*), and *IRunnableObject*. This is the essence of the content object in the container's process. Any great ideas to the contrary are indeed hogwash.

So in exactly what way are the default handler, a custom handler, and an in-process server different? The difference lies in the completeness of the implementation of their respective objects. It's the same as the difference between the lowest-price economy car and the most expensive European luxury sports car—both have the same basic car structure: a body, a chassis, four wheels, a steering column, an engine and a transmission, and some seats inside. To make the most basic, lowest-priced car on the market, you have to be extraordinarily careful about what you put in the car so that no part is more expensive than necessary. In contrast, to make the most luxurious car, you spare no expense whatsoever. It is a fact that there is always a better car than the cheapest economy model and that there is no better or more complete car than the top-of-the-line luxury automobile.

If you choose to implement only a local server and use the default handler as is, there is nothing for you in this chapter. However, if you want some finer control over the implementation of certain in-process interfaces, or if you want to optimize specific member functions, then you might want to implement a custom handler. If you want to do more, you can go all the way to an in-process server for your object.

A custom handler is like the economy car: small, inexpensive (to load into memory, that is), and sporting minimal features. In other words, the handler implements only as much as it needs to get into the market, simply overriding specific member functions of specific interfaces and delegating all others to the default handler (which might ultimately end up in a local server). An in-process server is like a luxury car: there is no higher power to which to delegate requests on its interfaces; the in-process handler implements all of it.

I can tell by the look on your face that you are starting to feel the same way about these choices as you would if your only choice in automobiles were between a $4,500 car and a $45,000 car. Relax—you have more choices because any good dealer wants to sell you a car for a little more than what you think you can afford. Although the basic, most minimal handler is at one end of the spectrum and the complete in-process server is at the other, many options lie in between. Just as there are many models of cars to choose from between the two extremes, there are many choices for in-process object implementations. Every feature you add to the minimal handler brings you one step closer to luxury, and somewhere in the middle, the picture becomes very fuzzy as to whether your application is truly a handler or an in-process server, as shown in Figure 19-1. At any point between the two extremes, your product is still a car. (Below the low end, your product ceases to be useful as a car; above the high end, you are dabbling in unauthorized experimental sciences.)

There is one more aspect of all this that is comparable to luxury tax. At some point in car prices, luxury tax might kick in: suddenly you're paying an extra 10 percent. This is not a gradual change but a very sudden one. In the context of handlers and in-process servers, a handler is overqualified and must be called an in-process server when the handler no longer depends on a local server.

**Figure 19-1.**
*Between the minimalist handler and the complete in-process server lie many possibilities for handler/servers, all of which still have the same structure.*

That is the difference: a handler is designed to work in conjunction with a local server, whereas an in-process server operates exclusive of a local server. Handlers are designed to be smaller on disk—and therefore faster to load—and to provide only a few basic features. The handler can cut corners all it wants, delegating everything else to the default handler. The default handler then launches the local server as necessary. On the other hand, an in-process server is usually larger and implements the complete object, so it has no need for a local server.

Does that mean that implementing an in-process server is a prohibitive amount of work? Does that mean you have to implement all those interfaces yourself? Actually no, because just as a custom handler delegates much of its work to the default handler, an in-process handler can delegate a fair amount of work, especially work dealing with caching, to OLE's data cache service, which we saw in Chapter 11. Oh, yes, caching is still important because if the user opens a compound document on a machine without the in-process server, cached presentations must still be there for the purpose of the default handler. The in-process server must ensure, however, that it stuffs the cache itself because the cache cannot automatically reach out to a local server to obtain a rendering.

…three! Wait, don't tell me you just slept through all that!

## Why Use a Handler?

The two main reasons for implementing a handler to work with your local server are speed and document portability. First, an object handler can generally satisfy most of the requests a container might make of an object, such as drawing an object on a specific device or making a copy of the object in another *IStorage*. Object handlers might also be capable of reloading a linked file and providing an updated presentation to the container. An object handler generally does not have the capability of activating objects itself, especially where editing and user interface are concerned. A handler might be capable of playing a sound, for example, but it might not be capable of providing the user interface to manipulate the sound. Therefore, the handler has much less code than might be present in a local server because most of the code in such a server usually exists for editing. Imagine how small a word processor would be if all it had to do was read and display text but never edit it. That's the idea of a handler. The speed advantage comes from the fact that the handler is a small DLL optimized to perform specific actions, such as drawing and rendering presentations. Because it's a DLL, it is loaded much faster into a container's process than an EXE could be launched, and there are no cross-process calls to be made for most operations.

Portability is a little less tangible. To explain what I mean by portability, let me use the following scenario: A user on one machine has created an embedded object of class X using the local server for class X, and the user has saved that object in a container's file. In this case, let's say that besides the object's native data, the file also contains a cached screen presentation and a cached presentation for a PostScript printer.

Now let's say this document is sent to other users who do not have the local server for class X on their machines because they have no use for editing the object, only for viewing and for printing it. Because the container's file has cached presentations for this object, these users can open those files and view or print the object. However, this assumes that the cached presentations are compatible with the output devices these users want to send them to. If they have only 16-color displays and the cached presentation uses 256 colors, the screen display might be ugly. If their printer is only dot matrix, the only possible presentation to send to such a printer is the one for the screen because we know that sending PostScript data to a dot-matrix printer gets us nowhere. In either case, the output quality is poor.

There are two solutions to this. First, you could sell these secondary users copies of the local server, but why would they want to pay for extra copies merely to print? You wouldn't want to let them freely copy your server either. So that solution won't work. A different solution is much better. You can provide an object handler that can render a presentation for an object's data reasonably well on any display or printer and allow your customers to freely distribute this handler. Not only does this result in optimal output quality, but it allows the container not to cache any presentations at all if it wants, making the compound document file much smaller. Because the handler is simply a small piece of code that can only display and print objects, people do not need a full application for those purposes. You can allow users to copy this file, and they can put it on a floppy disk along with a document so that the recipient of the document has the tools necessary for optimized output. This is a big advantage for you and your customers — objects always show up nicely regardless of where they're created and where they're displayed. Such is document portability.

The bottom line with both benefits is that object handlers improve object performance and can be confidently licensed for free distribution to optimize output wherever the object happens to travel. Because a handler does not include editing capabilities (which would qualify it for luxury tax), people still have an incentive to purchase your full server.

Just as an aside, you could have a handler display some advertising whenever a user attempted to use a feature that requires the full server. For example, a handler typically passes *IOleObject::DoVerb* to the default handler, which would try to launch the local server. If that fails, the handler can display a message that says, "Because you'd really like to edit this object, why don't you call our toll-free number right now and have your credit card handy so that we can get this product into your hands by tomorrow morning for the incredibly low price of $149.95?"

## Why Use an In-Process Server?

An in-process server provides all the benefits that an in-process handler provides except that loading time is generally a little slower because the DLL is larger. Nonetheless, you still gain all the performance benefits of a handler. You can also license an in-process server DLL for distribution if you see fit, using simple registry entries or other licensing information to limit its functionality and to display advertising as desired.

The primary benefit of an in-process server is that all the speed and portability of a handler and all the editing capabilities of a local server are stored inside a single disk entity — true one-stop shopping for an embedded object. Accordingly, in-process servers are a great choice for OLE Controls as well as for other objects that provide a dialog box–type user interface that then appears to be a native part of the container application. The version of Polyline that we create in this chapter will have just such a user interface.

### Why Not Use an In-Process Handler or Server?

The biggest reason to avoid using an in-process module of any kind can be summed up in one word: interoperability. A handler or server can be loaded only into a container process of the same bitness: 16-16 or 32-32. In addition, there is no interoperability between OLE 2 in-process modules and OLE 1 containers, period. The only solution is to create different versions for each possible case you want to support. This is a pain, but that's the price of evolving operating systems.

The other issues that might put in-process modules out of your reach are various technical implementation issues. DLLs, because they have no message loop themselves, have a problem handling, for example, keyboard accelerators or MDI interfaces that would typically require changes to a message loop. Overall, there are a number of things that you cannot do from a DLL. If you have to do one of them, a DLL is not for you. In implementing the Polyline example for this chapter, I ran into such problems. I originally planned to make the Polyline in-process server look much like Cosmo when it opened an object for editing, including menus and so forth. The lack of accelerators, however, meant menus were only marginally useful. I was forced as a result to come up with a different user interface based on a dialog box. Although this works well, it is different, and that difference might be reason enough for you to avoid an in-process server yourself.

The other technical issue is that as a DLL, an in-process server must be loaded into an existing process to be usable: you can't run a DLL by itself. For this reason, in-process servers generally do not support linked objects, only embeddings. What you can do, however, is create a shell EXE wrapper that loads the DLL and provides a stand-alone user interface in which you can create and save files to make suitable link sources.

# Delegating to the Default Handler and Data Cache

We programmers generally do not like to make extra work for ourselves—if code has already been written somewhere, we use it. I'm not saying we're lazy; we simply like to be as resourceful as possible in finding reusable code. That's why a language such as C++ was invented in the first place and why OLE has the code-reuse mechanisms of containment and aggregation.

In writing handlers and in-process servers, there are a lot of interfaces to implement: *IOleObject*, *IDataObject*, *IPersistStorage*, *IRunnableObject*, *IOleCache2*, and possibly *IOleCacheControl*. Many of these, however, you can obtain through aggregation with the default handler or the data cache. A handler always aggregates on the default handler by calling *OleCreateDefaultHandler* (which takes arguments similar to *CoCreateInstance*), exposing many of the default handler's interfaces directly through aggregation and delegating other selected calls through containment as necessary. An in-process server aggregates on the data cache through *CreateDataCache*, again exposing some of its interfaces directly and delegating to others. The in-process server generally implements *IOleObject* and *IRunnableObject* by itself, exposes the caching interfaces directly, and delegates a good number of calls to the other three interfaces to the cache's implementation, especially for display aspects that the server doesn't want to manage directly.

We've already explored the behavior of the data cache in Chapter 11, where we articulated the specific functionality of its *IDataObject*, *IPersistStorage*, *IViewObject2*, *IOleCache2*, and *IOleCacheControl* interfaces. (Please refer to Tables 11-1 through 11-4 on pages 552 through 556 for a refresher on the data cache.) Remember that the data cache will never attempt to launch a local server itself. That's not part of its design! Nor does an in-process server ever need a local server, of course.

Running the local server is, however, part of the design of the default handler. To understand how we can make use of the handler we need to see how it behaves through all of these interfaces as well as through *IOleObject*. In general, an object handler will directly expose the default handler's *IDataObject*, *IRunnableObject*, *IOleCache2*, and *IOleCacheControl* interfaces (and possibly also *IOleObject* and *IPersistStorage*) through aggregation. Handlers designed for the express purpose of display and printing optimization will generally implement only portions of *IViewObject2* themselves and then delegate the remainder of that interface to the default handler. We'll see an example later in this chapter.

The default handler itself uses the data cache internally. In fact, the default handler generally exposes the cache's *IPersistStorage*, *IViewObject2*, *IOleCache2*, and *IOleCacheControl* interfaces. For *IPersistStorage*, the default handler will delegate the call to a running object and then to the cache; otherwise, it just delegates to the cache. In either case, the behavior of these interfaces through the default handler is identical to the behavior of the cache. That leaves us to examine *IOleObject* and *IDataObject* (which are covered in the next two sections) and *IRunnableObject*. This last interface has a simple implementation: if the object isn't running, calling *IRunnableObject::Run* will launch the server but all other members will fail. (*IsRunning* will return S_FALSE.) If the object is running, *Run* and *IsRunning* will succeed and other calls are forwarded to the object.

## Default Handler *IOleObject* Behavior

Only two member functions in *IOleObject* always attempt to run the local server and delegate the call: *DoVerb* and *Update*. All others either have minimal implementations or simply return an HRESULT, as shown in Table 19-1. Also, the default handler saves the information from *Advise, Unadvise, EnumAdvise, SetClientSite, GetClientSite,* and *SetHostNames* so that if and when it launches a local server, it can forward that information. When the server is running, all of these functions are delegated to the running object.

| Member Function | Action |
| --- | --- |
| *Advise* | Calls *CreateOleAdviseHolder* if an advise holder has not yet been created. In either case, delegates to *IOleAdviseHolder::Advise.* |
| *Close* | Meaningless without a running server, so it returns NOERROR. |
| *DoVerb** | Runs and delegates to the server. |
| *EnumAdvise* | Delegates to *IOleAdviseHolder.* |
| *EnumVerbs* | Delegates to *OleRegEnumVerbs* and returns. |
| *GetClientSite* | Returns the last *IOleClientSite* seen in *SetClientSite* and NOERROR. |
| *GetClipboardData* | Returns OLE_E_NOTRUNNING. |
| *GetExtent* | Attempts to locate the requested aspect in the cache and returns the size of that presentation if available. |
| *GetMiscStatus* | Delegates to *OleRegGetMiscStatus.* |
| *GetMoniker* | Calls *IOleClientSite::GetMoniker* if *SetClientSite* has been called with a valid *IOleClientSite* pointer. Otherwise, returns E_UNSPEC. |
| *GetUserClassID* | Returns the CLSID passed to *OleCreateDefaultHandler*, mapped to a new CLSID if emulation is active, and NOERROR. |
| *GetUserType* | Delegates to *OleRegGetUserType.* |
| *InitFromData* | Returns OLE_E_NOTRUNNING. |
| *IsUpToDate* | Returns OLE_E_NOTRUNNING. |
| *SetClientSite* | Saves the *IOleClientSite* pointer in an internal variable and returns NOERROR. |

**Table 19-1.**                                                                    *(continued)*
*Behavior of the default handler's* IOleObject *interface for a non-running object.*

**Table 19-1.** *continued*

| Member Function | Action |
|---|---|
| *SetColorScheme* | Returns OLE_E_NOTRUNNING. |
| *SetExtent* | Returns OLE_E_NOTRUNNING. |
| *SetHostNames* | Stores the strings in atoms and returns NOERROR. |
| *SetMoniker* | Returns NOERROR. |
| *Unadvise* | Delegates to *IOleAdviseHolder*. |
| *Update*[*] | Runs the server and delegates to it. |

* Launches the local server

## Default Handler *IDataObject* Behavior

The default handler's *IDataObject* delegates, for the most part, to the data cache. The only two functions that will run the object are *GetData* and *Get-DataHere*. These functions also connect the cache to the newly running object. The default handler's behavior is described in Table 19-2. As with *IOleObject*, the default handler will remember calls to *DAdvise, DUnadvise*, and *EnumDAdvise* and forward them when the object is run.

| Member Function | Action |
|---|---|
| *DAdvise* | Calls *CreateDataAdviseHolder* if an advise holder has not yet been created. In either case, delegates to *IDataAdviseHolder::Advise*. |
| *DUnadvise* | Delegates to *IDataAdviseHolder::Unadvise*. |
| *EnumDAdvise* | Delegates to *IDataAdviseHolder::EnumAdvise*. |
| *EnumFormatEtc* | Delegates to *OleRegEnumFormatEtc*. |
| *GetCanonicalFormatEtc* | Returns OLE_E_NOTRUNNING. |
| *GetData*[*] | If the object is not running, runs it and calls the cache's *IOleCacheControl::OnRun* to connect the cache to the object. |
| *GetDataHere*[*] | Same as for *GetData*. |
| *QueryGetData* | Delegates to the cache. |
| *SetData* | Delegates to the cache. |

* Launches the local server

**Table 19-2.**
*Behavior of the default handler's* IDataObject *interface for a non-running object.*

If the object is running, the default handler still maintains the advisory connections. For calls that it normally delegates to the cache, it will still ask the cache first. If the cache fails, the default handler will delegate to the running object. All other calls are delegated to the running object directly.

# Implementing an Object Handler

Let's now look at a basic handler implementation using HCosmo (Cosmo Handler, found in CHAP19\MCOSMO) as an example. This handler is structured the same as any other in-process module, with *DllGetClassObject, DllCan-UnloadNow*, a class factory (these three items are in HCOSMO.CPP), and an object that implements the correct interfaces (FIGURE.CPP). Its REG file contains only two entries; these are meant to modify the entries of Cosmo in Chapter 18. Specifically, HCosmo changes Cosmo's InprocHandler32 key and removes OLEMISC_RECOMPOSEONRESIZE from Cosmo's MiscStatus bits. With a handler we can recompose directly without having to run the local server at all.

HCosmo implements the handler object by using its own version of the class *CFigure*, matching the class name we used in Chapter 18's Cosmo. This object creates an instance of the default handler during initialization and obtains *IOleObject, IViewObject2, IDataObject*, and *IPersistStorage* pointers from it. HCosmo delegates many function calls to these interfaces and directly exposes the default handler's *IOleCache2, IOleCacheControl*, and *IRunnableObject* interfaces (from within *CFigure::QueryInterface*).

HCosmo's purpose in being a handler is to optimize output through *IViewObject2::Draw* in a minimal sort of way—but in a way that demonstrates the idea nonetheless. To that end, we implement most of *IViewObject2* for DVASPECT_CONTENT and DVASPECT_THUMBNAIL, leaving DVASPECT_ICON to the default handler. We implement *IOleObject::GetExtent* (to call *IViewObject2::GetExtent*) and *IOleObject::DoVerb* (to show a message), delegating the remainder of *IOleObject* to the default handler. We fully implement *IPersistStorage* as well so we can make copies of the object. In addition, all of the member functions in this interface call the default handler so it can maintain the cache properly. This implementation of *IPersistStorage* also handles conversion and emulation for Polyline figure data.[1]

---

1. It does not implement OLE 1 conversion and emulation support, however.

The other interesting part of the *CFigure* class in HCosmo is that it implements *IAdviseSink* so that it can receive notifications from Cosmo itself. This interface is not exposed to the container but is connected explicitly to the local object when it becomes a running object. We'll see later why this is important.

## Obtain a Default Handler *IUnknown*

When initializing the handler object, you should create a default handler instance using *OleCreateDefaultHandler*, passing your CLSID and a pointer to your object's controlling *IUnknown* because you must aggregate on the handler in this situation. You get back an *IUnknown* pointer to this default object according to the aggregation rules. You need to pass your own CLSID so that the default handler can implement various functions using your registry entries.

After you have this default handler's *IUnknown*, you should query for *IOleObject*, *IPersistStorage*, and *IViewObject2* (and also perhaps *IDataObject*). You can later delegate to these interfaces, calling the controlling unknown's *Release* after each query according to the aggregation rules we saw in earlier chapters. This is much more efficient than calling *QueryInterface*, delegating the function, and calling *Release* every time you need to delegate. HCosmo does all this in *CFigure::Init* (called from *IClassFactory::CreateInstance*) after allocating its own interface implementations:

```
BOOL CFigure::Init(void)
    {
    LPUNKNOWN       pIUnknown=(LPUNKNOWN)this;
    HRESULT         hr;
    DWORD           dwConn;
    FORMATETC       fe;

    if (NULL!=m_pUnkOuter)
        pIUnknown=m_pUnkOuter;

    [Create interface implementations.]

    m_cRef++;

    hr=OleCreateDefaultHandler(CLSID_CosmoFigure, pIUnknown
        , IID_IUnknown, (PPVOID)&m_pDefIUnknown);

    if (FAILED(hr))
        return FALSE;
```

```
//Now try to get other interfaces to which we delegate.
hr=m_pDefIUnknown->QueryInterface(IID_IOleObject
    , (PPVOID)&m_pDefIOleObject);

if (FAILED(hr))
    return FALSE;

pIUnknown->Release();

hr=m_pDefIUnknown->QueryInterface(IID_IViewObject2
    , (PPVOID)&m_pDefIViewObject2);

if (FAILED(hr))
    return FALSE;

pIUnknown->Release();

hr=m_pDefIUnknown->QueryInterface(IID_IDataObject
    , (PPVOID)&m_pDefIDataObject);

if (FAILED(hr))
    return FALSE;

pIUnknown->Release();

hr=m_pDefIUnknown->QueryInterface(IID_IPersistStorage
    , (PPVOID)&m_pDefIPersistStorage);

if (FAILED(hr))
    return FALSE;

pIUnknown->Release();
m_cRef--;

//Set up an advise on native data so we can keep in sync.
SETDefFormatEtc(fe, m_cf, TYMED_HGLOBAL);
m_pDefIDataObject->DAdvise(&fe, 0, m_pIAdviseSink, &dwConn);

return TRUE;
}
```

When we want to free this default handler object, we need to call the controlling unknown's *AddRef* and then call *Release* through each *m_pDefI\** that we obtained earlier, again according to aggregation rules. This is done in *CFigure::~CFigure*.

Otherwise, everything about this code should look familiar by now, except for the part at the end, which sets up a data change advise connection.

The default handler will connect our *IAdviseSink* here to the local object when the latter becomes a running object. We use this connection to synchronize with the local object as described in "Synchronizing with a Local Server" in Chapter 11 on page 551 and "Synchronized Swimming with Your Local Server" later in this chapter. Note that I don't save the connection key from *DAdvise* because I won't need to call *DUnadvise* until I release *m_pDefIData-Object*, which will terminate the connection for me.

## Expose Default Handler Interfaces in *QueryInterface*

As with any aggregation relationship, we need to expose select interfaces from the inner object through our own *QueryInterface*, along with those interfaces we implement ourselves. To do this, *CFigure::QueryInterface* delegates to the default handler's *IUnknown* for the caching interfaces and *IRunnableObject*, returning other object pointers for the remaining interfaces:

```
STDMETHODIMP CFigure::QueryInterface(REFIID riid, PPVOID ppv)
    {
    *ppv=NULL;

    if (IID_IUnknown==riid)
        *ppv=this;

    if (IID_IPersist==riid || IID_IPersistStorage==riid)
        *ppv=m_pImpIPersistStorage;

    if (IID_IOleObject==riid)
        *ppv=m_pImpIOleObject;

    if (IID_IViewObject==riid || IID_IViewObject2==riid)
        *ppv=m_pImpIViewObject2;

    if (NULL!=*ppv)
        {
        ((LPUNKNOWN)*ppv)->AddRef();
        return NOERROR;
        }

    if (IID_IDataObject==riid || IID_IOleCache==riid
        || IID_IOleCache2==riid || IID_IOleCacheControl==riid
        || IRunnableObject==riid)
        return m_pDefIUnknown->QueryInterface(riid, ppv);

    return ResultFromScode(E_NOINTERFACE);
    }
```

As we discussed earlier about aggregation, you do not want to blindly delegate requests for unrecognized interfaces to the inner object's *QueryInterface* unless you specifically have a reason to do so.

Whatever the case may be, you can see here that the figure object in HCosmo exposes all of those interfaces that a container will expect: some from the default handler, others from the figure object itself. In addition, *CFigure::Release* will destroy the object when the reference count is 0, decrementing the global object count so *DllCanUnloadNow* works properly.

## Implement *IPersistStorage*

We now have an exciting opportunity to start changing specific pieces of each interface to suit our purposes. *IPersistStorage* is once again the best place to start because it's always called first on an embedded object. As stated before, our reason for implementing this interface is to provide container-side storage handling capabilities. The container can use these to make copies of the object without the local server being present. HCosmo includes a complete implementation of this interface, which also delegates to the default handler for cache handling. Delegation occurs in all the functions as it does in *IPersistStorage::InitNew*:

```
STDMETHODIMP CImpIPersistStorage::InitNew(LPSTORAGE pIStorage)
    {
    if (PSSTATE_UNINIT!=m_psState)
        return ResultFromScode(E_UNEXPECTED);

    if (NULL==pIStorage)
        return ResultFromScode(E_POINTER);

    //Good time to initialize our data
    m_pObj->m_pl.wVerMaj=VERSIONMAJOR;
    m_pObj->m_pl.wVerMin=VERSIONMINOR;
    m_pObj->m_pl.cPoints=0;
    m_pObj->m_pl.rgbBackground=GetSysColor(COLOR_WINDOW);
    m_pObj->m_pl.rgbLine=GetSysColor(COLOR_WINDOWTEXT);
    m_pObj->m_pl.iLineStyle=PS_SOLID;

    //Make sure these aren't filled with trash.
    memcpy(&m_pObj->m_plContent,   &m_pObj->m_pl, CBPOLYLINEDATA);
    memcpy(&m_pObj->m_plThumbnail, &m_pObj->m_pl, CBPOLYLINEDATA);

    m_pObj->m_pDefIPersistStorage->InitNew(pIStorage);

    m_psState=PSSTATE_SCRIBBLE;
    return NOERROR;
    }
```

Here we're setting up the initial storage with default data, after which we tell the default handler to initialize itself and the cache by calling the same member function through *CFigure::m_pDefIPersistStorage.* We follow the same procedure with all the other *IPersistStorage* members but completely ignore the return values. We do this because what really matters is whether the operation succeeded on our own data. The default handler's return values describe whether the operation succeeded on the cache. If the cache fails, big deal—it's just a bonus in the first place. The object's own data is more important.

If a handler implements *IViewObject2::Draw* for any given aspect in such a way that it never delegates *Draw* to the default handler, the cache doesn't need to contain a presentation for that aspect. Your handler is entirely responsible for generating presentations for that aspect. If a compound document is taken to another machine, on which not even your handler is present, the object will appear blank in the container. Another good reason to license handlers for free distribution.

A last note about *IPersistStorage* is a call to *OleIsRunning* within *IPersist-Storage::Save*:

```
STDMETHODIMP CImpIPersistStorage::Save(LPSTORAGE pIStorage
    , BOOL fSameAsLoad)
    {
    HRESULT          hr;

    ⋮

    if (OleIsRunning(m_pObj->m_pDefIOleObject))
        {
        hr=m_pObj->m_pDefIPersistStorage->Save(pIStorage
            , fSameAsLoad);

        if (SUCCEEDED(hr))
            m_psState=PSSTATE_ZOMBIE;

        return hr;
        }
    ⋮
    }
```

*OleIsRunning* tells us whether the local object connected to this handler is running. If it is, HCosmo completely delegates to the default handler, which saves the cache and calls the local object's *IPersistStorage::Save*. This ensures that we don't wastefully save our data twice and that what we save in the handler does not conflict with what the local object decides to save. This is especially important if the local object is incrementally accessing the storage and has already written some changes there, changes that a call to *Save* in the handler might obliterate. We want to avoid conflicts with the running server, so *OleIsRunning* is just what we need here.

## Implement *IViewObject2*

Now comes one of the most frequent uses for object handlers: optimizing drawing for particular devices. Your implementation of *IPersistStorage* loads the data to draw, and your *IViewObject2* handles all the drawing and other visual aspects. If you implement *IViewObject2::Draw* for any given aspect, you also need to implement *Freeze, Unfreeze, SetAdvise,* and *GetAdvise* for the same aspect. This makes *IViewObject2* the most complicated interface in your handler, as you can see from the amount of code shown in Listing 19-1.

```
IVIEWOBJ.CPP
[Constructor, destructor, IUnknown members omitted]

STDMETHODIMP CImpIViewObject2::Draw(DWORD dwAspect, LONG lindex
    , void *pvAspect, DVTARGETDEVICE *ptd, HDC hICDev
    , HDC hDC, LPCRECTL pRectBounds, LPCRECTL pRectWBounds
    , BOOL (CALLBACK * pfnContinue) (DWORD), DWORD dwContinue)
    {
    RECT            rc;
    POLYLINEDATA    pl;
    PPOLYLINEDATA   ppl=&m_pObj->m_pl;

    RECTFROMRECTL(rc, *pRectBounds);

    //Delegate iconic and printed representations.
    if (!((DVASPECT_CONTENT | DVASPECT_THUMBNAIL) & dwAspect))
        {
        return m_pObj->m_pDefIViewObject2->Draw(dwAspect
            , lindex, pvAspect, ptd, hICDev, hDC, pRectBounds
            , pRectWBounds, pfnContinue, dwContinue);
        }

    /*
     * If we're asked to draw a frozen aspect, use data from
     * a copy we made in IViewObject2::Freeze. Otherwise, use
     * current data.
     */
```

**Listing 19-1.**

*(continued)*

*Implementation of the* IViewObject2 *interface in HCosmo.*

**Listing 19-1.** *continued*

```
    if (dwAspect & m_pObj->m_dwFrozenAspects)
        {
        //Point to data to actually use.
        if (DVASPECT_CONTENT==dwAspect)
            ppl=&m_pObj->m_plContent;
        else
            ppl=&m_pObj->m_plThumbnail;
        }

    //Make copy so we can modify it.
    memcpy(&pl, ppl, CBPOLYLINEDATA);

    /*
     * If we're going to a printer, check if it's color capable.
     * If not, use black on white for this figure.
     */
    if (NULL!=hICDev)
        {
        if (GetDeviceCaps(hICDev, NUMCOLORS) <= 2)
            {
            pl.rgbBackground=RGB(255, 255, 255);
            pl.rgbLine=RGB(0, 0, 0);
            }
        }

    m_pObj->Draw(hDC, &rc, dwAspect, ptd, hICDev, &pl);
    return NOERROR;
    }


STDMETHODIMP CImpIViewObject2::GetColorSet(DWORD dwDrawAspect
    , LONG lindex, LPVOID pvAspect, DVTARGETDEVICE *ptd
    , HDC hICDev, LPLOGPALETTE *ppColorSet)
    {
    return ResultFromScode(S_FALSE);
    }


STDMETHODIMP CImpIViewObject2::Freeze(DWORD dwAspect, LONG lindex
    , LPVOID pvAspect, LPDWORD pdwFreeze)
    {
    //Delegate any aspect we don't handle.
```

*(continued)*

**Listing 19-1.** *continued*

```
    if (!((DVASPECT_CONTENT | DVASPECT_THUMBNAIL) & dwAspect))
        {
        return m_pObj->m_pDefIViewObject2->Freeze(dwAspect, lindex
            , pvAspect, pdwFreeze);
        }

    if (dwAspect & m_pObj->m_dwFrozenAspects)
        {
        *pdwFreeze=dwAspect + FREEZE_KEY_OFFSET;
        return ResultFromScode(VIEW_S_ALREADY_FROZEN);
        }

    m_pObj->m_dwFrozenAspects |= dwAspect;

    /*
     * For whatever aspects become frozen, make a copy of the
     * data. Later, when drawing, if such a frozen aspect is
     * requested, we'll draw from this data rather than from
     * our current data.
     */
    if (DVASPECT_CONTENT & dwAspect)
        {
        memcpy(&m_pObj->m_plContent, &m_pObj->m_pl
            , CBPOLYLINEDATA);
        }

    if (DVASPECT_THUMBNAIL & dwAspect)
        {
        memcpy(&m_pObj->m_plThumbnail, &m_pObj->m_pl
            , CBPOLYLINEDATA);
        }

    if (NULL!=pdwFreeze)
        *pdwFreeze=dwAspect + FREEZE_KEY_OFFSET;

    return NOERROR;
    }


STDMETHODIMP CImpIViewObject2::Unfreeze(DWORD dwFreeze)
    {
    DWORD        dwAspect=dwFreeze - FREEZE_KEY_OFFSET;
```

*(continued)*

**Listing 19-1.** *continued*

```
        //Delegate any aspect we don't handle.
        if (!((DVASPECT_CONTENT | DVASPECT_THUMBNAIL) & dwAspect))
            return m_pObj->m_pDefIViewObject2->Unfreeze(dwFreeze);

        //Aspect to unfreeze is in key.
        m_pObj->m_dwFrozenAspects &= ~(dwAspect);

        /*
         * Since we always kept our current data up-to-date, we don't
         * have to do anything here such as requesting data again.
         * Because we removed dwAspect from m_dwFrozenAspects, Draw
         * will again use current data.
         */

        return NOERROR;
        }


STDMETHODIMP CImpIViewObject2::SetAdvise(DWORD dwAspects
    , DWORD dwAdvf, LPADVISESINK pIAdviseSink)
    {
    //Pass on through anything we don't support.
    if (!((DVASPECT_CONTENT | DVASPECT_THUMBNAIL) & dwAspects))
        {
        return m_pObj->m_pDefIViewObject2->SetAdvise(dwAspects
            , dwAdvf, pIAdviseSink);
        }

    if (NULL!=m_pObj->m_pIAdvSinkView)
        m_pObj->m_pIAdvSinkView->Release();

    m_pObj->m_dwAdviseAspects=dwAspects;
    m_pObj->m_dwAdviseFlags=dwAdvf;

    m_pObj->m_pIAdvSinkView=pIAdviseSink;

    if (NULL!=m_pObj->m_pIAdvSinkView)
        m_pObj->m_pIAdvSinkView->AddRef();

    return NOERROR;
    }
```

*(continued)*

**Listing 19-1.** *continued*

```
STDMETHODIMP CImpIViewObject2::GetAdvise(LPDWORD pdwAspects
    , LPDWORD pdwAdvf, LPADVISESINK *ppAdvSink)
    {
    if (NULL==m_pObj->m_pIAdvSinkView)
        {
        return m_pObj->m_pDefIViewObject2->GetAdvise(pdwAspects
            , pdwAdvf, ppAdvSink);
        }

    if (NULL==ppAdvSink)
        return ResultFromScode(E_INVALIDARG);
    else
        {
        *ppAdvSink=m_pObj->m_pIAdvSinkView;
        m_pObj->m_pIAdvSinkView->AddRef();
        }

    if (NULL!=pdwAspects)
        *pdwAspects=m_pObj->m_dwAdviseAspects;

    if (NULL!=pdwAdvf)
        *pdwAdvf=m_pObj->m_dwAdviseFlags;

    return NOERROR;
    }


STDMETHODIMP CImpIViewObject2::GetExtent(DWORD dwAspect
    , LONG lindex, DVTARGETDEVICE *ptd, LPSIZEL pszl)
    {
    HDC         hDC;
    int         iXppli, iYppli;
    RECT        rc;

    /*
     * We can answer for CONTENT/THUMBNAIL, but try server for
     * others. In addition, always delegate if server is running
     * since it has a window to define the size.
     */
    if (!(((DVASPECT_CONTENT ! DVASPECT_THUMBNAIL) & dwAspect)
        !! OleIsRunning(m_pObj->m_pDefIOleObject))
        return m_pObj->m_pDefIOleObject->GetExtent(dwAspect, pszl);
```

*(continued)*

**Listing 19-1.** *continued*

```
/*
 * The size is in rc field of POLYLINEDATA structure,
 * which we now have to convert to HIMETRIC.
 */

hDC=GetDC(NULL);
iXppli=GetDeviceCaps(hDC, LOGPIXELSX);
iYppli=GetDeviceCaps(hDC, LOGPIXELSY);

RECTSTORECT(m_pObj->m_pl.rc, rc);
pszl->cx=(long)MulDiv(HIMETRIC_PER_INCH
    , (rc.right-rc.left), iXppli);

pszl->cy=(long)MulDiv(HIMETRIC_PER_INCH
    , (rc.bottom-rc.top), iYppli);

ReleaseDC(NULL, hDC);
return NOERROR;
}
```

Let's look at the simpler member functions before we jump into *Draw*. First, *GetColorSet* is unimportant for this handler (and for Cosmo as well), so we simply return S_FALSE to say we have nothing. Next, *SetAdvise* and *GetAdvise* handle a container's *IAdviseSink* to which we must send *OnViewChange* notifications when any data change occurs in our object that requires us to repaint. We delegate both of these calls to the default handler for DVASPECT_ICON and DVASPECT_DOCPRINT because we rely on the cache to handle those aspects for us in all other parts of the handler. That leaves us in *SetAdvise* to save the advise aspects, the flags, and the *IAdviseSink* pointer, to which we'll later send notifications, as described in "Synchronized Swimming with Your Local Server" later in this chapter. We need to hold all of these arguments so that we can return them through *GetAdvise,* as shown in the listing. Remember to call *AddRef* on the *IAdviseSink* pointer when you save a copy in *SetAdvise* (and release it before overwriting it) as well as to call *AddRef* on the pointer when returning a copy from *GetAdvise.*

NOTE: A container can call *SetAdvise* with a NULL *IAdviseSink* pointer. This means that the container is terminating the connection. Be sure you don't attempt to call *AddRef* on this pointer without checking for NULL.

*Freeze* and *Unfreeze* are a pair of functions that the container uses to control when a presentation is allowed to change. A change in the presentation, however, does not mean that you freeze underlying data; a freeze affects only one aspect. In HCosmo's case, a freeze on DVASPECT_CONTENT cannot freeze the data because DVASPECT_THUMBNAIL is drawn from the same data, and it is not frozen. Therefore, we must make a snapshot of the frozen data so that when we're asked to draw that aspect, we use the frozen copy instead of the current data. This allows the current data to change as needed. This also allows *IPersistStorage::Save* to write the current data without having to consider a frozen view aspect, which should not affect storage in any way.

Your implementation of *Freeze* must somehow remember that the aspect is frozen and make a snapshot of the data. HCosmo's code performs a bitwise OR operation to add a new aspect to the list of currently frozen aspects in *CFigure::m_dwFrozenAspects*. We then take a snapshot of the current data, putting it in either *CFigure*'s *m_plContent* or *m_plThumbnail* structure, depending on the aspect. *Draw* will later use all of this to determine exactly which data to use. In addition, *Freeze* must return some sort of key that can be passed later to *Unfreeze*. A good key is the aspect plus some random number to make the number meaningless to the caller. For example, I use FREEZE_KEY-_OFFSET, which I define in HCOSMO.H as 0x0723.[2] When this key is later passed to *Unfreeze*, we subtract the offset to yield an aspect and remove that aspect from *m_dwFrozenAspects*. When *Draw* is called subsequently, we see that the aspect is not frozen and will therefore draw from the current data. (We can assume *Draw* will be called because a container that thaws a view object will generally want to update immediately.)

Also, when working with *Freeze* you should first check to see whether the requested aspect is already frozen and return VIEW_S_ALREADY_FROZEN if it is. It must still return a key, however, which the caller can later pass to *Unfreeze*.

In the *GetExtent* member of *IViewObject2*, we delegate to the default handler for those aspects we do not support directly. In addition, we always delegate if the local object is running because that local object (we know) has a window to define its size accurately. Otherwise, we calculate the object's extents in HIMETRIC units and return.

---

2. If you can figure out where I got this number, I congratulate you on your resourcefulness. But don't expect any prizes; its meaning is entirely personal.

This brings us to *Draw*, which generally calls either *CFigure::Draw* (FIGURE.CPP) for DVASPECT_CONTENT and DVASPECT_THUMBNAIL or the default handler's *IViewObject2::Draw* for any other aspect. The latter check happens first, so we can ignore those cases.

For content and thumbnail aspects, we now have to see whether they are frozen. If they are, we use the data we copied in *Freeze* instead of the current data. In Listing 19-1, *Draw* sets the pointer *ppl* initially to the current data. Later, if the aspect is frozen, *Draw* points *ppl* instead to the snapshot of that aspect. In this way, *Draw* can copy whatever *ppl* points to into a temporary POLYLINEDATA structure so that we can now do a few device optimizations. HCosmo doesn't do anything fancy with devices, but it does provide an example of how to render differently for a printer and for the screen. If the *hICDev* parameter in *Draw* is non-NULL, that means the data is going to a device other than the screen. If that is true, *Draw* checks for the number of colors the device supports. If it's a black-and-white device with only two colors, we force the background color of the rendering to be white and the line color to be black, which avoids potentially ugly dithering or large black blocks on the printer. (I can't say that this is the best thing to do, but it's just an example.)

*IViewObject2::Draw* then calls *CFigure::Draw* with the temporary POLY-LINEDATA structure, which might be a frozen aspect or data modified for a printer. In any case, *CFigure::Draw* draws the image with a bunch of GDI calls. While we don't need to see all the code here, I do want to point out one bug I encountered when writing it. This code was originally taken from the full Cosmo's WM_PAINT handling of the Polyline window. Because Polyline was always in its own window, its client area always started at (0,0). This meant that I did not have the code in place to handle cases in which the upper left corner was not (0,0). When I first compiled HCosmo with this *IViewObject2* implementation, it continually drew in the upper left corner of the container instead of in the container's site. Not good. I had to be sure that HCosmo's implementation of the drawing code would work for any rectangle.

After implementing *IViewObject2*, you now have a handler that can load, save, and display or print your object's data to a device without requiring a local server. After you have debugged your drawing code, you might want to create a compound document and copy it to another machine. Then you can open it again with and without your handler installed in the registry. This will give you an indication of what will happen in the absence of both a handler and a local server.

### Fiddling Around in *IOleObject*

If your handler is present on a machine without the local server, a container's calls to *IOleObject::DoVerb* will fail. If your handler simply delegates all of *IOleObject* to the default handler, nothing else will happen. What you can do, however, is intercept this call and see whether it fails first. In response to failure, you can display a message telling the user what to do to get real server code:

```
STDMETHODIMP CImpIOleObject::DoVerb(LONG iVerb, LPMSG pMSG
    , LPOLECLIENTSITE pSite, LONG lIndex, HWND hWnd, LPCRECT prc)
    {
    HRESULT       hr;

    hr=m_pObj->m_pDefIOleObject->DoVerb(iVerb, pMSG, pSite, lIndex
        , hWnd, prc);

    if (FAILED(hr))
        {
        MessageBox(hWnd, TEXT("Local server not present.\nIf\
I wanted to make money\nI would put some advertising here.")
            , TEXT("Cosmo Handler"), MB_OK);
        }

    return hr;
    }
```

This is a wonderful way to sneak in some free advertising! But it does require that you override all the rest of the *IOleObject* member functions—which are many—to do nothing more than delegate to the default handler. If you choose to do this, you should also override the *GetExtent* member to call your own *IViewObject2::GetExtent*.

# Synchronized Swimming with Your Local Server

So now everything looks great and is less filling too, until you activate the object and start making changes in the server. Wait a minute! The changes you make in the server are not reflected in the container as they were before. What's going on? Well, you have a handler, and whenever the container calls *OleDraw* or *IViewObject2::Draw*, it's going to the handler. The handler, however, doesn't know about the changes you've been making, so how do you keep the handler and the running server in sync?

When we implemented Cosmo in Chapter 18, we sent *IAdviseSink::On-DataChange* notifications to all advise sinks that came into our local object's *IDataObject* implementation. Where do these notifications go? The simple answer is that they go to any advise sink with a connection to the running object. By default, the only advise sink with a connection to the running server is the cache. Well, the handler can also connect itself to data change notifications. This means that it can request a new copy of the object's native data rather than a new graphical rendering from the server, as the cache does. (Thus, the local object must support the native format through *IDataObject-::GetData.*) As I mentioned in Chapter 11, we don't worry about *IAdviseSink-::OnViewChange* notifications because they matter only in the relationship between the handler and the container.

However you decide to implement the *IAdviseSink* interface to pass to the local object's *IDataObject::DAdvise* function is up to you, but its *Query-Interface* should supply only *IUnknown* and *IAdviseSink* pointers. In HCosmo, I actually make this interface part of *CFigure* itself, but I hobble its *Query-Interface* to return only its own interface pointer.

Now, this *IAdviseSink* pointer is the same one we passed to the default handler's *IDataObject::DAdvise* in *CFigure::Init.* We did not specify ADVF_NO-DATA, however, so our implementation of *OnDataChange* will automatically receive new renderings from a running instance of the object in Cosmo. We use the data passed to update our data in the handler so the new call to *IViewObject2::Draw* will work properly:

```
STDMETHODIMP_(void) CImpIAdviseSink::OnDataChange(LPFORMATETC pFE
    , LPSTGMEDIUM pSTM)
    {
    //Get new data first, and then notify container to repaint.
    if ((pFE->cfFormat==m_pObj->m_cf)
        && (TYMED_HGLOBAL & pSTM->tymed))
        {
        PPOLYLINEDATA       ppl;

        ppl=(PPOLYLINEDATA)GlobalLock(pSTM->hGlobal);
        memcpy(&m_pObj->m_pl, ppl, CBPOLYLINEDATA);
        GlobalUnlock(pSTM->hGlobal);

        /*
         * Now tell container that view changed, but only
         * if view is not frozen.
         */
```

*(continued)*

```
            if (pFE->dwAspect & m_pObj->m_dwAdviseAspects
                && !(pFE->dwAspect & m_pObj->m_dwFrozenAspects))
                {
                //Pass this on to container.
                if (NULL!=m_pObj->m_pIAdvSinkView)
                    {
                    m_pObj->m_pIAdvSinkView->OnViewChange(pFE->dwAspect
                        , pFE->lindex);
                    }
                }
            }
        }

    return;
    }
```

Remember that because all calls to *IAdviseSink* are asynchronous, you cannot call back to the local object from within this function (or you'll see RPC_E_CANTCALLOUT_INASYNCCALL).

Another point to remember is that the container will pass its own *IAdviseSink* pointer to our very own *IViewObject2::SetAdvise*. We kept this pointer for those aspects we care about. We are therefore responsible for calling the site's *IAdviseSink::OnViewChange* when we have new data to draw. Thus, we must make that call within our own *IAdviseSink::OnDataChange*, as shown in the preceding code.

Finally, be sure to use the best storage medium for sending data between a handler and a local server. If the data is small, TYMED_HGLOBAL is fine, but large data should use a shareable medium such as TYMED_ISTORAGE or TYMED_ISTREAM to minimize the amount of data that must be copied.

## Year-End Bonuses

If you followed the HCosmo example in the previous sections, you now have a complete basic handler that is fully functional for rendering your object on a variety of displays, without depending on the cache or a local server. Anything else you do now is an added benefit to your handler—like giving it an extra paycheck at the end of the year.

There are many possibilities for improvement. You might want to implement *IDataObject::GetData* and *GetDataHere*, for example, to further reduce the need to launch a local server. After all, you already know how to draw your data in the handler, as well as how to save it to an *IStorage*, so you'd need to add only a bit of code to draw into a metafile or bitmap and to save into a different *IStorage*. You might think of ways to reduce your dependence on the cache, possibly managing it all yourself. You might consider adding features through a custom interface, given that you have a DLL and can provide a custom interface without the need for marshaling support. These new interfaces can do whatever you like. You can also implement a Play verb in *OleObject::DoVerb* if your object supports that sort of concept, again greatly improving performance and reducing your need for a server.

But eventually you cross the line. Give the handler too much extra pay and it decides to buy a yacht—for which it has to pay luxury tax. At that point, it ceases to rely on a local server for anything by implementing all of *IDataObject* and all of *IOleObject*, thus providing full editing services. The handler is now qualified to be an in-process server. But before it is confirmed as such, there are a number of points to consider.

## Notes on Implementing an In-Process Server

In Chapter 18, we saw how to implement a complete local server, and in the last section we saw how to implement an in-process handler. Now we can bring the two together in a single in-process server, as I have done with the Polyline component (CHAP19\POLYLINE). Because we've seen most of the implementation already, this section will highlight specific issues that I faced when modifying this sample. When implementing an in-process server for content objects yourself, be sure to use OLE's caching services through *CreateDataCache* and not through *OleCreateDefaultHandler*.

Let me point out that modifications made to Polyline for OLE Documents have not affected its usefulness to Component Cosmo (last seen in Chapter 13). In fact, the only change necessary for CoCosmo is to have it use CLSID_Polyline19 instead of CLSID_Polyline10, as it has been doing in *CCosmoDoc::Init*.[3] If I hadn't changed Polyline's CLSID, CoCosmo would require no changes at all! This shows that support for OLE Documents does not interfere with the general operation of the object as a general purpose component. Although a container can now use Polyline's embedded objects, CoCosmo can still use exactly the same in-process server as before. That's the beauty of the *QueryInterface* mechanism and interface separation.

---

3. The CHAP19\COCOSMO directory contains a README.TXT describing the changes necessary to make a new version of CoCosmo.

Much of Polyline's implementation is a cross between the code we've seen in this chapter for HCosmo and the code we saw in the last chapter for Cosmo itself. One of the more interesting points to note is that because Polyline cannot run stand-alone, it really can't create the same user interface as Cosmo does for editing a figure. I originally set out to do just this, but I soon discovered that it is difficult to manage a top-level pop-up window with a menu, a toolbar, and document windows within a DLL. For that reason, Polyline uses a dialog box–style user interface to display its figure from *IOle-Object::DoVerb*, as we'll see in a moment. First let's look briefly at how this version of Polyline differs from the one we saw in Chapter 10:

- The *CPolyline* class now manages additional interface pointers as well as pointers to the default handler *m_pDef<Interface>*, exactly as the *CFigure* class in HCosmo does. It also maintains the window handle of the dialog box we use to implement *IOleObject::DoVerb*. These additional variables are initialized to NULL in the *CPolyline* constructor and set to their real values in *CPolyline::Init* through *QueryInterface* on an *IUnknown* as returned from *CreateDataCache*.

- RESOURCE.H now contains many more identifiers for additions to POLYLINE.RC: an icon (for the default icon), strings we use in the user interface, and a dialog box used for object activation.

- The *SendAdvise* function added to *CPolyline* takes a notification code and calls the appropriate member function in *IOleClientSite*, *IOle-AdviseHolder*, or *IDataAdviseHolder* (as we implemented for Cosmo in Chapter 18). The most frequent notification that required a number of changes in Polyline is *OnDataChange* (generated by calling *CPolyline::SendAdvise* with OBJECTCODE_DATACHANGED). Any member function in *IPolyline10* (IPOLYLIN.CPP) that changes data, such as *LineStyleSet* and *ColorSet*, has been modified to send data changes, as has *CPolyline::DataSet*. In addition, we send this code when the user clicks in the Polyline window, thus adding a point to the figure.

- Member functions of *IPersistStorage* (IPERSTOR.CPP), in addition to their normal operation, now call the default handler's *IPersistStorage* to allow the cache to do what caches do.

942

- Polyline's *IDataObject* now implements *GetDataHere* for CFSTR_EMBEDDEDOBJECT.

- An implementation of *IViewObject2* is added. This is virtually identical to the one for HCosmo shown in Listing 19-1 earlier.

- *CPolyline*'s *QueryInterface* now includes the additional interfaces *IViewObject2*, *IRunnableObject*, and *IOleObject*. It also returns the default handler's *IOleCache2* interface but no others.

- Polyline creates its activation dialog from within *IRunnableObject-::Run* in a way that it can place the figure in a window to determine the object's extents. This dialog is not initially visible.

- Most of the implementation of *IOleObject* is identical to implementations we have already seen. The exception is *DoVerb*, which makes the dialog created in *IRunnableObject::Run* visible or hidden, depending on the verb. *PolyDlgProc* in POLYWIN.CPP handles the messages that come to the dialog from the various controls inside it.

These last two changes are most important because they deal with the special needs of activating an in-process object. Again, Polyline uses a dialog in which to display its figure because of the difficulty of creating a normal application user interface from within a DLL. This is actually a good thing — it doesn't make sense to display a user interface that's part of a stand-alone application for a module that cannot run stand-alone at all.

The better user interface for an in-process server is a dialog box, which makes your object look a lot like a part of the container application. Because you are invoking this dialog box from a DLL that has already been loaded, a window such as this will appear quite quickly after the end user activates the object in the container. This further reinforces the idea that the dialog box is tightly integrated with the container. Dialog boxes also give you quite a bit of support, such as keyboard mnemonics for controls, that you would not otherwise get without your own message loop.

Polyline actually creates its dialog box, shown in Figure 19-2 on the next page, with *CreateDialogParam* inside *IRunnableObject::Run*, which will be called whenever the object enters at least the running state. At this time, Polyline can create a figure window within that dialog and give the figure a definite size so that implementations of *IViewObject2::GetExtent* and *IOleObject::GetExtent* can return something meaningful.

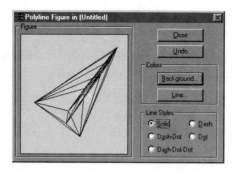

**Figure 19-2.**
*Polyline's dialog box user interface for editing an embedded object.*

*IOleObject::DoVerb* then needs only to make this window visible or invisible, depending on the verb. *DoVerb* will create the dialog by calling *IRunnableObject::Run* if for some reason that dialog is not yet active or has been closed. A call to *IOleObject::Close* will destroy the dialog box itself, although the Polyline object remains loaded.

When we make the dialog visible, we also center it on the screen instead of letting it be placed in relation to the container window. This is because the default placement of a dialog box will typically cover the upper left portion of the container's client area, just where a site is usually found. The dialog box covers the object in the document. When I had Polyline working in this way, I found that the first thing I did after activating the object was move the dialog box out of the way. I expect other users would be frustrated by the same thing. Centering the dialog on the screen will generally keep the site visible, your server more usable, and your customers more satisfied.

Other than that, the dialog box processes commands the same way any other dialog box does, changing Polyline's line style or invoking the Choose Color dialog box to change background and line colors. It also sends the appropriate notifications when closing the dialog box, as we would when closing a document window in a server application. We don't need to call *IOleClientSite::SaveObject* because we aren't unloading the server; we're simply closing the dialog box. We had to do this in a local server because the application would generally shut down when the user interface went away, and that would mean the data was lost as well. But because this is an in-process server, it's going to stay in memory along with the object's most current data, data that will be used in subsequent calls to *IViewObject2::Draw* and the like. When the container wants to actually save the object, it calls *OleSave*, which will call our *IPersistStorage::Save*, in which we'll save our current data. Therefore, no *SaveObject* call is necessary.

# Summary

The structures of an in-process object handler and an in-process server for embedded content objects are essentially identical. The only real difference is the relative completeness of the object implementation within the server. An object handler can implement almost nothing specific to an object, leaving most of the functionality to the default handler. (If there is nothing specific to do for the object, the default handler is sufficient.) An object handler thus depends on a local server to complete the implementation. At the point at which a handler no longer depends on a local server, it is a complete in-process server and contains the full object implementation itself. This dependency distinquishes a handler from a server.

The content object implemented in any sort of in-process module must expose *IOleObject, IDataObject, IPersistStorage, IViewObject2, IOleCache2, IRunnableObject,* and, for handlers, *IOleCacheControl.* Object handlers generally expose these interfaces through aggregation with the default handler, which is accomplished through the API function *OleCreateDefaultHandler.* The handler object implements an interface itself only when it has a reason to override one or more specific member functions in that interface, for example, for display optimization, speed, or document portability. On the other hand, a complete object implemented in an in-process server will provide most of these interfaces itself, relying on OLE's data cache for only a few of them (and for various display aspects). In this case, the object aggregates the data cache through the API function *CreateDataCache.* The behavior of the data cache's various interfaces was described in Chapter 11. This chapter covers all the interfaces exposed by the default handler.

This chapter also examines the implementation of an object handler for Cosmo, showing how to use the default handler as well as how to synchronize data between the object in the handler and the object in the local server when the server is running or active. Synchronization relies on the handler object exposing an *IAdviseSink* through which it receives data change notifications from the object in the local server. The handler object turns these data changes into *IAdviseSink::OnViewChange* notifications to the container. The container will then call the handler object's *IViewObject2::OnDraw.* In this chapter, we illustrate a full implementation of this interface.

We also examine the changes made to the Polyline component (last seen in Chapter 10) to make it an in-process server for content objects. This involves not only adding the necessary interfaces to the Polyline object, but also designing a user interface for the object's active state. In this case, Polyline uses a dialog box–style interface, making it look very much like part of the container itself, a perfect illustration of seamless integration between container and object, one of the goals of OLE Documents.

**C H A P T E R  T W E N T Y**

# Linking Containers

In many books and articles, including this one, you'll find references to other books and articles. These references identify the sources of particular information that either elaborates or reinforces the ideas presented in a book. Usually a book will quote from or present a short summary of the external information and then include a reference to the source.

Writers make references for two reasons. First, lawyers and copyright laws prevent wholesale duplication and plagiarism of another author's work—so you can't simply copy text from someone else's book and take credit for it yourself. The second reason is sheer efficiency. I've read books in which every 30-page chapter has 50 to 70 references to other works—a "Notes" section at the end of a book can take up more than a quarter of the book's total page count. If we didn't have references, writers would have to copy text from other sources into their own text, probably increasing the size of a book by a few orders of magnitude. Without references, books would be too large to hold, too expensive to print, too expensive to buy. Yes, references are a good thing.

Creating a compound document is much like writing a nonfiction book. While writing, authors pull in material from other sources as direct quotations (within the limits of fair use laws), embedding that text in the book itself. This is quite similar to creating an embedded content object in a document, as we've seen in the last three chapters. However, you will have already realized that embedding large amounts of data, especially large graphics and such, will rapidly increase the size of the compound document. There comes a point at which it might be too large to handle, just like an enormously thick book. In addition, maintaining a separate copy of data isn't always what you want in a document—for example, when you want a document that shows current sales data from a central database.

Authors have a similar need. In this book, I refer to the *OLE Programmer's Reference* as the source for the most up-to-date information on specific interfaces and API functions. Instead of quoting from a specific version of the documentation, I can simply refer to whatever the current version is. So in writing, references allow an author not only to keep book size smaller but also to refer to current information, whatever that might be. The external information is specifically named by the stylistic standards of the citation—title, author, periodical, page, publisher, and so on. The citation is thus a *link* to the information.

In OLE Documents, linking is the ability to store in a compound document a mere reference to external information. We call this reference a *linked content object*. In the "Analogy of the Cookie Jar" (Chapters 9 and 17), a linked object is a note or a treasure map inside the cookie jar that tells you where to find the cookies. As we know from Chapter 9, OLE's intelligent treasure map is a moniker. The citation or link from a compound document to the linked object is simply a moniker that names the location of the linked object's persistent data or the process to retrieve it. That moniker, instead of the object's data, is then stored persistently in the compound document, thus reducing the size of the compound document itself. In linking scenarios, the default handler generally provides the appropriate interfaces to what the container sees as the linked object. When asked to activate the linked object, the default handler asks the moniker to bind itself through the same mechanisms we saw in Chapter 9. Once activated, the user can work with the object in its own user interface, the same as for embedded objects.

In this chapter, we'll see the architecture involved in creating and managing linked objects, which includes additional OLE interfaces and more user interface. Much of the user interface concerns the standard Links dialog box (part of the OLE UI Library), which allows a user to update, break, or repair links to external data. This is necessary because currently it is patently difficult to have a compound document automatically track the movements of data to which it maintains links, just as it is difficult to automatically change citations in a book when the title of another book changes. We'll see, however, that there is a promising future for automatic link tracking on the computer.

This chapter looks at linking containers, as we add these capabilities to Patron. Chapter 21 looks at both linking servers and other link sources in the context of Cosmo as well as at support for what is called *linking to embeddings,* which we'll demonstrate with Patron. A link to an embedded object in another compound document is like a reference to one author's quotation that appears in another author's book. This is necessary in OLE Documents when the embedded object is the only source for the data, just as in writing it is necessary when you have no other source information for that particular quotation. You simply make the best reference you can.

# The Basic Architecture of Linking

If anything is central to the idea of linked content objects in OLE Documents, it is a moniker that provides the link between what is stored in a compound document and the real object's data that exists somewhere else. A linked object, for the most part, appears to a container the same as an embedded object—it still maintains a cache, still requires its own storage object, and still makes use of the container's site. Because a linked object is so much like an embedded object, it is best to implement embedding support in a container or server first and then implement linking. Linking is mostly an extension of embedding.

There are two major differences between a linked object and an embedded object. The first is that a linked object has two additional interfaces. One is *IExternalConnection* (for linking to embedding support), and the other is *IOleLink*, through which the container can manipulate the moniker that defines the link. The second difference is that the object's native data does not exist in the compound document itself. Instead, the object's storage contains the serialized moniker that names an external location where that data does exist. This relationship is illustrated in Figure 20-1.

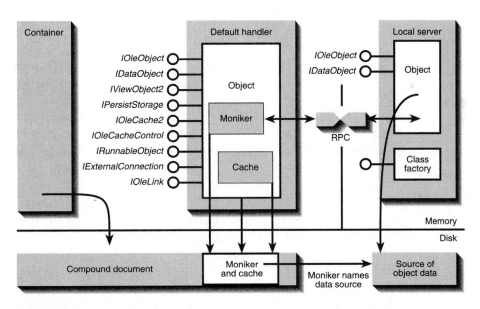

**Figure 20-1.**
*The container, cache, and handler for a linked object still use the object's storage to store the cached presentations and the moniker that names the location of the object's native data.*

The object's storage, like that for an embedded object, still contains all the cached presentations and other object information. Linking simply means that the object's native data is replaced with a serialized moniker.

The following sections look at the three primary parts of OLE Documents that make linking work. In the first we'll see where linked objects come from in the first place. Next we'll see the details of *IOleLink* and the standard Links dialog box in which the user can manipulate that link. Finally we'll look at issues surrounding link tracking.

## Where Do Linked Objects Come From?

The short answer to this question is that given a moniker, a container can create a linked object that manages that moniker. But where does the container get a moniker? In OLE Documents, this can happen in a number of ways:

- A full server that has a known file open copies a moniker to the clipboard. The container retrieves this moniker through a Paste Link operation (using a specific menu command or the Paste Special dialog box).

- The server provides a moniker in a drag-and-drop operation, which the container accepts for dropping when the user holds down the Shift and Ctrl keys (as mentioned in Chapter 13).

- The container creates a moniker itself using a filename obtained from the Create From File form of the Insert Object dialog box.

In all these cases, a container must specifically support linking by enabling the necessary options. With both the clipboard and drag and drop, the moniker appears in a data object as the format CFSTR_LINKSOURCE (the string "Link Source"), which is a stream (TYMED_ISTREAM) containing a moniker serialized with *OleSaveToStream* followed by the source object's CLSID written with *WriteClassStm*. So when a container checks whether a data object has usable formats in any transfer operation, it should also look for this link-source format to know whether a paste link or a drop link is possible in addition to other transfer operations. The standard Paste Special dialog box handles this by enabling the Paste Link button when the necessary data is available. This button uses the OLE API function *OleQueryCreateLinkFrom-Data*, which a container also uses to determine whether a link can happen through drag and drop.

When a container creates a linked object from the contents of a data object, as happens in the first two cases above, it calls the OLE API function *Ole-CreateLinkFromData*. This extracts the moniker from CFSTR_LINKSOURCE and builds a linked object (using the class defined by the trailing CLSID in the link-source data) around it. Of course, the server that supplies the moniker must have the necessary structure itself to support binding to that moniker— for example, implementations of *IPersistFile* and *IOleItemContainer,* as we'll see in Chapter 21. Almost all of the work for a linking server involves the moniker binding requirements.

The third way to create a linked object is through the Insert Object dialog box. In this case, a container must leave out the IOF_DISABLELINK flag when calling *OleUIInsertObject.* When the user selects Create From File in that dialog, he or she will now see a Link check box, as shown in Figure 20-2. When the dialog returns and the user has selected the Link check box, the container passes the filename to *OleCreateLinkToFile,* which creates a File moniker with that string and wraps a linked object around it.

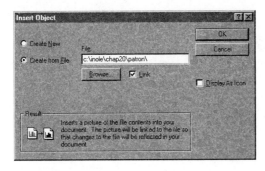

**Figure 20-2.**
*The Link check box as it appears in the Insert Object dialog box.*

Besides using the three methods described here, a container might obtain a moniker through some other means. Whatever the case, it can create a linked object with that moniker by calling *OleCreateLink* directly, which is used internally within the other creation calls mentioned above.

The result of creating any linked object is an instance of a handler in the container's process that manages the moniker and any other linking information. The handler in question is almost always OLE's default link handler, which provides an object with exactly those interfaces shown in Figure 20-1 on page 949. However, a link-source application can specify the use of its own custom link handler by providing the CFSTR_CUSTOMLINKSOURCE format ("Custom Link Source") and an in-process object implementation that supports all the necessary interfaces. Use of a custom link handler is rare, so we will not see any more about it in this book. See the *OLE Programmer's Reference* for more detailed information.

Before we take a look at the linked object in more detail, note that the CFSTR_LINKSOURCE format usually travels with CFSTR_LINKSRC-DESCRIPTOR ("Link Source Descriptor"), which is the same as CFSTR_OBJECTDESCRIPTOR, as we saw in the previous chapters. It is given a different format so that separate information can be supplied for embedded and linked objects in a data transfer operation.

In addition, the user interface guidelines for OLE recommend that a container implement a Show Objects command, which outlines embedded objects with a solid line and linked objects with a dashed line, giving the user an easy way to distinguish the two, as shown in Figure 20-3.

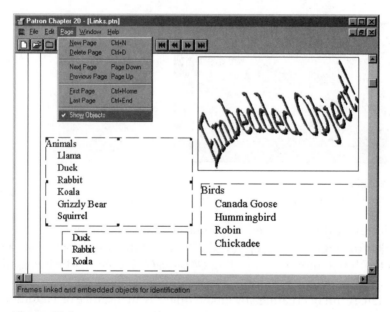

**Figure 20-3.**
*The effect of the Show Objects command for linked and embedded objects.*

Obviously, a container needs a way to determine which type of object it has in each site. Simply said, it queries for *IOleLink*, the presence of which unmistakably marks an object as linked.

## *IOleLink* and the Links Dialog

The *IOleLink* interface is the essence of linked objects. It defines what a linked object can do differently from an embedded object.

```
interface IOleLink : IUnknown
    {
    HRESULT SetUpdateOptions(DWORD dwUpdateOpt);
    HRESULT GetUpdateOptions(DWORD *pdwUpdateOpt);

    HRESULT SetSourceMoniker(IMoniker  *pmk, REFCLSID rclsid);
    HRESULT GetSourceMoniker(IMoniker **ppmk);

    HRESULT SetSourceDisplayName(LPCOLESTR pszStatusText);
    HRESULT GetSourceDisplayName(LPOLESTR *ppszDisplayName);

    HRESULT BindToSource(DWORD bindflags, IBindCtx *pbc);
    HRESULT BindIfRunning(void);

    HRESULT GetBoundSource(IUnknown **ppunk);
    HRESULT UnbindSource(void);
    HRESULT Update(IBindCtx *pbc);
    };
```

With what you know about monikers, you can probably guess what half of these functions do. Both *SetSourceMoniker* and *GetSourceMoniker* allow the container to change the link, which is necessary if the link is broken. *SetSourceDisplayName* and *GetSourceDisplayName* are more or less wrappers for *MkParseDisplayName* and *IMoniker::GetDisplayName. BindToSource* is a wrapper for *IMoniker::BindToObject,* and *BindIfRunning* first checks the running object table and binds only if the moniker is already there. *GetBoundSource* extracts a running object's pointer from the running object table, and *UnbindSource* simply disconnects the linked object from a running object to stop the flow of automatic updates.

*SetUpdateOptions* and *GetUpdateOptions* deal with the flags OLEUPDATE-_ALWAYS and OLEUPDATE_ONCALL, which are mutually exclusive. OLE-UPDATE_ALWAYS means that the link is an *automatic* or *hot link,* a link for which changes in the source are reflected in the linked object's presentation in the container. In other words, the linked object will actively send *IAdviseSink::OnViewChange* notifications to the container when this option is set. OLEUPDATE_ONCALL makes a *manual* or *warm link.* Here the user must manually ask to update the linked object's presentation. This is exactly what *IOleLink::Update* is for.

Almost all code that calls this interface is concentrated in the standard Links dialog, shown in Figure 20-4. Using this dialog, the user can view the links in the compound document, modify the update options, force an update, run the server and have it open the linked data, change the moniker (by entering a new display name in a File Open type of dialog), or even break the link entirely, converting the linked object to a static one.

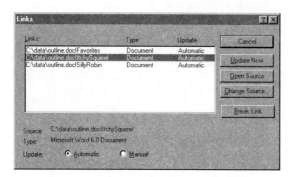

**Figure 20-4.**
*The standard Links dialog box provided by the OLE UI Library.*

The majority of a container's linking support is found in its support for this dialog. What isn't there, besides linked object creation and the Show Objects command, are two other conveniences for the end user. First, when opening a compound document, the container should update, if necessary, all linked objects marked OLEUPDATE_ALWAYS, displaying the Links dialog box if one or more of those links cannot be updated. The second convenience is that the container should ensure that all linked objects are automatically reconnected to their running sources, if possible, by calling *IOleLink::BindIfRunning* when loading those linked objects.

I said "update, if necessary," so how does OLE or a container determine whether a linked object is actually up-to-date with its source? This is probably the hardest problem to solve as far as linking is concerned. Also, with today's operating systems, in which we have at best file time stamps with which to guess when data might have changed, the solution is imperfect. Determining whether a linked object is up-to-date can be as expensive as simply updating it anyway. It is often necessary to run the source server itself and ask it about the update status.

That aside, most of the container's handling of a linked object is otherwise identical to its handling of an embedded object. Linked objects have verbs that are the same as any others, and activating the object results in the same thing. Activation, however, occurs through moniker binding; specifically, the default link handler calls the moniker's *BindToObject* and asks for *IOleObject*. Through this interface, it can then ask the object to execute a verb. If for some reason the link is broken, however, the binding process will fail, and the user has to repair the link.

## Link Tracking: Absolute and Relative Paths

One of the primary functions of the Links dialog box is to allow the user to repair broken links. This happens whenever the source of the linked data, for example a file, moves independently of the compound document. For example, if I create a link to the file C:\DATA\OLE\NEWFOR95.XLS and store it in the file C:\DATA\BOOK\CHAP20.DOC, I will break the link if I move the source file to C:\OLEDATA\NEWFOR95.XLS or otherwise rename it. In other words, the moniker that is serialized in the compound document for this link contains the original path. That path becomes invalid when I move or rename the source document. Attempting to activate the linked object in the compound document will now fail because C:\DATA-\OLE\NEWFOR95.XLS no longer exists.

This does not happen, however, when the relative path between the compound document and the link source remains the same. For example, the relative path between the document C:\DATA\BOOK\CHAP20.DOC and the linked file C:\DATA\OLE\NEWFOR95.XLS is the path ..\OLE\NEWFOR-95.XLS. Thus, we could move the entire C:\DATA directory into C:\OLE-DATA, preserving the entire directory structure, and not break any links. We might also move the entire tree to another drive altogether. In any case, the links stay intact.

OLE accomplishes this by maintaining two monikers for a linked object: one has an absolute pathname for the file portion of the link (if it exists), and another contains a relative pathname in the file portion. This is why *IMoniker* has the member functions *RelativePathTo* and *CommonPrefixWith*, as we saw in Chapter 9. Having both relative and absolute references to a source file maintains connections in many circumstances.

However, a link source might move independently of the compound document, in which case the link is broken. Under current operating systems, the user must manually repair these links through the Links dialog box. That is, the user must search for the new location of the file. When the user finds it, the code in the Links dialog will create a new moniker and store it in the linked object with *IOleLink::SetSourceMoniker*.

Microsoft plans to provide much more automatic link tracking, as shown in Figure 20-5 on the following page. This will relieve the user from such a tedious chore. Link tracking will require that the system know when any file moves, what compound documents have links to that file, and where the monikers for those links are stored in the compound document itself. Windows NT already has a file system that knows when files move, so that problem is solved. The work that remains is to keep an index of which documents contain links to what other sources. Then, when the sources change, the system can automatically create a new moniker and write it over the old one in the compound document. This does require that the (outdated) moniker be accessible in the compound document file itself so that the system doesn't have to launch an application to have it open the file. This is another great reason to use a compound file for an application's storage needs: the system could easily browse through all the elements in a compound file looking for the right moniker stream. It could then update the moniker automatically and efficiently without ever having to load the file itself or run the application that created it.

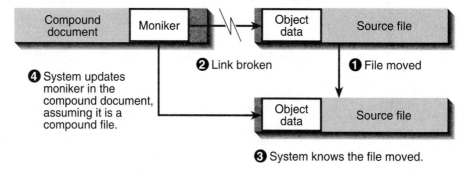

**Figure 20-5.**
*How automatic link tracking would work.*

# Linking Containers Step by Step

Within the framework of the support for embedded objects that we built in Chapter 17, we can use the following steps to add support for linking to the Patron sample (CHAP20\PATRON):

1. Enable links in the Insert Object dialog box.

2. Enable linking from clipboard and drag-and-drop operations.

3. Distinguish between linked and embedded objects with the Show Objects command.

4. Manage a file moniker for the document, call *IOleObject::SetMoniker*, and partially implement *IOleClientSite::GetMoniker*.

5. Invoke the Links dialog, which involves implementing the *IOleUILinkContainer* interface, changing link sources, and breaking links intentionally.

6. Update links on loading a document.

After following these six steps, you will have a container ready to link to any source, including the version of Cosmo we'll see in Chapter 21.[1]

## Enable Links from Insert Object

The first way in which we can obtain linking information is to use the Insert Object dialog box, provided we do not specify IOF_DISABLELINK. Chapter 17's version of Patron included this flag, so we remove it now. If the user selects the Link check box and provides a filename, the *dwFlags* field of the OLEUIINSERTOBJECT structure, on return from *OleUIInsertObject*, will contain the value IOF_CHECKLINK. From this we know to call *OleCreateLinkToFile* as opposed to *OleCreateFromFile* as we did in Chapter 17. In this case, Patron passes the flag TENANTTYPE_LINKEDFILE along with the filename all the way down to *CTenant::Create* (TENANT.CPP), which then calls *OleCreateLinkToFile*:

```
//In CTenant::Create
switch (tType)
    {
    [Other cases]

    case TENANTTYPE_LINKEDFILE:
        hr=OleCreateLinkToFile((LPTSTR)pvType, IID_IUnknown
            , OLERENDER_DRAW, NULL, NULL, m_pIStorage
            , (PPVOID)&pObj);
        break;

    ⋮
    }
```

As with *OleCreateFromFile*, the first argument to *OleCreateLinkToFile* is the filename in question. In both cases, OLE creates a file moniker and attempts to bind it so that the server associated with the file must again implement *IPersistFile* to support this operation. If that fails, both functions will attempt

---

1. These linking features give the container the ability to work with OLE 1 linking servers as well.

to create a package object whose display is always an icon. Whereas *OleCreate-FromFile* makes a package with the contents of the entire file, *OleCreateLink-FromFile* creates a package with just the name of the file inside. This is embedding and linking in its most primeval stages. Keep in mind, however, that *OleCreateLinkFromFile* will create an *embedded* package that stores the linked filename inside it. That is, the container will not see the package itself as a link. But a link of some sort is still involved, in the form of an embedded filename.

You may remember from Chapter 17 that a container does not initially activate an object created with *OleCreateFromFile*. The same applies to objects created with *OleCreateLinkToFile*. Only blank objects created with *OleCreate* should be activated immediately.

## Enable Linking from Clipboard and Drag-and-Drop Operations

In the same way that Patron creates embedded objects from both clipboard and drag-and-drop operations with *OleCreateFromData*, we can now create linked objects by using *OleCreateLinkFromData*. To accomplish this, we need to modify our pasting and our drag-and-drop code to handle CFSTR_LINK-SOURCE and CFSTR_LINKSRCDESCRIPTOR. These formats are registered in the *CPatronDoc* constructor and are saved in the variables *m_cfLinkSource* and *m_cfLinkSrcDescriptor*.

Now we need a function such as *CPatronDoc::FQueryPasteLinkFromData* to check whether we can create a link from a data object:

```
BOOL CPatronDoc::FQueryPasteLinkFromData(LPDATAOBJECT pIDataObject
    , LPFORMATETC pFE, PTENANTTYPE ptType)
    {
    HRESULT         hr;

    if (NULL==pIDataObject)
        return FALSE;

    hr=OleQueryLinkFromData(pIDataObject);

    if (NOERROR!=hr)
        return FALSE;

    if (NULL!=pFE)
        SETDefFormatEtc(*pFE, m_cfLinkSource, TYMED_ISTREAM);

    if (NULL!=(LPVOID)ptType)
        *ptType=TENANTTYPE_LINKEDOBJECTFROMDATA;

    return TRUE;
    }
```

You can see that *OleQueryLinkFromData* returns S_FALSE or NOERROR, so we have to compare the return value to NOERROR to test whether data is available. When the data is available, Patron fills a FORMATETC structure as appropriate for CFSTR_LINKSOURCE and indicates the type of tenant we can create from this data, specifically TENANTTYPE_LINKEDOBJECT-FROMDATA. *CTenant::Create* uses this flag to call *OleCreateLinkFromData*:

```
//In CTenant::Create
switch (tType)
    {
    [Other cases]

    case TENANTTYPE_LINKEDOBJECTFROMDATA:
        hr=OleCreateLinkFromData((LPDATAOBJECT)pvType
            , IID_IUnknown, OLERENDER_DRAW, NULL, NULL
            , m_pIStorage, (PPVOID)&pObj);
        break;

    ⋮

    }
```

With this code in place, we can add the clipboard and drag-and-drop functionality to make use of it. Now, because the link-source format is typically the lowest in the order of available formats, it is unlikely that a Paste command by itself will create a linked object. We need to give the user other ways to perform a paste link. The first way is the Paste Special dialog box, which is the topic of the next section. Then we'll look at modifications to our drag-and-drop code to support linking as well.

## Paste Link and Paste Special Commands

To repeat myself, users must have an explicit command with which to perform a paste link, as opposed to using a higher available clipboard format. There are two standard ways to present this command. The first is to enable linking in the Paste Special dialog box; the other is to create a Paste Link item on the Edit menu to give the user an explicit command. In Patron, we'll implement only the former because the result of both commands is the same.

In Chapter 17, you might have noticed that the Paste Special dialog box has a Paste Link button that has been disabled up to this point. To enable this feature, we need to add linkable entries in the OLEUIPASTESPECIAL data structure. You can see how we do this in the code on the following page.

```
BOOL CPatronDoc::PasteSpecial(HWND hWndFrame)
    {
    OLEUIPASTESPECIAL    ps;
    OLEUIPASTEENTRY      rgPaste[6];
    UINT                 rgcf[1];        //For ps.m_arrLinkTypes

    [Code to initialize other rgPaste[0] through rgPaste[4]]

    SETDefFormatEtc(rgPaste[5].fmtetc, m_cfLinkSource, TYMED_ISTREAM);
    rgPaste[5].lpstrFormatName=PSZ(IDS_PASTELINK);
    rgPaste[5].lpstrResultText=PSZ(IDS_PASTEASLINK);
    rgPaste[5].dwFlags=OLEUIPASTE_LINKTYPE1 | OLEUIPASTE_ENABLEICON;

    //Types we can Paste Link from the clipboard
    rgcf[0]=m_cfLinkSource;
    ps.arrLinkTypes=rgcf;
    ps.cLinkTypes=1;

    ⋮

    uTemp=OleUIPasteSpecial(&ps);

    ⋮
    }
```

The Paste Special dialog box will enable the Paste Link option if it encounters an OLEUIPASTEENTRY structure containing CFSTR_LINK-SOURCE (such as the one shown in the preceding code, in *rgPaste[5]*) and if the data object from the clipboard also contains CFSTR_LINKSOURCE.

The next step might seem a little strange because the Paste Special dialog box is designed to handle more than one type of link information, such as (dare we say it) DDE links. You'll notice that the CFSTR_LINK-SOURCE entry in the preceding code has the flag OLEUIPASTE_LINK-TYPE1. This flag indicates that this entry is attached to the first clipboard format in the OLEUIPASTESPECIAL structure's *arrLinkTypes* field. This field is a pointer to an array of UINTs in which each element is some sort of link format. In our example, the array *rgcf* has only one entry, CFSTR_LINK-SOURCE, so we indicate an array length of 1 in the *cLinkTypes* field. If we wanted to support another link-source format—say, an old DDE link—we would add that clipboard format to *rgcf*, increase *cLinkTypes*, and add another OLEUIPASTEENTRY structure with the flag OLEUIPASTE_LINKTYPE2, and so on. The Paste Special dialog box in the OLE UI Library supports up to eight link formats.

Now, if the user chooses Paste Link in the dialog and clicks OK, the *fLink* field in OLEUIPASTESPECIAL will be TRUE on return from *OleUIPasteSpecial*. In this case, we pass the clipboard's data object to *CPatronDoc::PasteFromData* with TENANTTYPE_LINKEDOBJECTFROMDATA, which calls down to *CTenant::Create*, as shown earlier. We also handle the cases in which the user chose Display As Icon, of course.

### Drag-and-Drop Linking Feedback

The other way a user can create a linked object from existing data is to drop a data object into a compound document directly. As we learned in Chapter 13, OLE Drag and Drop specifies that the Shift+Ctrl key combination changes the semantics of a drag-and-drop operation to DROPEFFECT_LINK. Until now, Patron has supported only DROPEFFECT_COPY and DROPEFFECT-_MOVE. Now we can add the code to check for the Shift+Ctrl combination as well. When a drop occurs and the latest effect is DROPEFFECT_LINK, we can toss the data object given to *IDropTarget::Drop* (DROPTGT.CPP) to *CPatron-Doc::PasteFromData*. It is so useful to have centralized functions like this!

To handle all of this, Patron initializes the flag *m_fLinkAllowed* in *IDrop-Target::DragEnter* by calling *OleQueryCreateLinkFromData*:

```
//Check whether we can link from this data object as well.
ppg->m_fLinkAllowed
    =(NOERROR==OleQueryLinkFromData(pIDataSource));

//We never allow linking by a drag operation in the current document.
ppg->m_fLinkAllowed &= !ppg->m_fDragSource;
```

If this flag is FALSE, we never allow DROPEFFECT_LINK. Otherwise, we check for Shift+Ctrl elsewhere in the *IDropTarget* implementation with code such as the following:

```
*pdwEffect=DROPEFFECT_MOVE;

if (grfKeyState & MK_CONTROL)
    {
    if (ppg->m_fLinkAllowed && (grfKeyState & MK_SHIFT))
        *pdwEffect=DROPEFFECT_LINK;
    else
        *pdwEffect=DROPEFFECT_COPY;
    }
```

With these few minor changes, you now have a complete set of means through which a user can create a linked object in the container. At this point, you should be able to run a suitable server application (one that supports linking), create and save a file, copy some data to the clipboard, and then try to use Paste Link in your container or drag and drop data from that source. What should appear in your container is an object that looks like an embedded object from the same server. Activating it shows the object in the server with the server's normal user interface (no special changes as there were for embedding). As with embedding, changes made to the data in the server should be reflected in your container by virtue of your *IAdviseSink* receiving *OnViewChange* notifications.

## Implement the Show Objects Command

Because embedded and linked objects look so much alike for most things a user might do with them in the container, it helps to have a way to differentiate the two. The Show Objects command allows the user to turn on and off extra graphical effects: solid lines drawn around embedded objects and dashed lines around linked objects, as shown in Figure 20-3 on page 952. The command itself, which is a toggle, should generally appear on an Edit menu but can appear elsewhere. In Patron, it is located on the Page menu, and some interaction between the frame and document objects (*CPatronFrame::UpdateMenus* in PATRON.CPP and *CPatronDoc::ShowOrQueryObjectTypes* in DOCUMENT.CPP) controls whether this menu item is checked. I'll leave it to you to follow the sequence of code for this.

Anyway, when you select this item, the frame routes the command down to *CPage::ShowObjectTypes*, which loops over all tenants in the page and calls *CTenant::ShowObjectType*. This function either includes or removes the flag TENANTSTATE_SHOWTYPE in the tenant's state flags:

```
void CTenant::ShowObjectType(BOOL fShow)
    {
    BOOL        fWasShow;
    DWORD       dwState;
    RECT        rc;
    HDC         hDC;

    fWasShow=(BOOL)(TENANTSTATE_SHOWTYPE & m_dwState);

    dwState=m_dwState & ~TENANTSTATE_SHOWTYPE;
    m_dwState=dwState | ((fShow) ? TENANTSTATE_SHOWTYPE : 0);
```

```
/*
 * If this wasn't previously shown, just add line;
 * otherwise, repaint.
 */
if (!fWasShow && fShow)
    {
    RECTFROMRECTL(rc, m_rcl);
    RectConvertMappings(&rc, NULL, TRUE);
    OffsetRect(&rc, -(int)m_pPG->m_xPos, -(int)m_pPG->m_yPos);

    hDC=GetDC(m_hWnd);
    UIShowObject(&rc, hDC, (TENANTTYPE_LINKEDOBJECT==m_tType));
    ReleaseDC(m_hWnd, hDC);
    }

if (fWasShow && !fShow)
    Repaint();

return;
}
```

If the state changes, the tenant immediately calls the helper function *UIShowObject* (in INOLE.DLL, INOLE\UIEFFECT.CPP), which calls the Windows function *Rectangle* with the appropriate pen type according to the type of object. A tenant with a linked object will have the type TENANTTYPE-_LINKEDOBJECT, as used in the preceding code.

*CTenant::Draw* also calls *UIShowObject* whenever it repaints the object later. This works well for existing tenants, but when we create a new tenant on the page, we have to be sure it knows about the current Show Objects state. So *CPage::TenantCreate* now calls *CTenant::ShowObjectType* as a step in its tenant initialization process. The *m_fShowTypes* flag in *CPages* contains the current state of the menu item.

In addition, tenants will be loaded and unloaded as you move from page to page in a Patron document. Whenever Patron loads a tenant, it also tells it about the current state of Show Objects so it can immediately reflect the proper user interface.

When you test this feature in your own container, be sure to verify that newly created and loaded objects react appropriately to the current state of Show Objects. I forgot to do this when I first wrote Patron, but fortunately it's not one of those bugs that is hard to find and fix.

## Manage a File Moniker, Call *IOleObject::SetMoniker*, and Implement *IOleClientSite::GetMoniker*

Linked objects always appreciate knowing exactly where they live so they can manage their absolute and relative monikers. The container's part in this is to provide a file moniker for its document through *IOleClientSite::GetMoniker* and to give all your linked (and embedded) objects that same moniker through *IOleObject::SetMoniker*. To do this, we first need to create the moniker, which we do in *CPatronDoc::Rename*. This is called whenever a document is assigned a known filename (loading or saving a file). This function then passes that moniker down to all its tenants through *CPages::NotifyTenants-OfRename*, which calls *CPage::NotifyTenantsOfRename*, which calls each tenant's *CTenant::NotifyOfRename*. (Most of this code was already in place in Chapter 17 for calling *IOleObject::SetHostNames*; we're now including a moniker.)

```
//DOCUMENT.CCP
void CPatronDoc::Rename(LPTSTR pszFile)
    {
    LPMONIKER    pmk;

    CDocument::Rename(pszFile);

    //Give a moniker to linked objects in tenants.
    if (NULL!=pszFile)
        {
        CreateFileMoniker(pszFile, &pmk);
        m_pPG->NotifyTenantsOfRename(pszFile, pmk);

        //No need for us to hold on to this.
        pmk->Release();
        }

    return;
    }


//TENANT.CPP
void CTenant::NotifyOfRename(LPTSTR pszFile, LPMONIKER pmk)
    {
    [Unmodified code to call IOleObject::SetHostNames]

    ⋮
```

```
if (NULL!=pmk)
    {
    if (NULL!=m_pmkFile)
        m_pmkFile->Release();

    m_pmkFile=pmk;
    m_pmkFile->AddRef();

    m_pIOleObject->SetMoniker(OLEWHICHMK_CONTAINER, pmk);
    }

return;

}
```

Along with the moniker, we pass the flag OLEWHICHMK_CONTAINER (WHICHMK reads as "which moniker") to *SetMoniker* to identify the moniker as the one naming the container document. Another possibility, which we'll use in Chapter 21, is OLEWHICHMK_OBJFULL. This describes the moniker as naming the object itself within the container document, useful for linking to embeddings.

The container may see some of these same flags in calls to its own *IOle-ClientSite::GetMoniker*, which might also include OLEWHICHMK_OBJREL. This asks for a moniker naming the object relative to the document, which is basically OLEWHICHMK_OBJFULL sans OLEWHICHMK_CONTAINER.

A basic linking container needs to handle only the OLEWHICHMK_CONTAINER case in *IOleClientSite::GetMoniker* for now. This flag supplies the information necessary for the linked object to maintain its relative moniker to the link source:

```
STDMETHODIMP CImpIOleClientSite::GetMoniker(DWORD dwAssign
    , DWORD dwWhich, LPMONIKER *ppmk)
    {
    *ppmk=NULL;

    switch (dwWhich)
        {
        case OLEWHICHMK_CONTAINER:
            //This is just the file we're living in.
            if (NULL!=m_pTen->m_pmkFile)
                *ppmk=m_pTen->m_pmkFile;

            break;
        }
```

*(continued)*

965

```
if (NULL==*ppmk)
    return ResultFromScode(E_FAIL);

(*ppmk)->AddRef();
return NOERROR;
}
```

The other moniker types are important for linking to embedding scenarios that we'll see in Chapter 21. For now, this code allows you to perform an experiment to see how linked objects can track a link source.

First create a file from some server and save it in a subdirectory. Then create a linked object to that source, and save your container document in a subdirectory that shares some elements with the source file but is not in the same directory as the source. If you activate the object now, the server will run appropriately and load the file. No problem.

Now go to another directory or another drive and re-create the same directory structure as the one in which you have the original container and source files. Copy the container document and the link-source files here, and then delete the original files so that any absolute pathnames in any file monikers are now invalid. Now run your container again, reload the file containing the link, and activate the linked object. Guess what? It still worked. The server still found and loaded the source file. The relative file moniker still contained a valid path because you preserved the directory structure.[2]

When a linked object finds an invalid absolute moniker but a valid relative moniker, it updates the absolute moniker to point to the new location, re-creating the absolute path from the relative moniker. To do this, OLE asks the container for the absolute path to its document through *IOleClientSite::GetMoniker(OLEWHICHMK_CONTAINER)*. To prove that this works, save your container document (to save the moniker) and move that file to a random location so that you invalidate the relative moniker but not the updated absolute moniker. Loading the file and activating the linked object will still work, and in the process OLE will update the relative moniker (which precipitates another call to *GetMoniker*).

Keep in mind that whenever moniker changes such as these occur, the container must save the linked object again or the new monikers will not be written to storage. The container is not notified of these changes, so you'll need to call the object's *IPersist::IsDirty* function to see whether the object needs to be saved.

---

2. Under OLE 1, this experiment would have failed because you would have broken the absolute pathname, which is all that OLE 1 linked objects maintained.

## The Links Dialog Box and the *IOleUILinkContainer* Interface

Now we come to what I consider the ugliest part of implementing a container application: the Links dialog box. This dialog is supposed to show *all* links in the current document. In Patron, I found this difficult to implement because I open only one page at a time, and opening all the pages at once only for this dialog would be a major change to the application architecture. So instead, Patron shows only the links in the current page.

As rich as this dialog is, we're fortunate that it's implemented in the OLE UI Library through *OleUIEditLinks*, which takes an OLEUIEDITLINKS structure. The only custom field (not common to all the OLE dialogs) in this structure, *lpOleUILinkContainer*, is a pointer to an interface named *IOleUILink-Container*, which is defined in OLEDLG.H for the express purpose of the Links dialog box:

```
interface IOleUILinkContainer : IUnknown
    {
    DWORD   GetNextLink(DWORD dwLink);
    HRESULT SetLinkUpdateOptions(DWORD dwLink, DWORD dwUpdateOpt);
    HRESULT GetLinkUpdateOptions(DWORD dwLink
        , DWORD *lpdwUpdateOpt);
    HRESULT SetLinkSource(DWORD dwLink, LPOLESTR lpszDisplayName
        , ULONG lenFileName, ULONG *pchEaten, BOOL fValidateSource);
    HRESULT GetLinkSource(DWORD dwLink, LPOLESTR *lplpszDisplayName
        , ULONG *lplenFileName, LPOLESTR *lplpszFullLinkType
        , LPOLESTR *lplpszShortLinkType, BOOL *lpfSourceAvailable
        , BOOL *lpfIsSelected);
    HRESULT OpenLinkSource(DWORD dwLink);
    HRESULT UpdateLink(DWORD dwLink, BOOL fErrorMessage
        , BOOL fErrorAction);
    HRESULT CancelLink(DWORD dwLink);
    };
```

This interface is the way the Links dialog box calls back to the container to tell the container to perform actions in response to the end user's actions in the dialog box itself. You can see direct analogs between controls in the dialog (Figure 20-4 on page 954) and the member functions of this interface. *GetNextLink* is what the dialog uses to enumerate the container's linked objects in order to populate the list box. This is a better mechanism than something like messages or a hook procedure. The table on the following page describes when each function is called.

| Function | When Called |
|----------|-------------|
| *GetNextLink,* *GetUpdateOptions,* *GetLinkSource* | All three of these functions are used to fill the dialog box. The dialog box manages a DWORD for each link in the list box, and *GetNextLink* is the function called repeatedly to obtain those DWORDs. Typically, this will be some pointer. When the dialog box initially fills the list box, it will, after calling *GetNextLink*, call *GetUpdateOptions* and *GetLinkSource* to obtain additional information to create the list box items. |
| *SetLinkUpdateOptions* | Called when the user selects the Automatic or Manual option button. |
| *SetLinkSource* | Called when the user makes changes in the Change Source dialog box. |
| *OpenLinkSource* | Called when the user chooses Open Source. |
| *UpdateLink* | Called when the user chooses Update Now. |
| *CancelLink* | Called when the user chooses Break Link. |

To invoke the Links dialog box, we'll need an implementation of this interface. Patron's implementation comes from *CIOleUILinkContainer*, defined in PAGES.H and implemented in IUILINK.CPP. The header comments in the source file itself describe the arguments and necessary behavior of each member. Let me also point out that *CIUILinkContainer* uses the value *IID-_IOleUILinkContainer* in its *QueryInterface* function. I could leave this out because the OLE UI Library is the only client of this object, and it never calls *QueryInterface*. In addition, OLE doesn't define this IID itself—I've defined it for my own uses in INC\BOOKGUID.H with one of my own values. Basically, no standard IID is assigned to this oddball.

As seems typical with my code, a few weird things deserve explanation. First is the extra protected function I've added to *CIUILinkContainer*. Named *GetObjectInterface*, the function merely queries for an interface pointer from a tenant identified by the DWORD *dwLink*. For Patron, every DWORD identifier in this interface is a pointer to a *CTenant*. Because most of what we use in *IOleUILinkContainer* is a pointer to *IOleLink*, the *GetObjectInterface* function exists to clean up the code everywhere else.

Next, because this is a stand-alone object, it maintains some of its own variables, such as *m_pPage*, a pointer to the current page from which we can obtain tenant pointers; *m_iTenant*, which is used to implement *GetNextLink*; and *m_fDirty*, which is a public variable in *CIOleUILinkContainer* and operates in such a way that after invoking the Links dialog box, the code in *CPatronDoc* can see whether anything happened in the dialog box that would make the document dirty. This is a little inelegant, but it provides an efficient way for the document to know whether any changes occurred.

There's also *m_pDelIUILinks*, which has to do with the other strange part of this code: a call to *CoCreateInstance* with *CLSID_LinksAssistant* found in *CIOleUILinkContainer::Init*. This CLSID refers to a component (named Links Assistant) that I implemented to help me—and ultimately you—implement the *IOleUILinkContainer* interface. The source code for this component is found in CHAP20\LNKASSIS and is compiled as LNKASSIS.DLL. You must be sure to register this component to make Patron work properly. (Patron's REG files include the entries as well, for convenience.)

```
BOOL CIOleUILinkContainer::Init(void)
    {
    HRESULT     hr;

    hr=CoCreateInstance(CLSID_LinksAssistant, NULL
        , CLSCTX_INPROC_SERVER, IID_IOleUILinkContainer
        , (PPVOID)&m_pDelIUILinks);

    return SUCCEEDED(hr);
    }
```

Links Assistant essentially provides default implementations of most of the *IOleUILinkContainer* member functions to which we can delegate, as you'll see in the IUILINK.CPP code. (Yep, we like delegation; it makes life easier.) I created this object because, in my opinion, the developers of the original OLE UI Library were in a hurry and put a greater burden on the container's implementation of *IOleUILinkContainer* than necessary. Links Assistant contains the container-independent parts of this interface that I think could have been built into the dialog in the first place. Take a look at the source code if you're interested in the grungy details. I won't show any of it here.

That leaves us to look at the interesting parts of *IOleUILinkContainer*. First, *GetNextLink* is an iterative function that is called in order to fill the list in the dialog box. The first call passes a 0 in *dwLink*, meaning "Return the first linked object." What it returns is again a DWORD that all the other functions are passed to identify which object is being manipulated. *GetNextLink* returns a 0 when there are no more links. Patron is concerned only with keeping an index of the current tenant to return (*m_iTenant*), and when this function is called, it gets the tenant pointer and checks to see whether it's an embedded or a linked object by means of the function *CTenant::TypeGet*. (Note that Links Assistant can't implement this function, so it simply returns an error.)

```
STDMETHODIMP_(DWORD) CIOleUILinkContainer::GetNextLink(DWORD dwLink)
    {
    PCTenant        pTenant;

    //If we're told to start sequence, set index to 0.
    if (0L==dwLink)
        m_iTenant=0;

    /*
     * On each subsequent call, find next linked object in
     * this document and return it. Be sure index is
     * incremented for next time this function is called.
     */
    for ( ; m_iTenant < m_pPage->m_cTenants; m_iTenant++)
        {
        if (m_pPage->TenantGet(m_iTenant, &pTenant, FALSE))
            {
            if (TENANTTYPE_LINKEDOBJECT==pTenant->TypeGet())
                {
                m_iTenant++;
                return (DWORD)pTenant;
                }
            }
        }

    //If we hit end of list, this tells dialog to stop.
    return 0L;
    }
```

*SetUpdateOptions* and *GetUpdateOptions* do little more than call the same named functions in *IOleLink*. *SetUpdateOptions,* however, sets the dirty flag if the change succeeds.

*SetLinkSource* is called when the user changes the source of the link. The implementation of this function is somewhat complex, so most of the meat is down in the Links Assistant object. If the change was successful, we set *m_fDirty* so that the rest of the application knows. We also must remember whether this change worked for the implementation of *GetLinkSource*. We do this here with a public flag in *CTenant* named *m_fLinkAvail*, which was added to *CTenant* specifically for this interface. It's part of *CTenant* because we need to maintain one value for each object, not for the *IOleUILinkContainer* interface as a whole. With this flag, we start by assuming that the new source is not valid, but if Links Assistant succeeds in changing the source, we can mark it as available. The reason we need to remember is exposed in *GetLinkSource*, which is called whenever the Links dialog box needs to update the list box entry for an object. *GetLinkSource* returns a flag indicating whether the link source is available, which is simply *CTenant::m_fLinkAvail*, and another flag indicating whether the object is currently selected in the container, which the application determines by calling another new function, *CTenant::FIsSelected*. The rest of the information needed from *GetLinkSource* is handled by the code in Links Assistant. If you say this object is unavailable, the rightmost column of the list box entry will read *Unavail*. If you say the object is selected, that entry, as well as any others that you say are selected, will be selected when the dialog box is initially displayed. The selected flag is meaningless anytime thereafter, however.

*OpenLinkSource* is another way of saying "activate with OLEIVERB-_OPEN." So that's what we do. *UpdateLink* is not quite as simple: Links Assistant calls *IOleObject::IsUpToDate*, and if it returns S_FALSE, Links Assistant calls *IOleObject::Update*, which might launch servers to obtain the update. Because the presentation might have changed, we should repaint the container site as well as update the tenant's *m_fLinkAvail* according to the success of the update. If the argument *fErrorMessage* is set, we're also responsible for displaying some meaningful error message on failure.

The last function in this interface, *CancelLink*, is meant to convert a linked object to a static object—that is, it causes the object to lose the ability to be activated and disconnects the object entirely from its link source. Links Assistant disconnects the object by calling *IOleLink::SetSourceMoniker(NULL)*, which forces the linked object to forget about its source completely, although the object still maintains any cached presentations. We want to keep those presentations, however, because a static object still needs something to show for itself.

Removing an object's ability to be activated is handled by yet another new function in Patron, *CTenant::ConvertToStatic*. I use this function to mark the object as static, which effectively prevents the tenant from activating it. This makes the object appear to be static, although it's still a linked object as far as OLE is concerned:

```
BOOL CTenant::ConvertToStatic(void)
    {
    m_tType=TENANTTYPE_STATIC;
    return TRUE;
    }
```

The catch in all of this is that we must remember that this object is static when we reload it. Patron handles this situation with a flag in its storage and code in *CTenant::ObjectInitialize* that calls *IOleLink::GetSourceMoniker*. Because we set the moniker to NULL, this call will return NULL as well, and we use that condition to reinitialize the object as static.

So that does it for implementing the *IOleUILinkContainer* interface. Now let's see where we use it.

## Invoke the Links Dialog Box

After all the work to implement *IOleUILinkContainer*, invoking the dialog box is rather painless. This should be done in response to a Links command that should appear on your Edit menu, enabled only when links are available. Patron also includes this item on the right-mouse-button pop-up menu for an individual object (which is not part of the OLE user interface guidelines, simply my own design). In both cases, the function *CPage::FQueryLinksInPage* ultimately determines whether links are available by looking for tenants of type TENANTTYPE_LINKEDOBJECT. If at least one object is available, the Links item is enabled. Selecting Links invokes *CPatronDoc::EditLinks*.

*CPatronDoc::EditLinks* first obtains the *CIOleUILinkContainer* through *CPages::GetUILinkContainer*, which initializes that object with the current page's *CPage* pointer. On return, that object pointer is stored in an OLEUI-EDITLINKS structure that is passed to *OleUIEditLinks*. On return from this function, the *m_fDirty* flag in *CIOleUILinkContainer* indicates to the document whether anything changed.

## Update Links on Loading a Document

Two final requirements make a linking container complete. First, you should call *IOleLink::BindIfRunning* whenever you load a linked object. This is done automatically, for some odd reason, if you pass your *IOleClientSite* pointer to *OleLoad*. Patron does not do this, so we make the call explicitly in *CTenant::ObjectInitialize*:

```
BOOL CTenant::ObjectInitialize(LPUNKNOWN pObj, LPFORMATETC pFE
    , DWORD dwData)
    {
    HRESULT         hr;
    LPOLELINK       pIOleLink=NULL;

    ⋮

    if (SUCCEEDED(pObj->QueryInterface(IID_IOleLink
        , (PPVOID)&pIOleLink)))
        {
        LPMONIKER   pmk;

        hr=pIOleLink->GetSourceMoniker(&pmk);
```

```
        if (FAILED(hr) || NULL==pmk)
            m_tType=TENANTTYPE_STATIC;
        else
            {
            m_tType=TENANTTYPE_LINKEDOBJECT;
            pmk->Release();

            //Connect to the object if source is running.
            pIOleLink->BindIfRunning();
            }

        pIOleLink->Release();
        }

    ⋮
    }
```

The second requirement is to update any automatic links when you load them from storage. This ensures that objects appear as current as possible in the document. So when opening a document (or in Patron's case, a page), we must check to see whether the document contains any automatic links. If it does have any, we call *OleUIUpdateLinks*. This function displays a dialog box with a progress indicator, as shown in Figure 20-6.

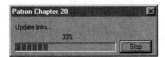

**Figure 20-6.**
*The Update Links dialog box displayed through* OleUIUpdateLinks.

*OleUIUpdateLinks* is a bit different from other OLE UI functions in that it doesn't take a structure pointer. The reason for this is basically that the function does not provide for customization. What *OleUIUpdateLinks* does take, however, is a pointer to your *IOleUILinkContainer* interface, an HWND of the owner window, a caption for the title bar, and a count of how many links it has to update. As shown beginning on the following page, Patron invokes this dialog inside *CPage::Open* after it has loaded all tenants.

```
        ⋮

UINT                    cLinks;
LPOLELINK               pIOleLink;
LPUNKNOWN               pIUnknown;
UINT                    uRet;
OLEUIEDITLINKS          el;
PCIOleUILinkContainer   pIUILinks;
HWND                    hWndDoc;

        ⋮

//First, count the number of automatic links.
cLinks=0;

for (i=0; i < m_cTenants; i++)
    {
    if (TenantGet(i, &pTenant, FALSE))
        {
        DWORD       dw;

        pTenant->ObjectGet(&pIUnknown);
        hr=pIUnknown->QueryInterface(IID_IOleLink
            , (PPVOID)&pIOleLink);
        pIUnknown->Release();

        if (FAILED(hr))
            continue;

        pIOleLink->GetUpdateOptions(&dw);
        pIOleLink->Release();

        if (OLEUPDATE_ALWAYS==dw)
            cLinks++;
        }
    }

//If we have any automatic links, invoke the update dialog.
if (0==cLinks)
    return TRUE;

//Create an IOleUILinkContainer instantiation.
if (!m_pPG->GetUILinkContainer(&pIUILinks))
    return TRUE;     //Guess we can't update; oh well.
```

```
hWndDoc=GetParent(m_hWnd);
LoadString(m_pPG->m_hInst, IDS_CAPTION, szCap, sizeof(szCap));

if (!OleUIUpdateLinks(pIUILinks, hWndDoc, szCap, cLinks))
    {
    /*
     * If updating failed, ask to show Links dialog. NOTE:
     * OleUIPromptUser has variable wsprintf argument list
     * after hWnd parameter!  Use appropriate typecasting!
     */
    uRet=OleUIPromptUser(IDD_CANNOTUPDATELINK, hWndDoc, szCap);

    if (IDC_PU_LINKS==uRet)
        {
        //Display Links dialog.
        memset(&el, 0, sizeof(el));
        el.cbStruct=sizeof(el);
        el.hWndOwner=hWndDoc;
        el.lpOleUILinkContainer=(LPOLEUILINKCONTAINER)pIUILinks;
        OleUIEditLinks((LPOLEUIEDITLINKS)&el);
        }
    }

m_pPG->m_fDirty=pIUILinks->m_fDirty;
pIUILinks->Release();

⋮
```

Our first task is to count how many automatic links are on this page (which is the document for Patron's purposes) by checking the types of all tenants on the page and incrementing the variable *cLinks* for each. If *cLinks* is 0 at the end, there are no links and there's nothing we need to do. Otherwise, we instantiate the *IOleUILinkContainer* interface, using exactly the same implementation we created for the Links dialog box. This was completely intentional, but note that *OleUIUpdateLinks* will use only the *GetNextLink* and *UpdateLink* members of that interface. We also grab the window handle of the document and a caption string and finally call *OleUIUpdateLinks.*

The progress dialog box will update its indicator bar and the displayed percentage every time it finishes updating a link. If it fails on any one of them, it will finish updating the remaining links, but it will then return FALSE instead of TRUE. A FALSE return value means the application should display the message shown in Figure 20-7 on the following page. This gives the user the option of going directly to the Links dialog box to correct any problems. The OLE UI Library even has a function named *OleUIPromptUser* to create this prompt (because *MessageBox* can't provide a Links button), which returns IDC_PU_LINKS if the user chooses the Links button. In response, the application invokes the Links dialog box exactly as before, passing our *IOleUILinkContainer* object.

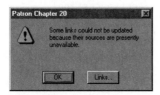

**Figure 20-7.**
*The message displayed from* OleUIPromptUser (IDD_CANNOTUPDATELINK).

One last item, and then we're finished. Be sure to update your document's dirty flag after calling *OleUIUpdateLinks* because things might have changed that do require a save.

So now you can link to the world, no matter how complicated the moniker. If links are broken, you can repair them with the Links dialog box. Your container stays current with all automatic links by updating them as you load those objects. You want to be sure now that this last feature works and that it can properly invoke the Links dialog box when necessary.

## Summary

The linked object feature of OLE Documents is built on top of the basic architecture for embedded objects, as described in earlier chapters. Whereas an embedded object stores all of its native data in the container's compound file directly, a linked object stores its native data somewhere else and provides the container with a moniker that refers to that other storage location. This moniker is then serialized in the compound document, providing the "link" between the document and the object's data. Cached presentations are also saved in the compound document exactly as they are for embeddings, in case the link becomes invalid.

Invalidating a link is not difficult in current file systems, in which files can move independently of one another without the operating system necessarily knowing of the event. Microsoft plans to provide the ability to track links between compound documents and the sources of object data so that when the source moves, OLE can automatically update the moniker inside a compound document in order to preserve the link.

This chapter deals primarily with the view of a linked object as seen by a container; in this situation, the object contributes the interfaces *IExternal-Connection* and *IOleLink* alongside all the other embedded object interfaces. It is the presence of *IOleLink* that differentiates a linked object from an embedded one. Through this interface, a container can choose between automatic (hot) and manual (warm) links for a linked object, as well as update the object, change the source of the object's data (used to repair broken links), and intentionally break the link itself. All these functions are exposed to the user through the standard Links dialog box, provided in the OLE UI Library. Most of the work in implementing a linking container, as is illustrated in this chapter using Patron as an example, comes from the necessary support for this dialog box.

Of course, a container must have a way to create linked objects in the first place. It can do so any time that it has a moniker referring to a source of data. The container might have a moniker itself, or it can obtain one from the clipboard or by means of a drag-and-drop operation. (The moniker is serialized in a stream and identified with the CFSTR_LINKSOURCE format.) OLE provides API functions to create a linked object from a moniker or from the data available in a data object. Containers use both the Insert Object and Paste Special dialog boxes in order to give the user the means to create such linked objects.

Containers also provide a Show Objects command that outlines linked objects with a dashed line and embedded objects with a solid line, giving the user a way to see the types of objects in a compound document. In addition, containers also automatically update any linked objects in a document when that document is loaded to ensure that presentations are up to date. Once again, all of these features are demonstrated in the Patron example accompanying this chapter.

## CHAPTER TWENTY-ONE

# Link Sources and Linking to Embeddings

*The history of The Valley has never lacked the dramatic element, and in this, the latest episode, it has held to its traditions. For consider the circumstances. This was to be our final season in The Valley. Six full seasons we had excavated there, and season after season had drawn a blank; we had worked for months at a stretch and found nothing, and only an excavator knows how desperately depressing that can be; we had almost made up our minds that we were beaten, and were preparing to leave The Valley and try our luck elsewhere; and then—hardly had we set a hoe to ground in our last despairing effort than we made a discovery that far exceeded our wildest dreams. Surely, never before in the whole history of excavation has a full digging season been compressed within the space of five days.*

—Howard Carter, from *The Discovery of the Tomb of Tutankhamen*

In the early years of the twentieth century, Egyptologists were busy scouring the Valley of the Kings in the Egyptian desert, hoping they would find the undiscovered tombs of the pharaohs before tomb robbers plundered their rich history. The Valley had already, centuries earlier, surrendered the tombs of kings such as Ramses VI and Seti II. In the area of the tombs, Howard Carter and other archaeologists found clues indicating that there might be other, still-hidden, tombs. One name that appeared in a few circumstances was that of the boy-king Tutankhamen. By the fall of 1917, Carter and his benefactor, Lord Carnavon, had decided to begin a systematic search of the rubble in the area in which they hoped to find Tutankhamen's tomb. In Carter's words, "The difficulty was to know where to begin, for mountains of rubbish thrown out by previous excavators encumbered the ground in all directions, and no sort of record had ever been kept as to which areas had been properly excavated and which had not."

Six long seasons they dug, finding nothing. All their hopes were spent. All their work had gone for naught. All the time spent piecing together clues to figure out even where to dig had gone unrewarded. But on the morning of November 4, 1922, Carter arrived at the site to find a strange silence, a void of activity that suggested something unusual, perhaps something extraordinary. A mere 13 feet downhill from the well-known entrance to the tomb of Ramses VI, Carter's workers had uncovered a step cut in the rock. Subsequent clearing unearthed 16 steps leading down to a sealed doorway, the seal unbroken since it was applied millennia earlier. But was it the tomb Carter was searching for? Or was it merely the tomb of a noble? Further painstaking work revealed that Carter had indeed discovered the tomb of King Tutankhamen. Carter's discovery enabled the modern world to behold all the wonderful treasures that had lain locked beneath the desert for over 3000 years.

In searching for the tomb, Carter had a most difficult time. While he was drawing his sketchy treasure map, he really didn't know where the treasure was. Even after he completed his map, he put in many passionate years of toil trying to follow it, searching and hoping for a tomb beneath the sand. Few of us would have such patience and perseverance—certainly not modern computer users. They simply do not want the hassle of tracking down the sources of linked objects.

Fortunately, computers are much more precise than Carter's rudimentary tools when it comes to creating and following treasure maps to the source of a link. In the best traditions of object-oriented programming, if you want a map to some treasure, you simply ask the treasure to make one for you. That's precisely what happens with a link source. The source is responsible for providing monikers that other components can use to reconnect (bind) to that source—the moniker is a treasure map that knows how to follow itself and bring back the treasure. We saw in Chapter 20 how a container makes use of a moniker in a linked content object. Now we can investigate the means through which a source provides a moniker to name its own treasures. In Chapter 9, we explored the moniker binding process in detail; here we'll see the additional support a source must provide to make linking work in the context of OLE Documents.

First we'll update the Cosmo sample from Chapter 18 so that it provides a simple file moniker as its link source. Then we'll enhance Patron so that it supplies a File!Item!Item moniker to support linking to embeddings. In this way, Patron itself becomes a server to the embedded objects contained within its documents, and the moniker names specific objects on a specific page in a specific document. Patron's document and page objects—up to now, nothing more than internal C++ objects—become OLE objects with the necessary interfaces to support moniker binding. This is nontrivial work, but it's certainly not as difficult as digging through rubble for six years. And to end users, the treasures held in embedded objects are often more valuable than the treasures of an Egyptian pharaoh.

# Server-Side Linked Objects

In Chapter 20, we saw that a container creates a linked content object using a moniker that it obtains either from the clipboard, from a drag-and-drop operation, from a filename, or through some other means not specified as part of OLE Documents itself. As far as the client is concerned, the linked object that wraps this moniker is almost the same as an embedded object, except that it also has the interfaces *IOleLink* and *IExternalConnection*. We also saw that activating a linked object basically means binding the moniker and asking for *IOleObject* in return.

This gives us the requirements for any local server that wants to support linking to its own objects:

■ The server must support binding for whatever moniker it provides through data transfer operations, following the details we discussed in Chapter 9. This usually involves at least file moniker support through *IPersistFile*.

■ The object named by the moniker must implement *IOleObject* and *IDataObject* to support OLE Documents. This differentiates a linking server for OLE Documents from a link source of any other kind. In this case, *IPersistStorage* is not necessary because the object saves its native data to its own storage by using whatever means it wants and does not need access to the object storage in the compound document.

The simplest linking scenario involves a single file moniker to describe the link. The version of Cosmo we'll create in this chapter supports this type of linking. A file moniker, if you remember, requires some implementation of *IPersistFile*, which must be implemented on the object named by that moniker. This file object must also implement *IOleObject* and *IDataObject*, as shown in Figure 21-1 on the following page. In Cosmo, the Figure object we implemented in Chapter 18 is already attached to the document and already supports most of these interfaces by virtue of its embedding support. Here we'll need to add *IPersistFile* and complete the implementation of *IOleObject::SetMoniker* and *IOleObject::GetMoniker*. In addition, we need to register the Figure object in the running object table, which is required for any link source.

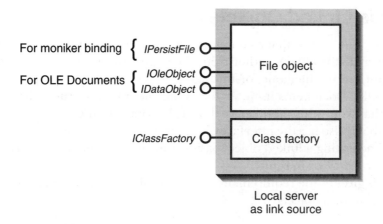

For moniker binding { *IPersistFile*

For OLE Documents { *IOleObject*
                    *IDataObject*

File object

*IClassFactory*

Class factory

Local server
as link source

**Figure 21-1.**
*A linked object in a local server named with a file moniker must implement*
*both* IOleObject *and* IDataObject *to support OLE Documents and*
IPersistFile *to support moniker binding.*

Some servers might want to support linking to a specific portion of a
file—for example, a paragraph in a document, a range of cells in a spreadsheet, or a small part of a larger drawing. In these cases, the server provides a
File!Item moniker to name what we call *pseudo-objects* in that larger data set.
When a container wants to talk to a specific pseudo-object, it will bind that
File!Item moniker. The server's implementation of *IOleItemContainer::GetObject*
will then create a structure for the pseudo-object and provide the container
with *IOleObject* and *IDataObject* interfaces for that structure. Pseudo-objects
don't exist as individual entities before that time, and they are not persistent
individually because they are saved with the larger file. In addition, the data
that makes up multiple pseudo-objects might overlap. For example, the cell
ranges R1C5:R10C8 and R3C2:R12C10 overlap, as shown in Figure 21-2. This
same spreadsheet is the source of a vast number of potential pseudo-objects.
Wildcard monikers exist so that a server like this need not register every
pseudo-object as individually running.

A server that supports linking to items in this way must implement
*IPersistFile* and *IOleItemContainer* on the document, or file object, named by
the File portion of the composite moniker. Whatever object is returned from
*IOleItemContainer::GetObject* is the pseudo-object. This defines a server structure, as shown in Figure 21-3.

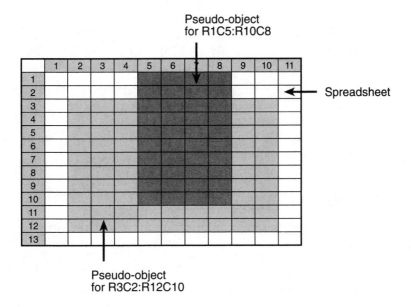

**Figure 21-2.**
*Pseudo-objects are named portions of a file to which a container can link with a File!Item moniker. In the source file, pseudo-objects can overlap.*

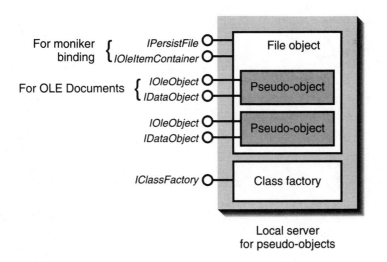

**Figure 21-3.**
*The structure of a server that supports linking to pseudo-objects.*

The implementation of the pseudo-object structure is the same as that for a file object in a simple server such as Cosmo. The server itself must register a wildcard moniker for the file and for all items within it after it has opened the file. It must also be sure to implement *IOleItemContainer::ParseDisplayName* to support the Change Source feature of the container's Links dialog box.

We won't see a sample of a pseudo-object server in this chapter because we can go one step further, using Patron to demonstrate linking to embeddings and a File!Item!Item linking case.

# Linking to Embeddings

Consider a typical word processor with an open report containing an embedded table with the latest sales figures, as shown in Figure 21-4.

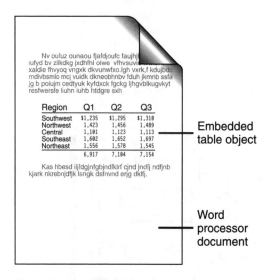

**Figure 21-4.**
*A typical word processor document that contains an embedded table object.*

Because the table is an embedded object, its data exists only in that embedded object. If the table were linked, its data would exist in another source. In this case, however, the table is the sole source for that data. Now suppose we want to add a chart to the report to show the numbers in that table graphically. We could create a new chart object and manually reenter all the numbers in the table to fill out the chart, but that would be tedious and detrimental to our quest for enlightenment. What we would really like to do is use the embedded table as a link source for the chart, as shown in Figure 21-5.

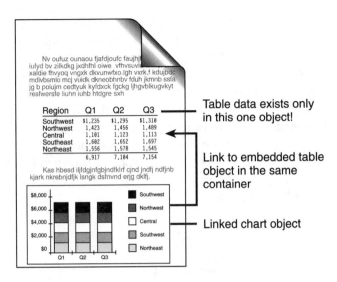

**Figure 21-5.**

*Linking a chart to an embedded table. In this example, the table is the only source for the data.*

This demonstrates linking to embeddings because embedded objects are valid sources of data as much as any other source outside the compound document. To make this work, the container itself has to provide link-source data when copying the embedded object to the clipboard or in a drag-and-drop operation. That means that the container must provide a moniker to name the embedded object inside the compound document, just as a linking server would name a pseudo-object in its own file. Keep in mind that the embedded object must support this sort of linking. The bit OLEMISC_CANTLINKINSIDE tells the container that such support is not present.

If the container can create a moniker to name the embedded object, any other container—even the original container itself—can now create a link to that embedded object by using the moniker (obtained from a Paste or a drop operation). Creating a chart that is linked to a table, for example, might require a sequence of steps that involve the creation of a new chart object followed by a call to its *IOleObject::InitFromData* function so that it can obtain the link-source data. In one way or another, the chart object can now obtain an *IDataObject* pointer for the table object. Through this pointer, the chart can extract the necessary data to render its own presentations.

Of course, the linked object doesn't always end up in the original container, but that linked object must still support activation. In this case, activation means that we must launch the original container and have it load *and activate* the embedded object. Thus, the container needs to support all the

985

binding mechanisms necessary for whatever moniker it uses to name the embedded object. This includes a class factory, an *IPersistFile* implementation, and any number of *IOleItemContainer* implementations. But the container doesn't implement the object itself—when asked for an interface pointer, it returns one from the embedded object.

We will demonstrate linking to embeddings with this chapter's version of Patron, which provides a File!Item!Item moniker to name an embedded object in a certain page of a certain document. Accordingly, Patron has to support binding for this moniker through the structure shown in Figure 21-6. Obviously, this will add some complexity to the application, but most of it is the result of moniker binding support.

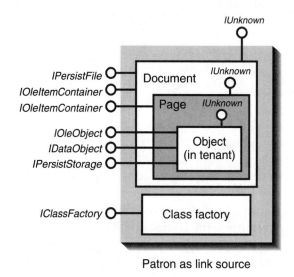

Patron as link source

**Figure 21-6.**
*The structure of Patron as a source for links to embedded objects.*

Linking to embeddings does make one demand on in-process servers for embedded objects. To show this, we'll update Polyline. First Polyline has to implement the moniker-related functions in *IOleObject*. It must then register itself as running within *IRunnableObject::Run*, using the container's name for embedding as obtained from the container's *IOleClientSite::GetMoniker(OLEWHICHMK_OBJFULL)*. At this time, the in-process object must also call the container's *IOleContainer::LockContainer* with TRUE. Now it is up to the in-process object to start a shutdown of the container in which it lives when a remote link to the object is released. To do so, the object implements *IExternalConnection* and calls its own *IOleObject::Close* function within *IExternal-*

*Connection::RemoveConnection. IOleObject::Close* then calls *IOleContainer::Lock-Container(FALSE)*, which causes the container to start its own shutdown. Through all of this, the other linking container can silently retrieve an update of the embedded object through the intermediate container, ensuring that everything is brought into and taken out of memory as necessary.

# A Simple Link Source for Content Objects: Cosmo

As described earlier, this chapter's version of Cosmo supports linking through a single File moniker, so the content object to which a container can link is an entire figure that makes up a single file. In this simple case, the changes required to support linking are not that extensive, as the following steps indicate:

1. When opening a file, create a file moniker and register it with the running object table. Remember to revoke the moniker from the table when closing the document. We saw how to do this in Chapter 9.

2. Re-create and reregister the file moniker when the document is renamed. This also means that you need to send the *OnRename* notification to any advise sinks obtained through *IOleObject::Advise*.

3. Call *IRunningObjectTable::NoteChangeTime* when the object is modified.

4. Include the CFSTR_LINKSOURCE and CFSTR_LINKSRC-DESCRIPTOR formats when copying data to the clipboard or through drag and drop. Do not provide these formats for a clipboard Cut operation because cutting removes the data that would be linked to in the first place.

5. Implement moniker binding support by implementing *IPersistFile* (as we already know from Chapter 9). *IPersistFile::QueryInterface* must return any of the other object's interface pointers. Note that file moniker binding requires an association between the server's file type and its CLSID, as needed by *GetClassFile* (also described in Chapter 9). In addition, we do not change the server's user interface when activating a linked object in *IOleObject::DoVerb*.

6. Implement *IOleObject::SetMoniker* and *IOleObject::GetMoniker*, and remove OLEMISC_CANTLINKINSIDE.

The following sections look at these steps more closely.

## Create, Register, and Revoke a File Moniker

Cosmo manages its file moniker in the *m_pMoniker* variable of its *CCosmoDoc* class. It creates and registers this moniker only when it has a known filename for the document itself. A new, untitled document is not registered as running. When you load a file with a known name or save a file, Cosmo ends up in *CCosmoDoc::Rename.* Here we revoke and release any old moniker and then create and register a new one for the new filename:

```
void CCosmoDoc::Rename(LPTSTR pszFile)
    {
    LPMONIKER    pmk;

    //We don't need to change base class, just augment....
    CDocument::Rename(pszFile);

    //Unregister old moniker (m_dwRegROT set to 0).
    INOLE_RevokeAsRunning(&m_dwRegROT);

    ReleaseInterface(m_pMoniker);

    if (NULL!=pszFile)
        {
        CreateFileMoniker(pszFile, &pmk);

        if (NULL!=pmk)
            {
            m_pMoniker=pmk;      //pmk AddRef'd in CreateFileMoniker
            INOLE_RegisterAsRunning(m_pFigure, m_pMoniker
                , 0, &m_dwRegROT);

            m_pFigure->SendAdvise(OBJECTCODE_RENAMED);
            }
        }

    return;
    }
```

The helper functions from INOLE.DLL, *INOLE_RegisterAsRunning* and *INOLE_RevokeAsRunning,* are wrappers for calls to *IRunningObjectTable.* (See INOLE\HELPERS.CPP.) A side effect of *INOLE_RevokeAsRunning* is that it sets our registration key to 0 to indicate a successful revoke. *INOLE_RegisterAsRunning* will actually call *INOLE_RevokeAsRunning* for us if *m_dwRegROT* is nonzero when we make the call. I'm not using this feature here; I want to show the steps explicitly.

When we change the name of the running object in this way, we have to advise any linked objects connected to this source that the name has changed. This is the purpose of calling *IAdviseSink::OnRename*. Containers themselves don't care about this notification, but the linking handler does. It uses the notification to inform the container of changes to the source.

Anyway, Cosmo sends this notification through *IOleAdviseHolder::Send-OnRename*, passing the new moniker, which gets forwarded to the necessary advise sinks:

```
//In CFigure::SendAdvise, FIGURE.CPP
case OBJECTCODE_RENAMED:
    m_pMoniker=m_pDoc->m_pMoniker;  //For IOleObject::GetMoniker
    m_dwRegROT=m_pDoc->m_dwRegROT;

    if (NULL!=m_pIOleAdviseHolder)
        m_pIOleAdviseHolder->SendOnRename(m_pMoniker);

    break;
```

In response to this, the linking handlers will update their internal monikers so that the link remains intact.

## Call *IRunningObjectTable::NoteChangeTime*

Whenever you make a change to Cosmo's Polyline figure, it calls *CPolyline-AdviseSink::OnDataChange* in DOCUMENT.CPP. This sets the dirty flag in the document by calling *CCosmoDoc::FDirtySet*, which in turn calls *CFigure::Send-Advise(OBJECTCODE_DATACHANGED)*. We send *IAdviseSink::OnDataChange* notifications as necessary, but we also call *IRunningObjectTable::NoteChange-Time*:

```
case OBJECTCODE_DATACHANGED:
    if (NULL!=m_pIDataAdviseHolder)
        {
        m_pIDataAdviseHolder->SendOnDataChange
            (m_pImpIDataObject, 0, 0);
        }

    if (0!=m_dwRegROT)
        INOLE_NoteChangeTime(m_dwRegROT, NULL, NULL);

    break;
```

The helper function *INOLE_ NoteChangeTime* takes the registration key from *IRunningObjectTable::Register* and calls the running object table for us. Its other two arguments are a FILETIME structure and a filename. If we pass NULL for the FILETIME, *INOLE_ NoteChangeTime* will use the current time or try to obtain it from the filename:

```
STDAPI_(void) INOLE_NoteChangeTime(DWORD dwReg, FILETIME *pft
    , LPTSTR pszFile)
    {
    IRunningObjectTable     *pROT;
    FILETIME                ft;

    if (NULL==pft)
        {
        CoFileTimeNow(&ft);
        pft=&ft;
        }

    if (NULL!=pszFile)
        GetFileTimes(pszFile, pft);

    if (FAILED(GetRunningObjectTable(0, &pROT)))
        return;

    pROT->NoteChangeTime(dwReg, pft);
    pROT->Release();
    return;
    }
```

Using the current time is good enough for Cosmo.

## Provide Link-Source Formats in Data Transfer

With the addition of the CFSTR_LINKSOURCE and CFSTR_LINKSRC-DESCRIPTOR formats to Cosmo's data transfer objects, we enable containers to link to a Figure object. Cosmo registers these formats in the *CCosmoDoc* constructor and saves them in *m_cfLinkSource* and *m_cfLinkSrcDescriptor*. We add these formats to those stored in the transfer object in *CCosmoDoc-::TransferObjectCreate*. This function calls *CCosmoDoc::RenderMedium* to render the data itself. As mentioned in Chapter 20, CFSTR_LINKSOURCE is a stream containing a serialized moniker; CFSTR_LINKSRCDESCRIPTOR is an OBJECTDESCRIPTOR structure:

```
BOOL CCosmoDoc::RenderMedium(UINT cf, LPSTGMEDIUM pSTM)
    {
    [Case for CF_EMBEDSOURCE]
```

```
/*
 * CFSTR_OBJECTDESCRIPTOR and CFSTR_LINKSRCDESCRIPTOR are the
 * same formats, but copy link source only if we have a moniker.
 */
if (cf==m_cfLinkSrcDescriptor && NULL==m_pMoniker)
    return FALSE;

if (cf==m_cfObjectDescriptor || cf==m_cfLinkSrcDescriptor)
    {
    SIZEL   szl, szlT;
    POINTL  ptl;
    RECT    rc;
    LPTSTR  psz=NULL;

    m_pPL->SizeGet(&rc);
    SETSIZEL(szlT, rc.right, rc.bottom);
    XformSizeInPixelsToHimetric(NULL, &szlT, &szl);

    SETPOINTL(ptl, 0, 0);

    //Include moniker display name now if we have one.
    if (m_pMoniker)
        {
        LPBC    pbc;

        CreateBindCtx(0, &pbc);
        m_pMoniker->GetDisplayName(pbc, NULL, &psz);
        pbc->Release();
        }
    CoTaskMemFree((void *)psz);
    pSTM->hGlobal=INOLE_AllocObjectDescriptor
        (CLSID_CosmoFigure, DVASPECT_CONTENT, szl, ptl
        , OLEMISC_RECOMPOSEONRESIZE, PSZ(IDS_OBJECTDESCRIPTION)
        , psz);

    pSTM->tymed=TYMED_HGLOBAL;
    return (NULL!=pSTM->hGlobal);
    }

if (cf==m_cfLinkSource)
    {
    if (NULL!=m_pMoniker)
        {
        FORMATETC   fe;
        HRESULT     hr;
```

*(continued)*

```
                pSTM->tymed=TYMED_NULL;
                SETDefFormatEtc(fe, cf, TYMED_ISTREAM);
                hr=INOLE_GetLinkSourceData(m_pMoniker
                    , (LPCLSID)&CLSID_CosmoFigure, &fe, pSTM);

                return SUCCEEDED(hr);
                }
            }

        return FALSE;
        }
```

We don't, of course, copy either link format if we have no moniker. If we have a moniker, we include the moniker's display name in CFSTR_LINK-SRCDESCRIPTOR, using our helper function *INOLE_ AllocObjectDescriptor* to create the data. To create CFSTR_LINKSOURCE, we use the helper function *INOLE_GetLinkSourceData*, which creates a stream in global memory, saves the moniker to the stream with *OleSaveToStream*, and saves the object's CLSID with a call to *WriteClassStm*.

As for the placement of the linking formats on the clipboard, they should always be after other formats, even after simple formats such as CF_TEXT. The reason is that linking almost never happens by default when a container pastes. It almost always happens when the user explicitly asks the container to perform a Paste Link operation. Keep the link data at the lowest spot on the totem pole.

## Implement *IPersistFile* and Activate the Object

After you copy link-source data to the clipboard, containers can create a linked object from it.[1] After all, it only takes a moniker to create the linked object. If you copy the link-source data now and try to activate the object, your server will be launched, provided *GetClassFile* can map your file moniker contents to your CLSID. Unfortunately, activation will not succeed because we haven't implemented *IPersistFile* yet. That is the next step, and the implementation is different from the ones we saw in Chapters 8, 9, and even 14. (In Chapter 14, Cosmo implemented *IPersistFile* support for accessing a file as an automation object.) Here we implement this interface as part of Cosmo's *CFigure* class alongside *IOleObject* and *IDataObject*. So after we've loaded the file, we'll be queried for *IOleObject*. When we've returned that interface, we should see a call to *IOleObject::DoVerb*, in which we activate our user interface.

---

1. Including OLE 1 containers, which see your moniker as OLE 1 link-source data.

Because we're editing a linked object, however, we do not—repeat, do not—modify the server's user interface when we show the window (as we did for embeddings in Chapter 18). With linked objects, end users need to know that they are working with a file, so they need File menu commands through which they can save or rename the file. In Chapter 18, we only switched the user interface around from within *IOleObject::SetHostNames*. Well, that function is never called for a linked object in a local server, so we never have to bother the UI. No problem!

## Implement *IOleObject::SetMoniker* and *IOleObject::GetMoniker*

The last step for making a complete linking server is to fill in the implementation of *IOleObject::SetMoniker* and *IOleObject::GetMoniker*. Implementing *SetMoniker* is important if you want to support linking to embeddings—that is, when your object doesn't include OLEMISC_CANTLINKINSIDE. This function is not called for one of Cosmo's linked objects but rather for an embedded object that is being linked to inside its container. *SetMoniker* tells us to register as running the full moniker naming this object in the container:

```
STDMETHODIMP CImpIOleObject::SetMoniker(DWORD dwWhich
    , LPMONIKER pmk)
    {
    LPMONIKER       pmkFull;
    HRESULT         hr=ResultFromScode(E_FAIL);

    if (NULL!=m_pObj->m_pIOleClientSite)
        {
        hr=m_pObj->m_pIOleClientSite->GetMoniker
            (OLEGETMONIKER_ONLYIFTHERE, OLEWHICHMK_OBJFULL
            , &pmkFull);
        }

    if (SUCCEEDED(hr))
        {
        if (NOERROR==pmkFull->IsRunning(NULL, NULL, NULL))
            {
            pmkFull->Release();
            return NOERROR;
            }

        //This will revoke the old moniker if m_dwRegROT is nonzero.
        INOLE_RegisterAsRunning(m_pObj, pmkFull
            , 0, &m_pObj->m_dwRegROT);
```

*(continued)*

```
          //Inform clients of new moniker.
          if (NULL!=m_pObj->m_pIOleAdviseHolder)
              m_pObj->m_pIOleAdviseHolder->SendOnRename(pmkFull);

          pmkFull->Release();
          }

      return hr;
      }
```

This code works in conjunction with our call to *INOLE_ NoteChangeTime* earlier. Cosmo maintains two registration keys (*m_dwRegROT*) from *IRunning-ObjectTable::Register*: one in *CCosmoDoc* and the other in *CFigure*. The former is used when Comso is handling a linked object. In that case, the variable in *CFigure* has a copy of the variable in *CCosmoDoc*. If we're embedded and *SetMoniker* is called, the document variable is 0 and the *CFigure* variable is the one from the registration shown in the preceding code. In either case, we'll always call *IRunningObjectTable::NoteChangeTime* for the right moniker in the right circumstances.

*IOleObject::GetMoniker* is used when Cosmo is servicing a linked or an embedded object, and it returns the full moniker to the object in either case. For linking, this is the document moniker; for embedding, this is the moniker we can get from the container:

```
STDMETHODIMP CImpIOleObject::GetMoniker(DWORD dwAssign
    , DWORD dwWhich, LPMONIKER *ppmk)
    {
    HRESULT            hr=ResultFromScode(E_FAIL);

    *ppmk=NULL;

    if (NULL!=m_pObj->m_pMoniker)
        {
        *ppmk=m_pObj->m_pMoniker;            //Document file moniker
        m_pObj->m_pMoniker->AddRef();
        }
    else
        {
        //Get full container:object moniker if we're embedded.
        if (NULL!=m_pObj->m_pIOleClientSite)
            {
            hr=m_pObj->m_pIOleClientSite->GetMoniker
                (OLEGETMONIKER_ONLYIFTHERE, OLEWHICHMK_OBJFULL
                , ppmk);
            }
        }

    return (NULL!=*ppmk) ? NOERROR : hr;
    }
```

And with that, we have completed the implementation of a simple link-source server.

---

### Closing a Linked Document Without Saving

When a user activates a linked object in a container, changes made to the object in the server are immediately reflected in the object image in the container site. Users usually save their file and then close the server when they have finished making changes. It is possible that a user can close the file and *not* save changes, in which case the image of the object in the container does not reflect what is actually in the source data. This is in fact the expected behavior of such linked objects, and it is a very difficult problem to handle in another way. It requires the server to reload its original data and update clients again before closing, which might not be all that easy. Furthermore, the same problem exists when links are broken—that is, when the site image in the container does not match the actual source data. So the container—and the cache in OLE—try to maintain an updated presentation within reasonable bounds. To deal with this, a container can try to detect this situation and revert its cache to some previous state, but that too is difficult. This is one update problem that simply doesn't have a good solution today.

---

# Linking to Embeddings: Patron

To name an embedded object within a page in a document, this chapter's version of Patron (CHAP21\PATRON) uses a File!Item!Item moniker. The File is the document filename, the first Item is the page name, and the second Item is the tenant name. As a source for this kind of moniker, Patron enables other containers to link to embedded objects within a compound document.

In the Link Source sample in Chapter 9, we demonstrated how to bind File!Item and File!Item!Item monikers in which the item monikers contained the names of elements within the source's compound file. Because Patron's file structure is almost the same, much of the code for *IPersistFile* and the two necessary *IOleItemContainer* implementations is quite similar to the code in Link Source. In Patron, the page name has the form "Page *n*," which corresponds to the name of the page's storage element in the file. The tenant name has the form "Tenant *n*." This identifies the tenant's storage element, in which an embedded object resides.

To this end, Patron now implements a class factory for its document objects (in ICLASSF.CPP) and implements both *IPersistFile* (IPERFILE.CPP) and *IOleItemContainer* (IOLECONT.CPP) interfaces on that document object. Patron already writes its CLSID into its documents, so finding the CLSID associated with the name in the file moniker isn't a problem. Patron's Page objects (PAGE.CPP) also now implement *IOleItemContainer*, sharing most of the code with the document's version of this interface, just as we did for Link Source many moons ago.

Because we've seen most of this sort of code already, the following sections highlight those areas of specific concern for a linking to embedding container. First we have to create and manage the monikers that name the embeddings as well as the document and the page. Doing this includes registering the monikers in the running object table. Then, whenever we copy an embedded object (one that does not have OLEMISC_CANTLINKINSIDE) to the clipboard or in a drag and drop, we have to include the moniker in CFSTR_LINKSOURCE data as well. Once another container creates a linked object with this moniker, our problem is mostly one of binding support.

## Create and Manage Monikers

Patron maintains three monikers within its various objects: a File moniker naming the document, a File!Item moniker naming the page, and a File!-Item!Item moniker naming each tenant. All of this starts in *CPatronDoc-::Rename*, in which we first learn of the document name itself:

```
void CPatronDoc::Rename(LPTSTR pszFile)
    {
    LPMONIKER   pmk;

    CDocument::Rename(pszFile);

    //Unregister old moniker (m_dwRegROT set to 0).
    INOLE_RevokeAsRunning(&m_dwRegROT);

    if (NULL==pszFile)
        return;

    CreateFileMoniker(pszFile, &pmk);

    if (NULL!=pmk)
        {
        LPMONIKER   pmkAll;
```

```
INOLE_RegisterAsRunning(this, pmk, 0, &m_dwRegROT);

//Give a moniker to linked objects in tenants.
m_pPG->NotifyTenantsOfRename(pszFile, pmk);

//Register a File!"\" wildcard moniker as well.
CreateItemMoniker(TEXT("!"), TEXT("\\"), &pmkAll);

if (NULL!=pmkAll)
    {
    LPMONIKER    pmkWild;

    INOLE_RevokeAsRunning(&m_dwRegROTWild);
    pmk->ComposeWith(pmkAll, FALSE, &pmkWild);

    if (NULL!=pmkWild)
        {
        INOLE_RegisterAsRunning(this, pmk, 0
            , &m_dwRegROTWild);
        pmkWild->Release();
        }

    pmkAll->Release();
    }

//There's no need for us to hold on to this.
pmk->Release();
    }

return;
    }
```

First we create a file moniker and register that moniker as running. Then we pass this moniker down to the current page through *CPages::Notify-TenantOfRename*, which calls *CPage::NotifyTenantsOfRename*. After this, we create a File!"\" wildcard moniker and register it as running too. Thus, all pages in this document are marked as running. An external client can retrieve the document object's pointer, query for *IOleItemContainer*, and call *IOleItem-Container::GetObject* to look up any page in the document.

Patron's document object does not hold on to its file moniker because we never have occasion to use it outside this renaming sequence. It does hold the registration value that comes back from *IRunningObjectTable::Register*. *CPatronDoc::FDirtySet* uses this value to call *IRunningObjectTable::NoteChange-Time* as needed.

This is not to say that the file moniker is not needed elsewhere. The page and tenants hold on to a copy of this moniker for their own needs, such as creating CFSTR_LINKSOURCE data, passing the moniker to *IOleObject-::SetMoniker*, and implementing *IOleClientSite::GetMoniker.* This means that we have to pass down this document moniker to the page and tenants, as described earlier. This lands us in *CPage::NotifyTenantsOfRename*:

```
void CPage::NotifyTenantsOfRename(LPTSTR pszFile, LPMONIKER pmk)
    {
    PCTenant    pTenant;
    UINT        i;
    LPMONIKER   pmkPage;
    LPMONIKER   pmkAll;
    OLECHAR     szTemp[32];

    //Save file moniker.
    if (NULL!=m_pmkFile)
        m_pmkFile->Release();

    m_pmkFile=pmk;
    m_pmkFile->AddRef();

    //Create page moniker to send to tenants.
    GetStorageName(szTemp);
    CreateItemMoniker(TEXT("!"), szTemp, &pmkPage);

    for (i=0; i < m_cTenants; i++)
        {
        if (TenantGet(i, &pTenant, FALSE))
            pTenant->NotifyOfRename(pszFile, pmk, pmkPage);
        }

    /*
     * Register a File!Page!"\" wildcard moniker as well.
     * Notice that page is already marked as running
     * with document's wildcard moniker.
     */
    CreateItemMoniker(TEXT("!"), TEXT("\\"), &pmkAll);

    if (NULL!=pmkAll)
        {
        LPMONIKER   pmkWild=NULL;
        LPMONIKER   pmkTemp=NULL;

        INOLE_RevokeAsRunning(&m_dwRegROTWild);
        pmk->ComposeWith(pmkPage, FALSE, &pmkTemp);
```

```
        if (NULL!=pmkTemp)
            {
            pmkTemp->ComposeWith(pmkAll, FALSE, &pmkWild);
            pmkTemp->Release();
            }

        if (NULL!=pmkWild)
            {
            INOLE_RegisterAsRunning(this, pmk, 0
                , &m_dwRegROTWild);
            pmkWild->Release();
            }

        pmkAll->Release();
        }

    //If anything held on to this, it called AddRef.
    pmkPage->Release();
    return;
    }
```

Here we do much the same thing as we did in *CPatronDoc::Rename*—we create a moniker naming the page, hand that moniker and the file moniker to each tenant in the page, and register a wildcard moniker for all the tenants in the page. This wildcard moniker has the form File!Item!"\", of course. Note that the page has no need to register itself as running because the wildcard moniker we registered in the document has already accounted for the page. This applies to the tenants as well: because the page registers a wildcard moniker for all its tenants, all those tenants are already marked as running.

We still need to tell embedded objects of the document's file moniker, however, by calling *IOleObject::SetMoniker*. This occurs in *CTenant::Notify-OfRename*:

```
void CTenant::NotifyOfRename(LPTSTR pszFile, LPMONIKER pmkFile
    , LPMONIKER pmkPage)
    {
    [Code to call IOleObject::SetHostNames omitted]

    ⋮

    if (NULL!=pmkFile)
        {
        if (NULL!=m_pmkFile)
            m_pmkFile->Release();
```

*(continued)*

999

```
                    m_pmkFile=pmkFile;
                    m_pmkFile->AddRef();

                    m_pIOleObject->SetMoniker(OLEWHICHMK_CONTAINER, pmkFile);
                    }

            if (NULL!=pmkFile && NULL!=pmkPage)
                {
                LPMONIKER    pmkTenant=NULL;
                LPMONIKER    pmkRel=NULL;
                HRESULT      hr;

                //Create moniker for this tenant.
                GetStorageName(szObj);
                hr=CreateItemMoniker(TEXT("!"), szObj, &pmkTenant);

                if (SUCCEEDED(hr))
                    {
                    //Create relative moniker--no pathname.
                    pmkPage->ComposeWith(pmkTenant, FALSE, &pmkRel);
                    pmkTenant->Release();

                    if (SUCCEEDED(hr))
                        m_pIOleObject->SetMoniker(OLEWHICHMK_OBJREL, pmkRel);

                    //Hold on to relative moniker.
                    ReleaseInterface(m_pmk);
                    m_pmk=pmkRel;
                    }
                }

        return;
        }
```

We call *IOleObject::SetMoniker* twice: once with OLEWHICHMK_CON-TAINER (the document moniker) and once with OLEWHICHMK_OBJREL (the Page!Tenant moniker). This gives a linked object all the information it needs to maintain both its absolute and its relative monikers, as described earlier.

You'll notice that the tenant holds on to the document-relative moniker in the variable *m_pmk*. This is used later for implementing *IOleClientSite::GetMoniker*, which must now support all the various OLEWHICHMK_* options:

```
STDMETHODIMP CImpIOleClientSite::GetMoniker(DWORD dwAssign
    , DWORD dwWhich, LPMONIKER *ppmk)
    {
    *ppmk=NULL;

    switch (dwWhich)
        {
        case OLEWHICHMK_CONTAINER:
            //This is just the file we're living in.
            if (NULL!=m_pTen->m_pmkFile)
                *ppmk=m_pTen->m_pmkFile;

            break;

        case OLEWHICHMK_OBJREL:
            //This is everything but the filename.
            if (NULL!=m_pTen->m_pmk)
                *ppmk=m_pTen->m_pmk;

            break;

        case OLEWHICHMK_OBJFULL:
            //Concatenate file and relative monikers for this one.
            if (NULL!=m_pTen->m_pmkFile && NULL!=m_pTen->m_pmk)
                {
                return m_pTen->m_pmkFile->ComposeWith
                    (m_pTen->m_pmk, FALSE, ppmk);
                }

            break;
        }

    if (NULL==*ppmk)
        return ResultFromScode(E_FAIL);

    (*ppmk)->AddRef();
    return NOERROR;
    }
```

Most of the preceding code applies equally well to any link-source server that wants to provide linking to pseudo-objects or to other portions of a file, a database, or other material. Managing the monikers that name items and supplying those monikers through *IOleObject* and *IOleClientSite* are requirements of all types of link sources in OLE Documents.

## Source the Composite Moniker

In our discussion of Cosmo earlier in this chapter, we saw how to present a moniker in the CFSTR_LINKSOURCE format and how to provide the CFSTR_LINKSRCDESCRIPTOR format in clipboard and drag-and-drop operations. Patron does more or less those same things in its function *CTenant::CopyLinkedObject*, which is called from *CPage::TransferObjectCreate* in any clipboard or drag-and-drop operation:

```
void CTenant::CopyLinkedObject(LPDATAOBJECT pIDataObject
    , LPFORMATETC pFE, PPOINTL pptl)
    {
    HRESULT             hr;
    LPMONIKER           pmk;
    DWORD               dwStat;

    //If we don't have full moniker, no linking is allowed.
    if (NULL==m_pmk)
        return;

    //If object doesn't support this, return.
    dwStat=0;
    m_pIOleObject->GetMiscStatus(m_fe.dwAspect, &dwStat);

    if (OLEMISC_CANTLINKINSIDE & dwStat)
        return;

    [Other code omitted]

    m_pIOleObject->GetUserClassID(&clsID);
    hr=m_pIOleObject->GetMoniker(0, OLEWHICHMK_OBJFULL, &pmk);

    [Create CFSTR_LINKSOURCE and CFSTR_LINKSRCDESCRIPTOR with pmk.]
        ⋮
    }
```

For the most part, this is exactly what any link source does to create the necessary formats, which we usually make available only when we have a known filename. (This is the reason for the validation of *m_pmk* in the code above.) For a container that supports linking to embeddings, there is another condition: the object must support the feature itself. This means that the moniker implements *IOleObject::GetMoniker* for OLEWHICHMK_OBJFULL, which usually does little more than call *IOleClientSite::GetMoniker*. Anyway, if a server does not implement *GetMoniker*, it will mark itself with OLEMISC-_CANTLINKINSIDE as returned from *IOleObject::GetMiscStatus*. The absence of this bit means that the object also understands what to do with monikers it receives through *IOleObject::SetMoniker*—for example, register that moniker as running, as we saw in Cosmo earlier.

## Support Binding for Linking to Embeddings

Because we are familiar with class factories, *IPersistFile*, and *IOleItemContainer* already, we don't need to examine all of Patron's code related to these matters. Instead, we'll just take a peek at those parts that are unique to a container.

The first of these is that the Patron's page implementation of *IOleItem-Container::GetObject* returns not a pointer to the tenant named by the item in question but an interface pointer for the embedded object in that tenant. The following code is taken from *CImpIOleItemContainer::GetObject* in IOLE-CONT.CPP:

```
if (TenantFromName(pszItem, &pTenant))
    {
    pTenant->ObjectGet(&pObj);

    /*
     * If we're asked for immediate or moderate, work only
     * if object is already running.
     */
    hr=IsRunning(pszItem);   //This is the function below.

    if ((BINDSPEED_IMMEDIATE==dwSpeed
        || BINDSPEED_MODERATE==dwSpeed) && NOERROR!=hr)
        hr=ResultFromScode(MK_E_EXCEEDEDDEADLINE);
    else
        {
        //IMPORTANT:  Be sure that this object is running first.
        OleRun(pObj);
        hr=pObj->QueryInterface(riid, ppv);
        }

    pObj->Release();
    }
else
    hr=ResultFromScode(MK_E_NOOBJECT);
```

You can see that Patron first checks whether the embedded object is already running when BINDSPEED_IMMEDIATE and BINDSPEED_MODERATE are specified in the bind context. If not, we return MK_E_EXCEEDEDDEADLINE. Otherwise, if the object is already running or if we have as much time as we want, we run the object and query for whatever interface the external container linking to this embedding has asked for. The call to *OleRun* (which doesn't affect an already running object) is vital, especially for objects from in-process servers. This call ensures that the object will be completely registered in the running object table and that any necessary remoting stubs and proxies will be created for it when we return an interface pointer to the remote container.

It is also important for a container to implement *IOleItemContainer::Lock-Container*, which Patron does in the same manner as *IClassFactory::LockServer*:

```
STDMETHODIMP CImpIOleItemContainer::LockContainer(BOOL fLock)
    {
    if (fLock)
        g_cLock++;
    else
        {
        g_cLock--;
        g_cObj++;
        ObjectDestroyed();
        }

    return NOERROR;
    }
```

When an embedded object is activated as a link through our container, it will call *LockContainer(TRUE)* to ensure that the container—and thus, the embedded object itself—remains in memory as long as the other linking container requires it. When that linking container has finished with the object, it will release that object's interface pointers. The object then has to tell the embedding container (which is Patron here) that it no longer needs to stay in memory if all it's doing is servicing the link to the embedding. This is the same behavior that we implemented in a simple embedding server in Chapter 18: when the user closes the embedded object, the server terminates itself. Here Patron is acting as a server in the same manner, only for some other server's embedded objects. So when the server closes itself, it will call *LockContainer(FALSE)* to tell the container that it too can terminate. Patron increments its global object count and then fakes an object destruction by calling *ObjectDestroyed* (in PATRON.CPP), which checks for the necessary shutdown conditions as usual:

```
void ObjectDestroyed(void)
    {
    g_cObj--;

    //No more objects, no locks, no user control; shut down application.
    if (0==g_cObj && 0==g_cLock && IsWindow(g_hWnd) && !g_fUser)
        PostMessage(g_hWnd, WM_CLOSE, 0, 0L);

    return;
    }
```

## Round Out *IOleClientSite*

We need two more pieces of implementation before we can call a linking to embedding container complete. Remember *IOleClientSite::GetContainer*? When a container supports linking to the objects in its document, this function must return the *IOleContainer* interface for the immediate container of the objects themselves. In Patron's case, this is the *IOleItemContainer* interface on the page object—remember that *IOleItemContainer* is derived from *IOle-Container*. Patron's implementation of *IOleClientSite::GetContainer* does the following:

```
STDMETHODIMP CImpIOleClientSite::GetContainer(LPOLECONTAINER FAR
    *ppContainer)
    {
    PCPage  pPage;

    *ppContainer=NULL;

    m_pTen->m_pPG->IPageGetFromID((DWORD)-1, &pPage, FALSE);

    if (NULL!=pPage)
        {
        return pPage->QueryInterface(IID_IOleItemContainer
            , (PPVOID)ppContainer);
        }

    return ResultFromScode(E_FAIL);
    }
```

The function *CPages::IPageGetFromID* conveniently returns to us the current *CPage* pointer, through which we can call *QueryInterface*.

The other change we must make is a modification to *IOleClientSite::Show-Object*. In Chapters 17 and 20, this container function was responsible only for bringing the object into view. Because Patron can now be launched with *-Embedding* on the command line, the main window might not be visible. Thus, to truly show the object, *ShowObject* must now also make the frame window visible:

```
STDMETHODIMP CImpIOleClientSite::ShowObject(void)
    {
    HWND      hWnd, hWndT;

    m_pTen->ShowYourself();

    //For linking to embeddings, now show main window.
    hWndT=GetParent(m_pTen->m_hWnd);
```

*(continued)*

```
while (NULL!=hWndT)
    {
    hWnd=hWndT;
    hWndT=GetParent(hWnd);
    }

ShowWindow(hWnd, SW_SHOWNOACTIVATE);
return NOERROR;
}
```

The use of SW_SHOWNOACTIVATE in the *ShowWindow* call means that Patron will not be brought to the foreground when we show the main window. This prevents Patron from obscuring the linking container that the user is working in. We want to make the intermediate container visible but not obnoxious.

A final note about containers and linking to embeddings is that unbeknownst to the container, OLE will establish advises between the other linking container and the embedded object in the running server. When you make a change to the object in the server, you will see the object change in both containers, as a user would expect. What appears to be happening is that the user makes a change to the embedded object, and that change is reflected in the immediate container. This amounts to a change to the object in the container that the second container is linked to, so the change is also reflected in the second container. But the immediate container doesn't have to do anything to make this happen: OLE will automatically connect the embedded object to the linked object in the second container.

## Linking to Embeddings Support in Polyline

Supporting linking to embeddings as an object is quite simple for a local server such as Cosmo: it needs only to implement *IOleObject::SetMoniker* properly because the default handler will automatically call the container's *IOleContainer::LockContainer* to handle proper shutdown. When the object is implemented from an in-process server such as Polyline, the object itself has to register its full moniker as running and also handle the shutdown conditions by calling *LockContainer* at the appropriate times. You can make these calls either in *IRunnableObject::Run* or in *IOleObject::SetClientSite*. Polyline uses the latter case (in IOLEOBJ.CPP) because it does not have any client site pointers by the time *IRunnableObject::Run* is called:

```
STDMETHODIMP CImpIOleObject::SetClientSite
    (LPOLECLIENTSITE pIOleClientSite)
    {
    if (NULL!=m_pObj->m_pIOleClientSite)
        m_pObj->m_pIOleClientSite->Release();

    m_pObj->m_pIOleClientSite=pIOleClientSite;

    if (NULL!=m_pObj->m_pIOleClientSite)
        {
        HRESULT         hr;
        LPMONIKER       pmk;
        LPOLECONTAINER  pIOleCont;

        m_pObj->m_pIOleClientSite->AddRef();

        hr=m_pObj->m_pIOleClientSite->GetMoniker
            (OLEGETMONIKER_ONLYIFTHERE, OLEWHICHMK_OBJFULL, &pmk);

        if (SUCCEEDED(hr))
            {
            INOLE_RegisterAsRunning(this, pmk, 0
                , &m_pObj->m_dwRegROT);
            pmk->Release();
            }

        hr=m_pObj->m_pIOleClientSite->GetContainer(&pIOleCont);

        if (SUCCEEDED(hr))
            {
            m_pObj->m_fLockContainer=TRUE;
            pIOleCont->LockContainer(TRUE);
            pIOleCont->Release();
            }
        }

    return NOERROR;
    }
```

Polyline revokes the running object table registration in its destructor, *CPolyline::~CPolyline.*

Now all we need to know is when to call *IOleContainer::LockContainer-(FALSE)* to start container shutdown. We make the call when the linking container (the one linking to this embedded object) releases all of its connections to this object. To know when this happens, we must implement *IExternalConnection*, which Polyline does in IEXTCONN.CPP, as shown on the following page.

```
STDMETHODIMP_(DWORD) CImpIExternalConnection::AddConnection
    (DWORD dwConn, DWORD dwReserved)
    {
    if (EXTCONN_STRONG & dwConn)
        return ++m_cLockStrong;

    return 0;
    }

STDMETHODIMP_(DWORD) CImpIExternalConnection::ReleaseConnection
    (DWORD dwConn, DWORD dwReserved, BOOL fLastReleaseCloses)
    {
    if (EXTCONN_STRONG==dwConn)
        {
        if (0==--m_cLockStrong && fLastReleaseCloses)
            m_pObj->m_pImpIOleObject->Close(OLECLOSE_SAVEIFDIRTY);

        return m_cLockStrong;
        }

    return 0L;
    }
```

When the last external strong lock disappears, we call our own *IOle-Object::Close* to handle our shutdown. In that function, we check the *m_fLock-Container* flag set in *IOleObject::SetClientSite*. If that flag is TRUE, we unlock the container to have it shut down as well:

```
STDMETHODIMP CImpIOleObject::Close(DWORD dwSaveOption)
    {
    [Other handling as usual]

    if (m_pObj->m_fLockContainer)
        {
        //Match LockContainer call from SetClientSite.
        LPOLECONTAINER  pIOleCont;

        if (SUCCEEDED(m_pObj->m_pIOleClientSite
            ->GetContainer(&pIOleCont)))
            {
            pIOleCont->LockContainer(FALSE);
            pIOleCont->Release();
            }
        }

        ⋮
    }
```

# Summary

To support linked objects in OLE Documents, any server or source of such links must provide a moniker that names the absolute location of the object's data. A source provides this moniker through data transfer mechanisms such as the clipboard and drag and drop. The moniker must name an object that implements the *IOleObject* and *IDataObject* interfaces, but this object doesn't actually need to exist until a container wants to bind to it.

As the source of a moniker, a linking server must also implement all the necessary binding support for whatever monikers it gives away, as explained in Chapter 9. This support typically represents the bulk of the implementation of the *IPersistFile* interface, one or more implementations of *IOleItemContainer*, and the management of the running object table (potentially with wildcard monikers). Such work is especially apparent when a container wants itself to be a source for the embedded objects and to that end implements a feature called "linking to embeddings." This gives the user the ability to link to data that exists only in an embedded object in some other compound document, a perfectly reasonable thing to do.

This chapter examines the implementation of a simple linking server using the Cosmo sample as a demonstration. Cosmo provides the ability to link to a "figure" that is the contents of an entire file and that requires only a file moniker to name it. This chapter also demonstrates a container that supports linking to embedding using the Patron sample. For this feature, Patron provides a File!Item!Item composite moniker to name an object on a page in a document. This process illustrates both complex binding support as a link source and the necessary steps to implement such linking as a container. Both the Cosmo sample provided here and an update to the in-process Polyline server support linking to embedding as well. Polyline requires an implementation of *IExternalConnection* to make the relationship with its container work properly, illustrating one of the primary uses for the interface.

## CHAPTER TWENTY-TWO

# In-Place Activation (Visual Editing™) and In-Place Containers

Long ago, in an era of greater simplicity, when the OLE Design Specification was only 50 pages long, there was a new idea called *in situ editing*. Instead of forcing you to edit an embedded object in a separate server window, in situ editing—an extension of normal activation—let you edit an object while remaining in the context of the compound document. The Latin phrase *in situ* means "in the natural or original position." Simple enough.

But the marketing types at Microsoft looked at *in situ editing* and, with good, sound intentions, changed it to *in-place editing*. OK, that's cool. The change got rid of that funny Latin stuff and made the term more comprehensible to us programmers who didn't break 600 on the SAT verbal. Everyone understood and was happy to get working on it.

In a burst of pure reason, marketing figured that the word *editing* was much too specific for compound documents because certain objects—for example, video objects—are more apt to be *played* in place instead of being *edited*. This led to the term *activation,* so this new idea was rechristened *in-place activation*. But that wasn't the end of the matter. Marketing just can't leave well enough alone.

Along came the tide of "Visual This" and "Visual That"—Visual Basic, Visual C++, and so on and so forth. Everything suddenly had to be *visual* in some way. It was cool. It would hook end users the same way free T-shirts hook hungry programmers at software development conferences. Marketing rode the wave and brought on *visual editing,* even going as far as to slap on the prominent trademark symbol(™).

Of course, with this latest term, the word *editing* again reared its ugly head, but then the name changes stopped. I fully expected *visual editing* to give way to *visual activation,* and after *visual* fell out of vogue, *visual activation* would revert to *in situ activation* and then back to *in-place activation* because us programmers *still* can't break 600 on the SAT verbal.

So I stick with the name *in-place activation* for the technology that is the subject of this chapter and the next, calling it *in-place* simply for convenience. We'll start this chapter with a look at a typical in-place session for an embedded object, given that both the container and the object (and the object's server) support this capability. This will show us the in-place interfaces that are involved and how they work together to merge the user interface in a way that looks a little weird at first, but one that has proved itself in usability testing. Much of in-place activation is about merging the object's user interface with the container's. Doing this brings the object's tools to the object instead of taking the object to the tools.

We'll also examine some additional considerations, including keyboard accelerators, context-sensitive help, Undo operations, and the ability to have multiple in-place objects active at the same time. In this chapter, we'll see the implementation steps for an in-place–capable container, using Patron once again as our sample. Chapter 23 will explore the object side of the picture. These two chapters set the stage for OLE Controls because controls, being self-contained units of functionality, are almost *always* in-place active. And with controls, the term *in-place activation* certainly fits because I have a hard time understanding how I would *visually edit* a control. Maybe I still need to learn Latin.

## Motivations

In-place activation is about document-centric computing—the notion that end users want to concentrate on the task at hand—the document—and to be free from having to remember which application to use at what time for what reason. As my mother would say, "I just want it to work! I just want to write a letter!" End users want to be sure that they use the best tools for the job without having to think too much about finding those tools.

Here's a case in point: while I was writing this chapter for the first edition of *Inside OLE,* Microsoft held a usability contest in which representatives from other companies were asked to create the most usable ATM—Automatic Taco Machine. No, seriously. The goal was to create an interface that would allow anyone to walk up to the ATM and, without ever having seen the device before, quickly and easily order a taco with any number of options. From what I heard, contestants exploited pull-down menus, pointing devices, three-dimensional beveled button controls, and all the other glitz we're used to seeing on a desktop computer. The entry that won was a simple design with a touch screen. You knew at a glance how to order a taco by pressing one spot on the screen; by pressing others you could specify exactly what kind of taco you wanted. No glitz. Just plain common sense.

Why did this win? Because it was, for lack of a better term, taco-centric. The purpose of the device was to allow an end user to order a taco. Period. The winning design did exactly that—no more, no less. It's not so much that it could do the right thing, but that it was designed in such a way that the only thing you could possibly do with it was the right thing. If this sort of idea interests you, Donald Norman's wonderful book *The Design of Everyday Things* (formerly *The Psychology of Everyday Things*) is a must-read. Norman would be the first to point out that the other designs failed because they paid so much attention to aesthetics that usability was flushed straight down the toilet. Sure, the menus and 3-D buttons were neat, but they didn't work. They would, however, probably win some prize for artistry.

In-place activation addresses the idea that we want the content in a document to look, feel, and act as if it were an integral part of that document. The basic activation concept that we've seen in Chapters 17 and 18 only partially achieves a document-centric model. It's a great start to have OLE automatically launch another application and to have the object automatically load its native data and show its user interface for editing. In this way, the user never has to leave the document to launch another application. However, having other applications show up on the screen in their own pop-up windows is still rather application-centric. These windows can obscure the compound document itself in such a way that the user might forget about the context in which he or she is working. In addition, users can be confused about where the real data exists. When an object is activated, its data or image is visible both in the server and in the container. Sure, the container draws a hatch pattern over the image in its own document, but confusion is still possible.

What in-place activation achieves is to bring all the necessary editing and other manipulation facilities from the object's own user interface to the container itself. That is, in-place activation is a means through which the object and the container merge their user interface elements: the container retains control of document-oriented elements, and the object gains control of content-oriented elements. Thus, the object can display its own menu items, toolbars, windows, and other devices in place in the container. When this happens, the user sees only one image of the object—the image in the document. And because no other pop-up windows appear, the user continues to work within the context of the document itself.

> ## In-Place Activation: For Embeddings Only
>
> In-place activation architecture, although technically capable of activating both linked and embedded objects in place, should be used only to activate embedded objects. The reason is strictly one of user interface. When a user edits the source data for a linked object, he or she is working with shared data. Changing the source can potentially change many other linked objects in other documents. If a linked object is activated in place, the user might not realize that he or she is altering shared data and thus other documents. On the other hand, editing an embedded object changes only that object's data, which is entirely contained in the compound document itself. However, if you are building a closed system in which you control all the containers and objects, you can activate links in place if you want. The restriction must be followed on open systems to maintain consistency.

# How In-Place Activation Works

In-place activation uses a series of well-defined protocols through which the container and the object communicate. OLE itself does hardly anything except route some messages to the proper windows. So in-place activation depends almost entirely on a container and an object communicating with each other through the OLE-defined interfaces *IOleInPlaceFrame*, *IOleInPlaceUIWindow*, *IOleInPlaceSite*, *IOleInPlaceObject*, and *IOleInPlaceActiveObject*.

In this section, we'll first see where these interfaces are placed and then take a quick look at the member functions they contain. We'll also see how they are used by following an entire in-place–activation session.

## In-Place Interfaces for Containers

For a container to support in-place activation, it must implement the *IOleInPlaceSite* interface on its site object alongside *IOleClientSite* and *IAdviseSink*. The presence of *IOleInPlaceSite* tells embedded objects that its container is in-place capable. In addition, the container must also create a frame object that implements *IOleInPlaceFrame*. This object is separate from the site, and only one frame exists per container. Through *IOleInPlaceFrame*, an object merges its top-level user interface (such as menu items and toolbars) with the container's. If the container can provide separate document windows, as MDI applications can, each document must be an object that implements *IOleIn-PlaceUIWindow*. Through this interface, the object can display user interface tools inside document windows. The overall structure of an in-place–capable container is shown in Figure 22-1. If the container does not have separate document windows, *IOleInPlaceUIWindow* is not needed.

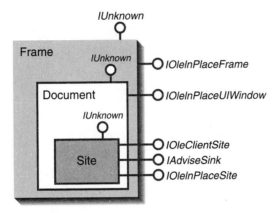

In-place–capable container

**Figure 22-1.**
*The structure of an in-place–capable container.*

All of these interfaces are derived from a common base interface named *IOleWindow*. It represents operations common to all parts of the container:

```
interface IOleWindow : IUnknown
    {
    HRESULT GetWindow(HWND *phwnd);
    HRESULT ContextSensitiveHelp(BOOL fEnterMode);
    };
```

*GetWindow* returns the handle of the window associated with whatever object is attached to this interface. A frame object would return the container's frame window, a document object would return the document window, and a site object would return whatever window is most closely associated with it, such as the document or some other client-area window.

*ContextSensitiveHelp* tells the object involved to enter or exit a mode in which mouse clicks, menu selections, and other user actions display help for that action instead of performing the action itself. The *fEnterMode* flag is set to TRUE when you should enter the mode, FALSE to exit the mode.

The other in-place interfaces are derived from *IOleWindow* as shown in the following code. *IOleInPlaceFrame* also derives from *IOleInPlaceUIWindow*:

```
interface IOleInPlaceSite : IOleWindow
    {
    HRESULT CanInPlaceActivate(void);
    HRESULT OnInPlaceActivate(void);
    HRESULT OnUIActivate(void);
    HRESULT GetWindowContext(LPOLEINPLACEFRAME *ppFrame
        , LPOLEINPLACEUIWINDOW *ppDoc, LPRECT prcPosRect
        , LPRECT prcClipRect, LPOLEINPLACEFRAMEINFO pFrameInfo);
    HRESULT Scroll(SIZE scrollExtent);
    HRESULT OnUIDeactivate(BOOL fUndoable);
    HRESULT OnInPlaceDeactivate(void);
    HRESULT DiscardUndoState(void);
    HRESULT DeactivateAndUndo(void);
    HRESULT OnPosRectChange(LPCRECT prcPosRect);
    };

interface IOleInPlaceUIWindow : IOleWindow
    {
    HRESULT GetBorder(LPRECT prcBorder);
    HRESULT RequestBorderSpace(LPCBORDERWIDTHS pBW);
    HRESULT SetBorderSpace(LPCBORDERWIDTHS pBW);
    HRESULT SetActiveObject(LPOLEINPLACEACTIVEOBJECT pActiveObject
        , LPCOLESTR pszObjName);
    };

interface IOleInPlaceFrame : IOleInPlaceUIWindow)
    {
    HRESULT InsertMenus(HMENU hMenuShared
        , LPOLEMENUGROUPWIDTHS lpMenuWidths);
    HRESULT SetMenu(HMENU hMenuShared, HOLEMENU hOLEMenu
        , HWND hWndActiveObj);
    HRESULT RemoveMenus(HMENU hMenuShared);
    HRESULT SetStatusText(LPCOLESTR pszStatusText);
    HRESULT EnableModeless(BOOL fEnable);
    HRESULT TranslateAccelerator(LPMSG pMsg, WORD wID);
    };
```

In general, the members of *IOleInPlaceSite* represent the various events and requests that an in-place object sends to or requires of the container. *IOleInPlaceSite::GetWindowContext* is the function that the object uses to obtain its pointers to the other interfaces on the container's frame and document objects. Through *IOleInPlaceUIWindow*, the object can negotiate with the container for space in a document window for tools. It also provides the document with an *IOleInPlaceActiveObject* interface, which we'll see in the next section. Finally, an object can do everything with a document window that it can do with a frame window, so *IOleInPlaceFrame* is derived from *IOleInPlaceUIWindow*. The added member functions represent frame-specific user interface elements, such as the menu, the status line, and keyboard accelerators.

These, then, are the interfaces through which an in-place object accesses the services of an in-place container. Let's now look at the interfaces that a container uses to communicate with an in-place object.

## In-Place Interfaces for Objects

The presence of *IOleInPlaceObject* marks an object as in-place capable. Otherwise, an in-place–capable object appears to a container as any other embedded object does. This interface is always available through *QueryInterface* with any of the object's other interfaces. When an object becomes in-place active, it also provides an implementation of *IOleInPlaceActiveObject*, which is conceptually located on a separate object altogether, as shown in Figure 22-2. Typically, as we'll see in Chapter 23, this interface is implemented on the object itself, but with a *QueryInterface* that doesn't respond to any interfaces other than *IUnknown* and *IOleInPlaceActiveObject*.

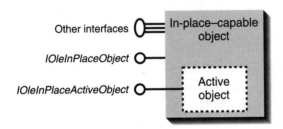

**Figure 22-2.**
*The structure of an in-place–capable object.*

As with the container interfaces, both *IOleInPlaceObject* and *IOleInPlace-ActiveObject* are derived from *IOleWindow*, as shown in the code on the following page.

```
interface IOleInPlaceObject : IOleWindow
    {
    HRESULT InPlaceDeactivate(void);
    HRESULT UIDeactivate(void);
    HRESULT SetObjectRects(LPCRECT prcPosRect, LPCRECT prcClipRect);
    HRESULT ReactivateAndUndo(void);
    };

interface IOleInPlaceActiveObject : IOleWindow
    {
    HRESULT TranslateAccelerator(LPMSG pMsg);
    HRESULT OnFrameWindowActivate(BOOL fActivate);
    HRESULT OnDocWindowActivate(BOOL fActivate);
    HRESULT ResizeBorder(LPCRECT prcBorder
        , LPOLEINPLACEUIWINDOW pUIWindow, BOOL fFrameWindow);
    HRESULT EnableModeless(BOOL fEnable);
    };
```

For the most part, these interfaces consist of various notifications that the container will send to the object when important things happen in the user interface. These events include deactivation of the object, resizing the object, performing an Undo operation, detecting a keyboard accelerator, changing window activation, resizing a window, and displaying or removing some sort of modal window.

## In-Place–Active States vs. UI-Active States

If you look carefully at the interfaces described in the previous two sections, you'll notice that some member functions are given names such as *InPlace-Activate* while others are named *UIActivate*. This reflects the fact that in-place activation adds two object states to those we first discussed in Chapter 17. The additional states are *in-place active* and *UI active*. The active state we've been describing is the state in which an object's user interface is visible in a separate window. A call to *IOleObject::DoVerb* with OLEIVERB_SHOW brings an object into this active state. (This is true for any other verb that implies a show operation, such as OLEIVERB_PRIMARY.) In-place activation defines two standard verbs through which a container can tell an object to enter the in-place–active or UI-active state: OLEIVERB_INPLACEACTIVATE and OLEIVERB_UI-ACTIVATE. The functions *IOleInPlaceObject::InPlaceDeactivate* and *IOleInPlace-Object::UIDeactivate* reverse these state transitions, as shown in Figure 22-3.

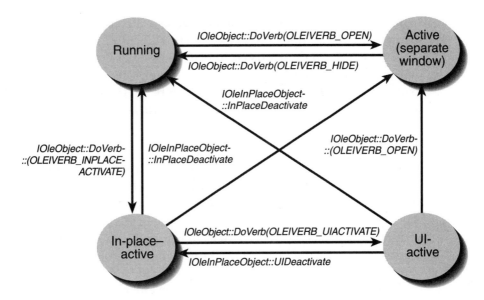

**Figure 22-3.**
*In-place–active and UI-active state transitions for in-place–capable objects.*

When an object is in-place active, it has a window of its own inside the container's document window. This enables the object to respond directly to mouse clicks and control its own rendering. The container also has the object's *IOleInPlaceActiveObject* pointer. However, an in-place–active object does not have any other user interface available. Only one UI-active object can have its toolbars, menus, and keyboard accelerators active at a given time. When the user clicks the mouse inside an in-place–active object's window, that object becomes the UI-active object. This causes the user interface for the previous UI-active object to be deactivated, but that object's in-place state is not fully deactivated. It remains in-place active if it wants.

In this manner, in-place activation allows a container to manage multiple in-place–active objects at the same time, but only one of them is also UI active. This is perfect for dealing with a form full of elements such as OLE controls; only the control with the keyboard focus needs to be UI active. All others will be in-place active, and a single mouse click on any control will make it the UI-active one.

Objects that support both of these states, which is optional, usually mark themselves as OLEMISC_ACTIVATEWHENVISIBLE. This means that a container should keep those objects in-place active, but not UI active, whenever they are visible to the end user. (This is usually whenever those objects are loaded.) Some of those objects might also be marked OLEMISC_INSIDE-OUT, which is a special case that we'll return to later.

## Where Does It All Start?

Now that we've seen the interfaces involved and where they are implemented, we can follow an in-place session from start to finish to see how these interfaces are used. Let's say we have a container—Patron, for example—in which we have opened a compound document containing an embedded graphic from a server such as Cosmo. This is shown in Figure 22-4. We now want to change that graphic, so we double-click on the graphic to activate it, at which time the container calls *IOleObject::DoVerb(OLEIVERB_PRIMARY)* as it always has. With the basic form of activation we've seen in previous chapters, the object would open in a separate window, in which we can make changes.[1]

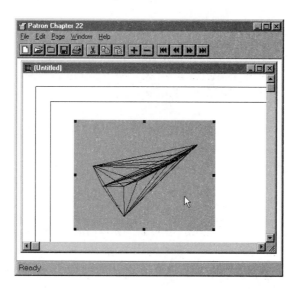

**Figure 22-4.**
*An example of a container with a compound document in which an embedded object lives.*

---

1. The exceptions are video objects and the like, which can use the *hWnd* and RECT arguments passed to *DoVerb* to temporarily play inside the container window.

In-place activation thus begins with a container's innocent call to *DoVerb*. At this point, we do not know whether in-place activation will actually happen. That is for the object to decide.

When an in-place–capable object receives a call to *DoVerb* (for verbs other than OLEIVERB_OPEN, which expressly means "activate in a separate window"), the object first checks whether the container is also in-place capable. It does this by asking the *IOleClientSite* pointer passed as an argument to *DoVerb* whether it supports *IOleInPlaceSite*. If the site fails this query, it is simply not in-place capable, and the object proceeds to activate normally. This shows again the power of *QueryInterface* to perform feature negotiation. Through this simple query, an in-place–capable object determines, at run time, whether it can use in-place activation. Thus, an in-place–capable object remains entirely compatible with in-place–capable containers that are not, but it's integrated better with in-place–capable ones.

Why, however, does the object query the *IOleClientSite* pointer passed to *IOleObject::DoVerb* rather than the pointer from *IOleObject::SetClientSite*? The former *IOleClientSite* pointer allows the container to activate an object in place in a different site from the one that manages the object otherwise. The container might want to activate an object in place in a specific location in its user interface outside the compound document itself. This alternative site is called the *active site,* and its *IOleClientSite* pointer is the one that shows up in *DoVerb* as the *pActiveSite* argument.

For whatever site is being used, the object will know that the container is in-place capable when the container returns an *IOleInPlaceSite* pointer. With this pointer, the object must now check whether in-place activation is allowed on this particular object at this particular time by calling *IOleIn-PlaceSite::CanInPlaceActivate*. This call separates the container's general in-place support for all objects—expressed by its support for *IOleInPlace-Site*—from its ability to activate a specific object in place. A container will, for example, refuse to activate the embedded object in place if the object is being displayed as an icon or if the object is linked and not embedded. If *CanInPlaceActivate* returns S_FALSE, the object is activated in a separate window.

If the container says that in-place activation is allowed, however, the object can start the full activation process by first calling *IOleInPlaceSite-::OnInPlaceActivate*, which tells the container to allocate any necessary structure for handling the in-place process. This process generally involves three steps: moving the object's editing window to the container, merging container and server menus into one shared set of menus, and creating editing tools (toolbars and so on) for the object in the container window. To accomplish these things, the object needs the container frame's *IOleInPlace-Frame* interface and the container document's *IOleInPlaceUIWindow* (if available). It retrieves these by calling *IOleInPlaceSite::GetWindowContext*. As interfaces on separate objects, they are not available through the site's *QueryInterface*!

## Your Window or Your Life

Besides the container's other interface pointers, *IOleInPlaceSite::GetWindow-Context* also returns two rectangles: a position rectangle that describes where the object must initially appear in the container window and a clipping rectangle that describes the space in which the container can display anything. With this information, the object takes whatever editing window it has (Cosmo's Polyline window, for example) and physically moves it to the container by calling the Windows API function *SetParent*. The parent window handle is obtained by calling *IOleInPlaceSite::GetWindow*. The object then moves the editing window to the position rectangle, clips it to the size of the clipping rectangle, and makes it visible. Because the position rectangle is usually the same as the rectangle occupied by the site, the editing window appears on top of the site.

Now that this window is visible, it gets whatever messages are generated by various mouse actions performed in it. If the user clicks the mouse—presto! WM_LBUTTONDOWN comes into the editing window's message procedure. Cosmo's Polyline window adds a point to its figure on such an event. Certainly, the user could do a lot with the object in its window at this time. But as shown in Figure 22-5, the only visual changes are the absence of the container's selection handles and a possible change in the mouse cursor. Compare Figures 22-4 and 22-5. What is different? Did anything happen? Not much—not enough to let users know that they're now supposed to be working on the figure and not on the container. We need some subtle indications that something changed, in addition to potential changes in the menus and toolbars.

To solve this problem, we need to indicate that the object has changed from the loaded state to the in-place–active state. The user interface guidelines for OLE Documents recommend that an object create a small hatched border around itself in the container, which can also include object-managed grab handles, as shown in Figure 22-6. To create this border, an object typically creates a special *hatch window* that is larger than the object's position rectangle on all sides by the width of the border.[2] The object uses this window

2. The border width is read from the [windows] section of WIN.INI using the key OleInPlace-BorderWidth. The default value is 4 pixels.

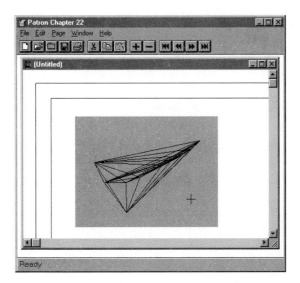

**Figure 22-5.**
*What Patron would look like if all that Cosmo did for in-place activation was
move its Polyline window into Patron. There's no magic here!*

as the parent of the editing window and then places the hatch window itself
into the container, offset left and up from the position rectangle by the border
width. The object occupies exactly the position rectangle, leaving the hatch
window with a small space in which to draw the hatching and grab handles.
Mouse clicks in the hatch window are always mouse clicks in the hatched border or on the grab handles, which the object can manage as necessary.

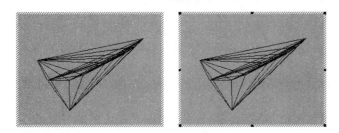

**Figure 22-6.**
*The hatched border that an object creates around itself when activated in
place, with and without sizing handles.*

If an object resizes itself with these grab handles while in place, it
should call *IOleInPlaceSite::OnPosRectChange*, which in turn calls *IOleInPlace-
Object::SetObjectRects* with an updated position and clipping rectangle. As

we'll see in Chapter 23, a hatch window helps the in-place object manage this clipping rectangle and the one it obtains from *IOleInPlaceSite::Get-WindowContext*. In any case, what the user will now see is something such as that shown in Figure 22-7.

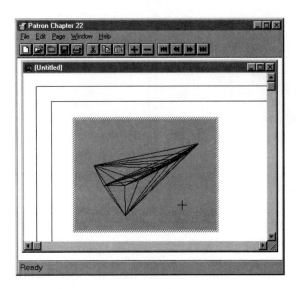

**Figure 22-7.**
*What Patron looks like after Cosmo has created its hatching around the object.*

At this point, an object is completely in the in-place–active state. This is as far as we go if we're handling OLEIVERB_INPLACEACTIVATE. If we're fully activating the user interface, the object now calls *IOleInPlaceSite::On-UIActivate* to warn the container. The object passes its *IOleInPlaceActiveObject* pointer to the container by calling *IOleInPlaceFrame::SetActiveObject* and, if the container has a document, *IOleInPlaceUIWindow::SetActiveObject*.[3] Because the container cannot query for this interface through the object itself, these calls to *SetActiveObject* are the only way the container obtains this pointer. Through this pointer, it must now notify the UI-active object of various events.

To complete UI activation, the object now creates a shared menu and displays its tools in the container. The next two sections describe the processes involved.

---

3. The *pszObjName* argument to *SetActiveObject* is not used and can be NULL. Some time ago, the user interface guidelines recommended that a container display this string in its document or frame caption bar. This is no longer the case, although you might still see applications that use the older form of the UI. The container should now ignore the argument completely.

## Socially Adept Menus

I call these menus socially adept because they're good at mixing. OK, bad pun.

The next phase in integrating the object's user interface with the container's is creating a mixed, or shared, menu that the container displays in its frame window. This menu is composed of pieces from the normal menus of both container and object. In a nutshell, the container retains possession of menus that have to do with the document. It provides the File menu, the Window menu (if the container supports MDI), and any other menus that pertain to document and container functions (such as Patron's Page menu). The object provides the Edit menu and the Help menu and can add any other menu necessary to manipulate the object while it is activated in place. (Examples are Cosmo's Color and Line menus.) This makes sense, but the question is how to take two sets of menus and merge them into one programmatically, as shown in Figure 22-8.

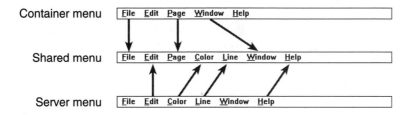

**Figure 22-8.**
*How container and server menus can merge to create one shared menu.*

How this works (and it does work) is that both container and object control three menu *groups,* and each group can have as many individual pop-up menus as desired. The container controls groups named File, Container, and Window; the object has groups named Edit, Object, and Help. The shared menu is the alternating combination of these groups: File, Edit, Container, Object, Window, and Help, as shown in Figure 22-8. (The Color and Line menus are both in the Object group.)

The object initiates the process for building this menu by creating a new, blank menu through the Windows function *CreateMenu.* It passes this menu to the container's *IOleInPlaceFrame::InsertMenus* function along with a pointer to a structure named OLEMENUGROUPWIDTHS, which is simply an array of six integers. Inside *InsertMenus,* the container calls the appropriate Windows API function, either *AppendMenu* or *InsertMenu,* to build its half of the menu. After Patron executes *InsertMenus,* for example, the menu will appear as follows:

```
File   Page   Window
```

On return from *InsertMenus*, the object inserts its own menu items for each of its groups between those contributed by the container. The container will have stored the width—the number of items—of each of its groups in the OLEMENUGROUPWIDTHS array. The elements at indexes 0, 2, and 4 contain the widths of the File, Container, and Window groups, respectively. In the Patron example above, each array element would contain the value 1.

The object now inserts its own groups between those of the container by using the Windows function *InsertMenu*, carefully controlling the position of each new item. The object inserts each menu item in its Edit group after the File group but before the Container group, using the width of the File group as the base offset for items in the Edit group. The base offset of the items in the Object group is the width of the File, Container, and Edit groups combined. Likewise, the starting offset for the Help group is the combined widths of all the other groups.

The object completes the OLEMENUGROUPWIDTHS array by storing the number of menus in its groups in array elements 1, 3, and 5. It then creates a *menu descriptor* by calling *OleCreateMenuDescriptor*, passing the new menu's handle and the width array. The object then passes that descriptor, the new menu handle, and a window handle to receive messages generated from the object's menus to *IOleInPlaceFrame::SetMenu*. At that time, the container displays the shared menu, as shown in Figure 22-9, and passes all the

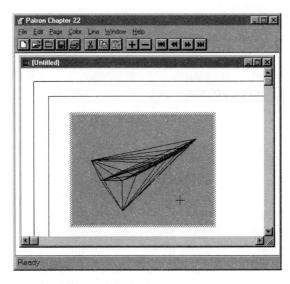

**Figure 22-9.**
*Patron displaying a menu it shares with Cosmo.*

information to *OleSetMenuDescriptor*, which is the key to making all this work. *OleSetMenuDescriptor* creates a message hook on the container's main window so that it can watch the messages generated from this shared menu (WM_COMMAND, WM_MENUSELECT, and so on) and redirect them to the object's window handle. OLE determines who owns which menu by checking the position of the menu generating the message against the group widths array stored in the descriptor. No magic!

## A Stop by the Hardware Store

*Hi there! Welcome to Hank's Hardware Heaven! We have everything! We have plumbing. We have lighting. We have paints, wallboard, industrial appliances, and 387 types of electrical tape! You want tools? We have tools! Lots of tools! Screwdrivers, wire cutters, wrenches, tape measures, drills, sanders, planers, jigsaws, band saws, hacksaws, power saws, table saws, radial arm saws! We have every conceivable drill bit, every conceivable lathe tool, every...*

*Oh, pipe down. Can you just point me to the toolbars?*

*Huh? Toolbars? Ain't got none of those....Better try the object down the street.*

The remaining user interface problem that we need to address is the toolbar. If you look back to Figure 22-9, you'll notice that Patron's toolbar is still visible and accessible. For the most part, that's fine because it provides easy access to commands such as File Open, File Save, Edit Copy, and Edit Paste, as well as the commands that also appear on the Page menu. There are two problems with this, however. First, while the object has the user's attention, none of its tools (if it has any) are visible. The second problem is that Edit commands are available on both the menu and the toolbar. The commands on the menu, however, are dispatched to the object, while those on the toolbar end up in the container, which still owns the toolbar. Although the end user sees the same commands on the toolbar and the menu, the commands behave differently. Not good.

For these and other fine reasons, in-place activation gives ownership of toolbars to the in-place object. The exception is the status line at the bottom of the window, which the container maintains for consistency.[4] To achieve this, the object has to negotiate with the container for space in the frame or document windows using the *RequestBorderSpace* member function of *IOleInPlaceUIWindow* (which is part of *IOleInPlaceFrame* as well).

---

4. Chapter 25 will describe some current work to better integrate toolbars so that the container can keep some of its own tools available.

The object first calls *RequestBorderSpace* in the appropriate interface, passing a BORDERWIDTHS structure (defined as a RECT). The structure's *left*, *right*, *top*, and *bottom* fields indicate the amount of space the object wants to allocate from each side of the window. Here the container can decide whether it wants to surrender that space to the object, and the container has every right to say no. If the container surrenders the space, the object then calls *IOleInPlaceUIWindow::SetBorderSpace*, at which time the container repositions its windows (like an MDI client) to make space for the object's tools. The object calls *IOleInPlaceUIWindow::GetBorder* to determine the actual dimensions of the container window and creates its tools as children of the container window to fit. After all this is done, the object has whatever tools it wants inside the container's frame (and document) window. Cosmo itself creates a single toolbar in the frame window, as shown in Figure 22-10. At this point, Cosmo is completely in-place activated.

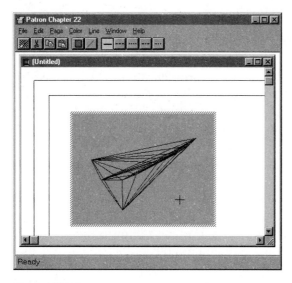

**Figure 22-10.**
*Cosmo fully in-place activated in Patron.*

If a container denies an object's call to *RequestBorderSpace*, the object can adjust its request and try the call again until the container accepts it. If an obstinate container refuses to grant an object space for its tools, it's not the end of the world. The object can always display those tools in a floating pop-up window because popups don't require permission from the container. A flexible object would generally be able to display its tools in a popup or on a toolbar on any side of a window in such a way that it would be able to work well in any container. If it does so, it has to enable and disable these pop-up windows inside *IOleInPlaceActiveObject::EnableModeless*. A container will use *EnableModeless* to simulate what Windows does automatically for a window hierarchy owned by a single application—when a modal window is displayed, all the others are disabled. With in-place activation, some of these windows are not owned by the container, so *EnableModeless* is used to communicate the necessary behavior for those windows.

Besides pop-up tools and toolbars in the frame and the document window, the object is also allowed to create *object adornments,* which are additional tools attached to the outer edges of the editing window. For example, table or spreadsheet objects might want to display row and column headers. A text-editing object might want to display style information to the left of the text. In these cases, the object simply makes its in-place window larger, always keeping the editing space the same size as the container site—that is, the same size as the object that is displayed in the container when the object is not active. The only restriction to these object adornments is that they cannot reach outside a clipping rectangle provided by the container under any circumstances. The object must obey out of courtesy—there are no police to stop you, but end users would most likely complain about the visual problems that disobedience would cause.

## Manipulations of an In-Place Object

When an object is both in-place active and UI active, various events can occur that might be processed by the object, the container, or both.

First are mouse events. When the mouse pointer is over the in-place object's editing window (when the object is both in-place active and UI active), all mouse messages go directly to that window, including WM_MOUSEMOVE, WM_SETCURSOR, and WM_LBUTTONDOWN. If the user now clicks an in-place–active object, it should become UI active. When the mouse pointer moves out of the object's window, it moves into the hatched area. If the user double-clicks here, the object should deactivate its in-place user interface and become active in a separate window—the semantics of OLEIVERB-_OPEN. If you are using a hatch window, you have an easy way to detect this mouse event.

If the user moves the mouse out of the hatched area and into the container document's area, the container will now receive messages. If the user clicks on the document itself—outside any objects—this signals the container to deactivate the object by calling *IOleInPlaceObject::InPlaceDeactivate* or *IOleInPlaceObject::UIDeactivate* if the object is marked with OLEMISC_ACTI-VATEWHENVISIBLE. (We'll see what happens here in a moment.) If the user happens to move the mouse to another in-place–active object and then single-clicks, that object becomes UI active. If that object is not in-place active and the user double-clicks, the container deactivates the UI-active object and activates the new one.

The second type of event is a keyboard event. According to the user interface guidelines, the UI-active object always has first crack at keystrokes. This is guaranteed by the UI-active object always having the focus. The container is responsible for calling the Windows function *SetFocus* to change the focus to the object window whenever the document containing that object becomes the currently active document. The container obtains the object's window handle by calling *IOleInPlaceObject::GetWindow*. Although focus takes care of normal keystrokes, it does not take care of accelerators. This requires some special treatment on behalf of the container and the server. The container must modify its message loop to call the current UI-active object's *IOleIn-PlaceActiveObject::TranslateAccelerator* before doing any of its own translation. This call actually applies only to in-process objects that would otherwise have no chance of handling accelerators because they have no message loop to call their own. When a local object is UI active, its own message loop is the active one, so it must call *OleTranslateAccelerator* after checking for accelerators itself but before calling *TranslateMessage* and *DispatchMessage*. *OleTranslateAccelerator* will call *IOleInPlaceFrame::TranslateAccelerator* if it finds that the accelerator pressed is in the container's accelerator table. This accelerator table is the other piece of information that an object receives from *IOleInPlaceSite-::GetWindowContext*.

This brings up another point: both container and server need to load and process different accelerator tables when they're involved with an in-place–active object. The container will want to disable its accelerators for any menu command that is not currently available—that is, for anything outside the File, Container, and Window menu groups. The server must do the same so that it doesn't attempt File Save or Window Tile operations as an in-place object.

Speaking of menu commands, we already saw how OLE uses the menu descriptor to route messages from the shared menu to the container or the object. One message is WM_MENUSELECT, which causes many applications to change the text in their status lines. When an object receives such a message, it can display appropriate text in the container's status line by calling *IOleInPlaceFrame::SetStatusText*. Also, an object can determine whether the container even has a status line by calling *SetStatusText* with NULL and watching for failure. If the call fails, the object can create a status line as an in-place tool if it wants.

A status line is one form of help that is not associated with the object's Help menu. The other form of help is context-sensitive help, initiated by pressing Shift+F1 (and possibly by choosing a menu command as well). If the container detects a request for context-sensitive help, it calls *IOleInPlaceActive-Object::ContextSensitiveHelp* to instruct the object to enter that help mode. If the object detects the keystroke, it can call the same member function on all three of the container interfaces.

Undo is another common application feature that has some special considerations for in-place activation. For example, performing an Undo operation immediately after an in-place object has been activated should mean "deactivate," just as an Undo operation immediately after a deactivation should mean "reactivate." If an Undo is the first event that occurs after an object is activated in place, the object calls *IOleInPlaceSite::DeactivateAndUndo*; otherwise, it calls *IOleInPlaceSite::DiscardUndoState* to let the container free the memory it was holding in case *DeactivateAndUndo* was called. In the same way, if an in-place object is deactivated and the first thing that happens in the container is an Undo, the container calls *IOleInPlaceObject::ReactivateAndUndo*. If anything else happens after a deactivation, the container calls *IOleObject::Do-Verb(OLEIVERB_DISCARDUNDOSTATE)*.

Something else that can happen with in-place activation is that the position rectangle that an object is given might actually extend past the edge of the container window. In that case, the object can call *IOleInPlaceSite::Scroll* to have the container show more of the object. This is useful for a spreadsheet object, for example, because the user might move the cell selection outside the visible region using the arrow keys. The user might also scroll the container document directly, in which case the container calls *IOleInPlaceObject-::SetObjectRects* to let the object know the new position. If the object allows resizing while in place, it calls *IOleInPlaceSite::OnPosRectChange* with the new rectangle it wants. In response, the container calls *IOleInPlaceObject-::SetObjectRects* to let the object know its allowable position rectangle and the clipping rectangle.

If the object is too small, the user can open the object in the full server window as if in-place activation never existed. This is done by calling the object's *IOleObject::DoVerb* with OLEIVERB_OPEN, which always causes it to activate in another window and never to activate in place. Besides double-clicking in the hatched border, the object should also provide an Open item on its Edit menu and watch for a Ctrl+Enter accelerator. Both means are also defined in the user interface guidelines.

## Pulling the Plug: Deactivation

At some point during its lifetime, an object will need to remove all of the user interface it created during UI activation and remove from the container the window that is created for the in-place–active state. The container controls which type of deactivation happens by calling either *IOleInPlaceObject::UIDeactivate* or *IOleInPlaceObject::InPlaceDeactivate*.

UI deactivation means that the object first calls *IOleInPlaceSite::OnUIDeactivate*, then removes its tools, and then unravels the shared menu. In-place deactivation implies UI deactivation if the object is UI active. UI deactivation is followed by the removal of the object's window from the container, a call to *IOleInPlaceUIWindow::SetActiveObject* with NULL, a call to *IOleInPlaceSite::OnInPlaceDeactivate*, and finally the release of the container's in-place interface pointers.

### Yes, This Really Works

I want to share a few things that Microsoft learned about in-place activation in usability tests involving test subjects who were accustomed to working with Microsoft Word and Microsoft Excel. The usability testers created a simulation in which an Excel spreadsheet object would be activated in place inside Word. At first, the usability designers thought some serious confusion might occur when the menus and toolbars began to switch around. What they actually found was quite surprising. When subjects activated the spreadsheet object in place, they immediately recognized Excel's row and column headings that appeared around the object. Without noticing what had happened, they went along using Excel's toolbar and formula bar (which had quietly appeared in place of Word's toolbar and ribbon) as well as Excel's menus (which had quietly merged with Word's). Only after doing their jobs (that is, manipulating the spreadsheet) for a number of minutes did the subjects begin to notice that things had changed. This was a surprise because the testers thought it would be obvious that stuff was switching around. But because the users were focusing so intently on the object they wanted to edit, they weren't even looking at the menus or the toolbar. When the object changed from a simple presentation to something that looked like an Excel spreadsheet, their Excel training kicked right in without a hitch.

On the whole, deactivation is simpler than activation. When the container deactivates an object, that container knows that it has regained control of the toolbar space, so it simply makes its tools visible again. Unwinding the menu is accomplished by the object removing its menu items, calling *IOleIn-PlaceFrame::RemoveMenus*, and then calling the Windows function *DestroyMenu* to match the earlier *CreateMenu*. Removing the in-place editing window is simply a matter of calling *SetParent* with one of the server's own window handles.

## Outside-In vs. Inside-Out Objects

In-place activation supports two different activation models—*outside-in* and *inside-out*. So far, we've been discussing the outside-in model, in which a user must double-click an inactive (loaded) object to make it UI active. If that embedded object contains other embeddings, the user has to double-click the next object down to activate that nested embedding in place, and so on.

Objects that are marked as OLEMISC_ACTIVATEWHENVISIBLE can completely avoid the need for a double click as long as the container supports the flag. But this is still an outside-in activation model—activation of the topmost object happens automatically, but the user might still need to double-click to get deeper into nested embeddings.

Some objects might want to support the inside-out activation model by marking themselves with the OLEMISC_INSIDEOUT flag. In this model, a single click on the object causes it to be activated in place. Furthermore, that inside-out object checks whether the mouse was clicked over a nested embedding that is also inside-out. If so, it activates the nested object, which then continues to do the same for however many nested objects there happen to be. In an inside-out activation model, the user can single-click to get to the innermost embedding in a stack of nested objects. This is the reason for the MSG structure passed to *IOleObject::DoVerb*; each object in the stack has to know where the mouse was clicked in order to know whether to activate another object.

Inside-out capability allows you to create content objects that act as data native to the container application, in which single clicks typically behave this way. Inside-out activation does require that the objects involved be small and fast to load, because you don't want to make users wait 10 seconds every time they click the mouse somewhere!

Finally, some objects might mark themselves as both OLEMISC_ACTI-VATEWHENVISIBLE and OLEMISC_INSIDEOUT. If the container supports the first flag, the latter is somewhat irrelevant because the object will see the single click itself. If the container doesn't understand the difference between the in-place–active and UI-active states, but it does understand OLEMISC-_INSIDEOUT, the object can still work with a single click.

> ### A Note About Handlers
>
> If you plan to support in-place activation for an object in a local server that already works with an in-process handler, that handler must expose the necessary in-place interfaces to the container through aggregation with the default handler. The handler must also forward *IOleObject::DoVerb* calls properly for in-place activation to occur.

# In-Place Container Step by Step: Patron

In-place activation is really an extension of embedding, so what we need to do to make a container in-place capable is add UI support to what is already present for embedding. We have a few interfaces to implement and a number of places where we need to add a small amount of code to make everything work smoothly. These are the steps that we'll use to make Patron (CHAP22-\PATRON) in-place capable:

1. Prepare the container application to handle the effect of creating shared menus, switching toolbars, and handling accelerators while an object is active in place.

2. Implement skeletal *IOleInPlaceFrame, IOleInPlaceUIWindow,* and *IOleInPlaceSite* interfaces.

3. Activate and deactivate the object.

4. Contribute the container's half of the shared menu.

5. Negotiate tool space and handle window repositioning when an object requests space.

6. Give the object a chance to process accelerators; be sure to disable all accelerators that are not applicable during an in-place session.

7. Handle all the remaining events—switching between document windows, resizing a frame or document window, scrolling a document, and an assortment of other small features. These are the little tweaks that make everything work.

This last step is rather nebulous. Many bits and pieces of work are necessary to round out an in-place container. This is another reason why the Microsoft Foundation Classes (MFC) are a powerful tool for working with

OLE Documents—the framework includes many of these little considerations by default, leaving you to implement only those parts that need customization.

The sections that follow include a number of sidebars noting experiences I had that caused me to regularly beat my head against a table, wall, or other sufficiently hard surface while I was developing this chapter's Patron sample. Not all of them are about bad stuff, however. Some are merely comments about tricky parts of the implementation. I hope they can prevent you from developing the same sort of flat spot as I inflicted on my forehead.

## Prepare the Container

You should keep in mind three primary considerations when designing and implementing an in-place–capable container.

First, you have limited command availability: not all of your menus will be available, you might not have your toolbars available, and you will not have first crack at accelerators. So ask yourself some questions. What functions do you want to have available during an in-place session? Are those functions on menus that you will retain during the session? Are there commands that are available only on a toolbar so that they will be inaccessible during the session? What accelerators correspond to menu items that you will not retain? Do you need to define separate menu and accelerator resources to load during a session? Can you modify your editing toolbar in such a way that if you are allowed to retain it during a session, you can remove those commands that you do not retain? Your answers to these questions might lead to significant code changes, but those are best done now, before attempting to work with in-place activation any further.

The second consideration is that you will be sharing the menu with the object. This means that your particular menu items can appear anywhere on the menu. You cannot depend on any particular item having any particular position. This will likely affect WM_INITMENU and WM_INITMENU-POPUP message handling—applications typically use the menu positions passed with these messages for enabling or disabling specific menu items—for example, Edit Paste. To work independent of specific positions, either you'll need to maintain an array of the current positions of the top-level items that you place in the shared menu or you'll need to modify your code to work solely on menu handles, which are also passed with WM_INITMENU-[POPUP] messages and provide a much more robust way to identify a specific menu item.

The third consideration is the negotiation of space for the object's in-place tools. How easily can your container handle foreign tools in the frame and document windows? Can you resize whatever window occupies the client area of your frame and document windows? Can you resize them in any direction? Can you resize them while keeping the contents at the same absolute screen position? How small can they be? Is there a point at which you would restrict the border space allowed for an object? Are there spaces in the frame or document client areas that should never be overlapped by an object (especially those areas that are drawn and not separate windows)? Do your tool windows use WS_CLIPSIBLINGS to keep them from interfering with object tools? Do you have a status line? When the frame or document window is resized, do you always resize the client to a specific position?

Grist for the mill. During an in-place session, you are responsible for respecting the space you allow an object, which means not drawing over it, keeping your client-area windows inside the space left over after the object's allocations, and ensuring that you resize the client windows correctly when the frame or document is resized. Thinking about the impact of sharing space on an arbitrary basis, and modifying your container code to handle it, is well worth the effort now before things get complicated.

## Implement Partial In-Place Container Interfaces

To build any other in-place–activation code, we'll need at least stub implementations of *IOleInPlaceSite*, *IOleInPlaceFrame*, and, if applicable, *IOleInPlace-UIWindow*. Each interface is part of the appropriate container-side object. Patron implements the first as a contained class in *CTenant* (through *CImp-IOleInPlaceSite* in IIPSITE.CPP), the second as part of *CPatronFrame* (in PATRON.CPP), and the third as a contained class in *CPatronDoc* (*CImpIOleIn-PlaceUIWindow* in IIPUIWIN.CPP). The *GetWindow* member of the site interface returns the pages window that occupies a document's client area—in other containers this might be simply the document window itself. The same member function in the other two interfaces returns the frame and document window handles as appropriate.

We don't need to implement every part of these interfaces right away. We'll get to everything in turn. At this point in our implementation, we need to do the following:

1. Implement the trivial *GetWindow* function of each interface.

2. Implement *SetActiveObject* in the frame and document interfaces to save the *IOleInPlaceActiveObject* pointer passed to each.

3. Implement the *IOleInPlaceSite* members of *CanInPlaceActivate*, *OnInPlaceActivate*, *OnInPlaceDeactivate*, and *GetWindowContext*.

4. Return E_NOTIMPL from everything else for the time being.

The following sections will look at steps 2 and 3 in more detail. You'll also need to ensure that each object, site, document, and frame supports the correct interfaces in *QueryInterface*. Each object will need to respond to *IOle-Window* as well as to the specific interface in question. In addition, the frame's implementation will need to respond to *IOleInPlaceUIWindow* because that is the base interface of *IOleInPlaceFrame*.

---

### EXPERIENCE: The Site Requires
### Access to the Frame and the Document

A site object will generally need access both to frame and document variables and to member functions because the interaction between the in-place object and the site will involve user interface elements for the frame and the document. This is especially true because *IOleInPlaceSite::GetWindowContext* must return interface pointers for the frame and document windows. For this reason, Patron stores its *CPatronFrame* pointer in a global variable, *g_pFR*. Not the best design, but it works.

---

### Implement *SetActiveObject* for the Frame and the Document

The *SetActiveObject* member in *IOleInPlaceUIWindow* (and thus *IOleIn-PlaceFrame*) is the function that the container uses to obtain the UI-active object's *IOleInPlaceActiveObject* interface, which the container must hold for later calls that we'll make to it. In Patron, both *CPatronFrame* and *CPatronDoc* have a member variable *m_pIOleIPActiveObject* for this purpose.

*SetActiveObject* will be called with both NULL and non-NULL pointers.[5] When NULL is passed, release whatever interface pointer you have. When non-NULL is passed, release the old pointer, save a copy of the new one, and call *AddRef* through that new pointer, as shown in the code at the top of the following page.

---

5. Again, ignore the *pszObjName* argument, which is no longer used.

```
if (NULL!=m_pIOleIPActiveObject)
    m_pIOleIPActiveObject->Release();

//NULLs m_pIOleIPActiveObject if pIIPActiveObj is NULL
m_pIOleIPActiveObject=pIIPActiveObj;

if (NULL!=m_pIOleIPActiveObject)
    m_pIOleIPActiveObject->AddRef();
```

### Implement Crucial *IOleInPlaceSite* Members

*IOleInPlaceSite* is the critical path of communication between an in-place object and the container, so for now we'll need to do most of our work in this interface. In Patron, the three members *CanInPlaceActivate*, *OnInPlaceActivate*, and *OnInPlaceDeactivate* are typical and rather short:

```
STDMETHODIMP CImpIOleInPlaceSite::CanInPlaceActivate(void)
    {
    if (DVASPECT_CONTENT!=m_pTen->m_fe.dwAspect)
        return ResultFromScode(S_FALSE);

    if (TENANTTYPE_EMBEDDEDOBJECT!=m_pTen->m_tType)
        return ResultFromScode(S_FALSE);

    return NOERROR;
    }

STDMETHODIMP CImpIOleInPlaceSite::OnInPlaceActivate(void)
    {
    //m_pIOleIPObject is our in-place flag.
    m_pTen->m_pObj->QueryInterface(IID_IOleInPlaceObject
        , (PPVOID)&m_pTen->m_pIOleIPObject);
    return NOERROR;
    }

STDMETHODIMP CImpIOleInPlaceSite::OnInPlaceDeactivate(void)
    {
    m_pTen->Activate(OLEIVERB_DISCARDUNDOSTATE, NULL);
    ReleaseInterface(m_pTen->m_pIOleIPObject);
    return NOERROR;
    }
```

For most containers, *CanInPlaceActivate* will not be too complex. Patron disallows in-place activation (returning S_FALSE) when the object is not embedded or is being displayed using an aspect other than DVASPECT-_CONTENT. Other containers can use other conditions, of course.

*OnInPlaceActivate* and *OnInPlaceDeactivate* tell the container to put itself in or take itself out of an in-place state. Patron's state consists entirely of the object's *IOleInPlaceObject* pointer (saved in *CTenant::m_pIOleIPObject*), which is managed in these two functions. Patron queries for and saves the pointer when the object is activated, releasing it when the object is deactivated. The pointer, which we need for making other function calls later, doubles as a flag to tell us whether we are handling an in-place session at the time. We'll come back to the *IOleObject::DoVerb* call later when we discuss Undo operations.

*IOleInPlaceSite::GetWindowContext* is the hairy beast of the group, requiring more code because it has more arguments to mess with. This function stores pointers to the container's *IOleInPlaceFrame* and *IOleInPlaceUIWindow* interfaces in two out-parameters (*ppIIPFrame* and *ppIIPUIWindow*), specifies the initial position and clipping rectangles for the object (in *prcPos* and *prc-Clip*), and fills an OLEINPLACEFRAMEINFO structure with accelerator information:

```
STDMETHODIMP CImpIOleInPlaceSite::GetWindowContext
    (LPOLEINPLACEFRAME *ppIIPFrame, LPOLEINPLACEUIWINDOW
    *ppIIPUIWindow, LPRECT prcPos, LPRECT prcClip
    , LPOLEINPLACEFRAMEINFO pFI)
    {
    PCPatronDoc     pDoc;
    RECTL           rcl;

    *ppIIPUIWindow=NULL;

    *ppIIPFrame=(LPOLEINPLACEFRAME)g_pFR;
    g_pFR->AddRef();

    pDoc=(PCPatronDoc)SendMessage(GetParent(m_pTen->m_hWnd)
        , DOCM_PDOCUMENT, 0, 0L);

    if (NULL!=pDoc)
        {
        pDoc->QueryInterface(IID_IOleInPlaceUIWindow
            , (PPVOID)ppIIPUIWindow);
        }

    //Now get rectangles and frame information.
    m_pTen->RectGet(&rcl, TRUE);
    RECTFROMRECTL(*prcPos, rcl);

    //Include scroll position here.
    OffsetRect(prcPos, -(int)m_pTen->m_pPG->m_xPos
        , -(int)m_pTen->m_pPG->m_yPos);

    SetRect(prcClip, 0, 0, 32767, 32767);
```

*(continued)*

```
    pFI->cb=sizeof(OLEINPLACEFRAMEINFO);
#ifdef MDI
    pFI->fMDIApp=TRUE;
#else
    pFI->fMDIApp=FALSE;
#endif

    pFI->hwndFrame=g_pFR->Window();

    pFI->haccel=g_pFR->m_hAccelIP;
    pFI->cAccelEntries=CINPLACEACCELERATORS;

    return NOERROR;
    }
```

Patron stores the global *CPatronFrame* pointer *g_pFR* as the *IOleInPlace-Frame* pointer (calling *AddRef*, of course) because *CPatronFrame* inherits from the interface directly. We have to ask the document for its *IOleInPlaceUIWindow*, however.

The container is responsible for returning two rectangles here. The position rectangle tells the object exactly which rectangle it occupies in the container in *device units* (pixels). In Patron's case, this is the rectangle for the tenant implementing this site, offset for the current scroll position. The object will use this position rectangle as the area in which it displays its data, surrounding that area with any adornments it wants. If this area is not the same as the object's own extents, the ratio of the two determines the scaling factor. An object can choose to resize itself to fit in this rectangle, or it can choose to not change its scale and provide scrollbars or other devices as necessary.

The second rectangle, the clipping rectangle, specifies where the object can legally display anything — including adornments outside the object's data area. The object is downright criminal if it dares to place anything outside the clipping rectangle. This is the law to prevent the object from overlapping parts of the container's own UI — such as sibling toolbars — that are visibly outside the document area itself. Patron actually makes no restrictions because the object's window will be clipped to the pages window that occupies the usable client area of the document (and which is moved to accommodate any document tools the object creates). So we store the maximum rectangle (0–32,767 in both extents) in *prcClip*, again in device units. Keep in mind that the position rectangle can be larger than or extend outside the clipping rectangle. The object will scale to the position rectangle, but it will be displayed only in the intersection of the position and clipping rectangles.

The OLEINPLACEFRAMEINFO structure that you fill here provides the object, if it comes from a local server, with the information it requires for calling *OleTranslateAccelerator*. In-process objects do not use this information. *OleTranslateAccelerator* needs to know whether the container uses MDI (so that it can call *TranslateMDISysAccel* appropriately), as well as the window to receive accelerator commands. The accelerators you include here should be only those you want active during an in-place session. (Patron's accelerators are listed for the identifier IDR_INPLACEACCELERATORS in PATRON.RC.)

The *cb* field in OLEINPLACEFRAMEINFO indicates the version of the structure itself. (Later revisions of OLE might change the structure.) The object will fill this field before calling *GetWindowContext*. This means that the container must not modify the field but rather use it to store the right information in the right part of the structure.

With only this level of implementation, a container can activate an object to the point shown in Figure 22-7 on page 1024. Trouble is, we have no code in the container to deactivate the object! So we'd better add support for the rest of an object's activation needs.

## Activate and Deactivate the Object

As described earlier, any call to *IOleObject::DoVerb*, except for OLEIVERB-_OPEN, can start in-place activation. To fully support in-place objects, a container needs to include a MSG structure telling the object what mouse message caused the activation. In Patron, activating an object with a double click occurs in *CPage::OnLeftDoubleClick* (in PAGEMOUS.CPP), which creates a MSG structure with WM_LBUTTONDBLCLK in it. This structure is sent to *CTenant::ActivateObject* along with OLEIVERB_PRIMARY, which then sends the structure to *IOleObject::DoVerb*. Because Patron also supports inside-out objects, it sends a WM_LBUTTONDOWN message with OLEIVERB_UI-ACTIVATE within *CTenant::Select* (which is called whenever the user clicks on a tenant to select it).

In other activation cases, such as those in response to menu commands, we don't need to send a message structure at all. This also applies for objects marked OLEMISC_ACTIVATEWHENVISIBLE. As you can see in *CTenant-::Load*, Patron will call *DoVerb(OLEIVERB_INPLACEACTIVATE)* for such an object so that it is always at least in-place active. In this case, we do not need to send a message to *DoVerb* either.

So now how do we deactivate the object? This should happen whenever the user clicks *either* mouse button outside the object. Patron picks up these events in *CPage::OnLeftDown* or *CPage::OnRightDown* (in PAGEMOUS.CPP). The appropriate function then calls *CTenant::DeactivateInPlaceObject*, which in turn calls *IOleInPlaceObject:: InPlaceDeactivate*, as shown in the code on the following page.

```
void CTenant::DeactivateInPlaceObject(BOOL fFull)
    {
    if (NULL!=m_pIOleIPObject)
        {
        if ((OLEMISC_ACTIVATEWHENVISIBLE & m_grfMisc) && !fFull)
            m_pIOleIPObject->UIDeactivate();
        else
            m_pIOleIPObject->InPlaceDeactivate();
        }

    return;
    }
```

*InPlaceDeactivate*, unless told otherwise, only deactivates the UI for an object marked OLEMISC_ACTIVATEWHENVISIBLE, which leaves it in-place active only. Otherwise, we deactivate the object, returning it to the running state. (See the following sidebar.)

Clicking outside the object is not the only event that can cause deactivation. Basically, you should deactivate if any event occurs that would create or activate a different object (such as a drag-and-drop operation) or that would require the object to be in the loaded state (such as closing the document or application). This latter case is handled in *CTenant::Close*, which calls *CTenant::DeactivateInPlaceObject* before calling *IOleObject::Close*.

When the user clicks inside an object with the activate-when-visible property, the object will call the container's *IOleInPlaceSite::OnUIActivate* function, at which time you should deactivate the object that was UI active. If that other object has the activate-when-visible property, you call only its *IOleInPlaceObject::UIDeactivate* function, as shown in the preceding code.

## EXPERIENCE: The Object Is Still Running

After you deactivate an in-place object, that object will still be in the running state, not the loaded state. *IOleObject::Close* is required to change the state. OLE does this to ensure quick reactivation by eliminating server load time. Therefore, the object's state is not reset between in-place activations. If you crash your container while debugging it, a local server might remain in memory with an undetermined state and a hidden window. You'll need to use a tool such as PVIEW to terminate the server so that you can run your container again with a fresh state.

## Mix-a-Menu: Shaken, Not Stirred

Now that we can activate and deactivate an object, it's time to start allowing the object to merge its user interface with the container's. To handle the shared menu, we need to implement the *InsertMenus, RemoveMenus,* and *Set-Menu* members of *IOleInPlaceFrame.* In addition, we need to do a little work now in *IOleInPlaceSite::OnUIDeactivate* to handle menu switches correctly.

### IOleInPlaceFrame::InsertMenus

The container has the easy part in creating the shared menu—it gets to stuff an empty menu with its own items whenever the object calls *IOleInPlace-Frame::InsertMenus.* (The poor object has to work with a partially populated menu.) Patron's implementation (PATRON.CPP) copies menu handles from its normal top-level menu for the File, the Container, and the Window groups and adds those items to the shared menu by calling the Windows API function *InsertMenu.* (Windows has no problem with multiple top-level menus sharing items.)

```
STDMETHODIMP CPatronFrame::InsertMenus(HMENU hMenu
    , LPOLEMENUGROUPWIDTHS pMGW)
    {
    InsertMenu(hMenu, 0, MF_BYPOSITION | MF_POPUP, (UINT)m_phMenu[0]
        , PSZ(IDS_FILEMENU));
    InsertMenu(hMenu, 1, MF_BYPOSITION | MF_POPUP, (UINT)m_phMenu[2]
        , PSZ(IDS_PAGEMENU));

    pMGW->width[0]=1;
    pMGW->width[2]=1;

#ifdef MDI
    InsertMenu(hMenu, 2, MF_BYPOSITION | MF_POPUP
        , (UINT)m_hMenuWindow, PSZ(IDS_WINDOWMENU));

    pMGW->width[4]=1;
#else
    pMGW->width[4]=0;
#endif

    return NOERROR;
    }
```

Conveniently, all of Patron's pop-up menu handles are already stored in the *CPatronFrame* array *m_phMenu.*[6] Patron uses strings from its stringtable for the item names. Because we are working with a clean menu, we can use constants to specify the positions of these items. We need to store only the width of our groups in the OLEMENUGROUPWIDTHS array.

---

6. Patron uses *m_phMenu* in processing WM_INITMENUPOPUP messages for enabling and disabling menu items. See *CPatronFrame::UpdateMenus* (in PATRON.CPP). That function works without a hitch even with a shared menu.

### *IOleInPlaceFrame::RemoveMenus*

By the time *RemoveMenus* is called, the object has already finished the more tedious work of removing its menus from the shared menu. So when we get the menu back at this point, all we have to do is remove the items we know we added. The best way to implement this function is to walk through the menu, removing any pop-up menu handles we recognize:

```
STDMETHODIMP CPatronFrame::RemoveMenus(HMENU hMenu)
    {
    int         cItems, i, j;
    HMENU       hMenuT;

    if (NULL==hMenu)
        return NOERROR;

    cItems=GetMenuItemCount(hMenu);

    for (i=cItems; i>=0; i--)
        {
        hMenuT=GetSubMenu(hMenu, i);

        for (j=0; j<=CMENUS; j++)
            {
            if (hMenuT==m_phMenu[j])
                RemoveMenu(hMenu, i, MF_BYPOSITION);
            }
        }

    //The menu should now be empty.
    return NOERROR;
    }
```

This defensive programming practice eliminates the possibility that any of our popups remain on this menu after we've finished with it, because as soon as we return, the object usually calls *DestroyMenu* on the whole shared menu. If any popups still exist, they too are destroyed. This doesn't bode well if those popups are also on our normal menu. Because we can't ensure that the object cleans up its pop-up menus properly, we should be sure we clean up ours.

### *IOleInPlaceFrame::SetMenu*

This frame function is called for either of two reasons: to display a shared menu or to tell the container to reinstate its original menu. The latter happens during an object's UI deactivation. Patron handles this call as follows:

```
STDMETHODIMP CPatronFrame::SetMenu(HMENU hMenu
    , HOLEMENU hOLEMenu, HWND hWndObj)
```

```
{
HRESULT          hr;
PCPatronClient   pCL=(PCPatronClient)m_pCL;

if (NULL==hMenu && NULL==hOLEMenu)
    {
    m_hWndObj=NULL;

    //Prevent redundant calls, or debug warnings on startup.
    if (NULL==m_hMenuTop)
        return NOERROR;

    hMenu=m_hMenuTop;
    m_hMenuTop=NULL;
    }
else
    {
    m_hMenuTop=m_hMenuOrg;
    m_hWndObj=hWndObj;
    }

pCL->SetMenu(m_hWnd, hMenu, m_hMenuWindow);
hr=OleSetMenuDescriptor(hOLEMenu, m_hWnd, hWndObj, NULL, NULL);
return hr;
}
```

If you receive a non-NULL menu handle in this function, you will also get a non-NULL HOLEMENU, which is merely a value you pass through to *OleSetMenuDescriptor*—this will either install or deinstall OLE's menu filtering, depending on whether a shared menu is present. OLE will send messages for the object's menus to the *hWndObj* window.

If *hMenu* and *hOLEMenu* are NULL, you should reinstall your normal menu. In the preceding code, Patron has its original top-level menu in *m_hMenuOrg* and saves the current top-level menu in *m_hMenuTop*. If we are reinstating the original menu, we set the argument *hMenu* to *m_hMenuTop*. Then, regardless of which menu we display, *CPatronClient::SetMenu* will make it visible (through the Windows API functions *SetMenu* and *DrawMenuBar*).

### IOleInPlaceSite::OnUIDeactivate

The last thing to do for menu handling is to implement part of *IOleInPlaceSite::OnUIDeactivate*. This function has to reinstate the container's original menu as part of the deactivation process. Any shared menu has already been disassembled by this time. The reason we reinstate the menu ourselves is that not every object will call *IOleInPlaceFrame::SetMenu.*[7] In Patron, *IOleIn-PlaceSite::OnUIDeactivate* calls an internal function, *CPatronFrame::ReinstateUI*, which calls another internal function, *CPatronFrame::ShowUIAndTools.* Among other things, this function calls our own *CPatronFrame::SetMenu(NULL, NULL, NULL)*, the interface member itself.

Once you have completed this implementation, test your shared menu with the object, activating and deactivating a few times to be sure things work correctly. (See the following sidebar.) If you experience problems with menu placement or command routing, check your *IOleInPlaceFrame::InsertMenus* code and be sure that you're filling OLEMENUGROUPWIDTHS correctly.

---

### EXPERIENCE: Menu Destruction—Just Do It (Right)

When developing Patron and Cosmo for this chapter and for Chapter 23, I had a really weird problem. The shared menu displayed in the first activation was perfect. On the second activation, however, the top-level menu appeared fine but no drop-down portions of the menu appeared. Hmmm. On the third activation, I got a bunch of vertically cascaded menu items on the top-level menu instead of the usual horizontal menu bar! What was going on? This was a real head-banger. I tried all sorts of combinations, but the problem was actually in the object's (Cosmo's) menu destruction code, in which Cosmo was not removing one of its own menu items properly.[8] When Cosmo called *DestroyMenu* to clean up the shared menu, it was destroying one of its own popups. Now the menu had an invalid handle in it that was still used to create the shared menu the next time around. Invalid menu handles cause all sorts of neat problems. If you encounter menu weirdness while writing a container program, try modifying your *RemoveMenus* function to remove all items on the menu, regardless of their origin. If that fixes it, the menu is not being cleaned up properly. If your container is removing its menus properly, the problem is most likely in the object's code. This is especially likely when you're developing containers and objects simultaneously! Otherwise, I hope you have a phone number for the object's lead developer!

---

7. Chapter 23 recommends that objects do make this call.

8. The problem turned out to be a constant, CMENUS, in Cosmo's RESOURCE.H file, which was incorrectly compiled assuming SDI for an MDI version of Cosmo. The bug was in the make file, of all places, which didn't define an MDI symbol properly!

## Negotiate Tool Space

Those pesky little objects are now going to make demands on the container for their own in-place tools. But being the good citizens that we are, we'll negotiate with the objects by implementing the *IOleInPlaceUIWindow::RequestBorderSpace* function for both our frame and our document windows. Negotiating objects will fill a BORDERWIDTHS structure and pass it to this function for your consideration. If you accept, you'll get a call to *IOleInPlaceUIWindow::SetBorderSpace* to actually allocate the space. Some objects might simply call *SetBorderSpace* first, and you have to handle that case. Anyway, if *SetBorderSpace* succeeds, the object will most likely then call *IOleInPlaceUIWindow::GetBorder* to ask for the size of the window in question. These functions all work on device units (pixels) and not HIMETRIC units, as many other parts of OLE do. Everything we do here is oriented toward the screen, so we don't need any fancy units.

Within *SetBorderSpace*, a container needs to reposition its various windows when asked to make space for tools. A container should try its best to keep the object in the same absolute position on the screen. After we look at the three member functions, we'll see what this means for our container.

### GetBorder

This function is relatively easy to implement. Simply return the client-area rectangle for the appropriate window if you have no restrictions about where an object can place tools. The rectangle represents the space (the amount can be negotiated) from which the object can make requests for the space it needs and also provides the object with the dimensions it should use when creating tools. Any space you do not include in the rectangle is strictly off-limits to the object. Patron itself makes no restrictions for its document window, but it excludes the status line area for the frame window, as we can see in the following code:

```
//From IIPUIWIN.CPP
STDMETHODIMP CImpIOleInPlaceUIWindow::GetBorder(LPRECT prcBorder)
    {
    if (NULL==prcBorder)
        return ResultFromScode(E_INVALIDARG);

    GetClientRect(m_pDoc->m_hWnd, prcBorder);
    return NOERROR;
    }

//From PATRON.CPP
STDMETHODIMP CPatronFrame::GetBorder(LPRECT prcBorder)
```

*(continued)*

```
{
if (NULL==prcBorder)
    return ResultFromScode(E_INVALIDARG);

GetClientRect(m_hWnd, prcBorder);
prcBorder->bottom-=CYSTATSTRIP;  //Height of status line

return NOERROR;
}
```

### RequestBorderSpace

Implementing this function can range from quite trivial to extravagantly complicated, depending on how picky you want to be about giving away border space. If you are not picky at all, simply return NOERROR from this function, as Patron does.

If you have some restrictions, you need to check each of the values in the BORDERWIDTHS structure passed to this function. BORDERWIDTHS has the fields *left*, *top*, *right*, and *bottom*, which specify how much space the object wants on each side of the window in question (frame or document). If you can grant the space, return NOERROR; otherwise, return INPLACE_E_NO-TOOLSPACE.

### SetBorderSpace

Two important things happen inside *SetBorderSpace*: if the container can grant the request, it should move its windows around to make room for the object's allocation and then remember those allocations so that it can resize its client-area windows properly when resizing the frame or document window.

Objects are allowed to call *SetBorderSpace* directly without first calling *RequestBorderSpace*—so don't assume a particular calling sequence. It's easy to have your *SetBorderSpace* call your own *RequestBorderSpace* to validate the object's request, returning INPLACE_E_NOTOOLSPACE to deny the request. The object must resort to negotiation at that point.

At the same time that it holds the object's request, the BORDER-WIDTHS pointer passed from the object can be NULL or the structure to which it points can contain zeros. In the former case, the object is telling us that it doesn't need any tools itself and that we can leave all of our tools visible. Most OLE Controls do exactly this (as does the Polyline sample from Chapter 23). If we're given a BORDERWIDTHS full of zeros, the object doesn't want anyone's tools to appear, so we have to remove all of ours (excluding the status line) even though the object isn't going to create its own.

When you know what border space to allocate on all four sides of the window in question, you need to remember those allocations in case the user resizes the window. Patron's *CFrame::SetBorderSpace* saves these values, which are used later in the WM_SIZE case of *CPatronFrame::FMessageHook* to resize the client-area window (managed in the *CPatronClient* class) so that it doesn't overlap any of the object's tools. This is pretty basic code.

The trickiest aspect of *SetBorderSpace* is the initial resizing and repositioning of the client-area window, which is generally necessary to accommodate the object's space request. The trick is that you should, if at all possible, keep the object's window in the same place on the screen regardless of what other windows you need to move around. The reason for this is that the user will be staring at the object in the document. The less you have to move that object, the less disconcerting the user interface changes will be to the user. This means that new object tools might overlap the object itself, but that is better than always shifting that embedded object around on the screen and giving the end user a case of the jitters.

Inside *CPatronFrame::SetBorderSpace*, Patron calculates the current position of the site (and therefore the object) and calculates the number of pixels, in both horizontal and vertical directions, that we'll have to scroll everything in the document to counter any change in the position of the client-area window. In other words, if we have to move the client-area window down by 10 pixels and right by 18, we need to move everything in the document up by 10 pixels and left by 18, because as children of the client-area window, the document's elements would otherwise move with the parent.

Unless the new border space requests require no repositioning of the client-area window, Patron's *SetBorderSpace* function calls *CPatronClient::MoveWithoutFamily* (in CLIENT.CPP), passing the new rectangle that the client window should occupy along with the differences between the old window position and the new one. *MoveWithoutFamily* moves the client window first and then moves all its children in the opposite direction. Truly the parent is leaving its family behind, as you can see in the following code:

```
void CPatronClient::MoveWithoutFamily(LPRECT prc, int dx, int dy)
    {
    RECT        rc;
    HWND        hWndFrame;
    HWND        hWnd;
    POINT       pt;

    hWndFrame=GetParent(m_hWnd);
    SendMessage(hWndFrame, WM_SETREDRAW, FALSE, 0L);

    ShowWindow(m_hWnd, SW_HIDE);
    SetWindowPos(m_hWnd, NULL, prc->left, prc->top
        , prc->right-prc->left, prc->bottom-prc->top
        , SWP_NOZORDER | SWP_NOACTIVATE);
```

*(continued)*

```
//Move all children of client.
hWnd=GetWindow(m_hWnd, GW_CHILD);

while (NULL!=hWnd)
    {
    GetWindowRect(hWnd, &rc);
    SETPOINT(pt, rc.left, rc.top);
    ScreenToClient(m_hWnd, &pt);

    if (pt.x!=dx && pt.y!=dy && !IsZoomed(hWnd))
        {
        //Move window in opposite direction of client.
        SetWindowPos(hWnd, NULL, pt.x-dx, pt.y-dy
            , rc.right-rc.left, rc.bottom-rc.top
            , SWP_NOZORDER | SWP_NOACTIVATE | SWP_NOSIZE);
        }

    hWnd=GetWindow(hWnd, GW_HWNDNEXT);
    }

SendMessage(hWndFrame, WM_SETREDRAW, TRUE, 0L);
ShowWindow(m_hWnd, SW_SHOW);

return;
}
```

The use of WM_SETREDRAW on the frame prevents the user from seeing some serious jitters. Without it, the user would see all the windows first move with the client and then move back one by one. To avoid this, we disable repaints and hide the client before moving anything. After moving everything, we reenable repaints and force an update by showing the client again.

---

## EXPERIENCE: The Jitters and *DeferWindowPos*

*BeginDeferWindowPos*, *DeferWindowPos*, and *EndDeferWindowPos* will not move a collection of container windows together, as we need to do here. These functions turn into no-ops when the windows you send to *DeferWindowPos* are not all siblings. Thus, you cannot use these functions to move a parent window and its children at the same time. *EndDeferWindowPos* indicates that the process worked (returns TRUE), but nothing actually happens. Hence the solution used in Patron.

---

> ### EXPERIENCE: Take Care
> ### with *IOleClientSite::ShowObject*
>
> In Chapter 17, Patron first implemented *ShowObject* to scroll an object into view if less than a quarter of it was visible. Such an action can easily ruin all the effort you put into keeping that object steady when activating in place, so if you've seen a call to *IOleInPlaceSite::OnInPlaceActivate*, don't scroll your document if any part of the object is visible—scroll only if the entire object is completely out of view.

### Repaint Optimizations

Switching the user interface around can cause considerable flickering and flashing as tools appear and disappear. Consider, for example, the case in which the container has an in-place object fully activated—user interface and all—so that the object's shared menu and tools are displayed. Now the end user immediately jumps over and double-clicks on another in-place object. Without any optimizations, the first object's tools disappear, the container's tools reappear, and then the second object is activated, causing the container's tools to disappear again and the new tools to appear. Blech! We'd like to prevent any excess work in making these changes, which applies to switching menus around as well.

The *OLE Programmer's Reference* documents some techniques for minimizing repaints that affect *IOleInPlaceSite::OnUIActivate* and *OnUIDeactivate*. It also suggests the creation of frame-level functions to add or remove specific user interface elements. In Patron, these are implemented as *CPatronFrame::ShowUIAndTools* and *CPatronFrame::ReinstateUI*. (The variable *m_fOurTools-Showing* determines whether *CPatronFrame::FMessageHook* will take the UI-active object's border space requests into consideration when processing WM_SIZE, as described earlier.)

```
void CPatronFrame::ShowUIAndTools(BOOL fShow, BOOL fMenu)
    {
    HWND    hWndTB;

    //This is the only menu case....Restore our original menu.
    if (fMenu && fShow)
        SetMenu(NULL, NULL, NULL);

    hWndTB=m_pTB->Window();
    ShowWindow(hWndTB, fShow ? SW_SHOW : SW_HIDE);
```

*(continued)*

1051

```
if (fShow)
    {
    InvalidateRect(hWndTB, NULL, TRUE);
    UpdateWindow(hWndTB);
    }

m_fOurToolsShowing=fShow;
return;
}


void CPatronFrame::ReinstateUI(void)
    {
    BORDERWIDTHS    bw;

    ShowUIAndTools(TRUE, TRUE);
    SetRect((LPRECT)&bw, 0, m_cyBar, 0, 0,);
    SetBorderSpace(&bw);
    return;
    }
```

These functions are then used within *IOleInPlaceSite::OnUIActivate* and *IOleInPlaceSite::OnUIDeactivate*, which themselves involve a number of Patron's functions. The code is rather lengthy, so here's a description of the process instead:

- When the user clicks or double-clicks on a tenant other than the UI-active one, we end up in *CTenant::Select*. This calls *CTenant::DeactivateInPlaceObject*, which we've already seen. No matter what type of object is in the tenant, we'll at least deactivate its UI.

- UI deactivation calls *IOleInPlaceSite::OnUIDeactivate*, which returns immediately if the variable *g_fSwitchingActive* is TRUE. (See below.) If we're also shutting down the object, we call *CPatronFrame::ReinstateUI* and we've finished.

- Otherwise, *IOleInPlaceSite::OnUIDeactivate* checks whether there's a double-click message in the message queue (calling *PeekMessage*). If not, it calls *CPatronFrame::ReinstateUI* and we've finished as usual. Also, because the user might have double-clicked on another in-place–capable object, we defer changing the UI by setting the variable *CPages::m_fAddUI*.

- If another object becomes UI active in response to this double click, we end up in *IOleInPlaceSite::OnUIActivate*. This first sets *CPages::m_fAddUI* to FALSE because *CPage::OnLeftDoubleClick* will check this flag later, and if it is still TRUE, *CPage::OnLeftDoubleClick* will, only then, call *CPatronFrame::ShowUIAndTools* to reinstall Patron's normal user interface. By setting the flag to FALSE here, we avoid Patron changing any of the frame UI itself, leaving that to the newly activated object.

■ *IOleInPlaceSite::OnUIActivate* then calls *CPage::SwitchActiveTenant* to change the selected tenant without trying to deactivate the previously selected tenant again—it has already been deactivated. While this is going on, *g_fSwitchingActive* is set to TRUE.

■ *IOleInPlaceSite::OnUIActivate* calls *CPatronDoc::NoObjectFrameTools* to determine whether there are any other object's tools visible at this time. It then passes the result (TRUE if there are no tools) to *CPatronFrame::ShowUIAndTools*, with the second argument set to FALSE (so as not to affect the menu). So, if no object tools are visible, the frame will now show its own. This handles the case in which we did indeed activate a new object, but that new object has no tools itself, so we need to display the container's.

I admit that this isn't perfect. For one thing, it's single-threaded because we make use of a global variable. Second, the check for a double click doesn't include a check for a single click on an inside-out object. You would still see some flicker in that circumstance. Finally, this code uses functions and variables in almost every internal object inside Patron: *CPatronFrame*, *CPatronDoc*, *CPage*, *CPages*, and *CTenant*. Not the cleanest model because such optimizations were an afterthought and had to deal with the existing structures and the permissions each had to access the other. Certainly this could stand improvement, but I hope it will give you a good idea of what is needed to support these optimizations.

## Testing It All

It's a good idea to stop here and test everything you've done by using a few different in-place–capable objects. Check that all the menus, toolbars, and other user interface elements show up correctly and that you can keep those objects fixed when shifting around the tools. A good test to see whether you've repositioned windows correctly is to drag a document window (assuming an MDI container) around and watch where the mouse is allowed to go. If you resized your client-area window to not overlap any of the object's tools, the mouse will be restricted to the visible client area. Otherwise, you'll see that you can move the mouse into the area occupied by tools and leave the document window there, perhaps with its caption bar completely hidden!

Also try resizing the frame window to be sure that the client is still resized properly by using the same test. You will notice after resizing the frame (or the document) that the object's tools are not resized to match. That's some of the polish we'll add in the section "Round the Corners: Other Miscellany" later in this chapter. But first let's handle accelerators.

## Provide In-Place Accelerators and Focus

As described earlier, a UI-active object always has first crack at accelerators and keystrokes. If the UI-active object is an in-process object, the container's message loop will pick up accelerators first. To accommodate this possibility, the container must call *IOleInPlaceActiveObject::TranslateAccelerator* in its message loop before translating any of its own accelerators. If the object uses the keystroke, the container must now also use it. Patron handles this in its *CPatronFrame::MessageLoop*, in which *m_hAccel* contains its normal accelerators and *m_hAccelIP* contains those accelerators that are available with a UI-active object:[9]

```
WPARAM CPatronFrame::MessageLoop(void)
    {
    MSG     msg;

    while (GetMessage(&msg, NULL, 0, 0))
        {
        HACCEL      hAccel=m_hAccel;

        //Always give object first crack at translation.
        if (NULL!=m_pIOleIPActiveObject)
            {
            HRESULT         hr;

            hAccel=m_hAccelIP;
            hr=m_pIOleIPActiveObject->TranslateAccelerator(&msg);

            //If object translated the accelerator, we're done.
            if (NOERROR==hr)
                continue;
            }
        if (!m_pCL->TranslateAccelerator(&msg))
            {
            //hAccel is either normal or in place.
            if (!::TranslateAccelerator(m_hWnd, hAccel, &msg))
```

9. In C++, *::TranslateAccelerator* calls the globally named Windows API. We need this because *CPatronFrame* has a *TranslateAccelerator* member function that would be called if we left off the *::* at the beginning of the function name. Don't feel bad if you didn't know this already—I had to ask other people how to do this when writing this code.

```
            {
            TranslateMessage(&msg);
            DispatchMessage(&msg);
            }
        }
    }

return msg.wParam;
    }
```

If *IOleInPlaceActiveObject::TranslateAccelerator* does not process the key-stroke, we can resume our message loop as usual. This function is set up in such a way that when we're not servicing an in-place object, we use our normal accelerators. When we have an *IOleInPlaceActiveObject* pointer, however, which is the in-place session flag for Patron's frame, we use the in-place accelerators.

Now, if the object is implemented in a local server, its message loop will pick up the keystroke messages first. The server processes its own accelerators immediately, but if it doesn't use a particular message, it must pass the message to *OleTranslateAccelerator* along with the OLEINPLACEFRAMEINFO structure it received from our own *IOleInPlaceSite::GetWindowContext* and the *IOleInPlaceFrame* pointer obtained at the same time. The OLEINPLACEFRAME-INFO structure holds our container's in-place accelerators, and *OleTranslateAccelerator* uses this table to determine whether the keystroke matches any accelerator in the table (or one for an MDI Window menu if the structure's *fMDIApp* flag is set). If a match is found, *OleTranslateAccelerator* passes the message and the command ID to *IOleInPlaceFrame::TranslateAccelerator*; otherwise, it returns to the server's message loop with S_FALSE so that the server can process the message.

As the container is given the command ID, implementing *IOleInPlaceFrame::TranslateAccelerator* is fairly easy: just invoke the correct command. (Patron does this through *CPatronFrame::OnCommand*.) An MDI container should also call *TranslateMDISysAccel* to handle the Window menu:

```
STDMETHODIMP CPatronFrame::TranslateAccelerator(LPMSG pMSG, WORD wID)
    {
    SCODE       sc;

    if ((IDM_PAGENEWPAGE <= wID && IDM_PAGELASTPAGE >= wID)
        || IDM_OPENOBJECT==wID || IDM_ENTERCONTEXTHELP==wID)
        || IDM_ESCAPECONTEXTHELP==wID)
        {
        //wID properly expands to 32 bits.
        OnCommand(m_hWnd, (WPARAM)wID, 0L);
        sc=S_OK;
```

*(continued)*

1055

```
    }
#ifdef MDI
  else if (TranslateMDISysAccel(m_pCL->Window(), pMSG))
      sc=S_OK;
#endif
  else
      sc=S_FALSE;

  return ResultFromScode(sc);
  }
```

There is one more step to make accelerators work properly. Whenever there's a UI-active object, the container must ensure that the object has the keyboard focus so that keyboard messages are marked for the correct window. The object will initially take the focus itself when it becomes UI active, but if the user switches away from the container and back again, the container will receive a WM_SETFOCUS message. Window's default processing of this message will set the focus to the frame window, which is not what we want. To set it to the UI-active object, the container must call *SetFocus* on the window returned from *IOleInPlaceActiveObject::GetWindow*:

```
case WM_SETFOCUS:
    if (NULL!=m_pIOleIPActiveObject)
        {
        HWND     hWndObj;

        m_pIOleIPActiveObject->GetWindow(&hWndObj);
        SetFocus(hWndObj);
        }

    break;
```

> **NOTE:** Avoid the temptation to pass the ill-named *hWndObj* argument from *IOleInPlaceFrame::SetMenu* to *SetFocus* because this might be the frame window handle of the object's server. If that were the case, your container would never get the focus at all. If you tried to reactivate your container's frame window, you would see it briefly flash active but then become inactive again when you made this *SetFocus* call. To bypass any problems, always use the window handle from *IOleInPlaceActiveObject::GetWindow*.

## Round the Corners: Other Miscellany

To finish up a complete container, we need to make a number of minor modifications, some of which are required and others of which are optional:

■ (Required) Call *IOleInPlaceActiveObject::OnFrameWindowActivate* and
*OnDocWindowActivate* when your frame and document windows
receive WM _ ACTIVATEAPP and WM _ MDIACTIVATE messages.
Switching document windows might also mean restoring your
container's normal UI.

■ (Required) Call *IOleInPlaceActiveObject::ResizeBorder* when either
your frame or your document window is resized so that the UI-active
object can adjust its tools.

■ (Required) Call *IOleInPlaceObject::SetObjectRects* whenever you scroll
the document or otherwise change the position and clipping rectangles of the object in relation to the document window (the
object's parent). Also implement *IOleInPlaceSite::OnPosRectChange*
and *IOleInPlaceSite::Scroll*.

■ (Required) Implement minimal context-sensitive help support in
case the server supports it, even if you don't.

■ (Required) Provide minimal Undo support by calling *IOleObject-
::DoVerb(OLEIVERB_ DISCARDUNDOSTATE)* when making a change
after deactivation and by implementing *IOleInPlaceSite::Deacti-
vateAndUndo*.

■ (Optional) If you have an Undo command, call *IOleInPlaceObject-
::ReactivateAndUndo* if the command is given immediately after
deactivation. Also implement *IOleInPlaceSite::DiscardUndoState*.

■ (Optional) Provide a Ctrl+Enter accelerator to generate a call to
*IOleObject::DoVerb(OLEIVERB_OPEN)*.

■ (Optional) If you have a status line, implement *IOleInPlaceFrame-
::SetStatusText*.

■ (Optional) If you have modeless pop-up windows that are typically
shown as part of your user interface, show/enable or hide/disable
these when *IOleInPlaceFrame::EnableModeless* is called. You can
tell an object to do the same by calling *IOleInPlaceActiveObject-
::EnableModeless* when displaying a modal user interface yourself.

The following sections briefly discuss each of these modifications.

### Call *IOleInPlaceActiveObject::On[Frame | Document]WindowActivate*

For the frame window, process the WM_ACTIVATEAPP message and call *IOleInPlaceActiveObject::OnFrameWindowActivate* if you have a UI-active object from *IOleInPlaceFrame::SetActiveObject*. The argument to *OnFrameWindowActivate* is a BOOL indicating whether the frame window is becoming active (TRUE) or inactive (FALSE). You can see a demonstration of this in *CPatronFrame::FMessageHook*.

Document switching is a little more complex, but it applies only to an MDI application. You need to process the WM_MDIACTIVATE message and check whether there is a UI-active object in the document at all. If there is, you need to call *IOleInPlaceActiveObject::OnDocWindowActivate* with a BOOL indicating activation (TRUE) or deactivation (FALSE) of the window itself. In response, the object will deactivate or activate its own UI (calling *IOleInPlaceSite* members accordingly). On the other hand, if a document window is becoming active and does not have a UI-active object in it, the container should reinstate its own frame UI. All of this occurs in *CPatronDoc::FMessageHook*, which calls *CPatronFrame::ReinstateUI* when activating a document without a UI-active object. The result is that switching documents will switch the necessary UI, depending on the contents of the documents.

### Call *IOleInPlaceActiveObject::ResizeBorder*

Because a UI-active object initially calls *IOleInPlaceUIWindow::GetBorder* to obtain the dimensions with which to create its in-place tools, a container has to tell the UI-active object when those dimensions change by calling *IOleInPlaceActiveObject::ResizeBorder*. The container passes the new size of the window (a RECT), the appropriate *IOleInPlaceUIWindow* pointer for the frame or document window, and a flag, *fFrame*, to indicate which window was resized. In response, the object will renegotiate for tool space and resize its tools as necessary. Patron makes these calls from within the WM_SIZE cases of *CPatronFrame::FMessageHook* and *CPatronDoc::FMessageHook*, calling *GetClientRect* to determine the rectangle and passing the other arguments as appropriate.

Be careful with the *fFrame* argument. When I first wrote this code, my document passed a TRUE and all sorts of wild things started happening as the object was resizing its frame tools to the dimensions of the document window. It was a hard bug to find, so give your implementation a little extra care.

## Call *IOleInPlaceObject::SetObjectRects* and Flush Out *IOleInPlaceSite*

Remember when we implemented *IOleInPlaceSite::GetWindowContext*? This function returned initial position and clipping rectangles to the object. If you scroll the document, however, you change these rectangles and must pass new values to all in-place–active objects, not only the UI-active object, by calling *IOleInPlaceObject::SetObjectRects* for each. Whenever Patron detects that scrolling has occurred, it will call *CPage::ScrolledWindow*, which loops over all the tenants in the page, calling *CTenant::UpdateInPlaceObjectRects* in each. This function calculates the new position rectangle based on the current scroll position and calls *IOleInPlaceObject::SetObjectRects* if that tenant holds an in-place–active object.

*CTenant::UpdateInPlaceObjectRects* also handles calls that come into *IOleInPlaceSite::OnPosRectChange*. An object will call this with a rectangle whenever it needs a larger position rectangle in the container. This might be in response to the user resizing the object with its own grab handles or to the object executing some command to change a scaling factor.

You can handle this in the container in two ways. Both methods end in a call to *IOleInPlaceObject::SetObjectRects* once again. First, you can restrict the object's size to the size of the site or to whatever other limit you want to enforce. In this case, you'll call *SetObjectRects* again with the rectangle of your choice. The object can choose to display (or remove) scrollbars as adornments, or it can scale the object as it sees fit. The other method is to let the object grow by passing whatever rectangle the object passed to you back to *IOleInPlaceObject::SetObjectRects*. In any case, the container controls the space the object occupies in the container, but the object controls how the object decides to use that space for scaling or whatever.

Besides the end user scrolling the document directly, the object can ask the container to scroll programmatically by calling *IOleInPlaceSite::Scroll*. This is useful when the object knows that it is clipped by the document window but the end user has done something to indicate that he or she would like to see that part of the object. Thus, Patron implements this function as follows:

```
STDMETHODIMP CImpIOleInPlaceSite::Scroll(SIZE sz)
    {
    int        x, y;

    x=m_pTen->m_pPG->m_xPos+sz.cx;
    y=m_pTen->m_pPG->m_yPos+sz.cy;
```

*(continued)*

```
SendScrollPosition(m_pTen->m_hWnd, WM_HSCROLL, x);
SendScrollPosition(m_pTen->m_hWnd, WM_VSCROLL, y);
return NOERROR;
}
```

The *SendScrollPosition* macros (INC\BOOK1632.H) here cause the document to scroll, which will generate calls to *IOleInPlaceObject::SetObjectRects* once again.

## Implement Minimal Context-Sensitive Help Support

Even if a container does not understand context-sensitive help, it must support an object that does. This means that a container must implement accelerators for Shift+F1 (enter mode) and Esc (exit mode) and process them as follows. (*fEnterMode* is TRUE on Shift+F1 and FALSE on Esc.)

1. Call your own *IOleInPlaceFrame::ContextSensitiveHelp(fEnterMode)*.

2. If your application is an SDI application, have the frame implementation call *IOleInPlaceActiveObject::ContextSensitiveHelp(fEnterMode)*.

3. If your application is an MDI application, have the frame implementation call *IOleInPlaceUIWindow::ContextSensitiveHelp(fEnterMode)* for each document. Patron does this in *CPatronClient::CallContextHelpOnDocuments*.

4. For MDI documents, have their *IOleInPlaceUIWindow* implementations call *IOleInPlaceActiveObject::ContextSensitiveHelp(fEnterMode)*.

If the object detects Shift+F1 or Esc, it will call your *IOleInPlaceSite::ContextSensitiveHelp*, which should be implemented as follows:

- If your application is an SDI application, call your document window's *IOleInPlaceUIWindow::ContextSensitiveHelp(fEnterMode)*.

- If your application is an MDI application, call the frame window's *IOleInPlaceFrame::ContextSensitiveHelp(fEnterMode)*, which will propagate the mode to all the documents.

There are some special considerations for an application that is both a container and a server and that has its own object embedded within itself. See the *OLE Programmer's Reference* for more details.

## Provide Minimal Undo Support

Even if the container does not have an Undo command (à la Patron), it still has two small responsibilities in that regard. First, it must implement *IOleInPlaceSite::DeactivateAndUndo* by calling *IOleInPlaceObject::InPlaceDeactivate*:

```
STDMETHODIMP CImpIOleInPlaceSite::DeactivateAndUndo(void)
   {
   m_pTen->m_pIOleIPObject->InPlaceDeactivate();
   return NOERROR;
   }
```

Second, whenever the object is deactivated, the container should call *IOleObject::DoVerb* with OLEIVERB_DISCARDUNDOSTATE. Why do we do this? Read on. It's important if you have an Undo command of your own—or if you are just exceptionally curious.

### Support Your Own Undo Command

Applications that support Undo operations generally save some Undo information whenever a change takes place. An application such as this will have this state when it activates an in-place object. If the first thing a user does afterward is choose an Undo command, the object will call your *IOleInPlaceSite::DeactivateAndUndo*. At this time, you deactivate the object and undo the last change in the container. You do this because activation and deactivation are not considered separate undoable actions, so the container reverses the last action that occurred before the Undo. If the user makes any changes to the object, it will call the container's *IOleInPlaceSite::DiscardUndoState*, at which time you can discard the last change state. Thus you hold the Undo state only as long as needed.

Now let's go the other direction. Suppose we just deactivated an object in a container and the user chooses Undo. We need to undo the deactivation and tell the object to undo its last change (which is one reason the object remains running after being deactivated). So the container calls *IOleInPlaceObject::ReactivateAndUndo*. If you make some other change before the Undo occurs, you have to tell the object to discard whatever Undo state it might have by calling *IOleObject::DoVerb(OLEIVERB_DISCARDUNDOSTATE)*.

The *fUndoable* flag passed to *IOleInPlaceSite::OnUIDeactivate* tells the container whether the object supports this sort of Undo at all.

### Provide an Open Accelerator

If you want, you can add a Ctrl+Enter accelerator for in-place activation that would generate a call to *IOleObject::DoVerb(OLEIVERB_OPEN)* to take an object from the in-place–active state to the open state. The object will generally also provide a way to do this on its own menus, so don't add a menu item, simply add the accelerator. Of course, you can use this accelerator all the time if you want, even outside in-place activation.

### Implement *IOleInPlaceFrame::SetStatusText*

If the container has a status line, it remains visible all through an in-place session. You also need to give the UI-active object a way to display status information. This is the purpose of *IOleInPlaceFrame::SetStatusText*, in which you take whatever text the object gives and display it in your status line, as Patron does here:

```
STDMETHODIMP CPatronFrame::SetStatusText(LPCOLESTR pszText)
    {
    m_pSL->MessageSet(pszText);
    return NOERROR;
    }
```

If an object calls *SetStatusText* with NULL, it is asking whether you have a status line at all. If you don't, return E_FAIL, which allows the object to display its own status line as an in-place tool.

### Show or Hide Modeless Pop-Up Windows

If a container has any modeless pop-up windows, an object might ask that you hide or disable them (your choice) by calling *IOleInPlaceFrame::EnableModeless(FALSE)*. It will later call this function with TRUE to show and enable those same windows. You can ask the object to do the same through *IOleInPlaceActiveObject::EnableModeless*, typically when you display some modal dialog box in which you want to disable anything else that appears to be part of the container. So both *EnableModeless* functions allow either container or object to enter a modal state and have that state apply to both.

## Summary

In-place activation, also called visual editing, is a user interface extension of the embedding feature of OLE Documents. It provides a more document-centric computing model through a set of interfaces and protocols that a container and an embedded object use to merge their various user interface elements and display those elements in the container's frame and document windows directly. In this way, the user never leaves the document to work with content objects. Microsoft's usability tests have shown that end users work very well with this model.

Unlike a basic embedded object, which is activated in a separate window, an in-place–capable object literally creates a window inside a container's document. The object can provide adornments such as row and column headings that surround its editing space. But a window is not sufficient to provide all the facilities necessary for a user to work with the object, so the container and object work together to merge other user interface elements. This involves the creation of a shared menu on which items from both the container and the object are available, a negotiation process through which the object is granted space in the container to create toolbars and other frame window and document window adornments, a protocol for handling both the container and the object's accelerators, and a variety of other small concerns such as handling Undo operations, context-sensitive help, window resizing, window activation, status lines, and modeless pop-up windows.

To do all of this, a container implements the interface *IOleInPlaceSite* on its site object alongside *IOleClientSite* and *IAdviseSink*. The presence of *IOleInPlaceSite* marks the container as in-place capable. The container also creates objects that represent its frame and document (if applicable) windows, implementing the interfaces *IOleInPlaceFrame* and *IOleInPlaceUIWindow*. The object, on the other hand, implements *IOleInPlaceObject* to indicate its in-place support, and when activated in place, it provides an implementation of *IOleInPlaceUIActiveObject*. In-place activation is accomplished primarily by the communication between container and object through all these interfaces—OLE itself provides only message filtering and additional helper functions. This is one example in which rich integration is achieved directly between a client and a component with minimal overhead from the system.

In-place activation introduces two additional object states: in-place active and UI active. A UI-active object has full control over the user interface elements shared with the container, whereas an object that is only in-place active has a window in the container's document but nothing else. Many OLE controls fall into this latter category, and although only one object can be UI active at any given time, there can be any number of in-place–active objects. In addition, objects can mark themselves to become in-place active whenever they are visible or to indicate that they support a single-click activation model referred to as *inside-out*.

This chapter demonstrates the container side of in-place activation by adding support for this feature to the Patron sample. Patron works in conjunction with in-place–capable versions of Cosmo and Polyline, provided in Chapter 23.

CHAPTER TWENTY·THREE

# In-Place Objects

*ACTIVE INGREDIENT: tetrahydrozoline hydrochloride, 0.05%*

Many medicines contain only a tiny amount of the key ingredient. For example, I have on my desk a small bottle of eye drops that I grabbed from the medicine cabinet. Of the 14.7 ml of liquid in this bottle, only a minuscule 0.00735 ml is the active ingredient; the rest is water. The addition of only a small amount of an active ingredient turns the liquid in the bottle into something of real value.

Compound document content objects are often the same way—the presence of a little feature can distinguish one from the rest of the crowd. If a content object is merely a small bottle of water, what will set it apart from the ocean of other content? A little bit of an active ingredient, such as in-place activation. Compared with the rest of a content object, the percentage of extra code necessary to implement in-place support is extremely small. Overall, it's nothing like what we had to do to create a container application in Chapter 22. Most of the work for activating an object in place, as you might imagine, is in building up and tearing down the in-place user interface, such as the shared menu and the in-place tools that we discussed in the first half of Chapter 22. Some objects need no such user interface, making the entire process even easier.

Because Chapter 22 already discussed the mechanics of in-place activation, this chapter is concerned with implementation. We'll add in-place capabilities to Cosmo and to Polyline, both of which we last saw in Chapter 21. As we'll see, almost the same steps apply to both local and in-process servers and their objects. One difference is that Polyline is marked as an activate-when-visible object, allowing you to explore that feature with Patron from Chapter 22. So if you're ready, let's see what we can accomplish with just a few drops of the programming equivalent of tetrahydrozoline HCl.

# In-Place Objects Step by Step

First you need an embedded object. Got one? Great, let's make it in-place capable by adding *IOleInPlaceObject* to the interfaces the object already has and providing an implementation of *IOleInPlaceActiveObject*. Well, let's not jump in quite so fast. There are crocodiles in the river. In-place activation carries some heavy implications for your object and server. So when implementing in-place activation, you should address these implications before adding anything related to in-place interfaces. Most of these implications have to do with the fact that you are going to be placing windows and menu items in a container application, so you have to check for assumptions that exist in your server windows exclusively. This may or may not be a major issue for you, but I hope to have you thinking about it before you get in too deep.

Given that deflating remark, here's how we'll progress through this chapter:

1. Prepare your object for the implications of in-place activation.

2. Implement skeletal *IOleInPlaceObject* and *IOleInPlaceActiveObject* interfaces and create some stubs for a few useful internal functions in your object.

3. Modify *DoVerb* to begin activation for the appropriate verbs and to provide for simple deactivation. This excludes most of the user interface.

4. Create, manage, and disassemble the shared menu.

5. Negotiate and create your in-place tools.

6. Modify your accelerators and your message loop to share the keyboard with the container.

7. Complete your implementation of the two in-place interfaces and add small fragments of code to round out your in-place object. This section, like the one in Chapter 22, is the catchall for the little fish that tend to slip through big nets. Here we'll also look briefly at inside-out objects.

The following sections describe these steps using Cosmo (CHAP23-\COSMO) as an example. This chapter also includes an in-place–capable version of Polyline (CHAP23\POLYLINE) that behaves almost exactly the same way as Cosmo except that it doesn't have any menus or toolbars. Polyline is a simpler case of an in-place object, which makes a nice foundation for creating an OLE control in Chapter 24.

I have not provided an updated version of the HCosmo handler that we saw in Chapter 19. The registry files used for Cosmo in this chapter specify the default handler as the InprocHandler32 entry. If you encounter odd problems when working with Cosmo here, check the handler entry and be sure it specifies the default handler.

## Drivers, Prepare Your Objects

In-place activation has two notable effects on the elements of an object's user interface:

- Menu items will be displayed in a shared menu in another application.

- Tool windows displayed in the container will have parent windows that don't understand them (which is common with adolescents).

Many of the issues that I raise here are similar to the concerns for containers that we looked at in Chapter 22. You might find it beneficial to read the section "Prepare the Container" on page 1035 if you have not already done so.

When you activate in place, you need to share the menu with the container. The menus you typically display for an object in a server will not all be available, nor will the keyboard accelerators assigned to them. This means that you'll need to use a different accelerator table while in place and move critical commands to menus in your Edit, Object, and Help menu groups. A typical problem is how to deal with a File Import command, which is a good command to have when editing. Consider how you might move this item to your Edit menu as a command such as Import From File. (I didn't do this with Cosmo.) You'll need to take steps such as these for similar menus.

Your object will still receive messages for the menus you place in the shared menu set, including WM_INITMENUPOPUP. Typically, you will still use this message to enable or disable certain items, such as Edit Paste. Oftentimes an application will use the absolute position of a menu item for enabling and disabling. But because the absolute position of each popup you might process will most likely change in the shared menu, you can no longer compare the index of the pop-up menu in this message with a constant. For example, the Edit menu is usually at index 1, so many applications have code that says, "If the pop-up menu is in position 1, enable or disable the Paste command." You have two ways to deal with this. The first is to keep an array of integers that holds the current position for each menu you have showing. The second technique is to depend solely on the menu handles that are passed with messages such as WM_INITMENUPOPUP. I will demonstrate this approach later in this chapter by creating an array of HMENU messages on startup and comparing the *hMenu* in the message with those in this array.

The other big impact on an object is that you are going to place a number of windows in the container's user interface as children of container windows. But because you have no control over those parent windows, you should ask yourself a few questions. Do the windows you intend to use send any messages to the parent window? Many of the standard Windows controls do exactly this—but you don't want them sending unexpected messages to the container's windows! Do your windows make assumptions about what other windows exist? Do your windows use WS_CLIPSIBLINGS? They should because you are going to share space with unknown sibling windows, and you do not want to overlap them visually. Can your windows be independently resized outside a WM_SIZE message in another window? At some point, the container application might ask your application to take just such an action in your *IOleInPlaceActiveObject* implementation, so be prepared. How will your editing window react if it cannot be shown completely? Can it handle the clipping rectangle that the container will specify?

The biggest problem is the first one mentioned here: windows that send messages to their parent. In this case, you need to redirect those messages by either rewriting the code for those windows or wrapping those windows with code that can forward the messages to another window altogether.

### Implement Skeletal In-Place Interfaces and Object Helper Functions

In-place activation for a server generally affects only the object in question, leaving most of the rest of the server unaffected. Cosmo's embedded object is implemented in *CFigure*. To this we need to add the *IOleInPlaceObject* interface (IIPOBJ.CPP) and provide an implementation of *IOleInPlaceActiveObject* (IIP-AOBJ.CPP). We'll implement the latter as part of *CFigure* as well, but its *QueryInterface* is hobbled so as not to respond to any interface but itself. I've included this interface with *CFigure* because most of what we need to do in it concerns the object. But we could have implemented it with a separate object altogether.

At this point, it is useful to start implementing a set of centralized functions to do most of the work involved with in-place activation. For this reason, I've added a number of internal (but public in C++) member functions to *CFigure* that will be called from the in-place interfaces:

```
class CFigure : public IUnknown
    {
    ⋮
    public:
      ⋮

        HRESULT    InPlaceActivate(LPOLECLIENTSITE, BOOL);
        void       InPlaceDeactivate(void);
        HRESULT    UIActivate(void);
        void       UIDeactivate(void);
        BOOL       InPlaceMenuCreate(void);
        BOOL       InPlaceMenuDestroy(void);
        BOOL       InPlaceToolsCreate(void);
        BOOL       InPlaceToolsDestroy(void);
        BOOL       InPlaceToolsRenegotiate(void);

        void       OpenIntoWindow(void);
        BOOL       Undo(void);
    }
```

*InPlaceDeactivate* and *UIDeactivate* will contain the same code we need in the *IOleInPlaceObject* functions of the same name, so we can have the interface simply call *CFigure* directly:

```
STDMETHODIMP CImpIOleInPlaceObject::InPlaceDeactivate(void)
    {
    m_pObj->InPlaceDeactivate();
    return NOERROR;
    }

STDMETHODIMP CImpIOleInPlaceObject::UIDeactivate(void)
    {
    m_pObj->UIDeactivate();
    return NOERROR;
    }
```

Why bother with these and functions such as *CFigure::InPlaceActivate?* The reason is that we might need to call them from multiple locations—for example, *IOleObject::DoVerb* and *IOleInPlaceObject::ReactivateAndUndo*. In Cosmo, *CFigure* has more access to the rest of the application than the interface implementations themselves, so we end up with cleaner code in the bargain. Also, *InPlaceActivate* is the only function that takes any arguments—an *IOleClientSite* pointer (generally the one passed to *IOleObject::DoVerb*) and a BOOL flag indicating that we want to activate the UI as well.

## Implement Simple Activation and Deactivation

As described in Chapter 22, *IOleObject::DoVerb* is the function in which in-place activation starts. First, then, we need to decide which verbs will try to activate an object in place. For example, a Play verb will not need to activate an object in place because it can temporarily play in the container already. Merging the user interface isn't necessary. We'll need to define the behavior for all our supported verbs as well as any standard ones according to Table 23-1.

| Verb | Behavior |
|------|----------|
| OLEIVERB_PRIMARY | Attempt full in-place UI activation if appropriate for this object. |
| OLEIVERB_SHOW | Attempt full in-place UI activation. On failure, open the object in a server window as usual. |
| OLEIVERB_HIDE | Fully deactivate the object if it's currently active in place; otherwise, hide the server window as usual. |
| OLEIVERB_OPEN | Do not attempt to activate in place. Always open in a server window. |
| OLEIVERB_INPLACE-ACTIVATE | Activate in place without UI activation, or fail if in-place activation by itself is not possible. |
| OLEIVERB_UIACTIVATE | Activate the object UI. (Implies activation in place first.) |
| OLEIVERB_DISCARD-UNDOSTATE | Free any Undo information you are holding. (See "Provide Undo Support" on page 1095.) |

**Table 23-1.**

*In-place–activation behavior for standard verbs.*

We can see how Cosmo handles these in its *DoVerb* implementation:

```
STDMETHODIMP CImpIOleObject::DoVerb(LONG iVerb, LPMSG pMSG
    , LPOLECLIENTSITE pActiveSite, LONG lIndex, HWND hWndParent
    , LPCRECT pRectPos)
    {
    ⋮
    switch (iVerb)
        {
        case OLEIVERB_HIDE:
            if (NULL!=m_pObj->m_pIOleIPSite)
                m_pObj->InPlaceDeactivate();
```

```
    else
        {
        ShowWindow(hWnd, SW_HIDE);
        m_pObj->SendAdvise(OBJECTCODE_HIDEWINDOW);
        }
    break;

case OLEIVERB_PRIMARY:
case OLEIVERB_SHOW:
    //If already in-place active, nothing much to do here.
    if (NULL!=m_pObj->m_pIOleIPSite)
        return NOERROR;

    if (m_pObj->m_fAllowInPlace)
        {
        if (SUCCEEDED(m_pObj->InPlaceActivate(pActiveSite
            , TRUE))) return NOERROR;
        }

    //FALL-THROUGH

case OLEIVERB_OPEN:
    /*
     * If already in-place active, deactivate and
     * prevent later reactivation.
     */
    if (NULL!=m_pObj->m_pIOleIPSite)
        {
        m_pObj->InPlaceDeactivate();
        m_pObj->m_fAllowInPlace=FALSE;
        }

    /*
     * With all in-place stuff gone, we can go back to
     * our normal open state.
     */
    ShowWindow(hWnd, SW_SHOWNORMAL);
    SetFocus(hWnd);

    m_pObj->SendAdvise(OBJECTCODE_SHOWOBJECT);
    m_pObj->SendAdvise(OBJECTCODE_SHOWWINDOW);
    break;

case OLEIVERB_INPLACEACTIVATE:
    return m_pObj->InPlaceActivate(pActiveSite, FALSE);
```

*(continued)*

```
    case OLEIVERB_UIACTIVATE:
        return m_pObj->InPlaceActivate(pActiveSite, TRUE);

    case OLEIVERB_DISCARDUNDOSTATE:
        //This program doesn't hold a state, but if yours does,
        //free it here.
        break;

    default:
        return ResultFromScode(OLEOBJ_S_INVALIDVERB);
    }

return NOERROR;
}
```

If Cosmo fails to activate in place for OLEIVERB_SHOW or OLEI-VERB_PRIMARY, it tries to open the object in a window as usual. This always happens with OLEIVERB_OPEN, so opening an object in a separate window from an in-place–active state is tricky because it requires deactivation first, after which we can show Cosmo's main window. After we're open in the main window, we cannot return to the in-place–active state unless the user closes the window and reactivates the object in the container. We must also guard against additional calls to *DoVerb* while we're open so that we don't attempt to become in-place active again. The *m_fAllowInPlace* variable controls this.

Now, to make any of these verbs work as advertised, we need to do a little work in our *InPlaceActivate* and *InPlaceDeactivate* helper functions.

## Basic In-Place Activation (sans UI)

The steps for basic activation are similar to steps we used in Chapter 22:

1.  Using the *IOleClientSite* pointer passed to *IOleObject::DoVerb*, query for *IOleInPlaceSite*. If that interface is available, call *IOleInPlaceSite::CanInPlaceActivate*. If that call succeeds, call *IOleInPlaceSite::OnInPlaceActivate*.

2.  Call *IOleInPlaceSite::GetWindowContext*, use the window context returned to change the parent and position of your editing window, show the window in the container, and call *IOleClientSite::ShowObject*.

3.  Call *IOleInPlaceFrame::SetActiveObject* and *IOleInPlaceUIWindow::SetActiveObject* to give the container your *IOleInPlaceActiveObject* pointer.

4.  If you want to fully activate the UI as well, call your own *UIActivate* helper function. The function does nothing at this point, but you'll want to call it later, so you might as well add it now while you're thinking about it.

You can see these steps implemented in Cosmo's *CFigure::InPlaceActivate*:

```
HRESULT CFigure::InPlaceActivate(LPOLECLIENTSITE pActiveSite
    , BOOL fIncludeUI)
    {
    HRESULT             hr;
    HWND                hWnd, hWndHW;
    RECT                rcPos;
    RECT                rcClip;

    if (NULL==pActiveSite)
        return ResultFromScode(E_INVALIDARG);

    //If already active, activate UI and we're done.
    if (NULL!=m_pIOleIPSite)
        {
        if (fIncludeUI)
            UIActivate();

        return NOERROR;
        }

    hr=pActiveSite->QueryInterface(IID_IOleInPlaceSite
        , (PPVOID)&m_pIOleIPSite);

    if (FAILED(hr))
        return hr;

    hr=m_pIOleIPSite->CanInPlaceActivate();

    if (NOERROR!=hr)
        {
        m_pIOleIPSite->Release();
        m_pIOleIPSite=NULL;
        return ResultFromScode(E_FAIL);
        }

    m_pIOleIPSite->OnInPlaceActivate();
    m_fUndoDeactivates=TRUE;

    m_pIOleIPSite->GetWindow(&hWnd);
    m_pFR->m_frameInfo.cb=sizeof(OLEINPLACEFRAMEINFO);

    m_pIOleIPSite->GetWindowContext(&m_pIOleIPFrame
        , &m_pIOleIPUIWindow, &rcPos, &rcClip
        , &m_pFR->m_frameInfo);
```

*(continued)*

```
m_pFR->m_pIOleIPFrame=m_pIOleIPFrame;

m_pHW->HwndAssociateSet (m_pFR->Window());
m_pHW->ChildSet(m_pPL->Window());    //Calls SetParent
m_pHW->RectsSet(&rcPos, &rcClip);    //Positions Polyline

hWndHW=m_pHW->Window();
SetParent(hWndHW, hWnd);             //Move hatch window.
ShowWindow(hWndHW, SW_SHOW);         //Make us visible.
SendAdvise(OBJECTCODE_SHOWOBJECT);

if (fIncludeUI)
    return UIActivate();

return NOERROR;
}
```

As we discussed in Chapter 22, the query for *IOleInPlaceSite* and the call to *IOleInPlaceSite::CanInPlaceActivate* are made to ensure that the container is both in-place capable and willing to activate this particular object in place. Failure in either case means that we activate the object in a separate window, remaining fully compatible with non-in-place containers. Success in Cosmo means that *CFigure::m_pIOleIPSite* is set to a non-NULL value. This variable is used in other places around the code to determine whether we're in-place activated.

If we can proceed to in-place activation, we call *IOleInPlaceSite::On-InPlaceActivate* so that it can initialize whatever state it wants. We also want to remember that the next Undo command we see should deactivate us, so we set our *m_fUndoDeactivates* variable to TRUE.

Our next task is to get all the information we need to work with the container by calling *IOleInPlaceSite::GetWindow*, which will be the parent of our editing window, and by calling *IOleInPlaceSite::GetWindowContext*. The call to *GetWindowContext* provides us with the position rectangle that the object's data area should occupy, a clipping rectangle, the container's *IOleInPlace-Frame* and *IOleInPlaceUIWindow* pointers, and the container's OLEINPLACE-FRAMEINFO structure, which holds the container's accelerators.[1] We'll need this information in our frame's message loop later on, so Cosmo stores this filled structure directly in its *CCosmoFrame* (*m_pFR*) object along with the container's *IOleInPlaceFrame* pointer, which our frame will need as well.

---

1. The object must fill the *cb* field of the OLEINPLACEFRAMEINFO structure before calling *GetWindowContext* to identify the version of the structure desired.

Next we need to take our editing window, which in Cosmo is the Polyline window referenced through *CFigure::m_pPL*, and move it to the container as a child of whatever window we get from *IOleInPlaceSite::GetWindow*. We don't actually place the Polyline window in the container alone: the Polyline window is a child of a special hatch window that is implemented in the sample code's CLASSLIB framework as *CHatchWin* (CLASSLIB\CHATCH-.CPP). *CFigure* creates a *CHatchWin* object in *CFigure::Init*, storing the pointer in *m_pHW* for our use here. The hatch window itself doesn't send any messages to its parent window but rather to an "associate" that we set with *CHatch-Win::AssociateSet*. This ensures that our in-place window will not send spurious messages to the container.

This hatch window, in its WM_PAINT processing, draws the border hatching around the object (as described in Chapter 22) using our INOLE-.DLL helper function *UIDrawShading* (INOLE\UIEFFECT.CPP). The width of the border is read from the OleInPlaceBorderWidth entry in WIN.INI (with a default of 4 pixels). In addition, the hatch window manages the position and the clipping rectangles that we obtain from the container. Basically, we make the Polyline window a child of the hatch window (*CHatchWin::Child-Set*). Then we tell the hatch window through *CHatchWin::RectsSet* to size the Polyline window within it to the position rectangle (*rcPos*) and to size itself according to the intersection of the position rectangle and the clipping rectangle (*prcClip*):

```
//From CLASSLIB\CHATCH.CPP
void CHatchWin::RectsSet(LPRECT prcPos, LPRECT prcClip)
    {
    RECT    rc;
    RECT    rcPos;

    //Calculate rectangle for hatch window; then clip it.
    rcPos=*prcPos;
    InflateRect(&rcPos, m_dBorder, m_dBorder);
    IntersectRect(&rc, &rcPos, prcClip);

    SetWindowPos(m_hWnd, NULL, rc.left, rc.top, rc.right-rc.left
        , rc.bottom-rc.top, SWP_NOZORDER | SWP_NOACTIVATE);

    /*
     * Set rectangle of child window to be at m_dBorder
     * from top and left but with same size in prcPos.
     * The hatch window will clip it.
     */
```

*(continued)*

```
SetWindowPos(m_hWndKid, NULL, rcPos.left-rc.left+m_dBorder
    , rcPos.top-rc.top+m_dBorder, prcPos->right-prcPos->left
    , prcPos->bottom-prcPos->top, SWP_NOZORDER | SWP_NOACTIVATE);

return;
}
```

The cumulative effect is that the object window is always scaled to the position rectangle but at the same time the position rectangle is clipped to the window's parent. (The hatch window has WS_CLIPCHILDREN for this purpose.) As the hatch window clips itself to the clipping rectangle, the object is also clipped to the clipping rectangle while still showing the proper scaling. The hatch window keeps itself slightly larger than its child window by the hatch border width on all sides, subject, of course, to the container's clipping rectangle.

After the hatch window is positioned with the Polyline window inside it, we can move it to the container with *SetParent*, make it visible with *ShowWindow*, and call *IOleClientSite::ShowObject* to let the container know our application is visible. This last call allows the container to scroll our application into view if it is scrolled out of view at the time.

We should now also implement both *IOleInPlaceObject::GetWindow* and *IOleInPlaceActiveObject::GetWindow* to return the topmost window that was moved into the container. In Cosmo, this is the hatch window:

```
STDMETHODIMP CImpIOleInPlaceObject::GetWindow(HWND FAR *phWnd)
    {
    *phWnd=m_pObj->m_pHW->Window();
    return NOERROR;
    }

STDMETHODIMP CImpIOleInPlaceActiveObject::GetWindow(HWND FAR *phWnd)
    {
    *phWnd=m_pObj->m_pHW->Window();
    return NOERROR;
    }
```

This works well because when the object is UI active and the container gets a WM_SETFOCUS in the frame, the container calls *SetFocus* on whatever window is returned from the UI-active object's *IOleInPlaceActiveObject::Get-Window*. That means it will call *SetFocus* on the hatch window, which will call *SetFocus* on our editing window. This is exactly how things should happen.

As the final step, *CFigure::InPlaceActivate* calls *CFigure::UIActivate* if we're going that far. We'll see what happens here shortly.

## Object Adornments

The hatch window is a special case of what are called *object adornments*, or additional user interface elements that appear outside the position rectangle of the object but inside the clipping rectangle. A spreadsheet object might display row and column headings, for example. The position rectangle defines the space that the object's data area should occupy, so adornments are not affected by that rectangle. If you need additional space for similar adornments, you can expand whatever windows you place in the container to accommodate them as long as those windows stay within the container's clipping rectangle and the object area stays the same size as the position rectangle, at least initially. No matter what adornments you add, the hatched border should always surround the object and all adornments.

### Basic Deactivation (sans UI)

Deactivation basically means reversing anything we did in the activation phase, in the opposite order. Where we previously obtained an interface pointer, we release it here. Where we called *SetParent* to move a window to the container, we call *SetParent* here to bring it back to the server. Deactivation involves the following steps:

1. Call the *UIDeactivate* helper function to remove menus and tools.

2. Call *SetParent* to move the hatch window and editing window back to the server.

3. Call *IOleInPlaceSite::OnInPlaceDeactivate*, release the pointers obtained from *IOleInPlaceSite::GetWindowContext*, and release the *IOleInPlaceSite* pointer obtained from *QueryInterface*.

We can see these steps implemented in the code for Cosmo's *CFigure::InPlaceDeactivate*:

```
void CFigure::InPlaceDeactivate(void)
    {
    RECT        rc;

    UIDeactivate();

    SetParent(m_pPL->Window(), m_pDoc->m_hWnd);
    m_pHW->ChildSet(NULL);
```

*(continued)*

```
//Be sure the hatch window is invisible and owned by Cosmo.
ShowWindow(m_pHW->Window(), SW_HIDE);
SetParent(m_pHW->Window(), m_pDoc->m_hWnd);
GetClientRect(m_pDoc->m_hWnd, &rc);
InflateRect(&rc, -8, -8);

SetWindowPos(m_pPL->Window(), NULL, rc.left, rc.top
    , rc.right-rc.left, rc.bottom-rc.top
    , SWP_NOZORDER | SWP_NOACTIVATE);

if (NULL!=m_pIOleIPSite)
    m_pIOleIPSite->OnInPlaceDeactivate();

m_pFR->m_pIOleIPFrame=NULL;
ReleaseInterface(m_pIOleIPFrame);
ReleaseInterface(m_pIOleIPUIWindow);
ReleaseInterface(m_pIOleIPSite);

return;
}
```

When we set Cosmo's Polyline window as a child of the hatch window, we repositioned it in relation to its parent. When we move it back to Cosmo's document window now, we have to adjust this relative position again. If we're deactivating because of OLEIVERB_OPEN, we'll be showing the document window in the server, so the Polyline window better appear in the right place!

Also, in-place deactivation takes the object back only to the running state, not to the loaded state. That means that a local server such as Cosmo will still be running. (An in-process server such as the Polyline sample in this chapter will always be in memory anyway.) Because the object has not been destroyed, you cannot assume that in-place activation will give you a chance to reinitialize your object's variables. So you need to be sure they are set back to whatever state you expect in *IOleObject::DoVerb*. For Cosmo, we set the *m_p-IOleIPSite* pointer to NULL so that we can activate in place again.

At this point in our implementation, we could compile our code, test it with a container, and see many of the in-place–activation steps take place. When you click outside the object in the container, you can trace through the deactivation steps.[2] What's missing are the extra pieces of user interface, which we'll now build in Cosmo.

---

2. As an extra debugging measure, you might also display your server window during this time so that you can watch the editing window disappear from within the server document on activation and reappear on deactivation.

## UI Activation and Deactivation

After we have the in-place–activation state handled, we can add the UI-active state. Cosmo handles the state through *CFigure::UIActivate* and *CFigure::UIDeactivate*, which are called from *IOleObject::DoVerb(OLEIVERB_UIACTIVATE)* and *IOleInPlaceObject::UIDeactivate*:

```
HRESULT CFigure::UIActivate(void)
    {
    if (NULL!=m_pIOleIPSite)
        m_pIOleIPSite->OnUIActivate();

    SetFocus(m_pHW->Window());

    if (NULL!=m_pIOleIPFrame)
        {
        m_pIOleIPFrame->SetActiveObject(m_pImpIOleIPActiveObject
            , PSZ(IDS_INPLACETITLE));
        }

    if (NULL!=m_pIOleIPUIWindow)
        {
        m_pIOleIPUIWindow->SetActiveObject(m_pImpIOleIPActiveObject
            , PSZ(IDS_INPLACETITLE));
        }

    InPlaceToolsCreate();
    InPlaceMenuCreate();
    return NOERROR;
    }


void CFigure::UIDeactivate(void)
    {
    InPlaceToolsDestroy();
    InPlaceMenuDestroy();

    if (NULL!=m_pIOleIPFrame)
        m_pIOleIPFrame->SetActiveObject(NULL, NULL);

    if (NULL!=m_pIOleIPUIWindow)
        m_pIOleIPUIWindow->SetActiveObject(NULL, NULL);

    if (NULL!=m_pIOleIPSite)
        m_pIOleIPSite->OnUIDeactivate(FALSE);

    return;
    }
```

The most critical parts of these functions are the calls to *IOleInPlaceSite-::OnUIActivate* and *OnUIDeactivate*, which let the container know when to initialize or uninitialize its own UI-active state. The next step is to pass your *IOleInPlaceActiveObject* implementation to both *IOleInPlaceFrame::SetActiveObject* and *IOleInPlaceUIWindow::SetActiveObject* (if applicable)[3] during UI activation, passing NULL pointers to deactivate. In addition, UI activation should include setting the focus to your in-place window so that you can receive keyboard accelerators. The call to *SetFocus* here gives the hatch window the focus, which in turn gives it to Cosmo's Polyline window.

### Assemble and Disassemble the Menu

Cosmo encapsulates menu creation and destruction in *CFigure::InPlaceMenuCreate* and *CFigure::InPlaceMenuDestroy*. As described in Chapter 22, creation of the menu involves these steps:

1. Create a new menu with the Windows API function *CreateMenu*.

2. Call *IOleInPlaceFrame::InsertMenus* to have the container make its contribution, also passing it the OLEMENUGROUPWIDTHS array, in which the container stores the number of items in each of its groups.

3. Call the Windows API *InsertMenu* to add your own menu items to the shared menu in the appropriate places and to fill in the remainder of the OLEMENUGROUPWIDTHS array.

4. Call *OleCreateMenuDescriptor* with the menu handle and the OLEMENUGROUPWIDTHS array.

5. Call *IOleInPlaceFrame::SetMenu*, passing the menu handle, the menu descriptor from step 4, and the handle of the window to receive messages generated from your items on this menu, typically your frame window.

If you have an object that doesn't need a shared menu at all, which is the case for this chapter's version of Polyline, you need to call only *IOleInPlaceFrame::SetMenu(NULL, NULL, hWnd)*, in which *hWnd* is the object's window. This call tells the container to keep its own menu active.

Cosmo, however, does use a shared menu. It assembles the menu as shown in the following:

---

3. Cosmo includes a title string for itself to remain backward compatible with older containers that still use the string for changing the caption bar. All in-place–capable objects should do this.

```
BOOL CFigure::InPlaceMenuCreate(void)
    {
    HMENU              hMenu, hMenuT;
    UINT               uTemp=MF_BYPOSITION | MF_POPUP;
    UINT               i;
    OLEMENUGROUPWIDTHS  mgw;

    for (i=0; i<6; i++)
        mgw.width[i]=0;

    //We already have pop-up menu handles in m_pFR->m_phMenu[].

    //Create new shared menu and let container do its thing.
    hMenu=CreateMenu();
    m_pIOleIPFrame->InsertMenus(hMenu, &mgw);

    //Add our menus, remembering that container
    //has already added its menus.
    InsertMenu(hMenu, (WORD)mgw.width[0]
        , uTemp, (UINT)m_pFR->m_phMenu[1], PSZ(IDS_MENUEDIT));

    //Add Open item to Edit menu.
    AppendMenu(m_pFR->m_phMenu[1], MF_SEPARATOR, 0, NULL);
    AppendMenu(m_pFR->m_phMenu[1], MF_STRING, IDM_EDITOPEN
        , PSZ(IDS_MENUOPEN));

    InsertMenu(hMenu, (WORD)mgw.width[0]+1+(WORD)mgw.width[2]
        , uTemp, (UINT)m_pFR->m_phMenu[2], PSZ(IDS_MENUCOLOR));

    InsertMenu(hMenu, (WORD)mgw.width[0]+1+(WORD)mgw.width[2]+1
        , uTemp, (UINT)m_pFR->m_phMenu[3], PSZ(IDS_MENULINE));

    //Window menu position changes between MDI and SDI.
#ifdef MDI
    hMenuT=m_pFR->m_phMenu[5];
#else
    hMenuT=m_pFR->m_phMenu[4];
#endif

    InsertMenu(hMenu, (WORD)mgw.width[0]+1+(WORD)mgw.width[2]+2
        +(WORD)mgw.width[4], uTemp, (UINT)hMenuT, PSZ(IDS_MENUHELP));

    //Tell OLE how many items in each group are ours.
    mgw.width[1]=1;
    mgw.width[3]=2;
```

*(continued)*

```
mgw.width[5]=1;

m_hMenuShared=hMenu;
m_hOLEMenu=OleCreateMenuDescriptor(m_hMenuShared, &mgw);

m_pIOleIPFrame->SetMenu(m_hMenuShared, m_hOLEMenu, m_pFR->Window());
return TRUE;
}
```

You can see how Cosmo uses the container's group widths in OLEMENU-GROUPWIDTHS to position our own Edit, Object, and Window groups correctly. Also, we complete this array by filling elements 0, 2, and 4.

Cosmo takes advantage of the capability of Windows to have multiple menus share the same pop-up handles. During an in-place session, Cosmo puts the same Edit, Color, Line, and Help menus on the shared menus that it displays on its own menu bar, using the same pop-up handles that are stored in its *CCosmoFrame::m_phMenu* array. This saves us the trouble of re-creating each pop-up menu all over again, but it means that we have to be very careful when we disassemble the menu, as we'll see shortly.

Cosmo also makes a small addition to the Edit menu for in-place uses: an Open item, which causes the in-place–active object to deactivate and open in a full window. We'll see how to process this command later, but it is a nice addition for an object to provide.[4]

The object is responsible for maintaining the menu it creates here, so remember to save the handle with the object, as Cosmo does in *CFigure::m_hMenuShared*. The object must also save the menu descriptor, a variable of type HOLEMENU (such as *CFigure::m_hOLEMenu*) that it gets back from *OleCreateMenuDescriptor* so that it can destroy the descriptor later. But, of course, we still have to send the descriptor to the container through *IOleInPlaceFrame::SetMenu*, along with the handle of the window to which you want menu messages sent. Generally, this window is your frame window because it's already set up to receive menu messages.

When we deactivate the object's user interface, we'll need to disassemble this shared menu. If you have no menu in the first place, the object (Polyline, for example) has nothing to do. Cosmo, however, performs the following steps to dismantle the menu created in the code above:

---

4. If your application is an MDI multiple-use server, you should *not* modify a pop-up menu that is used from two top-level menus (that is, the shared menu and the server's normal menu) because you'll be modifying the menu anywhere it's used. Either abstain from such modifications or create a separate pop-up menu for the shared menu and make your modifications to it alone. Remember also that you need to save this menu handle so that you can enable or disable items in it while processing WM_INITMENUPOPUP.

1. Calls *IOleInPlaceFrame::SetMenu* with NULLs.

2. Calls *OleDestroyMenuDescriptor* to free the menu descriptor.

3. Removes each of its menu items from the shared menu.

4. Calls *IOleInPlaceFrame::RemoveMenus* to remove the container menus.

5. Calls the Windows API function *DestroyMenu* to free the menu itself.

Here's the code to do it:

```
BOOL CFigure::InPlaceMenuDestroy(void)
    {
    int         cItems, i, j;
    HMENU       hMenuT;

    //If we don't have shared menu, nothing to do.
    if (NULL==m_hMenuShared)
        return TRUE;

    //Stop container frame from using this menu.
    m_pIOleIPFrame->SetMenu(NULL, NULL, NULL);

    //Clean up what we got from OleCreateMenuDescriptor.
    OleDestroyMenuDescriptor(m_hOLEMenu);
    m_hOLEMenu=NULL;

    cItems=GetMenuItemCount(m_hMenuShared);

    /*
     * Walk backward down the menu. For each popup, see whether it
     * matches any other popup we know about, and if so, remove it
     * from shared menu.
     */
    for (i=cItems; i>=0; i--)
        {
        hMenuT=GetSubMenu(m_hMenuShared, i);

        for (j=0; j<=CMENUS; j++)
            {
            /*
             * If submenu matches any we have, remove it; don't
             * delete. Because we're walking backward, this
             * affects only positions of those menus after us, so
             * GetSubMenu call above is not affected.
             */
```

*(continued)*

```
                    if (hMenuT==m_pFR->m_phMenu[j])
                        RemoveMenu(m_hMenuShared, i, MF_BYPOSITION);
                }
            }

        //Remove Open item and separator from Edit menu.
        RemoveMenu(m_pFR->m_phMenu[1], 6, MF_BYPOSITION);
        RemoveMenu(m_pFR->m_phMenu[1], 5, MF_BYPOSITION);

        if (NULL!=m_pIOleIPFrame)
            m_pIOleIPFrame->RemoveMenus(m_hMenuShared);

        DestroyMenu(m_hMenuShared);
        m_hMenuShared=NULL;
        return TRUE;
        }
```

The trick here is to *remove* each menu item that you added before. I emphasize this because you will generally be sharing menu handles between this menu and your normal server's menu, so destroying those pop-up items is not a good idea. Cosmo ensures that it removes all of its items by removing any popup it recognizes in the shared menu (that is, any handle that is also stored in *m_phMenu*). It also removes the extra Open item we added in the assembly phase. After we've called the *IOleInPlaceFrame::RemoveMenus* function, we can call *DestroyMenu* to free the resource. Then we're finished.

It's extremely important that you remove all your menu items properly before calling *DestroyMenu* because that function also destroys any popups on that menu as well. If you experience weird problems when assembling or disassembling your shared menu, comment out your call to *DestroyMenu* and see whether the problem still exists. If it does, you are not cleaning up your menu properly. If you missed it earlier, go back and read the sidebar "EXPERIENCE: Menu Destruction—Just Do It (Right)!" in Chapter 22 on page 1046 for a description of what happened when I didn't do it right. I had one major-league hair-puller with this one, and it all turned out to be a bug in my make file, of all things.

### Create and Destroy In-Place Tools

To complete full UI activation, we now need to create any in-place tools we want, including toolbars or toolboxes on any side of the container's frame or document window. We can also create floating pop-up windows as needed. Again, be sure that none of these windows send unexpected messages to the container, which will be the parent window in many cases, and that any tools added to the frame or document windows use WS_CLIPSIBLINGS.

Cosmo demonstrates this part of UI activation by using a single toolbar. The toolbar is created in *CFigure::InPlaceToolsCreate*, which executes these steps:

1. Negotiate tool space with the container by calling the *RequestBorder-Space* function in *IOleInPlaceFrame* for frame-level tools and in *IOleInPlaceUIWindow* for document windows.

2. When the container accepts your requests, send those same numbers to the *SetBorderSpace* members of the appropriate interface.

3. Create your tools either as child windows of the container's frame or document window or as pop-up windows, and then make them visible. You can use the rectangle from the *GetBorder* function of the appropriate container interface to set the initial dimensions of the tools if necessary.

All units used here are device units (pixels) because we're dealing with windows whose dimensions are always in device units. Don't use HIMETRIC, which is used almost everywhere else in OLE. Anyway, here's Cosmo's implementation of its in-place tools:

```
BOOL CFigure::InPlaceToolsCreate(void)
    {
    BORDERWIDTHS    bw;
    HWND            hWnd;
    UINT            uState=GIZMO_NORMAL;
    UINT            utCmd =GIZMOTYPE_BUTTONCOMMAND;
    UINT            utEx  =GIZMOTYPE_BUTTONATTRIBUTEEX;
    UINT            i;
    HBITMAP         hBmp;
    RECT            rc;

    //We don't need anything on document, so send zeros.
    SetRectEmpty((LPRECT)&bw);

    if (NULL!=m_pIOleIPUIWindow)
        m_pIOleIPUIWindow->SetBorderSpace(&bw);

    if (NULL==m_pIOleIPFrame)
        return FALSE;

    //Reserve frame space.
```

*(continued)*

```
if (!InPlaceToolsRenegotiate())
    {
    //If container doesn't allow us any, don't ask for any.
    m_pIOleIPFrame->SetBorderSpace(&bw);
    return FALSE;
    }

//Create toolbar window.
m_pIOleIPFrame->GetWindow(&hWnd);

//If we already have a toolbar, just show it again.
if (NULL!=m_pTB)
    {
    ShowWindow(m_pTB->Window(), SW_SHOW);
    return TRUE;
    }

m_pTB=new CToolBar(m_pFR->m_hInst);

if (NULL==m_pTB)
    {
    SetRectEmpty((LPRECT)&bw);
    m_pIOleIPFrame->SetBorderSpace(&bw);
    return FALSE;
    }

m_pTB->Init(hWnd, ID_GIZMOBAR, m_cyBar);
g_pInPlaceTB=m_pTB;

//Ensure that tools are initially invisible.
ShowWindow(m_pTB->Window(), SW_HIDE);

//Tell toolbar whom to send messages to.
m_pTB->HwndAssociateSet(m_pFR->m_hWnd);

[Omitted code to create all individual tools]

//Make tools visible.
ShowWindow(m_pTB->Window(), SW_SHOW);

return TRUE;
}
```

Because we don't want any document tools, we tell this to the container by calling *IOleInPlaceUIWindow::SetBorderSpace* with a BORDERWIDTHS structure full of zeros. (Because the structure is the same as a RECT, we can use *SetRectEmpty* here.) This call means, "We want no space and no tools showing."

If we call *SetBorderSpace* with a NULL pointer, however, that tells the container, "We don't want any space, and you can leave your tools showing." An object that does nothing for the UI-active state should call *SetBorderSpace* with NULLs for the container's document and frame window as necessary.

Cosmo wants a toolbar in the frame window, so it negotiates for space in *CFigure::InPlaceToolsRenegotiate*. This separate function exists because we'll need it later in *IOleInPlaceActiveObject::ResizeBorder*:

```
BOOL CFigure::InPlaceToolsRenegotiate(void)
    {
    HRESULT         hr;
    BORDERWIDTHS    bw;

    SetRect((LPRECT)&bw, 0, m_pFR->m_cyBar, 0, 0);

    hr=m_pIOleIPFrame->RequestBorderSpace(&bw);

    if (NOERROR!=hr)
        return FALSE;

    //Safety net: RequestBorderSpace can modify values in bw.
    SetRect((LPRECT)&bw, 0, m_pFR->m_cyBar, 0, 0);

    m_pIOleIPFrame->SetBorderSpace(&bw);
    return TRUE;
    }
```

If this function returns FALSE, the container will not allow us space for our toolbar. In this case, Cosmo merely lives without the tools because everything is still available on the shared menu. Some other objects might not want to activate in place in such a situation and should deactivate everything done to this point (including the shared menu) and open as a normal embedded object. Still other objects can elect to place those same tools in a floating pop-up window, which the container cannot restrict.

If the container does allow us space, we create our toolbar using the window from *IOleInPlaceFrame::GetWindow* as the parent and the dimensions from *IOleInPlaceFrame::GetBorder*.[5] Cosmo's toolbar stretches across the container's frame window, so we use the horizontal extent from *GetBorder* for this dimension with the vertical extent that we negotiated for previously. In general, tools on the top or bottom of a window should be created with the horizontal

---

5. Cosmo saves a copy of the in-place toolbar in *g_pInPlaceTB* in such a way that when the user selects a line style from the menu, the *CCosmoFrame::CheckLineSelection* function can activate the appropriate button on the in-place toolbar as it does on the normal toolbar. You will see extra code in COSMO.CPP to handle this.

extent from *GetBorder* and the negotiated height. Tools on the side of the window should use their negotiated width and the vertical dimension from *GetBorder*.

After executing this code, the toolbar should be visible in the container. To remove it, we need only to destroy the toolbar because the container will reinstate its own when we call *IOleInPlaceSite::OnUIDeactivate*. Cosmo's *CFigure::InPlaceToolsDestroy* is straightforward:

```
BOOL CFigure::InPlaceToolsDestroy(void)
    {
    //Nothing to do if we never created anything.
    if (NULL==m_pTB)
        return TRUE;

    if (NULL!=m_pTB)
        {
        delete m_pTB;
        m_pTB=NULL;
        g_pInPlaceTB=NULL;
        }

    return TRUE;
    }
```

It is perfectly reasonable to simply hide your tools at this point in case the object becomes UI active again, but remember that you must always negotiate for space whenever the object becomes UI active. You can't assume that the container will allow the same tool space for each activation.

If you compile and run your object at this point, you'll see the user interface created and destroyed as necessary. Pretty cool! Now resize the frame or document windows in which these tools appear. Ugly, huh? Your tools didn't resize with the container windows. We have to implement the *IOleInPlaceActiveObject* interface to handle this. But before we do this, let's finish up the last major modification—accelerator support.

## Manage and Process Accelerators

The UI-active object always has first crack at accelerators. If the object is implemented in a local server, your own message loop will be the first to retrieve keystrokes headed for its window, in which case you process accelerators by calling the Windows function *TranslateAccelerator* as you always have. If you have an in-process object, however, the container's message loop will pick up the message and call your *IOleInPlaceActiveObject::TranslateAccelerator* function before it dares to translate the accelerator itself. This member of *IOleInPlaceActiveObject* is not called in a local object, so Cosmo leaves it empty. The

Polyline sample in this chapter doesn't do anything with it either because it has no accelerators.

Nevertheless, Cosmo, as a local server, has two other considerations for its message loop in order to handle accelerators properly. First, it must avoid calling the Windows function *TranslateMDISysAccel* if it is an MDI application because the Window menu is not available during an in-place session. Second, it must call *OleTranslateAccelerator* to give the container a shot at the accelerators before the server dumps the message to *TranslateMessage* and *DispatchMessage*. Therefore, Cosmo's message loop, *CCosmoFrame::MessageLoop,* appears as follows:

```
WPARAM CCosmoFrame::MessageLoop(void)
    {
    MSG     msg;

    while (GetMessage(&msg, NULL, 0,0 ))
        {
        //If we're in place, don't bother with MDI accelerators.
        if (NULL==m_pIOleIPFrame)
            {
            if (m_pCL->TranslateAccelerator(&msg))
                continue;
            }

        //Translate our accelerators.
        if (TranslateAccelerator(m_hWnd, m_hAccel, &msg))
            continue;

        if (NULL!=m_pIOleIPFrame)
            {
            if (NOERROR==OleTranslateAccelerator(m_pIOleIPFrame
                , &m_frameInfo, &msg))
                continue;
            }

        TranslateMessage(&msg);
        DispatchMessage(&msg);
        }

    return msg.wParam;
    }
```

The *IOleInPlaceFrame* pointer (*m_pIOleIPFrame*) and the OLEINPLACE-FRAMEINFO structure (*m_frameInfo*) passed to *OleTranslateAccelerator* are those obtained from *IOleInPlaceSite::GetWindowContext*. We saved these earlier in *CFigure::InPlaceActivate*.

NOTE: A local MDI and multiple-use server will have a more complex test to determine whether to call *OleTranslateAccelerator*. You *must* call the function with the *IOleInPlaceFrame* pointer and OLEINPLACEFRAMEINFO structure of the container that's involved with the in-place object in the *currently active* document.

## Rounding Third...and Heading for Home

We're now on the home stretch and have only to add little bits of code to complete our in-place object implementation. Some of the following steps are required, and some are optional:

1. (Required) Resize your tools on *IOleInPlaceActiveObject::ResizeBorder*.

2. (Required) Implement *IOleInPlaceObject::SetObjectRects* to update your editing window's position, and call *IOleInPlaceSite::OnPosRect-Change* and *IOleInPlaceSite::Scroll* if you need more room.

3. (Required) Implement *IOleInPlaceActiveObject::OnFrameWindow-Activate* and *IOleInPlaceActiveObject::OnDocWindowActivate* to handle UI changes appropriately.

4. (Required) Implement minimal context-sensitive help support in case the container supports it, even if you don't.

5a. (Required) Provide Undo support by calling *IOleInPlaceSite::Discard-UndoState* when making a change after activation and by implementing *IOleInPlaceObject::ReactivateAndUndo*.

5b. (Optional) If you have an Undo command, call *IOleInPlaceSite-::DeactivateAndUndo* if the command is given immediately after deactivation. Also implement *IOleObject::DoVerb* for OLEIVERB-_DISCARDUNDOSTATE.

6. (Optional) Call *IOleInPlaceFrame::SetStatusText* with messages for your menu items even if you don't have your own status line.

7. (Optional) Provide methods for opening the object into a server window from an in-place–active state.

8. (Optional) If you have modeless pop-up windows that are usually shown as part of your user interface, show/hide or enable/disable these windows when your *IOleInPlaceActiveObject::EnableModeless* function is called. You can also tell the container to do the same by calling *IOleInPlaceFrame::EnableModeless*.

Also, if you want to experiment with your object as an inside-out object, mark it with OLEMISC_INSIDEOUT and OLEMISC_ACTIVATEWHEN-VISIBLE (I've done the latter for the Polyline sample in this chapter) and then run the object with a container that supports inside-out objects. You'll see that such a container treats your application somewhat differently when it's marked with these bits, especially the latter bit, which is common with OLE controls.

Let's now look at each of these steps in more detail.

### Implement *IOleInPlaceActiveObject::ResizeBorder*

Whenever an end user resizes the container's frame window or document window, the container calls your *IOleInPlaceActiveObject::ResizeBorder* function with the *IOleInPlaceUIWindow* interface for the container's frame or document.[6] A flag indicates which one the pointer refers to. Within *ResizeBorder*, you must renegotiate for space for your object's tools and resize those tools to fit in that space:

```
STDMETHODIMP CImpIOleInPlaceActiveObject::ResizeBorder(LPCRECT pRect
    , LPOLEINPLACEUIWINDOW pIUIWindow, BOOL fFrame)
    {
    //The document case is uninteresting to us.
    if (!fFrame)
        return NOERROR;

    if (!m_pObj->InPlaceToolsRenegotiate())
        return ResultFromScode(INPLACE_E_NOTOOLSPACE);

    SetWindowPos(m_pObj->m_pTB->Window(), NULL, pRect->left, pRect->top
        , pRect->right-pRect->left, m_pObj->m_cyBar, SWP_NOZORDER);

    return NOERROR;
    }
```

This code from Cosmo first shows that as a result of not having any document tools, we can simply return NOERROR if the *fFrame* parameter is FALSE. Otherwise, we need to go through the *RequestBorderSpace* and *SetBorderSpace* process again, which is handled by *CFigure::InPlaceToolsRenegotiate*. To optimize, you can try calling *SetBorderSpace* first; only if that fails do you need to call *RequestBorderSpace* again. Either way works—containers expect this.

---

6. Remember that *IOleInPlaceFrame* inherits from *IOleInPlaceUIWindow*, but do *not* typecast this *IOleInPlaceUIWindow* to *IOleInPlaceFrame* because the additional frame members will not be in the vtable for the interface pointer you receive. Upcasting like this is playing with some serious fire.

When you've renegotiated for space, reposition your tools by using the rectangle passed to this function. This rectangle contains the same thing you would receive from a call to the container's *GetBorder* function.

### Implement *IOleInPlaceObject::SetObjectRects* and Call Container Position Functions

There will probably be situations in which your object is not entirely visible and the end user will want to see more of the object. This can occur in two ways. The end user might scroll the container document directly or might perform some action in your object that would require your application to bring more of itself into view.

When the user scrolls the container document, the container calls *IOle-InPlaceObject::SetObjectRects* with a new position rectangle and a new clipping rectangle. The object must resize its editing window to the new position rectangle, keeping it clipped to the clipping rectangle. Cosmo tells its hatch window to do this, using *CHatchWin::SetObjectRects*, as we saw earlier:

```
STDMETHODIMP CImpIOleInPlaceObject::SetObjectRects(LPCRECT prcPos
    , LPCRECT prcClip)
    {
    m_pObj->m_pHW->RectsSet((LPRECT)prcPos, (LPRECT)prcClip);
    return NOERROR;
    }
```

When *IOleObject::SetObjectRects* is called, you have no choice but to obey the restrictions of the container. However, that does not mean that you have no control over the size of your object. The object can itself provide grab handles in the hatch border (which are capable of producing mouse events that would show up in the hatch window's message procedure). If the user resizes the object in this way, you can expand the editing window to show more data. (This does not affect the container's site size, however.) When an object is resized in this way, calculate the new position rectangle of the editing area of the window—making sure that you exclude all object adornments and the hatch border—and call *IOleInPlaceSite::OnPosRectChange*. In this function, the container will determine whether it can give you this space, or at least a portion of it, and will call your *IOleInPlaceObject::SetObjectRects* in response. At that time, your application obediently resizes itself. Some containers will let your object grow as much as it wants. Others will never let it grow larger than the container site itself. It's your responsibility to determine how your application will respond in these cases. You can either scale your object to fit the container's specified position rectangle or add scroll bars to your in-place editing window if you cannot scale and cannot display all the object's data in the position rectangle. In any case, what you do with the position rectangle from *SetObjectRects* is your choice, as long as your object can fit into it somehow.

Scrolling can also occur when part of your object's window is clipped by the container's windows. For example, a table object with only half the cells visible might be clipped by the edge of the container's document window. The user might use the arrow keys to move the cell selection into one of the hidden cells. In that case, your object can call *IOleInPlaceSite::Scroll* to scroll the document programmatically. If the container scrolls, it will again call *IOle-Object::SetObjectRects* to tell the object its new position.

### Implement *IOleInPlaceActiveObject*
### Functions for Window Activation Changes

When an object is UI active in a container document, it has menus and tools displayed in the container's frame window. If that container has multiple documents, the object's user interface should no longer appear in the frame when the user switches to another document. Therefore, the container might need to ask an object to temporarily remove its UI or to reinstall it when document activation changes. For this reason, *IOleInPlaceActiveObject-::OnDocWindowActivate* is passed a BOOL indicating whether the document is becoming active or inactive. In response, the object must either show or hide its UI-active state:

```
STDMETHODIMP CImpIOleInPlaceActiveObject::OnDocWindowActivate
    (BOOL fActivate)
    {
    HWND        hWndTB;

    if (NULL==m_pObj->m_pIOleIPFrame)
        return NOERROR;

    hWndTB=m_pObj->m_pTB->Window();

    if (fActivate)
        {
        m_pObj->m_pIOleIPFrame->SetActiveObject(this
            , (*m_pObj->m_pST)[IDS_INPLACETITLE]);

        m_pObj->m_pIOleIPFrame->SetMenu(m_pObj->m_hMenuShared
            , m_pObj->m_hOLEMenu, m_pObj->m_pFR->Window());

        if (m_pObj->InPlaceToolsRenegotiate())
            {
            RECT    rc;
```

*(continued)*

```
                m_pObj->m_pIOleIPFrame->GetBorder(&rc);
                SetWindowPos(hWndTB, NULL, rc.left, rc.top
                    , rc.right-rc.left, m_pObj->m_cyBar
                    , SWP_NOZORDER);

                ShowWindow(hWndTB, SW_SHOW);
                }
            }
        else
            {
            m_pObj->m_pIOleIPFrame->SetActiveObject(NULL, NULL);

            //Hide our tools, but do not call SetMenu.
            ShowWindow(hWndTB, SW_HIDE);
            }

        return NOERROR;
        }
```

The implementation of this function need not perform full UI deactivation or UI activation. To hide our UI, we simply need to call the frame's *SetActiveObject* with NULLs and hide our own tools. The container will then reinstate its tools, or if the document that is becoming active also has a UI-active object, that other object will reinstate its own tools. Hiding the object's UI requires no call to *IOleInPlaceFrame::SetMenu* because either the container will show its own UI or another object will display its shared menu.

When asked to show the object's UI, we call *SetActiveObject* again and reinstall the shared menu (which we saved in *CFigure* variables for this exact reason). We must also negotiate space for our tools again because conditions might have changed in the container since we were last active and the container might now refuse our tools.

Closely related to document switches is the function *IOleInPlaceActiveObject::OnFrameWindowActivate,* which tells the active object that the container's frame window has become active or inactive. An object has no set requirements here, but it can use this notification to perhaps show or hide modeless pop-up windows or control the activation of other user interface elements.

## Implement Minimal Context-Sensitive Help Support

Both containers and objects must provide at least some support for context-sensitive help even if they do not support that feature themselves. An object that doesn't support this help mode must avoid trapping the Shift+F1 and Esc accelerators—let them pass through to the container. If the container wants to enter the help mode, it will do so and call *IOleInPlaceObject::Con-*

*textSensitiveHelp(TRUE)* in your object. When this help mode is on and you do not support such help, ignore all mouse clicks in your object—that is, provide no help.

If an object does support context-sensitive help, it will trap Shift+F1 and Esc. On Shift+F1, enter the mode and tell the container by calling *IOleInPlace-Site::ContextSensitiveHelp(TRUE)*. When you detect Esc, stop the help mode and tell the container with *IOleInPlaceSite::ContextSensitiveHelp(FALSE)*.

## Provide Undo Support

Undo is another function that you might or might not support and your container might or might not support. Even if an object does not support Undo, the object must still reactivate itself in *IOleInPlaceObject::ReactivateAndUndo*. If your object has an Undo command itself, you not only reactivate yourself but also perform an Undo directly. Cosmo does the reactivation only because its Undo is really a Remove Last Point command, not a true Undo. (Cosmo does not maintain a last command variable to perform an Undo properly.) So it handles this case as follows:

```
STDMETHODIMP CImpIOleInPlaceObject::ReactivateAndUndo(void)
    {
    return m_pObj->InPlaceActivate(m_pObj->m_pIOleClientSite, TRUE);
    }
```

An object that supports the Undo command should maintain a flag such as *CFigure::m_fUndoDeactivates*, which is initially set to TRUE in *CFigure-::InPlaceActivate*. If the user selects Undo when this flag is set, call *IOleInPlace-Site::DeactivateAndUndo*, which will cause the container to deactivate the object. Cosmo does this in *CFigure::Undo*, which is called whenever Ctrl+Z or Alt+ Backspace accelerators are detected:

```
BOOL CFigure::Undo(void)
    {
    if (!m_fUndoDeactivates)
        return FALSE;

    m_fUndoDeactivates=FALSE;
    m_pIOleIPSite->DeactivateAndUndo();
    return TRUE;
    }
```

Cosmo clears *m_fUndoDeactivates* whenever the user makes any change whatsoever to the figure. This happens in *CFigure::SendAdvise* just before Cosmo sends off an *IAdviseSink::OnDataChange* notification, which also happens for any change to the object. In addition, if this is the first change to the object after activation, we must call *IOleInPlaceSite::DiscardUndoState* to tell the container that we will not be calling *DeactivateAndUndo* so that it can free any state it's holding.

The object can hold some Undo state itself in case the container calls *IOleInPlaceObject::ReactivateAndUndo*. (Cosmo does not maintain such a state.) If the container makes a change after deactivation so that it will not call this function, it calls *IOleObject::DoVerb(OLEIVERB_ DISCARDUNDOSTATE)*, at which time the object frees the state. *DoVerb* is used because once an object is deactivated, the container no longer has *IOleInPlaceObject* or *IOleInPlaceActive-Object* pointers but will have *IOleObject*.

The overall effect of this Undo handling is meant to create the illusion that the user is working with a single undo stack in the container, even though objects from other components are being activated. This is why *ReactivateAndUndo* and *DeactivateAndUndo* involve both the activation change and the Undo operation—activation changes themselves are not meant to be visually undoable operations.

### Call *IOleInPlaceFrame::SetStatusText*

As described in Chapter 22, the container maintains ownership of the status line throughout in-place sessions. If an object ever needs to display text in that status line, it can pass the string to *IOleInPlaceFrame::SetStatusText*. Cosmo does this whenever it detects WM_MENUSELECT messages in *CCosmoFrame-::FMessageHook*; the strings, of course, describe the functionality of the menu item in question. Cosmo has its own status line (which is hidden along with the rest of the server's main window) process the message and load the correct string. For an in-place object, we extract this string and send it to the container, making support for this feature quite simple:

```
BOOL CCosmoFrame::FMessageHook(HWND hWnd, UINT iMsg, WPARAM wParam
    , LPARAM lParam, LRESULT FAR *pLRes)
    {
    TCHAR           szText[128];

    if (WM_MENUSELECT!=iMsg)
        return FALSE;

    if (NULL==m_pIOleIPFrame)
        return FALSE;

    m_pSL->MenuSelect(wParam, lParam);
    m_pSL->MessageGet(szText, sizeof(szText));
    m_pIOleIPFrame->SetStatusText(szText);

    *pLRes=0L;
    return TRUE;
    }
```

You can see this interaction at work when you activate a Cosmo figure in place in the version of Patron from Chapter 22.

## Provide Techniques for Opening into a Window

I mentioned before that a container can call *IOleObject::DoVerb(OLEIVERB-_OPEN)* to end in-place activation and activate an object in a separate window. We saw earlier how Cosmo implements this verb. In addition, Cosmo provides the user with two other ways to do the same thing: through the Open item on the Edit menu and by picking up double clicks in the hatch border around the figure. You can also use a Ctrl+Enter accelerator for this purpose. (Cosmo does not.) In Cosmo, the menu selection and hatch border double click end up in *CFigure::OpenIntoWindow*, which calls our own *DoVerb* to deactivate and open into a separate window:

```
void CFigure::OpenIntoWindow(void)
    {
    if (NULL!=m_pIOleIPSite)
        {
        m_fUndoDeactivates=FALSE;

        m_pImpIOleObject->DoVerb(OLEIVERB_OPEN, NULL
            , m_pIOleClientSite, -1, NULL, NULL);

        m_fForceSave=TRUE;
        SendAdvise(OBJECTCODE_DATACHANGED);
        }

    return;
    }
```

We clear *m_fUndoDeactivates* so that an Undo command in the open Cosmo window will not attempt to in-place deactivate.

When I implemented the Open command in Cosmo, I encountered a couple of problems. The first was that the object would not be saved (through *IPersistStorage::Save*) after I opened it in a window and closed the window. The problem was that the object was not marked as dirty after such an operation. To correct this, I added the flag *m_fForceSave* to *CFigure* and set it to TRUE in *CFigure::OpenIntoWindow*. That causes the object to appear as dirty when closing, which generates the proper call to *IOleClientSite::SaveObject*. The other, related, problem was that the container site was blank when I opened the object into a window until that site was repainted. So in *CFigure::OpenInto-Window*, I immediately send an *OnDataChange* notification, which propagates to the container as *OnViewChange*, causing it to repaint the site.

### Show or Hide Modeless Pop-Up Windows

The final bit to complete an in-place object is to handle *IOleInPlaceActive-Object::EnableModeless* and call *IOleInPlaceFrame::EnableModeless*. As mentioned in Chapter 22, the container and the object use each other's *EnableModeless* to show/enable or hide/disable floating pop-up windows at various points in the in-place session. If you ever have occasion to tell the container to hide its pop-up windows (say, for example, when you display a modal dialog box), call *IOleInPlaceFrame::EnableModeless* with TRUE when showing the dialog box and with FALSE when closing the dialog box. The container will do the same thing for the same reasons with *IOleInPlaceActiveObject::Enable Modeless*. The use and implementation of these functions are, however, entirely optional.

# Summary

The addition of in-place activation to an embedded object server is only a small portion of the overall server structure but one that provides great user benefits. This chapter follows the implementation steps for adding in-place support to the Cosmo sample and also provides an in-place–capable version of the Polyline server.

The first step in such an implementation is to prepare the object and its server for the implications of merging user interface elements with a container. This can affect how the server deals with its menus, its toolbars, and its own child window classes. Assumptions that you can make when creating a stand-alone application no longer apply when in-place activation is involved. Simply said, menus, toolbars, and child windows might appear in a document or a frame window that is not owned by the server itself. This means that you have to be careful routing messages and specifying how the rest of the server code deals with these pieces of user interfaces.

The remaining steps mainly involve the implementation of *IOleInPlace-Object* and *IOleInPlaceActiveObject*, modifications to *IOleObject::DoVerb*, and all the work necessary to create the in-place UI, including keyboard accelerators. In addition, a number of small considerations require handling, such as Undo operations, context-sensitive help, window resizing and activation, document scrolling, object resizing, status line text, and the handling of modeless pop-up windows. In-place–capable objects can also choose to mark themselves with OLEMISC_ACTIVATEWHENVISIBLE and with OLEMISC-_INSIDEOUT. This choice really has little impact on the object itself. These flags primarily tell the container when to activate the object in the first place.

# PART VI

# OLE CONTROLS AND THE FUTURE OF OLE

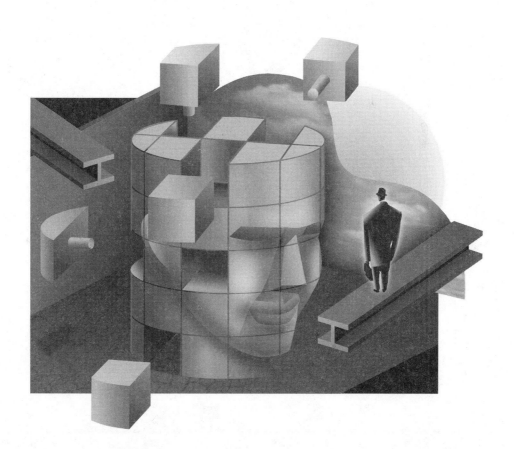

## CHAPTER TWENTY-FOUR

# An Introduction to OLE Controls

I awoke this morning to the sound of my alarm clock. As usual, I pressed the snooze button to get a few extra minutes of rest. After repeating this a couple of times, I finally turned off the alarm by moving a switch on the clock. Then I went to the bathroom, where I turned a doorknob to open the door and flipped a switch on the wall to turn on the light. I grabbed the handle on my shower door, moved the door aside, pushed up a round knob to turn on the shower, and rotated the knob to adjust the water temperature. When I left the bathroom, I flipped the light switch again to turn off the light, went downstairs, and then grabbed another handle to open the refrigerator to find some breakfast. After breakfast, I used a lever on the sink faucet to turn the water on and rinsed my dishes.

When I finally got to my study, I flipped one switch to turn on the desk light and rotated another knob to turn on a halogen lamp and adjust its brightness. Then I flipped a rocker switch to turn on my computer's monitor. On the screen appeared the applications I've been using to write this book. They too display an assortment of buttons, switches, and dials, as do the mouse and the keyboard I use.

All of these devices—buttons, switches, knobs, handles, dials, levers, and so on—are examples of *controls*. The first designers of graphical user interfaces created on-screen controls with the express purpose of imitating known mechanical controls. People, they thought, were used to mechanical controls, so they would naturally understand things that looked and behaved the same way on a computer screen.

A control, be it mechanical or computer-generated, is a device for transforming a human intent into a precise signal that triggers some response. The knob on my shower lets me carry out my intent to turn on water and adjust the temperature. The actions of lifting and twisting are transformed into the precise response of opening two valves and adjusting the mixture of water from the hot and cold water pipes. A push-button control on my computer screen transforms my mouse click into an event that triggers a specific piece of code. Pressing keys on my keyboard does exactly the same thing.

Through the design of a control, as well as the labeling or visual aspects of that control and the context in which it appears, an end user can decide what a control will do when activated in some way and whether using that control is an appropriate thing to do. By using controls, programmers build much of the user interface of an application. Controls are among the most powerful building blocks for creating applications, perhaps even more powerful than functional libraries.

In the early versions of Microsoft Windows, only a few controls were available: the push button (momentary switch), the radio button (mutually exclusive options), the check box (mutually inclusive options), the list box (variable list of exclusive or inclusive options), the edit control (text field), and the label and other static controls. Building a custom control—one of your own design—was difficult and did not allow you to extend the system very easily. Over time a few attempts have been made to make the creation of custom controls easier. Windows 3.0 introduced some standards for doing so, but they were weak. Visual Basic introduced the Visual Basic Extension, or VBX, which turned into a powerful but somewhat inelegant design for custom controls as well. When 32-bit operating systems became the norm, Microsoft discovered that the VBX standard did not carry over to 32-bit systems very well, so a new standard was called for.

The result is the technology named *OLE Controls,* in which an OLE control is the name we give a custom control built using OLE technologies. As you might remember from Figure 1-7 on page 26 in Chapter 1, OLE Controls builds on nearly every other technology in OLE, including in-place activation, OLE Automation, and Property Pages. For this reason, an OLE control is a superset of nearly any other type of component in OLE—you can use a control as a compound document content object, as an automation object, or simply as a data source. Because anything you can do in OLE is somehow encompassed in an OLE control, the OLE Controls technology is sometimes identified as what OLE is all about. Whether this is true, OLE controls—as COM components with a large number of interfaces—are powerful extensions of the existing component system. They also work well on both 16-bit and 32-bit operating systems.

Microsoft has great plans for using OLE Controls in future system shells. This will allow end users to quickly create their own user interface using existing controls or to build a new control based on those that already exist—all in a way that makes sense to the users. Microsoft's development tools are targeting the construction of applications, especially of the user interface, using OLE Controls, much as Visual Basic has done in the past. At the time of writing, Microsoft Access 2 already supports OLE Controls in building database forms.

However — and this is a big however — OLE Controls as a technology is still in its infancy at the time of writing this book. (This is especially true when OLE Controls is compared to the other technologies we've seen, which are generally more mature and solid.)[1] As a consequence, there is a conspicuous lack of well-known standards about what an OLE control should do at a minimum. The same is true for what sorts of features a container for OLE controls should have in order to take advantage of the content and functionality of most controls. In this chapter, we'll first examine the technical aspects of OLE Controls — which interfaces are used for what reasons, along with a few additional interfaces we haven't yet encountered. We'll then take a brief look at some samples: a version of Polyline enhanced to work mostly as a control and a version of Patron enhanced to work somewhat as a control container. What do I mean by "mostly" and "somewhat"? As I was writing this code, I had only a few standards to work with, so I cannot call these samples definitive or necessarily correct in all regards. They are certainly not complete as far as features go. My purpose for providing these samples is to give you an idea of how containers and controls interoperate through the OLE Controls technology.

This technology is indeed rich. As such, it in itself will be the topic of entire books.[2] Development tools such as the OLE Controls Development Kit (CDK), which comes with Visual C++, and the Microsoft Foundation Classes make the creation of a control nearly trivial. Visual C++ in particular provides a Control Wizard that automatically generates most of a control, leaving its specific features for you to implement yourself.[3] You basically never see the interfaces and the architecture that we'll discuss in this chapter.

So while we'll see the details of the technology and how a minimalist OLE control and control container manifest themselves in straight C++ code, we will generally not see how you would work with this technology yourself. Again, the samples provided here are simply for demonstration and are not intended to be model implementations. In the coming years, I'm sure that we'll see many great tools for building OLE controls and for building applications with them (as well as other components). As I've mentioned for the other complex OLE technologies, such as OLE Documents and OLE Automation, I encourage you to take advantage of these tools. After all, people use

---

1. This applies even to Connectable Objects, licensing, self-registration, Property Pages, and so on, which were originally defined for the purposes of OLE Controls. These simpler pieces of the puzzle are themselves stable and mature. What I'm talking about here is a full-blown control object, which combines many of these lesser technologies in a higher form.

2. Some are in the works at the time of writing, although not by this author.

3. Work is under way at the time of writing to provide control container support as well.

very powerful mechanical tools to efficiently fabricate the necessary mechanical controls we use in our day-to-day lives. At this point in the history of computing, we're ready to see a tremendous explosion in the number of on-screen controls and in the number of applications that are built with them.

# The Architecture of OLE Controls

What is an OLE control? In mundane terms, a control is mostly a collection of functionality and content (or information). It can also involve a specific and dedicated user interface that allows an end user to directly access the control's functionality and to directly manipulate its content. In addition, a control can be manipulated programmatically so that another piece of code can use it to perform specific tasks. Controls are, therefore, self-contained units of functionality and content that are independent of where they actually reside. That is, a control of a specific type in one container behaves the same as a control of the same type in another container.

An OLE control exposes its functionality through both incoming and outgoing interfaces. The incoming interfaces allow access to a control's content. This includes rendering data for the client of that control through either data structures or individual properties. A control's outgoing interfaces can include not only notifications of data changes or property changes but also custom *event sets*—notifications that a control sends when the user triggers an event in that control. A button control, for example, typically sends an event such as *OnClick* when the user presses it. An edit control might send events such as *OnChange* and *OnValidate*. OLE Controls classifies such events as requests, do events, or simple notifications.

Through events, then, a control transforms a user's actions into meaningful and precise triggers. Code in the container of that control (the container can be another control itself) picks up this event and executes some code in response. A container such as the Patron sample we'll see in this chapter does nothing more than play a user-selected sound in response to an event. More sophisticated containers, Microsoft Access or Visual Basic, for example, allow the user to attach custom code to an event. In either case, the user (or developer) determines exactly what happens when an event occurs.

Events are mechanisms to extend and modify a control's behavior when the control allows it. Certain events notify a container of a control's state change so that the container can cancel or modify that change. Other events ask the container to perform some action itself and give the container a customization capability similar to that which virtual functions give the implementer of a C++ derived class. Like virtual functions, a container might cancel, replace, or enhance the behavior of the operations that the customizable control supports. But unlike virtual functions, events ensure that the control always has a chance to maintain a consistent internal state without relying on the container to defer to it explicitly at some point. This gives the customizable object a higher degree of encapsulation.

A control's content, as I mentioned, consists of both data structures and individual properties. All of the content is usually persistent. The content provided through data structures is usually the data managed in the control itself, such as the text inside an edit control. Properties, on the other hand, are named characteristics and values that a control or a container can modify programmatically. Although some of these can expose bits of the control's actual content, most are used to expose a control's visual and behavioral aspects. Visual aspects include colors, fonts, label text, and so on. Behavioral aspects include operations such as telling a button whether it should behave as the momentary variety or as the push-on/push-off sort.

## Control and Container Requirements

If you take a control's functionality and content and add to them the other means necessary for a container to manipulate a control, you'll come up with five mechanisms that all controls must provide:

- Control properties. A mechanism through which the container can retrieve and modify properties as well as call a control's custom methods. The control must expose the names of properties as well as the names and parameters of its methods. This also includes a control-supplied user interface to allow end users to manipulate properties.

- Control events. A mechanism through which the control notifies the container of events that occur in the control.

- Control visuals. A mechanism through which the control draws itself but gives the container the responsibility to manage the control's position and dimensions.

- Control mnemonics. A mechanism through which the control can specify and process its keyboard mnemonics and accelerators, such as Alt key combinations and arrow keys.

- Control persistence. A mechanism through which the container can ask the control to save its current information into a storage or a stream object.

On the other side of the picture, a control container must provide various services to all controls within its form or document. Each control in the container is given its own *control site,* just as a content object is given a site in a compound document. These sites expose to the control container properties called *ambient properties* because they define the ambiance of the control's environment. By using ambient properties, the container can specify the default colors, fonts, alignment, and behavioral suggestions. Controls can choose to retrieve these properties from the container at run time to integrate themselves better into the form or document as a whole.

A container must also supply a control with event handlers—container-provided implementations of a control's outgoing interfaces that we can also refer to as *event sinks.* The container determines what other actions should be executed when the various functions in these event interfaces are called.

Besides dealing with properties and events, the container must also provide all the other facilities for object layout, ordering, and keyboard processing because only the container is aware of all the objects in a form and the relationships between those objects. It must also facilitate saving the document or form to a file for later reloading. If appropriate, the container can provide additional user interface features for the registration and creation of controls (for example, a dialog to add controls to the registry and a toolbar populated with buttons that represent the registered controls).

With these items in mind, we can draw up a list of the required mechanisms for a control container:

- Container layout. A mechanism through which the container can create, place, size, and order controls.

- Container form persistence. A mechanism through which the container can save and retrieve the persistent state of controls and the mapping of their events to container actions.

- Container ambient properties. A mechanism through which the container can expose ambient properties to all controls.

- Container event handlers. A mechanism through which the container can provide and expose event entry points to each specific control.

- Container extended controls. A mechanism through which the container can aggregate an OLE control into a container-implemented extended control. The container can then add its own methods, properties, and events to a control so that they appear as native control features to the rest of the container. This allows the container to treat all controls in a uniform fashion without regard to which piece of code implements a method, a property, or an event.

■ Container keyboard. A mechanism through which the container can inform controls of accelerator and other keyboard events as well as handle special purpose buttons, labels, and simple frame controls (a type of control that contains other controls).

In general, a container will also support different operational modes, named *design mode* and *run mode*. In design mode, the container is oriented toward assigning actions to control events, creating new controls, moving controls around in a form, and performing other tasks concerned with the form's design. A container can deactivate all controls at this time or simply tell controls to ignore user input. In run mode, also called *user mode,* the controls on the form are fixed in number and in position and any events a user sends trigger the actions assigned to those events in design mode. The container tells controls how to behave in each mode through ambient properties, as we'll see shortly.

## The Structure of OLE Controls and Containers

Nearly all of the requirements for both controls and control containers are fulfilled using OLE technologies that we've seen in this book. You can guess that properties are most likely handled through OLE Automation and that events are handled through connection points. The complete list of which technologies satisfy which requirements is shown in Table 24-1.

| Requirement | OLE Technologies Applied |
| --- | --- |
| Control properties | OLE Automation, Property Change Notifications, Property Pages, Connectable Objects (for change notification) |
| Control events | OLE Automation, Connectable Objects |
| Control visuals | OLE Documents (including in-place activation) |

**Table 24-1.** *(continued)*
*OLE technologies used to create OLE Controls.*

**Table 24-1.** *continued*

| Requirement | OLE Technologies Applied |
| --- | --- |
| Control mnemonics | OLE Controls (in-place activation handles accelerators for the UI-active control that has the focus) |
| Control persistence | Structured Storage, Object Persistence (any persistence model) |
| Container layout | OLE Documents, OLE Drag and Drop |
| Container form persistence | Structured Storage, Object Persistence |
| Container ambient properties | OLE Automation, OLE Controls |
| Container event handlers | OLE Automation, Connectable Objects |
| Container extended objects | OLE Controls |
| Container keyboard | OLE Controls |

The entries in Table 24-1 marked "OLE Controls" refer to the specific interfaces and protocols involved only with OLE Controls. The interfaces in question are *IOleControl*, *IOleControlSite*, and *ISimpleFrameSite*.

Structurally, an OLE control is a COM object, housed inside a server (as we saw in Chapter 5), that implements the following interfaces in addition to *IUnknown*:[4] *IOleObject*, *IOleInPlaceObject*, *IOleInPlaceActiveObject* (on a subobject if necessary), *IOleControl*, *IDataObject*, *IViewObject2*, *IRunnableObject*, *IExternalConnection* (if linking to embeddings is allowed), *IOleCache2*, *IDispatch*, *IConnectionPointContainer*, *ISpecifyPropertyPages*, *IProvideClassInfo*, and one or more of *IPersistStorage*, *IPersistStream*, or *IPersistStreamInit* (depending on the necessary persistence models). Besides implementing these interfaces, a control should also self-register and can optionally support licensing through *IClassFactory2*. Controls are usually marked with OLEMISC_ACTIVATEWHENVISIBLE, and each must include type information that describes its incoming and outgoing dispinterfaces. In addition, a control's coclass entry in its type information should also be marked with "control." Finally, a control must also support a connection point for each outgoing interface by virtue of implementing *IConnectionPointContainer*.

---

4. This list of interfaces assumes an in-process control. An in-process control can choose not to support caching by not exposing *IOleCache2*. At the time of writing, some of these interfaces did not support marshaling, so implementing controls in local servers was not possible. Typically, controls are in-process, which is why such support wasn't provided in the first place.

To the outside world, then, an OLE control appears as shown in Figure 24-1. It should be obvious that implementing an object with this many interfaces, along with type information, self-registration, licensing, and so on, is not exactly a trivial task. Although Microsoft chose to use existing technologies as a base and to provide maximum flexibility, it is up to tools like the CDK to make implementation less complex.

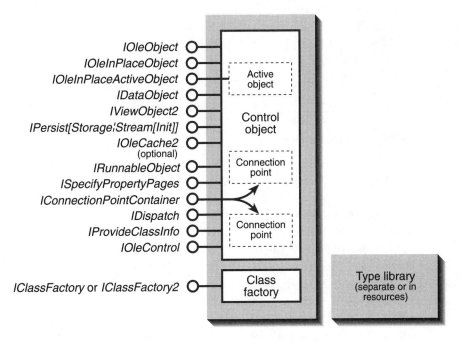

**Figure 24-1.**
*The structure of an in-process OLE control.*

Much of the implementation of an OLE control is to support OLE Automation and OLE Documents. The same applies to a control container, which, in addition to all of those site interfaces for an in-place–capable container that we've seen up to Chapter 22, implements *IOleControlSite*, *ISimpleFrameSite*, and *IDispatch* on the control site as well. (*IDispatch* exposes the container's ambient properties.) In addition, a site provides sink objects for however many event sets a control has, as well as a sink that implements *IPropertyNotify-Sink*. All of this is illustrated on the next page in Figure 24-2, which doesn't show that a container usually supports some of its own user interface for manipulating control properties and events.

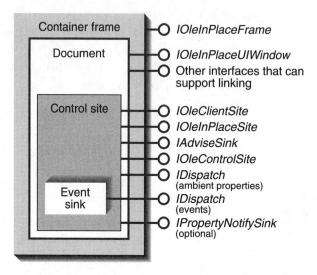

**Figure 24-2.**
*The structure of an OLE control container.*

As you might have noticed in several places in this book, many of the interfaces for both control and container were first defined expressly for OLE Controls. Controls were the first such components to really require licensing, general connection points, property pages, and so forth.

Because we've already explored the majority of these interfaces in previous chapters, we need to look at only the specific points that are relevant to OLE Controls, many of which are involved with the *IOleControl* and *IOleControlSite* interfaces. But before we do this, there are a number of other fine points to cover about control architecture, so the following sections discuss each in detail.

## *IOleClientSite::RequestNewObjectLayout* and MiscStatus Flags

Besides building on OLE Documents, OLE Controls adds more behavior to existing compound document functionality. First, a control container should implement *IOleClientSite::RequestNewObjectLayout*. In OLE Controls, a control that is only loaded or running uses this member function to tell the container that it wants to change its size, as opposed to using *IOleInPlaceSite::OnPosRectChange*, which works only for in-place–active objects. Inside *RequestNewObjectLayout*, the control container should get the new size by calling the control's *IOleObject::GetExtent* and pass it back to the control when convenient through *IOleInPlaceObject::SetObjectRects*.

Second, OLE Controls defines the verb OLEIVERB_PROPERTIES, which tells a control to display its own property pages through *IOleObject::DoVerb*. Typically, a control will show a Properties item on its verb menu as well. In doing so, an OLE control that can be inserted into a standard OLE Documents container (one that does not understand controls at all) gives the user access to those property pages without any modification to the container itself. Such controls usually display their property pages when handling OLE-IVERB_PRIMARY as well. In this way, activating a control from a noncontrol container still gives the user plenty of useful functionality, even if the container doesn't handle the control's events.

The other addition to OLE Documents is a set of control-specific Misc-Status flags that contain status information. Objects store this information in the registry; the information is returned by *IOleObject::GetMiscStatus*. Besides usually specifying OLEMISC_ACTIVATEWHENVISIBLE, a control can include any of the flags described in Table 24-2.

| MiscStatus Flag | Description |
|---|---|
| OLEMISC_INVISIBLE-ATRUNTIME | Indicates that the control has no run-time user interface but that it should be visible at design time. For example, a timer control that fires a specific event periodically would not show itself at run time, but it needs a design-time user interface so that a form designer can set the event period and other such properties. |
| OLEMISC-_ALWAYSRUN | Tells the container that this control always wants to be running. This means that the container should call *OleRun* when loading or creating the object. |
| OLEMISC-_ACTSLIKEBUTTON | Indicates that the control is buttonlike in that it can understand default and cancel properties, as described in "Keyboard Handling, Mnemonics, and *ISimpleFrameSite*" later in this chapter. |
| OLEMISC-_ACTSLIKELABEL | Marks the control as a label for whatever control comes after it in the form's ordering. Pressing a mnemonic key for a label control activates the control after it. |

**Table 24-2.**                                                    *(continued)*
*Control-specific MiscStatus bits.*

**Table 24-2.** *continued*

| MiscStatus Flag | Description |
| --- | --- |
| OLEMISC-_NOUIACTIVATE | Indicates that the control has no UI-active state, meaning that it requires no in-place tools, no shared menu, and no accelerators. It also means that the control never needs the focus. |
| OLEMISC-_ALIGNABLE | Indicates that the control understands alignment properties such as left, center, and right. |
| OLEMISC-_SIMPLEFRAME | Indicates that the control is a simple grouping of other controls and does little more than pass Windows messages to the control container managing the form. Controls of this sort require the implementation of *ISimpleFrameSite* on the container's site. |
| OLEMISC_SET-CLIENTSITEFIRST | Indicates that the control wants to use *IOleObject-::SetClientSite* as its initialization function, even before a call such as *IPersistStreamInit::InitNew* or *IPersistStorage::InitNew*. This allows the control to access a container's ambient properties before loading information from persistent storage.* |
| OLEMISC_IMEMODE | Marks the control as an Input Method Editor (IME). You can use an IME to enter information in large Asian character sets with a regular keyboard. A Japanese IME, for example, allows you to type a word such as "sushi," and when you hit the spacebar, the control converts that word to appropriate kanji or proposes possible choices. Containers sensitive to Asian languages use this bit to communicate IME-specific properties such as font and pop-up–window placement. |

\* At the time of writing, this bit was difficult to support from a container's perspective because neither *OleCreate* (and all variations), *OleLoad*, nor *OleLoadFromStream* currently understand this bit, and *OleLoadFromStream* doesn't understand *IPersistStreamInit*. Therefore, a container has to emulate the exact behavior of these functions to correctly handle this bit. However, the internal working of such functions is not documented, so this is difficult to do correctly. I hope Microsoft will soon update these functions in order to handle OLE controls more robustly or document their exact internal steps.

We'll see how some of these bits are used in the sections ahead.

## *IOleControl* and *IOleControlSite*

These interfaces extend the communication that usually occurs between a container and an object in OLE Documents for the purpose of handling control mnemonics, ambient properties, and extended controls:

```
interface IOleControl : IUnknown
    {
    HRESULT      GetControlInfo(CONTROLINFO *pCtrlInfo);
    HRESULT      OnMnemonic(LPMSG pMsg);
    HRESULT      OnAmbientPropertyChange(DISPID dispID);
    HRESULT      FreezeEvents(BOOL fFreeze);
    }

interface IOleControlSite : public IUnknown
    {
    HRESULT      OnControlInfoChanged(void);
    HRESULT      LockInPlaceActive(BOOL fLock);
    HRESULT      GetExtendedControl(IDispatch **pIDispatch);
    HRESULT      TransformCoords(POINTL *ptlHimetric
                    , POINTF *ptlContainer, DWORD dwFlags);
    HRESULT      TranslateAccelerator(LPMSG pMsg, DWORD grfModifiers);
    HRESULT      OnFocus(BOOL fGotFocus);
    HRESULT      ShowPropertyFrame(void);
    }
```

The *GetControlInfo* and *OnMnemonic* members of *IOleControl* and the *OnControlInfoChanged*, *TranslateAccelerator*, and *OnFocus* members of *IOleControlSite* are described later in this chapter under "Keyboard Handling, Mnemonics, and *ISimpleFrameSite*." We can mention that *IOleControlSite::OnFocus* notifies a site when its control either gains or loses the focus. *IOleControlSite::GetExtendedControl* gives a control a way to access a container's extended control and retrieve any properties it might have. (We'll cover this in more detail in the following section.)

That leaves only a few other methods to discuss briefly here. First is *IOleControl::OnAmbientPropertyChange*, which a container calls whenever it changes an ambient property. It passes the dispID of the property that changed (see the section "Standard dispIDs for Controls" later in this chapter for predefined dispIDs) or DISPID_UNKNOWN to indicate that multiple properties changed. In response, a control retrieves the new property (or properties) as necessary and updates itself. This notification mechanism doesn't involve connection points because there is little need for extensibility. Although control properties and events vary widely, the set of ambient properties is relatively small and varies little from container to container. And whereas a container needs notifications from many objects, a control needs notifications only from a single container. There's no need for overkill simply for ambient properties.

Whenever a control should display its property pages (for example, in response to OLEIVERB_PROPERTIES), it should first call *IOleControlSite::ShowPropertyFrame*. The reason for this is that the container might have an extended control built around the control that received the verb. Calling *ShowPropertyFrame* allows the container to include any of its own property pages along with those the control specifies through *ISpecifyPropertyPages::GetPages*. If the container returns an error from *ShowPropertyFrame*, however, the control should proceed to show its own property pages—do not expect the container to always implement the function.

*IOleControl::FreezeEvents* allows the container to turn off (freeze) and turn on (thaw) a control's events. When the events are frozen, the control will not fire them—it might queue them or discard them, but it won't fire them. The choice is up to the control itself.

The other two members of *IOleControlSite*—*LockInPlaceActive* and *TransformCoords*—generally have to do with events as well. *LockInPlaceActive(TRUE)* tells the container that a control wants to stay in the active state until *LockInPlaceActive(FALSE)* is called. This is primarily to prevent crashing problems when an in-place window is destroyed and messages are still coming to that window. A control will often call *LockInPlaceActive* before and after an event is fired if destroying the in-place window would cause problems.

*TransformCoords* handles the presentation of a uniform coordinate system to the container through all events, methods, and properties while allowing controls to choose whichever coordinate system they want. For example, if a MouseDown event is fired, the container should receive the coordinates in a system it understands instead of in whatever system the control is using. Windows programmers have always taken this for granted—any message or event coming from Windows had coordinates expressed in client-area units. But because events can come from any number of vastly different controls, all controls must take whatever coordinates they have in HIMETRIC and send them to *IOleControlSite::TransformCoords* to convert them to the container's units. Those units are then sent with the event itself.

## Extended Controls

To a container, an OLE control is already a convenient package of functionality and content set behind a large group of interfaces used for accessing those features. A control, however, will not maintain properties and support methods that are relevant only to the container. It would be beneficial, then, for the container to have a way to package its own custom properties and methods in a control so that those properties and methods appear as if they were native to the control itself. For example, a control does not maintain any information about its name or position within a container form. A container, however, might like to store this information as properties of that control. In this way, the rest of the container code can treat all properties as if they were native to the control itself.

An extended control is a partial control that wraps around another control through containment and aggregation in order to supply extended functionality that the control itself knows nothing about. In other words, the container provides its own extended control implementation that overrides specific interfaces on another control through containment and exposes the remaining interfaces through aggregation. This relationship is illustrated in Figure 24-3. An extended control typically augments the methods and properties exposed by a control by providing its own *IDispatch*. This interface implementation filters out container-specific dispIDs before passing the call to the control's *IDispatch*. If the extended control has its own events as well, it also implements *IConnectionPointContainer*. Other interfaces are overridden as necessary, in the same way that an in-process handler (as we saw in Chapter 19) overrides specific interfaces from the default handler as it sees fit. Whatever container code then communicates with the extended control sees it as nothing more than an ordinary control with added features.

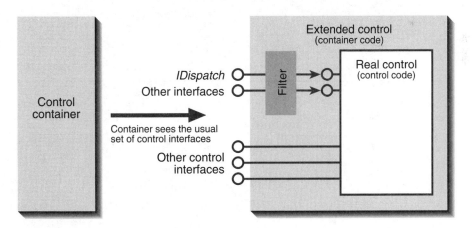

**Figure 24-3.**
*An extended control wraps around another control through containment and aggregation to support container-specific properties, methods, and events.*

This aggregation between control and extended control is one instance in which the extended control would delegate *QueryInterface* to the real control for all unrecognized interfaces. This allows the control to add new interfaces over time without requiring a change to the container or to the extended control itself. This works because the container, having intimate knowledge of its own extended control, knows exactly which interfaces the extended control will override. The container always knows that when it asks for *IDispatch*, for example, it will get the extended control's *IDispatch*.

A container doesn't have to implement extended controls if it has no reason to do so. In that case, *IOleControlSite::GetExtendedControl* should return E_NOTIMPL. Otherwise, this member function should return the *IDispatch* interface for the container's extended control managed by the site. A control can then access any properties of the extended control itself. (There are a few standards for this, as we'll see later in this chapter.) A control typically cannot depend on an extended property being present unless the control has intimate knowledge about the containers in which it will be embedded.

## Keyboard Handling, Mnemonics, and *ISimpleFrameSite*

As we saw in Chapter 22, in-place activation by itself allows keyboard accelerators to work only for the current UI-active object. While this is great for content objects, it doesn't work well for controls. When a form has multiple controls that are all in-place active, pressing keyboard mnemonics—Alt key combinations among others—should activate an appropriate control regardless of whether it's UI active.

To accommodate this need, both controls and containers require special handling. Controls have to make special considerations inside their implementation of *IOleInPlaceActiveObject::TranslateAccelerator*. Instead of simply processing its own accelerators, a control should decide whether it wants priority for the keystroke or whether it wants to give the container the chance first. When a control wants priority for a keystroke, it processes that keystroke first. If it wants to give the container priority, it calls *IOleControlSite::TranslateAccelerator* and then handles the keystroke if the container does not. For example, an edit control might want priority for a key combination such as Ctrl+C (Edit Copy) but might give the container priority for the Tab key. Because interpretations of specific keys vary from control to control, this mechanism allows the control to do what makes the most sense.

Now, of course, *IOleInPlaceActiveObject::TranslateAccelerator* applies only to the control that is UI active—the control with the focus. Mnemonics, however, have to apply to all controls in the form simultaneously, and the container is responsible for finding the right control to notify for any keystroke.

A control must therefore tell the container what keystrokes it wants. This is the purpose of *IOleControl::GetControlInfo*, which returns a CONTROLINFO structure to the container:

```
struct CONTROLINFO:
    {
    ULONG    cb;          //Structure size
    HACCEL   hAccel;      //Mnemonics table for the control
    USHORT   cAccel;      //Number of mnemonics
    DWORD    dwFlags;     //CTRLINFO_* flags
    };
```

```
#define CTRLINFO_EATS_RETURN  1  //Control processes RETURN key
#define CTRLINFO_EATS_ESCAPE  2  //Control processes ESC key
```

This structure contains a Windows accelerator table that describes the keystrokes a control wants to process.[5] The CTRLINFO_* flags let a control tell the container whether it processes the Enter or Esc key when the control has the focus, which is important for default and cancel button handling, as described later in "Default and Cancel Buttons." A control is allowed to change its mnemonics at run time, so it calls *IOleControlSite::OnControlInfo-Changed* to tell the container to reload the data if necessary.

When the user presses any key, the container first sends that keystroke to the current UI-active control. Otherwise, the container receives the WM_KEYDOWN or WM_SYSKEYDOWN message itself. The container can choose to eat certain keys itself, which usually involves the Enter and Esc keys. When the container doesn't use a key itself or doesn't choose to block it, the container searches each control's mnemonics table for a match. The order in which this happens is entirely the container's decision. When a match is found, the container calls the appropriate control's *IOleControl::OnMnemonic*, and the control then does whatever is appropriate for that keystroke.

There are, of course, some special cases for handling mnemonics. First of all, a control marked with OLEMISC_ACTSLIKELABEL doesn't process its own mnemonics. When a label's mnemonic matches a keystroke, the container should set the focus to (activate the UI of) whichever control is attached to that label in the form. (By "attached," I mean that the label gives a name to the other control.) This implies a container-managed order to the controls on the form other than the z-order (which handles only overlapping controls).

A user generally expects that the Tab key will move the focus from control to control, usually according to the visible order of the controls themselves,

---

5. An *accelerator table* is an array of ACCEL structures contained in global memory and is identified with the *hAccel* field in CONTROLINFO. The control always maintains ownership of this memory. The container should never attempt to free the memory itself.

ignoring those marked OLEMISC_INVISIBLEATRUNTIME, OLEMISC-_SIMPLEFRAME, OLEMISC_ACTSLIKELABEL, and OLEMISC_NOUI-ACTIVATE (for example, icons and pictures). Each control that can be tabbed to is called a *tab stop*. Usually, buttons, check boxes, list boxes, edit controls, combo boxes, and the like are tab stops.

When tabbing through the controls on a form you must pay attention to sets of exclusive buttons, such as radio buttons, a type of control in which only one button in the group can be checked at any given time. The Tab key navigates to this group as a single unit, and another Tab keystroke moves the focus to the control after the group. Inside the group, the arrow keys and the spacebar are used to change the selected option. The container is responsible for determining where the group starts and stops and is responsible for ensuring that only one button in the group is checked. The container determines whether any given control is an exclusive button by checking whether the type of the object's DISPID_VALUE property is OLE_OPTEXCLUSIVE.[6] With this information, it can determine where the group starts and stops in order to handle it appropriately. The container can also have its own user interface for assigning such boundaries.

When processing Tab keystrokes, a container must also take into account controls marked OLEMISC_SIMPLEFRAME. A simple frame control is one that groups other controls together — the Windows group box control is an example of this. A simple frame has its own window in the container and creates a group boundary so that the group acts as a single tab stop. When a simple frame receives Windows messages, it must pass those messages to the container through the interface *ISimpleFrameSite*:

```
interface ISimpleFrameSite : IUnknown
    {
    PreMessageFilter(HWND hWnd, UINT iMsg, WPARAM wp, LPARAM lp,
        LRESULT *plResult, DWORD *pdwCookie);
    PostMessageFilter(HWND hWnd, UINT iMsg, WPARAM wp, LPARAM lp,
        LRESULT *plResult, DWORD dwCookie);
    }
```

When the simple frame receives a message, it calls *ISimpleFrameSite::PreMessageFilter*. The container does what it wants with the message, stores a return value for the message in *\*plResult*, and stores some other piece of information (such as a pointer to a data structure) in *\*pdwCookie*. If the con-

---

6. The OLE_OPTEXCLUSIVE type has an identity of GUID_OPTIONVALUEEXCLUSIVE as defined in the OLE CDK header files. A container has to retrieve the type of the property and then retrieve the GUID for that type using *ITypeInfo* member functions. Along a similar line, OLE Controls defines the type OLE_TRISTATE for the handling of the selection state of check boxes.

tainer returns S_FALSE from *PreMessageFilter*, the control should not process the message itself. Otherwise, the simple frame can perform its own processing of the message, after which it calls *ISimpleFrameSite::PostMessageFilter*. The control passes to this function the same cookie that was returned from *PreMessageFilter*, allowing the container to pass information through the entire sequence of calls.

The container responds to the messages it receives in a variety of ways. The container might check for special keystrokes, implement its Tab key behavior, handle arrow keys in a special way, process WM_PAINT messages, and so forth. This chapter will not explore the uses of *ISimpleFrameSite*, so consult the CDK documentation for more information.

## Standard dispIDs for Controls

I mentioned earlier that OLE Controls defines a taxonomy for the classification of methods, properties, and events. Not only that, but OLE Controls defines a large number of standard dispID values beyond those we saw in Chapter 14. In defining these standards, OLE Controls uses the term *location* to describe which piece of code implements a particular method or property. The term *variety* describes how rigid a contract is defined for the property, method, or event in question. *Standard* properties have a specified behavior that must be followed. *Common* properties are more lax, as they have only a suggested behavior. *Other* properties, as you might guess, have no specific behavior and are entirely implementation-dependent. OLE itself doesn't define any methods, properties, or events in the common and other groups.

There are no less than 14 standard control properties. The names of the most interesting ones are listed in Table 24-3 on the next page. In addition, there are three standard methods—*Refresh*, *DoClick*, and *AboutBox*—and eight standard events—*Click*, *DblClick*, *KeyDown*, *KeyPress*, *KeyUp*, *MouseMove*, *MouseUp*, and *Error*. All of these have negative dispID values, indicating their standard status. This also applies to the 15 or so standard ambient properties (the interesting ones are described in Table 24-4) and a handful of standard extended properties, as described in Table 24-5. To avoid conflicts in the programmatic symbols for these dispIDs, all ambient properties are given symbols in the form DISPID_AMBIENT_<*property*>, as in DISPID_AMBIENT_FORECOLOR. All other symbols use DISPID_<*property*> as usual.[7]

---

7. I could not find a header file that defined symbols for the standard extended properties. According to the OLE Controls specification, DISPID_X_NAME is 0x80010000, DISPID_X_VISIBLE is 0x80010007, DISPID_X_PARENT is 0x80010008, DISPID_X_CANCEL is 0x80010037, and DISPID_X_DEFAULT is 0x80010038.

| Control Property | Type and Description |
|---|---|
| BackColor, ForeColor, FillColor, BorderColor | (OLE_COLOR) The control's color scheme. |
| BackStyle, FillStyle, BorderStyle, BorderWidth, BorderVisible, DrawStyle, DrawWidth | (short or long) Bits that define a control's visual behavior—solid or transparent, thick or thin borders, line style, and so forth. |
| Font | (IDispatch *) The font used in the control. This is an IDispatch pointer to a standard font object (see below). |
| Caption, Text | (BSTR) Strings containing the control's label (the caption) or its textual contents (the text). The caption does not necessarily name the control in the container. (See the extended Name property in Table 24-5.) |
| Enabled | (BOOL) Determines whether the control is enabled or disabled. (If disabled, the control is likely grayed.) |
| Window | (HWND) The window handle of the control, if it has one. |

**Table 24-3.**
*Standard control properties.*

| Ambient Property | Type and Description |
|---|---|
| BackColor, ForeColor | (OLE_COLOR) Provides controls with the default background and foreground colors. Use by a control is optional. |
| Font | (IDispatch *) A pointer to a standard font object (see below) that defines the default font for the form. Use by a control is optional. |
| LocaleID | (LCID) The language used in the container. Use by a control is recommended. |
| UserMode | (BOOL) Describes whether the container is in design mode (FALSE) or run mode (TRUE). A control must use this property to change its available functionality as necessary. |

**Table 24-4.**
*Standard ambient properties.*

*(continued)*

**Table 24-4.** *continued*

| Ambient Property | Type and Description |
|---|---|
| *UIDead* | (BOOL) Describes whether the container is in a mode in which controls should ignore user input. This applies irrespective of *UserMode*. A container might always set *UIDead* to TRUE in design mode and can set it to TRUE when it hits a breakpoint or such during run mode. A control must pay attention to this property. |
| *MessageReflect* | (BOOL) Specifies whether the container wants to receive Windows messages such as WM_CTL-COLOR, WM_DRAWITEM, WM_PARENTNOTIFY, and so on as events. |
| *SupportsMnemonics* | (BOOL) Describes whether the container processes mnemonics or not. A control can do whatever it wants with this information: for example, it would not underline characters it would normally use as a mnemonic. |
| *ShowGrabHandles, ShowHatching* | (BOOL) Describes whether a control should show a hatch border or grab handles (in the hatch border) when in-place active. Controls must obey these properties, giving the container ultimate control over whether the control or the container actually draws these bits of user interface. A control container might want to draw its own instead of relying on each control, in which case these ambients are always FALSE. |
| *DisplayAsDefault* | (BOOL) Describes whether a button control should draw itself with a thicker default frame. This property is exposed to buttonlike controls only. |

| Extended Property | Type and Description |
|---|---|
| *Name* | (BSTR) The container's name for the control. |
| *Visible* | (BOOL) The control's visibility. |
| *Parent* | (*IDispatch* ∗) The dispinterface of the form containing the control. |
| *Default, Cancel* | (BOOL) Indicates whether this control is the default or cancel button as described later under "Default and Cancel Buttons." |

**Table 24-5.**
*Standard extended control properties.*

The OLE_COLOR type is used for any color-related properties in OLE Controls. Usually it holds a standard COLORREF type, but it can also hold an index to a palette, a palette-relative index, or even a system color index appropriate for *GetSysColor*. The OLE Controls run-time DLL, the same DLL that supplies the *OleCreatePropertyFrame* and *OleCreatePropertyFrameIndirect* functions, provides *OleTranslateColor*, a function that converts an OLE_COLOR type to a COLORREF given a palette.

The standard font object is also implemented as part of the OLE Controls DLL. A font object is created with the OLE API function *OleCreateFontIndirect*, which takes a FONTDESC structure describing the font metrics. This function returns a pointer to either an *IFont* interface or an *IDispatch* interface (also called *IFontDisp*) through which the client can manipulate the font's properties or retrieve the corresponding HFONT that is used to draw text with that font. The container's ambient *Font* property supplies a font of this type (VT_DISPATCH specifically). A control's *Font* property also uses this kind of font object.

In a similar vein, a standard picture object is created with the API function *OleCreatePictureIndirect* or loaded from disk using *OleLoadPicture*. For this object, you can get a pointer to an *IPicture* interface or to an *IDispatch* pointer called *IPictureDisp*. Through this pointer, you can also manipulate the picture's properties.

For more information about these types and their interfaces, please refer to the CDK documentation.

## Default and Cancel Buttons

The design of Windows dialog boxes includes the concepts of the default button and the cancel button. The default button is activated when the Enter key is pressed and the control that currently has the focus is not itself a button. In other words, when a button has the focus, pressing the Enter key triggers that button. The cancel button is similar but simpler: when the Esc key is pressed, whatever button is marked as the cancel button is activated. Esc always affects the cancel button regardless of what control has the focus.

OLE Controls provides a means to duplicate this behavior. To begin with, controls that act as buttons (those that understand default and cancel operations) mark themselves with the bit OLEMISC_ACTSLIKEBUTTON. In design mode, a container provides the programmer with menu commands or some similar method to mark one such control with "default" and another control with "cancel." These commands should be enabled only if the selected control is marked with OLEMISC_ACTSLIKEBUTTON. Assigning default and cancel buttons is similar to marking one button as DEFPUSHBUTTON and giving another the identifier IDCANCEL in a typical Windows dialog.

What the container does with this information depends on a number of factors. Let's take the easy one first: the Esc key. When this key is pressed, the keystroke first goes to the UI-active control. If that control is marked CTRL-INFO_EATS_ESCAPE, we can be assured that it will process that keystroke. Note, however, that the button marked "cancel" in the container doesn't know that it's the cancel button, so it will not process this keystroke even if it is UI active. Anyway, if the UI-active control does not eat the Esc key, the container checks whether it has a button marked "cancel" and, if so, calls that control's *IOleControl::OnMnemonic*. Because the control knows it's a button (it's marked as such), it understands any mnemonic to mean "Press me" and will fire its primary event, even if the mnemonic isn't in its CONTROLINFO. That's part of being a button.

The default button is a little more complicated. First of all, there is an added UI element—a thick frame around the button that indicates that the button is the default. Second, the default button isn't always the one that the programmer marked. As a demonstration, open a typical Windows dialog box, such as File Open, and the initial default button will be the DEFPUSH-BUTTON in the template, in this case the OK button. Notice that the OK button doesn't have the focus, but it is still the default because it is marked as such. Now hit the Tab key until the Cancel button has the focus. Notice that it is now the default button because it has the thick frame. If you press Enter, you cancel the dialog. Well, don't cancel the dialog; instead, use the mouse to click on one of the list boxes. Notice that the focus goes to the list box and that the OK button once again becomes the default button.

This is the behavior OLE Controls allows you to duplicate, and it involves the *DisplayAsDefault* ambient property. Only one site in any given form or document should have this flag set to TRUE at any one time. When it is set, and the control in that site is a push button, the control will draw itself with a thick border. So first the container has to change this ambient property in its sites as focus changes between buttons as detected in *IOleControl::OnFocus*. If any button receives the focus, the container sets *DisplayAsDefault* to TRUE and calls *IOleControl::OnAmbientPropertyChange*. If the control with the focus is not a button, the container sets *DisplayAsDefault* to FALSE, notifies the control, and sets *DisplayAsDefault* to TRUE for the marked default button. Also, whenever any nondefault button loses the focus, the container must set that site's *DisplayAsDefault* to FALSE and notify the control.

Handling *OnFocus* and the *DisplayAsDefault* ambient property in this fashion treats the UI element more or less correctly. We still need to handle the Enter key and nonbutton controls that eat it. As with Esc, if the UI-active control eats the Enter key, it will specify CTRLINFO_EATS_RETURN. When such a control receives the focus, the container must turn off *DisplayAsDefault* for even the default button because the Enter key will never reach the container to be processed as a mnemonic.

## Events and Event Handling

A control can support as many event sets as it wants by describing their outgoing interfaces in its type information, marking each as a "source" in the control's coclass section. Only one of these source interfaces can also be marked "default," which makes it the control's primary event set.

Not all outgoing interfaces are event sets, as is the case with *IProperty-NotifySink*. Event sets are those interfaces that have meaning only to the particular control that defines them in its type information. A container that wants to process events in an event set and take action on them must somehow provide, usually at run time, an implementation of that particular interface. For this reason, controls almost always define an event set as a dispinterface. This allows a container to implement, at compile time, a sink object whose *IDispatch* can handle any arbitrary dispinterface at run time. The container uses the object's type information usually to display a list of events to the user or developer, allowing that person to assign actions to those events. The sink does little more than map an event dispID to some action to execute—it doesn't need to know the semantics of the event itself.

A simple container such as Patron can choose to support only a control's primary event set. Sophisticated containers should support all source interfaces that a control defines for itself, allowing a user or a developer to assign actions to all events.

OLE Controls classifies event types as *request, before, after,* and *do* events. A control sends a request event before the control does anything with the event itself, allowing the container to prevent further processing. *IPropertyNotify-Sink::OnRequestEdit* is an example. An edit control, as another example, might send an *OnValidate* event before processing every character typed into it, or it might send such an event before it loses the focus. The return value of such an event is obviously important. When a control doesn't allow the container a choice in the matter, it will send a before event prior to something happening. (The Windows message WM_INITMENUPOPUP is a good example; it is sent before a menu becomes visible.) Controls ignore any return code for such events. In the same manner, a control will ignore a return value for an after event, which is really only a notification to tell the container to do whatever it wants. Finally, a do event is one that allows the container to supplement or override the control's default behavior. Do events usually involve more complex arguments and return values.

Keep in mind that controls maintain no persistent state themselves for events—they simply fire events to any connected sinks. The actions taken on particular events are entirely an issue for the container, which must maintain the assignments as part of a form's persistent state. The container, of course, also provides whatever user interface or language mechanisms are appropriate for assigning actions to events in the first place.

## Control Persistence

I mentioned earlier that a control can choose to implement one or more of *IPersistStorage*, *IPersistStream*, and *IPersistStreamInit*. Because most controls maintain small data sets, they generally prefer and support stream-based persistence. Accordingly, a control container must be prepared to handle any one of these models, as the Component Cosmo sample in Chapter 8 demonstrated. CoCosmo's code prefers *IPersistStorage* over the others—most control containers will, however, prefer *IPersistStreamInit*, then *IPersistStream*, and then *IPersistStorage*. In addition, control containers must take OLEMISC-_SETCLIENTSITEFIRST into account as well.

A control can also choose to support multiple persistence models for maximum flexibility, but the container determines which model is given preference. Some containers may give storage-based persistence priority and others may use streams first. Either way, a control gets its chance to save its own data.

Be aware that stream-based controls will not automatically support caching because the data cache is entirely storage-based. In other words, a control implementing *IPersistStream[Init]* need not and cannot support *IOleCache2* itself or anything else to do with caching. This can markedly reduce the space required by the control as well as the time it takes to load a control in the first place. (This is because instantiating the cache does take a considerable amount of time.) The control should still be able to render a metafile or a bitmap for itself through *IDataObject::GetData* because a container might still want to cache presentations itself. Such a container can simply create its own data cache with *CreateDataCache* and manage it in a container-owned storage in which the control's own stream would be located.

A final note about persistence: Some containers do not store their forms in a binary format. Visual Basic, for example, saves a form as a straight-text file containing a description of the contents, including all control properties. A Visual Basic FRM file looks something like this:

```
VERSION 2.00
Begin Form ControlDialog
    Caption         =   "Some Form"
    ClientHeight    =   1665
    ClientLeft      =   7035
    ClientTop       =   1710
    ClientWidth     =   3795
    Height          =   2040
    Left            =   6990
    LinkTopic       =   "Form1"
    ScaleHeight     =   1665
    ScaleWidth      =   3795
    Top             =   1380
    Width           =   3885
    Begin CommandButton DoThings
        Caption         =   "&Do Things..."
        Height          =   495
        Left            =   240
        TabIndex        =   4
        Top             =   960
        Width           =   1095
    End
```

⋮

To support saving properties as text in this manner, OLE Controls specifies that a control should be able to provide a property set (as we discussed in Chapter 16) through its *IDataObject::GetData* member. It should also reinitialize itself with that same property set through *IDataObject::SetData*. This specific property set has the format ID *{FB8F0821-0164-101B-84ED-08002B2EC713}*, the contents of which are documented in the CDK.

## Control-Specific Registry Keys

To round out our discussion of the OLE Controls architecture, we'll cover two registry keys that a control should include. The first is simply named Control, which a control can include under its CLSID alongside entries such as

Insertable and InprocServer32. This is the only means by which to mark a registered object as an OLE control. Containers can use this key to populate an Insert Control dialog box.[8] Controls that are useful only to containers that know more about them might not include Control in the registry, requiring a container to know the control's CLSID ahead of time.

The second key is named ToolboxBitmap32. Its value is a path to a DLL or an EXE and a resource identifier such as is used for the DefaultIcon entry we saw for OLE Documents. This key allows a control container to extract a $16*15$ button face image for a registered control appropriate to display in a toolbar or tool palette (such as that which Visual Basic uses). Usually the module registered for ToolboxBitmap32 will be the same as the control's server module itself.

A control might or might not include the Insertable key under its CLSID. The key indicates that the control can be inserted into an OLE Documents container as a regular in-place–capable embedded object. This means that the control supports storage-based persistence and doesn't rely on a container to provide event sinks, extended controls, ambient properties, handling of control specific MiscStatus flags, or *IOleControlSite*. Including this key with a control means that you've made a conscious effort to test the control with noncontrol containers, that the control is prepared to work with a container, and that the control still provides value in such scenarios.

When a control does include Insertable, it should add Properties to its list of verbs. When this verb or OLEIVERB_PRIMARY shows up in *IOleObject::DoVerb*, the control should display its own property pages. This allows users of noncontrol containers to still manipulate the control and its state without requiring any interaction from the container.

An OLE control should generally be self-registering so that the control's DLL (or EXE) is all that one needs to copy to another machine in order to have a fully functional control (within the bounds of licensing, of course). Accordingly, a control container should provide some sort of user interface to invoke a control's self-registration facilities. This can amount to little more than a File Open sort of dialog or a more elaborate control browser— whatever is appropriate for the container.

---

8. At the time of writing, the OLE UI Library contained no standard implementation of this dialog.

# Notes on Patron as a Partial OLE Control Container

As an in-place–capable container for OLE Documents, the Patron sample from Chapter 22 is already well on its way to becoming an OLE control container. For this chapter's sample (CHAP24\PATRON), we'll try adding some control-related features to demonstrate a number of the concepts we've been describing. As elsewhere in our work with OLE Documents, implementing container features involves a good deal of user interface. Supporting OLE Controls is no exception.

Let me state again that Patron is *not* a complete control container by any stretch of the imagination. Patron merely demonstrates some of the techniques involved while leaving others unsupported. This sample doesn't implement any Tab key handling or tab order support, nor does it implement *ISimpleFrameSite*. It also does not handle default and cancel buttons, exclusive buttons, or labels. It doesn't have any way to call a control's methods or to manipulate its properties. Patron does not implement *IPropertyNotifySink*, demonstrate extended controls, provide a user interface for self-registering controls, use a control's toolbox bitmap, or deal at all with licensing issues. And finally, Patron ignores OLEMISC_SETCLIENTSITEFIRST and works only with controls that implement *IPersistStorage* and those marked "Insertable."

This last point deserves some clarification—Patron doesn't supply its own Insert Control dialog box, which normally would be populated with those objects marked with "Control" in the registry. Instead, it relies on the Insert Object dialog box we've used since Chapter 17. Therefore, Patron works only with controls marked "Insertable" and those that use the storage-based persistence model. If you'd like to play around with a control in Patron, you'll have to manually add the Insertable key and see what happens.

So does Patron do anything? What's left to demonstrate? Well, we still have a number of important pieces of a container—event handling, ambient properties, and keyboard mnemonics. The following list describes those parts of the OLE Controls technology that are demonstrated in this sample:

■ Patron supplies the ambient properties *UserMode, UIDead, Supports-Mnemonics, Font, BackColor, ForeColor, LocaleID, ShowGrabHandles,* and *ShowHatching*. The site's implementation of *IDispatch* is found in AMBIENTS.CPP. The interface does little more than copy values stored in Patron's *CTenant* class to the VARIANT out-parameters. The standard font object (14-point Arial) to return for the *Font* ambient property is managed in the *CPages* class, which creates the font inside *CPages::Init* with a call to *OleCreateFontIndirect*.

■ Patron provides menu items for switching between design mode and run mode, toggling the *UserMode* ambient property. In design mode, Patron deactivates all the controls and will return S_FALSE from *IOleInPlaceSite::CanInPlaceActivate*. In this mode, Patron supplies its own grab handles for sizing controls and its own drag-and-drop pick region for moving controls around in the document. Various classes in Patron, such as *CPatronDoc*, *CPages*, and *CTenant*, maintain duplicate flags named *m_fDesignMode* for the purpose of knowing which mode is in use. In the tenant, for example, this flag will suppress the initial activation of any object marked OLEMISC-_ACTIVATEWHENVISIBLE. When you switch to run mode, Patron will reactivate any such control and activate the UI of the currently selected one. When you create a new control in design mode, Patron does not initially activate it as usual for an embedded object because most controls have no open active state.

■ Patron also provides menu items for toggling the *UIDead*, *ShowGrab-Handles*, and *ShowHatching* ambient properties—you can watch what effect they have on various controls. The latter two properties are toggled together. All changes to ambient properties do, of course, generate a call to *IOleControl::OnAmbientPropertyChange*, which is centralized in the function *CTenant::AmbientChange*.

■ Patron's site object, implemented in the class *CTenant*, implements *IOleControlSite* (ICONSITE.CPP) and the *IDispatch* interface for ambient properties (AMBIENTS.CPP). Inside *IOleControlSite*, Patron implements the members *OnControlInfoChanged*, *LockInPlaceActive*, and *TransformCoords*. Having no extended controls, we have no need to implement *GetExtendedControl* and *ShowPropertyFrame*. Having no keyboard support—nor support for default and cancel buttons—allows us to return E_NOTIMPL from *OnFocus* and *Translate-Accelerator*.

■ The implementation of *IOleControlSite::LockInPlaceActive* simply increments or decrements a lock count. This affects *CTenant-::DeactivateInPlaceObject*, which will not deactivate a control when the lock count is nonzero. Instead, it sets a flag in *CTenant* named *m_fPendingDeactivate*. Whenever *IOleControlSite::LockInPlaceActive* decrements the lock count to 0, it will call *CTenant::DeactivateIn-PlaceObject* if *m_fPendingDeactivate* is set.

■ When Patron detects WM_KEYDOWN or WM_SYSKEYDOWN for Alt or Ctrl key combinations, it attempts to match a control's mnemonic in order to call *IOleControl::OnMnemonic*. This ends up in *CPage::TryMnemonic*, which loops through all controls on a page (using the current z-order), calling *CTenant::TryMnemonic*. This latter function will then scan the accelerator table in the control's CONTROLINFO structure as returned from *IOleControl::GetControl-Info*. If a match is found, we call *IOleControl::OnMnemonic*. Patron loads an object's CONTROLINFO structure initially inside *CTenant-::ControlInitialize*, replacing it whenever *IOleControlSite::OnControl-InfoChanged* is called.

■ Patron will call *OleRun* for any control marked with OLEMISC-_ALWAYSRUN. (See *CTenant::ObjectInitialize*.) Furthermore, code in *CTenant::Draw* and *CTenant::Select* suppresses drawing anything for a given control at run time when that control is marked OLEMISC-_INVISIBLEATRUNTIME. The tenant code will also avoid UI activation of controls marked OLEMISC_NOUIACTIVE.

■ Patron implements *IOleClientSite::RequestNewObjectLayout* to retrieve the control's new size. It passes the size to *CTenant::UpdateInPlace-ObjectRects*. This latter function generates the clipping rectangle and calls *IOleInPlaceObject::SetObjectRects*.

■ Patron allows you to assign a system sound to any control event through the Control Events dialog box shown in Figure 24-4. The Edit Events menu item is enabled whenever a control has events, which is determined through its type information. (This item is also placed on the right mouse button pop-up menu.) Although the actions you can assign to any event are limited, Patron does demonstrate how to handle a generic event set and how to save and load the action assignments persistently—with the limitation that it does not process event-specific arguments.

Patron best demonstrates the handling of an arbitrary event set. To display the dialog shown in Figure 24-4 (whose template is in EVENTS.DLG, by the way), we need some list of events and also to maintain a mapping from each event dispID to an action. We also need to implement an *IDispatch* that works with any event set to execute the action assigned to whatever event comes into *IDispatch::Invoke*. To receive these events in the first place, we have to find the type information for the event set. The following sections describe how Patron performs these steps.

**Figure 24-4.**
*Patron's Control Events dialog box in which the user can assign actions
(system sounds) to individual events. The events shown are those of the
Polyline control implemented in this chapter.*

## Initializing an Event Map

To handle the mapping between events and actions, Patron uses the class
*CEventMap* (EVENTS.CPP). Each instance of *CTenant* that contains a control
will manage an instance of *CEventMap*, which itself holds an array of EVENT-
MAP structures. All of these structures are defined as follows in TENANT.H:

```
//Event actions
typedef enum
    {
    ACTION_NONE=-1,
    ACTION_BEEPDEFAULT=MB_OK,
    ACTION_BEEPASTERISK=MB_ICONASTERISK,
    ACTION_BEEPEXCLAMATION=MB_ICONEXCLAMATION,
    ACTION_BEEPHAND=MB_ICONHAND,
    ACTION_BEEPQUESTION=MB_ICONQUESTION,
    ACTION_TAILING=-2
    } EVENTACTION;


typedef struct tagEVENTMAP
    {
    DISPID      id;             //Event ID
    EVENTACTION iAction;        //Action to take
    BSTR        bstrName;       //Event name (function only)
    } EVENTMAP, *PEVENTMAP;


class CEventMap
    {
    public:
        UINT          m_cEvents;
        LPTYPEINFO    m_pITypeInfo;
        PEVENTMAP     m_pEventMap;
```

*(continued)*

```
public:
    CEventMap(LPTYPEINFO);
    ~CEventMap(void);

    BOOL            Init(void);
    BOOL            Set(DISPID, EVENTACTION);
    EVENTACTION     Get(DISPID);
    void            Serialize(LPSTREAM);
    void            Deserialize(LPSTREAM);
};

typedef CEventMap *PCEventMap;

//Event stream in object storage
#define SZEVENTSSTREAM  OLETEXT("\003Event Mappings")
```

Each event map manages its own serialization and deserialization given any stream. Patron uses the stream name "\003Event Mappings," which it creates in the object's storage. Accordingly, we have to prefix the stream name with ASCII 3 to prevent an object from affecting this stream in any way.

Each EVENTMAP structure in an instance of *CEventMap* contains the name of an event (for displaying in the Control Events dialog box), the event's dispID, and whatever action is assigned to it. Regardless of the complexity of the container, these three elements will generally be present. A sophisticated container that allows a user to attach code to an event would, for example, replace the *iAction* field with a pointer to that code and would augment the structure with the names of an event's arguments for use elsewhere in that container's user interface.

You'll notice that the *CEventMap* constructor takes an *ITypeInfo* pointer. This pointer is eventually used to initialize the event map in *CEventMap::Init*. Here we cycle through the member functions of the interface described by *ITypeInfo*, storing each function name and dispID in a separate EVENTMAP structure (the BSTR name is freed in the *CEventMap* destructor):

```
BOOL CEventMap::Init(void)
    {
    LPTYPEATTR      pTA;
    UINT            i;

    if (NULL==m_pITypeInfo)
        return FALSE;

    if (FAILED(m_pITypeInfo->GetTypeAttr(&pTA)))
        return FALSE;
```

```
    m_cEvents=pTA->cFuncs;
    m_pITypeInfo->ReleaseTypeAttr(pTA);

    m_pEventMap=new EVENTMAP[m_cEvents];

    if (NULL==m_pEventMap)
        {
        m_cEvents=0;
        return FALSE;
        }

    for (i=0; i < m_cEvents; i++)
        {
        LPFUNCDESC      pFD;

        m_pEventMap[i].id=0;
        m_pEventMap[i].bstrName=NULL;
        m_pEventMap[i].iAction=ACTION_NONE;

        if (SUCCEEDED(m_pITypeInfo->GetFuncDesc(i, &pFD)))
            {
            UINT        cNames;
            HRESULT     hr;

            m_pEventMap[i].id=pFD->memid;

            hr=m_pITypeInfo->GetNames(pFD->memid
                , &m_pEventMap[i].bstrName, 1, &cNames);

            m_pITypeInfo->ReleaseFuncDesc(pFD);
            }
        }

    return TRUE;
    }
```

To get this far, of course, we need to retrieve the type information for at least the control's primary event set (the only one Patron uses). This is done through *ObjectTypeInfoEvents,* an internal function implemented in CONNECT.CPP:

```
BOOL ObjectTypeInfoEvents(LPUNKNOWN pObj, LPTYPEINFO *ppITypeInfo)
    {
    HRESULT             hr;
    LPTYPEINFO          pITypeInfoAll;
    LPTYPEATTR          pTA;
```

*(continued)*

```
    if (NULL==pObj !! NULL==ppITypeInfo)
        return FALSE;

    if (!ObjectTypeInfo(pObj, &pITypeInfoAll))
        return FALSE;

    *ppITypeInfo=NULL;   //Use this to determine success.

    if (SUCCEEDED(pITypeInfoAll->GetTypeAttr(&pTA)))
        {
        UINT        i;
        int         iFlags;

        for (i=0; i < pTA->cImplTypes; i++)
            {
            //Get the implementation type for this interface.
            hr=pITypeInfoAll->GetImplTypeFlags(i, &iFlags);

            if (FAILED(hr))
                continue;

            if ((iFlags & IMPLTYPEFLAG_FDEFAULT)
                && (iFlags & IMPLTYPEFLAG_FSOURCE))
                {
                HREFTYPE    hRefType=NULL;

                pITypeInfoAll->GetRefTypeOfImplType(i, &hRefType);
                hr=pITypeInfoAll->GetRefTypeInfo(hRefType
                    , ppITypeInfo);

                break;
                }
            }

        pITypeInfoAll->ReleaseTypeAttr(pTA);
        }

    pITypeInfoAll->Release();
    return (NULL!=*ppITypeInfo);
    }
```

This code employs straight usage of *ITypeInfo* member functions to look for an interface marked "source" and "default." The *ITypeInfo* pointer we use comes from another internal function in CONNECT.CPP, *ObjectTypeInfo*. This function simply queries for *IProvideClassInfo* and calls *IProvideClassInfo::Get-ClassInfo*. Nothing fancy.

## Event UI and the Events *IDispatch*

Now that we have an event map, we need a way to assign actions to be stored in the map and an implementation of *IDispatch* to trigger those actions when events occur. This is the point at which a container implementer should think about the possible uses of *IOleControl::FreezeEvents*, wrapping any risky non-reentrant event handling code with calls to *FreezeEvents(TRUE)* and *FreezeEvents(FALSE)*.

As I said earlier, each tenant that contains a control manages an instance of *CEventMap*. When you select the Events menu item, Patron invokes the Control Events dialog box, passing a pointer to the event map owned by the currently selected tenant. This pointer shows up in the dialog procedure *EventsDlgProc*, found in EVENTS.CPP. The dialog is really a user interface for working with the contents of an event map, which is used initially to fill the dialog's list box. Whenever you select an event in the list, the dialog procedure calls *CEventMap::Get* to retrieve the action assigned to that event's dispID and uses that action to check the correct radio button. When you change the selected sound assignment, the dialog calls *CEventMap::Set* to store it in the map for the event's dispID. Obviously, this user interface is simplistic, but it gives you an idea of how action assignment happens.

Given a populated event map, a tenant's implementation of *IDispatch* has something to work with. To receive events, of course, we first have to connect this *IDispatch* to the control as an outgoing interface. This involves retrieving the IID of the event set, going through the control's *IConnectionPointContainer* to find a connection point for that IID, and then passing our event sink interface to *IConnectionPointContainer::Advise*. All this happens with the functions *ObjectEventsIID* and *InterfaceConnect*, both of which are found in CONNECT.CPP. (The *InterfaceDisconnect* function is also used for terminating the connection.) Both functions are straightforward uses of their respective interfaces.

A tenant's event sink is implemented by using the class *CDispatchEvents*. A tenant will create an instance of this class as necessary. (See *CTenant::ControlInitialize*.) *CDispatchEvents* is derived from *IDispatch*, so it receives interface calls directly. Now, because an events interface is defined by the control itself, we have no need to implement any of the *IDispatch* members except *Invoke*. It would be crazy for a control that already knows the type information for its own outgoing interfaces to call *IDispatch::GetTypeInfo*, which would, if implemented, only turn around and ask the object for its type information. So Patron simply returns E_NOTIMPL from this function as well as for *GetTypeInfoCount* and *GetIDsOfNames*.

*Invoke* is where the fun happens. All we need to do is scan the event mappings held in whatever tenant is attached to the instance of *CDispatchEvents* that is called. If we find a match, we execute the action, which in our case means calling *MessageBeep*:

```
STDMETHODIMP CDispatchEvents::Invoke(DISPID dispIDMember, REFIID riid
    , LCID lcid, unsigned short wFlags, DISPPARAMS *pDispParams
    , VARIANT *pVarResult, EXCEPINFO *pExcepInfo, UINT *puArgErr)
    {
    HRESULT     hr;
    VARIANT     varResult;
    EVENTACTION iAction;
    UINT        i;
    PEVENTMAP   pEM;

    if (IID_NULL!=riid)
        return ResultFromScode(E_INVALIDARG);

    if(NULL==pVarResult)
        pVarResult=&varResult;

    VariantInit(pVarResult);
    V_VT(pVarResult)=VT_EMPTY;

    //Only method calls are valid.
    if (!(DISPATCH_METHOD & wFlags))
        return ResultFromScode(DISP_E_MEMBERNOTFOUND);

    iAction=ACTION_NONE;
    pEM=m_pTen->m_pEventMap->m_pEventMap;

    for (i=0; i < m_pTen->m_pEventMap->m_cEvents; i++)
        {
        if (dispIDMember==pEM[i].id)
            {
            iAction=pEM[i].iAction;
            break;
            }
        }

    if (ACTION_NONE==iAction)
        hr=ResultFromScode(DISP_E_MEMBERNOTFOUND);
    else
        {
        MessageBeep((UINT)iAction);
        hr=NOERROR;
        }

    return hr;
    }
```

I suspect that most event handling code for *Invoke* will look a lot like this. What you do after you find a matching dispID, however, and how you then execute the action will be a lot more complicated. This is especially true if you handle arguments that accompany the event, which a sophisticated container will do, as well as event return values. Such a container would be more interesting (and marketable) than a container that doesn't do anything more than beep, tweak, ding, and frazzle when you twiddle controls.

## Serialization and Deserialization of Event Mappings

After the end user has gone to the trouble of creating a form with controls, assigning actions to events, setting properties, and so on, you'd better be sure that you can save this information persistently and reload it when you load the object. As mentioned before, Patron stores its event mappings for each tenant in a stream named "\003Event Mappings" inside the object's storage.

The *CEventMap::Serialize* member, called from *CTenant::Update*, takes care of saving the information. This means writing the dispID/action pairs from its array of EVENTMAP structures and writing a terminator pair at the end of the list:

```
void CEventMap::Serialize(LPSTREAM pIStream)
    {
    EVENTMAP        emTemp;
    ULONG           cbWrite=sizeof(DISPID)+sizeof(EVENTACTION);

    if (NULL==pIStream)
        return;

    if (NULL!=m_pEventMap)
        {
        UINT        i;

        for (i=0; i < m_cEvents; i++)
            pIStream->Write(&m_pEventMap[i], cbWrite, NULL);
        }

    //Write terminating entry.
    emTemp.id=0;
    emTemp.iAction=ACTION_TAILING;
    pIStream->Write(&emTemp, cbWrite, NULL);

    return;
    }
```

Loading the event map for a control simply means reading these pairs back into memory, which happens in *CEventMap::Deserialize*. This function is called from *CTenant::ControlInitialize* (itself called from *CTenant::Load*) when a control is known to have events. The deserialization process ensures that the dispID still exists for the control in question and restores the assigned action if so.

```
void CEventMap::Deserialize(LPSTREAM pIStream)
    {
    if (NULL==pIStream)
        return;

    if (NULL==m_pEventMap)
        return;

    while (TRUE)
        {
        ULONG       cbRead=sizeof(DISPID)+sizeof(EVENTACTION);
        UINT        i;
        HRESULT     hr;
        EVENTMAP    em;

        hr=pIStream->Read(&em, cbRead, NULL);

        if (FAILED(hr))
            break;

        //If we hit the tail, we're done.
        if (ACTION_TAILING==em.iAction)
            break;

        //Assign action to ID if it exists.
        Set(em.id, em.iAction);
        }

    return;
    }
```

This code, which involves *CEventMap::Set*, does not assume that a control's events remain constant between instantiations. Before the tenant asks the event map to load its data from a stream, that event map will have already been initialized using the control's type information (as we do for a new control). Each call to *CEventMap::Set* will verify that the event dispID in question actually exists in the control's event set, and only then will it assign the action loaded from the stream.

If an event that used to exist is no longer available, Patron simply discards the action that was mapped to it. This is no big deal because the user hardly did any work to assign the action in the first place. However, if a user attached hard-written code to an event, we would not want to simply discard that code! That is a surefire way to annoy your users and draw fire from the popular press. So even though the code cannot remain attached to an event, you must still preserve it. Visual Basic, for example, copies the code to a global function. A sophisticated container will likely do something similar.

## Notes on Polyline as an OLE Control

The Polyline component that we've been creating in this book is the closest thing we have already to an OLE control: it is in-place capable, supports outgoing interfaces, and even has a custom interface that exposes its specific properties. It requires only a few specific additions, primarily involving additional interfaces. As with Patron, this chapter's Polyline sample (CHAP24-\POLYLINE) should not be considered a complete control. I'm providing it merely to illustrate how some of the control mechanisms appear in code. I'll leave it to the development tools to create truly complete implementations.

So what are Polyline's limitations? First of all, it's not a terribly useful control—it is much better suited to being a content object in a compound document. Nevertheless, we can use it to demonstrate control-like behavior. Second, Polyline has no accelerators and no mnemonics, so it doesn't demonstrate those aspects of control development. Third, none of its properties are bindable, so Polyline doesn't implement *IPropertyNotifySink* as an outgoing interface. Fourth, it doesn't support Save As Text. And finally, Polyline is not marked for self-registration as shipping controls should be—you'll need to use its REG file to properly register it. This REG file includes the Control key but does not include a ToolboxBitmap entry or mark Polyline with any of the control-specific MiscStatus flags.

These limitations do not mean that Polyline demonstrates nothing of interest. It already supports the connection point mechanism for outgoing interfaces, for example, which we added in Chapter 5. Polyline also demonstrates the handling of both storage-based and stream-based persistence, a feature we added in Chapter 8. Of course, it already implements *IDataObject*, *IViewObject2*, *IOleObject*, *IOleInPlaceObject*, *IOleInPlaceActiveObject*, *IRunnableObject*, *IExternalConnection*, and *IOleCache2*. To Polyline's existing implementation, I've added the features listed on the following pages; implementation of the additional interfaces can be found in CONTROL.CPP.

1. Polyline now supports OLE Automation through a dispinterface named *DIPolylineControl*. This interface exposes the properties *Back-Color*, *LineColor*, and *LineStyle*, with the custom methods *Clear* and *RemoveLastPoint*. These properties and methods reflect the relevant parts of the custom interface *IPolyline10*, which Polyline has carried throughout much of this book. This dispinterface is implemented using a custom interface, *IPolylineControl*, which is now another custom interface alongside *IPolyline10*. The addition of automation support, of course, means that Polyline also has type information. This is described in POLYLINE.ODL and exposed through the addition of *IProvideClassInfo*.

2. Polyline has always supported a custom outgoing interface named *IPolylineAdviseSink10*, with members such as *OnPointChange* and *OnColorChange*. For the purposes of becoming a control, a dispatch version of this interface, *DIPolylineAdviseSink10*, is defined in POLYLINE.ODL and is marked as the default source interface for the control. This interface is Polyline's primary event set. *IPolylineAdviseSink10* is itself marked as a source interface.

3. Polyline implements *ISpecifyPropertyPages* through which it returns only CLSID_PolylinePropPage (INC\BOOKGUID.H). This property page, shown in Figure 24-5, is implemented in CHAP24\POLYPROP and is structurally identical to the Beeper property page sample from Chapter 16. PolyProp simply uses a different set of controls and communicates with a different object. In particular, the property page applies changes through Polyline's custom interface, *IPolylineControl*. (This interface is also used to implement Polyline's incoming dispinterface through *ITypeInfo::Invoke*.)

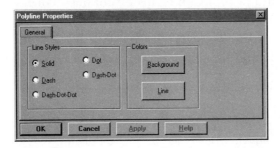

**Figure 24-5.**
*Polyline's property page.*

4. Polyline now supports a Properties verb in *IOleObject::DoVerb* (IOLEOBJ.CPP), which first attempts to call *IOleControlSite::Show-PropertyFrame*. Failing that, Polyline displays its own property page by calling *OleCreatePropertyFrame*. Polyline supports not only OLEI-VERB_PROPERTIES but also its own custom verb with the text "Properties…". It does this because the standard Properties verb has a negative value and will therefore not show up on verb menus by design.

5. Polyline implements *IOleControl* to round out its set of interfaces. Polyline has no accelerators, so *OnMnemonic* does nothing and *Get-ControlInfo* returns a structure containing no accelerators at all. However, Polyline does support event freezing and does reload ambient properties in *OnAmbientPropertyChange*.

6. On creation, Polyline retrieves the ambient properties *BackColor* and *ForeColor* (which are applied to the line color) along with *UIDead* and *ShowHatching*. Polyline's implementation of *IOleControl-::OnAmbientPropertyChange* will reload *UIDead* and *ShowHatching* when they change. The function *CPolyline::AmbientGet* is simply a wrapper for *IDispatch::Invoke(…, DISPATCH_PROPERTYGET,…)*, which is called on the container's ambient properties dispatch inter-face. The function *CPolyline::AmbientsInitialize* retrieves ambient properties and updates *CPolyline* variables as necessary. This latter function is called from within *IOleObject::SetClientSite* — in which the control first becomes aware of its container — and from within *IOleControl::OnAmbientPropertyChange* when it is called with DISPID_UNKNOWN.

7. Polyline supports the *UIDead* ambient property by ignoring WM_LBUTTONDOWN and WM_COMMAND messages that come into *PolyWndProc* (POLYWIN.CPP).

8. To support the *ShowHatching* ambient property, Polyline tells its hatch window, *CHatchWin* (implemented in CLASSLIB), to show or hide its hatching by calling *CHatchWin::ShowHatch*. To hide hatch-ing, the hatch window resizes itself so that it is the same exact size of the Polyline window it contains. This effectively hides the hatching. When told to show hatching again, the hatch window resizes itself to be slightly larger than the Polyline window within it, effectively making that hatch border visible once again.

Polyline implemented its outgoing dispinterface for events by playing a little trick on the rest of its code. In a number of places in its source code, Polyline is written to send notifications through its custom interface *IPolylineAdviseSink10*. Since Chapter 5, this interface was the only one supported through *IConnectionPointContainer*. In making Polyline an OLE control, I had to add support for another outgoing interface that would call the container's *IDispatch::Invoke*. To do this, I added a class, *CAdviseRouter* (CONTROL.CPP), that implements the custom interface *IPolylineAdviseSink10*. When members of that interface are called, *CAdviseRouter* turns around and calls *IDispatch::Invoke*. So when a control container asks to hook up its own event sink to Polyline, we simply give that sink's *IDispatch* pointer to an instance of *CAdviseRouter* and install that object as the sink that the rest of Polyline's code will notify. Not only was I able to make this change without modifying most of Polyline's existing code, but I also had a central place (*CAdviseRouter::Invoke*) to detect whether events were frozen (as flagged in the variable *CPolyline::m_fFreezeEvents*). If events are frozen, this notification router object will not bother to call the container, discarding the event instead.

We have seen almost all of the other features in one capacity or another in previous chapters, so there is little else for us to discuss. Polyline illustrates how an OLE control really brings many of the separate OLE technologies into one coherent package. An OLE control is the combination of a COM object with incoming and outgoing interfaces, a persistent object with multiple persistence models, a data object, a viewable object (that supports caching), an automation object with type information, an object with property pages, an embeddable in-place–capable content object, and an implementation of *IOleControl* to round out the feature set.

Technically speaking, an OLE control is rather complex. With all those interfaces and the protocols that a control must obey, you might think that controls would be fat and slow. On the contrary, Microsoft's engineers have found that an OLE control will consistently outperform a similar control written using straight Windows SDK techniques or using the VBX standard. The primary reason is that interface function calls, especially between a container and an in-process control, are almost always faster than sending or posting messages to a window. This really makes a difference in the core operations of a control: sending events, manipulating properties, and receiving method calls from a container. All of these operations have used Windows messages in the past. With OLE Controls, these operations are accomplished through *IDispatch::Invoke*, which is faster overall. Certainly, other aspects of OLE Controls are slower — creation, for example — but what matters most is run-time performance once the control is loaded.

These performance gains, combined with the benefits of multiple interfaces, licensing, self-registration, object-controlled persistence, and all of the other features we've seen, promises to make OLE Controls the control standard for the future. Microsoft is hedging its bets on this technology in many areas of its business, and as time goes by we'll see that OLE Controls will become even more powerful, more flexible, and more pervasive. It is a technology to watch, along with the rest of OLE.

# Summary

Many user interface elements on a computer are intended to mimic the behavior of the mechanical controls that abound in everyday life. Although operating systems such as Windows provide a base set of control objects, developers can create their own custom controls to extend the available set. In the past, several standards for writing custom controls have existed, but none were designed for extensibility and integration with arbitrary containers. The VBX standard for Visual Basic controls, for example, does not extend well to the 32-bit world. For that reason, Microsoft created OLE Controls, a new standard based on OLE.

A control implemented according to this standard is basically an OLE object that supports persistence, embedding, in-place activation, automation, outgoing interfaces (event sets), property pages, and keyboard mnemonics. To support these features, a control implements many interfaces, including *IOleObject*, *IOleInPlaceObject*, *IOleInPlaceActiveObject*, *IDispatch*, *IConnectionPointContainer*, *ISpecifyPropertyPages*, *IDataObject*, *IViewObject2*, *IProvideClassInfo*, *IRunnableObject*, any of the *IPersist\** interfaces (except *IPersistFile*), and the interface named *IOleControl*, which distinguishes a control from other types of objects.

In the same manner, a container for OLE controls must be capable of handling all these control features. It must also be capable of in-place activation as well as act something like an automation controller by assigning actions to control events that are handled inside event sinks. A container also provides an implementation of *IDispatch* to expose what are called *ambient properties*—characteristics of the container that apply to all controls. In addition, a container's site exposes the interface *IOleControlSite* to provide specific services to the control in that site.

For the most part, the OLE Controls technology uses many of the other technologies in OLE. Only the implementations of the *IOleControl* and *IOleControlSite* interfaces represent those functions that are relevant to controls. This includes, in addition to standard ambient properties, keyboard mnemonics, default and cancel buttons, additional MiscStatus bits, and a number of standard control properties, methods, and events.

This chapter explores the architecture of the OLE Controls technology and demonstrates parts of its implementation using the Patron and Polyline samples from previous chapters. Although controls are complex (and have a large number of interfaces), they are also quite powerful and will become more and more important in the future of component software.

## CHAPTER TWENTY-FIVE

# Future Enhancements and Component Software

*Since going backward is not the answer, how do we move forward?*
—Riane Eisler, *The Chalice and the Blade*

At the beginning of this book, I described OLE as an evolutionary step in computing technology. We've now examined all of OLE's present technologies and learned how they improve existing mechanisms and offer capabilities that have not been available before. In the first section of this chapter, we'll look back at the significant areas of OLE that we covered earlier.

Evolution, of course, simply doesn't stop—improvements and other changes continue to happen. OLE itself will continue to improve on the technologies we've seen and to expand into new areas. In the near future, you'll see enhancements of COM and OLE Documents and, further down the road, more enhancements of COM, OLE Automation, storage, OLE Controls, and OLE Documents and in many other areas. In addition, OLE will be applied to new problems that can be solved well with object-based architectures. For example, shell extensions in Windows 95 are basically simple COM objects with shell-specific interfaces. This chapter will also briefly examine many of the enhancements and additions that will be appearing in the future.

It is important to realize that with all these enhancements and additions you will not see another major version of OLE. Throughout this book, I've referred primarily to OLE as simply OLE. To be historically precise, OLE version 1 was Microsoft's first attempt at solving the compound document problem. OLE 2, which is primarily what this book discusses, improved on the capabilities of OLE 1 and also included the architecture for COM, storage, data transfer, drag and drop, OLE Automation, in-place activation, and so forth. Inherent in COM, however, is the capability to add new features incrementally through the definition of new interfaces. Because of this, talking about "OLE 3" isn't necessary because there basically won't be a major new version requiring the rewriting of applications and components. A new technology such as OLE Controls does not require a complete revision of the underlying COM and OLE architecture—new features and capabilities simply enhance the old.

But there is one question we have yet to answer in this book: "Why does OLE technology exist in the first place?" In other words, we need to make sense of OLE as a whole. We touched on some of the answers in Chapter 1, but there we focused on the more technical and architectural reasons. I freely employed the term *component software* without fully qualifying it, using only the example of compound documents to illustrate this idea.

The main purpose of this chapter, therefore, is to explore what component software means from a human perspective. How does component software affect the common computer user? How does it improve a user's productivity? How does it make the computer experience helpful and fun? We'll explore these questions first through the idea of document-centric computing, which is the reason behind OLE Documents. We'll see that the technology we have today is the first step down the road to an exciting computing environment, one in which users will truly concentrate on tasks rather than applications, which is the hallmark of document-centric computing.

We'll then go one step further, exploring what component software means not only to end users but to the computer industry as a whole. By taking a human approach, we'll see that component software can create what I believe to be an extraordinarily exciting future, filled with opportunity and growth for all programmers, developers, designers, and end users. I believe that component software is the key to a computing environment and industry in which everyone wins and in which we all work together in a partnership to solve real problems. It's an idea whose time has come, and OLE provides the means to make the idea a reality.

## What Is OLE? (A Reprise)

I've defined OLE as a unified environment of object-based services. OLE's services can be customized and its architecture arbitrarily extended through custom services. The overall purpose of such an extensible service architecture, as it is called, is to enable rich integration among components and the applications we know today. Rich integration empowers not only developers but also end users to build a custom application out of separate components, in much the same way that many custom electronic devices are built from smaller electronic components. The electronics industry has known how to work with components for many years. The software industry is just entering this arena. OLE is the first and strongest technology to actually make it possible.

At the core of OLE is the Component Object Model, or COM. COM defines the notion of *interfaces* — the means through which the client of an object communicates with the object. Each interface is a semantically related group of member functions. The interface as a whole represents a feature, and the member functions in that interface represent the various operations that make up that feature. When an object implements an interface, it provides a table of pointers to functions through which a client can access the object's implementation of the feature represented by the interface.

The concept of an interface fully supports the fundamental notions of object-oriented architecture: encapsulation, polymorphism, and reusability. In this concept, we recognize that inheritance, typically the bastion of what it means to be object oriented, is merely a means to the ends of polymorphism and reusability. In this book, I have endeavored to show that these two notions, along with encapsulation, are the truly important ones. When we realize the core needs of object orientation, we discover that inheritance is not the only means to polymorphism and reusability and that these other means have their appropriate uses depending on the problem one is trying to solve.

The fundamental problem that OLE solves is the integration of binary components, unlike programming languages, which primarily solve source code reusability problems. Accordingly, there are very few reasons to see OLE and programming languages as antagonists. Instead, they work together to achieve software solutions that have never been possible before.

Besides providing a means to make binary objects, OLE also improves on the basic object-oriented notions through the concept of the interface and the fact that the omnipresent *QueryInterface* function allows an object to implement multiple interfaces. Because each interface represents a feature, an object can provide support for as many features as it wants simply by implementing the appropriate interface. This idea is probably the most important contribution that OLE makes to object-oriented programming: What *QueryInterface* allows us to do is ask an object, at run time, whether it supports a particular feature. This allows us to write client code for that object that can respond to the absence or availability of a feature in an appropriate manner. The strength embodied in this capability is that whenever an object is updated to support a feature it had not supported before, any and all clients that are already aware of that feature, even those that are already running, can immediately take advantage of the presence of that feature on the updated object. OLE allows you to drop a new object implementation into a running system and have it be immediately integrated with existing clients. Not only that, but you can also make incremental changes to clients. When those clients are deployed in a running system, they can immediately take advantage of object features that they had not used before. We call all of this the robust evolution of functionality over time.

Interfaces allow an object's designer to factor that object's functionality and content into groups of a higher level than individual member functions. Traditionally, factoring an object's capabilities resulted in a set of member functions and data members for an object. Together, the functions and data members were referred to as the object's singular interface. OLE provides an entirely new means to factor an object's capabilities into discrete and higher-level features first and then to factor those features into the necessary functions and data members. This introduces a higher level of polymorphism than is traditionally understood with object-oriented programming—the notion of objects that conform to a prototype. A prototype is a definition of a *set* of interfaces in which all object classes that implement the same set of interfaces can be used polymorphically across those interfaces. So not only are two objects polymorphic along one dimension when they implement a single interface in common, but they are also polymorphic across multiple dimensions when they implement the same set in common. This means that applications and tools need to know only how to work with the prototype in order to work with any of the classes of objects that conform to that prototype. Whether those objects were created three years ago or will be created three years in the future doesn't matter. Combined with *QueryInterface*, this polymorphism solves the real-world problem of deployment of new components over time.

OLE's other major contribution to object-oriented computing is that a client can employ the services of an object without regard to the distance or boundaries between the client and the object. A client, as we've seen, always calls functions through an interface pointer that is meaningful to that client's own process. When the object is fully implemented inside a dynamic link library (DLL), such calls go immediately to the object's own code. When the object is "out-of-process"—that is, implemented inside an executable (EXE) on the same machine or any module on another machine altogether—an in-process proxy does whatever is necessary to communicate with the real object's implementation wherever it resides. This is called *Local/Remote Transparency*, with which a client can use interface pointers in its own process to access objects in other processes and on other machines. The client doesn't concern itself with the distance to the real object—OLE, particularly COM, makes it all transparent.

The idea of interfaces, along with Local/Remote Transparency, is at the center of OLE, even at the center of COM. Literally everything else in OLE is a service built on this core, a way to customize that service, or a means to create a custom service that extends the architectures. In this book, we've seen that OLE provides fundamental services for type information, custom service management, structured storage (Compound Files), naming and binding (monikers), data caching, and data exchange through the OLE Clipboard and OLE Drag and Drop. In addition, OLE provides a great number of minor services typically exposed through a few helper functions.

With these services in place, OLE provides the means for different components and clients to communicate on even higher levels of integration. These levels involve an object's incoming or outgoing interfaces (connectable objects), its persistent storage needs (the *IPersist\** interfaces), its formatted data structures (*IDataObject*), its display and printer renderings (*IViewObject2*), its individual late-bound methods and properties (*IDispatch*, OLE Automation, and property sets), its property pages (*ISpecifyPropertyPages*, *IPropertyPage*), its content appropriate for use in compound documents, and its ability to act as a custom control, which incorporates nearly every other OLE technology.

OLE is an incredible piece of technology, and it can be a very imposing one at that. At its core, OLE is elegant and simple, a generic set of mechanisms that improve the fundamental concepts of object-oriented programming. OLE also builds a great number of additional standards that open up a sometimes overwhelming number of possibilities. It has been our challenge to understand these possibilities and why they are important, looking at all the fine details that are necessary to make OLE work. For again, OLE is a technology aimed at component integration, and with potentially thousands of components and hundreds of ways to integrate them, the number of possible combinations is mind-boggling. But this is not a crisis; this is a tremendous opportunity. OLE has solved so many of the technical problems that only one question remains, one that I believe will become an ever more important question. What creative new software solutions can you achieve with OLE?

# Future Enhancements and Additions to OLE

With everything OLE already does, it can, of course, always do more. As I mentioned earlier, an evolutionary technology such as OLE keeps changing. When I wrote the first edition of this book during the first half of 1993, OLE 2 had just been released, and many of the technologies we've seen, such as Connectable Objects, Property Pages, and OLE Controls, did not yet exist. In 1994, Microsoft made a number of improvements to OLE Automation, implementing dual interfaces, for example, and also added the capabilities for OLE Controls. Incremental enhancements of this nature will continue well into the future.

For the short term (the next two years or so), I can offer a brief list of the enhancements that you can expect. Of course, I cannot guarantee the timing of any of this—these are simply the features that Microsoft considers a priority:

■ COM will support *distributed services,* which provide the ability to communicate with components and objects across network boundaries. In this book, we've already seen how some of this will work, but the details are not entirely available. Using RPC over a network is the easy part of working with remote objects. The tough parts have to do with security (restricting access to services), naming remote objects and their locations uniquely, providing for load balancing when the same service exists on multiple remote machines, and doing all of this as transparently as possible so that existing objects and clients can be deployed in a distributed manner without any code modifications whatsoever.

■ Marshaling interfaces across process or machine boundaries may happen automatically at run time based only on an IDL or ODL description. This would eliminate the need to create your own proxies and stubs with the MIDL compiler. Closely related to this is the intention to merge the IDL and ODL specifications to have one description language for all type information and marshaling needs.

■ There will be a richer classification of object types and their capabilities. Current specifications only classify objects using the Insertable and Control registry keys. As we've seen, there are no other standards for classifying an object, even as an object that supports OLE Automation, which is why I suggested the Programmable key in Chapters 14 and 15. You can well understand the future need to classify objects much more precisely—according to their capabilities—and the need for additional user interface standards that help users browse objects of a certain classification.

■ The structured storage model implemented today in Compound Files will eventually become the basis of a new object file system for Windows. This means that working with storage and stream elements will be exceptionally fast, that these elements will support reconciliation, and that a computer's entire namespace will be browsable as a uniform hierarchy through OLE interfaces. The entire network simply becomes an enormous root storage (with interfaces above and beyond *IStorage*), with substorages for each machine on that network, substorages for disk volumes and partitions—all the way down to individual substorages inside today's compound files.

Streams may appear at any point in the hierarchy to store extra information, including user-definable properties. Literally everything is browsable through the system shell, which will work with full-content filters in order to allow end users to quickly and easily search for information across the entire namespace no matter how deeply buried that information might be inside a file.

■ There will be an OLE-provided service for dealing with property sets more conveniently. Specific objects will encapsulate portions of a property set behind appropriate interfaces.

■ OLE Documents will be greatly enhanced to support even richer content than is possible today. First is the capability to create irregularly shaped content objects, be they in-place capable or not. Windows 95 and Windows NT 3.51 have built-in support for regional windows for this purpose. Second is the capability of container and content objects to negotiate menus and in-place tools to a much finer degree—down to the level of merging individual menu items and short segments of toolbars. Next is the capability to break objects into multiple pieces, whether rectangles or irregular regions. Thus, objects can span multiple pages or perform word wrapping as appropriate for the content. The latter allows content such as an equation to act like any other text in a word processor, even though the content is being managed by an entirely separate component. Along the same lines is the capability to display multiple views for an object. And finally, you'll see container-level search and replace and spell checking of an object's text without requiring the container to know where an object stores such text within itself.

These items are only those enhancements that Microsoft will make to the technologies we've already seen. Microsoft is also working on new systems technologies that will push OLE into even more areas than it exists in today.

One of the first places you will see (or have already seen) this expansion is the shell extensions to Windows 95, which are all based on COM objects of some sort that implement specific interfaces. For example, a Windows 95 "file viewer" is a simple COM object (with a CLSID and a server) that implements interfaces such as *IPersistFile* and *IFileViewer*. Other types of objects provide for extensions to object context menus, hooks for copy and move operations for directories and files, control over system icons, and custom extensions to object property sheets.

The way Windows 95 employs simple COM objects illustrates how useful such objects can be. Eventually you'll even see device drivers take advantage of COM's benefits for negotiating features through interfaces. Most device drivers today are simply DLLs that export specific functions—you can achieve the same end in COM with an in-process object for which all those functions are factored into meaningful interfaces. Over time, enhancements to device drivers will mean new interfaces to implement alongside existing interfaces. The ability to do this robustly is a tremendous improvement over current device driver models because most drivers have to be updated whenever a new version of the operating system is released. With an interface model, driver updates could happen incrementally.

Microsoft is also creating a specification for working with databases through OLE technologies, intended to augment and work with the Open Database Connectivity (ODBC) standard (which will, of course, continue to be fully supported). You can expect to see interfaces that can be used for purposes such as connecting to and managing databases, creating database schema, handling transactioning models, generating and executing queries, working with rows and columns (sorting, filtering, notifying), and so on.

Developers are working as well to create OLE-based multimedia technology for dealing with special content types and other needs unique to multimedia. And work is also going on related to accessibility, or providing ways for computers to work better with people who have various disabilities.

Of course, Microsoft cannot do everything by itself, and many areas of technology concern only a certain segment of the computer industry. For example, the WOSA/XRT specification we saw in Chapter 10 was the work of the Open Market Data Council, which involved representatives of more than 80 companies. Microsoft played only a supporting role in that effort, helping to guide the design to make appropriate use of OLE. But such a gathering of different companies with a common interest doesn't need Microsoft at all! Because COM already allows anyone to create his or her own custom interfaces with standard or custom marshaling, any group of people can get together, find solutions to their common problems, define interfaces to implement those solutions, and then use those interfaces to have their applications communicate and integrate with one another.

Indeed, a key design goal of OLE was the capability for any programmer to create, extend, or evolve an existing design without central coordination of his or her activity while still maintaining a true guarantee of robustness in the system. (In particular, the widespread use of GUIDs as a fundamental data type ensures that no two pieces of code will work together unless programmers intend that they do so.) What's important is that no changes to OLE or to the operating system are necessary. This means that no one needs to approach Microsoft and coerce them to add new APIs to the system or dedicate any other sort of resources. OLE empowers individuals in a partnership to create new designs for integration and interoperability. No one company dominates such a relationship because everyone involved is working for the common interest: integrating applications and components to solve customer problems.

For the longer term, it's hard to know what new additions and changes Microsoft will make and what sorts of technologies other groups might create themselves. There are so many interesting and exciting directions to pursue! In any case, Microsoft doesn't want to work in a vacuum, so they do welcome your ideas and requests. Let Microsoft know what your priorities are and what new features you would like to see. You can send electronic mail to *oleidea@microsoft.com,* or you can write a letter or send a fax to the attention of OLE Program Management. If you are involved in a third-party initiative and would like Microsoft's involvement in the effort, contact Microsoft through the OLESOLN forum on CompuServe or by e-mail at *i-stds@microsoft.com.*

## Document-Centric Computing

In the last section, I mentioned what some of Microsoft's future plans for OLE are at the time this book was written. In this and the next section, I offer my personal views of where we're headed with OLE. I cannot guarantee that Microsoft will pursue these ideas, but I believe that the ideas are a big part of the overall vision of OLE. This section discusses *document-centric computing,* in which users focus on their tasks instead of on applications. The final section of this chapter, and the book, concerns component software from a more general perspective.

In our discussions of OLE Documents, especially regarding in-place activation (Chapter 22), we saw that the primary purpose of compound document technology is to create a more document-centric computing environment. What OLE offers today is well along this path: through the Insert Object dialog box and in-place activation, end users never have to leave the document they're working on to incorporate a different sort of content into that document. The necessary tools come to the document instead of pieces of the document going to the necessary tools.

The reason why the document—and keeping the user focused on it—is so important is that a document represents a task. As I'm writing this chapter, I have a manuscript document open in a word processor. My current task is to write this chapter, not to use a word processor. The chapter document that I'm looking at is my task. No matter what I need to do to complete my task, document-centricity means that I can stay in the context of the task—that is, in the context of the document. If I needed to insert a type of content other than text, I could invoke the Insert Object dialog box, choose a content type, and have the necessary tools for creating that content show up in the document. You can easily imagine that the text I'm writing is itself simply one kind of content and that the container application is nothing more than a sophisticated shell for any type of content that you might want to place in it.

The Insert Object dialog box is an interesting piece of user interface. What it does is allow the user to specify an *intention*. When you choose an Equation type or a Sound type or a Chart type from the list in the dialog box, you're saying, "I want to create an equation" or "My intention is to now create a chart and place it at the insertion point in the document." The Insert Object dialog box is designed to help a user automatically map his or her intentions to the right tools to fulfill those intentions. Throughout the whole process, the user is focused on the document (the task) and its contents (the subtasks). Without Insert Object, the user would have to follow a disruptive thought process: "I want to create a chart at this point in the document. Now, what do I have that lets me create charts? Hmmm. I have an application to do that, but (checks Task Manager) it doesn't appear to be running. I guess I have to go look for it. (Switches to the system shell to look for an icon.) OK. There's GG&G Spreadsheet, and I know it can create a graph for me." At this point, the user runs the spreadsheet, selects File New Chart, and creates the chart. Now that user thinks, "OK, I have my chart. Where was I going to put it? Oh, yes, in my document. Now where did that get to? (Hunts around the desktop.) There it is. Now how do I get the chart into the document? Ah, yes, the clipboard." So the user copies the chart to the document, figures out where to save the original chart, closes the spreadsheet, and only then returns to the document to try to remember why he or she needed a chart in the first place.

You can see from this example that most of the user's time is spent hunting for the right application to match the user's intentions. Productivity is lost because application-centric computing forces a user to think about something other than the task at hand. The user's mental energies are spent in mapping intention to application, not in executing the task. What a waste.

The point is that the more a computer can help users map their tasks and intentions to the right tools, the more productive those users will become. Today's Insert Object dialog box for OLE Documents is only a first primitive step toward the complete realization of what we might call *intentional computing*.

## More Precise Classification

A first improvement would be to classify content objects more precisely than is done today. The Insert Object dialog box simply displays a flat list of any object marked "Insertable" in the registry. If you had three different charting packages on your machine, you'd see three different entries with "Chart" in them somewhere, entries that would not typically be listed together. The same thing applies to other content types. With better classification, a user might be presented with a list of individual generic content types such as Chart, Table, Text, Sound, Picture, Video, Control, and so on, as shown in the mock-up in Figure 25-1. In this manner, the list would be quite short, and selecting a content type from this generic list would invoke the user's preferred server for that type.

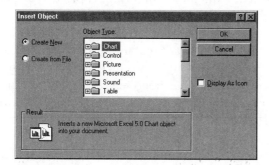

**Figure 25-1.**
*A mock-up of an Insert Object dialog box that displays generic content types.*

Now the user might want to select a specific server for a particular type, so each type listed in this dialog box could be expanded to show the individual servers that are registered for that type, as shown in Figure 25-2.

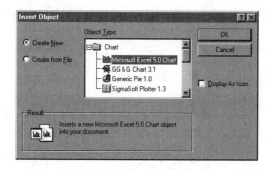

**Figure 25-2.**
*A mock-up of the selection of a specific type registered for a generic type.*

Through this sort of user interface, a user can quickly select a type of content without any extra complexity. But if the user wants to see all the information, there is still a way to access it.

## Task (Document) Templates

Now, a dialog box such as Insert Object represents only one level of user intention—the insertion of a content type into a document that itself already has a type. How did the user create the document in the first place? In general, this process is still application-centric: the user has to think, "I want to work on this task. What sort of applications do I have that let me work on a task like this?" The user then has to go looking for the right application, start that application, and create a new document of the appropriate type, possibly basing that new document on a template of some sort.

This process is less than optimal because the user must once again break the flow from intention to the fulfillment of that intention by searching for a program to run. This is the same problem that would occur in the absence of the Insert Object dialog box. Somehow we need to create a computing environment in which the user can quickly and easily map the task he or she intends to perform to some sort of task (or document) template that structures that task.

We want to give the user a way to say, "I want to start a new task, and this is the sort of task I want to perform." This is the essence of the File New command in most of today's applications. Some current major desktop applications already do something similar to this within the confines of their own document or file types. Consider, for example, Microsoft Word for Windows version 6. When you run Word without opening any documents, you'll be presented with an empty window frame in which only a few tools on the toolbars and only a few menu items are functional. In this mode, Word offers, besides access to Help, the File New, File Open, File Find File, File Templates, and File Exit commands, as shown in Figure 25-3.

Think for a moment about what you can accomplish at this point:

- Start a new task (File New)

- Continue work on an existing task (File Open)

- Find existing tasks (File Find File)

- Manage objects of some sort that each represent a specific task (File Templates)

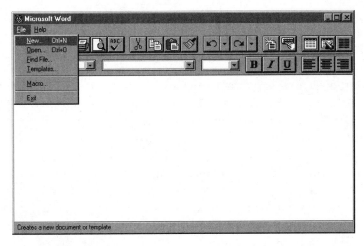

**Figure 25-3.**
*The available commands in Microsoft Word for Windows 6 when no documents are open.*

When you select File New in Word, you are presented with a dialog box that lists the current document templates installed on the machine, as shown in Figure 25-4. Take a close look at the contents of this list. Each item describes a task: the creation of an agenda, an award, a brochure, a calendar, a directory, a fax, a fax cover sheet, an invoice, a letter, and so on. This dialog box looks suspiciously like the Insert Object dialog box, does it not? It gives the user a way to map an intention, such as "I want to write an agenda for a meeting," to specific actions in a piece of software. Microsoft Word even provides template wizards to walk the user through much of the task, applying artificial intelligence

**Figure 25-4.**
*The list of document templates as presented by Microsoft Word when the user selects File New.*

heuristics to perform a great deal of the work involved in the task on the basis of a user's answers to a few questions. This is incredibly task-centric.[1]

I think, with new standards and extensions to OLE, we could accomplish this same level of task focus in a generic way for all task types, regardless of whether they involve text documents, spreadsheets, e-mail messages, database forms, or other content types. This idea applies equally well to the File Open, File Find File, and File Templates commands, which all give the user the means to map slightly different intentions to the actions to fulfill those intentions. Furthermore, these functions would not be part of any one application's frame but part of the operating system shell itself.

I say this because we are already seeing many of these features work their way into the system shell. Take, for instance, Windows Explorer in the Windows 95 shell. Explorer is a systemwide Find File user interface that allows the user to search for files based on many different criteria. The idea of the Explorer is that when you need to locate an existing task, you ask the computer to find it for you. You don't need to spend time navigating the directory structure of your network or hard drive looking for some obscure filename. (Long filenames help out here as well.) In short, a shell-level document search facility increases one's productivity by eliminating the time wasted in searching for files.

The result of any search will typically be a file list of some sort. Given long filenames, this list presents existing tasks that are described by the filename itself. A simple double click on one of the items in the list tells the shell to find the code associated with that file type, run that code, and have it load a file. We already know how to do all of these things using the file's extension, a CLSID, a file pattern, and so forth. In fact, the system shell could reduce the whole process to the creation and binding of a file moniker.

So through a user interface such as that in Explorer, and with a few future evolutionary enhancements such as full content searching, each application will no longer need to provide its own Find File capabilities, nor even its own File Open capabilities. With a shell-level user interface for selecting a new task, applications need no File New command themselves. At this point, there is no longer any reason to have applications as we know them today! This is because most of today's applications, especially the multiple-document applications such as Microsoft Word, are really nothing more than frames

---

1. The Windows 95 Start menu allows you to create something similar to this user interface already. You can create a folder that contains a number of document templates, each of which is given a long filename such as "Write a letter," "Send a fax," or "Draw a picture." Selecting one of these items launches the appropriate application and opens the template, which works with today's off-the-shelf applications. Although this requires some work on behalf of the end user, it does illustrate the idea of how task templates give the user a way to map intentions to software.

around a collection of documents. The functionality now provided by the frame is something that will eventually be provided by the system shell itself. Instead of having one application frame that manages text documents, another that manages spreadsheets, and another that manages e-mail messages, the system desktop itself becomes the frame that manages documents of all types in their own windows.[2]

I'm saying that what we now know as applications will become the servers for what I call *task template objects,* special flavors of OLE objects that implement interfaces specifically tuned to the management of a task. This means that an application such as Microsoft Word could simply become the server for a whole host of different template objects, as could all other applications. Each template type, appropriately classified, would be registered with the system along with its server. These registry entries would be the source of a system shell–level File New dialog that would list all the available task types on the system. When the user selected a task from such a list, the shell would basically create an instance of that type's CLSID, which would launch the server code for that type. Now, instead of the server displaying a document window inside some frame, it would simply display a document window, negotiating menu items and toolbar space with the system shell in order to provide the user with the appropriate commands for that task. When the user selected a piece of content to create using the Insert Object dialog box, the new content object would perform in-place negotiation with the document and the system shell (acting as the frame) to once again make commands and other tools available to the user.

The purpose of a shell-level File Templates command would be to help the user manage the tasks that are on a system, removing old ones, installing new ones, and so on. Given OLE controls and powerful end-user tools that work with them, users could even create their own templates — that is, define a custom task. This would also be the role of many corporate developers — creating business-specific task templates for use across their enterprise.

The big question, of course, is when and how this sort of task-centric computing environment will become fully implemented. What sort of interfaces will be involved with a task template object? How will it be integrated into a generic system shell? What services will the shell provide to templates? What other sorts of objects will be integrated with the shell? There are many such questions, most of which are very complex. Still, the process of creating the answers promises to be an exciting one.

---

2. Microsoft has been saying for some time that the multiple-document interface (MDI) is going to become obsolete in the future. To be precise, the need for MDI within a single application will become obsolete. It can be replaced by the idea of multiple documents on the desktop. MDI will still be valid for the system; it will simply become unnecessary for any application to use.

# Component Software and the Future of Computing

In Chapter 1, I defined component software as the practical and consumer-oriented realization of the developer-oriented principle of object-oriented programming. I described the benefits merely as the capability to add features to applications by purchasing components rather than by purchasing entirely new builds of feature-laden monolithic applications. In other words, instead of necessarily purchasing applications, end users would build their own custom applications to solve their own specific problems.

Why is this important? Think for a moment about how applications—the tools that are used to solve problems—are built today. A software vendor decides to create an application for a particular market segment. Designers from the company then use a variety of data gathering techniques to determine what problems need to be solved and what sorts of tools people would like to use to solve those problems. They send out surveys, hold focus groups, create and test prototype software, and so on. Eventually this data is collected and brought together in a functional specification. This specification drives the development of the software and, after a number of months or perhaps years, the software is fully developed and tested, ready to be sold in the software market in which people will generally purchase that release for the next year or two.

While this process is accepted as the standard today, look at the problems that are inherent in it. First, the data collected from surveys and similar methods depends greatly on the ability of target users to articulate exactly what they want. In other words, these collection methods assume that customers know what problems they want to solve and can articulate what those problems are as well as potential solutions. This is almost never a valid assumption, however, so it requires extremely careful design of surveys and other material (which has led to colleges offering degree programs in survey design). But no matter how you ask your target users what they want, they may or may not be able to articulate exactly what it is they need. And we all know, on a personal level, that what we say we want is not necessarily what we really do need. (For example, you say you *want* a sports car, but what you really *need* is basic transportation.)

So because data gathering techniques do not necessarily yield the correct data, applications built from that data will not necessarily solve the problems they intended to in the first place. Let's say, however, that such methods did yield the correct information (which is possible, simply unlikely). From the time a software development team receives this information to the time it can realistically deploy a solution is on the order of 3 to 6 months, minimum, even in a corporate setting. This reveals the second major shortcoming of our current design methods: by the time most software solutions are deployed, the problems that they intended to solve have most likely changed or become irrelevant. This is even more true when software is developed as a retail package and then sold for 18 to 24 months afterward. The problems addressed by the software at the end of its production cycle may already be 3 years old.

The most significant result of both the data gathering problems and the lag in deployment is that applications become more and more general purpose: single applications are designed to solve a wide variety of problems. Take, for example, Microsoft Office, which is composed of Microsoft Word, Excel, PowerPoint, Access, and Mail. Office is already sold as if it were a single product, and the integration capabilities provided through OLE blur the boundaries between the various pieces of Office.

This is not to say that general purpose tools are useless. In fact, they are very powerful and do many things that were not available in the past. But they have a hidden cost—user training. The more general purpose a tool becomes, the more training is necessary for users to learn how to apply that general tool to their specific problems. This is why there is still so much said about user-friendly applications and usability. This is why course catalogs for community colleges are littered with classes on using this or that application. This is why bookstores devote large amounts of shelf space to books that focus on using a specific application. The purpose of these after-market products is to help end users understand how to use general purpose tools to solve their specific problems.

But is this really what application software should be? After all, there is nothing sacred about our current software production methods. When I first used a computer, I didn't have any shrink-wrapped software at all—when I had a problem to solve, I sat down and wrote a program to solve it. If my first attempt at the program didn't solve my problem, I modified the program and tried again, until I got it right. When the problem was solved, I either dumped the program or saved it in case I might have a similar problem in the future and could modify the existing program to help solve it. Now, it occurred to a few people that other computer users might be willing to pay for a software solution, and this spawned the growth of the shrink-wrapped software industry, which has led to general purpose tools.

So what does all this have to do with component software? I believe that component software is the technological innovation that will spark a new explosion of growth in the software industry by empowering computer users to once again create their own custom applications for their own specific problems. In the future, using a computer will not entail starting an application but rather spending one or two minutes creating an application for whatever problem is at hand. This does not mean that end users will be writing C code—absolutely not! Instead, they will have high-level tools through which they can specify their exact problem—that is, specify their intentions. These tools will then assemble a solution—a very specific application—from a large pool of available components. If the application is not the perfect solution for the user's problem, the user can quickly modify it, again using a high-level tool, until it does solve the problem. Even when users don't fully articulate the problem initially, they can quickly go back and clarify their intentions. Within minutes, I believe, users will always end up with the right solution.

The result of this iterative problem-solving environment is that end users get exactly the applications they need exactly when they need them. In other words, a component software environment with appropriate high-level tools is one that avoids the problems of our current software development process. First, we eliminate the inaccuracies inherent in surveys, focus groups, and other data collection schemes. We also avoid misinterpretations by human beings trying to take all that data and formulate a functional specification, which is then subject to misinterpretation by a development team. Component software eliminates these processes by giving immediate feedback to users to tell them whether their stated problem was, in fact, their real problem. Second, component software eliminates the minimum 3-to-6-month lag between a user specifying a problem and a software solution being delivered. In the picture I'm painting here, a user specifies his or her intentions to a high-level tool that then cranks out an application within minutes.

Users are smart people. They know what problems they have to solve, but they are continually frustrated by their inability to articulate these problems to today's general purpose applications. Applications should solve problems, not simply be a tool to create solutions to problems. And most important, applications should not be problems themselves!

The future I see for component software is that given enough components and the appropriate types of tools to integrate those components, any end user will be able to sit down at a computer and quickly create a custom application for a specific problem—an application with all the power available in today's commercial applications. In the future, using a computer will mean stating problems and intentions and having the computer generate and execute a solution.

# Opportunity

You may or may not agree with the future I've described here. I cannot say that it is possible, nor can I guarantee that I've described it perfectly. Nevertheless, I believe it to be a worthy pursuit and the purpose of having an integration technology such as OLE in the first place. But OLE itself is simply the low-level plumbing that enables components to communicate. To realize a true component software environment requires a large number of components and a large number of tools—each appropriate for different types of end users—to integrate components into applications.

Herein lies the tremendous opportunity of component software: the market would no longer be one in which you must have a huge feature-laden application in order to compete. Instead, computing would be formed by a partnership of components that themselves come in many shapes and sizes. In other words, a component system, just as nature and society, requires diversity. There will be a great need for components that do nothing more than provide a service of some sort—a library of powerful functions for calculations, formatting, rendering, and so on. There will be a great need for components that encapsulate business processes—ones that incorporate specific functionality around specific content. There will also be a need for content-oriented components, things such as compound document objects and OLE controls, which are the types of components an end user might actually see.

There is not only a need for components but also a need for the development tools to build them and for the tools to integrate components together. Some tools will be targeted toward today's developers—the ones creating the low-level components in the first place. Others will be targeted toward corporate developers, who will pull together low-level, mid-level, and high-level components to build enterprise-wide solutions. Tools will also be targeted to end users for the purpose of building documents or high-level and specific applications. At this point in the history of the computer industry, we have only primitive tools—and very few of them. Where will the new tools come from? Perhaps from your own company.

Many of these components, and even some of the tools, will come from what I call the *componentization* of today's applications. When I look at the word processor I'm using to write this chapter, it has a tremendous amount of useful functionality and information that is available only to this one application. Componentization means making such elements available to everything else in the system in a reusable manner. OLE is *the* technology for doing this—once you analyze the functionality and content that is hidden within an application, most of the interfaces you'd need for creating objects that share that functionality and content have already been defined. New standard and custom interfaces, which fit so easily into the existing OLE architecture, will in time fill any gaps that exist. I fully expect that there's another book somewhere within this idea of componentization.

In any case, realizing true component software is going to take more work than one company can handle, but OLE is already here as the first step in the process. OLE is the beginning of a long evolution in the way we use computers and in the way in which we create, use, and sell software. But this is not merely about Microsoft's success—it's about yours. Component software is not just a way to reorganize existing market share between companies; it's an innovation that will lead to an explosive expansion of the entire software industry. There will be a great demand for many components and tools and, yes, even for shrink-wrapped component-based applications. I believe that this expansion of the market will happen faster than a company such as Microsoft can grow to fill in the gaps. This leaves a tremendous amount of room for new companies to emerge and for everyone to win.

# INDEX

## Special Characters

! (composite moniker notation), 446

• (composite moniker notation), 446

@ (display names), 470, 487

\ (root registry entry), 71

\ (wildcard item moniker), 456

{} (GUID notation), 69

32-bit vs. 16-bit platforms, 53

## A

absolute paths, links and, 955–56

accelerators. *See also* keyboard handling
  Ctrl+Enter, 1061
  in-place, 1030, 1054–56
  OLE controls, 1116–19

access
  incremental, 341, 368–69
  modes, 360, 361–63

activation, 47–48. *See also* deactivation
  content object states and, 819–21
  in-place objects, 1041–42, 1070–76 (*see also* in-place activation)
  linked objects, 992–93

active vs. UI-active states, 1018–20

*AddRef* function, 18, 82, 83–90

adornments, object, 1029, 1077

advise sinks. *See also* notifications
  connectable objects vs., 40n. 11, 196–97 (*see also* Connectable Objects)
  containers, 826–27
  data objects and, 40–41, 511–16
  implementing, 529–35
  in-process embedding handler, 938–40
  local embedding server, 907–10
  viewable objects and, 42, 550–51

aggregation, 19, 100, 101–5
  implementing, 137–41

alert object tables, 453

allocator objects, 108–12

ambient properties, 52, 1106, 1120–21

Animal sample, 100–105, 139–41

Anti-monikers, 39, 440–42

API functions, 23
  associating code with storage, 378–80
  BSTR types, 646
  COM, 31n. 5, 220
  compound file, 372–74
  dates, 646n. 2
  for finding CLSIDs and ProgIDs, 72
  GUID, 69
  interfaces and, 141–42 (*see also* member functions)
  memory allocation, 108–9
  moniker creation, 441–42
  obtaining first interface pointers for objects, 63–64
  OLE Clipboard, 566–68
  *QueryInterface* function vs., 91–92
  running objects, 666–67
  Safe Array types, 647
  type-conversion, 650–51

application objects, 716–18

*application* property, 715–16

arguments. *See* parameters

artificial reference counts, 90

ASCII 6, 37

asynchronous notifications and events, 302

at sign (@), 470, 487

attributes
  interface, 80–82
  ODL, 166–69
  type library and type library elements, 151–54

AutoCli2 sample, 795–97

AutoCli sample, 741–59
  as automation testing tool, 638
  calling dispinterfaces, 741–53
  custom and dual interfaces, 758–59
  function calls with arguments, 749–51
  function calls with named arguments, 752–53

nested classes, 130–33
nested lifetimes, 85–87
*NoteChangeTime* function, 989–90
notifications. *See also* events
asynchronous, and concurrency management, 302
connectable objects and, 29–31, 187–88 (*see also* Connectable Objects)
data objects and advise sinks, 40–41, 511–16 (*see also* advise sinks)
embedded or linked objects and, 49
embedding containers and, 838–43
linking servers, 989–90
local embedding servers, 907–10
in OLE Documents, 826–27
property change, 46–47, 775–77, 792–94
viewable objects and, 41–42, 550–51

## O

Object Components Framework (OCF), 60
Object Description Language. *See* ODL (Object Description Language)
object handlers. *See* in-process handlers
Object Linking and Embedding, 10–11. *See also* OLE
object managers, 6
object-oriented programming, 3–5, 14, 66n. 2, 252–56
objects, 4, 9, 12
adornments, 1029, 1077
advise sink (*see* advise sinks)
allocator, 108–12
application, 716–18
automation (*see* automation objects)
bind context, 433, 439, 456–61
C++ classes vs., 252–56
class, type, and prototype concepts, 64 (*see also* types)
class factory (*see* class factory objects)
classical definition of, 13–14
clients (*see* clients; consumers; containers)
collection, 662–65, 718–20
COM/OLE task requirements for using, 106–9
concepts, 14–19, 61–62, 142–43
connectable (*see* Connectable Objects)
connection point, 190, 192–95, 209–16

objects, *continued*
content (*see* content objects)
creating and initializing, from CLSIDs, 244–46
custom components (*see* COM (Component Object Model); custom components)
data (*see* data objects)
data advise holder, 514–16
data cache (*see* data cache objects)
data cache control, 556–58
designing hierarchies, 713–25
document, 720–22, 1037
documents collection, 718–20
drop source (*see* drop sources)
drop target (*see* drop targets)
embedded (*see* embedded objects)
emulation (*see* emulation)
enumerator, 62, 113–14, 508–11
error, 710–7
handlers (*see* in-process handlers)
identity issues, 64–73 (*see also* CLSIDs (class identifiers); GUIDs (globally unique identifiers))
implementing, in C and C++ (*see* EnumRect sample)
implementing, with multiple interfaces (*see* Query sample)
implementing reusable (*see* Reuse sample)
initialization and uninitialization, 106–8 (*see also* initialization)
inner vs. outer, 100, 103–4, 139–41
in-place (*see* in-place objects)
in-process, local, and remote, 32, 33–35 (*see also* Local/Remote Transparency)
inside-out vs. outside-in, 1033
interfaces and interface attributes, 73–82 (*see also* interfaces)
licensed, 247 (*see also* licensing)
lifetimes (*see* reference counting)
linked (*see* linked objects)
LockBytes, 370–72
memory management and, 108–9 (*see also* memory management)
message filter (*see* message filter objects)
methods, 15 (*see also* member functions)
multithreaded components and, 108
names (*see* monikers)
obtaining first interface pointer to, 63–64

## About the Author

During the production of this book, Kraig Brockschmidt was a software engineer in Microsoft's Developer Relations Group, where he was responsible for explaining new systems technologies—primarily OLE—to independent software vendors through books, papers, articles, and seminars at industry conferences. Since that time, he has joined the OLE team itself as a Program Manager, where he is now responsible for coordinating and driving the creation of future OLE technologies. He joined Microsoft in March 1988 and worked in the product support, applications, systems, and systems marketing divisions before joining the OLE team in March 1995. He holds a bachelor of science degree in computer engineering from the University of Washington.

The manuscript for this book was prepared and submitted to Microsoft Press in electronic form. Text files were prepared using Microsoft Word 6.0 for Windows. Pages were composed by Microsoft Press using Aldus PageMaker 5.0 for Windows, with text in New Baskerville and display type in Helvetica Bold. Composed pages were delivered to the printer as electronic prepress files.

*Cover Graphic Designer*
Rebecca Geisler

*Interior Graphic Designer*
Kim Eggleston

*Interior Graphic Artists*
Michael Victor
James D. Kramer
Jody Ivy

*Principal Compositor*
John Sugg

*Principal Proofreader/Copy Editor*
Shawn Peck

*Indexer*
Shane-Armstrong Information Systems

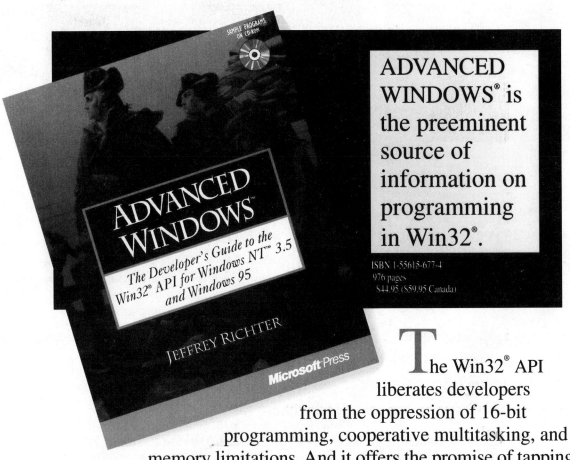

ADVANCED WINDOWS® is the preeminent source of information on programming in Win32®.

ISBN 1-55615-677-4
976 pages
$44.95 ($59.95 Canada)

The Win32® API liberates developers from the oppression of 16-bit programming, cooperative multitasking, and memory limitations. And it offers the promise of tapping into a rapidly expanding customer base of Windows NT™ 3.5 and Windows® 95 users. But there's more to making the 16-bit to 32-bit transition than just rowing across a river. Whether you're building a 32-bit application from scratch or porting an existing 16-bit application, ADVANCED WINDOWS offers the core information and sage advice you need to maximize performance and minimize the development cycle.

**_Microsoft_® Press**

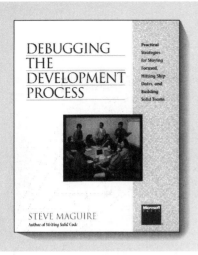